BUDGET TRAVEL
IN
AMERICA

FODOR'S TRAVEL GUIDES

are compiled, researched, and edited by an international team of travel writers, field correspondents, and editors. The series, which now almost covers the globe, was founded by Eugene Fodor in 1936.

OFFICES
New York & London

Fodor's Budget Travel in America:

Area Editors: STEPHEN ALLEN, JEANIE BLAKE, VICTOR BLOCK, DEAN BOSWELL, VERA BRADSHAW, CURTIS W. CASEWIT, EDGAR CHEATHAM, PATRICIA CHEATHAM, RALPH DANFORD, ALMA ESHENFELDER, PATSY FRETWELL, RALPH FRIEDMAN, HARRY E. FULLER, JR., PHIL HALPERN, MURRAY HERTZ, SHIRLEY ROSE HIGGINS, TONY HILLERMAN, DAVID HUNTER, IRIS SANDERSON JONES, ROBERT KAROLEVITZ, BERN KEATING, GLORIA HAYES KREMER, CANDACE L. KUMERFIELD, CAROLYN R. LANGDON, JANE E. LASKY, KAREN LINGO, BETTE McNEAR, JOHN MAXYMUK, IRA MAYER, LYLE NELSON, MONIQUE PANAGGIO, JOHN D. PHILLIPS, PAUL ROBBINS, ARCHIE SATTERFIELD, WILLIAM G. SCHELLER, WILLIAM SCHEMMEL, NORMA SPRING, RICHARD G. STAHL, BARC WADE, KATHARINE D. WALKER, JANE ZAREM, PAT ZIMMERMAN
Editor: DEBRA BERNARDI
Editorial Associate: ELENORE BODIE
Drawings: SANDRA LANG
Maps: DYNO LOWENSTEIN

FODOR'S

BUDGET TRAVEL
IN
AMERICA
1984

FODOR'S TRAVEL GUIDES

New York

All the following Guides are current (most of them also in
the Hodder and Stoughton British edition.)

CURRENT FODOR'S COUNTRY AND AREA TITLES:

AUSTRALIA, NEW ZEALAND AND SOUTH PACIFIC	ISRAEL
AUSTRIA	ITALY
BELGIUM AND LUXEMBOURG	JAPAN
BERMUDA	JORDAN AND HOLY LAND
BRAZIL	KOREA
CANADA	MEXICO
CARIBBEAN AND BAHAMAS	NORTH AFRICA
CENTRAL AMERICA	PEOPLE'S REPUBLIC OF CHINA
EASTERN EUROPE	PORTUGAL
EGYPT	SCANDINAVIA
EUROPE	SCOTLAND
FRANCE	SOUTH AMERICA
GERMANY	SOUTHEAST ASIA
GREAT BRITAIN	SOVIET UNION
GREECE	SPAIN
HOLLAND	SWITZERLAND
INDIA	TURKEY
IRELAND	YUGOSLAVIA

CITY GUIDES:

BEIJING, GUANGZHOU, SHANGHAI	PARIS
CHICAGO	ROME
DALLAS AND FORT WORTH	SAN DIEGO
HOUSTON	SAN FRANCISCO
LONDON	STOCKHOLM, COPENHAGEN, OSLO, HELSINKI, AND REYKJAVIK
LOS ANGELES	
MADRID	
MEXICO CITY AND ACAPULCO	TOKYO
NEW ORLEANS	WASHINGTON, D.C.
NEW YORK CITY	

FODOR'S BUDGET SERIES:

BUDGET BRITAIN	BUDGET ITALY
BUDGET CANADA	BUDGET JAPAN
BUDGET CARIBBEAN	BUDGET MEXICO
BUDGET EUROPE	BUDGET SCANDINAVIA
BUDGET FRANCE	BUDGET SPAIN
BUDGET GERMANY	BUDGET TRAVEL IN AMERICA
BUDGET HAWAII	

USA GUIDES:

ALASKA	HAWAII
CALIFORNIA	NEW ENGLAND
CAPE COD	PENNSYLVANIA
COLORADO	SOUTH
FAR WEST	TEXAS
FLORIDA	USA (in one volume)

MANUFACTURED IN THE UNITED STATES OF AMERICA
10 9 8 7 6 5 4 3 2 1

CONTENTS

THE SOUTH

CONTENTS

CONTENTS

THE PACIFIC ISLANDS

FACTS AT YOUR FINGERTIPS

LANGUAGE/30

For the Business or Vacationing International Traveler

In 24 languages! A basic language course on 2 cassettes and a phrase book . . . Only $14.95 ea. + shipping

Nothing flatters people more than to hear visitors try to speak their language and LANGUAGE/30, used by thousands of satisfied travelers, gets you speaking the basics quickly and easily. Each LANGUAGE/30 course offers:

- approximately 1½ hours of guided practice in greetings, asking questions and general conversation
- special section on social customs and etiquette

Order yours today. Languages available:

ARABIC	GREEK	JAPANESE	RUSSIAN
CHINESE	HEBREW	KOREAN	SERBO-CROATIAN
DANISH	HINDI	NORWEGIAN	SPANISH
DUTCH	INDONESIAN	PERSIAN	SWAHILI
FRENCH	ITALIAN	PORTUGUESE	SWEDISH
GERMAN	TURKISH	VIETNAMESE	TAGALOG

FACTS AT YOUR FINGERTIPS

13·06
5·34
2400
$2·30

WHAT WILL IT COST? The United States is not one of the world's cheaper countries for tourists, and many kinds of inexpensive accommodation that are helpful in other countries (such as pensions, Youth Hostels, government-run inns, and rooms in private houses) either do not exist or are underdeveloped here. Costs will vary somewhat by region (New York City is more expensive than rural Maine, for example), but the rise of nationwide, standardized hotel, motel and restaurant chains with their standardized facilities and prices has been a mixed blessing. Obviously, it is convenient to be able to reserve a room anywhere in the country, to have it ready even if you arrive late, and to know exactly what you may expect when you enter it. On the other hand, you may have removed yourself from a range of cheaper, local accommodations which may offer more personal service and regional atmosphere.

There has been a growing spread of budget motel chains which make a special effort to cut frills and prices both. There are now a number of these, and they are discussed in detail below in the section on *Hotels and Motels*.

A result of this spread is that the downtown areas of most cities still have some older hotels, formerly elegant, that have had to lower their prices to meet the competition of the newer places on the outskirts. Most guidebooks do not list these older and cheaper hotels (and many of them are being converted to condominium or co-op apartments) and you may have to spend a little more time hunting them out and checking their conditions. Often, however, they will prove quite adequate and may compare favorably with European, if not American, standards.

Two people can travel in the United States on a basic budget of about $90 a day (not counting gasoline or other transportation costs), as shown in the table below. This is an average; New York is the most expensive area, at about $100–115 a day; while in the Plains, Rockies, and Southwest, expenses can be kept closer to about $80 a day.

You can often cut expenses by traveling off-season when hotel rates may be lower; and in dealing out-of-season with smaller, locally owned motels you may be able to arrange reduced prices that the fixed policies of chain and franchise places do not permit. On the New England coast, for example, off-season prices are generally in effect from mid-October to mid-May, with peak season July 4 to Labor Day and the times in between as transitional. (However, many of the resort hotels in this area close completely during the off-season, so your choice will be more limited.) New England is also a region where, traditionally, rooms are available in many fine old private houses, some of them offering meals and run as inns, others providing breakfast only and usually called Guest Houses. In other parts of the country the term "Tourist Home" is often used. These places can be appreciably less expensive than the more modern and lavishly equipped motels. Larger towns and cities may have YMCA's and YWCA's with family accommodations, and there are government-supervised hotels, usually run by concessionaires, in some state and federal parks.

Another possibility, still not too well known, is college campuses. About 180 colleges and universities in 46 states and 7 Canadian provinces open their dormitories, cafeterias, and cultural and recreational facilities to vacationers outside of term time. Although requirements vary, usually reservations are required, pets are not allowed, eligibility is: "students, alumni, adults, families and prospective matriculants," baths are shared, prices per person per day are in the $5–15 range, weekly rates are available, and cafeteria meals are from $1–5. A directory of these opportunities is *Mort's Guide to Low-Cost Vacations and Lodgings on College Campuses,* US & Canada edition, available from Mort Barrish Associates, Inc., Research Park, State Rd., Princeton, N.J. 08540. Another source of information for campus accommodations is Campus Hotel Corporation, 95 W. 95 St., New York, N.Y. 10025, (212) 222-1400.

Because of the size of this country Youth Hostels here are much less developed than in Europe or Japan. There are about 200 hostels in the U.S., most of them in the compact areas that are New England and the Mid-Atlantic area, few in cities. Of equal interest with their possibilities as inexpensive lodgings are the conducted group hiking and bicycle tours that the American Youth Hostel Association offers. These vary from year to year, of course. See below under "Roughing It" for further details; and for complete up-to-date information write to: *American Youth Hostels, Inc.*, 1332 Eye St., N.W., 8th Floor, Washington, D.C. 20005; or, 132 Spring Street, New York, New York 10012.

YMCA's and YWCA's vary considerably from one city to another in age, equipment, lodgings, prices and policies. For complete listings write to: *National Council of YMCA's*, 291 Broadway, New York, New York 10007.

Another point to bear in mind is that the Interstate Highway System and the various State thruways are designed to speed you from city to city, not necessarily to show you a region's best scenery or local color and certainly not to take you to out-of-the-way resorts and quiet small towns where you may often find facilities that are older but more typical of the area, clean and attractive, run by local people, and definitely less expensive than more crowded places. When you look at your road map, ask yourself where people went before the Interstates were built. Route 1 up the coast of Maine is a good example, or the Boston Post Road through southern New England.

In planning your budget don't forget to allow a realistic amount for recreation and entertainment expenses such as sports equipment rental (boats, canoes, skis and boots, golf clubs, etc.); entrance fees to amusement parks, museums, galleries and historical sites; and tickets to movies, concerts, plays and exhibitions. You'll also need to include tolls for bridges and highways (this can add up to more than you think), souvenirs, extra camera film and perhaps some developing, and incidental medical fees that might not be covered by your insurance. Tipping will be another big extra; see below for a special section on where, when, whom and how much, and remember that in some situations this can raise your costs by up to 15–20%.

Typical daily budget for two people

Room at a moderate hotel or motel	$35.00
Light breakfast for two at coffee shop (incl. tip)	6.00
Lunch for two at an inexpensive restaurant (incl. tip)	10.00
Dinner for two at a moderate restaurant (incl. tip)	23.00
One sightseeing bus tour (two fares)	6.00
One evening cocktail for each of two persons (incl. tip)	6.00
Admission for two to one museum or historic site	4.00
	$90.00

According to this book's system of categories, a moderate hotel room, double occupancy, ranges from $25 to $40 (but with wide regional variations); a moderate restaurant dinner from $10–$15 per person. An inexpensive restaurant means that dinner will average under $10 per person.

These figures are a rough average for the entire country. Region by region, we suggest the following adjustments: *New England* - up 5%; *New York-New Jersey* - up 20%; *mid-Atlantic states* - up 5%, *South* - down 15%, *Midwest* - down 5%; *Rockies and Plains* - down 10%; *Southwest* - down 10%; *Far West* - no change. The figure for New York-New Jersey is skewed somewhat by including prices for its chief tourist area, New York City, and for several expensive resorts. Likewise, within a given region, conditions will vary somewhat. In the South, for example, Miami Beach between South Beach and Bal Harbor has a wide range of prices both in and out of season; and small towns on the Gulf Coast of North Florida's panhandle may be notably cheaper than the gaudier Atlantic Coast resorts. Generally, both hotels and motels are cheaper in the South and the West than in the rest of the country.

After lodging, your biggest expense will be food. To trim expenses, you might try picnicking. This will save you time and money; it will also help you to enjoy the scenery more as you travel toward your next destination. Most scenic highways and thruways now have well-maintained state picnic and rest areas equipped with tables, benches and trash cans, and often fireplaces, running water, and toilets.

Before you leave home put together a picnic kit. Sturdy plastic plates and cups will be cheaper in the long run than throw-away paper ones; and the same goes for permanent metal flatware rather than the throw-away plastic kind. Pack a small electric pot and two thermoses, one for water and one for beverages —or, one hot and one cold. If you go by car take along a small cooler. Bread, milk, cold cereal, jam, tea or instant coffee, bouillon cubes and instant soup packets, fruit, fresh vegetables that need no cooking, cold cuts, cheese, nuts, raisins, eggs (hard boil them in the electric pot in your room the night before)— with only things like this you can eat conveniently, cheaply, and well.

Even in restaurants there are a number of ways to control costs. 1) Always stop at the cash register and look over the menu *before* you sit down. 2) Order a complete dinner; à la carte almost always adds up to more, unless you see a big Chef's Salad and figure that's all you need. 3) If there is a salad bar or any kind of buffet or smorgasbord arrangement, fill up there and save on desserts and extras. 4) Ask for smaller portions, at reduced prices, for children. Most places are providing them now. 5) Go to a Chinese restaurant and order *one less* main dish than the number of people in your group. You'll still come away pleasantly full. 6) Ask for the Day's Special, House Special, Chef's Special, or whatever it's called. Chances are that it will be better, and more abundant, than the other things on the menu. 7) Remember that in many restaurants lunch may be a better bargain than dinner. 8) Below, in the section on restaurants, we suggest some chains that offer good value for your money.

If you like a drink before dinner or bed, bring your own bottle. Most hotels and motels will supply ice free or for very little, but the markup on alcoholic beverages in restaurants, bars, lounges, and dining rooms is enormous, and in some states peculiar laws apply anyway.

Camping, a mode of travel already very popular and highly developed in Europe, provides one of the cheapest and best ways of seeing some of the best parts of the entire country, its state and national parks. There are well over 4,000 campsites in America's National Parks, National Forests, and State Parks. Fees vary but are low; in the last several years advance reservations have become increasingly necessary for all the parks, so write ahead as early as possible, and make your plans with alternative choices in mind. For fuller information, write to: *National Parks Service,* U.S. Department of the Interior, Washington, D.C. 20240, or *National Forest Service,* U.S. Department of Agriculture, Washington, D.C. 20250.

SPECIAL TRAVEL RATES. All transportation companies (motor, rail, plane) offer special rates, seasonal and year-round. For example: Car rental companies have special rates for inexpensive, intermediate, and expensive cars, for daily hops, weekend jaunts, or extended trips. The major companies will let you rent a car in one city and drop it off in another for a modest service charge. Some also offer a 10% discount to holders of foreign passports. Car rental rate structures vary greatly. When comparing take into account whether the fees are a flat rate or subject to a per-mile charge.

Buses are already the least expensive way to go; and here there are two possibilities. The first is that the country's two major bus networks, Greyhound and Trailways, offer both sightseeing packages of their own and also various types of reduced fares. For example, there may be a 10% reduction on round-trip tickets. Special round-trip excursion fares are available between many cities if you agree to a pre-set time period. Children under 5 ride free; children 6–11 years old go for half fare. Special rates also obtain for friends and relatives, groups, and the handicapped (see below), for clergy and members of the Armed Forces. Hotel rooms may be available at special prices tied in with your bus ticket, too. *Greyhound's Ameripass* is available for 7 days, 15 days and 30 days at any time of the year, and will give you unlimited travel on any of its lines anywhere in the country. Rates in mid-1983 were: 7 days for $186.50, 15 days for $239.85, and 30 days for $346.45. Children as noted above; no Senior Citizen discounts. In addition, Ameripass entitles you to other discounts—on car rentals, some hotel accommodations, special sightseeing excursions, and a number of museums, theme parks, and other "attractions." *Trailways'* similar *Eagle Pass* gives approximately the same rates for the same periods. Each of these tickets may be extended for $10 a day up to a total of 30 days of extra travel. Furthermore, either pass may be used on buses of the other line, on a space-available basis.

The second is that the sightseeing packages offered by the many motor tour companies using their own buses on special-interest itineraries are so numerous and so diverse that surely you can find one of your choice that will be a bargain, dollar for dollar, over what you might see or do on your own. New England—7 days; Washington and Colonial Virginia—5 days; the Smoky Mountains—8 days; the Black Hills—7 days; the Pacific Coast—11 days; these are only a few examples. Packages generally include: transportation, lodging, baggage handling, some meals, some sightseeing and excursions, guide-escort service, and range in length from 4 to 31 days. *Bluebird, California Parlor Car Tours, Atpac Tours, Cartan Travel Bureau, Casser Travelcade Tours, East Coast Parlor Car Tours, Forlow Tours, Green Carpet Tours, Maupintour, Michaud Tours, Miller Tours, Percival Tours, Talmage Tours, Tauck Tours, Tour of the Month,* and *Yankee Holidays* are some of the leading firms in this type of travel. Your travel agent will be able to supply you with their addresses, brochures, and types of specialization on areas covered. Ask him to show you his copy of the leading directory in this field, the *Discover America Annual Sales Guide,* published by Travel Trade Magazine of New York.

Amtrak, the major American rail system serves about 500 communities in 44 states and offers connecting motor-coach and car-rental service to many others. It also has special rates, seasonally for some areas of the country, and year-round for other areas, as well as family rates, group rates, and a number of attractive package tours and excursions. Tickets may be bought not only at railway stations but also at downtown ticket offices in larger cities and from over 7,000 appointed travel agents throughout the country.

In many large cities and notable tourist areas, such as Boston, Niagara Falls or Washington, DC, *Amtrak* offers combinations of lodging, meals, local sightseeing, side trips, shopping discounts and car rental. For example, from Oakland and San Francisco, California, you can board a train for a Reno weekend, January through April. The all-inclusive rate covers round trip rail transportation, dance car and band, two nights first class accommodations, three breakfasts, one luncheon buffet, and a Reno hospitality coupon book. Ask also about Amtrak's *Rail, Road & City Adventure* packages. Seasonal offerings include autumn foliage trips and ski specials.

Amtrak's family plan ticket is good for unlimited rail travel on its routes and can begin on any day of the week. The ticket is for coach or first class trains where regular fare is $20.00 or more. The head of the family pays full fare, spouse and children from 12 to 21 get a 50% discount, and children from two to 11 get a 75% discount.

Airfares dropped sharply after deregulation in 1978, but recently fuel costs have been pushing them back up. The fare war which has ensued has its comic aspects. Even the airlines themselves do not know all the different promotional gimmicks they may have. (One company discovered that it had 18 different fares for the same run.) There is absolutely no way to know what will be available by the time you read this. In general, the lower the fare, the more limiting conditions there will be. "Supplemental" airlines make only major runs, sometimes use secondary airports (such as Newark and Oakland) and offer substantially lower fares than the bigger companies. *Capitol International Airways, World Airways,* and *Trans International Airlines* are three of these.

TIPPING. Basically, tipping is supposed to be personal, your way of expressing your appreciation of someone who has taken pleasure and pride in giving you attentive, efficient and understanding personal service. By and large, however, tipping has become a largely impersonal formula, and frequently an automatic demand. Standards of personal service are highly uneven here, so when you do in fact get genuinely good service feel secure in rewarding it, and when you feel that the service you get is slovenly, indifferent or surly, don't hesitate to show this by the size of your tip. Remember that in many places the help are paid very little and depend on tips for the better part of their income. This is supposed to give them the incentive to serve you well.

Although you will want to suit your tipping to the service you do in fact receive, here are some guidelines to follow. When in doubt, remember that the minimum tip for any service is 25¢, that 25¢ is the usual tip for miscellaneous small services, and that larger tips are rounded off to the nearest 5¢. In restaurants in this country the tips are not usually included in the bill but are decided by the guest and left on the table separately. Recently, in major resorts, tipping has become depersonalized to the point where guests receive printed lists of "suggestions" on how much to give. Such "suggestions" are rarely, if ever, too little. If you consider this impertinent, do not hesitate to say so. Some restaurants in major cities have also begun adding tips to checks—but you needn't feel obliged to pay them if the service has been subpar.

Many service people who may be tipped in other countries are *not* tipped here. These include: government employees, mailmen, airline personnel, store clerks, receptionists, bus drivers, elevator operators, gas station attendants, hotel clerks and managers, theater and movie ushers (although ushers at sports events may expect tips), and sightseeing guides at historical and artistic sites.

Restaurants: Waiters expect 15%; if the service is exceptional, leave 20%. Tip on the amount *before* taxes. Good captain service merits a dollar or two. In higher-priced places, the beverage waiter gets 15% of his separate bill. Coat checkers expect 25¢ per item in addition to the fixed house charge. Restroom attendants get 25¢. Tipping the maitre d' to get you a good table in a crowded place is officially discouraged, but it does happen, of course. Tipping at counters is not a universal practice, however many people do leave 25¢ on anything up to one dollar and 10% on bills over that. If you can find a cafeteria to eat in, of course you have saved 15% before you start.

Hotels and motels: For one-night stays in most hotels and motels you leave nothing. But if you stay longer, at the end of your stay leave the maid $1.25–1.50 per day or $7 per person per week for double occupancy or more. If the place is American Plan (meals included), leave your waiter or waitress either 15% of the bill or $1.50 per guest per day. If there have been various extra attendants (one for relishes, one for rolls, etc.) add a few extra dollars and give them to the captain or maitre d' when you leave, asking him to allocate the money.

For the many other services that you may encounter in a big hotel or resort, figure roughly as follows: doorman—25¢ to $1 for taxi handling, 50¢ to $1 for help with baggage; bellhop—50¢ per bag (or $1 per person or couple), more if you load him down with extras; parking attendant—50¢ to $1; bartender—15%; room service—10–15% of that bill; laundry or valet service—15%; pool attendant—50¢ per day; snackbar waiter at pool, beach or golf club—15% of the check; masseurs and masseuses—20%; locker attendant—50¢ per person per day, or $2.50 per week; golf caddies $2–3 per bag, or 15% of the greens fee for an 18-hole course, or $3 on a free course; barbers—15%; shoeshine attendants—50¢ to $1; hairdressers—15%; manicurists—$1.

Transportation: Give 25¢ for any taxi fare under $1 and 15% for any above; however, drivers in New York, Las Vegas and other major resort areas *expect* 20%. Limousine service—10%. Car rental agencies—nothing. Bus porters are tipped 25¢ per suitcase, drivers nothing. On charters and package tours, conductors and drivers usually get $5–10 per day from the group as a whole (but be sure to ask whether this has already been figured into the package cost). On short local sightseeing runs, the driver-guide may get 25¢ per person, more if you think he has been especially helpful or personable. Airport bus drivers—nothing. Redcaps—50¢ per suitcase. Tipping at curbside check-in is unofficial, but same as above. On the plane, no tipping.

Railroads suggest you leave 10–15% per meal for dining car waiters, but the steward who seats you is not tipped. Sleeping-car porters get about $1 per person per night. For a railway station baggage porter, 25–50¢ per bag depending on how heavy your luggage.

CREDIT CARD TRAVEL. There are three main types of credit card in this country. The general, or travel, shopping, and entertainment charge cards are issued by: *American Express Card Division,* 770 Broadway, New York, N.Y. 10003; *Carte Blanche,* P.O. Box 54116, Los Angeles, California 90054; and *Diners Club,* P.O. Box 5824, Denver, Colorado 80217. For one of these you pay a flat rate, about $35 per year, and interest charges, starting at 18% a year, apply only to certain types of purchase such as airline tickets and escorted tours if bills are not paid upon receipt. The principal bank cards are: *Visa* and *Mastercard;* these are issued through banks all over the country; inquire locally to see where they are available in your area. For these you pay a membership fee of about $15 to $20 in addition to a system of minimum monthly payments and of carrying charges or interest in excess of 18% a year. They are affiliated with many foreign banks, whose customers can use, for example, *Barclaycard* or *Sumitomo* card here. In addition, there are cards issued for more limited use, such as *Macy's, Montgomery Ward,* and *National Car Rental.*

To get either a charge or a credit card you will need to have a dependable job, a salary usually of at least $12,500 a year, and to furnish personal, family and financial information as well as personal references in order to establish your creditworthiness.

These cards have various advantages. Obviously they spare you the danger of carrying large amounts of cash, or even of Traveler's Checks, which can occasionally be awkward to cash without full identification. Cards can be used to draw extra funds in case of emergencies, or to take advantage of sales and special opportunities. For foreigners here, as for Americans abroad, charge cards can help to avoid losses due to unfavorable rates of exchange and commissions in hotels, restaurants and resorts or to the need to change large sums to pay small bills. For people traveling on expense accounts, or seeking tax deductions for business and professional expenses, they provide the records needed. They can make it easier to return unwanted merchandise to stores because the store simply makes out a credit slip to your card's account.

Despite these conveniences, there are various special restrictions and charges that apply in particular cases and which can raise your actual, final cost. Before you apply for a credit or a charge card, it is wise to talk with someone you know who has used one extensively and to obtain fully detailed information and examples of what your actual costs will turn out to be in every situation you can foresee. Another disadvantage is the loss you can incur if your credit card gets lost or stolen. Report this *immediately* to the company that issued it, or you may wind up paying for a spree for some complete stranger. Credit Card Service Bureau (P.O. Box 1322, Alexandria, Va. 22313) offers insurance coverage to all cards registered by its members and will notify all appropriate credit card companies for you if you report your cards stolen or missing.

WHEN TO GO. About 3,300 miles in length from Alaska to Texas and 2,900 in breadth from Maine to California, the United States covers over three and one-half million square miles and includes deserts, rivers, mountains, plains, forests, perpetual glaciers and tropical swamps, five inland seas and a great variety of climate, landscapes and resources. When you prefer to go will depend on what you like in the way of weather, sports, sightseeing, cultural events and local color. In this section we describe the advantages of the various seasons in each of the eight major regions. Be sure also to consult the sections on *Seasonal Events,* because America's pageants, fairs and festivals of every kind, from symphony and opera to corn-husking and pie-eating, should be an important part of your planning and enjoyment of this vast and varied country.

Every one of the 50 states maintains a tourist information office that provides free brochures, directories, and maps to help you plan your vacation. Because the amount of material is so great, you will get the best service if you follow four simple rules in making your request. First, be as specific as possible about your interests, season, and area. Second, inquire well in advance, and allow about one month for processing and mailing (3rd class) your reply. Third, make your request on a simple time-saving postcard. Fourth, be sure to give your return address.

Calendars of special events are usually published four times a year, by the seasons, so specify which one you want. Information on state-operated facilities such as parks and rest areas will usually be precise, objective, and reliable. Information on privately operated facilities such as hotels, motels, restaurants, camps, shops, theme parks, marinas, and "attractions" is usually promotional material put out by trade associations, and is of little help in judging quality.

If you call a toll-free 800 number, remember that outside of usual business hours you will probably get a general-information-type recorded announcement. Allow for differences in time zones, too, when calling.

NEW ENGLAND

New England attracts visitors all year round, with both downhill and cross-country skiing the lure in winter; a plethora of internationally acclaimed music, theater, and dance festivals in summer; spectacularly colorful fall foliage and a concurrent hunting season; and springs that are perfect for exploring the Appalachian Trail or other hiking and climbing paths. In recent years, the country-side of New England has come to be dotted with lovely, European-style country inns—some decorated with genuine European and American antiques and featuring *haute cuisine,* and others that are closer to what the English refer to as bed-and-breakfasts. The latter, generally called "guest houses," can usually be counted on for simple, clean accommodations even at the last minute on holiday weekends; the popularity of inns during high season (regardless of the time of year), however, makes advance reservations for weekends mandatory. The official summer season runs from July 4 to Labor Day when the coastal areas from Mystic, Connecticut, to Newport, Rhode Island, to Kennebunkport, Maine, are favorites for sunbathers, swimmers, sailers, fishers, and the like, while inlanders take part in the numerous cultural festivals that are to be found. Summer courses in the region's many excellent colleges and universities have also become a popular way to combine vacation, education, and local color with cutting expenses. For further information, write:

Connecticut: *Connecticut Department of Economic Development, Travel Director,* 210 Washington St., Hartford, Connecticut 06106, 800–243–1685.

Maine: *Maine Publicity Bureau,* 97 Winthrop St., Hallowell, ME 04347.

Massachusetts: *Massachusetts Department of Commerce and Development,* (Division of Tourism), 100 Cambridge St., Boston, Massachusetts 02202.

New Hampshire: *NH Office of Vacation Travel,* Box 856, State House Annex, Concord, NH 03301.

Rhode Island: *Rhode Island Department of Economic Development,* 7 Jackson Walkway, Providence, RI 02903.

Vermont: *Vermont Travel Division,* 61 Elm St., Montpelier, Vermont 05602.

NEW YORK

The unbelievably rich cultural life of New York City is probably unequaled anywhere else in the world, no matter the season. If time allows, though, you will want to keep in mind that the state of New York also has much to offer, and that while the Long Island beaches—from the Hamptons to Coney Island—represent one getaway on hot, muggy summer days, other alternatives include resort areas such as Lake George (popular in winter for skiing, as well) and Saratoga Springs. The latter remains popular among horse-racing enthusiasts but has increasingly drawn attention and crowds for its summer season of New York Philharmonic, City Ballet, and popular music concert series. Still other possibilities for peaceful retreat throughout the year are the Lake Placid–Saranac Lake part of the Adirondacks (scene of a recent winter Olympics), the Catskill mountain region in the central part of the state, and the Woodstock/New Paltz area (inhabited largely by artists, musicians, and writers) about 100 miles north of the city. Of course its natives insist that even the most humid of summer days on Manhattan Island are tolerable when visiting Central or Riverside Parks! Write:

New York: *New York Division of Tourism,* 99 Washington Ave., Albany, New York, 12245, 800–241–8444; in Canada, 1–800–268–7711.

New York City only: *New York City Convention and Visitors Bureau,* 2 Columbus Circle, New York, N.Y. 10019

MID-ATLANTIC STATES

In this region temperatures range from just below freezing, in the deep of winter, to the upper 80's in mid-summer. Humidity may be high in the river valleys and in the low-lying areas along the coast; Washington, the capital, is notorious for combining the disadvantages of both. Spring is spectacular in the mid-Atlantic region, with millions of blossoms bursting forth everywhere. Washington, in April, is as famous for its cherry trees as Tokyo or Kyoto. Azaleas, dogwood, camellias and apple blossoms follow each other through April and May. Summer can be enjoyable if you do as the local people do and slow down. It is in this region that you will first notice a very different pace to life from what you found in the North. The South really begins in Virginia, and you will begin to sense its different rhythm and flavor from Washington onward. Virginia has some good beaches and the scenic drives along the crests of the Appalachian mountains in the western part of the state are magnificent. In early spring and late fall county fairs attract visitors. Tourists and locals alike take advantage of the Farmers' Markets in Lancaster and Lebanon, Pennsylvania, year-round. The Christmas festivities in colonial Williamsburg, Va., and Bethlehem, Pa., are outstanding. There are winter sports in the Alleghenies and their foothills; and the region's colorful tobacco auctions go on year-round everywhere, especially in Virginia. For more precise information write to:

Delaware: *Delaware State Travel Service,* 630 State College Rd., Dover, Delaware 19901.

Maryland: *Maryland Office of Tourist Development,* 1748 Forest Drive, Annapolis, Maryland 21401, 800–248–5703 (outside Md.); 800–492–7126 (in Md. only).

New Jersey: *New Jersey Division of Travel & Tourism,* CN 384, Trenton, N.J. 08625.

Pennsylvania: *Pennsylvania Bureau of Travel Development,* Pennsylvania Department of Commerce, 415 South Office Building, Harrisburg, Penn. 17120.

Virginia: *Virginia State Travel Service, 6 N. 6th St., Richmond, Virginia 23219.*

District of Columbia: Washington Area Convention and Visitors Association, Suite 250, 1575 I St. NW, Washington, DC 20005.

West Virginia: *West Virginia Travel Development Division,* 1900 Washington St., Bldg. 6, Room B 564 State Capitol, Charleston, W. Va. 25305

THE SOUTH

Winter temperatures here average in the low 40's inland and in the 60's along the coast. Summer temperatures, modified by mountains in some places, by sea breezes in others, range from the high 70's to the mid 80's, with occasional low 90's; but because of the tempering effect of the Atlantic and Gulf breezes and the prevalence of air conditioning, summer is becoming increasingly popular with tourists who formerly thought of the South only as a winter resort. This is especially true of Florida. The inland heart of the region is the hills and mountains of the southern Appalachians; and in addition to their lakes and rivers, seven Southern states share a total of over 10,000 miles of salt water coastline, much of it in fine sandy beaches. The climate makes for lush, brilliant vegetation: Spanish moss, magnolia, roses, dogwood, iris, camellias, azalea, poinciana, poinsettia, orange blossoms and orchids in Florida, peach blossoms in Georgia. Fairs and festivals, art shows, parades and fiestas are mostly January to May and mid-September through October. For further information write to:

Alabama: *Alabama Bureau of Publicity and Information,* 532 South Perry St., Montgomery, Alabama 36130.

Arkansas: *Arkansas Department of Parks and Tourism,* 1 Capitol Mall, Little Rock, Arkansas 72201. 800–643–8383.

Florida: *Florida Division of Tourism,* Room 505, Collins Building, 107 W. Gaines St., Tallahassee, Florida 32304. 800–874–8660.

Georgia: *Georgia Tourist Division,* Georgia Bureau of Industry and Trade, P.O. Box 1776, Atlanta, Georgia 30301, 800–241–8444

Kentucky: *Kentucky Department of Tourism,* Capital Tower Plaza, 22nd floor, Frankfort, Kentucky 40601.

Louisiana: *Louisiana Office of Tourism, Inquiry Department,* P.O. Box 44291, Baton Rouge, Louisiana 70804.

Mississippi: *Mississippi Division of Tourism,* P.O. Box 849, Jackson, Mississippi 39205, 800–647–2290.

North Carolina: *North Carolina Travel & Tourism Division,* 430 N. Salisbury St., P.O. Box 25249, Raleigh, North Carolina 27611.

South Carolina: *South Carolina Tourism,* 1205 Pendleton St., Columbia, South Carolina 29201.

Tennessee: *Tennessee Tourist Development,* 601 Broadway, Nashville, Tennessee 37202.

MIDWEST

Late spring, summer and early fall are the best seasons in the Midwest, although winter provides ice skating, ice fishing, and more skiing than you might expect. In the north, mid-winter temperatures average in the 10-20 degree range, mid-20's in the central areas, and low to mid-30's in southern Illinois, Indiana and Ohio. Summer temperatures usually average in the mid-to-upper 70's, sometimes mid-to-upper 80's. However, every state in the Midwest (except Iowa) borders on at least one of the Great Lakes, and these waters do much to moderate summer heat and winter cold.

This is an agricultural region with a green-thumb population. In every city and town are gardens and parks that are proudly shown to visitors, and from mid-May through mid-July are flower festivals (tulip, lilac, rose, carnation, cherry, dogwood, magnolia, etc.), music, summer theater, showboats and colorful celebrations of the region's twenty or more ethnic groups. From mid-July to mid-September the calendar is solidly booked to state and county fairs, and then, in fall come the harvest and the foliage. Other festivals celebrate glass, pumpkins, turkey racing, bluegrass music and canal boats, to name only a few. The life of the Midwest is a panorama of genuine Americana that will delight foreigners and may well astonish Americans themselves who come from other parts of this country. For more specific information write to:

Illinois: *Travel Information,* 208 N. Michigan Ave., Chicago, Ill. 60601.

Indiana: *Indiana Tourism Development Division,* 440 N. Meridian St., Indianapolis, Indiana 46204.

Iowa: *Iowa Development Commission, Tourist Development Division,* 250 Jewett Bldg., Des Moines, Iowa 50309.

Michigan: *Michigan Travel Bureau,* 525 W. Ottawa, Lansing, Michigan 48933. 800-248-5703.

Minnesota: *Minnesota Tourist Information Center,* 480 Cedar Str., Hanover Bldg., St. Paul, Minnesota 55101, 800–652–9747 (Minnesota only) or 800-328-1461 (from out-of-state).

Ohio: *Travel Ohio,* P.O. Box 1001, Columbus, Ohio 43216, 800–282–5393 (Ohio only), 800–848–1300 (out of state).

Wisconsin: *Wisconsin Division of Tourism,* P.O. Box 7970, 123 N. Washington Ave., Madison, Wisconsin 53707. 800–362–9566 (Wisc. only) or 800-362-9566 (from Minnesota, Michigan, Iowa, and Illinois).

THE SOUTHWEST

This region, which runs from northern Missouri, with about the same latitude as Pittsburgh, to the southern tip of Texas, which is nearly parallel to Miami, has wide variations of temperature in all seasons. In general there is plenty of sunshine and low humidity except along the Gulf Coast. Arizona and New Mexico, though hot (up to 110–115°), are very dry, so 85° in St. Louis can seem worse than 105° in Tucson. Air conditioning is almost universal throughout the hotter parts of the region, especially in newer cities such as Houston and Phoenix. The biggest tourist season is late December through April, with February and March the peak months. Average temperatures in the winter months range from the mid-50's in the south to the 40's in the north. Summer highs are around 90 in the north to around 100 in the south (in June, July, August). However, anywhere away from the coastal plains, the summer nights can be chilly. For further information write to:

Arizona: *Arizona Office of Tourism,* 112 N. Central, Rm. 506, Phoenix, Arizona 85012.

Kansas: *Kansas Department of Economic Development,* 503 Kansas Ave., 6th floor, Topeka, Kansas 66603.

Missouri: *Missouri Division of Tourism,* P.O. Box 1055, Jefferson City, Missouri 65102, 800–392–0711 (Missouri only) or 800-325-0733 (out of state).

New Mexico: *New Mexico Travel Division,* Bataan Memorial Building, Santa Fe, New Mexico 87503, 800–545–2040.

Oklahoma: *Oklahoma Division of Tourism Promotion,* 500 Will Rogers Building, Oklahoma City, Oklahoma 73105.

Texas: *Texas Tourist Development Agency,* P.O. Box 12008 Capital Station, Austin, Texas 78711.

ROCKIES AND PLAINS

Running from Canada to New Mexico, this region naturally shows great variations in topography and temperature in all seasons. It can be 110° in the desert within clear sight of snow-covered mountains; but humidity is low and sunshine plentiful everywhere. Summer brings clear, hot days with temperatures ranging from the mid-80's in the north to around 100 in the south, with cool, often cold, nights. Winters average in the low 20's; spring and fall can go up to the high 80's. From Thanksgiving to mid-April there is some of the best skiing in the country in places like Aspen and Vail in Colorado and Alta and Snowbird in Utah. January and February are the best months for winter festivals, and June-July for rodeos and historical pageants. County and state fairs run from mid-July to early September and Nebraska has 61 in the single month of August. The region's cultural life in the sense of music, drama and the arts is largely concentrated in Kansas City, Denver, and the various university towns, and certain resorts in Colorado. For more specific information, write to:

Colorado: *Office of Tourism,* 500 State Centennial Building, 1313 Sherman St., Room 500, Denver, Colorado 80203.

Idaho: *Idaho Division of Tourism and Industrial Development,* Room 108, State Capitol Bldg., Boise, Idaho 83720.

Montana: *Montana Travel Promotion Unit,* Department of Commerce, 1424 Ninth Ave., Helena, Montana 59601, 800–548–3390.

Nebraska: *Nebraska Travel and Tourism Division,* P.O. Box 94666, 301 Centennial Mall South, Lincoln, Nebraska 68509.

North Dakota: *North Dakota Travel Division,* 1050 E. Interstate Ave., Bismarck, North Dakota 58505, 800–472–2100 (in state only), 800–437–2077 (out of state).

South Dakota: *South Dakota Division of Tourism,* 221 S. Central, Pierre, South Dakota 57501.

Utah: *Utah Travel Council,* Council Hall, State Capitol, Salt Lake City, Utah 84114.

Wyoming: *Wyoming Travel Commission,* Frank Norris Jr. Travel Center, Cheyenne, Wyoming 82002.

FAR WEST

With the cold Humboldt Current along its south coast and the warm Japan Current to the north, with America's highest, coldest mountains, thickest, wettest forests, and deepest, hottest, driest valleys, this region, stretching over 2,500 miles from north to south, has almost every natural and climatic condition you could ask for. In some places sea breezes can cause temperatures to vary up to 15 degrees in a single city. Southern California is in season all year-round as far as weather and tourism are concerned. January through March can be cold, windy and damp along the coast, so that is the season for skiing or hunting inland. California north of Sacramento is best in summer when temperatures range between 45 and 60 degrees. The state's mountains are always cool but its deserts, in the south, are usually too hot for even brief stays.

Oregon, Washington and Alaska are best in late spring, through summer and into early fall, though skiing is becoming more popular there. Nevada, largely desert, is best October through April. Southern Alaska and the coastal regions average 50 to 60 degrees in summer while inland valleys are cooler. The arctic north is hardly a tourist area yet. For more precise information write to:

Alaska: *Alaska Division of Tourism,* Pouch E, Juneau, Alaska 99811.

California: *California Office of Tourism,* 1030 13th St., Suite 200, Sacramento, California 95814.

Nevada: *State of Nevada Division of Tourism,* Department of Economic Development, 1100 East Williams, Carson City, Nevada 89701.

Oregon: *Oregon Travel Information Office,* Room 101A, Transportation Building, Salem, Oregon 97310.

Washington: *Washington Travel Information,* 312 1st Ave. N., Seattle, Washington 98109.

HAWAII

Hawaii is a land of perpetual spring, where the mean temperature fluctuates between 71 and 78 degrees from "winter" to "summer." Waikiki is the best-known area on the most popular island of Oahu, and it is the place for sunbathing among fellow travelers. The other islands offer a more tranquil vacation—on some you may never see other tourists—and can be reached via boat or helicopter. Write:

Hawaii Visitors Bureau, 2270 Kalakava Ave., Suite 801, Honolulu, Hawaii 96815.

 TIME ZONES. The continental United States is about 3,000 miles from east to west and stretches across four complete Time Zones: Eastern, Central, Mountain and Pacific. Alaska and Hawaii are separate cases, of course. Normally, this will cause no trouble. If you are driving, you will be able to adjust easily enough, an hour at a time, to local rhythms and conditions as you encounter them, and be annoyed only when a time zone cuts *through* a state, as in Kentucky, Tennessee, the Dakotas, Nebraska, Idaho, and bits of Kansas, Oregon and Texas. On long train trips you will have plenty of time to reset your watch and your mealtimes. Real inconvenience is likely only with plane schedules and long-distance phone calls.

 SEASONAL EVENTS. Even Americans themselves are likely to be astonished by the number, variety and exuberance of their festivals, fairs, contests, commemorations, parades and pageants, games, jubilees, days, weeks, weekends, celebrations, tournaments, tours, fiestas, shows, expositions, carnivals, frolics, races, derbies, rodeos, roundups, jamborees, "world" championships, sings, birthdays, bakes and homecomings. Surely there is much to be said for a country that can celebrate, among other things, cranberries, corn pone, swamp cabbage, chicken plucking, egg striking, dragon boats, Mozart, and the Holy Ghost.

There is no day in the year that does not have something going on, and hardly any inhabited place however small that has not found something to celebrate, exalt or commemorate, from favorite sons like *Jonathan Hager* (Hagerstown, Md., in mid-July) to local products like *apple butter* (Burton, Ohio, in mid-October), to remarkable attainments like *Watermelon Seed Spitting* (Paul's Valley, Okla., in late June). Apart from the major and legitimate holidays, there is a vast range of politically and commercially motivated non-events of the National-Eat-More-Kumquats-Week variety that can be largely ignored except when they reach such heights of inspired inadvertence as the simultaneous proclamations of National Music Week and National Noise Abatement Week.

"**Culture**" in the usual sense of music, dance, drama, painting, sculpture and literature is generally more abundant in the larger cities, and the opera, ballet, concert and gallery "seasons" in the major American cities are Fall, Winter and Spring just as they are in London, Paris, Stockholm or Tokyo. However, there is no American city of any size that has not by now a summer season as well, from the world-famous Boston Pops concerts, and Shakespeare in New York's Central Park, through al fresco symphony, opera, recitals, dance, light opera, musicals and "shows" in St. Louis, Cleveland, Miami, Chicago, Jacobs Pillow (Massachusetts), Marlboro (Vermont), Center Harbor (New Hampshire), Glens Falls (New York), and Lake Maxinkuckee (Indiana), to name only a few.

Much of this decentralized activity tends to center around resorts and college towns, but the fact that there are over 2,000 colleges and universities in the United States simply serves to indicate the vigor, abundance, and healthy distribution of the country's cultural and artistic life. Thus, New Hampshire's *Music Festival* (July-August) takes place in the heart of the state's Lakes Region with its many summer resort towns. Elsewhere, in late August and early September, the members of the *Society for Creative Anachronism* gather at the Snoqualmie Falls Forest Theater in Bellevue, Washington, to perform music, dances and sports of the 15th and 16th centuries in their *Renaissance Faire.* Some of the world's finest and most innovative *opera* is found in Santa Fe, New Mexico, some of America's best *theater* in Minneapolis, Minnesota. At this point, distinctions of amateur and professional erode completely, for most of the country's local performing arts groups combine people from all walks of life, local and imported, to produce remarkably sophisticated activity in quite unexpected places.

Festivals based on local and indigenous culture range all the way from painstaking preservations of aristocratic historical traditions like the *fox hunts, candlelight concerts* and *madrigal singing* of Virginia, through the various authentic *American Indian ceremonials,* to *historical pageants* like North Carolina's *Lost Colony of Roanoke.* There are expositions of rare and *historic handicrafts* and *traditional skills* like carding, dyeing, spinning, weaving and quiltmaking; *popular arts* like ballad singing, fiddling and folk dancing; *work skills* like log-rolling, steer roping, cabinet making, glass blowing and bread baking.

Many festivals celebrate very directly the local economy—*corn and rhubarb* in South Dakota, *maple syrup* in Vermont and Michigan, *tobacco* in Kentucky, *chicken* in Delaware, *oysters, cotton* and *rice* in Louisiana.

Sports. The range of events available includes not only football, skiing, yachting and other such familiar sights but also: wild cow milking (Colorado), chicken plucking (Florida), greased pig wrestling (Maryland, South Carolina), baseball on snowshoes (Minnesota), soccer played with firehoses (Washington), husband-calling (Tennessee), and fox-horn blowing (Virginia). There is *horse racing,* of course, but Americans also race king crabs in Alaska, terrapins in Arizona, shrimp boats in Florida, tricycles and bathtubs in Washington, wash tubs in South Carolina, sled dogs in New Hampshire, and lawn mowers in Indiana. As well as turkeys and canal boats. Frog jumping contests are held in Louisiana, Ohio, South Carolina and California. Ohio accepts contestants from foreign countries, and South Carolina's winning frog gets a free trip to California to compete for the national championship. The *National Cow Chip Throwing Contest* is held at Beaver, Oklahoma, in April, and politicians are given a special welcome. Other contests include hollerin', Easter egg fights, rolling pin throwing, and luring worms. Of particular interest in 1984 are the *Summer Olympics,* to be held in Los Angeles, July 28–August 12.

Fairs. Seriously, however, one of the finest ways to see a basic America that has held fast through all the changes of recent years is to attend some of the innumerable town, county and state fairs. Some of them, like the one in Reno, Nevada, with everyone wearing silk cowboy shirts on pain of paying a fine, are transparently commercial gimmicks; others, like the one in the little town of Lee, New Hampshire, in September, are unpretentious, totally genuine, and totally enjoyable. These fairs take place mostly in summer and fall, beginning, in the South and West, in July with rodeos and going on as late as November (in Arizona). The *Iowa State Fair* in mid-August, the *Eastern States Exposition* in Massachusetts in mid-September, and the *Texas State Fair* in mid-October are among the most notable. There are at least a few in every state in the country, and they are particularly numerous in the mid-West. The *Louisiana World's Fair* will be held in New Orleans, May 12–November 11, 1984.

Flower and foliage festivals are particularly popular through the mid-Atlantic and mid-West regions and include: tulip, rose, lilac, carnation, cherry, dogwood, magnolia, rhododendron, apple, daffodil and golden raintree, among others. Foliage viewing is, of course, for autumn, and is outstanding in New England and the Adirondacks, the second weekend in October usually being the best.

Ethnic festivals. Still another kind of festival celebrates the many ethnic strains that have contributed to this country's development, beginning with the American Indians and going on to Blacks, Asians and almost every country of Europe. In New York City, the Italian, Irish, Jewish, Puerto Rican and Chinese festivals are important. Through the mid-West are celebrations for Germans, Swedes, Swiss, Danes, Norwegians, Italians, Czechs, Poles, Slovaks, Ukrainians, Scots, Irish, and even Arabs (in Detroit). These festivals invariably feature local and ethnic cooking and sometimes the proportions of this can become awe-inspiring. Louisiana's late-October *Gumbo Festival* features a 4,000-gallon gumbo pot, and Ohio's mid-October *Circleville Pumpkin Show* features the largest Pumpkin Pie Ever Baked—over 260 lbs.

It is, in the last analysis, almost impossible to find any generalizations that can cover such variety and ingenuity. Every region, every season, every occasion, every product or activity imaginable—and then some—is likely to have its own festival somewhere in this country. Almost the only thing you can do is decide when you can travel, where you want to go, and then begin to check into what will be going on there then. In addition to the events listed state-by-state and interest-by-interest throughout this book, the various state tourist offices and local chambers of commerce are goldmines of information not only fascinating but sometimes overwhelming. For the months of June, July and August alone, Vermont, 43rd in size and 48th in population among the 50 states, lists over 450 events and attractions in a 32-page booklet that opens with the modest disclaimer, "Many Vermont events are not listed because information was not final at our printing deadline." (sic!) And a nationwide directory listing several thousand events is *Mort's Guide to Festivals, Feasts, Fairs and Fiestas,* published by Mort Barrish Associates, Inc., Research Park, State Rd., Princeton, N.J. 08540.

 HOLIDAYS AND BANK CLOSINGS. There are five major national holidays that are observed in all the 50 states. They are: *New Year's Day*—January 1; *Independence Day*—July 4; *Labor Day*—the first Monday in September; *Thanksgiving Day*—the fourth Thursday in November; and *Christmas Day*—December 25. The Congress, in the Uniform National Holiday legislation of 1971, arranged that national holidays falling on a Sunday should be observed on the following day, and that various others should in any case be observed on Mondays in order to provide the country with a number of three-day weekends.

Thus, in addition to the above, there are: *Washington's Birthday*—the third Monday in February; *Memorial Day*—the last Monday in May (not observed in Alabama and South Carolina); *Columbus Day*—the second Monday in October (not observed in Alaska, Iowa, Maine, Mississippi, Nevada, Oregon and South Carolina); and *Veteran's Day*—the fourth Monday in October (observed as Armistice Day on November 11 in 16 states).

Lincoln's Birthday is celebrated on February 12 in 23 states, on February 3 in Delaware and Oregon, and is not observed in the remaining 25 states. *Robert E. Lee's Birthday* is observed on January 19 or 20 in 11 Southern states; and *Confederate Memorial Day* comes in late April or early May in seven Southern states.

There are also various holidays that have a particular impact in certain areas. The *Jewish High Holy Days* of Rosh Hashanah and Yom Kippur, which usually fall in September, are important in New York City. Similarly, *Saint Patrick's Day,* March 17, is enthusiastically celebrated in Boston, and in New York City as well. New Orleans is world-famous for its *Mardi Gras* in February or March, and Louisiana celebrates *All Saints Day* on November 1. In Suffolk County, Massachusetts, March 17 is *Evacuation Day*. And so on.

Bank hours are usually 9 A.M. to 2 or 3 P.M., Monday through Friday. Some banks stay open one evening each week and a few are open on Saturdays. Many have also installed automated 24-hour "tellers"—computers able to accept deposits or give cash provided you have an account with that bank. Banks in particular regions close for local or regional holidays; and *all* banks close on: *New Year's Day, Lincoln's Birthday, Memorial Day, Independence Day, Labor Day, Columbus Day, Election Day* (which falls in the first week of November in even-numbered years), *Armistice Day, Thanksgiving Day,* and *Christmas Day.*

PLANNING YOUR TRIP. In the *Practical Information* sections for each of the separate states you will find detailed sources for information on general tourism, national and state parks, tours, gardens, festivals, sports, museums, historic sites and monuments, and much more.

If you would rather not bother making reservations on your own, a travel agent can be of help in suggesting vacation possibilities you hadn't thought of, for finding package tours that can save you time, money and planning, and for deciphering the increasingly volatile and complex fare structures of the nation's carriers.

"Package tours" usually touch upon a variety of important places, point out selected restaurants, offer tour guides, and present the possibility of meeting other people in the group for an all-inclusive rate. Tours of the fly/drive variety also are quite popular since they offer the "do-it-yourself" opportunity.

If you don't belong to an auto club, now is the time to join one. They can be very helpful about routings and offering emergency service on the road. The *American Automobile Association* (AAA), in addition to its information services, has a nationwide network of some 26,000 service stations which provide emergency repair service. Its offices are at 8111 Gatehouse Rd., Falls Church, Va. 20042. The *Exxon Touring Service,* 4550 Decoma, Houston, Texas 77092, provides information, low cost insurance, and some legal service. The *National Travel Club,* 51 Atlantic Ave., Travel Building, Floral Park, N.Y. 11001, offers information, insurance, and tours. If you plan the route yourself, make certain the map you get is dated for the current year. Some of the major oil companies will send maps and mark preferred routes on them if you tell them what you have in mind. Try: *Exxon Touring Service,* 1251 Avenue of the Americas, New York, N.Y. 10020 or 4550 Decoma, Houston, Texas 77092; *ARCO Travel Service,* P.O. Box 93, Versailles, Ky. 40383; *Texaco Travel Service,* P.O. Box 1459, Houston, Texas 77001; or *Mobil Travel Service,* P.O. Box 25, Versailles, Ky. 40383. The *AMOCO Motor Club* is at 1 North Charles St., Baltimore, Md. 21201. In addition, most states have their own maps, which pinpoint attractions, list historical sites, parks, etc. The addresses of the various state tourist information services have already been given above. City chambers of commerce and the convention and visitors bureaus also are good sources of information. Specific addresses are given under *Tourist Information* in the individual state chapters.

The tradition of free road maps at gasoline stations has almost totally disappeared in the U.S. today. Only Exxon provides them to any extent now. When you do find them there is usually a charge of at least 75¢. The alternative is, of course, a road atlas, purchased at a bookstore, and costing anywhere from $1.50 to $6.00. There are three major ones published in this country now: by Rand McNally, by Grossett, and by Hammond. Rand McNally also publishes a "Standard Reference Map and Guide" for each state individually. The Hagstrom Company is the country's leading publisher of city street maps.

Plan to board your pets, discontinue paper and milk deliveries, and tell your local police and fire departments when you'll be leaving, when you expect to return. Ask a kindly neighbor to keep an eye on your house or apartment; fully protect your swimming pool against intruders. Have a neighbor keep your mail, or have it held at the post office. Consider having your telephone temporarily disconnected if you plan to be away more than a few weeks. Empty your refrigerator and turn it off, turn off the hot water, and turn the thermostat down according to the weather. Look into the purchase of trip insurance (including baggage), and make certain your auto, fire, and other policies are up to date. Convert the greater portion of your trip money into travelers' checks. Arrange to have your lawn mowed at the usual times, and leave that kindly neighbor your itinerary (insofar as possible), car license number, and a key to your home (and tell police and firemen he has it).

TRAVEL AGENTS. The *American Society of Travel Agents, Inc. (ASTA)* is the world's largest professional travel trade association, composed of all elements of the travel business. ASTA was established in New York in 1931 to promote travel, to prevent unethical practices, and to provide a public forum for travel agents. It is the duty of every ASTA member agency to protect the public against any fraud, misrepresentation, or unethical practices. To avoid being victimized by fly-by-night operators who might claim better bargains, look for the ASTA member shield—the hallmark of dependable travel service. You'll find the shield on entrance doors, windows, and all office forms of the member agency you select.

ASTA membership indicates that the agent has been in business for a number of years—a minimum of three consecutive years is required—and is officially approved by the Society to sell tickets on behalf of airlines and cruise ships. ASTA agents also will arrange bookings for trains, buses, or car rentals. For further information write ASTA, 4400 McArthur Blvd. NW, Washington, DC 20007.

The best feature of the travel agent's role is that he does all your arranging, leaving you free to use your precious time elsewhere. But what should not be overlooked is his value in suggesting tailor-made vacations. Experienced agents have seen many tourist attractions firsthand and can suggest the best places for you—your purse, your age, your needs, and your desires. It is in the agent's best interest to help you avoid the problems or complexities of traveling.

For all this service, the travel agent does not charge you a fee. His fee is collected from the transportation carriers and hotels as a commission for promoting and making the sale. Your only charge might be for extra phone calls, cables, or other special services. On package tours and groups, the agent's and organizer's services are included in the total price. If an agent has to arrange a complex itinerary and perform myriad services, he may charge you, and you should discuss his charges in advance.

PACKING. What to take, what to wear. Don't try to pack at the last moment. Instead, begin in advance and make a list of things each member of the family will need; then check off the items as you pack them. You'll find it saves time and reduces confusion.

Be wise about packing. Regardless of how you plan to travel, it is less confusing to travel light—and less expensive, too. Check the climate and dress standards along your route and select clothes accordingly, sticking to the basic styles and colors which can be interchanged to create different outfits.

If you wear prescription glasses or contacts always take an extra pair or set; at the very least have a copy of your prescription. This is true of prescription sunglasses, too. A travel iron often comes in handy as do plastic bags (large and small) for wet suits, socks, etc. They are also excellent for packing shoes, spillable cosmetics, and other easily damaged items.

All members of the family should have sturdy shoes with nonslip soles. Keep them handy in the back of the car. You never know when you may want to stop and clamber along a rocky trail. Carry rain gear in a separate bag in the back of the car (so no one will have to get out and hunt for it in the middle of a downpour).

If you're stopping en route, you'll find it's convenient to pack separately those few things you'll need for just an overnight stay. If saves unloading the entire car, only to reload it the next morning.

Women will probably want to stick to one or two basic colors for their wardrobes so that they can manage with one set of accessories. If possible, include one knit or jersey dress or pants suit. The general consensus among well-traveled women is that a full-skirted traveling dress will show less wear and wrinkling. For dress-up, take along a couple of "basic" dresses you can vary with a simple change of accessories. That way you can dress up or down to suit the occasion.

Men will probably want a jacket along for dining out, and include a dress shirt and tie for the most formal occasions. Many restaurants in large cities, most hotels and resorts, and many motels require skirts for women and jackets and ties for men, especially for dinner. Don't forget extra slacks.

Apart from these general considerations, when you put together your traveling wardrobe you need to take the temperature and weather of the region you're traveling into account. Light, loose-fitting clothing is best for really hot areas. And if you're planning a lot of time in the sun, don't forget something sufficiently cover-up to wear over swimsuits en route to the pool, beach, or lakefront, and for those few days when you're getting reacquainted with sun on tender skin. For the cold and snow, you'll want a very warm coat, gloves, hat, scarf or muffler, and even galoshes. A slicker or an umbrella is a must.

INSURANCE. In planning your trip, think about three kinds of insurance: *property, medical,* and *automobile.* The best person to consult about insuring your household furnishings and personal property while you are away is your insurance agent. For Americans, he is also the person to consult about whatever special adjustments might be advisable in your medical coverage while traveling. Foreigners visiting the United States should bear in mind that medical expenses in this country may seem astronomical by comparison with those they are accustomed to at home, and that the kind of protection that some countries (Britain, for example) extend to their own nationals and foreigners alike does not exist here.

Every state has some sort of Financial Responsibility law establishing the minimum and maximum amounts for which you can be held liable in auto accidents. Most states require insurance to be offered, and 17 states require you to have it in order to register a car or get a license within their jurisdictions. In any case, it is almost essential to have at least third party coverage, or "liability insurance," as claims can run very high both for car repairs and particularly for medical treatment. Insurance premiums vary according to place and person; they are generally highest for males under 25, and for drivers who live in large urban areas.

One possibility is the *American Automobile Association* (AAA), which offers both group personal accident insurance (from $2,500 to $3,750) and bail bond protection up to $5,000 as part of its annual membership (fee $35). The AAA can also arrange the validation of foreign driving permits for use in the United States. Foreigners should consider getting their insurance before leaving their own countries since short-term tourists will find it difficult and expensive to buy here. For the AAA, write to *AAA,* 28 E. 78th St., New York City, N.Y. 10021; or *AAA,* 8111 Gatehouse Rd., Falls Church, Va. 20042. Travel insurance is also offered by the *Exxon Travel Club,* 4550 Decoma, Houston, Texas 77092; and by the *National Travel Club,* Travel Building, Floral Park, N.Y. 11001.

If you are over 50, write to the American Association of Retired Persons/ AIM, P.O. Box 2400, Long Beach, Calif. 90801 for information about its auto insurance recommendations and other travel services.

AMERICA BY CAR. The first precaution you should take is to have your car thoroughly checked by your regular dealer or service station to make sure that everything is in good shape. The *National Institute for Automotive Service Excellence,* which tests and certifies the competence of auto mechanics, publishes a directory of about 10,000 repair shops all over the U.S. which employ certified mechanics. It is available from *NIASE,* Suite 515, 1825 K Street N.W., Washington, D.C. 20006.

If you don't have a car of your own, there are a number of companies from which you can rent one. Perhaps it would be wise to first check the data of major companies individually, such as *Hertz*, 800–654–3131; *Avis*, 800–331–1212; *National*, 800–328–4567; *Dollar*, 800–421–6868; *Thrifty*, 800–331–4200; or *Budget*, 800–527–0700. Those telephone numbers are toll free for 24-hour information and rental service.

Most companies require a minimum age of 25, but under certain conditions will rent to a lower age group, usually not lower than 21.

Most companies also will honor certain major charge cards in lieu of a cash deposit. If cash is the means of deposit and payment, an advance cash deposit computed on the basis of the estimated rental charge is payable at the time of the rental. In addition, it is usually required for cash transactions that you fill out an application for verification by the rental company, which can be difficult after regular business hours and during weekends.

Be sure to check into the rent-it-here/leave-it-there information which allows you to rent the car in one place and drop it off at any other company location in the United States for a modest drop-off charge. Also check into special rates offered for different categories of cars, for weekends, holidays and extended trips. Rates and conditions can vary enormously; this is one area in which comparison shopping will pay off. In New York City, for example, it is cheaper to rent at the airport than in Manhattan—but chances are you won't want to have an automobile in Manhattan anyway.

Car rental companies generally charge a per day fee for insurance coverage. You should check the company of your choice for specifics, and if you're planning to rent for an extended period, whether it might not be more advantageous to purchase similar coverage independently. Here again, the services of a travel agent can save you time, money, and trouble.

In most cases, a valid driver's license issued by any state or possession of the United States; by any province of Canada; or by any country which ratified the 1949 Geneva Motoring Convention, is valid and is required to rent a car.

By Federal law, 55 mph is now the maximum speed limit. If the wide-open spaces of the nation's highways tempt you to go faster—don't. Not only will you save gas by observing the speed limit, you also may save your life. Government studies have shown a substantial drop in the number of highway deaths, directly attributable to the lowered speed limit. All the states use sophisticated speed detection devices, including radar and aircraft. So watch your speedometer!

Beware of the danger of highway hypnosis, especially prevalent on roads which stretch for miles without a break. Highway hypnosis results from steady driving over long distances at set speeds. Principal symptoms are drowsiness and the inability to concentrate on what you're doing. The cure: vary your speed occasionally, stop to stretch your legs, have a cup of coffee or tea, take a little exercise, take a brief nap.

There are four cross-country Interstate routes that bear the same number for their entire length: I-10 from Jacksonville, Florida to Santa Monica, California; I-40 from Greensboro, North Carolina to Barstow, California; I-80 from the George Washington Bridge, New Jersey, to San Francisco, California; and I-90 from Boston, Massachusetts to Seattle, Washington.

Except for terrain differences on the east coast, west coast, and mid-section of the country, driving conditions are basically the same. The major highways in the northeast section of the country are well-designed with frequent rest stops and gas stations. You'll soon learn that driving in the east can offer the same wide variety—albeit of a different kind—as driving in the west. You will encounter more than double the number of postings for speed limits for special conditions than you find elsewhere. Unmarked side roads should be inquired about or explored on foot if at all; they may be private or long out of use, hence unfit for modern autos.

In the South you will find, along with somewhat different scenery, the same sort of long, lonely stretches of straightaway as those in the central, west and southwest sections. There will be considerably more variety, however, to keep you alert, with gradual curves, for example, stretching for half a mile or more.

The Rockies and Plains provide a wide variety of scenery: the country of the Badlands of North and South Dakota, the mule-riding country of the Grand Canyon, the country of towering mountains interspersed with the broad flat spaces of the Plains—an area where the motorist can have virtually any driving experience he cares to meet.

Unless you venture onto exotic mountain roads, you should have little trouble with mountain driving. Today's mountain roads are engineered for the ordinary driver. They are normally wide, well graded, and safe. Be especially wary of exceeding the speed limits posted for curves. Keep to the right. If your normal driving is at low altitudes, have a garage mechanic check your carburetor. It may need adjusting for mountain driving. Use your motor for downhill runs—second or low gear—to save your brakes. If your car stalls, and your temperature gauge is high, it could mean a vapor lock. Bathe the fuel pump with a damp cloth for a few minutes.

California, with a motor vehicle registration of 16 million, easily outranks its two closest contenders, New York with 8 million registrations and Texas, with 10 million license plates. When you park in San Francisco, turn your wheels to the curb. If you park downhill, turn your steering wheel to the right to put your tires into the curb. If you park uphill, do the opposite. Turning your wheels to the curb in hilly San Francisco is the law, even on level stretches, because runaway automobiles have been a problem, and it's hard to tell where the hills end and the level stretches begin.

You will encounter stretches of desert driving in the Pacific states. The principal check before crossing the hot desert should be your tires. Put them at normal driving pressure or slightly below. Heat builds pressure. If your car seems to be bouncing too readily, stop to let your tires cool. If you have a good radiator, don't bother about extra water—except for Death Valley—but keep an eye on the water gauge. Be alert for sudden sandstorms and rainstorms. If you have a car radio, keep it tuned to local stations for information about unusual weather conditions. In spite of its dryness, there are occasionally deadly flash floods in the desert.

If you get stuck on any kind of road, pull off the highway onto the shoulder, raise the hood, attach something white (a handkerchief, scarf, or some other white cloth) to the door handle on the driver's side of the car, and sit inside and wait for help. This is especially effective on limited-access highways, diligently patrolled by state highway officers. A special warning to women stalled at night: Remain inside the car with doors locked, and make sure the Good Samaritan who approaches you is indeed a Good Samaritan. If you are a member of an automobile club and have access to a telphone, call the nearest garage listed in your service directory—or ask the operator for help. But by all means don't get out of your car and start walking along the highway looking for help. This is (a) dangerous and (b) illegal in some states.

TRAFFIC SIGNS AND ROAD MARKINGS. Since 1970, the United States has been moving more and more toward internationally accepted markings on road signs. This applies especially to the signs you most need to watch out for—those that get you in trouble when you miss them.

So, for "no left turn," or "no trucks," and other such prohibitions, you'll see the internationally familiar shapes and colors—the white background, black symbol, and the red circle with the diagonal slash. Usually, the prohibition symbolized on the sign will be repeated in words on a small sign just beneath it. You will sometimes find them as the only sign, without the accompanying international signal, in parts of the country that haven't caught up to the most modern standards yet.

America has adopted two other international regulatory signs, those for "yield" and "do not enter." The first is the inverted triangle with the red border. The second is a red circle with a white bar in the middle. America puts the words "do not enter" on the latter, unlike most other countries. One other regulatory sign is a yellow pennant, or sideways triangle, with the words "no passing zone." It marks the beginning of an area where you are not allowed to pass, and is located on the left hand side of the road.

American road signs are color-coded. Briefly: warnings are yellow; directions are green; recreational features are often brown; services are blue; construction sites are orange. Now, in more detail, warning signs—upcoming pedestrian crossings and traffic lights, slippery spots, low bridges, etc.—are yellow diamonds with black markings or symbols. Below these signs, the message is given in words, on a smaller, rectangular sign. Again, learn to read them, and look out for the old-fashioned yellow triangles with just words, no symbols. There are still quite a few around.

The only warning sign that departs from the shape mentioned above is that for a school crossing. The new sign is yellow, but instead of diamond-shaped, it is a pentagon with the point up—sort of the shape of a small house. Inside the sign are stick figures symbolizing children with school books.

Many of the symbolic shapes used in warning signs will be familiar to the international traveler. A rear view of a car with wiggly lines means "slippery when wet." A black triangle with a vehicle, usually a truck, going down one side means "hill." The pedestrian crossing is a stick figure walking between parallel lines.

When you begin to wonder if you are going in the right direction, or where you should turn to get someplace, start looking for a sign with a green background. They give directions. Green signs with exit numbers will help you off the highway by telling you the main towns and routes served by the upcoming exit, and how far away they are. Mileage markers alongside the road are green, too. Knowing that you are at mile 44 may help you in trip-planning. There are also green directional signs pointing to biking and hiking trails.

One special sign falls in this group. It has a brown background and gives information about routes to public parks and recreation areas. So, if you're looking for one of those, look for brown signs.

Signs telling you where to find services such as hospitals, restaurants, motels, telephones, and camping areas are blue. They have recognizable symbols for the service indicated, plus directional arrows, and often a word sign as well.

The color which tells you of road construction is orange. That includes detour signs, and orange striped barriers, and often the words "road construction 1500 feet."

As for pavement markings, the main thing to remember is never cross a solid line on your side of the road. If you see a dotted line on your side and a solid line beyond it, you may pass.

Here's a word of warning: In some foreign countries, it is the practice to pay the policeman the fine on the spot. *In America that is not done.* An attempt to do so can be misinterpreted as an attempt to bribe the police officer, and that can mean big trouble. In order to know what is the right thing to do, ask the policeman. Another source of information is the ticket itself. They almost always have instructions on the back.

 FLY/DRIVE VACATIONS. Among the many ways you can travel, the fly/drive package offers a bit more, or perhaps a different way, to satisfy a deeper curiosity. Most airlines, in conjunction with car rental companies, offer these combination opportunities to most parts of the country all year round. Fly/drive package rates and flexibilities vary considerably from one to another. Generally, they cover one or more cities plus the use of a rented car for the specified number of days.

Car usage also varies from one to another. For example, with some you can drive an unlimited number of miles, free. On others you get a specified amount of mileage free, and then must pay an additional charge per mile for the overage. Gas, generally, is not included.

Some packages offer plans for small groups and a choice of hotel accommodations. Some even offer motor homes, if you're interested in roughing it. Check into special children's rates.

Before booking, though, you should check with your agent about where you pick up the car (at airport or other station), and about the time it will take you to arrive at your hotel to meet your reservation. If you are not going to pick up the car at the airport, you should check ahead on airport limousines and bus and taxi service to your hotel. These are important details that should be included in or provided for by any good package-tour combination.

If you decide to fly to the destination and not drive while there, check into the substitutions some companies make with bus tours, rail tours, local sightseeing excursions, admissions to theme parks, museums, zoos, amusement parks, sports events, curiosities and "attractions," etc. There may be a number of such substitutions and fringe benefits in your package.

 AMERICA BY PLANE. A network of thousands of airline flights a day makes America only five and a half hours wide and two hours from top to bottom. Even with the limited time most vacations allow, you can see a lot of this country by flying from place to place.

Here are some typical distances and times to help you plan your travel in the United States: The distance from Boston, Massachusetts in the northeast of the country to Los Angeles, California on the West Coast is 2,600 miles. Flying time is about five and a half hours. From Chicago, Illinois in the north to New Orleans, Louisiana in the south is 837 miles. Flying time is two hours. Miami, Florida is a long way from Seattle, Washington—2,934 miles, but it takes only eight hours to fly. From the West Coast to Honolulu takes about five and a half hours, to Anchorage, Alaska, about four and a half. To Puerto Rico from Washington, D.C., expect to fly for three and a half hours.

Ten airlines link the major United States cities. These are called *trunk lines.* They are *American, Continental, Delta, Eastern, National, Northwest Orient, Trans World (TWA), United* and *Western.* However, deregulation has opened the air ways to literally dozens of other lines, many of which had formerly been limited to regional runs. Among the latter are *USAir,* in the Northeast; *Ozark,* mostly the central section, plus New York and Washington, D.C.; *Frontier,* midwest and west except the west coast; *Piedmont,* middle east, north to New York; *North Central,* Ohio to Kansas and points north; *Southern,* the southeast; *Texas International,* the southwest and Mexico.

Information on connecting flights between trunk and regional airlines is available from any of the airlines or your travel agent.

Once you get to Alaska, *Alaska Airlines, Wien Air Alaska,* a dozen commuter airlines, and a hundred "air taxis" help you get around—to almost anywhere in the state. Look at a map and see how big Alaska is, and you'll really appreciate the need for these flights.

You don't have to stay on the American Continent to stay in America. Try Hawaii, Puerto Rico, or the Virgin Islands.

To get to Hawaii from the mainland there are 8 airlines: *American, Canadian Pacific, Continental, Northwest Orient, Pan American, United* and *Western.* Within the island state, two carriers give regularly scheduled service: *Aloha Airlines* and *Hawaiian Airlines.* In addition, there are a number of commuter/air-taxi services, such as *Brandt, Island Pacific, OK, Air Ananda, Royal Hawaiian Air Service,* and others.

Pan American will get you to Hawaii (among other carriers), as well as to Guam and American Samoa. *Eastern Airlines* Caribbean service out of Miami, Florida will take you to the Virgin Islands.

Three major cities have time-saving helicopter flights to beat the heavy road traffic when you're in a rush.

In New York, *New York Airways* ties together LaGuardia and Kennedy Airports with Newark and two smaller airports in New Jersey, Morristown and Teterboro. *Chicago Helicopter Airways* links downtown to Midway and O'Hare International Airport weekdays, and provides a charter service. *SFO Helicopter Airlines* serves San Francisco International Airport, Oakland International Airport, Berkeley and Marin County.

Helicopter flights may be the fastest way to get around, but aren't the cheapest—unless they can be included as a connecting flight on your regular ticket. This is often the case. Check with your ticket agent. You may even fly free.

For getting to even more out-of-the-way places quickly, you can choose from more than 200 commuter airlines. They fly scheduled flights, mostly in two engine planes carrying four to 19 passengers. The more than 2,500 air taxi firms in America do not have regular schedules, but will fly you between any two points on a charter, contract, or demand basis. They'll even get you to hidden lakes in the woods you can't reach any other way.

Two classes of service, first class and coach, are the most commonly found. As in the rest of the world, first class is more spacious, meals more elaborate, drinks are free. Coach is the standard service. Meals are served at appropriate times. You pay for your drinks. This is comparable to the economy class on international flights.

A third type of fare seen recently on some airlines to some destinations is economy class. You sit in the same cabin as coach passengers, but you don't get food or beverages. So, bring your lunch. Still others offer business class (usually under a trade name) in which services fall somewhere between first and coach for a modestly higher-than-coach fare.

We note here: Major international credit cards are generally accepted by airlines. Best to check ahead, though.

Baggage allowances are now computed by size rather than weight. You may carry with you one piece of baggage no more than 9" high (so that it can fit underneath the seat ahead of you) and you may check through free one large piece where height, length, and width together total no more than 65", and one medium piece where dimensions total no more than 55".

Remember, also, to identify all your bags by firmly affixing your name to the outside and inside. The airlines will not accept them for checking otherwise. Name tags ensure a faster tracing of misdirected luggage. They also avoid the possibility of picking up someone else's bag.

AMERICA BY TRAIN. *Amtrak* is the semi-governmental corporation that has taken over passenger service on most of the nation's railroads. At present the system has some 26,000 miles of track linking over 500 cities and towns in 44 states (except Maine, New Hampshire, Oklahoma, South Dakota, Alaska, and Hawaii) and since mid-1979, under the pressure of soaring gasoline prices the number of passengers carried has risen sharply. Amtrak's equipment, at best, is among the most modern and comfortable anywhere in the world; not all of the equipment is up to this standard, however; and the condition of the tracks and the adequacy of the auxiliary services (stations, meals, punctuality, etc.) is highly uneven. In general the system seems to work best in the "Northeast Corridor," the Boston–New York–Philadelphia–Baltimore–Washington megalopolis, and in southern California, where distances are short and getting to and from airports is inconvenient and expensive. On medium and longer runs the advantages of rail travel are in the spaciousness of the cars (against the cramped immobility of bus and plane) and the chance to enjoy the changing American landscape.

Once again you can ride in relative comfort on trains with magic names—the *Broadway Limited* from New York to Chicago; the *Silver Meteor* from New York to Miami; the *Merchants Limited* between Boston and New York; the *Southern Crescent* from New York via Washington and Atlanta to New Orleans; the *Southwest Limited* (formerly the *Super Chief*) and the *San Francisco Zephyr.* You can ride *Turbo Trains* out of Chicago, the all-electric, high-speed *Metroliner* from New York to Washington, or take a trip clear across the continental United States without ever changing cars.

Some sample times are: New York to Washington, 4 hours; Chicago to San Francisco, 23½ hours; San Francisco to Los Angeles, 10 hours; New York to New Orleans, 29 hours. On some of the most popular runs, such as New York–Boston or New York–Chicago, there is a high speed Metroliner service which shaves about a third of the travel time off those trips. Still, it must be admitted that due to the deteriorated condition of many roadbeds even the best trains may run late.

The simplest is, of course, day coach. There you ride in reclining seats, which may be reserved, with ample leg room, never more than two abreast. Next up is the leg-rest coach with (of course) leg rests, head rests and deeper cushioning for the simplest kind of long distance nighttime accommodation. Slumbercoaches have lounge seats that convert into either a single bed or upper berths at night. For more space and privacy, a roomette gives a sitting room by day and at night a sleeping room with a full-length bed, and private toilet facilities. Bedrooms have two separate sleeping berths and private washing and toilet facilities. Superliner cars, operating between Chicago and the West Coast, also have family bedrooms that can sleep up to two adults and two children. Other types of special cars include dining cars, of course, and tavern lounges—an informal setting for a quiet drink, a game of cards, or just conversation. Some trains, especially where the scenery is best, have dome lounge cars, which give a great view of the countryside through high glass domes.

First class tickets are valid for parlor and club cars, and sleeping cars—the roomettes and bedrooms. Coach class tickets are for reserved and unreserved coaches, either day coach or leg-rest coaches. The reservation system is computerized and operates on a nationwide plan, available at 61 cities and travel destinations all over the country. With a single call to your Amtrak agent you can make your train reservation and at the same time get one day's lodging at a Holiday Inn and three days' unlimited-mileage-use of a Hertz compact rental car. Prices vary by city and season, rail fare not included, for from 1 to 4 persons. Extra nights at the inn are also available at reduced rates. Since this is per room and per car rather than per person, for a group that splits it the economy can be considerable. For brochures on the packages available in that part of the country you are interested in, write to *Amtrak Travel Center,* PO Box 311, Addison, Illinois 60101. If you want information on escorted and group rail travel as well, specify this.

Amtrak has about 75 different package tours to choose from, too, ranging from a weekend package in New York or Washington to a 24-day, coast-to-coast circle tour, plus 16 different Broadway show tours in New York City. A sample is the *Bonanza Americana,* out of Chicago stopping at Yosemite National Park, San Francisco, Big Sur, Los Angeles, Las Vegas, the Grand Canyon among other places and returning to Chicago after 16 days for $2,228 including *everything* (hotels, etc. . . . *75%* of all meals).

Because the Boston–Washington corridor is so heavily traveled, various special discounts up to 25 percent obtain on round-trip tickets, *with stopovers,* in this area. And in addition, an entirely different system of discounts applies to round trip fares anywhere *outside* the Boston–Washington corridor. A number of connecting rail and motor coach services are available locally out of the major cities along the Northeast Corridor—Boston, the south shore of Connecticut, Long Island from New York, New Jersey out of Newark or Philadelphia, and suburban Philadelphia and Washington.

Senior Citizens and the *Handicapped* receive 25% off all regular one-way fares of $40 or more except on Metroliners. Proof of age (65 and above), or of Handicapped status must be shown. Groups of 15 or more can save 15% on one-way fares, up to 25% on round-trip fares. There are also student group rates, and various special excursion fares.

Some sample round-trip coach fares in mid-1983 are: New York–Philadelphia $36 (2 hrs.); New York–Washington $64 (4½ hrs.); New York–Boston $69 (5 hrs.). Sample one-way coach fares: New York–Chicago $119; Chicago–San Francisco $229; San Francisco–Los Angeles $52. Be sure to check current fares before you book.

In Montreal, Boston, New York, Philadelphia, and Washington, Amtrak packages include rail fare, hotel reservations, and various combinations of meals, sightseeing, and theater tickets. Other money-saving packages may also be available.

Not all American trains have been updated. Some have been back-dated. Romantic old steam trains that have been restored and put back into special service now dot the country. Many feature events of local history on their runs. You can be chased by Indians, shop in colonial villages, or probe deep into the heart of a redwood forest on an old logging train. There are some very special trips into the past, to an era full of the romance of trains.

 AMERICA BY BUS. The most extensive and least expensive means of travel in America is the motor coach—the bus. More than 1,000 inter-city and suburban bus companies operate to about 15,000 cities, towns and villages in the United States, 14,000 of which have no other kind of intercity public transportation. The network totals over 277,000 miles of routes carrying 10,000 buses.

Two of these are major national lines, *Greyhound Lines* and *Trailways,* operating 6,700 buses between them, and covering the entire country with regularly scheduled routes. America's intercity buses carry over 350,000,000 passengers a year, more than Amtrak and all the airlines combined.

Reservation and ticketing procedures are basically the same for both. With more than 8,000 coaches on the road daily, you can go almost anywhere with little delay at connecting points. Reservations can be made for only a few trips. "Open date" tickets, good for travel any day, any time, are the rule. So, you just get your ticket, choose the time you want to travel, and show up early enough to get your bags checked in (15 minutes ahead in small towns, 45 minutes in cities).

Both companies offer bargain-rate passes for unlimited travel on any regularly scheduled route in the United States and Canada. These passes are available to both residents and visitors, so there are no restrictions about when and where you can buy them. If they are bought abroad, the period of validity begins on the first day of use in this country; if they are bought here, it begins on the day of purchase.

As of mid-1983, Greyhound's *Ameripass* is priced at $186.50 for 7 days, $239.85 for 15 days, and $346.45 for 30 days. Children 6 to 11½ travel for half fare, and those under 6 go free. Trailways' *Eagle Pass* has almost identical rates. Both passes may be extended indefinitely at a fixed rate of $10 per day. Furthermore, although the two companies do not stress the fact, either pass can be used on buses of the other company provided space is available. Greyhound also offers regional unlimited-mileage passes within California, Florida, and New England (including New York City and the New York–Albany–Montreal route).

Both companies offer discounts to travelers over 65; the rates change, however through the end of 1982 they were 10% on both companies. Two other special situations are: unlimited one-way travel with unlimited stopovers; and promotional discounts between particular points. These change frequently, so inquire specifically for the area and time that you are planning for.

The main U.S. office of Continental Trailways is at 1512 Commerce Street, Dallas, Texas 75201; that of Greyhound is Greyhound Tower, Phoenix, Airzona 85077.

Long-distance buses carry about 45 passengers. They are air-conditioned in summer, heated in winter. Baggage goes underneath, so the passenger compartment is up high, providing a better view through the big, tinted windows. Seats are the lounge chair type, with reclining backs and adjustable head rests. Reading lamps are individually controlled. Almost all long-distance buses have rest rooms.

Some sample, point-to-point times are: New York City to Washington, D.C. —four and a half hours; Los Angeles to San Francisco—nine hours; Chicago to New Orleans—24 hours. Buses must adhere to the recently imposed national speed limit of 55 mph.

A wide variety of tours is offered by the two national lines and many others. They are of three main types. First is the "city package," which includes hotel and sightseeing in one city or the immediate surroundings. Second is the "independent package," which combines inter-city travel on regular schedules with hotel and sightseeing in several cities or places of interest. Third is the "escorted tour," which is a scheduled departure for groups only during certain seasons of the year, leaving from major cities. These range from 4 to 31 days, and are led by an escort, usually only English-speaking.

Some representative one-way bus fares: New York City–Chicago $66.00; Boston–Philadelphia $42.00; Seattle–San Francisco $79.00. Be sure to check any special fares on for summer, weekend, low season and extended traveling.

Sightseeing is often an important part of the traveler's vacation. Even "independent types," who usually go it alone, find sightseeing bus tours one of the best ways to get oriented to a new city or area. The most familiar of the sightseeing bus companies is the *Gray Line,* actually an association of independent companies that cooperate with each other to make more than 11,000 motor coaches available all over the country for tours, circuits, and excursions of from

2 to 10 hours duration every day of the week. Gray Line and *American Sightseeing International* offer tours in virtually every major city and tourist area in the country. You may even get to ride on something else when you take your bus jaunt. Here are some examples from Gray Line: take a five-hour trip in New Mexico, and ride on the longest tramway in the western hemisphere at Sandia Crest; tour the Redwood Forest aboard California's Roaring Camp narrow gauge railroad; ride the giant log flume at Busch Gardens, Los Angeles.

 TRAVELING WITH CHILDREN. If the children are very young or the trip is a long one, you may want to have medical and dental checkups before your departure. The doctor may also want to advise special prescriptions or feeding formulas that should be taken along.

Minor medical problems can easily be handled with a good first-aid kit. Include the standard contents as recommended by the Red Cross, any special prescriptions required, spare glasses, a cough syrup, a stomachache remedy, a laxative, children's aspirin, an opthalmic ointment, and antidiarrheal tablets (they travel more safely than the liquid). One of the greatest triumphs of medical science, as far as traveling is concerned, is the individually packaged gauze pad pretreated with antiseptic and a mild local anesthetic (such as Clean and Treat, made by Pharmaco, Inc.). These are ideal for cleaning up the scrapes and scratches children are prone to. A tube of zinc oxide is a versatile aid for sun and wind burn, diaper rash, and minor abrasions. The dosage and directions for all medicines should be checked with the physician before departure. Pack the kit in a small shoulder bag so it can easily be kept handy.

The itinerary itself should take the youngsters into consideration. Because children's "biological clocks" are more finely tuned than adults', long trips should be divided into short segments to allow the children to adjust to time-zone changes. This also decreases the period of time in which children can repeat the age-old question "Are we there yet?"

In your sightseeing, try to include something of interest to children. Public parks, zoos, aquariums, amusement parks are perfect child-pleasers and often have special attractions for the kids. Beaches, circuses, forts, and aquariums also make big hits with tiny tourists. Many hotels and motels have baby-sitting services, day-care centers, playrooms, cribs and baby carriages to make things easier for the traveling family.

Tours and excursions for children should allow as much freedom as possible. Probably the ideal (though certainly not the only) way for a family with young children to travel would be in their own auto on their own schedule. Conveniently located camping sites offer children the space and freedom not found in hotels. Whenever possible, children should be able to set their own pace. A tightly scheduled and confined tour of more than a half-day's length is generally too restrictive.

Packing for children requires a little extra effort. Clothing should be as simple, comfortable, and versatile as possible. Wash-and-wear and stain-resistant fabrics will make life easier. One of the handiest items is a box of small premoistened towelettes for impromptu clean-ups of hands and face. If a child is not yet a good walker, it is a good idea to pack him too—in one of the back carriers that allows a parent to carry the child while keeping his own hands free or take along a collapsible stroller.

The times which try parents' and progenies' souls alike usually occur at the scores of times each day when the family is waiting for a plane, waiting for a meal to be served, waiting for everyone else to get ready to leave for an outing. The solution is deceptively simple: toys. A few small cars, a mini-doll, small notebooks and pencils, small puzzles and games could be kept on reserve in pocket or purse ready to be produced if boredom rears its ugly head. Easily portable collections of stamps, coins, jacket emblems, seashells, or minerals can also serve this purpose.

Hunger pangs have a way of striking children at the exact moment when food is not available. An offering of small snacks can help keep sunny dispositions from clouding.

In the end, of course, it is impossible to plan for every situation which may arise; indeed, the unpredictability of children is part of the charm of traveling with them. A little imagination on your part can turn an otherwise trying situation into a game. And however inconvenient and ill-timed their demands can be, children bring to traveling a freshness and sense of discovery that can make even the most hardened traveler alive to the places they visit.

 HINTS TO HANDICAPPED TRAVELERS. Important sources of information in this field are: 1) the books, *Travel Ability,* by Lois Reamy (pub. Macmillan) and sources *Access to the World: A Travel Guide for the Handicapped,* by Louise Weiss, Facts on File, 460 Park Ave. S., New York, NY 10016. 2) The *Travel Information Center,* Moss Rehabilitation Hospital, 12th Street and Tabor Road, Philadelphia, Pennsylvania 19141. 3) *Easter Seal Society for Crippled Children and Adults,* Director of Information and Education Service, 2023 West Ogden Avenue, Chicago, Illinois 60612; *Rehabilitation International USA,* 20 West 40 Street, New York, N.Y. 10018. In Britain, there are *Mobility International,* 62 Union St., London SE1 (403–5688); and *The Royal Association for Disability and Rehabilitation,* 25 Mortimer Street, London W. 1. (637–5400).

There are several other publications of interest, including *The Wheelchair Traveler,* c/o Douglass Annand, Ball Hill Road, Milford, N.H. 03055, which also lists sightseeing attractions. The President's Commission on Employment of the Handicapped, along with the Easter Seal Society, has put together a series of guide books for every major city in the United States and a special book called *Guide to the National Parks and Monuments.* Each book lists only those places that are reasonably accessible to the handicapped or are so well known that information is frequently requested. The Commission has also issued a guide to over 330 roadside rest area facilities considered "barrier free" for the disabled. Write to the Commission at Washington, D.C. 20210.

Lists of commercial tour operators who arrange or conduct tours for the handicapped are available from the *Society for the Advancement of Travel for the Handicapped,* 26 Court Street, Brooklyn, New York 11242. For more information and a catalog of the books available write to the Easter Seal Society. The Greyhound Bus system has special assistance for handicapped travelers; and TWA publishes a free 12-page pamphlet entitled *Consumer Information About Air Travel for the Handicapped* to explain all the special arrangements that can be had and how to get them. For rail travel, see *Access Amtrak,* a 16-page booklet published by the National Railway Passenger Corporation.

 HOTELS AND MOTELS. *General hints.* Don't take potluck for lodgings. You'll waste a lot of time hunting for a place, and often you won't be happy with what you finally find. If you don't have reservations, begin looking early in the afternoon. If you do have reservations (but expect to arrive later than 5:00 or 6:00 P.M.), advise the hotel or motel in advance. Some places will not otherwise hold reservations after 6:00 P.M. A hotel or motel will also usually guarantee a room regardless of your arrival time if you book using a major credit card. Of course, if you don't end up using the room in such instances, you are still charged the full rate (unless you cancel by a specified time). And if you hope to get a room at the hotel's *minimum* rates, be sure to reserve ahead or arrive early.

If you are planning to stay in a popular resort in season, reserve well in advance, and make a deposit. Most chains or associated hotels and motels publish directories of their memberships and will make advance reservations for you at affiliated hostelries along your route.

A number of hotels and motels have one-day laundry and dry-cleaning services, and many motels have coin laundries. Most motels, but not all, have telephones in the rooms. If you want to be sure of room service, however, better stay at a hotel. Many motels, even some in the heart of large cities, have swimming pools, as do many beachfront hotels.

Free parking is assumed at motels, motor hotels, country and resort hotels; you must pay for parking at most city hotels, though certain establishments have free parking, frequently for occupants of higher-than-minimum-rate rooms.

Baby sitter lists are always available in good hotels and motels, and cribs for the children are always on hand usually at a minimal cost. Cots to supplement the beds in your room also will involve a minimal cost. Better hotels and motels generally add a moderate charge for moving an extra single bed into a room.

Hotel and motel chains. In addition to the hundreds of independent hotels and motels throughout the country, there also are many that belong to national or regional chains. A major advantage of these chains is the ease of making reservations en route, or at one fell swoop in advance. If you are a guest at a member hotel or motel, the management will be delighted to secure you a sure booking at one of his affiliated hotels, at no costs to you. Chains also usually have toll-free WATS (800) lines to assist you in making reservations on your own, saving you time, worry and money. In addition, the chains publish directories giving detailed information and all their members so that you can, if you prefer this style of travel, plan your entire trip ahead with great precision, albeit less flexibility. Request free copies either through your nearest member motel or by the chains's WATS line. The insistence on uniform standards of comfort, cleanliness and amenities is more common in motel than in hotel chains. (Easy to understand when you realize that most hotel chains are formed by buying up older, established hotels while most motel chains have control of their units from start to finish.) However, individuality can be one of the great charms of a hotel.

Some travelers prefer independent motels and hotels because they are more likely to reflect the genuine character of the surrounding area. There are several aids to planning available in this sphere. The *Hotel and Motel Redbook,* published annually by the American Hotel and Motel Association, 888 Seventh Avenue, New York, N.Y. 10019, covers the entire world; *Hotel and Travel Index,* is published quarterly by Ziff-Davis. Both are expensive, hence best consulted at your travel agent's office. On a more modest scale, the AAA supplies, *to members only,* regional *Tour Guides* that list those establishments recommended by the Association. Members of the *AMOCO Motor Club* and of the *NRTA/AARP Motoring Plan* can get a certain amount of local information from these organizations.

The National Hotel & Motel Reservations Corporation now has an Independent Reservation System which provides a toll-free telephone number for prospective travelers to call to make room reservations around the country. In 47 of the 48 contiguous states the number is 800–317–9157; in Illinois, where the WATS line number originates, the number is 800–942–8888. The system handles only a few chain hotels, but includes most independent hotels and motels. If desired, recommendations will be offered.

Since the single biggest expense of your whole trip will be lodging, you may well be discouraged at the prices of some hotel and motel rooms, particularly when you know that you are paying for things that you neither need nor want, such as a heated swimming pool, wall-to-wall carpeting, a huge color TV set, two huge double beds for only two people, meeting rooms, a cocktail lounge, maybe even a putting green. Nationwide, motel prices for two people now average $40 a night; hotel prices run from $60–90; with the average around $70. This explains the recent rapid spread of a number of chains of budget motels whose rates average $20 for a single and $25. for a double, an advantage that needs no further comment. These are listed in detail below.

HOTEL AND MOTEL CATEGORIES

Hotels and motels in this guidebook are divided into two categories, arranged primarily by price, but also take into consideration the degree of comfort you can expect to enjoy, the amount of service you can anticipate, and the atmosphere which will surround you in the establishment of your choice. Failure to include certain establishments in our lists does not mean they are not worthwhile—they were omitted only for lack of space.

Although the names of the various hotel and motel categories are standard, *the prices listed under each category may vary widely.* Regionally speaking, the Northeast is the most expensive part of the country, followed by the Mid Atlantic states, the Midwest, the South Central states, the Plains and Far West, and the Southeast, in that order. Within a region prices vary: Mississippi is cheaper than Florida; Maine is cheaper than New York. Prices vary within a state: Syracuse will be cheaper than New York City. Average prices vary between chains; among the national (non-budget) motel chains, the upper price range is occupied by Hilton, Marriott and Sheraton; the middle range includes Holiday Inns, Howard Johnson, Quality Inns, and Travelodge; and the least expensive are generally Best Western, Ramada, and Rodeway (mostly in the South). Even within a given chain prices may vary startlingly: a Ramada Inn in one city may charge $24 for a double while one in another city in the same region asks $40. A Holiday Inn in one city may ask $28 for what is $76 in one elsewhere. Thus, as you travel you will have to apply any system of classifications on an ad hoc basis wherever you stop. *In every case, however, the dollar ranges for each category used in this book are clearly stated before each listing of establishments.*

Moderate: In hotels, each room should have an attached bath or shower, restaurant or coffee shop, TV available, telephone in room, heat and/or air conditioning, relatively convenient location, clean and comfortable rooms and public rooms. Motels in this category may not have attached bath or shower, may not have a restaurant or coffee shop (though one is usually nearby), and may have no public rooms to speak of.

Inexpensive: Nearby bath or shower, telephone available, and clean rooms are the minimum.

In the last few years, the soaring prices of hotel and motel accommodations have given rise to a number of chains of budget motels. A few of these are nationwide, most of them are still regional. However, as their prices, in mid-1981, average under $25 for a double, their advantage over ordinary hotels and motels is obvious. Grouped by region, they are as follows. The addresses and phone numbers of the central offices which supply free directories are given with the first listings.

Nationwide: *Budget Host Inns,* Box 16656, Fort Worth, Texas 76114, (817) 626–7064; *Days Inns of America,* 2751 Buford Highway NE, Atlanta, Georgia 30324, (404) 320–2000; *Friendship Inns International,* 739 South 4th Street West, Salt Lake City, Utah 84101, (801) 532–1800. *Best Value Inns,* 2602 Corporate Ave. E., Suite 125, Memphis, Tenn. 38132, (800) 238–2552

New England: *Susse Chalet, International,* 2 Progress Ave., Nashua, N.H. 03062 (800) 258–1980; *Econo-Travel Motor Hotel Corp.,* 20 Koger Executive Center, P.O. Box 12188, Norfolk, Virginia 23502, (800) 446–6900.

Mid-Atlantic (incl. N.Y. and N.J.): *Econo-Travel; Imperial 400 National, Inc.,* 1830 North Nash St., Arlington, Virginia 22209, (800) 531–5300; *Thr-rift Inns,* Ltd., P.O. Box 6160, Newport News, Virginia (804) 877–7536.

Southeast: *Coachlight Inns,* Route 5, 166C, Tyler, Texas 75706, (214) 882–6145; *Days Inns; Econo-Travel; Family Inns of America,* Box 10, Pigeon Forge, Tennessee 37863, (615) 522–7373; *Imperial 400; La Quinta Motor Inns,* P.O. Box 32064, San Antonio, Texas 78216, (800) 531-5900; *Motel 6, Inc.,* (213) 961–1681; 1156 7th Ave., Hacienda Heights, Ca. 91745; *Scottish Inns of America,* 1700 El Camino Real, San Mateo, California 94802, (800) 843–1991.

Midwest: *Days Inns; Econo-Travel; Exel Inns of America,* 4706 East Washington St., Madison, Wisconsin 53704, (608) 241–5271; *Family Inns of America; Friendship Inns,* 739 So. 4th West, Salt Lake City, Utah 84101, (800) 453–4511; *Imperial 400; Interstate Inns,* P.O. Box 760, Kimball, Nebraska 69145, (308) 235–4616; *La Quinta; L-K Restaurants & Motels, Inc.,* 1125 Ellen Kay Drive, Marion, Ohio 43302, (614) 387–0300; *Magic Key Inns,* 5 North First Avenue, Yakima, Washington 98902, (509) 248–7421; *Red Roof Inns,* Davidson Rd., Amlin, Ohio 43002, (614) 376–9961; *Regal 8 Inns,* P.O. Box 1268, Mount Vernon, Illinois 62864, (618) 242–7240; *Super 8 Motels,* 1700 El Camino Real, Suite 503, San Diego, California 94402, (800) 843–1991.

Southwest: *Coachlight Inns; Days Inns; Friendship Inns; Imperial 400; Interstate; La Quinta; Motel 6; Penny Lodge,* Fenelon, 14033 Rosencrantz, San Diego, California 92106, (714) 223–2285; *Regal 8.*

Rockies and Plains: *Econ-O-Tel of America,* Box 2603, Fargo, North Dakota 58108, (701) 282–6300; *Friendship Inns; Imperial 400; Interstate; La Quinta; Magic Key; Motel 6; Regal 8; Super 8.*

Far West: *California 6; Imperial 400; Magic Key; Motel 6; Penny Lodge; Regal 8; Super 8.*

Senior Citizens may in some cases receive special discounts on lodgings. The *Days Inn* chain offers various discounts to anyone 55 or older. *Holiday Inns* give a discount to members of the NRTA (write to National Retired Teachers Association, Membership Division, 406 Grand Ave., Ojai, California 93023) and the AARP (write to American Association of Retired Persons, Membership Division, 215 Long Beach Blvd., Long Beach, California 90802). *Howard Johnson's Motor Lodges, Marriott, Quality Inns, Ramada Inns, Rodeway Inns, Sheraton,* and *Treadway Inns* (a New England chain) are chains which have offered varying discounts to members of AARP and other Senior Citizens' organizations; however the amounts and availability of these discounts change so it is wise to check their latest status. The *National Council of Senior Citizens,* 925 15th St. NW, Washington, DC 20005, works especially to develop low-cost travel possibilities for its members.

Increasingly popular throughout the country but especially in New England and the Northwest since the late 1970s are traditionally styled country inns. *Architectural Digest* publishes beautifully illustrated and amply descriptive regional inn guides, under the title *Country Inns of America* (Knapp Press). Another reliable source is Norman T. Simpson's *Country Inns and Backroads* (Berkshire Traveler Press).

The closest thing America has to Europe's bed-and-breakfast is the private houses that go by the various names of Tourist Home, Guest Home or Guest House. These are often large, still fairly elegant old homes in quiet residential or semi-residential parts of larger towns or along secondary roads and the main streets of small towns and resorts. Styles and standards vary widely, of course, and private baths will be less common and rates will be pleasingly low. In many small towns such Guest Houses are excellent examples of the best a region has to offer of its own special atmosphere. In popular tourist areas, state or local tourist information offices or chambers of commerce usually have lists of homes that let out spare rooms to paying guests, and such a listing usually means that the places on it have been inspected and meet some reliable standard of cleanliness, comfort, and reasonable pricing. Their rates are generally under $20 per night for two persons. One directory is *Guide to Guest Houses and Tourist Homes U.S.A.,* published by Tourist House Associates of America, Inc., P.O. Box 335-A, Greentown, Pa. 18426.

In larger towns and cities a good bet for clean, plain, reliable lodging is a YMCA or YWCA. These buildings are usually centrally located, and their rates tend to run to less than half of those of hotels. Non-members are welcome, but may pay slightly more than members. A few very large Ys may have accommodations for couples, but usually the sexes are segregated. Decor is spartan and the cafeteria fare plain and wholesome, but a definite advantage is the use of the building's pool, gym, reading room, information services, and other facilities. For a directory, write to: *National Council of the YMCA,* 291 Broadway, New York, N.Y. 10007.

ROUGHING IT. More, and improved, **camping** facilities are springing up each year across the country, in national parks, national forests, state parks, in private camping areas, and trailer parks, which by now have become national institutions.

Farm vacations continue to gain adherents, especially among families with children. Some are quite deluxe, some extremely simple. For a directory of farms which take vacationers (including details of rates, accommodations, dates, etc.) write to *Adventure Guides, Inc.,* 36 East 57 Street, New York, N.Y. 10022 for their book *Country Vacations U.S.A.* 22 local offices of the Department of Agriculture supply information on farms in their areas. For the list itself, write to: Special Reports Division, Office of Governmental and Public Affairs, Room 460-A, United States Department of Agriculture, Washington, D.C. 20250.

Because of the great size of the United States, the distances involved, and the consequent domination of private automobiles, **Youth Hostels** have not developed in this country the way they have in Europe and Japan. In the entire 3½ million square miles of the U.S. there are upwards of 200 Youth Hostels, most of them in the compact areas that are New England and the Mid-Atlantic states. Other groupings are in Michigan, Ohio, central Colorado, and around Puget Sound in Washington. Elsewhere, not much. As they are, in any case, designed primarily for people who are traveling under their own power, usually hiking or bicycling, rather than by car or commercial transportation, they tend to be away from towns and cities and in rural areas, near scenic spots. Of equal interest with their possibilities for inexpensive lodgings are the conducted group hiking and bicycle tours that the *American Youth Hostel Association* offers. These vary from year to year, of course. For up-to-date information, write to: American Youth Hostels, Inc., National Administrative Offices, 1332 I St. NW, Washington, D.C. 20005; or, 132 Spring Street, New York, N.Y. 10012. Although the members are mainly young people, there is no age limit. Membership fees are: under 18—$7; 18 and over—$14; family—$21. You must be a member to use Youth Hostels; a copy of the Hostel Guide and Handbook will be included in your membership. (Since 1979, the *Handbook* for the U.S. has been commercially available in bookstores as well.) Accommodations are simple, dormitories are segregated for men and women, common rooms and kitchen are shared, and everyone helps with the cleanup. Lights out 11 P.M. to 7 A.M., no alcohol or other drugs allowed. In season it is wise to reserve ahead; write or phone directly to the particular hostel you plan to stay in. Rates vary from one hostel to another, but a rough national average is now about $3.50 per person per night.

The excellent topographical **maps** published by the Federal Government are available in some bookstores and usually in stores handling hiking, camping and backpacking equipment. Failing that, however, for states east of the Mississippi and including Minnesota, write to: Branch of Distribution, United States Geological Survey, 1200 South Eads Street, Arlington, Virginia 22202. For states west of the Mississippi and including Louisiana, the same agency at P.O. Box 25286, Federal Center, Denver, Colorado 80225.

Useful Addresses: *National Parks Service,* U.S. Dept. of the Interior, Washington, D.C. 20240; *National Forest Service,* U.S. Dept of Agriculture, Washington, D.C. 20250. For information on state parks, write *State Parks Dept., State Office Building* in the capital of the state in which you are interested.

The *National Campers & Hikers Assoc.,* 7172 Transit Rd., Buffalo, N.Y. 14221. Other hiking clubs are *Appalachian Trail (Maine-Georgia),* Appalachian Trail Conference, P.O. Box 236, Harpers Ferry, W.Va. 25425; *Nationwide,* Wilderness Society, 1901 Pennsylvania Ave. N.W., Washington, D.C. 20006; *New England,* Appalachian Mountain Club, 5 Joy St., Boston, Mass. 02108; *New York State,* Adirondack Mountain Club, 172 Ridge St., Glens Falls, N.Y. 12801; *Pacific Northwest,* The Mountaineers, 719 Pike St., Seattle, Wash. 98101; *Sierra Nevada,* The Sierra Club, 530 Bush St., San Francisco, Calif. 94108; *Vermont/New England,* Green Mountain Club, P.O. Box 889, Montpelier, Vt. 05602; *Western States,* Federation of Western Outdoor Clubs, 4534½ University Way N.E., Seattle, Wash. 98105. Commercial camping organizations include: *American Camping Assoc., Inc.,* Bradford Woods, Martinsville, Ind. 46151. Also *Kampgrounds of America, Inc.,* P.O. Box 30558, Billings, Mont. 59114. The great popularity of recreational vehicles in the past few years has led to the development of a kind of intermediate level of "camping" which provides the possibility of sampling the great outdoors in moderate doses from the safety and comfort of a little rolling home complete with all the gadgets. Great numbers of commercial "campgrounds" have appeared to cater to this market, and various directories have appeared to guide campers to them. Here are three, each one running to well over 600 pages: 1) *Wheeler's Recreational Vehicle Resort and Campground Guide, North American Edition (US, Canada, Mexico),* published annually by Print Media Services, Ltd., 222 South Prospect Avenue, Park Ridge, Ill. 60068 and distributed through Simon & Schuster; 2) *Woodall's Campground Directory,* Woodall Publishing Company, 500 Hyacinth Place, Highland Park, Ill. 60035; 3) *Rand McNally Campground and Trailer Park*

Guide, published annually by Rand McNally Company, 10 East 53rd Street, New York, N.Y. 10022.

DINING OUT. *General hints.* For large cities, reservations in advance whenever possible for mid-day and evening meals. In other areas remember that at dinner time most travelers have settled in a particular place for the evening and will quickly fill up the nearby restaurants. Most hotels and farm vacation places have set dining hours. For motel-stayers, life is simpler if the motel has a restaurant, as their hours are more accommodating to early and late traffic.

Although dress standards have become more casual, some restaurants are fussy, especially in the evening. For women, pants and pants suits are now almost universally acceptable. For men, tie and jacket remains the standard, although no longer in the guise of the more formal "suit." Shorts are almost always frowned on for both men and women with the exception of resort establishments, some of which might allow very casual dress at breakfast or lunch meals. If you have any doubt about accepted dress at a particular restaurant, call ahead. At fast-service places, turnpike restaurants, cafeterias, and roadside stands there are no fixed standards of dress. If you're traveling with children, you may want to find out if a restaurant has a children's menu and commensurate prices, as many do.

When figuring the tip on your check, base it *only* on the total charges for the meal, including cocktails and wine, if any. Do *not* tip on any taxes there may be.

RESTAURANT CATEGORIES

Restaurants located in large metropolitan areas are categorized in this volume by type of cuisine: French, Chinese, Armenian, etc., with restaurants of a general nature listed as American-International. Restaurants in less populous areas are divided into price categories as follows: *moderate* and *inexpensive.* As a general rule, expect restaurants in metropolitan areas to be higher in price, although many restaurants that feature foreign cuisine are often surprisingly inexpensive. Our price categories, unless otherwise stated, are for a complete dinner (appetizer or soup, entrée and dessert) but do not include drinks, tax or tip.

We should also point out that limitations of space make it impossible to include every establishment. We have, therefore, included those which we consider the best within each price range. Also consider that new places are established constantly, and our omission of a worthy one would only indicate an early publication date precluding mention.

Although the names of the various restaurant categories are standard in this volume, *the prices listed under each category may vary from area to area.* This is meant to reflect local price standards, and take into account the fact that what might be considered a moderate price in a large urban area might be more expensive in a rural region. *In every case, however, the dollar ranges for each category are clearly stated before each listing of establishments.*

Moderate: This category is indicative of a general reputation for good, wholesome food. Restaurants will have clean kitchens, adequate staff, better-than-average service, and air conditioning (when needed). They also will serve cocktails and/or beer where the law permits.

Nationwide average price: $10 up.

Inexpensive: This is the bargain place in town. It will be clean, even if plain. It will have, when necessary, air conditioning, tables (not a counter), a clean kitchen, and will make an attempt to provide adequate service.

Nationwide average price: under $10.

Budget Chains: *Inexpensive to Moderate:* There are now a number of restaurant chains, some nationwide, others regional, some of the crudest and most minimal fast-food-assembly-line type, others offering proper restaurant service and amenities, most of them having fixed and fairly limited menus, but all at budget prices. Often for the same, or less, money, you can do much better in a grocery or delicatessen by buying the makings for a picnic, as we have suggested earlier. This much said, here are some suggestions for restaurants and cafeterias (where, after all, you save 15% on the tip!), that can save you money. When you arrive in a town or city, look in the phone book under the names given below.

Nationwide: *Arthur Treacher's Fish 'n Chips* (for the Tuesday night special); *Far West Services* (individual restaurants are usually named *Moonraker* or *Plankhouse;* most numerous in California; lunch is a better bargain than dinner); *Holiday Inns* (for their all-you-can-eat-buffets); *Mr. Steak* (children's rates, Senior Citizen discounts, various specialties); *Red Barn Restaurants; Red Lobster Inns; Sambo's Restaurants; Sheraton Hotels* (for their all-you-can-eat-buffets); *Village Inn Pancake Houses* (try their other dishes, too).

Southeast: *Admiral Benbow's; Morrison's Cafeterias.*

Midwest: *Bishop's Buffets and Cafeterias; Bob Evans Farm Restaurants.*

Southwest and Far West: *Luby's and Romano's Cafeterias; Pancho's Mexican Buffets; Wyatt Cafeterias.*

 NIGHTLIFE. In the large cities the problem is never what to do in the evening but how to choose. Whether you like theater, music, dance, or the cinema, famous performers or undiscovered talent, ornate and multi-tiered opera houses, or the bare walls and wooden seats of a tiny cabaret, the city inevitably offers something to suit your taste. To find out what's going on in a city consult the local papers or entertainment magazines.

Outside the big cities, abundant entertainment is still available, at least in the on-season, in those regions that cater to tourists. Big-name shows and performers are often scheduled for the summer months. But in a small town or during the off-season, the problem of finding something to do may be more acute. You'll certainly not have a wide range of choices. Local festivals, larger rodeos, state fairs, and the like, may have entertainment associated with them; but most often nightlife in a small town, if it exists at all, is confined to the weekends and consists of the motel lounge or roadhouse-with-a-bandstand-in-the-corner variety. Your desk clerk or local residents are probably the best sources of information about what's going on.

 DRINKING LAWS. These vary from state to state, and there are sometimes differences between the individual counties of the same state. In general, however, you must be at least 18 years of age to buy or drink alcohol, although some states require that you be at least 21. Wine and hard liquor are rarely sold in package stores on Sundays, holidays, or after midnight any day; Nevada is a notable exception.

Some states prohibit the sale of mixed drinks; you may, however, bring your own bottle to a restaurant or club and they will supply glasses, ice, and mix. Some states which prohibit the sale of mixed drinks in public bars permit private clubs to do so. Often you can join these clubs on the spot for the price of your first drink, which you then get free. Unfortunately, these clubs can be difficult to locate without the benefit of an informed local guide. Sometimes liquor is not for sale at all—in locales known as "dry" areas—and sometimes only beer and/or wine are available.

Most bars close at the hour set by state law; there are, however, after-hours clubs where you can drink when the regular bars have closed, that is, in states which permit after-hours clubs.

On the whole, then, drinking laws are complex and sometimes confusing, so your best bet is to consult the rules which apply to each state separately.

SUMMER SPORTS. *New England's* 500-mile-long ragged coast provides abundant opportunity for many kinds of boating and excellent, if sometimes chilly, swimming. For the fisherman, there is everything from surfcasting to deep-sea fishing. The inland waters offer boating, canoeing, swimming, water skiing, and, of course, freshwater fishing. Hiking, mountain climbing, and horseback riding are popular ways to take in the region's beauty. And there are golf courses throughout.

In *New York and New Jersey,* you'll find yachting in Long Island Sound and body surfing along the Atlantic Coast, golf, especially at Great Gorge, and hiking in the hills and mountains. Fishermen take to the lakes, rivers, and streams or go out to sea. And hunters track down big and small game. For spectators there are baseball, hockey and thoroughbred and harness racing.

The lakes and golden beaches found in much of the *South* invite the swimmer, waterskier, skin- and scuba diver. Tennis and golf are played virtually everywhere. All forms of boating are popular including sailing. Freshwater fishermen take to lakes, rivers, and streams, while saltwater enthusiasts cast in the surf or fish the deep seas. For the spectator there is plenty of thoroughbred and harness racing, greyhound or stockcar races. And in Florida there is the excitement of *jai alai,* the lethally swift Basque version of handball.

Lake Erie's beaches, the Atlantic coast, and the lakes, rivers, and streams throughout the *mid-Atlantic* states provide ample opportunity for the water sport enthusiast and fisherman. Crabbing and clamming are popular in some areas. Hikers take the famous Appalachian Trail, a strenuous footpath which runs from Maine to Florida, or less demanding walks through the lush hills. Golf courses and tennis courts are everywhere. Spectators have thoroughbred races, horse shows, and major league baseball.

The Great Lakes and the Missouri and Mississippi rivers make boating of all types, including sailing, a popular pastime of the *Midwest.* And where there is water, there are sure to be swimmers and water-skiers. In gentle streams and quiet ponds anglers look to take a variety of freshwater fish, and there are several fisherman's dude ranches. Others take to the outdoors on golf courses, tennis courts, or the backs of horses.

In the *Rockies and Plains,* the water sport enthusiast takes to the lakes and reservoirs, the swimmer to the hot springs, the fisherman to the rivers and streams, and the canoer, kayaker, and rafter to the white-water rapids. The rugged mountains offer plenty of opportunity for hiking, backpacking, climbing, or horseback riding. Recalling the frontier heritage, rodeo is the most pervasive of spectator sports, attracting national champions. Golf and tennis is available in nearly every major city and resort.

The *Southwest's* lakes and the Gulf of Mexico offer excellent swimming, water-skiing, boating, and even sailing. Freshwater fishing lures literally millions to rivers and giant lakes, and sailfish and tarpon swim the deep seas of the Gulf. Sportscar racing, bullfighting (just over the border in Mexico), horse shows, and, of course, rodeos draw crowds of cheering spectators.

All along the coast of the *Far West* you'll find every variety of water sport and, in the north, clam digging. Inland there is golfing, swimming, boating, tennis, backpacking, rock-hounding, freshwater fishing, rafting down turbulent rivers, and panning for gold. You can even ski year-'round on Mt. Hood in Oregon and into July in some areas of Washington. For the spectator there is the fast-paced game of jai alai and thoroughbred and greyhound racing.

WINTER SPORTS. To many, *New England* has almost become synonymous with skiing. Facilities for both down-hill and cross-country are excellent and widespread. With skiing has come the resurgence of ice-skating, particularly in well-lighted rinks at night. Snowmobiling, ice-fishing, even sled dog-racing are included in the region's winter activities. In the late fall, hunters come to stalk big and small game with rifle or bow and arrow.

New York and New Jersey have many ski areas, not the least of which is Lake Placid in upstate New York. There are seasons for big and small game, and archery certificates are available if you want to give the animals a better chance. *New York Jets & Giants* football and *Knickerbockers* basketball attract thousands of devoted fans.

Skiers in the *mid-Atlantic* states head for the Pocono and Allegheny mountains of Pennsylvania, though even Virginia and West Virginia are not without slopes. Frozen lakes invite ice-boating and ice-fishing. Large and small game, waterfowl, even exotic birds await the hunter. And the spectator can thrill to professional football and basketball, & horse and auto racing.

In the *South,* where winters are less cold, fishermen are still out for both fresh-and saltwater varieties, and hunters bag big and small game. Even midwinter swimming, water-skiing, and skin-diving are possible. Spectators can choose from among rodeos, stockcar races (including Daytona and Sebring), greyhound and thoroughbred racing, horse shows, and even jai alai and polo. Football, especially the New Year's Day Bowl games, captures the attention of many.

Except in Iowa, skiing is available in the *Midwest,* and ice-skating and tobogganing are popular wherever there is a frozen pond or snow-covered hill. The hunter can go after large and small game; along the Mississippi Flyway duck hunting is exceptional. Basketball, college and professional football, and winter carnivals entertain spectators throughout the season.

The spectator in the *Southwest* can enjoy basketball, football, bowl games, thoroughbred racing, and polo matches and horse shows. Hunters look to bag small game and birds. Swimming in heated pools runs later than usual, and deep-sea fishermen go after record catches in the temperate Gulf. Taos, New Mexico, is one of the finest and most challenging ski areas in the country, and there is good skiing near Albuquerque and Santa Fe.

Skiing is without a doubt the major winter sport of the *Rocky Mountain* area. New facilities continue to be developed. Ski touring or cross-country skiing has become increasingly popular, and more and more people take up the sport of snowmobiling. Ice-skating, on frozen ponds or lakes or in year-round rinks, has its share of enthusiasts. Hunters in this region go out for large and small game and a variety of fowl.

The mountains that run throughout the *Far West* ensure an abundance of skiing, and there are hundreds of well-developed facilities. Ice-skating is popular and more readily available as you go farther north. For something unusual, you might look into the old Scottish favorite, curling, now practiced in Alaska.

In Southern California even the primarily summer sports of golf, tennis, water-skiing, swimming, and surfing are practiced year-round.

Entertainment for the spectator includes professional football, basketball, and ice hockey, as well as rodeos and horse shows.

 CHURCHES AND OTHER PLACES OF WORSHIP. For information about the location of the church, synagogue, or other place of worship of your choice and the hours of services, masses, or prayer, consult either the local newspaper, or the desk clerk at your hotel. He should also be able to tell you what is available in the immediate neighborhood and throughout the city.

Although you may not be interested in the religious services themselves, there are hundreds of churches throughout the United States that are of historical or architectural interest. Temple Square in Salt Lake City, the Vatican of the Mormons, is one such example. The Temple itself is closed to all but Mormons in good standing, but the Tabernacle is open, and the famous choir performs during Sunday services.

California and the Southwest were once part of the territory ruled by the Spanish. They left a trail of missions as evidence of their influence upon the religion and architecture of the region. In many of these, mass is still said in Spanish. Similarly, the Puritans left their mark on New England in the form of white, often austere meetinghouses and churches. Many of these remain and are outstanding examples of early American architecture. In smaller towns, particularly in the Midwest, different Protestant sects have competed on occasion to build the grandest church, frequently on opposite sides of the same street, or on opposite corners of an intersection. Their positions often tell you much about the relative importance of the sects' standings in the community.

MAIL. Stamps can be purchased at any post office in the United States, often from your hotel desk, or from coin-operated vending machines located in transportation terminals, banks, and some shops (stationers and drugstores, for example). They cost a little more if you get them from a machine—you pay for packaging and convenience—so for the sake of economy you may wish to buy as many as you think you will need when you find a handy post office. Postal rates are listed in the table below.

Post offices are usually open from 9 A.M. (0900 hours) to 5 P.M. (1700 hours), Monday through Friday, and until 1 P.M. (1300 hours) on Saturday. They are closed on national holidays. Substations and branch offices in the bigger cities observe the same hours, but the main central post office is often open 24 hours a day.

Stamped mail can be posted in the letter drops at the post office, in the letter chutes of some hotels and office buildings, in the blue mailboxes on many street corners, or you may leave it with your hotel desk, which will take care of posting it for you.

If you expect to receive mail while traveling, you can have it addressed to you in care of your hotel(s). If you don't know where you'll be staying, you can have mail from home sent to you at the main post office, in care of General Delivery, as, for example: Your Name, c/o General Delivery, Main Post Office, Miami, Florida, USA. All General Delivery mail must be collected in person, and you will be asked to show identification.

POSTAGE. There is no separate Air Mail rate for letters or postcards posted in the United States for delivery within the country or to Canada. Mail for distant points is automatically airlifted. The following are the postal rates in effect as of mid-1982, but they are subject to change—usually up, not down—so check when you buy stamps to be sure.

	Letters	*Postcards*
United States and Canada	20¢ 1st oz.	13¢
*Mexico		
Air Mail	20¢ 1st oz.	13¢
	20¢ 1st oz.	13¢
*Overseas		
Air to Europe	40¢ 1st ½ oz.	28¢
Air to Central America and Caribbean	35¢ 1st ½ oz.	19¢
Air to most other countries	40¢ 1st ½ oz.	28¢
Surface to Europe	30¢ 1st oz.	19¢
Surface to Central and South America	30¢ 1st oz.	19¢
Surface to most other countries	30¢ 1st oz.	19¢
Air Letter Forms to all countries	30¢	

*Subject to change.

TELEPHONE. Coin-operated public telephones are available almost everywhere: in hotel lobbies, transportation terminals, drugstores, department stores, restaurants, gasoline filling stations, in sidewalk booths, and along the highway. To use the coin telephone, just follow the instructions on the phone box. Local calls usually cost 10 or 20 cents and can be dialed directly. If you don't reach your party, your money is automatically refunded when you hang up.

For long-distance calls, dial "0" (zero) and have plenty of coins available, or reverse the charges. The operator may ask for enough change to cover the initial time period before she connects you. To place a call outside the United States, dial "0" and ask for the overseas operator.

In hotels, your switchboard operator will either place your outside call for you, or tell you how to dial directly from your room. The telephone charges will be added to your hotel bill and you will pay for them when you check out.

Charges are almost always several times what you would pay at a coin-operated booth.

TELEGRAPH. To send a telegram to a destination anywhere within the United States, ask for assistance at your hotel, or go to the nearest *Western Union* telegraph office. You'll find it listed in the classified section (yellow pages) of the telephone directory under "Telegraph." Overseas cablegrams can also be dispatched by Western Union, or by any cable company (also listed under, "Telegraph"). You can phone Western Union and have a telegram charged to your home telephone (U.S.A. only). Mailgrams are similar to telegrams, only they are delivered with the following day's mail and cost less than half what is charged for regular telegrams.

NATIONAL PARKS. A vacation unequaled elsewhere in the world is a week or two in one of the 40 national parks that preserve in beauty and naturalness the variety of landscapes and climates that make the United States so fascinating both to lovers of free space and clear air and to all kinds of students of the outdoors. There are glaciers and tropical swamps; volcanic mountains and parched, endless deserts; pounding seacoasts and tranquil rivers; Cliff Dwellers' ruins and geysers and medicinal springs. There are crashing mountain brooks alive with trout and rain forests where herds of elk brush silently through the luminescent yellow-green of heavy foliage. In the parks you can find nearly every kind of physical geography that the world provides—the mysterious sculptures in glowing red and orange and yellow stone of the Utah highlands, the endless vistas of flat grass in the prairies, the giant sequoias and redwoods.

With some 26½ million acres, the National Park Service has within the last half century managed to preserve about one percent of the total American land as it was before the coming of civilization so that future generations will forever have access to some parts of their country that are unfenced, unworked, unsullied by man's incessant urges to profit from his ground, change it, force his will upon it. The goal of the parks, according to former Director Newton B. Drury, is "to conserve them, not for commercial use of their resources, but because of their value in ministering to the human mind and spirit."

In spite of this goal of naturalness—the parks are like living museums that may forever show man how the world was before he and his machines took charge—there is plenty of space in the parks for people and much for them to do without so much as leaving a mark behind them. They hike, and camp out, and cook out, and take pictures, and fish, and study the trees and the flowers. They can study in fossils the passage of earlier living creatures and in some of the parks there are petroglyphs and ceremonial mounds that give intriguing clues to earlier civilizations of man. There is much to be learned on the nature trails—every park has these, clearly marked, sometimes even in braille (blind persons can touch and feel nearby trees and plants as they follow a rope strung along posts beside the path). Visitors centers provide museums displaying what is helpful in understanding the peculiarities of that particular park land; slides and movies do the same thing. You can learn as much or as little as you like.

Or you can just walk out into these open spaces and breathe and open your eyes to the original world taken straight, and then often return to a comfortable rustic lodge with a log fire glowing in a fieldstone fireplace—if it's the season for it. Many parks have bridle trails or pack trips (you can ride a mile down into the Grand Canyon on muleback), and several parks provide river float trips. In summertime, the busy season in most parks, rangers put on frequent programs of informal talks or guided tours. Some of the talks are given at dusk around a communal campfire and provide for many visitors the most memorable moments of their park vacations. Almost all the parks have towns near them that offer accommodations and other tourist needs, but within the borders of the parks you feel as if you could be a thousand miles away from the nearest outpost of that life you've left behind.

NATIONAL MONUMENTS AND OTHER PARK PROPERTY. Although the *national parks* are unquestionably the most important parts of our national trust of scenic wild lands, there is much more territory under the National Park Service administration that is designated as *national monuments, historic parks, national seashores,* and *national recreation areas.* The official distinction between a national park and the other properties is that the former have all been created by Acts of Congress, while the latter were either purchased by the government or deeded to it.

Many of the features of the national parks—visitor centers, campgrounds, ranger-led tours and campfire talks, nature trails and hiking and bridle paths—can also be found in the national monuments and other Federal lands, and many of them, in the opinion of some travelers, equal the national parks in magnificence of natural surroundings or in areas of specific interest.

Almost as impressive in value to the future of the country are the *national forests,* many of which also offer a variety of recreational opportunities. The woodlands cover almost 189 million acres of the country from Puerto Rico to Alaska to Hawaii in 154 national forests, among which a score have visitors centers similar to those of the park service.

For information on national parks, battlefields, and recreation areas, write to National Parks Service, Department of the Interior, Washington, D.C. 20240. For information on National forests and recreation areas, write to National Forest Service, U.S. Department of Agriculture, Washington, D.C. 20250.

INFORMATION FOR FOREIGN VISITORS

HOW TO GET TO THE UNITED STATES FROM ABROAD. Although air travel is considerably quicker than other means, and often less expensive, it's not always easy to arrange these days. Air fares are changing constantly, and the airlines' unceasing efforts to better each others' bargains can turn the simple task of buying a plane ticket into a difficult, confusing, and ultimately frustrating chore. To save yourself headaches, it's best to consult a travel agent. They are well equipped to keep up with all the latest offerings, and they charge no fee, their commissions being paid by the airlines themselves.

However you arrange your flight, here are some things to keep in mind. You'll pay the highest fares if you travel during peak summer months, but often less if you go during the off-season. Most airlines offer two basic fares: first class and economy. First class, of course, is by far the most expensive—up to three times the cost of the cheaper fares. In return for your investment you get all the on-board amenities the airlines can dole out (and shortened flight time on the Concorde, which sells only first-class seats). Moreover, first-class tickets are without restrictions; you may book, travel, and change flight plans at any time, and stop over as you wish. Economy (considerably less luxurious, but still restriction-free) is less expensive than first class, but still not cheap; stopovers may cost extra.

APEX (Advance Booking Excursion) is one of the best bargains available. It offers enormous reductions on the cost of first-class and economy tickets, though a number of restrictions are imposed in exchange for the savings.

Generally, APEX seats are round trip only, must be booked and paid for 21 days in advance, require at least a seven-day stay, and once booked, cannot be changed. Details vary from airline to airline, however; be sure to inquire fully.

Other possibilities include package tours, straight charters, and standby. A package tour usually includes an airfare (at a charter price) plus various land arrangements. An example would be the Self-Catering Vacations offered by Britain's *Twickenham Travel Ltd* (84 Hampton Rd., Twickenham, Middlesex), which provide furnished apartments or cottages; or the very inexpensive tours of the U.S. and Canada offered by *Sovereign Holidays* (West London Air Terminal, Cromwell Rd., London SW7). There are hundreds of these tours offered each year, and they change from year to year, so the most we can do here is advise you to see your travel agent for current offerings. Straight charters give you airfare only and leave you to make your own land arrangements. An excellent guide to these is *How to Fly for Less* published annually by Travel Information Bureau, 44 Country Lane Road, Farmingdale, N.Y. 11735, a concise, lucid, and complete survey together with an analysis and a directory of the charter flight business and how to use it to your advantage. Price postpaid (through 1982), $5. Standby fares operate, as of presstime, only between London and New York, with Los Angeles due for early approval and other gateway cities under consideration. The pioneer in this was Britain's now defunct Laker Airways, but several other companies have proclaimed their enthusiasm for service to the public and reluctantly followed suit, including TWA, Pan Am, Air India, British Airways, and El Al. It looks very promising; but if the ferment is creative it is also confusing. New promotional fares and competitive gimmicks appear and disappear so quickly that the airlines themselves sometimes lose track of what they have done. Inquire for the latest developments!

At international airports you will find exchange facilities and special visitor information booths. We suggest, however, that you have about $50 in U.S. currency, in small denominations, already on hand when you arrive, as exchange facilities in this country are still far from what they are in Europe and some other parts of the world.

Arrangements for getting from airports into the cities they serve vary; in some cases there is train service, but the choices are usually bus, limousine, and taxi, in ascending order of costliness. Unless you have cumbersome baggage, the bus will be cheapest. *Inquire carefully at the airport as to what is available and what it should cost, especially with regard to taxis.* Most drivers are honest, but every so often there is a flagrant abuse; and taxis are expensive in this country anyway. The three major airports serving the greater New York area—JFK, La Guardia, and Newark—all now have increasingly good public transportation by bus and special subway lines into downtown Manhattan. Major car rental companies also maintain services at all international airports. If you want to be assured that there will be a car waiting for you, particularly on weekends or holidays, you may wish to reserve one in advance of your arrival.

By Sea. The chances of traveling by ship across the Atlantic reduce each year. In the past, sea-lovers had a choice between ocean liners and freighters—the former hardly in the realm of budget travel. The possibilities for the more economically enticing freighter travel have been dwindling drastically. The few cargo ships making the trip and accepting passengers are booked several years ahead. Polish and Russian ships, the international political situation being what it is, are no longer open to citizens of the United States—and only rarely to others from the Western world. Nonetheless, the persistent can be rewarded with passage on the rare freighter offering relatively comfortable, one-class accommodations for a maximum of 12 people. For details, and to help you choose between the lines available, consult either of the following specialists: *Air Marine Travel Service,* 501 Madison Avenue, New York, N.Y. 10022, publisher of the *Trip Log Quick Reference Freighter Guide,* or *Pearl's Freighter Tips,* 175 Great Neck Road, Great Neck, N.Y. 11201. In England, *Pitt and Scott Travel* puts out a booklet entitled *Freighter Voyages,* which lists current cruises. Write to Pitt and Scott Travel, Shipping Dept., 3 Cathedral Place, London EC4M 7DT.

Among the alternatives to trans-Atlantic travel for those who wish to spend some time on the water are cruises along the Mississippi, around the Florida coast (usually to various Caribbean islands), "to nowhere"—two or three day jaunts on ocean liners, usually for gambling, or around the St. Lawrence Seaway. The details of these change with some frequency, and it is best to consult a travel agent for the latest information.

By rail. Visitors coming from Canada and Mexico may also enter the United States by rail, bus, or automobile. The National Railroad Passenger Corporation *(Amtrak)* is the principal rail carrier in the United States, operating passenger service to some 500 cities and towns in 44 states. Trains operate on frequent schedules and most are temperature controlled and equipped with dining cars or snack bars. Hand luggage is carried free, as are trunks in the baggage car. Rail terminals in the bigger cities house a wide variety of services, including waiting rooms, information and Travelers Aid centers, restaurants and snack bars, baggage lockers, barber shops, drugstores, newsstands, and public telephones.

From Mexico, the best rail connection is at Nuevo Laredo. Another good one is the Ciudad Juarez/El Paso gateway, where direct connections can be made between *Mexican National Railways* and *Amtrak* trains.

From Canada, you can board *Amtrak* trains directly at Montreal or Vancouver, but connecting services are provided through most major cities along the United States-Canada border.

By bus. Both *Greyhound* and *Continental Trailways,* the two largest motor-coach carriers, offer varied tours and passes including unlimited-travel, fixed-price tickets, and discounts on circle tours. For more details see *America by Bus,* earlier in this chapter, as well as the section on bus travel below. As with train travel, the best places for visitors *from Mexico* to make direct connections with major domestic bus services are Laredo and El Paso, although connecting service is also available out of Tijuana, Mexicali, Nogales, Ojinaga, Piedras Negras, and Matamoros.

Canadian visitors will have no difficulty making connections out of Vancouver, Winnipeg, Sault Ste. Marie, Toronto, Ottawa, Montreal, and other border cities.

By car. Arrival by private automobile affords the greatest personal flexibility in entering the United States at your own convenience and offers the additional opportunity to stop wherever, whenever, and however long you wish. Highways are excellent. You may bring your automobile into the United States free of duty for your own personal use. Citizens of most countries may tour in the United States with their own national license plates (registration tags). See *America by Car* section for details.

You may also choose to enter the United States by *private boat* or *plane.* Local air and marine authorities can advise you about the necessary documentation.

PHYSICAL FEATURES. The United States, excluding Alaska, lies between 25° and 50° latitude, or roughly from the northern border of France farther south even than the Pyramids in Egypt. Alaska is as far north as Sweden, Norway, and Finland. Europeans may find it helpful to bear in mind that the distance from New York to Washington, D.C. is about the same as that from London to Paris, from New York to Chicago as from London to Berlin, and from New York to Los Angeles greater than from London to Baghdad or from Lisbon to Moscow.

The continent itself is unequally divided by the chain of Rocky Mountains. Often rising over 14,000 feet, these form what is known as the Continental Divide, so called because the waters on one side of the chain flow eastward, those on the other westward. Between these peaks and the Pacific Ocean is a region made up largely of mountains and high plateaus, but the landscape is remarkably varied. In the states bordering the coast, there are rain forests, giant redwoods, glaciers, fiords, active volcanoes, scorching deserts, craggy mountain peaks, deep gorges, and turbulent rivers. In the Southwest, mountains forested with ponderosa pine and aspen overlook the mile-deep Grand Canyon. Much of it is desert, and mesquite cactus is as probable a backyard tree as any other; yet the Colorado and Rio Grande rivers flow here. The Rocky Mountain states themselves, composed generally of majestic peaks, forests, placid valleys, blue lakes, and deep canyons, contain such contrasting scenery as sand dunes, arctic tundra, waterfalls, curious rock formations, glaciers, hot springs, geysers, salt flats, and the Great Salt Lake.

East of the Rockies the land descends imperceptibly across the Great Plains. Beyond these lies mid-America, known more commonly as the Midwest. The land here is broad and flat with clusters of rolling hills but no mountains and, in the north, dense forests. The Mississippi River system, with such major branches as the Missouri, Ohio, and Arkansas, spreads like an enormous tree throughout this region.

Between the plains and the Atlantic Coast lies another range of mountains, the Appalachian and Blue Ridge. Older than the Rockies, these seldom rise above 5,000 feet. For the most part heavily wooded, they are shot through with lakes, valleys, and rolling farmlands. To the south of this range along the Gulf of Mexico is a subtropical region of palm-shaded beaches and trees thick with Spanish moss.

Along the Atlantic itself stretches a wide coastal plain. From Delaware to New York, the area bordering the ocean is largely populated, but inland is some of the world's richest farmland. Finally, in the northeast the plain gives way to New England's rocky coast and rugged mountains.

 IMMIGRATION AND CUSTOMS. There are a few simple travel formalities you will be asked to complete before you enter the United States. You will need a passport, usually a visitor's visa and, depending on where you come from, some kind of health record.

First you must have a current passport, which authorizes you to travel outside your own country. You will be asked to present it when you apply for a visitor's visa from the United States Embassy or Consulate nearest you, which you may do either in person or by mail. In some countries visa applications can also be obtained from the leading transportation companies and travel specialists.

Along with your application you will be required to supply one passport-size photograph of yourself, and some kind of evidence that you intend to return home after your visit. There is no special form for providing such evidence and the United States Embassy or Consulate will consider whatever you wish to submit. It might be a letter from your employer stating that you will be returning to your job, or from a community leader, such as a government, bank, school official, or a clergyman, describing ties in your community that would give you good reason to return.

As soon as your credentials are found to be in good order you will be issued a visitor's visa. The period of time it covers and the number of entries permitted will be specified on the visa.

WARNING! When you arrive in the U.S.A., the immigration officer may grant you less time here than your visa specifies. He may do this *without* telling you, simply by writing down an arbitrary date on your I–94 form, the white piece of paper which he will attach to your passport. This form shows the visa classification under which you have arrived, the date of your arrival, the purpose of your visit, and the latest departure date which the Immigration Service assigns to you. Be sure to make clear to him before he writes this in how long you want to stay and ask him to grant you that period of time or to explain why he has not. Later on, if you want to extend your stay, you must apply for an extension *at least one month* before your assigned departure date. Also, if you are 21 years old or more and happen to be in the United States over a January 1st, you must fill out a short alien registration card which you can get at any post office.

As the inflow of illegal immigrants seeking jobs in the USA has been increasing in recent years, Immigration authorities are getting tougher toward everyone, bona fide tourists included. Be sure to get this point settled before accepting your passport back at point of entry.

Exceptions: There are certain persons who are exempted from passport and/or visa requirements. The following, among others, are not required to present either passports or visas:

Canadian citizens, if arriving in the United States after a visit only in the Western Hemisphere. (Border-crossing cards are issued by the United States Immigration Service at Canadian border offices to facilitate admission).

British subjects residing in Bermuda or Canada, if arriving after a visit only in the Western Hemisphere.

Citizens of Mexico holding valid United States border-crossing cards, if arriving from Mexico or Canada.

Certain government and military travelers.

Holders of *Belgian* identity cards issued in lieu of passports are exempt from the passport requirement, but must have a valid visa.

Among those who need a passport, but who are excused from the visa requirement are:

British subjects residing in and coming directly from the Cayman Islands, and who are in possession of a political affiliation certificate and a clerk of court certificate.

Bahamian nationals residing in the Bahamas and coming directly to the United States on a precleared flight from Nassau.

Citizens of any country admitted to the United States on a single entry visa may visit Canada or Mexico for not more than 30 days and reenter the United States without a new visa, provided the reentry falls within the specifications of the original admission. If you remain in the United States more than 90 days in any one year, or if you have worked and earned here over $3,000 in one year, you should check with the U.S. Government Internal Revenue Service to see if you have to pay any taxes in this country. Your own country's Embassy or consulates can advise you on this too, as well as on whether or not your country has a tax exemption treaty with the U.S. so that you do not get taxed by both countries at the same time. Lists of cities having foreign consulates are given at the end of this section.

HEALTH REQUIREMENTS. Smallpox vaccination certificates are required only for persons who in the previous 14 days were in a country infected with smallpox. Additional vaccinations, for cholera or yellow fever, for example, might be required, depending on the areas in which you have traveled. These vary all the time, according to local conditions, so check carefully when you get your visa.

CUSTOMS. When you get to the United States, you will be processed through Customs, even if you have nothing to declare. United States citizens go through the same procedure. The Customs inspector will probably ask you to open your luggage, so it will save time if you have your keys handy.

All items intended for your own personal use (not including gifts or anything you plan to sell) can be brought into the United States duty and tax free. This includes anything from wearing apparel, jewelry, toilet articles, cameras, sports equipment, and other personal effects to baby carriages, bicycles, boats, and automobiles. Household effects and professional equipment or instruments may also come in duty-free if you have had them for more than one year. There is no limit on the amount of money you may bring with you, but if it's more than $5,000 you'll be asked to file a report with Customs.

You may also bring with you up to $100 worth of gifts, tax and duty free, provided you remain in the United States not less than 72 hours and have not claimed the exemption within the prior six months. Within this allowance, adults may bring one quart of alcoholic beverages (0.946 liters) for personal use.

Adults are also permitted 100 cigars as gifts, plus 50 cigars, or 200 cigarettes, or 3 pounds (1.359 kilograms) of tobacco for personal use. You may choose instead to bring a combination of cigars, cigarettes, and tobacco for personal use. Children are also allowed 100 cigars as gifts. Importation in any form of tobacco originating in Cuba is prohibited.

Articles accompanying you, in excess of your personal exemption, are subject to varying rates of duty, depending on the value of the item.

If you're thinking about bringing the family dog along on your trip to the United States, probably the best advice you'll get is "don't." No matter how well behaved, it can seriously limit your choice of transportation, lodgings, and itinerary.

But if you decide to, a certificate of rabies vaccination is required for dogs, signed by a licensed veterinarian and stating that the dog has been vaccinated at least 30 days prior to entry. Dogs without certificates must be vaccinated at the port of entry and quarantined for 30 days.

No vaccination is required for dogs coming from countries designated as rabies-free by the United States Public Health Service. These are currently listed as Australia, the Bahamas, Bermuda, Fiji, Great Britain, Iceland, Northern Ireland, Republic of Ireland, Jamaica, New Zealand, Norway, and Sweden. This list is subject to change as conditions warrant.

Cats are not required to have a rabies vaccination, but are subject to inspection on arrival and must be free of communicable diseases. All animals entering the United States are examined at the port of entry for evidence of disease, even if they have been certified. If an animal is not in apparent good health it may be subject to examination by a veterinarian at the owner's expense. If, as a result, the pet or other animal is excluded from entry, it must either be deported or destroyed.

Exception: Hawaii requires that all dogs and cats entering the state be quarantined at the owner's expense for 120 days, unless they are coming from Australia or New Zealand. This requirement applies even to guide dogs for the blind.

Dogs and cats entering the United States are subject to a Customs duty of 3 and one-half percent of their value, but the amount may be included in your $100 exemption.

Your travel agent or the United States Consulate can give you more detailed information about traveling with your pet. They can also advise about state and local regulations, which sometimes, as in the case of Hawaii, are more stringent than the federal regulations. Ask the consulate for the brochure entitled *So You Want to Import a Pet,* or write to the: Foreign Quarantine Program, U.S. Public Health Service, National Communicable Disease Center, Atlanta, Ga. 30333.

Also consult the Consulate if you plan to bring along any fruits, vegetables, plants, seeds, meats, or any plant or animal products. Many are admitted without restriction other than inspection, some are prohibited entry, and a few are generally prohibited but may, under certain conditions, be admitted.

The following indicates some of the things you are—and are *not*—permitted to bring into the United States.

Admitted: Bakery goods, candies, fully cured cheeses, medicinal cotton, fresh cut or dried flowers, canned or processed fruits, jams and jellies, Mexican jumping beans, rocks and minerals, dried spices, truffles.

Permit required: Fresh berries, corn, eggs, fresh fruit and vegetables (some kinds prohibited).

Prohibited: Pine branches, citrus peel, fresh dairy products, fresh meat, plants in soil, items stuffed with straw, sugarcane, packing materials made from plant and animal fibers.

As with all Immigration and Customs regulations, the above are subject to revision and modification. For latest details on this, ask your nearest U.S. Consulate for Program Aid No. 1083, *Traveler's Tips,* or write to: Quarantines, Department of Agriculture, Federal Center Building, Hyattsville, Md. 20782.

 SPECIAL FARES AND SERVICES FOR INTERNATIONAL VISITORS. Private and public agencies offer a number of special courtesies to international visitors, not least valuable of which are the bargain rates on transportation. Outlined below are some that are currently available, but modifications are frequent, new discounts are introduced as others are retired, so check with your travel agent for latest information.

Airlines. Some domestic airlines offer special "Visit USA" discounts of up to 40 percent off regular coach fares on travel within the continental United States. In order to qualify, you must live at least 100 miles (161 kilometers) outside the border of any state in the United States. These discounted tickets cannot be used in combination with other special airfares or excursions.

Visit USA tickets are valid for up to 1 year. Reservations must be made before you arrive in the U.S.A. and tickets must be confirmed within seven days of arrival, travel must begin no later than the 15th day after arrival.

Bus Services. Discount-priced international rates on point-to-point travel are available from either of the two giant American motorcoach companies, *Greyhound Lines* and *Trailways.* Both of them have more than 4,000 motorcoaches in operation every day. International rates are listed on a separate schedule, but discounts amount to around 10 percent off regular fares. Tickets must be purchased overseas from authorized agents or representatives. *Trailways* has "Visit USA" offices in: Luxembourg (c/o Bureau de Voyages et d'Emigration), Mexico City (Trailways), Johannesburg (c/o Global), Taipei (c/o Zion International, Ltd.), Tokyo (c/o Holiday Inns), Seoul (c/o Sharp, Ltd.), Sydney (c/o Henning International), Brussels (c/o Holiday Inns), Frankfurt (c/o Deutsches Reiseburo), Guatemala City (c/o IMC Consultores), and London (c/o Holiday Inns, 2 Old Brewery Mews, London NW 3. Tel. 794–5762).

Both companies also offer bargain-rate passes for unlimited travel on any regularly scheduled route in the United States and Canada. Passes are available to residents as well as visitors, so there are no restrictions about when or where you can purchase them. If you buy it after you arrive, its period of validity begins on the date of purchase. If you buy it at home, validity begins on the first day of use.

For rates and other conditions, see under *America By Bus* earlier in this section.

Accommodations. Many hotels and motels, both independent and chain-affiliated, offer special Visit USA reductions that can amount to as much as 35 percent off the average double room-rate. Some of the same facilities specialize in accommodating non-English-speaking travelers and will provide language and other helpful services. Hospitality packages providing for prepurchase of specified meals and accommodations at reduced rates are also available. Your travel agent can tell you which facilities offer discounts to international visitors.

Tour Packages. Tours originating outside the United States can also be great values. Tour operators, because of the volume of business they generate, are entitled to quantity discounts on travel services and accommodations and can offer a prepackaged itinerary at often far lower cost than you could if you tried to assemble it yourself. Such package tours are available in seemingly endless variety, and you're almost certain to find one going wherever you are. There are also special interest tours in abundance, and whether your own penchant is for horses or health, skiing or snorkeling, art, antiques, theater, music, cowboys and Indians, sports, the outdoors or whatever, you can probably find one that suits you—and perhaps meet some congenial traveling companions along the way. Again, your travel agent is the person to see.

Hospitality Programs. One of the pleasures of visiting other countries is the opportunity to get to know the people. A Visit USA program called *Meet Americans at Home* invites you to do just that. In many cities and communities you can arrange to visit an American family at home for a few hours by calling a telephone number you will find listed in a folder distributed by your travel agent.

Meet Americans at Home is a community activity and your hosts will be responsible citizens who have volunteered to help make your visit a pleasant one. Often they will speak your native language. It will probably be necessary for you to answer a few questions about your country of origin, occupation, hobbies, and special interests so that a meeting can be arranged that will be enjoyable and congenial for both you and your hosts.

If your travel agent does not have the Americans at Home folder, he can request it from: United States Travel Service, United States Department of Commerce, Washington, D.C. 20230.

Many cities also have other public and privately sponsored hospitality programs, some for specific nationals, some for all. They offer information, assistance, numerous small advisory services and sometimes operate a hospitality center where you can go and meet other travelers. They will also seek or supply language services for visitors who need them. You can find out about such programs from the Visitors and Convention Bureau in any major city. Some are also listed in the telephone book.

See "Interpreter Services" for other courtesies extended to international visitors.

For British Students. If you attend a university or college of further education it is possible to get a working visa (J1) for the summer months through the British Universities North America Club. There is a quota, so apply early. For information contact BUNAC, 30 Store St., London WC1.

INTERPRETER SERVICES. There was a time when you couldn't hope to travel comfortably in the United States without a passable acquaintance with English. A little bit still helps, especially outside the gateway cities, but recent efforts on the part of both public and private agencies have made language services far more readily accessible to international visitors who need them, or who just feel more comfortable communicating in their own language.

French, German, Spanish, and Japanese are the services most widely available, but in the major cities you should have little difficulty finding someone to interpret for you in any language.

Look for the *multilingual Golden Girls* who are now stationed at a number of international airports to assist you through Immigration and Customs. They will also help you to make transportation connections. At many ports of entry you will also find an information desk staffed by multilingual agents who will help you with local transportation or in locating various services. The *Travelers Aid Society* desk at city bus and railroad terminals can assist you in several languages.

You will find a plaque at the registration desk of many hotels, issued by the United States Travel Service, which indicates that French, Spanish, German and/or Japanese are spoken at the front desk, at the telephone switchboard and in the hotel dining room. Even if you don't see the plaque, you can ask to speak to someone in your own language. If the hotel has such a person on its staff, it will ask him to interpret for you.

Many sightseeing services offer conducted tours with multilingual tour guides, both day trips and longer excursions of two or three days to a week or more. Some provide each passenger with a tape recorded commentary in his own language. Many major tourist attractions will also provide interpreter services on request.

Large city department stores have multilingual employees who will be glad to assist you with your shopping, either by appointment or by request at the store. You will also often find smaller shops with signs in the window indicating what languages are spoken there.

A good source of information about local interpreter services is the city's *Visitors and Convention Bureau,* usually itself staffed by multilingual personnel. Ask your hotel desk where they are, or look them up in the telephone book. They will also advise you about where to go, what to see and do in the city.

In large metropolitan areas, the publishing offices of foreign language newspapers and magazines can frequently advise about interpreter services, too. For information about where to find them, or about foreign language radio programs, ethnic groups and organizations in the United States, you can contact the *American Council for Nationalities Service* at 20 W. 40th St., New York, N.Y. 10018. Tel. (212) 398–9142. The Council has member agencies in more than 30 cities which serve as centers of service and fellowship for all nationalities.

Many cities also maintain their own local service agencies, such as the *International Visitors Information Service* 1825 H Street NW, Washington, D.C. 20006, (202) 872–8747, which offer language assistance as well as information and hospitality services to international visitors.

If you are outside a metropolitan area and need assistance, you can call *Travel-Phone North America,* toll free from anywhere in the continental United States except Alaska. Staff members who speak German, French, Spanish, and Japanese, as well as English, are available to answer questions about the location of tourist attractions, which airlines and bus lines serve particular cities, and what hotels have interpreter facilities. They make hotel reservations anywhere in the country. They can also refer you to others who can answer such travel questions as how to find a guided tour in the area you wish to visit, where the nearest Visitors Bureau is, and what to do if you lose your passport. The Travel-Phone number is (800) 255–3050. Just dial and ask for the *Travel-Phone North America* desk. (In Kansas call [1–800] 322–4350.)

A second multilingual telephone service for foreign tourists is *Hotel, Auto, Tour, Air (HATA),* based in Madison, Wisconsin. Its number is 800–356–8392. HATA provides general information, emergency road service for users of Hertz rental cars (call 800–654–3131), and makes travel reservations.

International symbol signs, which circumvent any potential language problems, are more and more being used at international airports, along the highways, in hotels and restaurants.

If you want the reassurance of full-time interpreter service, you might want to consider a conducted tour package that includes your transportation, accommodations, and guide service on a prearranged itinerary—many times the choice of first-time visitors to the United States. Your travel agent can make all the necessary arrangements.

Interpreters are available at all major gateway cities. Some in-land cities have this service, too. Akron, Ohio; Buffalo, New York; Charleston, West Virginia; Cleveland, Ohio; Pittsburgh, Pennsylvania; Rochester, New York; and Youngstown, Ohio are examples. Languages covered are: Arabic, Chinese, Croatian, Czech, Dutch, Filipino, French, German, Hungarian, Italian, Japanese, Lithuanian, Polish, Rumanian, Russian, Serbian, Serbo-Croatian, Slovak, Turkish, and Ukrainian.

CURRENCY. The United States puts no limit on the amount of money you may bring into the country. For your own convenience, however, come with a supply of smaller bills, credit cards, and travelers checks (preferably in US dollars).

Denominations. The basic United States monetary unit is the dollar ($), which is equivalent to 100 cents (¢). Coins are minted in 1¢ (penny), 5¢ (nickel), 10¢ (dime), 25¢ (quarter), 50¢ (half dollar), and $1 denominations. Half dollars are rare and inconvenient; silver dollars are very rare; and the recent $1 coins are rather unpopular. Coin-operated telephones and vending machines accept nickels, dimes, and quarters. Try to keep a fair supply of coins in your pocket while you are in the United States. Shops usually dislike to supply change unless you make a small purchase; and in many cities you will need exact change to ride on the buses, as the drivers are not allowed to make change for you.

Paper currency is printed in $1, $2, $5, $10, $20, $50, $100, and $1,000 denominations. While the amount is clearly indicated on each bill, all are the same size and the same green color. To avoid mistakes, keep the different denominations separated in your purse or billfold; and when you pay for a small purchase with a large bill, state the amount of that bill. For example: "Two seventy-nine out of ten" means that you have paid for a $2.79 purchase with a $10 note and expect $7.21 in change. Two-dollar bills are not common, and in some parts of the country they are actively disliked. You will probably have trouble changing bills larger than $20s in many places.

Currency Exchange. Visitors who arrive by air can usually exchange their currency at the gateway airport. Not all exchange facilities offer 24-hour service, however, and we suggest that you have with you when you arrive about $50 in bills of various sizes to cover tips and your transportation into the city.

Some hotels in the United States, particularly in major gateway cities, will exchange or accept foreign currency, but many more will not. Unless you have been assured in advance that your hotel(s) will change your money for you, don't count on it. You will in any event get a slightly more favorable rate of exchange at the bank. Outside the downtown areas of larger towns and cities, most American banks do not handle foreign exchange, especially of the (in America) less common currencies, so plan accordingly. Visitors from Central and South America would do well to establish some kind of relationship with a U.S. bank in Miami before going on to other parts of the country. Banks are open Monday through Friday from 9 A.M. to 3 P.M. (0900 to 1500 hours), and *sometimes* later, except on national holidays.

When you do change your money, you can ask for the denominations you want. For day-to-day expenses, small bills are more convenient than large, preferably nothing larger than a ten. Many small shops and other small businesses, such as filling stations and fast-food establishments, will even refuse a fifty. Banks will also sometimes refuse to break a large bill unless you carry an account with them.

Travelers Checks. A handy alternative to carrying currency and the enduring hazards of exchanging it is travelers checks in United States dollar denominations, which are accepted as cash by most shops, restaurants, and other commercial establishments. You will receive your change in dollars. Almost any bank will also cash them for you, as will your hotel cashier. Your local bank can advise you about how to purchase and use travelers checks.

Letters of Credit. If you wish to have extra money available to you in case of emergency, or for some expensive serendipity, a letter of credit will do it for you. Your local bank can arrange for such a letter with its corresponding bank in the United States.

MEASUREMENTS. The United States, out of step with most of the rest of the world, does not widely use metric measures—at least not yet. The table below indicates the metric equivalents for the measures you will most likely encounter as a traveler. For table of equivalent garment sizes, see "Shopping."

United States Measure	Metric Equivalent
Weight	
Ounce	28.349 grams
Pound	0.453 kilograms

United States Measure	Metric Equivalent
Capacity	
Pint	0.473 liters
Quart	0.946 liters
Gallon	3.785 liters
Length	
Inch	2.540 centimeters
Foot	30.480 centimeters
Yard	0.914 meters
Mile	1.609 kilometers

 BUSINESS HOURS. With few exceptions, American business offices are open from 9 A.M. to 5 P.M. (0900 to 1700 hours) Monday through Friday. There is an hour's break for lunch anywhere between 12 noon and 2 P.M. (1200 and 1400 hours), but the schedule is staggered so that everyone doesn't leave at the same time. Business is often conducted over lunch among executives and salespersons and such working luncheons may extend to two or even three hours.

Hawaii is one exception to the general 9-to-5 rule. Business hours in the Islands tend to begin and end earlier than they do on the Mainland: 7:30 or 8 A.M. to 4 P.M. (0730 or 0800 to 1600 hours), an arrangement that permits residents to enjoy some of the outdoor activities that tourists find so attractive. The practice is also followed by some companies in California and other fair-weather areas.

Retail stores operate on a somewhat different time schedule than business offices. Most department stores and specialty shops in downtown areas are open Monday through Saturday from 9:30 or 10 A.M. until 5:30 or 6 P.M. (0930 or 1000 hours to 1730 or 1800 hours). Major department stores are also open until 9:00 P.M. (2100 hours) at least one night a week for the convenience of shoppers who can't get there during regular business hours. Late nights vary from city to city, but are often Monday/Thursday or Tuesday/Friday.

In tourist and resort areas, shops may be open seven days a week to accommodate visitors and vacationers, though hours may be shorter on Sundays.

If you're looking for snacks or sundries, city and suburban supermarkets, groceries, and delicatessens are usually open Monday through Saturday from 9 A.M. to about 9 P.M. (0900 to 2100 hours). Some are also open on Sundays, depending on the area, but often close earlier than on weekdays. Some are open 24 hours.

Drugstores usually operate Monday through Saturday from 8 or 9 A.M. (0800 or 0900 hours) often until late in the evening. In almost any big city neighborhood there is sure to be at least one open until midnight and all day on Sunday, but most of them aren't.

Banking hours are from (at least) 9 A.M. to 3 P.M. (0900 to 1500 hours), Monday through Friday. Museums are open from around 10 A.M. to 5 P.M. (1000 to 1700 hours), with local variations. Many are open on Sunday afternoons and some are closed on Mondays.

All banks, government and business offices in the United States are closed on national holidays, as are many retail outlets and services. Restaurants, motion picture theaters, and other entertainments are open, more often than not. Big downtown department stores are always closed on Thanksgiving, Christmas, and New Year's Day, but are often open on such other holidays as Columbus Day, Veteran's Day, and George Washington's Birthday—now traditionally sale days on which the stores offer particularly attractive bargains.

Reminder: Most of the United States observes Daylight Saving Time from April through October, during which period the clocks are set forward by one hour. Thus 12 noon Standard Time becomes 1 P.M. (1300 hours) Daylight Saving Time. It might be later than you think!

ELECTRICITY. The current in electric outlets in the United States is 110–115-volt, 60-cycle AC, as compared with the 220–240-volt DC or 220–240-volt, 50-cycle AC that is standard in some other parts of the world. Most small electric appliances—razors, electric hair curlers, dryers, and the like—will operate efficiently on the lower voltage. However, if your razor (or other electrically operated device) has a round-prong plug, you will need to bring along an adapter in order to connect it to American outlets, which accept only flat-prong plugs. In any case you won't have to carry a travel iron. One-day cleaning and even while-you-wait pressing service is available in all major cities.

SHOPPING. In a Budget Guide, the first rule for shopping and souvenir-hunting is obviously—DON'T. Instead of loading up on things, carry a notebook and keep a diary of your trip. This will fix your impressions and experiences much more clearly in your mind.

If you're looking for inexpensive novelties, color transparencies, or postcards, you'll find them in the souvenir shop at any self-respecting tourist attraction. For something a little more unusual, look for such locally crafted products as Rocky Mountain jade jewelry, buckskin jackets from Colorado, hand-stitched quilts from the mountains of West Virginia, leather cowboy boots from New Mexico, Indian basketry, jewelry and handwoven rugs from Arizona, miniature totem poles from the Northwest, red clay Indian pipes from Minnesota, Eskimo whalebone carvings from Alaska, leis from Hawaii, saddles, cowboy clothes, pottery, toys, and much more.

Products such as these are most generally available in the areas where they are crafted: at local shops and specialty stores, at crafts centers, and at state and county fairs. If your hotel is a large one, you might also find one or more boutiques in the shopping arcades that specialize in local handicrafts, although hotel shops tend to be very expensive.

Museums are another source for unusual gifts and souvenirs. Museum shops often offer excellent reproductions of some of their art objects at prices from reasonable to moderate.

Foreign visitors find that very practical everyday items are often cheaper and of better quality in the U.S. than at home. Favorite purchases are: cotton goods (towels, shirts, bedding), low-priced watches, cosmetics, sporting goods, phonograph records and tapes, clothing, luggage, pens, and sunglasses. Big cities, rather than small towns and rural areas, are the best place to shop for practicalities—both because of the variety of merchandise they offer and because they are most accessible to international visitors. Any city of even moderate size has so many different kinds of shops and stores that the very wealth of opportunity can be bewildering to a shopper from out of town. Audio and video equipment are also much cheaper in the U.S. than in Europe or, surprisingly, Japan; if you are interested in purchasing TVs or video tape recorders, however, be sure the one you want is compatible with the broadcast system back home.

The following is a guide to the shopping facilities in a typical American city. Most are easy to recognize, but if you want advice you can consult the desk at your hotel. Or ask any of the natives. They're friendly.

Specialty Shops. Many shops in the United States have very narrow specialties. They stock only one kind of merchandise, but in a complete range and assortment of models, sizes, colors, design, manufacture, etc. In any major city there are shops that specialize in books, records, sporting goods, radios and television sets, cameras, antiques, stationery, jewelry, clocks and watches, men's clothing, women's clothing, children's clothing, linens, shoes, toys, china, housewares, needlecraft, or you name it. You might sometimes have to venture off main thoroughfares to find the specialty shops you're looking for, but the effort can be worth it because of the large selection they offer—often unusual items that you can't easily find anywhere else.

Chain Stores. Somewhere in size between the specialty shops and the giant department stores are the chain stores, which operate under the same name throughout the country—names such as *J. C. Penney, Sears Roebuck,* and *Montgomery Ward.* They tend to specialize in ready-to-wear clothing, accessories, household goods, home appliances, hardware, and gadgets. They don't offer the range of choice in brand names that either the specialty shops or department stores do, but they generally offer very good value at a moderate price.

There are also low-cost chain stores, properly called variety stores, but locally known as "dime stores" or "five-and-tens." Anachronisms now, but at one time much of their merchandise did sell for 5 or 10 cents. Today the prices are up, but they still carry an inexpensive line of products that includes cosmetics, accessory items for men and women, stationery supplies, notions, hardware, toys, and games. Names by which you will recognize them include *K Mart, Kress, Lamston,* and *Woolworth.*

Department Stores. A department store in any major city in the United States tends to be very large and may have as much as 3 million square feet (more than 900,000 square meters) of selling space and carry up to 160,000 items in 150 or more separate departments. The enormous variety of its goods also covers a broad range of price and quality. Often the budget department is located in the basement, where merchandise is low cost, but can be of very good quality. Some stores also offer higher-cost merchandise that hasn't sold in its regular department upstairs at reduced prices in the basement, a practice that spawned the descriptive terms "bargain basement" and "bargain-basement prices."

Clearance sales are also conducted periodically throughout the store, often on national holidays when most government and commercial offices are closed. General sales are advertised in the newspapers, but you might find a clearance rack or counter or corner in many departments at any time during the year. It's worth looking over the merchandise, which often sells for one-fourth to one-third off, sometimes even at half the regular price.

Department stores also offer many small services for customers, such as shopping advice services, child care, rest rooms, wrapping and mailing, gift wrapping, etc. Often there is a restaurant where you can have lunch without leaving the building.

Discount Stores. Big discount stores offer substantial savings—20 to 25 percent—over what the same merchandise would cost at a department store or specialty shop. Most houses started as discount dealers in appliances, but many have expanded to clothing, sporting goods, records, photo equipment, and many other lines. They are often located outside the main shopping area, their decor is functional, they offer few amenities and a smaller selection than full-price stores do. By doing so they can reduce their operating costs and pass the savings along to customers. If you know what you want, you can often realize a substantial saving by purchasing it at a discount store. It is unlikely that they will be able to pack for export, or handle the shipping for you, so be prepared to carry your purchase with you. The warranties and repair services offered by discount houses are often much more limited than those given by regular dealers, however, so you may wind up losing money in spite of the lower initial cost, particularly if you do not get well-established brand-name merchandise. The atmosphere of large discount houses can be noisy and frantic in a way that interferes with calm judgment, too.

Factory Outlets. Run by the manufacturers themselves, these retail outlets sell their own products at prices below those charged by competing retail stores. Merchandise you can expect to find includes clothing, shoes, linens, furniture, pottery, china, and cigarettes. Like discount stores, factory outlets are frequently outside the shopping district and you'll probably have to go a bit out of your way to find them—a sightseeing opportunity in itself. If you have time, order a copy of *Factory Outlet Shopping Guide,* by Jean Bird, from P.O. Box 256-N, Oradell, N.J. 90649. Volumes run about 100 pages, large-size, softbound, and are available for: New England; New York and New Jersey; Pennsylvania; Washington, Maryland, Delaware and Virginia; and North and South Carolina. Bear in mind that to pursue this kind of shopping seriously you will need a car.

Shopping Centers. Enormous shopping centers are part of the suburban landscape all across the United States. Usually located a few miles outside the city, they house branch outlets of the big downtown department stores, at least one supermarket, fast food stands and ice cream parlors, and as many as 50 or more specialty shops offering perhaps as many kinds of merchandise. Surrounded by acres of parking space, the newer shopping centers are fully enclosed, heated in winter and air-conditioned in summer, with fountains, ponds, plants, and flowers in the walkways between the stores. If you have the opportunity you might want to sample what has become, in the suburbs, a way of life. Even smaller towns have their own modified versions of the suburban shopping center. Prices are comparable to those at the downtown stores.

Food and Drug Stores. You can buy food and beverages for between-meal snacks or picnics either at supermarkets or from neighborhood grocery stores. Supermarkets, which may carry anywhere from 6,000 to 8,000 items, are usually plentiful in and around the downtown area. The smaller neighborhood stores, fresh produce stands, bakeries, delicatessens, health food, cheese, and ethnic specialty stores are more often out of the way for visitors, but do sometimes offer unusual or gourmet items that are difficult to find elsewhere.

Sales Taxes. There are no federal sales taxes in the United States, but many states and a few cities do impose their own taxes on the retail price of merchandise. The combined state-city rate runs anywhere from 2 percent to as high as 8¼ percent of the purchase price. In most places if the merhcandise is sent outside the state, the tax is not charged. On any substantial purchase, you might save money by having it shipped home. You'll want to weigh the shipping charge versus the amount of tax you will save in making your decision. You might not always get a remission of the tax charge, since laws do vary from state to state, but it's worth asking.

You can also avoid sales taxes by shopping at the tax-free stores located at most international airports. Merchandise here is not subject to customs duties or sales or excise taxes, and you can save 25 to 50 percent or more compared to what you would pay in the city. Heavily taxed items such as liquor and cigarettes are especially favorable buys. Whatever you buy, you'll have to take it with you. Most tax-free shops are accessible only to those who can show a boarding pass for a flight whose destination is outside the United States.

SIZES. If you're shopping for shoes or clothing, the table below will help you find your way to the right size. Even so, it's best to try the item on since sizes do vary slightly from one manufacturer to another.

Men

Suits	United States	34	36	38	40	42	44	46	48	
	Metric		44	46	48	50	52	54	56	58
Shirts	United States	14	14½	15	15½	16	16½	17	17½	
	Metric		36	37	38	39	40	41	42	43
Shoes	United States	7	7½	8	8½	9	9½	10	10½	11	11½
	Metric		39	40	41	42	43	43	44	44	45	45

Women

Suits/ Coats/	United States	8	10	12	14	16	18	20	
Dresses	Metric		36	38	40	42	44	46	48
Blouses/ Sweaters	United States	32	34	36	38	40	42	44	
	Metric		40	42	44	46	48	50	52
Stockings	United States	8	8½	9	9½	10	10½	11	
	Metric		0	1	2	3	4	5	6
Shoes	United States	5	5½	6	6½	7	7½	8	8½	9

Metric	35	35	36	37	38	38	39	39	40
Gloves	Same designations								

*All size equivalents are approximate

TOBACCO. You are permitted to bring a limited amount of tobacco into the United States with you (see *Immigration and Customs*). Tobacco is heavily taxed in the United States, as are alcoholic beverages. In addition to government excise taxes there are state and local sales taxes. The rates vary from one area to another, so a pack of cigarettes you pay 55 cents for in one city might cost you 90 cents or more somewhere else. As a rule, though, cigarettes are less costly if you buy them by the carton (ten packs per carton) than by the pack, and most costly if you buy them from vending machines.

COSMETICS. Cosmetics are not subject to the same limitations as tobacco and you may bring with you whatever you think you'll need for your stay in the United States, tax- and duty-free. If you do need to make a purchase—lipstick, cleansing cream, face or eye makeup—the bigger metropolitan drug and department stores carry some imported cosmetic lines. Among them are *Eve of Roma, Lancome, Myurgia, Orlane, Mary Quant, Kanebo,* and *Shiseido.*

If you want to venture into American-made cosmetics, the domestic brands are excellent. Well-known labels include *Max Factor, Estée Lauder, Revlon, Helena Rubinstein, Ultima II,* and the hypo-allergenic lines *Almay* and *Clinique.*

Cosmetics can also be purchased in variety stores (such as the Woolworth chain), which carry such lower-priced lines as *Cutex, Flame-Glo, Maybelline, Helen Neushaefer,* and *Westmore.* They are also very good products, but are sometimes less expensively packaged than the higher-priced lines.

TELEPHONE. Post offices in the United States provide only postal services. They don't have the telephone and telegraph facilities that they do in some other countries. On the other hand, this country has more telephones per capita than any other country in the world, and the system functions superbly. The telephone is far and away the chief means of communication in the United States, and life in a city like New York would be physically impossible without it. Public telephones are everywhere, in every kind of public facility and commercial establishment—bus and train stations, air terminals, gas stations, the lobbies of office buildings, bars and restaurants, hotels, many shops, and in small booths along streets and highways. Each phone has a small plaque with operating instructions on it; the usual basic charge is 10¢ to 30¢ for three minutes.

Telegraph service in the United States has been in steady decline for many years now, and for domestic communications the telephone is much faster and more reliable. For overseas communications you can go through Western Union, the telegraph company, to either R.C.A. (Radio Corporation of America) or I.T.T. (International Telephone and Telegraph Company), both of which handle cables to other countries.

MEDICAL ASSISTANCE. Medical care in the United States is very expensive. A visit to the doctor's office can cost you $20 and up, more if laboratory tests, injections, drugs, or surgical supplies are required. If the doctor comes to treat or examine you in your hotel room, his fee will usually be not less than $35, usually more. If you must be hospitalized, your room and board alone can run well over $100 a day (over $200 in New York), with extra charges for lab tests, medication, doctors, special nurses, use of operating room, anesthetist, etc. The cost of even a short stay can be several thousand dollars.

With all this in mind you will probably want to take the precaution of purchasing insurance to cover your medical expenses in case of accident or illness during your trip. Many package tour and charter operators now offer insurance as part of their overall packages. By way of example, some may offer an inclusive policy covering medical expenses, personal accident, baggage, and certain cancellations, with provisions for extra coverage if needed, and the premium is payable with your deposit on any of its Self-Catering Vacations in the U.S. If your travel arrangements don't include such insurance, or if your present policy doesn't cover you outside your own country, then your best investment is in the low-cost holiday coverage available from certain of the big international insurance companies.

One such is *American International Underwriters,* which issues International Holiday Travel Insurance with accident and sickness coverage for about as little as \$30.00 for a 15-day visit. This buys you approx. \$4,000 worth of medical insurance and will also pay about \$12.00 per day on your hotel room if you are confined there by illness or injury.

You may elect to purchase greater coverage at proportionately greater cost. Plans are available for periods from seven to 180 days, with coverage from approx. \$4,000 to \$40,000, at premiums ranging from \$4 to \$115. The company will also provide personal effects and baggage coverage (only in combination with its accident and sickness policy) at modest extra cost. American International Underwriters offices in more than 130 countries can issue a policy for you, or write to: International Underwriters Inc., Investor's Building, Washington, D.C. 20036.

The only domestic private company still to offer short-term (30- to 60-day) insurance to foreign travelers is Mutual of Omaha, whose Foreign Visitors Plan may be bought through travel agents abroad and at some airports in the U.S.

Railway, bus, and air terminals in the United States also sell accident insurance policies on individual trips, available at insurance counters or from coin-operated vending machines.

More recently companies such as *MediCall* (c/o The Siesel Co., Inc., 845 Third Ave., New York, N.Y. 10022); *Assist-Card* (745 Fifth Ave., New York, N.Y. 10022); and *International Underwriters* (7653 Leesburg Pike, Falls Church, Va. 22043) have begun to offer actual medical assistance to the traveler through networks of affiliated doctors. Rates vary but are relatively inexpensive (\$25 for a single trip, \$75 for a year, with family rates often available).

If you do need a doctor or an ambulance while you are traveling in the United States, notify your hotel desk or, if you are outside the hotel, dial *Operator* from any telephone. The telephone operator can summon an ambulance, direct you to the nearest hospital, help locate a doctor, or refer you to a medical emergency service. Several cities also have an *emergency telephone number*—911—to call for an ambulance or the fire and police departments.

For people with a chronic illness, such as diabetes, or those taking a drug that might interfere with emergency treatment, or who are allergic to penicillin or other drugs sometimes given in emergencies—even for those who wear contact lenses—there are internationally recognized tags that can be worn on a bracelet or around the neck, specifying the condition. If any of them are yours, you should wear this little bit of jewelry, which can help avoid mistakes in case of emergency.

If you are under medication, you should bring along any pills or compounds that you are required to take, plus any necessary doctor's prescriptions. Your prescription will probably have to be rewritten by a United States doctor before a pharmacist can fill it in any event, but if you have it with you, it will often not be necessary for the doctor to reexamine you. Most towns have at least one drugstore that stays open evenings and on Sunday where you can have a prescription filled, or purchase emergency nonprescription drugs.

It's also a good idea, if you wear glasses or contact lenses, to carry an extra pair as a safeguard against the inconvenience of loss or breakage. You might also get a written copy of your lens prescription from your optometrist before you leave home—just in case you do need a new pair of glasses, or find a new frame that you especially like.

LEGAL AID. Unless you are deliberately engaged in illegal activity, it is unlikely that you will run afoul of the law in the United States. Traffic violations are always a possibility, of course, especially if you aren't thoroughly familiar with local regulations. For minor infractions, however, you often don't have to appear in court at all. You will simply be fined a set sum, depending on the nature of the violation (speeding, illegal turn, or whatever). Do *not* attempt to pay it to the officer who tickets you. He will suspect that you are offering a bribe—another, more serious offense. All fines must be paid, in person or by mail, to a clerk of the court.

If you do have to appear in traffic court, no legal representation is usually necessary, although if you are not fluent in English, you might want to have an interpreter with you.

You will need a lawyer if you run into more serious difficulty and find yourself accused of a criminal offense. If you are arrested, you will be permitted to make one telephone call to whomever you choose. You will probably choose to call your nearest consulate (or someone who can contact them for you) for assistance and advice about obtaining legal counsel or arranging for bail. If you are unable to pay a lawyer to defend you, you may ask to be assigned a public defender, whose services are free of charge.

AMERICA'S
VACATIONLANDS

CONNECTICUT

The Constitution State

Connecticut's four seasons offer year-round pleasure. Any spells of rain, fog or snow are usually short-lived and the climate is never extreme.

Connecticut is home to a cosmopolitan population. All branches of the military are represented here. Industrial employment is varied and includes shipbuilding, aeronautics, electronics, pharmaceuticals, tool-making, textiles and diverse manufacturing. The insurance business, centered in Hartford, employs many residents.

Farming, both poultry and dairy, as well as truck gardening, is becoming stronger than ever, perhaps due to the greater emphasis on good nutrition programs and home-grown products.

Numerous colleges and universities attract students from around the world—followed by parents, friends and peers—all acknowledging the stimuli to be found in this state.

Access to Connecticut is easy from almost anywhere. Amtrak has regular daily schedules in and out of the state. Bradley International Airport, just north of Hartford (in Windsor Locks), has regular domestic and international arrivals and departures. Commuter planes serve airports within the state as well as LaGuardia and Kennedy airports in New York. Regularly scheduled limousine service to airports is available in many parts of the state.

From Long Island and Fishers Island, N.Y., and Block Island, R.I., ferries accommodate people and cars en route to Connecticut.

Connecticut has an area of 5,000 square miles and 75 percent is forest or woodland.

There are picturesque villages and towns throughout the state, both on Long Island Sound and in the hills to the north.

With 96 boat or canoe launching sites (10 with access to salt water), bow and arrow as well as muzzle-loader and shotgun hunting seasons, six ski areas, more than 100 recreational areas (State Parks and Forests), and with more than 1,500 campsites in 20 campgrounds, Connecticut not only welcomes visitors but caters to them.

EXPLORING HARTFORD

The state's capital is one of Connecticut's largest and perhaps most interesting cities.

The first building one passes approaching the city from the south on I–91 is easily identified by its onion-shaped dome, topped by a gilded horse. The building is owned by the Colt Patent Firearms Company, which manufactured the famous Colt revolvers that "won the West."

Proceeding north along the Connecticut River, the highway turns into a maze of intersections leading into and out of downtown Hartford.

Entering the city via State Street, Constitution Plaza—a complex of office buildings, a hotel, TV studio, and a tree-dotted mall lined with shops and investment offices—is on the right. Across the street is the Phoenix Mutual Insurance Company's unique headquarters, which resembles a green glass boat.

Directly facing you as you proceed on State Street is the lovely Old State House (1796), a Colonial red brick masterpiece with a white dome, designed by Charles Bulfinch. The building is open to the public as a museum.

South on Main Street is the Travelers Insurance Company, one of the tallest buildings in New England. At night, its tower light welcomes travelers home. The Wadsworth Atheneum, built in 1842, is America's oldest art museum and is next on Main Street. Then come the Avery Memorial, and the adjoining Morgan Memorial, a museum with a fascinating gun room, an excellent collection of Middle Eastern and Oriental archeological relics and one of the largest exhibits anywhere of Meissen china. The gun room displays muskets, rifles, and Colt revolvers. The Avery boasts paintings by Rembrandt, Wyeth, Daumier, Gilbert Stuart, Picasso, Goya, Giordano, Cézanne, Whistler and Sargent. The statue on the lawn in front of the Morgan Memorial honors the young Connecticut schoolteacher, Nathan Hale, who was captured and hung by the British while spying on Long Island for Washington's forces.

The present state capitol sits dramatically atop the highest point in Bushnell Park, the "Central Park" of Hartford. While the governor and top officials have their offices in the gold-domed capitol, most state workers are housed in the State Office Building on the edge of the park.

Across the street in the imposing State Library, there is an interesting collection of early rifles and revolvers, and the table upon which President Abraham Lincoln signed the Emancipation Proclamation that freed all slaves during the Civil War.

Hartford's Civic Center offers major shows, entertainments and sports events. The shops, meeting rooms, boutiques, restaurants and parking garage for 4,000 cars are all awaiting the visitor. The Civic Center has brought new life to downtown Hartford, initiating new business and rejuvenating older enterprises. The Civic Center is home to Connecticut's NHL Hartford Whalers.

At 351 Farmington Avenue, on the few remaining acres of a tract once known as Nook Farm, you'll find the grand old Victorian home of Samuel Clemens (Mark Twain) and the neighboring house in which Harriet Beecher Stowe lived and worked. Today the venerable old Mark Twain House is much as it was when the Clemens family lived here. The south portico of the house is shaped like the wheelhouse of a Mississippi River steamboat, recalling for Clemens the happy years he spent on the river as a pilot. In a top floor room is the pool table upon which he worked when he wanted to escape the hubbub of the family below. The Harriet Beecher Stowe House, filled with Mrs. Stowe's furnishings, is also open to the public as a museum.

The Children's Museum of Hartford, one of the most complete in the country, is located in West Hartford. Youngsters are fascinated with the numerous exhibits, ranging from Colonial artifacts to natural history displays to planetarium shows.

PRACTICAL INFORMATION FOR HARTFORD

MUSEUMS AND GALLERIES: *Wadsworth Atheneum,* 600 Main St., 36 galleries of world-wide collections. A special gallery for sight and hearing impaired. *Connecticut Historical Society Museum,* 1 Elizabeth St. *Austin Arts Center,* Trinity College. *Joseloff Art Gallery,* University of Hartford. *Old State House* (1796), 50 State St. Bulfinch-designed brick and brownstone museum of state's legislative, governmental and judicial history.

Old Newgate Prison Museum, Newgate Rd., Rte. 20, East Granby. *Farmington Museum* (Stanley-Whitman House, c. 1660), High St., *Hill-Stead Museum,* 671 Farmington Ave., Farmington. *Old Academy Museum,* 150 Main St., Wethersfield.

HISTORIC SITES. *Mark Twain House* (1874), 351 Farmington Avenue, home of the famous author when he wrote his bestsellers. Next to it the *Harriet Beecher Stowe Home,* also open to the public. The *Butler-McCook Homestead* (1782), in the heart of downtown Hartford at 396 Main St., was occupied by four generations of one family and is furnished with original family possessions. The *Amos Bull Home,* 59 South Prospect St., houses offices of the Connecticut Historical Commission. *Hatheway House* (1760–1795), Simsbury, reflects three of Connecticut's 18th- and 19th-century architectural styles. *Ellsworth Homestead,* Windsor; *Noah Webster Birthplace,* 227 S. Main St., West Hartford, a salt-box house (about 1676), now a town museum.

In Wethersfield, the *Butolph-Williams House,* Marsh St.; the *Silas Deane House,* 209 Main St.; the *Joseph Webb House* (1732), 211 Main St., where

General Washington and Count de Rochambeau planned the Battle of Yorktown in May 1781.

TOURS. Visit *Constitution Plaza,* where the modern high-rise buildings look down on the *Old State House* (1796), an outstanding landmark-museum. *Trinity College Campus Tours* (free) can be arranged. The *Hartford Civic Center* has many shops, boutiques, and restaurants in downtown Hartford.

Special Interest Tours: Elizabeth Park, 915 Prospect Rd., has 99 acres of outstanding gardens, considered the most beautiful municipal rose gardens in the country.

Bus Tours: Gray Line has a 1½-hr. tour of the city.

Walking Tours: Hartford Convention and Visitors Bureau issues a pamphlet with recommended walking tours.

HOTELS AND MOTELS. Hartford area has hotel-motel chains as follows: *Howard Johnson,* 5; *Holiday Inns,* 2; *Ramada Inns,* 6; *Susse Chalet,* 1, and has added many modern accommodations in recent years. Rates are based on double occupancy in season; *Expensive:* over $60. *Moderate:* $35–60; *Inexpensive;* under $35. Always check for family and senior citizen rates.

HARTFORD. *Moderate:* **Koala Inn.** I–91, Exit 27. About 5 min. from downtown. Complimentary Continental breakfast.

Governor's House Best Western. 440 Asylum St. Urban. Family and weekend plans. Restaurant. Pets. Sauna.

Howard Johnson's Motor Lodge. Restaurant, bar, pool.

7 Weston St. Golf and Jai Alai nearby.

Inexpensive. **Susse-Chalet Inn.** 185 Brainard Rd. About 5 min. from downtown. One of chain.

EAST HARTFORD. *Moderate:* **Holiday Inn.** 363 Roberts. St. Branch of chain. Restaurant, bar, pool. Special family rates.

Ramada Inn. 100 E. River Drive, adjacent to Founders Bridge. Branch of chain. Dining room, bar. Continental nightly. Indoor heated pool, sauna, exercise room.

Inexpensive: **Howard Johnson's Motor Lodge.** 490 Main Street. About 10 min. from downtown Hartford. Branch of chain. Restaurant.

FARMINGTON. *Expensive:* **Hartford Marriott Hotel.** I–84, Exit 37. Full facilities including pools, health club.

Moderate: **Farmington Motor Inn.** Farmington Ave. Pleasant rooms, restaurant. Pool, sauna. Bar. Pets.

WINDSOR LOCKS. *Moderate:* **Bradley Ramada Inn.** 5 Ella Grasso Tpke. Near airport. Restaurant, bar. Indoor and outdoor pools, sauna. Limo service.

DINING OUT in the Hartford area includes everything from steak houses to a variety of ethnic restaurants. Price ranges: *Moderate,* $15–20; *Inexpensive,* under $15. Prices are based on a full meal, without alcoholic beverages.

Moderate: **Brownstone.** 124 Asylum St. Pleasant atmosphere in this restored "brownstone" with its antiques and stained glass. Entertainment. Continental menu.

Frank's. 159 Asylum St. Popular downtown restaurant. Extensive Italian-American menu.

The Last National Bank. 752 Main St. Restaurant in a former bank vault. American cuisine.

Inexpensive to Moderate: **Civic Center Restaurants.** Any of a dozen or more cater to every whim or appetite. Ethnic foods, deli sandwiches, counter or table service—even ice cream parlor delicacies. There is something here to suit the entire family.

Inexpensive: **Valle's Steak House.** 165 Brainard Road. Member of chain of family restaurants, well known for its quality beef and daily luncheon specials. Breakfast served. Free parking.

FARMINGTON. *Moderate:* **Benihana of Tokyo.** 270 Farmington Ave. Oriental décor. Hibachi preparation. Communal seating.

Corner House. In the Farmington Motor Inn. Seasonal specialties in a pleasant dining room. Entertainment nightly in the cocktail lounge.

EXPLORING CONNECTICUT

Bridgeport, second major city in the state, is principally a manufacturing center. Space-age-minded visitors may be interested in the city's Museum of Art, Science and Industry, with its Planetarium; circus fans will enjoy the P.T. Barnum Museum; and animal fanciers will want to stop at the Beardsley Park Zoo, "the biggest little zoo in New England." Carry on from Bridgeport to one of the loveliest theatrical settings in Connecticut, the American Shakespeare Theatre/Connecticut Center for the Performing Arts at Stratford. The building, modeled after the Globe Theater at Stratford-upon-Avon, England, is open primarily during the summer but does schedule special theatrical or musical performances occasionally in other seasons. At press time the future of the theater is somewhat uncertain.

New Haven

New Haven has a treasure trove of things to see, many of them connected with Yale University. A guided tour, or an individual walking tour, provides an overall view of the university. Next, visit the Art Gallery, the Peabody Museum of Natural History, or perhaps the Yale Center for British Art (from 1600s to 1900s), the Rare Book and Manuscript Library and the Yale University Library, which stages regular exhibits. New Haven's Long Wharf and Yale Repertory theaters are well known for their productions of both classical and experimental drama. They offer subscription series, and individual tickets are often available.

East of New Haven, along the shoreline, is Old Saybrook. A charming old town, it is where Yale University was spawned prior to locating in New Haven.

The Connecticut River towns on the west bank are located along Rte. 9: Essex, Deep River, Chester, Haddam, Higganum, Killingworth, and so on, to Middletown. (Rte. 9A runs parallel and is a more scenic "country" road.)

Essex is unspoiled and maintains an aura of its historic past. Homes have been kept to their colonial authenticity, and any which may have fallen into disrepair over the years have been nobly restored. The Essex Steam Railway attracts families for an old-fashioned train ride along the river and through the woods; the return to Essex may be on a sightseeing boat on the Connecticut River.

At Chester, a tiny old ferry is operated by the state. For a small fee, the ride across the river to Hadlyme and Rte. 82 gives an unusual opportunity to see the Rhenish castle high on the riverbank. It was built in 1914–19 by the actor William Gillette, famous for his portrayal of Sherlock Holmes. The castle and grounds are now state-owned and open to visitors. (mid-May–mid-October.)

Goodspeed Opera House in East Haddam, a landmark built in 1876 and restored in 1963, is the home of the American Musical Theatre. Many of the revivals and new musicals introduced at the Goodspeed later enjoy Broadway success. The wedding-cake architecture, right on the edge of the Connecticut River, is the focal point of "Goodspeed's Landing," an historic district.

Rte. 9 continues north through Middletown, home of Wesleyan University, to Hartford. Northwest of Hartford, via Rte. 44, lies Riverton—on State Rte. 20 at the far side of the People's State Forest. Here the Hitchcock Chair Factory, founded in 1818, is still making chairs modeled after the original design. Visitors can watch the "rushing" operation on chair seats through glass windows or visit the John T. Kenney Hitchcock Museum specializing in 19th-century furnishings and artifacts.

State 8 south, through Winsted and Torrington, is picturesque as it winds along through state forest areas, passing connecting routes to small rural towns on the way to the city of Waterbury, known world-wide for the fabrication of brass products such as paper clips, safety pins and uniform buttons.

Litchfield

The historic town of Litchfield should not be passed by en route south. State 118 will lead from State 8 right to the village green, which is dominated by a beautiful (reconstructed) white-steepled Congregational Church. North and South Streets contain some of the most magnificent colonial houses in America. The area has been declared an historic district by the state. The white clapboard homes with their black or green shutters must remain unchanged. Harriet Beecher Stowe, Henry Ward Beecher, and Ethan Allen were born on North Street.

Near Litchfield is Bantam Lake, largest natural lake in the state and a popular summer playground—public swimming at Sandy Beach and hiking, swimming, picnicking, camping and horseback riding at the 4,000-acre White Memorial Foundation, a bird and animal sanctuary. Lake Waramaug is also popular for watersports.

Sharon, Kent, Cornwall (with its one-lane covered bridge) and Canaan are lovely towns to explore in the northwest corner of the state; and farther south (toward Danbury) Roxbury, Bridgewater, Brookfield and New Milford are charming as well. Nearby are Candlewood Lake and Squantz Pond State Park, popular public swimming, boating and picnicking areas.

One aspect of the more technical side of Connecticut history is reflected in the area of Thomaston, Terryville, and Bristol. This is clock country, with two towns taking their names from pioneer clockmakers.

Seth Thomas started his clock works in Thomaston in 1812, after learning the trade with Eli Terry, who patented a clock with wooden works that became hugely successful. In Bristol, more than 1,600 clocks and watches, some dating back to 1790, are on display at the American Clock and Watch Museum. Terryville has a Lock Museum of America where over 18,000 locks and keys manufactured in Connecticut over a century ago are housed. Lake Compounce Amusement Park, Lake Ave., Bristol, has showboat tours of the lake, rides, games, swimming and picnic area. (Seasonal.)

Southeastern Connecticut

Those who follow American Indian lore will want to stop in Montville (north of New London), rich in the history of Uncas, chief of the Mohegans, born a Pequot. Reminders of Uncas are everywhere. Near the Mohegan Congregational Church is a small museum of Indian relics, the Tantaquidgeon Indian Museum. The frames of both a long house and a round house, the types of dwellings common to eastern Indians who didn't live in teepees as did their western counterparts, are on display in the yard.

Norwich was one of the earliest settlements in the state. There are many pre-Revolutionary homes around the Norwichtown Green, all handsomely restored and privately occupied. Mohegan Park has a memorial rose garden and small zoo. The Leffingwell Inn (1675), where Washington and his officers were frequent guests, is now a museum of Colonial times. The Slater Memorial Museum, particularly noted for its Indian and Japanese collections, is located on the grounds of the Norwich Free Academy. The Rose Arts Festival, in June, is a week-long celebration in Norwich, attracting thousands of visitors to its variety of programs.

New London and Environs

South on the Connecticut Turnpike, then on State 32, lies New London, one of Connecticut's earliest towns and one integrally connected with the sea. Like Nantucket and New Bedford in Massachusetts, New London was home for whaling ships. Whaling provided the fortunes that built the mansions of Yankee sea captains and ship owners, some of which still stand today. New London is the site of the U.S. Coast Guard Academy. Visitors may tour the grounds, stopping first to see the Visitors' Center, then visiting some buildings and the beautiful sailing vessel used in cadet training, *Eagle,* when she's in port. The Shaw Mansion (1756), now the New London County Historical Society, the Joshua Hempsted House (1678), and the Old Town Mill (1650, rebuilt in 1712), are only some of the historic buildings. The Lyman Allyn Museum has collections of Connecticut furniture, paintings, and sculpture.

For all its extensive shoreline, many Connecticut beaches are private or restricted to town residents. Those wishing to swim in salt water may stop at Ocean Beach Park, maintained by the City of New London and open to all visitors. The white sand beach is spacious. An Olympic-size pool, restaurants, snack bars, and boardwalk are additional features. Moderate entrance fees are charged. (The state maintains two beaches west of New London and east of New Haven—Rocky Neck in East Lyme and Hammonassett in Madison—as well as Sherwood Island in Westport.)

The Eugene O'Neill Memorial Theater Center is in Waterford, just west of New London's Ocean Beach Park. The Center is a living memorial to the playwright, whose summer home (and locale for several of his plays) was New London. The family summer place on Pequot Avenue, New London, called Monte Cristo Cottage, is now owned by the Center and is open to the public.

Harkness Memorial State Park, 235 waterfront acres, adjoins the O'Neill Center. Picnic facilities, a 42-room mansion and exquisite gardens attract families touring the area.

Just across the Thames River is the headquarters of the North Atlantic submarine fleet. The U.S. Navy Submarine Base is open to visitors by appointment only. A Submarine Memorial Museum is located on the east bank of the Thames River, in Groton, and a decommissioned submarine, USS *Croaker*, may be boarded.

Just east of Groton, in Mystic, the Age of Sail is recalled at Mystic Seaport Museum. The Seaport is a re-creation of an early 19th-century New England coastal village. The featured exhibit is the *Charles W. Morgan*, a venerable old ship which spent an incredible eighty years in pursuit of whales. The *Joseph Conrad*, a former Danish maritime training ship, is also permanently berthed at the Seaport and is headquarters for the Seaport Youth Training program. *Sabino*, one of the last passenger-carrying steamboats, is still operating daily tours on the Mystic River. A planetarium is an interesting complement to the tiny village scene.

The Mystic Marinelife Aquarium, just north of the Seaport, has natural displays of known, and less known, varieties of sea animals. An hourly dolphin, whale and seal show in the 1,400-seat marine theater is a daily bonus for visitors.

The Borough of Stonington is east of the village of Mystic and reached via Rte. 1. There are interesting landmarks, elegantly restored homes once owned by sea captains, and the less pretentious cottages of the fishermen. A visit to this elm-shaded area leaves lasting memories.

Northeastern Connecticut is not a tourist magnet, but is pleasant rural countryside and the home of the University of Connecticut (Storrs) and the Nathan Hale homestead (Coventry).

PRACTICAL INFORMATION FOR CONNECTICUT

HOW TO GET THERE. Connecticut is accessible via 26 airports, of which Bradley International (Windsor Locks) is the largest; *Amtrak* and local trains; *Greyhound, Trailway* and *Bonanza* buses; private car on 4,039 miles of state-maintained highways and roads; and ferry or private boat landings along the 253 miles of Long Island Sound shoreline.

TOURIST INFORMATION SERVICES. *Connecticut Department of Economic Development,* Hartford, 06106, has free Vacation Guide. Included in this publication is a comprehensive list of sites and attractions offering free admission. *Parks & Recreation Division,* State Dept. of Environmental Protection, Hartford, 06106, has list of parks, forests, campsites. *Connecticut Commission on the Arts,* Hartford, 06106, gives information on creative events. Hiking trail lists come from P.O. Box 389, East Hartford, 06108. *New England Tourist Information Center* in Olde Mistick Village, Mystic 06355; *Greater Hartford Convention & Visitors Bureau,* One Civic Center Plaza, Hartford 06103; *Bradley International Airport,* Windsor Locks. State-operated information centers are located along I–95, I–84, I–86, I–91 and the Merritt Parkway, but are open only during the summer.

MUSEUMS AND GALLERIES. Since the mid-1600's Yankee foresight has preserved much of historical interest. Yale University has the most comprehensive treasure house of arts and culture in its museums, including *Yale Art Gallery, Peabody Museum of Natural History.* In Bridgeport, visit the *Museum of Art, Science, Industry,* with its Planetarium, and the *P.T. Barnum Museum. Stamford Museum and Nature Center,* Stamford; *Bruce Museum of Natural History,* Greenwich; *Silvermine Art Guild,* Norwalk. *Litchfield Historical Society,* Litchfield; *Davidson Art Center,* Middletown. *Lyman Allyn Museum* in New London. Almost every city and town boasts a museum or gallery.

HISTORIC SITES. Note: Most historic buildings have limited hours; check first. *Lockwood-Mathews Mansion,* Norwalk. *Keeler Tavern,* Ridgefield, *Amasa Day House,* Moodus; *Nathan Hale Homestead,* Coventry, near Storrs. *Hyland House, Thomas Griswold House, Henry Whitfield House,* Guilford. *New Milford Historical Society and Museum,* New Milford. *Denison Homestead,* Mystic. *Shaw Mansion, Joshua and Nathaniel Hempsted Houses, Nathan Hale Schoolhouse, Old Town Mill,* New London. *Leffingwell Inn,* Norwich. *Groton Monument* and *Fort Griswold,* Groton; *Lighthouse Museum,* Stonington, *Thomas Lee House* in East Lyme, and *Fort Nathan Hale,* New Haven.

TOURS. *Yale University* has daily tours. *River cruises,* Essex and Haddam; *harbor cruise,* New Haven; *Valley Railroad,* Essex; *"Sabino" Mystic River cruise,* Mystic. Also nature tours at *West Rock Nature Center,* New Haven or *The Audubon Center,* Greenwich. *Gray Line* offers bus tours of some major cities.

DRINKING LAWS. Local option in towns; a few towns, therefore, are "dry" and some permit beer only. Packaged liquor, beer, and wine are sold at licensed liquor and drug stores. Beer by the carton is sold in supermarkets and grocery stores by permit. No package liquor sales Sundays, legal holidays. Liquor by the glass is available at specified times at licensed bars and restaurants.

SPORTS. *Golf:* There are 75 public golf courses and 9 semi-public courses in Connecticut, some among America's best. *Tennis:* Tennis courts are open to the public in many city parks and schools. Indoor tennis courts are found in many communities, and racquetball courts are on the increase. *Boating:* Boats can be rented in many state parks and at marinas along Long Island Sound. Launching ramps are provided by the state, both along the Sound and on the lakes. *Sportfishing:* Numerous charter boats leave ports in New London, Old Saybrook, and Noank. *Skiing.* There are six ski areas in the state. Largest is Mohawk Mt. in Cornwall. *Cross-country skiing* is offered at many state parks.

Bridgeport, Hartford, and Milford have *Jai Alai frontons,* and Plainfield Greyhound Park has dog races. Details from Tourism Div., Conn. Economic Dev. Com., State Office Bldg., Hartford, CT. 06106.

 WHAT TO DO WITH THE CHILDREN. Most of the parks in Hartford and New Haven have swimming pools, tennis, and often golf. In Hartford, the *Old State House* and *Mark Twain Memorial* interest children. Best *amusement parks* are at Lake Quassapaug, Middlebury, Lake Compounce, Bristol, and Ocean Beach Park, New London. All have swimming, boating, rides, and picnic groves. *Ocean Beach Park* in New London has a wide, white sand beach on Long Island Sound and a boardwalk, restaurant, and snack bars. The *Moran Zoo* and picnic area is also in New London. *Mystic Seaport Museum* and the *Mystic Marinelife Aquarium,* Mystic, are of interest to all ages. The *American Indian Archaeological Institute* in Washington is a research center for pre-historic man in the Northeast.

 HOTELS AND MOTELS. Accommodations are listed by price range for double occupancy, at peak season: *Moderate:* $35 to $65; *Inexpensive:* under $35. For information on **bed-and-breakfast** accommodations throughout the state, contact Nutmeg Bed & Breakfast, 56 Fox Chase Lane, West Hartford 06107, (203) 236–6698 or Bed and Breakfast, P.O. Box 216, New Haven 06513, (203) 469–3260.

AVON. *Moderate:* **Avon Old Farms Motel.** Medium size. Pool, pets, Old Farms Inn across Rte. 44.

BETHEL. *Moderate:* **Stony Hill Inn.** Medium-size motel with good restaurant, bar, pool, playground. Efficiencies available.

ESSEX. *Moderate:* **Griswold Inn.** A country inn in operation since 1776. Fine restaurant, bar.

FAIRFIELD. *Moderate:* **Merritt Parkway Motor Inn.** Exit 44E/45W. Restaurant and lounge. Playground. Outdoor pool.

HAMDEN. *Inexpensive:* **Sleeping Giant Motel.** Small motel near State Park and Quinnipiac College.

MADISON. *Moderate:* **Dolly Madison Inn.** Restaurant. Beaches nearby. Tennis and golf available in area.

MIDDLEBURY. *Moderate:* **Preston Hill Inn.** Preston Hill Dr. Restaurant and lounge with entertainment. Golf and tennis nearby.

MYSTIC. *Moderate:* **Days Inn.** 122 rooms and a swimming pool. Located on Route 27 near I–95 intersection. Restaurant.

NEW CANAAN. *Moderate:* **Hampton Inn.** Continental breakfast. Rail access and limo service.

NEW HAVEN. *Moderate:* **Howard Johnson's Motor Lodge.** 400 Sargent Drive. Restaurant, bar, pool. Pets.
New Haven Motor Inn. 100 Pond Lily Avenue. Pool, putting green. Pets.

NEW LONDON. *Moderate:* **Holiday Inn.** Restaurant, bar and entertainment. Steam baths in some rooms. Outdoor pool. Pets.

Inexpensive: **The Vaux Hall.** Restored Victorian home. Bed-and-breakfast plan.

NEW MILFORD. *Moderate:* **Homestead Inn.** Lovely old building (1816) with additional rooms in modern motel section. Restaurant nearby.

NORWALK. *Moderate:* **Silvermine Tavern.** 200-year-old New England inn. Rooms furnished with antiques. TV in parlor. Rural locale. Restaurant.

OLD SAYBROOK. *Moderate:* **Baldwin Bridge Motel.** On I–95. Refrigerators in rooms; restaurants nearby. Beach privileges.
Old Saybrook Motor Hotel. In center of town, set back from highway. Pool. Beach privileges. Restaurants nearby.
Howard Johnson's Motor Lodge. 24-hour restaurant. Other restaurants nearby. Indoor pool. Beaches nearby.

SALISBURY. *Moderate:* **White Hart Inn.** On Village Green. Picturesque, Victorian inn with fine restaurant, patio, bar.

SOUTHPORT. *Moderate.* **Pequot Motor Inn.** Exit 19, I–95. Nearby tennis and golf.

STRATFORD. *Moderate:* **Stratford Motor Inn.** Main St., Exit 53 off Merritt Pkwy. Large attractive motel, overlooking Housatonic River. Good restaurant. Boating, tennis, golf nearby. Pool, playground. Pets. Babysitting available. Laundry on premises. Shuttle to airport limo.

TORRINGTON. *Moderate:* **Yankee Pedlar Inn & Motor House.** Tradition-laden hostelry. Excellent restaurant, bar.

WATERFORD. *Moderate:* **Lamplighter Motel.** Double-decker. Restaurants nearby. Some efficiencies. Pool. Miniature golf.

 DINING OUT. Price range is for full dinners without wine or drinks, as follows: *Moderate,* $10–20. *Inexpensive,* under $10.

BRIDGEPORT. *Moderate:* **Fitzwilly's.** Light luncheon menu and special entrées at dinner. Open 11:30–midnight daily.

DANBURY. *Moderate:* **Bella Italia.** Unpretentious. Excellent Italian cuisine. Full meals as well as pizza.
Chuck's Steak House. One of chain. Char-broiled specialties. Salad bar. Beef and lobster tails. Also in Darien, East Haven, West Haven, Farmington, Hartford, Mansfield, Putnam, New London, Rocky Hill, Mystic.
Inexpensive. **Delmar.** Portuguese and Italian specialties. Open daily for lunch and dinner.

ESSEX. *Moderate:* **Griswold Inn.** Catering to travelers for 200 years. Seafood and New England fare. Music in bar nightly.

GEORGETOWN. *Inexpensive:* **Georgetown Saloon.** Steaks, chops, burgers and chili. Good food; excellent value. Live country western music weekends.

GREENWICH. *Moderate:* **Tracks.** Pub specialties: meat and fish. Open daily. Sunday brunch.

Hunan Gardens. Interesting Chinese décor. Varied Chinese menu with several specialties. Lunch and dinner. Also in Stamford and Westport.

HIGGANUM. *Moderate:* **Glockenspiel.** Bavarian cuisine, including all favorites. Desserts made on premises. Located near Rte. 9, on a running brook.

LITCHFIELD/BANTAM. *Inexpensive:* **New Bantam Inn.** Bantam. Pleasant restaurant in country setting. Continental menu.

MYSTIC. *Moderate:* **Sailor Ed's.** A landmark in the area for seafood. Noted for New England shore dinners. Seashore atmosphere.

NEW CANAAN. *Moderate:* **Gates.** Pasta and seafood specials. Lunch and dinner daily and Sunday brunch beginning at noon.

NEW HAVEN. *Moderate:* **Basel's.** Greek cuisine and wines. Live Greek music and dancing weekends.
Leon's. Fine Italian cuisine. Pasta, meat and seafood specialties, served in an attractive Mediterranean setting.
Annie's Firehouse Restaurant. Soups, sandwiches, salads. Dinner menu. Special desserts.
Inexpensive: **Fitzwilly's.** Light menu, sandwiches, soups, salads, and quiches. Lunch and dinner daily.

NEW LONDON. *Moderate:* **Chuck's Steak House.** Part of chain. Charbroiled specialties. Overlooking yacht basin on Thames River.
Fred's Shanty Seasonal. Outdoor eating overlooking the river. Burgers, chowders, seafood sandwiches.
Paisano's. A simple but attractive Italian restaurant in downtown New London. Daily specials at lunch and dinner.
Inexpensive: **Thames Landing Oyster House.** Raw shellfish bar. Dining room overlooks City Pier. Seafood specialties daily.
Whaler Restaurant on Captain's Walk. Downtown New London. Fast service, well-prepared luncheon specialties, catering to local business people. Dinners also served. Closed Sundays.

NORWALK. *Inexpensive:* **Little Anthony's.** Homestyle Italian cooking. Homemade pasta, family dining. Cocktails.
Loaves & Fishes. Fresh fish, shore dinners. Casual atmosphere. Bring the family.

OLD LYME. *Moderate:* **One Hundred Acres.** Open year-round and specializing in lobsters. Closed Mondays except July and August. Golf driving range, pitch & putt.

STAMFORD. *Moderate:* **Pellicci's.** Family-style restaurant. Italian cuisine and pizza.

STRATFORD. *Moderate:* **Fagan's.** Extensive seafood menu in relaxed atmosphere suitable for family dining.

WESTPORT. *Moderate:* **Chez Pierre.** Charming, informal bistro centrally located among Westport's shops and boutiques. French provincial menu.
Peppermill. Limited-menu steakhouse. Also lobster tails, barbecued chicken and prime ribs; salad bar. Children's portions.
Szechuan. Chinese cuisine. On Boston Post Rd., E. Near shops. Open seven days.

Inexpensive: **Arrow.** Family-oriented Italian restaurant near RR station. Full meals and pizza.

Damien's. Informal bistro near RR station. Unusual specialties; delicious burgers. Friendly bar.

WEST REDDING. *Inexpensive:* **The Country Emporium.** Small, informal restaurant adjacent to country store. Unusual pancakes and burgers on home-made "dilly" buns, sarsaparilla and orange crush.

MAINE

The Pine Tree State

To a lover of sea and scenery, the drive along the Maine seacoast on US–1 from Kittery all the way "down east" (northeast) to Eastport is a feast for the senses: crisp air, sparkling water, dark pines, the Atlantic crashing on rocky promontories, and quiet secluded harbor towns. On a straight line the coast of Maine is about 250 miles long, but if you follow the shoreline around the bays and harbors, capes and peninsulas, it is nearly 3,500 miles.

The coastal area from York Beach to Scarborough is very popular for summer vacations—long stretches of sandy beach and a variety of entertainment possibilities.

Portland, Maine's cultural and commercial center, is the gateway to Down East Maine. It is here that the shoreline changes to coves and capes, rocky coast, bays and peninsulas, and myriad offshore islands. Cruises around Casco Bay and its islands leave from the Custom House Wharf. Near the waterfront, in the Old Port Exchange district, old buildings and warehouses have been painstakingly restored and converted into an endless variety of shops.

Some of Maine's interesting and scenic towns are along Rte. 1 north of Portland: Freeport (home of L. L. Bean), Brunswick (Bowdoin College), Bath ("City of Ships") and Wiscasset (charming architecture). The Boothbays are very popular boating communities.

Rockland is a busy fishing port and an active business community. The Maine Seafoods Festival is held here in midsummer. Several windjammers that sail the Maine coast each summer depart from Rockland Harbor, as well as from Camden and from Rockport.

Camden, on Penobscot Bay, is a delightful town. Visitors are charmed by the pretty flower baskets on the lampposts. In summer, there are frequent musical and theatrical productions.

Mount Desert Island and Acadia National Park are the destination of many travelers to the Maine coast—and with good reason. The Mount Desert/Acadia National Park area reflects all the best aspects of the Maine coast and has some unique features of its own.

Almost 2,500,000 motorists annually visit Mount Desert Island and Acadia National Park. Along scenic drives, bicycle trails and footpaths, travelers stop to poke about, to see Thunder Hole, great ragged cliffs and caves, the fjord at Somes Sound (for this, be sure to take Sargent Drive, passenger cars only, out of Northeast Harbor) and to contemplate Jordan Pond. Glaciers, winds and sea have worked marvels here. Cadillac Mountain rises 1,530 feet and commands an unmatched view of both coastal and inland Maine. The summit is easily reached by car from Bar Harbor.

Bar Harbor is the commercial center of Mount Desert Island—its attractive village center is full of shops and restaurants, with a wide variety of accommodations available. There are festivals, concerts, and special events scheduled throughout the summer season.

Other points of interest in Maine: Augusta, the state capital and home of the State Museum; for campers and hikers, the vast wilderness areas of northern and eastern Maine are a sportsman's paradise; for four-season vacationing, the spectacular mountains in the Rangeley Lakes and Bethel areas are without parallel; and the Sebago-Long Lakes chain, a popular recreation area 25 miles northwest of Portland.

PRACTICAL INFORMATION FOR MAINE

HOW TO GET THERE. *By air:* There are direct flights from Boston to Augusta, Bar Harbor, Bangor, Portland, Rockland, Waterville, Auburn/Lewiston, and Presque Isle. In addition, smaller aircraft are accommodated at the many airfields located throughout the state.

By car: I–95 (which links up with four-lane Maine Tpke) cuts the state nearly in half diagonally. US 1 meanders "Down East" along the coast and then northward along the Canadian border. Primary access from Canada is through the province of Quebec via US 201.

By car ferries: Passenger-auto service from Bar Harbor and from Portland to Yarmouth, Nova Scotia.

By bus: Daily service from Boston, Mass., to Portland and along Rte. 1 to Calais. Canadian service available from Montreal to Bangor and to Portland, between Quebec and Augusta and from the Maritime Provinces along Rte. 1 to Bangor.

TOURIST INFORMATION SERVICES. Consult *The Maine Publicity Bureau,* 97 Winthrop St., Hallowell, Me. 04347; *New England Vacation Center,* Shop #2, Concourse Level, 630 Fifth Ave., New York, N.Y. 10020; and *InfoRoute USA,* Centre Capitol, 1200 McGill College Ave., Montreal, Quebec, Can. H3B4G7. There are additional Tourist Information Centers in Kittery, Portland, Augusta, Old Town, Bangor, Fryeburg, Bethel, Calais and Houlton.

STATE PARKS. In addition to Acadia National Park, 29 state parks provide excellent facilities and outdoor experiences. The season generally runs May 15–Oct. 15. Best known is *Baxter State Park,* with Mt. Katahdin, in Millinocket. Other major parks are *Aroostook,* Presque Isle; *Cobscook Bay,* Dennysville; *Lily Bay* (Moosehead Lake), Greenville; *Quoddy Head,* Lubec; *Sebago Lake,* Naples; *Rangeley Lakes,* Rangeley; *Warren Island,* Islesboro; *Grafton Notch,* Newry; *Camden Hills,* Camden; and the *Allagash Wilderness Waterway.*

MUSEUMS AND GALLERIES. Historical: *The Robert Abbe Museum of Stone Age Antiquities,* Acadia National Park; *Shaker Village,* Poland Spring; *Maine State Museum,* Augusta; *Fort Western,* Augusta; *Univ. of Maine Anthropology Museum,* Orono; *Acadian Village,* Van Buren.

Art: *Portland Museum of Art,* Portland; *Colby College Art Museum,* Waterville; *Bowdoin College Museum of Art,* Brunswick; *Wm. A. Farnsworth Museum,* Rockland.

Special Interest Museums: *Lumberman's Museum,* Patten; *Penobscot Marine Museum,* Searsport; *Boothbay Railway Village,* Boothbay; *Seashore Trolley Museum,* Kennebunkport; The *Jackson Laboratory,* Bay Harbor; *Peary-MacMillan Arctic Museum,* Brunswick, *Maine Maritime Museum,* Bath.

HISTORIC SITES. *York Village,* York, includes Emerson-Wilcox House (1740), Old Gaol Museum (1720) and several other 18th-century buildings. The *Wadsworth-Longfellow House,* Portland, was the poet's home. In Bristol, the *Colonial Pemaquid Restoration* is the site of 16th- and 17th-century archeological findings. *Fort Western,* in Augusta, and *Fort Halifax,* in Winslow-Waterville, were both stopping places on Benedict Arnold's march to Quebec.

TOURS. *By boat:* Out of Boothbay Harbor, excursion boats cruise the coastal waters and offshore islands. Boats leave Bar Harbor and Northeast Harbor for sightseeing trips around Mt. Desert Island.

By bus: A variety of bus tours are available in popular touring areas around the state: Rockland area, Portland, Boothbay Harbor, and Bar Harbor/Mt. Desert Island.

Walking tours are outlined for the capital city of Augusta, the Old Port section of Portland and the Marginal Way in Ogunquit.

Cable car Rides: Saddleback Mountain, double chair lift; Sugarloaf Mtn., gondola ride; Squaw Mtn. and Pleasant Mtn., chairlifts.

Fall foliage: Best viewing from mid-Sept. to early Oct.

WILDLIFE. *Baxter State Park,* 200,000 acres of wilderness, is a sanctuary for wild beasts and birds; *Acadia National Park,* the most important point for the Atlantic Flyway, has nature walks daily in summer; *Moosehorn National Wildlife Refuge,* Calais area; *Rachel Carson National Wildlife Refuge,* Wells (4,000 acres of coastal marsh area—habitat for a wide variety of birds, mammals and plants).

SPORTS. For the *fisherman,* this is the only state where Atlantic salmon may be caught. Saltwater fisherman go after cod, pollock, haddock, striped bass, mackerel, flounder, halibut and tuna. Charter boats are available at many coastal towns. Licenses are required for freshwater fishing, best of which are trout and bass. (Write to: Dept. of Inland Fisheries & Wildlife, State House, Augusta, Me. 04333).

Boating: The endless coastline and hundreds of miles of inland waterways offer opportunities for all types of boating. The coast is dotted with towns where boats are for hire and excursion boats embark. Rentals and guides are available at lakeside towns.

Flat-water and white-water *canoeing* are popular on lakes and streams for the beginner and expert. Best known region is the Allagash Wilderness Waterway.

White-water *rafting* has become popular, especially on northern reaches of the Kennebec and Penobscot rivers.

Hunting: In Oct., Maine's woods open for bow and arrow deer hunting; deer hunting with firearms opens generally for two weeks in Nov. Contact the *Dept. of Inland Fisheries & Wildlife,* Augusta, for licensing and for information on bear, bobcat, duck, geese, woodcock, pheasant and snowshoe rabbit hunting.

Skiing extends through Easter. Major ski areas are: Camden Snow Bowl, Camden; Squaw Mountain, Greenville; Sunday River, Bethel; Mount Abram, Locke Mills; Pleasant Mountain, Bridgton; Saddleback, Rangeley; and Sugarloaf USA, Carrabassett Valley, with Maine's only gondola. Major cross-country ski touring centers are located in Acadia National Park, Sunday River (Bethel), Carrabassett Valley, Squaw Mountain (Greenville). Other winter sports are *snowmobiling,* especially in the Allagash Wilderness Waterway area, *ice-fishing, snowshoeing* and *sled dog races.*

WHAT TO DO WITH THE CHILDREN. York Beach, Wells, and Old Orchard Beach all have amusement parks. *Seashore Trolley Museum* in Kennebunkport features open trolley rides. *Boothbay Railway Museum* offers rides on a narrow-gauge railroad. *Grand Banks Schooner Museum,* Boothbay Harbor, is a Grand Banks fishing dory to tour from stem to stern. *Gulf of Maine Aquarium,* Portland, has "hands-on" exhibits. Andre the Seal, Rockport, performs daily during the summer at 4 P.M.

CAMPING. Besides being less expensive, the mountains and lakes, woods and seashore of Maine are perfect settings for camping or for renting a cottage by the week. The Maine Publicity Bureau, 97 Winthrop St., Hallowell, Me. 04347, furnishes an annual listing of campgrounds and cottage rentals.

HOTELS AND MOTELS. Accommodations in Maine range from the expensive and sometimes spectacular resorts to simple hotels and motels in the small towns. Cottages, guest houses, delightful tourist homes and "bed and breakfast" inns abound and are often the most charming and least expensive alternative. Chambers of Commerce will be happy to send you names and addresses. Rates are based on double occupancy, in season: *Moderate* $30–45; and *Inexpensive* under $30. There is a 5% room tax throughout the state. Along the coast, many hotels and motels are open from May to Sept. or Oct. only, so it's best to check ahead.

BANGOR: *Moderate:* **White House Motel.** A Best Western motel; all the usual amenities. Quiet, spacious. Pool. Open year-round.

Inexpensive: **Woodland Terrace.** Attractive, secluded setting. Play area. Golf course. Breakfast available.

BAR HARBOR. *Moderate.* **Cadillac Motor Inn.** Pleasant motel close to town. Ideal for families. Convenient, comfortable, cordial. Some kitchenettes.
Frenchman's Bay Motel. Directly across from ferry slip. Golf privileges, tennis, and swimming. Sweeping views. Private beach.
Inexpensive: **McKay Cottages.** Guesthouse. Charmingly furnished. Walk to restaurants, shopping and waterfront.

BATH. *Moderate:* **Grane's Fairhaven Inn.** A country inn (1790) nestled in the hillside overlooking the Kennebec River. Hike in 27 acres of surrounding woods. Boating, beach, golf, restaurants nearby. Country breakfast available.

BETHEL. *Inexpensive-Moderate:* **Sunday River Inn.** Hostel accommodations; families and groups welcome. Family-style meals included. Open during ski season only.
Inexpensive: **L'Auberge.** Homelike country inn at edge of village. Spacious lawns and gardens.

BOOTHBAY. *Moderate:* **Captain Sawyer's Place.** The "yellow house" in the heart of town. An old sea captain's home remodeled into a charming guest house.
Ocean Point Motel. Motor lodge, inn and motel—charming seacoast setting, Down East hospitality, home-cooked food. Boat trips leave from wharf.
Thistle Inn. Old sea captain's home, in center of town, converted to a New England inn. Good food, friendly bar. Open all year.

CAMDEN. *Moderate:* **High Tide.** Overlooks Penobscot Bay, with private beach, play area. Cottages and family units available.
Inexpensive: **Snow Hill Lodge.** Open year-round. Coffee bar. (Just north of Camden, in Lincolnville.)

CASTINE. *Moderate:* **Pentagöet Inn.** Small, comfortable Victorian inn, right on the coast. Full dinner service.

ELLSWORTH. *Moderate:* **Brookside Motel.** Convenient in-town location, 20 minutes from Acadia National Park. Attractive, modern rooms; pool. Open all year.

FORT KENT. *Moderate:* **Jalbert's Allagash Camps.** Located in Allagash Wilderness Waterway area, reachable by canoe only. Comfortable cabins, tasty meals. Equipment and guides provided for a variety of deep-woods experiences, especially canoeing and fishing.

KENNEBUNK. *Moderate.* **The Kennebunk Inn.** Fine lodging and meals in historic inn. Cocktail lounge. Centrally located in village.

KENNEBUNKPORT. *Moderate:* **The Tides Inn By-the-Sea.** Quaint ocean-front lodging on beach. Sports nearby. Restaurant. Casual.

MONHEGAN ISLAND. *Moderate:* **The Island Inn.** Rather plain food and furnishings. Peace and quiet. No smoking. Appeals to birdwatchers, artists and fishermen.

MOOSE RIVER. *Moderate:* **Sky Lodge and Motel.** "Luxury in the Rough" in remote back country. Mountain and lake views. Excellent food. Pool, archery, rifle range. Rustic.

OGUNQUIT. *Moderate:* **Colonial Village.** Screened cottages, some with kitchens, and additional motel units—overlooking the ocean. Tennis, boating, pool.

PORTLAND. *Inexpensive:* **Susse Chalet,** Comfortable and predictable member of chain.

RANGELEY. *Moderate:* **Town & Lake Motel.** Modern lakeside family resort, offering private beach and play area. Swimming and boating; skiing (nearby) and snowmobiling.

TENANTS HARBOR. *Moderate:* **The East Wind Inn.** Restored 19th-century inn. Lovely view of the waterfront from the veranda. Perfect for a relaxing vacation. Hearty meals.

WALDOBORO. *Moderate:* **Moody's Motel.** Casual, relaxed motel, high on a hill with a wonderful view. Fine restaurant.

WELLS. *Moderate:* **The Grey Gull Inn.** Oceanfront rooms in a small Maine Coast "bed and breakfast" inn. Fine restaurant, cocktails. Open year-round.

WESTPORT. *Moderate:* **The Squire Tarbox Inn.** Very small restored country inn. Delightful and friendly. Antique furnishings. Sumptuous dining.

 DINING OUT. Seafood and Maine are virtually synonymous. No visit is complete without a meal or meals of lobster, clams, salmon and/or trout. Dinner price ranges are for complete dinners per person, exclusive of cocktails and wine, as follows: *Moderate* $10–15; *Inexpensive* under $10.

BANGOR. *Moderate:* **Pilot's Grill.** Family-owned and operated. Home-style cooking, featuring delectable lobster, steak and roast beef; well-rounded bill of fare. Children's menu.

BAR HARBOR. *Moderate:* **Brick Oven Restaurant.** Cozy turn-of-the-century atmosphere, reminiscent of Bar Harbor's golden era. Varied menu: lobster, seafood, beef, great salads, and tasty desserts.
Testa's. Grill Room and Garden Room. Steaks, shellfish, Italian specialties; inspired green salads, fresh fruit pies. Breakfast, lunch, and dinner. Children's portions.

BETHEL. *Moderate:* **Mother's.** Gingerbread house with wood stoves and bookshelves in the dining room. Lobsters and steamers are featured.

BOOTHBAY. *Moderate:* **The Blue Ship.** Seafood, steak, sandwiches and chowder. Homemade breads and pastries. Wonderful cinnamon buns for breakfast! Harbor view.
Inexpensive: **Ebb Tide.** Breakfast, sandwiches, chowders, seafood dinners. Homemade pies. Children's plates. Take-out available.

BRUNSWICK. *Moderate:* **Stowe House.** Enjoy prime ribs, steak, Maine seafood and other selections in this historic home of Harriet Beecher Stowe. Children's menu available.

CAMDEN. *Moderate:* **Peter Ott's Tavern & Steakhouse.** Dinner only, offering excellent steaks and seafood. Home-baked bread and homemade desserts. Informal.

FALMOUTH. *Inexpensive:* **Alan's Acre.** A real, honest-to-goodness diner serving "fast food" and homemade specials. Muffins, pies and chowders made on the premises. Breakfast and lunch only.

HALLOWELL. *Moderate:* **Mariah's.** Fine cuisine with French touch. Veal scaloppine, duckling with blueberry sauce, steaks and seafood.

KENNEBUNKPORT. *Moderate:* **Olde Grist Mill.** Dine in an historic (1749) tide-water mill filled with antiques. Traditional Maine dishes—from chowder to Indian pudding. Children's portions. Country store and gift shop adjacent.

OGUNQUIT. *Moderate:* **Ogunquit Lobster Pound.** Lobster, clams, steaks, deep-dish pies. Dine outdoors or in the rustic dining room.
Inexpensive: **Barnacle Billy's.** Perkins Cove. Dine outside by the cove or inside by the hearth. Lobster, chicken, and stews, sandwiches and salad plates. Scenic cruises from wharf.

OQUOSSOC (Rangeley Lakes). *Moderate:* **The Oquossoc House.** Restaurant and cocktail lounge. Charcoal-broiled steaks, seafood, daily specials.

PORTLAND. *Moderate:* **The Marketplace Restaurant** (So. Portland). Designed as a turn-of-the-century city market. Prime beef and seafood, New York-style cheesecake.
Inexpensive: **Cap'n Newick's Lobster House.** So. Portland. Complete seafood menu at family prices; also steaks and chicken. Informal.

SOUTHWEST HARBOR. *Moderate:* **Long's Downeast Clambakes.** Lobster, clams and corn—steamed in rockweed and served outdoors.

YORK. *Moderate:* **Bill Foster's New England Lobster & Clambake.** Clams, lobster and all the "fixin's" (or steak or chicken). Features an old-fashioned sing-along. Reserve ahead. Summer only.

YORK HARBOR. *Moderate:* **York Harbor Inn.** Varied menu—"Continental" selections, including stuffed mussels, pasta, veal, beef, and seafood. Children's portions; entertainment in the lounge.

MASSACHUSETTS

Boston, Berkshires and the Cape

A tour of Massachusetts properly starts in Boston—and on foot. The most historic sites are located along the Freedom Trail, a well-planned walk of only one and one-half miles. The tour leads through the heart of the historic old city, linking sixteen famous colonial, revolutionary, and other historic sites. As you follow the trail, which is marked by a red line, you will walk not only into the past of Boston, but into some of the most exciting chapters in the early history of the United States. Visit the Freedom Trail Information Center on the Tremont St. mall adjacent to the Boston Common for brochures and maps.

First stop is the Park Street Church, built in 1809. Henry James called it "the most interesting mass of brick and mortar in America." It was here that William Lloyd Garrison gave his first anti-slavery address (1828) and that *America* was first sung (1831), both on July 4th. The corner on which the church stands was once known as Brimstone Corner because at the time of the War of 1812 brimstone, a component of gunpowder, was stored in the church.

After leaving the church, walk up Park Street towards the gold-domed brick structure which faces Boston Common. This is the "new" State House, built on what was John Hancock's cow pasture and completed in 1798. It is an excellent example of the work of Charles Bulfinch, our first important native-born architect. Among the rooms open to visitors are the Archives Museum (annals of American history) and the Hall of Flags, a memorial to those who died in the Civil War and later conflicts in which America was involved. One of the more interesting artifacts housed in the State House is the "Sacred Cod," which hangs in the portal of the visitors' gallery. The 200-year-old carving pays homage to the fish on which Massachusetts built its colonial economy.

Boston Common, which you will enter after leaving the State House and crossing Beacon Street, is just that—land held in common by the people of Boston. It has never been anything but open land, although it once sloped much more sharply towards the crest of Beacon Hill. Earth taken from the top of this promontory (the hill was once itself as high as the top of the State House dome) was used to begin the landfill projects which changed the face of Boston in the 19th century. The town bought the 50-acre pasture which forms the Common from a hermit, Rev. William Blaxton, in 1634. Originally the land was set aside for the training of the local militia and the common grazing of cattle, and citizens of Boston may still graze their cows there—if they have any and are so inclined. The Common is where 17th-century Puritans set up stocks and pens to punish such crimes as swearing and failing to keep the Sabbath. A more permissive attitude prevails today, and just about every political and social viewpoint is represented by the soapbox orators and pamphleteers at the Park and Tremont entrance to the Common. Farther along Tremont is the Central Burying Ground, where artist Gilbert Stuart is buried.

From the Park Street Church, the Freedom Trail heads north along Tremont St. On the left is the Granary Burying Ground, once the site of Boston's granary which gave its name to the cemetery. The graves of John Hancock, Robert Treat Paine, and Samuel Adams, signers of the Declaration of Independence, are here, as are those of Paul Revere, Peter Faneuil, James Otis, many governors, Benjamin Franklin's parents, and victims of the Boston Massacre.

At the corner of Tremont and School Sts. stands King's Chapel, Boston's first Episcopalian church. The present building was completed in 1754, although the congregation was organized in 1686. In Colonial days the church was a royal favorite. Queen Anne donated the red cushions and George III supplied the communion plate. The burying ground beside the church was the colony's only cemetery for many years and contains the graves of Governor Winthrop and William Dawes, Jr. On the opposite corner is the Parker House hotel, which gave its name to Parker House rolls.

On the left as you head down School St. is Boston's old City Hall. A schoolhouse built near the hall in 1635 became Public Latin School, the first public school in the country. The Rev. Cotton Mather, Emerson, Hancock, and Samuel Adams are a few who studied there and went on to make their mark on American history. On the lawn of City Hall is a statue of Benjamin Franklin which was erected in 1856. One side of Franklin's face is smiling while the other is sober; sculptor Richard S. Greenough seems to have presaged Picasso in his ability to convey two sides of his subject's personality at once.

On the left where School St. meets Washington St. is the Old Corner Bookstore. Built in 1712–1715, the building was a meeting place for such writers as Emerson, Hawthorne, Longfellow, Oliver Wendell

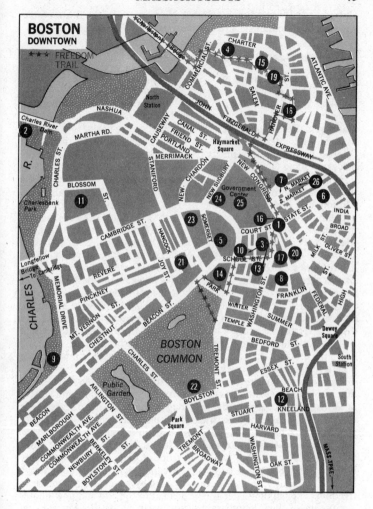

Points of Interest

1) Boston Massacre Site
2) Boston Museum of Science
3) Old City Hall
4) Copp's Hill Burying Ground
5) Court House
6) Custom House
7) Faneuil Hall
8) Franklin's Birthplace Site
9) Hatch Memorial Concert Shell
10) King's Chapel
11) Massachusetts General Hospital
12) Tufts New England Medical Center
13) Old Corner Book Store
14) Park Street Church and Old Granary Burying Ground
15) Old North Church (originally Christ Church)
16) Old State House
17) Old South Meeting House
18) Paul Revere's House
19) Paul Revere Statue
20) Post Office
21) State House
22) Central Burying Ground
23) State Office Building
24) John F. Kennedy Federal Building
25) New City Hall
26) Quincy Markets

Holmes, and Harriet Beecher Stowe. Now owned by the Boston *Globe* newspaper, it contains a literary museum and a bookstore.

The Tea Went Overboard

Across Washington St. is the Old South Meeting House. Here, the colonists held many mass meetings that culminated in the Revolutionary War. The plot for the Boston Tea Party took shape here and during the war the building was used by the British for practicing equestrian maneuvers. Returning along Washington St. to the north, turn right on State St. and enter the Old State House, once the seat of the British colonial government. From its balcony, citizens of Boston heard the news that King George III had been crowned. Here, too, the Declaration of Independence was first read in Boston on July 18, 1776. Below the balcony, mobs burned symbols of the hated British. Generals Gage, Clinton, and Howe planned the strategy for the battle of Bunker Hill in the building. Across State St. from the Old State House is a circle of cobblestones marking the site of the Boston Massacre when, on March 5, 1770, British soldiers fired into a taunting mob of colonists, killing five men. One was Crispus Attucks, the first black person to die in America's battle for liberty. In a rare show of cooperation, the British agreed to a trial of their soldiers involved in the massacre. Eager to prove their fair-mindedness, the colonists provided John Adams and Josiah Quincy, Jr. to conduct the defense. All but two were acquitted, and those convicted of manslaughter were branded on the hand and discharged from the army. That might have been the end of it, but Sam Adams got Paul Revere to do an engraving of the Redcoats shooting down the peaceful citizens of Boston. Widely circulated, it inflamed the populace against the British.

The old State House, now carefully restored, once again displays the lion and unicorn at the corners of its east gable. These ancient symbols of British imperial power flanked the current monarch, George III's descendant Queen Elizabeth, when she spoke from the building's balcony during her bicentennial good-will visit to Boston.

Continue down State St. and turn left at New Congress St. Dock Square and Faneuil Hall will be in front of you. The hall, originally built by Peter Faneuil as a market, is called the "Cradle of Liberty" because so many meetings were held here by advocates of American freedom. The building later was presented to the city and now houses a museum of flags, photographs, and weapons of the Ancient and Honorable Artillery Company of Boston. The great balconied hall on the upper floor is still used as a forum for public discussion and debate.

The ground floor of Faneuil Hall has been renovated as a part of one of the most talked-about urban "recycling" projects of recent years. Restaurants, food, and specialty shops dominate the three stately granite and brick arcades of the old Quincy Market, which stand behind Faneuil Hall; beyond this chic bazaar stretches the new waterfront park and the handsomely restored wharf buildings, several of which also house new shops and eating places. The view of the harbor makes this a favorite area for evening strollers.

The next point on the Freedom Trail is the Paul Revere House. Revere lived here from 1770 to 1780, and from here set out on his historic ride to Lexington in April, 1775. The house, probably the oldest wooden structure in Boston, was built in the 1670s and is furnished as it was when the patriot lived here.

From the Revere House it is a short walk (via Prince, Hanover, Bennett, and Salem Sts.) to Old North Church (1723), the oldest church in Boston. The two lanterns hung from its steeple on the night of April 18, 1775, signaled that the Redcoats were leaving for Lexington and Concord and started Paul Revere on his ride. In 1781, the old bells in the steeple rang out the good news that Cornwallis had surrendered at Yorktown. The Cyrus Dallin equestrian statue of Paul Revere graces the small park at the rear of the Church.

You are now in the middle of Boston's North End. As you will no doubt gather from the narrow, winding streets, this is the oldest part of the city. Since its heyday as an eighteenth-century residential neighborhood, this compact area has been home to waves of foreign immigrants. The last great influx, around the turn of the present century, was Italian, and it is an Italian flavor which continues to prevail here. Plan to arrive in the North End hungry—and if you are traveling in summer, try to take in one of the many street festivals with which saints' days are still celebrated.

Charlestown, the Bunker Hill Monument, and the *Constitution (Old Ironsides)* are on a Freedom Path across the Charlestown Bridge. Follow local signs to the Bunker Hill Monument. You can climb the spiral staircase of this 221-foot granite obelisk commemorating the first major battle of the Revolution and enjoy a grand view of historic Boston. Built in the early 19th century to commemorate the famous battle of June 17, 1775, the monument actually stands on Breed's Hill, where the misnamed battle was fought; Bunker Hill is just north of it. At the bottom of the hill can be seen the docks of the Charlestown Navy Yard and the tall masts of the *Constitution*. There are adequate parking facilities at the ship if you are driving. Walk up the gangplank onto the wonderfully preserved ship that never lost a fight. The 44-gun frigate first put to sea in 1798 and is the oldest commissioned ship of the U.S. Navy. Its copper sheathing and brass fittings came from the foundries of Paul Revere and Sons. The navy yard, now decommissioned, is being restored as a part of Boston National Historic Park.

Beacon Hill and Back Bay

No visit to Boston would be complete without at least a brief walk through the beautiful, gas-lit, tree-lined streets of Beacon Hill, past the brick townhouses where many of Boston's wealthy, socially prominent families lived throughout the nineteenth century.

The twin mansions at 39 and 40 Beacon Street were built around 1815, and house the Women's City Club. Call for tour schedules.

After you have walked the Freedom Trail through old Boston and have seen Beacon Hill relax as Bostonians do in the Public Garden. Then continue your walking tour of Boston with a stroll through the Back Bay, so called because it was once a backwater of the Charles River, before being filled and reclaimed. It is now a treasury of cultural institutions and Victorian architecture.

Two blocks west of the Garden, on Boylston St., is Copley Square, one of the most attractive public places in the nation. On the left as you enter the square is Trinity Church, designed by H.H. Richardson and built in 1877. Across the square is the Public Library, designed in the style of the Italian Renaissance. An interior courtyard and many art-works by Puvis de Chavannes, John Singer Sargent, Daniel Chester French, and others give it uncommon interest. The library has been expanded with a large addition designed by Philip Johnson. Copley Square is bounded on the south by the elegant old Copley Plaza Hotel and the new Copley Place development of hotels, shops, and apartments. Behind the hotel rises the 60-story John Hancock Tower, a thin rhomboid covered with reflective glass, designed by I. M. Pei. From the John Hancock Observatory on the 60th floor of the Tower, the highest man-made observation point in New England, you may have a panoramic view of eastern Massachusetts from New Hampshire to Cape Cod. Also worth your time are four observatory exhibits: "Boston 1775," "Cityflight," "Skyline Boston," and "Photorama." Fine views of the city may also be had from the top of the Prudential Tower, which stands at the center of a complex of shops, apartments, and a hotel between Back Bay and the architecturally interesting South End.

Cambridge

Across the Charles River from Boston is Cambridge, a city world-famed for its educational institutions. Harvard University, oldest in America, was founded in 1636. Center of collegiate life is the original campus, Harvard Yard, mellow with age and teeming with youth. The architecture of Harvard ranges from the red brick Georgian of Massachusetts Hall, the oldest building on the campus (1720), to the Visual Arts Center, designed two-and-a-half centuries later by Le Corbusier. In mid-course of Harvard's architectural evolution is University Hall, a handsome granite edifice designed in 1813 by Charles Bulfinch. Two Harvard attractions that should not be missed are the Fogg Art Museum and the University Museums, which include collections devoted to archeology and ethnology (the Peabody Museum), comparative zoology, minerals and geology, and botany (be sure to see the famous glass flowers).

Sharing the Charles River waterfront with Harvard is the Massachusetts Institute of Technology, founded in 1861 and now considered the world's leading school of science and engineering. M.I.T.'s architecture ranges from neo-classical to ultra-modern (see the Saarinen chapel and the auditorium).

Two of Cambridge's traditional landmarks are Christ Church, a beautiful Georgian edifice designed by Peter Harrison in 1761 and used during the Revolution as a barracks for Colonial soldiers, and the Longfellow House at 105 Brattle St., about half a mile from Harvard. George Washington used this house as headquarters in 1775. A young Harvard instructor, Henry Wadsworth Longfellow, bought the house in 1843 and lived here until his death in 1882. Open to the public, the house is furnished with the poet's furniture and books.

Lexington and Concord

Northwest of Boston by way of Arlington is the attractive suburb of Lexington. In the center of town is Lexington Green. Here, on April 19, 1775, 77 Minutemen stood up to 700 British soldiers and lost eight of their number in the opening skirmish of the Revolutionary War. Buckman Tavern, still standing on the Green, was the mustering place of the Colonials. Nearby is the Hancock-Clarke House, where John Hancock and Samuel Adams were awakened on the 18th of April in '75 by Paul Revere's announcement that the British were coming. British headquarters were in the Munroe Tavern at 1332 Massachusetts Ave. All these buildings, open to visitors and furnished as they were, will help you re-create the events of that day which made Lexington "The Birthplace of American Liberty."

At Minuteman National Historical Park you will see the famous Old North Bridge across the Concord River, with Daniel Chester French's equally famous statue of the Minuteman standing guard. Visit the Concord Museum on Lexington Road to see Paul Revere's signal lantern, relics of the battle, and a diorama of the Battle of Concord. And if you are here on Patriot's Day (the Monday closest to April 18th), see the battle re-enactment at Lexington and the parade over the North Bridge in Concord.

Concord is equally noted for its literary associations. You can visit Emerson House, the home of Ralph Waldo Emerson from 1835 to 1882; The Old Manse (just a step from Old North Bridge), originally the parsonage of Emerson's grandfather, later the home of Nathaniel Hawthorne; Orchard House, where Louisa May Alcott wrote *Little Women;* and Walden Pond, where Thoreau lived for two years before writing *Walden.* Another literary shrine is six miles out of Concord at South Sudbury. This is the Wayside Inn, made famous by Henry Wadsworth Longfellow's *Tales of a Wayside Inn.* Restored to its original state by Henry Ford, the Wayside Inn still receives travelers and offers them such New England delights as Indian pudding and deep-dish apple pie. You will enjoy strolling through the extensive gardens of this charming old inn. One of its attractions is the original schoolhouse to which Mary went followed by her little lamb. Uncounted Americans who know "Mary Had a Little Lamb" by heart are surprised to learn that this jingle concerned real characters. But this is typical of Boston and its suburbs, where American history, legend, and folklore come alive.

PRACTICAL INFORMATION FOR BOSTON AND CAMBRIDGE

HOW TO GET AROUND. *By air: Logan International Airport,* about 3 miles from Boston, is served by all major airlines. Facilities have been designed with handicapped travelers in mind. There is adequate taxi service to downtown Boston, as well as private bus service and Massachusetts Bay Transit Authority (MBTA) public transportation (bus and subway).

By boat: Service from Boston to Provincetown, daily in summer from Commonwealth Pier. Boats also leave Rowe's and Long Wharves for Nantasket beach.

By bus: Greyhound terminal is at Park Square; *Trailways* is at South Station. The MBTA operates local and suburban bus, subway, and trolley lines. Maps available at Park Street Station.

By train: Boston is the northern terminus of *Amtrak*'s northeast corridor, and is served several times daily by trains from Washington and New York. *South Station* is the point of arrival and departure for these trains. Trains also leave South Station for Springfield, Mass., Albany, N.Y., and points west. *North Station* is the terminal for rail service to the north shore and western suburbs. Contact Amtrak for information on budget excursion fares.

TOURS. *Gray Line of Boston,* departing from Park-Plaza, Sheraton-Boston, and Copley Plaza hotels, has a number of good tours covering historical and business sections; also other sites of interest.

SPECIAL INTEREST TOURS. *Harbor:* Bay State Cruises, 20 Long Wharf, and Massachusetts Bay Lines, 344 Atlantic Ave., offer tours of the inner and outer harbors, some with stops on Georges Island. Mass Bay Lines runs dinner and sunset cruises with live music.

Bicycle Tour: Planned and frequently ridden by famed heart specialist Dr. Paul Dudley White, marked 11-mi. path begins and ends at Eliot Bridge across Charles River.

Walking Tours: The City of Cambridge publishes Old Cambridge Walking Guide, available free at information center in Holyoke Center, Harvard Sq. or at Cambridge City Hall, Central Square. Included are Cambridge Common, Christ Church, the Longfellow House, and some of the historic buildings of Harvard.

The Harvard Information Center at Holyoke Center offers university maps and information on guided tours which leave twice each day and once on Saturdays from the Admissions Office, 8 Garden St. Saturday tours leave from Holyoke Center. Free guided tours of the M.I.T. campus depart weekdays from the Information Center, Building 7, on the Institute's Mass. Ave. campus. Call the Institute for details.

MUSEUMS. *Museum of Fine Arts.* 465 Huntington Ave. American, European, Oriental collections; period rooms, musical instruments, silver. Lectures, films, special children's programs. Be sure to see the Museum's new West Wing. *Isabella Stewart Gardner Museum,* 280 The Fenway. Home of Mrs. Gardner, patron of arts. Paintings, sculpture. Both the Museum of Fine Arts and the Gardner Museum are the site of frequent concerts of classical music given by local chamber ensembles. *Institute of Contemporary Art,* 955 Boylston St. *Fogg Art Museum,* Harvard Univ., 32 Quincy St., Cambridge. Paintings, drawings, sculpture, photography. *Peabody Museum,* 11 Divinity Street, Cambridge. Mayan and other ancient artifacts. *Busch-Reisinger Museum,* Kirkland Ave., Cambridge. On Harvard campus, specializing in art of Germanic countries from medieval through modern periods. Free concert programs weekly during school year. *Museum of Science,* Science Park. Natural history, physical science demonstrations, astronomy, medical science displays. *Charles Hayden Planetarium,* part of Museum of Science. 45-min. shows. *Children's Museum,* 315 Congress St., downtown Boston. Hands-on, "do-it-yourself" exhibits. *New England Aquarium,* Central Wharf. Hundreds of live specimens, including dolphins and sharks. *John F. Kennedy Library,* Columbia Point, houses late President's papers and effects; film on JFK's life shown daily.

HISTORIC SITES. *Freedom Trail:* Booklet outlining walking tour is available at Tremont St. Information Center; the Greater Boston Chamber of Commerce, 900 Boylston St.; and at points along the way.

John F. Kennedy National Historic Site, 83 Beals St., Brookline. Birthplace of Pres. Kennedy. *Bunker Hill Monument,* Monument Sq., Lexington & High St., Charlestown. Spiral staircase to top of 221-ft. obelisk. *The Longfellow National Historic Site,* 105 Brattle St., Cambridge, is a Georgian house (1759) which served as Gen. Washington's headquarters in 1775 and was Henry Wadsworth Longfellow's home. In Brookline, *Frederick Law Olmstead National Historic Site,* Warren St., commemorates life and work of great landscape architect. In South Boston, *Dorchester Heights National Historic Site* marks spot where Washington placed guns for siege of Boston. Information on other historic sites in area available at headquarters of *Boston National Historic Park,* on State St. opposite Old State House.

GARDENS. *Public Garden,* next to Boston Common, has formal gardens, rare trees, swan boats, and in spring a wondrous display of tulips. *The Arnold Arboretum,* Jamaica Plain, offers a non-stop, year round show of flowers, shrubs, trees. One of the best in the country.

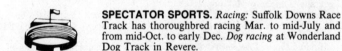

SPECTATOR SPORTS. *Racing:* Suffolk Downs Race Track has thoroughbred racing Mar. to mid-July and from mid-Oct. to early Dec. *Dog racing* at Wonderland Dog Track in Revere.

The Red Sox play *baseball* at Fenway Park; the Celtics, *basketball,* and Bruins, *hockey,* at Boston Garden; and the Patriots, *football,* at Foxboro Stadium.

SPORTS. *Boating* and *fishing* (on Charles and Mystic rivers, harbor bay, and inland lakes); *golf, tennis, horseback riding, in Franklin Park; ice skating* in winter.

WHAT TO DO WITH THE CHILDREN. Young people will enjoy the *Freedom Trail Walking Tour* or a sightseeing trip to *Paul Revere's House;* the site of the Boston Massacre; *Old Ironsides* (in the U.S. Naval Shipyard); and other highlights of the country's history. Other points of interest include: *Franklin Park Zoo* (Dorchester), *New England Aquarium, Children's Museum of Boston, Museum of Science* and the *Charles Hayden Planetarium,* as well as the swan boats in the *Public Gardens.*

HOTELS AND MOTELS. The following ranges pertain to double occupancy in both Boston and Cambridge hotels and motels: *Moderate,* $60–85; *Inexpensive,* $35–60; *Rock Bottom,* under $35.

BOSTON. *Moderate:* **Eliot.** 370 Commonwealth Ave. Small, renovated Back Bay hotel, corner Mass. Ave. Half-hour walk or subway to downtown sights.

Ramada Inn. 1234 Soldiers Field Rd., Brighton. Pool, play area nr. Pets. Restaurant, bar, entertainment, dancing. There is another Ramada Inn at Logan Airport.

Inexpensive: **1200 Beacon St.** 1200 Beacon St., Brookline. Restaurant, bar, entertainment, dancing. Free airport car.

Terrace. 1650 Commonwealth Ave., Brighton. All rooms with kitchenettes. Restaurant nr.

Rock Bottom: **Susse Chalet Motor Lodge.** 800 Morissey Blvd. Pool area. No pets. Restaurant nr. Just renovated. 15-minute drive to Harvard Square. Lowest prices around.

CAMBRIDGE. *Moderate:* **Harvard Motor House.** 110 Mt. Auburn St. Practically in Harvard Square. Direct access to public transportation.

Rock Bottom: **Susse Chalet.** 211 Concord Tpk. (Rte. 2). Not very close to Harvard or other Cambridge attractions, but lowest prices around.

DINING OUT. Boston is as good a place for gourmet dining and wining as you're likely to find. The cost of an a la carte dinner is the basis of our price range but does not include drinks, tax or tip. *Moderate,* $12–16; *Inexpensive,* under $12.

Moderate: **J.C. Hillary's.** 793 Boylston St., nr. Prudential Center. Steaks, stew, seafood, burgers. Sunday brunch. Bar.

Inexpensive: **Jacob Wirth's.** 31 Stuart St. Dark beer, wurst, heaps of kraut—a century-old Boston tradition.

No Name. 15½ Fish Pier. Fish, fish, fish. Broiled fish, fried fish, great fish chowder—all right off the boat. A local institution.

Brandy Pete's. 82 Broad St. A downtown bargain. Roast turkey, seafood, veal parmigiana.

Italian. Moderate: **Amalfi.** 10 Westland Ave. Veal and chicken specialties. Cocktails. Symphony Hall opp.

Inexpensive: **The Pushcart.** 61 Endicott Street. Not really a pushcart, but a tidy little restaurant. A plate of sausage, potatoes, and vinegar peppers will hold you for the day.

Middle Eastern. Inexpensive: **The Red Fez.** 1222 Washington St. This out-of-the-way spot near Dover "T" station has a good reputation. Try the *kibbe* or lamb with string beans.

Cafeteria. Inexpensive: **Fill-a-Buster.** 9 Park St. If you find yourself near the State House at breakfast or lunch time, stop here. Excellent Greek salad, falafel, hummus. No dinners.

CAMBRIDGE. *Moderate:* **Iruna.** Spanish cuisine; hearty stews, garlic soup. Ample servings and quiet atmosphere.

Peasant Stock. Off the beaten track, and with a limited menu, but featuring hearty, well-prepared meals, wines, and frequent after-dinner chamber music. 421 Washington St., Somerville (out Kirkland St. and just over the Cambridge line.)

T.T. the Bear's. 10 Brookline St., Central Sq. Seafood, steak, Italian dishes. Also, a cheeseburger hailed by the Boston *Globe* as the area's best.

Inexpensive: **Lucky Gardens.** 282 Concord Ave. Everything from vegetable dishes to Peking duck. Some spicy Szechuan dishes. Try the fried dumplings and scallion pancakes.

EXPLORING CAPE COD

Although you can make a complete circuit of the Cape in 2½ hours, it's really a place for relaxing. You can find all sorts of accommodations from guest houses to resort motels or housekeeping cottages. Reservations are a good idea between April and October; during high summer, though, they are a must. Winter Cape trips, while not for everyone, offer a wonderful sense of peace and solitude.

An interesting side trip along Route 3 includes Plymouth. The first permanent colonial settlement in the United States, Plymouth has become a national shrine visited annually by thousands. Since that historic day in December 1620 when the weary, weakened Pilgrims landed there in the *Mayflower,* Plymouth has grown and thrived and is now a busy city. But, thanks to the many restorations and museums, the imaginative visitor to Plymouth will find that sense of the past he seeks. Plymouth Rock now rests under a canopy of granite to protect it from souvenir hunters. A few yards from the hallowed boulder is the *Mayflower II,* a replica of the original ship. Built in England, it sailed across the Atlantic in 1957. Visitors are welcome aboard. From the Rock, climb the stairway leading to Cole's Hill. This is where the Pilgrims buried their dead by night, so that the Indians could not calculate the number of survivors. If it had not been for the friendship of Massasoit, the great chief of the Wampanoags, all would have perished. His statue stands near the sepulcher. Nearby is the First Parish Church, which was the Pilgrims' church organization. The original building was erected in 1683 and the present church is the fifth on this site. Walk up the stone steps beside the church to Burial Hill, which overlooks the square. The fort was built in 1622 and contained five cannons. It was also used as a meeting house and burial ground. You can pick out the graves of such settlers as Governor Bradford, Edward Gray, Thomas Clark, and John Cotton. Also of interest is the town brook, which furnished water to the Pilgrims. The town established Brewster Gardens nearby, on the site of the settlers' original gardens.

Another worthwhile spot to visit, the Pilgrim Hall Museum, has an interesting collection of Pilgrim relics and paintings. Next, travel to Plimoth Plantation, a re-creation of the original Pilgrim colony as it looked in 1627. Costumed men and women enact the day-to-day life of the Pilgrims there.

The Cape Cod Canal, which separates the Cape from the mainland, is crossed on Rte. 3 (on the Cape side, it is Rte. 6) by the Sagamore Bridge and on Rte. 28 by the Bourne Bridge. The canal was dug between 1909 and 1914 by the U.S. Army Corps of Engineers, 300 years after Myles Standish first proposed it to eliminate the dangerous trip around the shallows off Provincetown.

From the canal to the elbow (Cape Cod resembles a crooked arm), the Cape is traversed by three major roads: Rte. 6A on the north; Rte. 6, a two-lane highway down the middle; and Rte. 28 to the south. They all join at Orleans, and Rte. 6 continues to Truro and Provincetown. The three main highways traverse contrasting regions. Rte. 6 passes through the relatively unpopulated center of the Cape, which is characterized by an undulating landscape of scrub pine and scrub oak. It is generally the fastest route east and the most direct to the National Seashore.

The Southern Shore

The southern side of the Cape, reached by Rte. 28, is the most heavily populated and the major center for tourism. Its growth as a resort area has been abetted by its abundance of scenic harbors overlooking Nantucket Sound and its fine beaches. In the extreme southwestern corner is Woods Hole, where the car ferries depart for Martha's Vineyard and Nantucket. It is also the location of the Woods Hole Oceanographic Institute, the *Marine Biology Laboratory,* and the aquarium of the U.S. Bureau of Commercial Fisheries. Falmouth and the surrounding villages comprise one of the Cape's main commercial and resort areas. It was settled in 1660 by a group of Quakers and was an active center of trade and shipping. The bell in the Congregational Church was cast by Paul Revere. Mashpee, where Otis Air Force Base is now located, is the home of many descendants of the original Wampanoag Indians. There are also some cranberry bogs as well as beautiful Mashpee Pond and two nature reserves. Hyannis, with its fashionable satellite resort towns, is the commercial hub of tourism on the Cape. The Kennedy family compound is located behind a high fence in Hyannis Port. There are some fine sea captains' mansions in South Yarmouth.

Chatham is a typical Cape village, but is free of the commercialism that mars many towns and villages on the south shore of the Cape. Rigid zoning laws have helped to keep Chatham the way it was at the turn of the century. You can watch the boats unloading their catch around noon at the Fish Pier. The view of the ocean from the Chatham Lighthouse is spectacular. South of Chatham, trailing off from the "elbow" of the Cape, lies Monomoy, accessible only by boat. This fragile spit of land now enjoys protection as a federally designated wilderness area—although this political distinction did nothing to mitigate the ravages of the freak tides which accompanied the blizzard of '78. In the words of an Audubon Society official, there are now "two Monomoys." From Chatham, Rte. 28 curves north and joins 6 and 6A at Orleans on the northern part of the Cape. In Orleans you can follow Rock Harbor Road to the town landing where in 1814 the militia of Orleans routed a British landing party. Many citizens of Massachusetts, though, were opposed to the War of 1812 because of its adverse effect on trade. From Orleans go east on Nauset Beach Road to Nauset Beach, one of the finest along the east coast. From here, federally protected beaches stretch for 40 miles to Provincetown.

National Seashore

Three miles north on US 6 is the town of Eastham; just beyond the village is the headquarters of the Cape Cod National Seashore Project, established in 1961 to preserve the Cape's natural and historic resources. At Nauset, Marconi Station, Pilgrim Heights, and Province Lands, there are visitor centers and parking areas. Starting out on foot from these points, you can find superb ocean beaches, great rolling, lonely dunes, various types of swamps, marshes and wetlands, and all kinds of wildlife. The headquarters building in Eastham has displays, literature, and an auditorium for nature lectures. Rte. 6 continues on through Wellfleet, once the location of a large oyster industry, and, along with Truro, a colonial whaling and codfishing port.

Historically, Provincetown, or P-Town as Cape Codders abbreviate it, has an ancient quarrel with Plymouth. The Pilgrims' first landfall in the New World was at the tip of Cape Cod. The *Mayflower* remained off-shore for four or five weeks. P-Towners wonder why Plymouth, a Pilgrim afterthought, should get all the glory and fame, so the town has done everything possible to encourage the association of the Pilgrims with Provincetown. They erected a 252-foot stone tower to mark the place the Pilgrims landed, and built a historical museum to house an excellent collection of early relics. In summer, Provincetown attracts artists, playwrights, novelists, poets, and an unorthodox crowd of hangers-on, along with an equal number of tourists to watch them at work and play. Souvenir shops, art galleries, craft shops, and restaurants are jammed together along the narrow main street. The summer theatre in which Eugene O'Neill presented his first plays is still active.

The northern shore or Bay side of the Cape is different from the south shore and tends to be marshy. The water is far calmer than that of Nantucket Sound and the Atlantic, and the area is less developed. The towns have retained more of their original quality; main streets are lined with fine old shade trees and stately white clapboard mansions built by sea captains. Brewster has several such mansions as well as salt-box Cape Cod cottages. In West Brewster you can visit a working corn mill, a museum of natural history and Sealand of Cape Cod, which features a marine aquarium, seal pool, and trained dolphins. At Dennis's Scargo Hill, the highest spot in the mid-Cape, the view of the Bay is spectacular. Yarmouth and Yarmouth Port are particularly lovely old seafaring towns and some of the captains' homes are open to the public.

As you continue west on 6A, you will come to Barnstable, a lovely town of large old homes, many built when the town had a large trade in codfish, rum, and molasses. Great salt marshes extend into the bay. Sturgis Library, dating from 1644, is the country's oldest public library building.

Sandwich is the oldest town on the Cape and one of the most interesting and charming. It remains famous for the beautifully colored glass which bears its name and was produced there from 1825 until 1888, when labor-management disputes closed the factory. The *Sandwich Glass Museum,* Rte. 130, contains relics of the early history of the town as well as an outstanding collection of pressed and lace glass. You may visit the nearby Hoxie House, a 17th-century shingled salt-box cottage, and see Dexter's Gristmill in operation. Heritage Plantation is a complex of various museums and craft exhibits housed in a collection of old buildings, some real and some reproductions.

PRACTICAL INFORMATION FOR CAPE COD

 MUSEUMS AND GALLERIES. Cotuit: *Crocker House,* Main St. Americana. June–Oct. Barnstable: *Donald G. Trayser Memorial Museum,* Main St. Historical documents, marine exhibits. July–Sept.: Tues.–Sat.

Brewster: *Drummer Boy Museum.* Rte. 6A. Guided tours. Late May–mid-Oct. *New England Fire and History Museum,* Rte. 6A. Early fire engines. Daily, mid-June–mid-Sept. *Cape Cod Museum of Nat'l. History,* Main St. Animal, marine exhibits, nature trails. Daily summer; Tues.–Sat. winter.

Centerville: *Centerville Historical Society Museum,* Jct. of West Bay Rd., Parker Rd. Sea captain's home. Doll collection, ship models. Memorial Day–Christmas: Wed.–Sun.

Chatham: *Old Windmille* (1797), Shattuck Rd. Working mill with meal for sale July–Labor Day. *Railroad Museum,* Depot Rd., off Rte. 28. Thousands of models, photos. Late June to early Sept.

Eastham: *Old Grist Mill* (1793), Grist Mill Park. Late June to mid-Sept. *Schoolhouse Museum,* off Rte. 6. Early school house, Indian artifacts, farming tools. Also *Swift-Daley House.* Early June–Labor Day.

Falmouth: *Historical Society Museum.* Whaling, period furniture, tools, costumes. Garden. Mid-June to mid-Sept. *Saconesset Homestead Museum,* Rte. 28A, W. Falmouth. Restoration of 1678 house, 15 acres. Late May–Sept. 30.

Provincetown: *Pilgrim Memorial Monument,* Town Hill. Commemorates Pilgrims' first landing. Historical Museum has marine relics. *Mayflower* diorama. Open year-round.

Sandwich: *Historical Society, Sandwich Glass Museum,* Town Hall Sq. Examples of renowned Sandwich glass. April–Nov. *Hoxie House & Dexter's Grist*

Mill. Restoration of 17th-century home and mill. Mid-June–Oct. *Heritage Plantation,* Grove & Pine Sts. Round barn houses Barney Oldfield diorama, historic cars. *Military Museum* contains Lilly collection of miniature soldiers, antique firearms; Arts & Crafts Bldg. exhibits colonial tools, paintings. May to mid-Oct. *Yesteryears Museum,* Main & Rivers Sts. Dolls, doll houses, furnishings. Late May to mid-Oct.; by appt. rest of year.

Truro: *Truro Historical Society Museum,* South Highland Road. Also visit nearby Highland Light; tours in season to top of lighthouse.

Yarmouth: *Winslow Crocker House,* Rte. 6, Yarmouth Port. Period furnishings in restored late 18th-century house. June–Sept. Tues., Thurs., Sun. *Captain Bangs Hallet House,* Strawberry Lane, Yarmouth Port. Sea captain's home with original furnishings. July through Labor Day. Closed wknds.

TOURIST INFORMATION SERVICE. Free folders, brochures, and maps may be obtained from *Cape Cod Chamber of Commerce,* Hyannis, Mass. 02601; resort directories can be obtained at Chamber of Commerce booths in Bourne and Sagamore. For information about Cape Cod National Seashore, write Superintendent, Cape Cod National Seashore, South Wellfleet, MA 02663.

SPECIAL INTEREST TOURS. The Massachusetts Audubon Society and the National Seashore sponsor *Spring Wildlife Pilgrimages,* usually late May. Also, walking tours for bird watchers can be arranged at Audubon sanctuaries in Hatchville (Falmouth) and Wellfleet. For information, contact Mass. Audubon at Box 236, S. Wellfleet, MA 02663.

SPORTS. *Fishing:* Surf casting and deep-sea fishing are deservedly popular. Charter party boats can be hired for the day at Falmouth, Hyannis, Provincetown, Wellfleet, Oak Bluffs, and Nantucket. No license needed. *Surfing:* Nauset Beach, East Orleans, and White Crest Beach, Wellfleet, have special areas for the surfer. Special sections of Coast Guard Beach and Nauset Light Beach, Eastham, are also set aside.

HOTELS AND MOTELS. The Cape offers a wide range of accommodations, from luxurious seaside resorts to the most basic motel. Many close down completely during the off-season; others offer much lower prices. Our price rating is based on double occupancy, European plan, in season. *Moderate,* $45–60; *Inexpensive,* $30–45; *Rock Bottom,* under $30. For information on **bed-and-breakfast** lodgings, contact Bed and Breakfast Cape Cod, Box 341, W. Hyannis Port; or House Guests Cape Cod, 85 Hokum Rock Rd., RFD Dennis.

BASS RIVER. *Moderate:* **Village Green.** S. Shore Dr. Pleasant motel opp. beach. Pool, play area, Restaurant nr. Pets off season.

Inexpensive: **Pine Knot Motel.** Rte. 28. Some kitchens. Pool. Nr. golf, beach, restaurants.

BOURNE. *Moderate:* **Mashnee Village.** Mashnee Village Rd., 5 mi. W of bridge, off Rte. 28. Pool, tennis, play area. Beach. Cottages with kits. Bar. Pets.

Inexpensive: **Panorama Motor Lodge.** South Bourne Bridge Rotary, Rte. 28. Bar, pool.

BREWSTER. *Inexpensive:* **Inn of the Golden Ox.** Main St. and Tubman Rd. Pleasant guest rooms adjoining restaurant renowned for German cuisine.

Skyline. Mid-Cape Hwy., exit 9. No frills, but pleasant. No pets.

BUZZARDS BAY. *Inexpensive:* **Buzzards Bay Motor Lodge.** On private beach with dock. No pets.

Quintal's Motor Lodge. Rte. 28 at Bourne Bridge. Indoor pool, sauna, exercise room. Restaurant, lounge. Refrigerators in rooms. Open all year.

CHATHAM. *Moderate:* **Seafarer.** Rte. 28 and Ridgevale Rd. Spacious rooms, quiet location, ½ mile from beach. Some 2-room efficiencies. Restaurants, golf, tennis near.

CRAIGVILLE. *Moderate:* **Craig Village by the Sea.** Craigville Beach Rd. Cottages with fireplaces opp. beach. Pets off season only. Play area.

DENNIS. *Moderate:* **Lamplighter Motor Lodge.** Rte. 28, Dennis Port. Family motel with picnic and play areas. Pool. Restaurant nr.
Inexpensive: **Ocean View Lodge and Cottages.** Depot St. Motel and efficiency accommodations. TV lounge. Weekly rates avail. Nr. beach.

EASTHAM. *Moderate:* **Now Voyager.** Rte. 6, 3 mi. N of Nat'l. Seashore entrance. Comfortable quarters on wooded grounds. Pool, play area. Restaurant, bar.

FALMOUTH. *Inexpensive:* **Elm Arch Inn.** Off Main Street. Pool. Walking distance to beach. Colonial atmosphere.
Moderate: **Ox Bow Motel.** Nicely kept, nicely furnished. Heated pool. 2-day minimum stay in season.
Studio Motel. 113 Falmouth Heights Rd. Spacious rooms overlooking harbor. Restaurant nr.

HARWICH. *Moderate:* **Moby Dick.** Main St., S. Harwich. Pool, play area. Croquet and shuffleboard. Nr. golf courses. Efficiencies avail.
Stone Horse. Rte. 28, S. Harwich. Beautiful gardens. Pool, play area. Nr. beach, marina, golf. Coffee shop in season.

HYANNIS. *Moderate:* **Country Lake Lodge.** Rte. 132. On lake, with fishing, boating avail. Pool, play area. Restaurant nr. Some efficiencies.
Hyannis Star. Rte. 132 & Pine Needle Lane. Pool, play area. Pets. Motel rooms or full kitchen cottages. Wkly rates avail.
Hyannis Town House Motor Inn. 33 Ocean St. Restaurants, shops, beaches nr.
Hyannis Travel Inn. 16 North St. Pool. Free cont. breakfast.
Presidential Motor Lodge. On lake; water sports; convenient. Across street from new golf course.

NORTH TRURO. *Moderate:* **Horizons.** Rte. 6A. Beach Point. Long private beach. Pool.
Fore n' Aft. Rte. 6A. Private beach, pool. Cottage efficiencies or motel.
Inexpensive: **Whitman House.** Great Hollow Rd. Family-oriented inn. Pool, play area. Restaurant, bar. Wkly rates.

ORLEANS. *Inexpensive:* **Ridgewood Motel & Cottages.** Jct. Rtes. 28 & 39. Play area. Pool. Refrigerators in rooms. Picnic grounds with bbqs.

PROVINCETOWN. *Moderate:* **Best Western Chateau.** Bradford St., Rte. 6A. Pool. Comfortable rms. overlook dunes. Open May to Oct.
Bradford House & Motel. 41 Bradford St. Pleasant, centrally located. Restaurant nr. Mid-May to late Oct.
Breakwater. Shore Dr. Beach. Pool nr. Restaurant, bar next door. Open mid-Apr. to late Oct.

Cape Colony Inn. 280 Bradford St. Pool, play area. Open mid-May to mid-Oct.

Kalmar Village. Rte. 6A. Traditional Cape Cod cottages on a private beach. Motel rms. also avail. Laundromat on premises. Pool. Open mid-May–mid-Oct.

Masthead. 31 Commercial St. Cottages facing ocean, and attractive motel rms. Restaurant nr. Private beach.

Meadows Motel & Cottages. Bradford St. Ext. Efficiency cottages. 3 min. to beach.

Quality Inn Eastwood. 324 Bradford St. Heated pool, play area. Restaurant nr. Putting green, tennis.

SAGAMORE. *Inexpensive:* **Windmill Motel.** Mid-Cape Hwy. Pool; bicycle trails.

SANDWICH. *Inexpensive:* **Earl of Sandwich Motor Manor.** Rte. 6A. Charming small motel with Tudor décor.

YARMOUTH. *Moderate:* **Cape Sojourn.** Rte. 28, W. Yarmouth. Htd. indoor and outdoor pools. Whirlpool. Free morning coffee. Pkgs. avail.

American Host. Rte. 28, W. Yarmouth. 5 min. to Hyannis. Indoor/outdoor pools, miniature golf. Nr. beaches, tennis. Pkgs. avail.

Green Harbor On the Ocean. 182 Baxter Ave., W. Yarmouth. Pool, private beach. Very attractive. Cottages with sundecks. Some kitchen units.

Hunters Green. Rte. 28, W. Yarmouth. Heated outdoor/indoor pool. Nr. beaches, restaurants, shops, tennis.

Mayflower. Rte. 28. W. Yarmouth. Pool, play area. Restaurant adjacent.

Thunderbird Motor Lodge. Rte. 22, W. Yarmouth. 1 mi. from downtown Hyannis. Indoor and outdoor pools; saunas. Restaurant nearby.

Town 'n Country. Rte. 28. Outdoor, indoor, and kids pools. Putting green, play area, saunas. 2 restaurants adjacent. Pets.

 DINING OUT. Cape Cod is liberally dotted with interesting restaurants and inns. Although some restaurants are closed after the summer season, many are open the year round for those interested in seeing the Cape after the sun-worshippers have all gone.

Our ratings are based on the price of an à la carte dinner: but do not include drinks, tax and tip. *Moderate,* $12–16; *Inexpensive,* under $12.

BARNSTABLE. *Moderate:* **Mattakesse Wharf.** Barnstable Harbor. Seafood. Bar.

BUZZARDS BAY. *Moderate:* **The Windjammer.** 3131 Cranberry Hwy. Seafood. Own baking: popovers, breads, pastries. Bar.

CHATHAM. *Moderate:* **Captain's Table.** 580 Main St. Yankee cooking: chicken pie, fish.

The Impudent Oyster. 15 Chatham Bars Ave. Good offering of seafood and vegetarian selections.

FALMOUTH. *Moderate:* **Coonamessett Inn.** Jones Rd. & Gifford St. Lovely traditional dining room. Open for breakfast, lunch, dinner. Bar with pianist, trio, dancing.

HARWICH. *Moderate:* **Sword & Shield of York.** 554 Main St., Harwich Port. Pub-style restaurant featuring Yankee menu. Open for lunch, dinner yr. round.

HYANNIS. *Moderate:* **Mitchell's Steak and Rib House.** Rte. 28 opposite airport. Beef and seafood specialties. Bar; Irish music.

Mildred's Chowder House. Iyanough Rd., Rte. 28. Seafood specialties. Bar, entertainment.

Inexpensive: **Hearth & Kettle.** Main St. (also Falmouth and S. Yarmouth, both Rte. 28.) Open 24 hrs. Seafood, chowders. Reduced price entrees 12–6 P.M.

PROVINCETOWN. *Moderate:* **Tip for Tops'n.** 31 Bradford St. Seafood and Portuguese specialties, marinated pork chops, homemade puddings.

The Cottage. 149 Commercial St. Breakfast especially good. Try the blueberry pancakes.

Plain and Fancy. 149 Commercial St. Chicken Kiev; boeuf bourguignon. Children's menu. Open mid-May–mid-Sept.

Inexpensive: **Cookie's.** 133 Commercial St. Authentic Portuguese cooking. Piquant marinated fish dishes; kale soup; squid stew. A favorite with natives.

WELLFLEET. *Inexpensive:* **The Lighthouse.** Main St. Homemade chowder. Wine and beer.

YARMOUTH. *Moderate:* **Cranberry Moose.** 43 Main St. International cuisine in 200-yr.-old building. Paella, roasts, duckling.

La Cipollina. Rte. 6A, Yarmouthport. Italian cuisine.

Old Yarmouth Inn Restaurant. Rte. 6A. In historic inn. Curries and local specialties. Bar, dancing.

EXPLORING THE BERKSHIRES

On the outer edge of the northeast urban corridor, yet easily accessible from Boston, New York, and the north, stand the Berkshire hills. This is a region that combines a gentle, pastoral landscape with some of the finest cultural attractions in New England. The Berkshires have long been settled; but as in the quiet shires of old England, the terms between man and nature are relaxed.

Near Pittsfield is Mt. Greylock, occupying an 8,660-acre state reservation with bridle paths, picnic facilities, hunting, and camping. At 3,491 feet, Greylock is the state's highest peak, overlooking magnificent panoramas of western Massachusetts, the Hudson Valley of New York, and the Green Mountains of southern Vermont. Many foot trails, including the Appalachian Trail, cross the summit. After driving down the mountain, continue to State 2, driving west to Williamstown, one of the loveliest towns in New England and the site of Williams College (1793), which evolved from a free school. The attractive campus is well worth a walking tour. On South St. is the Sterling and Francine Clark Art Institute, one of the finest small museums in America. It boasts great paintings, including a memorable collection of Renoirs, rare silver, furniture, and china. The college's Thompson Memorial Chapel, a Gothic structure built in 1904, is on the north side of Main St. Its stained glass windows are seen to best advantage from inside. Diagonally across the street is the Lawrence Art Museum, identifiable by its octagonal form and Grecian rotunda. It houses fine collections of glass, pottery, bronzes, paintings, and sculpture.

Williamstown, with good restaurants, motels, and inns, is a delightful place to pause, with excellent skiing nearby as well as areas for hiking, riding, golfing, and foliage-watching. Another local feature is

Adams Memorial Theatre, regarded as one of the leading summer theatres in the nation.

If you travel from Williamstown to Pittsfield in summer, plan to stop at the Hancock Shaker Village. Each year as more buildings are restored and opened to the public, more fascinating objects attesting to the genius of these spiritually motivated people for coping with the material world are revealed. The Round Stone Barn, scrupulously restored, is an architectural treasure.

The easterly road south, Route 8, goes through Adams and Cheshire. Vistas in these towns sometimes resemble the English Lake District and sometimes the factories and row houses of a Dickens setting. The environs are lovely to drive through at foliage time. South of Savoy about a half mile to the left of Route 9, is Cummington Road and the William Cullen Bryant homestead, open to the public for a small fee.

Continuing west on Route 9, the ride down from the hills approaching the town of Dalton offers excellent views, particularly during foliage season. Pause here to visit the Crane Museum of paper making (no fee) housed in the Old Stone Mill on the banks of the Housatonic. At the foot of the hills, a well-marked road on the left leads to Wahconah Falls, a state park created around a waterfall in a clear, cold mountain stream. Continue west on Route 9, through Dalton to Pittsfield.

Pittsfield, the Berkshire County seat, is at the county's geographic center. It is also a center of commerce and industry in a most inviting setting surrounded by mountains. At the southern edge of town toward the great Berkshire cultural centers of Lenox, Lee, and Stockbridge is South Mountain with its fine vistas and seasonal programs offered by the South Mountain Chamber Music Concerts. Lenox, of course, is the home of the Tanglewood summer concerts. Here every summer on a 200-acre estate, students and famous performers, the Boston Symphony, and just plain music lovers gather to learn, enjoy, and perform. The main shed seats 6,000, but many prefer to listen outside on the great lawn, relaxing on blankets or their own folding chairs. Near Lenox is the Pleasant Valley Wildlife Sanctuary, a Massachusetts Audubon Society facility sheltering many living specimens of regional plant and animal life. In West Becket, take in the Jacob's Pillow Dance Festival and visit the school founded by the late Ted Shawn and continued by Walter Terry. Top dancers from all over the world give regular performances to packed houses. Also in Lee is the 14,000-acre October Mountain State Forest. The Appalachian Trail runs through it and there are facilities for fishing, camping, and other outdoor activities.

Stockbridge

Return via US 20 to Stockbridge. Stockbridge, to many the archetype of the New England small town, has a long history of attracting creative people. Here is where Jonathan Edwards spent the last eight years of his life writing theological treatises and serving as missionary to the Indians. The late playwright Robert Sherwood summered here, and the town provided inspiration for its most famous recent resident, Norman Rockwell, who died in 1978. Many Rockwell paintings are on exhibit in the Corner House's permanent collection. There's an inviting inn here (the Red Lion) and one of the nation's top summer theatres, the Berkshire Playhouse. Other places worth visiting are the Mission

House, Naumkeag Gardens, the Library, and Chesterwood, a 150-acre estate containing the studio of Daniel Chester French, sculptor of the famed Lincoln Memorial Statue and of Concord's Minuteman. Chesterwood, now a national trust, is located off 183, two miles west of Stockbridge.

A short scenic drive south from Stockbridge on US 7 takes you to Great Barrington, largest town and economic center of the south Berkshires. The townspeople seized the courthouse from the British in August 1774; it has been claimed that this was the first act of open resistance to the Crown in America.

PRACTICAL INFORMATION FOR THE

BERKSHIRES

 HOW TO GET THERE. *By car:* The Berkshires can be approached from several directions; from Conn. on US 7 and Mass. 8, along feeder roads off New York's Taconic Parkway, through Columbia and Rensselaer Counties, or from Vermont on Routes 7 and 8. The Mohawk Trail (part of Route 2) is the most spectacular.

By air: Bradley International, Windsor Locks, Conn. would be nearest, necessitating a drive from that point. *By train: Amtrak* offers service to Springfield and Pittsfield via Boston and Albany, and to Springfield via New York, New Haven, and Hartford; bus connections and car rentals are available at those points.

 MUSEUMS AND GALLERIES. Stockbridge: Chesterwood, studio of Daniel Chester French, sculptor of Lincoln Memorial statue, Washington, D.C., and Minuteman, Concord. Old Corner House. Major collection of Norman Rockwell's work, including many of the artist's magazine paintings. Williamstown: Sterling and Francine Clark Institute. Renoirs, Corots, Sargents, and many other masterpieces. Free. Closed Mondays. Pittsfield: *The Berkshire Museum.* Art, science and local history.

 STATE PARKS. Beartown State Forest, access from State 23 or 102 near Great Barrington. Camp and swim at Benedict Pond. Ski in winter. More than 8,000 acres. Mohawk Trail State Forest, State 2, near Charlemont. Fish for trout, take scenic photographs. Mt. Greylock State Reservation, near N. Adams. Mt. Greylock is highest mountain in Massachusetts. Hunt, ride, camp, ski on more than 8,000 acres. October Mountain State Forest, near Lee. Good camping, fishing. Largest Mass. forest of nearly 15,000 acres. Pittsfield State Forest, near Pittsfield. Sports galore, include skiing.

GARDENS. Stockbridge. Naumkeag Gardens. Exotic, with Chinese motif, moongate. Mansion belonged to Joseph Choate, Ambassador to England. Open July–Labor Day.

 MUSIC. Lenox. Berkshire Festival, Tanglewood. Summer festival begins early July. Performances in Music Shed, Fridays, Saturdays, Sundays. Pittsfield. South Mountain Concerts. A marvelous selection of chamber music, opera, and young people's concerts.

HOTELS & MOTELS IN BERKSHIRES. Our price rating is based on double occupancy. *Moderate,* $45–60; *Inexpensive,* under $45.

GREAT BARRINGTON. *Moderate:* **Briarcliffe Motor Lodge.** Rte. 7. Play area. Free morning coffee.

LEE. *Moderate:* **Laurel Hill.** Rte. 20. Free in-room coffee. Pets.
Morgan House. Small inn; shared baths. Antique shop on premises.
Inexpensive: **Gaslight Motor Lodge.** Rte. 20, E. Lee. On lake;.full water-sports.

LENOX. *Moderate:* **Lenox Motel.** Pittsfield Rd. 2 miles from ski area. Pool. Free in-room coffee.
Quincy Lodge. 19 Stockbridge Rd. Centrally located; breakfast avail.
Candlelight Inn. 53 Walker St. Small, quaint inn with good restaurant on premises. Expensive during Tanglewood season.

PITTSFIELD. *Moderate:* **Heart of the Berkshires.** 970 W. Housatonic St. Pool, play area.

SHEFFIELD. *Inexpensive:* **Ivanhoe Country House.** Undermountain Road. Secluded inn set amidst rolling hills. 1 room with fireplace. Continental breakfast brought to room.

SOUTH EGREMONT. *Moderate:* **Egremont Inn.** Fireplaced public rooms; outdoor sports, including cross-country skiing in winter. MAP.

STOCKBRIDGE. *Moderate:* **Pleasant Valley.** In-room coffee; restaurant nr.
The Inn at Stockbridge. Rte. 7. Circa 1900 country inn, 1 mile n. of town. Brkfsts, dinner wknds and holiday weeks. Cross-country skiing; pool.

DINING OUT IN THE BERKSHIRES. Our ratings are based on the price of an à la carte dinner but do not include drinks, tax and tip. *Moderate,* $11–17; *Inexpensive,* under $11.

GREAT BARRINGTON. *Moderate:* **20 Railroad St.** Stew, quiche; pub atmosphere.

LEE. *Moderate:* **Cork 'n Hearth.** Rte. 20. Steak, seafood, Italian dishes. Closed Tues.

LENOX. *Moderate:* **Ganesh Café.** 90 Church St. Soups, quiche, omelets, salad. Patio dining. Sunday brunch.
The Restaurant. 15 Franklin St. Cantonese duckling; marinated beef; shrimp.

PITTSFIELD. *Moderate:* **Yellow Aster.** Pittsfield-Lenox Rd. Eclectic menu. Colonial House; sun porch dining in summer. Bar. Closed Tues.

WILLIAMSTOWN. *Moderate:* **Country Restaurant.** Escalopé de veau Oscar.
Williams Inn. Pleasant restaurant; bar.
Inexpensive: **British Maid.** Crepes, omelettes, quiche. Fine homemade desserts. Full license. Entertainment wknds.

PRACTICAL INFORMATION FOR THE REST OF MASSACHUSETTS

 HOW TO GET THERE. *By Car:* Mass. Tpke. I–90 runs East to West from Boston to the New York border at W. Stockbridge, connecting with New York Thruway. Route 128 circles Boston from Gloucester to Braintree. Route 15 links Wilbur Cross with Mass. Pike at Sturbridge. I–91 runs north-south along the Connecticut River. *Car rental:* Avis, Hertz, National, and Budget have offices in key localities. *By bus:* Trailways and Greyhound serve the state. *By air:* Boston's Logan International is served by major airlines. Springfield is served by Bradley International, Windsor Locks, Conn. *By train:* Amtrak service from Washington, D.C., Philadelphia, Newark, New York, New Haven, and Providence to Boston; *Lake Shore Limited* leaves Chicago daily for Boston via Albany, N.Y., Pittsfield, Springfield, and Worcester. Also trains to Springfield from New York, New Haven, and Hartford.

 TOURIST INFORMATION SERVICES. Free folders, brochures, and maps can be obtained from Mass. Department of Commerce, Division of Tourism, 100 Cambridge St., Boston 02202. There is a Visitor's Information Center at Tremont St., Boston Common.

 MUSEUMS AND GALLERIES. Andover: *Addison Gallery of American Art,* Phillips Academy, Chapel Ave. Works of artists, glassware, sculpture, ship models. Framingham: *Danforth Museum.* Local art and history. Williamstown: *Sterling and Francine Clark Art Institute.* Renoirs, Sargents, Corots, other masterpieces in impressive marble bldg.

Salem: *Salem Witch Museum,* 19½ Washington Sq., N. Salem. Re-creations of witch trials. Witch House (1642), Essex St., is where witches were interrogated. *Peabody Museum.* Marine history, ethnology, and natural history. *House of the Seven Gables,* made famous in Hawthorne novel, is restored 17th-century home.

Springfield: *Springfield Armory Museum.* American military arms were made here for 174 years. Now houses world's largest small arms collection. *George Walter Vincent Smith Museum.* Oriental Art; excellent collection of carpets.

Sturbridge: *Old Sturbridge Village.* Restored 18th-century village. 36 old houses surround green on 200-acre site. Costumed guides explain exhibits, crafts. (Children will enjoy.)

 HISTORIC SITES. Massachusetts has a wealth of national historic sites, historical parks, and points of interest connected with great events of the past. In Concord the *National Minuteman Historical Park* commemorates the first skirmish of the Revolution. Visitor's Center has audio-visual program.

Adams National Historic Site, Quincy, was given to nation by the descendants of John Adams. Original furnishings. *The Salem Maritime National Historic Site,* Salem, includes visitor center in the Custom House, Derby St., and Derby House, which has been restored and furnished as a Salem merchant's home. *Saugus Iron Works* on Central St., Saugus, includes restorations of an ironmonger's house, blast furnace, forge slitting mill, and a museum. Also, visit *Deerfield,* site of Indian Massacres, 1675, 1704. Six Colonial homes are open. In Salem is the *Essex Institute,* displaying 300 years of history, including 5 period houses: Pingree House (1804), John Ward House (1684), Pierce-Nichols

House (1782), Crowninshield-Bentley House (1727), Assembly House (1782). *Pioneer Village,* Forest River Pk., has reproductions of 1630 village. (Open summers.) In Lowell, *Lowell National Historical Park* incorporates 19th-century mill buildings, interprets early U.S. industrial history. Trolley and canal boat rides, museums.

TOURS. *Gray Line,* 420 Maple St., Marlboro, MA 01752. Recent offerings include *Plymouth Pilgrimage;* tours of villages on Cape Cod; circuit of north shore, including Marblehead and Salem; Martha's Vineyard ferry-bus tours; also tours of Cambridge, Lexington, and Concord, 1-day excursions along the Massachusetts seacoast to New Hampshire and Maine, and 3-day fall foliage tours. Salem: *Michaud Bus Lines,* Jefferson St. Tours of North Shore. From New York, *Tauck Tours,* 475 Fifth Avenue. Vacations from Manhattan to Concord-Lexington-Sturbridge. *Continental Trailways* has escorted tour of Historical Boston, Marblehead, Salem, etc. *Peter Pan Bus Lines,* 1776 Main St., Springfield, offers excursions from Boston to the Eastern States Exposition, and from Boston and Springfield to Old Sturbridge Village.

DRINKING LAWS. Drinks available until 1 A.M. daily, midnight on Saturdays, if over age 20.

SUMMER SPORTS. *Golf:* Massachusetts has many fine courses, including the Kittansett Club, Marion; Salem Country Club, Peabody; Trull Brook Country Club, Tewksbury; and Taconic Golf Club, Williamstown. *Boating:* Charter, party boats available at all major ports. Larger lakes, ponds have ramps. Boats may be rented. *Fishing:* Excellent fresh-water fishing in many lakes and streams stocked by Division of Fish and Game. *Water Skiing:* Chaubunagungamaug Lake, 1,400-acre lake in Webster, is best. *Swimming:* There are pools, lakes, and beaches throughout the state.

WINTER SPORTS. *Skiing:* Novice-Expert trails include Brodie Mt., New Ashford with 1,250 drop, 12 trails; Berkshire East, Charlemont, with 1,150 drop, 12 trails, Jiminy Peak, Hancock, with 1,130 ft. drop, 20 trails; Catamount, S. Egremont, with 1,000 foot drop, 7 trails. Areas with shorter drops are: Butternut Basin, Gt. Barrington, with 975 ft. drop, 10 trails; Mt. Tom, S. Holyoke, with 840 ft. drop, 3 trails, and Bousquet, Pittsfield, with 750 ft. drop and 10 trails. *Cross-country skiing* is popular throughout the state, with trails near most towns and cities.

WHAT TO DO WITH THE CHILDREN. For the young set, there are summer *amusement parks* at Revere Beach, Revere; Paragon Park, Nantasket Beach; Salisbury Beach; Mountain Park, Holyoke; and Riverside Park, Agawam. *Edaville Railroad.* S. Carver, has train chugging through Cranberryland. *Zoos:* Franklin Park Zoo, Blue Hill Ave., Dorchester. Hundreds of animals and excellent aviary on 50-plus acres with picnic grounds. Forest Park, Springfield, has zoo, picnic grounds. Also *Stone Memorial Zoo,* Stoneham. *Old Sturbridge Village* re-creates an 18th-century farming village. *Dinosaur Land,* S. Hadley, exhibits assorted dinosaur prints. Children will also enjoy Storrowton Village, a collection of 18th-and 19th-century homes and shops moved to the grounds of the Eastern States Exposition in West Springfield. An authentic blacksmith shop operates here two days each week. *Whale watch* cruises are popular with both children and adults. Boats leave Macmillan Wharf, Provincetown, as well as Plymouth and Gloucester.

HOTELS AND MOTELS. Price categories are based on the following (double occupancy): *Moderate*, $45–60; *Inexpensive*, $30–45.

CONCORD. *Moderate:* **Colonial Inn.** 11 Monument Sq. Colonial inn on village square. Restaurant, bar.

LEXINGTON. *Inexpensive:* **Catch Penny Motor Lodge.** 440 Bedford St. Pool; restaurant.

STURBRIDGE. *Moderate:* **Publick House.** I–86, Exit 3. Charming, late 18th-century inn. Restaurant, bar, entertainment.

DINING OUT. *Moderate*, $11–17; *Inexpensive*, under $11.

SALEM. *Moderate:* **Folsom's.** 7 Dodge St. Fine selection of fresh fish. Seafood market on premises.

ANDOVER. *Moderate:* **Andover Inn.** On Andover Academy campus. Relaxed. Sundays: Rijsttafel—Dutch Indonesian buffet.

NEW HAMPSHIRE

The White Mountains and the Lakes

New Hampshire's highlights lie in three regions—the seacoast, the White Mountains, and the lakes region—each with historic sites, scenic beauty and well-developed tourist facilities.

Most compact is the seacoast region, 18 miles of coast and an extensive system of rivers and inland saltwater bays. Its gateway, historic Portsmouth (pop. about 30,000), was settled in 1630; 250 years of prosperity from fishing, shipbuilding and manufacturing endowed it with some of America's finest colonial mansions. Oldest of all is the Jackson House (1664) with its sweeping saltbox roof and somber siding. The Warner House (1716) is the earliest Georgian building in New England. Equally stately and graceful are the Moffat–Ladd (1763), Wentworth Gardner (1760) and Governor John Langdon (1784) houses, among others. The more modest lives of ordinary people—craftsmen, artisans, mariners, shopkeepers—are preserved in Strawbery Banke, a 10-acre restoration around Puddle Dock, the original port; some traditional crafts are still practiced here.

The beaches are all along shoreline Route 1A. Well-equipped state parks are at Wallis Sands and at 2-mile Hampton Beach. Less commercialized public beaches are found also at Rye and Seabrook. Elegant summer estates line the rocky bluffs at Great and Little Boars Heads.

Inland, Exeter (pop. 10,000) has a famous boys' prep school and many lovely houses along its elm-shaded streets. In Durham, the University of New Hampshire's Paul Creative Arts Center is particularly interesting for visitors; and in Dover, the Woodman Institute Museum preserves an original garrison farmhouse from 1675.

The 724,000 square-acre White Mountain National Forest covers most of north central New Hampshire. Beyond lies the relatively undeveloped and still unspoiled North Country. Three main passes cut through the mountains: Pinkham Notch in the east, Crawford Notch in the center, Franconia Notch in the west; and the scenic Kancamagus Highway crosses the entire range east-west.

There are four ways up 6,288-ft. Mt. Washington, tallest peak in the Northeast: hike, drive the 8-mile toll road, ride in specially engineered "stages" (vans), or try the puffer-belly Cog Railroad. The summit includes new million-dollar Summit House and superb views. In North Conway you can ride the Skimobile up Mt. Cranmore; and in Franconia Notch the Cannon Mountain aerial tramway takes you up above the state's most famous landmark, the Old Man of the Mountains, Hawthorne's "Great Stone Face." Here too is the Flume, a lovely river gorge 70 feet deep by 800 feet long with waterfalls and deep clear pools. North Conway is the gateway town to the region's forests, peaks, rivers, hiking trails, half-dozen major ski areas, campgrounds and year-round inns, motels, and guest houses.

Lake Winnipesaukee (72 square miles) dominates central New Hampshire. Laconia, site of the World Sled Dog Championships each February, is the chief town. Steamer cruises on the lake leave from Weirs Beach, Wolfeboro, Center Harbor and Alton Bay. Summers, the New Hampshire Music Festival gives chamber and orchestral concerts at Center Harbor and Meredith. Northeast of the lake, near Moultonborough, the Castle in the Clouds is a 6,000 acre area of great natural beauty with hiking trails and views of both the lake and the White Mountains. Weirs Beach has a water slide and its Boardwalk is scene of special events all summer.

Southwest New Hampshire is a land of lovely old villages with white churches and graceful homes grouped around village commons. Amherst, Antrim, Hillsboro, Henniker, Candia are a few of the many. Local and county fairs each summer showcase traditional fun in 20th-century setting.

In Concord, the state Capitol is architecturally and historically interesting, and the New Hampshire Historical Society shows traditional domestic interiors 1680–1720. Here too is the main showroom of the League of New Hampshire Craftsmen, at 36 North Main Street. Manchester, the state's largest city (pop. about 100,000), has an outstanding collection of American work in its Currier Gallery of Art, 192 Orange St. The Amoskeag Manufacturing Company was once the world's largest textile mill; in the Depression they went bankrupt. Now diversified, the area holds over 100 manufacturing and service companies.

PRACTICAL INFORMATION FOR
NEW HAMPSHIRE

HOW TO GET THERE. *By air:* From New York to Lebanon via *Command Airways;* Keene from New York via *Precision;* Lebanon from Boston on *Precision* and *Command.* Precision service also into Laconia, Manchester.

By car: From Boston take I–95 for Portsmouth and the seacoast, I–93 for Manchester, Concord, the Lakes and the White Mountains. From New York take I–95 to New Haven, Conn., then I–91 north along the Vermont–New Hampshire border, to reach White River Junction. From New York, 222 miles, 5 hours; from Chicago 903 miles, 21 hours; from Montreal 112 miles, 2½ hours. There is limousine service from Boston's Logan Airport to Portsmouth, Nashua, Manchester, and Concord.

By bus: From Boston: *Vermont Transit/Greyhound* to Manchester, Concord, and the Lakes, or to the North Country via Portland, Maine. *Michaud* to the Seacoast. *Trailways* to the Lakes and the North Country via either the Seacoast or Nashua, Manchester, and Concord.

By train: Amtrak serves White River Jct. from New York or Boston via Springfield, Mass., but the bus is faster, cheaper, and more frequent.

TOURIST INFORMATION SERVICES: Maps, recreational calendars and pamphlets on special facilities and activities from *New Hampshire Vacations,* Box 856, Concord, NH 03301. White Mountains News Bureau staffs a year-round Information Center at the jct. of I–93 and Rte. 3 in North Woodstock; or write Box 176, No. Woodstock 03262. Turnpike information booths at Dover, Hooksett, Hampton, Merrimack and Rochester toll plazas. The New England Vacation Center, 630 Fifth Ave., NYC 10020.

SEASONAL EVENTS. *Antiques Shows: Flea Market,* Lancaster, June; *Outdoor Antiques Market,* Amherst, Apr.–Oct.; *Annual Strawbery Banke Antiques Show,* Wentworth-by-the-Sea, July.

Arts and Crafts: Annual Craftsmen's Fair, Mt. Sunapee State Park, early Aug.

Fairs: New Hampshire Music Festival, Laconia-Meredith, July–August. *Old Home Week,* throughout the state, third week in Aug.; *State Fair,* Plymouth, Aug.; *Rochester Fair,* mid-Sept.; *Fall Foliage Festival,* Warner, Oct.; *Dartmouth Winter Carnival,* Hanover, February; *Sled Dog Derby* in Laconia.

Sports Events: Volvo International Tennis Tournament, North Conway, Aug.

MUSEUMS AND GALLERIES. Portsmouth's *Strawbery Banke* is the most ambitious; other valuable historical collections are in Claremont, Concord, Dover, Durham, Candia, Canaan, Keene, Manchester, Peterborough and Hampton. Art collections reward visitors in Hanover, Durham, Manchester, Rochester, Sharon, Cornish, Keene, and Belmont-Laconia.

HISTORIC SITES. Write to the State Historical Commission in Concord for details on the state's 29 historic sites, including Daniel Webster's birthplace, near *Franklin;* the state Capitol in *Concord;* the Franklin Pierce Homestead in *Hillsboro;* Shaker Village in *Canterbury;* Mystery Hill in *North Salem;* and the colonial mansions of *Portsmouth.*

TOURS. On Lake Winnipesaukee boat excursions may be boarded in season from Weirs Beach, Center Harbor, Wolfeboro, Alton Bay, Meredith, and Glendale. On Lake Sunapee there are cruises from Sunapee Harbor. From Portsmouth, July through September, cruises to the Isles of Shoals (reservations required). Salt water fishing from Rye Harbor. In summer, there are train rides daily from North Conway and three sites near Lake Winnipesaukee: Wolfeboro, Sanbornville, Wakefield.

DRINKING LAWS. State Liquor Stores are open Monday through Saturday; beer and wine are sold by grocers, hotels, clubs, and restaurants; beer, wine and liquor by the drink according to local option. Minimum legal age is 20.

SUMMER SPORTS. New Hampshire has 18 miles of *seacoast*, over 1,300 lakes and ponds for *boating* and 1,500 miles of streams for *fishing*. Public beaches, piers, launching areas and boat rentals available on all major lakes. Marked *hiking* trails cover the state, especially in the White Mountains; the Appalachian Mountain Club sells a White Mountain Guide (AMC, 5 Joy St., Boston 02108) and issues a free pamphlet, AMC Huts System, giving details.

WINTER SPORTS. There are two dozen major ski areas and more than 20 cross-country centers in New Hampshire. Snowmaking enables the areas, with the major ones in the White Mtns., to offer skiing from mid-December, sometimes from Thanksgiving, until Easter. Biggest are in the White Mtns.: Waterville Valley, Loon Mtn., Cannon Mtn. and Wildcat Mtn., but Bretton Woods, Attitash, and King Ridge show size isn't everything. Jackson has 125 miles of touring trails; Waterville and Bretton Woods have both hosted the national cross-country championships in recent years, and WV is a regular on the alpine World Cup schedule.

SPECTATOR SPORTS. These include *ski events, sled dog racing,* winter carnivals, *harness racing* in Hinsdale and *greyhound racing* in Seabrook, *yacht racing* off New Castle, *football* in the college towns of Durham, Hanover, Plymouth and Keene, and the *Volvo International Tennis Tournament* at North Conway during the first week of Aug.

WHAT TO DO WITH THE CHILDREN. Museums, playlands and theme parks are particularly abundant in the Lakes Region, at Weirs Beach, Alpine slides are at Attitash in Bartlett and Alpine Ridge in Gilford; the White Mtns. abound in family attractions (kids love to poke through and around the fallen boulders in Lost River at North Woodstock).

SHOPPING. For the best in modern and traditional work, the shops of the League of New Hampshire Craftsmen are open all year in Concord, Exeter, Hanover, Nashua, and North Conway—in season elsewhere. Typical New Hampshire products available everywhere include maple syrup and sugar, colonial furniture, hand weaving, ceramics, herbs and spices, and specialty foods.

HOTELS AND MOTELS. Some New Hampshire hotels rival the scenery for magnificence. Some are very reasonable, including even housekeeping facilities. If you can, stay awhile; many resorts offer less expensive rates for longer stays. Rates are based on double occupancy in season: *Moderate* $30 to $50 double; *Inexpensive*, under $30 double.

BARTLETT. *Inexpensive:* **North Colony.** Pleasant small motel near ski area. Seasonal rates, cafe 1 mile.

CLAREMONT. *Inexpensive:* **Cote's.** Bkfst. available, pets accepted.

COLEBROOK. *Inexpensive:* **Colebrook Country Club.** Pool, pets, cafe, entertainment, golf.
Northern Comfort. Some cottage units, kitchens. Cafe 1 mile.

CONCORD. *Inexpensive:* **Barwood Manor.** Rtes. 3 & 4, five mi. N in Penacook. Small, clean. Pets. Color, cable TV.

DOVER. *Moderate:* **Best Western In-Towne.** Pool, family rates, cafe next door.

FRANCONIA. *Moderate:* **Notchway.** Pool, cafe, fine views.

GILFORD. *Moderate:* **Saunders Bay Motel & Cottages.** Lakefront units, 30 kitchenettes, swimming, boating. Pool. TV.

GLEN. *Inexpensive–Moderate:* **Red Apple Inn.** Rte. 302. Nothing overly fancy, just comfy.

HAMPTON AND HAMPTON BEACH. *Moderate:* **Harris Sea Ranch Model.** Boardwalk motel. Family rates and kitchenettes available.
Town & Beach. Weekly rates, kitchens, heated pool.
Windjammer Motel. Ocean front units with beach.

HANOVER. *Moderate:* **Chieftain.** A small facility near Dartmouth College. Family rates and units.

HILLSBORO. *Inexpensive:* **1830 House.** Small motel, seasonal rates, continental bkfst in a delightful 18th-century house.
Valley Inn. Remodeled 125-yr.-old home. Some shared baths. Cafe, bar.

JACKSON. *Moderate:* **Covered Bridge Motel.** Brookside, bridgeside. Full breakfast service, no other meals. Heated pool, tennis, fishing. Color, cable TV.
Eagle Mountain House. An older, comfortable hotel on 400 acres overlooking Wildcat Valley. Sports, dancing, movies.

LACONIA. *Moderate:* **Best Western.** Large in-town motel; restaurant.
Hi-spot Motor Court. Overlooks the lake. Housekeeping units available. Beach. Color, cable TV.

LINCOLN-NORTH WOODSTOCK. *Moderate:* **Kancamagus Motor Lodge.** Some air-conditioning; Pool; near cafe.
Drummer Boy Motel. Rte. 3. Pool, lawn games.
Inn at Loon Mountain. Perfect spot for skiing, semi-secluded for summer. Hearty fare in restaurant, lively lounge.

NASHUA. *Moderate:* **Hannah Dustin Motel.** Pool, play area, picnic area, cafe next door.

Susse Chalet. Pool, secretarial and valet services.

NORTH CONWAY. *Moderate:* **Nereledge Inn.** Country bed-and-breakfast inn nearly two centuries old (c. 1787), only 8 rms. Colonial dining rm, traditional meals.

School House Motel. On "Motel Row," south of the village. Clean, comfy, close to everything. Color, cable TV.

Scottish Lion. Bed-and-breakfast. Pint-size Scottish shop, lounge, and even an adjacent art gallery.

PLYMOUTH. *Moderate:* **Tobey's Motel.** An older motel. Family units available.

PORTSMOUTH. *Inexpensive:* **River Bend Motel.** In Newington. Seasonal rates, good restaurant next door, some rms. with kitchens.

ROCHESTER. *Inexpensive:* **Cress Motel.** Some kitchens, free coffee, cafe nearby, playground, pets accepted.

RYE AND RYE BEACH. *Moderate:* **Orwood Lodge.** Small motel and cottages, nr. restaurants and shops.

Seafarer. Modern, small motel and housekeeping cottages overlooking ocean.

WATERVILLE VALLEY. *Moderate:* **The Resort at Waterville Valley.** This ski resort complex has accommodations in all price categories. Four-season resort (two ski areas, 50 miles of touring trails, 18 tennis courts) with variety of accommodations. Free shuttle circles valley in winter.

WEIRS BEACH. *Moderate:* **Lakeside Hotel and Motel.** Large family hotel, with cottages and kitchenettes, private beach at Lake Winnipesaukee.

Inexpensive: **Flamingo.** Weekly rates, pool, refrigerators, near cafe, bus and airport pickup.

Mother Bear & Cubs Cottages. Kitchenettes; close to the beach. Pets. TV.

St. Moritz Terrace Motel & Chalets. Rooms and efficiency family units with lovely view of lake. Beach.

WOLFEBORO. *Moderate:* **Clearwater Lodges.** Housekeeping cottages, on lake. Beach, water sports. Game room.

Winter Harbor Lodges. Weekly rates, private beach, recreation area, water sports; good family resort.

In New Hampshire there are Youth Hostels in Alton (569–9878), Danbury (622–0685), Grantham (863–1002), Keene (352–1909), North Haverhill (989–5656), Peterborough (924–6928), Randolph (466–9487) and Twin Mountain (846–5527). Concord has a YMCA, Nashua has a YWCA, Manchester has both.

DINING OUT. The clear mountain air can make a traveler hungry enough for two. Fortunately, New Hampshire can provide tasty New England food aplenty. Lobster, steak, turkey, ducklings, and homemade baked goods head most menus. The prices used are: *Moderate:* $10–20; *Inexpensive,* under $10. Of course, meals ordered á la carte will cost more. Listings are in order of price ranges.

ALTON BAY. *Moderate:* **Stage Coach Lobster House.** Nice view of bay. Features lobster and steak.

BARTLETT: *Moderate:* **W.W. Doolittle's.** Menu leans heavily toward steak and seafood. Oak and stained glass decor adds to warmth.

BETHLEHEM. *Moderate:* **Wayside Inn.** Continental cuisine specializing in veal dishes. Fully licensed.

BRETTON WOODS. *Moderate:* **Fabyan's.** Another recycled train depot. Steaks and seafood.

CONCORD. *Moderate:* **Brick Tower.** Open for breakfast, lunch, and dinner; Sat. night buffet. Seafood and steaks specialties, but nice selection of other dishes.
Mai Kai. Rte. 106. Polynesian-American cuisine.

EXETER. *Moderate:* **Exeter Inn.** Popular restaurant open from breakfast. Sun. for lunch & evening buffet. Bar.

FRANCONIA. *Moderate:* **Hillwinds.** Beehive at night during ski weekends. Hearty steaks, good shrimp.
Village House Restaurant. Meals until midnight. Tempting desserts.
Inexpensive: **Polly's Pancake Parlor.** Superb breakfasts.

GILFORD. *Moderate:* **B. Mae Denny's.** Victorian decor. Steakhouse.

HANOVER. *Moderate:* **Five Olde Nugget Alley.** Oversized burgers plus original dishes; e.g., Hovey's Grill is onions and peppers blanketed by melted cheese.
Inexpensive: **Lou's.** Right on Main St. More functional and filling than fashionable and flashy.

GLEN. *Moderate:* **Red Parka Pub.** Bouncy aprés-ski spot. Great steaks and shrimp. Lively entertainment.
Papa Mike's. Mexican eats.

KEENE: *Moderate:* **Hungry Lion.** Rte. 12. Steakhouse but fine lobster, too. Salad bar.

LACONIA. *Moderate:* **Hickory Stick Farm.** Country-style roast duckling and beef are specialties of this converted farm house. Open Memorial Day—Columbus Day.
King's. Authentic Chinese food, exotic drinks.
Pierside Restaurant. Greek, Italian, and seafood specialties.
Winnisquam House and Motor Inn. Fine home cooking served in Colonial dining room, breakfast and lunch served.

LEBANON. *Moderate:* **Owl's Nest.** Salad bar. Homemade soups. Seafood smorgasbord Fri. night. Umpteen Tiffany lamps.

MANCHESTER. *Moderate:* **Sheraton-Wayfarer.** Pleasant atmosphere for any meal. Buffet lunch.
The Millyard. Recycled woolen mill building. Steak, steak, and more steak. Scrod and scallops, too.
Inexpensive: **Copper Tray.** A thrifty gourmet's delight and very popular locally.

MEREDITH. *Moderate:* **Hart's Turkey Farm.** Specializes in family-style turkey dinners with home-grown birds, but has varied menu & take-out orders.

NASHUA. *Moderate:* **Green Ridge Turkey Farm.** Besides turkey raised on local farm, you will find chops, roast beef, seafood. Entertainment, dancing.

Inexpensive: **88 Restaurant.** Excellent and varied food. International Buffet on Wed.

NEW LONDON. *Moderate:* **Peter Christian's.** Excellent for lunch or dinner. Hearty sandwiches, fine steak dinners.

NORTH CONWAY. *Moderate:* **The Eating House.** A picturesque setting and an excellent menu of seafood specialties as well as steak.

Horsefeathers. Fun-filled atmosphere, prime locals' spot. Creative cuisine. Try the capuccino pudding.

Lobster Trap. Good family spot. Italian seafood is the specialty.

PLYMOUTH. *Moderate:* **Tobey's.** Specializing in New England dishes such as chicken pie, Yankee pot roast, and homemade pastries. Wine list.

PORTSMOUTH. *Moderate:* **Clarence's Chowder House.** You can fill up on a different chowder each day but Sun.

Oar House. Recycled grain warehouse with waterfront perch. You can get seafood everywhere, so try the ribs.

Puddle Dock Pub. Sandwiches, fondues, excellent dessert, small patio.

Pier II Restaurant. Varied menu emphasizing seafood. Upstairs bar and lounge.

Yoken's. Family-owned, with own bakery. Seafood specialties, nautical surroundings.

Warren's. On the water. Lobster supreme.

WATERVILLE VALLEY. *Moderate:* **Finish Line at Snow's Mtn.** Lunch and dinner daily. Late night sandwiches.

WEST LEBANON. *Moderate:* **China Light.** Has triggered a small rash of local Oriental restaurants, but this beats them all.

WOLFEBORO. *Moderate:* **General Wolfe Inn.** 1 mi. S on State 28. At this old New England inn, enjoy roast beef, baked stuffed shrimp and a variety of entrees. Bar.

Lakeview Inn & Motor Lodge. Distinctive food served in Early American dining room. Bar.

RHODE ISLAND

Newport's Museum Mansions

Colonial Newport, founded in 1639, is one of New England's most fascinating towns. The first Quakers in America settled here in 1657. Sephardic Jews came in the following year, establishing a center of Jewish culture which has endured for three centuries. With its salubrious climate and splendid bluffs overlooking the sea, Newport became America's first resort. Wealthy merchants came here for the summer as early as 1720. The resort reached its apogee at the end of the 19th century in the extravagant and tax-free "Gilded Age" when such wealthy families as the Vanderbilts, Astors, Belmonts, Berwinds and Fishes built a series of "cottages" along Bellevue Avenue. The cottages were often full-size, 70-room imitations of Italian palaces and French châteaux, aglitter with imported crystal chandeliers, mirrored walls, rose-colored marble, mosaic floors, gilded woodwork, and every conceivable sign of conspicuous consumption. Many of these opulent residences are now open to the public as "museum mansions." Considered the most stunning is "The Breakers," originally designed for Cornelius Vanderbilt. First among the Bellevue Avenue estates is "Kingscote," built in 1839 by Richard Upjohn for George Noble Jones of Savannah, Georgia. "The Elms," built for the late E.J. Berwind, Philadelphia coal magnate, by Horace Trumbauer, is known for its French garden and arboretum. William K. Vanderbilt's "Marble House," also known as the "Sumptuous Palace by the Sea," and the "Chateau-sur-Mer" are two other Bellevue Avenue museum cottages to ogle. A new addition on the grounds of Marble House is the colorful, restored Chinese teahouse. Oliver Hazard Perry Belmont's (a descendant of Commodore Perry) "Belcourt Castle," contains possibly the world's largest private collection of stained glass. Finally, there's "Rosecliff," a mansion designed by Stanford White, that was the setting for the motion picture "The Great Gatsby," and in 1978 "The Betsy."

Even with the seeming worship of opulence, the town is not without religious landmarks. Trinity Church, built in 1726, with its three-tier, wine-glass pulpit and well-preserved wooden structure has been called a supreme and matchless wonder of Colonial America. Newport also has America's oldest Seventh Day Baptist Church, built in 1729, and America's oldest synagogue, constructed in 1763. Touro Synagogue, designed by Peter Harrison, is done in Georgian style but modified to accommodate Sephardic ritual.

Returning to the secular world, other must-see's are: Hunter House, a National Historic Landmark built in 1748 and featuring Townsend and Goddard furniture; Beechwood; Hammersmith Farm; the Newport Casino, home of the International Lawn Tennis Hall of Fame; the Old Colony House; and White Horse Tavern, America's oldest tavern.

Block Island

About nine miles south of the mainland, Block Island is a summer beach resort and fishing center and well worth a one-day round trip. Take a picnic or eat at one of the seafood snack bars at Old Harbor. Visitors spend many pleasant hours on Block Island State Beach. Some deep-sea fishing for tuna, swordfish, bluefish, cod, striped bass and flounder is another interest. At the southeastern corner end of the island, you can see Mohegan Bluffs, spectacular cliffs of clay, which bear a strong resemblance to the chalk cliffs of Dover, England, rising almost 200 feet above sea level and stretching along the coast for about five miles.

Whittier's poem "The Palatine Light" commemorates the Palatine Graves area near Dickens Point, where the crew of an ill-fated Dutch ship lie buried. A man-made harbor, New Harbor, graces the western shore of the island. It was constructed by connecting the Atlantic with the Great Salt Pond by means of digging a channel across the narrow strip of land. Old Harbor, on the other side of the island, is where a small fishing fleet and pleasure boats dock.

PRACTICAL INFORMATION FOR RHODE ISLAND

HOW TO GET THERE. *By air:* Providence is served by major carriers, with connecting limousine service to major destinations. *By car:* New York to Providence via the New England Thruway (I–95). For the Narragansett seashore, exit at Connecticut Rte. 2 to R.I. Rte. 78, then follow US 1 to R.I. Rte. 108. Signs mark routes to Jamestown and Newport Bridges.

By rail: Providence is served by *Amtrak.* From New York, 4 hrs., Boston, 1 hr.

By bus: Greyhound and *Bonanza.*

By ferry: To Block Island from New London, Conn., Providence and Newport R.I., mid-June to about Labor Day. From Galilee (Point Judith), year-round.

TOURIST INFORMATION SERVICES. The Rhode Island Department of Economic Development, 7 Jackson Walkway, Providence, R.I. 02903, supplies reams of tourist information. Information, licenses and permits for State Parks and fishing streams from Division of Parks and Recreation, Dept. of Environmental Management, 83 Park St., Providence. Almost every town has its own chamber of commerce, some with visitor centers. The state maintains a visitor information center year-round at the Theodore Francis Green Airport. Rhode Island area code is 401; pay phones are 10¢.

SEASONAL EVENTS. One of the most important is Rhode Island Heritage Month, the annual May celebration commemorating the state's declaration of independence from Britain. In October a striped bass tournament is staged at Newport. Galilee is the scene of several deep-sea sports fishing tournaments for sword, shark, and giant bluefin tuna. The Newport Motor Car Festival is held in the middle of June, and the Narragansett Auto Fair at the end of July. Newport has a steady stream of yachting events, climaxed every few years by the America's Cup Race, and the annual "Christmas in Newport" events throughout December. Block Island Week Sailing Regatta is held in late June on odd-numbered years; it is the East Coast's largest yachting event. In even-numbered years a cruising class week is held in late June.

MUSEUMS AND GALLERIES. In Bristol, Haffenreffer Museum of Anthropology. In East Greenwich, the Varnum Military & Naval Museum. The Fire Museum, in Jamestown. In Newport, The International Lawn Tennis Hall of Fame and Tennis Museum. In Peace Dale, the Museum of Primitive Culture. Slater Mill Historic Site, Pawtucket. Tomaquag Valley Indian Memorial Museum, in Arcadia, includes a nature trail and ceremonial programs. For Newport mansions and castles, consult The Preservation Society of Newport County, 118 Mill St. Reduced combination tickets are available at their mansions.

HISTORIC SITES. History, Providence and Roger Williams have been synonymous since he stepped ashore in 1636. The Roger Williams Rock at Power, Williams and Gano Sts., the Roger Williams Spring at N. Main St. (now included in the currently developing Roger Williams National Memorial), the First Baptist Meeting House in America, and the Roger Williams Memorial all commemorate the founder. Historic homes in Providence include that of Stephen Hopkins, a signer of the Declaration of Independence, and the John Brown House, once visited by George Washington. The State House, which boasts the second largest unsupported marble dome in the world, houses Gilbert Stuart's full-length portrait of George Washington. Newport has its share of historic landmarks, including the Brick Market, in Washington Square; the Newport Historical Society and Marine Museum; the Redwood Library, the oldest library room in continuous use in the United States and the Naval War college Museum. The Babcock-Smith House, Westerly, was frequently visited by Benjamin Franklin.

TOURS. *Viking Tours* of Newport highlights at least 150 points of interest including the 10-mile Ocean Drive and a visit to a mansion. Arrangements are made for groups and parties. Viking also conducts walking tours of Newport. Viking and *Newport Harbor Tours* give tours of the historic waterfront. The M/V *Southland* has tours of Great Salt Pond (Galilee, Jerusalem area). Ranger-given seaside tours, Beaver Tail, Jamestown.

GARDENS. Formal Sunken Garden and labeled trees and shrubs at The Elms, modeled after the Chateau d'Asnieres near Paris, and rose garden at Rosecliff, both in Newport. The famous "Green Animals," Portsmouth, is considered one of the best topiary gardens in the country. The Winsor Azalea Garden, Cranston, is open late May (donation for historic preservation). Japanese Garden at Roger Williams Park. Blithewold Gardens and Arboretum, Bristol.

DRINKING LAWS. Minimum age is 20. Package stores closed Sun.

SUMMER SPORTS. *Swimming:* Good beaches are always nearby in Rhode Island. Recommended beaches are Scarborough State Beach, Roger W. Wheeler State Beach, East Matunuck State Beach, Misquamicut, Watch Hill, Block Island State Beach. *Fishing:* Fishing tournaments are sponsored by some sea-coast towns. Charter boats available for big game fish, the biggest fleets found at Galilee and Jerusalem. Skiff rentals are obtainable. License required only for fresh water.

HOTELS. Accommodations range from family-style cottages to luxurious seaside resorts. Price ranges are based on double occupancy, peak season, EP. Listings for price ranges: *Moderate:* $25–35; *Inexpensive:* under $25. A list of the state's **bed-and-breakfast** facilities is available from the R.I. Tourist Promotion Division, 7 Jackson Walkway, Providence, 02903.

Note: There are very few motels under $40 in Newport during the summer season.

NEWPORT. *Moderate* (off season): **Carlton Motel.** Aquidneck Avenue.
Gateway Motel, One Mile Corner.
Harbor-Base Motel, Coddington Highway.
In adjoining Middletown and Portsmouth: **Founders Brook Motel** and **Pines Motel.**
Guest House Association of Newport County, 849–7645.
Near Newport, in Jamestown, **Bay Voyage Inn.**

PROVIDENCE. *Moderate.* **Hi-Way Motor Inn.** 1880 Hartford Ave.; US 6, Johnston; $22, 2 persons, 1 bed. No other services, but convenient to area restaurants and downtown Providence.
Holiday Inn. 21 Atwells Ave. I-95, Exit 21. Large downtown hotel opposite Providence Civic Center. The Garden Room serves meals and The Cellar Lounge is a popular bar. Heated indoor pool. Pets.
New Yorker Motor Lodge. 400 Newport Ave., East Providence. Lounge. Breakfast only.
Wayland Manor. 500 Angell St. Has a good dining room for lunch and dinner. Bar. Located near good shops and attractive residential section.
Narragansett guest house information is available from Narragansett Chamber of Commerce, 783–7121.

RESTAURANTS. *Moderate:* $10–15; *Inexpensive:* under $10. Prices are for a complete meal but do not include drinks, tax or tip.

BLOCK ISLAND. *Inexpensive:* **Airport Restaurant.** Open year-round.
Barone's.
Ernie's Old Harbor.

NEWPORT. *Moderate:* **Salas Dining Room.** 343 Thames Street.
LaForge Casino Restaurant. 186 Bellevue Avenue.
The Mooring, Sayer's Wharf, off America's Cup Ave.
Chart House Restaurant, 22 Bowen's Wharf.
Inexpensive: **Mack Clam Shack,** 117 Long Wharf.

PROVIDENCE. *Moderate:* **Club Casablanca,** The Arcade, Westminster St.
Smith's 1049 Atwell's Ave., and Asquino's, 584 N. Broadway, (East Providence) are popular Italian restaurants.
Pot au Feu, 44 Custom House St., serves good French cuisine. Lower level, informal.
Near Providence, in Bristol, try the **Lobster Pot** for a Rhode Island Shore Dinner, specialty of the state.
In East Greenwich, **The Warehouse Tavern** on Greenwich Cove serves pleasant outdoor luncheons.

VERMONT

Green Mountains, Ski Heaven

Vermont is primarily rural; its man-made attractions are small, graceful, and scattered. Only Burlington has over 25,000 population, and the charm of this state lies in the way its historical and cultural heritage, its natural setting and recreational facilities, and the life of its people form an inseparable whole, unique in America. In 1970 the state enacted this country's most comprehensive and stringent development control law to ensure Vermont's intrinsic harmony and balance.

Some of the best scenery is in the 40 state parks and 34 state forests (information, maps, reservations, etc. from the Department of Forests, Parks and Recreation, Montpelier, 05602). Mt. Mansfield State Forest, near Burlington, surrounds Vermont's highest mountain (4,393 feet). Allis State Park, south of Montpelier, is well equipped for recreation; Monroe State Park is a bird, plant, and game sanctuary; and Emerald Lake State Park in Dorset has swimming and boating on a lake of unusual beauty. The department operates 35 public campgrounds with 2,200 campsites, 33 State Recreation Areas, and 13 major state beaches. There are also 73 private campgrounds. The Green Mountain National Forest in central and southern Vermont comprises 293,376 acres, served by US 4, US 7, and Rtes. 11 and 100. Twelve leading ski areas are within it, including Mt. Snow, Bromley, Sugarbush Valley and Sugarbush North, and Stratton Mountain resort. Summer camping, hunting, hiking on the 263-mile Long Trail and fishing in 3,233 acres of ponds and 349 miles of streams add to Vermont's attractions.

Particularly scenic are: the Mt. Equinox Skyline Toll Road near Manchester in the Southwest; Brandon Gap, a 2,170-foot-high pass north of Rutland; the 163-foot-deep Quechee Gorge near White River Junction; the toll road to the top of Mt. Mansfield; Lincoln Gap, a 2,424-foot-high pass 30 miles southwest of Montpelier; and the nearby Granville Gulf Reservation on Rte. 100, "six miles of wilderness forever"; the ferry rides across Lake Champlain; the view from 3,861-foot Jay Peak, just south of the Canadian border (aerial tram to the top); and McIndoe Falls, on the Connecticut River south of St. Johnsbury. Yet some of your loveliest memories of Vermont will be serendipitous —a chanced-upon harmony of hills and fields and forest with a white church spire or red barn set among them.

In the southwest corner of the state, historic Bennington has a fine regional museum, the 306-foot Bennington Battle Monument (elevator to the top), the lovely Old First Church (1805), the Parke-McCullough Mansion (National Historic Site), and Bennington College, known for its creative arts programs and progressive teaching methods. Rte. 7 into Manchester is lined with stately old homes and the large old Equinox Inn (now closed), where Abraham Lincoln stayed; just down the road is Hildene, his son's former estate and now a finely restored tourist stop. Nearby Dorset's elegance is simpler and quieter than Manchester's, and its inn is at the town's center on a handsome village green. Many writers, artists, and craftsmen have settled in this part of Vermont; and Marlboro, to the east, is the site both of an innovative liberal arts college and the renowned Marlboro Music Festival. Newfane, about 12 miles north of Brattleboro, is another lovely village; on the green are a fine Greek Revival courthouse, restored homes, two of the state's finest restaurants, and the Windham County Historical Society Museum. Grafton, too, has been restored to its colonial elegance.

In the central part of the state, Poultney, Middleton Springs, Castleton, Pittsford (which has four covered bridges), Weston, and Windsor all are attractive towns with Vermont flavor; and the community restoration program at Woodstock attracts year-round visitors from all over the world. Galleries, antique shops, boutiques occupy the eighteenth- and nineteenth-century houses. Power lines around the Green are buried for aesthetic appeal. The Romanesque-style public library (1885) has one of the best collections in Vermont, along with the Woodstock Historical Society, in the Dana House. Four of Vermont's eight Paul Revere bells are in Woodstock.

Montpelier is dominated by the State House, a simple Doric structure with an imposing gold-leafed dome. Nearby, the state office building houses the Vermont Historical Society Museum. North are the two ski mountains of the Stowe-Mt. Mansfield complex. Most of the area's 65 lodges stay open summers and offer tennis, golf, swimming, hiking, etc. Beyond lies Burlington, the state's largest city (population about 40,000). In 1842 Charles Dickens called it "an exquisite achievement of neatness, elegance and order." Parts of it still are. The Fleming Museum of the University of Vermont has a fine collection of American, ancient, and Oriental art; the city has fine views over Lake Champlain, and there are a number of historic site markers throughout the city. Don't miss the Shelburne Museum, a 100-acre park containing 35 historic buildings brought from all parts of the state to house an enormous and top-quality collection of American art, folk art, folk craft, and technology—samples of architecture, furniture, household articles, toys, quilts, carriages, farm implements, smithing and woodworking tools, country stores, a locomotive, a 220-ft sidewheel steamer—tens of thousands of articles beautifully displayed. A full visit will take two days; if time is short go directly to your special interest.

Main points of interest in the so-called Northeast Kingdom are St. Johnsbury; Lake Memphremagog, which straddles the U.S. and Canadian border; the nearly unspoiled quality of the region; Danville, site of dowsers' convention in mid-September; the Jay Peak winter and summer sports areas; and the scenic valley of the Connecticut River.

PRACTICAL INFORMATION FOR VERMONT

HOW TO GET THERE. *By air:* Major airfields are Burlington, Montpelier, Springfield, and Rutland in Vermont, and nearby Keene and Lebanon in New Hampshire. Airlines serving them are *Air North, Command Airways, United, USAir,* and *Precision.*

By car: From New York take the Thruway to Exit 24 to Rte. 7. Out of Troy, Rte. 7 to the Vermont border, at which point it becomes Rte. 9. I–91 from New Haven, Connecticut, through Massachusetts to southeastern Vermont. From Boston, I–93 to Concord, N.H., then I–89.

By bus: Vermont Transit Lines: from New York and Boston through *Greyhound;* from Montreal through *Voyageur.* Other connections are from Concord, Keene, and Portsmouth, N.H., and Portland, Me.

By train: Amtrak has two daily trains from Montreal and Washington (via New York), stopping at Brattleboro, Bellows Falls, White River Junction, Montpelier, Waterbury, Essex Junction, and St. Albans. The problem with Amtrak is its arrival in Vermont, i.e., very late at night from Montreal to New York and before dawn from New York, bound for Montreal. For further information contact any Amtrak office.

TOURIST INFORMATION SERVICES. Travel suggestions mailed free by the *Vermont Travel Division,* 134 State St., Montpelier, 05602. Literature is also available from Vermont Attractions, Box 7, Shelburne, 05482; Northeastern Vermont Development Association, Box 640, St. Johnsbury, 05819; Stowe Area Association, Stowe, 05672. Vermont Transit Co., Inc., 135 St. Paul St., Burlington, 05401, has information on bus service. Lake Champlain Transportation Co., King St. Dock, Burlington, 05401, will send information on Lake Champlain ferry service. Write the Dept. of Forests, Parks, and Recreation, Montpelier, 05602, for information on forests. Vermont Association of Private Campground Owners & Operators, Box 214, Middlebury, 05753, has information about private campgrounds. Long Trail hiking information can be obtained from the Green Mountain Club, Inc., P.O. Box 889, 43 State St., Montpelier, Vt. 05602. For information about the Appalachian Trail write the Appalachian Trail Conference, Box 236, Harpers Ferry, W. Va. 25425. In New York City, the New England Vacation Center is at 630 Fifth Ave., New York, NY 10020, (212) 307–5780; in Montreal, the Vermont Information Center is at 2051 Peel St., (514) 845–9840.

Within Vermont there are information offices in Barre, Bellows Falls, Bennington, Bradford, Brandon, Brattleboro, Burlington, Island Pond, Manchester, Middlebury, Montpelier, Newport, Rutland, St. Albans, St. Johnsbury, Swanton, Wells River, White River Junction, and Woodstock; on I–91 at Guilford, Putney, Westminster, White River Jct., Bradford, Lyndonville, and Coventry;

on I–89 at Fairfax, Georgia, Highgate Springs, Randolph, Sharon, and Williston; and on Rte. 4 at Fair Haven. For a full listing of lodgings, restaurants and attractions, write to the Vermont State Chamber of Commerce, Box 37, Montpelier, Vermont 05602 and ask for *Vermont's Gazetteer.*

 SEASONAL EVENTS. The ski season runs from Thanksgiving to Easter at most areas, although Killington usually starts in October, Sugarbush by early November; they both run into May along with Mt. Snow. Ski races, demonstrations, and cross-country meets take place through the winter, as do winter carnivals held at Brattleboro, St. Albans, Mt. Snow, Stowe, Ludlow, Brattleboro, and Middlebury College.

In the spring, the major event is sugaring. St. Albans celebrates the flow of syrup with the *Franklin County Maple Syrup Festival* in early April. The production of syrup and syrup products can be observed across the state from early March through at least mid-April.

Summer brings antiques, art and craft shows and demonstrations around the state. Barre holds a one-day *Heritage Festival.* Castleton celebrates *Colonial Day* and has open house in midsummer. The *Fleming Art Museum* and the *Southern Vermont Art Center,* in Burlington and Manchester respectively, host impressive exhibits. The *Annual Antique and Classic Car Show* is held in Bennington on the second weekend in September. The month-long *Stratton Mountain Arts Festival* opens in mid-September.

One of the most exciting events is the series of concerts given by the *Marlboro Music Festival* at Marlboro College during July and August; there also is a *Mozart Festival* in July and August in Burlington. The *Champlain Shakespeare Festival,* staged by professionals, begins in August and runs through October in the *University of Vermont's Royall Tyler Theatre,* Burlington. Summer theater throughout the state runs from mid-July into early September, at several theaters, notably the *Dorset Playhouse* and the *Weston Playhouse.*

Outing and canoe clubs sponsor *slalom championships* on West River, Jamaica, in May. There are numerous horse shows and events; a favorite event of those staged by the *Green Mountain Horse Association of South Woodstock* is the *100-Mile Trail Ride,* which originates at South Woodstock during the last weekend in August.

Fall Harvest and the turning leaves inspire festivals in all parts of Vermont. Some fairs are held in August before vacationers leave the state. *Addison County Field Days* in New Haven in August feature horse shows and cattle judging. A week-long *State Fair* is held in Rutland in September. At Tunbridge, a 4-day *World's Fair* is held in mid-September. Danville holds its annual *Dowsing Convention* in September. Montpelier has a *Square Dance Festival* in October and a *Statewide crafts fair* on Columbus Day weekend. An outstanding regional festival is the *Fall Foliage Festival of the Northeast Kingdom,* involving the villages of Walden, Cabot, Marshfield, Peacham, Barnet Center, and Groton, in early October. Warren has an *Oktoberfest,* and the *Stratton Mountain Arts Festival* continues during fall foliage time.

 MUSEUMS AND GALLERIES. Vermont's historic, cultural, and artistic memorabilia are preserved in 25 museums. Outstanding among them are: the *Bennington Museum,* on Rte. 9; Weston, on the Green, the *Farrar-Mansur House;* the *Shelburne Museum,* US 7, in Shelburne, 100 acres of Americana; *Pater Matteson Tavern Museum,* East Rd., Shaftsbury; *Brattleboro Museum and Art Center* in the recycled train depot; *Sheldon Museum,* Middlebury; *Walker Museum,* US 5, Fairlee; *Bixby Library Museum,* 258 Main St., Vergennes; *Wilson Castle,* Proctor.

HISTORICAL SOCIETIES. *Vermont Historical Society Museum,* Pavilion Office Bldg., Montpelier; *Grafton Historical Museum; E. Poultney Historical Society Museum; Dana House,* 26 Elm St., Woodstock; *Barre Historical Society Museum,* Washington St.; *Brookfield Historical Society Museum; Rokeby,* US 7, Ferrisburg; *Windham County Historical Society,* Newfane; *Peacham Historical Society Museum.*

ART MUSEUMS. *Wood Art Gallery,* 135 Main St., Montpelier; *Fleming Museum, University of Vermont,* Colchester Ave., Burlington; *Athenaeum Art Gallery & Library,* St. Johnsbury; *Southern Vermont Art Center,* Manchester; *Bundy Museum,* Waitsfield; *Chaffee Art Center,* Rutland; *Springfield Art & Historical Society.*

HISTORIC SITES. In 1961, the *Vermont Board for Historic Sites* was established to preserve the state's heritage. For a complete guide write to: Vermont Division of Historic Preservation, Montpelier, 05602.

TOURS. *Fall Foliage Tours:* The foliage period is usually September 25 to about October 15; color changes begin in the upper reaches of the Green Mountains and radiate southward. The *Vermont Travel Division,* Montpelier 05602, publishes a brochure with 13 proposed scenic tours along marked paved roads through the best areas.

DRINKING LAWS. Drinking in restaurants and hotels is legal; and alcohol is sold by the drink Mon.–Fri. 8 A.M. to 2 A.M., Sat. until 1 A.M., and Sunday from noon to 2 A.M. Minimum age is 19. Bottled beer and light wine to take out are sold at grocery stores with second-class licenses, open Mon.–Sat. 6 A.M. to midnight, Sunday 8 A.M. to 10 P.M. Bottled liquor is sold at state liquor stores and agencies.

SUMMER SPORTS. *Golf:* According to *Golf Digest* the following are the best courses in Vermont: *Mount Snow C.C.,* West Dover, a rolling course at 2,000 ft. *Haystack,* Wilmington. *New Desmond Muirhead* course with spectacular mountain scenery. *Lake Morey Inn & C.C.,* Fairlee, lakeside, rolling; site of annual *Vermont Open. Crown Point C.C.,* Springfield, flat, pretty. *Equinox Hotel & C.C.,* Manchester, superbly groomed, rolling course. *Manchester C.C.,* Manchester, attractive layout. *Stratton Mountain C.C.,* Stratton Mt., designed by Geoffrey Cornish. *Sugarbush C.C.,* Warren, Robert Trent Jones course. *Stowe C.C.,* Stowe, large, well-trapped green; open to guests of Stowe member lodges. *Woodstock C.C.,* Woodstock, Robert Trent Jones course in beautiful valley with brook. *Basin Harbor C.C.,* Vergennes, bordered by woodland and Lake Champlain; broad, rolling fairways. In addition, there are 11 18-hole courses and 26 9-hole courses, some of which are open only to guests of acceptable lodges. Inquire locally. The *Stratton Mountain Golf Academy* is located at that southern Vermont resort near Manchester.

Riding: From late May to late Sept., there are more than 30 riding events in Vermont, notably in *Arlington, Brookfield, Proctorsville, Woodstock, Killington,* and *Windsor.* For a complete listing of Vermont riding stables, write the Travel Division, Montpelier, 05602.

Mountain rides: North America's first Alpine slide, now three tracks, is at Bromley Ski Area near Manchester. Others are at Stowe and Pico Ski Area near Rutland. Gondola or chairlift rides are available at Stowe, Killington, Jay Peak.

Boating: Canoe, sailboat, rowboat, and motorboat rentals are available throughout the state. In most state parks, rowboats and canoes are for rent. Canoeing is best in the spring, when the waters are high. *Lake Champlain* is a favorite area for summer boating; other good spots are: *St. Catherine, Seymour, Bormoseen, Memphremagog, Dunmore, Fairlee, Caspian.* For a complete listing of boat rental areas write the Travel Division, Montpelier, 05602.

Hunting and fishing: The hunting season begins in October and ends in November. Fishing starts in the early part of April and extends through September. All licenses are available from local town or city clerks. Nonresidents must prove that they hold licenses in their home states, or that they have previously held licenses in Vermont, or that they have passed a hunting safety course. Contact the Vermont Fish & Game Dept., Montpelier, 05602.

WINTER SPORTS. Alpine and cross-country skiing, skating, snowshoeing, ice fishing are things to do during the winter. Vermont has more than 20 ski areas; for details, write to the Vermont Travel Division, Montpelier 05602, or Vermont Ski Areas Assn., 26 State St., Montpelier 05602.

Cross-country skiing is available at 60 touring centers. Among the best: *Blueberry Hill, Goshen; Woodstock Ski Touring Center; Stratton Mountain Ski Touring Center; Living Memorial Park, Brattleboro; Trapp Family Lodge, Stowe.*

Ice skating: There are rinks at *Killington, Middlebury Snow Bowl, Mount Snow,* and *Sugarbush Valley* ski areas.

WHAT TO DO WITH THE CHILDREN. *Santa's Land, U.S.A.,* north of Putney (I–91 and US 5), includes *Santa's Alpine Railroad;* open May to Christmas, daily. The *Shelburne Museum* (US 7), south of Burlington, comprises 35 early American buildings on 100 acres; open daily, mid-May to mid-October and Sundays in winter. The *Springfield Public Library,* 43 Park St., has a special children's room. The *Discovery Museum,* 51 Park St. (878–8687) combines hands-on fun with exploration and education. *Dana House,* Woodstock, has a children's room with doll exhibit and doll houses.

HOTELS AND MOTELS. Accommodations in Vermont are excellent, with many establishments serving both the winter sportsman and the summer loafer. As Vermont's tourism infrastructure has grown, so has its quality and sophistication. Off-season rates understandably are lower, but a winter vacation need not be limited only to skiing. Prices are based on double occupancy, European Plan (no meals) unless indicated.

Listings are based on the following price ranges: *Moderate:* $30–50; *Inexpensive,* under $30. There are *Youth Hostels* in Colchester (878–8222), Craftsbury Common (586–2514), Fairlee (333–9766), Rochester (767–9384), Warren (496–3744), Waterbury Center (244–8859), and Woodford (442–2547). Burlington has a *YMCA* and a *YWCA.*

We have listed, generally under *Inexpensive,* some of the many excellent Guest Houses and Tourist Homes to be found in Vermont, a state where this type of lodging flourishes. There are many more of these than we have space for here, and as they are both characteristic of New England and generally *Inexpensive,* or at most, *Moderate,* we refer you to the several detailed directories listed in the section on Hotels and Motels in the beginning of this volume, under Planning Your Trip. There are over 60 recommended establishments in Vermont.

ARLINGTON *Inexpensive:* **Cut Leaf Maples Motel.** 20 rms., 12 baths, seasonal and family rates, and MAP available. Play area, cafe.

Valhalla. Rte. 7. Outdoor pool. Weekly rates available.

BARRE. *Moderate:* **Sir Anthony.** Pool, dining room, bar, seasonal rates.

Inexpensive–Moderate: **Arnholm's.** Antique furniture, free coffee, cafe near. Picnic area. Closed Nov.–April.

Knoll. Small (15 rms.) motel, cafe nearby. Air-conditioning, parking, lawn games, picnic area.

BENNINGTON. *Moderate:* **Catamount Motel.** Charming Colonial decor. Pleasant spacious rooms. Restaurant near. Pool, play area.

Hillbrook Motel. Situated away from the hwy. with nice view. Restaurant near. Pool, play area. Pets allowed.

Inexpensive: **Pleasant Valley Motel.** Rte. 9. Small, set back from hwy. Pool. TV.

Swiss Village. Exit 2 off Rte. 7. Pool, water slide, play area.

BRANDON. *Inexpensive-Moderate:* **Adams.** One- and two-room cottages. MAP available. Pool, cafe, pleasant rooms, quiet, off highway.

BRATTLEBORO. *Inexpensive:* **Susse Chalet.** At I–91, Exit 3. Member of New England's major budget chain. Pool, laundromat, valet, serving and secretarial services, emergency automobile service, air-conditioning.

BURLINGTON. *Moderate:* **Bel-Aire,** 111 Shelburne Rd. Seasonal rates, TV, free coffee. Cafe and coin laundry nearby.

Brown, 165 Shelburne Rd. Pool and playground. Cafe and coin laundry nearby. Weekly and seasonal rates. Some suites.

Grand View, ½ m. S. of exit 17 on I–89. Some kitchen units. Weekly and seasonal rates.

Redwood Master Hosts Inn. Well-appointed rooms. Near colleges, golf course, Shelburne Museum.

Inexpensive: **Econo Lodge.** South Burlington off I–89 at Exit 14. Near Univ. of Vt., Shelburne Museum, airport. Pool.

Huntington. Downtown medium-sized hotel. Near theaters, restaurants, and stores.

Traux Tourist Home, 32 University Terrace. 4 comfortable guest rooms near the university. Children welcome.

DORSET. *Moderate:* **Dorset Inn.** Medium size with bath or combination bath, restaurant, bar. Terrace for steak cookouts. Pool.

MANCHESTER. *Moderate:* **The Inn at Manchester.** On US 7. Beautifully renovated mansion. Breakfasts served in cheerful dining room. Tennis and golf privileges; pool.

Toll Road Motor Inn. Convenient to all outdoor sports. Pool. Restaurant nearby. Golf privileges.

Weathervane Motel. Beautiful setting and locale, just south of village on Rte. 7, large rooms, pool. Many extras, including free bicycles, antique shop, honeymoon suites.

Inexpensive–Moderate: **Skylight Lodge.** Family-like atmosphere with dormstyle bunks or modest but cozy rooms. Last of original owners from post-World War II era, just as skiing was getting started at Bromley.

Inexpensive: Motels: **Stamford, Sunderland.**

MARLBORO. *Moderate:* **Whetstone Inn.** Small, 170-year-old country inn with pleasant rms. Friendly atmosphere. Kitchen units, weekly rates.

MIDDLEBURY. *Moderate:* **Blue Spruce.** US 7. Homey. Color, cable TV.

Greystone Motel. US 7. Small, clean. Pets. Color, cable TV.

Inexpensive: **Waybury Inn.** Rte. 125. Colonial charm (1810), fireplaces. Excellent dining, lounge.

MONTPELIER. *Moderate:* **Brown Derby.** Restaurant, bar, entertainment.

Tavern Motor Inn. More functional than fancy. Close to state offices and capital. Two dining rooms. Bar.

RUTLAND. *Moderate:* **Rutland Travelodge.** Well-appointed rooms. Indoor pool, saunas, No pets.

    Woodstock East Motel. US 4. Kitchenettes, free coffee. Pool. Color, cable TV.

    Inexpensive: **Country Squire Motel** in N. Clarendon, nr. junct. Rte. 103 and US 7; and **Green-Mont,** 138 N. Main St.

SPRINGFIELD: *Moderate:* **Abby Lynn Motel.** Good location at jct. of Routes 106 and 10. Near airport. Outdoor pool. TV.

    Inexpensive: **Pa-Lo-Mar Motel.** Rte. 11. Small, kitchenettes. Coffee shop. Heated pool, picnic area. Color, cable TV.

STOWE. *Moderate:* **Country Squire Motor Lodge.** On State 100. Attractive rms. with balconies. Restaurant nr. Pets. Play area.

    Scandinavia Inn. Pool, sauna, cafe, golf privileges, some fireplaces in rooms.

    Green Mountain Inn. Another former stagecoach stop (1833) but with modern annex. Restaurant, lounge.

    Inexpensive–Moderate: **Golden Kitz Lodge.** Rte. 108. European-style pension. BYOB.

WAITSFIELD. *Inexpensive–Moderate:* **Bagatelle.** Modern guest rooms in main building, sleeping bag room in back section. Restaurant, lounge.

WHITE RIVER JUNCTION. *Inexpensive.* **Susse Chalet.** At I–89—I–91 interchange. Pool, laundromat, valet, serving and secretarial services, emergency automobile service, air-conditioning. Restaurant and health center adjacent. Also: **Pleasant View,** ¼ m. west on Rte. 4.

WOODSTOCK. *Moderate:* **Ottauquechee Motel.** Small motel situated in appealing country area. Rooms are neat, tastefully furnished. Library.

 DINING OUT. Restaurants in Vermont take pride in local specialties, such as roast turkey, clam chowder, griddle cakes with maple syrup, maple-cured ham, maple butternut pie, rum pie, and country-style sausage. Price ranges are based on a full dinner, but remember that á la carte meals will bring your tab up. Listings are based on the following price ranges: *Moderate:* $10–20; *Inexpensive,* under $10.

ARLINGTON. *Inexpensive:* **West Mountain Farm.** A cozy inn on a 145-acre estate. Roast beef and steak dinners are specialties. Bar. Children's portions. Open year-round, but closed Tues. Outdoor dining in season.

BENNINGTON. *Moderate:* **Heritage House.** Small family restaurant, proud of its Vermont dishes, especially the roast turkey, steak. Clam chowder on Fri. Weekday luncheon buffet. Open all year.

    Publyk House. Rte. 7A. Remodeled barn. Rustic decor with view of Mount Anthony. Steaks, salad bar, kids' portions.

    Inexpensive: **Geannelis' Restaurant.** Rte. 9. Excellent breakfasts, fine sandwiches.

    Shirkshire, 663 Main Street.

BRATTLEBORO. *Moderate:* **Common Ground.** 25 Elliot St. Gourmet natural foods menu. International vegetarian meals on the terrace in good weather. Closed Tues. nights.

    Country Kitchen. Dark paneled rooms. Small bar. Steaks, seafood. Children's portions. Reservations.

BURLINGTON. *Inexpensive:* **Ben & Jerry's Homemade.** St. Paul & College Sts. Vegetarian sandwiches, salads, crepes, homemade soups, ice cream.

Carbur's. 119 St. Paul St. Dazzling array of sandwiches on 25-page menu. Especially good for families.

Lincoln Inn, 4 Park St., Essex Junction. Family-owned, baking on premises, specialties—steak, lobster, turkey.

The Tower. US 2. Country-style breakfasts, and then Italian fast foods— pizza, subs, etc. Other locations in Barre, Essex Junction.

What's Your Beef, 152 Paul St., Semi-á la carte, children's portions, steak and seafood.

DORSET. *Moderate:* **Dorset Inn.** New England meals. Wed. steak cookouts. Sun. buffet. Children's portions. Bar. Open mid-June–mid-Oct.

LAKE MOREY (FAIRLEE). *Moderate:* **Lake Morey Inn.** This large resort features traditional New England fare with continental flourishes. Sun. night buffet. Bar. Open daily early June–mid-Oct. for breakfast, lunch and dinner.

Rutledge Inn. Colonial decor, own baking, special desserts, children's portions. Open mid-June to Labor Day.

MANCHESTER. *Moderate:* **Colburn House.** Yankee foods. Bar. Open for breakfast, lunch, and dinner.

Sand Trap Restaurant. Excellent for relaxing lunch. Homey setting.

Quality Restaurant. Wide choice of New England cooking, featuring steak, chicken, or fish. Pleasant atmosphere. Paintings for sale. Note original oil painting of proprietor by Norman Rockwell. Bar. Children's portions. Open daily except Tues. Nov.–Apr.; also closed Dec. 25.

Inexpensive: **Garlic John's.** Italian specialties, children's portions, bar, chef-owned.

MARLBORO. *Moderate:* **Skyline Restaurant.** 100-mile view from summit of Hogback Mt., opposite *Marlboro Inn.* Vermont specialties. Try waffles or griddle cakes with homemade sausage. Children's portions. Chef-owned.

MIDDLEBURY: *Moderate:* **The Dog Team Tavern.** Charming atmosphere. Popular spot. Menu posted on a blackboard. Children's portions. Bar. Closed Mon.

Middlebury Inn. Situated on the Green, this colonial inn has been a long-time favorite with Middlebury College families. Children's portions. Cocktails in *Snow Bowl* and *Pine Room.*

MONTGOMERY CENTER. *Inexpensive–Moderate:* **Brown Derby.** Steak, seafood, children's plates, entertainment, dancing.

MONTPELIER. *Moderate:* **Lobster Pot.** Large restaurant featuring lobster, seafood, and chicken specialties. Bar. Children's portions. Open weekdays; and Sun. July, Aug., and Sept.

Inexpensive: **The Brown Bag.** Elm St. Superb sandwiches.

NEWPORT. *Moderate:* **The Landing.** Right on Lake Memphremagog. Steaks plus the obvious: fresh fish, seafood.

NORWICH. *Moderate:* **Norwich Inn.** 1 mi. from Dartmouth College. This country inn serves Vermont foods such as maple-cured ham, country sausage, and pancakes in *Four Seasons Dining Terrace.* Bar.

Carpenter Street. Different special every night. Oriental night is Wednesday.

QUECHEE: *Moderate:* **Dana's by the Gorge.** US 4. Fine soups, hefty burgers; excellent luncheon stop but crowded around noon.

RUTLAND. *Moderate:* **Kong Chow Restaurant.** 48 Center St. Chinese and American dishes.

Sirloin Saloon. Rte. 7. Steak, seafood. Children's portions.

Vermont Inn. Charming farm house with cozy fireplaces. American and continental cuisine. Bar. Children's portions. Closed Tues. and May.

Vincent's. Italian food, seafood, children's plates, own baking.

ST. JOHNSBURY. *Moderate:* **Aime's Restaurant.** Distinguished for 30 years. Seafood, beef specialties. Homemade pastry. Children's portions. Bar.

Rabbit Hill Motor Inn & Motel. Attractive dining room overlooks the Connecticut River and White Mts. Menu features veal parmigiana, baked stuffed shrimp. Homemade pastries. Bar. Closed Tues. in winter.

SPRINGFIELD. *Moderate:* **Hartness House.** Country inn on former residence of Gov. James Hartness. New England meals are served daily. Bar. Buffet on Tues. and Wed. Look for *Underground Lounge.*

Penelope's. Première eatery in town. Soup 'n sandwiches at lunch, fish or fowl for dinner.

The Paddock. Seafood, beef, own baking, children's portions, pleasant converted-barn decor.

STOWE. *Moderate:* **Green Mountain Inn.** Dine in a charming colonial inn with friendly atmosphere. Menu features crabmeat au gratin. Homemade pastries. Bar. Limited wine list. Children's portions. Closed Apr. 15–June 1, Oct. 30–Dec. 15.

Spruce Pond Inn. Renovated farmhouse. Specializes in brook trout. Homemade soups, pastries. Bar. Children's portions. Closed Mid-Apr.–late May; late Oct.–Mid-Dec.

Inexpensive: **The Shed.** Danish cooking, own baking, beef, chicken and shrimp specialties. Al fresco in season. Lunch and dinner; sandwiches to take out from the rustic bar on the other side of building. Known locally as "The Ho Jo Room" because of barnboard décor, like so many other restaurants.

WAITSFIELD/WARREN (SUGARBUSH VALLEY). *Moderate:* **Edison's Studio.** Rte. 100; Waitsfield. Off-beat place to enjoy pizza, sandwich, and a beer while watching movies at night.

The Phoenix. Sugarbush Village. Antique decor, international cuisine. Super desserts.

Sam Rupert's. Just down the access road from Sugarbush's South Village base area. Fresh fish from the Boston docks and thick steaks.

Inexpensive: **The Deli.** Also on the access road. An overgrown variety store which produces hefty sandwiches, especially ideal for skiers who want to side-step the higher prices of on-mountain cafés and eat in-between runs while going up the chairlift.

Mooselips. Rtes. 17 & 100. Waitsfield. Italian meals, pizza.

Odyssey. Sugarbush Village. More Italian eats. Unpretentious. Fine sandwiches, burgers.

WESTON. *Moderate:* **The Inn at Weston.** This small country inn offers imaginative meals, with everything fresh and homemade. Reservations for dinner.

Inexpensive: **Vermont Country Store Restaurant.** Old-fashioned dining rooms, specializing in Vermont foods (chicken, sausage, ham, and griddle cakes).

WEST WINDSOR. *Moderate:* **Jeremiah's Pub.** Cozy, rustic atmosphere in oversized log cabin. Limited menu but excellent French onion soup and quiche. Hefty salads.

WILMINGTON/WEST DOVER (MOUNT SNOW). *Moderate:* **Poncho's Wreck.** So. Main St., Wilmington. Varied assortment, from Mexican to seafood, steak to fowl.

WINDSOR. *Moderate:* **Windsor Station.** In recycled train station. Your basic steakhouse menu.

WOODSTOCK: *Moderate:* **Kedron Valley Inn.** Just five miles down Rte. 106 from the Green. Nothing fancy but sumptuous, homey dining in the main building (1824). Recommended: the Vermont turkey or Saturday-night buffet.

New England Inn. Quiet atmosphere, excellent sirloin in a converted turn of the century Victorian-style home.

NEW YORK

City, Island and Fabulous Upstate

New York City is easy to explore with the aid of a city map which you can pick up at the New York Convention and Visitors' Bureau at the south side of Columbus Circle. The bus systems and the more than 500 miles of subways will take you to almost any sight you want to see; for in-town touring, a car is an expensive handicap. You will find walking the most rewarding way to come to know the city and its people, to savor its flavor, and to make little discoveries of your own.

The Battery Park area, where the city's history began, is an excellent starting point for lower Manhattan. Bus and subway systems converge here at Bowling Green, the little "Green before the fort" where early burghers bowled on summer evenings. Within a small radius are some of the city's most historic sites.

The Statue of Liberty

After a ten-minute ferry ride from Battery Park to Liberty Island, you will find National Park guides on hand to answer questions and provide a free souvenir pamphlet detailing the statue's history. An elevator will take you up ten floors to the balcony which runs around the top of the pedestal. For the stout of heart and strong of limb there is a staircase spiraling up twelve more stories to Liberty's crown for a stratospheric view. Rest platforms are located every third of the way up, where you can also cross over and climb back down if you have a change of heart about making it all the way to the crown. When you come down, be sure to see the Museum of Immigration, which highlights the history of the settling of the U.S. Allow yourself at least two-and-a-half hours for the ferry ride and tour of Liberty Island. Plans for renovating Miss Liberty may close the site temporary in 1984.

Battery Park

On your return to Battery Park, you might find a circular stroll rewarding; the handsome Marine Memorial is especially worthy of a few moments. Stand behind the memorial—an eagle on a black marble pedestal facing a corridor of huge granite slabs engraved with names of those who gave their lives to the sea—and you will see the Statue of Liberty dramatically framed.

The Victorian gray building, with its gay red window frames and bright green roof (near the park's exit), is the home of the city's fireboats; and the round brownstone building near the entrance to the the park is the Castle Clinton, built in 1811 to defend New York against British attack. In 1823 the fort was ceded to New York City and transformed into Castle Garden, which served as a theater and public center. From 1855 to 1890 the castle was used as the nation's principal immigrant depot, more than 7,000,000 "tempest-tost" souls passed through its gate into a bright new world until Ellis Island became the new depot. After years of being closed, Ellis Island is now open to the public once more. From 1890 till 1924, this served as the processing center for new arrivals. Opposite Bowling Green is the Customs House, an ornate Maine granite edifice studded with statuary by Daniel Chester French, which reflects the sprawling, rococo period of building at the turn of the century. The streets here are narrow, cut up, and squeezed awry by the confluence of the Hudson and East rivers. If there is one place you'll need a street map to guide you, it is here. Tucked in among them are a few historic buildings which have managed to escape destruction or have been cleverly reconstructed.

One is Fraunces Tavern on Pearl Street, a block east of the Customs House. Erroneously called "the oldest building in Manhattan," it is in fact an excellent reconstruction dating from 1907. Its square proportions, hipped roof edged with a light balustrade, regular window spacing, and white portico are perfect examples of the Georgian Colonial style favored in the early 18th century. Built of brick—which likely saved it from going up in flames during the disastrous fires of the Revolution—and turned from a residence into a successful business building (which staved off demolition)—it has had a long, colorful history. The building was erected in 1719 as a residence for Etienne de Lancy, a wealthy Huguenot. His grandson turned it into a store and warehouse in 1757, and in 1762 it was sold to Samuel Fraunces, a west Indian, who renovated it, making it the Queen's Head Tavern. Taverns in those days were often used as meeting halls, and it was at Fraunces Tavern that the Chamber of Commerce of the State of New York was founded in 1768 to help press the fight against the Stamp Act and the tax on tea. Here, too, George Washington called his officers together in the tavern's Long Room to bid them farewell.

The Sons of the Revolution in the State of New York purchased the property in 1904, faithfully re-created the original building, and today use it as their headquarters. A restaurant and bar occupy the first floor. On the floors above you can view the Long Room, where Washington made his adieus, and wander through a small museum of relics from the Revolutionary period, paintings and prints depicting historical events. (Closed on weekends.)

South Street Seaport

New York City gained much of its prominence and wealth as a major seaport. A non-profit organization with a membership of more than 25,000 people established the South Street Seaport Museum, covering a four-block area around the former Fulton Fish Market in lower Manhattan, in remembrance of the city's early seafaring days. The museum gallery is located at 16 Fulton Street, a book shop is located nearby (at the corner of Fulton and Water Streets), and a model shop and print shop are both located at 207 Water Street, a short walk north from Fulton Street. The primary goal of the museum organization is to restore the historic buildings in the four-block area and ten early vessels. Several are undergoing the process of restoration and are located at a pier where Fulton Street meets South Street. The flagship of the seaport is a four-masted German bark, the *Peking*. Other vessels open to the public include the original *Ambrose Lightship*, built in 1904, and the *Lettie G. Howard*, an 1893 fishing schooner. A new shopping and restaurant mall is also being created here as part of the overall effort to revitalize lower Manhattan.

Wall Street

Wall Street, which is only seven blocks long, follows what once was the walled northern boundary of the original Dutch colony and became a financial center soon after the Revolutionary War. Today the New York Stock Exchange has over 1,500 member firms, and up to 60 million shares have been traded daily behind the ornate façade on Broad Street, around the corner from Wall Street. Visitors are welcome to the second-floor gallery (weekdays until about 3:30) where you can look down on the Exchange floor and listen to a recording describe what all the frantic business is about. Guides take you on a tour and demonstrate how a sale is recorded on ticker tape.

Around the corner from the Exchange is a handsome Greek Revival building, on the corner of Wall and Nassau Streets. It is Federal Hall National Memorial built in 1842 on the site of New York's first City Hall. Here, freedom of the press and freedom of speech were won by John Peter Zenger in 1735, the first Congress convened, and on April 30, 1789, General Washington was inaugurated president. It was here that the Congress adopted the Bill of Rights. Administered by the National Park Service, Federal Hall is filled with permanent exhibits.

At the head of Wall Street, fronting on Broadway, is one of New York's richest landlords, Trinity Church. The present church building, erected in 1846, is the third to occupy this site. Its graveyard dates from even before 1697; if the gate is open you can seek out the final resting places of Alexander Hamilton, Robert Fulton, and others who figured in the city's early history.

North of Trinity Church on Broadway and Fulton Streets is one of the city's few remaining examples of Colonial architecture, St. Paul's Chapel, one of many Trinity built throughout the city. When it was erected in 1766, it stood in a field outside the city. Townspeople complained that it was much too far to go to church; yet it is only a five-block walk from Trinity. On either outer aisle you will find a handsome box pew. One was the special preserve of the governors who worshipped here in the comfort of upholstered chairs and draft-deflecting canopies. The pew on the left was also used by George Washington. Original William and Mary chairs in bright red satin brocade give the pew an air of elegance seldom seen in churches. Duncan Phyfe, whose cabinet shop was around the corner from the chapel, fashioned the handsome sofa you can see in the rear of the church. The altar, its railing, and a great deal of ornamentation in the church is the work of Major Pierre L'Enfant, the designer who later planned the city of Washington, D.C.

Directly behind St. Paul's is the gigantic World Trade Center, operated by the Port Authority of New York and New Jersey. The Center takes up 16 acres of lower Manhattan and nine million square feet of office space is included in two 110-story buildings surrounding a landscaped five-acre plaza. The first hotel to be erected in lower Manhattan this century, the Vista International, is at the Center. A trip to the 107th-floor observation deck is worthwhile.

City Hall

Return to Broadway and stroll up to City Hall. It is both a museum and a municipal capitol. Architecturally it is considered one of the finest public buildings in America. During the period between 1803 and 1811 when it was being built, construction costs rose to $538,000—a shocking amount in those days. The Common Council members, pinching pennies wherever they could, decided considerable money could be saved by using marble on the front and sides only. Brownstone would be used to face the back. Most of the city's population lived south of the park and it would be a waste to use marble where it seldom would be seen. In 1956, the outside was faced in limestone on all four sides.

Chinatown

On leaving City Hall, walk around to its rear and over to the tall-towered Municipal Building. A passageway through its arch will bring you out on Park Row, near the approach to the Brooklyn Bridge, the city's oldest span. From here, it is but a five-minute walk north to Chinatown. It is tiny, encompassing something like nine square blocks. Thousands of Chinese are crowded into tenements lining the narrow, crooked streets. Pseudo pagodas crowning their roofs, bright banners garlanding the streets, and temple bells help create an aura of China's civilization all around. Emporiums have modern adding machines but prefer to do their bookkeeping with the beaded abacus; apothecary and herb shops still compound family medicinal formulas. Stalls and shop windows are piled high with exotic displays of condiments and herbs, snow peas, bean curd, shark fins, duck eggs, dried fungi, squid, and other ingredients used in delectable Chinese dishes. In keeping with the Oriental theme, even the sidewalk telephone booths have been designed as tiny pagodas. The juncture of Worth and Mott Streets, across from Chatham Square, is the gateway to Chinatown. A Chinese Museum is located at 7 Mott Street, and for a small admission fee, you can view exhibits of Chinese coins, costumes, deities, and dragons. There are displays of flowers, fruits, chopsticks, and incense with explanations of their history and the symbolism attached to each. The museum also supplies you with a walking-tour map which is most helpful in identifying the Buddhist Temple, Christian churches, Chinese theaters, and other local attractions. Chinese symbols and English appear on most signs. There are dozens of shops to browse through. Jade and ivory carvings, good luck charms, slitted brocade dresses, tea sets, and sweets are to be had for generally lower prices than those uptown.

The Bouwerie, The Bowery

Just north of Chinatown, in the shadow of the Williamsburg Bridge, is the Bowery. Once an Indian trail used by Peter Stuyvesant to ride to his *bouwerie,* "farm," the thoroughfare grew into a fashionable amusement and theater center in the early 19th century then went into a decline as people moved uptown to new neighborhoods. For almost a century the Bowery has been the "street of forgotten men." You'll see them curled up in doorways or sprawled on the street, a newspaper or hat cushioning their heads, sleeping off an ever-present hangover. There are beds in flophouses above gin mills and pawn shops, but the bed that used to cost 25¢ a night now goes for $1.45 or even more. The men here live by panhandling and on the charity of such organizations as the Salvation Army.

The Lower East Side

Between the Bowery and the East Village is probably New York's most integrated area; the mile-square area (bounded roughly on the south by Canal Street and on the north by 7th Street) is the most dramatic example of the blending of many races, religions, and cultures in the world. Here, immigrants were crammed into ghettos and English was treated as a foreign language. Only those with the greatest stamina survived and those with the greatest will succeeded in escaping from it. From here came Alfred E. Smith, a son of Irish immigrants, who became governor of New York State. Several sons of Jewish immigrants made the climb to success, too. Among them were Senator Jacob Javits, composer George Gershwin, comedian Eddie Cantor. A little Italian boy made it also—Jimmy Durante. The Lower East Side was, and in a way still is, an enclave which is sufficient unto itself.

"The Village"

Greenwich Village is not an entity but rather a collection of little villages. Its heart is Washington Square, at the end of Fifth Avenue, and its extremities reach out farther each year. Roughly, it is bounded by Houston Street on the south, 13th Street on the north, Hudson Street on the west—although much of the area between Hudson (the street) and Hudson (the river) has been restored and taken on a "village" look. Its eastern boundary now extends to Lafayette Street and the vague beginnings of the East Village, where some of the Bohemians have migrated. Today's Village residents are largely career people—business executives, lawyers, doctors, teachers, writers and artists—who have been drawn by its small town neighborliness and convenient location to the city's business centers, and live in old houses they have renovated. You'll see little clusters of these tidy row houses on tree-shaded side streets, their tiny rear gardens bright with blooms and redolent of steak and chicken barbecuing over charcoal grills.

The Village also is home to a large segment of New York's Italian population. Their province, usually called Little Italy, south of Washington Square, is a tangle of shops strung with tangy cheeses, breads, red peppers, garlic, bunches of oregano and rosemary. Hordes of housewives stream in from all parts of the Village to thump the melons, poke through the endive, and argue a bit about prices before making their selections.

In the early '20s the Village was a lively and bawdy place, a Montmartre in the midst of Manhattan. Since the turn of the century, it has been a center of creativity and intellectual curiosity which nurtured some of America's greatest writers and artists: Henry James, Edith Wharton, O. Henry, E. E. Cummings, Maxwell Bodenheim, Rockwell Kent, and many others. To explore the area, a detailed map is mandatory. Even then, it is difficult to find your way without asking directions. You'll find the Villagers friendly and willing to help you out of the maze.

South of Houston

SoHo has fast become one of New York's most exciting and desirable neighborhoods. The area's century-old cast-iron buildings that housed the notorious "sweat shops" in the late 1800s, have been converted into fashionable and functional lofts and studios for many of the city's art community. Floor space is at a premium in New York, and SoHo's buildings offer the kind of room many artists, photographers, and sculptors need for their work.

Dozens of fine art galleries crowd SoHo's streets, and new restaurants and shops seem to pop up almost weekly. The area is still busy with light industry on weekdays, but on weekends, SoHo becomes a very busy cultural center. You'll see artists in their paint-splattered work clothes walking side-by-side with beautifully dressed patrons or buyers. SoHo has become so overrun with visitors, in fact, that many of the early residents (the artists) are leaving in search of quieter quarters. But for the visitor to New York, whether art lover or not, SoHo is a must.

Focal Point of the Village

Washington Arch, at the foot of Fifth Avenue, is the best point to start a stroll through the most colorful and historic Village areas. Choose a Sunday in spring, summer, or fall for one of the town's best known free entertainments. The fountain in the square is a meeting place for jazz musicians, guitar players, and pluckers of home-made instruments. Sunday strollers are apt to include young parents with toddlers, a multitude of dog-walkers and arms-around-each-other couples of all ages, in all manner of dress.

The fountain is a good vantage point for viewing the red brick, white-trimmed houses which line the square's north side. Built around 1830, they remained a fashionable center of New York for a generation, sheltering members of old New York's aristocracy and a long-gone way of life so vividly described in Henry James's *Washington Square.* Edith Wharton lived in the old Boorman house on the northeast corner of the square, a setting which inspired her novel *The Age of Innocence.* At No. 3, John Dos Passos wrote *Manhattan Transfer* and artist Norman Rockwell painted his own brand of "primitives." Rose Franken, author of *Claudia,* lived at No. 6 before this, while other lovely, patrician homes began to vanish.

New York University, which has been here since the 1830's, owns and leases about four-fifths of the land around the square. In its original building, which stood at 100 Washington Square East, Professor Samuel F. B. Morse developed the telegraph and Samuel Colt invented the single-shot pistol. When its student body began bursting the seams of the campus buildings on and around the square, the university reluctantly gave notice to artists and writers along Genius Row, and the row of garrets has been replaced with the Georgian-style Law School at the southwest end of the square and modern Roman Catholic Holy Trinity Chapel. Other N.Y.U. additions are the Hagop Kevorkian Center for Near Eastern Studies and Bobst Library. Up the street, the tall brick and glass Loeb Student Center covers the site of Madame Blanchard's boarding house, whose boarders included Theodore Dreiser, Eugene O'Neill, Zona Gale, Frank Norris, O. Henry, and many other literary greats.

Midtown

Midtown Manhattan, which ranges roughly from 34th to 59th Streets and river to river, is a center of superlatives. The biggest buildings, best restaurants, most art galleries, brightest lights, greatest concentration of big business, largest complex of theaters and concert houses, best bargain basements, most exclusive couture houses, and the most specialized services are all here.

Midtown does not readily lend itself to cut-and-dried walking tours. It is an area to be explored according to one's whims and particular interests. There are museums which specialize in collections of modern art, contemporary crafts, folk art, primitive art, costumes of all nations, re-runs of old silent movies, and lecture programs. There are scores of foreign tourist information centers and airline ticket offices with information and advice to inspire your next vacation. There are awesome views to be seen from observatories atop midtown's tallest buildings, a world to explore underground, a hundred little personal discoveries to be made, world-renowned stores, and countless small specialty shops. The most famous shops are located between 34th and 57th Streets on the showcase avenues, Fifth and Madison. Three of the city's greatest attractions are in this midtown area: Times Square; Rockefeller Center; and the United Nations.

The Great White Way starts at Times Square, a point where meandering Broadway crosses 42nd Street and Seventh Avenue. It is a monument to the vision and the gambling spirit of three men: Oscar Hammerstein I, an impresario who in 1894 sank a two-million-dollar fortune, and then some, into building the first theaters here; August Belmont, a financier who more than matched Hammerstein's gamble by extending the subway to bring the crowds uptown to the new theater district; and publisher Adolph S. Ochs, who built the Times Tower in 1904 as the new headquarters for his influential newspaper, *The New York Times*.

The theater district has tarnished since the glamorous pre-Depression days; Times Square has taken on a midway bazaar-like look, with its soft drink and pizza stands, pinball and shooting galleries, racy lingerie and fake "fire sale" shops. Many of the old prestige theaters now feature X-rated movies, and ladies of the evening roam the streets along with a hodge-podge of derelicts and eccentrics. Within the radius of a few blocks in the 40's, however, there still remains surely the greatest concentration of dramatic and musical productions you will find anywhere in the world. This tight little center of entertainment offers a rare opportunity for last-minute shopping. If you've neglected to order theater tickets in advance, check with the Times Square Ticket Service ("Tkts.") office at 47th Street and Broadway, where tickets for cultural events from concerts to legitimate theater are usually available for on, off, and even off-off Broadway performances. They are always to be had for half the box-office price plus a minimal service fee. Incidentally, right near this ticket mecca in the small triangular-shaped Duffy Square is a city-run visitors information center where you can pick up brochures and ask for tourist advice. A half-price ticket booth for concerts and dance events is located in Bryant Park, 42 St. between Fifth and Sixth Avenues.

The Avenue of the Americas

Sixth Avenue, also known as the Avenue of the Americas, is changing as glittering new skyscrapers take the place of older edifices. Bryant Park, located between 40th and 42nd Streets behind the New York Public Library, is a green and relaxing spot to visit and rest. Named in 1884 for William Cullen Bryant, poet and journalist, it is a gathering place for impromptu public speeches and their eclectic sort of audience. The park is also an excellent vantage point from which to view one of the city's more unusual new skyscrapers. Located between the Avenue of the Americas and Fifth Avenue, with entrances on 42nd and 43rd Streets and adjacent to the Graduate Center of CUNY, the Monsanto Building slopes gently upward, narrowing from its base to its towering roof, producing the rather uneasy effect of a hill carved from glass and stone. A similar one curves inward from both 57th and 58th Streets, also between Fifth Avenue and the Avenue of the Americas.

Walk north from 42nd Street and you'll see many other recently constructed buildings. At 1133, corner of 43rd Street, is the Kodak Exhibition Center where you might stop in to see the exhibits in its downstairs gallery. Now a short detour east on 44th towards Fifth

Avenue to the Algonquin Hotel and restaurant still operating at No. 59. Behind its rather unimposing Renaissance façade many noted literary figures have wined, dined, and talked the hours away: Dorothy Parker, Harold Ross, and Robert Benchley, among others. At 47th Street, you just might be tempted to take another detour east for a look at the block-long area known as the city's diamond center—it's obvious why when you see the countless glittering shop windows.

For the next three blocks on the Avenue, west side, you'll be passing three of the newer skyscraper members of the Rockefeller Center community: the 45-story Celanese Building; the 51-story McGraw-Hill building, home of *The New York Experience;* and the 54-story headquarters of Exxon.

Radio City Music Hall, on the east side of the avenue at 50th Street, is a primary attraction. It is the largest indoor theater in the world, with a seating capacity of six thousand. Near the brink of collapse in 1978, it has been revived, and its future seems at last secure. The Christmas "spectacular" is a city tradition upheld in fine form; during the rest of the year similarly elaborate stage shows alternate with pop concerts, ice shows, and other special events. Two major television and radio network headquarters are located a couple of blocks beyond—CBS between 52nd and 53rd Streets and designed by Eero Saarinen, and ABC at 54th Street. Both are on the east side of the avenue. On 55th Street, almost to Seventh Avenue is the New York City Center, 131 West 55th Street; and two blocks north along Seventh Avenue, around the corner of 57th Street, is Carnegie Hall.

If you have an artistic bent, backtrack to 53rd Street and turn east towards Fifth Avenue. On this one block you'll find the handsome sculpture garden and avant garde works of the Museum of Modern Art, at 11 West 53rd Street, the Museum of American Folk Art at 49, and the American Craft Museum at 44.

On Columbus Circle at Central Park is architect H. Van Buren Magonigle's "Maine Memorial" with figures by sculptor Attilio Piccirili. That massive building over to the northwest is the New York Coliseum, where exhibitions of varying interests and degrees of interest are held. On the south side of the circle is the New York Convention & Visitors Bureau, in the building which resembles a large refrigerator.

Rockefeller Center

Rockefeller Center is a city-within-a-city; you could easily spend a whole day within its complex of twenty-one buildings. Many of its residents—it has a daytime population of 240,000—never leave from their arrival in the morning until they go home. There is no need to, for the center has just about everything one could ask for. There are almost thirty restaurants, several shoe repair shops, drugstores, chiropodists, dentists, oculists, gift and clothing shops, bookstores, hairdressers, barbers, banks, a post office, movie theaters, schools, and subway transportation to all parts of the metropolis. Consulates of 20 foreign nations have offices in the center, as do twenty airlines, railroad and steamship lines, and 58 state and other travel information bureaus. A shop-lined concourse, an underground passageway almost two miles long, ties together all its buildings.

The Channel Gardens—six formal beds running from Fifth Avenue to the Lower Plaza—with their ever-changing seasonal plantings, draw millions of visitors. Artists, designers, and sculptors work year-round to devise new and dramatic floral patterns for the 10 seasonal displays. The showings run consecutively, starting with thousands of lilies at Easter and ending with the greatest Christmas tree of all. The Lower Plaza, where you can ice skate from the end of September through April, and dine *alfresco* in warm weather, is a kind of ceremonial town square where distinguished visitors are greeted, occasional concerts given, and special events commemorated with colorful ceremonies. From the Observation Roof of the 70-story RCA building, at 30 Rockefeller Plaza, you'll be treated to a spectacular view. A visit to the observatory is included in the guided tour of Rockefeller Center's highlights, an hour-long educational stroll which takes you to a landscaped roof garden, the interior of the Music Hall, the famous murals and art works scattered throughout the center, and along the concourse of shops of all nations. When in doubt about what to see and where it is, visit the center's information booth in the main lobby at 30 Rockefeller Plaza, just behind the statue of Atlas at the Fifth Avenue entrance.

Fifth Avenue

New York's most famous thoroughfare, Fifth Avenue, was originally Millionaire's Row. The Astors, Vanderbilts, and numerous others built fine mansions here after the Civil War. The dividing line between East Side and West Side, it is still the most fashionable avenue in the city. With dozens of high quality shops and department stores lining it from 34th to 59th Street, a stroll along here is very pleasureable. The Empire State Building stands at 34th St.; walk north from there (after visiting the observation tower 102 floors up), and you'll take in the best of New York. At 59th Street and Central Park South you'll see Grand Army Plaza and F. Scott Fitzgerald's old haunt, the fine Plaza Hotel.

The United Nations

New York City grew from a metropolis to a cosmopolis in 1952, when the United Nations moved into its elegant new home overlooking the East River between 42nd and 48th Streets.

Acres of parkland make the U.N. grounds a pleasant place to stroll and watch the busy river traffic of freighters, tankers, and pleasure boats plying the rolling Hell Gate waters.

The visitors' entrance to the United Nations Headquarters is at the north end of the marble and limestone General Assembly Building, at 45th Street and First Avenue. There is a museum-like quality to the vast lobby with its free-form multiple galleries, soaring ceiling, and collection of art treasures contributed by member nations.

Visitors are welcome to attend most official meetings and admission is free. Tickets to the meetings are issued in the lobby fifteen minutes before meetings are scheduled to start. Because there is no advance schedule of meetings for any given day, and since they may be cancelled or changed at the last minute, the majority of tickets available to individual visitors are issued on a first-come, first-served basis.

At most meetings, speeches are simultaneously interpreted in Chinese, English, French, Russian, and Spanish and there are earphones at each visitor's seat with a dial system to tune in the language of your choice.

Taking the hour-long guided tour through the headquarters buildings is the most satisfactory way to see all the meeting rooms, to learn the aims, structure, and activities of this world body, and to appreciate fully the art works and exhibits displayed. To lunch with the delegates, stop by the information desk in the main lobby and ask about making a table reservation in the Delegates' Dining Room. Tables for visitors are in short supply and are assigned on a first-come basis. The earlier you make the reservation, the better.

On the lower concourse there is a coffee shop for a quick snack and lounges to rest. Here, too, are several shops which offer books, art, and handicraft products of the U.N.'s member nations.

Up in Central Park

Central Park, an 840-acre oasis of rural beauty in the midst of a concrete jungle of midtown spires, runs from 59th to 110th Street and from Fifth Avenue to Central Park West (an extension of Eighth Avenue). Masterfully designed by Frederick Law Olmstead and Calvert de Vaux, the park was designated a National Historic Landmark in 1965. A stroll through the park will reveal the woodland terrain of New York as it might have been in the days of the Dutch settlers, before dredges and bulldozers leveled the hills and rocky outcroppings to erect a fence of apartment houses. If you take a drive down through the park from the north end at dusk, just as lights begin to sparkle in windows and the last rays of the sun silhouette the spires at the south end, you will be rewarded with a strikingly beautiful sight. Or hire a carriage—they park across the street from the Plaza Hotel—and take a leisurely turn around the ponds, lakes, and woodlands.

The park is a many-splendored melange of fountains and ponds, statues and monuments, promenades and wooded paths. On warm weekdays, office workers find a favorite rock by the pond, spread out their lunches, and share them with the water birds. In the winter, they skate at Wollman Memorial Rink. On Sundays, families come to picnic, play softball, pitch horseshoes, ride the merry-go-round, fly kites, row boats, ride bicycles on the curling, car-free drives, and absorb enough sun and fresh air to last them through another week of molelike living. Off the 64th Street entrance on Fifth Avenue is a small zoo with a splendid collection of birds, wild animals, and a seal pond.

Lincoln Center

Lincoln Center for the Performing Arts is an elegant four-block cultural world, located between 62nd and 66th Streets west of Broadway, on the West Side. Get acquainted with the buildings by taking one of the guided tours, or wander around the open plazas and parks on your own. Standing on Broadway, the building you see to the left of the large central fountain plaza is the New York State Theater, home of the New York City Opera and the New York City Ballet. On the right is Avery Fisher Hall, home of the New York Philharmonic.

Between the two stands the Metropolitan Opera House with its two colorful Marc Chagall windows depicting motifs and themes relating to music. It houses The Metropolitan Opera company and has the Center's largest seating capacity: for over 3,700 people in its main auditorium. Tucked behind Philharmonic Hall is the charming Eero Saarinen-designed Vivian Beaumont Theater, sadly shuttered as discussions over possible renovations and programming policies continue. And in back, with an entrance on Amsterdam Avenue, is the Library and Museum of the Performing Arts, a branch of the New York Public Library. Also on these grounds is the Guggenheim Bandshell for alfresco concerts. Across 65th Street is the Juilliard School campus which includes Alice Tully Hall, a Lincoln Center facility noted especially for its chamber music presentations.

The American Museum of Natural History

If you are interested in tracing the history and growth of New York, visit the New York Historical Society's headquarters at 77th Street and Central Park West. A block or so north is the American Museum of Natural History, founded in 1869 "for the purpose of encouraging and developing the study of natural science, advancing the general knowledge of kindred subjects, and of furnishing popular instruction." It has been operating for over a century and houses tens of millions of zoological, geological, anthropological, and botanical specimens that are studied by scientists, students, and scholars from all over the world.

To make the most of your visit, pick up a guide book and check off the exhibits you want to see first. Two of the museum's greatest attractions are the 94-foot life-size model of a blue whale on the first floor and the two huge halls' worth of dinosaur fossils on the fourth floor. Other highlights include the 64-foot long Haida Canoe, made from the trunk of a single cedar tree; the Hall of the Biology of Man, which is devoted to the evolution, structure, and function of man as an organism; reconstruction of the extinct dodo; the recently completed exhibition of the Courtship of Birds; the collection of mammals; the Northwest Coast Indian Hall; the Hall of Man in Africa; and the demonstration-participation lectures in the new People Center where onlookers are invited to try on costumes or play instruments, for example, of cultures around the world.

A connecting passageway takes you to the Hayden Planetarium, at 81st Street and Central Park West, the department of astronomy of the American Museum of Natural History. The planetarium has numerous exhibits: murals of lunar landscapes, eclipses, and the aurora borealis; collections of meteorites (some weighing up to thirty-four tons); ancient Chinese, French, and German astronomical instruments.

East Side Museums and Galleries

On the Fifth Avenue side of Central Park and on the side streets of Madison Avenue in the '70s is the city's greatest concentration of art galleries and museums. You might work your way up Fifth Avenue to 92nd Street, then over to Madison Avenue and down to the '60s. A good starting point is the Frick Collection on Fifth Avenue at 70th Street, a splendid example of French classic architecture (formerly the home of Henry Clay Frick), enclosing a peaceful glass-roofed courtyard; the private collection of fine paintings, ornaments, and furnishings will give you an idea of the scale of living enjoyed by New York society before the income tax.

Across the way, facing Fifth Avenue between 80th and 84th Streets, is the Metropolitan Museum of Art. The neo-Renaissance design of this imposing structure infringing on the reaches of Central Park was taken from the Columbian Exposition (Chicago World's Fair) of 1893. The museum houses one of the most comprehensive collections in the world, more than a million art treasures representing the work of 50 centuries. The whole of it cannot be enjoyed in one visit; so it would be best to ask for a floor plan at the information booth and choose the galleries which hold the most interest for you. There are also Acoustiguides for rent here; the recorded tour takes approximately 45 minutes. Its departments include Egyptian Art, Near Eastern Art, American painting, sculpture, furniture, armor, and arms.

Frank Lloyd Wright's Spiral

One of the most extraordinary buildings in New York is the Solomon R. Guggenheim Museum at 88th Street, a six-story spiral staircase designed by the late Frank Lloyd Wright, which provides a quarter-mile of ramp, its walls hung with an ascending collection of contemporary art. It's best to take the elevator to the top and meander down. At 91st Street the former house of steel tycoon Andrew Carnegie is now the Cooper-Hewitt Museum of Design. One block north is the luxurious former home of banker Felix N. Warburg, whose widow presented it to the Jewish Theological Seminary to be used as a museum. The Jewish Museum has become the repository of the most extensive collection of Jewish ceremonial objects in the United States and also is one of the three most important in the world, the other two being in Jerusalem and Prague.

In the midst of all this art is yet another great museum, the Whitney Museum of American Art at Madison Avenue and 75th Street. The building itself is at first startling. Given slightly less than one-third of an acre on which to build, architect Marcel Breuer's solution was to turn the traditional ziggurat (or "wedding cake") design upside down, with the second, third and fourth floors each projecting fourteen feet farther out over the street than the one below.

From here, to the fine Museum of the City of New York at 103rd Street. The museum's collections are extensive and cover a wide variety of fields, reflecting both the city of today and yesteryear. Its decorative arts collection includes outstanding examples of costumes, furniture, and silver.

The West Side Again

The rocky ridge that begins in Central Park rises gradually as it travels uptown through Harlem and Morningside Heights to the precipitous lookout at Washington Heights. One of the most scenic drives in the city is along Riverside Drive, which follows the Hudson River shoreline from 72nd Street up to Inwood, at the northern tip of Manhattan. Along the route you will pass the boat basin, at 79th Street, where large yachts anchor. Next the Soldiers and Sailors Monument comes into view, a handsome Italian Carrara marble "silo" circled by twelve Corinthian columns. The 392-foot Gothic tower of Riverside Church can be seen a mile to the north. Its 72-bell carillon is the largest in the United States and its range of tonal quality is superb. The largest bell, the *Bourdon,* weighs more than twenty tons, while the smallest weighs only ten pounds.

World's Largest Church

Directly east, if you want to make a detour at this time, is the Church of St. John the Divine, on Morningside Heights (Amsterdam Avenue and 112th Street). Started in 1892, it will be the largest Gothic cathedral in the world when it is finally completed. The campus of Columbia University fills the center of the Heights and just north of it are those of Union Theological Seminary and the Jewish Theological Seminary.

General Grant's Tomb is at 123rd Street, and at about this point Riverside Drive begins to skirt Fort Washington Park. At 155th Street you might want to make another short detour east to Broadway to visit a unique cultural center which houses five special-interest museums. Here you'll find the Museum of the American Indian-Heye Foundation, which has an outstanding collection of Indian art and relics of North and South America. The Hispanic Society of America has a museum of ancient and modern Spanish culture. At the American Numismatic Society, you can see a vast collection of coins and medals, and the country's most comprehensive library on the subject. A large collection of historic maps is displayed at the American Geographical Society, and at the American Academy of Arts and Letters, you can view the memorabilia of many famous artists, writers, and musicians.

Heading north and west, pick up Fort Washington Avenue and follow it to Fort Tryon Park. This is the brow of Manhattan; from this vantage point, you have an uninterrupted view of the magnificent sweep of the Hudson River up to the Tappan Zee, the precipitous Palisades shoreline of New Jersey, the graceful arc of George Washington Bridge, and the far reaches of the Bronx beyond Spuyten Duyvil.

Set in the midst of this woodland park is The Cloisters; sections of medieval European monasteries have been connected by a charming colonnaded walk and merged with a French Romanesque chapel, a chapter house of the 12th century, and a Romanesque apse which is on loan from the Spanish Government. Among the museum's most notable treasures are the *Hunt of the Unicorn* tapestries, which are considered to be among the world's greatest.

Sailing Around Manhattan

The Circle Line lecture trip leaves from Pier 83 on the Hudson River, at 43rd Street and 12th Avenue. Heading south you pass Manhattan's lower West Side. The ferry rounds the island's southern tip, giving a superb view of the Statue of Liberty and of the Wall Street skyline. Heading up the East River, you'll pass under three very different spans to Brooklyn: the Brooklyn, Manhattan, and Williamsburg bridges. A glimpse of fashionable Brooklyn Heights is available and you may see, a mile or so upriver, a huge U.S. Navy cruiser or carrier in dry dock at the Brooklyn Navy Yard. Looking back to the Manhattan side, you'll have passed Chinatown and the lower East Side and now be closing in on the United Nations Building at 44th Street and 1st Avenue. On your right will be the Delacorte Geyser and Roosevelt Island with its new housing developments. The bridge overhead is the stolid Queensborough or "59th Street."

Then it's upstream under the Triborough Bridge (linking Manhattan to Queens and the Bronx). After several smaller spans, you'll see on the right refurbished Yankee Stadium. Rounding the northern tip of Manhattan through the Spuyten Duyvil cut, the cruise slips past Columbia University's boathouse, Inwood Hill Park, and the Henry Hudson Bridge. Once again, you're on the Hudson River flanked on the west by the towering Palisades of New Jersey. On the east you'll see The Cloisters and the heights of Fort Washington Park as you approach the George Washington Bridge, Grant's Tomb, Riverside Church, and the Soldiers and Sailors Monument. Midtown towers come into view as you head back to the dock past rebuilt luxury-liner piers between 54th and 45th Streets. It's a cruise you'll long remember. It lasts about 3 hours, and a guide narrates the scenes along the way. The cruises run from mid-April through early fall.

Brooklyn

Shortly after the West India Company settled Manhattan they sailed over to the "broken lands" southeast of the Battery to negotiate with the Indians for the purchase of the whole western end of Long Island. Their first parcel in Brooklyn (Breuckelen—broken land) was acquired in 1636. On Ilpetonga (high sandy bank) where the Canarsie Indians had lived in community houses some of which were a quarter of a mile long, wealthy merchants built elegant homes. From the heights they could watch their clipper ships round Red Hook and berth at the waterside warehouses. They called the area Clover Hill. Today it is known as Brooklyn Heights. Their homes have been partitioned into studios and apartments which are handsomely restored by artists, writers, and people who enjoy the Victorian atmosphere and one of the most exciting views in the world. This view alone makes a trip to Brooklyn worthwhile.

Flatbush Avenue, a few blocks from Brooklyn Heights, will lead you southeastward to the monumental Grand Army Plaza with its 80-foot high memorial arch. A little beyond the Plaza to your left are the huge Brooklyn Museum and the beautiful Botanic Garden. The Museum's collections of primitive and prehistoric art are world renowned: North and South American Indian handicrafts; works from Oceania, Indonesia, and Africa. There is a notable collection of American painting and sculpture from Colonial times to today. Its collection of Egyptian antiquities on the third floor is considered outstanding. One floor below is a fine collection of bronzes and porcelains from China, as well as changing exhibitions from the museum's wealth of over thirty thousand prints and drawings. Up on the fourth floor the costume galleries and the series of American interiors from the 17th century to the present are also of special interest.

The 50-acre Botanic Garden behind the museum, with more than ten thousand trees and plants, is especially noted for its Garden of Fragrance, one of the few gardens in the world planted and maintained for the blind. The plants were selected primarily for their fragrance and shape so that the blind might enjoy nature's beauty by the sense of smell and touch.

To the south of the Botanic Garden is Prospect Park, a 500-acre expanse of woods, meadows, footpaths, bridle trails, and tree-shaded drives designed by the same men who did Central Park, Olmstead and de Vaux. Here you can visit the Lefferts Homestead, a Dutch Colonial farmhouse which was built in 1776 and originally stood at 563 Flatbush Avenue. When the Lefferts family bequeathed it to the city the home was moved to the park as a museum.

The Bronx

The New York Botanical Garden's flower displays spread over 230 rolling acres of the northern half of Bronx Park. In its center is a forest primeval of hemlocks, one of the very few virgin tracts to have survived the axe in the East. West of Hemlock Forest is a turn-of-the-century museum building which houses an herbarium, library, auditorium, and exhibition halls. Across from the museum are a four-acre garden with hundreds of rock-loving plants, and the Conservatory, an elaborate complex of greenhouses with orchids, poinsettia, and other brilliant tropical plants. Behind the Conservatory, you'll come upon the vast Rose Garden, several thousand plantings of more than 160 rose varieties.

The Bronx Zoo—the southern half of Bronx Park—is built with moats rather than iron bars to give the illusion of a walk through the African Veldt while elephants, deer, lions, ostriches, peacocks, and other wild life roam around at will. The 252-acre zoo is one of America's largest and, for the foot-weary, there are an aerial tramway that passes directly over the African Plains, the Great Apes House, and Goat Hill, as well as a guided train tour and the "Bengali Express," a monorail that circles the Asian area.

PRACTICAL INFORMATION FOR

NEW YORK CITY

HOW TO GET THERE. *By air:* New York City is served by virtually every major (and most minor) airlines at the following airports: *John F. Kennedy,* in southeastern Queens; *LaGuardia,* in northern Queens; and *Newark,* in nearby New Jersey.

By bus: The *Port Authority Building* (Eighth Ave. and 40th St., Manhattan) is the central terminal for buses serving parts of New Jersey, the Hudson Valley area, Putnam and Dutchess Counties, the Berkshires, and the Poconos, as well as for the *Greyhound* and *Trailway* giants which serve every region of the United States. The central number for passenger information is (212) 564–8484.

By car: The Lincoln Tunnel from New Jersey, and the Midtown Tunnel and Queensboro Bridge from Long Island, are the most direct arteries to mid-Manhattan. The Holland Tunnel from New Jersey, and the Battery Tunnel from Brooklyn, reach lower Manhattan. The George Washington Bridge from New

Jersey, and the Triborough Bridge from Queens and the Bronx, give access to upper Manhattan.

The Verrazano-Narrows Bridge from Staten Island, and the Brooklyn-Queens Expressway from Queens, will get you to Brooklyn.

From New England, the New England Thruway leads to the Bruckner Expressway in the east Bronx, which you may use to get to Queens (Bronx-Whitestone or Throgs Neck Bridges), Manhattan (Bruckner Expressway and Triborough Bridge), or the west Bronx (Cross-Bronx Expressway). From upstate New York the New York (Thomas E. Dewey) Thruway extends via the Major Deegan Expressway (both I–87) to the south Bronx and the Triborough Bridge. The bridge gives access to both Queens (Grand Central Parkway) and Manhattan (Franklin D. Roosevelt Drive).

By train: Long distance *Amtrak* and *Conrail* routes reach New York from Chicago and the West, Washington, Florida and the South, plus Boston, Montreal and Toronto, and all terminate in the city at either Grand Central Station (42nd to 46th Sts. on Park Ave.) or Penn Station (31st to 33rd Sts., Seventh to Eighth Aves.). Suburban lines stretch about 75 to 100 miles north and east.

HOW TO GET AROUND. *By subway:* During daytime hours the subways are best for speed, thrift, and convenience. A pocket atlas, obtainable at book stores and some magazine kiosks, superimposes subway routes onto the street maps. Once you've targeted the proper stop, check a map of the subway system which you can get at any token booth or at the *New York Visitors' Bureau,* Columbus Circle. Subways are not recommended for late-night travel, especially for women traveling alone. Fare: 75¢ in tokens, but subject to unexpectedly sudden increases.

By bus: Free route maps are available at the *Convention and Visitors' Bureau,* Columbus Circle. The ordinary bus fare is 75¢ and you must have exact change or a token when boarding.

By ferry: The famous ride from the Battery to Staten Island carries cars as well as people on a glorious voyage through the New York Harbor—and for all of 25¢!

From the airports: The Carey Bus Co. will bring you into Manhattan near the Grand Central Terminal ($3.50). You can also take the "Train from the Plane," a super-express subway from JFK Airport to Manhattan via Sixth Avenue ($5.00).

By taxi: There are well over 30,000 yellow (licensed) cabs in New York. The driver, by law, may not refuse to take any "orderly" passenger anywhere in the five boroughs, Nassau, Westchester or to Newark Airport (the last three destinations entitle him to twice the fare shown on the meter). Neither may he charge each passenger separately when there is more than one passenger. These rules, along with the phone number (212) 747–0930 of the city's *Taxi and Limousine Commission,* are posted inside each cab. On the back of the roof-light, you'll find the vehicle's medallion (identification) number. Sharing of taxis is allowed between the airports and a few midtown Manhattan hotels. Some yellow medallion cabs are also entitled to a 50¢ surcharge between 8 P.M. and 6 A.M.

On foot: New York is a walker's delight—up and down the avenues, through distinctive neighborhoods such as Soho or Chinatown, or even across the Brooklyn Bridge. Parks aren't recommended after dark unless there are special events taking place; otherwise, well-soled shoes are all you need. Walking tours are outlined in the section on *Historic Sites.*

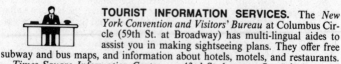

TOURIST INFORMATION SERVICES. The *New York Convention and Visitors' Bureau* at Columbus Circle (59th St. at Broadway) has multi-lingual aides to assist you in making sightseeing plans. They offer free subway and bus maps, and information about hotels, motels, and restaurants.

Times Square Information Center, on 43rd St. between Seventh Ave. and Broadway (212) 245–1212, offers maps listing many of the city's attractions in a variety of languages.

A *Guided Tour and Information Desk* at 30 Rockefeller Plaza (212) 489–2947 is open daily, except Christmas Day, and offers multi-lingual guided tours of Rockefeller Center, including a backstage tour of Radio City Music Hall.

New York, The Village Voice, and the *New Yorker* are weekly publications featuring a wealth of information on current entertainment and cultural events.

The city's daily papers, *The New York Times, The New York Post,* and *The Daily News* also list current attractions.

 SEASONAL EVENTS. *January* brings the National Boat Show and the Greater New York Auto Show to the New York Coliseum, while one of the big Ice Shows occupies Madison Square Garden.

Madison Square Garden features the Westminster Kennel Club's annual Dog Show early in *February,* and follows it with the National Antiques Show. This is also the time that the Chinese New Year celebration fills the streets of Chinatown.

The Money Show is held at the Coliseum in *March.* The parade season begins with the festive St. Patrick's Day extravaganza.

The Easter Parade originates around St. Patrick's Cathedral. All through *April* Madison Square Garden hosts the "Greatest Show on Earth," Ringling Brothers, Barnum and Bailey's Circus. The Greek Independence Day parade is the best-attended one of the month.

In *May* visit the Washington Square Outdoor Art Exhibition. The major parade honors the Armed Forces. The Circus continues.

June is the time for the Feast of St. Anthony of Padua, held on Sullivan St. between Houston and Spring Sts. The New York Philharmonic presents a program at Avery Fisher Hall. And *"Shakespeare in the Park"* begins its summer season at Central Park.

July brings fireworks on the city's rivers and ballfields in honor of Independence Day. The Newport Jazz Festival fills the city with music early in the month at many local concert halls and outdoor amphitheaters.

The Yankees and Mets usually hold their annual Old Timers' Day ceremonies in *August.* Late in the month the artists of Greenwich Village bring out their wares again for the second installment of their annual show.

The St. Gennaro Festival centers around Mulberry and Grand Sts. At this mid-*September* gala, Italian-Americans honor the patron saint of agnostics. Uptown German-Americans parade on Steuben Day.

In *October* the Coliseum presents a College Fair for high school students, and the International Wine and Cheese Festival. Three parades march this month: on Pulaski Day, Columbus Day, and Hispanic Day.

In *November* the Coliseum helps you get a head start on winter with the International Ski and Winter Sports Show and also presents a second chance for devotees of the National Rod and Custom Car Show. Thanksgiving Day brings the fabled Macy's Parade with huge balloon representations of comic book and TV cartoon characters. It is the traditional opening of the Christmas season in New York. The National Horse Show comes to Madison Square Garden, usually before mid-month.

Christmas displays in department store windows are almost an art form in New York. Fifth Avenue is their main gallery; *December* their month. Rockefeller Center has its Christmas Tree and illuminated Channel Gardens, as well as its ice-skaters and carol-singers. Finally, New Year's Eve finds Times Square jammed with hundreds of thousands of celebrants who count out the old year and noisily ring in the new.

 PARKS. Manhattan's *Central Park* has 840 acres that include lakes for boating, trails for horseback riding, playfields, a green for lawn bowling, and a skating rink. The roads that circle through it are travelled by cars during weekday rush hours and pedaled by bicyclists the rest of the time.

On the West Side is *Riverside Park,* stretching along the Hudson River from 72nd St. up to the tip of the island.

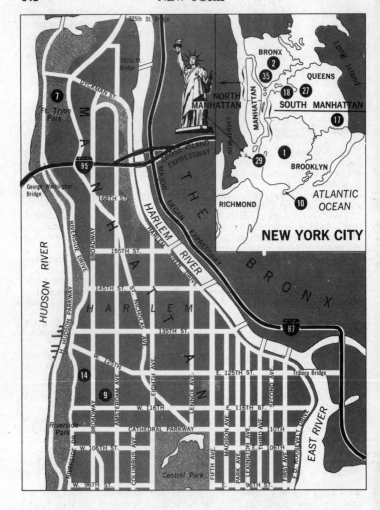

Points of Interest

1) Brooklyn Museum
2) Bronx Zoo
3) Carnegie Hall
4) Central Park Zoo
5) Chinatown
6) City Hall
7) Cloisters
8) Coliseum
9) Columbia University
10) Coney Island
11) Empire State Building
12) Gracie Mansion
13) Grand Central Station
14) Grant's Tomb
15) Guggenheim Museum
16) Hayden Planetarium
17) Kennedy International Airport
18) La Guardia Airport

19) Lincoln Center for the Performing Arts
20) Madison Square Garden
21) Metropolitan Museum of Art
22) Museum of Modern Art
23) Museum of Natural History
24) Pennsylvania Station
25) Rockefeller Center
26) St. Patrick's Cathedral
27) Shea Stadium
28) South Street Seaport
29) Statue of Liberty
30) N.Y. Stock Exchange (Wall St.)
31) Theater District (Broadway)
32) United Nations
33) Whitney Museum
34) World Trade Center
35) Yankee Stadium

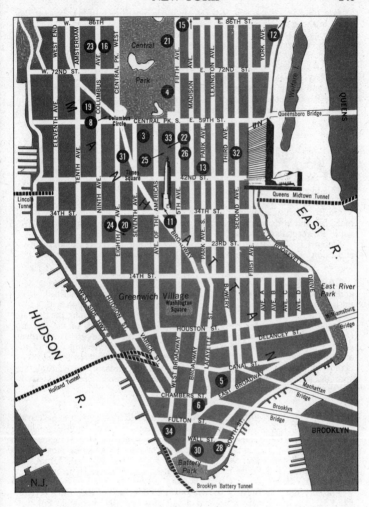

Van Cortlandt Park is a cool retreat in the northwest Bronx. *Pelham Bay Park* in the east Bronx is almost entirely surrounded by water.

Queens' most notable parks are *Cunningham, Kissena* and *Flushing Meadow,* all in the central part of the borough.

Prospect Park's 500 acres in Brooklyn include lakes and a boathouse.

Fort Wadsworth on Staten Island is one of the quieter green spaces in New York City, situated under the Staten Island end of the Verrazano-Narrows bridge and commanding an impressive view of the New York harbor.

The Parks Department sponsors drama, film, poetry, music, and dance at various parks throughout the summer. Call (212) 472–1003 for their current plans.

 ZOOS. The *Bronx Zoo,* located near the intersection of Pelham and Bronx River Parkways, is one of the largest in the world. The *Flushing Meadow Zoo* is near the N.Y. World's Fair's former Hall of Science and Shea Stadium. In Manhattan's Central Park you'll find a small *children's zoo,* and next to it, at 65th and Fifth Ave., a larger zoo for kids of all ages.

On Brooklyn's Coney Island is located the *New York Aquarium* where mammals, fish and birds from the world's water environments are displayed and fed, while Prospect Park houses both regular and children's zoos.

Staten Island's *Barrett Park Zoo,* not far from the ferry terminal, claims a collection of snakes and reptiles which is world famous.

GARDENS. *New York Botanical Garden,* directly north of the Bronx Zoo, and the 50-acre *Brooklyn Botanic Garden* in Prospect Park are described earlier in this chapter. The pond-and-hill garden is a landscape of symbols with a tori, or gate, in the pond, a shrine on top of the hill and caves echoing the delicate sound of five tiny waterfalls. The second is an exact replica of the Ryoanji (Buddhist) Temple Garden of Kyoto, one of the most famous abstract gardens of contemplation in the Far East, with a replica of the viewing wing of the ancient Ryoanji Temple. Another unique feature of the Brooklyn Botanic Garden is its Fragrance Garden for the Blind. The plants, in raised beds, are specially selected for identification by taste, touch, or smell; the plaques describing the flowers are in Braille.

 MUSEUMS AND GALLERIES. Art abounds here in all its variegated magnificence—much of it housed in buildings which are of great architectural interest themselves. In addition, there are myriad art galleries, most of the better ones clustered near Madison Avenue in the '50s, '60s, and '70s, as well as newly founded galleries in the SoHo district just below Houston St. and Greenwich Village.

The incredible vastness of the *Metropolitan Museum of Art,* Fifth Ave. at 82nd St., is actually many museums in one. It is not only impossible, but even undesirable, to see its collection of 5,000 years of art and culture all at once. Be choosy if your time is short; otherwise plan a return visit. The museum publishes a monthly calendar of events which you may write for. Floor plans, helpful staff members, a cafeteria restaurant, and numerous special services are available.

The *Museum of Modern Art* at 11 W. 53rd St. is the world's most outstanding museum devoted entirely to modern art in all media. There are examples of every creative movement from the gradual birth of modern art to the explosive designs of the 1960s, and an extremely pleasant sculpture garden for eating or just musing on Henry Moore. The museum's excellent film program includes documentaries, avant-garde experiments, and classics. Tickets are free with museum admission, and you must apply for them in person at the museum. There are also gallery talks three times a week, a lively schedule of lectures and events, and a bookshop. Films and talks are free once you've paid the admission charge. Due to construction its shows will probably be curtailed during 1983.

The *American Museum of Natural History,* Central Pk. W. at 79th St., is probably the largest and most fascinating museum of its kind in the world.

Almost everything is on view here, from giant dinosaur skeletons to the reproduction of a rain forest. There are frequent lectures and movies, as well as a bookshop and cafeteria. Annexed to it is the Hayden Planetarium.

The *Museum of the City of New York,* Fifth Ave. and 103rd St., covers almost every aspect of the development of a small Dutch town into a booming metropolis of skyscrapers and neon. A small scale model shows the early island of Manhattan, and the Dutch Galleries include a life-size reconstructed portion of Fort Amsterdam, from whose bastion you have a 360° view of the city skyline (painted) as it was in 1660. From April to October the museum sponsors a series of guided walking tours around New York neighborhoods on certain Sunday afternoons. From October to May there are special programs of events. Call (212) 534–1672, or write for schedules of these and the walking tours.

Note: Many more museums are listed in *Fodor's New York,* one of the multi-volume series on the U.S.A.

Bronx. *Bartow-Pell Mansion Museum and Garden* is at Pelham Bay Park. The mansion, built in 1842, is a Greek Revival restoration with sunken gardens, period furnishings, paintings, and a 200-volume library containing books on architecture, gardening and herbs. Small admission for adults.

Brooklyn. *Brooklyn Museum,* Eastern Parkway and Washington Ave., has an outstanding collection of ancient Egyptian art, and galleries devoted to the primitive arts of Africa, Japan, and Indonesia. The Hall of the Americas has exhibits of American primitive art. Also on view are the arts of India and the Orient. The museum has concerts, films, and lectures (write or call (212) 622–4433 for a schedule), and there is a cafeteria and a Gallery Shop in the building.

Manhattan. *The Cloisters.* Fort Tryon Park. Parts of 5 medieval monasteries are reassembled here. Exhibits include the famed unicorn tapestries.

Flushing, Queens. The *Hall of Science* in the U.S. Space Park of the former New York World's Fair contains full-sized manned orbital space vehicles, a Planetarium, a Chick Hatchery, a children's museum, and a cafeteria. Closed until spring 1984.

Staten Island. *Staten Island Institute of Arts and Sciences* is at 75 Stuyvesant Place. The science and ecology exhibits show plants, animals, and insects typical of Staten Island. The arts part of the museum contains paintings, graphics, and decorative arts.

 HISTORIC SITES. *The Harbor.* If you are conducting your own walking tour of sites and sights, you might want to start out where the city did. Henry Hudson, employed by the Dutch East India Company, sailed his ship, the *Half Moon,* into the harbor in 1609 and the area's inclusion in what Europeans called the "New World" dates from then.

Battery Park. On Tuesdays at noon (from the end of June to early September) your explorations can be accompanied by the brassy beat of a Battery Park Band Concert.

Bowling Green, many believe, is where Peter Minuit bought the island of Manhattan from the native Algonquins. The original 1771 fence around the green is intact today.

Fraunces Tavern Restaurant at the corner of Broad and Pearl Sts. is one of the few reconstructed colonial buildings in the city. Built in 1719 as a handsome private house for Etienne de Lancey, it was bought in 1762 by Samuel Fraunces. He ran it as the Queen's Head Tavern, and it was there, in the second floor dining room, that General Washington gave the farewell dinner to his officers. Souvenirs of the occasion are on the third floor *Museum of the Revolution,* open Monday through Friday and Washington's birthday. The ground floor restaurant is open for lunch and dinner weekdays and Washington's birthday.

While at Battery Park you will no doubt want to visit the *Statue of Liberty.* Special ferries leave from Battery Park every hour on the hour daily. Tel. (212) 269–5755 for information on schedules. Fare includes admission to the statue.

Lower Manhattan. Trinity Church was given a grant of land by Queen Anne in 1705 covering much of lower Manhattan, much of which the church still owns. It is one of the wealthiest and most historic churches in New York. Alexander Hamilton and Robert Fulton are buried in the church's graveyard.

City Hall, completed in 1811 and renovated in 1956, is both museum and municipal capital. Open Monday to Friday, 10 A.M. to 3 P.M.

Greenwich Village. The Village was the city's first residential suburb, started in the late 1730's when people fled "north" to escape the plague. Washington Square was designated as a potter's field and public execution ground. By 1826, when it became a drill ground for militia, some 10,000 bodies, victims of the plague or the gallows, had been buried there.

Washington Arch was first built in 1889 when the city celebrated the centenary of Washington's inaugural. The present version was designed by the famous Stanford White, and built in 1895.

Midtown and Uptown. The *Pierpont Morgan Library,* 36th St. between Park and Lexington Aves., in the classic Italian Renaissance style, was the financier's private library, office, and personal museum. The library is one of the most opulent rooms in the world.

The Other Boroughs. Bronx. *Van Cortlandt House,* Van Cortlandt Park, was built in 1748 and has furnishings and household goods which reflect both its Dutch and British owners.

Queens. *Bowne House,* 37–01 Bowne St., Flushing, is known for the Flushing Remonstrance. John Bowne, advocate of religious freedom when New York was still New Amsterdam, lived in this house built in 1661. It contains 17th-century furnishings, a pewter collection and Bowne family memorabilia.

Brooklyn. *Brooklyn Heights,* a picturesque 50-block architectural delight with brownstone, brick, and old wooden houses high on a bluff overlooking New York Harbor, has recently been designated New York's first "historic district." The New York Landmarks Commission calls the Heights "by far the finest remaining microcosm of our city as it was more than 100 years ago." Wander through the streets and you can trace the evolution of the New York townhouse; wooden and brick Federal style, Greek Revival, Gothic Revival, Romanesque Revival and Renaissance Revival.

Staten Island. *Conference House* at the south end of Hylan Blvd. in Tottenville was built in 1680, and held the only peace conference during the Revolutionary War.

 MUSIC. *Lincoln Center,* Broadway and W. 65th St., is the musical heart of New York City. Within the Lincoln Center complex are: *Avery Fisher Hall,* home of the New York Philharmonic Orchestra, which performs throughout the year except August. Twice a summer they perform in the Sheep Meadow at Central Park, and at least once in a park in every borough.

The *Metropolitan Opera Company* performs at the Metropolitan Opera House from September through April. They perform in Central Park and other city parks at no charge in June and July.

The *Juilliard Building,* with *Alice Tully Hall,* features chamber music by its own Juilliard School students, the renowned Juilliard String Quartet, and visiting performers.

Carnegie Hall at Seventh Avenue and 57th Street is a much-loved city landmark that presents classical symphonic concerts and occasional pop music programs.

The *Guggenheim Bandshell* in Damrosch Park (Lincoln Center) has outdoor concerts in the summer. The Goldman Band performs popular and light classical music on summer evenings.

The *New York City Opera* performs at the New York State Theater as does the *New York City Ballet.*

The biggest non-classical event in the city is the *Newport Jazz Festival,* held for about a week and a half that usually includes the Independence Day weekend.

Pop and rock concerts are presented all over town, all year long; the biggest attractions fill *Madison Square Garden* for several nights.

DANCE. New York has, in versatile Lincoln Center and the revitalized Brooklyn Academy of Music, facilities for every variety: classical ballet to avant-garde dance theater, African to Far Eastern. Prominent regular New York performers include George Balanchine's world famous *New York City Ballet,* the *American Ballet Theater,* the *Joffrey Ballet Company,* and the *Alvin Ailey Dance Company.* For performance schedules (of visiting companies as well), contact Lincoln Center, the box office at the City Center Theater or BAM.

TOURS. The traditional bus rides are still available from midtown (*Gray Line,* (212) 397–2600, is prominent in this field). A fresher perspective and less confining atmosphere are found on boat and helicopter trips. The famous *Circle Line,* (212) 563–3200, leaves from 43rd St. and the Hudson River and goes all the way around Manhattan. *Island Helicopters,* (212) 895–5372, provides flights as short as five minutes if you're interested in an aerial view. An excellent and inexpensive weekend alternative are the two self-guided culture bus loops operated by the city transit authority, (330–1234).

SPECIAL INTEREST TOURS. *Adventure on a Shoestring,* (212) 265–2663, plans a variety of unusual and offbeat tours and behind-the-scenes visits. If you've never been in a trans-oceanic port before, the busy piers and luxury liners may prove fascinating indeed. The newspaper shipping pages list departure schedules and if you call the line for its visiting policy, you'll be ready to stroll around the decks while passengers are being taken aboard.

Two traditionally popular guided tours shouldn't be forgotten: the *United Nations,* First Ave. and 42nd St., and the *New York Stock Exchange,* 20 Broad St.

STAGE. In New York City, the theater district—as almost all the world knows—is situated around the bright lights of Broadway and the streets in the mid-40's. Elsewhere in the city, uptown and down, are scattered the other theaters whose productions are known as "off-Broadway" and are more likely to give avant-garde productions. "Off-off-Broadway" are even more avant-garde productions and are often held in places not originally designed as playhouses. Most impressive is the Joseph Papp New York Shakespeare Festival Theater on Lafayette St. near Astor Place. The theater holds above 4 different stages, and most of the productions are of new or up-and-coming American playwrights.

An important new development for the benefit of playgoers is in Duffy Square, the narrow area of W. 47th St. between Broadway and Seventh Ave. and at the World Trade Center. Here, at booths named "Tkts," you may buy, at half-price, any unsold or otherwise available seats for performances on the same day or night for Broadway, off-Broadway, music, dance and special programs. A similar booth for half-price concert and dance tickets is located in Bryant Park, 42 St. between Fifth and Sixth Avenues.

SPECTATOR SPORTS. *Baseball,* April through early October, features the Mets at Shea Stadium, in Flushing, Queens, and the Yankees at the handsomely refurbished Yankee Stadium in the Bronx.

Football. The Jets play at Shea Stadium during the fall, except that there are never any home games until the Mets have finished their baseball schedule. The Giants, an old team that recently gave up New York for friendlier financial climes in New Jersey, play at the new and impressive Giants Stadium just across the Hudson River in East Rutherford.

Basketball's Knicks play at Madison Square Garden. Nassau Veteran's Memorial Coliseum in Uniondale, Nassau County, L.I., is home for the Islanders *hockey team* while their National Hockey League neighbors, the Rangers, play in the Garden. Each of these three teams has a regular season running from early October to early April.

Flat and harness tracks draw millions of horse racing enthusiasts each year. The thoroughbreds run at Aqueduct and Belmont, both in Queens, and at the Jersey Meadowlands. The Belmont Stakes, mid-June jewel in the Triple Crown for three-year-olds, highlights the flat racing schedule. Working folks benefit from the night-time programs of standard bred harness races at Yonkers and Roosevelt Raceways, where elaborate parlay opportunities fan the hopes of busy wagerers.

Soccer fans in the New York area journey out to East Rutherford, New Jersey, just 15 min. from Manhattan, where the aptly named New York Cosmos play professional rivals in Giants Stadium.

Madison Square Garden has long hosted the Millrose Games, one of America's great *track and field* meets, and has the equipment for putting on almost any kind of sporting event or entertainment attraction.

 SPORTS. The sports most participated in by New Yorkers are probably jogging and bicycling, since they require no in-place equipment, just some park space. Central Park in Manhattan and Prospect Park in Brooklyn have automobile roadways which are reserved for walkers, runners, and pedalers during daylight hours on weekends, and you can find plenty of places to rent a bike on the nearby side streets and avenues.

For specific details about your favorite athletic pastime, be it golf, skating, fishing, or horseback riding, contact the *New York Convention and Visitors Bureau* at their Columbus Circle office.

 SHOPPING. It may come as no great news that huge numbers of visitors come to New York City solely to shop. There is probably no city on earth that possesses the number and diversity of shops that New York can proudly claim. If you can't find it in New York, the chances are it just doesn't exist.

Women's Clothing: Bargain Hunting: For the indescribable thrill of "real" bargain shopping at a manufacturers' outlet, *Loehmann's* (Fordham Rd. and Jerome Ave. in the Bronx) is the granddaddy of the best buys.

Resale stores carry "gently used, good things" culled from the best private wardrobes—chances are some of their offerings have never been worn. The best-known shop is *Ritz Thrift Shop,* 107 W. 57th St.

Men's Clothing: The four weekdays that follow Labor Day is the time when *Barney's,* the largest men's store in the world, holds its famous warehouse sale. All department and specialty stores also have sizable men's departments catering to all sorts of tastes.

Most of the best discounters are on Fifth Ave. between 14th and 23rd Sts. where men's clothing manufacturers have existed for many years. *Harry Rothman* at 111 Fifth Ave. is the oldest of these value-oriented retail clothiers.

Uptown, at Third Ave. and 86th St., is one of the largest stores for jeans, work shirts, and western wear, known as *The Gap* (branches all over the city). But for the wildest selection of all, you've got to head way downtown. *Hudson's* is the grandfather of all the so-called Army & Navy stores, though their merchandise encompasses a far wider range than just military surplus.

For the truly adventurous, however, there is no more interesting shopping experience than a tour of the Greenwich Village boutiques, particularly the used clothing shops on lower Second Ave.

Children's Clothing: Every one of the major department and specialty stores has a children's department that generally reflects its basic position on the adult fashion ladder. Of all these stores, however, *Macy's* rates as the top choice, if only because of its huge selection.

For bargains, there's no place better than *Nathan Borlam* at 157 Havemeyer St. in Brooklyn, where name brands are available at very low prices, and bargains are easily recognizable because the original labels are all left in. Open only Sunday through Thursday.

Books: *Daltons* (666 Fifth Ave.), *Scribner's* (49th at Fifth), and *Barnes and Noble* (18th St. on both sides of Fifth Ave., plus an impressive, huge discount book store on Fifth Ave. and 49th St.) have the largest general selections, although academic and privately printed works on consignment are easier to find in the many shops near the college campuses, especially Columbia (Broadway and 116th St.) All have smaller branches spread around the city.

Literature lovers who are searching for hard-to-find classics should try the famous *Gotham Book Mart,* on 47th St. between Fifth and Sixth avenues.

The hub of the used book market (these include mint-condition reviewer's copies and unsold remainders) is along Fourth Ave. between 9th and 14th Sts. The best shop of this sort, with the largest selection, is the *Strand* at Broadway and 12th St.

Records: *Sam Goody's* and *King Karol* have numerous locations around town; Greenwich Village has *Discophile;* and the *Record Hunter,* Fifth Ave. and 43rd St., concentrates on classical music and foreign labels. *Jimmy's* and *J&R* are big discounters.

If you're looking for an old album that even the original issuing company doesn't have in its warehouse, try the *Record Exchange* (Seventh Ave. and 55th St.) The largest single inventory of records (of all types and descriptions) is probably the *Colony Record Center* (1619 Broadway), and their proud boast is that they can get any record ever made.

 WHAT TO DO WITH THE CHILDREN. Children will enjoy much of what fills this chapter. In addition, theaters for children are rapidly growing in number. Some of the best are the *Bil Baird* (59 Barrow St.) for puppet shows; *Courtyard Playhouse* (137A W. 14th St.); *South St. Seaport* (South and Fulton Sts.); and in the *Magic Towne House,* 1026 Third Ave., featuring magicians and clowns. Others include the *Fire Department Museum* at 104 Duane St., downtown, for a colorful display of fire engines and exhibits, and the *Hayden Planetarium* at 81st St. and Central Park West to really see the stars and planets in fascinating reproductions.

 HOTELS AND MOTELS. Those accustomed to the motel situation in almost all other parts of the United States may be taken aback by (1) the paucity of motels in the city and (2) the lack of or limited parking areas at those that do exist. The $13.95–21.95 you might pay at a budget motel elsewhere is about what you'd pay for a single at the YMCA or YWCA in Manhattan; and no matter how much or how little you anticipate paying, it is always best to have made a reservation prior to your scheduled arrival. That way you're assured of a room—and that the rate will be confirmed.

Another important suggestion in selecting a hotel or motel to suit your needs: If you have the luxury of planning ahead, consult a travel agent or, if you can get a copy ahead of time, the *Sunday New York Times Travel Section.* We've listed some hotels for you to choose from, including the range of rates for a *double* room—i.e., for two persons. Many of these hotels, however, offer special packages for visitors—particularly for non-expense-account sightseers. Most of these deals are built around weekend stays at reduced rates (when there are fewer businesspeople in town) and often include theater tickets to top Broadway shows, a bus tour, a bottle of wine or champagne on arrival, Sunday brunch (and the *Times*—a tradition among New Yorkers themselves) or other similar amenities. In comparing these packages, however, be aware that in order to bring the numbers down to eye-catching appeal, some advertise the rate per person, based on double-occupancy. Others give you the full weekend rate, all-inclusive. In other words, read the fine print carefully.

Because of the unique nature and diversity of New York City, we advise you to give consideration to geographic location as well as price and appointments. Getting around the city can be time-consuming and expensive; thus a few extra dollars per night to be in the area in which you plan to spend most of your time (the theater district, Lower Manhattan, the Upper East Side, etc.) may well save you money in the long run. For budget-minded travelers, we have selected a small group of hotels and motels with rooms for $60 and under, double-occupancy, as of mid-1983; however, be aware that when a hotel says it has a range of rooms from $60 to $115, most are going to be toward the higher end of that range, which is another reason for making advance reservations whenever possible.

Chelsea. 222 W. 23rd St.; 243–3700. Totally unique, with a long history of sheltering creative talent—including the likes of Mark Twain, Thomas Wolfe, Virgil Thomson, Arthur Miller, and Dylan Thomas. Funky and not for everyone, but definitely New York. 400 rooms. *$45.*

Empire. 44 W. 63rd St. at Broadway; 265–7400. Opposite Lincoln Center, the Empire is surprisingly modest—popular for organized tours and among visiting musicians and performers. Weekly rates available. 600 rooms. *$60–75.*

Gorham. 136 W. 55th St.; 245–1800. Central midtown location offering relatively large, neat, and quiet rooms. Most also have kitchenettes. *$60–75.*

Iroquois. 49 W. 44th St.; 840–3080. Right next door to the posher Algonquin, this is an adequately serviceable family favorite. Weekly rates are even more attractive than the daily ones. *$45.*

Mansfield. 12 W. 44th St.; 944–6050. Just off Fifth Ave., and not far from Times Square. There are no pretensions and the quarters are agreeable. The staff is particularly good for a hotel in this price range. 200 rooms. *$44–48.*

Murray Hill. 42 W. 35th St.; 947–0200. A small hotel offering quiet in a busy neighborhood. Pleasant, large rooms. Near *Altman's* and *Lord & Taylor,* but not in Murray Hill district itself. 140 rooms. *$50.*

New York Sheraton. Seventh Ave. and 56th St.; 247–8000. The lobby is as busy as a train station, but you can't beat it for convenience. 1600 rooms. *$57–105.*

Roger Smith. 501 Lexington Ave.; 755–1400. Unexceptional businessman's hotel near Grand Central. Adequate and comfortable, but hardly distinguished. 200 rooms. *$60–77.*

Royalton. 44 W. 44th St.; 730–1344. Quiet, dignified hotel right in the midst of the Times Square panoply. Good value for the price. 175 rooms. *$58–85.*

Seymour. 50 W. 45th St.; 840–3481. Pleasant, older hotel, somewhat modernized, with large rooms. 250 units. From *$50.*

Sheraton City Squire. 790 Seventh Ave.; 581–3300. Modern, attractive, and close to the hub of the city's activities—and with an indoor swimming pool. 700 rooms. *$57–110.*

Shoreham. 33 W. 55th St.; 247–6700. Just off Fifth Ave. and splendidly located for shopping activities, the Museum of Modern Art, and Broadway. The rooms are modest but clean and each has its own pantry. 150 rooms. From *$60.*

Taft. Seventh Ave. and 50th St.; 247–4000. Very large old hotel close to most theaters. Unpretentious, to be generous, and the rooms are modest. 1300 rooms. *$60–65.*

Travel Inn Motor Hotel. 515 W. 42nd St.; 695–7171. Off the mainstream near the Lincoln Tunnel but convenient to the 42nd St. crosstown bus. Pool. Parking. 250 rooms. *$54.*

Wales. 1295 Madison Ave. (near 92nd St.); 876–6000. Close to the Metropolitan Museum of Art—but a mite uptown from the heart of the city. Clean and functional rooms, some with views of Central Park. 100 rooms. *$32–50.*

Wellington. 871 Seventh Ave.; 247–3900. Central to theaters, shopping, and concert halls, the rooms are contemporary but the hotel rundown. Provides most of the services of more expensive establishments to compensate. 700 rooms. *$54–60.*

ROCK BOTTOM AND LOWER. It is difficult to recommend most other hotels and motels in the $60 and under range without telling you to look at what you're getting before you make a reservation—not a practical way of doing things when planning ahead. Many YMCAs and YWCAs, however, have rooms at reasonable rates—beginning with singles at $13 a night. Sometimes they are limited to students and other young people, but check with the individual Y for specifics. Unfortunately, they tend not to be among the cleaner accommodations around. Also, as with regular hotels, it is essential to make reservations well in advance for weekends, holidays and other peak periods. Among the possibilities in Manhattan (see the Yellow Pages for those in the other boroughs), with approximate prices:

Allerton House, 302 W. 22nd St.; $20 and up single, women only. **Martha Washington Hotel,** 29 E. 29th St.; $20 single, women only. **William Sloane House YMCA,** 356 W. 34th St.; $15 single, $20 double; men and women. **West Side WMCA,** 5 W. 63rd St.; $18 single, men and a limited number of women. **Vanderbilt YMCA,** 224 E. 47th St.; $16 single, $22 double. Though they say they only accept men, they do also accept groups of women. **McBurney YMCA,** 215 W. 23rd St.; $13 single, men only. **International House of New York,** 500 Riverside Dr.; $75 per week, men and women. Accepts transient graduate students from May through August only.

THE OUTLYING BOROUGHS. The following motels near JFK and La Guardia Airports are convenient for overnight stopovers. Prices indicated for these not inexpensive but generally reliable establishments are for doubles: **Hilton Inn at JFK,** 322–8700, *$71–108;* **Holiday Inn of La Guardia,** 898–1225, *$80–85;* **International TraveLodge at JFK,** 995–9000, *$65–79;* **Howard Johnson's Kennedy Airport,** 659–6000, *$65;* **Sheraton Inn La Guardia,** 446–4800, *$90.*

Two other nearby possibilities that bear mentioning for their close driving proximity to the city: **Capri Whitestone,** 555 Hutchinson River Parkway at the Bronx Whitestone Bridge tollgate, 597–0600; and **Van Cortlandt,** 6393 Broadway at 256th St., 549–7272. Both have doubles available for under *$30.*

 DINING OUT. There is really no single comment that can effectively describe the phenomenon of eating out in New York City. Put at its simplest, there is a dining experience in the Big Apple to satisfy any palate (no matter how exotic one's tastes) and any budget.

You can cover the globe gastronomically in New York—which coincidentally is probably the way you'll go easiest on your budget. You can feast reasonably on steaks at Farnie's or the Blue Mill Tavern, but you can be transported to the far reaches of India by heading over to East 6th St. between First and Second Aves. where about a dozen friendly, inexpensive family-run eateries offer outstanding curries and tandoori specialties. Indeed, the Lower East Side is a gourmand's-eye-view of the melting pot that is New York, with Russian, Polish, Ukrainian, and Jewish fare available at very reasonable prices, even if the setting tends toward the simple.

Similarly, while there is no dearth of Chinese or Italian restaurants in midtown, the budget traveler could not do better than to head down to Mott St. in Chinatown or Mulberry St. in Little Italy to dine. The food will be authentic, in many instances exceptionally well-prepared, and you'll get a taste of New York's ethnic diversity at no extra cost.

The city is filled with such ethnic pockets, and its restaurants spill over with the flavor of the Old World, Asia, the Orient. The far east Seventies and Eighties of Manhattan are known as the Yorkville area, and offer Slavic and German eateries galore. Greek and Thai restaurants have found a home north of the skin-flick houses on Eighth Ave. from 48th to 56th Sts. West 46th St. has taken on a decidedly Brazilian flavor, and mid-Manhattan looks like Tokyo East, with the smell of sushi and tempura coming out of just about every other doorway.

None of which is to say you should deny yourself the luxury that is to be had at some of New York's finest establishments. By remembering a few little "tricks," you can dine in splendor without going into lifelong debt. For example, many of the city's finest restaurants—and the splendid Four Seasons heads the list!—offer special pre-theater dinners at prices that are a third to half less than the same meal ordered during prime serving periods. The menu selections are generally a little more limited, and you must usually be seated between 5 and 6 P.M., but service, preparation, and surroundings are at the same high standards for which these restaurants are noted.

Then, too, lunches are often 10–20 percent cheaper than the same dinners would be. Nor is it written that you must order courses as suggested on the menu at luncheon or dinner. If you are two or three people, for example, there is no reason why you can't order a selection of appetizers (which in at least some cases are scaled down portions of entrées), a salad, and a dessert—all to be shared. You get to sample several different items and the check—even if there is a "plate charge"—is within reason. Weekend brunches can also be an economical way to sample ordinarily more expensive places' fare.

We have broken down our restaurant listings first by area, so that you can find a place to sample some of New York's culinary delights whether you are in midtown or on the Southern end of the island. (For more detailed suggestions, or for places above 59th St., consult *Fodor's New York City.*) In addition, we have divided these restaurants by price—those said to be *moderate* are places where a three-course meal (appetizer, main course, dessert) will run approximately $12–15; *inexpensive* establishments should cost under $10 per person excluding beverages—and by type of cuisine.

Midtown (34th to 59th Street)

American/International. Moderate: **Joe Allen's.** 326 W. 46th St.; 581–6464. Theater hangout that's casual and reliable for salads, quiches, burgers—and famous faces.

Maestro Café. 58 W. 65th St.; 787–5990. Convenient to Lincoln Center, a little hectic, but they'll get you out in time for your curtain.

Brazilian. Moderate: **Brazilian Pavilion.** 316 E. 53rd St.; 758–8129. Traditional cuisine in a modern setting, with seafood, steaks, and excellent black bean soup. Closed Sun.

Inexpensive: **Brazilian Coffee Restaurant.** 45 W. 46th St.; 719–2105. *Feijoada* is on the menu Wed. and Sat., with shrimp dishes and codfish always good. Closed Sun.

British. Inexpensive: **English Pub.** 900 Seventh Ave. at 57th St.; 688–4725. Duly pub-like, with Shepherd's pie and directly across the street from Carnegie Hall.

Chinese (best value is Chinatown—see below). *Moderate:* **Hunam,** 845 Second Ave.; 687–7471. Devilishly spicy when so requested and a sterling example of the cuisine in a pleasant setting.

Peng Tengs. 219 E. 44th St.; 682–8050. Specialties of the Peking, Szechuan, and Hunan provinces. Weekend *dim sum* lunches are inexpensive and satisfying.

Delicatessen. Moderate-Inexpensive: **Stage.** 834 Seventh Ave.; 245–7850 and **Carnegie,** 854 Seventh Ave.; 757–2245. The best way to do it is to order one sandwich and a side of fries or cole slaw for two—splitting is still plenty.

French. Moderate: **Le Biarritz.** 325 W. 57th St.; 245–9467. Simple, country-style French fare in a leisurely and decorous atmosphere. Dinner only Sat. and Sun.

Pierre Au Tunnel. 250 W. 47th St.; 582–2166. Small and unpretentious, and a favorite among theater goers. The food is hearty and comes in ample portions. Closed Sun.

Greek. Inexpensive: **Molfetas.** 307 W. 47th St.; 840–9594. Cafeteria-style restaurant (with some table service) offering lamb, fish, moussaka, and the like.

Pantheon. 689 Eighth Ave. near 44th St.; 664–8294. Meats may be overcooked, but that doesn't stop the hungry. Portions are generous and the preparation authentic.

Indian (best value is downtown—see below). *Moderate:* **Akbar India,** 475 Park Ave. at 58th St.; 838–1717. Tandoori specialties in an especially attractive setting.

Inexpensive: **Madras Woodlands.** 310 E. 44th St.; 986–0620. Vegetarian fare from the south of India, with excellent combination platters for wide sampling.

Irish. Moderate: **Landmark Tavern.** 626 Eleventh Ave. near 57th St.; 757–8595. On the outskirts of the theater district, but a favorite for more than a century.

Italian (best values are in Greenwich Village or in Little Italy—see below). *Moderate:* **Trattoria,** in the Pan Am Bldg., Lexington Ave. at 45th St.; 661–3090. Cheerfully gaudy but fine for simple pastas and antipasti. (Best bets are really in Little Italy.) Closed Sat. and Sun.

Inexpensive: **Guido's.** 511 Ninth Ave. at 39th St.; 244–9314. Old-style family-run restaurant hidden behind a macaroni factory—but well worth searching out.

Manganero's. 492 Ninth Ave. near 38th St.; 947–7325. Best hero sandwiches around—especially sausage and peppers, or mixed antipasti.

Japanese. Moderate: **Rock Garden of Tokyo.** 34 W. 56th St., 245–7936. Attractive and unharried, with a grill built into every table.

Inexpensive: **Fuji.** 238 W. 56 St.; 245–8594. Small, reliable and friendly, with sushi bar or Western seating, convenient to Carnegie Hall and the theaters.

Korean. Moderate. **Arirang House.** 28 W. 56th St.; 581–9698. Spicy grilled beef and the sourest of pickles in a darkly mystical setting.

Seafood. Inexpensive: **Oyster Bar.** Grand Central Station; 490–6650. Oysters, clams, and crabs for grab in the midst of the rush hour—and still exhilirating. Closed Saturday and Sunday. Dining room more expensive.

Thai. Moderate: **Siam Inn.** 916 Eighth Ave. near 55th St.; 489–5237. Chilies and coconut milk are used unsparingly and the results are marvelous—and the small room crowded.

Downtown (below 34th St., including Greenwich Village, Chinatown, and Little Italy)

Chinese (remember, Chinese food is almost always served family-style, for sharing. Order approximately one dish less than the number of people in your party—or take the leftovers home. All of the following represent excellent value, and will almost always run less than $10 per person.)

In Chinatown: for traditional Cantonese cooking take your pick among **Bo Bo** (20½ Pell St; 962–9458), where the house dinner is good for novices, or **Hong Fat** (63 Mott St.; 962–9588), which will satisfy your cravings 24 hours a day. For Peking Duck without ordering ahead, try **Peking Duck House** (22 Mott St.; 962–8208). For the spicier Hunan and Szechuan dishes there are **Hunan House** (45 Mott St.; 962–0010) and **Szechuan Taste** (23 Chatham Sq.; 267–0672). Mandarin is the specialty at the popular **Say Eng Look** (5 E. Broadway; 732–0796).

Dairy. Moderate: **Ratner's Dairy Restaurant.** 138 Delancey St.; 677–5588. A legend in its own time for blintzes, real Russian black bread, potato pancakes, and the like.

Inexpensive: **Arnold's Turtle.** 51 Bank St.; 242–5623. Small storefront restaurant in residential West Village where vegetables—in salads and casseroles—rule.

B&H Dairy Restaurant. 127 Second Ave.; 777–1930. A tiny coffee shop—and there is almost always a line.

Delicatessen. Inexpensive: **Second Ave. Kosher Deli.** 156 Second Ave.; 677–0606. Free pickles, cole slaw and peppers, well-stuffed sandwiches and none of midtown's inflated prices. Half-sandwiches for seconds, too!

Pastrami & Things. 297 Third Ave.; 683–7185. Generally acknowledged as indeed having the best pastrami in a city of pastrami connoisseurs.

Greek. Inexpensive: **Z.** 117 E. 15th St.; 254–0960. Price not withstanding, this is probably the best Greek restaurant in the city. Always bustling. Closed Mon.

Indian. With one or two exceptions, all the restaurants on East 6th St. between First and Second Aves. in the Village are owned by the same family, with similar (though not without variation) menus and inexpensive prices. **Mitali** (334 E. 6th St.; 533–2508) is one favorite, but you can almost never go wrong anywhere on the block. The neighborhood, though, is for the adventurous.

Italian. Moderate in the Village: **Caffè Da Alfredo** (17 Perry St.; 989–7028, closed Mon.), **Trattoria da Alfredo** (90 Bank St.; 929–4400, closed Tues.), and **Tavola Calda da Alfredo** (285 Bleecker St.; 924–4789) are all under the same ownership—and each is outstanding. Reservations well in advance are necessary at the first two, but the experience is exceptional, especially given the low prices. More in the heart of the Village are **Monte's** (97 MacDougal St.; 674–9456, closed Tues.) and **Livorno** (216 Thompson St.; 677–9515), both serving southern Italian fare.

Inexpensive in the Village: **Bleecker Luncheonette,** corner Bleecker and Cornelia; no phone. Patrons willingly wait to partake of the meatballs and peppers, or homemade manicotti. Closes at 7 P.M.

Little Italy is, alas, coming up in prices, with fancy new establishments pushing out the older family-run ones. Some remaining mainstays of moderate cost: **Angelo of Mulberry St.** (146 Mulberry; 226–8527) and **Forlini's** (93 Baxter St.; 349–6779).

Inexpensive: **Puglia's** (189 Hester St.; 226–8912), where cafeteria-style tables feed hundreds nightly, and where the atmosphere is absolutely (and wonderfully) chaotic. For seafood, hit **Umberto's Clam House** (129 Mulberry St.; 431–7545) or its less-known but much celebrated rival, **Vincent's** (119 Mott St.; 226–8133).

Japanese. Moderate: **Bizen,** 171 Spring St.; 966–0963. German husband tends bar and serves, Japanese wife cooks, and a setting that is latter day crafts-and-Bohemian. An incongruous but most agreeable SoHo combination.

Inexpensive: **Shoei,** 27 W. 8th St.; 228–6688. Very pleasant with authentic cooking in the heart of the Village.

Mexican. Moderate: **El Coyote,** 774 Broadway at 9th St.; 677–4291. Considerably more than a taco parlor and probably the single most favored of the city's Mexican haunts.

Seafood. Moderate: **Jane St. Seafood Café.** 31 Eighth Ave.; 243–9237. Narrow, intimate West Village setting with a gourmet touch in the kitchen.

Inexpensive: **Sloppy Louie's.** 92 South St.; 952–9657. In the heart of the fish market and a favorite among nearby Wall Streeters. Community tables and closed on weekends—but worth a trip.

Southern. Inexpensive: **West Boondock,** 114 Tenth Ave.; 929–9645. Sawdust on the floor, good free jazz and down-home cooking—but take a cab at night.

Steakhouses. Moderate: **Blue Mill Tavern.** 50 Commerce St.; 243–7114. On a quaint old Village street, where the most simply prepared is always the best.

Farnie's Second Ave. Steak Parlour. 311 Second Ave.; 228–9280. Does its best—which is pretty good—to compete with better-known and more expensive brethren.

Thai. Inexpensive: **Thailand,** 106 Bayard St.; 349–3132. Justly celebrated as the finest example of Thai cuisine in the city—especially the curries, fried fish and crab dishes. Also happens to be the cheapest! Closed Mon.

Ukrainian. Inexpensive: **Ukrainian Restaurant and Caterers** (140 Second Ave.; 533–6765) fills with local regulars but are more than cordial to new faces. Pirogi (stuffed dumplings), blintzes, stews, and boiled meats are the specialties.

EVERYWHERE. *McDonald's, Burger King, Kentucky Fried Chicken,* and *Arthur Treacher's Fish and Chips* are among the national fast-food franchises to be found at various locations around the city, with the local *Steak and Brew* chain (now emphasizing salads, too) also relatively modest in price.

DESSERTS. Aside from the *Häagen-Dazs, Baskin-Robbins, Sedutto's* and *Bassetts* specialty ice cream shops cropping up all over the city, and the "gourmet cookie" outlets such as *David's,* there are numerous Italian coffee houses on Mulberry St. in Little Italy and along MacDougal St. in Greenwich Village. The most authentic (and, alas, expensive, though portions can be shared) Art Deco ice cream parlor is the **Agora,** 87th St. at Third Ave.; 369–6983, which coincidentally is also a clothing boutique.

EXPLORING LONG ISLAND

Long Island, 1,723 square miles and a population of over seven million, extends 120 miles east by northeast from New York Harbor. Although its westernmost half is an increasingly crowded jumble of residential suburbs for New York City, the eastern section still has unspoiled open spaces. The history and growth of the Northeast can be traced on a tour of Long Island—the ceremonial dances at the annual Shinnecock Indian Powwow in Southampton at the end of the summer; 18th-century Dutch windmills and English salt-box houses; a pre-Civil-War farm village restoration; late 19th-century mansions such as the Vanderbilts' in Centerport; and the bedroom communities, industrial complexes, and vacation colonies of today.

Excellent fishing, public golf courses, State Parks, outdoor art shows and historical museums, the sandy beaches of its South Shore and the pebble beaches of its North Shore, have made Long Island one of the Empire State's most popular vacationlands.

To get out to eastern Long Island, take the straight Long Island Expressway or the several auxiliary highways that roughly parallel it. The Expressway goes all the way to Riverhead. The Long Island Railroad conducts guided tours to various places of interest from mid-May to mid-November on weekends; on weekdays in July and August. The New York State Division of Tourism makes available a possible traveler's itinerary in a list of suggested three-day tours of the state. A good place to start might be at Great Neck, the beginning of Nassau County's well-to-do North Shore.

At Kings Point, on Little Neck Bay, the United States Merchant Marine Academy may be visited by the public daily from 9 to 5; and although their sailing and steam vessels will intrigue mariners more than landlubbers, the Regimental Review, held on most Saturdays in May, June, September, and October, weather permitting, will interest everyone.

You might like to walk through Adelphi University in Garden City, one of the first fully planned communities. Garden City also has the Episcopal Cathedral of the Incarnation, featuring some beautiful hand-carved mahogany and rare marble. Old Westbury Gardens, on Old Westbury Road, is the former estate of the late John Phipps, sportsman and financier, and was made available to the public in 1959. Like an 18th-century English "great park" with a stately Georgian mansion, the Gardens' flowers and trees present a continually changing picture with the seasons. Be sure to wear comfortable walking shoes, as there are miles of paths winding through the 100-acre grounds.

On the North Shore

Heading back up towards the Sound and 25A, you're on your way to Glen Cove, Oyster Bay, and Huntington. Oyster Bay is renowned as the summer home of Teddy Roosevelt, although his estate, Sagamore Hill, is really down the road in Cove Neck. It is today furnished as it was when TR himself lived there, stuffed with such paraphernalia as elephant tusks from the Emperor of Ethiopia, rugs from the Sultan of Turkey, and the sword and pistol that Roosevelt brandished up San Juan Hill during the Spanish-American War. Built in 1884, it served as the family home until it was opened to the public in 1950, two years after the death of the late President's widow. Down along the water between Cove Neck and Oyster Bay are other attractions for the sightseer. About a mile east of Oyster Bay the Theodore Roosevelt Memorial Sanctuary and Trailside Museum maintained by the Audubon Society, contains the sort of nature exhibits that the conservationist President would have enjoyed immensely. He is buried in nearby Young Memorial Cemetery. Before continuing east, you might like to visit the Planting Fields Arboretum State Park. This four-hundred-acre estate, formerly the home of the late William Robertson Coe, now houses one of the largest collections of labeled trees, shrubs, bulbs, and flowering plants in the country. Visitors may guide themselves around the grounds at their leisure every day of the year except Christmas Day.

Leaving the Oyster Bay area and heading east again along 25A, the traveler can stop in Cold Spring Harbor for a look through the Whaling Museum of what was once one of Long Island's leading whaling ports. Huntington is famous as the birthplace of the great American poet Walt Whitman. Turning south from 25A for a mile along State 110 will bring you to his boyhood home, now an Historic Site owned and administered by New York State; manuscripts, publications, and pictures of Whitman are on display. A church dating back over 315 years will interest many, but the other major points of interest in Huntington are the Heckscher Museum, with a collection of European and American paintings and frequent special exhibits, and the Powell-Jarvis House, over three hundred years old, which features period rooms and a pottery collection in an old farmhouse.

It's a short hop east to Centerport, where the forty-three-acre estate of the late William Vanderbilt is now a museum and planetarium with beautifully kept gardens. The Vanderbilt Museum has a staggeringly complete collection of marine life, wildlife diorama, and natural habitat groups. The mansion, a 24-room structure of Spanish-Moroccan design, has a fascinating array of items from 13th-century Portuguese handiworks to 17th-century Florentine carved walnut furniture to a $90,000 organ hidden behind an enormous Aubusson tapestry.

At Riverhead the Island splits into the North and South Forks. Although rising land prices and soaring taxes have greatly reduced Long Island's farming area, there is still a lot concentrated around Riverhead and the two forks, and Suffolk is the leading agricultural county of New York State in dollar volume. Thanks to Suffolk County, New York is one of the country's top potato growing states. A thriving business is also done in greenhouse products and strawberries, cauliflower and peaches. But Long Island is really noted for the ducks served in restaurants all over the nation.

The North Fork

Taking State 25 out the North Fork, the traveler comes into the town of Cutchogue, where the 1650 Old House is considered the finest example of English architecture in this country. Greenport, a little further on, once a major whaling port, still bustles with dockside activity. The North Fork was the center of the oyster industry on Long Island at the turn of the century. From Greenport, you can take the short ferry ride to Shelter Island, a beautiful and lush island. A drive around it takes about an hour. The North Fork is also a paradise for sportsmen. Miles of sandy beaches offer clean, calm water both in Long Island Sound and Peconic Bay, so swimming, sailing, skin diving, and fishing are also popular here. Audubon groups find this area good for bird watching, since it is along the migratory routes of many species. There are golf courses and many fine horse trails. Finally, at the end of State 25, we reach Orient Point. The town itself is a provincial village, reminiscent of New England with its Cape Cod houses. Here are an Indian burial ground, the oldest Congregational Church in the state, and Orient Point State Park, perhaps the most strangely beautiful spot on all of Long Island. It's a strange mixture of barren sand and dirt washed up onto the beach, desolate rocks, long eerie strands of seaweed, birds who don't see enough people to be frightened of them, and nothing but water beyond.

The South Fork

Sag Harbor was a great whaling port during the 19th century, and celebrates an Old Whalers Festival each summer, with activities centered around the Long Wharf, built in 1770. In 1789, President George Washington named it a port of entry for the United States. For many years, it cleared more tonnage than any other port in the nation. Sag Harbor preserves the flavor and nostalgia of the old days of the sailing ships, and there are even today a church shaped like a sailor's spyglass and a whaleboat in front of the Masonic Temple. Inside the Suffolk County Whaling Museum you'll see relics of the whaler's trade, and nearby is the Custom House, the first in New York, which houses a number of historic documents.

Montauk is perhaps the liveliest fishing town on Long Island; boats for hire will take deep-sea anglers out for tuna, bluefish, or a host of other varieties. Surf-casters will find Montauk a paradise, also, as do bird watchers, hikers, bathers, and sailors. A couple of points of interest to visitors are the Montauk Lighthouse, built in 1795. (Although it is not permissable to climb to the top, a new museum in the lighthouse has an interesting display of nautical artifacts;) Deep Hollow Ranch, built in 1774 when the area was an important cattle grazing area, and at which TR and his Rough Riders stayed on their way to war; and Hither Hills State Park, which has camping, fishing, a children's area, picnic tables, a bathhouse, showers, and areas for trailers and tents.

Turning back from Montauk, heading west towards New York City, travelers may stop off at their leisure in the Hamptons, a dozen or more small communities along the South Shore, starting at Amagansett, rimming Shinnecock Bay, and subsiding at Westhampton. Easthampton is one of the more fashionable summer vacation colonies. Old Hook Mill, built in 1806 of oak and hickory brought from Gardiners Island, is the only one of the windmills in the area still in working order. Easthampton is also the site of Clinton Academy, the first academy chartered in the state, which now houses an historical museum featuring exhibits of Indian relics, whaling gear, early farming tools, and shipwreck mementos. The real charm of the area, however, can be found in a quiet drive along country lanes and wide sandy beaches around Southampton, after we turn off State 27A. Just outside the township is the Long Island Automotive Museum, which claims to be the largest in the world devoted exclusively to motor cars.

On to Quogue, Hampton Bays, and Westhampton, all offshoots of Southampton, but with a more bohemian atmosphere. Many of the summer residents are writers, artists, and musicians, although in recent years an increasing number of executives have been coming in. Quogue has a 200-acre Wildlife Refuge run by the state's Department of Environmental Conservation, while Westhampton has one of the finest beaches anywhere in the world.

Fire Island

Other than a parking lot at Smith Point County Park, south of Shirley, there are no roads on this forty-mile strip of sand dunes and barrier beach. The 25,000 persons who summer here in a dozen established communities wish to keep it that way. The United States Congress established the Fire Island National Seashore in 1964. It offers excellent facilities at several spots on the island to those who do not own or rent property there. A ten-year plan was begun in the summer of 1966 to build facilities for swimming, hiking, nature tours, bicycling, and water sports, with all public areas accessible by ferry. Robert Moses State Park at the westernmost tip of Fire Island is reached by bridge from a point a few miles west of Bay Shore.

We now wind our way westward, eventually reaching Great River and the Bayard Cutting Arboretum, a 643-acre gift to the Long Island State Park Commission on which can be seen just about every variety of tree and plant imaginable, some in hothouses.

Jones Beach State Park, along the Atlantic shore south of Wantagh, is a 2,500-acre expanse of sand and woods accommodating over 100,-000 bathers, with parking space for 23,000 cars in its fourteen lots. It is best reached early in the day. Jones Beach, the largest state park on the Atlantic Coast, features ocean and salt-water pool swimming, fishing facilities, restaurants, a two-mile boardwalk, athletic fields, and the famous $4 million Marine Theater, where theatrical spectaculars and water shows are presented during the summer months.

North and somewhat east by the Seaford–Oyster Bay Expressway are Bethpage State Park and the town of Bethpage, where a 2½-acre farmer's market offers over 300 indoor booths, as well as a children's amusement park and a carnival atmosphere that children and adults alike will enjoy. The farmer's market is held every Friday and Saturday, and on the Fourth of July. Old Bethpage is a nice restoration village with various activities and craft demonstrations in the same area.

PRACTICAL INFORMATION FOR LONG ISLAND

HOW TO GET AROUND. *By car:* Most highways alternate between limited-access sections and double-duty stretches as the main streets of towns and villages. They usually have names as well as numbers, so asking directions may elicit a confusing, though well-intentioned answer. By all means, have a map along.

Towns on the South Shore are served directly by State 27A, called *Merrick Road* in the western half of the island; *Montauk Highway* in the eastern. It is a winding and busy thoroughfare. A bit to the north, but requiring less perseverance, is State 27, called *Sunrise Highway*. It runs as far out as Southampton, then joins State 27A for the last lap to Montauk. The *Southern State Parkway* runs from Kennedy Airport to East Islip. Down the center, take the *Long Island Expressway* from Manhattan to Riverhead. Thereafter, take State 25 to the north fork and Orient Point or State 24 southeast for a link-up in Hampton Bays with State 27 to Montauk. The northern routes out of the city: Queens Boulevard, State 25, becomes *Jericho Turnpike* in Nassau County. It takes a fairly straight inland path northeast to Orient Point. Northern Boulevard, State 25A, becomes *North Hempstead Turnpike* and serves the North Shore communities— Great Neck, Huntington, Port Jefferson and Wading River—before dissolving into State 25 ten miles west of Riverhead. The *Northern State Parkway* continues from the city's Grand Central Parkway.

By train: The Long Island Railroad reaches almost every town, and makes the run to Montauk from Manhattan in less than 4 hours. From Manhattan, the line operates out of Penn Station (31st–33rd Sts. between 7th and 8th Avenues). There are also stations in Woodside, Queens and downtown Brooklyn. Most trains headed for Suffolk pass through Jamaica, Queens, and it's about even money you'll have to make a change there. The best way to get information is to go to Penn Station and consult timetables. Or try calling one of the stations on Long Island close to your destination.

MUSEUMS. Centerport: *Vanderbilt Museum.* Little Neck Rd., off State 25A. Marine and wildlife exhibits in mansion on former Vanderbilt estate.

Cold Spring Harbor: *Whaling Museum.* Main St. Exhibits and relics to show the whaling industry during its boom, including a fully equipped whaleboat from a 150-year-old brig.

East Meadow: *Museum in the Park.* Eisenhower Park, between Old Country Rd. and Hempstead Tpke. Changing exhibits trace the history of Nassau County.

Huntington: *Heckscher Museum.* Prime Ave. Fine collection of European and American art.

Port Washington: *The Polish-American Museum.* 5 Pulaski Pl. Arts and antiques from Poland, along with displays that show the important roles the Polish played in the shaping of American history.

Sag Harbor: *Suffolk County Whaling Museum.* Main St. Tools, pictures, oddities of the fascinating whaling era on Long Island.

Stony Brook: *The Museums at Stony Brook.* Main St. off State 25A and continuing onto State 25A itself. An historic grouping of the best; an art museum, carriage museum, several period buildings, a crafts center, and museum shop.

HISTORIC SITES. Bay Shore: *Sagtikos Manor.* State 27A. Built in 1692, this home was one of the centers of pre-Revolutionary War aristocracy. Period furnishings and antiques throughout its 42 rooms.

Cutchogue: *The Old House.* A mid-17th-century house filled with tools, household goods and furniture of that grand era.

East Hampton: *"Home Sweet Home."* 14 James Lane. Salt-box house, circa 1660, where John Howard Payne, the composer of "Home Sweet Home" lived. Lots of Payne mementos; windmill on the site.

Great Neck: *Saddle Rock Grist Mill.* On Bayview Ave. off State 25A. Tide-powered mill, built in 1702, which still grinds corn meal for visitors.

Huntington: *Powell-Jarvis House.* 434 Park Ave. The oldest house in the village, with grand antiques, pottery, and paintings on display. *Walt Whitman Birthplace.* On Walt Whitman Road, a by-pass off State 110, 1 mile north of Northern State Parkway. The poet of "Leaves of Grass" was born here in 1819. All period furniture and mementos of his day.

Oyster Bay: *Raynham Hall.* W. Main St. Built in 1738, this was the home of Robert Townsend, spy of George Washington. The unsuspecting British used it as military headquarters during the Revolution. *Sagamore Hill.* Cove Neck Rd. The very impressive Summer White House of Theodore Roosevelt. Filled with his trophies and personal possessions.

Sag Harbor: *Old Custom House.* Garden St. A lovely old landmark that was the first custom house in New York State (1789) and Long Island's first post office (1794).

TOURS. The Long Island Railroad offers day-long tours from Penn Station, Brooklyn or Long Island's Jamaica Station. Their "Around Long Island Tour" includes the train to Westhampton, a bus ride to Greenport and ferry rides to Shelter Island and Sag Harbor, a visit to Montauk Point and return. Tickets and information from the Long Island Railroad Tour Dept., Jamaica, N.Y. 11435. Tickets are also on sale during the week of the trip at Penn, Flatbush Ave. and Jamaica Stations.

GARDENS. Albertson: *Clark Garden* (Nassau branch of the Brooklyn Botanic Garden). Reflecting ponds, running streams; wild flower, herb and rock gardens; Hunnewell Rose Garden; white pine groves, dogwood, hemlock. Picnic areas. Great River: *Bayard Cutting Arboretum.* 690 acres of trees, shrubs, and wild flowers, some growing since 1887. Open Wed.–Sun. Old Westbury: *Old Westbury Gardens.* Group of 18th-century gardens on former John S. Phipps estate. Richly furnished Georgian mansion an added attraction. Upper Brookville: *Planting Fields.* This magnificent 409-acre estate, once owned by William R. Coe, is open all year, but magnolias and bulb display are April features, with blossoming azaleas, rhododendron, and dogwood at their best in May & June. Grounds open daily.

SPORTS. *Swimming. Jones Beach State Park,* Wantagh Pkwy. *Hither Hills State Park,* Montauk, offers bathing, fishing and picnicking. Superb *public beaches* at East Hampton, Fire Island, Patchogue, Quogue, Sayville, Shelter Island, Southampton and Westhampton Beach, all on the Atlantic side. Most beaches on Long Island Sound are private. *Note:* Swimming at some beaches may be considered unsafe because of pollution. Better check ahead of time.

Fishing, water sports and sailing. Charter boats and marina facilities available at many places in Montauk, Sag Harbor and Shelter Island. The public dock in East Hampton provides excellent fishing. Unmatched salt-water fishing and freshwater angling at the Hamptons.

Golf. Bridgehampton, *Poxabogue Course,* 9 holes. Commack, *Commack Hills Course,* 18 holes. Farmingdale, *Bethpage Color Courses,* five 18-hole courses. Huntington, *Dix Hills Course,* 9 holes. Northport, *Crab Meadow,* 18 holes. Rocky Point, *Tall Tree,* 18 holes.

SPECTATOR SPORTS. *Pro Hockey* (the NHL New York Islanders) play from Oct. to March at the Nassau Veterans Memorial Coliseum in Uniondale. There is *harness racing* at Roosevelt Raceway in Westbury. Aug. & Sept. bring annual *Horse Shows* at Piping Rock Club, Locust Valley, and C.W. Post College show grounds, Jericho Turnpike, Old Brookville. *Sports car racing* at Bridgehampton is a weekend feature from May to Sept.

HOTELS AND MOTELS on Long Island number about 600 altogether. Most motels have swimming pools, restaurant, cocktail lounges, and television; a few have beauty shops, massage rooms, and saunas. Most do not allow pets. At the western end of Long Island, most are open all year; at Montauk and the Hamptons, the majority close for the winter.

Prices for double-occupancy rooms in this region are: *Moderate* $35 and over *Inexpensive* under $35.

BAY SHORE. *Inexpensive:* **Bay Shore Motor Inn.** Attractive and comfortable rooms.

EAST HAMPTON. *Moderate.* **Bassett House Inn.** Comfortable rooms, some with fireplaces. Rural inn atmosphere.

FREEPORT. *Inexpensive.* **Freeport Motor Inn.** 46 rooms in 2-story units. Restaurant, cocktail lounge. Continental breakfast included in low rate.

GREENPORT. *Moderate.* **Townsend Manor Inn.** Nice accommodations in this renovated 18th-century home on the water. Pool, dining room, bar.

HEMPSTEAD. *Moderate.* **Coliseum Motor Inn.** Large motel with 110 air-conditioned rooms near Nassau Veterans Memorial Coliseum. Dining room, cocktail lounge, pool.

MONTAUK. *Moderate.* **Ronjo.** 36 rooms, many with kitchen units. Two pools, playground, grills, picnic tables. Restaurant nearby.

RONKONKOMA *Inexpensive:* **Eden Rock.** Veterans Memorial Highway. Nicely maintained rooms, Continental breakfast included; adults preferred.

 DINING OUT on Long Island stacks up with the finest anywhere in the state. The cuisine here accentuates seafood, Long Island Duckling, and beefsteaks, but ethnic specialties are excellent and easy to find. Categories reflect the cost of a mid-priced meal at each establishment. Included in the meal are hors d'oeuvres or soup, entree and dessert. Not included are drinks, tax and tip.

The categories are: *Moderate* $15. and up, and *Inexpensive* under $15.

BAY SHORE. *Moderate:* **Hisae at Old Gil Clark's.** A nice blend of East and West here, with seafood, fish and Oriental specialties.

EAST HAMPTON. *Moderate:* **Spring Close House.** Enjoy terrace dining in summer at this intimate spot. Specialties are scampi and roast duck.

GARDEN CITY. *Moderate.* **The Hunt Room.** Good food served in pleasant surroundings.

JERICHO. *Moderate:* **Maine Maid.** Duck, lobster and cordon bleu are specialties.

LINDENHURST. *Inexpensive:* **Barnacle Bill's.** Seafood and steak on the water. Informal attire.

MATTITUCK. *Moderate:* **Old Mill Inn.** Patio tables and candlelight in this early 19th-century building. Menu features fresh seafood.

NORTHPORT. *Moderate:* **Karl's Mariners Inn.** Home baking, seafood, L.I. duckling, sauerbraten. On the waterfront.

MONTAUK. *Moderate:* **Gosman's.** Overlooking the harbor and open on all sides, magnificently situated. It has several large dining rooms where family-style dinners feature fresh seafood.

PORT WASHINGTON. *Moderate:* **Louie's Shore.** Patio dining. Own baking, seafood, L.I. duckling, steaks, etc. On Manhasset Bay.

SAYVILLE. *Moderate.* **Lake House Restaurant.** Attractive place, good American cooking. Dinner only.

SOUTHAMPTON. *Moderate:* **Balzarini's.** Northern Italian-American cuisine, with veal, seafood in season, pasta and desserts all home-made. Family-owned with quiet, roomy dining area.

STONY BROOK. *Moderate:* **Three Village Inn.** Antiques displayed in an Early American setting. Well-prepared shrimp and clam dishes.

EXPLORING THE HUDSON VALLEY, WEST-CENTRAL NEW YORK, AND THE CATSKILLS

The Hudson Valley

Three main regions conveniently divide most of the state's remaining tourist attractions. These are: the Hudson River Valley, the Capital District, and the West-Central/Finger Lakes Region.

As important rivers go, the Hudson is not long; it rises in a lonely pond in the Adirondacks and flows only 315 miles to New York Harbor and the sea. Yet without it neither the city nor the state of New York would exist as we know them today. This is the highway up which much of America's early history advanced: Henry Hudson in 1609, crucial campaigns of the Revolution in 1776, Robert Fulton's first steamboat in 1807, and the Erie Canal in 1825. The river is lined with splendid mansions; some of the important ones open to the public are: the Jay Homestead in Bedford Village, the Van Cortlandt Manor in Croton-on-Hudson; Boscobel in Garrison; the Brett Homestead in Beacon; the Roosevelt and Vanderbilt estates in Hyde Park; and others in Hudson, Kinderhook, Coxsackie, Kingston, New Paltz, Newburgh, North Tarrytown, Hastings and Yonkers. West Point offers the US Military Academy; and there are a number of parks and recreational areas all along the river. Highways are excellent, and there is train and bus service to main points. For more details, write to the Hudson River Valley Association, 150 White Plains Rd., Tarrytown, N.Y. 10591.

Albany

In Albany, the principal sight is the Rockefeller Empire State Plaza, a $2 billion extravaganza, that now makes the capital one of the most brilliant, beautiful, and efficient in the world. But, with all that's new, like the nearby Tower Building with its 44th-floor observation deck and panoramic view, don't forget the old, most notably the Capitol, an imposing edifice resembling a French château. Albany's leading museums are the Albany Institute of History and Art, and the New York State Museum (in the Empire State Plaza), both with regional paintings, silver, furniture, displays on the natural history and Indian groups of the region, and changing exhibits of art, as well as research libraries.

The Schuyler Mansion, Cherry Hill, and the Ten Broeck Mansion are the most important of the capital's stately old homes.

West-Central and Finger Lakes

Western New York state, with Rochester, Syracuse, Rome and Utica, was the creation of the Erie Canal which, in 1825, linked the Hudson River with the Great Lakes and the center of the continent. Its main geographical feature is the lovely Finger Lakes, center of a rich agricultural area (vineyards), much fine scenery and over twenty State Parks. Fifty miles south of Rochester, in Letchworth State Park, the Gorge of the Genesee River is a 17-mile long, 600-foot-deep canyon full of spectacular rapids and falls. Rochester, the state's third largest city, is noted for photographic equipment, of course, and for a fine music school and several good museums. New York's famous wine region is between lakes Canandaigua and Keuka, and Naples and Geneva are the towns to work from. Ithaca, at the end of Cayuga Lake, is the home of Cornell University and of some rather extraordinary topography— hills and deep, scenic gorges. Syracuse is the site, in August–September, of the New York State Fair; and Cooperstown, on Otsego Lake, is the baseball shrine par excellence.

The Catskills

Grossinger's, the Concord, lox and bagels—right? No. The Borscht Belt cliché began to go out in the fifties. There are still large numbers of Italian, Irish, Greek, Polish, and Jewish guests, but sectionalism has broken down so much that this area is now attracting Americans of all origins. The famous resorts, with their all-inclusive environments, are doing better than ever. Alternatively, with horse trails, county fairs, camping areas, skiing, hiking, fishing, canoeing, historic sites, a host of State Parks, and so many other fine things to do, you can have a marvelous time without ever coming near them.

Quiet country inns offer the chance to enjoy the countryside, savor good food in a myriad of styles, and haunt back roads for antiques. Any time of the year is good for a Catskills vacation, as new facilities are making this area one of the most popular ski centers in a state which has more ski areas than any in the country.

A good entrance to the Catskills is over the Thruway to Kingston. Like many other early towns, it was burned during the 17th century by the mountain Indians and rebuilt within a stockade by Peter Stuyvesant, only to be looted and set aflame by the British during the Revolution. For the third time it rose from the ashes to become a prosperous village, visited by George Washington, and the meeting place of New York's first Senate.

South of Kingston in High Falls is the Delaware & Hudson Canal Museum, an interesting and worthwhile trip for anyone interested in the history of the canals that made the Empire State great.

PRACTICAL INFORMATION FOR THE HUDSON VALLEY, WEST-CENTRAL NEW YORK, AND THE CATSKILLS

HOW TO GET THERE. *By car:* Interstate 81 goes through New York, passing through Binghampton, Syracuse, and Watertown. Interstate 87 connects New York City, Kingston, Albany and Glens Falls, and continues north to Montreal. Interstate 95 connects New York City to East Coast cities from Bangor to Miami. Interstate 90 traverses the state from Pennsylvania to Massachusetts, passing through Buffalo, Rochester, Syracuse, Utica, and Albany.

By air: The airports handling interstate traffic (besides New York's) are at: White Plains, Rochester, Binghamton, Elmira, Ithaca, Buffalo, Syracuse, Poughkeepsie, and Albany.

By train: Amtrak has good service to the larger cities in New York State. Buffalo, Rochester, Syracuse, Utica, Albany, Poughkeepsie are on the New York City–Toronto line. *Conrail* has service to Westchester County, Albany and towns along the Hudson from New York.

By bus: Trailways and *Greyhound* have terminals in nearly every major city.

TOURIST INFORMATION. The New York State Division of Tourism publishes the *"I Love New York State Travel Guide,"* an all-purpose, 72-page booklet in full color with just about everything the casual traveler needs to know. Other literature includes pamphlets and folders on boating, hiking trails, horseback-riding trails, county fairs, ski areas, historic sites, museums, suggested tours, children's attractions, lists of events by date and area, scientific exhibits, campgrounds, and dude ranches. All literature of the New York State Division of Tourism is free, and available from their main office at 99 Washington Avenue, Albany 12210. There are branch offices in: Binghamton, Buffalo, Elmira, Kingston, Jericho on Long Island, New York City, Ogdensburg, Rochester, Syracuse, and Utica.

STATE PARKS. The state of New York has over 150 state parks, forests, and recreation areas, plus numerous private and public campgrounds, many of which have excellent facilities for the camper. Usually there is a nominal fee for the use of a camp site. In most places there are toilet and cooking facilities, complete with running water.

DRIVING LAWS. The speed limit is 55 miles per hour unless otherwise posted. Motorists must show proof that they have $10,000/$20,000/$5,000 liability insurance with a company that covers New York State. Check with your insurance agent. Out-of-state drivers may drive in New York State if they are at least 16 years old. Drivers under 18, however, may not drive at any time in New York City or Nassau County, and may not drive elsewhere in the state between the hours of 8 P.M. and 5 A.M. unless accompanied by a parent or guardian.

SPORTS. Saratoga Springs is the scene of *thoroughbred racing* in August, *harness racing* April–November. The *Eastern States Speed Skating Championships* are held in January. Many fine public 9-hole and 18-hole *golf* courses dot the countryside including Albany, Amsterdam, Canajoharie, Cobleskill, Hoosick Falls, Saratoga Springs, Schenectady, and Troy. *Skiing* can be found at numerous resorts throughout the area. Some are Royal Mountain (in Johnstown), Maple Ski Ridge (Schenectady), and Belleayre Mountain (Pine Hill). A list of ski areas is available from the New York State Division of Tourism.

Boating. Popular along *Lakes Erie* and *Ontario* and in the *Finger Lakes* region. Any of these lakes could be a starting point for a cruise along New York's famed barge-canal system. Splitting the state horizontally, the historic *Erie Canal* crosses to the *Hudson River* which flows southward to the Atlantic and is connected by the *Champlain Canal* to *Lake Champlain.*

Gliding and *soaring.* Elmira and *Harris Hill* are the centers of motorless flying.

Sports Car racing. Annual Grand Prix of U.S. Formula 1 for World Championship of Drivers Road Race held at Watkins Glen in October.

Ice boating, ice fishing, ice skating. Popular on many lakes and rivers in winter.

 DRINKING LAWS. The minimum age is 19. You may purchase any type of liquor at private package stores during the week, but the stores are closed on Sundays. Bars are open six full days a week, and on Sundays after 12 P.M.

AROUND WESTCHESTER AND THE HUDSON VALLEY

 HOTELS AND MOTELS. Categories for this region are: *Moderate* $25 and up, *Inexpensive* under $25. Many are charming, some are quietly sited, and several are worth a special trip.

CANAAN. *Moderate:* **Berkshire Spur.** In a scenic hillside location, it's convenient to Tanglewood.

CATSKILL. *Inexpensive:* **Catskill Starlight.** Rates are for late June–Labor Day; even lower during remainder of year.

HIGHLAND FALLS. *Moderate:* **Palisade.** State 218, 1 mi. S. Convenient to Storm King, West Point, and Bear Mountain.

HYDE PARK. *Inexpensive:* **Hyde Park.** It has well-kept rooms, café across the road. Pets are limited. Rates are lower after Labor Day.

NEWBURGH. *Moderate:* **Howard Johnson's Motor Lodge.** 75 air-conditioned rooms in 2-story complex. Swimming pool, tennis court.

PEEKSKILL. *Inexpensive:* **Peekskill Motor Inn.** Nicely appointed rooms. Restaurant, cocktail lounge, pool.

POUGHKEEPSIE. *Moderate:* **Best Western Red Bull Motor Inn.** This is a nicely furnished two-story inn. Pool, pets allowed, restaurant.

DINING OUT. Cost categories are comparisons between medium-priced meals from all the menus listed. In this wealthy region, the categories are as follows: *Moderate* $10 up, and *Inexpensive* under $10. Included in these prices are hors d'oeuvres or soup, entree and dessert. Not included are drinks, tip, and tax.

CANAAN. *Moderate:* **Queechy Lake Inn.** Lots of good American food at this picturesque restaurant, hung over an arm of the lake. Stuffed shrimps are a specialty. Bar.

CENTRAL VALLEY. *Moderate:* **Gasho of Japan.** The original timbers of a Japanese 15th-century Samurai warrior hideout have been reassembled with traditional rice rope and wood pegs. Tableside hibachi cooking. Oriental gardens.

CHATHAM. *Moderate:* **Jackson's Old Chatham House.** Rustic tavern atmosphere. Excellent American fare, with emphasis on homemade soups, breads, and charcoal-broiled steaks.

PEEKSKILL *Moderate:* **Monte Verde.** Former Van Cortlandt mansion features Continental specialties, overlooks Hudson.

AROUND THE CAPITAL DISTRICT AND SARATOGA AREA

HOTELS AND MOTELS. Double-occupancy rates are categorized as follows: *Moderate* $20–25 and *Inexpensive* under $20. Good base from which to start an Adirondack excursion.

ALBANY. *Moderate:* **Holiday Inn.** You have a choice of three of the H.I. properties here. Each has all the amenities you have grown to know, plus new special units for the handicapped. You'll find the Inns at 1614 Central Ave.; on State 32, one mile south of town; and on US 9.

HOWES CAVE. *Inexpensive:* **Howe Caverns.** The location opens up a spectacular view. Closed mid-October. to mid-May.

SARATOGA SPRINGS. *Inexpensive:* **Best Western Playmore Farms.** This is a very comfortable family-style lodge with a swimming pool and playground.

SCHENECTADY. *Inexpensive:* **Imperial "400" Motel.** Small and pleasant spot, with a heated swimming pool. Continental breakfast is included in the rate.

SHARON SPRINGS. *Inexpensive:* **Horseshoe.** Small but nice motel near the beautiful spa and recreation center below Canajoharie.

DINING OUT. All the places recommended below can be categorized *Moderate,* with mid-priced full-course dinners costing between $8 and $10. Not included in the prices are drinks, tax and tips.

ALBANY. Century House. Colonial décor and the service is good. Own cheese cake, duckling, and frogs' legs specialties. Dinner only.

Jack's Oyster House. An extensive menu of well-prepared dishes features seafood, delicious pastries.

L'Auberge Des Fougeres. Excellent French dishes, intimate atmosphere. Own soups, pastries.

COBLESKILL. Bull's Head Inn. Beef filets or brook trout. Own baking, too, in this pleasant 1802 edifice with early American decor.

DUANESBURG. The Hub. Quaint spot serves nicely prepared food, cocktails.

GREENWICH. Wallie's of Greenwich. Good, substantial meals are served up in a pleasant atmosphere.

JOHNSTOWN. Union Hall Inn. A landmark, this inn has been serving the public for more than 175 years. Dinner only.

SARATOGA SPRINGS. Country Gentleman. Generous portions of good food. Reservations advised, jacket required weekends. Dinner only.

AROUND WESTERN AND CENTRAL NEW YORK

HOTELS AND MOTELS. Cost categories for double-occupancy rooms in this region are: *Moderate* $30 up and *Inexpensive* under $30.

BATH. *Moderate:* **Ramada Inn.** Attractive accommodations in the heart of the Finger Lakes. Swimming pool, restaurant, cocktail lounge.

BINGHAMTON. *Moderate:* **Holiday Inn-SUNY.** Swimming pool, kennels, nice rooms. Restaurant.

GENEVA. *Moderate:* **Chanticleer Motor Lodge.** Relax in the heated pool and sauna bath. Restaurant, cocktail bar.

ITHACA. *Moderate:* **Collegetown Motor Lodge.** Nicely decorated rooms in convenient location. Restaurant on premises.

ROCHESTER. *Moderate:* **TraveLodge Colony East.** Minutes from downtown and close to the museums. 140 well-appointed rooms.
TraveLodge Airport. Comfortable accommodations here directly opposite the airport.

SYRACUSE. *Moderate:* **Syracuse Airport Inn.** Hancock Airport, 5 miles North of the city. Heated swimming pool, restaurant and cocktail lounge.

VICTOR. *Moderate:* **Trenholm East Inn.** Conveniently located in a quiet eastern suburb of Rochester, this property has a restaurant, lounge with entertainment and dancing, and a swimming pool.

DINING OUT. Price categories are determined by comparing costs for full-course dinners from the middle range of each menu sampled. For this region, the categories are: *Moderate* $10 up and *Inexpensive* lower than $10. Included in these prices are hors d'oeuvres or soup, entree and dessert. Not included are drinks, tax and tip.

AURORA. *Moderate:* **Aurora Inn.** Dining with a view of Owasco Lake. Charming atmosphere in this old inn makes you glad you came.

BINGHAMTON. *Moderate:* **Vestal Steak House.** Generous portions of well-prepared seafood and prime ribs distinguish this locally popular establishment.

ELMIRA. *Inexpensive:* **Moretti's.** Friendly family atmosphere in an establishment that has been in the clan for over 55 years. Very nice selection of American and Italian dishes. Dinner only.

HONEOYE FALLS. *Moderate:* **The Mill.** Steak house in a restored 150-year-old grist mill serves delicious dinners.

ITHACA. *Moderate:* **Taughannock Farms Inn.** Converted farmhouse offers good food and relaxed dining. Reservations advised. Dinner only.
Inexpensive: **The Station.** Popular spot for steaks and seafood, served nicely in a converted 19th-century railway station.

MOUNT UPTON. *Moderate:* **The Old Mill.** 18th-century mill overlooking the Unadilla River. Menu features delicious chicken, beef, shrimp. Own baking. Dinner only.

NAPLES. *Moderate:* **Vineyard.** State 245 at State 21. Locally popular outdoor restaurant. Listen to music while dining on well-prepared dishes, homemade pastries. Salad bar. Menu features stroganoff and local wines. Cocktail lounge. Dinner only, closed during winter.

ROCHESTER. *Moderate:* **Cartwright Inn.** Country dining in delightful surroundings. Menu features live lobsters, special desserts.
Spring House. This well-known dining room sets out lobster thermidor and excellent baked Alaska.

SYRACUSE. *Moderate:* **Valle's Steak House.** One in an excellent chain, serves steaks, lobster, stuffed shrimp. Cocktails, own baking.

UTICA. *Moderate:* **Hart's Hill Inn.** View of valley from tables near windows. Menu features fine regional fare.

WATKINS GLEN. *Moderate:* **Town House.** Attractive establishment has nice atmosphere. Crab, ribs, duckling specialties. Dinner only.

WAVERLY. *Moderate:* **O'Brien's.** An incredible place, with its own salad dressings, sausage, cheese, baking, and desserts. Specialties are turkey, aged beef, seafood.

AROUND THE CATSKILLS

HOW TO GET THERE. *By car:* The Quickway (State 17) runs from Exit 16 on the Governor Thomas E. Dewey Thruway to Binghamton through the Catskills south of the Forest Preserve. Exits 16–21 from the Thruway will also take you into the Catskills.
By bus: Adirondack Trailways has very complete coverage of the Catskills. Their main office is at 18 Pine Grove Ave., Kingston 12401. *Greyhound Short Line* (Hudson Transit), and *Monticello Transit* also have service to the Catskills.

TOURIST INFORMATION. Catskills Resort Association, 10 Hamilton Ave., Monticello 12701. Sullivan County Public Information Center, 100 North St., Monticello, NY 12701.

MUSEUMS. Middletown, *Empire State RR Museum,* picnic grounds; scenic ride, June to mid-Oct., Sat. & Sun. Narrowsburg, *Fort Delaware,* Museum of American Frontier. Prattsville, *Zadock Pratt Museum.* Rock carvings represent life of the village founder.

 HISTORIC SITES. Roxbury, Burroughs, Memorials, state-owned historic sites, in Memorial Field. Grave and "Boyhood Rock" of John Burroughs, his farmhouse birthplace and summer cottage, "Woodchuck Lodge," are nearby. Open when the family is in residence.

TOURS. Pine Hill: Belleayre Mountain Chairlift. Late June–Labor Day, daily; Labor Day–Oct., weekends (depending on foliage). Picnic area at summit.

 SUMMER SPORTS. Outdoor activities include golfing and hiking. There are beautiful courses everywhere. *Golf:* Liberty, *Grossinger's Hotel,* a private course extending privileges to guests of hotels and motels, 18 holes; *Sullivan County Course,* 9 holes; Roscoe, *Twin Village,* 9 holes; *Tennanah Lake,* 18 holes; Windham, *Windham Course,* 18 holes. *Hiking:* Slide Mountain, Catskill State Park. *Fishing:* Phoenicia, trout fishing capital of the Catskills, Schoharie Creek through Catskill State Park. *Races:* Monticello Raceway, at jct. State 17 and State 17B. Harness racing, spring, Mon.–Sat; summer daily.

 WINTER SPORTS. There are too many areas to list them all. The New York State Division of Tourism makes available lists of *ski areas* throughout the state. A few of the popular ones in the Catskills are Belleayre (in Pine Hill), Big Vanilla (Woodridge), Holiday Mountain (Monticello), Hunter Mountain (Hunter), Scotch Valley (Stamford), Ski Minnewaska (Lake Minnewaska), and Highmount (in Highmount). Other areas have tobogganing, sleighing, and skating.

 WHAT TO DO WITH THE CHILDREN. *Catskill Game Farm* between Cairo & Palenville. Carson City, between Cairo & Palenville, *Old Wild West Town,* with picnic area.

 HOTELS AND MOTELS are so plentiful and varied that you can stay anywhere you like in the Catskills. Price categories for double occupancy rooms in this region are: *Moderate* $21–30, and *Inexpensive* $20 and under. Call first to be sure the place you want accepts guests other than by the week.

BARRYVILLE. *Moderate:* **Reber's.** Bavarian-style architecture has provided large comfortable rooms overlooking the Delaware River. Heated pool, barber shop. Pets are allowed.

DELHI. *Inexpensive:* **Buena Vista.** Relax in attractive, well-kept rooms. Pets are allowed, cribs are free, breakfast is available.

LIVINGSTON MANOR. *Inexpensive;* **Willowemoc.** Hunting and fishing nearby, pets limited, coffee in rooms. Comfortable.

MIDDLETOWN. *Moderate:* **Middletown Motel.** Pleasant place to stay, with pool, restaurant and cocktail lounge.

MONTICELLO. *Moderate:* **Holiday Mountain Motor Lodge.** Seasonal skiing and hunting attract many to this fine motel. Restaurant and cocktail lounge, pool, very nicely furnished rooms. Reservation deposit; three-day minimum weekend stay in summer.

Patio. In center of village, with pool, café, 500 acres of private hunting grounds, fishing nearby.

STAMFORD. *Moderate:* **Red Carpet Motor Inn.** Large attractive rooms in two-story motel. Swimming pool, café, dancing, and entertainment.

 DINING OUT in the Catskills means eating in the hotel to most travelers, but there are plenty of excellent independent restaurants, too. Many of the hotels and resort hotels in the Catskills specialize in both kosher and non-kosher cuisine, with separate menus. Prices: *Moderate* $10–15 for a complete dinner, not including drinks, tax and tip.

BARRYVILLE. *Moderate:* **Eldred Preserve.** Trout from an indoor pond, among other nice things.

MIDDLETOWN. *Moderate:* **Archie's Inn.** Wide menu variety in a very old house; atmospheric.

WOODSTOCK. *Moderate:* **Deanie's.** Ribs, seafood, and home baking. Locally popular. Dinner only.

EXPLORING THE ADIRONDACKS AND
THOUSAND ISLANDS

A Jesuit missionary was the first white man to see Lake George's blue waters, in 1646. Today, most of the islands—there are more than one hundred in the thirty-two-mile lake—are state-owned and available for camping and picnicking. Lake George Beach, a public facility with every amenity, can accommodate six thousand bathers along its sandy half-mile; and in and around the village are accommodations for 25,000 visitors. In summer, strollers, shoppers and automobiles jockey for space, while the lake buzzes with motorboats, and even planes. Visitors have a choice of boat tours, speedboat rides, and moonlight cruises. The historically minded will enjoy Fort William Henry, a restored fort of the French and Indian War, which stands on a nineteen-acre plot in the village and commands the head of the lake. Rebuilt from original plans, it is a museum of Colonial America with mock military drills and demonstrations of musketball molding, and cannon and flintlock firing. What you will be unable to avoid is the barrage of commercial amusements (for children and adults alike) that has sprouted here in recent years. Performing dolphins, duck races and Greta Garbo's Duesenberg, among other "attractions."

Three Forts

At Ticonderoga, on Lake Champlain, is the fort made immortal to Americans in 1775, when it was taken from the British by Ethan Allen and his Green Mountain Boys "in the name of Jehovah and the Continental Congress." Today, the fort has been restored and contains a museum. A nearby blockhouse, Fort Mount Hope, has also been restored, and features the ruins of a colonial warship. At Mt. Defiance, a toll road follows a British military trail to the summit for a spectacular panoramic view of the entire area, and at Ticonderoga you can take a ferry across Lake Champlain and back for a delightful scenic ride. Nearby is the Crown Point Reservation, a National Historic Landmark, where the French built their southernmost outpost in 1731, and where the British later constructed a fort of their own.

Ausable Chasm

Opened in 1870, Ausable Chasm is one of America's oldest organized attractions. The Ausable River plunges through a cut several hundred feet deep and a mile and a half in length. There are spectacular waterfalls, rushing rapids, and massive rock formations carved into strange shapes by millions of years of erosion. The chasm can be explored on stairways, walks, and footbridges, and the trip ends with a boat ride "shooting" one of the (safer) rapids.

Plattsburgh, site of an important victory over the British in the War of 1812, is the largest city in Clinton County, and has a number of spots of interest to vacationers. The Kent-Delord House Museum is one. An 18th-century home and British headquarters during the War of 1812, today it contains historical exhibits, and is furnished as it was when occupied by the Kent and Delord families, with china, glassware, silver, and furniture of the period.

Lake Placid is a beautiful resort community sitting in a bowl surrounded by some of the Adirondack's highest peaks. It has every imaginable facility for both winter and summer sports. It was chosen twice—in 1932 and in 1980—as the site for the Winter Olympic Games. Unique among its attractions is the mile-long Olympic bobsled run on Mt. Van Hoevenberg, seven miles south of town along State 73. Heavy iron racing sleds rush down the mountainside at speeds of close to one hundred miles an hour, and climb twenty feet of glare ice on the curves.

Lake Placid is a year-round resort, and there is always something going on, be it the New York State Junior Ski Jumping Championships, an annual Winter Carnival, a cross-country race, the annual Ausable River Canoe Race, a golf tournament, or a square dance festival. Near Lake Placid is the John Brown Farm, where the body of the militant abolitionist, hanged for his part in a raid to free slaves, lies a-mould'rin' in the grave. Throughout the Adirondack region are many marked sites denoting stations along the Underground Railroad, an escape route for runaway slaves.

Lake Resorts

Saranac Lake lies ten miles west of Lake Placid and here, too, can be found an abundance of sports facilities. The Dickert Memorial Wildlife Collection is the natural history wing of the Saranac Lake Library. It features volumes of Adirondack lore, maps and photographs, and a variety of mounted birds, game, and fish. The Stevenson

Cottage, where author Robert Louis Stevenson hoped to be cured of his tuberculosis, is maintained as a literary shrine, and is open to visitors. The annual Winter Carnival at Saranac Lake has been held here since before the turn of the century. There are boat races in July, an annual show and sale of antiques at the Town Hall, and an August Paint and Palette Festival. To the west is Tupper Lake, a popular resort, where a chair lift will carry you on a three-thousand-foot ride to the summit of Big Tupper. Skiing, hunting and fishing, boating and swimming, hiking and camping, and looking at the scenery all have their devotees here. The Adirondack Museum, at the intersection of State routes 30 and 28, is a superb place: It has twenty buildings and is outdoors as well as indoors. Exhibits of paintings, maple sugaring, horse-drawn transportation, and tools, along with its dioramas of life in the 19th century, tell the complete story of Americans' relationship to the Adirondacks.

The Thousand (and More) Islands

Thousand Islands is no exaggeration. In fact, there are more than eighteen hundred of them, some mere points of rock, some large enough for an entire village. Most can accommodate a home or summer camp, and there are numerous old stone houses and mansions on them. A good place to begin is at Natural Bridge. Here travelers can go on an underground boat trip along the subterranean Indian River, and see fascinating natural rock formations while a guide expounds on geology and the natural history of the area. Sackets Harbor, on the shores of Lake Ontario, was a War of 1812 battlefield and military cemetery. It has probably the only navy yard in the world at one time commanded by a woman. Regional history and artifacts are displayed at the Pickering-Beach Historical Museum. Sackets Harbor was defended during the War of 1812 by Jacob Brown, and his home, the 150-year-old stone Brown Museum in neighboring Brownville, has portraits and mementos of this early settler. A railroad museum in the town features a restored New York Central depot, with displays and photographs. Stone Mills, also in the vicinity, has an agricultural museum housed in an 1837 stone church, which shows antique farm tools and implements, and holds an annual summer crafts fair.

Along the Seaway

At Cape Vincent the waters of Lake Ontario flow into the St. Lawrence. Here are a state-owned aquarium, the ruins of an old fort, the Tibbits Point Lighthouse, and a fisheries station of the State Department of Conservation. The stretch of the St. Lawrence between Cape Vincent and Ogdensburg is an angler's delight, with bass, pickerel, pike, and muskellonge all ready to give you a run for your money. Fishing isn't the only water activity around; there's lots of swimming, too, and scenic boat tours of the islands on the sightseeing vessels that depart frequently from many of the towns along the river. At Alexandria Bay is the Thousand Islands Bridge, from which motorists can see two hundred of the islands, part of a seven-mile span of uniquely beautiful scenery between E Pluribus Unum and Maple Leaf Country. Here also, on Heart Island, is German-style Boldt Castle, planned by a wealthy hotel owner for his wife, and left uncompleted after an expenditure of over $2 million upon her death in 1902. The grieving widow just left it there, and it stands today, eerie, vacant, and full of crates of the marble and rare woods that were to have been installed. At Ogdensburg, the Frederic Remington Art Memorial, housed in an 1809 mansion, contains the largest single collection of the noted artist's paintings, bronzes, and sketches of the Old West. There is also a re-creation of his last studio. The town itself was founded in 1748, and northern New York's oldest settlement. Massena, the power plant and shipping center of the North Country, is the place to see the famed St. Lawrence Seaway at its most spectacular. From Barnhart Island some of the locks and other engineering marvels of the Seaway are visible. You can see the great Moses-Saunders Power Dam, one of the world's largest hydroelectric plants, and take tours in the administration building. From a grandstand, you can watch the Dwight D. Eisenhower Lock raise or lower seagoing ships thirty-five feet. Air flight tours are available from Massena Airport, and cover about twenty miles of the St. Lawrence Seaway.

PRACTICAL INFORMATION FOR THE
ADIRONDACKS AND THOUSAND ISLANDS

HOW TO GET THERE. *By Car:* I–87 (Adirondack Northway) through the eastern Adirondacks from Albany to Plattsburgh. State 30 (Adirondack Trail) travels north from I–90 at Amsterdam through the heart of the Forest Preserve. For the Thousand Islands take I–81 through Syracuse or State 12 from Utica and along the St. Lawrence on the American side from Wellesley Island to Morristown.

By air: Air North flies to Plattsburgh and Saranac Lake–Lake Placid. In the Thousand Islands area, Air North serves Massena, Ogdensburg, and Watertown.

By bus: Greyhound and *Adirondack Trailways* have service throughout the Adirondack and Thousand Islands areas.

By train: Amtrak heads north right through the mountains, with several stops enroute to Rouse's Point at the Canadian border. It does not quite reach the Thousand Islands but does reach Utica and Syracuse.

TOURIST INFORMATION. Write to the Adirondack Park Association, Adirondack, NY 12808, and the St. Lawrence County Chamber of Commerce, Canton, N.Y. 13617.

MUSEUMS AND GALLERIES. Blue Mountain Lake: *Adirondack Museum.* Indoor and outdoor exhibits relating to the history of Adirondacks. Elizabethtown: *Adirondack Center Museum and Colonial Garden.* Exhibits relating to the area. Glens Falls: *Hyde Collection.* Museum of old masters. Ogdensburg: *Frederic Remington Museum.* Collection of works by America's foremost artist of the Old West. Saranac Lake: *Dorothy Yepez Gallery without walls.* Changing exhibits. *Stevenson Cottage.* Robert Louis Stevenson literary shrine. Watertown: *Jefferson County Historical Society Museum.* Regional history.

HISTORIC SITES. Canton: *Silas Wright House and Museum.* Restored rooms of mid-1800s era. Fort Edward: *Old Fort House Museum.* Historic exhibits. Lake Placid: *John Brown Farm.* Home and grave of the abolitionist. Lake George: *Fort William Henry.* A restored fort of the French and Indian War. Ticonderoga: *Fort Ticonderoga.* A museum and restored fort and dungeon.

TOURS. Alexandria Bay: *Boat Trips.* Hourly May, June, Sept., less often in Oct.; *Boldt Castle.* On Heart Island. Tour boats stop here. May–Oct; *Ausable Chasm.* Tour of gorge, climaxed by boat ride through the "flume." Mid-May–mid-Oct. Lake George: *Boat Trips.* Daily sightseeing trips, speedboat rides and moonlight sails. Lake Placid: *Boat Trips.* Daily from George & Bliss dock, May–Oct. *Seaway and Power Development Bus Tour.* Guided tour covers locks, Robert Moses State Park, N.Y. State Power Authority Building, power dam. Leaves Chamber of Commerce parking lot. Natural Bridge: *Natural Bridge Caverns,* ¼ mile boat trip on Indian River, which flows underground. North Creek: *Carnet Mines Tour,* Tour of open pit mine. Tupper Lake: *Big Tupper Chair Lift.* Scenic 3,000-ft. ride to summit. Picnic area, hiking trails.

SUMMER SPORTS. "Long Path," challenges hikers. In the Adirondacks, it begins at Lake Placid. The New York State Division of Tourism has listings of major attractions throughout the Adirondacks and Thousand Islands, as well as guides of the main hiking and horse trails through the region.

WINTER SPORTS. There are countless ski areas in the Adirondacks and Thousand Islands area. Whiteface Mountain, in Wilmington, 4,867 feet high, has a vertical drop purported to be the highest in the East, over a dozen slopes, and three chair lifts. Lake Placid has all winter sports, including the Mt. Van Hoevenberg Olympic Bobsled Run. The area is the scene of many winter carnivals, skating and skiing championships.

WHAT TO DO WITH THE CHILDREN. Lake George: Storytown, U.S.A., theme park with rides, etc. Animal Land, Wilmington. Santa's Workshop. Nativity pageant, puppet shows, rides, magic shows, tame animals.

HOTELS AND MOTELS. Cost categories for double occupancy rooms in this region are *Moderate* $20–30 and *Inexpensive* $19 and under.

ALEXANDRIA BAY. *Moderate:* **Alexandria.** Quiet, attractive rooms, landscaped grounds; reservation deposit.

LAKE GEORGE. *Moderate:* **Deep Dene.** Well-run motel among trees, nice rooms, and lake front with beach.

LAKE PLACID. *Moderate:* **Art Devlin's Olympic Motor Inn.** Gorgeous mountain view, many rooms with patio or balcony. Deposit required.
    Northway. Comfortable, back from highway, large pleasant rooms, reservation deposit.

PLATTSBURGH. *Moderate:* **Pioneer.** A grove of evergreens is the setting for this excellent motel. Reservation deposit.

SARANAC LAKE. *Moderate:* **Lake Side.** Continental breakfast. Reservation deposit.

TUPPER LAKE. *Moderate:* **Shaheen's.** Nice rooms, heated pool, restaurant, deposit required.
Inexpensive: **Tupper Lake.** Friendly motel has well-kept rooms. Heated pool. Reservation deposit.

 DINING OUT. Establishments are categorized according to the price of a dinner from the middle range of their menus. For this region: *Moderate* $7 and up, *Inexpensive* below $7. Included are hors d'oeuvres or soup, entree and dessert. Not included are drinks, tax, and tip.

ALEXANDRIA BAY. *Moderate:* **Cavallario's Steak House.** Food served and cooked extremely well. Steaks, lobster, Italian dishes, own baking. Dinner only.

LAKE GEORGE. *Moderate:* **Ridge Terrace.** Dine in a rustic log cabin on lovely grounds, and enjoy good German and American cooking. Salad bar, meat cooked on the open hearth.

LAKE LUZERNE. *Moderate:* **The Hitching Post.** Specialties change daily, but the baked stuffed shrimp is always good in this pleasant log building. Dinner only.

SARANAC LAKE. *Inexpensive:* **Hotel Saranac of Paul Smith's College.** The name is a mouthful, and so are the meals, which feature home baking.

EXPLORING THE NIAGARA FRONTIER

New York's Niagara Frontier is more than just Niagara Falls. Here also are two of the Great Lakes, galleries and museums, rich farmlands, orchards and vineyards, and many structures from an era when this was the frontier of the nation itself. Native Americans regarded the Falls as a sacred shrine, and heard in the waters' roar the voices of their gods. In 1678, Father Louis Hennepin, a French missionary, became the first European to visit them, and now the Falls are international, with the State of New York and the Province of Ontario cooperating to preserve the surroundings of this natural wonder.

In its thirty-six-mile run from Lake Erie to Lake Ontario, the Niagara River drops 326 feet, more than half of it in this single plunge. Actually, there are three falls: the American Falls, 182 feet high and 1,075 feet wide; the Canadian (Horseshoe) Falls, 176 feet high and 2,100 feet wide; and the Bridal Veil Falls. They move upstream about a foot each year. What makes Niagara unique is that you can stand next to it, descend to the bottom, and even ride almost into it. Start on the U.S. side. The three crests are all visible from Prospect Point, where an observation tower gives a panoramic view of the entire scene. Goat Island, in the middle of the river is a seventy-acre park where you can stroll along the very edge of the Falls. "Viewmobile" sightseeing cars circulate around the principal points of interest, and you can get on and off anywhere. From Goat Island you may take a helicopter to survey the Falls from above. And try to see them after dark, when they are colorfully lighted up—it is an entirely different spectacle.

A magnificent way to view them is from the bottom looking up. The Prospect Point Observation Tower elevators descend into the gorge, where you board the *Maid of the Mist* and approach to within yards of the Falls. From here also, giant rafts depart on a White Water Tour of downriver rapids. An elevator on Goat Island takes visitors to the Gorge Walkway, which ends under Terrapin Point below Horseshoe Falls, or to the Cave of the Winds, where you trek across the base of Bridal Veil Falls.

U.S. and Canadian citizens may cross the river and pass customs and immigration with few formalities. The Canadian side offers the highest panoramic towers: the Seagram Tower, 525 feet above Horseshoe Falls; the Oneida Tower, 450 feet; and the Niagara International Center, which features exhibits of science, industry, and government, 775 feet. There is also a Canadian landing at which you may board the *Maid of the Mist.* On U.S. soil, visit Devil's Hole, Whirlpool, and other state parks in the area which offer bathing, camping, colorful foliage, winter sports, hiking and picnicking.

Buffalo, at the eastern end of Lake Erie, and at the western terminus of the Barge Canal, is an important commercial port as well as a leading manufacturing, railroad, steel, and grain center.

The area was first claimed by the French, in 1679. But the opening of the Erie Canal in 1825 made it a major American city, and the development of a steam-powered grain elevator in 1843 helped its grain-processing industry and march towards prosperity.

Today, over a million people live in metropolitan Buffalo; they enjoy an excellent philharmonic orchestra, one of America's finest art galleries, the only inland naval park, and an assortment of nightclubs, and theaters, and top professional sports teams. Forming an almost unbroken ring around the city is a series of parks, over three thousand acres, offering swimming, golf, riding, and tennis.

Lockport, in the heart of the orchard country, was settled around a series of locks of the Erie Canal; they still operate, raising and lowering the water more than sixty feet for barges and pleasure craft.

PRACTICAL INFORMATION FOR THE NIAGARA FRONTIER

HOW TO GET THERE. *By car:* Buffalo is on I–90, the Governor Thomas E. Dewey Thruway. From Buffalo take I–90 to Niagara Falls.

By air: Altair, American, Eastern, New York Air, People Express, United, and *USAir* have frequent service to Buffalo.

By bus: Buffalo and Niagara Falls are served by *Blue Bird, Canada Coach, Trailways* and *Greyhound,* among others.

By train: Buffalo is on *Amtrak's* "Niagara Rainbow" route.

TOURIST INFORMATION. Niagara Falls Convention and Visitors Bureau, 300 Fourth St., Niagara Falls 14303; The Buffalo Convention and Tourism Board 107 Delaware Ave., Buffalo, N.Y. 14202.

 MUSEUMS AND GALLERIES. Buffalo: *Albright-Knox Art Gallery,* 1285 Elmwood Ave., in Delaware Park has an outstanding contemporary collection. *Buffalo & Erie County Historical Society,* located on Nottingham Court, off Elmwood Ave., features Indian, pioneer and early craft exhibits. *Buffalo Museum of Science,* Humboldt Park, for astronomy, botany, zoology, geology and the natural sciences.

Niagara: *Niagara's Wax Museum of History.* 333 Prospect St., shows wax figures, displays.

 TOURS. Lackawanna: *Our Lady of Victory National Shrine,* State 62 & Ridge Rd. Summer guided tours. *Cave of the Winds.* Trip from Goat Island down elevator to base of Falls, etc., charge includes rain gear and guide service. *Helicopter Ride. Maid of the Mist.* Boat ride almost into the Horseshoe Falls. Fee includes use of rain gear. *Observation Tower.* Elevator also descends to the gorge. *Niagara Power Project.* Lewiston Rd., State 104, 4 mi. N. *Power Vista,* Observation Bldg., animated models, films. Balcony views of U.S. and Canadian Falls.

 SPORTS. *Golf:* Batavia: Terry Hills, 9-hole course. Buffalo: Delaware Park, 18-hole course. South Park, 9-hole course. Grand Island. Beaver Island, 18-hole course. Niagara Falls: Hyde Park, three 18-hole courses.

SPECTATOR SPORTS. Buffalo Bills of the National Football League, Buffalo Sabres of the National Hockey League, and the Buffalo Stallions of the Major Indoors Soccer League. Many colleges engage in varsity athletics.

 WHAT TO DO WITH THE CHILDREN. Buffalo: Delaware Park Zoo has a Children's Zoo. Grand Island: Fantasy Island, Thruway Exit N–19 is an amusement park. Niagara Falls: Oppenheim Zoo on Niagara Falls Blvd; Niagara Falls Aquarium, 701 Whillpool St.

 HOTELS AND MOTELS. Cost categories for double-occupancy rooms in the region are: *Moderate* $30 up and *Inexpensive* $34 and below.

BUFFALO. *Moderate:* **Holiday Inn Midtown.** Comfortable downtown motel, with guests under 12 free.

LOCKPORT. *Moderate:* **Sheraton Motor Inn.** State 78, 1 mi. S. of town. Attractive rooms. Facilities include indoor heated pool, sauna, health club. Pets limited. Restaurant and cocktail lounge.

NIAGARA FALLS. *Moderate:* **John's Flaming Hearth Motor Inn.** 443 Main St., across from the Rainbow Bridge. Restaurant and cocktail lounge.

Niagara Falls actually has more than 3,000 rooms on the American side, including several new downtown motels, and scores of motels at modest prices along US 62 between Niagara Falls and Buffalo. In addition, the Canadian side offers numerous accommodations. Most have a summer rate and an off-season rate.

NORTH TONAWANDA. *Inexpensive:* **The Packet Inn.** 84 Sweeney St. Nicely furnished rooms; café, bar, entertainment.

 DINING OUT. In the Niagara Frontier, and especially around Buffalo and Niagara Falls, there are many good restaurants. Medium-priced full-course dinners at the restaurants listed occupy only one category: *Moderate,* under $12. Included are hors d'oeuvres or soup, entree and dessert. Not included are drinks, tax and tip.

BUFFALO. Royal Knight. Background music, American favorites like prime rib, chicken or pork chops.

LOCKPORT. The Cozy Clipper. This relaxed dining spot features seafood and steak specialties.

NIAGARA FALLS. John's Flaming Hearth. 443 Main St. Steak and lobster specialties, interesting desserts. Locally popular.

DELAWARE

America's First State

From the north, whether it's over the Memorial Bridge from the New Jersey Turnpike or down I–95 from Philadelphia, all roads lead to Wilmington, largest city in the state. Settled by Swedes who landed in 1638, Wilmington has not forgotten its heritage; in fact, it maintains a strong tie with Sweden through its sister city, Kalmar.

Willingtown Square, in the heart of the city, is a conclave of six 18th-century houses which have been moved to this site beside the Market Street Mall and are being used as a series of museum displays, workshops, and offices. Modern inside, these small buildings have been completely restored to their original appearance on the outside.

Across the Mall is Old Town Hall (1798), restored even to the basement cells which made up the jail. The Mall itself, after years of planning and construction, is a charming place to stroll, shop, or stop at a sidewalk cafe for a bite to eat. Dominating the Mall, the Grand Opera House, one of the finest in America, has been renovated with funds donated by Delaware citizens. It's the scene of year-round cultural events.

The Brandywine Zoo, in the heart of Wilmington, is a delight to visit. Well-kept and attractive, it is open daily with special prices for children and seniors.

Six miles northwest of Wilmington on Del. 52 (Kennett Pike) is the world-famous Henry Francis du Pont Winterthur Museum, with 14 rooms open for a nominal fee. The remaining 100-odd rooms may be seen by appointment.

Traveling south on US 13, follow the signs to New Castle, a delightful town designed by Peter Stuyvesant and preserved, house by house, by individuals who live in them. On occasion these private homes are open to the public, but any time of year the visitor may tour the Amstel House, the Old Dutch House, the elegant George Read II House, and the Old Court House of 1732.

Driving west from New Castle on Del. 273, you'll pass through Christiana, with its two ancient inns scheduled for restoration. These were coach stops during the Revolutionary period, and Washington is supposed to have stayed in them many times. Turn left in Christiana on Old Baltimore Pike and you'll come to Cooch's Bridge, scene of the only Revolutionary War battle fought in Delaware, and where the Stars and Stripes were first flown in land battle.

Take a left on Del. 896, then a right on US 13 to Odessa, with its three historic buildings maintained by Winterthur Museum and worth a stop. On down the road, you'll find Dover, the capital of Delaware, which grew around the site of a county courthouse and prison laid out by William Penn in 1683. The green, center of this complex, still remains, and Delaware's capitol buildings are quite beautiful, somewhat like a college campus with ivy-covered brick walls. Stop by the Visitor Center in the State House annex on Federal Street for information on the buildings to be seen, or join a tour there.

A relaxing, enjoyable ride aboard one of three sleek bay liners comprising the Cape May-Lewes Ferry will take you across the Delaware Bay to Cape May, N.J. and a world of gingerbread and Victoriana. It's a 70-minute ride, and you can buy a meal aboard.

Back in Lewes, pick up Del. 14 south to Rehoboth Beach, a favorite playground for Washingtonians. Here you'll find all kinds of hotels, motels, guest houses, and inns; there's a boardwalk, ocean swimming, and the fishin's good. If you go much farther south, you're in Maryland.

PRACTICAL INFORMATION FOR DELAWARE

 HISTORIC SITES. *Lewes Historic Complex.* At 3rd and Shipcarpenter streets, Lewes. *Thompson Country Store; Rabbit's Ferry House,* a small 18th-century farmhouse. Open June 15 through Labor Day, Tuesdays through Saturdays, 10 A.M. to 5 P.M. Admission: tours, $1.50; individual buildings, 50¢. *Cooch's Bridge.* Off State 896, south of Newark.

Old Swedes Church, Wilmington. Believed to be the oldest Protestant church still in use in America. Guide service. *Fort Christina,* Wilmington. Built by Swedes after landing in Delaware in 1638. *Caesar Rodney Statue,* Rodney Square, Wilmington. Depicts horse and rider making famous trip from Dover to Philadelphia to break the tie vote on Independence, July 2, 1776. *Fort Delaware* State Park, Pea Patch Island. Reached by launch from Delaware City.

Great Cypress Swamp. Trussum Pond, near Laurel. Northernmost natural stand of cypress in U. S. Follow signs from Trap Pond State Park (Del. 24 west of Laurel) for best view.

Mason-Dixon Monument. West of Delmar via Del. 54. Double crownstone erected in 1768 by Charles Mason and Jeremiah Dixon at the southern end of the north-south portion of the Mason-Dixon Line, which resolved boundary disputes between Calvert and Penn families.

Bombay Hook National Wildlife Refuge. Off Del. 9, north of Leipsic. 15,110-acre haven for migrating and wintering waterfowl. Open daily sunrise to sunset.

 MUSEUMS AND GALLERIES. *Henry Francis du Pont Winterthur Museum.* 14 rooms in south wing open Tues.–Sun. and holiday Mons. To see main museum (some 100 rooms) write Reservations Office, Winterthur Museum, Winterthur, Del. 19735. 6 miles northwest of Wilmington on Kennett Pike (Del. 52). *Delaware Art Museum.* 2301 Kentmere Pkwy., Wilmington. *Old Town Hall* and *Willingtown Square,* downtown Wilmington on the Market St. Mall. Guide service. *Rockwood Museum.* Off Washington St. Extension, Wilmington. Fine Victorian home built by one of founders of city, maintained by New Castle County. For appointment, telephone (302) 571–7776; guides usually on duty. Built in style of English country manor, with park-like landscaping.

Old Court House. New Castle. Delaware's colonial capital and the county seat for many years, now a state museum. *Old Dutch House Museum,* New Castle. Said to be oldest house in state. *Amstel House,* New Castle. Fine examples of early Delaware furnishings. *George Read II House,* The Strand, New Castle. Outstanding example of Georgian architecture, formal gardens. Built by son of a signer of the Declaration of Independence. *Corbit-Sharp House, Wilson Warner House, John Janvier Stable,* Odessa. Maintained by Winterthur Museum.

Hagley Museum, near Wilmington. Preserved and restored site of the original powder works of the Du Pont Company. *Eleutherian Mills,* home of E. I. duPont de Nemours (1803), on hill overlooking Hagley, open year-round.

Delaware State Museum, Dover. Housed in four separate buildings with exhibits on many phases of Delaware life. Especially interesting is the Eldridge Reeves Johnson collection of old talking machines and records. *Woodburn,* the governor's mansion, Dover. Open Saturdays, 2:30–4:30 P.M., except during Jan., Feb. *Agricultural Museum.* Delmarva farm living. On U.S. 13 just south of Del. State College. Special seasonal events.

Island Field Archeological Museum, South Bowers Beach. Site of prehistoric cemetery, still being excavated. Open March 1—Nov. 30. *John Dickinson Mansion,* Kitts Hummock Road near Dover. Dickinson has been called the Penman of the Revolution. House was built in 1740 by his father, Samuel. Fine restoration. *Barratts Chapel,* near Frederica, is called the Cradle of Methodism in America.

Historic complex, Lewes. Includes *Marine Museum, Lightship Overfalls,* several other buildings. *Zwaanendael Museum,* Lewes. Charming example of Dutch architecture housing Dutch artifacts.

 HOTELS AND MOTELS in Delaware range from plain, comfortable roadside establishments in the country to the luxury (and high prices) of some Rehoboth Beach hotels.

The price categories in this section are for double occupancy: *Moderate* $25 up, and *Inexpensive* below $25 (not including taxes). For a more complete description of these categories see the Hotels and Motels section of *Facts at Your Fingertips* at the front of this volume.

DOVER. *Moderate:* **Quality Court South.** Heated pool, restaurant.
Ramada Inn. N. duPont Highway. Pool, restaurant, entertainment.
Inexpensive: **Caravan.** Pool, restaurant adjacent.
Capitol City. Pool. Snack room, washer, dryer.
Towne Point. Color TV, pool, adjacent restaurant.

GLASGOW. *Inexpensive:* **Clay's Motel.** US 40. Restaurant across highway. Small, clean.

WILMINGTON. *Moderate:* **Dutch Village.** Pool, adjacent restaurant.

El Capitan Motor Hotel. 1807 Concord Pike. Near museums, restaurant next door, pool. Near I–95 exit 8N.

Gateway Motor Inn. Pool, some waterbeds.

Park Plaza. Some efficiency units, pets OK. Restaurant adjacent.

Skyways Motor Lodge. Pool, kiddie pool, restaurant.

Tally Ho. US 202 north of city. Pool, restaurant, entertainment. Free morning coffee & donuts.

 DINING OUT in Delaware often means chicken, since the state raises a great deal of poultry; it can also mean crabmeat, often in some exotic form—crab Imperial, crab cakes or deviled crabs. You might also want to sample stuffed crab, or baked, steamed or soft shell crabs.

Restaurant price categories are as follows: *Moderate* $5 up and *Inexpensive* below $5. Not included are drinks and tips. There is no sales tax in Delaware.

DOVER. *Inexpensive — Moderate:* A host of fast-food spots along US 13.
Inexpensive: **Orient Express.** Rte. 113, south end of town. Good Chinese menu, open 7 days. Take-outs.

LEWES. *Moderate:* **DiLeo's.** On the canal. Unique Italian dishes, seafood, everything fresh to order. (Formerly *Ianire's.*)

NEWARK: *Moderate:* **Arner's Family Restaurant.** Next to airport. Very popular for lunch, dinner. Fine salad bar.
Dragon's Den. Excellent Chinese food. On Cleveland Avenue.
Iron Hill Inn. At I–95. German food and seafood, German band weekends.
Inexpensive: **Ivystone II.** Family fare, children's menu, 32 kinds of pie. In Newark Shopping Center.
Klondike Kate. Old mining-town atmosphere. Dinners, omelets, soup du jour, glorified hamburgers. On Main Street.

NEW CASTLE. *Moderate:* **Rebel Cork Irish Pub** at the Arsenal. Lunch, dinner, Irish music on weekends. In old armory building as you enter town.

REHOBOTH BEACH. *Moderate:* **Avenue.** Homemade rolls and pastries.
Crab Pot. Seafood, take-out menu.
Sir Boyce's Pub. Nice atmosphere, good seafood, super prime ribs. On main highway near Dewey Beach.

ST. GEORGES. *Inexpensive:* **Ches Del.** Just south of St. Georges Bridge on US 13. Chicken and slippery dumplings (a Peninsula specialty) served on Wednesdays. Homemade soups, desserts. Children half-price. Open for breakfast daily.

SMYRNA. *Moderate:* **Wayside Inn.** duPont Highway and Mt. Vernon St. Good homemade pies.
Inexpensive: **Smyrna Diner.** On duPont Highway. Clean; good food. Open early and late.

WILMINGTON. *Moderate:* **Del Rose Café.** 1707 Delaware Ave. Friendly atmosphere, excellent Italian dishes. Favorite of locals.
Ground Round. 1101 Phila. Pike. (Also in Newark and Dover.) Good beef, fun atmosphere.
Hearn's. 2008 Market St. Pleasant, old, established family restaurant. Lunch, dinner, cocktails.
Oscar's. On Market St. Mall. Featuring Sunday brunch, great sandwiches, homemade soups. Once an elegant candy company, the décor has been preserved.

Inexpensive: **Charcoal Pit.** 2600 Concord Pike. Open 7 days. Great hamburgers, steak sandwiches.

Inexpensive: **Post House Restaurants.** 1722 Penna. Ave., 43rd & Market, 105 N. Union, and 145 E. Main St. (Newark). Open 6:30 A.M. to 10 P.M.

H. A. Winston & Co. In Independence Mall, Concord Pike. Great variety of gourmet hamburgers, fun décor. (You'll find Winston's in Newark and Dover, too.)

MARYLAND

Baltimore, the Bay and the West

You can drive from Washington to Baltimore over US 1, I-95 or the Baltimore-Washington Parkway. You may be surprised to find yourself in one of the most vibrant of U.S. cities. Center of much activity in Baltimore is the redeveloped Inner Harbor, 95-acre recreational park and plaza, site of a continuing series of ethnic festivals, concerts, art shows and other activities during much of the year. Serving as a reminder that Baltimore has been a seaport since Colonial days, the Inner Harbor setting includes the U.S. Frigate **Constellation,** which was built in 1797 and is the oldest United States Navy ship afloat as well as a national historic landmark. There are also a World War II submarine; a public marina, tour boats, and rental sail and paddleboats. Harbor Place is a two-story, glass-enclosed collection of restaurants, shops, boutiques and food markets that jumps with activity day and night. The National aquarium in Baltimore is two piers away.

Be sure to see Ft. McHenry, a national monument and historic shrine where the original Star-Spangled Banner flew—visited by over half a million people a year.

The Flag House, home of Mary Pickersgill, who made the Star-Spangled Banner (all 1,260 square feet of it), is also open to the public. Mt. Vernon Place is the site of the first completed architectural monument to George Washington, begun in 1815 and completed in 1829.

Mt. Vernon Place is known as one of the most beautiful city squares in America.

The Walters Art Gallery houses works of art spanning 6,000 years. Peale Museum, opened in 1814 and devoted to Baltimore life, is also extremely interesting. The Baltimore Museum of Art, which has a huge collection of classic and modern work, and the Baltimore & Ohio Railroad Museum are both intriguing. The latter is the greatest collection of old locomotives in the world.

At the Maryland Historical Society you will find a vast collection of exhibits relating to state history. Among these is the original manuscript of the "Star-Spangled Banner" which, incidentally, was not written on "an old envelope," as a popular legend has it.

The Methodist Museum of the Lovely Lane Methodist Church has a comprehensive collection of records and exhibits pertaining to the history of American Methodism. Mount Clare, the magnificent home of Charles Carroll, the barrister who wrote the Maryland Declaration of Independence in 1776, is open to the public, too.

Saint Elizabeth Seton House, where the founder of the American Order of the Sisters of Charity made her home in 1806, is open, as is the Edgar Allan Poe House, where the poet lived while he was courting his future wife. The Lloyd Street Synagogue, dating from 1845, is distinguished for its architectural beauty. So is the Basilica of the Assumption of the Virgin Mary, the first Catholic cathedral in the United States (1806).

National Social Security Headquarters, located on Security Blvd. (Baltimore Beltway, I–695, Exit 17), offers an interesting educational tour featuring its vast complex of sophisticated electronic data-processing equipment.

PRACTICAL INFORMATION FOR BALTIMORE

HOW TO GET THERE. *By car:* Baltimore is on I–95 40 mi. north of Washington and 90 mi. south of Philadelphia. From Hagerstown in the west I–70 runs to the city, as does I–83 from Harrisburg, Pennsylvania, to the north.

By air: Baltimore-Washington International Airport, 10 mi. south of the city, is served by numerous airlines, including *American, Allegheny, Delta, Eastern, Ozark, Piedmont, TWA, United* and *USAir.*

By train: Baltimore is on the *Amtrak* line. The station is at 1500 N. Charles St. (800) 523–5700.

By Bus: The *Trailways* bus terminal is located at 210 W. Fayette St. *Greyhound* is at Howard and Centre Sts.

TOURIST INFORMATION. The Baltimore Office of Promotion & Tourism, 110 W. Baltimore St., Baltimore 21201, will be glad to answer any questions. The phone number is (301) 752–8632.

TOURS. Guided historic tour of Baltimore, including Fort McHenry, B&O Museum, Star-Spangled Banner Flag House, Washington Monument and Mount Vernon Place, are offered by several companies, including *American Excursions, Baltimore Rent-A-Tour, Gray Line,* and *Mini-Tours.*

Baltimore Patriot Harbor Cruises operates the *Patriot* and *Defender* cruise ships around the inner harbor and to Fort McHenry, departing from Constellation Dock, Pratt St.

GARDENS. Spring begins in Baltimore when the *Sherwood Gardens* bloom, usually in mid-May. Follow the crowd to hundreds of thousands of flowers at 204 E. Highfield Rd., just east of 4100 block N. Charles St.

HISTORIC SITES. *Edgar Allan Poe House,* 203 Amity St. In this tiny house, the melancholy poet lived and courted his cousin, who later became his wife. His grave is in nearby Westminster Churchyard. *First Unitarian Church.* North Charles St. at Franklin St. Built in 1819, it is considered the birthplace of the Unitarian Church.

Ft. McHenry, foot of Fort Ave. Overlooking Baltimore harbor, this starshaped fort with brick walls 20 feet thick withstood the might of the British fleet on Sept. 13–14, 1814. Francis Scott Key, witnessing the bombardment and the flag at dawn, was inspired to write what became the National Anthem.

Lexington Market, Lexington and Eutaw Sts. One of the oldest markets in the nation (1803), it has now been modernized but still has stallkeepers whose fathers and grandfathers had stalls there before them. *Lloyd St. Synagogue,* Lloyd St. off 1100 E. Baltimore St. Third oldest synagogue in the United States is now a museum.

Mount Clare Station, Pratt and Poppleton Sts. The first passenger and freight station in the United States, it was here that Samuel F. B. Morse's first telegraph message, "What hath God wrought," was received. It now is the entrance to the B&O Railroad Museum, which contains fine examples of early steam engines.

Tyson St., 900 block north. A slum for a century, this is now Baltimore's most colorful block, with its circa 1830 houses renovated by arty folks right after World War II.

Washington Monument, Charles and Monument Sts. Laid out in 1830, this gracious square is known for its fountains and mini-parks, the Washington Monument, and surrounding architecture, including elegant townhouses, Walters Art Gallery and Peabody Conservatory of Music.

MUSEUMS AND GALLERIES: *Baltimore Museum of Art.* This popular institution has achieved national stature for its collection of Picasso, Matisse, and Cézanne. *Walters Art Gallery,* Charles and Centre Sts. Ranks among the most comprehensive American art museums. *Peale Museum,* 225 N. Holiday St. The oldest museum building in America, it features portraits and Baltimore memorabilia. The *National Aquarium in Baltimore,* largest in the U.S., is located at the Inner Harbor.

SPORTS. A favorite way to spend a Saturday afternoon or a weekday evening out is to eat peanuts and hot dogs while watching the Orioles play nine innings of *baseball* or a twilight doubleheader at Memorial Stadium. The old Indian game of *lacrosse* is the national sport of Canada, but Baltimore is the game's unofficial capitol. A rough sport, games are played at most high schools and colleges. Landscaped with dogwoods and pines, Pine Ridge is generally rated as the best of the *golf courses* owned by the city. It's on Dulaney Valley Rd. near Loch Raven. With nearly 50 *yacht clubs* around the Chesapeake Bay area, there is hardly a weekend that does not feature a sailboat race. They continue right up through the "frostbite season." A good vantage point is along the sea wall inside the U.S. Naval Academy grounds in Annapolis.

Memorial Stadium still lives up to its nickname as "the world's largest outdoor insane asylum" whenever the Baltimore Colts play *football.* With spring meets starting in January and fall meets ending in December, there is almost continuous *horse racing* at one of the following tracks: Laurel (Rte. 198 off I–95 about midway between Baltimore and Washington, D.C.); Bowie (Rte. 197 from the Baltimore-Washington Expy.); Pimlico, in Baltimore, and Timonium (I–83 just north of Baltimore). Transportation is provided daily by Baltimore Motor Coach buses from Civic Center. No reservations needed.

In winter, the Baltimore Blast indoor soccer team, and Skipjacks ice hockey team, attract large crowds to the Civic Center.

WHAT TO DO WITH THE CHILDREN. *Baltimore and Ohio Railroad Museum.* Poppleton and Pratt Sts. A collection of replicas and original iron horses from America's first railroad.

Children's Zoo in Druid Hill Park. Besides the usual zoological attractions, there are farm animals and various playground apparatus.

Children's Creative Center, 608 Water St. This unusual recycling center features an ever-changing stock of "affordable" goodies, including paper and fabrics, buttons, spools, foam scraps and industrial surplus.

Among attractions in the Inner Harbor area are the popular *National Aquarium* in Baltimore, *Science Center,* shops and eateries of *Harbor Place,* U.S. frigate *Constellation* and a *World War II submarine,* and *rental boats.*

HOTELS AND MOTELS in Baltimore characterized with few exceptions by the ultramodern atmosphere. Almost all of the old-line establishments, with traditional plush accommodations, have closed in the last few years. It is wise, therefore, to check these listings carefully and to make advanced reservations always.

All hotels and motels listed are in the *moderate* price range. Based on double occupancy, the range is $25–35.

Eleanor D. Corner House. 128 W. Franklin St. No-frills YWCA bed-and-breakfast for women and families.

Harbor City Inn (Best Western). 1701 Russell St., Exit 7 from Baltimore-Washington Expy. Modern, handsome.

Howard House. 8 N. Howard St. Basic accommodations.

DINING OUT in Baltimore can involve some serious exploring. Though one hears a lot about Maryland's traditional dishes—spoon bread, beaten biscuits, terrapin soup, oyster stew—the truth is that it's not so easy to find them on menus. However, those whose business it is to know say that the equal of Baltimore's Maryland roast turkey, Maryland fried chicken, crab cakes, or fried Chincoteague oysters is nowhere to be found. Oyster crackers are hard to find these days, but you can still stand in Lexington Market and eat succulent bivalves raw as the stall-keeper shucks them, along with a seemingly endless variety of other regional and ethnic specialties.

Restaurant price categories are as follows: *Moderate,* $10–15; *Inexpensive,* below $10. These prices are for hors d'oeuvres or soup, entree, and dessert. Not included are drinks, tax, and tips.

Moderate: **American Café.** Harbor Place. Light American fare, overlooking the harbor.

Bertha's. S. Broadway at Lancaster St. Try the mussels, other seasonal delights at this Fells Point spot.

Bud Paolino's. 3919 E. Lombard St. Crabs are king. Also steaks, Italian specialties.

Burke's. 36 Light St. Pub-style.

DeNitti's. 906 Trinity St. One of many good eating places in "Little Italy."
Frazier's. 857 W. 33rd St. Huge selection.
Ikaros. 4805 Eastern Ave. Hearty moussaka, other Greek food.
Owl Bar. In the Belvedere Hotel, Charles and Chase Sts. Salads and snacks.
Phillip's Harbor Place. Seafood served in a Victorian setting. Crowded, but worth the wait.
P. J. Cricketts. 206 W. Pratt St. Pub atmosphere, across from the Convention Center.
Inexpensive: **Lexington Market.** Lexington and Eutaw Sts. Countless stalls serve everything from egg rolls to seafood, corned beef to bratwurst.
Lighthouse. 10 Park Ave. Seafood, near the Civic Center.
Pub Down Under. 201 N. Charles St. Soups and sandwiches.

EXPLORING MARYLAND

Annapolis

Your first stop on the Western Shore will be Annapolis, founded in 1649, and the capital since 1695. Its historic area (a National Historic Landmark District) contains the State House (1772), William Paca House and Garden (1765), Hammond-Harwood House (1774), Chase-Lloyd House (1771), Brice House (1773)—all Registered National Historic landmarks. The United States Naval Academy is open daily for visiting. A harbor boat operates from the city dock late spring through fall.

Then go south on US 301. If your trip is made between March and May, you will be able to see the world's greatest loose-leaf tobacco auctions along your way, weekday mornings at Upper Marlboro, Waldorf and La Plata, and at nearby Hughesville on State 5. Visitors are welcome at the warehouses and there is no charge.

Take 301 and State 6 west to Port Tobacco, one of the oldest inhabited sites in the country. Today half a mile from the river, this quiet town was once the port through which southern Maryland's vast tobacco crop was shipped abroad. It had a customs house, extensive wharves, warehouses, a courthouse, churches, and taverns. Then, due to the change of shoreline, it eventually lost its waterfront, and died. You will see a handful of buildings now, and a public square that is almost, but not quite, empty.

Maryland's Not-So-Wild West

In the town of Frederick, the National Historic District includes the beautiful Court House Square; tomb of Francis Scott Key in Mt. Olivet Cemetery, plus numerous other historic homes and attractions. The Visitor's Center at 19 E. Church St. is open daily year-round, and May–October offers guided walking tours.

A few miles east of Frederick on State 144, off I-70, is New Market, called the "Antiques Capital of Maryland." It is a tiny village that is entirely supported by the sale of antiques. More than four dozen shops line its brief street, all of high quality.

South of Frederick is Stronghold, a private estate, the grounds of which are open to the public, and well worth seeing. They include

Sugarloaf Mountain, a steep and lofty elevation, on the slopes of which are overlooks and picnic grounds along a well-planned drive. One reaches Stronghold by going south on I–270 to State 109 West via Comus.

Go by US 40 or Interstate 70 to Hagerstown. In the City Park there see the Hager House, built by the founder of the city in 1739. This building combines the aspects of a mansion and a fort, reminding the modern traveler that in 1739 this area was the American "West."

On the field of Antietam on September 17, 1862, the Union Army repulsed the first Confederate attempt to invade the North. The field, a National Monument and Historic Battlefield Site, can be reached by State 65 out of Hagerstown. There is a Visitors Center and Museum, a good place to begin your tour.

Leave Hagerstown and proceed west via I–70. A highway sign will direct you to Ft. Frederick State Park. Here is a huge stone fort of the French and Indian War period (1756). The structure and reconstructed barracks remind you vividly of the dangers of frontier existence.

The above is an outline of one possible tour. It is not the full list of what there is to see in the Old Line State, but it will give you an idea of how much is waiting for you should you go there.

PRACTICAL INFORMATION FOR MARYLAND

HOW TO GET THERE. *By car:* I–95 enters the state near Wilmington, Del. passing through Aberdeen and Baltimore and leaving the state at Washington, D.C. I–70 connects central Pennsylvania and Baltimore, entering Maryland at Hancock. The primary north-south routes on the Eastern Shore are US 301, which enters the state from Middletown, Del., and US 13 from Laurel, Del. US 13 goes through Salisbury into Virginia, where it leads to the Chesapeake Bay Bridge-Tunnel connecting Cape Charles and Cape Henry, Va.

By air: There is scheduled air service to Baltimore (Baltimore-Washington International Airport), Hagerstown, and Washington, D.C. Numerous airlines fly to Baltimore and Washington, D.C. *USAir* flies to Hagerstown and Salisbury.

By bus: Greyhound and *Trailways* are the major carriers to Maryland, and Baltimore is the major terminal.

By train: Amtrak has service to Wilmington, Delaware, Baltimore, BWI Airport, Washington, D.C. and western Maryland.

TOURIST INFORMATION. Maps, brochures, and information of all kinds are available from the Division of Tourist Development, Maryland Department of Economic & Community Development, 1748 Forest Dr., Annapolis 21401. (301) 269–3517. Call toll-free (800) 638–5252; within Maryland, (800) 492–7126.

NATIONAL PARKS AND FORESTS. *Chesapeake and Ohio Canal.* Stretching from Georgetown in the District of Columbia to Cumberland, along the Maryland bank of the twisting Potomac River, this is the longest of all national parks, 185 miles. An idea of George Washington's, the canal was started by President John Quincy Adams on July 4, 1828—the same day the Baltimore and Ohio Railroad was begun.

Catoctin Mountain Park, just three miles west of Thurmont, includes the site of Camp David, the Presidential retreat. For the public there is a seven-mile scenic drive, twelve miles of well-marked hiking trails, two picnic areas, and a modern camp for five-day family camping from mid-April to October.

MUSEUMS AND GALLERIES, *Calvert Marine Museum,* Solomons. A museum dedicated to preservation of local marine history, featuring a lighthouse, boat models, bay boats, paintings, and other exhibits.

Washington County Museum of Fine Arts, in City Park, Hagerstown. The only real art museum in the state outside Baltimore. Features a new exhibit every month and Sunday afternoon concerts in fall and winter.

Chesapeake Bay Maritime Museum, on State 33 off US 50, in St. Michael's. Established in 1965 to keep alive the memories, romance, and artifacts of America's great inland sea, the museum has an impressive collection of boat models, name boards, figureheads, waterfowling guns and decoys, a lighthouse and several sailing craft which can be boarded.

HISTORIC SITES. *Central Maryland,* all within an hour's drive from Baltimore. *Clara Barton House,* MacArthur Blvd. in Glen Echo, three mi. north of District of Columbia line. Home of the Civil War nurse who founded the American Red Cross, built for her by the grateful survivors of the 1889 Johnstown flood who used lumber from emergency barracks erected while she was director. Served as Red Cross Headquarters from 1897 to 1904.

Great Falls of the Potomac, on State 189 near Potomac, Md. A spectacular sight the year round. The *Chesapeake and Ohio Canal,* which skirted the falls in 1828, is restored at this point. The canal begins in the Georgetown area of Washington, D.C. and reaches 184 miles to Cumberland along the Maryland shore of the Potomac River.

Southern Maryland. Annapolis. The capital of the Old Line State offers much for the visitor to see and all of it within easy walking distance. Included are the State House, oldest in America in continuous legislative use; many 18th-century mansions which are Registered National Historic Landmarks; the bustling waterfront; and the United States Naval Academy. *Old State House,* St. Mary's City, Rte. 5. A replica of the original built in 1676, was erected in 1934 as part of tercentenary celebration. *Sotterley,* three mi. east of Hollywood, State 235. Many Marylanders say this is their favorite house. Overlooking the Patuxent River, the long, low structure built in 1711–27, has a notable Chinese Chippendale stairway and other fine woodwork. Since it never deteriorated, it never had to be restored. It's still surrounded by a plantation-size farm. *London Town* on the South River, off State 2, the site of a once-thriving seaport, consists of a mid-18th-century Publik House inn, reconstructed colonial log tobacco barn, visitors' center, and 10-acre woodland gardens.

Eastern Shore. The Eastern Shore of Maryland, nine counties on the Delmarva Peninsula, is the area most often associated with Maryland by out-of-staters.

Wye Mills, on State 404 off US 50. Here is the location of the Wye Oak, Maryland's official tree, said to be over 400 years old. Nearby is a restored 18th-century grist mill which ground flour for George Washington's army, a one-room schoolhouse, and restored Wye Church (1721).

Oxford-Bellvue Ferry, one of the last in Maryland, is the oldest continuous ferry in the nation, having made its first crossing of the Tred Avon River in 1760. The present diesel-driven barge carries six cars. Reached from Easton via St. Michaels Rd. to Royal Oak or from Easton via Oxford Rd. Oxford is a charming waterside village, where log canoe and sailboat races are held many summer weekends.

Ocean City, eastern terminus of US 50, is Maryland's only oceanside resort. White clapboard hotels and boarding houses face the Atlantic on one side and Sinepuxent Bay on the other in the oldest section, but its northern end now has all the glitter of Atlantic City. Beautiful wide beach. Three amusement parks. Deep-sea and bay fishing available.

TOURS. *Historic Annapolis,* Inc., Old Treasury, State Circle, Annapolis, 21401, conducts several walking tours. So does *Three Centuries Tours of Annapolis,* P.O. Box 29, Annapolis 21404, (301) 263–5327. Sightseeing water cruises are offered by *Chesapeake Marine Tours,* P.O. Box 3350, City Dock, Annapolis 21403.

GARDENS. *Lilypons,* a 300-acre tract of exotic water plants and ponds, 8 miles south of Frederick, off State 85, features water lilies named after such famous personalities as Colonel Lindbergh and Dorothy Lamour.

DRINKING LAWS. Minimum age is 21 for all alcoholic beverages. It is best to inquire locally about drinking restrictions, but most bars, restaurants, and hotels are open from 6 A.M. to 2 A.M. except Sundays (when hours are shorter) and election days.

HOTELS AND MOTELS in Maryland range from deluxe to inexpensive, and include resorts over a century old and the latest in up-to-the-minute motels. Price categories for double-occupancy rooms in Maryland are divided into the following ranges: *Moderate,* $25–30; and *Inexpensive,* under $25.

ANNAPOLIS. *Inexpensive:* **The Gables.** 1422 West St. A tourist home with clean, comfortable—but unair-conditioned—rooms
Thr-rift Inn. 2542 Riva Rd. Annapolis-Crownsville exit off US 50. Clean, few-frills accommodations.

EASTON. *Inexpensive* **Econo-Travel Motor Hotel.** US 50 in town. Color TV, restaurant adjacent.

ELKRIDGE. *Inexpensive:* **Econo-Travel Motor Hotel.** 5895 Bonnie View Lane.

ELLICOTT CITY. *Moderate:* **Forest Motel.** 10021 Baltimore National Pike. Restaurant and pool.

FREDERICK. *Inexpensive:* **Dan Dee Motel.** US 40 W. Dining room.

GRANTSVILLE. *Inexpensive:* **Little Meadows.** Small, secluded.

HAGERSTOWN. *Moderate:* **Friendship Inn Mid-Town.** 16 N. Prospect St. Children under 8 free.
Hagerstown Motel. US 11 off I–81 at Maugans Ave. Exit. Heated pool.

JESSUP. *Moderate.* **Econo Lodge.** Baltimore-Washington Parkway and Rte. 175. Swimming pool, restaurant.

JOPPA. *Moderate:* **Lakeside Motel.** I–95 Exit 3–A (south) or 4 (north). Private fishing and swimming lake.

LAUREL. *Moderate:* **Valencia Motel.** US 1 in town. Pool, picnic grove. Winner of National Housekeeping award.

LEXINGTON PARK. *Inexpensive:* **A&E Motel.** Great Mills Rd. In historic St. Mary's County.

OCEAN CITY. *Moderate:* **The Admiral.** 9th St. and Baltimore Ave. Also, some apartments.

Belmont-Hearne. Dorchester and Boardwalk. American Plan available.

Misty Harbor Motel. 25th St. and Philadelphia Ave. Pool, bayside docks.

ODENTON. *Moderate.* **General's Red Carpet Inn.** Rte. 175. Restaurant, lounge.

SALISBURY. *Moderate.* **Days Inn.** Two miles N on US Rte. 13. Handicap facilities.

Temple Hill Motel. Three miles S. on S. Salisbury Blvd. off US 13. Room coffee, heated pool.

Thr-rift Travel Inn. N. Salisbury Blvd. Clean accommodations.

WILLIAMSPORT. *Inexpensive:* **Days Inn.** 310 East Potomac St.

YOUTH HOSTELS. *Cambridge.* 1311 Race St. Homelike atmosphere; 10 beds. *Knoxville.* 16 mi. W. of Frederick on Sandy Hook Rd. Open summers only.

 DINING OUT In Maryland this can involve not only fine local dishes, but also the pleasure of a country drive; if you have the time you should definitely try to sample some of the more out-of-the-way places. Restaurant price categories are as follows: *Moderate,* $10–15; *Inexpensive,* below $10. These prices are for hors d'oeuvres or soup, entrée, and dessert. Not included are drinks, tax, and tips.

ANNAPOLIS. *Inexpensive:* **Burger King.** Main St. and Conduit. Typical hamburger chain.

Little Kitchen. 18 Market Space. Sandwiches, seafood platters.

Market House. Market Space. Take-out hot and cold sandwiches, raw bar.

Old Towne Seafood Shoppe. 105 Main St. Fresh, well-prepared dishes.

BETHESDA. *Inexpensive-Moderate:* **Hot Shoppes.** 7500 Wisconsin Ave. Good food, pleasant family atmosphere.

CHEVY CHASE. *Inexpensive:* **Hot Shoppes Cafeteria.** In Barlow Building on Wisconsin Ave., just outside District of Columbia.

EASTON. *Moderate:* **Easton Manor Restaurant.** US 50. Good Eastern Shore cuisine.

EDGEWOOD. *Moderate:* **House of Hess.** 1709 Emmorton Rd. American food, seafood. Breakfast, lunch and dinner.

FREDERICK. *Moderate:* **Dan-Dee Country Inn.** US 40, five mi. W. Family-style dinners.

Peter Pan Inn. Family recipes.

FROSTBURG. *Inexpensive:* **Barton's Restaurant.** Rte. 220 S. Near Frostburg State College.

GRANTSVILLE. *Moderate:* **Penn Alps.** Pennsylvania Dutch cuisine.

HAGERSTOWN. *Moderate:* **Nick's Airport Inn.** Middleburg Pike, 5 mi. N. on US 11. Steaks, prime rib, seafood.

OCEAN CITY. *Moderate:* **Francis Scott Key.** Colonial atmosphere.

Pirate's Den Coffee Shop. 32nd St. at Baltimore Ave. Good for breakfast and lunch.

Inexpensive: **English Diner.** 21st St. and Philadelphia Ave.

Hall's Coffee Shop. 306 S. Baltimore Ave. Not fancy, but wholesome food.

Happy Jack Pancake House. 403 S. Baltimore Ave. Breakfast and lunch.

House of Pasta. On the Boardwalk at S. Division St. Good Italian specialties.

OXFORD. *Moderate:* **Pier Street Marina and Restaurant.** Historic site.

ROCKVILLE. *Inexpensive-Moderate:* **Hot Shoppes.** Congressional Plaza Shopping Center on Rockville Pike.

NEW JERSEY

From Beauty Pageants to Gambling

The many faceted state of New Jersey is an ideal holiday destination for residents and visitors to the nearby metropolitan areas of New York City, parts of Connecticut, Philadelphia and Wilmington, Delaware.

All parts of this state are well within a full gasoline tank, with most of the state accessible via a round-trip tankful. In these energy-conscious days, this is indeed an important consideration.

In addition, most New Jersey destinations are served via either bus or rail service, and even air service via local airlines, making it easy to spend an economical holiday in this state.

What's Your Interest?

You name it and you'll find it in the wide-ranging facilities available in the Garden State. From backpacking on part of the Appalachian Trail to casino gambling in Atlantic City, there's virtually no limit to the sports and fun facilities available.

There's surf boarding at Avon-by-the-Sea and other points where the surf runs high at times, sailing on many lakes, bicycling along planned trails and historic restorations in what was one of the original land grants of the United States.

You can enjoy the best in theater, comedy, ballet and opera by top talent from Broadway, Hollywood and television at one of many state summer theaters. For example, there's the Garden State Arts Center just off the Garden State Parkway in Holmdel, and an hour's drive from New York City.

The most visible New Jersey attraction is casino gambling in Atlantic City. With nine casinos operating, there is a wealth of fine dining and entertainment available.

Perhaps the biggest one-day travel bargain available today is the Atlantic City casino trip offered by various bus lines from major New Jersey cities and from the New York Port Authority Bus Terminal. For a nominal fee you are transported to Atlantic City in a plan subsidized by the various casinos.

Several Bus Lines in New Jersey, New York and Pennsylvania are offering special casino one-day bus trips with the fare reimbursed in quarters upon arrival in Atlantic City. These low-priced trips vary according to the casino destination; others may offer food and drink, one of the glamorous shows, or even a box of saltwater taffy.

Atlantic City, however, is a small part of New Jersey, which offers a great deal of vacation, sports and exploration. It ranges from mountains in the northwest to historic sites and the famed Jersey Shore, which boasts among the finest sand beaches in the world.

Other than the 48 miles along its northern boundary with New York, New Jersey is washed on all sides by water. Except for the Hawaiian Islands, it is the most completely water-locked state in the union. The western and southern border is the Delaware River, flowing from the New York state line to Delaware Bay. On the east is the Hudson River, New York Bay, and the Atlantic Ocean. Just behind most of this 127-mile ocean front is the gentle Intercoastal Waterway, a series of bays, inlets and marshy streams.

Whether they move by boat or wheels, travelers will find beach and water facilities to meet just about any need, be they fishermen, swimmers, boatsmen, or just plain vacationers. From Sandy Hook, at the entrance to New York Harbor, to Cape May on the Delaware Bay this beach front provides unusual attractions for millions of vacationers each year.

Sandy Hook is part of the Gateway National Recreation area. Its history goes back to 1609, when Henry Hudson tied up here before exploring the river which bears his name. Since that time it has played an historic part in the protection of New York Harbor—through the Revolution, the Civil War, and the development of the port and the city as world leaders. National Park guides can explain the history, including that of the Twin Light Houses, built in 1828. For purely recreational purposes there are swimming, fishing, nature trails, and picnicking.

Quaint towns, posh resort areas, and just plain fun spots pop up all along the shoreline. Short-stay facilities are available along the main shore highways. Detailed information may be obtained from either the town's visitors' agency or from the Department of Labor and Industry, Tourism, CN384, Trenton, N.J. 08625.

Two major toll roads cross the Garden State, providing quick access to virtually every attraction. The Garden State Parkway runs from the New York State border, where it connects with the New York State Thruway, all the way south to the Delaware Bay at Cape May, where you can take the ferry to Lewes, Delaware on your way to Washington, D.C., Virginia and on to Florida.

The other major toll road is the New Jersey Turnpike, which runs on a westerly slant from just above the Lincoln Tunnel connection at its northern end to a crossing below Wilmington, Delaware. You can leave the turnpike at the Philadelphia exit to pick up the Pennsylvania Turnpike on your way out west.

West across the state, out of New York City, I–80 is a six- to eight-lane highway which crosses New Jersey to Delaware Water Gap, one of the state's most delightful mountain settings and a national recreation area. Beyond this one-hour's drive, I–80 continues across the country to San Francisco.

Trenton and Princeton

The state capital is Trenton. Most of the interesting spots can be seen on a walking tour from the capitol building.

Princeton, the home of Princeton University, has more residents in *Who's Who* per capita than any other municipality in the country. There are tours of the university campus, the Educational Testing Service, and the Institute for Advanced Study, where Albert Einstein did his research.

The middle sector of the state has several towns of historic and investigative interest. New Brunswick is the site of Rutgers, the state university; Menlo Park is the home of Edison's Laboratory; Flemington has the highly interesting restored Liberty Village; Camden has the Walt Whitman homestead and the Campbell Museum.

Newark and the North

Newark is the third oldest of the major American cities, and New Jersey's largest. A visit should include the Newark Museum. Paterson is the city selected by Alexander Hamilton as the model for an industrial community and was built according to his ideas around the Great Falls of the Passaic River, 70 feet high and in the center of town.

A drive along the Hudson River in Bergen and Hudson Counties, offers a superb view of the New York City skyline. The Palisades cliffs tower above the river and there are trails and some driveways to scenic points.

The northwestern corner of the state looks much like New England, with rolling hills, lakes, and forests. Points of greater interest are the Franklin Mines, where you can scavenge for minerals and keep what you find, and the 10,000-acre Wawayanda State Forest in Sussex County. The 5,830-acre Worthington Forest, just above the Delaware Water Gap, intersects the Appalachian Trail and is nestled in the Kittatiny Range of mountains. At McAfee is the Great Gorge Vernon Valley ski area and year-round resort.

Even back in the early 1900s, New Jersey was the summer home for many families whose breadwinners commuted to them on weekends while they lived away from the hot, crowded city.

Accommodations range from the super luxury hotels, which represent many big chain operations such as Hilton and Sheraton to many independent motels, to a smattering of charming historic inns.

Also available are summer-long rentals of homes or economical efficiency units where you may enjoy a home away from home with some meals you prepare yourself. (The most desirable long-term rentals are usually booked well in advance.) For information on rentals in the areas in which you are interested, write to the suggested addresses at the end of this chapter.

PRACTICAL INFORMATION FOR NEW JERSEY

TOURIST INFORMATION. Tourism, CN384, Trenton, N.J. 08625.

CAMPING. Among the budget vacation possibilities is camping, which can be a truly different holiday. The tenting equipment is a one-time investment that will pay for itself over and over again. Above all, it provides a fun holiday. For those who have never camped, it is often possible to rent equipment for your first camping experience.

Camping is an entirely different world. You are close to nature, free from regular work routine and are away from everyday cares. Of course, there is the kitchen detail, but the whole family usually participates in the non-routine preparation of meals and snacks. The fisherman of the family may even provide the main course. From nearby farms you may enjoy the freshest vegetables possible. Imagine corn cooked within minutes of being picked. There is no comparison with that bought at a local supermarket after it has been days in transit to the eventual consumer.

Campers can go on their own or with a group of friends to share in this different way of life. Camping is especially fun for youngsters, as there are always pools, ponds or lakes for swimming and boating. There will be memorable times; the fragrance of campfires, breakfast cooking in the early dawn or roasting marshmallows over the open fire, for example.

You can sightsee in the area of the campsite and explore historical places. There are many different social activities offered at campsites, such as square dancing, horseback riding, hayrides and other group activities.

Here in the great open outdoors, there are usually movies in the evenings under the stars, and some campsites will feature covered-dish dinners, when each camp group brings a favorite dish to share with others. On Sundays, there are frequently religious services nearby.

Planning ahead can assure a delightful holiday. Make your reservations in advance to campsites. A booklet listing campgrounds in New Jersey as well as New Jersey State Forests, Parks and Recreation Area campgrounds, is available free from: The Division of Travel and Tourism, CN384, Trenton, N.J. 08625.

MUSEUMS AND GALLERIES. The *New Jersey State Museum* in the Cultural Center, Trenton, adjacent to the state capitol, has a varied and changing series of exhibitions featuring Jerseyana; also a planetarium and an auditorium where lectures, slides, and films are presented. Write the museum in advance for programs and tickets—205 West State St., Trenton, N.J. 08625. The *Newark Museum* has a Junior Museum. *Paterson Museum* has John P. Holland's original submarine from 1878. The S.S. *Ling,* a World War II submarine, has been reactivated and is docked as a museum in a special berth at Borg Park, 140 River St., Hackensack.

Thomas Edison's Laboratory—for 44 years—is in West Orange.

Three unique iron-making villages, preserved and reconstructed, are located in state parks: The 78-room *Ringwood Manor* in Ringwood State Park; *Batsto Village,* where cannons were made during the Revolutionary period, in the Southern Pine Barrens near Hammonton, and *Allaire State Park* in Farmingdale, site of the historic Howell's Iron Works.

Major libraries are the *Harvey Firestone Library* at Princeton University, with over two million volumes, including the writings of Woodrow Wilson, William

Faulkner, and F. Scott Fitzgerald, and *Rutgers University Library,* with its Walt Whitman papers.

HISTORIC SITES: Much of the Revolutionary War was fought in New Jersey and several historic battlefields and headquarters are spread and marked throughout the state. Among the more important and interesting: *Washington Crossing State Park* on the Delaware above Trenton, marks the spot where Colonial troops, under General Washington, crossed the river and attacked and defeated the British at Trenton on Christmas night, 1776. After Trenton, General Washington marched on Princeton and once again defeated the British (see Battle Monument there), then set up winter quarters in Morristown, where he also spent the following winter. A well-preserved and presented series of encampments in and around the town offers a splendid panorama of the days of the Revolution.

FISHING. New Jersey's coastal waters have most species of saltwater fish known in North America: tuna, striped bass, marlin, kingfish, swordfish, flounder, albacore and blue fish. Charter fishing boats are available along the coast, with the principal headquarters at Asbury Park, Briell, Long Beach Island, Atlantic City, the Wildwoods, and Cape May. No license is required for deep-sea and surf fishing. Inland fishing offers trout, pickerel, bass, and sunfish. Licenses are required.

HIKING. The Appalachian Trail runs across the high section of the state, providing excellent backpacking possibilities. The Palisades, along the Hudson, offer some routine mountain climbing on a small but risky scale.

WINTER SPORTS. There's plenty of nearby skiing, especially for the novice or out-of-condition skier. When temperatures are below 32 degrees, the snow-making machines keep the slopes covered at Great Gorge Ski/ Vernon Valley in the hilly northern part of the state. Also at the Arrowhead ski area in Monmouth County. And for cross-country skiing and snowshoeing try the trails at the Stokes State Forest in the northwest part of the state. Other winter sports include ice-boating on the lakes or the Navesink River, ice skating everywhere and even sleigh-riding behind a spirited horse.

SPECTATOR SPORTS. The largest spectator sports attraction in New Jersey is the *Meadowlands,* just four miles west of the Lincoln Tunnel if you're driving. Or you may take the Maplewood Equipment bus lines from the Port Authority Bus Terminal in New York City.

There you may see the standardbred horses trot and pace from mid-January to early August, while the thoroughbreds race from September to the end of December.

The outdoor stadium houses both the *Giants* football team and the *Cosmos* soccer team. The indoor Brendan Byrne Arena houses 20,000 spectators and is home of the *New Jersey Nets* basketball team. The complex also features concerts, tradeshows, and other sports and recreation.

For information on coming events, write the *New Jersey Sports Authority,* Public Affairs Office, East Rutherford, N.J. 07073.

WHAT TO DO WITH THE CHILDREN. *Six Flags Great Adventure* is a combination theme park and safari land on 1,100 acres in the middle of Jackson Township. Located off Exit 7A of the N. J. Turnpike, it is just 75 minutes from New York City. With thousands of wild and exotic animals, it has thrill rides for everyone and over four hours of shows plus a special Kiddie Kingdom section. *Turtleback Zoo* in West Orange offers miniature train rides and animals to see; *Wild West City*, Netcong, offers a bit of the Old West with plenty of action.

Also see *Storybook Land* at Cardiff, 10 miles west of Atlantic City; ride the *Black River and Western Railroad* at Flemington, and try the rides on all Boardwalks, be they in Asbury Park, Atlantic City, or Ocean City. These are just a few of the family-oriented attractions to be seen.

DRINKING LAWS. Legal drinking age is 21. On-the-premises consumption seven days a week. Liquor stores closed Sundays.

HOTELS AND MOTELS. *Moderate*, $30 and up; *Inexpensive*, under $30, all based on double occupancy. Accommodations in Atlantic City may be more expensive.

ATLANTIC CITY. Situation in flux due to casino boom. Write Convention and Tourist Bureau, 16 Central Pier, Atlantic City NJ 08401, for up-to-date information. Tel. (609) 345–7536. One motel likely to maintain fairly moderate rates, even during the summer season, is the *Flamingo*, 3100 Pacific Ave. Weekend reservations required.

CAMDEN (Cherry Hill). *Moderate.* **Best Western Country Squire Motor Lodge,** Cherry Hill. *Inexpensive:* **Bel-Air Motor Lodge,** Maple Shade. **Quality Inn.** Moorestown.

FLEMINGTON. *Moderate:* **Flemington Travel Inn.**

HAMMONTON. *Moderate:* **Winslow Motor Lodge.** Near Winslow and Wharton State Forest.

HIGH POINT STATE PARK. *Moderate:* **High Point Motor Lodge.** RD 4, Sussex.

PRINCETON. *Moderate:* **Holiday Inn.**

TRENTON. *Moderate:* **Trenton Motor Lodge.**

WILDWOODS AND CAPE MAY. More than 10,000 rooms available. Prices cover a wide range and are variable for seasonal and holiday fluctuation. Write: The Cape, Cape May County Department of Public Affairs, P.O. Box 365, Cape May Court House 08210 (609) 886-0901.

DINING OUT. *Moderate*, $7.50–12.50; *Inexpensive*, under $7.50. Prices are for a complete dinner but do not include drinks, tax or tip.

ATLANTIC CITY. *Moderate:* **Abe's Oyster House,** seafood; **The Easy Street Pub,** meat, seafood; **Flying Cloud Café,** seafood; **The Front Porch,** French cuisine; **Le Grand Fromage,** cheese, salads, seafood, meats, chicken, *nouvelle cuisine;* **Al Troiano's Lido,** seafood, meats, poultry; **Los Amigos,** Mexican food; **Orsatti's Warwick Restaurant,** seafood, steaks, Italian; **Shumsky's,** accent on

Jewish dishes; **12 South,** sophisticated sandwiches. *Inexpensive:* **The White House Sub Shop,** hoagies. Local landmark.

CAPE MAY. *Moderate:* **Lobster House.** Feasts on a fishing schooner.

CHATHAM. *Moderate:* **The William Pitt,** 1760 Colonial house.

COLLINGSWOOD. *Moderate:* **The India Palace.** Authentic Indian cuisine. Sagami Japanese Restaurant. Fine Japanese food.

FLEMINGTON. *Moderate:* **Spread Eagle Inn,** Colonial times and food.

LAMBERTVILLE. *Moderate:* **Lambertville House.** Candlelight dining in Early American setting.

MORRISTOWN. *Moderate:* **Black Horse Inn** and **Wedgwood Inn.**

OAKLYN. *Inexpensive–Moderate:* **The Spaghetti House.** Homemade pasta.

PRINCETON. *Moderate:* **Nassau Inn.** Colonial atmosphere.

PARAMUS. *Moderate:* **Old Salt.** Fine seafood in a salty setting.

SPRING LAKE. *Inexpensive–Moderate:* **Old Mill Inn.** Special Senior Citizen's dinners, 3–5 P.M.

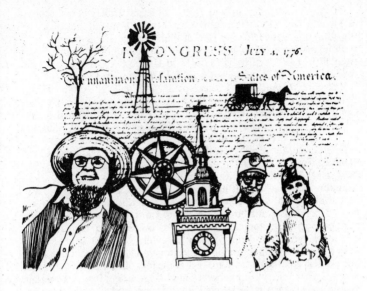

PENNSYLVANIA

Philadelphia, Pittsburgh and the Poconos

Whether it be in the restored Independence National Historical Park, the "most historic square mile in America," or the narrow, cobblestoned streets of Society Hill, or the 8,400 acres of Fairmount Park, a visitor to Philadelphia will find an incredible number of new things to see and do while visiting this historic city.

A good start would be to begin a walking tour at Independence Hall, a red brick Georgian structure, built between 1732 and 1741 as the colonial capitol of Pennsylvania. It was designed by Andrew Hamilton, a lawyer best remembered for his defense of newspaper editor John Peter Zenger in the colonies' first fight for freedom of the press. Nobody dreamed at the time that representatives of a defiant Continental Congress would gather here, that they would ratify the Articles of Confederation, commission George Washington commander in chief of the American armed forces, and sign the Declaration of Independence and the Constitution of the United States—all in this historic hall.

Perhaps the most famous historical treasure connected with Independence Hall is the cracked Liberty Bell, one of the cherished symbols of American freedom. Made in England in 1751, the bell cracked while it was being tested in Philadelphia. Recast, it rang when the Declaration of Independence was signed. It rang also—but cracked again—when knelling for Chief Justice John Marshall. The bell was moved into its own building in front of Independence Hall in 1976.

On one side of Independence Hall is Congress Hall, where Congress met from 1790 to 1800 (legislative chambers authentically restored); on the other side is the Old City Hall of Philadelphia. The Supreme Court Building, constructed in 1789–91, housed the nation's Supreme Court from 1791–1800. Nearby is the Second United States Bank, built between 1819 to 1824, and known as the Old Custom House.

Carpenters' Hall, at 320 Chestnut St., originally the guild hall for Philadelphia's carpenters, served as the meeting place for the First Continental Congress in 1774. The First Bank of the United States, founded by Alexander Hamilton in 1795 when he served as Secretary of the Treasury, is on S. 3rd St.

On 2nd St., between Market and Arch, stands the Georgian Christ Church. Founded in 1695, with the present structure built between 1727 and 1754, it ranks as the oldest of the city's churches. Both Franklin and Washington had family pews at Christ Church, and in its burial ground is Franklin's grave. Although it is impossible to list all of Franklin's contributions to the town, in addition to the Philosophical Society, he founded the *Saturday Evening Post,* the University of Pennsylvania, and Pennsylvania Hospital.

For general strolling around the visitor should see the old homes on Society Hill and the restored market at the foot of Pine St., Head House Square, where every summer weekend brings an outdoor flea market. Barely a block away is the revived South St. area and all its crafts shops, cafés, and charm.

New Philadelphia

The visitor who has finished his tour of old Philadelphia should not miss the attractions at the other end of town. The principal shopping streets are Market St. and the now closed-to-vehicles Chestnut St., with handsome fashionable department stores. Recently opened is the new 125-store Gallery Mall at Market Street between 8th and 10th streets. The latest, most charming redevelopment area in Philadelphia is New Market, at Head House Square in Society Hill. Bordered by Front and 2nd, and Pine and Lombard streets are hundreds of historic nooks and contemporary crannies. One may relax, browse, wander, dine or shop in this historic and picturesque neighborhood facing the Delaware River. Another popular outdoor market is the Italian Market, on 9th St., from Wharton to Christian, where neighborhood merchants sell every variety of food. Open every day but Sunday (Saturday is the day to go!), the visitor is afforded the opportunity to bargain for his meals among hundreds of streetside stands and intimate shops.

Beyond City Hall and Penn Center, where the Tourist Center is located, Benjamin Franklin Parkway begins. Here is the oldest natural history museum in the United States, the Academy of Natural Sciences. The Franklin Institute, a museum of mechanics and applied science, is next door. The Free Library is across Logan Circle. Next along the boulevard comes the Rodin Museum, which houses, barring France, the largest collection of the 19th-century sculptor. In front of the museum is a replica of "The Thinker." The Museum of Art is at the junction of Benjamin Franklin Parkway and Spring Garden St. in Fairmount Park. It houses an extremely fine collection of American art, including works by Thomas Eakins, Gilbert Stuart, Charles Peale, and Thomas Sully.

Also in Fairmount Park are a number of handsome colonial houses. Most impressive of these homes are Mt. Pleasant and Strawberry Mansion. At Robin Hood Dell East and Mann Music Center, in the park, summer concerts are performed in open-air for over 10,000 people.

In 1682 William Penn landed his ship, the *Welcome,* on the left bank of the Delaware River. That spot, now known as Penn's Landing, has today become the largest freshwater port in the world. Penn's Landing offers an exciting and scenic array of majestic sailing vessels (Admiral Dewey's USS *Olympia,* and the 18th-century Portuguese fishing vessel, the *Gazelo Primeiro,* docks at the landing summer months only), World War II submarine USS *Becuna,* unique restaurants, museums, landscaped gardens, and much more.

A short walk away, discover one of the most exciting, inviting, delighting places in Philadelphia: NewMarket at Head House Square, in Society Hill. NewMarket is hundreds of historic nooks and contemporary crannies. A visitor has a chance to relax, dine, wander, and shop in one of America's most historic neighborhoods. The Gallery, at 9th and Market Streets, offers 125 stores and ethnic restaurants.

PRACTICAL INFORMATION FOR PHILADELPHIA

HOW TO GET AROUND. *By bus:* The fare is 75 cents, exact change. Maps of the bus system are available at newsstands.

By subway: Fare is 75 cents, with exact change. Lateral transfers for 15 cents.

By taxi: Yellow Cab is major carrier in town.

From the airport: Bus to downtown hotels. Yellow Cab limousine and regular cab are more expensive.

TOURIST INFORMATION. The Convention and Visitors Bureau is at 1525 J. F. Kennedy Blvd., downtown, 215–568–6599. Special Events Information: Philly Fun Phone 568–7255.

CITY PARKS. *Fairmount Park,* with 8,400 acres, is the largest city-owned park in the world and houses America's oldest zoo and the Philadelphia Art Museum. Along the Parkway one may also visit the Franklin Institute and the Academy of Natural Sciences. The wide, lovely boulevard is the scene of many activities: biking, hiking, tennis, picnicking, and sculling. It has more cherry blossoms than Washington, D.C., a huge azalea garden, and eight Colonial houses.

MUSEUMS AND GALLERIES. The *Academy of Natural Sciences,* 19th and Franklin Parkway, is the nation's oldest museum of its kind, with a two-story-high dinosaur, fossils, and children's museum. The Franklin Institute, 20th and Franklin Parkway, has 6,000 exhibits including a beating heart to walk through. The *Rodin Museum* on the Franklin Parkway, contains the largest collection outside France of the sculptor's works. The *Philadelphia Museum of Art* is a major assemblage of medieval, renaissance, and modern art. It is one of the world's leading museums and offers tours in eight languages.

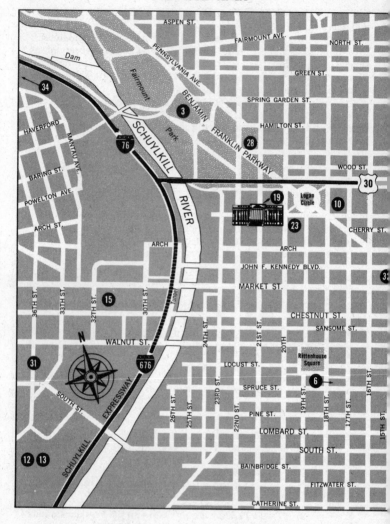

Points of Interest

1) Academy of Music
2) American Philosophical Society
3) Philadelphia Museum of Art
4) Antique Row
5) Arch Street Friends Meeting House
6) Art Alliance
7) Atwater Kent Museum
8) Betsy Ross House
9) Carpenter's Hall

10) Cathedral of St. Peter and St. Paul
11) City Hall
12) Civic Center
13) Convention Hall
14) Congress Hall
15) Drexel University
16) Elfreth's Alley
17) Forrest Theater
18) Franklin's Grave

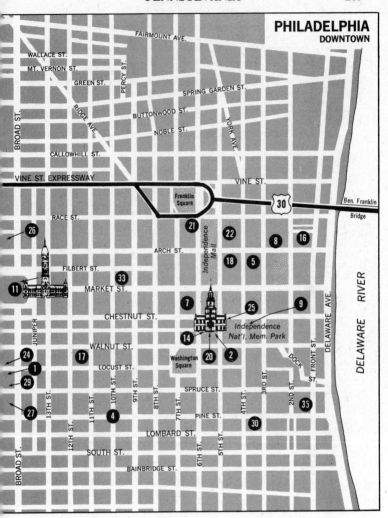

PHILADELPHIA
DOWNTOWN

19) Franklin Institute and Fels Planetarium
20) Independence Hall and Mall
21) Franklin Court
22) U.S. Mint
23) Moore College of Art
24) New Locust Theater
25) Old City Hall
26) Pennsylvania Academy of Fine Arts
27) Phila. College of Art

28) Rodin Museum
29) Shubert Theater
30) Theater of Living Arts
31) University of Pennsylvania
32) Visitors Bureau
33) The Gallery
34) Zoological Gardens
35) New Market

The *Pennsylvania Academy of Fine Arts,* Broad and Cherry Sts., is noted for its collection of American portraits from Revolutionary times to the present. The *University Museum,* 33rd and Spruce, has an extensive collection of ancient and primitive archeological and anthropological pieces from all over the world. Other museums are: the *American Swedish Historical Museum,* in South Philadelphia; the *Atwater Kent Museum* on S. 7th St., which tells Philadelphia's history; the *Barnes Foundation,* in nearby Merion and open by appointment, has a world-famous impressionist collection. The Norman Rockwell Museum, 601 Walnut St., displays different forms of works covering sixty years of this artist's career. The Brandywine River Museum, in nearby Chadds Ford, is primarily devoted to the paintings of three generations of the Wyeth family.

Numerous galleries and antique shops are in center city on Spruce, Pine, and the lower end of South St. Among those to see are the *Works* sculpture gallery and *Photopia* photography gallery.

TOURS. The *U.S. Mint,* 5th and Arch, is the largest of the country's three mints. *City Hall,* larger than the U.S. Capitol and fashioned after the Louvre in Paris, has guided tours and an elevator ride to the top, with a view of the city. The acoustically perfect *Academy of Music* is home of the Philadelphia Orchestra and is a national landmark. *Masonic Temple* on Broad St., has separate rooms for Corinthian, Ionic, Italian Renaissance, Norman, Gothic, Oriental, and Egyptian architectural periods. *Philadelphia Stock Exchange* is the nation's oldest. For free group tour information (Acme Bakery, Nabisco, U. S. Post Office, others), call 568–6599.

SIGHTSEEING. Visitors can see the attractions of Philadelphia in different ways. *Gray Line Tours* offers a variety of narrated sightseeing tours in air-conditioned, deluxe buses. *Philadelphia Carriage Tours* takes you through Philadelphia's colonial neighborhoods in restored 19-century horse-drawn carriages. The *Fairmount Park Trolley Buses* use Victorian trolleys to take visitors through the Park, its museums, and attractions.

GARDENS. *Bartram's Gardens,* 54th and Elmwood, is the nation's first botanical garden. *Morris Arboretum,* Chestnut Hill, is a research center for the University of Pennsylvania. The *Schuylkill Valley Nature Center,* at 8480 Hagy's Mill Rd., has a wildlife reserve and nature museum. *Longwood Gardens,* Kennett Square, for exquisite blooms.

SPORTS. Philadelphia has every major sport: *football* Eagles, *baseball* Phillies at Veterans Stadium. Fever, *indoor soccer,* at Spectrum; Stanley Cup champion *hockey* Flyers and *basketball* 76ers at the Spectrum arena; and *racing* at Keystone and Liberty Bell track. Major *college basketball* games are at the Palestra. Philadelphia also hosts the U.S. Professional Indoor Tennis Championships, Jan. or Feb; the Penn Relays in April; the Dad Vail Regatta in May; the IVB-Philadelphia Golf Classic in July; and the Army-Navy football classic held at JFK Stadium late November or early December.

WHAT TO DO WITH THE CHILDREN. A good double treat is the *Academy of Natural Science* and *Franklin Institute* across the street from each other. (Children's Nature Museum explores fossil caves, dinosaur footprints.) *Please Touch Museum,* 1910 Cherry Street. The *Philadelphia Zoo* has a special Children's Zoo on its grounds. *Schuykill Valley Nature Center* has trails where live animals can be fed by children. The *zoo* has a special children's section. The *Philadelphia Orchestra* has children's concerts at the Academy of Music and Robin Hood Dell. Temple's Theatre Dept. produces children's theatre on Saturdays. 1619 Walnut St., Stage Three.

HOTELS AND MOTELS are rated: *Moderate,* $30–35; *Inexpensive,* under $30. For information on **bed-and-breakfast** accommodations, contact Bed & Breakfast of Philadelphia, P.O. Box 101, Oreland 19075.

Moderate: **Holiday Inn.** Independence Hall. 4th and Arch. Convenient to historic areas.

Penn Center Inn, 20th & Market Sts.

Treadway Motor Inn. 4200 Roosevelt Blvd. In northeast section.

Also **Holiday Inns** at: Airport, 18th & Market Sts., and at University City (36th & Chestnut Sts.).

Philadelphia Best Western. City Line Avenue.

Philadelphia Centre Hotel. 1725 Kennedy Blvd.

Also **Sheraton Hotels** at: 9461 Roosevelt Blvd., Airport, King of Prussia, and Wilmington, Del.

Inexpensive: **Cresheim Arms,** Allens Lane and Bryan. Located in historic Germantown section of city. Quiet atmosphere.

DINING OUT. Restaurants are classed as: *Moderate,* $10–15; *Inexpensive,* under $10, this is for a complete meal without drinks.

Moderate: **Dante's.** 10th and Christian Sts. Center of Italian section. Tasty dishes, reasonable prices.

La Diet. 1634 Ludlow St. Center city locale. Calorie count beside every dish. Also has take-out service.

Imperial Inn. 941 Race St.,,, heart of Chinese section. Exotic Far East cuisine.

Oyster House. 1516 Sansom St. Seafood specialties, wines and spirits.

Inexpensive: **Triangle Tavern.** 10th and Reed Sts. Popular South Philadelphia restaurant. Italian dishes. 40s live music.

Bourse. Independence Mall East. Third floor of renovated mall features international potpourri of restaurants.

Eden. 1527 Chestnut and 3701 Chestnut Street. Unusual cafeteria.

Mayflower. 220 N. 10th St. Mandarin, Szechuan and Cantonese.

Stroli's Bar. 1528 Dickinson. Homemade pasta, real Italian atmosphere.

Cafes and Cabarets: **The Library.** 2 Bala Cynwyd Plaza. Sophisticated disco.

Grendel's Lair Cabaret. 500 South St. Dinner, drinks, intimate revues.

Corned Beef Academy. 121 S. 16th St., good, fast deli.

EXPLORING PITTSBURGH

Every city impresses people differently. Pittsburgh prevails in its own style. To most of the nation, "Pittsburgh" suggests steel, red hot from the furnace, the tense luxury of executive suites, and barges easing up the Ohio River. These images project strength, energy, and ambition, which accurately depict Pittsburgh's atmosphere.

The heritage of civic-minded men of wealth becomes especially apparent as we move into the Oakland section. In or near Schenley Park are two large universities, Carnegie-Mellon and the school-in-a-skyscraper, Pittsburgh University's Cathedral of Learning. The area also includes Phipps Conservatory, exhibiting botanical wonders; the Pittsburgh Playhouse and America's first community-supported TV station, WQED; fine art on the inside of the Frick Building and the outside of Gothic St. Paul's Cathedral. In the neighborhood are the Heinz Chapel, with its superb stained glass windows, and the Stephen Foster Memorial, which holds a special program every January commemorating the works of the American composer.

PRACTICAL INFORMATION FOR PITTSBURGH

HOW TO GET AROUND. *By bus:* Minimum fare is $1, but varies for different zones within city. *By taxi:* Cabs are expensive, $1 to start the meter. *From the airport:* Yellow Cab limousine to downtown. Good airport bus service.

TOURIST INFORMATION. Pittsburgh Convention and Visitors Bureau, 4 Gateway Center, answers all questions. 412–281–7711.

MUSEUMS AND GALLERIES. The city goes all out on its 3 Rivers Arts Festival, held annually, outdoors, throughout Gateway Center. The *Frick Museum,* 7227 Reynolds Ave., Homewood, has an exquisite collection of French, Italian, and Flemish Renaissance paintings. *Henry Clay Frick Fine Arts Building,* in Schenley Park, houses the Lochoff Collection of fine Renaissance works and an old Italian-style cloister.

The *Pittsburgh History and Landmarks Foundation* preserves the history of Allegheny County. The *Old Post Office Museum,* 701 Allegheny Square West, is a restored Italian Renaissance building featuring changing historical exhibits of architecture, fashions, and nostalgia. Andrew Carnegie established the *Carnegie Institute* at 4400 Forbes Ave., housing a library, museums, art gallery, and music hall—the focal point of culture in the Oakland section. Its *Museum of Natural History* has over 5 million items including a 20-foot skeleton of a tyrannosaurus dinosaur. Nearby in Oakland, the *Cathedral of Learning* has 19 international rooms, each furnished in the style of the country it represents. Most contemporary art can be seen at the *Pittsburgh Center for the Arts,* 6300 5th Ave., with exhibits changing monthly. Other galleries include the *Art Institute of Pittsburgh,* 526 Penn Ave.; The *Kingpitcher Gallery for Contemporary Art,* 5219 5th Ave.; and the *Pittsburgh Plan for Art,* 407 S. Craig Street.The *Stephen Foster Memorial Hall,* Forbes and Bigelow, has the songwriter's memorabilia. The *Historical Society of Western Pennsylvania,* 4338 Bigelow, has an early America firearms collection.

HISTORIC SITES. Pittsburgh, focal point of the French and Indian War, unfortunately has only one landmark still standing, the Block House of *Ft. Pitt.* Dating from 1764, it is in Point State Park, at the conflux of Pittsburgh's three great rivers. Not far from the blockhouse is the Fort Pitt Museum, a unique reconstruction of the Monongahela bastion. A few miles north of Pittsburgh is *Old Economy,* on Ohio River Blvd., in Ambridge, site of the Harmony Society's 19th-century experiment in communal living.

TOURS. *Gateway Clipper,* Station Square Dock, operates cruises on the three rivers. Inquire for schedules, generally May–September.

GARDEN. *Phipps Conservatory,* Schenley Park, is a tropical forest of exotic plants with rare blooms under glass and an orchid collection. Second largest of its kind in the country. Spring & fall flower shows are fabulous. The *Conservatory-Aviary,* West Park at W. Ohio and Arch Sts., displays exotic and domestic birds and plants in native habitat settings.

SPORTS. Three Rivers Stadium provides headquarters for the 1979 World Champion Pittsburgh Pirates and the Super Bowl champion Pittsburgh Steelers. The Pittsburgh Spirit soccer team plays at the Civic Arena. The NHL Penguins play in the Civic Arena. The Pitt Panthers, the number-one team in the nation in 1977, play major college-level football. Boyce Park Ski Area has beginner and intermediate slopes. Allegheny County boasts it has more golf courses than any other U.S. county.

About 1½ hours east from the city limits are a host of ski resorts that dot the Laurel Mountains—Seven Springs, Hidden Valley, White Mtn., and Bear Rock. For those more adventuresome, white-water rafting is at nearby Ohiopyle on the Youghiogheny.

WHAT TO DO WITH THE CHILDREN. The *Carnegie Museum* and its dinosaurs are always a delight. *Buhl Science Center* has working displays. *Highland Park* has a regular and children's zoo. The *Arden Trolley Museum* in nearby Washington is open weekends. *Kennywood Park,* 4800 Kennywood Blvd. in W. Mifflin, has four roller coasters, Kiddieland, gardens, and picnic areas. *White Swan Park,* 3 mi. SE of Greater Pittsburgh Airport, has amusement rides, miniature golf, and picnic areas. *Lovelace Marionettes,* at 5888½ Ellsworth Ave., Shadyside, will delight children and adults. The *Pittsburgh Puppet Theater* and the *Conservatory Children's Theater* both run in the summer.

HOTELS AND MOTELS. *Moderate,* $30–35; *Inexpensive,* under $30. Rates are based on single room double occupancy.

Moderate: **Howard Johnson Motor Lodge,** opposite the Greater Pittsburgh International Airport.

Holiday House. 3755 William Penn Highway, Monroeville. Supper club.

Quality Inn Redwood. Banksville and Potomac (5 minutes from downtown). Piano bar.

Sheraton Motor Inn. 624 Lysle Rd. in McKeesport suburb.

Inexpensive: **Conley's Motor Inn.** 3550 William Penn Highway, Monroeville. Pool, restaurant.

Tonidale Motor Inn. Rts. 22–30, W. Oakdale, between downtown and airport.

Viking Motor Lodge. Banksville Road. Five minutes from downtown. Entertainment nightly.

DINING OUT. Restaurants are classed as: *Moderate,* $10–15; *Inexpensive,* under $10. This is for a complete meal without drinks.

Moderate: **Alexander Graham Bell's.** Market Square. Telephones on every table.

Samreny's. 4808 Baum Blvd. Lebanese, in University area.

Sarah's. 52 S. 10th. Eastern European cuisine; only one like it in town.

3 Lions Law & Finance Bldg. Downtown gathering spot. Convenient location.

Inexpensive: **Johnny Garneau's.** 6th St., downtown. Smorgasbord or regular cuisine.

Nello's Golden Lion. Italian in McKee's Rocks, suburb.

Smithfield Cafe. Smithfield St. Downtown. Organ music Fri. and Sat.

Wiegand's Cafe. 422 Forland St. German cuisine.

EXPLORING PENNSYLVANIA

The Poconos

The Pocono Mountains resort area is a vast playland of some 2,400 square miles in northeast Pennsylvania, and only a few hours away from New York or Philadelphia. This popular retreat for eastern city dwellers is dotted with lakes, mountains, streams (Pocono is an Indian word meaning "stream between the mountains"), and fine hotels. It offers outstanding fishing, golfing, hunting, swimming, skiing, camping and hiking on the Appalachian trail. And for honeymooners, the Poconos offer nine special honeymoon resorts that cater only to newlyweds as part of the area's claim to be the America's Honeymoon Capital.

The Delaware Water Gap is a famous scenic entrance to the Poconos. This deep, tree-covered gorge is especially beautiful when leaves turn in autumn, and when the mountain laurel blossoms in the spring. Just west and north of the gap are the resort areas of: Stroudsburg; Big Pocono State Park with a view atop Camelback Mountain (also a winter ski center); and Mount Pocono center. Promised Land State Park, with excellent camping facilities, is the center of the Pocono game country, and some wild deer are tame enough to wander into campsites. Nearby is Lake Wallenpaupack, Pennsylvania's largest lake and regional watersports center. Near Milford are the bluffs of Coykendall's Pool, where thousands of swallows roost from April to August. In Bushkill are the region's largest waterfalls, Bushkill Falls—the "Niagara of Pennsylvania."

Valley Forge

A necessary stop when leaving or entering the Philadelphia area is Valley Forge. Here Washington's ill-clad, poorly fed, badly supplied Continental Army suffered through the cold winter of 1777–78, after the British had occupied Philadelphia. It was at this hallowed spot, Valley Forge, that victory and defeat walked side by side and were scarcely distinguishable. Today, Valley Forge is a 2,300-acre national park, with historic displays and relics. History-minded visitors will find a host of other fascinating attractions in and around Valley Forge country. There's the birthplace of Daniel Boone, and Mill Grove, restored first home in America of naturalist John James Audubon. Another important historic site is Washington Crossing State Park, further north, along the Delaware River, where Washington made the historic fording in 1776 en route to battles at Trenton and Princeton. The park has an observation tower and some still standing Revolutionary period houses. Washington Crossing is also a good jumping off point for a tour of Bucks County, one of the state's largest and loveliest, noted for rolling farm lands and the artists' town of New Hope.

Northwest Pennsylvania

Presque Isle, at the northwest tip of the state, holds an important place in American history, for it was in Presque Isle Bay that Oliver Hazard Perry, in 1813, constructed ships that met the British in combat in the Battle of Lake Erie. In nearby Erie, the commodore's flagship, the U.S.S. *Niagara,* is docked. Erie has the Perry Memorial House, also known as Dickson's Tavern, which served as Perry's quarters before the battle and later was a "station" of the Underground Railroad before the Civil War. Erie also has a replica of the blockhouse in which Revolutionary hero "Mad" Anthony Wayne died in 1806.

Between Erie and Pittsburgh is Titusville, where Edwin L. Drake drilled the first productive oil well on August 27, 1859. Replicas of the early riggings still stand. Also on the road towards Pittsburgh, in Ambridge, is the 19th-century religious community of Old Economy with many original structures open to visit. A final site in the western end of the state is Ft. Necessity, a National Battlefield, in Uniontown. In 1754, at the age of 22, George Washington lost his first battle at the fort during the French and Indian campaign. Washington's commanding officer, General Braddock, is buried here.

Gettysburg and Central Pennsylvania

In the middle of the state is Gettysburg National Battlefield, perhaps the nation's most famous Civil War monument. It was here, on July 3, 1863, that the continent's greatest artillery battle was fought, and General Lee was forced to retreat. Lincoln delivered his famous address on November 19, 1863.

York is another central Pennsylvania attraction. This city served as the colonial capital between September 1777 and June 1778 and was a leading weapons producer. North is Harrisburg, the state capital. The city is abustle when the legislature sits, and also has pleasant walks and gardens on the banks of the Susquehanna River. The Italian Renaissance capitol building was modeled after St. Peter's in Rome. Barely 12 miles away, following the delicious aroma, is Hershey, one of the last company towns in America. Planned and laid out by Milton Hershey in 1903, the former Lancaster caramel manufacturer decided to make chocolate here. The town now has a resort hotel, motor lodge, convention center, Hersheypark and Chocolate World (free), gardens with 42,000 roses and 30,000 tulips, a museum and a community center built by Hershey. Two streets in town are Chocolate and Cocoa Aves.

Pennsylvania Dutch Country

In and around Lancaster is the renowned Pennsylvania Dutch country. This is a world apart from modern America. The Amish farmers sport full beards and broad black hats; their wives don bonnets and all work is done without the use of power tools or conveniences. Lancaster itself, founded in 1718, was capital of the U.S. for one day on September 27, 1777, and is still regional center for farm produce and open air markets. The religious inhabitants of the region are collectively called the "plain people" and include the Amish, the Brethren or Dunkards, and the Mennonites. All vary, to some extent, in their beliefs, conservatism, somber dress, but all are master farmers of the very rich soil. Pennsylvania Dutch cooking is unique and based on the idea of seven sweet and seven sour dishes that comprise a delicious smorgasbord—pickles, relishes, apple butter, dumplings, pretzels, molasses, and shoofly pie to name a few. Other sites in the area are James Buchanan's house in Lancaster and the Pennsylvania Farm Museum at Landis Valley.

PRACTICAL INFORMATION FOR PENNSYLVANIA

 HOW TO GET THERE. *By car:* From New York on the east, I–95 runs to Philadelphia; in the northeast, I–81 passes through Binghamton, N.Y. to Scranton and Harrisburg. I–80 and Pennsylvania Tpke. bisect the state on east-west axis. I–79 runs from Erie to Pittsburgh and Morgantown, W. Va.

By train: Amtrak serves Philadelphia, Harrisburg, Lancaster, and Pittsburgh.
By bus: Greyhound, *Trailways, Lake Shore System* serve selected cities.
By air: Philadelphia and Pittsburgh have major airports.

TOURIST INFORMATION. The Bureau of Travel Development, Pennsylvania Dept. of Commerce, 416 Forum Bldg., Harrisburg, Pa. 17120.

  MUSEUMS AND GALLERIES. In Gettysburg: *Gettysburg National Museum,* largest collection of Civil War relics; *Hall of Presidents,* at National Cemetery has life-sized wax figures of all Presidents; *Lincoln Room Museum,* where he finished address; *Horse and Buggy Museum;* and *Gettysburg Observation Tower.* In Chadds Ford, Chester County, the *Brandywine River Museum,* housing works of the famous Wyeth family. York, one time capital of the United States, has over 300 original *Currier and Ives* lithographs.

In Strasburg, near Lancaster, state-operated *railroad museum,* with Strasburg Railroad nearby. *Pennsylvania Farm Museum,* north of Lancaster with rural America collection. Doylestown, Bucks County, has *Mercer Museum of Early American Tools and Implements* and *Moravian Pottery and Tile Works Museum.* At *Reading Public Museum and Art Gallery,* fine exhibitions of art, science, and commerce. Dutch folk art. A glimpse into the life of Christopher Columbus after he made his historic voyage may be had in central Penna. at the *Boal Estate,* in Boalsburg. *Colonial Pennsylvania Plantation Farm,* Media, Pa. 18th-century farm life in Ridley Creek State Park.

 HISTORIC SITES. *Washington Crossing State Park,* near Buckingham, was the General's embarkation point for battles of Trenton and Princeton. New Hope has *Parry House* from 1700s and the *New Hope–Delaware Canal Locks* and the *Barge Landing* (1890). Erie is site of *Ft. Le Boeuf* from French and Indian Wars; the *Wayne Blockhouse,* last home of "Mad" Anthony Wayne; and Oliver Hazard Perry's U.S.S. *Niagara* and *Perry Memorial House.* Near Lancaster are two Amish farms, *Amish Farm and House* and Amish *Homestead.* *Pennsbury Manor* in Morrisville, is a re-creation of William Penn's house of 1699–1701. Offers the largest collection of 17th-century antiques in Pennsylvania. In Fallingston are three hundred years of American architectural history. *Gettysburg National Military Park* encompasses numerous museums, tours, monuments, and points of interest.

TOURS. *Casser, Parker, Tauck, Greyhound, Gray Line,* and *Trailways* all run out of New York to Pennsylvania Dutch country and other areas.

Walking Tour of Pennsylvania Capitol (every ½ hour), or Self-Guided Walking tour of Harrisburg. Call 717–787–6810.

Free tour of Mill Grove, home of James Audubon. Free tours of Valley Forge (bike rentals available). Free tour of Peter Wentz Farmstead. Centre Point, off Route 73. 18th century gardens.

DRINKING LAWS. Legal age is 21. Bottled liquor only sold in state stores.

SUMMER SPORTS. Some of the best known *golf courses* are Hershey, Shawnee-on-Delaware, Pocono Manor, Merion, Oakmont, and Ligonier. Williamsport annually hosts the World Series of *Little League Baseball.* Major league *baseball* in Philadelphia and Pittsburgh. *Flat horse racing* at: Liberty Bell, Keystone, Philadelphia; Commodore Downs, Erie; and Penn National, near Hershey. *Harness racing* at: Liberty Bell; Pocono Downs, between Scranton and Wilkes-Barre; and the Meadows, Meadowlands. Lakes and streams throughout the state provide excellent *fishing.* Licenses required. Pennsylvania has miles of *hiking* trails including the Horse Shoe Trail and a section of the Appalachian Trail. Lakes and rivers also abundant for *canoeing, sailing, boating, white water rafting, and swimming.* Sand *beaches* on Lake Erie. More than 100 state parks bring Pennsylvania near its goal of "a state park within 25 miles of every Pennsylvanian." For campground directory, write to Bureau of Travel Development, 416 Forum Bldg., Harrisburg, Pa. 17120. For information on state parks, write: Pennsylvania Bureau of State Parks, P. O. Box 2063, Harrisburg, Pa. 17120.

WINTER SPORTS. The Pocono Mountains have the northeast Pennsylvania centers for *skiing* at Big Boulder, Camelback, Buck Hill, Pocono Manor, Jack Frost, Elk Mountain, and Shawnee Mountain. Other winter sports: *ice-skating, tobogganing, ice-boating, ice-fishing.* In northwestern Allegheny Mountains, skiing at: Seven Springs, Laurel Mountain, Hidden Valley, Bear Rocks, and Blue Knob. Other ski areas scattered throughout the state. *Hockey* popular in Philadelphia and Pittsburgh.

WHAT TO DO WITH THE CHILDREN. Parks featuring fairy tales and characters from children's literature: *Sesame Place,* Langhorne; *Storybook Forest,* Ligonier; *Dutch Wonderland,* Lancaster; *Moon Valley Park,* Milford, *Pocono Action Park,* Tannersville, *Memorytown,* Mt. Pocono. *Fairyland Forest,* Conneaut Lake Park. Underground caves and caverns: *Indian Caves,* Spruce Creek; *Laurel Cavern,* Uniontown; *Crystal Cave and Onyx Cave,* Kutztown; *Indian Echo,* Hummelstown, near Hershey; *Lost River Caverns,* Bethlehem; *Penn's Cave,* Centre Hall. Coal mines with tours: *Seldom Seen Valley Mine,* St. Boniface; *Pioneer Coal Mine Tunnel,* Pottsville, and Railroads: *East Broad Top Railroad, Strasburg Rail Road,* the *W.K. & S.,* Kempton; and the *Gettysburg Railroad.* Good zoos in Philadelphia and Pittsburgh. Amusement Parks include *Dorney Park* in Allentown, and *Hersheypark* in Hershey. While in Hershey, visit Hershey's *Chocolate World.* Near Altoona, there is the *Forest Zoo* and an *Animal Safari and Game Preserve.* The sight of rattlesnakes being milked of their venom attracts thousands to the *Pocono Reptile Farm,* near Bushkill. The "Grand Canyon of Pennsylvania" is upstate near Wellsboro.

HOTELS AND MOTELS. *Moderate,* $25–35; *Inexpensive,* below $25, double occupancy.

ERIE. *Moderate:* **The Bel-Aire Motel.**
Howard Johnson's. Conveniently located.

Niagara. View of Erie Harbor.
Spartan Inns of America. Popular.

GETTYSBURG. *Moderate:* **The Holiday Inn.**
Quality Inn Larson's. Next to General Lee's old home.

YORK. *Moderate:* **Yorktowne.** Midtown.
Inexpensive: **Modernaire.** Small, with pool.

HARRISBURG. *Moderate:* **Congress Inn.** Pleasant accommodations.

 DINING OUT. Restaurants are grouped as: *Moderate,* $10-15; *Inexpensive,* $10, this is for a complete meal without drinks.

ERIE. *Moderate:* **Barnacle Bill's Eastern Shore.** Seafood.

GETTYSBURG. *Moderate:* **Dutch Cupboard.** Pennsylvania Dutch menu.
Farnsworth House Dining. Original Civil War decor, over 100 bullet holes visible.
Inexpensive: **Hickory Bridge Farm.** Restored early American farmhouse.

HARRISBURG. *Expensive:* **The Gazebo Room.** Near the capitol.
Inn 22. Steaks, ribs, shrimp.
Penn-Harris Motor Inn.
Inexpensive: **Castiglia's.** Pasta.

LANCASTER. *Moderate:* **Stock Yard Inn.** Ribs, steak, seafood.
Two Pennsylvania Dutch "family style" restaurants are **Good n' Plenty** in Smoketown, and **Plain and Fancy** in Bird-in-Hand. Both feature family-style eating and incorporate the notion of seven sour and seven sweet courses. Good home cooking.
Inexpensive: **The Willows.** Dutch cooking, good for families.

NEW HOPE. *Moderate:* **Hacienda.** 36 W. Mechanic St. Attractive decor, interesting menu.
Inexpensive: **Mother's.** N. Main Street. Extremely good food at modest prices.
The Ritz. Mechanic Street. Informal atmosphere, part-outdoors.

VALLEY FORGE. *Moderate:* **The Buoy I.** Lancaster Pike, Paoli (10 minutes from Valley Forge). Fish specialties highlight a diverse menu.
Valle's. Rte. 202 and Henderson Road, King of Prussia (5 minutes from Valley Forge). Large selection of meat and seafood dishes.
Victoria Station. Rte. 202 and Henderson Road, King of Prussia. Attractive decor, good family fare.

 POCONOS HOTELS AND MOTELS offer so many types of accommodations and plans at each of the large resorts that prudent vacationers will want to examine them in detail by sending for brochures. The categories used for the survey in this section are, for double occupancy: *Moderate* $25–35 and *Inexpensive* $25 and lower.

CANADENSIS. *Moderate:* **Laurel Grove Inn and Cottages.** This establishment has a 9-hole golf course and all-weather tennis facilities. Heated pool, rec room, live music.

Linder's Hillside Lodge. State 390, 1 mi. N of town. One of the newest in the area, it's in an attractive woodland setting. Motels and cottages available. Tennis courts, golf nearby; entertainment and dancing, 3 meals daily. There's a heated swimming pool.

Inexpensive: **Goose Pond Run Lodge.** Housekeeping cottages, fully equipped kitchen, fireplace.

CRESCO. *Moderate:* **Crescent Lodge.** State 191 at State 940. Tennis, other indoor and outdoor games. Golf, riding, and skiing nearby. Restaurant and cocktail lounge.

Moderate: **Naomi Cottages.** State 390, 1 mi. N of town. In a secluded area, this motel has tennis, shuffleboard, and a rec room. There's a coin laundry; early check-out time.

DELAWARE WATER GAP. *Moderate:* **Howard Johnson's Motor Lodge.** Near exit 53 from I-80. Heated pool, cocktail lounge. Fishing, hunting, golfing, skiing nearby.

EAST STROUDSBURG. *Inexpensive:* **Paramount Motel.** US 209 Business. This in-town establishment is next door to a restaurant and provides a pool and some games. Good place to locate if your interest in the Poconos is exploring rather than resort living.

MOUNT POCONO. *Inexpensive:* **Hawthorne Inn and Cottages.** W of State 611, 1 mi. S of town. Swimming pool, tennis, playground, golf, riding, Cellar Bar. Open June 22 to Sept. 4.

STROUDSBURG. *Moderate:* **Yoga Spa Retreat.** Slim diet programs for men and women.

Sheraton Pocono Inn. 1220 W. Main St. Indoor courtyard with pool, sauna, gift shop, recreation room, indoor putting green, swimming pool, coffee shop, restaurant, cocktail lounge.

There are nine Honeymoon or "Couples Only" resorts in the Poconos:

Cove Haven, Lakeville.
Birchwood, E. Stroudsburg.
Mt. Airy Lodge, Mt. Pocono.
Paradise Stream, Mt. Pocono.
Penn Hills, Analomink.
Pocono Gardens Lodge, Cresco.
Pocono Palace, Echo Lake.
Strickland's, Mt. Pocono.
Summit, Tannersville.

 DINING OUT in the Poconos means one thing above all else—Pocono Mountain trout, the specialty of many restaurants in this area. In addition to trout, of course, are many other foods associated with Pennsylvania, including Pennsylvania Dutch cuisine. The vast recent growth of hotels, motels and inns in the area has resulted in a similar proliferation of restaurants, and you can now get almost any kind of dish. US highways, such as 6 and 209, are dotted with truck stops and these are at their best around breakfast time.

Price categories for the region are: *Moderate* $10–15 and *Inexpensive* under $10. These prices include first course or soup, entrée and dessert. Not included are drinks, tip and the Pennsylvania 6% food tax. For a more complete explanation of price categories, see *Facts at Your Fingertips* at the beginning of this volume.

BUSHKILL. *Moderate:* **Fernwood Gaslight Lounge Restaurant.** On US 209, 1½ mi. SW of town. Dinner, music, dancing, and entertainment nightly.

EAST STROUDSBURG. *Moderate:* **Peppe's Ristorante.** Complete luncheon and dinner menus, cocktails from the Carriage Pub. At Eagle Valley Mall, junction of Business 209 and 477.

GREENTOWN. *Moderate:* **White Beauty View Resort.** State 507, Lake Wallenpaupack. Dining room open to public, specializes in Italian and American cooking. Spectacular, expansive view of the lake from dining rooms and cocktail bar.

HAWLEY. *Moderate:* **Perna's.** State 590, 3 mi. SW of town. Hawley is on the northern edge of the Pocono region and you'll see more nature and fewer resorts driving around here. At this locally popular chef-owned restaurant, you'll enjoy the homemade Italian dishes.

MOUNT POCONO. *Moderate:* **Highland Inn.** State 611. Completely renovated, cocktail lounge. Features home-cooked food. Private dining room for groups. Opens at noon. Rustic fireside lounge.

POCONO PINES. *Inexpensive:* **King of the Poconos.** Hearty breakfast fare.

STROUDSBURG. *Moderate:* **Beaver House.** 1001 N. 9th St. (State 611, 1 mi. N of town). Six dining rooms. Maine lobsters, sirloin steaks, shore dinners. Cocktails. Open at mealtimes only.
Inexpensive: **Historic Henryville House.** State 191 at 715, 6 mi. N of town. Authentically restored Victorian inn. Museum rooms open to public. All food and pastries are prepared on the premises.

TANNERSVILLE. *Inexpensive:* **Inn at Tannersville.** Good, varied menu.

VIRGINIA

Where America Began

A tour through Virginia is easily begun on the Atlantic Coast. First stops on the Eastern Shore are Chincoteague and Assateague islands, home of the Chincoteague ponies, thought to have originally swum ashore from a shipwreck in the 16th century. Besides the ponies, Assateague is a National Seashore and Chincoteague National Wildlife Refuge is a sanctuary for more than 250 kinds of birds. Winter flocks include honking snow geese and whistling swans, while summer brings egrets, herons, and ibises.

Continuing south travelers must cross the unique seventeen-mile Chesapeake Bay Bridge-Tunnel to reach Norfolk, its neighboring beaches, shipyards, and water-sports centers. Norfolk has the world's largest naval base and is home port to over one hundred ships of the Atlantic and Mediterranean fleets. Boat tours of the harbor are available during the summer season. A marked tour route of this historic city includes the Chrysler Museum, the General Douglas MacArthur Memorial, the Gardens-by-the-Sea, St. Paul's Church which still has a British cannonball embedded in its wall, and the Adam Thoroughgood House, an English-style brick home dating from the 1600s. Southeast of Norfolk is Virginia Beach, a popular resort with a wide range of activities. Nearby is Seashore State Park, and historic Cape Henry.

Across the bay from Norfolk are Hampton and Newport News. Fort Monroe, surrounded by a moat in Hampton, housed such prisoners as

Indian chief Black Hawk and Confederate president Jefferson Davis, and would have been a great spot from which to have watched the Civil War clash of the *Monitor* and *Merrimac* ironclads. The Newport News Shipbuilding and Dry Dock Company, which built the *United States* passenger liner and nuclear-powered aircraft carrier *Enterprise*, is actually in Hampton. Newport News has the well-known Mariners Museum.

Jamestown—Williamsburg—Yorktown—Famous Homes

Three of America's most historic sites are linked by the Colonial Parkway. Jamestown, settled in 1607, was the first permanent English Settlement in the New World. Today only the old church tower and outlines of foundations remain. Adjacent to the historic site is Jamestown Festival Park with a reconstructed stockade, and full size replicas of the three tiny ships that brought the first settlers.

A few miles away is Williamsburg which became the Colonial capital in 1699. It is a living museum of restored and reconstructed 18th-century buildings, many of which are open to the public. All visits to the area should begin at the Colonial Williamsburg Information Center to see an interpretive film.

Yorktown should include a tour of the battlefields plus a visit to the National Park Service Visitor Center to illustrate the final decisive battle of the American Revolution. In October 1781 the American and French forces defeated the British under Cornwallis, and ended British rule in the colonies.

The trip between Yorktown and Richmond passes through the historic James River plantation country. Carter's Grove near Williamsburg is considered one of the most beautiful. Among the great estates are: Sherwood Forest, the home of President John Tyler; Belle Air, one of America's oldest frame dwellings, built in 1670; Colonel William Byrd II's plantation in Westover; and Berkeley, ancestral home of Declaration of Independence signer Colonel Benjamin Harrison and two United States Presidents, William Henry Harrison and Benjamin Harrison.

Virginia's northern neck, lying between the Rappahannock and Potomac rivers, is noted for producing presidents, aside from its stately plantations. James Madison came from King George County and George Washington and James Monroe came from Westmoreland County, as did Robert E. Lee. Further along is Fredericksburg, a frequent target for both sides in the Civil War. In and around the area were bloody battles, including those at Chancellorsville, the Wilderness, and Spotsylvania Court House. Further north is Mt. Vernon, the home of George Washington. Nearby is Gunston Hall, the home of George Mason. A visit to this area should also include historic Alexandria. Take a walking tour after a visit to Ramsay House, the Visitor Center at 221 King Street.

Richmond and Charlottesville

In Richmond the two most revered structures are the capitol, designed by Thomas Jefferson, and St. John's Church, built in 1740–41, where Patrick Henry made his famous liberty-or-death speech to the

Second Virginia Convention in 1775. Down the hill from St. John's is Richmond's oldest dwelling, the Old Stone House, built about 1737 and now a memorial to Edgar Allan Poe, who lived in Richmond for 26 years. Also see the house Chief Justice John Marshall built about 1790 and occupied until his death in 1835.

About sixty miles west of the Virginia capital is Charlottesville, which might be more appropriately named Jeffersonville. Jefferson's architectural accomplishments here include the University of Virginia campus, Ash Lawn, the estate of James Monroe, and Monticello, his home which he spent 41 years building.

West of Charlottesville the character of the land changes, as perhaps does the character of the people. The Blue Ridge Mountains form the great divide in Virginia, with the Skyline Drive wriggling 105 miles along the range's backbone through Shenandoah National Park. At Afton, the scenic road becomes the Blue Ridge Parkway and winds 217 miles more to the North Carolina line.

The Shenandoah Valley

Beyond the Blue Ridge are the Allegheny Mountains and between the two ranges lies the Shenandoah Valley. At the head of the Valley, in northwest Virginia, is Winchester. Here sixteen-year-old George Washington worked as a surveyor for Lord Fairfax. His headquarters at Cork and Braddock Streets is now a museum. Winchester is the site of the annual Apple Blossom Festival.

At Lexington is Washington and Lee University, named for George Washington, who endowed it, and Robert E. Lee, who was its president from the close of the Civil War to his death in 1870. On the campus is the Lee Chapel, housing the Valentine recumbent statue of Lee and a crypt in which are buried the general and members of his family.

Washington and Lee's neighbor is the Virginia Military Institute, "the West Point of the South," where Stonewall Jackson taught before he found fame and death as a Confederate General. VMI is the site of the research library and museum honoring another distinguished alumnus, George C. Marshall, Chief of Staff during World War II. A talking map with moving lights traces the highlights of World War II.

The Valley offers an array of natural formations, the most renowned being Natural Bridge, on Interstate 81 and US 11, and twelve miles south of Interstate 64. It rears 215 feet above Cedar Creek and is ninety feet long and from fifty to one hundred feet wide. Along the edge of the Valley are numerous caves. Luray Caverns is popular for its colorful formations and the unusual stalacpipe organ. Among other historic sites in the Valley is the birthplace of Woodrow Wilson at Staunton, and the Battlefield Park at New Market.

Deep in the southwest corner is Cumberland Gap, the gateway through the Alleghenies traversed by settlers pushing into the Northwest Territory and westward to the Mississippi. Cumberland Gap Historical Park touches Virginia, Kentucky, and Tennessee and commemorates the thousands who passed through, including the likes of Daniel Boone back in 1775.

PRACTICAL INFORMATION FOR VIRGINIA

HOW TO GET THERE. *By car:* I–95 parallels US 1, runs north-south, passes through Washington, D.C., Richmond, and Petersburg. I–81 runs northeast-south-west in the western part of the state. I–64 runs east-west. US 13 gives direct access to the Tidewater area. Tolls at Chesapeake Bay Bridge-Tunnel.

By air: Washington, D.C., Richmond, Newport News, (serving Williams-burg), Norfolk, Bristol, Roanoke, Charlottesville, Lynchburg, and Danville. Regular scheduled air service available to other cities in state.

By train: Amtrak serves Washington, Alexandria, Fredericksburg, Rich-mond, Petersburg, and Charlottesville. Also direct service to Williamsburg, and Newport News.

By bus: *Greyhound* and *Trailways* throughout the state. A wide variety of motor coach tours to and through Virginia from many major cities in the Northeast. Consult your travel agent.

TOURIST INFORMATION. Virginia State Travel Service, 202 N. Ninth St. Suite 500, Richmond 23219. Telephone (804) 768–2051.

Ten Highway Travel Information Stations are located near state lines and are open seven days a week. There are more than 500 Virginia travel publications and maps on hand. All services and publications are free. *Facilities provided are barrier-free for the physically handicapped.*

MUSEUMS AND GALLERIES. In Richmond: *The Virginia Museum of Fine Arts,* the nation's first state-supported museum; *White House of the Confederacy; Edgar Allan Poe Museum;* the *Science Museum of Virginia* features a planetarium/space theater. and *Valentine Museum* for historic and costume treasures. In Newport News, the nationally known *Mariners Museum.* Norfolk has the *Hermitage Foundation Museum,* the *Chrysler Museum,* and the *Douglas MacArthur Memorial Museum.* Big Stone Gap has the *Southwest Virginia State Museum.* The *Abby Aldrich Folk Art Collection* in Williamsburg has America's largest collection of primitive paintings.

HISTORIC SITES. *Alexandria:* Take a walking tour of Old Town that begins at the Ramsey House. This is George Washington's town, and many of the historic sights are associated with his life here. A short distance south via the George Washington Memorial Parkway is his estate, Mt. Vernon, overlooking the Potomac.

Appomattox: Where General Lee surrendered to General Ulysses S. Grant at McLean House on April 9, 1865.

Arlington: Arlington National Cemetery, with the Tomb of the Unknowns; the Iwo Jima Marine Corps Memorial; and the Pentagaon (free tours) are military historical sights. Also see Arlington House, built by the adopted son of George Washington, and later the home of Robert E. Lee.

Charlottesville: Thomas Jefferson's University of Virginia, Monticello and Ashlawn, James Monroe's country home designed by Jefferson.

Fredericksburg: Fredericksburg and Spotsylvania National Military Park encompass four Civil War battlefields: Fredericksburg, Chancellorsville, the Wilderness, and Spotsylvania Courthouse.

Jamestown: A walking tour of the historic site includes an orientation at the visitor center operated by the National Park Service. Also visit Jamestown Festival Park and see the reconstructed fort, and the replicas of ships that brought the first settlers.

Norfolk: A marked tour route includes the Chrysler Museum, the General Douglas MacArthur Memorial, St. Paul's Church, and the Adam Thoroughgood House, dating from the 1600's.

Petersburg: National Battlefield Park was the site of Lee's last stand before surrender at Appomattox. The city underwent a 10-month siege in 1864–65.

Richmond: Capital Square has the capitol building designed by Jefferson with a life-size statue of George Washington. Nearby is Robert E. Lee's Civil War House. St. John's Church was locale for Patrick Henry's liberty-or-death speech. Chief Justice John Marshall's house is also open for visiting.

Williamsburg: A tour of the restored and reconstructed colonial capital should begin with the movie "The Story of a Patriot" at the information center. Highlights of a tour include the Capitol, the Governor's Palace, Bruton Parish Church, and the Craft Shops.

Yorktown: The battlegrounds where Cornwallis was defeated, ending the American Revolution. Start your tour at the visitors' center.

SPORTS. *Swimming* in the tidewater is superb along the Atlantic coast beaches. Over 400 *golf* courses throughout the state. Virginia offers *riding* opportunities and horse shows and hunt club events. Licenses needed for freshwater *fishing* and *hunting.* Skiing at: Mountain Run, Newmarket; Wintergreen, Massanutten near Harrisonburg; Cascade Mountain at Fancy Gap; Homestead, Hot Springs; Bryce Mountain near Basye.

DRINKING LAWS. Liquor sold through Alcoholic Beverage Commission stores unless prohibited by local option. Mixed drinks at licensed restaurants and hotels. Drinking age is 19 for beer, and 21 for all other drinks.

WHAT TO DO WITH THE CHILDREN. Jamestown, Williamsburg, and Yorktown have programs for children, with both historical and amusement value. State battlefields' features encourage climbing and touching of relics. Barter Playhouse at Abingdon schedules matinees and still swaps tickets for vittles, a custom from the Depression. Amusement parks at the Old Country Busch Gardens, Williamsburg. Kings Dominion near Ashland is a popular theme park, with rides, a scaled-down model of the Eiffel Tower, and a Lion Country Safari. The Science Museum of Virginia in Richmond permits children to be involved with many of the exhibits.

HOTELS AND MOTELS. *Moderate:* $30–40; *Inexpensive:* below $30. (See also Washington, D.C. listings for Virginia suburban hotels.)

Due to rapidly escalating rates, some of the following listings will not seem to be in a budget category. However, these listings are ones that will be as moderate as any in their particular areas. There are at least two chain motels with accommodations spread in major tourist areas—Days Inns (800–241–7200) and Econ-Travel Motor Hotels (800–446–6900 outside Virginia; within Virginia (1–800–582–5882). Note off-season winter rates available for many oceanfront motels/hotels in Virginia Beach area.

ABINGDON. *Moderate:* **Empire Motor Lodge.** N. on US 11.

BUENA VISTA. *Moderate:* **Barnes Motel.** Pool, restaurant.

CHARLOTTESVILLE. *Moderate:* **Cardinal Motel.** **Econo Travel Motor Hotel.** At Jct Rte. 250 Bypass US 29N.

CULPEPER. *Moderate:* Sleepy Hollow Motel. Opposite Culpeper Shopping Center.

DANVILLE. *Moderate:* **Shamrock Motel,** Pool.

FRONT ROYAL. *Moderate:* **Cool Harbor/Budget Host Motel.** S of I–66 on US 340 and 522.

NORFOLK. *Moderate:* **Econo-Travel.** East of town.

RICHMOND. *Moderate:* **Cardinal Motel.**
Days Inn. 3 locations in area.
Econo-Travel Motor Hotels. Three in town.

VIRGINIA BEACH. *Moderate:* **Econo-Travel Motor Hotels.** Two in town.

WILLIAMSBURG. *Moderate:* **King William Inn.** Central location.
Inexpensive: **Motel 6.** US 60, 3030 Richmond Rd. Plain, comfortable.

YORKTOWN. *Moderate:* **Tidewater Motel.** N. on Rte. 17. Kitchenettes.

 DINING OUT IN VIRGINIA. *Moderate:* $10–15; *Inexpensive:* under $10. For the budget-minded traveler, complete meals are generally featured during luncheon at prices that are considerably lower than evening dinner. Drinks, tax and tip not included.

ALEXANDRIA. *Inexpensive:* **S & W Cafeteria.** In Landmark Shopping Center, Duke St. exit from I–95. Family dining.

ARLINGTON. *Inexpensive:* **Hot Shoppe Cafeteria.** In Crystal Plaza, ½ mi. S of I–95 on US 1.

CHARLOTTESVILLE. *Inexpensive:* **Michie Tavern.** Formerly run by Patrick Henry's father. Fried chicken.

FREDERICKSBURG. *Inexpensive:* **Allman's Pit Cooked Bar-B-Q.** A plain counter-type roadside eatery known for very good barbecue.
Anne's Grill. 1609 Princess Anne St.
The 2400 Diner, 2400 Princess Anne St., popular locally.

LYNCHBURG. *Inexpensive:* **S & W Cafeteria.** S. on Business US 29, varied fare.

RICHMOND. *Moderate:* **Morrison's Cafeteria.** Off I–64 at Glenside Dr. & Broad St. Popular chain.

SMITHFIELD. *Inexpensive:* **Smithfield Inn.** Good meals.

TYSONS CORNER. *Inexpensive:* **Hot Shoppe Cafeteria.** In Tyson's Shopping Center just off I–495.

WILLIAMSBURG. (Reservations advisable at all listed restaurants.) *Moderate:* **Christina Campbell's Tavern.** Seafood.
Inexpensive: **Motor House.** At information center.

YORKTOWN. *Moderate.* **Nick's Seafood Pavillion.** Seafood cooked to order.

WASHINGTON, D.C.

Favorite Tourist Target

Start a Washington walking tour—and leisurely walking is by far the best way to explore this city—from Lafayette Square directly in front of the White House. Bear in mind, however, that covering the vast distances outlined in the suggested walking tour may be practical for only the most intrepid (and fit) hiker. By all means consider riding the Tourmobile to cover at least a part of your downtown explorations. The new Metro subway route is also worthy of study. (See more details in the *Practical Information* section.) Whatever you decide to do, obtain a good map to help you plot your route.

At the National Geographic Society headquarters, 1145 17th St., N.W., is the society's Explorers Hall, a permanent exhibition that tells the story of 75 years of adventure and discovery by more than 200 pioneering expeditions in many fields and many lands. The society's building is the work of Edward Durell Stone, who also is the architect of the Kennedy Center for the Performing Arts. His building for the National Geographic Society is among Washington's most distinguished non-government buildings. It's only about five blocks north of Lafayette Square, a pleasant stroll up 16th St. which takes you first to St. John's Church, called the "Church of the Presidents" because every president, starting with Madison, has attended it. It's a beautiful little church, erected in 1816 from a design by Benjamin Latrobe, and now almost dwarfed by the big buildings around it.

Welcome to the White House

Probably the first of the great Washington attractions in which you will wish to spend time is the White House, just south of Lafayette Square. The line for the regular tours (10 A.M. to noon, Tuesday through Saturday, until 2 P.M. through the summer) sometimes extends for hundreds of yards. During the peak spring and summer seasons visitors must obtain an entrance ticket for a specific time, obtainable at the blue tent on the Ellipse on the south side of the White House. Should you wish to wait there, you will be provided with entertainment and a place to sit. The yearly total of visitors is more than 1.5 million. Tourists are taken through only the public ground-floor rooms. The presidential living quarters are on the second and third floors, and tourists do not see the offices, the kitchens, press room, and so on.

What you do see are the most famous rooms. The East Room, the largest of all, is a lofty, dignified salon of white and gold with touches of blue. It is associated with splendid and solemn events: weddings and funerals, receptions and small concerts or recitals. President John Adams' wife, Abigail, hung her laundry in it. Today it is mainly the public audience chamber.

The Green Room, named for the wall coverings of moss-green watered silk, is done in a graceful and delicate American Federal style. It's a fashionable parlor such as Adams or Jefferson might have known. Furniture includes a particularly striking New England sofa, originally the property of Daniel Webster.

The oval-shaped Blue Room was designed as the most elegant architectural feature of the President's house. The White House's first wedding took place here when President Grover Cleveland married Frances Folsom in 1886.

The Red Room, called the "President's Ante-Chamber" in the original plans, is hung in cerise silk with gold scroll borders and is furnished as an Empire parlor of the early 19th century.

The State Dining Room, second largest in the White House, is used for official luncheons and dinners. Much of the design is English Regency, with a mantel decorated with carved buffalo heads. One hundred and forty guests may be seated here for lunch or dinner.

As you leave the White House note the great variety of old trees. Across Pennsylvania Avenue you will see Blair House, the official guest house of the President. It is here that visiting heads of state stay when on a visit to Washington. President Truman and his family lived here from 1948–52 during the $5,800,000 renovation of the White House, after the discovery that the venerable mansion was "standing up purely from habit."

The Washington Monument

Waiting for the elevator at the Washington Monument is a likelihood during most of the year, and the line usually encircles the base of the monument. Try to arrive early. Winter hours are from 9 to 5; summer hours are 8 to midnight. You may no longer walk up the 898 steps, but you can walk down them, and many do so. The 555-foot shaft, believed to be the tallest masonry structure in the world, is the dominant landmark in the city. It stands straight and clean against the skyline and can be seen from almost any direction. It's almost due south of the White House and a pleasant few minutes' stroll around the Ellipse and across Constitution Ave.

The Washington Monument is the centerpiece of Washington's grandest vista, the axis of its grand design. To the east is the great, green corridor of the Mall, sweeping to the Capitol. To the west across the Reflecting Pool, bearing the shimmering image of the monument's soaring shaft, is the Doric Parthenon of the Lincoln Memorial. We suggest you walk through Constitution Gardens, a 45-acre park bounded by Constitution Avenue and the Reflecting Pool. Be sure to visit the most recent addition to the monuments on the Mall, the Vietnam War Memorial. The simple V-shaped black wall is etched with the names of the 57,692 Americans who died in the war.

The Lincoln and Jefferson Memorials

About the Lincoln Memorial, Roger Angell wrote of the "tired, infinitely distant eyes" of Lincoln and of the "great hands" and of "the soft light falling through the marble ceiling." The best time to visit the Lincoln Memorial, many agree, is late on a rainy night when you are likely to be alone with your thoughts, but Washingtonians urge visitors to go to the memorial both by night, when it is floodlighted, and by sunlight. As at the Washington Monument, you have a magnificent view—in one direction back across the Reflecting Pool and the Mall; in the other, the fabled Potomac River and the Arlington Memorial Bridge. In a direct line is another memorable specimen of the Doric— Arlington House, also called the Custis-Lee Mansion, home of Robert E. Lee, high on a hill in Arlington National Cemetery. Just below the mansion, before the leaves are in full leaf, the eternal flame which marks the grave of President John F. Kennedy may be seen.

From the Lincoln Memorial it's another good hike across West Potomac Park to the Tidal Basin, famed for its flowering Japanese cherry trees, which usually bloom in early April. Around the basin to the east, swan boats may be rented. On the south shore of the basin stands the Jefferson Memorial. The exterior and the setting of this John Russell Pope classic are superlative. The Memorial was built in the Pantheon form which Jefferson himself favored in designing his own Monticello and the University of Virginia rotunda. Its rounded form accents the spire of the Washington Monument to the north and the rectangular perfection of the Lincoln Memorial, which forms the other apex of the triangle of monuments to the west.

After completing your walk around the Tidal Basin you will see, just off Ohio Drive, a boat dock for Washington Boat Line tours. Every hour on the hour *The Spirit of '76*, a 64-foot boat seating 125 people, picks up its passengers for a comfortable and fascinating narrated tour of the Potomac River, with a stop in Georgetown where you may disembark and catch a later boat on the half hour for the return trip. Your complaining feet will thank you for the rest as you cruise along in climate-controlled comfort, all the while seeing the capital from a new angle.

Treasury Ruins the Plan

Heading toward the Capitol from the White House area, you come first to the Treasury building, built in 1842 and the oldest of the government department buildings. When Andrew Jackson designated its site next to the White House, he disrupted the L'Enfant plan, which provided that Pennsylvania Ave., the city's main ceremonial street, should lead directly from the Capitol to the White House. As a result of this, inaugural and other parades must dogleg around the Treasury Building. On either side of the building are statues of two famous early secretaries of the treasury: Alexander Hamilton, the first of them, on the south side; Albert Gallatin on the north. A new museum tracing the history of the Bureau of Alcohol, Tobacco, and Firearms from Colonial days to the present may be visited on weekdays. Entrance is on 12th Street between Pennsylvania and Constitution avenues.

Walk south on 15th St. to the Commerce Department's entrance at 1400 Pennsylvania Ave. In the impressive Great Hall visitors may obtain helpful sightseeing information. Children will want to see the fish in the National Aquarium in the basement. The Patent Office Search Room, with models of famous patented devices, also intrigues many visitors. Commerce is the first of a complex of buildings called the Federal Triangle, between Pennsylvania and Constitution Aves. The others, east along Pennsylvania Ave., are the District Building, housing District of Columbia municipal offices; the Post Office Department, where philatelists may buy stamps at face value in Room 1315; Labor Department; Internal Revenue Service; Department of Justice; the National Archives; and the Federal Trade Commission. You will probably want to stop by the imposing J. Edgar Hoover FBI Building, between 9th and 10th streets on Pennsylvania Ave., for the popular hour-long tour emphasizing the past achievements of the Bureau.

The National Archives, a handsome building modeled after the Pantheon, houses America's most precious documents, including the Declaration of Independence, the Bill of Rights, and the Constitution. There are special facilities for students and researchers, but most visitors make only a brief stop to see the documents, which are protected by one of the world's most elaborate burglar-alarm systems. Sealed in glass containers filled with inert gas, they also are protected against deterioration. Of special interest is former President Richard Nixon's 11-word letter of resignation addressed to Secretary of State Henry Kissinger, on display at the information desk near the entrance.

On the south side of Constitution Ave., opposite the Federal Triangle on one side and facing the Mall on the other, are, heading east, the Smithsonian's Museum of American History (formerly called the Museum of History and Technology), the venerable Museum of Natural History, formerly called the National Museum; and the handsome National Gallery of Art and its new East Building.

The Biggest Elephant

Near the top of everyone's must-visit list, the Museum of American History displays in striking fashion some of the Smithsonian's collections, including the famous collection of first ladies' inaugural gowns and the original American flag, which Francis Scott Key so proudly hailed flying from Fort McHenry during the War of 1812. In the great rotunda of the Museum of Natural History stands the biggest elephant of record, 13 feet high, killed in Africa in 1955. This museum also houses the 44½-carat Hope Diamond, largest blue diamond in the world, and a fabled 330-carat sapphire, plus the gold nugget found by James Marshall that launched the 1848 California gold rush. The National Museum of American Art (formerly called The National Collection of Fine Arts), once housed here, has been moved to the fine old Patent Office Building at 8th and G Sts. N.W., also housing the National Portrait Gallery.

The finest collection of art in Washington—and one of the very best in the world—is the National Gallery of Art, completed in 1941, and designed by John Russell Pope. The beautiful rose-white marble building and one of the collections within it was the gift of Andrew Mellon, the Pittsburgh financier who was Secretary of the Treasury under Hoover. It also houses the collections of Dale, Kress, and Widener. Corridors from the great rotunda lead to some 100 exhibit halls. Sightseers often plan their tours so as to have lunch at the cafeteria here. A favorite time for Washingtonians is Sunday evening (except during the summer months), when visitors may also enjoy the free concerts of the National Gallery Orchestra under its permanent conductor, the composer-musicologist Richard Bales. Allow extra time to enjoy the spectacular new East Building of the National Gallery of Art, a must for every visitor.

Heading on east along Constitution Ave. you'll almost have reached Capitol Hill. At the very foot of the hill, at the eastern end of the Mall is one of the biggest statuary groupings in the country, the Grant Memorial. The bronze of General Grant is said to be the second largest equestrian statue in the world, topped only by the one of Victor Emmanuel in Rome, and that by only a half an inch. Also at the western foot of the hill are statues of President Garfield and Chief Justice John Marshall. At Constitution Ave. and 1st St. stands the memorial to Senator Robert A. Taft, a 100-foot-high bell tower, with a solitary bronze figure of Taft at its base.

Capitol Hill itself encompasses not only the 131 acres of the Capitol grounds, but in general terms also includes the two Senate Office Buildings to the north of it, the three House Office Buildings to the south, the Library of Congress and Supreme Court to the east, plus the surrounding residential and business area, which includes a half-dozen hotels. At the northernmost edge is the monumental Union Station, now being converted back to its original purpose, that of a rail terminal and gateway for passengers arriving in the nation's capital.

The Capitol—Monument on a Pedestal

L'Enfant, a French engineer who served under Washington in the Revolutionary War, selected what was then called Jenkins' Hill as the Capitol site, calling it "a pedestal waiting for a monument." Today it holds some of the country's most important buildings. The 535 members of Congress who convene in its two houses are served by more than 7,500 staff employees. The Capitol is a complicated labyrinth and few indeed are the native Washingtonians who can find their way easily about. Conducted tours through the building lasting 40 minutes are given from 9 A.M. to 5 P.M. in summer, 9 A.M. to 3:30 P.M. the rest of the year. Tours leave from the Rotunda every few minutes. There is no charge.

The Capitol building is 751 feet long, 350 wide, and from the base to the top of the Statue of Freedom on the dome it is 287 feet high. The 19-foot-high statue itself looks roughly like Pocahontas but the sculptor, Thomas Crawford, who did his work in Rome, said he had a freed Roman slave in mind. The cast-iron dome on which she stands weighs 4,455 tons, and engineers say it expands and contracts according to outside temperatures as much as four inches a day.

The most impressive room in the Capitol is the Rotunda under the great dome. As you stand in the Rotunda look up at Constantino Brumidi's fresco glorifying Washington. Although some of the figures are 15 feet tall, they appear life-sized from below. Directly below is the spot where most recently the flag-draped caskets of Presidents John F. Kennedy, Dwight Eisenhower, Lyndon B. Johnson and Senator Hubert H. Humphrey lay in state as have those of other statesmen and honored servants of the republic, as a mark of the nation's esteem. The dome rises to 180 feet above the Rotunda's floor.

The 10-ton bronze "Columbus Doors" leading to the Rotunda are masterworks portraying the story of Columbus' discovery. Of the eight huge oil paintings hanging on the walls by far the most important are those done by John Trumbull, aide-de-camp to General Washington. They are: the Declaration of Independence; the Surrender of Lord Cornwallis; the Surrender of General Burgoyne at Saratoga; and George Washington Resigning His Commission. "My one ambition," Brumidi wrote, "is that I may live long enough to make beautiful the Capitol of the one country on earth in which there is liberty." He was only able to complete a third of his 300-foot-long circular frieze, however, before he died after a fall from the scaffold. A pupil, Filippo Costaggini, took eight years to complete eight other sketches left by Brumidi. The final gap in the frieze wasn't completed, however, until 1953, by Allyn Cox. The frieze depicts scenes from American history. Brumidi fell as he was painting Penn's treaty with the Indians. The last scene painted was the Wright Brothers' first powered flight in 1903.

From the Rotunda the next stop is Statuary Hall; it was originally the legislative chamber of the House of Representatives. It is renowned for its reverberating acoustics. A slight whisper uttered in one part of the hall may be heard distinctly across it, a phenomenon which delights modern tourists much more than it did the legislators. When Statuary Hall was set up, each state was invited to contribute two statues of native sons or daughters they considered sufficiently worthy of the honor. Their weight, however, strained the beams supporting the floor, and now there's a limitation of one favorite son per state within the hall. The other statues have been placed in the Hall of Columns or elsewhere in the building. Just outside Statuary Hall is a statue of Will Rogers, the humorist who gained fame making jokes at Congress' expense. Recently opened are the old Senate chamber, and below it the original Supreme Court chamber.

America's Most Famous Bean Soup

Should you wish to watch Congress in session, from either the House or Senate gallery, for longer than the few minutes allowed on your escorted tour, you need a pass from a congressman or senator. While getting the passes you might also obtain permission to lunch in one of the Capitol restaurants, where the bean soup has been a popular specialty for years. It's made and served every day by special order of Congress! A must for every young visitor to the Capitol is to ride on one of the subways connecting the Capitol with the Senate and House office buildings on either side. If you wish to watch a congressional committee meeting—and they, incidentally, are often more interesting and livelier than what transpires in the actual legislative sessions—watch the morning newspaper for a listing of the meetings, specifying which ones are public. Taxpayers who have a penchant for snorting in righteous indignation particularly like to look over the Sam Rayburn House Office Building, which cost about $75 million, as compared with a total $12 million spent for the first two.

You'll hear less indignation about another expanding institution on the Hill, the Library of Congress. It all began with a $5,000 appropriation in the early 1800s to stock one room in the Capitol. Now it's generally believed to be the largest and most important library in the world with over 75 million items on 320 miles of bookshelves covering 35 acres of floor space. It offers both permanent and special exhibitions of manuscripts and documents. A unique feature is the Coolidge Auditorium endowed concert series. Some of these concerts are played on the library's collection of rare Stradivarius instruments. The library's musicology section also has one of the world's finest collections of folkmusic recordings. The original building is of ornate Italian Renaissance design with an interesting copper dome and Neptune Fountain outside. The annex is of severe, functional modern design. A handsome building just around the corner of 201 E. Capitol Street S.E. is the Folger Shakespeare Library, containing the largest Shakespearian collection in the world. It also has a model of the Globe Theater, in which many of Shakespeare's plays were first performed in 17th-century London, plus a large exhibition gallery with a wide assortment of Elizabethan-era relics. You may attend a play presented by the Folger Theatre Group, but plan ahead—tickets are hard to come by.

Just north of the Library of Congress on 1st St. is the Supreme Court Building. It is impressive in a way beyond anything else on Capitol Hill. Designed by Cass Gilbert and constructed of the whitest of white marble, its rows of Corinthian pillars and its sculptured pediment look much as the proudest temples in Rome must have appeared when those temples were gleaming new and Rome was in her glory. The Court meeting inside is equally impressive in a way even the Senate could never be. Visit here if you can when the Court is in session, arriving early enough for the opening ceremonials at 10 A.M. to hear the ancient call of the bailiff crying: "Oyez, oyez, oyez . . . ," as the black-robed figures of the Supreme Court justices file in one by one, intoning, "God save the United States and this Honorable Court." The best day of the week to visit the Supreme Court from a standpoint of excitement is Monday, which is "Decision Day." You could very well be present when an important decision is announced. (Court recesses from June to October.)

From the Supreme Court retrace your route back 1st St. S.E. to Independence Ave., turn right and stroll down past the three House Office Buildings (Cannon, Longworth and Rayburn), and just beyond 1st St. S.W. see the U.S. Botanic Gardens, the favorite spot on the Hill for all who take their gardening seriously.

Just across Independence Ave. from the gardens is the graceful bronze Bartholdi Fountain, a creation of F. Auguste Bartholdi, sculptor of the Statue of Liberty.

Strolling west on Independence Ave., you pass the Department of Health and Human Services. It's a modern building without much character, but inside, on its second floor, is the Voice of America of the U.S. International Communication Agency. (Main office of the information agency, appropriately, is at 1776 Pennsylvania Ave., N.W.) The Voice of America broadcasts in 37 languages over a network of 114 transmitters. You can get an excellent idea of its operation in a 40-minute tour. Beyond it, heading west, are the National Aeronautics and Space Administration and the Department of Transportation. They are part of an extensive new southwest complex of buildings resulting from redevelopment.

The Smithsonian

Walk another block west, and across the street you'll see the towers and turrets of Washington's most interesting architectural curiosity—and one of its most cherished treasures—the main building of the Smithsonian Institution, built in 1852 with funds willed by Englishman James Smithson, who had never even seen America. The institution now administers numerous divisions ranging from the adjacent Freer Gallery of Art to the National Zoological Park (Washington Zoo, Connecticut Ave. at Cathedral Ave., N.W.). In the great Main Hall of the Smithsonian are exhibits showing the great scope of the Institution's work. The Smithsonian has been called "the nation's attic," and it contains, at last count, something over 70 million catalogued items. In the Smithsonian's new $41 million National Air and Space Museum are the two exhibits that most visitors wish to see: the Wright Brothers' plane, the 1903 *Flyer*, the first heavier-than-air machine to fly; and Charles Lindbergh's *Spirit of St. Louis*, the little monoplane in which he made that historic New York-to-Paris nonstop flight, which charted the way for today's commuter-like world-spanning jets. (Later Orville Wright nicknamed the first plane the "Kitty Hawk.") Allow some extra time to see the remarkable film "*Living Planet*," shown about every 45 minutes. Charge is 50 cents for adults, 25 cents for children. A filmed flight-oriented tour of America's history is projected onto a giant screen, and six-track stereo with eleven speakers makes an indelible impression on your hearing and memory. In the Albert Einstein Spacearium, "*Cosmic Awakening*" will show how the human concept of the universe has changed over the past 200 years, and how it is likely to change in the next century.

Making Money—by the Bushel

A few blocks south on 14th St., S.W. is the Bureau of Engraving and Printing, where the government designs, engraves, and prints paper money, bonds, and stamps. It is said that the face value of money printed here averages some $40 million a day. You can actually see the money being printed from the visitors' gallery.

If you've done this tour-around-Mall in one day (and a lot of people do), you probably will want to soak your feet in hot water rather than go out on the town that night. You'll still, however, have seen only a part of Washington.

Back on your bench in Lafayette Square again, map yourself a tour of Foggy Bottom and Georgetown in the morning and wind up with a tour of "Embassy Row" in the afternoon.

From the square walk west on Pennsylvania Ave., then turn left on 17th St. past what is now called the Executive Office Building. This was originally called the War, Navy, and State Building, and all three of these important departments were housed here until the Pentagon was built. Patterned after the great Louvre Museum in Paris, it was built in 1875. Those who work in the Executive Office Building like it even more because of the high ceilings and general feeling of spaciousness. Because of security it is not open to tourists. Here are housed the offices of the Vice President, a Presidential "hideaway" suite, and offices of assistants to the President and commissions working on special projects for the President.

Continuing on south on 17th St. you'll find the headquarters of the American Red Cross in an appropriately gleaming white building. The Red Cross Museum tells the story of this humanitarian organization's worldwide activities. In the courtyard is the statue of a nurse, a memorial to the hundreds of nurses who were killed serving in World War I. There is also a Tiffany window of glowing colors on the second floor.

Another block south is the national headquarters of the Daughters of the American Revolution, whose annual convention is a Washington feature each spring. Memorial Continental Hall faces 17th St. between C and D Sts., N.W. Connected to it but facing 18th St. is Constitution Hall, seating almost 4,000, where most of Washington's major concerts were held before construction of the Kennedy Center. Continental Hall contains one of the largest genealogical libraries in the world, and you might go there to look up your own family tree—for a fee. There are also an historic museum and 28 period rooms representing various states.

Along 17th St. the House of the Americas (formerly called the Pan American Union) also faces Constitution Ave. This is the headquarters of the Organization of American States, representing 21 American republics. It is the oldest international organization in the world. The building's interior patio maintains a year-round tropical atmosphere. Lush trees and plants from South and Central America grace the patio, and in the center is a lovely fountain in the Spanish-American manner. In the rear of the building is still another garden, centering around a statue of the Aztec god of flowers, Xochipilli. There is also a Hall of Heroes containing busts of the founders of the American republics and

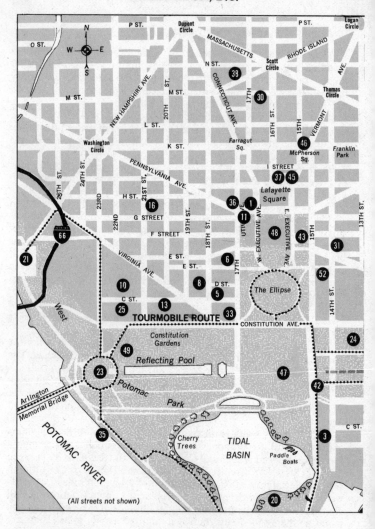

Points of Interest

1) Blair House
2) Botanical Garden
3) Bureau of Printing & Engraving
4) Capitol
5) Constitution Hall
6) Corcoran Art Gallery
7) Department of Energy
8) Department of Interior
9) Department of Justice
10) Department of State
11) Executive Office Building

12) FBI (J.E. Hoover Building)
13) Federal Reserve Board
14) Ford's Theater
15) Freer Gallery of Art
16) George Washington University
17) Government Printing Office
18) Hirshhorn Museum & Sculpture Garden
19) House Office Bldgs.
20) Jefferson Memorial
21) John F. Kennedy Center

22) Library of Congress
23) Lincoln Memorial
24) Museum of American History
25) National Academy of Sciences
26) National Air & Space Museum
27) National Archives
28) National Collection of American Art & National Portrait Gallery
29) National Gallery of Art

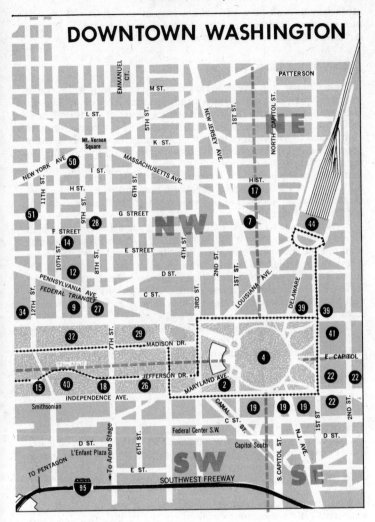

DOWNTOWN WASHINGTON

30) National Geographic Society
31) National Theater
32) Natural History Museum
33) Organization of American States
34) Post Office
35) Potomac Boat Tours Dock
36) Renwick Gallery
37) St. John's Church
38) St. Matthew's Cathedral
39) Senate Office Buildings
40) Smithsonian Institution
41) Supreme Court
42) Sylvan Theater
43) Treasury Department
44) Union Station
45) Veterans' Administration
46) Washington Convention & Visitors Association
47) Washington Monument
48) White House
49) Vietnam Veterans Memorial
50) Washington, D.C. Convention Center
51) Metro Center
52) Department of Commerce Visitors Center

other heroes. You may also take a look at the impressive council meeting room, and there usually are interesting exhibits in the Modern Art Museum, entrance 201 18th St. N.W.

Bolivar, the Liberator

From Constitution Ave., you turn north again on 18th St. In a small triangular park on your left is a handsome statue of Simon Bolivar, liberator of many South American republics. North of this is the Interior Department Building, which covers two blocks between 18th and 19th, C and E Sts. Besides a museum, explaining the work of the entire department, the building contains a most interesting craft shop displaying and selling works of American Indians—pottery, jewelry, rugs, etc. Just north of the building is Rawlins Park, which is one of Washington's loveliest jewel-like parks, especially beautiful when its tulip-tree magnolias are in bloom, generally in late March. In the center its pool is filled with water lilies.

Facing Rawlins Park to the northeast is Octagon House, which served as the temporary White House in 1814–15 for President James Madison and his wife, Dolly, after the British burned the White House. Actually, the building has not eight sides, as its name implies, but six! It and an adjoining new building are the national headquarters of the American Institute of Architects, which offers guided tours daily except Monday and has interesting exhibits on the development of architecture.

Going east from Rawlins Square along E St., you cross Virginia Ave. and enter what was once strictly a workingman's section of the city, called Foggy Bottom because of the mists from the nearby Potomac River. Here, at 2201 C St., now stands the second largest building belonging to the U.S. Government, the State Department Building.

Federal Charms

Georgetown has no government buildings of note, nor any memorials, but to many it is the most charming part of the city. To your left from Pennsylvania Ave. as you enter the section is the old Chesapeake and Ohio Canal. Beginning at Lock 3 at 30th Street and Thomas Jefferson Street you may walk along the Canal's towpath. North of Pennsylvania Ave. and M St., with which Pennsylvania merges, is one of Washington's finest residential sections and seat of Georgetown University. It's a pleasure to walk along any of the brick sidewalks under the bower of trees covering its narrow streets, looking at the beautiful Federal-period homes, many of which are even more striking inside, and hide gems of gardens behind tall brick walls. Georgetown's equivalents of Main St. are M St., on which are most of the restaurants and night clubs and several galleries, and Wisconsin Ave., which intersects M at the heart of the section. Along Wisconsin Ave. are many of the fine unusual shops for which Georgetown is noted. Most of the fine Georgetown homes, of course, are closed to the public, but some are opened, as are the embassies, for special charity tours. Two fine old homes which tourists can and should visit are Dumbarton House, 2715 Q St. N.W., headquarters of the Society of Colonial Dames of America; and Dumbarton Oaks, 3101 R St. N.W., which also contains a notable museum of Byzantine art and is the property of Harvard University (closed Mondays). The exquisite gardens covering 16 acres may be visited daily between 2 and 4:45 P.M.; entrance is on R Street. Both the Museum and the gardens are closed on holidays and in inclement weather.

A good way to circle from Georgetown into "Embassy Row" along Massachusetts Ave. N.W. is to cross Rock Creek Park on the unique, curving Buffalo Bridge at Q St. (It's so named because of the big life-sized buffalo sculptures at either end.) After crossing this delightful bridge, turn left on 23rd St. and you are right in the middle of the biggest concentration of Washington's embassies. On your left is that of Turkey. Across the street is Romania's. Then you're at Sheridan Circle, around which are the embassies of Ireland, Greece, Kenya, and Korea. Between Sheridan Circle and the Naval Observatory to the west are a score of embassies, the most notable being the great mansion of the British government. Just past the British Embassy, and on the same side of Massachusetts Avenue, is the towered Victorian mansion on the grounds of the Naval Observatory. It serves as the official residence of the Vice President. Heading south again toward town you will pass on your left the beautifully tiled edifice of Iran. In the center of this array, serving the embassies of the Moslem countries, is the striking Mosque and Islamic Center, with a 162-foot-high minaret.

Winding through this section of the city is another of Washington's greatest treasures, Rock Creek Park. This park, which snakes through the whole length of the city alongside the stream for which it is named, offers an escape from the city within minutes. Stroll along Rock Creek Park to where the stream flows into the Potomac River and you will arrive at Washington's newest major tourist attraction, the John F. Kennedy Center for the Performing Arts. Here is a building on a grand scale, 630 feet long and 300 feet wide. Guides will tell you the Washington Monument could be laid in the Grand Foyer, which runs the length of the building, with 75 feet to spare. The total area is big enough for four football fields. No athletic events are held here, however. Inside are an opera house, concert hall, two dramatic theaters, and film theater, plus three restaurants. We recommend that you take a tour between 10 and 1 P.M., Monday through Saturday. You will see rooms not open to the general public.

PRACTICAL INFORMATION FOR

WASHINGTON, D.C.

HOW TO GET THERE. *By Car:* I–95 is the major access route from the north or south, I–270 from the northwest. From the eastern shore of the Chesapeake take US 50 over the toll bridge, through Annapolis and into Washington.

By plane: Washington National Airport handles the city's domestic traffic. Dulles International Airport, 25 miles away in Virginia, serves the larger jets and all international traffic. Baltimore-Washington International Airport (BWI), near Baltimore, is a 45-minute ride to downtown D.C. Air taxi service between Dulles and BWI is available. The 25-minute Federal Shuttle ride costs $35.

By train: Washington is served by *Amtrak* and the *Southern Railway System.*
By bus: Washington is a major terminal for *Trailways* and *Greyhound.*

HOW TO GET AROUND. *By car:* Never set forth without a map. Acquaint yourself with the general layout of the city, including the Virginia and Maryland suburbs. Circle your sightseeing objectives on your map. Try to avoid driving between 7:30 and 9 A.M. and 4:30 and 6 P.M., as commuters burden the main arteries and bridges during these hours. Be prepared for many NO LEFT TURN signs in the downtown area and confusion at the traffic circles. Read with care the parking signs before leaving your car. Some meters are for 20-minute parking only, most are for an hour, and occasionally you will find one for two hours. If you leave your car parked along a main street after 3 P.M., the police will cart it off to the nearest precinct headquarters. Two-hour parking on the Mall is allowed, but finding your niche will be time-consuming. A new garage below the National Air and Space Museum (Independence Ave. between 4th and 7th Sts., S.W.) provides parking for Mall visitors. Sunday in the city provides you with relatively traffic-free avenues and easier parking. A nighttime tour of the floodlit monuments is unforgettable.

By tourmobile: We highly recommend sightseeing the Tourmobile way. You enjoy a narrated tour of all the principal monuments and points of historical interest along the way, dispense with driving and parking worries, and go at your own pace, getting on and off as often as you like at no extra charge. Call Landmark Services at 554–7950 for detailed information.

By taxi: Taxis charge according to a zone plan displayed in each cab. There are no metered cabs. For trips beyond the downtown area or to suburbia, check with the driver before you board the cab.

By boat: Highly recommended is the *Washington Boat Line* Tours, which leave from a pier near the Lincoln Memorial every hour on the hour during the summer months. The firm offers trips on its 353-passenger cruise ship to Mount Vernon and back from March 13 to Labor Day. Call 554–8000 for schedules.

By bus: Metrobus provides bus service for Washington, Maryland, and northern Virginia areas. Fares within D.C. are 60 cents (more during rush hours) and increase by zone. Ask your driver and have exact change.

By subway: Each Metro station's entrance is marked by a brown four-sided pylon with an "M" at the top. The basic fare is 75 cents (more during rush hours) but it increases by zone. On weekends and holidays the fare is 75 cents no matter how many zones you pass through. The fare is collected by an electronic collecting system and each passenger must have a farecard for entry and exit. Metro branches go out to National Airport, the Pentagon, Arlington Cemetery, RFK Stadium, and to Maryland and Virginia suburbs. Buses from outlying areas feed into the rail system. Suburban branches still under construction. Metro operates 6:30 A.M. to midnight, Mon. through Sat., and from 10 A.M. to 6 P.M., Sun. For information call 633–2437.

TOURIST INFORMATION SERVICES. Contact the Washington Convention and Visitors Association, 1575 Eye St., N.W., Washington, D.C. 20005 (Tel. (202) 789-7000) for pamphlets and brochures on hotels, motels, restaurants and sightseeing here and in the environs. Open Mon.-Fri., 9–5.

Opened in March 1983 is the Washington Visitor Information Center in the Great Hall of the Commerce Department, 1400 Pennsylvania Ave., N.W, (789-7000). Volunteers from Travelers Air, IVIS (see below), and the National Park Service provide sightseeing information. The White House Historical Association sells its publications here.

IVIS, the International Visitors Information Service, 801 Nineteenth St., N.W. (Tel. (202) 872–8747) stands ready to help foreign visitors with free maps in foreign languages and some multilingual pamphlets. IVIS also maintains a Language Bank to help visitors with a language problem and serves as the Washington coordinator of the Americans-at-Home Program.

The *Washington Post* and the new *Washington Times* carry information on movie, theater, sports, and cultural events. Look for the "Day's Activities in Congress" column in the *Post* for a list of House and Senate Congressional hearings, all open to the public unless marked *Executive*. Friday's *Post* publishes "Weekend," a supplement detailing cultural activities for the week.

The monthly *Washingtonian* magazine ($1.95) covers in detail music, dance, theater, films, museums and exhibitions, lectures, sports, and night life in its "Where and When" section, and readers absorb Washington's special flavor by reading its feature articles.

  MUSEUMS AND GALLERIES. *Anderson House Museum,* 2118 Massachusetts Ave., was once an elegant private home and now serves as the headquarters of the Society of the Cincinnati. Open Tues.–Sat., 1–4 P.M.

Corcoran Gallery of Art. 17th St. and New York Ave., N.W. American art from colonial days to the present, and a representative group of European works. Free. Closed Monday. Open Thurs. evening until 9 P.M.

B'nal B'rith Museum. 1640 Rhode Island Ave., N.W. Closed Jewish Holy Days and holidays. In Klutznick Hall are exhibits showing the contribution Jews have made to the development of our democracy. Open Sun.–Fri., 10 A.M.–5 P.M.

D.A.R. Memorial Continental Hall. 17th and C Sts., N.W. *Museum* at 1776 D St., N.W. Period rooms and lovely antiques. Open Mon.–Fri., 10 A.M.–4 P.M. Sun., 1–5 P.M.

Dumbarton Oaks Collection. 1703 32nd St., N.W. (Georgetown). Collections from Early Christian and Byzantine periods and pre-Columbian art—a jewel of a museum in a perfect setting. Open daily 2–5 P.M.; closed holidays.

Hillwood Museum, 4155 Linnean Ave., N.W. The home of the late Marjorie Meriweather Post is open for tours Mon., Wed., Fri., and Sat. On display is an outstanding collection of Russian works of art. The gardens alone merit a visit. Reservations must be made well in advance; call (202) 686–5807. $7 for adults; children under 12 not admitted.

Interior Department Museum. C St. between 18th and 19th Sts., N.W. Free. Indian exhibits and work of Interior Dept. The National Park Service furnishes data regarding the national parks, monuments, and other reservations under its jurisdiction. Open Mon.–Fri., 8 A.M.–4 P.M.; closed holidays.

Marine Corps Museum and Historical Center. Navy Yard, 9th and M Sts., S.E. Special exhibits in an unusual setting. Open Mon.–Sat., 10 A.M.–4 P.M.; Sun., noon–5 P.M.

National Archives. 7th St. and Pennsylvania Ave., N.W. The Declaration of Independence, the Constitution, and the Bill of Rights handsomely displayed. Open daily 10 A.M.–5:30 P.M.

Phillips Collection. 1600 21st St., N.W. Works of the French Impressionists and post-Impressionists, including Degas, Monet, Manet, Renoir, Van Gogh, and Cezanne. Traditional and contemporary American painters are also represented. Closed Mon. Open Sun. 2–7 P.M.

Textile Museum. 2320 S St., N.W. Outstanding collection of rugs and textiles. The shop sells needlepoint and crewel original transfers taken from objects in museum collection, canvas, and wool. Open Tues.–Sat., 10 A.M.–5 P.M.

Truxton-Decatur Naval Museum. 1610 H St., N.W. Exhibits on naval history: prints, models, and paintings. Free. Open daily 10 A.M.–4 P.M.; closed holidays.

Smithsonian Institution. Jefferson Dr. between 9th and 12th Sts., S.W. *Note: Smithsonian Museums on the Mall* (except for the Freer Gallery) are open daily 10 A.M.–5:30 P.M. Free. The following are Smithsonian museums:

Arts and Industries Building. 9th St. and Jefferson Dr., S.W. Recreation of The Philadelphia Exposition of 1876. Newly restored to original appearance.

Freer Gallery of Art. 12th St. and Independence Ave., S.W. Free. No tours. Paintings, ceramics, pottery, manuscripts, and sculpture from the Near and Far East are shown in this delightful small museum built around a central courtyard. The Freer houses one of the largest collections of the works of Whistler.

Hirshhorn Museum and Sculpture Garden, Independence Ave. at 8th St., S.W. Nicknamed "The Doughnut on the Mall," the Hirshhorn, opened in 1974, houses a collection of over 6,000 works of art by European and American artists dating from the late 19th century to the present. Outdoor sculpture garden with delightful vistas of the Mall. Outdoor cafeteria in summer.

Museum of African Art. 316–318 A St., N.E. Traditional African sculpture and modern art showing African derivation. Open Mon.–Fri., 11 A.M.–5 P.M.; Sun., noon–5 P.M.

National Museum of American History. Between 12th and 14th Sts., N.W., on Constitution Ave. Imposing new building containing gowns of the First Ladies, the Star-Spangled Banner, famous inventions, early automobiles, locomotives, stamps; cultural and technological development of the United States from Colonial times. Cafeteria.

National Air and Space Museum. Independence Ave. and 6th St., S.W. Opened July 4, 1976. Dramatic displays of aircraft, including *The Spirit of St. Louis,* the Wright brothers' plane, and the Apollo II command module. Movie "Living Planet" and Spacearium. Cafeteria.

National Collection of American Art and the National Portrait Gallery. 8th and G Sts., N.W. Especially noteworthy are the 445 paintings of George Catlin's Indian Gallery, the "Art: U.S.A." collection of S. C. Johnson and Son, Inc., and the always outstanding special exhibits.

National Gallery of Art. 6th St. and Constitution Ave., N.W. A daily schedule of events appears on bulletin boards at either entrance. If time permits, take introductory tour of the gallery. LecTour (taped lectures) may be rented for 25¢. Get free brochure of gallery with map showing the location of paintings by school and period. Don't miss the new *East Gallery,* a spectacular building designed by I. M. Pei, and adjacent to the *National Gallery of Art.*

National Museum of Natural History. 10th St. and Constitution Ave., N.W. Hall of Dinosaurs, Hall of Gems (see the Hope Diamond).

Renwick Gallery. 17th St. and Pennsylvania Ave., N.W. near White House. Victorian building filled with Americana.

 HISTORIC SITES. Some of the most interesting historic sites are little known. Open to the public is the *Woodrow Wilson House,* located at 2430 S St., N.W. Here Wilson, 28th President of the United States, retired at the end of his second term and died three years later, Feb. 3, 1924. The house contains furnishings, portraits, books, memorabilia, and other effects belonging to the Wilsons. Open Tues.–Fri., 10 A.M.–2 P.M. Admission $2 for adults.

A fine early Federal house open to the public is *Dumbarton House* in Georgetown, now headquarters for the National Society of Colonial Dames. Dating from 1799, this red brick mansion contains authentic period pieces and an outstanding collection of silver and china. 2715 Q St., N.W. Open Mon.–Sat., 9 A.M.–noon. Free.

Decatur House, a block from the White House and overlooking Lafayette Square, was designed in 1818 by famed architect Benjamin Latrobe. This elegant Georgian town house is at the corner of H St. and Jackson Pl., N.W. Open Tues.–Fri., 10 A.M.–2 P.M.; weekends, noon–4 P.M. Admission $2 for adults.

Arlington House (also known as the Custis-Lee Mansion). In Arlington Cemetery. Home of Robert E. Lee, commander of the Confederate Army during the Civil War. A Tourmobile stop. Open daily 9:30 A.M.–4:30 P.M. Free.

Arlington National Cemetery. Across Memorial Bridge from the Lincoln Memorial: the Tomb of the Unknowns (change of guard every hour on the hour), the Amphitheater, Arlington House, and the graves of President John F. Kennedy and his brother, Senator Robert F. Kennedy. No cars allowed. Take Tourmobile or walk. Especially lovely in early spring. Open daily 8 A.M.–5 P.M.; 8 A.M.–7 P.M., Apr.–Sept.

The Capitol. On Capitol Hill. Tours leave from the Rotunda every 15 minutes. Free. Explore this vast building on your own after the 45-minute tour; take a ride on the underground subway to the Senate and House Office Buildings. Should you wish to spend more time in the House or Senate gallery than the few minutes allowed on your tour, you must get a pass from the office of your

Senator or Congressman. See the lighted Capitol at night, and during the summer attend a concert at the West Front. Open daily 9 A.M.–4:30 P.M.; tours, 9 A.M.–3:45 P.M. (free).

The Library of Congress, 1st St. and Independence Ave., S.E., ranks among the great libraries of the world, with 75 million books, periodicals, photographs, and microfilms housed in over 320 miles of shelves. On permanent exhibition are a three-volume, 1455 edition of the Gutenberg Bible, and Thomas Jefferson's "rough draft" of the Declaration of Independence. Tours of this ornate, Italian Renaissance style building are conducted almost every hour, 9 A.M. to 4 P.M. Should you be exploring the Library on your own, be sure to take the elevator to the Visitors' Gallery above the second floor for a spectacular view looking down on the Main Reading Room. Open Mon.–Fri., 9 A.M.–4 P.M.; tours.

The *Folger Library,* 201 East Capitol St., S.E., houses the world's largest collection of Shakespeareana and an extraordinary collection of material in English dealing with the 17th and 18th centuries. The *Exhibition Hall* reproduces the great hall of an Elizabethan palace. The *Shakespearean Theater* is a full-size replica of a public playhouse of Shakespeare's day, except that it does not open to the sky. Plays are presented by the Folger Theater Group—call for information. Open Mon.–Sat., 10 A.M.–4 P.M.

Jefferson Memorial. On the south bank of the Tidal basin. Honors Thomas Jefferson, third President, the author of the Declaration of Independence and the Bill of Rights. It is particularly lovely at cherry blossom time and on a summer night. Parking at an adjacent parking lot. Gift shop. Open 24 hours a day.

Lincoln Memorial. West Potomac Park at the foot of 23rd St., N.W. The statue of Lincoln is imposing by day, unforgettable by night. Walk around the portico for fine view of the Potomac River and Arlington Memorial Bridge, Arlington House across the river, with just below, the eternal flame marking the grave of President Kennedy. Gift shop. Parking on Ohio Drive. Open 24 hours a day.

Mount Vernon. Mount Vernon, Va. (16 miles south of Washington, D.C.— allow a half day for the trip). Washington's home on the Potomac. Outbuildings and gardens in a lovely setting. The grave of George and Martha Washington is just below the mansion. Open daily Mar.–Oct., 9 A.M.–5 P.M.; Nov.–Feb., 9 A.M.–4 P.M. Adults, $3.

Supreme Court, 1st St. and Maryland Ave., N.E. Court is in session Oct.–June. Tours. Open Mon.–Fri., 9 A.M.–5 P.M.

Vietnam Veterans Memorial, N.W. corner of Constitution Gardens. Dedicated November 13, 1982, the two long walls of polished granite contain the names of 57,692 Americans killed in the war.

Washington Monument. On the Mall at 15th St., N.W. 555-foot obelisk: elevator ride to top for fine view. Open daily 9 A.M.–5 P.M.; longer hours in summer.

The White House. 1600 Pennsylvania Ave., N.W. Every president has lived here except Washington. Eight of 132 rooms are on display. In summer, tickets for tour distributed on Ellipse. Closed Sun. and Mon. Open 10 A.M.–noon other days.

TOURS. The larger companies—*Diamond, Gray Line, White House, and Blue Line* amongst others—will pick you up at hour hotel or motel 30 minutes before the scheduled time of your tour's departure, and return you without extra charge. *Tourmobiles,* smooth-riding shuttle trams carrying 88 passengers, provide an efficient way to sightsee in the principal Mall-Monument area, and Arlington Cemetery. Call 554–7951 for information. From June 1 to Sept. 15 a Mount Vernon tour is available. Made-to-order group tours are offered by the *National Fine Arts Associates,* 4801 Massachusetts Ave., N.W., Washington, D.C. 20016. Call (202) 966–3800.

SUMMER SPORTS. There are three public *golf courses* open year-round from sunrise to sunset—East Potomac Park, Langston Park, and Rock Creek Park, with rental bags and clubs. *Rowboats, swan boat rides, canoes,* and *pedal boats* are for hire at the north end of the Tidal Basin, 15th St. and Maine Ave., S.W. Both *Thompson's Boat Center* at Rock Creek Parkway and Virginia Ave., N.W., and *Fletcher's Boat House,* 4940 Canal Rd. (on the C. and O. Canal Tow Path) will rent you a canoe, rowboat, or bicycle.

WINTER SPORTS. For a list of *ice skating* rinks in and around the city, consult the Yellow Pages. The finest new facility is right on the Mall. Skate at the National Sculpture Garden Ice Rink on Constitution Avenue between 7th and 9th Sts., N.W. Skates for rent. Music and great views. Once every few years the C. and O. Canal freezes over, and the scene is one from an old Dutch painting. Equally picturesque are the rare occasions when the public is allowed to skate on the Reflecting Pool at the base of the Washington Monument.

SPECTATOR SPORTS. During the fall season the *Washington Redskins* play at R.F.K. Stadium. In August, attend a Redskin preseason exhibition game, when getting a ticket is no problem.

Racing fans may enjoy horse racing almost year-round within easy driving distance of Washington. Laurel, Maryland, tracks (18 miles), Bowie (20 miles), and Pimlico (40 miles—near Baltimore) operate in spring and fall, and a harness racing season is held at Laurel and Rosecroft. The new *Washington Federals* (546–3337) of the U.S. Football League will play nine games March–July at R.F.K. Stadium. *Polo games* are played at different locations during the summer and fall, usually on Sundays. *Cricket* enthusiasts may attend games played by members of the British Commonwealth Cricket Club on the polo grounds of West Potomac Park from April to October, usually at 2 P.M. Saturdays and Sundays.

The pro ice hockey team, the *Capitals,* plays at the Capital Centre in Landover, Md. from October to early April. The pro basketball team, the *Washington Bullets,* plays at the Capital Centre from October to April. The D.C. National Bank International Tennis Tournament is held the last week in July at the tennis stadium in Rock Creek Park.

WHAT TO DO WITH THE CHILDREN. Washington abounds in things to do which have special appeal to children. Many of these activities, sights, or excursions will delight the parents as much as their offspring. The *National Zoo,* 3000 Connecticut Ave., N.W. has two panda bears, Ling Ling and Hsing Hsing. Other attractions for children in Rock Creek Park (where the zoo is located) are *Pierce Mill* at Tilden St. and Beach Drive, N.W., the only operating grist mill in Washington, and the *Nature Center,* near Military and Glover Rds., where a planetarium is the stellar attraction.

In the lower lobby of the Department of Commerce Building at 14th and E Sts., N.W., the *National Aquarium* displays live specimens of food and game fishes from the inland waters of the United States in a small area just right for children. Fee.

The *Capitol Children's Museum,* 800 3rd St., N.E. (near M St.) has wonderful "hands-on" exhibits through which children learn by doing. Closed Mondays.

The *Federal Bureau of Investigation* is only a few blocks away (between 9th and 10th Sts. on E Street, N.W.). Tours are free. Allow one hour.

The *Bureau of Engraving and Printing* at 14th and C Sts., N.W., provides the opportunity to view the printing of postage stamps and paper money on a 25-minute self-guided tour, with taped commentaries explaining the steps you are observing.

The *Smithsonian Natural History Building* at 10th St. and Constitution Ave., N.W., displays the Fenykovi elephant, estimated to have weighed 12 tons while alive, in the giant rotunda. See, too, the Hall of Dinosaurs, the Hall of Indians, and the Hall of Gems. Equally popular are the exhibits at the new *Museum of American History* at 13th St. and Constitution Ave., N.W., showing the cultural and technological development of the U.S.

Explorers Hall at the National Geographic Society, 17th and M Sts., N.W., offers a well-displayed potpourri of fascinating exhibits of National Geographic researches and explorations.

Tours of the Potomac by boat leave every hour on the hour from the dock on Ohio Drive near the Lincoln Memorial. Call 554–8000 for schedule of boat trips to Mount Vernon. Or board *The Spirit of '76* on the half hour from the foot of Wisconsin Ave. in Georgetown. April–October.

Less time-consuming would be a *swan boat ride* at the Tidal Basin, where, at the north end, rowboats, canoes, and paddle boats may be rented.

Children of all ages enjoy the *Washington Doll's House and Toy Museum* at 4236 44th St., N.W., a half hour bus ride from downtown.

 HOTELS AND MOTELS. With more than 20 million visitors to Washington each year, tourism has become the capital's principal industry, and demand for hotel space often exceeds space available. Be sure to write or phone in advance for confirmed reservations.

Downtown in the District of Columbia is where the majority of hotels are located. Some of them were built many years ago and show the signs of old age, but many are undergoing face-lifts. For this reason it is difficult to rate some of the accommodations, as they will vary considerably from room to room. Motels have been listed at all the major approaches to the city, and none of those listed is more than 35 minutes by car from downtown Washington.

Double-occupancy lodgings in Washington are categorized as follows: *Moderate,* \$50–70; *Inexpensive,* under \$50.

Moderate. **Park Central Hotel.** 705 18th St., N.W. A smallish (250 rooms) in-town hotel centrally located just two blocks west of White House and two blocks from subway stop. Roof garden and restaurant.

Inexpensive. **Bellevue Hotel.** 15 E St., N.W. Within walking distance of Capitol Hill area; near National Visitor's Center and subway. Smallish with "Quad" rooms for groups. Cafeteria and Pub. Near subway.

Harrington Hotel. 11th and E Sts., N.W. Large, older downtown hotel; good for families; excellent cafeteria.

Hawthorne Hotel, 2134 G St., N.W., A modest, clean, and comfortable hotel located downtown on the George Washington University Campus.

The Kalorama Guest House. 1854 Mintwood Place, N.W. A European style bed-and-breakfast guest house in the attractive embassy district of downtown Washington. Six rooms; resident host.

Motels and Hotels Outside City

ARLINGTON. *Moderate.* **Holiday Inn Key Bridge.** Has pool and restaurant.
Hospitality House, on US 1 in Crystal City near National Airport.
Iwo Jima Motor Motel, on US 50 near Roosevelt Bridge.
Quality Inn Central, on US 50 at Court House Road.
Stouffer's National Center Hotel, in Crystal City near National Airport.

ALEXANDRIA. *Moderate:* **Best Western Olde Colony.** 1st and N. Washington Sts. Colonial Virginia architecture. Free continental breakfast.
Guest Quarters. 100 S. Reynolds St. Suites only with kitchens. Pool, playground, coin-op laundry. Ideal for families.
Holiday Inn of Old Town, 480 King St., colonial style in the heart of Old Town.
Inexpensive. **Quality Inn-Towne.** 808 N. Washington St., modest.
Virginia Motel. 700 N. Washington St., pleasant.

BETHESDA. *Moderate:* **Bethesda Motor Hotel.** 7740 Wisconsin Ave., N.W.; near NIH.

Holiday Inn. 8120 Wisconsin Ave., N.W. 270 rooms with notable restaurant, The Peppermill.

Linden Hill Hotel. 5400 Pooks Hill Road. 1½ mi. N of I–495, exit 19. Off Wisconsin Ave. Apartment-hotel with pool, tennis courts; sauna; excellent restaurant. 150 rooms.

Ramada Inn. 8400 Wisconsin Ave., N.W., convenient to NIH and Bethesda Naval Hospital.

United Inn of America. 8130 Wisconsin Ave., N.W. Near National Institutes of Health and beltway.

FAIRFAX. *Moderate:* **Quality Inn.** 11180 Main St. at Germantown Rd on Rte. 50. 118 rooms; pool.

Inexpensive: **White House,** 9700 Lee Highway. 2½ mi. E on US 29. Small, 56 rooms. Pool; a restaurant nearby.

FALLS CHURCH. *Moderate:* **Best Western Village House Motor Hotel.** *Inexpensive.* 245 N. Washington St. On US 29, 1 block N of junction State 7. Small; 65 rooms. Pool, restaurant.

Quality Inn Governor. 6650 Arlington Blvd. 1 mi. W of Seven Corners on US 50; 2½ mi. E of I–495, exit 8E. Medium size, 124 rooms. Pool and restaurant.

SILVER SPRING. *Moderate:* **Holiday Inn.** 8777 Georgia Ave. 1 mi. S of I–495, exit 21 at Silver Spring Shopping Plaza. Pool; restaurant and dancing; 231 rooms.

Howard Johnson's. 2715 University Blvd., Wheaton. 160 rooms; pool.

 DINING OUT. In the past few years the number of fine restaurants has increased tremendously, with an ever-growing variety of cuisines serving authentic dishes from Europe, Asia, and Latin America.

For mid-priced dinners on each menu, the following *approximate* categories apply: *Moderate* $10–$15 and *Inexpensive* under $10. Prices are for a complete dinner including soup, entreé, and dessert (not included are drinks, tax and tip).

Moderate: **Adam's Rib.** 2100 Pennsylvania Ave., N.W. Variety of cuisines—Greek, American, French dishes—and fish.

Billy Martin's Carriage House. 1238 Wisconsin Ave., N.W. In the heart of Georgetown. American fare, including seafood.

Evans Farm Inn. On Madison Hwy., use McLean Exit No. 123 from Beltway. The seven-mile drive to McLean, Va. is well worth the trip. Distinctively American dishes, such as plantation chicken, roast duckling, spoon bread, and many others.

Gusti's. 19th and M Sts., N.W. Lasagna al Forno, fettucine, scampi, calamari, and other Italian standards are the favorites, and the homemade spumoni is essential for dessert. Alfresco dining in mild weather.

Joe and Mo's. 1211 Connecticut Ave., N.W. Hearty, straightforward American food; beef and seafood always on menu, along with two or three daily specials.

The Roundtable, 4859 Wisconsin Ave., N.W. A neighborhood family-type restaurant with few frills, but good food, reasonably priced.

Inexpensive. **Martin's.** 1264 Wisconsin Ave., N.W. Unassuming Georgetown restaurant with a down-to-earth menu.

Kennedy Center. *Encore Cafeteria (Inexpensive)* serves simple food with little variation, but if it's summertime you'll enjoy the terrace. *Curtain Call Café,* in a more intimate setting, offers good food at a *Moderate* price. (Same menu for lunch and dinner.)

CAFETERIAS. *Inexpensive:* **All States Cafeteria.** 1750 Pennsylvania Ave. N.W. Cafeteria service.

American Café. 1211 Wisconsin Ave., N.W.; 227 Massachusetts Ave., N.E.; 5252 Wisconsin Ave., N.W. More restaurants than cafeterias, these restaurants are all attractive, with good soups, salads, sandwiches and desserts.

Café Sorbet. 1810 K St., N.W. A bright, crowded French café with a range of inexpensive to moderate dishes.

Chamberlin's Cafeteria. 819 15th St., N.W. Just plain good food, southern style cooking, and homemade baked goods.

Hot Shoppes. Food for the whole family at locations all over town (see Yellow Pages).

Kitcheteria. In the Harrington Hotel, 11th and E Sts., N.W.; great for families.

National Gallery of Art. Constitution Ave., and 6th St., N.W. Handsome new dining room; ground floor of the Gallery. Get there early for lunch to avoid the long line. (Other good government cafeterias are also open to the public in the Smithsonian Air and Space Museum, Museum of American History, National Portrait Gallery and in the Commerce, Health, Education and Welfare, Interior, State and Supreme Court Buildings.)

Sholl's. 1433 K St., N.W. and 1990 K St., N.W. Vegetables, pies and puddings outstanding, as are the moderate prices.

CHINESE. *Moderate:* **Empress.** 1018 Vermont Ave. (near 15th and K Sts., N.W.) Award-winning cuisine; Mandarin and Szechuan dishes. Peking duck available without advanced notice.

China Coral. 6900 Wisconsin Ave., Chevy Chase, Maryland. Your trip to the suburbs will be rewarded by "the best in Chinese seafood from the seven seas."

FRENCH. *Moderate:* **L'Escargot.** 3309 Connecticut Ave., N.W. Good French cuisine at fair prices; unpretentious neighborhood restaurant.

Le Gaulois, 2133 Pennsylvania Ave., N.W. Small, but French cooking at its best at moderate prices.

Inexpensive. **Bread Oven,** 1220 19th St., N.W. Breakfast, lunch & dinner; daily specialties. Crowded, noisy; good cheeses, coffees, teas & pastries.

Chez Odette. 3063 M St. in Georgetown. Small, quiet, and unassuming, with plain French food. Try the chicken Di jon.

GREEK. *Inexpensive:* **Astor Restaurant.** 1813 M St., N.W. Authentic Greek food, reasonable prices. Booths. Deservedly crowded.

ITALIAN. *Moderate:* **Gusti's.** 1837 M St., N.W. A long-established traditional Italian restaurant with many rooms and a good sidewalk café.

Pines of Rome. 4709 Hampden Lane, Bethesda, Md. Southern Italian favorites served in an informal setting; popular, and justifiably crowded.

Inexpensive: **Anna Maria's.** 1737 Connecticut Ave., N.W. Small restaurant with no pretensions; fine veal dishes, open until 4 A.M. Mon.–Sat.

A. V. Ristorante. 607 New York Ave., N.W. Good southern Italian specialties served in a setting lacking in amenities and ambience.

MIDDLE EASTERN. *Moderate:* **Iron Gate Inn.** 1734 N St., N.W. Located in former stable, with outdoor dining in summer, this unusual restaurant offers couscous, hummous, pita bread, and delicious shishkebabs.

SEAFOOD. *Moderate:* **Aux Fruits De Mer.** 1329 Wisconsin Ave., N.W. A small, crowded Georgetown restaurant serving outstanding fish dishes; a friendly place with a loyal following.

Flagship. 900 Water St., S.W. Gigantic restaurant on waterfront; all meals cooked to order.

Hogate's Spectacular Seafood Restaurant. 9th St. and Maine Ave., S.W. Another restaurant on waterfront.

VIETNAMESE. *Inexpensive:* **Vietnam-Georgetown.** 2934 M St., N.W. Consistently fine specialties including crispy rolls, grilled shrimp on sugar cane, asparagus and crabmeat soup.

WEST VIRGINIA

Mountains and Commerce

It is known as the Mountain State, its motto is "Mountaineers are always free," and its state animal is the black bear. These emblems would indicate that West Virginia is a rugged place, an interesting state to visit. It is. What's more, such a trip can be relatively inexpensive.

At the start of the Civil War, there was no West Virginia. The state of Virginia extended from the Potomac west to the Ohio. But early in the conflict, Union victories in western Virginia incited the mountain men to rebel against the Tidewater aristocrats. They formed their own state and placed it in the Union.

Relics of this fight for control are found throughout the Allegheny Mountains, which tower over most of West Virginia. They are visible from Civil War battle sites, coal-mining areas, and feud-ridden backwoods.

In these mountains, the visitor can explore with back packs or on trail rides. He can float wild rivers (the New and the Gauley at Thurmond, for instance). He can visit caves and see strange plant life in the Spruce Run–Seneca Rocks National Recreation Area near Riverton. He can fish, hunt, camp, climb mountains—even see or try jousting, like a knight of old, at Moorefield, Petersburg, and Elkins.

For historic interest there are Indian burial mounds—the largest, Grave Creek, near Moundsville. Harper's Ferry, in the Maryland-Pennsylvania area, is scenically beautiful and historically important as the scene of John Brown's Raid. This old town at the juncture of the Shenandoah and Potomac rivers is being restored.

There are good highways throughout the state, including a turnpike, and byways to take you into backwoods spots where you can visit the hill people and the mining towns and even locate the area of the legendary Hatfield-McCoy feud near Logan.

In Charleston, the state capitol is recognized as one of the most beautiful Italian Renaissance buildings in the nation; the state museum is a storehouse of historic treasures and frontier artifacts.

In Wheeling, industrial tours can be arranged through the Chamber of Commerce. Oglebay Park has museums and year-round recreation facilities, including a ski area. Southward, on the Ohio River in Point Pleasant, the Point Pleasant Monument State Park marking a preliminary skirmish often called the first battle of the American Revolution.

PRACTICAL INFORMATION FOR WEST VIRGINIA

TOURIST INFORMATION. For maps, calendars of events, and other information write Office of Economic and Community Development, Travel Development Division, State Capitol, Charleston 25305.

MUSEUMS AND GALLERIES. *Exposition Coal Mine,* Beckley. Working equipment demonstrates mining techniques; miners are guides. *Pearl S. Buck Birthplace,* Hillsboro. Many original furnishings. *Jefferson County Museum,* Charles Town. John Brown memorabilia. *Willow Glen,* Wheeling. Huge mansion built by coal baron has Italian Renaissance furniture, Tiffany lamps, bedroom suite French gave Benjamin Franklin. *Huntington Galleries,* Huntington. Displays of paintings, ceramics and fabrics, art and craft shop.

Sunrise, Charleston. Restored mansion has art gallery, planetarium, live animal fair, garden center, children's museum.

DRINKING LAWS. All liquor stores in West Virginia are state-owned. Minimum legal drinking age is 18. Liquor sold by the drink in private clubs. Many hotels, motels, resorts and restaurants offer short-term club memberships enabling guests to order mixed drinks.

SUMMER SPORTS. *Boating.* Many state parks. *Diving.* Bakerton Quarries, *Baker;* Stoney River Dam, *Grant County;* Cheat Lake near *Morgantown;* Quarry Run near *Mont Chateau;* Bull Run, *Masontown;* Monongahela River near *Morgantown;* Tygart Lake State Park; New River, *Peterstown;* Sutton Lake; Summersville Lake.

Fishing. Statewide. Trout, black bass, muskie, other species year-round.

Horseback riding. Babcock, Blackwater Falls, Cacapon, Lost River, Mont Chateau, Pipestem, Watoga State Parks. Oglebay Park, Wheeling.

Mountain climbing. Seneca Rocks; Snowshoe Resort, Slatyfork.

WINTER SPORTS. *Ice-skating.* Blackwater Falls State Park, Coopers Rock State Forest, Wheeling Municipal Park, Pipestem State Park. *Skiing.* Chestnut Ridge, Morgantown; Canaan Valley State Park; Oglebay Park, Wheeling; Snowshoe Resort, Slatyfork; Alpine Lake, Terra Alta. *Tobogganing.*

Blackwater Falls State Park; and Oglebay Park, Wheeling, where there is also *sleigh riding.*

Trapping and hunting. Statewide. Mid-Sept. through Feb. Small game, fowl. Bow and arrow season for deer, bear, turkey. Many farms board hunters.

SPECTATOR SPORTS. *Auto racing.* West Virginia International Speedway, Ona, near Huntington. *Basketball.* West Virginia Univ., Morgantown; Marshall Univ., Huntington. *Tennis.* Pro/AM Tournament, Snowshoe Resort, Slatyfork. Mar., Sept. *Hydroplane racing.* Bluestone Lake, Hinton.

Football. West Virginia Univ., Morgantown.

Horseracing. Charles Town Race Course and Shenandoah Downs, Charles Town; Wheeling Downs, Wheeling.

Ice skating meet. Morgantown. Jan.

Skiing meet, state championships, Morgantown. Jan.

WHAT TO DO WITH THE CHILDREN. Huntington. *Camden Park.* Wild animal zoo, miniature golf, amusement rides, roller skating, penny arcade, boat and train rides. Charleston. *Sunrise.* Children's museum. Exhibits, live animals, displays, class instruction, planetarium.

Bluefield. *Ridge Runner Railroad.* Miniature replica of 1863 steam locomotive and three coaches; station modeled after 1890 depot; ¾-mile run, June–Aug.

Cass. Ride old steam locomotive to top of Bald Knob for spectacular view. In Cass are a *Civil War Museum, Cass Country Store,* and horse-drawn *Cass Stagecoach Line.* In nearby Green Bank is the *National Radio Observatory,* with tours of the installation.

Lewisburg. *Lost World Caverns.* Scenic trails wind amid fanciful stalagmites, stalactites, hex stones.

Wheeling. *Jamboree USA.* Live radio shows of country music presented by WWVA at Capitol Music Hall, 1015 Main St.

HOTELS AND MOTELS. Price categories for double occupancy will average: *Moderate* $25–45; *Inexpensive* under $25.

BECKLEY. *Moderate.* **Best Western Motor Lodge.** 1939 Harper Rd. (on WV 3 & I–77).

Honey in the Rock Motel. 2315 S. Faxette.

Laurel Lodge. 1909 Harper Rd.

Twin Falls Lodge. In Twin Falls State Park, 25 m. S.W. via WV 16, 54, then W. on WV 97.

Inexpensive. **Pagoda Motel.** 1114 Harper Rd.

BERKELEY SPRINGS. *Inexpensive:* **Park Haven Motor Lodge.** 9¾ mi. S. on US 522.

BLUEFIELD. *Moderate:* **Brier Motel.** 3206 E. Cumberland.

Econo-Travel Motel. 3400 Cumberland Rd.

Highlander Motel. 3144 Cumberland Rd.

CACAPON STATE PARK. *Moderate:* **Cacapon Lodge.** In Cacapon State Park, 10 mi. S. of Berkeley Springs.

CHARLESTON. *Moderate:* **El Rancho Motel.** 2843 MacCorkle Ave. (St. Albans).

Smiley's. 6210 MacCorkle Ave. S.W. (St. Albans).

Red Roof Inn. Putnam Village Shopping Center (Hurricane).

Inexpensive: **Town 'n Country.** 7203 MacCorkle Ave. (St. Albans).

CHARLES TOWN. *Moderate:* **Towne House.** E. Washington St.

CLARKSBURG. *Moderate:* **Town House West.** US 50, at Wilsonburg Rd. exit.

DAVIS. *Moderate:* **Blackwater Lodge.** In Blackwater Falls State Park, 3 mi. S.W. off WV 32.

GAULEY BRIDGE. *Moderate:* **Glen Ferris Inn.** 1½ mi. W., at Glen Ferris. **Hawks Nest Lodge.** In Hawks Nest State Park, 1 mi. W. on US 60.

HINTON. *Inexpensive:* **Coast to Coast Motel.** 1 mi. S. on WV 3, 20. **Sandman Motel.** 2 mi. S. on WV 3, 20.

HUNTINGTON. *Moderate:* **Uptowner Inn.** 1415 4th Ave.

LEWISBURG. *Moderate:* **General Lewis Inn.** 301 E. Washington St. **Old Colony Inn.** 1 mi. N. on US 219. **Sunset Terrace.** ½ mi. W. on US 60.

MARTINSBURG. *Inexpensive:* **Windewald Motel.** 1022 Winchester Ave,

MORGANTOWN. *Moderate:* **Coliseum.** 3506 Monongahela Blvd. **Mountaineer.** 452 Country Club Rd.

PARKERSBURG. *Inexpensive.* **Econo Lodge.** 6333 Emerson Ave. *Inexpensive:* **Parkersburg-Williamstown Days Inn.** I-77 & WV 31.

WHEELING. *Moderate:* **Econo Lodge.** At Exit 11, on I-70 at Dallas Pike, Triadelphia. **Comfort Inn.** 2501 National Rd. E.

WHITE SULPHUR SPRINGS. *Moderate:* **Best Western Old White Motel.** 865 E. Main St. **Colonial Court.** 1 mi. E. on US 60.

 DINING OUT. Price categories: *Moderate:* $10–17.50. *Inexpensive:* under $10. Prices are for a complete dinner but do not include drinks, tax or tip.

BERKELEY SPRINGS. *Inexpensive.* **Coolfont Recreation Center.** Rte. 9 W. All meals. All-you-can-eat buffets. Non-smokers' section. **The Country Inn,** 207 S. Washington St.

CHARLESTON. *Moderate:* **Smiley's,** 6210 MacCorkle Ave. **The Cornerstone,** 3103 MacCorkle Ave. SE., **Kanawha City Motor Lodge.**

DAVIS. *Moderate:* **Blackwater Lodge.** Blackwater Falls State Park.

FAIRMONT. *Moderate:* **Muriales.** 1742 Fairmont Ave. Italian. **Tiffany's.** In the Continental Key Club, Rte. 19, N. Fine seafood, Italian specialties.

HARPER'S FERRY. *Moderate:* **Cliffside Inn.** 2 mi. S.W on US 340.

HUNTINGTON. *Moderate:* **Rebels and Redcoats Tavern.** 626 Fifth St. W. One of state's finest wine selections. Lamb, quail, seafood, Bombay of beef are specialties.
Inexpensive: **Bailey's Cafeteria,** 410 9th St.

LEWISBURG. *Moderate:* **General Lewis Inn,** 301 E. Washington St.

PARKERSBURG. *Moderate:* **Point of View.** Overlooking historic Blennerhassett Island. Popular Sunday brunch, luncheon specialties, as well as flaming dishes prepared at tableside.

SHEPHERDSTOWN. *Moderate:* **The Bavarian Inn.** Overlooks Potomac River. Bavarian, Continental specialties, personalized service.

WHEELING. *Moderate:* **Eric's Steak House,** Waddle Run Road.

WHITE SULPHUR SPRINGS. *Moderate:* **Valley Barn.** Rte. 92 N.

ZELA. *Moderate:* **Country Road Inn.** Near Summersville. Superb Italian specialties, including homemade pasta, desserts; everything is made from scratch.

ALABAMA

More than Cotton

Birmingham, Alabama's largest city, is a good base for touring the state. Dominating the metropolis is the 55-foot-tall cast iron figure of Vulcan surveying the city from a pedestal 124 feet high. *Vulcan,* the Roman god of fire and forge, was designed for the Louisiana Purchase Exposition in St. Louis. It was made of Birmingham iron, cast in its foundries and overlooks the city as a monument to an industry.

Arlington is Birmingham's only antebellum home and tells a story of a bygone era as it stands in quiet memory. It was built by slaves of handmade bricks and hand-hewn timbers, and later became the headquarters for Union General Wilson. On display are authentic period furniture, a plantation kitchen with authentic utensils, a 19th-century garden and a museum.

Nearby, in the wooded areas of beautiful Lane Park, are Birmingham's zoo, Botanical and Japanese Gardens.

US 78 northwest intersects with Route 5 at Jasper. Route 5 continues north to Phil Campbell and the Mysterious Dismals Wonder Garden, then US 43 north to Tuscumbia, the birthplace and early home of Helen Keller. "Ivy Green," built by her grandfather in 1820, still stands. Helen Keller was born a normal child here in 1880, but two years later typhoid fever tragically deprived her of both sight and sound, beginning the greatest drama in Ivy Green's long history.

Much the same now as it was then, the many significant places and things—Whistle Path, the pump, her personal effects—have been kept intact for the visitor. Her story is retold each summer when William Gibson's play, "The Miracle Worker," is staged at the site.

Sheffield, north off US 43, is the principal railroad and industrial center of the Muscle Shoals area. Your chief interest, however, will be the Wilson Dam, largest of the TVA dams and a National Historic Monument, 5 miles northeast on State 133. Its great bulk—4,500 feet in length, 137 feet in height and 101 feet thick at the base—creates Wilson Lake, and miles of shoreline popular for aquatic vacation activities.

Huntsville

US 72 A east goes to Huntsville, once a cotton field and now the home of the Alabama Space and Rocket Center, located just southwest off US 231. Here, you can ride or operate 60 do-it-yourself space-age devices, including some used to train astronauts. Bus tours available to nearby Marshall Space Flight Center, NASA's largest facility.

Huntsville's link to the past is Twickenham, a 12-block, 300-structure district on the National Register of Historic Places. In the area 159 buildings are said to have historic and architectural significance and 12 are listed in the Historic American Buildings Survey of 1935. Twickenham is the founding place of Huntsville and the cornerstone of Alabama.

US 72 continues to Scottsboro and northeast through mountainous terrain to Bridgeport, gateway to the Russel Cave National Monument, which lies about 8 miles northwest off US 72 via County 75 and 91. The cave has a possibly unparalleled continuity of cave life for some 8,000 or more years. At the Visitor Center, displays show man's use of the cave from prehistoric times, covering Archaic, Woodland, Hopewellian, Mississippian, and historic cultures.

Montgomery and Mobile

The prime point of interest in Montgomery, the state's capital, is the historic State Capitol building, one of the Southland's most beautiful. Inside, the state's rich, historical background has been caught by an artist's brush in great, colorful murals; indeed, a visual experience. Conveniently across from the Capitol is the two-story First White House of the Confederacy which contains personal furnishings of Jefferson Davis and his family. The capitol building is surrounded by other state office buildings including the *Archives* and *History Building*.

Among the city's historic buildings are those in the Old North Hull Historic District, including a tavern, church, log cabin, grange hall, doctor's office, and 1850s town house.

The busy port city of Mobile overlaps past and present on the western bank of the Mobile River at the top of Mobile Bay. Old mansions and grillwork balconies of many pre-Civil War buildings overlook boulevards fanning out from Bienville Square at the center of the city and lead through flower-gardened residential sections.

Most highly publicized of gardens in the Mobile area is Bellingrath Gardens and Home on an 800-acre spread 20 miles south of town on

US 90 and then Bellingrath Rd., in the hamlet of Theodore. The Ile-aux-Oies River laces through some 65 acres of forests and gardens planted in azaleas.

To reach Pleasure Island and romp along the Gulf of Mexico, US 90 east from Mobile connects with either US 98 or State 59 going south.

PRACTICAL INFORMATION FOR ALABAMA

HOW TO GET THERE. *By air:* Birmingham direct on *American, Delta, Eastern, Republic, United, US Air;* Huntsville-Decatur on *Republic, United;* Mobile on *Eastern, Republic, American, Continental, Republic;* Montgomery on *Delta, Republic, Atlantic Southeast.* Dothan and Tuscaloosa on Republic. Anniston on *Atlantic Southeast, Piedmont,* and *Republic.*

By car: I–59 from Chattanooga, Tenn., to Birmingham; I–20 from Atlanta, Ga., to Birmingham; both to Tuscaloosa; I–85 from Atlanta, Ga., to Montgomery; I–65 from Tenn. to Mobile; and I–10 from New Orleans, La. to Mobile.

By bus: Greyhound, Trailways.

By train: Amtrak into Birmingham, Anniston, Eutaw, Livingston and Tuscaloosa.

TOURIST INFORMATION SERVICES. Montgomery, 36130: Alabama Bureau of Publicity and Information, State Highway Bldg.; Alabama State Parks, State Administrative Bldg.; Alabama Travel Council, 660 Adams Ave.; all local Convention & Visitors Bureaus, Tourist Information Centers or Chambers of Commerce. Toll-free information (except in-state, Alaska, Hawaii), 800-633-5761. In Alabama call 800–392–8096.

MUSEUMS AND GALLERIES. Birmingham: *Museum of Art.* 2000 8th Ave. north; *The Red Mountain Geological Museum,* 2230 15th Ave. S. Mobile: *Fine Arts Museum of the South,* Langan Park. Montgomery: *Museum of Fine Arts,* 440 S. McDonough St.; *Tumbling Waters Museum of Flags,* 131 S. Perry St.

HISTORIC SITES. Dauphin Island: *Fort Gaines* stands at entrance to Mobile Bay, near scene of 1864 Battle of Mobile Bay during which Admiral Farragut defeated Confederates. Gulf Shores: *Fort Morgan,* twin fort defending entrance to Mobile Bay, captured by Union forces during Mobile Bay campaign. Alexander City: *Horseshoe Bend National Military Park,* where Andrew Jackson defeated the Creek Indians to break their strength during the War of 1812. Wetumpka: *Fort Toulouse,* erected by the French in 1717 to defend their trade with the Indians from British interlopers. Site includes a nature trail and the William Bartram Arboretum.

TOURS. *Gray Line Tours* offers variety packages around Mobile. In the Sheraton Inn at 301 Government Street.

DRINKING LAWS. Liquor sold by drink in licensed places; by miniature bottles in restaurants and lounges, which also sell beer. Most metropolitan areas are "wet." Some counties are "dry." Minimum age: 19 years. No Sunday sales.

SPORTS. *Boating:* Rental boats in many state parks, and from marinas and fish camps. *Fishing:* Fresh water rivers and lakes, plus Gulf of Mexico for saltwater angling. License required at nominal cost. *Golf: Golf Digest* rates C.C. of Birmingham; Jetport G.C., Huntsville; and Langan Park G.C., Mobile, and the golf courses at the Grand Hotel at Point Clear. For other courses write Alabama Bureau of Publicity and Information, State Highway Bldg., Montgomery 36130.

Hunting: Obtain information from Alabama Department of Conservation, Game and Fish Division, Montgomery 36130.

SPECTATOR SPORTS. *Basketball* via college teams. *Football* heavies at Birmingham's Legion Field Stadium, site of the Hall of Fame Bowl in December; Senior Bowl game, Mobile in Jan.; and Blue-Gray game, Montgomery in Dec. *Horse Shows:* Decatur, Montgomery, and Selma, Sept. into Nov. *Rodeo:* Montgomery and Opp in Mar.; Athens in Aug. *Greyhound Racing:* year-round at Greentrack in Eutaw, Feb.–Dec., Mobile.

WHAT TO DO WITH THE CHILDREN. Birmingham: Birmingham Zoo, 2630 Cahaba Rd., US 280. Mobile: U.S.S. *Alabama,* Battleship Pkwy., US 90. Montgomery: W.A. Gayle Planetarium, 1010 Forest Ave.

HOTELS AND MOTELS. Most of the motels and hotels in Alabama, especially those along the Gulf Coast, boast various indoor and outdoor recreational facilities. Listings are in order of price category based upon double occupancy: *Moderate:* –$25 to $35; *Inexpensive:* under $25. For a more complete explanation of hotel and motel categories see *Facts at Your Fingertips* at the front of this volume.

ALEXANDER CITY. *Moderate:* **Horseshoe Bend.** Restaurant, pool.

BIRMINGHAM. *Moderate:* **Holiday Inn.** Complete. 6 locations.
Motel Birmingham. Pleasant rooms, pool. 7905 Crestwood Blvd.
Passport Inn. Convenient to campus of Univ. of Ala. in Birmingham.
Primeway Inn. All facilities. 195 W. Oxmoor Rd.
Southern Motor Inn. All facilities. 1313 3rd Ave. N.

DECATUR. *Moderate:* **The Decatur Inn.** Olympic pool, restaurant.
Red Carpet Inn. Restaurant, pool (heated).

FLORENCE. *Moderate:* **Florence TraveLodge.** Short-order restaurant open 24 hours, pool (heated).
Quad Cities Inn. Pool. Pets allowed.

FLORENCE-MUSCLE SHOALS. *Moderate:* **Lakeview Inn.** Pets permitted. Restaurant.

GADSDEN. *Moderate:* **Holiday Inn.** Café; laundry; airport transportation.

GULF SHORES. *Moderate:* **Oleander.** Off-season rates. On water. Half mile from state park.

GUNTERSVILLE. *Moderate:* **Lake Guntersville State Resort Park.** Resort inn, restaurant.
Inexpensive: **Bel Air Motel.** Kitchenette units available.

HUNTSVILLE. *Moderate:* **Barclay Motel.** Two locations, all facilities.
Kings Inn Motor Hotel. Restaurant, pool, nightly entertainment.
Inexpensive: **Brooks Motel.** Pool; restaurants nearby.

MOBILE. *Moderate:* **Beverly Motel.** Restaurants nearby. **Holiday Inn.** Four
locations.
Howard Johnson's. Pool, restaurant.
Days Inn. One of chain; pool, restaurant.
Family Inns of America. Pool. Children under 12 free.
Inexpensive: **Motel 6.** Pool. Pets allowed.

MONTGOMERY. *Moderate:* **The Diplomat.** Pool; restaurant; kids under 16
free.
Inexpensive: **Scottish Inns.** 2 locations. Pool, restaurant usually open only
in mornings.
Motel 6. Pool, adjacent restaurant.
Town Plaza Motel, restaurant next door.

YOUTH HOSTELS. Mobile: *YMCA,* 61 South Conception St.; *YWCA.* 1060
Government St. Montgomery; *YMCAs* at: Central Branch, 761 South Perry St.;
East Montgomery Branch, 3407 Pelzer Ave.; Cleveland Ave. Branch, 1202
Cleveland Ave.; and a *YWCA* at 204 South Lawrence St.

 DINING OUT in Alabama leans toward traditional
Southern dishes, including Southern fried chicken, ham
steak with red gravy, and chicken pan pie. The Gulf
Coast is noted for creole specialties, so be sure to ask for
Gulf flounder, shrimp, and other special seafoods and gumbos. In river towns
try catfish caught fresh from the Tennessee River.

Restaurants are in order of price category. Price categories and ranges for a
complete meal, excluding drinks, are as follows: *Moderate:* $10–15; *Inexpensive:*
under $10. For a more complete explanation of restaurant categories see *Facts
at Your Fingertips* at the front of this volume.

BIRMINGHAM. *Inexpensive:* **Cathay Inn,** Homewood. Exceptional Manda-
rin and Szechuan cuisine.
Steve Leontis Smokehouse. Best barbecue in town.
La Paree. 2013 5th Ave. North. Luncheon specials.
Lloyd's. Best barbecue out of town. 5301 Hwy. 280 S.
Battle Cafeteria. Self-serve buffet, Hoover Mall, Hwy. 31 S.

DECATUR. *Inexpensive:* **Gibson's.** Barbecue and Brunswick stew.

FLORENCE. *Moderate:* **Lakeview Inn Restaurant.** Regional specialties.
Inexpensive: **Starkey's Cafeteria.** Southern food, atmosphere.

GADSDEN. *Inexpensive:* **The Embers.** Specialty, seafood.

GUNTERSVILLE. *Inexpensive:* **Reid's.** Specialties, catfish, vegetables and
desserts.

HUNTSVILLE. *Moderate:* **The Fogcutter.** Steaks, seafood, salad bar. Locally
popular.

MOBILE. *Moderate:* **Constantine's.** Outstanding seafood.
Eight Kings. European cuisine.
Inexpensive: **Morrison's Cafeteria.** 3282 Springdale Plaza.

MONTGOMERY. *Moderate:* **Riviera.** Good, entertainment, open all day.
Inexpensive: **Elite.** Steaks and seafood. Locally popular for more than 60 years.
Morrison's. Cafeteria.

FLORIDA

Where the Sun Spends the Winter

Today's Florida is a subtropical playground, home and workplace for some nine million people, vacationland throughout the year for the seekers of something—wildlife, high life, low life; the quiet, noisy, lively, sedate, simple, luxurious, or a combination; in sum, the good life. More of them come in summer than winter. July and August are the peak months, when the school's-out family trade heads for the summer beach resorts of northern Florida from Pensacola to Apalachicola; to the Sun Coast area of Tampa and St. Petersburg, or central Florida's newest fun-tier, the Orlando–Walt Disney World area.

The winter visitors stay longer, spend more, and are concentrated in the bottom half of the state, where it's warmer than anywhere else in the continental United States. Average January temperatures are 71 degrees in the Florida Keys and 69 on the mainland southern tip, compared to 54 in the northwest Panhandle.

As an alternative to the high-priced winter season, late-April through May offers dependably warm but not hot weather; many of the subtropical flowers and trees are at their gaudiest then, and the mid-summer tendency toward brief but almost daily showers has not yet begun. Labor Day through November provide the other bonus period, at low hotel rates like those of late spring.

On a bare-bones budget during your Florida foray, you can: (1) Plan ahead. Even in the toniest South Florida towns you can find budget motels with cooking facilities. (2) Picnic once or more a day. The parks are everywhere, many with grills. (3) Have lunch rather than dinner in the most expensive restaurants. Look for Early Bird dinners, usually before 6:30 or 7. Even the better restaurants may have them. (4) Drink during Happy Hour. Many lounges have such generous hot and cold hors d'ouevres free during these hours; you won't need dinner. (5) Carry some way of heating water in your room. It can make morning coffee, soup for lunch, or midnight snack, instant freeze-dried "camper" meals. (6) Fish in saltwater. No license is needed. Then grill and eat the catch. You're never more than 60 miles from the sea in Florida. (7) Stay put. Many hostelries discount stays of one week or more. (8) Leave pets home. You'll pay extra for them in many hotels or you may be refused at many others.

Guide to Miami Beach

To get to Miami, just go south. You can't miss it—and you shouldn't. There's Miami Beach and Coral Gables, Hialeah and Miami Springs, the core city of Miami proper, and Biscayne Park, West Miami, North Miami, South Miami, Miami Shores, and others. Put them all together and they still spell Miami, the magic word.

Over four million visitors a year come to this little (7.2 square miles) island just across Biscayne Bay from mainland Miami. There is a permanent population of more than 96,000, but the island can accommodate three times this many visitors. One-fourth of all the hotels in Florida are situated here in a slender strip of architectural virtuosity. The 360 hotels have 29,083 rooms ranging from $25 to $150 a day during the winter season, about half that, or less, in summer. There are also 47,866 apartment units in 2,571 other buildings, but this isn't all, for in truth the beach and the hotels extend northward more than a hundred additional blocks: Surfside and Bal Harbour, the county's Haulover Park with a public beach and a marina, and the oceanfront motels—fancy, gaudy, pretty, monstrous, prim, ostentatious—side by side in a battle for attention all the way to the county line. The entire string, top to bottom, should be seen at least once. Start by taking A1A from Hollywood and Hallandale. The Sheraton Bal Harbour (formerly the Americana) at 97th Street and Collins Avenue, will be the first of the large, convention-oriented luxury hotels you will see, and Collins Avenue, for the next ninety-seven blocks, *is* Miami Beach, the beach, and the mailing addresses of Miami Beach, Surfside, Bal Harbour, and Sunny Isles. For the purposes of our listings, we're combining them all under Miami Beach. The effect is a blinding, kaleidoscopic, gaudy extravagance. Most of the spectacle is new since World War II. For a number of years after the war, Miami Beach built more new hotels than all the rest of the world combined.

Getting around in Miami by automobile is fairly simple, but can run into a lot of mileage. The street numbering system is centered at Miami Avenue and Flagler Street, and is divided into quadrants surrounding that point—northeast, northwest, southeast, and southwest. Streets run north and south, as do terraces. The avenues and places run east and west. There are exceptions: Coral Gables has its own system of Spanish-named avenues, However, the basic system prevails generally, as far as 215th Street on the north, 360th Street on the south, and 217th Avenue on the west. If you want to get to Northwest South River Drive or Southwest North River Drive, however, it's perhaps best to take a cab.

Miami Beach's massive $64-million beach restoration project is now finished, promising 10.5 miles of 300-foot-wide sand from Government Cut north to Haulover Park. The entire beach is public but you'll find easier access, and parking, by using parks rather than trying to sneak through hotels.

From 79th to 87th streets, North Shore Open Space Park is Miami Beach's newest attraction, a 32-acre oceanfront recreation area. Environmental restoration includes man-made sand dunes, masses of sea grapes and sea oats, and a variety of flowers, plants and trees. Along with the beachfront for water sports, the park is equipped with winding boardwalks, picnic areas, bicycle paths, and shaded pavilions.

Downtown Miami

Biscayne Boulevard is the city's best-known thoroughfare. Since it is also US 1, it will send you to Key West or Canada if you stick with it, but, for our purposes, it is Miami's downtown "show" street. Stately royal palms line its eight traffic lanes, divided by four parking lanes, between Southeast First Street and Northeast Fifth Street. On the west are tall, showy hotels and business buildings; on the east is Bayfront Park, a worthy daytime destination but best avoided now at night, with the charter fishing fleet docked on the Bay. On the north end of the park is the city's auditorium and access to the Port of Miami on Dodge Island where cruise ships leave for all points of the Bahamas and Caribbean ports of call. At the south end of the park; at the foot of Flagler Street, is the Miami Public Library.

Since 1961, Miami has added a whole new dimension. It is called "Little Havana," an exciting area of excellent restaurants, nightclubs, and shops which, for the English-speaking visitor, provides the flavor and feel of a foreign country. It centers around SW 8th Street and W. Flagler Street where most of Miami's more than 450,000 Cubans work and live, an area of "old Miami" two-story homes and aging commercial buildings. Little Havana is no hybrid; it's a completely Cuban world with hundreds of open front cafés, restaurants, oyster bars, bookstores, tobacco shops, and grocers. About all that is missing from Old Havana are the cries of lottery ticket vendors and the covered arcades. Prices in Little Havana can be ridiculously low for good Cuban dishes in some of the smaller niches to downright expensive in the fancier supper clubs. There are also excellent Cuban-Chinese restaurants in the area. Although Miami has been overburdened recently with a surge of refugees from the various Caribbean Islands, which has made the crime rate rise, it is still a big attraction for tourists. As with any other city in this world, be cautious about walking alone with a wallet or handbag full of money on deserted streets late at night.

Close to downtown, at NW Third Street and 14th Avenue, is the Orange Bowl, where the Miami Dolphins and University of Miami Hurricanes play football. It's simpler to park downtown and take a special bus or cab on game days, for parking facilities are limited.

Just past the Miami Marine Stadium on the Rickenbacker Causeway on Virginia Key is Planet Ocean, a showcase of seven multi-media panoramic theaters, 100 dazzling exhibits—including an iceberg—and a real submarine for youngsters to view inside. The multi-million-dollar ocean science center is world headquarters for the non-profit International Oceanographic Foundation which includes theme exhibits on the Ocean Reservoir of Life, The Restless Sea and Weather Engine. At present, one of the most popular exhibits, recounted on television monitors and model ships, recounts the history of the gold-laden Spanish galleons and the hurricanes that scattered these ships over the coral reefs, spewing their treasures on to the Keys and the Caribbean.

Across the street is the popular Miami Seaquarium, with its performing killer whale and dolphins, and Lost Islands exhibit.

A bridge connects Virginia Key to Key Biscayne, the area's favorite recreation spot. During the summer months, the rates at the outstanding Sonesta Beach Hotel & Tennis Club on Key Biscayne plunge so low, including special weekend rates, that families should not miss the fun of staying here. The "Just Us Kids" program for the little ones is supervised by trained counselors. The northern half of the 4½-mile-long island is county-owned Crandon Park, which offers a marina, 2½ miles of uncluttered beach, landscaped parking areas, barbecue pits, and sports facilities. The middle third of the island consists of privately owned homes, apartments, and hotels and the southern third, Cape Florida, is a state park.

Back to the mainland, and just a few blocks south (follow the signs) is another county facility, Villa Vizcaya, the former home of James Deering of the International Harvester fortune. Deering collected art works abroad for twenty years before beginning work in 1912 on what is, in reality, an Italian Renaissance palace. With up to one thousand craftsmen at work, it took five years to complete the 69-room main palace and formal gardens, 10 acres with clipped hedges, fountains, reflecting pools, and statuary in seven separate areas. As a breakwater, there is a stone version of Cleopatra's barge. Inside, architects faced the problem of accommodating a frescoed ceiling here, a sideboard from a 15-century Italian church there, or the tapestry that hung in Robert Browning's villa in Asolo, Italy. What it all cost, Deering didn't say, but estimates range up to $10 million pre-World War I dollars. The "Sound and Light" performances at Vizcaya are spectacular; check the schedules at the hotel desk to see this worthwhile show.

Across from the Vizcaya entrance is the Museum of Science, on original Vizcaya grounds. The Space Transit Planetarium at the east end of the museum aims to make every viewer feel like an astronaut; visitors blast off and go on a reeling simulated space ride. A 65-foot dome makes it the third largest planetarium in the country.

Coconut Grove is Miami's Bohemian section and at the same time the home of some of the area's oldest families, the original settlers and local aristocracy who came down before the various boom times. It is a village within the city, private, discreetly cosmopolitan, charming, part Greenwich, Connecticut, and part Sausalito, California, with overtones of Tahiti. To reach it, go south on Miami Ave., which becomes Bayshore Drive.

Residential Gables

Coral Gables is something else again. From U.S. 1, look for SW 22nd St., and head west to the Spanish-towered and columned city hall where they'll give you a map and notes for a series of self-guided tour signs on the street that will hit all the high spots for twenty rambling miles of points such as the Venetian Pool, the University of Miami, the villages (little compounds of homes in Dutch, French, and Chinese architecture), the plazas, and entranceways.

Coral Gables is an example of what can be done to keep a city the way most of the residents want it. Every street was planned and plotted when it all began in the '20s. Now every new building must be approved by a board of architects and erected according to a strict zoning code. There are no billboards, no cemeteries, no trailer parks, and industry must be clean, smokeless, and within a designated area.

PRACTICAL INFORMATION FOR MIAMI AND MIAMI BEACH

HOW TO GET THERE. *By air:* You can reach Miami on direct flights from all major American cities via *Continental, Delta, Eastern, Northwest Orient, TWA, Pan Am, Ozark, Piedmont, Republic, USAir, American* or *United.* Eight companies serve Miami from cities within Florida, plus the all-jet *Air Florida.* With all the deregulation which began in 1979, more and more airlines have extended routes to Miami, so do check with an ASTA travel agent. Now *Air Florida* also flies from Washington, D.C., Philadelphia, New York, the Caribbean, Central America, the Bahamas, and Europe.

Air Canada, Delta and *Eastern* have direct flights from Montreal; *Eastern* from Ottawa; *Air Canada* or *Eastern* from Toronto. There are connecting flights from Calgary, Edmonton, Halifax, Hamilton, and Vancouver.

There are over 750 flights weekly from 48 Latin American cities.

British Airways, Pan Am and others have direct flights from London; Pan Am also has direct flights from Paris, Frankfurt, Amsterdam. *Aeromexico* has a Paris–Madrid–Miami flight. Iberia has Madrid–San Juan–Miami flights. *Lufthansa* flies from Frankfurt; *El Al* has direct service from Tel Aviv; *Eastern* flies from Haiti, Dominican Republic, Cancun, Merida, Aruba and more. *Aeromexico* and *Mexicana* fly to Mexico City, Merida, Cancun.

By train: Amtrak has regular service. Even before streamlining by Amtrak, the *Seaboard Coast Line,* a Miami to New York run, was one of the last truly luxury trips by train still available in the U.S. Now it is even better. Coach fare is cheaper than by air; sleepers are much more expensive. Approximately a 24-hr. journey.

By car: From the northeast I–95 (not yet completed in some parts) is your fastest route; A1A the beautiful, leisurely way; US 1, the slow, sure way.

By bus: Trailways or Greyhound will get you there.

By boat: The Intracoastal Waterway parallels the coastline and runs 349 mi. from Jacksonville to Miami.

HOW TO GET AROUND. Take the airport limousine to your hotel, if it is a major one. You will save about $4 or $5 on the trip. *Taxis* charge over $1 for the initial 1/9 of a mi. and the rates keep going up. At press-time, each additional 2/9th mi. was 20 cents. Renting a car is your best bet; there's a great supply and rates are reasonable.

TOURIST INFORMATION. *Metro Dade County Dept. of Tourism,* 234 W. Flagler St., Miami 33130, and *Miami Beach Visitor and Convention Authority,* 555 Seventeenth St., Miami Beach 33139.

SEASONAL EVENTS. *January:* New Year's Night, *Orange Bowl football game, International Travel Camping Show,* Miami.

February: Doral Open Golf Tournament, late Feb. to early Mar., at Doral Country Club. *Sidewalk Art Show,* Coral Gables. More than 200 artists participate, Feb. 15 to 17. *Grand Prix* auto race, *Miami Boat Show* and *Grove Arts Festival,* all mid-Feb. *Vizcaya Art Show,* 3251 S. Miami Ave., last Sun. in Feb.

March: Carnaval Miami, Hispanic festival, held the first two weekends in March. *Exhibition games of the Baltimore Orioles,* and *Youth Fair,* both mid-Mar. to early Apr. *Museum of Science's Annual Around the World Fair* at Tropical Park Race Track.

June: Poinciana Festival, early June.

July: Fourth of July Parade, Key Biscayne, floats, marching units, and bicycles. *Bowling Tournament of the Americas,* Miami. Amateur bowling champions from nations of the Western hemisphere vie for top honors, July 8 to 14.

November: Jr. Tennis Championships, Coral Gables, for youngsters 8 to 12, regarded as tune-up for Jr. Orange Bowl Tennis Tournament.

December: Orange Bowl Festival, one of the nation's most celebrated festival and sporting events. King Orange Jamboree Parade highlights New Year's Eve in downtown Miami, terminating with the football classic on New Year's Night. *Junior Orange Bowl* activities in Coral Gables.

MUSEUMS AND GALLERIES. Historical: *Cape Florida State Recreation Area,* 1200 S. Crandon Blvd., Key Biscayne. Seminole history. Restored Cape Florida Lighthouse. *Historical Museum of Southern Florida,* NW 2nd Ave. and 1st St. Maintained by nonprofit Historical Association of South Florida. Closed Mon.

Art: *Bass Museum of Art,* 2100 Collins Ave., Miami Beach. Paintings, sculpture, vestments and tapestries. *Bacardi Art Gallery,* 2100 Biscayne Blvd. Exhibitions by local, national, and international artists. *Dade County Center for Fine Arts,* NW 1st St. and 2nd Ave. *Lowe Art Museum,* 1301 Miller Dr., Coral Gables. Becoming one of the finer galleries in the South. *Metropolitan Museum and Art Center,* 1212 Anastasia Ave., Coral Gables. Art treasures, splendid building. *Virginia Miller Galleries,* Coconut Grove, fine art and artifacts. *Monastery Cloister of Saint Bernard,* 16711 W. Dixie Hwy., North Miami Beach. Built in Segovia, Spain, in 1141, it was disassembled and brought to the U.S.

Special Interest: Museum of Science, 3280 S. Miami Ave., Miami. Recently upgraded. Dynamic hands-on scientific exhibits/dioramas. Museum has extensive displays of Florida wildlife. Planetarium is adjacent to the Museum of Science. Afternoon and evening show daily. Weekly programs in Spanish. Programs change every 5 to 6 wks. *Planet Ocean,* just past the Marine Stadium on Rickenbacker Causeway, Key Biscayne. The mystique of the oceans is explored in seven multi-media theaters and through over 100 exhibits. The ocean showplace includes an iceberg, and a submarine for children to enter. Spectacular theme areas, including the Gulf Stream, NOAA Hurricane Center, and ship models are just a few of the fascinations here.

Others: Miami Wax Museum, 13899 Biscayne Blvd. Miami from Columbus to the astronauts in life-size wax sculptures. *International Design Center,* North Miami Ave. at 42nd St., Miami. A grouping of art centers that offer glimpses of interior design and the technical construction of architectural and decorating innovations.

HISTORIC SITES. *Vizcaya,* Dade County Art Museum, 3251 S. Miami Ave., Miami. An Italian palace, created by an American millionaire with a Hollywood imagination. *Art Deco Historic District,* the largest single concentration of Art Deco architecture in U.S., situated in a 10-block area in S. Miami Beach.

TOURS. *Nightclub tours: Leblang's Tours,* 216 71st St., Miami Beach; *Grayline Tours,* 587–8080, *American Sightseeing,* 871–4992, *A-1 Lines,* 573–0550, or see the bell captain at your hotel.

By boat: Island and Casino Tours. Cruise ships leave from Dodge Island port in Miami, and Port Everglades in Fort Lauderdale. The casinos at Freeport and Paradise Island are the favored destinations. Island life lures nongamblers, also, to Nassau, Haiti, Bimini and Jamaica. The *Nikko Gold Coast Cruises* offers five sightseeing tours: Everglades, Seaquarium, Millionaires' Row, Villa Vizcaya, Gold Coast Combination. Sails from Haulover Park Docks and Miami Beach.

Check into *Trolley Tyme Tours* with passenger pickup along Miami Beach on "Lolly the Trolley." Various day and night tours; children's rates.

By air: Cruise at fine camera height in a *helicopter* from Gold Coast Helicopters, 15101 Biscayne Blvd., or 3000 Interama Blvd., or try *glider-sightseeing* from the Miami Gliderport, operating from Nov. to May and located on Krome Ave. and SW 162nd St. Soaring instructions.

Everglades by airboat. Along the Tamiami Trail, on US 41 about 17 mi. W. of downtown Miami, airboat operators will whisk you off on small craft with aircraft motors and guarded propellers. These were developed for fishing and hunting forays into the remote wilderness areas. Four to twelve persons can pile aboard and the normal sightseeing tour costs only a nominal fee.

Other Tours: American Sightseeing Tours offers one-day and extended tours to Walt Disney World, shuttle service, group sightseeing, special tours, school charters and race track service, 1000 NW LeJeune Rd. *Burnside–Ott,* at the Opa Locka Airport, offers air tours with professional pilots and late-model aircraft. Paddleford Packet's *Viking Explorer* cruises between Miami and Flamingo with stops in the Keys (Nov–April).

GARDENS. The Cloud Forest, part of the Miami Beach Garden Center and Conservatory (a rapidly developing horticultural complex), is operated by the city without admission charge. On Washington Ave. 2 blocks N. of Lincoln Road Mall (follow in to the west). The air inside the dome is changed very frequently, but it's so hot no visitor can stay very long. The Cloud Forest plants thrive in a droopy-hot atmosphere like that in the backwaters of the Amazon. This is a compact display with many rarities. The conservatory was recently given one of the world's larger orchid collections.

Fairchild Tropical Garden, 10901 Old Cutler Rd., Miami, is always open from sunrise and the "largest tropical botanical garden in America," holds the Fairchild Ramble in early Dec. It's a benefit bargain hunt with unimaginable goods—bobcat skin, a 90-year-old baby buggy, a Japanese party set that cost the lady who gave the party $2,500. The garden itself, founded by a tax attorney, is spread out on 83 acres south of Matheson Hammock Park. Leave US 1 at SW 112th St. and take a short jog on SW 57th Ave. before turning left on Old Cutler Road. Hourly tours on a little train. Admission fee.

Other horticultural things to see: the *Miami Flower Show* is in mid-Mar. *Garden of Our Lord,* St. James Lutheran Church, 110 Phoenetia, Coral Gables, displays many exotic plants mentioned in the Bible. *Japanese Garden,* Watson Park, on the MacArthur Causeway, features statues of Hotei, arbor, teahouse, stone lanterns, pagoda, ornate main gate, rock gardens, and waterfall lagoon. *Redland Fruit and Spice Park,* 35 mi. SW of Miami, in Homestead. Intersection of Coconut Palm Dr. (SW 248th St.) & Redland Rd. (187th Ave.). A 20-acre tropical showplace featuring fruit, nut, and spice-producing plants from around the world. Guided tours Wed. at 3:30 are free.

About a 30-minute drive from Miami Beach, green-thumbers will be delighted with the *U.S. Subtropical Horticultural Research Unit.* The Ladies Garden Club sponsors free tours Tuesdays and Thursdays from 10 A.M. to 2 P.M. Tropical fruits, such as mangos, and a splendid variety of rare plants are grown here.

SPORTS. Because of the semitropical climate there is no division of sports activities into summer or winter in the greater Miami area. Instead, we will list them alphabetically. *Bicycling:* There are about 100 mi. of well-marked secondary routes adjoining thoroughfares for safe, scenic cycling. Grey-nolds Park is a good starting point in the north part of the Miami area. Bike paths wind through picnic grounds, around a lake with boat rides and fishing. Coconut Grove has excellent bike paths, winding through the oldest and most historic section of Miami. Route maps are provided by local chambers of commerce, the Coral Gables Community Development Dept. and Dade Metro Dept. of Tourism. Numerous shops offer loaners; bicycles can be included in some auto rental arrangements.

Boating: Miami has berthing for over 4,000 boats and takes anything up to a 180-ft. yacht. Miamarina is the city's newest and most modern marine facility with all the downtown advantages. It offers 178 slips for pleasure craft and space for 30 commercial craft, such as charter and sightseeing boats. Circuit voyages out of Miami go through the Keys, Fort Myers and Okeechobee Waterway. As for distance on the Intracoastal Waterway, Jacksonville to Miami is a 349-mi. trip and it's 158 mi. inside the Keys from Miami to Key West. Competitive boating includes a speed classic at the Marine Stadium on Rickenbacker Causeway and, in mid-Jan., a 9-hr. endurance race. There's an 807-mi. race from Miami to Montego Bay and races from St. Petersburg to Fort Lauderdale and Miami to Cat Cay in late Feb. The Lipton Cup yacht race is considered by yachtsmen to be a warmup for the great Miami-Nassau race; both are held late Feb. or early Mar.

Fishing: Deep-sea fishing: You can charter boats for trolling, drift-fishing or bottom fishing. Since they carry up to six persons, you can share the costs. The deep blue of the Gulfstream is their beat for the big gamefish, marlin, sail, wahoo, dolphin and tuna. Key Largo, south of Miami in the Florida Keys, is great sport-fishing haunt. There are about 200 licensed fishing guides to take you to the Upper Keys and into the flats of Florida Bay.

Freshwater fishing: Most famous freshwater fishing in Greater Miami is the Tamiami Canal, extending from west edge of Miami along US 41. The canal is 50 ft. wide, 50 mi. long with plenty of parking and fishing spots along the banks. Skiffs and hired guides are available along the Tamiami Trail for trips into the Everglades. The *Miami Herald's* Metropolitan Miami Fishing Tournament, one of the world's largest, runs each year from mid-Dec. to mid-Apr. Despite the skill and knowledge of local anglers, a majority of the average annual 50,000 entries of fish contesting for citations and trophies are made by visitors from all parts of the world.

Golf: The greater Miami area has over 45 golf courses. Greens fees are low on summer weekdays at most 18-hole municipal courses. Many courses offer reduced "twilight" rates, which take effect daily between 3 P.M. and 6 P.M., depending on the season.

The Doral C.C., Miami, with its five courses, ranks among the third ten of America's 100 greatest golf courses, according to *Golf Digest,* which also recommends: *Lejeune Melreese G.C.,* with a gently rolling terrain: *Vizcaya G. & C.C.,* nicely landscaped with palm trees; *C.C. of Miami,* a fine resort course; *Miami Lakes Inn & C.C.,* a challenging course; *King's Bay & C.C.,* a challenging, scenic course open to members and hotel guests; *Fontainebleau Hilton C.C.,* a Mark Mahannah course with seven lakes, rolling fairways (all in Miami). Also: *Miami Shores C.C., Miami Shores,* for members and their guests only; *Miami Springs G. & C.C., Miami Springs,* former site of the Miami Open; *Bay Shore Municipal,* Miami Beach, a municipal course with rolling fairways, mounds and lakes; *Key Biscayne G.C.,* Key Biscayne, a unique Robert Von Hagge course, with tough tests; *Palmetto* G.C., S. Miami, a municipal course with 13 water holes; *Biltmore* G.C., Coral Gables, a municipal course with some tricky water holes; and

Normandy Shores G.C., Miami Beach, on the Isle of Normandy in Biscayne Bay.

Ice Skating: Nearest facility is in Ft. Lauderdale: Sunrise Ice Skating Center, NW 88 Ave.

Water sports: Water-skiing schools, jumps, and towing services are located along beaches and causeways. *Skiing* lessons consist of approximately three 1-hr. sessions. Boats with tow equipment and fuel can be rented. *Surfing* is practiced in Florida, although the local surfers are a frustrated lot—the waves are seldom large enough. However they do their best at Haulover Beach Park and South Miami Beach, where there are special areas reserved for surfers. There are miles of sand beaches for *swimming.* Crandon Park and Cape Florida State Park on Key Biscayne; Haulover Beach on Collins Ave., north of Bal Harbour; Lummus Park on Miami Beach; Matheson Hammock, 2 mi. south of Miami on Old Cutler Rd., Tahiti Beach in South Miami, are among the many choice spots. Another favorite swimming spot is the Venetian Municipal Pool, 2701 DeSoto Blvd., formed from the coral quarry which was mined to build the city of Coral Gables. The pool is reminiscent of a Venetian Palazzo, with shady porticos, loggias and towers.

Windsurfing: Miami Windsurfing, 7524 SW 53 Ave., also lessons at Diplomat Hotel, Fontainebleau Hilton, Thunderbird.

Biggest splash for water-sport enthusiasts is the new North Shore Open Space Park, a $10-million, 32-acre oceanfront recreation area, from 79th to 87th Streets, Miami Beach. There are also bicycle paths, winding boardwalks, and picnic areas.

A number of local firms specialize in scuba and skindiving instructions and excursions to sunken hulls, reefs and underwater gardens. Fowey Rock Light area, just south of Key Biscayne, is among the best for *underwater photography.* Other fine locations are Haulover, Elbow Light, Pacific Light, Carysfort Light and John Pennekamp State Park. Skindivers should observe State Conservation laws regarding crawfish (Florida lobster) and other regulations on *spearfishing.* Crawfish may not be taken by spearing. There are no special restrictions on the use of spearguns in Dade and Broward counties, but they are prohibited in Pennekamp Park and within one mile of US 1 in the lower keys. Diver flags are required.

 SPECTATOR SPORTS. *Baseball:* In Miami, the Baltimore Orioles work out at the Miami Stadium, 2301 NW 10th Ave., beginning Feb. 15, with exhibition games starting Mar. 15. *Football:* The Miami Dolphins, under Coach Don Shula, won their first World Championship in 1973 and repeated in 1974—not bad for a team formed in 1966. They play in the Orange Bowl, as do the Univ. of Miami Hurricanes.

Racing: There are three horse racing tracks and one harness racing track in South Florida. *Hialeah Park,* 4 E. 25th St., is open Mar. to mid-Apr. The grounds also feature an aquarium, rare birds, flamingoes, English carriages, riding regalia, snacks and souvenirs, and a tram ride. *Gulfstream Park Race Track,* US 1, Hallandale; mid-Jan. to Mar. Miami's *Calder Race Course,* NW 27th Ave. at 210th St., has two seasons: May to Nov. and mid-Nov. to mid-Jan. All three tracks are within easy reach of Miami and Miami Beach. Special buses run from Miami Beach to Pompano Beach for harness racing at *Pompano Park.* Dog racing (greyhounds, of course), a Florida staple, at *Biscayne,* 320 NW 115th St.; Flagler, 410 NW 38 Ct.; Hollywood, 831 N. Federal Hwy. No minors allowed.

Jai-alai: A dangerous combination of handball, tennis and lacrosse, jai-alai requires great nerve, endurance and savvy—and lends itself to betting. The sport derives from Spain and 17th-century Basques. Players use a pelota (virgin-rubber ball covered with goatskin) and a cesta (curved basket of imported reed) which straps to the wrist. Nightly except Sun., Apr. to Dec. *Miami Jai Alai Fronton,* 3500 NW 37 Ave. Both *Dania Jai-Alai* and Miami Frontons offer excellent dining. One can see the games live or on closed-circuit TV.

WHAT TO DO WITH THE CHILDREN. A number of sea zoos have been created in Florida, and they are probably the most exciting of all diversions for youngsters—and perhaps parents, too. The largest and most famous is the *Miami Seaquarium* located beyond the Rickenbacker Causeway (follow US 1 to the sign with the circling shark), south of downtown. It has been there 20 years, and it is often crowded for the show in the porpoise tank. But there are also the shark show, the killer whale show, the penguin–seal–pelican show (for this you sit in an inclined grandstand), and the show down below in the great tank when the divers vacuum the bottom and feed the establishment's biggest captive. Daily 9 to 5.

Metrozoo, 124000 SW. 152nd St., Miami. A sunny, green, open and free animal preserve with no cages. Eventually, it will be the country's largest.

Planet Ocean, just past Marine Stadium on Rickenbacker Causeway. Newest addition to the Virginia Key ocean-science community, which includes The Rosenstiel School of Marine and Atmospheric Sciences of the University of Miami, and the Miami Seaquarium. A multi-million-dollar ocean-science showplace with more than 100 exhibits, including a Hurricane Center, ship models; an iceberg, a submarine for children to climb into and inspect, and more. The mystery and magic of the oceans are explored in exhibits and multi-media panoramic theaters. Open seven days a week.

Serpentarium, US 1, 126th St. and Dixie Hwy., South Miami. Cobras and other snakes, tortoises, crocodiles, iguanas. Cobra venom extraction. Daily 9 to 6. *Parrot Jungle,* 11000 SW 57th Ave. Birds perform all kinds of tricks. Winding trails through natural hammock to Flamingo Park, 9:30 to 5.

Monkey Jungle, about 20 mi. S. of Miami on U.S. 1. Monkeys cavort without being caged. Enclosures for visitors. Shows.

Miami Beach hotels, especially the most luxurious ones, have satisfying programs for the teenager and younger child. Usually they're free, all day every day if you like, summer, Christmas, Easter vacations. All the "club" activities are supervised by special counselors. At Omni International Hotel, the "Treasure Island" entertainment center is fun. Also in the mall are six first-run theaters for young film buffs.

HOTELS AND MOTELS. To the first-time visitor, the hotels of Miami Beach will seem like one continuous city. The Flabbergast Hotels, as they have been called, are the prototypes for much of the resort architecture around the world. To the honeymooner, beautiful; to the yearning secretary, a fable; to the social reformer, a parody; but nearly all are comfortable and superbly equipped.

What the hotels charge varies wildly, coming to a peak in mid-December, January, February. The labels attached here have meaning mostly as a way of establishing one or another as a bit more expensive than its neighbor. Many modestly rated establishments are the equal in comfort and location of those that—usually because of a later construction date—have a higher standard price.

Vacationers have a choice of hundreds of hotels and motels in the Miami and Miami Beach area, ranging from the most luxurious to merely modest. Restaurants, nightclubs, shops, and stores are usually close by the hotels, while tennis courts and golf courses are within easy driving distance. The vast majority of hotels have swimming pools for guests and the larger ones maintain free recreational programs.

Rates vary according to season and quality of room. The lowest rates are in the summer, which usually begins in May and continues until Nov. 1. This is the period for bargain hunters, when you can acquire pleasing and even downright sumptuous accommodations for around $30 a day per person.

We have listed hotels and motels alphabetically in categories determined by double, in-season rates: *Moderate,* from $50–70, *Inexpensive,* from $30–50.

MIAMI: *Moderate:* **Danker's Inn.** 5890 SW 8th St. 3-story motor inn with pools, play area, restaurant. Free airport transportation.

Holiday Inn. 10 locations, each with heated pool, restaurant, bar.

Howard Johnson's. 7 locations, each with pool, restaurant, bar.

Inexpensive: **Arrowhead Motel.** 1050 Brickell Ave. Fam. rates avail. Some kitchen units.

Siesta Motel, 5101 Biscayne Blvd.Small, attractive motel with kitchen units.

Willard Garden Hotel. 124 N.E. 14th St., Unusual do-it-yourself hotel popular with backpackers, budgeters. Make your own bed, carry your own bag. Unique, tight security. Near OMNI, discount shopping, economy restaurants. Beach 5 minutes by bus.

MIAMI BEACH. *Moderate:* **Bancroft.** 1501 Collins Ave. Pool, beach, game area.

Beacharbour Resort. 18925 Collins Ave. Pools, beach, game area. Restaurants, bar.

Holiday Inn. 6 locations, all with usual comforts of this chain.

Lombardy. 6305 Collins Ave. Pool, beach. Restaurant nr. Fam. rates avail.

Shore Club Hotel. 1901 Collins Ave. Restaurant, bar, dancing, entertainment.

Aztec Resort Hotel. 159th St. at Collins. Outside FL 800–327–0241. 3-block beach, adult and kiddy pools, MAP available, lounge, entertainment. Some kitchenettes.

Singapore Resort Motel. 96th at Collins. Outside FL 800–327–4911. Full-block beach, sundeck, heated pool, dining room, dancing, entertainment, tennis, social director.

Inexpensive: **Rodney,** 94th St. on the ocean. Rooms, efficiencies, and apts. Tennis, pool.

Shorecrest Hotel. 1535 Collins. Coffee shop, kitchenettes.

Garden of Allah Motel, Indian Creek Dr. and 65th St.

Golden Sands. 6901 Collins Ave. Pool, pets, Restaurant, bar.

Waldman Hotel. 4299 Collins Ave.

DINING OUT. The several thousand places to dine in Miami and Miami Beach range from gourmet restaurants to sandwich shops. Some of the Cuban restaurants in Miami are among the finest anywhere. The area offers a full range of foreign restaurants, with entrées from seafoods to roast beef, turkey or steaks. Florida lobster, or crawfish, is a big favorite in these parts. You can dine on succulent Everglades froglegs, pompano or conch chowder. Stone crabs are a native south Florida delicacy, and fresh shellfish, lobsters and oysters are flown in daily.

Restaurants are listed by cuisine and price category. Dinner in a *moderate* restaurant $8–12, in an *inexpensive* restaurant, under $8. Prices do not include drinks, tax or tip. Cafeterias and hamburger houses fall into the inexpensive category, with an adequate dinner selection costing perhaps $1.50 to $3. A la carte dining will of course be more expensive.

American International. Moderate: **County Store.** 2880 Florida Ave., Coconut Grove. Several dining rooms decorated with antiques; good selection of seafoods, chicken Kiev, flaming shish kebab.

Inexpensive to Moderate: **Tony Roma's A Place for Ribs.** Baby back ribs, chicken and ribs and more. Great luncheon specials. 15700 Biscayne Blvd.; 180th St. & Collins Ave.; also Coral Gables and South Miami.

Inexpensive: **Gulf Stream,** Jordan Marsh Dept. Stores, 1501 Biscayne Blvd. Casseroles, salads, homestyle baking.

Hofbrau Bar. 172 Giralda. Tasty sandwiches, lots of atmosphere.

Sally Russel's Part I. 68 W. Flagler. A varied menu of meat and fish.

Cafeteria. Inexpensive, **Biscayne Cafeteria,** 147 Miracle Mile, Coral Gables. Long lines in season, but ample and filling.

Italian. Moderate: **Raimondo.** 4612 S. LeJuene Rd. Try the zuppa di pesce al Peppino. Special orders by reservation. Intimate atmosphere.

Barbecue. Inexpensive, **Swiss Chalet.** 101 Miracle Mile, Coral Gables (it's a local chain). Chicken, ribs to eat in or take out. Cocktails, beer, wine.

Latin American. Moderate: **El Baturro.** 2322 NW 7th St. (Miami). Interesting items dot an extensive menu, and the specialties are the paella and the sautéed red snapper. Music is live.

Madrid. 2475 Douglas Rd. Spanish food. Try delicious white bean soup.

Minerva Spanish Restaurant. 265 NE 2nd St. Convenient location downtown. Popular long before Cuban refugees arrived.

OK Restaurant. 1164 W. Flagler. Typical of Cuban restaurants with meat counter in back, sidewalk coffee bar in front. Daily specials.

Oriental. Moderate: **Canton.** 6661 S. Dixie Highway. Cantonese and Mandarin food.

Tiger Tiger Teahouse. 5716 S. Dixie Hwy. Mandarin, Tsechway, Shanghai, and Mongolian dishes. Jin jo shrimp and cashew chicken are specialties.

Polynesian. Moderate: **Rusty Pelican.** Off Rickenbacker Causeway, nr. Key Biscayne. Open-hearth cooking. Succulent Polynesian spareribs.

Seafood. Moderate: **Port of Call.** 14411 Biscayne Blvd. (Miami). The owners are fishermen themselves, and it is partially their own catch that graces the tables. The bouillabaisse is something special.

MIAMI BEACH. *American International. Inexpensive:* **Black Angus.** 17700 Collins Ave. and other locations. Old West decor and sixgun-quick hotdogs, sandwiches.

Enrico & Paglieri. 18288 Collins. Italian vineyard decor. All the antipasto you can eat, then on to the pastas and steaks.

Bagel Nosh. All-hours eating, deli-style specialties.

Pub. 2301 Collins Ave. Steak, chicken ribs, and seafood in a pleasant spot.

Italian. Moderate: **Gatti's Restaurant.** 1427 West Ave. Continental food with Italian accent. Chicken à la tetrazzini a specialty. 5:30 to 10:30. Closed Mon. and May 1 to Nov. 1.

Jewish. Moderate: **Wolfie.** 2 locations: 2038 Collins Ave.; 195 Lincoln Rd. Stuffed cabbage, cheesecake, smoked whitefish.

Seafood. Moderate: **New England Oyster House.** 5 locations. Native and imported seafood.

EXPLORING THE REST OF FLORIDA

Jacksonville, the first city you'll see in Florida if you enter from the north via I–95 or from the west on I–10 is Florida's under-priced, under-appreciated budget Big Apple—as long as you don't expect it to be Tahiti in January. Summers here are *the* season, so prices in spring, winter, and fall are temptingly low even though temperatures are almost always mellow. The city has youth, sizzle, history, and variety. There are fine restaurants, the most modern hotels, endless beach (Jax Beach), and culture that won't quit.

It's an un-Florida city that has been here for centuries. Side trips include St. Augustine, the site of a French Huguenot settlement in 1516, a gracious plantation home with the ruins of slave quarters, the big fleet at Mayport. For information on this bargain bonanza write the Visitors and Convention Bureau, 206 Hogan St., Jacksonville FL 32202.

Oldest City

For St. Augustine, the nation's oldest city, you'll need time . . . and a separate guide book. Recommended is *St. Augustine's Historical Heritage,* a publication of the *St. Augustine Historical Society.* There are numerous illustrations, an excellent map, and a well-written text. Try the information center on San Marco Ave. as you near the city gates.

Walk through the narrow streets and see a tiny stone cottage here, an elaborate cathedral there, a massive stone fortress yonder, each from a different layer of history. From the first Spanish period, the mission of Nombre de Dios was founded on the same day as the city, its Shrine of Nuestra Señora de la Leche is a tiny jewel of a chapel. Built of coquina rick covered with ivy, it was restored in 1918, following the design of the original. The Cathedral of St. Augustine—from the second Spanish period—was completed in 1797, restored after a fire in 1887. The Llambias House reflects the English period, as does the Prince Murat House, named for Napoleon Bonaparte's nephew who lived there. Ralph Waldo Emerson was a guest in 1827. The St. Francis Inn, once known as the Dummitt House, was a headquarters for Civil War spies, before that a jail just after Florida became a U.S. territory, before that a barracks for English soldiers . . . and before that the first church of the Franciscans, in 1577.

So there's the oldest school, oldest house, oldest store—some of the best history-hunting in the U.S. mixed with the inevitable tourist clap-trap. Castillo de San Marcos, the quadrangular, moated fortress just opposite the old city gates, isn't finished yet. It has been a national monument since 1924, and it now is being improved by restoration of some of the inside rooms together with the reconstruction of the Cubo Line, the ancient town wall which extended from the Castillo to the San Sebastian River. There's a souvenir reminder of the Old City again, 14 miles south at Matanzas Inlet. The stone fort, built in 1742 to protect the inland waterway approach to St. Augustine, is a national monument; daily visiting hours are from 8:30 A.M. to 5:00 P.M.

The Ormond-Daytona Complex

Only a couple of miles south is Marineland of Florida, a commercial attraction presenting displays of marine specimens, porpoise acts, a performing whale, and below-the-water ports for viewing the ocean's creatures, some bizarre, some brilliantly colored. It's an interesting and wholesome attraction. Half an hour more on route A1A will put you in the first of the major tourist-oriented resorts on this route—the Ormond Beach–Daytona Beach Complex geared almost totally to entertainment of the fun-seeking tourists.

Walt Disney World

Orlando was settled, after the Seminole Wars, by former volunteers who decided to stay after the withdrawal of the army. Later, new blood was added by English settlers who bought land for as little as $1 an acre. They came to grow citrus, but they also brought a way of life with them, and had organized a polo team by 1884. For many years Orlando, with its well-ordered beauty, was a favorite winter vacation and retirement center for middle-aged or older people who found its climate, location, and atmosphere "just right." Today, Orlando is having a hard time retaining that old atmosphere. Cape Canaveral and the Kennedy Space Center are only 65 miles away; and some 3,000 people a day commute to the Cape, and more than 11,000 work at the Glenn

L. Martin Company's 22 building plant on the outskirts. Population of Orange County in 1950 was 114,000; now it is three times that. Its location makes Orlando an excellent hub for one-day touring in almost any direction. (A hotel/motel explosion since Walt Disney World opened has added 20,000 new rooms.)

Twenty miles south, for instance, on four-laned US 17–92, is Kissimmee, home of the famous Silver Spur Rodeo held in February and July. It's of special interest to the budget traveler because Kissimmee–St. Cloud is Disney's bedroom—offering hundreds of spacious, available rooms at un-Disney prices. For a list, write the CVB, P.O. Box 2007, Kissimmee FL 32741.

Plan at least two days for WDW—one for the Magic Kingdom and another for the world-of-tomorrow EPCOT Center. You can buy a package admission, or separate tickets. Located on US 192, just west of I–4, Walt Disney World offers golf, boating, swimming, camping, hiking, water-skiing, horseback riding, canoeing, and night life as well as the thrills and excitements of the theme park. For the budget-minded: there is no admission fee to enter Walt Disney World Village at Lake Buena Vista, which is filled with interesting shops and restaurants. Sea World and Circus World, both premier attractions shouldn't be missed, and the area also offers Wet 'n' Wild, Stars Hall of Fame, and much more.

Cape Canaveral

Cape Canaveral (named Cape Kennedy after the assassination of the late President, then renamed Cape Canaveral once again a decade later), the Kennedy Space Center, the Merritt Island moon-launch site, Patrick Air Force Base Missile Test Center—together the jumping-off place for our epochal strides into space—are aligned along a forty-mile strip of erstwhile deserted sandpits. Should there be any major space ventures, these will be advertised days in advance. In the meantime, you may wish to visit other nearby attractions. During past blast-offs, there would be a "caravan" route to Cocoa Beach, several miles south of Cape Canaveral for the best view.

There used to be plenty of experts around to make sure you were looking at the right launching pad. Neophytes have been known to keep their binoculars trained on a 165-foot-tall object, painted with black and white stripes, throughout a countdown only to stand befuddled as it sat there motionless while everyone was screaming at the liftoff. What they had observed with such dedication is the Cape Canaveral Lighthouse, which hasn't moved an inch in almost a hundred years.

If there's no blast-off scheduled, you can tour the main launching area for the Atlantic Missile Range and the pad from which astronauts are shot into space, and/or NASA's moon-launch area on Merritt Island. The only authorized guided tours of the area are NASA Tours, operated by TWA Services, Inc., regularly throughout the day from the Visitors Information Center. Operational activity at the space center makes the tours subject to change. While it won't really put you very close to things, the moon-launch tour will certainly give you something to look at. This is the Vertical Assembly Building, the world's largest building in terms of enclosed space—129 million cubic feet. The VAB will permit assembly of four space vehicles as large as the Apollo moonshot rocket and is fifty-two stores high, covering eight acres. Nearby stand the giant mobile launchers, in which the missiles are transported to the launching pad three miles away. You will also see the launch complexes and a small space museum.

On Sundays you can drive your own car around the space center at no charge. Be sure to stop at the Visitors Information Center, located at the space center, six miles east of US 1, south of Titusville. It has splendid free exhibits, movies and detailed lectures on the space program. For those who can't take the weekend tours, there's a display of missiles at Patrick Air Force Base, just south of Cocoa Beach.

The Everglades

The beauty of Everglades National Park escapes some people, but it wouldn't if they'd slow down enough to really look at it. At first, there seems a sameness, a monotony to the landscape. But there are subtle blendings of plant and animal life in cycles that began, ended, and began again thousands of years ago. At the Royal Palm Hammock visitors' center, Park Rangers can tell you what to look for and can show it to you through exhibits and color movies. But the vastness, the variety, the shadings do not appear in miniature representations. You can only see them in their larger-than-life actuality.

Branching off from the main road are various viewing areas and trails which sample the complexity of the Everglades. Pa-hay-okee overlook is elevated to give you perspective on a sea of grass stretching endless miles. Gumbo Limbo Trail leads you through a tropical density where you can see only a few feet through the dark foliage. At Taylor Slough, alligators, water birds, ducks, turtles, otter, deer, panther, black bear, and bobcats congregate. You will see some of them. The Anhinga Trail is a boardwalk which reaches out over a slough, in which the visitor can observe the everyday life and death drama of the glades.

About the time you have become convinced that you are near the outer limits of civilization, that only you, the road, and your strange vehicle remain as outcroppings of the man-made universe, you will reach Flamingo and the familiar world of martinis and steaks and air conditioning. Flamingo has a lodge, a dining room for 200 guests, a drugstore, a marina, rental boats, groceries, gas, tires, oil, and all the accoutrements you suspected were far behind you. From here you can go on to see more of the park—and there is much more to see than you have, to this point—but from here you go by boat, and with a guide, of necessity. Morning and evening excursion boat tours can accommodate the mildly curious; those with their own or rented craft may join the Saturday Ranger-conducted boat-a-cades which ramble along 65-mile tours.

There are picnic and camping areas at Flamingo and Long Pine Key. The Flamingo campsites hold 60 mobile homes and 171 tents or trailers; a small store sells groceries, fishing supplies, and sundries. Long Pine Key has 108 camp units, each including a picnic table, cookout grill, and a paved strip for trailer or tent, with drinking fountains and comfort stations close by. You can fish all year here and do pretty well. You won't even need a license for saltwater fishing. But no hunting of any kind at any time is allowed. (You may, of course, defend yourself against the mosquitoes, but they are the hunters in this case.)

A long, furious controversy has surrounded the "flood control project" in the park. It has cost hundreds of millions and, according to opponents, controls flooding in only a minor way. They consider it land reclamation in disguise, a publicly subsidized move, benefiting landowners and real estate men. They have raised fears that loss of water, without replenishment, could destroy the park and hurt tourism.

To Key West

The best way to see Key West is via the Conch Tour Train or Old Town Trolley, trams which ramble some 14 miles in a 1½-hour viewing of such sites as Harry Truman's Little White House, Ernest Hemingway's home, Audubon House, the turtle kraals, the shrimp fleet, art centers, and all the attractions open to visitors. Audubon House was the Geiger House when the artist stayed there in 1831–32 sketching Keys birdlife. It's been restored and contains some of Audubon's work, plus a mixture of furnishings much like those the original owner salvaged from shipwrecks. Ernest Hemingway lived in Key West during much of his most productive writing period, working on *The Green Hills of Africa, To Have and Have Not, The Snows of Kilimanjaro* and *For Whom the Bell Tolls.* Hemingway was attracted by the old (1851) house's grillwork. He furnished it heavily with Spanish antiques and rebuilt the kitchen to put all the appliances several inches higher. A wealthy couple bought the house in 1961, intending to make it their home, but as they discovered more and more artifacts and Hemingway memorabilia they decided instead to make it a museum. The town's atmosphere seems to stimulate writers. Tennessee Williams, John Dos Passos, and Robert Frost also worked here. No charge, of course, for Key West's daily sensational show, the sunset, attracting all kinds of characters, locals and visitors to Mallory Square.

If you plan to tour west across Florida on the Tamiami Trail, avoid metropolitan Miami traffic by switching to US 27 at Florida City, then turn west on US 41. The Tamiami Trail connects Miami with Tampa, sweeping through Everglades country for 100 miles to the West Coast at Naples, then angling northward, generally inland from the "quiet coast" of Florida.

Along the Tamiami Trail

The Tamiami Canal, which parallels the road on the north, was dug to supply fill for the roadbed and automatically presented prime freshwater fishing grounds the length of the route. Most of the Seminole villages along the Trail are semi-tourist attractions, ranging in scope from a couple of elevated huts, called *chickees,* to an elaborate restaurant-marina-souvenir shop-filling station complex. Airboat rides are exhilarating once one gets over the shock of skimming along over an inch or two of water or perhaps only some damp sawgrass. Access to the western portion of Everglades Park is via the Shark Valley entrance. Birdwatchers will want to see this section, which includes Duck Rock, home of some 75,000 white ibises during the summer months.

For an adventure, head north on State 29 and you will reach Corkscrew Swamp Sanctuary, a 6,000-acre preserve featuring thousands of rare birds, elevated walkways through the heart of a jungle, and giant bald cypress trees—700 years old and 130 feet high.

Gulf-central Florida yields to no other section of the state in tempting visitors. There are lovely beaches all along the generally serene Gulf Coast, centers of art and architecture such as Sarasota, metropolitan blandishments with a subtropical flavor in the Tampa-St. Petersburg area, Old World color in the Greek colony at Tarpon Springs, New World agronomy in the rolling citrus grove centers of Lakeland and Winter Haven.

Sanibel and Captiva Islands, accessible via US 41, are the seashell fancier's idea of paradise because of the supply of left-handed welks, spiny periwinkles, large cockles, and coquina. Sanibel, connected to Captiva on the north end by a small bridge, was considered the ultimate in tropical splendor mixed with blessed privacy when only a ferry gave access to the mainland at Punta Rassa, but a toll causeway now makes the 3½-mile trip simple and quick. The $3 (roundtrip) toll, a concession to islanders who want privacy after all, keeps the traffic down.

The new high-speed Interstate 75 is open from Naples to the mid-U.S.A.

Culture-happy

Sarasota is noted for its beautiful beaches on the connecting keys and also as a cultural center. The John and Mabel Ringling Museum of Art, owned and operated by the state, contains one of the nation's outstanding collections of Baroque and Renaissance paintings: the *Rubens* collection is America's finest. Contemporary and modern art also are on display. Near the museum is the state-acquired Asolo Theater, a gem of an 18th-century interior from the castle at Asolo, Italy, which is in almost constant use for appropriate presentations: opera, concerts, and an eight-month season of plays.

The grandiloquent Ringling mansion on Sarasota Bay, and Ringling Museum of the Circus, also are part of the overall museums, which may be entered separately or with a combination ticket for all. The culture doesn't linger in the past, however. Such outstanding architects as Paul Rudolph and Victor Lundy have contributed greatly with churches, homes, shops, and schools, and I.M. Pei designed buildings for the Oxford-like New College, which had Dr. Arnold Toynbee on the faculty for the first handpicked class of 94 scholars. The intellectual life is contagious. Little theater groups, art schools, concerts, and art shows permeate all strata of the population. And everybody shares the "regular" niceties of sun, beaches, fishing, golf, tennis, patio socializing, and the like.

Bradenton has its own offshore key, Anna Maria. At the mouth of the Manatee River, five miles west of Bradenton, is De Soto National Memorial Park. Just across the river on US 41 or 301, turn east for a couple of miles to reach the Gamble Mansion, a plantation-style antebellum museum. Judah P. Benjamin, Confederate Secretary of State, hid out here briefly after the South lost the war and eventually made it to England where he became a successful barrister.

The Sunshine Skyway

Either 41 or 301 will take you to Tampa, but for a spectacular view and a quick entry into St. Petersburg switch to US 19 north, just outside Palmetto. You will cross the 15-mile Sunshine Skyway (toll: $1 per car) and save 45 miles.

Because of an accident, the bridge needs massive repairs and will handle only 2 lanes for some years to come. When you enter St. Petersburg from the south, a "semicircle" radiates from the Municipal Pier, the yacht-clustered marina and on to Central Avenue. The Pier, scene of most racing regattas (St. Petersburg is considered the boating capital of the U.S.A.), is also dominated by the unique, inverted pyramid building. The five levels include a window-walled seafood restaurant, the Isle of Nations with ethnic entertainment and boutiques. Because it was named one of the healthiest cities in the good old days, retirees flocked here, but now only 25 percent of the population is above retirement age.

At the Vinoy Basin, next to the city pier, you can (shades of Captain Bligh) crawl aboard the famed sailing ship *Bounty.* Major show business personalities star at the Bayfront Center. St. Petersburg and the connecting seven beach communities are now known as the Pinellas Suncoast and includes St. Pete Beach, Clearwater Beach, Dunedin, Holiday Isles, Madeira Beach, Treasure Island, Tarpon Springs. The beaches are easy to reach by a modern system of causeways. Your first chance is via the Pinellas Bayway on the left soon after you reach the mainland southern tip of St. Petersburg. This offers access to some newly opened islands to the south, such as Mullet Key.

Fort de Soto (1898) has become one of the Gulf Coast's most popular parks. An excellent beach, picnic sheds, barbecue pits, excellent camping areas, and prime mackerel and tarpon fishing help attract more than a million visitors a year and entrance is free. In 1978, the fort's cannons were dedicated as a National Historic Landmark. The ocean beaches north of Mullet Key (turn west onto State 699 if returning from Mullet Key) are known collectively as the Holiday Isles, including Indian Rocks Beach, Redington Beach, etc. All told, there are 28 miles of beach and beachfront accommodations range from luxury hotels and motels and condominium apartments to weathered frame beach houses that may be rented by the week or month.

St. Petersburg Beach (re-named St. Pete Beach for its younger image) is connected to the mainland by Corey Causeway (free) and has one of the best, wide white-sand beaches anywhere. (The civil objective is to give St. Petersburg the lively image it now deserves. But first, one has to emphasize that St. Petersburg, and the connecting island of St. Pete Beach, are entirely two different places.) The National Historic Landmark "pink palace" the Don CeSar Beach Resort Hotel adds a beautiful Spanish accent to the skyline. Two penthouse-topped hotels, the St. Pete Beach Hilton and Schrafft's Sandpiper Resort are among the most popular of the beachfront hotels. Clearwater Beach also has glamorous hotels, and budget "Mom and Pop" motels on the bay side.

Diving for Sponges

Tarpon Springs' sponge industry began in 1905, with the perfection of deep-sea diving equipment. The Greeks moved up from Key West where they had been hooking sponges with long poles from boats. Synthetic sponges and plastics have made inroads on the sponge industry now, of course, but there are still a score of boats working the offshore beds. The Sponge Exchange, where the "catch" is auctioned, is interesting, or you may prefer a sponge diving exhibition from boats at the docks.

US 19, a mile west of Tarpon Springs, can bring you south again, but check your map and decide which route you wish to take to Tampa. From St. Petersburg, the superhighway I–275, via the Howard Frankland Bridge, is the fastest. Tampa is now Florida's third largest city—it has breweries and cigar factories, plus a busy deep-water port and an excellent future. The citrus industry added shipping and canning, World War II brought shipbuilding, and the postwar years have brought a little of everything. Breweries supply one of the state's most popular tourist attractions. Busch Gardens, a 300-acre theme park, is a tropical garden with one of the world's largest aviaries. At least a thousand African animals (including tigers) live freely among the 150,-000 trees, plants, and lakes. There's also a Swiss chalet-type restaurant, sky-ride, and a monorail which passes over an animal-inhabited man-made Africa. You can tour the brewery and grounds on your own. One paid admission includes everything, from the fine areas of the Dark Continent to the thrilling rides (Python, Mamba, Flume, etc.), and the beer is on the house. For an extra admission, you can visit Adventure Island, with white sand beach, pools with surf as high as three to five feet, flumes and all sorts of fun and games. Timbuktu is an exciting part of the Dark Continent, with thrilling rides, game areas, amphitheater for porpoise and dolphin shows, restaurants, etc. A few more blocks north on 30th Street to the Schlitz Brewery for another tour and complimentary draught. On the way a turn west onto Broadway will yield a sample of Ybor City and the Latin Quarter of Tampa, Spanish architecture and some of the nation's best Spanish restaurants.

Lakes and Cypress Gardens

Another Florida, distinctly different from the beach—keys—ocean experience, rises into view with rolling hills and lakes east of Tampa. This is the rich citrus and farming area around Lakeland, Winter Haven, Lake Wales, and Bartow. Tourism is considerable, for many winter visitors prefer the soft inland air, redolent with orange blossoms, to the tangy salt atmosphere near the ocean. Too, there is a reassuring permanence to quiet residential streets, long-established parks, and city squares. The visitors come and go, but when they go there is no void; life goes on at a neat clip, buoyed by the citrus industry, the farms, the cattle ranches, the phosphate mines, the general prosperity of stable communities.

Tampa has experienced tremendous growth in recent years, especially in the addition of resort facilities. Take I–4 east from Tampa 35 miles to Lakeland; there are eleven lakes, large and small, within the city limits. Water-skiing, fishing, and boating are popular, but there are also fine golf courses, and major league baseball exhibitions in the spring when the Detroit Tigers train here.

On the shores of Lake Hollingsworth is Florida Southern College, said to have the largest single concentration of Frank Lloyd Wright buildings anywhere. On the same lake are held the crew races, a popular campus sport among the smaller Florida colleges that do not have football, and powerboat races. The Orange Cup Regatta, in late January or early February, attracts the fastest boats on the racing circuit, and scores of world records have been set here. In the heart of the city, along Lake Mirror, is the Civic Center with its bowling greens, shuffleboard courts, a recreation center, and tennis courts. Lakeland also is the headquarters for the Florida Citrus Commission, the state agency which oversees quality control. Polk County, of which Lakeland is the largest city, produces a third of the state's crop. Packing houses, canneries, and frozen-concentrate plants dot the area. Large trailer trucks, filled to overflowing with oranges, stream along the roads during the busiest season, from mid-September to May.

Winter Haven can be reached quickly from either Lakeland (via US 92) or Bartow (via US 17) and from Winter Haven it is only five miles to Cypress Gardens. Perhaps as much as any place in Florida, Cypress Gardens proves what imagination, promotion, and a pliant Mother Nature can do. What was once only a swamp well off the beaten track has been prodded, drained, and manicured into 164 acres of botanical flamboyance with over 11,000 varieties of flowers and plants in more than a dozen gardens of the world. In 1979, millions of dollars worth of new attractions were added, including "Southern Cross Roads" and "The Living Forest" exhibits. Cypress Gardens also features exciting water-skiing and hang-gliding competitions. The Florida Sports Hall of Fame is located here.

An Area of Sundry Attractions

Near Cypress Gardens, Lake Wales and the Bok Tower are accessible via US 27. Edward Bok, wealthy editor of the *Ladies Home Journal* and a Pulitzer Prize winner in 1920, established the free Mountain Lake Sanctuary on the slope of Iron Mountain. It is 324 feet above sea level, the highest point in peninsular Florida and a refuge for birds and man, as well as a proper setting for the carillon tower that now serves as his memorial. Lovely gardens surround the 205-foot tower, and there are "blinds" for visitors to observe or photograph the birdlife. A pool reflects the image of the tower, and carillon concerts are given several times weekly. There is no tourist access to the tower's top. Serenity is the attraction. Lake Wales is also the scene, from early February to mid-April, of the Black Hills Passion Play, presented four times a week in a 3,500-seat amphitheater with a stage more than 100 yards wide.

Thirty miles south of Lake Wales—again by US 27 or Alternate 27—is Sebring, famous for its annual twelve-hour speed and endurance sports car races which are held in March. Nearby, Sun 'n' Lake Resort has tennis, golf, water sports, restaurant, entertainment facilities, and spacious villas. Otherwise, Sebring is just a quiet spot for fishing, hunting, golf, and outdoor pursuits. The nearby Highlands Hammock State

Park has catwalks into a cypress swamp area, as well as guided tour and small museum.

North Central Florida

North of Orlando is the outdoorsman's jackpot: Ocala National Forest. There are 31 varied recreation areas within these 362,000 acres of lakes and rolling hills; they offer swimming, camping, trailer sites, fishing, and scenery by the mile. In fact, there are 65 miles without a stoplight on State 19, which offers a north-south "vistaway" all the way from Palatka, north of the forest. Another state road, 40, is east-west and crosses 19 in the middle of the forest. Two favorite spots are Alexander Springs, near the southern entrance, and Juniper Springs, near the crossroads. Alexander Springs bubble up a torrent of 76 million gallons of 74-degree water every day of the year, and there's a white sand beach, picnic area, refreshments, a bathhouse, boats for rent, nature trails, and nearby camping and trailer sites equipped with electricity, water, and sewers. Juniper Springs offers the same, basically, plus a 13-mile (downstream) canoe rental trip. One can just laze along, drifting, through a subtropical forest, finally reaching a waterway park back beside State 19. The Forest Service people take the canoe back by trailer.

Silver Springs, surrounded by over 100 acres of landscaped grounds, has attracted visitors for centuries. Included is a Wild Waters playground, Jungle Cruise, Deer Ranch, Reptile Institute, and Early American Museum.

Back to the Old South

Just north of Lake City on US 41, at White Springs, is the Stephen Foster State Folk Culture Center near the Suwannee River. Carillon recitals from the 200-foot tower feature the composer's work four times daily. Foster never even saw the Suwannee, of course, picking the name for its beauty. As it happened, he picked a good one. The rambling Suwannee, from the Georgia line to the Gulf, is a beautiful stream, and the 243-acre park at the Memorial sets it off well. The Florida Folk Festival, with two thousand or more folk dancers, singers, craftsmen, and tale tellers, is held during the first week in May each year.

West on US 90 is Tallahassee, the state's capital. Ralph Waldo Emerson noted in 1827 that the city was a "grotesque place . . . settled by public officers, land speculators, and desperadoes." Today however, Tallahassee is pleasant, though not as quiet as in earlier times. Rolling hills, giant oaks strewn with Spanish moss, and pre-Civil War mansions help Tallahassee retain its Old South look, while modern buildings climb skyward at Florida State. The Chamber of Commerce headquarters building, "The Columns," was built in 1835 and served as a financial and professional center, as well as one of the city's finest brick residences in earlier years. A skyscraper state capitol building was completed in 1975. Tallahassee (the name means Old Fields in Apalachee Indian) has one of the state's most spectacular floral extravaganzas at Maclay State Park, about five miles north of town on US 319. There are 308 acres of garden and recreation area with pools, formal arrangements of flowers bracketed by blooming trees, a walled garden, and a Camellia Walk flanked by 12-foot-high camellias. Adjacent in the recreation area are picnic shelters with grills, swimming, and a boat ramp. Near the airport is the Tallahassee Junior Museum's Pioneer Village, which presents typical farm buildings and implements of Northwest Florida farm life, circa 1880. South on highway 61, you can enjoy Wakulla Springs, with its glass-bottomed boats and wildlife refuge, and St. Marks, with its state museum and lighthouse.

The Miracle Strip

Start southward to reach Florida's expanse of beach, 100 miles extending from Apalachicola to Pensacola and modestly termed the Miracle Strip: the sand is pure white quartz variety, and the offshore formation provides a good surf.

Panama City is a sort of Southern Atlantic City, complete with roller coaster and convention hall, but the fishing is better than Jersey's. The city claims as its share 23 miles of beach, a portion of it in St. Andrews State Park, with a 450-foot fishing pier to help pedestrian anglers get out there with the bigger ones. Sport fishing of all types is a big attraction, and the city's marina is home port for a considerable fleet of charter craft.

US 98 is the east-west coastal route, and in truth, the Miracle Strip extends eastward of Panama City all the way to Port St. Joe and Apalachicola. Westward from Panama City via US 98 there remain some relatively unpopulated seashore vistas, by Florida standards at least, but you will have little trouble finding accommodations almost anywhere along the route.

The last city on this tour is Pensacola. It's a young, go-ahead town thanks to the Naval Air Station. There's a new theme park here, LaFitte's Landing. For beachside accommodations, try Pensacola Beach or camp at Fort Pickens State Park.

Driving from Fort Walton Beach on US 98, you can cross over to Santa Rosa Island on State 399 at Navarre and continue to Fort Pickens and the outstanding Gulf Islands National Seashore, where overnight beachfront camping is permitted. To reach Pensacola itself, take State 399 to US 98. Buses tour the Naval Air Station, Fort San Carlos and Fort Barrancas, the Naval Aviation Museum, Sherman Field, home of the Blue Angels precision flying team, the giant aircraft carrier U.S.S. *Lexington* (on holidays you can go aboard), and the Old Pensacola Lighthouse, built in 1825 and still working.

PRACTICAL INFORMATION FOR FLORIDA

WALT DISNEY WORLD

MUSEUMS. *Orlando: John Young Science Center,* 810 E. Rollins, is a museum and planetarium with you-can-touch science exhibits, a realistic trip to the stars, cosmic concerts Friday, Saturday. Daily except Christmas.

SPORTS. There's sailing and canoeing from Barrett's Marina (rentals and lessons), 4503 N. Orange Blossom Trail. Canoeing, camping, and fishing from Katie's Wekika River Landing in Santord, 25 mi. from downtown Orlando.

WHAT TO DO WITH THE CHILDREN. *Walt Disney World* is divided into 6 sections: *Fantasyland,* with Cinderella's Castle, Mickey Mouse revue, and Captain Nemo subs; *Main St. USA*—a study in nostalgia; *Tomorrowland,* preview of the future; *Adventureland* with jungle cruises, luau, tree house; *Frontierland,* a recreation of the Old West; Liberty Square with colonial shops, Hall of Presidents and a haunted house. EPCOT, Walt Disney's ultimate dream, is a world of tomorrow. Buy a package ticket. There are motels, camping sites, tours, special package tours. The waterpark *Wet 'n' Wild* is ten minutes from Walt Disney World. *Walt Disney World Village* at Lake Buena Vista has boutiques, craft shops, marina with paddle boats, *Empress Lily* riverboat for lunch, dinner. No admission fee for the village. Orlando's *Sea World* is a 125-acre-park with killer whale and dolphin shows, pearl diving exhibitions. It's at 7007 Sea World Dr.

 HOTELS. Based on single room double occupancy, rates are *moderate,* $50–75, *inexpensive* under $50, highest season.

KISSIMMEE–ST. CLOUD. Quickest, most uncrowded, best-buy accommodations for Disney World area. For a complete list, from very inexpensive to deluxe, write the Convention and Visitors Bureau, P.O. Box 2007, Kissimmee FL 32741.

Moderate. **Larson's Lodge.** 2009 W. Vine St. and 6075 Space Coast Parkway. 800–327–9074. In Florida call collect: 305–846–2713. Packages available off-season. Pets allowed, restaurant, game room, gift shop, shuttle bus, laundry room.

Ramada Inn Southwest. 2950 Reedy Creek Blvd. 800–327–9127 U.S.; 800–432–9195 Florida. Packages available which include tickets to attractions. Pool, lounge, game room, shuttle buses, laundry room.

Sheraton Lakeside Inn. 7711 W. Hwy. 192. Mini-golf; packages including attractions, pool, game room, shuttle, restaurant. Pets allowed.

Inexpensive. **Comfort Inn.** 7501 W. Hwy. 192. A Quality Inn with 280 rooms, restaurant, lounge, game room, pool. Children under 17 free.

Days Inn. Three locations. Call 800–555–1212 for toll-free numbers in your state. Disney West is at 7980 W. Hwy. 192; Disney East 5840 Hwy. 192; Kissimmee, 2095 Hwy. 192. Each has pool, restaurant, playground.

Eastgate Motor Inn. 900 E. Hwy 192. Packages available, restaurant, pool. 42 rooms.

Fiesta Inn. 402 Simpson Rd. 198 rooms. Call collect 305–846–1530. Pets allowed. Pool, restaurant, game room, laundry room.

Flamingo Motel. 801 E. Hwy 192. 15 rooms. Call collect 305–846–1935. Packages available. Pets allowed.

Holiday Inn. Four locations in and near Kissimmee/Disney World. U.S. except Tennessee telephone 800–238–8000 for information and reservations. All have pool, restaurant, laundry room.

Howard Johnson's. Three locations. Information and reservations 800–654–2000. Pool, restaurant, laundry room.

Econo Lodge Inn at the Gate. 8620 W. Hwy. 192. 800–327–9077 U.S. In Florida dial 800–432–9101. Packages, pool, pets allowed, indoor mini-golf, shuttle bus.

 RESTAURANTS. For the best buys in dining, try the Kissimmee/St. Cloud area where there are at least 58 restaurants in the *Inexpensive* category. That means you can get soup or appetizer, entrée, dessert, but not including drinks, tax, and tips, for under $5.00. *Moderate* means $5.50 to $9.00.

KISSIMMEE–ST. CLOUD. *Moderate.* **Catfish Place.** 2324 E. Hwy. 192, St. Cloud. Great hush puppies, frogs' legs, catfish.

Lake Marian Restaurant. Hwy. 523, Kenansville. Nothing fancy, just local color and all the crispy catfish you can hold.

People's Place Courtyard. 220 Broadway, Kissimmee. Gracious setting, steaks, crêpes, quiche. Sunday brunch; dinner 5 to midnight. Friday and Saturday dinners until 2 A.M. Open Monday–Thursday, 11 A.M. to midnight.

Twin Dragons. 4002 W. Hwy. 192. Oriental, of course, but the wonton soup is extra-special and a lot of people like the all-you-can-eat buffet.

Fat Boy's Barbecue. 1606 W. Hwy. 192. Floridians know their open-pit barbecue and this Fat Boy's is a favorite. Chicken, beef, ribs, baked beans.

Big Bicycle Buffet. Hyatt Hotel, 6375 W. Hwy. 192. Unique "theme" buffets which change every few weeks. You might stoke up on Western chuckwagon favorites, a German Oktoberfest, seafood, or whatever tickles the chef's fancy. An adventure.

Inexpensive. **Alice's Restaurant.** 321 S. Bermuda is great for breakfast but you'll find honest home cooking here three meals a day. Save room for the homemade pie.

Bill Chen's Magic Wok. Mill Creek Mall. Modestly priced Oriental classics; a popular take-out.

Brown's Café. 14 Broadway. A local hangout in front of the pool room where in-the-know natives come for down-home cooking.

Mrs. Mac's. 122 E. Broadway. Family restaurant favored for homemade pies, chicken, steaks.

CAPE CANAVERAL AREA

MUSEUMS. *Kennedy Space Center,* open daily 8 to dark. *The Air Force Space Museum* is open to the public for drive-through tours Sun. only from 9 to 3.

TOURS. *Kennedy Space Center Tours.* Guided tours of Kennedy Space Center are operated by TWA. Tours depart regularly from Visitor Information Center, 6 mi. E. of US 1, S. of Titusville. Also special tours for the handicapped.

HOTELS. Prices for a single room, double occupancy rate range from *moderate,* over $50 but less than $75, to *inexpensive,* under $50.

COCOA. *Moderate:* **Howard Johnson's.** 860 N. Cocoa Blvd. Pools. Pets. Restaurant.

Quality Inn. 3220 N. Cocoa Blvd. Pool, bar, dancing, entertainment.

COCOA BEACH. *Moderate-inexpensive:* **Holiday Inn Merritt Island.** 260 E. Merritt Island Causeway. Tennis court, pool. Near fishing, beach. Nice dining room, lounge with Happy Hour. Near Information Center for Space Center.

Inexpensive: **Polaris.** 5600 N. Atlantic Ave. Pool, beach, play area. Pets. Restaurant, bar, dancing, entertainment.

MELBOURNE. *Inexpensive:* **Holiday Inn.** 2 locations of this popular chain: East: 440 S. Harbor City Blvd. West: 10900 W. New Haven Ave.

Host of America. 420 S. Harbor City Blvd. Restaurant, bar, dancing, entertainment.

TITUSVILLE. *Inexpensive:* **L-K Motor Inn.** 3755 Cheny Hwy. (I-95 at Rte. 50). Pool, restaurant with budget menu, lounge, game room, scheduled transport to town. 10 miles to golf, Cape.

RESTAURANTS. Prices for a complete dinner range from *moderate,* $8–12, to *inexpensive,* under $8. Drinks, tax, and tips not included.

COCOA. *Moderate:* **Dixie.** 301 Forest Ave. Their Greek salad is renowned. Dancing.

COCOA BEACH. *Moderate:* **Bernard's Surf.** S. Atlantic Ave., very good seafood.
Hong Kong House. 5450 N. Atlantic Ave. Good selection of Chinese dishes.
Ramon's. 204 W. Cocoa Beach Causeway. Prime ribs, seafood. Caesar salad.

TITUSVILLE. *Moderate:* **Sand Point Inn.** Seafood delights in an attractive weathered wood building, jutting out over Indian River. Worth splurging.

THE EVERGLADES

 TOURS. Everglades Jungles Cruises leave from City Yacht Basin, Fort Myers, for a 3-hr. trip up Caloosaka-chee River to the Everglades. Birds, rookeries, wild or-chids and alligators can be seen. If you have the time, take a five-day Shanty Boat Cruise from Caloosakatchee River into Everglades. There's time allotted to explore by swamp buggy and air boat and to visit heron and egret rookeries. Departs on Mon. from Orange River Dock. Nov. to Apr. and July at 9:30 A.M., returns Fri. No children under 16. For reservations write Rte. 1, Box 336, Fort Myers 33905 or tel. 694–3401.

 HOTELS. Prices for a single room, double occupancy rate range from *moderate,* over $25, to *inexpensive,* under $25.

EVERGLADES. *Moderate:* **Flamingo Inn.** State 27, 47 mi. SW of Home-stead. Pool, play area. Bicycles avail. Great bird watching in park.
Rod and Gun Club Lodge. US 41, 35 mi. E. of Naples. Sportsman's retreat which can be reached by car, boat, airplane. Charter boat and skiff fleet, dock.

FLORIDA CITY. *Inexpensive:* **Tropical Inn Motel & Apts.** 905 W. Palm Dr. Special fam. units. Take-off point for Everglades.

THE REST OF FLORIDA

 HOW TO GET THERE. *By air:* Major airlines serve Daytona Beach, Gainesville, Jacksonville, Miami, Or-lando, Panama City, Sarasota-Bradenton, Tallahassee, Tampa-St. Petersburg-Clearwater, Titusville, and West Palm Beach. From Toronto and Montreal you can reach Jacksonville, Miami, Sarasota-Bradenton, Tallahassee, West Palm Beach. From San Juan, direct flights to Miami, Tallahassee, and Orlando. With all the 1979 deregulation, many airlines were awarded Florida routes and new airports have been expand-ing, so do check with an ASTA travel agent before planning your trip. Best buy: People Express Newark–Jacksonville. There's now direct service to foreign countries from several Florida airports.
By train: Amtrak has service to Miami, Orlando, Winter Haven, Tampa, Clearwater, St. Petersburg, W. Palm Beach, Ft. Lauderdale and Hollywood.
By car: The speedy way to the main East Coast resort area and Central Florida from the northeast is I–95. The beautiful, leisurely way is AIA. The frustrating, stoplighted way is US 1. To the west coast take I–95 to Petersburg Virginia, then I–85 to Atlanta and I–75 as far as Tampa.
By bus: Trailways and Greyhound provide good service. In addition, 13 other lines operate from out of state to various cities within Florida.

TOURIST INFORMATION. *Visitor Centers* dispensing information are at Pensacola (I–10), Jennings (I–75), Hilliard (US 1 and 301), Yulee (I–95), and on the Suncoast at 688, north of St. Petersburg, just as you exit off US 275 and the Howard Frankland Bridge.

Florida Division of Tourism, 126 Van Buren St., Tallahassee, Fl 32301.

Florida Dept. of Natural Resources, 3900 Commonwealth Blvd., Tallahassee, 32304.

Visitor Information Center, 75 Kings St., St. Augustine 32084.

St. Petersburg Beach Visitors' Bureau, 6990 Gulf Blvd. St. Pete Beach, 33706; *Pinellas Suncoast Tourist Development Authority,* St. Petersburg/Clearwater Airport, Clearwater, 33520.

Broward County Tourist Development Council, 111 SE 6th St., Ft. Lauderdale.

Every Florida community has a chamber of commerce eager to give free information to visitors, upon written request.

 STATE PARKS. Despite the often justified concern that Florida is rapidly becoming overdeveloped, there are vast areas which remain in a natural condition. Happily, many of those areas will remain so permanently, as state parks. There are 47 in all, some in the midst of crowded urban areas, others remote and relatively wild; some of historical or cultural interest, others built around outstanding scenic or natural features. For complete information write to Florida Parks/Recreation Division, 3900 Commonwealth Blvd., Tallahassee 32303.

 MUSEUMS AND GALLERIES. There are **historical collections** in these cities: Pensacola, *Pensacola Historical Museum,* 405 S. Adams St.; St. Marks, *San Marcos de Apalache State Museum,* US 319S; St. Petersburg, *Haas Museum & Grace S. Turner House & Village,* 3511 2nd Ave.; Tallahassee, *Division of Archive, History & Record Management,* 401 Gaines St. (Capitol building); Tampa, *Tampa Municipal Museum,* in the south wing of the U. of Tampa's main building.

Florida's major **art museums** are: Daytona Beach, *Museum of Arts and Sciences,* 1040 Museum Blvd.; Fort Lauderdale, *Fort Lauderdale Museum of the Arts,* 426 E. Las Olas Blvd.; Gainesville, *University Gallery,* U. of Florida, SW 13th St. at 4th Ave.; Jacksonville, *Cummer Gallery of Art,* 829 Riverside Ave.; *Jacksonville Art Museum,* 4106 Blvd. Center Dr.; Orlando, *Loch Haven Art Center, Inc.,* 2416 North Mills Ave.; Palm Beach, *The Society of the Four Arts,* Four Arts Plaza; Pensacola, *Pensacola Art Association,* 407 S. Jefferson St.; St. Augustine, *Pan American Building,* 97 St. George St.; St. Petersburg, *Museum of Fine Arts,* 255 Beach Dr. N.; Tallahassee, *Florida State University Art Gallery,* Fine Arts Bldg.; *Tampa Museum,* 601 Doyle Carlton Dr. (adjacent to Curtis Hixon Convention Center); Tampa, *Florida Center for the Arts,* U. of S. Fla., 4202 E. Fowler Ave. West Palm Beach, *Norton Gallery,* 1451 S. Olive Ave.; Winter Park, *Morse Gallery of Art,* Holt Ave., Rollins College.

Special Interest: Bradenton: *South Florida Museum and Bishop Planetarium,* 201 10th St. W., The Civil War, two World Wars, and the Seminole days are recaptured in exhibits. Tues. to Fri. 10 to 5; Sat. 10 to 5 and 7 to 9; Sun. 1 to 5.

Crescent City. *Pioneer Settlement,* living and operating daily like an early-Florida homestead.

Cross Creek: *Marjorie Kinnan Rawlings State Museum,* 20 mi. SE of Gainesville on State 325. Home of the writer whose works include *The Yearling* and *Cross Creek.* Guided tours daily 9 to 5.

Fort Walton: *Temple Mounds Museum.* US 98 downtown Fort Walton Beach. Best preserved Indian mounds in Florida. Tues. through Sat. 11 to 4; Sun. 1 to 4; Thurs. 6 P.M. to 8 P.M.

Key West: *Hemingway Home & Museum,* 907 Whitehead. Mementoes and mounted specimens of the Hemingway safaris. Daily 9 to 5. Adults $1; children

50¢. *Fish Museum,* Mallory Sq., Chamber of Commerce Bldg. Big game fish exhibits. Mon. to Fri. 9 to 5; Sat. 9 to 12.

Palm Beach: *Henry Morrison Flagler Museum,* 71 Whitehall Way. Tues. to Sun. 10 to 5.

Pensacola: *Naval Aviation Museum,* U.S. Naval Air Station. Bus tours leave the main gate daily for a 2-hr. tour of the Air Station. The Museum is open Tues. to Sat. 8:30 to 4:30.; Sun. 12:30 to 4:30. Free.

Perry: *Forest Capital State Cultural Museum,* 1 mi. S. of Perry, in largest timber producing area in state.

St. Augustine: *Museum of Yesterday's Toys,* in the Rodriquez Avero House, 52 St. George St. Collection of toys dating from the 17th century. Mon. to Sat. 9 to 5; Sun. 1 to 5. *Oldest Store Museum,* 4 Artillery Lane. Over 100,000 mementoes of yesteryear. Mon. to Sat. 8:30 to 5:30; Sun. 1 to 5:30.

St. Petersburg: *St. Petersburg Historical Museum,* 335 2nd Ave., NE. Pioneer life, Timuca Indian artifacts. Mon. to Sat. 11 to 5; Sun., holidays 2 to 5.

Sarasota: *The Ringling Museums* include the Museum of Art, the Asolo Theater, the Museum of the Circus, and the residence itself. Mon. to Fri. 9 A.M to 10 P.M.; Sat. 9 to 5; Sun 1 to 5.

Sarasota: *Bellum's Cars & Music of Yesterday.* US 41N. Features 150 antique, classic and race cars, and over 1,000 mechanical music machines. Blacksmith shop and country store. Mon. to Sat. 8:30 to 6.

Stuart: *House of Refuge,* Hutchinson Island. Tues. to Sun. 1 to 5. Adults 50¢; under 12 free. Closed Mon.; *Elliott Museum,* State 5, Hutchinson Island. Daily 1 to 5.

Tallahassee: *Tallahassee Junior Museum,* 3945 Museum Dr. Housed in 1880 farm. Pre-Colombian Indian artifacts, costumes, agriculture. Outdoor museum. Tues. to Sat. 9 to 5; Sun. 2 to 5. Closed Mon., state holidays and one wk. at Christmas.

Florida is a state rich in history and there are many more museums. Hours and prices vary, so phone ahead for last-minute information. Many musuems change exhibits often; others have yearly special festivals.

HISTORIC SITES. Apalachicola: *John Gorrie State Historic Memorial,* Ave. D & 6 St. Bradenton: *DeSoto National Memorial,* 75th St. Bushnell: *Dade Battlefield State Historic Site,* on US 301. Cedar Key: *Cedar Key State Memorial,* State 24. Crystal River: *Crystal River State Archeological Site,* off US 19, 98. Ellenton: *Gamble Mansion State Museum,* US 301, 4 mi. NE of Bradenton. Fort Myers: *Edison House Museum,* 2341 McGregor Blvd. Homosassa Springs: *Yulee Sugar Mill State Historic Site.* 5 mi. W. of US 19 on State 490. Jacksonville: *Fort Caroline National Memorial,* 12713 Ft. Caroline Rd. Key West: *Audubon House,* Whitehead & Greene Sts. New Smyrna Beach: *New Smyrna State Historic Site,* 1 mi. W. on State 44. Olustee: *Olustee Battlefield State Historic Site,* off US 90, 2 mi. E. of Port St. Joe: *Constitution Historic Memorial.* On US 98. Rattlesnake Island: *Fort Matanzas National Monument,* 14 mi. S. of St. Augustine. St. Augustine: All of St. Augustine is, in fact, one enormous historic site, with the early days of American development written indelibly in crumbling or reconstructed stone. The Visitor Information Center has a free, first-rate movie. Then take the free Visitors Guide and decide what to see in person. The *Historic St. Augustine Preservation Board* has strip tickets to all the historic buildings. Be sure to see *Castillo de San Marcos,* located on site of an original Spanish fort.

St. Petersburg: *Madeira Bickel Mound.* Terra Ceia Island off US 41 S. of St. Petersburg. *Heritage Park* and new *Pinellas County Museum* opened July 1977, at 125th St. and Walsingham Road in Largo, heading west on Ulmerton Road from St. Petersburg, and turning south on 125th St.

Tallahassee: *Natural Bridge State Historic Site; Prince & Princess Murat Home of Bellevue.*

TOURS. *Gray Line Tours (Also known as A-1 Lines)* operate at Miami, Miami Beach, Fort Lauderdale, Hollywood, Tampa and Sarasota. *American Sightseeing Tours* offers a variety of combination trips. Check local yellow pages for telephone numbers.

Pensacola offers a tour of the *Naval Aviation Museum, Sherman Air Field* (base of the Blue Angels supersonic precision team), the survival exhibit where demonstrations indicate how to live from Arctic Circle to steamiest hotlands. Also on the tour: *Fort San Carlos,* and *Fort Barrancas,* built by Spanish in the 16th century, and the old Pensacola lighthouse, built in 1825, and still operating.

By Boat: From the downtown St. Petersburg Marina at Vinoy Basin, the *Steven Thomas* cruises out to the Skyway Bridge and Bay. The *Captain Anderson* sails out of Dolphin Village, St. Petersburg Beach, for dinner cruises from October to spring. From Clearwater Beach Marina, the *Captain Memo* sails out to a private island under the command of Captain Memo costumed as a pirate. In Sarasota there are also 2-hr. narrated boat cruises. The *Cheerio* leaves daily except Sat. *Bay Queen,* Sanford, cruises St. Johns River, and *Island Queen,* Riviera Beach.

St. Augustine's sightseeing cruise takes 1½ hrs., leaves from Municipal Yacht Pier, Avenida Menendez. In Titusville, boat tours leave from Westlands Marina daily. Winter Park has a narrated tour of the canals and lakes to view estates, azaleas, Rollins College, etc. There's also a 2-hr. narrated cruise on the *Commodore II* leaving from Bill King's Marina in Marathon, Oct. to May and July to Labor Day. And at Homosassa Springs, US 19, there is a scenic boat trip to view fish and waterfowl.

Glass-bottom boats will open a whole new world at Silver Springs and at Wakulla Springs.

Key Largo has a 2-hr. boat trip to the coral reefs daily if the weather is good and Key West a 2-hr. reef cruise on the *Fireball* from the Gulf to the ocean daily, if clear. Take a glass-bottomed boat tour of the John Pennekamp Coral Reef State Park. Skeletons of old ships lie here with tropical fish swimming among them. The remarkably visible reef has 40 kinds of coral and is 21 mi. long. The trip lasts 2½ hrs. and leaves three times daily. Those willing to take the underwater tour can hire diving equipment on the spot—tank with air, masks, fins, snorkel.

Jungle Queen cruises, leaving from Fort Lauderdale's huge and beautiful Bahia Mar Yacht Basin, has two sailings daily. The *Jungle Queen* passes Venetian Isles, winds through Fort Lauderdale, takes in exotic gardens, tropical bird grounds, alligator wrestling, Seminoles and their chickees, Dania Waterway, Broward International Airport, Hollywood Intracoastal Waterway, Port Everglades and Stranahan River. The *Paddlewheel Queen* also offers an interesting sightseeing cruise and a dinner-entertainment cruise from Fort Lauderdale.

 DRINKING LAWS. City and county establish their own closing times for bars and nightclubs. Package liquor stores are under control of State Beverage Commission. Supermarkets can't sell wine past 1 o'clock on Sundays in some counties. Minimum age in Florida is 19.

 SPORTS. The state's subtropical climate makes sports possible all year. For that reason, they are listed alphabetically and not by season. Florida is high on participant sports—fishing, hunting, tennis, even boccie. It is the great winter training ground for big league baseball. In addition, there are sports exotica for the tourist and the gambler—jai alai, polo, racing with dogs, horses, sulkies, sailing and powerboat events. Shuffleboard is everywhere.

Boating: There are 2,200 miles of tidal shoreline, thousands of navigable lakes and rivers. Under the out-of-state reciprocity system, Florida grants full recognition to valid registration certificates and numbers from other states for 90 days. Persons staying longer must register their vessels with the county tax collector. Write the Florida Department of Natural Resources in Tallahassee for a boating directory. This gives route maps, lists marine facilities and tells where all ramps are located.

Fishing: The question isn't where—because it's everywhere. No license is needed for saltwater, but a freshwater license is necessary. You have the choice of fishing in canals, lakes, rivers, by ocean pier, or by ocean-going yacht.

Freshwater equipment may be used in saltwater, but must be cleaned afterwards to prevent corrosion. If you're able, buy big gear after arrival, when you know what you want to catch. Shops that sell or rent tackle are everywhere.

Water Sports: Florida keeps pace, with water-ski schools, skindiving shops and surfing-supply houses. Dozens of local restrictions exist on where and when water skiers may be towed, and many areas are off limits to divers (too dangerous), so inquiries should always be made.

Surfing: Florida waves are rarely conducive to first-class sport. Mobile surfers spend hours, going from Miami to Fort Pierce, and higher, seeking the best water. Cocoa Beach is a favored spot.

Sailboarding. This exciting sport is taught in most resorts and communities. Rentals available everywhere.

Lobster diving. Use only your hands—it's a state law. Spears and hooks aren't allowed, skindivers wear a mask, swim fins, cotton gloves, possible a snorkel, to go after the lobsters. They're found at any depth from three feet on. In daylight, the lobster hides but can be spotted under logs or rocks by his antennae. The antennae break off easily, so the diver must get a grip on the front body shell. First he twists, then he pulls. Watch out for the morey eel, barracuda, and the black, pincushiony sea urchin.

Golf: Florida is a golfer's paradise, with some of the finest courses in the U.S. According to *Golf Digest* the *Seminole G.C.,* North Palm Beach, ranks among the first ten of America's 100 greatest courses; *Pine Tree G.C.,* (Florida's toughest) Delray Beach, among the second ten; *PGC National G.C.,* Palm Beach Gardens, among the third ten; *Bay Hill Club,* Orlando, among the fourth ten; *Innisbrook G. & C.C.,* Tarpon Springs, among the fifth ten; *Walt Disney World G.C.,* Lake Buena Vista, among the second fifty. The *Mangrove G.C.,* a public course in St. Petersburg, is rated among the nation's top courses. *Bardmoor* and *Isla del Sol* in St. Petersburg are also among the best.

Others recommended by *Golf Digest* are located in: Amalia Island, Ponte Vedra Beach, Sawgrass, Tallahassee, Pensacola, St. Augustine, New Smyrna Beach, Daytona Beach, Ormond Beach, Cocoa Beach, Titusville, two in Vero Beach, Ft. Pierce, Stuart, Port St. Lucie, Tequesta, Lost Tree Village, N. Palm Beach, four in W. Palm Beach, Palm Beach, Royal Palm Beach, two in Lake Worth, Lantana, two in Boynton Beach, two in Delray Beach, six in Boca Raton. Coral Springs, four in Pompano Beach, Plantation, Lauderhill, seven in Ft. Lauderdale, six in Hollywood, Homestead, Biscayne Village, N. Key Largo, Marco Island, four in Naples, Rotondo West, four in Fort Myers, Cape: Coral, two in Lehigh Acres, Englewood, two in Punta Gorda, Port Charlotte, N. Port Charlotte, two in Venice, Captiva Island, six in Sarasota, Palma Sola, Sun City, Lake Placid, two in Sebring, three in Clearwater, five in Tampa, Leesburg, five in St. Petersburg, Dunedin, Williston Highland, two in Orlando, Sanford, Howey-in-the-Hills, Crystal River, Wildwood, Ocala and two in Panama City Beach.

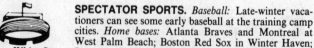

SPECTATOR SPORTS. *Baseball:* Late-winter vacationers can see some early baseball at the training camp cities. *Home bases:* Atlanta Braves and Montreal at West Palm Beach; Boston Red Sox in Winter Haven; Chicago White Sox at Sarasota; Cincinnati Reds at Tampa; Detroit Tigers at Lakeland; Kansas City Royals at Fort Myers; L.A. Dodgers at Vero Beach; Minnesota Twins at Orlando; St. Louis Cardinals and New York Mets at St. Petersburg; New York Yankees at Fort Lauderdale; Phillies at Clearwater; Toronto Blue Jays at Dunedin; Pittsburgh at Bradenton; Houston at Cocoa; and Texas Rangers at Pompano Beach.

Car racing: The Feb. "Daytona 500" has attracted as many as 110,000 spectators. Short and long stock car events precede the "500." Drag and sports car races are held at Lakeland International Raceway. Auto races in Tampa,

Mar. to Nov. Stock car races at W. Palm Beach, Feb. to Nov. Also special events at Sunshine Speedway in St. Petersburg (Evel Knevel has raced here).

Dog racing: Greyhound tracks are at Hollywood (Nov.–March); Key West (Dec.–April); Miami (Biscayne July–Sept.; Sept.–Nov.; West Flagler, May–July, Nov.–Jan.); Bonita Springs (Dec.–April); St. Petersburg (Jan.–May); Sarasota (May–Sept.); Daytona Beach (June–Sept.); Sanford-Orlando at Longwood (Dec.–April); Jacksonville (3 tracks, all year); Ebro (Panama City area, May–Sept.); Monticello (May–Sept.); Seminole Park, in Casselberry, (mid-April–Sept.). No minors allowed at parimutuel facilities.

Horse racing: Tampa has mid-winter racing at Tampa Bay Downs, Jan. to Mar. Gulfstream Park in Hallandale runs mid-Jan. to Mar. There is harness racing at Pompano Beach, with races mid-Dec. to mid-Apr. and Seminole Park, in Casselberry, runs mid-Apr. to Sept. There is quarter horse racing at Gator Down Racing, Pompano, June to Sept. In Hollywood, the Calder Race Course has thoroughbred racing from May to mid-Nov. and has incorporated the former Tropical Park season, mid-Nov. to early Jan.

Jai Alai is played at Dania, Daytona Beach, Tampa, W. Palm Beach, Quincy (nr. Tallahassee), Fern Park (near Orlando), Orange Lake, Ocala-Gainesville, Fort Pierce, Melbourne, Miami, and Winter Park.

Soccer: The Tampa Bay Rowdies play at Tampa Stadium. The Strikers play in Ft. Lauderdale. Jacksonville has its Tea Men.

National Football League: The Tampa Bucs play at Tampa Stadium, the site of Super Bowl 1984.

Polo: At Palm Beach Polo and Country Club, West Palm Beach, from Dec. through April. 18 mi. w. of Palm Beach on a 1,650-acre complex of 9 polo fields, clubhouse, stadium. Prince Charles was here in 1980.

 WHAT TO DO WITH THE CHILDREN. One of the best marine shows is at *Marineland* of Florida, 18 mi. S. of St. Augustine. Six performances daily. The *Gulfarium,* E. of US 98 on Okaloosa Island, nr. *Fort Walton Beach,* has fish and scuba diving shows in their reef tank; trained porpoises in the main tank. Miami's *Seaquarium* has a shark channel, killer whales, porpoise and sea lion shows. A monorail circles the 60-acre garden. The trained porpoises for many of the Orlando *Sea World* shows come from *Flipper's Sea School* Key West. You can see them at their lessons daily from 10 to 4. *Ocean World,* 1701 SE 17th St. Causeway, Ft. Lauderdale, also has performing porpoises, a seal pool and shark moat.

The *Theater of the Sea,* in Islamorada, offers hr-long "bottomless" boat tours in addition to trained porpoise shows and the aquarium. You can also take a charter boat to visit underwater coral gardens and wreck of a Spanish galleon.

There's lots to see at the Tarpon Springs sponge docks. *Spongeorama,* 510 Dodecanese Blvd., gives sponge-diving exhibitions, shows movies and exhibits about the sponge industry, and offers a self-guided tour of the boats. Miami's mammoth new, cageless Metrozoo will be the nation's largest when fully completed.

On the landward side of the nature-lover's coin are animal refuges. Tiny key deer, 25 in. high, can be photographed at the *National Key Deer Refuge* off State 940 on Big Pine Key. Tame deer may be fed at *International Deer Ranch,* Silver Springs. The visitor is caged, the monkey free at *Monkey Jungle,* 3 mi. W. of US 1 in Goulds, 20 mi. S. of Coral Gables. In Tarpon Springs visit *Noell's Ark Chimpanzee Farm,* US 19. The *Jacksonville Municipal Zoo,* on Trout River off N. Main St., features animals and birds from many lands; famous for its black leopards. Islands for bears and lions. Miniature railroad.

Over 100 lions and other African wild animals roam at large in *Lion Country Safari,* on US 98 in West Palm Beach. You can rent an explanatory tape and tape recorder. *"Jungle Larry's African Safari"* in Naples is a 200-acre tropical garden with exotic birds, waterfowl, chimp shows, and a lion and tiger training school. *Sarasota Jungle Gardens* has an awesome number of tropical plants in wild jungle and formal gardens, exotic birds, chimp acts, and bird shows. It's at 3701 Bayshore Rd. There are a bird walk, guided boat tours, a sundown train trip to a bird rookery, and native wildlife at Myakka River State Park, 17 mi. E. of Sarasota. *St. Augustine's Alligator Farms,* on Anastasia Island, features alligator wrestling and a zoo of Florida wildlife. *Gatorland Zoo,* Kissimmee, features alligators, crocodiles, giant tortoises, zebras. Train ride.

Costumed Indians make dolls, do beadwork and make baskets at *Seminole Okalee Indian Village,* 6073 Sterling Rd., West Hollywood. Arts and crafts center, small zoo and alligator wrestling. The Seminole Indian Reservation is on State 721 W. of Brighton. Exhibits at *Temple Mound and Museum,* US 98, Fort Walton Beach, tell story of Indian culture, religion.

Circus buffs will have a heyday at the *Ringling Museums,* a complex of 4 bldgs. on 68 acres on US 41, 3 mi. N. of Sarasota. The circus museum covers circus history from ancient Rome to the present day with collections of hand-bills, posters, costumes, wagons, etc. The *Ringling Residence* is a fabulous Venetian Gothic building; the *Museum of Art* has both a fine collection of contemporary work and a renowned collection of baroque art; the *Asolo Theater* is a reassembled Venetian theater. Venice is winter quarters for *Ringling Bros.— Barnum & Bailey,* with a rehearsal hall and arena on Airport Ave.

Circus World in Haines City (near Orlando) is a big, fun place, where you can walk the tightrope, be painted up like a clown, or be a circus performer, under professional supervision, of course. Under the Big Top, there's an excellent panorama film, special shows, and all the excitement of the circus. For roller coaster fans, The Roaring Tiger ride is a thriller!

Weeki Wachee Spring features underwater ballet by "mermaids" in a specially designed auditorium 16 ft. below the surface. Comfortable sightseeing boats with commentary by the "captain" make regular trips down the Weeki Wachee River. There's also an Exotic Trained Bird Show with macaws and cockatoos skating, playing cards and doing other unbirdlike tricks. The Springs are 12 mi. W. of *Brooksville* at the jct. of State 50 & US 19.

Cypress Gardens, in Winter Haven, has water skiing, aquarama shows, walk through aquarium, zoo, Living Legend audio-visual show with life-size wax figures; boat tours of the canals and exquisite gardens.

Six Gun Territory, Silver Springs, is a recreation of an Old West Frontier town. Steam train, gondolas, rides, gunfights, Indian dances add to the fun. Rides and shows are included in fee. The new *Wild Waters,* with flumes and surf-tipped pools, was completed at Silver Springs in '78. *Petticoat Junction,* 10 mi. W. of Panama City at Long Beach Resort, also features cowboy and Indian fights, steam engine rides. Mar. to Labor Day. *Atlantis,* the world's largest water theme park, is now open in Ft. Lauderdale. Wave pool, water slides, and rapids. In nearby Pompano Beach, the famous Goodyear Blimp winters. Rides are no longer offered but you can take a good look at the blimp and tour a museum. *Busch Gardens,* on Busch Blvd., Tampa, is an adventure into The Dark Continent, with a 200-acre prairieland, (Serengeti Plain) where hundreds of animals roam freely, including lions, zebras, rhinos, etc. The animals are observed in their natural habitat from the skyride or the monorail. In the Moroccan Village, snake-charmers, magicians, and exotic dancers are just part of the entertainment. Walk through the well-known Bird Garden, take an exciting ride on The Python, the Monstrous Mamba, or the Log Flume. A fascinating Jungle Cruise was added in '78. Adults can tour the Anheuser-Busch Brewery and have some free "suds" while the youngsters enjoy, enjoy. Busch's Campgrounds are adjacent, for a stay within the sound of the lions' roars. In 1979, Timbuktu was added to the Dark Continent, with more thrilling rides, an amphitheater, restaurants, game area; also the new Adventure Island, with white sand beach, pools for surfing, flumes, picnic grounds and "the ultimate water experience."

Also of interest to the pirate-adventure lover, in St. Petersburg, adjoining Municipal Pier, is MGM's replica of *The Bounty,* the mutiny ship. There's also a *Tahitian village,* dioramas. At the Million Dollar Pier, children can feed the pelicans. Nearby Haas Museum has interesting displays for kids, including a banyan tree to climb.

There are many museums which will interest children. Among them: *South Florida Museum & Bishop Planetarium,* 201 10th St. W., Bradenton. *Museum of Arts and Sciences,* in Jacksonville at 1025 Gulf Life Dr. Ecology, wild life, Timaqua Indians, Planetarium shows. *John Young Museum and Planetarium,* 810 E. Rollins Ave., Orlando.

The *Museum of Yesterday's Toys*, 52 St. George St., St. Augustine, displays over 4500 dolls, other toys and accessories. Guided tours of house, garden. *Oldest Store Museum* in St. Augustine carries turn-of-the-century merchandise. The *Zorayda Castle*, 83 King St., St. Augustine, was inspired by the Alhambra in Spain. Kids will also appreciate the *Ripley's Believe It or Not Museum*, 19 San Marco Ave. In Winter Haven, the *Museum of Old Dolls and Toys* at 1530 6th St. displays 3-century-old dolls, mechanical banks. Sarasota's *Bellum's Cars & Music of Yesterday*, 5500 N. Tamiami Trail, has antique cars, mechanical music boxes.

Tallahassee's Junior Museum, 3945 Museum Dr., is a restoration of a pioneer farm with blacksmith shop, farm house, smokehouse, etc.; 4 museum bldgs, nature trails. The *Junior Museum* features Seminole Indian culture, and a man-in-space display.

Ralph Heath's Suncoast Seabird Sanctuary, 18328 Gulf Blvd., Indian Shores, about a ten-minute drive from St. Pete Beach, is open 7 days a week during daylight hours. Admission is free to see how injured seabirds receive tender loving care. Or the children may want to adopt a bird! At least 500 birds of 40 different species live here.

Waterslide sites include the *Wet 'n Wild* watersport theme park in Orlando, the *Zoom Flume* in Panama City, *Water Boggan* in Pompano Beach, *Hawaiian Slip Waterside* in Kissimmee, *Okaloosa County Water Slide* in Fort Walton Beach.

Roger Brown's Miniature Horse Farm, a 15-acre attraction at Pompano Beach, features races and special performances of these tiny horses.

Alligatorland Safari Zoo, Kissimmee, is an animal jungle compound. The Fort Myers *Wildlife Park* has exhibits and bird and wildlife shows. It's adjacent to the captivating (and free) Shell Shop.

Sunken Gardens, 1825 4th St., St. Petersburg, delights the children with more than 5,000 plants and flowers, an orchid arboretum, colorful native and exotic birds, a King of Kings exhibit, a colossal gift shop. *Tiki Gardens*, 19061 Gulf Blvd., Indian Rocks Beach, outside of St. Pete, is a veritable Polynesia, with Tiki gods, gardens, comical monkeys, and strutting peacocks outside a restaurant-gift shop complex. *London Wax Museum*, 5505 Gulf Blvd., St. Pete Beach, is a fascinating display of almost 100 of the most famous and infamous people, plus a Chamber of Horrors.

 HOTELS AND MOTELS. In Florida more than any other state, your entire schedule of activities will probably revolve around where you stay. If you want active sports, you will want one kind of hotel; if you prefer to lounge on the beach, you will prefer another. Rule of thumb on prices; the farther from the ocean, the cheaper the room. Good buys can be found up and down US 1 on the east coast. In many locations, such as the Pinellas Suncoast along the Gulf of Mexico, offseason prices are as much as 50 percent cheaper, making an expensive hotel a summer bargain.

We have listed hotels and motels alphabetically in categories determined by double-occupancy in-season rates: *Moderate*, $50–70; *Inexpensive*, $30–50.

BRADENTON. *Inexpensive:* **Days Inn.** US 301 & State 64. A good operation, featuring popular Tasty World restaurant. Pets.

CLEARWATER. *Inexpensive:* **Days Inn.** US 19 & State 590. Well-kept. Pool, play area.

CLEARWATER BEACH. *Moderate:* **Bel Crest Apt. Motel.** 706 Baywater Blvd. Pretty bay view. Fishing dock. Heated pool. Efficiencies, too.

DAYTONA BEACH. *Moderate:* **TraveLodge on the Beach.** 301 S. Atlantic. Restaurant, bar, enterprise 800–255–3050.

Inexpensive: **Days Inn.** Four locations in area. A good buy. Pool, play area, gift shop, gas station.

DEFUNIAK SPRINGS. *Moderate.* **Ramada Inn.** Restaurant, lounge, all amenities of this popular chain.

DELRAY BEACH. *Moderate:* **Candlelight Motor Lodge.** 3356 N. Federal Highway (US 1). Small motel. Heated pool. Convenient; refrigerators in rooms.

FORT LAUDERDALE. *Inexpensive:* **Anchorage Resort Apts.** 1760 E. Los Olas. Weekly only. Efficiency or 1-bedroom apt. Owners speak Spanish, some French, accept leading overseas currencies.
Casa Carmeleta, 2300 NE 33rd. On ICW, 2 blocks to beach. Pool. Hotel room or apt. to 3 brs.
Gold Coast. 545 N. Atlantic. On ocean. Pool. Apts. available.
Marine Terrace Hotel. 527 N. Birch Rd. Rooms have refrigerator; efficiencies have full kitchen. 1 block to ocean.
Spindrift Motel. 2501 N. Ocean. Heated pool. Rooms have refrigerators. Efficiencies available. No pets.
Seville-Beachdale. 3020–3021 Seville St. Near shops, restaurants, entertainment. Rooms have refrigerators/efficiencies available.

FORT MYERS. *Inexpensive:* **Fountain Motel.** 7490 McGregor Blvd. S.W. Near fishing, marinas, golf. Kitchens avail.
Sabal Motel. 1652 N. Tamiami Tr. Each unit has kitchen, cable TV, cross-ventilation if you don't like a/c. Near shopping, etc.

FORT MYERS BEACH. *Inexpensive:* **Carousel Motel.** 6230 Estero Blvd. Gulfside, beach. Near golf, tennis. Motel rooms, efficiencies, apts.
Eventide. 1160 Estero. Pool, beach. Efficiencies available.

FORT PIERCE. *Moderate:* **Holiday Inn.** Two locations. Pool, restaurant; playground. Family-oriented.
Inexpensive: **Colony Motor Court.** 1007 S. Federal Hwy. Small motel with restaurant nearby.

FORT WALTON BEACH/DESTIN. *Moderate:* **Howard Johnson's.** 314 Miracle Strip Pkwy. SW. Fishing pier, dock, restaurant, bar, entertainment, dancing.
Sandestin Resort Inn (Formerly *Sheraton*), on Florida Gulf. 18 holes of championship golf, 9 tennis courts. Fishing, sailing, lawn games. Two pools. Near Indian Temple Mount Museum and other attractions.
Marina Bay Resort. 80 Miracle Strip Pkwy SE. Pool, fishing, boating. Family rates avail.
Inexpensive: **Fort Walton.** 185 Miracle Strip Pkwy. Pool. Pets, Restaurant nr.

HOLLYWOOD. *Inexpensive.* **Jo-Lin Apt. Hotel.** 2634 Johnson St. Rooms, studios. apts. Kingside pool, friendly bunch, potlucks, bingo, barbecue.

JACKSONVILLE. *Inexpensive:* **Heart of Jacksonville,** 901 Main St.
Jacksonville Airport Hilton. P.O. Box 18069.
Ramada Inn West. I–10 at Lane Ave.
Quality Inn Golfair. I–95 at Golfair.
Holiday Inn Airport.
Econolodge Motel. 2300 Phillips Hwy.

JACKSONVILLE BEACH. *Inexpensive:* **Howard Johnson's Ocean.** 1515 N. 1st St.
Holiday Inn Oceanfront. 1617 N. 1st St.
Best Western of Neptune. 1401 Atlantic Blvd.
Tabb's Seasite, 1023 N. 1st St.

Sea Horse Motel. On the ocean at Neptune Beach.
Towels Motel. 435 N. 3rd St.
Seabreeze, 117 N. 1st St.
Beachcomber. 411 S. 1st St.
Bennett's Beach Motel. 363 Atlantic.

KEY WEST. *Moderate:* **Southernmost Motel.** 1319 Duval St. Pleasant, small. Short walk to sights. Some efficiencies.

LAKE WALES. *Moderate:* **River Ranch Resort.** At Yeehaw Junction between Lake Wales and Okeechobee. Wild West action in Florida, with horseback riding, cookouts, rodeos, square dancing, archery, hunting. Boating and fishing. Pool. Golf. Western café, Wild West saloon. Rustic, comfortable.
Inexpensive. **Emerald.** 522 S. Scenic Hwy. Pool. Pets. Restaurant nr.

LAKE WORTH. *Inexpensive:* **Martinique.** 801 S. Dixie Hwy. Free morning coffee & rolls.
Lago Motor Inn. 714 S. Dixie Hwy. Some units have wet bars, refrigerators. Near downtown, golf, Bryant Park.
Midnight Sun. 1030 S. Federal Hwy. Pool.

MARINELAND. *Moderate:* **Marineland Quality Inn.** Hwy. A1A. Oceanfront. Pools. Marina. Tennis courts, putting green. Playground. Good restaurant, cocktails.

NAPLES. *Inexpensive:* **Bay Villa.** 3350 Kelly Rd. All units have electric kitchen, front-door parking. Heated pool, free boat ramp.

OCALA. *Moderate:* **Holiday Inn.** Half a dozen locations here. Telephone 800–238–8000 for details, rates, reservations.
Inexpensive: **Days Inn.** I–75 & State 40. Usual good standards. Pool, gift shop, gas station. Tasty World restaurant.
Sheraton Country Inn. 3620 SW. Broadway. Restaurant, bar, dancing, entertainment wknds.

ORLANDO. *Moderate:* **Days Inn.** Name any motel or hotel chain and it's likely you'll find one or more of them here. Most are in the inexpensive-to-moderate range year-round.

ORMOND BEACH. *Moderate:* **Argosy Motel.** On SR A1A. 1255 Ocean Shore Blvd. Small motel on beach.
Holiday Inn. I–95 and US 1. Playground, pool. Restaurant, cocktails.

PENSACOLA. *Moderate:* **Rodeway Inn.** 710 N. Palafox St., also on SR 297. Restaurants, cocktails, entertainment. Pool (heated).
Inexpensive: **Days Inn.** I–10 & US 29N. Another branch of this dependable chain. Pool, play area, gift shop, gas station.

POMPANO BEACH. *Inexpensive:* **Surfside Motel.** 710 S. Ocean Blvd. Heated pool; refrigerators; efficiencies. Family-oriented.

ST. AUGUSTINE. *Moderate:* **Continental Inn.** 1 Dolphin Dr. Pool, dick, fishing pier. Restaurant.
Holiday Inn. 2 locations, each with pool, restaurant, bar, dancing entertainment in season: I–95: I–95 at State 16; US 1: 1300 Ponce de Leon Blvd.
Inexpensive: **Days Inn.** Two branches of good chain. State 16. Pool, play area, gift shop, gas station. Also I–95 at State 16.
Lantern Lodge. 345 San Marco Ave. Pool, sauna. Morning coffee free.

Red Carpet Inn. I–95 Pleasant 2-story motel. Restaurant.

ST. PETE BEACH. *Moderate:* **Beachcombers Resort Motel.** 6200 Gulf Blvd. On beautiful beach. Family-oriented activities. Some efficiencies.

ST. PETERSBURG. *Moderate:* **Holiday Inn.** 3 locations, each with pool, restaurant, bar, entertainment: North: 5005 34th St.; South: two Inns on 34th St.

SANFORD. *Inexpensive:* **Holiday Inn.** Off I–4. 800–238–8000. Restaurant, lounge, entertainment.

SARASOTA. *Moderate:* **Howard Johnson's Airport.** 6325 N. Tamiami Trail. Attractive rooms with patios or balconies.
Inexpensive: **Cadillac Motel.** Pool (heated), play area. Restaurant nearby.

SANIBEL ISLAND. *Moderate:* **Hurricane House.** 2939 W. Gulf Dr. Beach-front cottages, each with kitchen. Heated pool, tennis, badminton, horseshoes. **Beachview Cottages.** 306 W. Gulf. On Gulf. Kitchens, Heated pool. Week minimum holidays.

SEBRING. *Inexpensive:* **Clayton's.** Pets. Pool, beach. Restaurant, bar.

TALLAHASSEE. *Moderate:* **Holiday Inn.** 2 locations, each with pool, restaurant, bar, entertainment, daning, airport transportation: Apalachee: 1302 Apalachee Pkwy. Downtown: 316 W. Tennessee St.

TAMPA. *Moderate:* **Admiral Benbow Inn.** 1200 N. Westshore Blvd. Heated pools, sauna. Restaurant, lounge, entertainment.
Causeway Inn. Campbell Causeway. Large pool. Live entertainment, restaurant.
Holiday Inn. 4 locations, all with pool, restaurant, bar. Near Airport, 4500 Cypress St. (newest) North: 400 E. Bearss Ave.; East: 2708 N. 50th St.; West: 4732 N. Dale Mabry (US 92). Fishing, picnic area.
Quality Inn. 2 locations, each with pool, restaurant: North: 210 E. Fowler Ave.; South: 3693 Gandy Blvd.
Ramada Inn. Two locations: 2522 N. Dale Mabry and I–75 at Busch Blvd. Pool (heated). Restaurant, bar, entertainment, dancing.
Inexpensive: **Days Inn.** Two branches of popular chain. Busch Blvd. & 30th St. and I–4 & State 579. Both have pool, play area, gift shop, gas station. Pets. Tasty World restaurant.

TREASURE ISLAND. *Moderate:* **Island Inn.** 9980 Gulf Blvd. Colorful, small beach resort. Family-oriented activities. Snack bar. Management's cook-outs.
Thunderbird. 10700 Gulf Blvd. Beachfront. Heated pool, sundeck. Some efficiencies. 24-hour coffeeshop, restaurant. Lively lounge, entertainment, dancing.
Inexpensive: **Buccaneer.** 10800 Gulf Blvd. Treasure Island. On white sand beach. Heated pool, free breakfast. Kitchen units avail.

WEST PALM BEACH. *See Lake Worth.*

WINTER HAVEN. *Moderate:* **Banyan Beach Motel.** 1630 6th St. NW. Dock, boats, fishing.
Inexpensive: **Landmark Motor Lodge–Best Western.** U.S. 17 at S.R. 544. Pool, bar, lounge, 2 blocks to shopping.

DINING OUT. Eating your way across Florida may not be good for the waistline—or the budget. It's hard to find a city without at least one superior eating place. Restaurant categories in the listing below reflect the cost of a medium-priced dinner at each establishment. Included are hors d'oeuvres or soup, entree and dessert. Not included are drinks, tax and tip.

Price ranges for Florida are *Moderate:* $8–12 and *Inexpensive:* below $8.

BRADENTON. *Moderate:* **Pete Reynard's.** 5325 Marina Dr., Holmes Beach. Fisherman's platter, steak & prime ribs.
Inexpensive: **Morrison's Cafeteria.** Fourteenth St. Fast, quiet service, cafeteria style.

CAPE CORAL. *Inexpensive:* **Willy's Restaurant.** Cape Coral Shopping Plaza. Home cooking.

CLEARWATER. *Moderate:* **Kapok Tree Inn.** 923 McMullen Booth Rd. Dazzling estate, landscaped gardens. Must be seen. Lunch, dinner, cocktails. Children's menu.
Inexpensive: **Fish House.** On US 19. Daily to 10 P.M. Opens 11:30 A.M. Lunch, dinner, cocktails.
Morrison's State Rd. 60.
Robby's Pancake House. 1617 Gulf to Bay Blvd. Eat this American favorite, fillingly and inexpensively, until 9 P.M.

DAYTONA BEACH. *Moderate:* **Chez Bruchez.** 304 Seabreeze Blvd. Delicious pastries, plus French or American food. Children's menu.
Julian's. 88 S. Atlantic Ave. Opens at 4 P.M. for dinner. Sensibly priced.

DUNEDIN. *Moderate:* **Bon Appetit.** On Marina. Go at breakfast, lunch or early-bird dinner.

FERNANDINA BEACH. *Moderate:* **Palace Saloon.** Florida's oldest (1878). Antique decor. Boiled shrimp with hot tomato sauce only food served. Great drinks. Try 22-ounce Pirate's Punch, if you dare.

FORT LAUDERDALE. *Moderate:* **Ambry.** 3016 E. Commercial Blvd. Favorite with the young because of wine cellar atmosphere.
Café de Geneve. S. Andrews Ave. across from Broward General. Authentic Swiss dishes, especially the fondues, veal. Cozy ambiance.
Ernie's Booze & Barbecue. 1843 S. Federal Hwy. Conch chowder, conch fritters, Bimini bread. Crowded during college vacations.
Yesterday's. Oakland Pk. at the Intracoastal. Three seatings nightly. Filling feasts and a nice view of the passing water scene.
Patricia Murphy's Candlelight Restaurant. In Bahia Mar Yachting Center. Beautiful views. Good home-style food and popovers. Children's menu. Lunch, dinner. Cocktail lounge.
Inexpensive: **Rustic Inn Crab House.** 4331 Ravenswood Rd. Family recipes including a unique garlic crab. A 50-year local tradition.
Wolfie's. 2501 East Sunrise Blvd. Deluxe delicatessen. Own bakery (try the strawberry cheesecake).
Yum Yum of Siam. 3856 N. University. Thai food, beer, wine. Closed Monday.

FORT MYERS. *Inexpensive:* **Western Sizzling Steak House.** 5601 S. Tamiami Trail. Family priced. 17 selections on menu.
Perkins, 8580 S. Tamiami Trail. Diverse menu.

JACKSONVILLE. *Moderate:* **Stricklands.** Mayport, near Jacksonville. Fishing village atmosphere. St. Johns River views. Fresh snapper and local seafoods.

Inexpensive: **Beach Road Chicken Dinner.** 4132 Atlantic Blvd. For years a local favorite for its lip-licking fried chicken and traditional trimmings.

Bono's Pit Barbecue. 4907 Beach Rd. Renowned for smoky, tangy ribs, chicken, beef with your choice of sauces.

KEY WEST. *Inexpensive:* **Fourth of July.** 1110 White St. Cuban specialties, conch fritters. Take-out service.

Half Shell Raw Bar. At the foot of Margaret St. Local hot spot for real conch chowder, just-shucked oysters, draft beer. Oyster-eating records made here.

LAKE WALES. *Moderate:* **Highlander Restaurant.** North Ave. Orange-creme spread, home-made pastries.

MADEIRA BEACH. *Moderate:* **Richards.** 5001 Duhme Rd. Acropolis-style statuary, lavish gardens, lagoons. Ornate dining rooms. Cocktail lounge in Indian bridal tent. Salad bar.

Inexpensive: **Captain's Galley.** Near Medeira Shopping Mall, across from Santa Madeira ship. Broiled grouper, strip steaks, varied menu. Cozy with water views. Cocktails.

Santa Madeira Brown Derby. On Intracoastal Waterway at end of Madeira Shopping Mall. Newly built replica of Spanish galleon. Seafood, beef, chicken, salad bar. Cocktail lounge.

PALM BEACH. *Moderate:* **Angelique,** 237 Worth Ave. Singing staff serves up 3 meals a day from fragrant French kitchen.

Inexpensive: **Clematis St. Café.** 531 Clematis St. Fresh, natural foods. Open only for lunch but you won't need dinner after their supersize sandwiches and desserts.

Hamburger Heaven. Not just another burger barn. Fat, fancy burgers festooned with a feast of toppings.

PLANT CITY. *Moderate:* **Branch Ranch.** Thonotassa Rd., off I–4. Worth the drive from Tampa—or anywhere. Serves chicken, ham, chicken-ham combination. Vegetable dinner has chicken pot pie as side dish. Everything is home grown.

POMPANO BEACH. *Moderate:* **Gentleman Jim's.** 2031 NE 36th St., Lighthouse Point. Cheese soup, salads, beef, and seafood.

Inexpensive: **Perry's.** 235 S. Federal Hwy. Greek specialties. Early-bird specials and lunches are real bargains.

SARASOTA. *Moderate:* **Marina Jack.** 2 Marina Plaza. Attractive site overlooking bay. Wide variety in menu.

Inexpensive: **Main Bar.** Across from Maas Brothers. Extra-special sandwiches, salads, and beer.

ST. PETERSBURG. *Moderate:* **Aunt Hattie's.** 625 1st St. Chicken & dumplings, seafood. Victorian décor.

Moderate-Inexpensive: **Fish House.** South Pasadena Avenue. Artistically decorated with aquarium walls, antiques, greenery. Good values for seafood.

Inexpensive: **Belmark Restaurant.** 1001 1st Ave. N. Neat cafeteria. Daily luncheon specials (like Friday's baked sea bass) under $3, and no charge for seconds.

Duff's Famous Smorgasbord. 1440 34th St. N. All you can eat from the groaning board at lunch or dinner, under $5.

Gigi's. Pasadena Shopping Center. Manicotti and music. Budget-priced luncheons. Attractive decor.

Morrison's Cafeteria. At four locations: 391 34th St. N.; Pasadena Shopping Center; 8050 Gateway Mall; 202 Pinellas Square Mall. Lunch and dinner under $3.

Ted Peters Smoked Fish. 1350 Pasadena Ave. S. Lunch or early dinner al fresco, at rustic tables. Smoked mullet, smoked mackerel, clam chowder, German potato salad. Good hamburgers, too. Beer, soft drinks. Closed Tuesdays.

ST. PETE BEACH. *Inexpensive:* **Brown Derby.** 6000 Gulf Blvd. in front of Sandpiper resort. Pleasant Tiffany-shaded decor. Help-yourself salad bar with lunch and dinner. Unbelievably priced for such good food, atmosphere, service. Double drinks and free canapes in Luv Pub at Happy Hour. Always crowded.

TAMPA. *Inexpensive:* **Mel's Hot Dog Stand.** Busch Blvd. near Busch Gardens. Chicago-style kosher specials for hot dog connoisseurs.

Silver Ring. Seventh Ave., Ybor City, a couple of blocks west of famous Columbia Restaurant. Shop might not look appealing but the large Cuban sandwiches (ask for a special) are considered the best.

TGI Friday's. Hyde Park section of Tampa. Fun and games harking back to turn of century. Same menu lunch and dinner. Cocktails.

TARPON SPRINGS. *Moderate:* **Louis Pappas Riverside Restaurant.** 785 Anclote Blvd. On the sponge docks. Flavorful Greek and American foods.

TIERRA VERDE *Moderate:* **The Good Times.** 1130 Pinellas Bayway. Continental specialties, rostbraten Esterhazy, veal roast Florentine, roast duckling. Special desserts. Lunch, dinner.

GEORGIA

Cities, Seashore and Hills

There's a revolving lounge atop a hotel in Atlanta from which you can *almost* see the city grow. New buildings are springing up at every compass point; old ones are being removed to make way for progress. A few years ago the Atlanta newspapers published a photograph of the skyline in the early '60s—another, of the same spot in the '70s. Two entirely different cities.

Scarlett O'Hara said: "Atlanta is full of pushy people." Pushy, ambitious, determined—whatever the word, since the early Reconstruction days following the Civil War, Atlanta has had a winning combination which is still excelling.

Much of the charm of legendary southern hospitality is tenaciously guarded, cherished. New tides of energy are surging everywhere, but the past remains as real as the present.

The Cyclorama, famous three-dimensional panoramic painting of the Battle of Atlanta, located at Grant Park, has been restored and reopened to the public. The Swan House on the grounds of the Atlanta Historical Society is an example of Italian Palladian architecture, and an interesting collection of mementos from Georgia's past are housed in contemporary McElreath Hall. Adjacent is the Tullie Smith farmhouse, which looks essentially as it did in 1840's. Nearby, Georgia's governor resides in a new mansion, a show place, opened for tourists several times each week.

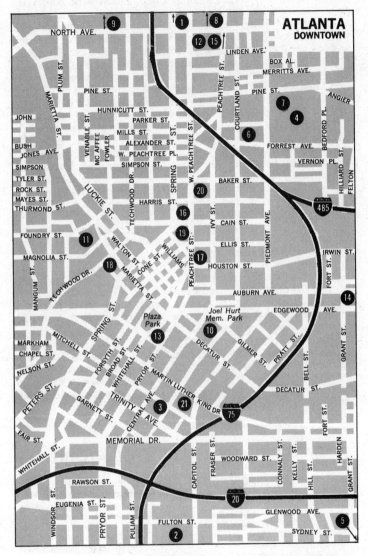

ATLANTA DOWNTOWN

Points of Interest

1) Atlanta Historical Society
2) Atlanta Stadium
3) City Hall
4) Civic Center
5) Cyclorama
6) Emory University School of Dentistry
7) Exhibition Hall
8) Fox Theater
9) Georgia Institute of Technology
10) Georgia State University
11) Georgia World Congress Center
12) High Museum of Art
13) Five Points Rapid Rail Station
14) Martin Luther King grave
15) Memorial Arts Center
16) Merchandise Mart
17) Georgia-Pacific Center
18) Omni Hotel and Megastructure
19) Peachtree Plaza Hotel
20) Hyatt Regency Atlanta Hotel
21) State Capitol

Six Flags Over Georgia, a family entertainment park, covers 331 acres, has over 100 attractions, rides, and live shows—all for one admission price. Rides include the Dahlonega runaway mine train, the log flume, and the Jean Ribaut riverboat adventure. The park has sections, one for each of the six flags which have flown over Georgia—French, Spanish, English, Confederacy, United States, and Georgia. The park boasts two hair-raising roller coasters, including the triple-loop Mind Bender. Thunder River, opened in 1982, is an exciting raft trip on a whitewater river. One of the most popular rides is The Great Gasp, a 40-foot free-fall parachute drop, that ends with a slow and controlled perfect landing, and a "great gasp" from partakers.

Stone Mountain, the world's largest mass of exposed granite, is surrounded by a 3,200-acre park. A massive Confederate carving features General Robert E. Lee with General Stonewall Jackson and Confederacy President Jefferson Davis. Lee's likeness is 138 feet from the top of his head to his horse's hoof. His face measures twenty-one feet, his nose, five feet. The stars on his collar are bigger than dishpans and the sword, measuring fifty-eight feet in length and four feet in width, weighs one hundred tons. The giant granite dome, which rises 650 feet above the surrounding plain, stands about twenty miles east of downtown Atlanta and is visible from the top of many of the city's larger buildings. A cable-car lift rises from the base of the mountain to the summit 2,600 feet distant. Two glass-enclosed cable cars, each carrying fifty passengers, afford a superb view. A replica of the famous Civil War locomotive, "The General," pulls vintage coaches along a seven-mile ride that circles the base of the mountain. A Memorial Building contains a museum featuring Sherman's famous "March to the Sea," depicted in a sixty-foot relief map. Magnolia Hall, an authentic antebellum plantation, was moved from its original site at Dickey, Ga., carefully furnished and restored. There is an antique automobile museum, a steamboat operating on an adjoining lake, a marina, a carillon with concerts daily, excellent fishing, horseback riding, golf, and camping.

PRACTICAL INFORMATION FOR ATLANTA

HOW TO GET THERE. *By air:* The world's second busiest airport, Atlanta has domestic service from *Delta, Eastern, Frontier, Northwest Orient, Ozark, Piedmont,* and *Republic.* International service is available on *Bahamasair, British Caledonian, Delta, Eastern, KLM, Lufthansa,* and *Sabena. By car:* I–85, I–75, and I–20 will all get you to Atlanta. *By train:* Atlanta may be reached by *Amtrak's* Crescent, with daily passenger service between New Orleans and Washington, D.C. *By bus: Greyhound, Trailways,* and several other companies serve Atlanta.

MUSEUMS AND GALLERIES. *Georgia Dept. of Archives and History,* 330 Capitol Ave. SE.: history of Georgia depicted in stained-glass windows. *Cyclorama,* Grant Park: huge canvas Battle of Atlanta recently restored. *Swan House,* 3099 Andrews Dr. NW: period rms. on first floor. *Governor's Mansion,* 391 W. Paces Ferry Rd.: Federal furnishings in elegant home. *Emory Museum,* Bishop's Hall, Emory Univ., S. Oxford Rd. NE in Druid Hills:

Far Eastern, African, Near Eastern, American Indian artifacts. *High Museum of Art,* Memorial Art Center, 1280 Peachtree St. NE: contains Western art from early Renaissance to present. *Georgia State Museum of Science and Industry,* 4th fl. State Capitol Bldg.: displays, dioramas. *Fernbank Science Center,* 156 Heaton Park NE.: observatory, exhibit hall, forest and reference library. Third largest planetarium in the nation, open daily.

HISTORIC SITES. *Wren's Nest,* 1050 Gordon St. SW: home of Joel Chandler Harris, creator of Uncle Remus stories. *Martin Luther King, Jr.* is entombed beside the Ebenezer Baptist Church, 413 Auburn Ave. NE. *Zero Mile Post,* nr. Decatur St. under Central Ave. Bridge, marks the southwestern terminus of the Western & Atlantic RR and is the birthplace of the city of Atlanta.

TOURS. *By bus:* Tours range from 3 to 5 hours and include downtown, Ga. Tech, Peachtree St., Lenox Sq., Emory U., Cyclorama, Druid Hills, State Capitol, Stone Mountain. Operators are *American Sightseeing; Gray Line; Arnel; Tour Gals; Atlanta Convention Planners; Presenting Atlanta Tours; Guidelines.*

HOTELS AND MOTELS. Atlanta's accommodations should prove pleasant for even the most discriminating traveler, and cover a wide, diverse range. Listings are in order of price category. Based on double occupancy without meals in the peak season, the ranges are as follows: *Moderate:* $35–50; *Inexpensive:* under $20–35. For a more complete explanation of hotel and motel categories see *Facts at Your Fingertips* at the front of this volume.

Moderate: **Harley Hotel.** I–285 at Camp Creek Pkwy., near Atlanta Airport. Beautiful guest rooms, restaurant, lounge, health club.

Holiday Inn. Pool, play area, restaurant. 6288 Old Dixie Hwy., Jonesboro; 4422 Northeast Expwy., Doraville; 1810 Howell Mill Rd. NW.; 4225 Fulton Industrial Blvd.; Hapeville; Airport; I–75 Perimeter; 175 Piedmont Ave.; 4300 Snapfinger Woods Dr.; 1944 Piedmont Circle; I–85 at Monroe Dr.; 2360 Delk Rd., Marietta.

Howard Johnson's. Six locations. Pool, restaurant. 1377 Virginia Ave., East Point; 2090 N. Druid Hills Rd.; 1701 Northside Dr. NW; 5793 Roswell Rd. NW; 759 Washington St. SW. 100 10th St. NW at I–75-I–85.

Master Hosts Inn. N.W. 2375 Delk Rd, 100 rooms.

Ramada Inn. Four locations. Pool, restaurant. 845 N. Central Ave., Hapeville. 180 rooms. I–85 North at Monroe Dr. (448 rooms); I–20 East at Candler Rd. (194 rooms); 305 Industrial Circle S.W. at Six Flags (153 rooms).

Stone Mountain Inn. 1 mi. S. of 78 Stone Mountain exit. In Stone Mountain Park.

White House Motor Hotel. 219 rooms. 70 Houston St., NE.

Inexpensive: **Days Inns and Days Lodges.** Several in metro Atlanta.

Days Inn. Ten motels, 6 lodges in Atlanta area.

DINING OUT in Atlanta can mean the usual fine fare to be found in most large American cities, but it can also mean good Southern cooking—often in re-created rural surroundings. Restaurants are listed by price category as follows: A complete dinner may cost up to $15 in *Moderate:* and up to $10 in *Inexpensive.* Drinks, tax and tip not included. A la carte meals will bring the tab up. For a more complete explanation of restaurant categories see *Facts at Your Fingertips* at the front of this volume.

Moderate: **Aunt Fanny's Cabin.** 375 Campbell Rd. (Smyrna). Southern-style cooking and plantation entertainment.

Dailey's. 17 International Blvd., downtown. Excellent American/Continental dishes. Handsome brick-walled décor, friendly service.

Herren's. 34 Luckie St., downtown. Long established favorite for seafoods, steaks.

Theda's. 1026 N. Highland Ave. Stylish restaurant/bar in a lively midtown neighborhood. Continental cuisine.

Inexpensive. **The Colonnade.** 1879 Cheshire Bridge Rd. Very friendly place for American and Southern cooking.

El Toro. Eight locations. The city's best Mexican food.

Mary Mac's. 224 Ponce de Leon Ave. Atlantans flock here for fried chicken, Southern-style vegetables.

Peking. 3361 Buford Hwy. (Northeast Plaza). Excellent Szechuan, Mandarin-style Chinese cuisine.

The Varsity. Landmark drive-in famous for chili dogs. North Ave. at I–75-I–85.

EXPLORING GEORGIA

An awareness of history combined with an appreciation of the state's abundant natural resources is evident throughout Georgia.

Savannah preserves its past with care, and much of the downtown remains as General Oglethorpe, Georgia's founder, planned it.

Historic houses include Telfair Academy of Arts and Sciences, site of the royal governor's mansion; the Green-Meldrim Home, headquarters of General Sherman during his Savannah occupation; the birthplace of Juliette Gordon Low, founder of the Girl Scouts; Davenport House, 19th-century Georgian structure; Owens-Thomas House, designed by William Jay.

Savannah's most glorious season is spring, when millions of azaleas and dogwood bloom, and historic private homes are open to visitors. The city's St. Patrick's Day celebration is one of America's largest and most exuberant. Interesting shops, taverns, and restaurants are housed in the old cotton warehouses along the Savannah River.

South from Savannah is Brunswick, a port town and gateway to Georgia's Golden Isles. Jekyll, a state-owned island, has beach fronting the Atlantic Ocean, a restored village, and four golf courses. St. Simons is a beach resort with much history, including Fort Frederica and Christ Church.

In sharp contrast to these islands is the primordial atmosphere of the famed Okefenokee Swamp, adjacent to Folkston and Fargo. Here visitors on boat tours may enjoy the quiet natural surroundings of the primitive wilderness area, or visit flora and fauna exhibits, as well as bird walks, nature trails, and an observation tower.

Westward is Waycross and the entrance to Okefenokee Swamp Park, which features wildlife shows and boat trips. There is also an Interpretative Center, an Ecology Center, and Pioneer Island exhibits. The swamp is the headwater for both the Suwannee River and the St. Mary's. Stephen Foster State Park, on State 177 north of Fargo, pays tribute to the famed composer.

In Columbus, often called "Fountain City" because of the many fountains at its parks, office buildings, and on residential lawns, visit the Museum of Arts and Crafts with its Yuchi Indian exhibit.

At the Fort Benning Infantry Museum follow the evolution of the infantry from the French and Indian War to the present.

South of Columbus is Georgia's peanut country, centering on Americus and Plains but best known as the land of President Jimmy Carter.

Pine Mountain is home of the famed Callaway Gardens, a 2,500-acre resort noted for its wildflowers of the Southern Appalachians. There are scenic drives, walking trails, display greenhouses, sixty-three holes of golf, a 175-acre fishing lake, horseback riding, quail hunting on a 1,000-acre preserve, and skeet and trap shooting.

Franklin D. Roosevelt chose the Pine Mountain area for his second home because of the curative qualities of the mineral waters at Warm Springs and because of the peaceful atmosphere. He came here in 1924 for treatment of his infantile paralysis. His modest white frame dwelling, the Little White House, where he died in 1945, has been operated as a shrine for more than 30 years, remaining just as he left it. Nearby Franklin D. Roosevelt State Park was established in his honor.

Georgia has two national forests, the Chattahoochee and the Oconee. The Chattahoochee covers 687,000 acres in northern Georgia and the Oconee more than 100,000 in the central part of the state. Both have scenic hiking trails, mountains, stream and lake fishing, and ample camping facilities.

PRACTICAL INFORMATION FOR GEORGIA

HOW TO GET THERE. *By air:* Direct flights on most major airlines to Atlanta, Augusta, Macon, Savannah, Columbus, Albany, Athens, Moultrie, and Valdosta. *By car:* A number of interstate highways enter Georgia from South Carolina, Tennessee, Alabama, Florida, and North Carolina.

By train: Amtrak serves Atlanta from New Orleans, New York and Washington; Amtrak also serves Savannah, Thalman, Waycross, and Valdosta from Washington, New York and Florida.

By bus: Trailways and Greyhound.

TOURIST INFORMATION. Twelve *Tourist Information Centers,* located on highways and at Atlanta Airport. Additional information: *Game & Fish,* Dept. of Natural Resources, 270 Washington St., Atlanta 30334; *State Parks,* Dept. of Natural Resources; *Tourist Division,* Georgia Department of Industry and Trade, P.O. Box 1776, Atlanta 30301. U.S. Forest Service, P.O. Box 1437, Gainesville, Ga., for camping information.

MUSEUMS AND GALLERIES. *Thronateeska Heritage Museum* in Albany has Indian artifacts, science and art exhibits; *Augusta Museum* has archeological, historical, natural science exhibitions; *Harris-Pearson-Walker House,* Augusta, is the site of a Revolutionary War battle. In Columbus visit the *Confederate Naval Museum,* and in Fitzgerald, see the *Blue and Grey Museum.* In Washington, *Washington-Wilkes Historical Museum* displays antebellum furnishings and Civil War relics.

Georgia Museum of Art, on campus of U. of Georgia, Athens, and the *Gertrude Herbert Memorial Art Institute* in Augusta, which has a small permanent collection of works from Renaissance to present. The *Macon Museum of Arts and Science and Planetarium* exhibits regional contemporary art, as well as scientific displays.

New Echota near Calhoun is a restored 220-acre site of Cherokee Indians; at the Indian museum in *Kolomoki Mounds State Park* near Blakely, 18 exhibits interpret artifacts and culture of moundbuilders. Near Eatonton is Rock Eagle Effigy, a 10-ft.-high mound of milky quartz shaped like an outstretched bird with a 120-ft. wingspread, created approx. 6,000 years ago. 10,000 years of Indian settlement are reviewed at *Ocmulgee National Monument* near Macon.

HISTORIC SITES. Visit the infamous Confederate prison at *Andersonville National Historical Site. Chickamauga,* site of one of the Civil War's fiercest battles, is near the Tennessee border. *Fort Pulaski,* 15 mi. E. of Savannah, was built during colonial days, and *Fort King George,* in Darien, was the first settlement in what is now Georgia. *Fort McAllister,* 17 mi. south of Savannah.

Among restored houses are *Eagle Tavern,* 8 mi. S. of Athens, at Watkinsville, on US 129, and *Traveler's Rest,* 6 mi. NE of Toccoa, off US 123, a restored plantation house and stagecoach inn. *Callaway Plantation,* W of Washington on US 78, has restored houses, hewn log kitchen with utensils, craft demonstrations, working farm. The *Little White House,* Warm Springs, is preserved as it was during Pres. Franklin D. Roosevelt's occupancy. *Liberty Hall,* Crawfordville, home of Alexander H. Stephens.

TOURS. In *Columbus,* the two-hour *Heritage Tour* covers five historic houses and Springer Opera House. *Athens, Macon, Fort Gaines,* and *Sparta* offer do-it-yourself maps of historic sites. *Thomasville* Chamber of Commerce sponsors tours daily of plantations, historic homes, and gardens of the immediate area. Tours of *Okefenokee* are available at the Suwannee Canal Recreation Area, 7 mi. SW of Folkston. A boat tour of the swamp operates from the Okefenokee Swamp Park near Waycross.

A number of sightseeing companies provide several tours of Atlanta and the surrounding areas.

DRINKING LAWS. Min. age is 19. Liquor store hours: 8 A.M. to 11:30 P.M. daily except Sun. and election days. Cocktails are served every day in Atlanta, Savannah, Augusta, and Columbus, but not on Sunday in most other areas.

SUMMER SPORTS. *Waterskiing, fishing, swimming,* and *sailing* are chief summer participant sports. See *car races* at the Atlanta International Raceway. Callaway Gardens hosts the Masters Water-Ski Tournament, and Augusta National, the *Master's Golf Tournament.* The Atlanta Braves play at the Atlanta Stadium.

Fishing: Anglers are challenged at Lake Lanier, above Atlanta, and Lake Allatoona, south of Lanier. Clark Hill, Hartwell, and Savannah Bluff reservoirs near Augusta are well-stocked. In addition, there are many mountain lakes and streams.

Golf: 131 public courses and a host of private ones. Atlanta has three excellent public courses.

Tennis: Popular throughout Georgia. Atlanta has America's largest lawn tennis association. Racquetball is on the rise.

Running and Jogging: Many towns have marked paths. In July, the Peachtree Race in Atlanta attracts 25,000 runners.

WINTER SPORTS. *Skiing* is found at *Sky Valley Ski Area,* northeast from Dillard on Rte. 246; here are beginner, intermediate, and expert slopes, a lodge, and double-chair lift.

Hunting: Game is abundant on 22 public preserves. Dogs, guides, transportation, and dressing of game available at moderate fees.

SPECTATOR SPORTS. The *Atlanta Falcons* play in the Atlanta Stadium; fans also enjoy the *Yellow Jackets* from Georgia Tech and the *Bulldogs* from the U. of Georgia. The *Hawks* of the NBA play in the 16,000-seat Omni coliseum, downtown.

WHAT TO DO WITH THE CHILDREN. Pan for gold at *Crisson's,* 3 miles north of Dahlonega on Wimpy Rd., Apr. 12-Nov. 7; visit *Atlanta Zoo* in Grant Park; *Stone Mountain Park,* 16 mi. E. of Atlanta on US 78, has a game ranch and antebellum plantation. *Six Flags Over Georgia,* on I–20 outside of Atlanta, is a 331-acre theme park.

HOTELS AND MOTELS in Georgia run the gamut from the deluxe resort on Sea Island to the inexpensive, but attractive, motels found along many of the state's major highways.

Accommodations are listed according to price categories, based on double occupancy in the peak season, without meals: *Moderate:* $25–35; *Inexpensive:* $20–30. For a more complete explanation of hotel and motel categories see *Facts at Your Fingertips* at the front of this volume.

ATHENS. *Moderate:* **Downtowner.** Pool, restaurant.
Howard Johnson's. Family rates.
Inexpensive: **Bulldog Inn.** Pool. Pets.

AUGUSTA. *Moderate:* **Continental Airport.** Opp. airport terminal. Pool, sauna, restaurants.
Holiday Inn. 1602 Gordon Highway. There are 143 rooms. Pools, restaurant.
Thunderbird Inn. 919 15th St. Has 121 rooms. Pool, restaurant.
Inexpensive: **Econo-Travel.** Pleasant.

BRUNSWICK. *Moderate:* **Holiday Inn.** Two locations. 2307 Gloucester St.; I–95, US Hwy 341.
Ramada Inn. Two locations. 3241 Glynn Ave.; US 341 at I–95.

COLUMBUS. *Moderate:* **Heart of Columbus.** 1024 4th Ave. There are 68 rooms. Pets. Restaurant.
Holiday Inn. Two locations: near the airport at 2800 Manchester Expressway; and at 3170 Victory Drive. Pool, pets, restaurant.
Quality Inn of Columbus. 1011 4th Ave., with 180 rooms. Heated pool.
Sheraton-Ralston Inn. Heated pool. Pets.
Inexpensive: **Motel 6.** Heated pool.

FOLKSTON. *Moderate:* **Johnson Motor Lodge.** Pool. Fishing. Restaurant.
Quality Inn Tahiti. At state line on US 1, 23, 301.

HELEN. *Moderate:* **Helendorf Inn.** 305 Main St. There are 34 rooms.

JEKYLL ISLAND. *Moderate:* **Seafarer.**

MACON. *Inexpensive:* **Macon Travelodge.** Pool, restaurant.

MARIETTA. *Moderate:* **Bon Air Best Western,** U.S. 41. Family and seasonal rates.

PINE MOUNTAIN. *Moderate:* **Callaway Cottages.** Family recreation park.

ST. SIMONS. *Moderate:* Queen's Court.
Craft's Ocean Courts.

SAVANNAH. *Moderate:* **Days Inn.** 201 W. Bay St. Attractive, opened in 1982. 196 rooms. 24-hour restaurant.
　Downtowner. 201 Oglethorpe Ave. Pool. Restaurant.
　Heart of Savannah. Pool.
　Holiday Inn. Two locations. 121 W. Boundary St. just S of Talmadge Bridge; at Jct US 17 & I–95.
　Howard Johnson's. Two locations. 224 W. Boundary St.; Rte. 204 at I-95.
　Best Western Riverfront Motor Inn. 412 W. Bay St. Good restaurant. 200 rooms.
　Ramada Inn. US 17 at I–95.
　Inexpensive: **Days Inn.** Two locations. US 17, Richmond Hill; 114 Mall Blvd. (GA 204).

VALDOSTA. *Moderate:* **Holiday Inn.** Pools, play area, pets, restaurant, bar.

WAYCROSS. *Moderate.* **Holiday Inn.** US 1 & 23. Pool, restaurant, lounge. 145 rooms.
　Inexpensive: **Pine Crest.** US 1, 23, ¼ mi. S. of US 84. Pool.

 DINING OUT in Georgia usually means fine Southern-style foods in a rural atmosphere, or charming plantation house, or sophisticated French cuisine in an elegant urban dining room. Many worthwhile restaurants may be found at the hotels we have listed. Our price categories are for a complete dinner; *Moderate* will run about $15; *Inexpensive,* below $10. Drinks, tax and tip not included. A la carte meals will, of course, bring the bill up. For a more complete explanation of restaurant categories see *Facts at Your Fingertips* at the front of this volume.

ATHENS. *Inexpensive:* **Davis Bros. Cafeteria.** 2012 Milledge Ave. Fried chicken.

AUGUSTA. *Moderate:* **Town Tavern.** Popular, attractive.

BAINBRIDGE. *Inexpensive.* **Jack Wingate's Lunker Lodge.** GA 310 at Lake Seminole. Excellent fresh seafoods, barbecue. Locally very popular.

BRUNSWICK. *Inexpensive:* **Kody's** or **The Wharf** for Southern cooking and local seafoods.

COLUMBUS. *Moderate:* **Black Angus.** Steak. Seafood.
　Inexpensive: **Morrison's Cafeteria.** In Cross Country Shopping Center.

DILLARD. *Inexpensive:* **The Dillard House.** Landmark for family-style Georgia mountain cooking.

JASPER. *Moderate:* **The Woodbridge Inn.** Very good continental dishes and comfortable accommodations in rustic mountain surroundings.

MACON. *Moderate.* **Len Berg's.** downtown. Nicely prepared Southern dishes.

ST. SIMONS ISLAND. *Moderate:* **The Crab Trap.** Excellent local seafoods, popular with residents and summer vacationers.

SAVANNAH. *Moderate:* **Johnny Harris Restaurant.** 1651 Victory Dr. Savannah landmark for barbecue, fried chicken.

Inexpensive. **Mrs. Wilkes.** 107 W. Jones St. Excellent Southern cooking, served boardinghouse style. Very popular locally.

Palmer's Seafood. GA 367, near Savannah Inn and Country Club. Tasty, simply prepared crabs, oysters, shrimp.

SOPERTON. *Inexpensive:* **Sweat's Barbecue.** Ga. 29, just off I–16. Excellent barbecue, Brunswick stew.

THOMASVILLE. Mom and Dad's. Restored house, specializes in Italian food, next to Rose Test Gardens.

KENTUCKY

Horses, Caves and Lakes

Kentucky offers numerous choices for the budget traveler. Consider these sights, sites, shrines and activities, most of them inexpensive or free:—Thoroughbred horses; great horse farms; Churchill Downs, home of the Kentucky Derby, at Louisville; and the lavish $27-million Kentucky Horse Park at Lexington, which features a horse museum, riding concessions, horse-drawn tours, special equine events and celebrations, model working farm.

—Tremendous caves, topped by Mammoth Cave National Park, and awesome canyons like the 1,600-foot-deep gorge in Breaks Interstate Park near Elkhorn City, called the "Grand Canyon of the South."

—The country's largest recreation area—Land Between the Lakes, a 170,000-acre, 40-mile-long facility between Lake Barkley and Kentucky Lake, free to the public.

—An ancient buried city at Wickliffe, near the confluence of the beautiful Ohio and mighty Mississippi rivers.

—Pioneer country, including memorials to Daniel Boone: Cumberland Gap National Historical Park, Daniel Boone National Forest (with its Red River Gorge), the Daniel Boone Festival at Barbourville, and his grave in Frankfort.

—Shrines at the birthplaces of the Presidents of the opposing sides in the Civil War—Abraham Lincoln and Jefferson Davis.

—Shakertown at Pleasant Hill, near Harrodsburg, the restoration of a 19th-century communal religious society. You can also enjoy distinctive dining and lodging in some of the 27 restored buildings.

—Well-known whiskey distilleries at Bardstown, Frankfort, Lexington, Louisville, Owensboro, Paris (in Bourbon County, for which Kentucky whiskey is named).

—Rugged eastern Kentucky's dramatically beautiful Appalachian Mountains, which you can explore by leisurely drives along the Daniel Boone and Mountain Parkways.

Mammoth Cave

Cave City is appropriately named. Nearby are any number of caverns, the largest of which is Mammoth Cave, one of the nation's 37 national parks. The underground passages at Mammoth total 180 miles on five levels. A variety of tours range from a half-mile to five miles. In addition to the weird formations, unusual phenomena in the cave include sightless fish and other water denizens. Aboveground, the park embraces more than 50,000 acres of recreation land, including the Green River, on which cruise boat trips can be made.

Lakes

Kentucky Lake, with a shoreline of approximately 2,400 miles, and Lake Barkley, with 1,200 miles, are the state's largest. Recreation is at its best along these two bodies of water. The Tennessee Valley Authority, which built the dams creating them, is now developing the intervening area as the Land Between the Lakes.

PRACTICAL INFORMATION FOR KENTUCKY

HOW TO GET THERE. *By air: USAir, American, Delta, Eastern, Ozark, Piedmont,* and *TWA.* Major airports at Louisville and Lexington. *By bus: Greyhound, Trailways, ABC Coach Lines, Bowling Green-Hopkinsville Bus lines, Crown Transit, Gulf Transport Co., Illini-Swallow Lines, Lake Shore System, Short Way Lines, Southeastern States, Inc.*

TOURIST INFORMATION. *Kentucky Dept. of Tourism,* Fort Boone Plaza, Frankfort, KY 40601.

PARKS. *Mammoth Cave National Park,* near Cave City; *Cumberland Gap National Historical Park,* 20,170 acres near Middlesboro; *Breaks Interstate Park,* which Kentucky shares with Virginia; *Daniel Boone National Forest,* eastern Kentucky, covers nearly 800,000 acres; *Land Between the Lakes,* an expansive recreational area between Kentucky Lake and Lake Barkley.

Kentucky has one of the nation's finest state park systems. Conveniently located in every section of the state, 43 state parks and historic shrines in beautiful natural environments offer camping, picnicking, a wide choice of outdoor recreation. Sixteen have attractive resort lodges and/or cottages.

MUSEUMS AND GALLERIES. Historical: *Kentucky Library and Museum*, Bowling Green; *Columbus-Belmont Battlefield State Park Museum*, Columbus; Civil War. Art: *J.B. Speed Art Museum*, Louisville. Special interest: *Barton Museum of Whiskey History*, Bardstown; *Appalachian Museum*, Berea; *Wondering Woods*, reconstructed 1900s town, Cave City; *Shakertown* at Pleasant Hill, Harrodsburg; *John James Audubon State Park Memorial Museum*, Henderson; *Headley-Whitney Museum*, Lexington; *American Saddle Horse Museum, Kentucky Railway Museum, Churchill Downs Museum, Museum of Natural History and Science, Rauch Memorial Planetarium*, Louisville. *National Museum*, Boy Scouts of America, Murray.

HISTORIC SITES AND HOUSES. *Abraham Lincoln Birthplace National Historic Site*, Hodgenville; *Federal Hill*, "My Old Kentucky Home" site, Bardstown; *Lincoln Heritage House*, Elizabethtown; *Jefferson Davis Monument and Shrine*, near Hopkinsville; *Mary Todd Lincoln House, Waveland State Shrine, Hopemont*, and *Ashland*—Henry Clay's estate—Lexington; *Brennan House, Farmington*, and *Locust Grove*—George Rogers Clark's last home—Louisville.

SPECIAL INTEREST TOURS. *Horse breeding farms:* Many horse farms throughout the state welcome visitors. Arrangements should be made in advance. For free guide, "Kentucky—Where the Horses Are," write Kentucky Dept. of Tourism.

SPORTS. *Fishing and hunting:* Fishing is great in hundreds of lakes, rivers and streams. For information on both sports contact Department of Fish and Wildlife Resources, Frankfort 40601. *Golf:* There are some 200 courses in the state, 17 in state parks. *Water Sports:* Many of the state parks offer boating, swimming, and water skiing.

SPECTATOR SPORTS. *Horse racing* is the big thing. The Kentucky Derby at Churchill Downs, Louisville, takes place on the first Saturday in May; however, tickets are difficult to obtain. Other races occur here late Apr.-June, mid-Oct.-late Nov. Other racetracks: Keeneland and the Red Mile in Lexington, Latonia in Covington. University of Kentucky *football* and *basketball* games are held at Frankfort.

HOTELS AND MOTELS. Accommodations are listed according to price categories, based on double occupancy. *Moderate* $25–40, *Inexpensive* under $25.

BARDSTOWN. *Inexpensive to Moderate:* **Best Western General Nelson.** 411 W. Stephen Foster. Dining room, cocktail lounge, pool. Under 12 free in room with parents.

Holiday Inn. 31 E. South and Bluegrass Pkwy. Dining room, cocktail lounge, live entertainment.

Moderate: **Holiday Inn.** I-65 & KY 90. Medallion Dining Room. Gift shop. Game room. Cable TV.

Quality Inn. I-65 at KY 90, 70. Restaurant, pool, playground. Water slide and golf nearby. Family and senior citizens plans, facilities for handicapped. Ladies sportswear shop (factory outlet) on premises.

CAVE CITY. *Inexpensive to Moderate:* **Best Western Kentucky Inn.** I-65 & KY 70, 90. Dining room, pool. Pets. Handicapped facilities.

Oasis Motor Inn. (formerly Howard Johnson's). ¾ mi. W on KY 70. Color TV, pool, café.

Inexpensive: **Cave City Motel.** US 31 W, 1 mi NE of I–65 exit 53. Color cable TV, pool, tennis. Pets.

Cave Land Motel. US 31 W, 1 mi NE of I–65 exit 53. Pool, wading pool, playground. Pets.

Jolly's Motel. US 31 W, 1 mi NE of I–65 exit 53. Color TV, pool, playground. Pets. Restaurant nearby.

ELIZABETHTOWN. *Moderate:* **Best Western Cardinal Inn.** 642 E. Dixie Hwy. Dining room, pool, playground, pets.

Days Inn. I–65 & US 62. Dining room, service station. Pets. Handicapped facilities.

Inexpensive: **Lincoln Trail.** 905 N. Mulberry St. Pool, coffee shop nearby.

Motel 6. I–65 & US 62. Pay TV, free crib. Pool. 24-hr. café nearby.

FRANKFORT. *Moderate:* **Days Inn.** I–64 & US 127S. Dining room, free in-room movies.

LEXINGTON. *Moderate:* **Days Inn.** 1675 N. Broadway. Dining room, service station, handicapped facilities. Pets.

Quality Inn Northwest. 1050 Newton Pike. Restaurant, lounge. Pool.

LOUISVILLE. *Moderate:* **Admiral Benbow Inn.** 3315 Bardstown Rd. Color TV. Pool. Free crib. Senior citizen rates; bellhops. Restaurant, lounge, dancing & entertainment.

Holiday Inn. 4805 Brownsboro Rd. Golf, indoor tennis, pool. Color TV. Lounge, live entertainment.

Inexpensive to Moderate: **Best Western Middletown Manor.** 12010 US 60, at Middletown. Dining room, lounge, pool, playground. Tennis courts nearby.

Louisville/La Grange Days Inn. I–71 & KY 53. Dining room, some special weekend rates.

Red Roof Inn. 9330 Blairwood Rd. Color TV. Pets.

Motel 6. 3304 Bardstown Rd. Color TV, pool. Café nearby.

PADUCAH. *Moderate:* **Days Inn.** I–24 & US 60W. Dining room, service station. Handicapped facilities. September Days Club honored.

 DINING OUT. Categories for complete dinners excluding drinks, tax and tip: *Moderate,* $10–$15; *Inexpensive,* under $10.

BARDSTOWN. *Moderate:* **Jones' Kentucky Home.** Best Western General Nelson Motel. 411 W. Stephen Foster Ave. Fried chicken, country ham, child's plates.

Old Talbott Tavern. 107 W. Stephen Foster Ave. Luscious regional specialties in historic 1799 building.

The Old Stable. 116 W. Stephen Foster Ave. Inside, old barn wood and copper; outside, a charming sidewalk café.

BEREA. *Moderate:* **Boone Tavern.** Dining room, a student-managed project of Berea College, features lunch and dinner specialties such as Kentucky ham, blackberry dumplings, spoon bread. Children's portions. No tipping.

COVINGTON. *Moderate:* **Mike Fink's Restaurant.** Foot of Greenup St. Dining aboard an Ohio River sternwheeler; delicious lunch and dinner specialties.

LEXINGTON. *Moderate:* **Darryl's 1891 Restaurant.** US 27, 1 blk S. of New Circle Rd. Lunch, dinner, salad bar.

The Little Inn. 1144 Winchester Rd. Prime ribs, steak are specialties. Salad bar, child's plates, weekday luncheon buffets. Locally popular.

Inexpensive: **Blue Boar Cafeteria.** Turf Land Mall.

Morrison's Cafeteria. 2305 Lexington Rd.

LOUISVILLE. *Moderate:* **Bauer's Since 1870.** 3612 Brownsboro Rd. Hearty fare, locally popular.

Bill Boland's Dining Room. 3708 Bardstown Rd. Regional specialties in charming 1809 farmhouse.

Hasenhour's. 1028 Barrett Ave. German, Kentucky specialties, steaks, ribs. Continental dining in The Atrium, also on the grounds.

Inexpensive to Moderate. **Hoe Kow.** 12101 Shelbyville Rd. Excellent selection of Cantonese specialties. Very popular locally.

Inexpensive: **Blue Boar Cafeteria.** 5000 Shelbyville Rd.

PADUCAH. *Moderate:* **Stacey's.** 1300 Broadway. Steaks, prime ribs, smorgasbord luncheons.

SHAKERTOWN AT PLEASANT HILL. *Moderate:* **Trustees' Office Inn.** Just off US 68. Shaker and Kentucky specialties in a gracious atmosphere of antiques. Hearty buffet breakfasts. No tipping. Reservations requested.

LOUISIANA

New Orleans and the Bayous

New Orleans is the home of a unique attraction: the French Quarter, or *Vieux Carré* ("Old Square"), the original town laid out by the French. There is nothing quite like the atmosphere of these narrow streets, lovingly restored old buildings, flower-filled patios, antique shops, coffee bars, world-famous restaurants, and a few remaining places where authentic New Orleans jazz is still played. Within its area of about a square mile, strict legal ordinances have preserved the Quarter's special character. The facades, of French and Spanish design, are painted in their original colors. After over 200 years this harmony of graceful iron grillwork, intimate courtyards, and classic French lines remains undisturbed. Neatly bounded by Decatur St. and the Mississippi River on one side, and by the Canal, North Rampart, and Esplanade on the other three, the creation of the architects Latrobe, Galliers, De Pouillys, and Dakins—the Quarter is just the right size for a leisurely walking tour.

Starting at Canal and Royal, the tourist first notices, down Canal toward the river, the massive granite structure of the Customs House, whose cornerstone was laid in the 1840's by Henry Clay. This square-block building marks the original riverbank, now moved further off by means of landfill. The stretch of Canal between Royal and Exchange Alley was once a rendezvous where unemployed sailors ("monkeys") used to borrow money ("wrench") from friends with jobs; hence the nickname "Monkey Wrench Corner." Continue down Royal St. to the Old Bank of Louisiana, now the home of the Greater New Orleans Tourist Commission (No. 334 Royal St.). Free tourist information can be obtained here. At this point, you should continue down Royal St. until you reach St. Peter, turn toward the river. The Arsenal (No. 615) was built in 1839 and houses a collection of 19th-century firefighting equipment. Jackson House (No. 619) has a collection of Louisiana Folk Art, considered the best single collection of this genre in the country.

Facing on Chartres is the Cabildo, originally the Spanish colonial legislature, now a museum displaying furnishings and portraits. Next door is the St. Louis Cathedral. Behind the Cathedral is St. Anthony's Garden, an attractive spot where Creoles once met for duels. On the other side of the Cathedral is the Presbytere. This museum features a collection of costumes and fashions, one of the largest in the South. The park in front of the Cathedral is Jackson Square, the center of the French Quarter. Flanking it are the Pontalba Apartments, reputed to be the oldest apartment building in America. The 1850 House, 523 St. Ann St. in the Lower Pontalba, is now a state museum with period furnishings and décor.

Beyond the French Quarter

The Louisiana Superdome, opened on August 3, 1975, is the world's largest enclosed stadium-arena, covering 52 acres and reaching 27 stories high. It seats more than 80,000 and houses major sports events, including the Sugar Bowl football games; leading entertainers, circuses, trade shows. Tours of the Superdome are conducted daily.

The Garden District, which is bounded by St. Charles Ave., Louisiana Ave., Jackson Ave., and Magazine St., is one of the city's most elegant sections, featuring old mansions, most in Greek Revival style. For exploring without a car, take the St. Charles Ave. streetcar, which runs along the edge of the Garden District, past Tulane and Loyola Universities, to the place where the avenue meets the Mississippi River levee.

PRACTICAL INFORMATION FOR NEW ORLEANS

 HOW TO GET THERE. *By air:* There are direct flights to New Orleans from cities within the U.S.A. on *Continental, Delta, Eastern, Ozark, Pan Am,* and *United Airlines.*

By car: I–10 connects Baton Rouge, Lafayette, Houston, and points west with New Orleans. It also comes in from Mississippi and the east. I–55 connects New Orleans with Jackson, Miss., Memphis, Tenn., and points north. I–59 also comes from Mississippi into New Orleans.

By train: Amtrak will get you to New Orleans.

By bus: Greyhound and *Trailways,* can get you to New Orleans.

HOW TO GET AROUND. *By car: Avis, Budget, Hertz, National,* and *Thrifty* all have rental offices within or near the airport. *By bus:* The "Streetcar Named Desire" has been replaced by a bus. *By trolley:* St. Charles Ave. is served by trolley. It is a fun and economical way to go from the business district to uptown.

SEASONAL EVENTS. The *Louisiana World's Fair* will be held in New Orleans May 12–November 11, 1984. For information contact Louisiana World's Exposition, 804 S. Front St., New Orleans 70130. *Carnival* climaxes on *Mardi Gras* (Shrove Tuesday), the forty-first day before Easter Sunday, not counting Sundays. Two-week *Spring Fiesta* is held beginning first Friday after Easter, during which tours of the French Quarter, Garden District, and plantation homes are arranged. Parade, street dancing, and outdoor art show add to fun. *Jazz and Heritage Festival* celebrates crafts, food, and music in mid-Apr. There are jazz, ragtime, gospel, blues, country, and Cajun music concerts and river cruises.

MUSEUMS AND GALLERIES. *The Historic New Orleans Collection,* 533 Royal St. *Louisiana State Museum,* 751 Chartres St., housed in 1791 Presbytere, is a complex of eight buildings, seven of which are open to the public: The Cabildo, Presbytere, 1850 House, Madame John's Legacy, U.S. Mint, Jackson House and the Arsenal. *New Orleans Museum of Art,* Lelong Ave., City Park. Closed Mon. and holidays. *Gallier House,* 1118–32 Royal St. Decorative art museum. Pitot House, 1440 Moss St., on Bayou St. John near City Park, an 18th-century plantation furnished in the Federal style. Open on Thursdays only.

Special Interest: La Maritime Museum, located in International Trade Mart. Exhibits relating to area sea events. *Pharmaceutical Msueum,* 519 Chartres St. Built in 1847, the museum reflects early history of New Orleans medicine. *Confederate Museum,* 929 Camp St. Relics pertaining to military history; Civil War memorabilia. *Louisiana Wildlife and Fisheries Museum,* 400 Royal St. Natural history museum.

HISTORIC SITES. In New Orleans the *Vieux Carré (Old Square)* represents a concentration of historic sites, with the apex at Jackson Square, where the old *St. Louis Basilica* has housed the Catholic See of New Orleans continuously since 1794. It was around this square that Bienville had engineers lay out the city in 1718. Uptown, the *Garden District's* great homes are still maintained as showplaces of the antebellum period. *U.S. Custom House,* 423 Canal St., four-story 1849 building of granite, on site once occupied by Ft. St. Louis. Used as an office by Gen. Benjamin F. Butler during the Union Army's occupation of New Orleans. *Chalmette National Historical Park,* St. Bernard Hwy., State 39, site of the Battle of New Orleans in the War of 1812. Closed Christmas and Mardi Gras.

TOURS. *Bus. Gray Line* offers tours covering various sections of city. Night-life tours cover the Bourbon St. area, various clubs, and cafés; make reservations. Tours of French Quarter and Garden District are offered. Southern and Dixieland are among the other companies offering a regular tour. *Boat. MV Voyageur* leaves from foot of Canal St. for cruise into Intercoastal Waterway, through Bayou Barataria, and return through Harvey Canal; five hrs. Harbor cruise to Chalmette Battlefield, 2 hrs. *Mark Twain,* diesel-powered replica of sternwheeler steamboat, leaves Canal St. Dock for bayou trip. 5 hrs. *S.S. President,* large sidewheel steamboat, offers harbor cruises, 2½ hours daily, leaving Canal St. dock; Sat. night cruises with jazz band, drinks, dancing. *On*

foot. Friends of the Cabildó conducts tours of interiors and gardens of Garden District antebellum homes.

 GARDENS. During the blooming time of camellias (late Nov.–Mar.) and azaleas (late Feb.–Apr.) New Orleans becomes a huge garden, with concentrated displays in almost all parks. Along the country roads of St. Tammany Parish, across the causeway from New Orleans, the tung trees and azaleas bloom profusely in late March. *Longue Vue House and Gardens,* 7 Bamboo Rd., is an 8-acre city estate featuring a 20th-century mansion and magnificent gardens. Open to the public. *City Park* has a conservatory featuring bromeliads and formal gardens built during the depression and now recently renovated.

 SHOPPING. The French Market has recently undergone a renovation and, in addition to the Moon Walk park area and a parking lot for cars, there are a half dozen shops and boutiques. In one shop you can watch pralines being made daily; you can purchase cookery equipment and spices; there's a candle shop, a toy store, and several snack spots as well as a seafood house and the Farmer's Market, where shopping for fresh fruits and vegetables has been a tradition since New Orleans' earliest days. On weekends, the area next to the Farmer's Market is the Flea Market and attracts thousands of tourists and locals.

 WHAT TO DO WITH THE CHILDREN. *Pontchartrain Beach Amusement Park* has rides and shows. It opens in late March and closes after Labor Day. The *Audubon Park and Zoological Gardens* features a special petting zoo for children and rides on the elephants. The *Louisiana Nature Center,* 11,000 Lake Forest Blvd., shows the dependence of humans on the environment. It has nature trails and exhibits.

 HOTELS AND MOTELS. Minimum night stays are required at Carnival and during the Sugar Bowl football and sports events at the New Year. Listings are in order of price category. Based on double occupancy without meals, price categories and their ranges are *Moderate:* $55–70; *Inexpensive:* under $55.

Moderate: **Holiday Inn.** There are seven locations in the New Orleans area. All have restaurant, lounge. pool.

Howard Johnson's Motor Lodge. At two locations: **East,** 4200 Old Gentilly Rd. & I–10 at Louisa St. exit; **Airport-West,** 6401 Veterans Memorial Blvd., Metairie.

Lamothe House. 621 Esplanade Ave. Small but special. Restored mansion with antique furnishings, balconies overlooking courtyard. Advance reservations.

LaQuinta Motor Inn. Two locations. Pool, 24-hour adjoining restaurant. Children under 12 free.

Quality Inn. 4104 Chef Menteur Hwy. There are three locations in New Orleans area. All have restaurant, cocktail lounge, pool, and color TV.

Ramada Inn. At four locations. Restaurant, lounge, pool.

Scottish Inn. Three locations. Pool, café, bar.

Landmark French Quarter Motor Lodge. 920 N. Rampart. Sidewalk café; restaurant, bar, pool.

DINING OUT. Fine Creole cooking is a treat in New Orleans, but other cuisines can also be found here. Classic French fare is also a specialty. See the previous hotel listings for some other good restaurants. Price categories and ranges (for a complete dinner not including drinks, tax or tip) are as follows: *Moderate:* $10–20; *Inexpensive:* under $10. Listings are in order of price category.

Moderate: **Castillo's Mexican Restaurant.** 620 Conti St. Mexican cuisine. Mouthwatering specialties: nopalitos, puerco en chile Colorado and chilmole Yucateco. Children's portions. Closed holidays.

Charlie & Naomi's Steak House and Bar. 4501 Dryades St. Chicken, trout and steak are featured at this pleasant dining spot. Closed Sun., holidays.

The Embers. 700 Bourbon St. Charbroiled steaks are their specialty.

Felix's. 739 Iberville St., between Bourbon and Royal Sts. Seafood is their specialty. Closed, Sun., Christmas, Mardi Gras.

Kolb's. 125 St. Charles. Authentic Bavarian decor. Schnitzel à la Kolb, imported draft beer. Est. 1899.

T. Pittari's. 4200 S. Claiborne. Creole cuisine, lobster, beef.

Sclafani's. 1315 N. Causeway Blvd. Italian, American, and Creole dishes served in a Louisiana plantation-styled dining room.

Tujagues. 823 Decatur St. Locally popular. Well-prepared Creole and French dishes served family style. No menu choice.

Turci's. 3218 Magazine St. Italian, American menu. Their homemade ravioli is delicious. Children's portions. Reservations advised.

Inexpensive: **Camellia Grill.** 626 So. Carrollton Ave. Pecan waffles are rich and delicious.

Casamento's. 4330 Magazine St. Oyster "poorboys" are a specialty. Closed mid-June to mid-September.

COFFEE HOUSES. Across the square from St. Louis Basilica and down the street are the outdoor coffee houses of the French Market. Although the famed *Morning Call* coffee house has moved to Fat City, the *Cafe Du Monde,* next to the entrance to the Moon Walk (here you can watch the ships and barges make their way along the Mississippi), and the *Cafe Maison,* located a few shops over, offer the weary tourist some of that special New Orleans coffee (cafe au lait) and mouth-watering *beignets* (square, puffy doughnuts always freshly made). Open 24 hours a day the year round. *La Marquise Pastry Shop,* 625 Chartres St., is a favorite spot for French pastries. *The Gumbo Shop,* 630 St. Peter St., is a local favorite for breakfast.

Baton Rouge

The Indians called it *Istrouma*—a tall cypress marking the boundary between tribal hunting grounds. In 1699 someone in the Iberville-Bienville party pushing up to the Mississippi marked the spot on his map: *le baton rouge* ("the red staff"). A good place to take a first look is from the observation platform atop the 34-story capitol building, overlooking the 27 acres of formal gardens on the capitol grounds. Main points of interest in the city are: the Old Capitol, with its hand-wrought iron fence, spiral staircase, and prism skylight, a blend of Norman, Gothic, and Moorish styles; the Louisiana State University campus; Southern University, the nation's largest predominantly black university, on bluffs overlooking the river; the Arts and Science Center, at the former Governor's Mansion (exhibits of art, natural history, and anthropology); and the zoo, a 140-acre expanse with walkways through forest settings for over 500 animals. LSU Rural Life Museum depicts life in rural South in 19th century, including typical plantation buildings. On Foster Road, just off Comite Drive Wide is the Cohn Memorial Arboretum, which encompasses 16 acres and features over 120 varieties of shrubs.

Acadian Lafayette

Lafayette, a fast-growing city that bills itself as the "Capital of French Louisiana," is a good base from which to explore Acadiana. A museum and center for tourist information is now housed in the 1848 Charles Mouton House.

The 800-acre campus of the University of Southwestern Louisiana has a Maison Acadienne dedicated to the perpetuation of French and Acadian traditions. Lafayette's Mardi Gras celebration is second only to New Orleans' gala festival, and draws upwards of 100,000 people.

Every September there is the Festival Acadiens, which celebrates Acadian culture, music, arts, crafts, and food. From April to September, it's thoroughbred racing at Evangeline Downs.

Southeast of Lafayette is St. Martinville, one of the oldest and most charming small places in Louisiana. Settled in the eighteenth century by Acadian and French royalist refugees, the town became an early center of culture and elegant living where richly dressed nobles attended luxurious balls and operas; often it was spoken of as "Le Petit Paris." The old church on Main St. dates from 1832, but the Evangeline Oak, on the banks of Bayou Teche at the foot of Port St., is the most popular tourist attraction in town. Across the street is the Convent of Mercy, a very old building, once a trading post, now a school run by the Sisters of Mercy. At the edge of St. Martinville is the attractive Longfellow-Evangeline State Commemorative Area. The Acadian House Museum, dating from about 1765, records the Acadian story of expulsion from Nova Scotia and settlement in Louisiana. Cajun crafts are displayed and sold in a reproduction of a typical small farmhouse. Camping sites, picnic shelters with tables and grills, a pool, and restaurant are also in the park.

Fourteen miles south of St. Martinville on State 182 is New Iberia. Shadows-on-the-Teche, a stately mansion in the heart of town, now the property of the National Trust for Historical Preservation, was built in 1830. Moss-draped trees and a formal garden of roses, camellias, azaleas, and other flowering shrubs adjoin a handsome lawn sloping to the banks of the Bayou Teche. The Acadian Regional Tourist Information Center is quartered in a plantation cabin built of native cypress about 1880. At 541 E. Main is the Gebert Oak, a magnificent specimen planted in 1831. Attractions in the area include the Justine Plantation (1822), the Loreauville Heritage Museum, Jefferson Island plantation house and gardens, Avery Islands 200-acre Jungle Gardens, and Cypremont Point seaside recreational area.

Lake Charles, Louisiana's third seaport, is the center of an important petrochemical empire.

Natchitoches

Natchitoches, a charming river town and farm center, is the oldest town in the Louisiana Purchase territory, established in 1714—four years before New Orleans—as a French outpost and trading center. Front St. on Cane River provides the most charming prospect of any town in Louisiana. Many old buildings and antebellum homes remain along the river and side streets. During the Christmas season streets, buildings, riverbanks, and bridges blaze with over 140,000 lights.

Monroe on the Ouachita ("Washitaw") River is one of Louisiana's oldest settlements, established in 1785 as Ouachita Post. In the nineteenth century, Monroe was a center of cotton production and export. After the discovery that the entire parish of Ouachita rested upon a vast pool of natural gas, Monroe and West Monroe (across the river) became a thriving industrial region. Attractions in Monroe include Ft. Miro (marked only by commemorative plaque), Layton Castle, Stubbs House, and Filhiol House. The Masur Museum is an attractive art gallery with educational and cultural exhibits, and there is a Little Theatre housed in the new Strauss Playhouse. The Louisiana Purchase Gardens and Zoo has a 100-acre park with formal gardens, moss-laden oaks, and winding waterways.

Shreveport

Shreveport, founded in 1832, is one of the country's leading oil and gas centers and a natural center for the so-called "Ark-La-Tex" area. There are three major annual events at Shreveport. In fall, the State Fair attracts half a million visitors during its 10-day run, with music (the city considers itself a country-western capital), auto races, rodeo exhibitions, arts and crafts displays, carnival rides, band concerts, and fireworks. Adjacent to the fairgrounds, the Louisiana State Exhibit Museum contains dioramas, an art gallery, historical murals, and archeological relics. Another big event is the 10-day Holiday in Dixie each April. It is a round of flower shows, sports competitions, an air show, carnival, treasure hunt, pet show, two fancy-dress balls, and a grand finale parade. The city's brochure promises 10 days "packed with a sort of leisurely frenzy!" Then there's the Red River Revel held in the fall—"a celebration of the arts," on the riverfront.

Just across the Red River in Bossier Parish is Louisiana Downs, one of the state's most successful tracks. Its season runs from June to November.

PRACTICAL INFORMATION FOR LOUISIANA

 HOW TO GET THERE. *By air:* New Orleans may be reached from cities within the U.S.A. on direct flights of: *Continental, Delta, Eastern, Ozark, American, Pan Am, Southwest,* and *United* airlines; Baton Rouge on direct flights of: *Delta, Royale,* and *Republic;* Monroe on direct flights of: *Royale* and *Republic;* Alexandria on *Delta* and *Royale;* Lake Charles on *Royale;* and Shreveport on *Delta* and *Royale.*

To New Orleans, *Delta* has direct flights out of Caracas, Venezuela; *Aviateca* and *Taca* have direct flights out of Mexico City.

By car: From Picayune, Miss., you can get to New Orleans via I–59; I–55 will take you from McComb, Miss., south to Kentwood and Hammond; I–20 comes in from Vicksburg, Miss., and cuts through the state west to the Texas state line. I–10 enters the state at Vidor, Texas, and goes through the state to Slidell. In the northern part of the state I–20 comes into Shreveport from Texas and continues east to the Mississippi state line. US 71 comes in from Texarkana,

Texas/Ark., goes south to Shreveport and then east to Alexandria. US 61 enters the state at Woodville, Miss., goes south to Baton Rouge and then east to New Orleans.

By train: Amtrak to New Orleans from Chicago, New York, and Los Angeles.

By bus: Greyhound and *Trailways* provide frequent service. In addition, Baton Rouge and New Orleans can be reached by about a dozen other companies.

TOURIST INFORMATION SERVICES. The *Greater New Orleans Tourist and Convention Commission* at 334 Royal St. will help you plan. The *Chamber of Commerce* at 334 Camp St. is also helpful. For the rest of the state, inquiries to specific chambers of commerce of cities and towns and to the *Louisiana Tourist Development Commission,* Box 44291, Baton Rouge 70804. *State Tourist Information Centers* are found at several gateway points. *Louisiana Wildlife and Fisheries Commission,* 400 Royal St., New Orleans 70130 will supply fishing and hunting regulations. *Forest Service,* Southern Region, 50 7th St., N.E., Atlanta, Ga. 30323, offers information on national forests.

SEASONAL EVENTS. The annual *Cajun Pirogue* (Indian log canoe) *Race* is held south of New Orleans on Rte. 45 near *Lafitte* each year at varying times that the Louisiana Tourist Commission, 334 Royal St., can identify. *Spring: Mardi Gras* is the most famous seasonal event in the state, with all-out, 2-week celebration in *New Orleans,* and *Shrove Thursday* celebrations in *Houma* and *Lafayette.* In March *Lafayette* annually observes the *Azalea Trail;* and in September, *Festival Acadiens; Lake Charles* has a *House and Garden Tour;* Shreveport, a 10-day, *Holiday in Dixie* festival celebrating the Louisiana Purchase. Balls, parades, water shows, art exhibits are part of the festivities. Lake Charles celebrates *Contraband Days* late May to early June with a water sports carnival.

Summer: The Morehouse rodeo takes place in *Bastrop* in June; the *KC fishing rodeo* in *Houma,* $3, is also in June, while *Ruston* celebrates its *Peach Festival* late in the month. *Many* has its *Arts and Crafts Festival* the first weekend in June. *Houma's Tarpon Rodeo* takes place in July. *Winnsboro* has a *Deep South Rodeo,* three nights in mid-Aug.

Fall: This is the time of harvest festivals: *Sugar Cane Fair and Festival* in *New Iberia,* Sept. The *International Rice Festival* and the *Frog Derby* in Reyne; *Sauce Piquante Festival* and *Pirogue Races* in *Raceland; Yambilee Festival* in *Opelousas* all take place in Oct. *Natchitoches* offers its *Historic Plantation Tour* the second weekend in Oct.

Winter: Sugar Bowl Festival begins right after Christmas, culminating in Sugar Bowl football classic on New Year's Day. *Battle of New Orleans* is celebrated in January at *Chalmette National Historical Park.*

NATIONAL PARKS AND FORESTS. Campsites and trailer space, as well as picnicking facilities, are available throughout the nearly 600,000 acres of the Kisatchie National Forest in central and northwest Louisiana. Eleven recreation centers, open year-round. There is a nominal charge for campsite or trailer parking. Most campsites are located on lakes or streams; and all have fireplaces and sanitary facilities. A nominal charge is made for fishing, for duck hunting, and for boats. Reservations should be made through the Forest Services, U.S.D.A., Box 471, Alexandria.

Chalmette National Historical Park, east of New Orleans on State 46, commemorates the last battle of the War of 1812.

STATE PARKS. There are 25 state parks and commemorative areas in Louisiana; all but 3 permit picnicking, 10 permit camping. *Audubon Memorial State Park,* near *St. Francisville* on State 965, is the site of Oakley Plantation House, a museum of Audubon memorabilia, with period furnishings. Formal garden, picnicking, hiking trails. *Bogue Falaya Wayside Park, Covington,* has a natural beach, picnicking on its 13 acres. *Ft. Jesup State Monument,* 6 mi. east of *Many* on State 6, is the site of the antebellum garrison. Replica of two-story brick and frame building and an original army field kitchen. Museum, picnicking. *Ft. Pike State Monument,* US 90, 30 mi. east of New Orleans, picnicking. *Lake D'Arbonne State Park,* off Rte. 33 west of Rte. 15 near *Farmerville,* 90-acre wooded lakeside area with picnicking, boating, water skiing. *Longfellow-Evangeline State Park,* 3 mi. northeast of *St. Martinville* on Rte. 31, on banks of Bayou Teche, has restored Acadian house, kitchen garden, craft shop, replica of Acadian cottage. Museum, picnicking, swimming, boating, fishing.

 MUSEUMS AND GALLERIES. *Lafayette Museum,* 1122 Lafayette St., *Lafayette,* was home of Gov. Alexandre Mouton. Furniture, historical documents, portraits, Indian artifacts. Tours.

Imperial Calcasieu Museum, 204 W. Sallier St., *Lake Charles,* contains Victorian period furnishings, Gay Nineties barber shop, glass, crystal. Tour.

Louisiana State Exhibit Museum, 3015 Greenwood Rd., *Shreveport,* tells history of state through murals, dioramas, glass, china, paper money, Indian artifact collections.

In *Baton Rouge,* the *Old Arsenal Museum* houses historical exhibits in building used by federal troops during Civil War. The *Rural Life Museum,* Burden Research Center on LSU campus, is comprised of blacksmith shop, general store, overseer's cottage typical of 18th- and 19th-century plantation life.

Loreauville Heritage Museum, 9 mi. northeast of New Iberia in *Loreauville,* is a 40-unit village and farm, telling history of territory.

Special Interest Museums. In *Baton Rouge,* LSU's *Geoscience Museum* is open daily 8 A.M. to 5 P.M.; *Museum of Natural Science,* Foster Hall. *Louisiana Arts & Science Center & Planetarium,* 502 North Blvd., houses paintings, sculpture, cultural, historical, scientific exhibits.

Natural History Museum & Planetarium, 637 Girard Park Dr., *Lafayette,* maintains an environmental trail, changing exhibits.

 HISTORIC SITES. Throughout Louisiana are numerous antebellum homes, many open to the public. *Oakley Plantation,* on Hwy. 965, east of St. Francisville, is where Audubon became acquainted with the wildlife of the Feliciana countryside. It is now in a 100-acre Audubon Memorial State Park. *Rosedown,* on State 10, east of St. Francisville, has antique furnishings, seventeenth-century gardens. *Cottage Plantation,* on U.S. 61, 9 mi. north of St. Francisville, was started in 1795. On grounds are smokehouse, school, slave cabins. In White Castle, *Nottoway Plantation,* the largest plantation house in the South, has overnight accommodations. Reservations a must. *Destrehan Manor House,* the oldest remaining plantation home on the lower Mississippi, is on River Road, 8 mi. above the N.O. International Airport. *Derbigny Plantation* is a fine old Louisiana cottage on River Road near Oak Ave., above Westwego.

St. Martinville, east of New Orleans on US 90, is center of legends surrounding Longfellow's *Evangeline.* In the churchyard of *St. Martin of Tours Catholic Church,* 133 S. Main St., is the grave of the poem's heroine, Emmeline Labiche. The *Evangeline Oak* still stands at the end of Port St. *Evangeline Museum,* 429 E. Bridge St., and *Longfellow-Evangeline State Park's Acadian House Museum,* St. Martinville, reconstruct Acadian life.

Edward Douglass White Memorial, 5 mi. north of *Thibodaux,* on State 1, includes restored homestead of Chief Justice of Supreme Court.

Oak Alley, on River Rd. near Vacherie, is a Greek Revival mansion, built in 1830s. Live oaks line a corridor from the house to the river.

Parlange Plantation, on LA 1, 5 mi. south of New Roads, was built in 1750. *Houmas House,* on LA 942 in Burnside, is a magnificent Greek Revival mansion.

Near *Franklin* are two outstanding houses. *Oaklawn Manor,* 5 mi. off US 90, has a large grove of live oaks and lovely gardens. *Albania Mansion,* near Jeanerette, 14 mi. from Franklin on US 90, features a three-story spiral staircase.

In *Natchitoches, Rogue House,* Riverbank Dr. near Keyser Ave. Bridge, is an excellent example of pioneer Louisiana construction.

Shadows on the Teche, 117 E. Main St., *New Iberia,* is a gracious two-story, 16-room town house set among live oaks. *Justine,* originally built in Franklin in 1822, was added to twice and moved to New Iberia by barge. Furnished in Victorian period.

In *Reserve, San Francisco Plantation* house is 2 mi. upriver on State 44. Eighteenth-century furnishings, landscaped grounds.

TOURS. *Louisiana Lagniappe Tours* offers trips of Baton Rouge and nearby plantations. *Delcambre,* 15 mi. west of New Iberia on Rte. 14, offers tours aboard paddlewheeler *Cajun Belle. Passe Partout Touring Co.* in *Lafayette* has a variety of offbeat tours through Cajun country.

GARDENS. Avery Island's *Jungle Gardens,* off State 329 via a toll road, is a 300-acre paradise, with camellias blooming Nov. to April, iris Mar. to July, azaleas late Feb. to late Apr. Also featured are tropical plants, sunken gardens, a Chinese garden with a centuries-old Buddha, and a bird sanctuary where egrets nest.

Hodges Gardens, 15 mi south of *Many* on US 171, is a 4,700-acre garden in a forest. There are experimental areas, wildlife refuge, wild and cultivated gardens in bloom year-round. In Dec. there's a Christmas light tour that is free. Picnicking, boating, swimming, and fishing also available.

Rosedown Plantation and Gardens, St. Francisville, is a magnificently restored antebellum home with seventeenth-century-style French formal gardens.

In *Monroe, Louisiana Purchase Gardens* is a 140-acre garden and zoo with over 8,000 plants and 800 animals. Fall to spring.

In *Shreveport,* the *Barnwell Center Botanical Gardens* are open daily. *American Rose Center* open during summer. *Walter Jacobs Nature Trail,* open to public.

DRINKING LAWS. Liquor sold by package and drink at stores or establishment with a license. Sunday sales optional in some locations. Much of northern Louisiana is dry. None may be imported from another state. The minimum age is 18.

SPORTS. *Fishing,* both fresh and saltwater, is a year-round sport. Spanish and king mackerel, jewfish, marlin, bluefish, cobia, speckled trout, pompano, red snapper, and common jack are found in the coastal areas and Gulf of Mexico. Tarpon fishing below Houma and Grand Isle is becoming increasingly popular. Crayfish are found inland. Bass fishing is highly popular on huge man-made lakes. Boats, tackle, and bait are available everywhere. Nonresident fishing license costs $6; a 7-day license, $3. No license is required for saltwater fishing.

Hunting, concentrated generally within Dec., requires a nonresident license for 3 days, $10; for a season, $25. Visitors, who are residents of Arkansas, Texas, Mississippi, Alabama, and Florida, must pay an even higher fee. Louisiana's coastal marshes provide a winter home for ducks, turkey, wildfowl using the Mississippi flyway. Turkey, squirrel, and deer inhabit the pine hills and swampland.

Licenses and information available from Wild Life and Fish Commission, 400 Royal St., New Orleans 70130.

Swimming is available at the following recreation areas: Bogue Falaya Wayside, Covington; Chemin-A-Haut, near Bastrop; D'Arbonne Lake, Farmerville; Fontainebleau, Mandeville; Grand Isle, off Rte. 1; Lake Bistineau, south of Doyline; Lake Bruin, northeast of St. Joseph; and at Cotile Reservoir, 20 mi. west of Alexandria.

Golf is popular throughout the state. *Alexandria: Bringhurst Park,* off Masonic Dr., 9 holes. *Lafayette: City Park Golf Course,* Mudd Ave. and 8th St. 18 holes. *Shreveport: Andrew Querbes Park,* Gregg and Fern Sts., 18 holes; *Lakeside,* Milam St., *Huntington,* Pines Rd., 18 holes; *New Orleans; Lakewood Country Club* sponsors Greater New Orleans Open every spring.

SPECTATOR SPORTS: New Orleans' *professional football* team, Saints, and Tulane University's football team play at the Super Dome. LSU's athletic teams play in Baton Rouge. *Racing:* Thoroughbred, quarter horseracing at *Evangeline Downs,* Lafayette, from Apr.-mid-Sept. Parimutuel betting. *Fair Grounds Race Track,* New Orleans, was established in 1872. Parimutuel betting. Thanksgiving-late Mar. *Jefferson Downs Race Track,* 44th St. and Williams Blvd., Kenner, has races Apr.-June, mid-Sept.-late Nov. Quarterhorses and thoroughbreds race at *Delta Downs* in Vinton for most of the year. Thoroughbreds race at *Louisiana Downs,* Bossier City, from late spring into the fall.

WHAT TO DO WITH THE CHILDREN. *Louisiana Purchase Gardens and Zoo,* off I-20, *Monroe,* exhibit rare animals in modern buildings, some glass-fronted, some moated. Nocturnal animals are shown under red lights. The entertainment section has a Lewis & Clark Railroad, boat rides, and other amusement rides. Adults 75¢; children 4 to 12, 50¢; under 4, free. Rides, 35¢.

Hamel's Park in Shreveport is a small but good amusement park with several outside and inside rides, including train and roller coaster.

HOTELS AND MOTELS. Most of the state's establishments are less expensive outside New Orleans. There are many "chain" motels along I-10 and I-12. Based on double occupancy without meals, price categories and ranges are as follows: *Moderate:* $30-45; *Inexpensive* under $30.

BATON ROUGE. *Moderate:* **Days Inn.** Pool, restaurant.
Inexpensive: **Alamo Plaza Hotel Courts.** Free continental breakfast.

LAFAYETTE. *Moderate:* **Rodeway Inn.** Pool, restaurant.
Holiday Inn. Two here: north and south. Each has pool, restaurant, and bar.
Inexpensive: **Imperial "400" Motel.** Downtown. Pool.

NATCHITOCHES. *Moderate:* **Revere Inn Motel.** Restaurant across the street.
Tourist Inn. Hwy. 6 E.

SHREVEPORT. *Moderate:* **Ramada Inn.** Pool, restaurant, lounge, dancing.
Rodeway Inn. Pleasant rooms.
Inexpensive: **Days Inn.**

DINING OUT in Louisiana often means the same fine Creole cooking you can experience in New Orleans. Price categories and ranges, for a complete dinner, are as follows: *Moderate:* $7-15; *Inexpensive:* under $7.
Drinks, tax and tip not included.

ALEXANDRIA. *Moderate:* **Herbie K's.** Specialties: oysters on half shell, other seafood, and steaks.
Inexpensive: **Casa Pepe's Colonial Restaurant.**

BATON ROUGE. *Moderate:* **Piccadilly Cafeteria.** A local favorite.
Inexpensive: **The Gumbo Place.** Cajun dishes.

LAFAYETTE. *Moderate:* **Don's Seafood House.** The seafood is excellent.
Inexpensive: **Dwyer's Café.**

NATCHITOCHES. *Inexpensive:* **Lasyone's Meat Pie Kitchen.**

OPELOUSAS. *Moderate:* **The Palace.** Gumbo, crawfish, seafood, and steaks are specialties.

MISSISSIPPI

Heartland Dixie

Oxford, 27 miles south of Holly Springs on State 7, is the site of the University of Mississippi (Ole Miss). It was also the home of the late William Faulkner, 1949 Nobel Prize winner for literature, and is the "Jefferson" featured in so many of his novels. Medals and prizes awarded to Faulkner and interesting historic relics are on display in the Mississippi Room of the Library on the Ole Miss campus.

Jackson, Mississippi's capital, on US 51, is well worth investigation. It played an important role in the Confederacy until 1863, when the Federal Army captured, burned and looted the town. During its rebuilding, Jackson contended with hordes of "Carpetbaggers," indicative of the entire South's problems, and it was here that Jefferson Davis last spoke to a vanquished South. Buildings connected to the past and present state government are important attractions. The Old Capitol, which houses the State Historical Museum and is an excellent example of Greek Revival architecture, has been completely restored. You can inspect the reconstructed governor's office with its ornate, authentic period furnishings, as well as the Hall of Representatives, the scene of many important events in state and national history.

Few cities live more intimately with the past than does Vicksburg, on US 61 and Interstate 20, the site of one of the Civil War's fiercest battles. Today the Vicksburg National Military Park surrounds the city. Two main avenues, Confederate and Union, wind through the

321

1,330-acre park, following the main defensive position of Southern forces and the lines of Northern troops. At the park's entrance, the Visitors' Center offers a pictorial display of the 47-day battle which ended with the Confederate surrender on July 4, 1863. On the park grounds, you can examine 898 historical tablets, 274 markers, 230 commemorative monuments, nine memorials, three equestrian statues, 150-odd busts and relief portraits, and 128 cannons.

Among the antebellum houses in Vicksburg, three are of particular interest. McRaven was owned by John Bobb when General U.S. Grant marched into Vicksburg. When Federal troops refused to leave his yard, Bobb threw a brick at them. He later was shot to death while walking alone in his garden, and this first incidence of violence against the civilian populace during Vicksburg's occupation caused an outraged Grant to have the guilty soldiers court-martialed and hanged. Cedar Grove is a restoration project of the Little Theater group, and mute testimony to the siege can be seen in its walls where Federal warships attempted to level the house with cannonballs but failed. Planters Hall, the third showplace, has had a varied career. It was erected in 1832 as a bank, converted into a residence by the McRae family in 1848, and later bought by the Vicksburg Council of Garden Clubs for use as a museum.

Thirty miles south of Vicksburg on US 61 is Port Gibson. Tombstones in Port Gibson's cemeteries tell interesting tales of American history. Harmon Blennerhasset, associate of Aaron Burr in the Burr Conspiracy, is buried in the Protestant Cemetery, and the Catholic Cemetery holds the grave of Resin P. Bowie, inventor of the famed bowie knife, first used by his brother, Jim, of Alamo fame. Ten miles from Port Gibson on Old Rodney Road lie the ruins of Windsor, one of the most extravagant antebellum mansions of Greek Revival style in the state. Built in 1861 and consisting of five stories and an observatory, it burned in 1890, when a careless swain showing off a newfangled cigarette at a house party threw the glowing butt into a pile of shavings in the corner of the ballroom. Nearby is the ghost town of Rodney—a town which died when the river moved away. Not far from there is Grand Gulf Military Park, where Grant landed his troops and doomed Vicksburg by taking it from the rear.

Natchez, farther south on US 61, is your introduction to an antebellum town where time seems to have stood still. The past is treasured here, but this is also a manufacturing center, and modern buildings mingle with the dominating 18th- and 19th-century structures. Undoubtedly more people visit Natchez during its annual Spring Pilgrimage (March and April) and Fall Pilgrimage (October 5 through 22), than at any other time. The Pilgrimage was established in the 1930s by farsighted ladies, and many antebellum houses are open daily, some only during the Pilgrimage. The rest of the year a roster of mansions rotate the duty of staying open for visitors so that some are always available. For details, contact the Natchez-Adams County Chamber of Commerce, 300 N. Commerce St. 39120. On Ellicott's Hill stands Connelley's Tavern, reputedly the spot where Aaron Burr planned his defense against a charge of treason. A treacherous attorney in the pay of bandits also supposedly hung about the tavern to pick up from careless conversation hints of loot to be lifted from travelers on the Natchez Trace by his gang. Beginning about 10 miles north of Natchez on US 61 is a long segment of the old Natchez Trace, now paved and maintained as a part of the federal park system. Along the Trace are Mount Locust, a restored hostelry, Emerald Mound, a magnificent 12-acre Indian mound, and the ghost town of Rocky Springs.

PRACTICAL INFORMATION FOR MISSISSIPPI

HOW TO GET THERE. *By air: Delta, American* and *Republic* have direct service into many cities in the state. *Rio* connects Memphis–Greenville; *Royale* flies New Orleans–Natchez–Jackson. *Air South* connects New Orleans/Gulfport. *Jamaire* connects Memphis/Greenwood. *By car:* I–55, US 45 and US 61 go from north to south; US 82, I–20, I–10, US 84 and US 90 run from east to west. *Car rental: Avis, Hertz, Budget,* and *National* in major cities. *By train: Amtrak* from Chicago to New Orleans. *By bus: Greyhound* and *Trailways. By ferry:* from St. Joseph, La., to Port Gibson.

TOURIST INFORMATION. Contact the *Mississippi Dept. of Tourism Development,* P.O. Box 22825, Jackson, 39205; the *Mississippi Park Commission,* 717 Robert E. Lee Bldg., Jackson 39201; individual city chambers of commerce; and *Natchez-Adams County Chamber of Commerce,* 300 N. Commerce St., Natchez, re: antebellum homes open to public.

MUSEUMS AND GALLERIES. *Brice's Cross Roads Museum,* Baldwyn. *Winterville Indian Mounds Museum & State Park,* Greenville. *Grenada Historical Museum,* Grenada. *State Historical Museum,* in the Old Capitol, Jackson. *Old Spanish Fort,* Pascagoula. *Natchez Trace Parkway,* Visitor Center, Tupelo. *Park Museum,* Vicksburg National Military Park.

Art: *Kate Freeman Clark Art Gallery,* Holly Springs. *Municipal Art Gallery,* Jackson. *Mary Buie Museum,* Oxford. *Museum of Art,* Meridian. The *Lauren Rogers Memorial Library and Museum of Art* at Laurel deserves special mention, for it houses many canvases of the masters, including Homer, Whistler, Corot, de Hoog, and Daumier.

Special interest: *Mississippi Museum of Natural Science,* Jackson. *Military Museum,* Port Gibson. *Dunn-Seiler Museum* (geology) at Mississippi State University, Starkville. *Art Center Planetarium,* Jackson.

Others: *Old Country Store,* Lorman, *River Museum and Hall of Fame,* Vicksburg. *Florewood River Plantation State Park,* Greenwood. *Grand Village of the Natchez Indians,* Natchez.

HISTORIC SITES. *Brice's Cross Roads National Battlefield Site,* off Rte. 370, Bladwyn. *Beauvoir* (Jefferson Davis Shrine), Biloxi. *Friendship Cemetery,* Columbus. *Corinth National Cemetery,* Corinth. *Ship Island,* by excursion boats from Biloxi and Gulfport. *Tupelo National Battlefield,* Tupelo. *Vicksburg National Military Park & Cemetery. Grand Gulf Battlefield,* Port Gibson. *Emerald Indian Mound,* ghost town of *Rocky Springs,* Natchez Trace Parkway. *Old Spanish Fort,* Pascagoula.

TOURS. Schedules vary with seasons and days. *By boat: Sailfish Tour Boat,* 1½ hr. shrimping and oystering expedition from Biloxi. *Magnolia Blossom Sternwheeler,* from Old Place Plantation, Gautier. *Jefferson Davis Cruises,* from Vicksburg.

SPORTS. *Swimming:* The world's longest man-made beach runs from Biloxi to Henderson Point. Other beaches are at Pascagoula, Ocean Springs, Bay St. Louis, Waveland and on offshore islands. *Boating:* Most towns on waterways have launching ramps. There is powerboating in the Mississippi Sound and many rivers and bayous. Small sailboat rentals are available in Biloxi. *Fishing:* Year-round saltwater and deep-sea fishing coast-wide. Freshwater fishing is excellent in the state's many streams and lakes, particularly good in reservoirs behind dams, and spectacular in the oxbow lakes that border the Mississippi River.

SPECTATOR SPORTS. The *Shrimp Bowl* Football game is held at Biloxi in early December; football is king throughout the state all fall. Major golf tournaments are held at Pass Christian, Hattiesburg, and Greenwood.

WHAT TO DO WITH THE CHILDREN. *Vicksburg National Military Park* and the *Park Museum* are teeming with mementos of the Civil War. At Biloxi is *Six Gun Junction* combined with the *Deer Ranch* where children pet the animals. At Gulfport is the *Marine Life Aquadome.* At Meridian and Tupelo are fish hatcheries with guided visits. The *Jackson Zoo* has a petting section and a Chimneyville Choo Choo train ride. At Vicksburg the Jefferson Davis boat ride follows the route of attacking Union gunboats.

HOTELS AND MOTELS. Along the Gulf Coast are several resort hotels with full beach and sports facilities. Inland hostelries are more modest. Hotels and motels are listed alphabetically within categories based on double-occupancy, in-season rates. Family rates are available at almost all listings. Rates run $3 to $4 higher during Pilgrimages. *Moderate:* $45–50; *Inexpensive:* $30.

BILOXI. *Moderate:* **Holiday Inn, Howard Johnson's, Quality Inn-Emerald Beach, Ramada Inn** are only slightly less opulent than the top rankers—and only slightly less expensive.

CLARKSDALE. *Inexpensive:* Both **Holiday Inn** and **Best Western Up-Town** offer entertainment and other amenities unusual in houses charging so little.

COLUMBUS. *Moderate:* **Ramada Inn** has dancing and entertainment despite modest fees.

CORINTH. *Moderate:* **Holiday Inn** and **Ramada Inn,** kennels at former, entertainment at latter.

GREENVILLE. *Inexpensive:* **Riverview Inn** has evening entertainment. *Inexpensive:* **Holiday Inn** has modest but adequate amenities.

GREENWOOD. *Moderate:* **Holiday Inn** offers heated pool, kennel, entertainment and dancing. **Ramada Inn** has heated pool, entertainment, dancing.

GULFPORT. *Moderate:* **Best Western** (formerly Downtowner), **Holiday Inn** and **Sheraton Gulfport** somewhat more lavish than most motels in their respective chains.

HATTIESBURG. *Moderate:* **Holiday Inn** has a kennel for pets.

JACKSON. *Moderate:* **Coliseum Ramada Inn, Executive Plaza, Regency, Holiday Inn–North, Holiday Inn–Southwest, Howard Johnson's** and **Sheraton** are all considerably more luxurious than the average of their respective chains. All offer entertainment and dancing.

Passport Inn and **Quality Inn** I–55 North are scarcely less luxurious than more expensive neighbors. Both excellent bargains.

LONG BEACH. *Moderate:* **Ramada Inn.** Entertainment, dancing, tennis, putting green.

MERIDIAN. *Moderate–Inexpensive:* Two **Holiday Inns, Howard Johnson's** and **Ramada Inn** typical comfortable chain operations. **Holiday Inn–Northeast** and **Ramada Inn** sometimes offer entertainment and dancing.

NATCHEZ. *Moderate:* **Ramada Inn.** Entertainment and dancing. Superb view of Mississippi River.

Inexpensive: **Holiday Inn. Prentiss,** entertainment and dancing.

All Natchez inns add a few dollars to fees during Pilgrimage.

OXFORD. *Moderate:* **Admiral Benbow** and **Holiday Inns** offer usual chain amenities. **Rodeway Inn** has entertainment and dancing. Football weekends pose space problems.

PASCAGOULA. *Moderate:* **La Font Inn,** heated pool, lifeguard in summer, playground. Some rooms have sauna.

Longfellow House. Par-3 course, full golf privileges, tennis, Olympic pool, dancing, entertainment including dinner theater on weekends. Pleasant grounds. Cottages available. Best buy in area.

STARKVILLE. *Inexpensive:* **Holiday Inn** with heated pool and kennel for pets.

TUPELO. *Inexpensive:* **Ramada Inn.** Entertainment, dancing, beauty shop.

Inexpensive: **Natchez Trace Inn.** Playground, entertainment, dancing.

VICKSBURG. *Moderate:* **Holiday Inn** and **Ramada Inn** have music and dancing. **Downtowner** houses the Old Southern Tea Room.

 DINING OUT. Mississippi offers many traditional Southern specialties, as well as all the standard American favorites. Along the Gulf coast, try shrimp prepared in the Creole manner, and hot gumbos or other seafood specialties. Among the Southern items to be found on many Mississippi menus: hush puppies, grits, country-style ham, and of course, Mississippi River catfish.

For other worthwhile restaurants, be sure to re-check hotel listings. Restaurants are listed in order of price category. Price ranges and categories for a complete meal are as follows: *Moderate:* $6.50–12.50; *Inexpensive:* $4.50–6.50.

BILOXI. *Moderate.* **Mary Mahoney's.** Chic surroundings, fine cuisine.

Inexpensive: **Baricev's.** Seafood plates from that same day's catch.

Sea n' Sirloin. Try stuffed sirloin.

GREENWOOD. *Inexpensive:* **Webster's.** Charming decor and very good food.

GULFPORT. *Inexpensive:* **Angelo's.** European cuisine.

HOLLY SPRINGS. *Inexpensive:* **Hitching Post.** Steak and seafood.

JACKSON. *Moderate:* **Crechale's.** Jam-packed hole-in-the-wall. Excellent. **Dennery's.** Oyster specialties.
Le Fleur's. Excellent raw oyster bar. Rivals Bernard's for best table in town.
Sundancer. Lively. Best buy in town.

MENDENHALL. *Inexpensive:* **The Hotel Mendenhall Revolving Tables.** Glorious old-style boardinghouse cooking.

MERIDIAN. *Inexpensive:* **Weidman's.** A pleasant surprise.

NATCHEZ. *Moderate:* **Carriage House.** Southern cooking.
Cock of the Walk. Catfish in wicked old Natchez-Under-the-Hill.
Side Track. Converted railroad depot overlooks Mississippi River.

OCEAN SPRINGS. *Moderate:* **Trilby's.** Creole menu. Seafood.

OXFORD. After years of mediocre-to-poor dining, the town now offers a wealth of sound and inexpensive restaurants at **The Deli, the Gin,** and **the Warehouse.** Cajun gumbo at **Audie-Michael's** matches the original Louisiana product.

PASCAGOULA. *Moderate:* **Longfellow House.** Prime ribs, seafood, and steak amid pleasant surroundings.

PORT GIBSON. *Moderate:* **The Depot.** Turn-of-century, railroad ambiance. Daily specials based on market availability of ingredients.

TUPELO. *Inexpensive:* **Hunter's.** Man-sized portions.

VICKSBURG. *Moderate:* **Velchoff's.** Seafood.
Walnut Hills. Lazy Susan roundtable.

NORTH CAROLINA

Blue Ridge, Smoky Mountains and the Sea

The Cape Hatteras National Seashore embraces seventy miles of oceanfront between Nags Head on Bodie Island and the village of Ocracoke on the southern tip of Ocracoke Island. Focal point of the National Seashore is Cape Hatteras itself, where the tallest lighthouse in the United States—208 feet—protects shipping from the treacherous Diamond Shoals. In earlier times Diamond Shoals was called the Graveyard of the Atlantic and, according to legends of the area, the original residents of Nags Head used to tie lanterns on the necks of their horses to lure ships into the shoals and then prey upon them for their profitable salvage.

Almost all of Ocracoke Island is on the National Seashore. Ocracoke and the central coast are virtually uninhabited Outer Banks of Portsmouth, Core, and Shackleford, destined for preservation in the natural state as the Cape Lookout National Seashore. The development of seaside beach and fishing resorts and the National Seashore has ended more than two centuries of isolation for the Outer Banks between Kitty Hawk and Ocracoke. Important fishing centers are at Oregon Inlet and Hatteras Village, the site of Gamefish Junction, where Gulfstream and cold northern currents meet, and where northern and southern species of fish abound. As to other natural endowments, within the National Seashore there is Pea Island National Wildlife Refuge on Hatteras Island, flocking point of shore birds and migratory waterfowl. Here over one half the world's population of greater snow geese can be seen between early November and late January.

The central coast swings southwest from Hatteras to Morehead City, one of the state's two ocean ports, the center of the maritime province of Carteret County. Morehead City has the state's largest fleet of charter fishing boats. Nearby resorts on Bogue Island offer advantages of both ocean and sound recreation activities. Wilmington, a historic port and permanent mooring of the battleship USS *North Carolina,* is a hub of beaches, plantations, and recreation for the southeastern coast. Wilmington greets Spring with its annual Azalea Festival. Topsail, Wrightsville, Carolina, Long, Ocean Isle and Sunset beaches are tamer than the Outer Banks, but offer the same activities.

Raleigh–Durham–Chapel Hill

Raleigh, the capital, is the southeastern apex of the Research Triangle Park formed by North Carolina State University in Raleigh, the University of North Carolina at Chapel Hill, and Duke University in Durham. Visitors can tour the historic capitol, the North Carolina Art Museum, and the Museum of Natural History, and see the equestrian statue in Capitol Square honoring the three Presidents born in North Carolina: Andrew Jackson, Andrew Johnson, and James K. Polk. Durham is an industrial center, the home of Duke University, and a tobacco center spurred by the Duke family, which may be to the gold leaf what the Carnegies have been to steel. The University of North Carolina's famous alumnus Thomas Wolfe once described Chapel Hill as a place that "beats every other town all hollow." U.S. astronauts use the university's Morehead Planetarium in preparing for their space flights. North of Chapel Hill is historic Hillsborough, established in 1754 and the site of the hanging of six of the Regulators whose uprising against the British culminated in defeat at the Battle of Alamance on May 16, 1771.

Other major cities in the Piedmont are Charlotte, Greensboro, Burlington, High Point, and Winston-Salem, each important as trade and tobacco centers.

Blue Ridge Parkway

The Blue Ridge Parkway is a high-altitude route for pleasure travel between Shenandoah National Park in Virginia and the Great Smoky Mountains National Park entrance near Cherokee. The scenic drive illustrates the history, geology, and culture of the mountains. There are campgrounds, picnic areas, and scenic overlooks. Highest sections may be closed in winter.

Half of the Great Smoky Mountains National Park is within the state, with the Great Smokies Divide zigzagging from northeast to southwest for 71 miles along the North Carolina–Tennessee line.

Great Smoky Mountains National Park

At the North Carolina entrance to this 800-square-mile park there is an excellent pioneer farmstead maintained by the rangers. Just outside this entrance the town of Cherokee, the capital of the Cherokee

Indian reservation, has a street lined with shops purveying Indian-made crafts. The park has some 150 miles of roads, half of them paved, and 700 miles of horseback and hiking trails. At the highest point in the park, Clingman's Dome, an evergreen rain forest can be explored with the help of a self-guiding trail. Trout streams are open to fishing from May through August. Some roads are closed because of snow in the 5,000- and 6,000-foot-high ridges but otherwise the park is open all year—it gets over 8-million visitors annually.

The main North Carolina entrance is on US 441 near Cherokee and the southern terminus of Blue Ridge Parkway. Oconaluftee Ranger Station, with Pioneer Exhibits and Farmstead, at the Park entrance, is open daily. Tent and trailer camping allowed at developed campgrounds; rough camping by permit from rangers. Pets must be kept leashed or restricted at all times. Marked hiking trails include 70 miles of Appalachian Trailway along the crest of Great Smokies Divide. Livery stable concessionaires rent horses from June through Aug. Trout fishing mid-May to Sept. US 441 is the transmountain highway through the Park. At Newfound Gap on the North Carolina-Tennessee line, it intersects with a paved Park road to Clingman's Dome, highest peak in the Great Smokies. Tourist accommodations at Waynesville, North Carolina, and at Gatlinburg, Tennessee, among others.

PRACTICAL INFORMATION FOR NORTH CAROLINA

HOW TO GET THERE. *By air:* Raleigh-Durham, Charlotte, Greensboro, Asheville, Fayetteville, Goldsboro, Hickory, Jacksonville, Kinston, New Bern, Rocky Mount, Wilmington, and Winston-Salem are all served from outside the state.

By rail: Amtrak goes to Rocky Mount, Wilson, Raleigh, Fayetteville, Hamlet, and Southern Pines/Pinehurst.

By car: I–95, I–85, I–77 run north-south. I–40 goes east-west. I–26, and I–77 comes in from South Carolina.

By bus: Greyhound and *Trailways.*

TOURIST INFORMATION. *North Carolina Travel Division,* Dept. of Commerce, Raleigh, 27611. *Park Superintendent,* Cape Hatteras National Seashore, Box 457, Manteo, 27954.

MUSEUMS AND GALLERIES. Historical: *North Carolina Hall of History,* Raleigh; *Cornwallis House,* Wilmington; *Museum of the Albemarle,* Elizabeth City. *Greensboro Historical Museum.*

Art: Asheville Art Museum; Mint Museum of Art, Charlotte; *Duke University Museum of Art,* Durham; *North Carolina Museum of Art,* Raleigh; *Piedmont Craftsman,* Winston-Salem; *Museum of Early Southern Decorative Arts,* Winston-Salem; *St. John's Art Gallery,* Wilmington.

Special-interest museums: *Country Doctor Museum,* Bailey; *Museum of the Cherokee Indian,* Cherokee; *Hampton Mariner's Museum,* Beaufort; *World Golf Hall of Fame,* Pinehurst; *Discovery Place* (science museum), Charlotte, NC.

HISTORIC SITES. *Thomas Wolfe Memorial, Asheville; Ft. Fisher State Historic Site,* Carolina Beach; *Wright Brothers Nat. Memorial,* Kill Devil Hills; *Roanoke Island Historical Park,* Manteo; *James K. Polk Birthplace,* Pineville; *Old Salem,* Winston-Salem. *Historic Bath State Historic Site,* Bath.

TOURS. *By boat:* Southport–Ft. Fisher Ferry. Car and passenger ferry from Cedar Island–Ocracoke; Hatteras–Ocracoke.

DRINKING LAWS. Local option on county-by-county basis. In "wet" counties or municipalities imbibers must be at least 21.

SUMMER SPORTS. *Water sports:* Bathing season begins in May and runs into late autumn on beaches, rivers, lakes. Intercoastal Waterway for 265 miles in state; consult Inland Waterway Guide, Ft Lauderdale, Fla. *Fishing:* Deep-sea, salt-water centers at Nags Head, Morehead City, Oregon Inlet, Hatteras, Wrightsville, Southport, with blue marlin the big game. Freshwater requires a license.

Golf: Over 300 courses. According to *Golf Digest,* Pinehurst #2 in America's top 10, C.C. of North Carolina in top 30, Grandfather in Linville and Red Fox in Tryon in top 100.

Horseback riding and hiking all throughout the state: Appalachian Trail through Smokies. Pisgah and Nantahala Parks.

WINTER SPORTS. *Hunting:* Bear, boar, deer, small-game animals, ducks, etc. Consult *Wildlife Resources Commission,* Raleigh. *Skiing:* Appalachian Ski Mt., Hound Ears, Mill Ridge, Seven Devil Sugar Mtn., Beech Mtn., all near Banner Elk. Also, Cataloochee Ski Slopes, Waynesville; High Meadows at Roaring Gap, and Wolf Laurel near Mars Hill.

SPECTATOR SPORTS. *Charlotte Motor Speedway* in May and October and North Carolina Motor Speedway with NASCAR events. *Greater Greensboro Open* is a PGA tour stop. Duke, UNC, N.C. State, Wake Forest Davidson are among major colleges playing most sports.

WHAT TO DO WITH THE CHILDREN USS *North Carolina* Battleship Memorial, Wilmington; *Tweetsie Railroad,* Blowing Rock; *Cherokee Indian Reservation; Grandfather Mtn.,* Linville, with mile-high swinging bridge; *Discovery Place,* "hands on" science museum, Charlotte; *Caro-Winds,* theme park, south of Charlotte; *Frontierland,* Cherokee; *Oconaluftee Indian Village,* Cherokee; *Daniel Boone Railroad Park,* Hillsborough; *North Carolina Museum of Life & Science,* Durham; *Ghost Town* in Maggie Valley.

HOTELS AND MOTELS Throughout the state you will find economy motel chains; i.e., Econolodge, Hotel 6, Scottish Inns, Cricket Inns, Days Inn. Accommodations listed fall in the following price ranges: *Moderate* $30–40; *Inexpensive:* under $30.

ASHEVILLE. *Moderate:* **John Yancey Motel.** Year-round comfortable motel.

Mountaineer Inn. 155 Tunnel Rd.

ATLANTIC BEACH. *Moderate.* **Flemings.** Attractive motel. Restaurant. *Inexpensive:* **Bel-Air Motel.** Year-round, pool, kitchenettes. Seasonal rates.

BLOWING ROCK. *Moderate:* **Parkway Motel.** Year-round 20 units, kitchens.

Azalea Garden Motel. Attractive landscaping.
Inexpensive: **Village Inn.** Restaurant nearby.

CHAPEL HILL. *Moderate:* **Carolina Inn.** Comfortable old inn run by the university.

Holiday Inn. North of town. Pools, restaurant, and bar.
Inexpensive: **University Motor Inn.** On N.C. 54. Restaurant and pool.

CHARLOTTE. *Moderate:* **Holiday Inn.** Five locations in town.
Cricket Inn. 4115 Glenwood Dr. Lounge, pool, restaurant.
Inexpensive: **Days Inn.** Large motor inn. Two locations. W. Woodlawn and Sugar Creek Rd.

CHEROKEE. *Moderate:* **Boundary Tree Motor Court.** Operated by Cherokee Indians.

Drama Motel. On Oconaluftee River.
Holiday Inn. Has trout fishing.

DURHAM. *Moderate:* **Downtowner Motel.** Downtown.
Inexpensive: **Days Inn of America.** Another of chain.
Dutch Village Motel. 2306 Elder St. Facilities for handicapped, near Duke & Veteran's Hospitals.

GREENSBORO. *Moderate:* **Smith Ranch Motel,** 2210 Randleman Rd. Clean and comfortable.
Inexpensive: **Cricket Inn.** I–85 & Elm St.
Days Inn. I–40 at airport exit.

NAGS HEAD. *Moderate:* **Cabana East.** Year-round. Pool; kitchens.
Travelers Inn Motor Lodge. All-year facility, with kitchens.

OCRACOKE. *Moderate:* **Pony Island Motel.** Year-round, restaurant.

RALEIGH. *Moderate:* **Best Western South.** Convenient, clean, nr. restaurants.

Plantation Inn. On Hwy 1 N. Lovely setting. Excellent dining. Putting green.
Ranch Motel. On Hwy. 70. Very good restaurant, lounge and pool.

SOUTHERN PINES. *Moderate:* **Howard Johnson's Motor Lodge.** Access to nearby facilities.

Pinehurst Motor Lodge. Near shopping area.
Sheraton Motel. Typical of the chain. Very comfortable.
Inexpensive: **Charlton Motel.** Lakefront, year-round, kitchens.

WILMINGTON AND WRIGHTSVILLE BEACH. *Moderate:* **Heart of Wilmington.** 311 N. Third St. Pool, restaurant.

Hilton Inn. Across from scenic U.S.S. *North Carolina* battleship. Near restored area.
Silver Gull Motel. Year-round, kitchenettes. Seasonal rates; on beach.
Inexpensive: **El Berta Motel.** Year-round.
Motel 6. 2828 Market St. Facilities for handicapped.

WINSTON-SALEM. *Moderate:* **Sheraton Motor Inn.** Good facilities and near shopping center and mini-mall.
Inexpensive: **Travel Host of America.** US 52N. Lounge, pool, and good restaurant.

DINING OUT IN NORTH CAROLINA. Prices are for a complete dinner but do not include drinks, tax, or tip. *Moderate:* $10 up; *Inexpensive:* under $10. Among North Carolina's specialties are country-cured ham, hot biscuits, chess pie, barbecue, strawberry pie, and candied yams.

ASHEVILLE. *Inexpensive:* **S&W Cafeteria.** Excellent food.
  Mom's Kitchen. Tunnel Rd. One of best mountain-country breakfasts in area.

BLOWING ROCK. *Moderate:* **Sunshine Inn.** Now year-round. Food is very good and plentiful.

BOONE. *Moderate:* **The Daniel Boone Inn.** Family style. Chicken, ham biscuits, fresh vegetables are specialties.

CHAPEL HILL. **Carolina Coffee Shop.** E. Franklin St. 1922 Chapel Hill landmark. Closed Mondays. Informal dining and excellent food.
  Carolina Inn. Excellent cafeteria in this old inn.

DURHAM. *Moderate:* **Hartman's Steak House.** Steak.
  Inexpensive: **Bullock's Bar-B-Cue.** Specialty of the area.

GREENSBORO. *Moderate* **Darryl's 1808.** 2102 N. Church St. Period restaurant and tavern.
  Stamey's Bar-B-Que. Two locations. 908 S. Main St., and 2206 High Point Rd. Good eating.

MONROE. *Moderate:* **Friendship Inn and Hilltop Restaurant.** Southern-style food. Excellent.

RALEIGH. *Moderate:* **Ballentine's Cafeteria.** In Cameron Village. Well known for southern-style vegetables.
  Neptune's Galley. Good seafood, steamed oysters.
  Inexpensive: **Barbecue Lodge.** Located in Mini City, Hwy 1 N. Pork & chicken barbecue, brunswick stew and cornsticks.
  Canton Restaurant. Featuring oriental cuisine.

WILMINGTON AND WRIGHTSVILLE BEACH. *Moderate:* **Cortley's Old Fashioned Deli.** Located in restored waterfront area of The Cotton Exchange in Wilmington.
  The Mediterranean. On Wrightsville Beach. Seafood and Italian. One of the best.
  Inexpensive: **Ballentine's.** Cafeteria with Southern specialties. (Wilmington).

WINSTON-SALEM. *Moderate:* **Salem Tavern.** In Old Salem.
  Staley's Charcoal Steak House. Steaks, chops.
  Inexpensive: **K & W Cafeteria.** Two locations: 720 Coliseum Dr., and in Parkway Plaza off I–40 at Knollwood Exit. Breakfast, lunch, dinner.
  Tuesday's. A delightful period restaurant, located in Hanes Mall.
  Zevely House. Quiche is one of the specialties of the house. Informal atmosphere. Enjoy brunch or lunch in one of the oldest restored houses in the city.

SOUTH CAROLINA

*Charleston, Myrtle Beach, Hilton Head Island
and More*

Charleston, important as a major seaport and industrial center, is above all the "Mother City of the South," a treasure trove of beautiful eighteenth- and nineteenth-century houses, gardens and churches. Several exquisitely restored houses are open year round. Many others welcome visitors during the annual month-long spring Festival of Houses. In spring, too, famous Cypress, Magnolia and Middleton Place Gardens offer a feast of color. Magnolia and Middleton Place remain open year round, brilliant in summer with oleanders, hydrangeas, hibiscus, roses, magnolias and crape myrtle. Middleton Place's Plantation Stableyards also offers fascinating glimpses of a working 18th-century plantation. Magnolia has a petting zoo with rare mini-horses. Nearby is Drayton Hall, considered the nation's finest untouched example of Georgian architecture. Boone Hall, on a 738-acre estate, is a beautiful plantation with original slave houses and ginhouse.

In broad and beautiful Charleston Harbor stands Fort Sumter, where the Civil War began. For Revolutionary War buffs, there's Fort Moultrie on Sullivan's Island, site of the first decisive American victory over the British. Another permanent resident of this historic city is the aircraft carrier *Yorktown,* famed "Fighting Lady" of World War II, berthed at Patriots Point across the Cooper River. Also here are the nuclear-powered *NS Savannah,* destroyer *Laffey,* and submarine *Clamagore.*

Charles Towne Landing is a beautiful state park on the coastal site where the state's earliest English colonists settled in 1670. Archeological remnants of the first settlement have been unearthed and a handsome contemporary visitor center vividly depicts three centuries of South Carolina history. Creatures indigenous to the 1670s roam the Animal Forest. You may also board *The Adventure,* replica of an eighteenth-century West Indies trading ketch, moored in the harbor.

Myrtle Beach

Hub of the 55-mile stretch of broad, sun-splashed Atlantic beach known as the Grand Strand, Myrtle Beach is a popular family vacation center with wide ranges of accommodations for every budget. You'll enjoy virtually every water-related activity, excellent golf courses, tennis, sports fishing, special events ranging from fishing tournaments to flower shows, plantation tours and musical festivals.

Beaufort

Beaufort is a city where British merchants made fortunes in cotton and indigo. This is the South of stately old homes with spacious porches and old-fashioned gardens set amid moss-bearded oaks. The landscape varies from high bluffs, densely wooded with subtropical growth, to sloping sandy beaches. The natural harbor here is one of the finest on the coast. One of the offshore islands, Hunting Island, is a state park where deer, raccoon, and flocks of local and migratory birds and waterfowl can be found. This scenic, wooded 5,000-acre island offers fine beaches, nature trails, facilities for picnicking, camping, fishing.

Columbia

State capital, largest city, and home of the University of South Carolina, Columbia is in the midlands. Its three-story State House shows Civil War scars of General Sherman's artillery, and has a statue of John C. Calhoun, famed antebellum statesman. Riverbanks Zoological Gardens, one of the nation's most modern, is notable for areas where creatures roam freely.

Greenville

Hub of industrial Piedmont, "textile center of the world," this prosperous city is also a cultural center. The ultra-modern Greenville County Art Museum boasts the nation's most complete collection of Andrew Wyeth paintings. The Art Gallery of Bob Jones University has one of the Southeast's major collections of religious art.

National Forests, Wildlife Refuges

Francis Marion National Forest, on the coastal plains north of Charleston, was named for the "Swamp Fox," hero-general of the American Revolution. Indians, Spanish, and French explorers roamed the area, following waterways flanked by moss-covered gums, cypress and tall loblolly pines. Camping, picnicking, boating, fishing, and hiking trails are available.

Cape Romain National Wildlife Refuge, northeast of Charleston, is an unspoiled island marsh and sea area, a haven for shell collectors and bird watchers. Savannah National Wildlife Refuge, among the nation's oldest, teems with wildfowl, deer, raccoons and alligators. Santee National Wildlife Refuge is a major sanctuary for thousands of Canada geese and other waterfowl.

PRACTICAL INFORMATION FOR SOUTH CAROLINA

 HOW TO GET THERE. There's air service to Charleston, Columbia, Greenville-Spartanburg and Myrtle Beach. Principal routes through South Carolina are I-95, I-85, I-20, I-26. U.S. 17, the "coastal highway," parallels the shoreline. *Greyhound* and *Continental Trailways* buses serve the state and *Amtrak* goes into Dillon, Florence, Kingstree, Charleston, Yemassee, Clemson, Camden, Columbia, Denmark, Spartanburg, Greenville, and Clemson.

TOURIST INFORMATION. The South Carolina Division of Tourism, Box 71, Columbia, SC 29202, will supply detailed information.

 MUSEUMS AND GALLERIES. Charleston: *Charleston Museum* has fine collections of arts, crafts, furniture, textiles from state's early days. *Gibbes Art Gallery* displays notable Oriental collections, paintings, prints, sculptures, miniatures. *Hunley Museum* focuses on Confederate naval history, has replica of Confederate submarine *Hunley. City Hall Council Chamber* is a mini-museum of relics and paintings, including Trumbull's famous portrait of George Washington.

Columbia: *Columbia Museums of Art and Science* feature fine collection of Renaissance art from Kress Foundation; also include aquarium, nature garden, planetarium.

Rock Hill: *The Museum of York County* is one of nation's finest regional natural history museums. Maurice Stans African Hall has world's largest collection of mounted African animals in environmental settings.

Clemson: *Keowee-Toxaway Visitors Center* has fascinating ultra-modern three-dimensional energy displays, offers nature trails, picnicking along lake shore. Admission is free.

 HISTORIC SITES. *Camden,* state's oldest inland town, is site of Historic Camden, restored Revolutionary era settlement with lovely old houses, remains of forts, small animal farm. *Historic Pendleton District,* dating from 1789, is three-county area encompassing historic houses, early agricultural museum. It includes Fort Hill, on Clemson University campus, home of John C. Calhoun.

At *Cowpens National Battlefield,* British sustained one of worst disasters in southern Revolutionary War campaign, starting Cornwallis on road to ultimate defeat.

Kings Mountain National Military Park, site of crucial Revolutionary battle, is off SC 216, just south of I-85.

Andrew Jackson State Park is north of Lancaster in heart of scenic Waxhaw Hills where "Old Hickory," seventh U.S. President, was born. Exact birth spot is disputed—both Carolinas claim him!

TOURS. *Fort Sumter Tours* offers boat rides, guided tours of the national monument. *Gray Line* has boat tours of Charleston harbor, several motorcoach tours of city and area. There are several other bus, limousine, carriage, bicycle, cassette and individually guided tours of Historic Charleston.

DRINKING LAWS. Mixed drinks (sold by "mini-bottles") may be ordered in licensed restaurants, hotels, and motels. State package liquor stores sell by the bottle except Sundays and holidays. Legal age is 21, 18 for beer and wine.

SPORTS. With 36 fine courses, the Grand Strand is one of the east coast's major golf centers. Add to this the dozen-plus fine championship courses of the resort islands and state resort parks, and duffer and pro alike can choose from miles of fairways, hundreds of traps and hazards. In the state's mild climate, golf is a year-round sport.

For fishing buffs, there are rainbow and brown trout in the mountainous areas of the western counties, striped bass in the Santee-Cooper Lakes. Surf casting is popular all along the Grand Strand and in the islands, and charter boats offer deep-sea fishing in the Gulf Stream from Charleston and the islands.

Top spectator sports include the spring Carolina Cup and autumn Colonial Cup steeplechase events in Camden, the late March Sea Pines Heritage Golf Classic on Hilton Head Island and the Labor Day Southern 500 Stock Car Race in Darlington.

SPECIAL EVENTS. Late May to early June, Charleston is annual site of *Spoleto Festival USA*, major international festival of performing and visual arts, founded by famed composer Gian Carlo Menotti as counterpart to annual Spoleto, Italy, festival.

WHAT TO DO WITH THE CHILDREN. A "family fun mecca," Myrtle Beach offers *Magic Harbor,* an entertainment park with kiddie rides, ice skating revue, country music, puppet shows, water slide; *Pipeline Water Slide & Gay Dolphin Arcade; Ripley's Believe It or Not Museum. Brookgreen Gardens* at nearby Murrells Inlet has hundreds of sculptures in beautiful garden setting, picnic areas, wildlife park.

HOTELS AND MOTELS. Price categories and ranges, based on double occupancy, are: *Moderate:* $31–40; and *Inexpensive:* $20–30. Prices subject to change, of course!

BEAUFORT. *Moderate:* **Best Western Sea Island Motel.** 1015 Bay St. Convenient downtown location. Swimming pool, color TV. Dining room, cocktails.

Inexpensive: **Lord Carteret Motel.** 301 Carteret St. In center of city. Refrigerators, color TV, kitchenettes, in-room movies.

The Pines Motel. Jct. US 21 & SC 170. Color cable TV, pool. Large landscaped grounds. Hot sandwiches, soft drinks on premises; near restaurants. Pets. A Budget Host Inn.

CHARLESTON. *Moderate:* **Best Western Dorchester.** I–26 at Dorchester Rd. Restaurant, lounge, pool, entertainment. Cable TV.

Heart of Charleston. 200 Meeting St. Pool, coffee shop, cocktail lounge.

La Quinta Motor Inn. 2499 La Quinta La., Charleston Hgts. Pool, color TV. Restaurant nearby.

Vagabond Inn. 1468 Savannah Hwy. (US 17S). Pool, playground. Movies. Pets. Coin laundry. Dining room, lounge, entertainment.

Days Inn. 2 locations: 3016 W. Montague Ave., at I–26, 6 mi. N. on US 17 bypass, Mt. Pleasant, SC. Restaurant, handicapped facilities. Pets. September Days Club honored.

Inexpensive: **Econo Travel Motor Hotel.** 3 locations: 4500 Arco Lane (I–26 & W. Montague) Montague Ave., Exit 213A, 5169 Rivers Ave. (Rte. 52, 78, & Van Buren Ave.), 2237 Savannah Hwy. (US 17). Free crib, color TV. Some no-smoking rooms. Restaurants near.

COLUMBIA. *Moderate:* **Downtowner Motor Inn.** 1301 Main St. Pool, pets, dining room, cocktails.

Matador Motor Inn. 322 Bush River Rd., at I–126, I–26. Color TV, pool. Dining room, cocktails, disco.

Tremont Motor Inn. 111 Knox Abbott Dr. (Cayce, SC). Color TV, some refrigerators. 24-hr. dining room, cocktail lounge. Coin laundry, pool, putting green, playground. Pets.

Inexpensive to Moderate: **Howard Johnson's.** 2 locations: I–26 & I–20; 2½ mi. S. on US 21, 176, 321. Pools, playgrounds, color TV. Restaurants, lounges.

Inexpensive. **Days Inn.** I–26 & SC 302 (Airport Exit). Dining room, service station. Handicapped facilities. Family rates, September Days Club honored. Near Riverbanks Zoo.

Econo Travel Motor Hotel. 2 locations: 127 Morninghill Dr. (I–26 & Bush River Rd., exit 108), 1617 Charleston Hwy. (SC 321, 21, S. of SC 302 & 321). Free crib, color TV. No-smoking rooms available. Restaurants next door.

GREENVILLE. *Moderate:* **Holiday Inn.** 2 locations: 27 S. Pleasantburg Dr.; I–85 at Exit 46. Both have dining rooms, entertainment, pools, color TV, kennels. Golf, tennis, racquetball, sauna.

Howard Johnson's Central. 10 Mills Ave. Restaurant, lounge, cable TV. Waterbeds available.

Inexpensive: **Econo Lodge.** 536 Wade Hampton Blvd.

MYRTLE BEACH. *Moderate:* **Jade Tree Motor Inn.** 5308 N. Ocean Blvd. Oceanfront. Pool, surf fishing, golf privileges. Dining room, lounge.

Ocean Spray Motel. 1304 S. Ocean Blvd. Family oriented. Pools, restaurant adjacent.

Inexpensive–Moderate: **Shangri La Motel.** 2700 N. Kings Hwy. Color cable TV, pool. Pets. Some efficiencies. Restaurant adjoins.

Inexpensive: **Lakeside.** 6805 N. Kings Hwy. Pool, playground, putting green, lawn games, picnic tables, grills, game room. On private lake, near restaurants and beach.

 DINING OUT. The categories and price ranges for a complete dinner are: *Moderate:* $10–15; *Inexpensive:* under $10. Not included are drinks, tax and tip. Coastal seafood is superb. Don't miss such local specialties as she-crab soup, benne (sesame) seed wafers!

CHARLESTON. *Moderate:* **Henry's.** 54 Market St. Superb Low Country specialties, including stuffed mackerel, flounder, she-crab soup. Low-key atmosphere, a great local favorite.

Swamp Fox Room-Francis Marion Hotel. King at Calhoun Sts. American cuisine.

Inexpensive-Moderate: **Lorelei.** Shem Creek, US 17N. Family dining, seafood specialty.

Trawler. US 17N, Mt. Pleasant. Family dining, seafood specialty.

COLUMBIA. *Moderate:* **The Lion's Head.** 741 Saluda Ave. Beef specialties, children's menu.

Market Restaurant. 1205 Assembly St. Beef and seafood specialties, children's menu. Near State Capitol.

Inexpensive: **Morrison's Cafeteria,** Dutch Square Mall; **S & S Cafeteria,** 1411 Gervais St.

MYRTLE BEACH. *Moderate:* **Crab House.** U.S. 17 N. on Restaurant Row. All-you-can-eat seafood. Casual dress.

The Rice Planters. 6707 Kings Hwy. N. Superb Low Country specialties in attractive rustic setting decorated with artifacts, antiques from rice planting era.

Sea Captain's. 3002 N. Ocean Blvd. Superb seafood in charming ocean front setting. Also at Murrells Inlet, SC

Steven's Oyster Roast. SC 9, North Myrtle Beach. Classic country cooking: steamed, fried oysters; fish; shrimp right off the boat. Great local favorite.

Inexpensive: **Dino's House of Pancakes.** 2702 Hwy. 17 N. Serves complete breakfast and lunch daily—omelettes, waffles, pancakes, eggs, sandwiches.

The Farm House. Kings Hwy. & 5th Ave. N., downtown. All you can eat country menu—ham, fried chicken, beef stew, 14 vegetables, hot biscuits, corn sticks, fruit cobbler!

Morrison's Cafeteria. Myrtle Square Mall. Fine home-cooked food, desserts. One of regional chain.

Western Steer Steak House. 2 locations: 512 Hwy. 17 S., 8000 Hwy. 17 N. Steaks, steak & seafood platters. Children's menu.

TENNESSEE

Frontier Country, the Smokies, and Nashville

The wide sinewy Mississippi River rolls the entire length of Tennessee's western boundary. The Great Smoky Mountains National Park barricades its southern border with some of the highest crests east of the Rockies. The Cumberland Gap and the state of Kentucky range along the northern side. In between are the sites of some of the bloody battles of the Civil War and a birthplace of the atom bomb which ended World War II. Some of this country's great frontiersmen were born or lived here, Davey Crockett and Daniel Boone among them. Here, too, the Tennessee Valley Authority (TVA) spawned the dams and lakes which made engineering and ecological history in addition to delightful recreation areas. And across Tennessee rise some unusual cities—Memphis, Knoxville, Nashville, and Chattanooga.

Tennessee is a state with many rare sights and sites, an area that offers a great deal to a traveler on a budget. Its four major cities are each uniquely attractive. The state also presents a magnificent outdoor playground featuring the Smokies and picturesque, man-made lakes impounded by TVA dams. Interstate 81 comes into the state from the east at the twin cities of Bristol, straddling the Tennessee-Virginia line. This is one of the most popular gateways to the state.

Nearby is South Holston Lake, impounded by a TVA dam. At Johnson City are two more TVA dams and lakes, Boone and Fort Patrick Henry. On US 11E, near Limestone, is Davey Crockett Birthplace Park. Farther north, Tennessee shares the Cumberland Gap area with Kentucky and Virginia. Boone and frontier companions hacked the "Wilderness Trail" out of this mountainous country in 1775.

Knoxville

From the east, I–81 and I–40 take you into Knoxville, site of the gala 1982 World's Fair. Approach it from the west via I–40, from north or south via I–75. An industrial city with a rich historical background, it played a strategic role in the Civil War and today houses the University of Tennessee and TVA headquarters. Knoxville's earliest link to the past is the Blount Mansion, built for the territorial governor, William Blount. Several homes of early settlers are also open to visitors. The Confederate Memorial Hall is a large house of pre-Civil War times that was the headquarters for Confederate Gen. James Longstreet during the siege and battle of Knoxville. The 70-acre World's Fair site is now an attractive permanent recreation area welcoming visitors to the heart of the city.

Great Smoky Mountains

Before heading west from Knoxville, travelers should visit Oak Ridge, 15 miles west on Rte. 52. The activities in this town were probably the best-kept secret of World War II. It was here that much of the atom bomb was produced. Today there are guided tours, demonstrations, and exhibitions at the American Museum of Science and Energy, conducted by the U.S. Atomic Energy Commission.

From Knoxville, you can continue west on I–40 to Nashville or, better still, take I–75 southwest to Chattanooga, then I–24 northwest to Nashville. If you are a shun-piker you will find any number of interesting roads heading in the same direction and, at the same time you can visit places such as Athens (fishing and game hunting), Dayton (Scopes Trial of 1925), Lynchburg (distillery tours), Murfreesboro (Oaklands Mansion and Stones River National Battlefield, both Civil War memorials).

South of Knoxville, US 411 takes the traveler to Gatlinburg, an attractive town nestled amid the Smokies that serves as the major entrance to the park. Extensive virgin forests and masses of wildflowers cover the towering, brooding mountains. The park is a natural habitat for wild animals. Bears are plentiful, and frequently come to the roadside. Motorists are cautioned not to get out of their cars when these picturesque animals approach.

Three "don't miss" spots in the park are the observation points at Newfoundland Gap and Clingman's Dome—the views from both are impressive—and Cades Cove, a settlement in the western part of the park where life as it was in the early-settlers' days is depicted.

Gatlinburg is a bustling resort town full of neon, motels, restaurants, shops, and "shoppes." There is a sky lift here that carries sightseers up Crockett Mountain for good views of this Appalachian area. Some 150 motels and inns are spread about town, and campgrounds seem to thrive in every pocket of land in the area. Six miles north of Gatlinburg is Pigeon Forge, where the kiddies who are not impressed with mountains can ride a narrow-gauge railroad or visit Silver Dollar City.

Chattanooga

A city set in the midst of steep mountain ridges, Chattanooga grew from the spot where three Indian trails joined. In 1837, Cherokee Indians, being removed forcibly to lands west of the Mississippi, began here their "Trail of Tears." Three great battles of the Civil War were fought in the mountainous terrain nearby. The Chattanooga National Military Park, nine miles south and across the Georgia border, marks the bloody struggles of Chickamauga and Missionary Ridge. This is the oldest and largest military park in the country. The battle of Lookout Mountain, called the "Battle Above The Clouds," was fought on the slopes of this rocky, 1,700-foot bastion. Visitors may ride or hike to the top, or take the world's steepest incline railroad to Point Park, where there is a museum and observatory. Rock City Gardens, high up on the slopes, offers ten acres of flora and some amazing scenic views. Inside the mountain are Ruby Falls and the Lookout Mountain Caverns. And at the foot of the mountain is Confederama, with some 6,000 tiny figures depicting the battle fought here.

Nashville

Nashville has often been called the Athens of the South. Contributing factors are the city's Greek-style architecture, its many institutions of learning, and its churches and religious headquarters. These characteristics were not around in the early days. Nashville, the state capital, was originally settled in 1779 by James Robertson, and a group of pioneers who built Fort Nashborough on the west bank of the Cumberland River. That log stockade has now been reconstructed at First Avenue and Church Street. Thirteen miles east of the city, you can tour one of the nation's most beautiful historic houses, The Hermitage, home of President Andrew Jackson; six miles south of Nashville, off US 31, is Travellers' Rest, which Jackson and other early Americans visited.

By the 1830s, log construction in Nashville was being replaced by limestone and marble, and the buildings were taking on the classic Greek look. Near Centennial Park is a replica of the Parthenon, which stands atop the Acropolis of Athens. It is the only one of its kind in the world. The state capitol, completed in 1855, is another impressive example of this Greek influence.

There is nothing Grecian about the Grand Ole Opry, the longtime musical venture which has made Nashville the capital of country music. Ryman Auditorium, home of the Opry for many years, is now a museum. Performances now take place at the Grand Ole Opry House at Opryland U.S.A., 2800 Opryland Drive, about six miles northeast of the city. Every Friday and Saturday night the nation's oldest continuous radio show is presented here. Write or phone Grand Ole Opry, 2808 Opryland Drive, Nashville 37214—615-889-3060—for reservations and information. Order tickets well in advance, especially for summer performances. Opryland, itself, is a 120-acre theme park, emphasizing live musical productions and also featuring rides, games, shops, restaurants. For further information: 2802 Opryland Drive, Nashville 37214; 615-889-6611.

Memphis

I–40 takes you from Nashville to Memphis, largest city in the state. In Pee Wee's Saloon on Beale Street, W.C. Handy blew those first lonesome notes and became the "Father of the Blues." And, in a Memphis recording studio, the late Elvis Presley launched the career that made him "King of Rock 'n' Roll."

The Mississippi River sweeps past Memphis, presenting the opportunity for trips on the "Father Of Waters." Short cruises are available on the *Memphis Queen II, Memphis Queen III,* and the *Belle Carol.* The *Delta Queen,* a modernized, historic old paddlewheel steamer that cruises the Mississippi and Ohio Rivers, stops at Memphis, and longer trips on these two rivers can be made. Information can be obtained from Delta Queen Steamboat Co., 322 E. 4 St., Cincinnati, Ohio 45202.

Recently opened on Mud Island in the broad river is the impressive new Mississippi River Museum, a \$63-million, 50-acre complex dedicated to life on the Lower Mississippi.

PRACTICAL INFORMATION FOR TENNESSEE

HOW TO GET THERE. *By air:* Direct flights on several major airlines to Memphis, Nashville, Knoxville and Chattanooga. *By car:* Six interstate and several U.S. highways enter and criss-cross the state from Alabama, Arkansas, Georgia, Kentucky, and Mississippi. *By bus:* Good service provided by several lines. *By train:* Amtrak serves Memphis and Dyersburg on the route between Chicago and New Orleans.

TOURIST INFORMATION. Fourteen welcome centers are conveniently located on the interstate highways entering Tennessee. Information about major attractions, events, state parks may be obtained from the Tennessee Department of Tourist Development, P.O. Box 23170, Nashville 37202; about the Great Smokies from Park Superintendent, Great Smoky Mountains National Park, Gatlinburg 37738; about TVA recreational sites and activities from Tennessee Valley Authority, Knoxville 37902.

PARKS AND FORESTS. There are nine national projects—Great Smoky Mountains National Park; Cherokee National Forest; Stones River National Battlefield (Murfreesboro); three national military parks, Chickamauga-Chattanooga, Fort Donelson (Dover), Shiloh (Savannah); Natchez Trace Parkway (Nashville to Natchez, Miss.); Cumberland Gap National Historical Park (Harrogate); and Andrew Johnson National Historic Shrine (Greenville).

Tennessee offers some 44 state parks, among the country's finest. Accommodations range from modern motels to primitive campsites. For full information contact Tennessee Department of Tourist Development, P.O. Box 23170, Nashville 37202. Camping is also available in the TVA's Land Between the Lakes (Tennessee Valley Authority, Knoxville 37902) and the Cumberland Gap National Historical Park.

TOURS. *By car:* Drive through Reflection Riding, 300 acres in Chattanooga with historical details and nature trails. Battlefield tours near Chattanooga, Dover, and Savannah. *By bus: Gray Line* tours of Chattanooga, Great Smokies (from Gatlinburg, Knoxville), Memphis, Nashville. *By rail:* The Incline Railway, Lookout Mountain, Chattanooga. *By Boat:* Nashville, *Captain Ann;* Memphis, Mississippi River excursions on *Memphis Queen II, Memphis Queen III,* or *Belle Carol,* and river cruises on *Delta Queen; By ski lift:* Ski Lift, Crockett Mountain, Alpine Tramway, Gatlinburg. *Grand Ole Opry Sightseeing Tours* features varied tours of the area, some including a trip backstage at the Grand Ole Opry. Contact Opryland Information Center, 2802 Opryland Dr., Nashville 37214; 614–889–6611.

MUSEUMS AND GALLERIES. Nashville: *Tennessee State Museum,* 5th and Deaderick; *Cumberland Museum and Science Center,* 800 Ridley Ave.; *The Upper Room,* 1908 Grand Ave.; *Country Music Hall of Fame and Museum,* 4 Music Square, East (The Museum is located at the end of "Music Row," a street that is a center of America's music publishing business.); The Parthenon, Centennial Park. Memphis: *Magevney House,* 198 Adams Ave.; *Brooks Memorial Art Gallery: Chucalissa Indian Village and Museum.* Chattanooga: Confederama, foot of Lookout Mountain; *Hunter Museum of Art: Cravens House,* on Lookout Mountain; *Chattanooga Choo Choo and Terminal Station,* 1400 Market St.; *National Knife Museum,* 7201 Shallowford Rd. Knoxville: *Dulin Gallery of Art,* 3100 Kingston Pike; Harrogate: *Lincoln Museum,* campus of Lincoln Memorial University.

MUSIC. Memphis is the home of the blues; Nashville the home of country music's "Nashville Sound." *Music Village U.S.A.* (Music Village Blvd., P.O. Box 819, Hendersonville 37075; 615–822–1800) is an entertainment complex, showcasing country music stars. Though not yet fully completed, visitors can already see top country entertainers perform.

SPORTS. With more than 600,000 acres of water and 10,000 miles of shoreline, the state offers limitless opportunities for fishing, boating, and water-skiing. Hunting, horseback riding, and golf are also popular sports. Hiking and back-packing in the mountains are superb. Skiing at Ober Gatlinburg Ski area.

SPECTATOR SPORTS. The Liberty Bowl football game in Memphis. College football at Knoxville (University of Tennessee) and Nashville (Vanderbilt), Danny Thomas Memphis Classic Golf Tournament. NASCAR stock car racing, Tennessee State Fairgrounds, Nashville, April to October.

LIQUOR. Package, 8 A.M. to 11 P.M. and by the drink at licensed establishments. No Sunday sales or on most holidays. Nashville, Memphis, Knoxville, Chattanooga, Clarksville, and Oak Ridge are among the cities permitting liquor by the drink. Legal age 19.

HOTELS AND MOTELS. Prices based on double occupancy in peak season, in these categories: *Moderate:* $35 –45; *Inexpensive:* under $35.

ATHENS. *Moderate:* **Best Western Snuffy's.** 2620 Decatur Pk. **Holiday Inn** (formerly Sheraton). I–75 & Mt. Verd Rd.

BRISTOL. *Moderate:* **Holiday Inn South.** 536 Volunteer Pkwy. S. (US 11E–19).

Inexpensive: **Econo-Travel Motel.** 912 Commonwealth Ave.
Siesta Motel. 1970 Lee Hwy.
Shamrock Motel. Lee Hwy., 6 ½ mi. NE on US 11, ¼ mi. N of I–81 Exit 5.
(Last 3 are in Virginia half of city.)

CHATTANOOGA. *Inexpensive:* **Days Inn.** 1401 Mack Smith Rd.
Holiday Motel. 5011 Dayton Blvd.
Chanticleer Lodge. 1300 Mockingbird Lane, Lookout Mountain, TN.

COOKEVILLE. *Inexpensive:* **Days Inn.** I–40 & TN 111.
Eastwood Inn. 1646 E. Spring St.

GATLINBURG. *Moderate:* **Creekside Motel.** Willow & Sycamore Lanes.
Circle K Motel. Baskins Creek Rd.
Gatlinburg Econo Lodge. 167 Parkway (US 441).
Inexpensive: **L Ranch Motel.** TN 73, Rt. 1, Cosby, TN.

GREENEVILLE. *Inexpensive:* **Star Motel.** Hwy. 11 E Bypass.

JACKSON. *Moderate.* **Quality Inn.** I–75 & US 25 W.
Thunderbird Motel (Friendship INN). US 45 S.

KNOXVILLE. *Moderate:* **Best Western of Knoxville.** I–75 & Merchant's Rd.
Inexpensive: **Days Inn/Concord.** I–75-I–40 & Lovell Rd.
Red Roof Inn. 5640 Merchants Center Blvd.

MEMPHIS. *Moderate:* **Admiral Benbow Inn.** 4720 Summer Ave.
Best Western Lakeland. I–40 E.
Best Western Riverbluff Inn. 340 W. Illinois St. Overlooks Mississippi River.
Inexpensive: **Days Inn.** 3 locations: I–55 & Brooks Rd., I–240/I–40 & 5301 Summer Ave., I–55 & E. Shelby Dr. exit, 1970 E. Shelby Dr.

MURFREESBORO. *Moderate:* **Best Western Wayside Inn.** I–24 & US 231.
Inexpensive: **Days Inn.** 2036 S. Church St. **Motel 6,** 114 Chaffin Place.

NASHVILLE. *Moderate:* **Madison Square Motel.** 118 Emmitt Ave.
La Quinta. 2001 Metro Center Blvd.
Quality Inn Bell Road. I–24 & Bell Rd.
Inexpensive: **Days Inn.** 4 locations: I–65 & Trinity La.; Old Hickory Blvd. at I–40, Hermitage, TN; 1101 Bell Rd., Antioch, TN. I–24 & Murfreesboro Rd. **Motel 6.** 95 Wallace Rd.

RESTAURANTS. Price ranges: *Moderate:* $10–15; *Inexpensive:* under $10. Prices are for a complete dinner but do not include drinks, tax or tip.

CHATTANOOGA. *Moderate:* **Chattanooga Choo Choo Restaurant.** Terminal Station, 1400 Market St.: **Town and Country,** 110 N. Market St.
Inexpensive: **Fehn's.** 600 River St.; **Gula's,** 1516 McCallie Ave.; **Magic Seasons Family Restaurant.** 1305 Patten Rd.

GATLINBURG. *Moderate:* **Ogle's Buffet Restaurant,** Crossroads Mall, US 441; **Pioneer Inn,** 373 N. Pkwy.

KNOXVILLE. *Moderate:* **Arthur's,** 4661 N. Broadway; **Copper Cellar & Cappuccino's,** 7316 Kingston Pike; **Regas Restaurant & The Gathering Place,** 318 Gay St.; **Steak & Ale (formerly Jolly Ox),** 8314 Kingston Pike.

Inexpensive: **Morrison's,** Kingston Pike; **Ramsey's,** 16th & White Ave.; **S & S,** 4808 Kingston Pike. All are cafeterias.

MEMPHIS. *Moderate:* **Doebler's Dock,** 110 Wagner; **Four Flames,** 1085 Poplar Ave.; **Jim's Place East,** 5560 Shelby Oaks Dr.; **Joy Young,** 861 White Station Rd.

Inexpensive: **Britling's** and **Morrisons** Cafeterias. Several locations throughout city.

MONTEAGLE. *Inexpensive.* **Jim Oliver's Smoke House Restaurant.** Sewanee Rd. (just off I-24, Exit 134). Fabulous barbecue, fried chicken, country ham, steaks, ribs, catfish, and much more in attractive rustic setting. Adjacent trading post has specialty, handcraft, antique shops.

NASHVILLE. *Moderate:* **Brass Rail Stables,** 206 ½ Printers Alley; **Praline's,** Maxwell House Hotel, MetroCenter Blvd.; **Silver Wings,** Hilton Airport Inn, 1 International Plaza; **Sperry's,** 5109 Harding Rd.

Inexpensive: **B & W** Green Hills, Village Dr.; **Morrison's,** 3 locations: One Hundred Oaks Shopping Center, Rivergate Mall, Hickory Hollow Mall. **Po Folks.** 3737 Nolensville Rd.

ILLINOIS

Surprising Colossus of the Midwest

A visit to Illinois should begin with Chicago, the nation's second largest city. Just mention that destination and some people still raise their eyebrows while visions of Elliot Ness, Al Capone and Bugs Moran in big black Packards race through their imagination. That happened about 40 years ago, and though that side of the city may resurface occasionally, Chicago is a whole new scene.

After years of standing shyly on the sidelines nursing a Second City complex, Chicago has emerged as a glamorous, sophisticated Cinderella. Visitors are discovering what locals have always known—that Chicago is special, with a vibrant, friendly personality all its own. And, wonder of wonders, beside a great wealth of attractions and excellent hotels and restaurants, its buses run, its garbage is collected and the nitty gritty of daily life continues to function.

Many cities have allowed their waterfronts to become an unappealing clutter of piers, shabby warehouses, and dockyards. Fortunately Chicago had the good sense to prevent this and develop its lake frontage. Yacht harbors, sand beaches, and beautiful parks stretch along the city's world-famed shoreline, creating an eye-opening backdrop for the tall buildings of its dramatic, ever changing skyline. The lakefront extends north of the central area along the city's Gold Coast and past affluent suburbs. It extends south to a vast complex of steel mills, oil refineries and diversified industrial plants. Chicago is the only inland city with combined lake, river and ocean traffic. Freighters from all over the world, plying the St. Lawrence Seaway, meet Great Lakes carriers, river barges and other vessels from the Mississippi and other rivers and canals of the Inland Waterway.

Chicago continues to experience a building boom with skyscrapers reaching above the lower cloud levels. Sears Tower at the southwest edge of the Loop is the world's tallest building. It rises 109 stories to a height of 1,468½ feet, occupies a full city block of about 129,000 square feet, houses nearly 17,000 employees, and has a power capacity equal to the requirements of Rockford, the state's second largest city. It is the first building to use a modular construction system. It has an observation level 1,350 feet above ground level. Sears Tower is 100 feet higher than the New York World Trade Center, and nearly 325 feet higher than Chicago's John Hancock Center.

Hancock Center, known locally as Big John, at 875 N. Michigan Avenue, is the world's fifth tallest building and the world's largest combined office and apartment building. It has 100 stores and reaches 1,100 feet above ground level. The first 34 floors accommodate offices and parking space. Above these are 750 apartments on 49 floors, beginning with the 44th. An observation area facing all four directions is just below a restaurant on the 95th floor.

Another new skyscraper is the Standard Oil Building at 200 E. Randolph. It has 80 stories and a height of 1,136 feet, making it the world's fourth tallest building.

Breathing space has been provided by landscaped plazas built in connection with many of the giant buildings. The plaza at the Civic Center in the Loop is a popular strolling and resting place in the heart of the inner city. The plaza is dominated by a huge steel Picasso sculpture, which has caused much controversy and frequently gives rise to the question, "What is it?" Only Picasso knew for sure whether it was anything but a giant spoof, and he carried the secret to his grave.

The Loop is an area bounded by Wabash Avenue on the east, Wells Street on the west, and Van Buren and Lake Streets on the south and north, and so named because it is "looped" by elevated tracks.

Chicago is in the process of an explosion in imaginative building taking place on air rights over 83 acres of land between Randolph Drive and the Chicago River, Michigan Avenue and Lake Michigan. The Prudential Building, the Standard Oil Building, Hyatt Regency Hotel and other buildings already have been erected. So Chicago continues in its century-long tradition as an innovator in architecture. In fact, Chicago can best be described as an enormous outdoor museum of architectural standouts dating back to 1893, when the "Chicago School" of architecture started creating revolutionary new concepts in building. Chicago is noted for its excellent museums covering history, science, and art of many cultures and a wide range of periods and styles. A generous listing is provided under the heading "Museums and Galleries" in the Practical Information section.

PRACTICAL INFORMATION FOR CHICAGO

HOW TO GET AROUND. *By bus:* Chicago has an extensive bus system that will take you long distances for a modest fee. For 10¢ extra you can get a transfer that allows you to spend an hour shopping or sightseeing before you ride back. Get a map of the system from the *Chicago Convention and Tourism Bureau,* McCormick Place on the Lake, Chicago 60616; write ahead for one, or pick one up from the Visitor Information Center in the old Water Tower. CTA Culture Bus operates every Sunday and holidays mid-April through September on 3 routes departing the Art Institute for over 30 museums and cultural attractions, 11 A.M. to 5 P.M.

By subway: Subway maps are also available from the Chicago Tourism Bureau, and the same fare structure applies. If you need information on public transportation, call C.T.A. 24-hour Information at 312–836–7000.

From the airports: O'Hare Airport, at Mannheim and Kennedy Expressways, is the world's busiest airport. *Continental Air Transport* will take you to downtown Chicago. The stops for the limousine are listed by hotels, so just get out at the hotel nearest your destination. A rapid transit train under construction at press time should be completed in 1984, offering direct service to Chicago.

By car: If you must travel by car in the city, get a good road map and be wary of parking regulations; they are strictly enforced.

TOURIST INFORMATION. Contact the *Chicago Convention and Tourism Bureau,* McCormick Place on the Lake, Chicago 60616, 312–225–5000. New Chicago *Visitor Information Center* is in historic Water Tower. State Division of Tourism has walk-in information center at 208 N. Michigan Ave. and the Conservation Dept. at 160 N. LaSalle St. Visitor Eventline offers 24-hour phone information on activities (tel. 225–2323). Chicago Assoc. of Commerce & Industry has Visitors Center at 130 S. Michigan Ave. *International Visitors Center* is at 116 S. Michigan Ave. (332–5875). In a language emergency call 332–1460. *HOT TIX* half-price ticket booth sells day-of-performance tickets at Daley Center downtown. Call hotline after 11A.M. weekdays, 10 A.M. Sat, 977–1755.

SEASONAL EVENTS. *January* brings the Boat, Travel and Outdoor Show, and March a grand and glorious St. Patrick's Day parade come rain, sleet or snow. They put dye in the Chicago River to turn it green for the day. *May* illuminates Buckingham Fountain in Grant Park with a nightly show of various colored water designs and a colorful circus wagon parade. A Taste of Chicago is a taste sampler's July 4th holiday favorite. Chicagofest is a week-long celebration every *August,* climaxed by a Venetian Nights Water Parade. *Summer* through *mid-September,* for 40 summers now, the Ravinia Festival presents a varied musical program at Highland Park. *October* brings an Autumn Fair at Navy Pier, focusing attention on dress and customs of our ancestors in their native lands. Santa Claus arrives for the State Street parade, generally Thanksgiving weekend. And for *Christmas* there is a Flower Show at the Garfield and Lincoln Park Conservatories.

MUSEUMS AND GALLERIES. The *Field Museum of Natural History,* in Grant Park at 12th St., is the world's largest museum of natural-history exhibits. It has a dazzling collection of precious and semiprecious stones. Trace the history of man through exhibits.

The *Oriental Institute* at the University of Chicago has exhibits dating back to 3000 B.C. Closed Mon. Free. Artifacts from Egypt, Mesopotamia, Syria, Palestine.

Art Institute of Chicago is truly one of the great art museums of the world. Noted for its Impressionist collections, Thorne miniature rooms, garden restaurant, Children's Museum. Free Thursday.

Adler Planetarium, near the Field Museum, is a great observatory on the lakefront and offers a dramatic view of the city's skyline.

John G. Shedd Aquarium, across Lake Shore Drive from the Field Museum, contains an impressive collection of freshwater and sea creatures. Facilities for handicapped. Daily.

Chicago Historical Society, in Lincoln Park at Clark St. and North Ave., has everything to acquaint you with Chicago's history. Particular emphasis is placed on Abraham Lincoln, Illinois pioneer life and the Chicago Fire.

Chicago Academy of Sciences, 2001 N. Clark St., is well worth a visit. Daily.

Museum of Science and Industry, in Jackson Park, is a magnet that attracts kids and senior citizens alike with its 14 acres of exhibits in engineering, industrial and medical progress. Tour a simulated operating coal mine, a Nazi submarine, an antique car display, Main Street of Yesterday. A must for all ages. You can spend days here.

Museum of Contemporary Art, 237 E. Ontario St., may give you a different viewpoint on modern art.

Ukrainian Institute of Modern Art, 2320 W. Chicago Ave., has special showings by appointment. Closed Mon. and Wed. Free.

Polish Museum of America, 984 N. Milwaukee Ave., has notable stained glass, Polish and American art, sculptures. Daily 1–4. Free.

Balzekas Museum of Lithuanian Culture, 4012 S. Archer Ave., has the largest amber and armor collections. Daily 1–4:30.

DuSable Museum of African-American History, 740 E. 56th Pl., has rotating exhibits and documents pertaining to the history of Black Americans.

Ripley's Believe It or Not Museum, 1500 N. Wells St., shows fabulous exhibits or oddities collected by Robert L. Ripley during his foreign travels. Daily.

USS Silversides, behind the Naval Armory at Randolph St., is city's first floating museum. Open spring into winter. Restored WWII submarine.

HISTORIC SITES. The picturesque *Water Tower* at Michigan and Chicago Avenues is one of the few buildings on the Near North Side that was not destroyed by the great Chicago fire of 1871, which made ruins of a large part of the city, including the central business district.

The Auditorium Theatre (1889) is one of the city's restoration jewels.

The *Pullman Community,* near 111th St. and Cottage Grove Ave., is a quaint reminder of the paternalistic outlook of the railway-sleeping-car inventor.

The lobby of *The Rookery,* 209 S. La Salle St., was designed by Frank Lloyd Wright in 1905. The building is the oldest remaining steel-skeleton skyscraper in the world. Chicago has 14 homes designed by Wright, including *Robie House,* 5757 S. Woodlawn. Suburban Oak Park has over 2 dozen more, with guided tours of home and studio where he lived and worked for 20 years.

Old Town, running from 1200 to 1700 north on Wells St., includes some of Chicago's finest restored Victorian residences. It is a cosmopolitan area colored with distinctive shops, restaurants and pubs. The entrance to the famous 19th-century Piper's Alley at 1608 is marked by a large Tiffany lamp.

Prairie Ave. Historic District, former "Millionaires' Row," now undergoing restoration. Glessner House there is a 35-room Romanesque mansion.

TOURS. Chicago and nearby areas of interest are covered in tours offered by *Chicago Gray Line,* 400 N. Wabash Ave., and *American Sightseeing Tours,* 33 E. Monroe. They offer various specialized tours such as tours for women, nightclubs, the plush suburbs, after-dark, and Chinatown.

There are boating tours on Lake Michigan by the *Mercury Scenicruiser,* and *Wendella Streamliner.* All offer views of the photogenic shoreline and skyline, and leave from the Michigan Avenue Bridge and pass through locks at the mouth of the Chicago River into the lake. New 400-passenger *Star of Chicago* cruises city's scenic shoreline for lunch and dinner, offering varied entertainment.

 GARDENS. *Garfield Park Conservatory.* 300 N. Central Park Ave., offers exceptional flower shows and is considered largest in world under one roof. *Lincoln Park Conservatory* is well worth a visit. Both are open daily 9–5 and free. *Morton Arboretum,* 25 miles west of Chicago Loop on State 53 near the east-west tollway, offers an escape to the tranquil life. It's a nature lover's paradise with 4,800 species of living plants and trees. The conservatory has a plant clinic, lectures and field trips. Spring garden walks are offered by many North Shore and city residential communities. Inquire locally. New *Botanical Gardens* north of Skokie Lagoons near Glencoe is worth the trip. *Shakespeare Gardens* on Northwestern University's Evanston campus is planted with flowers Shakespeare wrote about in his plays.

 SPECTATOR SPORTS. *Baseball.* Chicago Cubs play at Wrigley Field on the North Side, Chicago White Sox at White Sox Park on the South Side. *Basketball.* Chicago Bulls play at Chicago Stadium, which also is host to many college games and tournaments. Loyola, De Paul and Northwestern usually field strong, exciting teams. *Football.* Chicago Bears now play at Soldiers Field in fall and winter, Chicago Blitz in spring and summer. Northwestern plays Big Ten and other teams at Dyche Stadium in Evanston. *Hockey.* Chicago Black Hawks play at Chicago Stadium. Chicago Sting soccer team, plays at Soldier's Field.

Horse racing. Flat racing at Arlington Park and Hawthorne. Harness racing, mostly nights, at Sportsman's Park, and Maywood Park.

Tournaments. Western Open Golf Tournament is held in early summer. Sailors hope for a breeze the third weekend in July for Chicago-to-Mackinac boat race. College All-Star vs. Super Bowl Champion football game held late July or early August in Soldiers Field. Norge Ski Jump at Fox River Grove has tournament in January. Polo matches at the Chicago Armory and at Oak Brook.

 WHAT TO DO WITH THE CHILDREN. *Colleen Moore's Doll House,* model trains, baby chicks, etc., get smallfrys' attention at the Museum of Science and Industry. Every child should see the *Adler Planetarium, Shedd Aquarium* and *Field Museum of Natural History,* all near Soldiers Field. *Lincoln Park Zoo* has a small operating farm. Both Lincoln Park and the *Brookfield Zoo* have children's zoos'. Marriott's *Great America* north at Gurnee is the state's biggest new attraction. *Art Institute* has a *Junior Museum.*

 HOTELS AND MOTELS in the Chicago area range from inexpensive to deluxe, with some surprising budget finds. We have listed establishments in the downtown area, some well-known ones away from the central business district, and selected motels and hotels in the nearby suburbs.

The price categories in this section, for double occupancy, will average: *Moderate* $55–85, *Inexpensive* under $55.

Moderate: **Allerton.** 701 N. Michigan Ave. Conveniently located. Very posh area.

Bismarck. 171 W. Randolph St. Garage, entertainment. Near Civic Center.

Windemere House. 1642 E. 56th St. Across from Museum of Science and Industry.

Chicago Motor Inn. 601 W. Diversey. Close to Lincoln Park.

La Salle Motor Lodge. 720 N. La Salle. Park next to your room.

Ohio House. La Salle & Ohio Sts. Near Merchandise Mart. 2-story motel, at-door parking, near heart of city, free courtesy car to Loop.

O'HARE AIRPORT AREA. *Moderate:* **Holiday Inn.** Four locations: 3801 N. Mannheim Rd.; 1900 N. Mannheim Rd.; Touhy Ave. & Mannheim Rd; 1000 Busse Hwy., Elk Grove Village.

Rodeway Inn O'Hare, 5615 N. Cumberland. Convenient, free parking.
TraveLodge. Mannheim Rd. N of Higgins Rd. Comfortable.

EVANSTON. *Moderate:* **Orrington.** 1710 Orrington Ave. By Northwestern.
Inexpensive. **Bed & Breakfast/Chicago.** 1316 Judson Ave. (312) 328–1321. $25–75 double with breakfast. Some hosts multilingual. Contact for information on 70 different locations in homes and apartments in Evanston, Chicago.

LAKE FOREST. *Moderate:* **Deerpath Inn.** 255 E. Illinois Rd. Quaint inn.

OAK PARK. *Moderate:* **Carleton Hotel and Motor Inn.** 1110 Pleasant St. Near business area.

 DINING OUT in Chicago can be exotic and memorable, expensive or inexpensive, depending on your taste and your purse. There are many great steakhouses. Restaurants are listed by type of cuisine.

Price categories are as follows: *Moderate* $13–20, *Inexpensive* $8–12. These prices are for hors d'oeuvres or soup, entree and dessert. Not included are drinks, tax and tips.

American-International. Moderate: **Carson's Grill.** (Carson Pirie Scott & Co.) 36 S. Wabash. Good Value.
Cafe Bohemia. 138 S. Clinton St. Wild game from buffalo to bear.
Chicago Claim Company. 2314 N. Clark. Old West goldmining decor.
Ireland's. 500 N. LaSalle St. Seafood favorite.
Miller's On Kinzie. 33 W. Kinzie. Terrific vintage atmosphere.
Sally's Stage. 6335 N. Western. Conversation stopper. Waitresses on roller skates, mechanical bull for kids, games, contests.
Inexpensive: **R.J. Grunts.** 2056 N. Lincoln Park West. Lively menu, fun atmosphere.
D.B. Kaplan's Delicatessen. 7th floor. Water Tower Place. Sandwiches, endless ice cream.
Lawrence of Oregano. 662 W. Diversey. Hearty portions; strawberry pie.

Chinese. Moderate: **Chiam.** 2323 S. Wentworth. Exotic Oriental atmosphere.
Lee's Canton Cafe. 2300 S. Wentworth Ave., Chinatown. Good.

French. Moderate: **Jacques Garden.** 900 N. Michigan Ave. Parisienne garden atmosphere with fountain and flowers.

German. Inexpensive: **Berghoff.** 17 W. Adams. Gemutlichkeit setting, exceptional German food. Since 1898. A bit of old Heidelberg.
Brown Bear. 6318 N. Clark St. Good, pleasant. Lots of atmosphere.
Golden Ox. 1578 N. Clybourn. Munich mood. Zither music.
Greek. Inexpensive: **Parthenon.** 314 S. Halsted St. Lamb is special.

Italian. Moderate: **Agostino's.** 7 E. Delaware Pl. Fine food.
Como Inn. 546 N. Milwaukee. Mediterranean personality. A fun place.

EXPLORING ILLINOIS

To begin a tour of the state from the Chicago metropolitan area, start north on US 12 to the 960-acre Chain O'Lakes State Park, the largest

Points of Interest

1) Adler Planetarium
2) Art Institute and Goodman Theater
3) Auditorium Theater
4) Blackstone Theater
5) Buckingham Fountain
6) Chicago Civic Center (Richard J. Daley Center)
7) Chicago Theater
8) City Hall
9) Civic Opera House
10) Sears Tower
11) De Paul University (Downtown Campus)
12) Field Museum
13) Fort Dearborn original site
14) John Hancock Center
15) Lakefront Tower
16) Water Tower Place
17) Chagall Mosaic (First National Plaza)
18) Tribune Tower
19) Orchestra Hall
20) Roosevelt University
21) Shedd Aquarium
22) Shubert Theater
23) Soldier Field
24) Northwestern University
25) University of Illinois

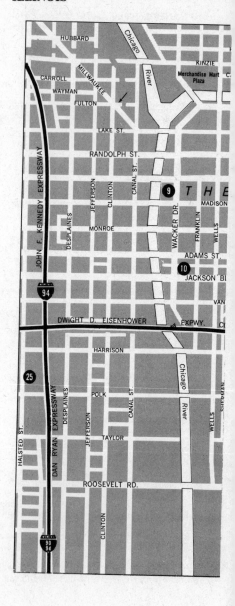

CHICAGO
DOWNTOWN

single concentration of lakes in the state, offering boating and fishing—even fishing through the ice in winter.

West to Galena, the town that time forgot, once a bustling city whose lead and zinc deposits made the future seem limitless in the 1820s when a cluster of cabins was all Chicago could boast of. It climbed to a population of 15,000 by 1860 but now counts only about 4,000 residents. Much of the town was built on the bluffs, and most of the early buildings are still in use. This remarkably preserved slice of history is definitely worth a detour. A hilly, rolling landscape enhances its architectural treasures.

Ulysses S. Grant lived briefly in Galena, tending his father's harness and leather store, before leaving to lead the North to victory in the Civil War. His career as Commanding General of the Army, Secretary of War, and President gave him and his family little time to occupy the home local citizens presented him after the war. His son eventually deeded it to the state, which restored it and made it a state memorial in 1955.

The next stop is Rock Island, one of the Quad Cities—along with Moline, East Moline, and Davenport, Iowa—which constitute a busy commercial and industrial center on the Mississippi. Here you can tour Arsenal Island, a Civil War ordnance depot and prisoner-of-war camp, now housing (at Rock Island Arsenal) much of the nation's present small-arms stock. There is a replica of the blockhouse at Ft. Armstrong.

Inland to the east are Tampico and Dixon, the typically Midwest towns where President Ronald Reagan was born and grew up. His second floor birthplace, at 111 Main St., Tampico, is undergoing restoration. There is a museum on the first floor and a "Reagan Country" gift shop selling souvenirs. Nearby Dixon's Chamber of Commerce at 74 Galena Ave. directs visitors past his former home at 816 S. Henepin and the park where he was a lifeguard. Melick Library at Eureka College in Eureka (between Bloomington and Peoria), where he attended college, has an 800-piece memorabilia collection chronicling his Illinois career and motion picture achievements.

Along the Mississippi, here and there winding its way into Iowa, runs a string of highways called the Great River Road. It passes through Nauvoo, one of the state's great historic sites. Joseph Smith led the main body of the Church of Jesus Christ of Latter Day Saints (Mormons) from Missouri to this point in 1839 and established it as the church's capital. In a few short years they had built a busy and prosperous community of 20,000, the largest in Illinois. But fear and suspicion of Mormonism was deep-seated in the countryside, and when Joseph Smith and his brother Hyrum were taken into "protective custody" in the Hancock County jail at Carthage in 1844, a lynch mob took them from the jail and killed them. Two years later Brigham Young led the Mormon community from Nauvoo on the long overland trip that led to the Utah Territory and Salt Lake City.

Three years later Etienne Cabet, a French lawyer and political figure with Utopian dreams, established a community of French and German followers known as Icarians in Nauvoo. Although Cabet's dream of a Utopian community withered and died, the grape vines that his followers planted flourished, and do to this day, with a symbolic "Wedding of the Wine and Cheese" festival being held every Labor Day weekend.

The Land of Lincoln

Even more than Kentucky, where he was born in a log cabin, and Indiana, where he grew to manhood, Illinois claims Lincoln as its own. Aside from the centers of population and the usual reasons of business, education, culture and spectator sports that attract masses of people, the Lincoln story is the great key to Illinois as a tourist state. Almost every locale throughout central Illinois boasts some Lincoln association.

The story begins on the west bank of the Wabash River across from Vincennes, Indiana, where young Abe's family entered the state on their way toward a farm site near Decatur, now the Lincoln Homestead State Park. And south of Charleston is the Lincoln Log Cabin State Park, graced by a reproduction of a two-room cabin Lincoln's parents built the year he left home to make his own way in the world.

The village of New Salem, now Lincoln's New Salem State Park, knew Lincoln as the gangly young man who arrived in 1831, his sole possessions the clothing he wore. Here he tended a store and the post office, studied surveying and law, and in 1837 was elected to the legislature, then moved to Springfield to establish himself as a lawyer.

Springfield is the heart of the land of Lincoln. Here he married and practiced law, except for the two years he spent in Congress. Many old buildings still stand, among them the Lincoln home, the building where he had his law office, the impressive restored Old State Capitol fronted by a mall, and others, including an old railroad station that recalls his moving farewell to neighbors and friends as he left for the national capital for the last time. His tomb in the Oak Ridge Cemetery is open to the public, for Lincoln does, indeed, "belong to the ages," as his Secretary of War, Stanton, said in the epitaph you will find there.

PRACTICAL INFORMATION FOR ILLINOIS

HOW TO GET THERE. *By car:* I–80, in the northern part of Illinois, and I–70, in the south, are the major east-west highways. I–90 and I–94, north of Chicago, and I–57, south of Chicago, are the major north-south highways into Illinois. *By train:* Amtrak serves Chicago from major cities throughout the United States and connections from Canadian rail systems. Check for schedules and costs with your travel agent or nearest Amtrak passenger station.

By air: Chicago's O'Hare airport is served by numerous major airlines including *Northwest, United, American, Delta, Trans World, Continental Jet America, Capitol, Piedmont, US Air, Midway, Ozark, Republic,* and *Eastern.* Local ("trunk") airlines flying to Chicago are: *Air Illinois, Mississippi Valley, Simmons, Midstate.*

By bus: Greyhound, Trailways, and many other bus lines serve Illinois. Consult a travel agent or the carriers directly: *Greyhound* at 74 W. Randolph, *Trailways* at 20 E. Randolph, Chicago.

TOURIST INFORMATION. The *Office of Tourism,* Department of Commerce and Community Affairs, 222 S. College St., Springfield 62706, can be helpful. They also have offices at 2209 West Main St., Marion, and at the walk-in *Illinois Adventure Center,* 208 N. Michigan, Chicago. Dept. of Conservation has one at 160 N. LaSalle St., Chicago, as well as their main office at 655 State Office Bldg., Springfield. The Chicago Association of Commerce & Industry welcomes tourists to its *Visitors Bureau* at 130 S. Michigan. The Tourism Council of Greater Chicago has a *Visitors Information Center* in the historic Water Tower.

MUSEUMS AND GALLERIES. The Rock Island Arsenal houses the *John Browning Memorial Museum of Firearms,* including those developed by Browning. Wed. –Sun. 11–4, free. The *William Jennings Bryan Museum* in Salem was the birthplace of the golden-voiced orator. Daily except Thurs., 11–4, free. *G.A.R. Memorial Museum,* 629 S. 7th St., *Illinois State Museum of Natural History and Art* and the *Illinois State Historical Library* in the Old State House are among the many interesting museums in Springfield.

HISTORIC SITES. In Cahokia the state's first courthouse is a *State Memorial.* Daily 9–5, free. Cahokia also has some of the state's most important Indian mounds. In Carthage the *Old Jail* is a sober reminder of the lynching of two Mormon leaders, leading to the Mormon trek to Utah. In nearby Nauvoo, many buildings have been restored. The Mormon story is shown in pictures and lectures at a new Visitors Center. Free guide service. Galena has many buildings of historical interest, including the *Ulysses S. Grant* home, built by grateful citizens. *Carl Sandburg's* home is a Galesburg landmark, and Springfield has a wealth of Lincoln landmarks, including his home, law office, restored State Capitol where he gave his "house divided" speech, tomb, and nearby New Salem State Park. *Magnolia Manor* is a Cairo mansion, Springfield has *Vachel Lindsay's* home, *John Deere's* restored blacksmith shop and house are in Grand Detour, *Edgar Lee Masters'* boyhood residence still stands in Petersburg.

DRINKING LAWS. Liquor can be purchased at any privately owned liquor store weekdays during regular business hours. Restaurants, bars and nightclubs have different closing hours depending on the license they hold. Minimum age is 21.

SPECTATOR SPORTS. *Basketball.* Bradley University and the University of Illinois vie with Southern Illinois University at Carbondale and Northern Illinois University at DeKalb. *Football.* Northwestern University, the University of Illinois, Southern Illinois University and Northern Illinois University offer first-class teams. Saturdays, Sept.–Nov.

Horse racing. Thoroughbred racing at Cahokia Downs near East St. Louis and Fairmount Park in Collinsville. Harness racing at Springfield State Fair and many county fairs. *Tournaments.* State basketball tournament, the Sweet Sixteen, in March at Champaign–Urbana.

WHAT TO DO WITH THE CHILDREN. *Santa's Village* near Dundee is a popular spot for the kids. *Quinsippi Island,* in the Mississippi River at Quincy, has a small-gauge steam-train ride to the 130-acre recreation park. An excursion boat and cable car are in operation. Marriott's *Great America* at Gurnee is the state's biggest new attraction for families.

HOTELS AND MOTELS outside the Chicago metropolitan area cover a broad price range. Economy-minded chains are building low-cost motels along the interstates and other principal routes especially for the traveler who is not interested in extras. The price categories in this section, for double occupancy, will average: *Moderate* $35–50, *Inexpensive* under $35.

CHAMPAIGN–URBANA. *Moderate:* **Lincoln Lodge Motel.** Next to a park. *Inexpensive:* **Regal 8 and Motel 6.** Both offer bargain rates.

DIXON. *Moderate:* **Chalet.** A bargain in President Reagan's hometown.

GALENA. *Inexpensive:* **Grant Hills Motel.** Picnic tables and grill.

LA SALLE. *Moderate:* **Starved Rock Lodge.** Woodsy, rustic setting. Recently refurbished to accommodate handicapped.

OREGON. *Inexpensive:* **White Pines Lodge.** Old-style log cabins, picnic facilities. Surrounded by beauty of White Pines Forest State Park.

PETERSBURG. *Inexpensive:* **New Salem Lodge.** Attractive. Closed winters. Across from New Salem State Park. Rustic, frontier flavor.

SPRINGFIELD. *Moderate:* **Mansion View Lodge.** Across from Governor's mansion.
Inexpensive: **Days Inn, Regal 8** and **Motel 6** all offer good dollar value.

DINING OUT reflects the state's fertile land bordered by fish-filled waters and a German and Central European influence in the northern part of the state. Establishments are categorized according to the cost of a full-course dinner from the medium-price range of their menus: *Moderate* $9–14, *Inexpensive* $6–9. Included are hors d'oeuvres or soup, entree and dessert; not included are drinks, tax and tips.

BLOOMINGTON. *Moderate:* **Central Station Restaurant.** New look for old firehouse.

CHAMPAIGN. *Moderate:* **The Round Barn.** Actually a restored barn.

GALENA. *Moderate:* **Stillman Manor Inn.** 1858 Victorian mansion.

GURNEE. *Moderate:* **Rustic Manor.** Rambling log restaurant built around re-created mill, appealing frontier décor. Near Marriott's Great America.

LINCOLN. *Moderate:* **Heritage Inn.** Delightful, Early American setting. **Lincoln Depot.** In original train depot. Terrific soup and salad bar.

MOLINE. *Moderate:* **Boar's Head.** Red snapper, beef. Old English mood.

PETERSBURG. *Moderate:* **New Salem Inn,** State Park. Home-baked treats. Waitresses in Ann Rutledge costume. Marvelous Lincoln-era atmosphere.

QUINCY. *Moderate:* **Stipp's.** Fresh fish, barbecued ribs. Try the catfish.

ROCKFORD. *Inexpensive:* **Bishop Buffet.** Cafeteria. Delicious desserts. Colonial character.

SPRINGFIELD. *Moderate:* **Clayville Country Kitchen Restaurant.** At old stagestop. Early pioneer recipes.
Inexpensive: **Heritage House Smorgasbord.** 4 mi. S on Rt. 66. A full plate of midwest favorites. Good for hungry families.

WHEELING. *Moderate:* **94th Aero Squadron.** Decor is an unusual one, including old plane and ambulance, moat and sandbagged hallway. Put on headsets and listen to takeoffs and landings at Palwaukee Airport, visible through picture windows.

WOODSTOCK. *Moderate:* **The Old Courthouse.** Popular country kitchen in refurbished courthouse in the old square. Eat in the vault, browse through boutiques after dessert.

INDIANA

Hoosier Heartland

Downtown Indianapolis boasts the state's tallest building, the 504-foot-high Indiana National Bank Tower, as well as the elegant gold-domed State Capitol, built in the late 1880s with the finest Indiana limestone.

The hub of the city is Monument Circle, adorned with the lofty Soldiers and Sailors Monument, which has an observation platform at its top. From here, the web of streets fans out to include such worthwhile attractions as the John Herron School of Art, the Benjamin Harrison Memorial Home, Children's Museum, Scottish Rite Cathedral and the James Whitcomb Riley home.

Indianapolis' main attraction, however, is located five miles west of the center. This is the two-and-a-half-mile oval, the Indianapolis Motor Speedway, which plays host to the world-famous Indianapolis 500 held around Memorial Day. Crowds of 300,000 and more pay from $10 general admission to $50 for box seats, in order to see the fastest cars in the world roar around the track. Since the first race was held in 1911, twelve drivers have been killed. Controversy over the safety of the track is perennial.

During the "500" Festival Month, 30 days of hoopla preceding the big race, the city bursts with civic activities: a parade, coronation ball, Festival of the Arts, and much more. Motels and hotels charge higher rates and are still jammed. During State Fair time, usually the 10 days preceding Labor Day, Indianapolis also swings at a faster tempo. The rest of the year, one might aptly describe it as a wholesome, family-fun town.

PRACTICAL INFORMATION FOR INDIANAPOLIS

SEASONAL EVENTS. May 1 is the opening of the mammoth *"500 Festival."* Events happen all month and become a regular frenzy the week before the big race. The *Romantic Music Festival* in Clowes Memorial Hall during the first week in May is a fine festival of Romantic music. Reservations required.

MUSEUMS AND ART GALLERIES. *Museum of Art.* Permanent collection of paintings, featuring 19th-century works, sculptures, textiles, graphics and silver. *Connie Prairie Pioneer Settlement and Museum,* 10 mi. NE in Noblesville. Good restoration of early 19th-century Indiana village. *State Library and Historic Bldg.* Extensive collection of material on state history and development, genealogical aids.

SUMMER SPORTS. Biggest single spectator sport by far is the world-famous *Indianapolis 500,* held around Memorial Day. The world's top racing drivers go for gold and glory in front of some 250,000 spectators or more who jam the grandstands and infield. Grandstand tickets are sold out months in advance. General admission (no seat) is available at about $10 a person.

WHAT TO DO WITH THE CHILDREN. *Children's Museum.* One of the best of its kind in the nation, with more than 30,000 exhibits ranging from an Egyptian mummy to an original log cabin. *Indianapolis Zoo,* in George Washington Park, displays animals in their native habitat, exhibits of native Indiana animals and children's zoo.

HOTELS AND MOTELS. Price categories for double occupancy will average as follows: *Moderate* $30–35; and *Inexpensive* under $30. Prices subject to change, so inquire ahead. Rates may be higher during the Indianapolis "500 Festival."

Moderate. **Day's Inn.** 5151 Elmwood Dr., 6 mi. SE at I–465, Emerson St. exit. Pool, playground.
    Ramada Inn-East. 3525 N. Shadland. 7 mi. NE on State 100.
    Inexpensive. **American Inn-North.** 7202 E. 82nd St., 14 mi. NE on I–69, Castleton exit.
    Cloverleaf Motel. 6915 E. Washington St., 7 mi. E on US 40 at State 100.
    Red Roof Inn. 5221 Victory Dr., 6 miles southeast off I–465, Emerson St. Exit.

DINING OUT. Price categories are as follows: *Moderate* $8–15; *Inexpensive* under $8. These prices are for hors d'oeuvres or soup, entrée and dessert. Not included are drinks, tax and tips.

Moderate. **J. Ross Browne's.** Good seafood, nautical decor.

Hollyhock Hill. Fried chicken. Family style.
J. Pierpont's. Steak, seafood. 19th-century decor. Jackets required.
Key West Shrimp House. Seafood and steak.
San Remo. Nicely prepared Italian fare.
Inexpensive. **Block's Terrace.** In Block's Department Store. Liquor served.
Heritage House Smorgasbord. Chicken, ham, roast beef, home baking.
Laughner's. Popular cafeteria. Chicken, roast beef.

EXPLORING INDIANA

Along the beach in Indiana Dunes State Park, a high ridge of sand has accumulated, held together by vegetation. Behind the ridge are the dunes, sparkling sandy slopes, all sizes and shapes, some stationary and some shifting. Loftiest of these miniature sand-mountains is Mt. Tom, 190 feet high and more than 100 acres. Plant growth amidst the dunes is almost tropical in its luxuriance. Wild flowers include 26 members of the orchid family and more than a thousand species of plants and trees thrive here. The area is also directly in the migration path of thousands of birds.

A good portion of the well-kept farms in the lake country belong to Indiana's sizable Amish and Mennonite sects. Their biggest concentrations are in and around Berne and Goshen. At Nappanee, just south of Elkhart on US 6, is Amish Acres, a working Amish farmstead. Guided tours are available year round.

To the east is the heart and shopping mart for the Indiana lake district, bustling Fort Wayne, which has scrambled upwards from a crude military outpost into the most surprising, cosmopolitan city in Indiana.

Terre Haute, atop a plateau along the Wabash River, is a historic city with several interesting birthplaces open to the public. Southwest of Vincennes, one can visit original buildings in the restored village of New Harmony, founded in 1825 by an experimental "Utopian" society that eventually failed, but not before founding the first free public school and first free library. Rustic Nashville, set in the hills of Brown County, is noted for its art colony and the Brown County Playhouse, which is operated May–October by students from Indiana University in nearby Bloomington.

Lincoln Land

Between the ages of 14 and 21 Lincoln lived in the hills and forests of what is now Spencer County. Here, young Abe split rails, went to school a little, cleared land, wrestled with other boys of the rough pioneer village and read everything he could get his hands on, from the *Bible* to the *Arabian Nights.* By the time he was twenty-one and the family moved to Illinois, Lincoln was matured in mind and body.

PRACTICAL INFORMATION FOR INDIANA

HOW TO GET THERE. *By car:* Though Indiana ranks 38th in size among the 50 states, it ranks about seventh in highway mileage. More than 96 percent of the state's roads are paved. Highways, towns and other points are well marked, so getting around the state by car is never a problem. *Hertz, Avis, National, Budget* and other rental car agencies are found in most major cities and at airports.

By bus: There is good bus service, with *Greyhound* and *Continental Trailways* the major lines. There are several other smaller companies, such as *Indiana Motor Bus.*

By air: USAir serves the most Indiana cities (seven) with regular service, using mainly DC-9's. *Ozark* and other airlines also serve the state.

By train: Indiana fares well in national *Amtrak* passenger rail service with trains from Indianapolis, Fort Wayne and other cities to both the East and West coasts and other points. (Routes are being reviewed and may be discontinued.)

By taxi: All airports and almost all cities over 10,000 population have taxi service.

TOURIST INFORMATION SERVICES. For general travel information write to the *Tourist Division,* Indiana Department of Commerce, 440 N. Meridian St., Indianapolis, IN 46204.

MUSEUMS AND ART GALLERIES. Bloomington: *Dailey Collection of Hoosier Art* and Thomas Hart Benton Murals. Fort Wayne: *Lincoln Library and Museum.* Extensive collection of Lincoln lore and memorabilia, including books, letters, photographs and paintings.

South Bend: *Notre Dame Memorial Library,* with 13 floors, has facilities for seating thousands all at once, and has a potential for housing two million volumes; proclaimed as one of the world's greatest college libraries. Most famed is the 3,000-volume Dante collection.

SUMMER SPORTS. There is golf throughout the state, and boating, principally in the northern lakes district. Fishing is good in the south-central area where trout are often cooperative in many clear streams. The state also stocks hundreds of miles of streams and lakes with fish. Riding is another popular sport, particularly in the many fine State Parks. Hunting is good in the northern and central corn fields, where pheasant and Hungarian partridge are the chief game. A non-resident hunting license is $37; a non-resident fishing license is $3 a day, $12.50 a year.

WINTER SPORTS. Major college football and basketball draw huge crowds at Notre Dame, Purdue and Indiana University, and the latter has produced dominant swimming and diving squads for over a decade. Popular ski areas include Mt. Wawasee, US 6 near Peru; The Pines, near Valparaiso and Ski Valley, Inc., 5 mi. W of LaPorte.

WHAT TO DO WITH THE CHILDREN. Evansville: *Mesker Zoo,* northwest of the city in Mesker Park, keeps most of its animals behind hidden moats, eliminating cages and bars. Monkeys frolic aboard copy of Columbus' flagship, the Santa Maria, cast in concrete in the middle of a lake.

Lincoln City: *Lincoln Boyhood National Memorial.* Visit Lincoln Living Memorial Farm, area similar to what young Abraham Lincoln lived on for 14 years of his youth.

Santa Claus: *Santa Claus Land,* in town offers varied commercial attractions with children's rides, wax museum, circus acts and rides, deer farm, snacks, Santa Claus and gift shop. Located between Evansville and New Albany.

HOTELS AND MOTELS. Hotels and motels in Indiana offer the traveler a wide range of accommodations, from elaborate facilities to the plain, but comfortable rooms to be found at most roadside motels in the countryside. The price categories in this section, for double occupancy, will average as follows: *Moderate* $25–30, and *Inexpensive* under $25.

ANGOLA. *Moderate:* **Potawatomi Inn.** Delightful scenic setting in Pokagon State Park.

BLOOMINGTON. *Inexpensive.* **Motel 6.** 126 S. Franklin Rd. near junction US 48 and State 37 Bypass. Pool. TV 75 cents extra.

COLUMBUS. *Moderate.* **Lee's Inns.** At I–65 and State 46W. Under 18 free.

EVANSVILLE. *Inexpensive:* **Jackson House.** 20 Walnut St., 1 mi. E of US 41. Pool.

Esquire Motel. 1817 State 41N (Business Route), 2½ mi. N. Under 12 free.

FT. WAYNE. *Moderate.* **Day's Inn.** 3527 W. Coliseum Rd. Playground, coffee shop.
Econo-Travel. 1401 W. Washington Center Rd. Coffee shop next door.
Red Roof Inn. 2920 Goshen Rd., off I–69 at US 30–33 exit.

GARY. *Moderate.* **Red Roof Inn.** 4 miles south on US 30. Under 12 free.

TERRE HAUTE. *Moderate:* **Pick of Terre Haute.** 4800 Dixie Bee Rd. Pool. Dancing.
Regal 8 Inn. 3 mi. S on US 41 at I–70. Indoor pool.

Bargain-priced accommodations can be found in *Indiana State Park* inns. Rates begin as low as $10–20 single and $12–25 double per night, often without private bath. A room with bath, a modern motel-type unit, runs about $18 for two. For the most part the rooms are plain, clean and lack such frills as phones, radios or television. The inns, themselves, however, are attractive and park activities are varied.

Abe Martin Lodge. Brown County State Park. Nashville. Spacious and comfortable.

DINING OUT. Restaurants in Indiana have long prided themselves on their homestyle cooking. In recent years, however, the Hoosier State has developed many fine Continental-style dining rooms with good wine lists. Restaurant price categories are as follows: *Moderate* $10–15; *Inexpensive* under $10. These prices are for hors d'oeuvres or soup, entrée and dessert. Not included are drinks, tax and tips.

BROOKVILLE. *Inexpensive:* **The Mounds.** 4 mi. SE on US 52. Long noted for home cooking, served family-style.

EVANSVILLE. *Inexpensive:* **F's Steakhouse.** Steak, lobster, children's plates.

FT. WAYNE. *Moderate:* **Zoli's Café Continental.** American and Hungarian specialties.

MORRISTOWN. *Moderate:* **The Kopper Kettle.** US 52. Home cooking, generous portions. Between Indianapolis and Rushville.

NASHVILLE. *Inexpensive:* **Nashville House.** Native specialties.

TERRE HAUTE. *Inexpensive:* **Goodie Shop Cafeteria.** Very popular.

VINCENNES. *Moderate:* **Marone's. Formosa Gardens.** Chinese. Pleasant surroundings.

IOWA

The Beautiful Land

From the Missouri River on its western border to the Mississippi River on the east, Iowa stretches out in a patchwork of fertile plains and forested hills. Des Moines, its largest city, is the commercial and cultural heart of the state. Begin with a tour of the capitol, which overlooks the city. The gilded dome, one of the largest of its kind, rises 274 feet above the ground floor. Carved stone and wood, the work of individual skilled craftsmen, decorate the interior in unexpected places. Art work, mural paintings, intricate mosaics, and a huge post-World War I mural photograph ornament the walls. Across the street is the Iowa State Historical Museum and Archives. Organized in 1892, the department's fine collection of historic artifacts preserves Iowa history from the earliest geological time, through the days of the Indians and pioneers, to the present. The building also houses important collections —genealogical, medical, historical—of the state library.

Other points of interest in Des Moines and surrounding Polk County include the Heritage Village on the Iowa State Fairgrounds; the Des Moines Botanical Center; and Terrace Hill Mansion, one of America's finest examples of Victorian architecture. Built in 1869, it is now the Iowa governor's residence and is open to the public for tours. Both within and near the city are numerous parks, many with lakes and camping and swimming facilities.

The way from Fairfield to Iowa City, and the University of Iowa, leads through Amish country in Washington County (IA–1 via Kolona), where Amish farmers settled in 1846. Known as "the plain people," the Old Order Amish live much as their ancestors did a century ago, rejecting most modern conveniences. Motorists should watch out for horse-drawn vehicles on area roads. At Iowa City the state's first permanent capitol, built in 1840, still stands at the center of the University of Iowa campus.

In southeast Iowa take a scenic journey up the Great River Road, which hugs the banks of the Mississippi River. At Keokuk the River Museum is housed aboard an old double helical paddle-wheel towboat, the *George M. Verity,* dry-docked on the riverfront. The next principal city upriver is Burlington, which celebrates its heritage each June with Steamboat Days. Crapo Park and adjoining Dankwardt Park in Burlington include a hundred acres of natural stone bluffs, deep ravines and majestic panoramas of the Mississippi River.

Northeast Iowa

Beautiful northeast Iowa is known for its tree-studded hills and rushing trout streams, some of the state's best canoe routes. Entering on I–80 you'll be in the Davenport-Bettendorf area. Turning north along the Great River Road takes you to LeClaire, the birthplace and early home of William F. "Buffalo Bill" Cody. A museum dedicated as a memorial to Indians, pioneers, and steamboat days sits along the waterfront adjacent to the dry-docked sternwheeler *Lone Star,* restored to its original condition as a working barge tow, and open for tours. The museum contains displays associated with Buffalo Bill's Wild West shows, Cody's rifles, Indian artifacts, and memorabilia of riverboat days.

At Clinton, the completely restored triple-deck sternwheeler *City of Clinton* from May to Oct. serves as a theater for summer stock. The 193-foot showboat was acquired from West Virginia in 1966. Its steam-driven engines, turbines, generators, and huge paddle-wheel shafts are intact and open for inspection.

If you head west from Davenport along Interstate 80, at West Branch, the Herbert Hoover Presidential Library-Museum, operated by the National Archives and Records Service, houses papers, personal correspondence, books, manuscripts, audio-visual materials, plus memorabilia of the first president born west of the Mississippi River. In the auditorium films are shown several times daily during the summer.

Adjoining the grounds of the Library-Museum is Herbert Hoover National Historic Site. Here, the two-room Hoover Birthplace Cottage, restored in 1938, holds some possessions of the Hoover family. This cottage, built 1871 by Jesse Clark Hoover, remains on its original site, and a replica of the blacksmith shop operated by the president's father stands behind the cottage. Across the street is the old Quaker Meeting House Herbert Hoover attended as a boy, and the graves of President and Mrs. Hoover are on a hillside about a quarter of a mile southwest of the birthplace cottage.

Continuing westbound on I–80, a key stopover is the Amana Colonies, seven Old World villages, the first of which, Amana, was founded in 1854 in the Iowa River Valley by the Inspirationalists under the leadership of Christian Metz. They established their own industries to supply the villages with all the essentials of life, and the excellence of Amana products soon attracted national attention. Tours are provided through Amana factories and workshops, which produce fine furniture, woolens, baked goods, wines and meat specialties in the Old World tradition. In 1932 the original communal organization of the colony was changed to capitalism, and today the new ways blend with the old. The Amana refrigerator was invented and is manufactured here. Amana restaurants are famous for excellent meals served family style.

Guided tours are available of the Amana Heim and Blacksmith Shop Museum Complex in the village of Homestead. Another outstanding attraction, the Museum of Amana History in Amana, portrays the early communal life of the colonies. For a guide map and business directory, write the Amana Colonies Travel Council, Amana, Iowa 52203.

Western Iowa

In northwest Iowa, Fort Dodge is a good starting place. The Fort Dodge Historical Museum, Stockade, and Fort include a replica of a government fort built in 1850 as quarters for the U.S. Sixth Infantry, which protected the early settlers from hostile Sioux. The replica was built to the exact specifications of the original drawings. Two original log cabins, the first hotel, and the first post office in Fort Dodge were used in re-creating the old fort.

The Estherville area is the gateway from the east to Iowa's leading resort area—the Iowa Great Lakes—consisting of Spirit Lake, West Okoboji, and East Okoboji. Dozens of smaller lakes dot this region; all are of glacial origin, dating back about 12,500 years. The beautiful Okobojis make up one of only three blue water lakes in the world. There are ample tourist facilities as well as camping and other outdoor recreational areas.

Two excellent state parks are the Lewis and Clark just south of Sioux City and Lake Manawa near Council Bluffs. Ample camping facilities are available in these parks as well as at Wilson Island near DeSoto National Wildlife Refuge, west of the town of Missouri Valley. The DeSoto Refuge is a public-use area, and a major feeding and resting place for geese and ducks migrating along the Missouri River Valley. Up to 200,000 snow and blue geese stop here during their flights between Arctic nesting grounds and Gulf Coast wintering areas. Up to 225,000 ducks, mostly mallards, also congregate. The peak migration months are March and April, and October and November. Artifacts recovered from the sunken steamboat *Bertrand* (1865) are on display in a new visitors' center and museum.

PRACTICAL INFORMATION FOR IOWA

HOW TO GET THERE. *By car:* Interstate 80 from the east and west, Interstate 35 from the south and north through the center of the state, and Interstate 29 from the south and north through the western section of the state. *By air:* The main carriers to Des Moines are *United, Republic, TWA, Frontier, Ozark* and *American Central.*

By train: The only rail transportation through the state runs east and west with stops at Burlington, Mt. Pleasant, Ottumwa, Osceola, Creston and Fort Madison. Service is operated by *Amtrak,* which can supply information and schedules.

By bus: Trailways, Greyhound (east and west) and *Jefferson* (north and south) have very good coverage throughout the state.

TOURIST INFORMATION. Tourism Division, *Iowa Development Commission,* 250 Jewett Building, Des Moines, Iowa 50309.

WINTER SPORTS. *Skiing* (Alpine and cross-country), *snowmobiling* and *ice-fishing* are increasingly popular pursuits. *Hunting:* In addition to pheasant hunting, Iowa has good quail, partridge, grouse, duck, goose, rabbit, squirrel, raccoon, fox, and coyote hunting open to both resident and nonresident hunters. Nonresident fees are substantially higher than resident fees, but not excessive for the amount of game available to the hunter.

Unfortunately, neither deer nor turkey hunting, both excellent, are open to nonresidents. Complete information on hunting seasons, bag limits, and licensing requirements and fees is available from the Superintendent of Information and Education, *Iowa Conservation Commission,* Wallace State Office Bldg., Des Moines, Iowa 50319. Specify the type of game you are interested in, and handy pamphlets on where to find and how to hunt it will be provided free.

SUMMER SPORTS. Fishing, boating, water-skiing, and sailing have long been popular in the Iowa Great Lakes Region in upper northwest Iowa, and at Clear Lake in north-central Iowa. They have also taken hold at such large reservoirs as Red Rock near Knoxville, southeast of Des Moines, Lake Rathbun near Centerville, in south-central Iowa, Saylorville near Des Moines, and Coralville near Iowa City. The state's many major rivers also offer excellent fishing, boating and water-sport opportunities. In addition, the Mississippi River on the state's eastern border is a tremendous water playground, with houseboating and river boat excursions highlights.

Canoeing: Canoe rentals are available in cities and towns adjacent to the more easily accessible rivers. Good camping at state, federal, county, and privately owned campgrounds.

Information on fishing, boating, sailing, water sports, and canoeing Iowa rivers is free from the Superintendent of Information and Education, *Iowa Conservation Commission,* address above, and from the Tourism Division, *Iowa Development Commission,* address above.

SPECTATOR SPORTS. Professional baseball is in Des Moines, where the *Iowa Cubs* of the American Association take to the diamond each spring. *Football, basketball* and top-ranked collegiate *wrestling* are available at the University of Iowa (Big Ten) at Iowa City, Iowa State University (Big Eight) at Ames and the University of Northern Iowa, Cedar Falls. Drake University in Des Moines not only has Mo. Valley Conference sports but is the site each

April of the nationally prominent *Drake Relays,* featuring top amateur college, university and high school track and field events for men and women.

MUSEUMS AND GALLERIES. The *Cedar Rapids Art Center* houses the world's largest collection of works by Iowa native Grant Wood, as well as many other contemporary paintings and prints.

The *Davenport Putnam Museum* features a Riverboat section and a Pioneer room of Indian and early-settler artifacts.

The *Des Moines Art Center* has an excellent collection representing American and European painting and sculpture of the past 200 years. The *Center* itself is by Eliel Saarinen. An addition by I.M. Pei houses sculpture.

The *Des Moines Center of Science and Industry* offers exhibits on space, environment, photography, and science, plus the *Sargent Planetarium.*

The *Salisbury House* in Des Moines is a replica of a King's Country House in Salisbury, England. Most of the interior materials were taken from the home built in 1579 by Christopher Weeks, mayor of Salisbury, England. The 42-room Salisbury House now is headquarters of the Iowa State Education Association, and guided tours can be arranged by contacting the ISEA at 4025 Tonawanda Drive, Des Moines, Iowa 50312. Weekdays, self-guided mini-tours.

DRINKING LAWS. State-run liquor stores are open daily except Sundays and legal holidays. Beer may be purchased in grocery stores until 2:00 A.M. except on Sun., when hours are noon to 10 P.M. Bars and restaurants are permitted to sell mixed drinks and beer from Sun. noon to 10 P.M. The legal drinking age in Iowa is 19.

WHAT TO DO WITH THE CHILDREN. *Living History Farms* on I-80 west of Des Moines features a pioneer village and three working farms: the Pioneer Farm of 1840, the Horse-Powered Farm of 1900 and the Farm of Today and Tomorrow. There are crafts demonstrations, hayrides and special events every weekend. *Adventureland,* just east of Des Moines, is a theme park with over 100 rides and daily live entertainment.

HOTELS AND MOTELS in Iowa are easy to find, and there are many fine smaller motels and hotels that are family-operated businesses and provide that personal warmth that only an individual innkeeper can give. The price categories in this section, for double occupancy, one bed, are approximately as follows: *Moderate* $30–40, and *Inexpensive* under $30. (Hotel-motel tax in some cities.)

AMANA COLONIES. *Inexpensive:* **Die Heimat Motor Hotel.** In village of Homestead off I-80. Restored 1858 hotel, many rooms furnished with antiques. Small, family-operated. Continental breakfast available.

AMES. *Inexpensive:* **New Englander.** Pool and children's play area, restaurant nearby.
New Frontier. Pool. Restaurant nearby. In-room coffee.
Silver Saddle. Restaurant nearby. Pool.

BETTENDORF. *Inexpensive:* **Twin Bridges Motor Inn.** Pool, restaurant.

BURLINGTON. *Moderate:* **The Holiday.** Indoor pool, restaurant, lounge.

CEDAR RAPIDS. *Moderate:* **Best Western Village Motor Inn.** Restaurant. Live entertainment.
Inexpensive: **Howard Johnson's Executive Motor Inn.** Restaurant. Pool.

Red Roof Inn. Restaurant nearby. Noted for hospitality and cleanliness.

CENTERVILLE. *Moderate:* **Motel 60 and Villa** 7 mi. from Lake Rathbun. Saunas. Some efficiency suites. Fish-cleaning facilities.

CLEAR LAKE. *Moderate:* **Holiday Motor Lodge.** Restaurant. Lounge. Entertainment. Pool.
Inexpensive: **Blue Horizon.** Private verandas overlook beach on Clear Lake. Swimming, dock, and fishing. Restaurant nearby.

COUNCIL BLUFFS. *Moderate:* **Best Western Frontier Motor Lodge.** Restaurant, pool, whirlpool, sauna.

DAVENPORT. *Inexpensive:* **Bronze Lantern Motel.** Family-owned. Pool.
Moderate: **Clayton House.** Restaurant, lounge. Indoor and outdoor pools. Overlooks the Mississippi River.

DES MOINES. *Moderate:* **Best Western Bavarian House Motel.** Indoor pool. Excellent restaurant.
Rodeway Inn. Off I–80 Merle Hay Exit. Pool, lounge, restaurant.
Inexpensive: **Redwood Motel.** Small. Family-owned. 3 mi. from Adventureland.

DUBUQUE. *Inexpensive:* **Julien Motor Inn.** Restaurant, lounge. Family-owned.

EMMETSBURG. *Inexpensive:* **Suburban Motel.** Supper club adjacent.

FORT DODGE. *Moderate:* **Holiday Haus Motel.** Pool. Restaurant and lounge with live entertainment.

IOWA CITY. *Moderate:* **Alamo Friendship Inn.** Oversized beds. Free continental breakfasts and suppers. Restaurant adjacent.
Inexpensive: **Hawkeye Lodge.** Near university campus, restaurant, and 18-hole golf course. Continental breakfast included in rates.

KEOKUK. *Moderate:* **Keokuk Motor Lodge.** Picturesque grounds. Mississippi River and dam 3 miles away. Restaurant nearby.

OSKALOOSA. *Inexpensive:* **Best Western Traveler Motel.** Restaurants nearby. Old-fashioned hospitality by owner. Three miles from Nelson Pioneer Farm & Craft Museum.

STORM LAKE. *Inexpensive:* **Best Western Motel Vista.** Restaurant near-by. In-room coffee.

 DINING OUT in Iowa is no longer a meat-and-potatoes affair. Although you can still find country-style cookery in this land of plenty, today numerous restaurants serve gourmet and international dishes. Iowa's famous beef and pork are on almost all menus. Restaurant price categories in this section will approximate: *Moderate* $10–15; *Inexpensive* under $10. These prices may or may not include soup and dessert but do not include alcoholic drinks, tax, and tips.

AMANA COLONIES. *Inexpensive:* **Bill Zuber's Restaurant; Colony Inn; Colony Market Place; Ox Yoke Inn; Ronneburg Restaurant.** All known for excellent German-American food served family-style.

BETTENDORF. *Inexpensive:* **Bishop Buffet** at Duck Creek Plaza. Cafeteria. Quality food.

CEDAR FALLS. *Inexpensive:* **Bishop Buffet.** Excellent selection of entrées, salads, vegetables and desserts. In College Square Shopping Center.

CEDAR RAPIDS. *Inexpensive:* **Bishop Buffet.** Cafeteria. Quality Food.

DES MOINES. *Moderate:* **Babe's.** 417–6th St. Downtown. A tradition. Italian-American cuisine at its finest.
Chicago Speakeasy. 1520 Euclid. Clever prohibition-era décor. Mon. night special, excellent prime rib (generous cut) and other specials Tues., Wed., Thurs. Good salad bar.
Inexpensive: **Baker Cafeterias.** (Sherwood Forest, 7400 Hickman; Colonial at 5030 N.E. 14th.) Wholesome, well-prepared foods. Home-made bakery goods.
Bishop Buffets. Merle Hay Plaza and Wakonda Shopping Center. Cafeterias. Good food, reasonably priced.

DUBUQUE. *Moderate:* **Leiser's Supper Club.** Three miles north of Dubuque on US 52. Prime rib, lobster tails, chicken, catfish.

IOWA CITY. *Moderate:* **Iowa River Power Company.** Outstanding food served in unusual surroundings of a converted power plant. Hoover Presidential Library not far away.

MALCOM. *Inexpensive:* **Dickey's Prairie Home Restaurant.** Home cooking, family style. Buffet nightly and Sunday.

MARQUETTE. *Moderate:* **Pink Elephant Motel & Supper Club.** Sweeping view of the Mississippi River. Shrimp steamed in beer is a specialty.

STORM LAKE. *Inexpensive:* **Ken-A-Bob Buffet.** Very popular well-established cafeteria, noted for home cooking.
Cobblestone Inn. Good food in an early American environment.

WINTERSET. *Inexpensive:* **Gold Buffet.** All you can eat from extravagant buffet tables.

MICHIGAN

Detroit and the Land between the Lakes

The top of the downtown Renaissance Center is a good place to get a feel for Detroit. The Metropolitan Detroit Convention and Visitor's Bureau is below you at Suite 1950, 100 Renaissance Center. The Visitor Information Center is on the street below near Hart Plaza.

A minibus stops at RenCen on its regular run through the downtown area. Old English streetcars run along nearby streets. A new mall has been built along Washington Boulevard from Michigan Avenue to Grand Circus Park. Another has been completed in the center of shopping activity along Woodward Avenue, a few blocks north of the river.

Six blocks north is a small area called Greektown, a favorite downtown spot for Greek food, belly dancing, nighttime street life or little ethnic shops. A major restoration of Trapper's Alley is underway, including shops, artist studios and restaurants. About three miles north at Grand Boulevard and Woodward Avenue is the New Center, site of the Fisher Theatre and General Motors world headquarters.

The Cultural Center

A few blocks south of the New Center, Wayne State University shares the Woodward Avenue area with a dozen cultural institutions, most of them free. The Detroit Institute of Arts has 35,000 works in

101 galleries, including two contemporary wings. The Detroit Public Library has its own walking tour, which includes the Burton Historical Collection and the National Automotive History Collection. You can walk the streets of 18th- and 19th-century Detroit in the Detroit Historical Museum at Woodward and Kirby. Kirby is also the site of the Children's Museum and the International Institute. Other cultural institutions in the area include Your Heritage House, a black museum; Detroit Community Music School; and the Detroit Science Center. A new Afro-American Museum is near Farnsworth.

Belle Isle

Belle Isle, east along Jefferson Avenue, has been a favorite place for family picnicking, canoeing and ball games for 100 years. It includes a conservatory, aquarium, nature center, carillon, the Dossin Great Lakes Museum, and the exciting Safari Trail Zoo for children.

Ford Country

Michigan Avenue runs 12 miles west to the heart of Dearborn (faster traffic chooses the Edsel Ford Freeway, I–94 West). On the northwest corner of Michigan and Southfield is a monorail or "people mover" running from the bronzed glass Hyatt Regency Hotel to Fairlane Town Center, one of North America's newest and largest shopping centers.

Southwest of this corner is the "skyline" of the largest indoor-outdoor museum in the world. Henry Ford Museum has 14 acres of technology and decorative arts under one roof. Greenfield Village has 260 acres of reconstructed village streets where homes and businesses of the past have been restored.

PRACTICAL INFORMATION FOR DETROIT

HOW TO GET AROUND. *By Car:* Always refer to current highway numbers and a current map. Names associated with highways are: I–75, south to north, is the Seaway Freeway, Fisher Freeway, Chrysler Freeway. I–94 is the Edsel Ford Freeway. U.S. 10, the John Lodge Freeway, merges with Northwestern Highway and with I–696, Walter Reuther Highway. I–96, the Jeffries Freeway, joins I–275 (no name) for a few miles. M–85 is Fort Street; M–1 is Woodward Avenue; M–3 is Gratiot; M–102 is, east to west, Vernier, Base Line, Eight Mile, Grand River and M–102 Expressway. U.S. 24 is Telegraph Road.

By bus: Maps of bus routes are obtainable at the D.S.R. booth on Woodward Ave. between Michigan Ave. and State St. in downtown Detroit, and at the Visitor Information Center. The booth also has general maps of the area.

By taxi: The taxi rate is $.90 the moment you get into the cab and $1 for each additional mile.

From the airport: Greyhound buses run from Metro airport to downtown hotels and cost $4.75.

By train: SEMTA train downtown, north to Pontiac. *Amtrak* to New York City via Toledo, to Chicago via Ann Arbor, and to Toronto via Port Huron.

TOURIST INFORMATION. Visitor Information Center, 2 East Jefferson.

MUSEUMS AND GALLERIES. The *Detroit Historical Museum* centers its displays around the city of Detroit: Here you may see the city as it existed 100 years ago reflected in the exhibits and pictures.

Also in the city is the *Detroit Institute of Arts.* World famous, this excellent gallery has examples from almost every culture of note in the world. The south wing, opened in June 1966, houses a permanent African art and artifacts exhibit. Kresge Court dining area, with regular concerts, was recently renovated.

In Dearborn is the *Henry Ford Museum* and *Greenfield Village,* a reconstructed 19th-century outdoor village.

At Bloomfield Hills are the *Cranbrook Institutes,* including the museum of the Cranbrook Academy of Art. Here you will find an excellent collection of fine arts, well displayed and featuring many of the contemporary artists of the area. *Cranbrook Science Museum* is a fine stop for adults and children.

HISTORIC SITES. At 6325 W. Jefferson is the *Fort Wayne Military Museum.* The military feeling of 100 years ago is captured in the exhibits and fortifications in this unique museum. The actual stone barracks and the small museum with Indian memorabilia are just two of the many excellent displays which you may see.

TOURS. *Charter Bus Unlimited* offers city tours. *Gray Line* has three-to-seven-hour tours of the city and suburbs at $15 to $19. One bus tour goes to Greenfield Village, where you can walk through history to see the homes, clothes, and crafts of pioneer settlers. Time is given for one to walk leisurely around the grounds. Mini-buses circle the downtown area. Trolleys tour downtown, including the only double-decker open-air trolley in the U.S. And the Detroit "waterline" can be seen on a sightseeing cruise to Boblo Island. Or on moonlight cruises on the river.

WHAT TO DO WITH THE CHILDREN. The *Belle Isle Zoo and Aquarium* has a Safari Trails Zoo; and children may ride a miniature railroad through naturalistic terrain at the *Detroit Zoological Park* in Royal Oak. Take the riverboat to *Boblo Island Amusement Park.* Visit *Detroit Science Center,* downtown, and *Kensington Children's Farm and Village,* adjacent to Kensington Metro Park northwest of the city. Children will also love the *Henry Ford Museum* and *Greenfield Village* in Dearborn.

HOTELS AND MOTELS in Detroit range from the ultra-sophisticated to the plain, comfortable facilities of less expensive motels. The price categories in this section, for double occupancy, will average: *Moderate* $45, *Inexpensive* $35.

Moderate: **Barclay Inn.** 145 S. Hunter Blvd. and Maple Rd., Birmingham. 45 minutes from downtown Detroit. Exclusive area near good restaurants and shopping.

Dearborn Travelodge. 23730 Michigan. Families.

Falcon Inn. 25125 Michigan Ave., Dearborn. Just west of US 24. Greenfield Village nearby. There's a restaurant.

Presidential Inn. 17201 Northline, Southgate. Off I–75. 20 minutes from downtown. Heated pool, sauna, playground, cocktails, entertainment.

Village Motor Inn. Birmingham. Central to elegant suburban main street.

Inexpensive: **Sagamore.** 3220 N. Woodward Ave., Royal Oak. Has a restaurant, and the Detroit Zoo is nearby.

Shorecrest Motel. 1316 E. Jefferson. Restaurant. Clean, secure, friendly. Close to Rennaisance Center and river.

Suez. 3333 E. 8-Mile Rd., Warren. 20 minutes from downtown Detroit.

Telegraph House. 23300 Telegraph, Southfield. Clean suburban motel.

DINING OUT in Detroit provides the traveler with a wide range of restaurant styles and variations on standard menus. Restaurant price categories are as follows: *Moderate* $8–12, *Inexpensive* $5–8. These prices are for hors d'oeuvres or soup, entrée, and dessert. Not included are drinks, tax, and tips.

Moderate: **Carl's Chop House.** 3020 Grand River. Prize-winning beef. Popular with locals and conventioneers.

Mayfield Chop House. 1422 Griswold. Fresh seafood daily. Good steaks.

Sheik Café. 316 E. Lafayette. Best Lebanese food in town.

Inexpensive: **Magic Pan.** Five locations for crepes and house wine, in shopping malls.

Peabody's. 154 S. Hunter, Birmingham. Hearty, informal; good prices for a fine dinner. Be prepared to stand in line. Cocktails.

Porter Street Station. 1400 Porter, off Trumbull. Former warehouse in old Corktown.

Traffic Jam and Snug. 4268 Second Blvd. Quiche and pies on campus.

American-International. Moderate: **Joey's Stables.** 8800 W. Jefferson. American-Bavarian.

Seafood. Inexpensive: **Ivanhoe Cafe.** 5249 Joseph Campau. Great Lakes perch.

Italian. Expensive: **Roma Cafe.** 3401 Riopelle. Excellent variety of pastas.

Oriental. Inexpensive: **Chung's.** 3177 Cass Ave. Cantonese.

Greek. Inexpensive: **Hellas,** 538 Monroe, Greektown near RenCen. Detroit's favorite late night ethnic neighborhood.

Other Inexpensive. **Sinbads,** 100 St. Clair, Detroit. No reservations. Where socialites, sailors and just plain folks mix. East on riverfront.

Woodbridge Tavern, 289 St. Aubin. Old saloon with porch. Deli, sandwiches, pizza.

Olga's Kitchen, Renaissance Center and malls citywide. Plants everywhere. Beef and lamb on Greek bread.

Butchers' Inn, Eastern Market. Get a 10¢ beer for breakfast!

EXPLORING MICHIGAN

Even a sampling of Michigan, the 23rd largest state, should include stops in big-city Detroit, in the lower and the upper peninsula. A corridor of cities runs westward from Detroit to Lake Michigan: Lansing, Ann Arbor, Battle Creek, Grand Rapids, Kalamazoo, Muskegon. A shorter corridor runs north through the General Motors complex at Flint to the tri-city area of Saginaw, Bay City and Midland. Above the Bay City Midland line, small towns and inland lakes dot the highways running to the Mackinac Bridge. Beyond the bridge is the Upper Peninsula, a proud and sparsely settled region of forested recreation areas. The land gets hillier and rockier going north, and by the time you hit the Lake Superior shore on the northern side of the U.P., you are in the land of the Pictured Rocks and the Isle Royal National Park.

Traveling Toward Lake Michigan

Ann Arbor, 40 miles west of Detroit, is an ongoing fiesta of music, theater, art and special events related to the University of Michigan. A monthly calendar, available city-wide, lists the events. Tour the campus, dine in the many student hangouts or the sophisticated eateries, and check out the interesting shopping. Another university town, Lansing, is also the state's capital and has a vital part in automobile manufacturing. Michigan State University, the state's first land grant college, is in nearby East Lansing and has one of the nation's most beautiful campuses.

From Lansing, travel west on I–96 to Grand Rapids, once known for furniture and now for its outdoor sculpture and exciting downtown renewal as well as the Gerald R. Ford Museum.

West of Grand Rapids is the city of Holland, home of an annual Tulip Time Festival where, for four days in May, the city remembers its Dutch heritage with wooden shoe dancing, parades, and pageants, as townspeople, dressed in authentic Dutch costumes, scrub the streets with long-handled brooms. With good luck and good weather, you may arrive in time for the city's thousands of tulips to burst into bloom.

Further south on I–94 are the cities of Battle Creek, home of Kellogg's cereals and Kalamazoo, home of two of Michigan's finest universities. Spend an afternoon poking through some of Kalamazoo's wonderful antique stores. Also nearby is Jackson, with its Michigan Space Center and its computerized musical fountain. Driving west, you reach two major industrial cities: Muskegon and Benton Harbor. You have come to the shores of Lake Michigan.

This is boating and summer home country, whether you drive south toward Benton Harbor and on past the Indiana lakeshore dunes to Chicago, or north through Muskegan, Ludington, and Manistee to the hiking, camping, and glorious dunes of Sleeping Bear National Lakeshore. Ride dune buggies outside the park.

The Lakeshore leads north into the state's busiest resort area. Follow tiny towns, ferries, fruit stands and fruit farms around the Leelanau Peninsula to Traverse City, which celebrates a cherry festival in summer and a frozen cherry festival in winter. From this city overlooking Grand Traverse Bay you can reach 11 Lower Peninsula ski resorts and you can drive north along the shore through Charlevoix to Petosky and Harbor Springs. Or travel 15 miles southwest of Traverse City to the National Music Camp at Interlochen; there is a campsite on one side of the road and wonderful musical events on the other.

Take a ferry boat from Charlevoix to Beaver Island, 35 miles out in the lake. This island was once the kingdom of James Strang, a self-proclaimed monarch who ruled his Mormon colony for nine years. When he decreed that all women must wear bloomers, he had gone too far. Someone shot him and ended the only kingdom on U.S. soil.

At Petoskey, a retirement resort with fine shops (whose owners close their doors in October and spend the winter in Florida's Naples and West Palm Beach), you will, if you are lucky, find one of the famed Petoskey stones at the beach. Bay View, near here, a small settlement of Victorian cottages with Chattaqua-like summer programs, is now on the National Register of Historic Places.

Only 35 miles north and east of Petoskey and the Little Traverse Bay is the Mackinac Bridge, connecting the two peninsulas of Michigan. Before you cross the five-mile long suspension bridge, go to see the restored Fort Michilimackinac under the bridge. Then take the ferry to Mackinac Island in the Straits of Mackinac.

Mackinac Island

Ferries, operating on an hourly basis, take you across the straits in ten or twenty minutes. Dominated by the long, white pillared porch of the Grand Hotel, the island is three miles long and two miles wide. Tour the former fur-trading post operated by John Jacob Astor and English military fort by rented bicycle, horse and carriage or saddle horse. There are no automobiles on the island.

The Upper Peninsula

The fee for crossing the bridge is $1.50 for passenger cars. Take I–75 north of St. Ignace and stop at the locks at Sault Ste. Marie. Pleasure and commercial boats move through these locks all day and tourists may watch the process. The Upper Peninsula is a place to be outdoors. Tourist highlights include Isle Royale National Park—offshore in Lake Superior; the waterfalls Laughing Whitefish, Douglas Houghton, and especially Tahquamenon Falls; the Pictured Rocks; eight major ski areas; and the National Ski Hall of Fame. There are also ski jumping competitions, mine tours, and camping in both wonderful wilderness parks and those with full facilities.

PRACTICAL INFORMATION FOR MICHIGAN

HOW TO GET THERE. *By car:* Major routes into Michigan are I–75, I–94, and Canada's Rte. 401, which approaches from Toronto and the east. Detroit Federal highways include US 23 and US 131.

By train: The major *Amtrak* run is from Chicago to Detroit via Kalamazoo, Battle Creek and Jackson.

By bus: Direct *Trailways* service will get you to Detroit only. *Greyhound* has fairly extensive routes into Michigan. The southern third of the state is so thickly settled that intrastate lines pick up where the Big Two leave off. *Indian Trails* has daily bus service from Bay City–Saginaw–Flint to Chicago via Lansing, Battle Creek.

By air: Twenty Michigan cities have regularly scheduled flights in and out. *Republic* and *United* have good service to Detroit. Commuters include *Wright and Simmons Airlines.*

TOURIST INFORMATION. General information for the state may be obtained from the Michigan Travel Commission, P. O. Box 30226, Lansing, MI 48909; Metropolitan Detroit Convention and Visitor's Bureau, 100 Renaissance Center, Suite 1950; the East Michigan Tourist Association, 1 Wenonah Park, Bay City 48706; West Michigan Tourist Association, 136 Fulton East, Grand Rapids 49503; Travel and Tourist Association of Southeast Michigan, 64 Park St., Troy 48084; and the Upper Peninsula Travel and Recreation Association, P. O. Box 400, Iron Mountain 49801. There is also a Chicago office: 55 E. Monroe St., Chicago, Ill. 60603.

MUSEUMS AND GALLERIES. The *Grand Rapids Art Museum* has a collection of master prints of all eras, as well as American and German Expressionist paintings.

Voight House in Grand Rapids is a Victorian-era museum with original furnishings. The *Gerald R. Ford Presidential Museum* opened in 1982 in Grand Rapids.

Also check out the tiny *Besser Museum* in Alpena; *Hackley Art Gallery* in Muskegon; *Ski Hall of Fame* in Ishpeming; a fine music museum at Interlochen; and the museums in universities statewide.

Monroe, Manistee, and Marquette are just a few of the other localities with interesting museums.

Michigan Space Center in Jackson has space modules and displays from Apollo, Mercury and Gemini flights, plus a Moon Room and Astrotheater.

HISTORIC SITES. Perhaps the most unusual historical fact concerning Michigan is that at one time *Beaver Island* in Lake Michigan was ruled by a "king"! This tiny monarchy of more than 100 years ago still shows evidences of its Mormon ruler.

Another deserted community is the *ghost town* of Fayette, now restored as a state park.

The bloody Indian wars which erupted in this area are still remembered: there are no fewer than five restored or preserved forts in the state.

TOURS. Capsule tours by *Greyhound, Indian Trails* or *Trailways* are excellent for acquainting you with the different attractions of the state. One way to enjoy Michigan is by water, and there are several conveyances available for different bodies of water. An easy means of seeing wilderness, maybe a deer drinking, or a duck teaching its young to swim, is by canoe. Michigan has literally hundreds of places where canoes can be rented, along streams with names like Tittabawassee, Manistee, Pere Marquette. And one of the country's famed trout streams, the Au Sable, probably has more canoe liveries and canoe traffic than any other. One could engage a guide and special trout longboat for a no-effort trout trip on this clear, pine-banked river.

If you want a little more boat between you and the water, take the two-hour cruise down the Au Sable River on the *River Queen,* a paddlewheeler from the days when they trafficked up and down the river in great numbers. The boat leaves from the Five Channels Dam near Oscoda. It is advisable to make reservations a few days in advance.

DRINKING LAWS. The legal age is 21. Sales by the drink or in package stores are allowed 7 A.M.–2 A.M. except Sunday, when, at local option, they may begin at 2 P.M.

SUMMER SPORTS. Water sports, golf, and tennis are all enjoyed by millions each year. Trails for hiking, biking, and horseback riding are becoming more abundant, and gliding and skydiving also are gaining adherents. More than any of those, hunting and fishing are the recreations that attract people to the state because of the species that abound here.

WINTER SPORTS. Downhill (Alpine) and cross-country (Nordic) skiing and snowmobiling are the biggest cold-weather favorites and land-development patterns reflect this fact. Some hunting seasons occur with snow on the ground, and ice-boating and ice-fishing demonstrate that Michigan's thousands of lakes are never wasted.

SPECTATOR SPORTS. The most popular college and professional team sports are baseball, football, basketball, soccer, and hockey. Fast-proliferating rival tours in golf and tennis as well as track and field, all kinds of auto racing, and winter sports keep the fan busy.

WHAT TO DO WITH THE CHILDREN. Historic sites and amusements abound outside the Detroit area. *Fort Michilimackinac,* in Mackinaw City, holds the remains from the fur-trading and Indian days. A little to the south, at Ossineke on the northeastern shore of Lake Huron, they may wander through a *prehistoric forest* which includes full-sized dinosaurs. South of Baldwin is a gigantic statue of *Paul Bunyan,* with displays of early logging days. In the southwestern corner of Michigan, the twin cities of St. Joseph and Benton Harbor have beaches. Coloma has a *Deer Forest.* The little town of Holland has lots of transplanted Dutch people and customs which are interesting; the children will surely enjoy the *Dutch village,* the wooden-shoe factory, *Windmill Island Park,* and *Deerland Zoo.* At *Deer Acres,* near Bay City, children can feed the deer and also enjoy the Mother Goose characters and a fire engine ride. Don't miss the authenticity and fun at the *Michigan Space Museum* in Jackson, or the ferry to *Mackinac Island.* New attractions are *Historic Crossroads Village* and *Huckleberry Railroad,* just north of Flint, operated by the Genesse County Parks & Recreation Department. Season is May through September. It is a bona-fide reproduction village and the railroad ride is one of few left in Michigan.

HOTELS AND MOTELS in Michigan include such diverse establishments as the resort hotels of Mackinac Island and the state's simple but nicely furnished accommodations along the highways. The price categories in this section, for double occupancy, will average: *Moderate* $35, *Inexpensive* $28.

ANN ARBOR. *Moderate:* **Bell Tower Hotel.** 300 S. Thayer. Near central campus. Small, popular; good restaurant.
   Inexpensive. **Best Western Wolverine Inn.** 3505 S. State at I–94. Near shopping mall.

BATTLE CREEK. *Moderate:* **Village Inn.** Heated Pool.

CADILLAC. *Moderate:* **Caberfae Ski Resort.** Dinner theater.

CEDAR. *Moderate:* **Sugar Loaf Mountain Resort.** Skiing, golf, tennis, boating.

GRAND RAPIDS. *Moderate:* **Midway Motel.** Heated pool.

HARBOUR SPRINGS. *Moderate:* **Harbor Inn.** 19th-century lakeside resort being restored.

HOLLAND-SAUGATUCK. *Moderate:* **Wooden Shoe.** Pool, café, laundromat.

HOUGHTON. *Moderate:* **Kings Inn.** Downtown, near Isle Royale boat docks.

MACKINAC ISLAND. *Inexpensive:* **Yoder's Bayview.** Tourist home. Nostalgic.

MACKINAW CITY. *Moderate:* **Chippewa Motor Court.** Beach, picnic grill.

PETOSKY. *Moderate:* **Perry-Davis Hotel.** Old sprawl of white clapboard restored beside the lake in downtown Petosky.

ST. IGNACE. *Moderate:* **Straits Breeze Motel.** Lake view.

SAULT STE. MARIE. *Moderate:* **Ramada Inn.** Restaurant.

TRAVERSE CITY. *Moderate:* **Days Inn.** Heated pool. Restaurant. New housekeeping units.

 DINING OUT. Michigan's people are well known for their love of wholesome food, and around the state there are many moderately priced establishments serving fine meals. German and Scandinavian restaurants and dining rooms serving fresh fish from Michigan's abundance of waterways are almost everywhere.

Restaurant price categories are: *Moderate* $9, *Inexpensive* $5–9. These prices are for hors d'oeuvres or soup, entree, and dessert. Not included are drinks, tax, and tips.

ANN ARBOR. *Moderate:* **Old German.** Gemutlicheit.

BENTON HARBOR. *Moderate:* **Holmsted.** Home cooking.

CHARLEVOIX. *Moderate:* **Grey Gables Inn.** Dinner only.

CLARE. *Inexpensive:* **Dougherty's.** Smorgasbord in main street hotel, with pots of blue cheese for the salad.

ESCANABA. *Moderate:* **House of Ludington.** Once a grand hotel, now renovated as an elegant, turn-of-the-century dining room.

GRAND RAPIDS. *Moderate:* **Granny's Kitchen.** Family atmosphere.
Inexpensive: **Schnitzelbank.** Oompa-pa good.

HOLLAND. *Moderate:* **Dutch Village.** Dutch cuisine.

HOUGHTON. *Moderate:* **The Library.** Locals and university students love the sandwiches.
Inexpensive: **Rushnen's Suomi Bakery and Restaurant.** Fresh pastries daily. Breakfast all day.

MARQUETTE. *Moderate:* **Northwood Supper Club.** Country setting overlooking fish pond and woods. Summer patio. Sunday brunch. Try the whitefish.

MCMILLAN. *Moderate:* **Helmer House.** In Manistique Lakes district of UP. Turn-of-the-century roadhouse. Fresh fish. Antique clocks everywhere.

ST. IGNACE. *Moderate:* **Georgian House.** Fine view.

ST. JOSEPH. *Moderate:* **Holly's Landing.** Rustic. Comfortable.

SAULT STE. MARIE. *Moderate:* **Knife and Fork.** Ramada Inn. Wednesday smorgasbord.

Inexpensive: **The Antler's Bar.** Bells ring, noisemakers blare, kids clap. Fish, steak and memorabilia.

MINNESOTA

Twin Cities and 15,000 Lakes

Minneapolis and St. Paul, Minnesota, may be directly across the Mississippi River from each other, but in no way are they "Twin Cities." Local residents consider them about as much alike as New Orleans and New York, San Francisco and Des Moines, or Tokyo and Leningrad.

St. Paul, the older city, is the state capital. It is Irish and Catholic. It is a smaller version of Boston, and fairly conservative, with the older Yankee influences still dominating the town. It is the end of "the East."

Minneapolis is a beautiful city. It has 11 lakes within the city limits, and they are still clean enough for swimming. Minneapolis has one of the finest park systems in the U.S., and its 156 parks are havens of greenery. They contain bikeways and hiking paths, flower gardens, wildlife areas, and numerous athletic facilities. Minnehaha Falls, in Minnehaha Park, was made famous by Henry Longfellow in his poem, *Song of Hiawatha* (though he'd never actually seen it himself). Minneapolis has twice been voted an "All-American City." Its combination of enlightened urban renewal, industrial progress and cultural pursuits is matched by few cities.

St. Paul is more small-town and more beautiful in some ways than Minneapolis. You can take a drive down Summit Avenue, a boulevard lined with stately old mansions. It is on this street that F. Scott Fitzgerald ran down the steps of his home, raced along the avenue, and shouted, "It's done! It's finished!" He was talking about *This Side of Paradise.*

The theatrical scene in Minneapolis and St. Paul is hard to beat. For example, there are the renowned Guthrie Theatre, one of the nation's foremost repertory organizations; numerous community theatres; and the Old Log Theatre, on the shores of beautiful Lake Minnetonka.

PRACTICAL INFORMATION FOR
THE TWIN CITIES

HOW TO GET AROUND. *By car:* The Belt Line (I–494 and I–694) encircles the Twin Cities, while I–35 bisects the metro area from north to south.

Minneapolis streets follow in numerical or alphabetical order, but there is no such logical order to St. Paul streets.

By bus: The basic fare is 60¢. Trips between the cities or to suburbs cost 60¢ to $1.25. Children and senior citizens ride for less at specified times.

By taxi: The base rate is $1.95 for the first mile and $1.10 per each additional mile.

From the airport: Limousines stop at all the major downtown hotels and many suburban motels, especially those along I–494 near the airport.

MUSEUMS AND GALLERIES. At the *Walker Art Center* in Minneapolis, on Vineland Place, there is a quality collection of modern American art. The *Minneapolis Institute of Art,* 2400 Third Avenue South, contains local and international paintings, sculpture, and artifacts from many periods. Private Minneapolis galleries, open to the public, that sell works by regional and international artists include *WARM Gallery, By Design, Barry Richard Gallery, Groveland Gallery,* Peter M. David Gallery.

In St. Paul's *Minnesota Historical Society,* at 690 Cedar Ave., the days of the pioneers graphically come to life. Nearby is the fascinating *Science Museum of Minnesota* where cultural and craft demonstrations are often scheduled.

HISTORIC SITES. *Sibley House* and *Faribault House* in Mendota and the *Alexander Ramsey House* in St. Paul represent the Northwest in the mid-1800s. The *Gibbs Farm Museum,* 2097 W. Larpenteur Ave., St. Paul, displays facets of mid-19th-century farm life. The *F. Scott Fitzgerald home,* 599 Summit Ave., St. Paul, is not open to the public, but do drive by. At *Ft. Snelling,* perched on the bluffs at the confluence of the Mississippi and Minnesota rivers, visitors are greeted by persons who dress and speak as if they were living in the 1800s. The *Minnesota Valley Restoration Project,* southwest of the Twin Cities near Shakopee, is a collection of original buildings gathered from various areas of Minnesota in which period items and crafts are displayed.

TOURS. Regularly scheduled tours of the Twin Cities are offered by *Gray Line* (summers only) and *Magic Carpet Tours.* Maps of self-guided walking tours of downtown Minneapolis are available at the Information Center in the IDS Crystal Court. Free tours of business and industrial firms range from a look at the Minneapolis Grain Exchange to the Betty Crocker Kitchens. Cultural centers such as Orchestra Hall and the Walker Art Center offer tours. Reservations are suggested. You can also cruise the Mississippi aboard the sternwheelers *Jonathan Padelford* or *Josiah Snelling,* or choose two other sternwheelers: *Queen of the Lakes* on Lake Harriet or *Lady of the Lake* on Lake Minnetonka.

WHAT TO DO WITH THE CHILDREN. Visit the "Touch and See" room of the *Bell Museum of Natural History,* 17th and University Aves. S.E., and the *Children's Museum,* 700 N. 1st St., Minneapolis; *The Science Museum of Minnesota* and the *McKnight 3M Omnitheater,* 30 E. 10th St., St. Paul; The *Children's Theater,* 201 E. 24th St., Minneapolis; St. Paul's *Como Zoo* and *Conservatory;* the *Minnesota Zoological Garden* in suburban Apple Valley; the *State Capitol* or *Gibbs Farm Museum* in St. Paul; and the *Minnesota Valley Restoration Project* or *Valleyfair Amusement Park,* both near Shakopee.

HOTELS AND MOTELS. The price categories, for double occupancy, average as follows: *Moderate* $46–65, and *Inexpensive* under $46.

Moderate: **Curtis Hotel.** Older, established hotel within walking distance of downtown and Nicollet Mall at 10th St. and 3rd Ave. S.

Fair Oaks Motel. Pleasant rms. 2 mi. S of downtown, just off I-35 at 2335 Third Ave. S. Near Mpls. Institute of Arts.

Guest House Motel. Close to loop at 704 Fourth Ave. S. Attractive rooms.

Inexpensive: **Cricket Inn of Plymouth.** I-494 and Hwy. 55. Modern rooms. Restaurant adjacent.

ST. PAUL. *Moderate:* **Golden Steer.** 1010 S. Concord St. Pleasant rooms.

Cricket Inn. Comfortable rooms ten minutes from fairgrounds.

Northernaire. Nice rooms ten minutes from downtown.

Inexpensive: **Bleick House Bed and Breakfast Inn.** Renovated 110-year-old home near downtown. Antique and period decor. Includes continental breakfast.

DINING OUT in the Twin Cities frequently means steaks, although there are plenty of exotic restaurants featuring everything from sukiyaki to baklava. Restaurant price categories are as follows: *Moderate* $10–15 and *Inexpensive* under $10. Prices are for a complete meal, excluding drinks, tax and tip.

Moderate: **Black Forest Inn.** 1 E. 26th St., Minneapolis. Hearty German fare, Informal atmosphere.

Chi Chi's. I-494 and Nicollet Ave. Mexican specialties. Lively happy hour.

The Good Earth. 3460 W. 70th St. in Edina. Vegetarian dishes and scrumptuous desserts on imaginative menu.

The Nankin. 2 South 7th St., Minneapolis. Splendid Cantonese fare.

Venetian Inn. 2814 Rice St., St. Paul. Southern Italian specialties.

Inexpensive: **Becky's Cafeteria.** 1934 Hennepin Ave., Minneapolis. Classy cafeteria decorated with antiques. Home-style cooking.

The Brothers. In all the Dale shopping centers and downtown. Delicatessen with scrumptuous desserts.

Haberdashery. 1501 Washington Ave. S., Mpls., and 395 Wabasha, St. Paul. Sandwiches, omelettes and all the peanuts you can shell.

The Pantry. 7545 Lyndale S. and 5101 Arcadia Ave. Imaginative sandwiches and homemade soups and desserts.

EXPLORING MINNESOTA

The strongest pull for the typical vacation visitor to Minnesota is the still-unspoiled North Country, where the fish come big and the fish stories bigger, and the local lore is a mixture of Indian legends and tales of Paul Bunyan.

Traveling northeast from the Twin Cities, a North Country tour begins at Duluth, the international port city on Lake Superior. On a warm summer day, you'll suddenly feel a cool, caressing breeze. That's the first dividend of the North Country—natural air conditioning.

Duluth itself has some interesting sights for those who tarry before heading northward. The city shoreline on Lake Superior runs 24 miles, and the buildings here seem to spill downhill from the bluffs that rise 600 feet above the lake.

Duluth attractions include the Canal Park Marine Museum, St. Louis County Heritage and Arts Center, Tweed Art Gallery, Skyline Drive, Glensheen Mansion, Harbor cruises, Duluth Zoo, and Leif Erikson and Enger parks.

Less than an hour's drive from Duluth is Two Harbors, Minnesota's first iron-ore port. Massive ore-loading docks contrast in size with the diminutive Three Spot, the 1887-vintage woodburning steam locomotive that is enshrined near the railway station.

Continuing on, you'll pass Gooseberry Falls on your way to Split Rock Lighthouse, perched on a sheer cliff just short of Beaver Bay. Now a state park, Split Rock Lighthouse is being restored to its 1930s appearance.

Further on, at the halfway point to the Ontario border, a high curving bridge crosses the Manitou River. From here, a footpath leads to a mighty 80-foot waterfall.

Some of the region's outstanding scenery is in Cascade State Park. The Cascade River flows through the beautiful 2,300-acre park and pours into Lake Superior over a series of dazzling waterfalls.

Grand Marais, 11 miles ahead, is a fishing and tourist center. It also serves as a jumping-off point for a delightful shunpike over the Gunflint Trail into a wilderness area of Superior National Forest. Beyond Grand Marais is Hovland, where there's a junction with another wilderness trail offering a side trip into Superior National Forest.

Minnesota has extensive national parks and forests. Voyageurs National Park, the state's first, is on the Kabetogama peninsula, just south of International Falls. Isle Royale National Park, actually located in Michigan, is more easily reached from harbors in Minnesota. At Isle Royale, visitors will find over 100 miles of trails for hikers (no automobiles are transported to the island), as well as boating excursions.

Chippewa National Forest, comprising over 641,000 acres, has more than 2,000 lakes, including some of the largest in the state. For information, write to: Forest Supervisor, Chippewa National Forest, Cass Lake, Minnesota.

Superior National Forest covers more than three million acres and has close to 2,000 lakes. It borders on Canada's Quetico Provincial

Park, and the two regions cover 3,400 square miles. For information, write: Forest Supervisor, Superior National Forest, Duluth, Minnesota.

Within Superior Forest is one of the famed, relatively new National Forest Wilderness areas. The name is apt; there are no public roads, no big recreation areas, no timber-cutting operations. The Superior Wilderness contains the Boundary Waters Canoe Area, possibly the most famous of the country's canoeing regions. It runs for nearly 200 miles along northeastern Minnesota's boundary with Canada. Travel permits are required.

State parks include Interstate State Park, south of Taylors Falls; Itasca State Park, north of Park Rapids; Judge C. R. Magney State Park, east of Grand Marais; Mille Lacs Kathio State Park, west of Onamia; Savanna Portage State Park, north of McGregor; Minneopa State Park, west of Mankato; and Camden State Park, southwest of Marshall.

Grand Portage Trail

At the easternmost point of Minnesota's North Shore is Grand Portage State Park. The first white settlement in Minnesota, the village of Grand Portage is steeped in regional history. The Grand Portage Trail, carved through the heart of the park, is kept cleared for hikers and cross-country skiers who would like to follow the path of the old-time voyageurs.

From Grand Portage, visitors can head for Isle Royale, Michigan, one of the nation's most primitive national parks. Twenty-two miles from the Minnesota mainland, the island is a paradise for nature lovers. Wildlife is abundant; the largest herd of moose in North America resides here.

Sportsman's Paradise

A major port of entry between Canada and Minnesota, International Falls is a crossroads for sportsmen traveling to and from the great walleye-populated waters of Rainy Lake, the isolated smaller lakes on both sides of the border, and huge Lake of the Woods, famous for its muskies and walleyed pike. International Falls is also one of the country's major centers of the wood-pulp products industry.

Rochester and the Mayo Clinic

Rochester has come a long way since Dr. William W. Mayo settled here in 1855. Besides taking a tour of the huge clinic and its fascinating medical museum, you can visit Mayowood, the home of Drs. C. H. and C. W. Mayo. This handsome mansion, set on 10 acres, contains period antiques and mementos. Guided tours are arranged through the Olmsted County Historical Center and Museum; call in advance. Mayo Park houses the Rochester Art Center, Civic Auditorium, and Civic Theatre; professional dramatic productions, children's theater, and concerts are scheduled. Within a short distance of Rochester are parks and recreation areas for sports activities and picnicking.

PRACTICAL INFORMATION FOR MINNESOTA

HOW TO GET THERE. *By car:* The two main east-west arteries are I–90, which skirts the southern border, and I–94, running diagonally from Fargo, North Dakota, in the northwest, through the Twin Cities to Eau Claire, Wisconsin in the southeast. I–35 runs north to south through the Twin Cities.

By air: Northwest Orient, Western, United, USAir, Eastern, American, Ozark, Pan Am, Texas International, Air Wisconsin, Mississippi Valley and *Republic.*

By bus: Greyhound and *Jefferson* are the transcontinental lines serving this area.

By train: Two *Amtrak* routes cross Minnesota: the Empire Builder from Winona in the southeast through St. Paul to Fargo, ND; and the North Star, from St. Paul to Duluth in the northeast.

TOURIST INFORMATION. The Minnesota Tourist Information Center, 240 Bremer Bldg., 419 N. Robert, St. Paul 55101, can furnish you with information about the state and its tourist facilities. Contact individual chambers of commerce for more specific information.

Tourist Information Centers, run by the Minnesota Dept. of Transportation, are located at Thompson Hill (near Duluth); Dresbach, just north of LaCrescent on I–90; Moorhead, at the North Dakota-Minnesota border on I–94; Beaver Creek on I–90; and south of Albert Lea on I–35.

MUSEUMS AND GALLERIES. At the *St. Louis County Heritage and Arts Center* in Duluth, 2222 East Superior St., you can see relics from the history of Duluth. Visitors can view the inactive Glen open pit mine from a glass-enclosed walkway extending out over the mine at the *Iron Range Interpretative Center* on Hwy. 169 southwest of Chisholm. At 1832 East 2nd St., Rochester has the *Mayo Medical Museum.* Life-size dioramas of Indian life are featured in the *Mille Lacs Indian Museum* in Onamia. Minnesota's interpretive centers are especially informative and entertaining. Each contains documents, period items, photographs and slide presentations on particular persons or eras. Centers are located at: *Fort Ridgely,* south of Fairfax; *Grand Mound,* west of International Falls; *Lindbergh House,* in Little Falls; and the *Lower Sioux Agency,* east of Redwood Falls.

HISTORIC SITES. The lives of several famous Minnesotans are recorded in their restored homes: the *Mayo House* in Le Sueur; the *Folsom House* in Taylors Falls; the *Comstock House* in Moorhead; and the *Kelley Farm* southeast of Elk River. Other sites range from the prehistoric *petroglyphs* etched in rock near Jeffers to the *Harkin Store* northwest of New Ulm with its shelves stocked with 1800s wares to the *North West Company Fur Post* near Pine City to the *Grand Portage National Monument* northeast of Duluth, the home ground of the French voyageurs.

DRINKING LAWS. Legal age is 19. Cocktail lounges and bars close at 1 A.M.

SUMMER SPORTS. Minnesota, "land of sky blue waters," is a little bit of heaven for the avid sportsman. So extensive are its forest and prairie and so numerous are its lakes that the hunter can always find new trails to traverse, and the fisherman can fish for a lifetime without visiting all the lakes.

The sportsman can enjoy every kind of water sport in addition to riding, camping, hiking, tennis and golf.

Northern Minnesota's low mountains are heavily wooded, while the middle and southern sections are gentle hills and prairies. The Arrowhead District of the northeast, so called because of its shape, is a renowned resort and sports area. The Detroit Lakes section, in the west, is famous for its excellent fishing.

Every kind of *fresh water fish* can be found in Minnesota waters. There is even deep-sea fishing for lake trout in Lake Superior.

Hunting is excellent. The hunter can find deer, pheasant, grouse, and other game.

The *Department of Natural Resources,* Centennial Building, St. Paul, can supply information on all sporting activities in state parks.

One of the United States' great areas for *canoeing* is the Quetico Reserve in the Superior National Forest. The Chippewa National Forest is also a wooded land of many lakes.

Visitors to the Twin Cities will find an assortment of sports activities throughout the year. Both cities are on the Mississippi and have lakes within their limits. Nearby are Lake Minnetonka and White Bear Lake. The cities offer golf courses and nature reserves, as well as hiking and cycling along scenic woodland park trails.

 **WINTER SPORTS.** In this state, winter sports rival the summer ones for popularity. *Ice skating, hockey, skiing, ski touring, bobsledding, curling, sleigh riding, snowshoeing, ice boating, ice fishing, sled dogging, inner tubing* and *snowmobiling* are enthusiastically enjoyed by residents and visitors alike.

For details on where you can enjoy these winter sports, send for the free *Minnesota Winter Guide.* Write: Minnesota Department of Economic Development, 240 Bremer Bldg., 419 N. Robert, St. Paul 55101.

 HOTELS AND MOTELS in Minnesota run the gamut from deluxe resort-style facilities in the lake regions to commercial hotels in the larger cities to comfortable, family-run motels. The price categories in this section, for double occupancy, average as follows: *Moderate,* $35–45; *Inexpensive,* under $35. Rates vary by season in resort areas.

ALEXANDRIA. *Moderate:* **Viking Motel.** Across from airport. Restaurant and pool.

BEMIDJI. *Inexpensive:* **Bel Air Motel.** NW of town. Pleasant rooms.

BRAINERD. *Moderate:* **River View Motel.** Rooms plus efficiencies and two-room units.
Inexpensive: **Thrifty Scot Motel.** Nice rooms.

DULUTH. *Moderate:* **Best Western Downtown.** Convenient, next to skywalk. Free continental breakfast.
Inexpensive: **Spirit Motor Inn.** Close to Spirit Mountain.

GRAND MARAIS. *Moderate:* **Cascade Lodge.** Rooms and cottages facing Lake Superior.

GRAND RAPIDS. *Moderate:* **Rainbow Inn.** Very nice rooms and restaurant.

INTERNATIONAL FALLS. *Inexpensive:* **Falls Motel.** Clean, attractive rooms.

MANKATO. *Inexpensive:* **Cliff Kyes.** Nice rooms.

ROCHESTER. (Many of the hotels here have provisions for the handicapped and free transportation to the Mayo Clinic.) *Moderate:* **Gas Light Inn.** Nice rooms.
Center Towne Travel Inn. Downtown. Pool, laundromat, free parking.
Inexpensive: **Beverly Motel Apartments.** Equipped kitchenettes. Near Mayo.
Carlton. Good, older hotel. Downtown.
Silver Lake Motel. Nice rooms and some efficiencies.

ST. CLOUD. *Inexpensive:* **Gateway.** Attractive rooms with patios.
Inexpensive: **Kleis.** Comfortable rooms.
Travel Wise Motel. Nice rooms.

 DINING OUT. Minnesota's rivers and "10,000 lakes" abound with good things to eat—pike, trout and bass. Many restaurants are situated along the water's edge, nature thus providing beautiful views as well as good food. But if North Woods fresh-water fish is not to your taste, this is a land of farms, too, and the Minnesotans know how to bake and how to broil steaks.

Restaurant price categories (average) are as follows: *Moderate,* $8–10; and *Inexpensive,* under $8. Prices are for a complete meal, excluding drinks, tax and tip.

BEMIDJI. *Moderate:* **Snider's Restaurant.** Homemade pastries. Home—style meals.
Inexpensive: **Perkin's Cake & Steak.** Full menu, from pancakes to shrimp. Open 24 hours.

BRAINERD. *Moderate:* **Lumbertown Dining Room** at Madden Inn. Family-style dining in rustic setting.

DULUTH. *Moderate:* **Carlton House.** Meals and railroad museum under same roof.
Grandma's Saloon & Deli. Great sandwiches and ice cream drinks. Summer beer garden.
Pickwick Restaurant. Lake view. Old Heidelberg atmosphere.

FARIBAULT. *Moderate:* **Lavender Inn.** Generous portions. Complete menu. Adjoins art gallery.

GRAND MARAIS: *Moderate:* **Cascade Lodge.** Excellent food amid North Woods atmosphere.

HASTINGS. *Moderate:* **Mississippi Belle.** Showboat setting with full menu and delicious pies.

ROCHESTER. *Moderate:* **Carter's.** Homemade soups and BBQ ribs daily; plus dinner specials.
Green Parrot Café. Family restaurant with varied menu.

WINONA. *Moderate:* **Hot Fish Shop.** Steak, seafood.

OHIO

Best of the Midwest

Situated on the shores of Lake Erie at the mouth of the Cuyahoga River, within 500 miles of half of the populations of the United States and Canada, the largest city in Ohio was founded by Moses Cleaveland in 1796. The Civil War occasioned a great need for iron and steel, and set Cleveland on its way to industrial preëminence. Ore deposits in the upper Great Lakes and vast nearby fields of coal made the fantastic growth of the city inevitable. The Irish were the first to arrive, followed by the Welsh and English, a few French and Dutch. Then came masses of Poles, Germans, Czechs, Hungarians, Jews, Serbs, Italians, Slavs and more, until 63 different cultures were represented in Cleveland, each with its own customs, languages, costumes and foods.

The nation's ninth largest metropolitan area sprawls along the lake for 45 miles on either side of the Cuyahoga and runs inland for an average of 10 miles.

The Cleveland Art Museum is the leading attraction of the park-like University Circle area. Here are also found the Museum of Natural History; Severance Hall, the acoustically perfect home of the renowned Cleveland Orchestra; Western Reserve Historical Museum; and Case Western Reserve University. Still other points of interest are: the Health Education Museum, first in the nation; Dunham Tavern, a converted stagecoach house now filled with antiques; the Cleveland

Zoo, one of the country's top five; and the General Electric Lighting Institute, at Nela Park.

In addition to a two-hour boat tour up the Cuyahoga River and through the harbor and lake, there is a guided tour of the city daily, departing from Public Square and downtown hotels. The Cleveland Playhouse houses a professional repertory company and three theaters. The Hanna Theater and the interracial Karamu House are frequently visited by Broadway road companies, and Cleveland is also the home of several little theater groups. For those whose tastes run to things musical, there are the Blossom Music Center, summer home of the Cleveland Orchestra, which also presents excellent rock, jazz and popular concerts, and the Beck Center for the Cultural Arts in Lakewood. And for sports fans Cleveland offers more than twenty public and semi-private golf courses, thoroughbred, and harness racing, ski areas, boat launching ramps, and plenty of fine tennis courts, riding areas, wildlife sanctuaries, and other recreational facilities.

PRACTICAL INFORMATION FOR CLEVELAND

HOW TO GET THERE. There are several good ways to get to and from Cleveland. Interstates 71, 77, 80 and 90 are excellent. Railway service is poor, but *Greyhound* and *Trailways* provide satisfactory bus service. Cleveland is served by 11 major airlines operating in two airports, Burke Lakefront and Cleveland Hopkins International.

HOW TO GET AROUND. *By taxi:* In downtown Cleveland, taxis are readily available on the street. *By bus:* The downtown local shuttle (the bus is orange and marked "Local") is cheap. The longer-range "Express Service" costs more. *From the airport:* Public Rapid Transit operates between the airport and downtown Cleveland. The trip from Hopkins International to Public Square takes about twenty minutes and is about 50¢. A cab ride from the airport to downtown will cost you about $12.00.

TOURIST INFORMATION. The *Convention and Visitors Bureau of Greater Cleveland*, 1301 E. 6th St., Cleveland 44144, (216) 621–4110, has information on all facets of Cleveland life. Group tours can be arranged by contacting the bureau. Call (216) 621-8860 for a recorded message on current events, shows.

MUSEUMS AND GALLERIES. The *Cleveland Museum of Art*, 11150 East Boulevard, overlooks the Fine Arts Gardens in University Circle. It is the second wealthiest museum in the nation, topped only by the Metropolitan Museum in New York. Closed Mon., July 4, Thanksgiving, Christmas, and New Year's Day.

Cleveland Health Education Museum, 8911 Euclid Ave., first health museum in the U.S., opened in 1940. Exhibits show how the human body works, the transparent woman, and model of electronic human brain brought from New York World's Fair. Closed Thanksgiving, Christmas, and New Year's Day.

Also in Cleveland are the *Temple Museum of Jewish Religious Art & Music*, the *Howard Dittrick Museum of Historical Medicine*, the *Natural Science Museum*, the *Romanian Folk Museum*, the *Dunham Tavern Museum*, the *Western*

Reserve Historical Society Library & Museum, and the *Afro-American Cultural and Historical Society.*

Short trips from Cleveland will take you to *Geauga County Historical Museum* in Burton, *Fairport Harbor Museum* (Fairport), *Pioneer Farm and Home Museum* and the *Dudley Peter Allen Memorial Art Museum* in Oberlin, the *Great Lakes Historical Museum* in Vermilion, and the Museum of *Lake Erie Junior College* in Bay Village.

 GARDENS. For *Cleveland Cultural Gardens,* enter at East Blvd. and Superior Ave., continue toward St. Clair on East Blvd. in Rockefeller Park. Open all spring, summer, and fall. A chain of 19 cultural gardens that combine landscapes and sculpture typical of the cultures of the Polish, German, Hebrew, Italian, Lithuanian, Slovak, Yugoslav, Czech, Hungarian, Greek, Russian, Irish, American Colonial, Ukrainian, and Finnish who represent the national backgrounds of Cleveland's citizenry. The gardens were inspired by the success of the first, a *Shakespearean Garden,* dedicated Apr. 14, 1916, oldest Shakespeare garden in the country. Free.

Also in Cleveland are the *City Greenhouse* and the *Cleveland Fine Arts Garden* and the *Garden Center of Greater Cleveland.*

 SUMMER SPORTS. In baseball, the *Cleveland Indians* represent the American League, and in football there are the *Cleveland Browns,* who play at Lakefront Stadium. In basketball, there are the *Cleveland Cavaliers,* and in hockey, the major league *Cleveland Barons. Thistledown Race Track* is on Warrensville Center Road. *Northfield Race Track* has trotters.

WINTER SPORTS. Several good skiing areas can be found just outside of Cleveland in the nearby *Cuyahoga Valley* and *Alpine Valley.*

 WHAT TO DO WITH THE CHILDREN. *Cleveland Zoo,* in Brookside Park off W. 25th Street, features lions and tigers without cages or bars, birds in natural habitat, Children's Farm, Kiddieland Park and touring trains. Open daily year-round 9:30 A.M. to 5 P.M. Sundays and holidays in summer to 7 P.M.

Sea World features the world's first trained killer whale, a Hawaiian village, and a Canadian lumberjack show. Located SE of the city on State 43, 7 miles off Ohio Turnpike Exit 13. Open daily 9 A.M. to 10 P.M. Memorial Day to Labor Day.

 HOTELS AND MOTELS in Cleveland are plentiful and afford the traveler any kind of accommodation he or she may desire. Downtown hotels, offering good locations and all facilities, compete with motels in and around the city.

The price categories in this section, for double occupancy, will average as follows: *Moderate* $30 and up, *Inexpensive* under $30. For a more complete description of these categories see the *Hotels & Motels* part of *Facts at Your Fingertips.*

Inexpensive. **Gold Coast Inn.** 11837 Edgewater Dr. One block from Lake Erie.

Lakewood Manor. 12019 Lake Ave., Lakewood, just W of I–90 Bishop Rd. exit.

Red Roof Inn. 6020 Quarry Ln., Independence, 7 mi S, on I–77 Rockside exit. Café next door.

DINING OUT in Cleveland can be exciting, and the quality of food served in those spots featuring entertainment competes favorably with that in restaurants specializing in cuisine only. There are several fine Italian kitchens, but beef seems to top the menus in establishments favored by Clevelanders.

For other worthwhile restaurants, check hotel and nightclub listings. If you plan to eat out on a holiday, make sure you call to see if the establishment will be open. Restaurants are categorized according to a mid-priced meal in each.

Restaurant price categories are as follows: *Moderate* $10–15, *Inexpensive* under $10. These prices are for hors d'oeuvres or soup, entree, and dessert. Not included are drinks, tax and tips.

Moderate. **Pier W.** Good seafood with view of lake and city.
James Tavern. Early American menu.
Inexpensive: **Bali Hai.** Chinese and Polynesian food.
Earth By April. Seafood, vegetarian dishes.
Miller's Dining Room. Family-operated and popular.

EXPLORING OHIO

With the start of the 19th century, Cincinnati became a boom town because of its strategic location on the increasingly busy Ohio River and the introduction of the steamboat to the waterways of the West. German influence is still strong in the Ohio Valley today, an area which brings to mind the Rhine wine country. The Queen City is an engaging mélange of mosaics that are partly Midwest, partly European, with a touch of the South added for accent.

Conservative politically and cosmopolitan socially, Cincinnati today is similar in many ways to San Francisco, even to being situated on many hills. Cincinnatians enjoy the good things, and their city's restaurants well deserve their national recognition. The city is no laggard culturally, with fine collections housed in both the Taft Museum and Cincinnati Art Museum. The Cincinnati Summer Opera performs during the summer, and the Cincinnati Symphony Orchestra and Cincinnati Ballet Company perform during the winter. Many nightclubs here and across the river in Kentucky re-create the atmosphere of the French Quarter in New Orleans. Garden lovers will appreciate the Irwin M. Krohn Conservatory in Eden Park, and the Mount Airy Arboretum. And the hills come alive with the sounds of music during the traditional May Festival, a two-week program of music. During the summer, the river steamboat *Delta Queen* takes passengers in air-conditioned comfort on five-, seven- and ten-day trips on the Ohio River and 20-day cruises all the way to New Orleans, and the *Showboat Majestic* presents comedy and musicals at the Public Landing at the foot of Broadway. At Riverfront Stadium, sports fans can watch the Cincinnati Reds and the Cincinnati Bengals. Arena sports, circuses and other shows are staged at Riverfront Coliseum.

One of the largest amusement parks in the Midwest, Kings Island, is north of Hamilton County Cincinnati on I-75. Six theme areas, centering around a replica of the Eiffel Tower, are International Street, Rivertown, Hanna-Barbera Land, Wild Animal Safari, Oktoberfest, and turn-of-the-century Coney Island. Near the park are the College Football Hall of Fame and the Jack Nicklaus Sports Center.

Toledo

Toledo is the home of the world-famous Jeep, as well as scales manufacturers, one of the country's finest art museums, and an equally outstanding zoo. The museum is known for its collections of glass, paintings, sculpture, and decorative arts. Attractions at the zoo, which opened in 1899 with one woodchuck, include the Museum of Science and Natural History, a large fresh-water aquarium and the children's Wonder Valley, plus a second woodchuck.

Country of Plain Folk

The Amish are divided into two sects: The severe Old Order forbids owning cars, using electricity and strongly opposes any ostentation, worldly pleasures and all forms of violence; the more progressive Mennonites may own automobiles and also avail themselves of modern conveniences and comforts. Theologically, however, there is little difference between the two.

You'll see crowds of both Mennonites and Amish throughout Holmes, Wayne and Tuscarawas counties, among the nation's finest agricultural sections, and the shrewd, hard-working and self-sufficient Amish have contributed much to this standing. Largest town in Holmes County is Millersburg, which is also the county seat. The town's business district accommodates its many Amish customers with long hitching rails to which the farmers tie their horses while they shop. The Amish also have country auctions, just about the only social activity they allow themselves outside of their weddings and wakes. During summer, these auctions are held on Tuesday afternoons in Farmerstown and on Thursday afternoons in Kidron. Mostly produce is sold at these auctions.

Columbus

Columbus, unlike the other large cities in Ohio, has less than three percent foreign-born citizens. With its rapid growth in the last few years has come a similar change of pace and face in the downtown area. Buildings that stood since the Civil War have been torn down in the last two years, replaced by office buildings, hotels, and motels. One thing that hasn't changed is the staid old limestone capitol, considered the purest example of Doric architecture in the United States. Completed in 1861, its walls are 12 to 15 feet thick, stronger by far than the Ohio State Penitentiary, just a few miles away. Columbus is full of points of interest. One of the newest is the Ohio Historical Center, with its central museum and archives, and collection of archeological, historical, and geological material. The main branch of Ohio State University is located here with its 80,000-seat stadium, 900,000-volume Ohio State Library, and horticultural gardens. Blossom browsers enjoy the Park of Roses in Whetstone Park with its 425 varieties of roses, and the Franklin Park Conservatory, part of the 1893 Chicago World's Fair, with its array of exotic tropical and sub-tropical flora. Ohio

Village is a reconstructed Ohio county seat, vintage 1800-1850, with 14 buildings and demonstrations of commercial crafts of that era. Seven miles north in Worthington is the Ohio Railway Museum. Also north of the city on State 23 are the Olentangy Caverns, the only three-level caves in Ohio. Just a mile south of the center of Columbus is a restored German village, home of the Oktoberfest in the fall. Restaurants and sausage houses here offer regional food, and shops and bazaars sell hand-crafted items. During the summer months, thoroughbred racing is presented at Beulah Park in neighboring Grove City and harness racing at Scioto Downs. Golfers, anglers, hikers, ice skaters, and picnickers can pursue their own interests at the seven reservations in Columbus' Metropolitan Park System.

Dayton and Airplanes

There will be no doubt in your mind as you drive through the modern downtown area of Ohio's fourth largest city: Dayton is a progressive town. Her greatest contribution to the world came with the success of the Wright brothers. Their first experiments with flying machines here led directly to their historic flight in North Carolina at Kitty Hawk.

At the city's Carillon Park are many transportation exhibits, including a restored Wright brothers' plane, a Conestoga wagon, a Concord coach, and Newcom Tavern, Dayton's oldest building. The park includes an actual section of the Miami-Erie Canal, fitted with one of the original locks.

The Air Force Museum at Dayton's Wright-Patterson Air Force Base is located in Fairborn, 11 miles east of Dayton. More than 20,000 items are on display as well as more than 150 historic airplanes and spacecraft. These include aircraft from World Wars I and II such as the German ME 109, the Russian Yak and Japanese Zero. Animated displays explain how jets and rockets work.

Other attractions include the Dayton Museum of Natural History, which also houses a planetarium; the Paul Lawrence Dunbar Homestead, home of the famous black poet; and the Dayton Art Institute.

PRACTICAL INFORMATION FOR OHIO

HOW TO GET THERE. *By car:* The major east-west highways into Ohio are I–90, I–80 and I–70. On the north-south axis are I–77, I–71, and I–75.

By train: Amtrak serves Cincinnati and Columbus. For information on *Amtrak* tours write to Amtrak Travel Center, P.O. Box 474, Riverdale, Maryland 20840. (Routes are being reviewed and are subject to discontinuation.)

By bus: Greyhound and *Trailways* provide service from all over America to Ohio.

By air: Cleveland, Toledo, Lima, Akron, Columbus, Dayton, and Cincinnati are all served by major carriers.

TOURIST INFORMATION SERVICES. *Ohio Office of Travel and Tourism,* Box 1001, Columbus 43216: information on Ohio's festivals, history, gardens, Mound Builders, farm vacations, historic inns and mills, highway maps and much more. *Ohio Division of Parks and Recreation,* Department of Natural Resources, Publishing Center, Fountain Sq. Columbus 43224. *Guide to State Parks,* and camping information. *Lake Erie Islands and Peninsula Vacationland Association,* Port Clinton: brochure containing tourist map of area pin-pointing attractions and listing cottage information in the area. In Cincinnati: The Cincinnati Convention & Visitor's Bureau, 200 West Fifth St., Cincinnati 45202.

MUSEUMS AND GALLERIES. Canton has the *National Pro Football Hall of Fame,* just north of Fawcett Stadium and Cincinnati has the new *College Football Hall of Fame,* north off I-75 at King's Island exit. In Dayton, see the *Air Force Museum,* Wright-Patterson Air Force Base. *Carillon Park,* on US 25, is a series of historical exhibits dealing with early modes of transportation, displayed in a charming village museum. Others in Dayton are the *Dayton Art Institute,* the *Newcom Tavern,* and the *Dayton Museum of Natural History.*

The *Toledo Museum of Art* contains a world-renowned collection of glass. Toledo also has a good *Museum of Science and Natural History.* The *Jonathan Hale Homestead and Western Reserve Pioneer Village* depicts Western Reserve life from 1800 to 1850.

In Cincinnati there are: *Taft House Museum,* an outstanding example of Greek Revival architecture. It houses a priceless collection of portraits; French Renaissance painted enamel plaques and dishes; jewelry and watches from many countries; and almost 200 Chinese porcelains. You may also visit the *Jewish Museum of Hebrew Union College,* the *Museum of Natural History,* the *Cincinnati Art Museum,* the *Cincinnati Fire Department Museum,* the *Contemporary Arts Center, Stowe House,* and the *Christian Walschmidt House. Grant's Birthplace and Museum* is 15 miles east at Point Pleasant.

HISTORIC SITES. *Fallen Timbers Park,* on US 24 just southwest of Maumee; free. *Flint Ridge State Memorial,* 3 miles N. of Brownsville off US 40 on State 668; *Fort Recovery State Memorial* is on State 49 at the small town of Fort Recovery; *Schoenbrunn Village,* 2 miles S. of New Philadelphia on State 8 and US 250; *Roscoe Village,* an old canal town on the north edge of Coshocton; *Serpent Mound* (4 miles northwest of Locust Grove off State 73), built of stone and clay, curls like an enormous snake for 1,335 feet—the largest and most remarkable effigy mound in America; free *Zoar Village* on State 212 is in a small, peaceful community.

Ohio contains more remains of the ancient race of Indians known as the *Mound Builders* than any other state east of the Mississippi River. Eleven of these mounds are maintained as State Memorials by the Ohio Historical Society. One group is administered by the National Park Service as a National Monument. Serpent Mound, discussed above, is in this group. For a complete listing of Ohio's state memorials, write the Ohio Historical Society, Ohio Historical Center, Columbus, 43211.

DRINKING LAWS. Bars remain open until 1 or 2:30 A.M. daily, with most larger cities serving on Sun. by local option. Liquor may be purchased by the bottle in state stores from 11 A.M. to 6 P.M. Mon.-Sat. Age limit is 21 years, except for beer, 19 years.

SUMMER SPORTS. There are more than 100,000 acres of inland lakes, 36,000 acres of Sandusky Bay, and 7,000 miles of streams where water enthusiasts can enjoy boating, fishing, swimming, water skiing, canoeing, and scuba diving. There are more than 200 golf courses available to visitors. Hunters roam 10 million acres of farm lands and a half-million acres of licensed shooting preserves. Hikers and backpackers use the 478-mile *Buckeye Trail.* There are 200 miles of bridle trails through state forests, as well as primitive campgrounds for horsemen. Special bikeways have been built for cyclists who want to take a self-guided tour through scenic and historic areas of the state.

WINTER SPORTS. There are at least ten small ski areas. Two of the best are *Snow Trails* and *Clear Fork Valley* near Mansfield. Ice skaters join anglers and boaters who use Ohio's many rivers and lakes for winter sports activities.

SPECTATOR SPORTS. During fall and winter, the *Cleveland Browns* and the *Cincinnati Bengals* play professional *football.* In Columbus, the Buckeyes of Ohio State University draw huge crowds to their Big Ten college games. Other fine collegiate teams include *Miami, Bowling Green, Ohio University, Dayton, Western Reserve,* the *University of Cincinnati* and *Xavier. The Toledo Golddiggers* offer professional *ice hockey.* A top winter game is *basketball,* which finds many college teams participating, while the *Cleveland Cavaliers* offer professional play.

In major league *baseball* are the *Cincinnati Reds* and the *Cleveland Indians.* The *Toledo Mud Hens* are part of the International League. *Racetracks* are located in 16 Ohio communities, including Cincinnati, Cleveland, Columbus, Grove City, and state and county fairgrounds. The *Mid-America Sports Car Course* at Mansfield is rated as one of the most competitive in the country. Trapshooters come from all over the world to compete in the *Grand American Trapshooting Tournament* held at Vandalia in late August.

WHAT TO DO WITH THE CHILDREN. Vacationers can drive their cars through *African Lion Safari* and see lions, zebras, and plains game near Port Clinton. *Sea World* features the world's first tame killer whale, a Hawaiian village, and a Canadian Lumberjack Show, SE of Cleveland. A miniature Disneyland is located at *Cedar Point* on Lake Erie. There are more than 200 things to do and see, including a cable car ride, riverboat cruises, stage shows, and crafts on the historic Frontier Trail. The *Toledo Zoo* features the nation's largest fresh water aquarium, a children's zoo, a 12-foot cobra in its Reptile House. In Cincinnati: the second oldest zoo in the country, the *Zoological Gardens,* is located at Vine and Erkenbrecher Streets. A miniature Eiffel Tower stands in the amusement park at *Kings Island,* located 23 miles north at the junction of Kings Mill Road and I-71. It features International Street, Oktoberfest, Rivertown, Coney Island and the Happy Land of Hanna-Barbera.

HOTELS AND MOTELS in Ohio, outside the metropolitan areas of Cleveland and Cincinnati, range from deluxe to inexpensive, and can provide the traveler with any kind of accommodation from the dignified, older downtown hotel to the brighter, newer motel along the roadside. The price categories in the section, for double occupancy, are: *Moderate,* around $30; *Inexpensive,* under $30.

CINCINNATI. *Moderate.* **LaQuinta.** 11335 Chester Rd., 15 mi. N at I-75 Chester Rd. exit. Pool, coffee shop.

L-K Penny Pincher Inn. I-75 Donaldson Road-Airport Exit, 8 mi. S in Erlanger, Ky. Pool, 24-hour café.

Inexpensive. **Bargaintel Florence.** One block W of I-75 exit 180. Coffee shop next door.

Red Roof Inn. 2 locations: 11345 Chester Rd. at I-75 exit 15 and 8 mi. NE on I-71, Ridge Rd. Exit.

COLUMBUS. *Moderate.* **Homestead.** 4182 Main St. Pool, playground, café.
Inexpensive. **Bargaintel.** 10 miles east at I-70, Brice Road Exit. Pool.
Knight's Inn. 10 miles east at I-70, Brice Road Exit. Pool, 24-hour coffee shop.
Red Roof Inn. Three locations with same rates: 10 miles east on I-70; 7 mi. N. on I-71, Morse-Sinclair Exit, and 7 miles west on I-70.

DAYTON. *Inexpensive:* **Knight's Inn.** 10 mi. S on I-75 exit 44 at State 725. Pool, café.
Red Roof Inn-North. 7 mi. N. on I-75, exit 60.

LEBANON. *Moderate:* **The Golden Lamb.** Ohio's oldest hotel still accommodates a few guests in antique-furnished rooms, so phone ahead and relax in the peaceful atmosphere.

MANSFIELD. *Moderate:* **L-K Motel.** Shelby, 12 mi. No. on State 39.

OXFORD. *Inexpensive:* **Oxford Motel.** 1 mi. W. on US 27. Pool.

 DINING OUT. While the Midwest is generally steak and fried chicken country, seafood and foreign dishes are also popular. Hot cinnamon rolls, watermelon pickles, and hash brown potatoes are part of the country cooking in the small-town restaurants throughout the state.

Restaurant price categories are as follows: *Moderate* $10-15; *Inexpensive* under $10. These prices are for hors d'oeuvres or soup, entrée and dessert. Not included are drinks, tax and tips.

AKRON. *Moderate:* **Tangier.** Outstanding lamb, Mideast fare, Exotic décor, floor shows.
Tavern in the Square. Built 1860s. Steaks, prime rib.
Inexpensive: **Art's Place.** Excels in fried chicken, prime rib.

BURTON-WELSHFIELD. *Moderate:* **Welshfield Inn.** An historic inn, once a stop on the underground railroad.

CANTON. *Inexpensive.* **Roadhouse 77.** Prime rib, seafood, own baking.

CINCINNATI. *Moderate.* **Lenhardt's.** Viennese and Hungarian specialties in University of Cincinnati area.
Rockwood Pottery. In former pottery atop Mt. Adams; noted for its burgers.
Inexpensive. **The Colonnade.** Downtown cafeteria with home cooking. Lunch only.
The Cricket Tavern. Popular downtown family place with complete dinners.
T.G.I. Friday's. Huge menu, bargain prices. North of city at I-75 and I-275.
The Old Spaghetti Factory. Charming, good food. Downtown.

COLUMBUS. *Moderate:* **Kahiki,** Polynesian, Chinese, and American specialties.
Oliver's Tavern. Barbecued ribs, seafood. Old English décor.
Inexpensive **Ricardo's.** Italian-American fare, entertainment.

COSHOCTON. *Moderate:* **Old Warehouse.** Quaint dining room in restored Roscoe Village.

DAYTON. *Moderate:* **King Cole.** French-American menu.
Inexpensive: **Anticoli's.** Italian specialties.

MANSFIELD. *Moderate.* **Castle Keep.** London broil, own baking.

MARIETTA. *Moderate.* **The Gun Room.** Excellent for price. Interesting setting in Lafayette Hotel of steamboat era.

MILAN-NORWALK. *Inexpensive:* **Milan Inn.** A historic "Inn of Fine Foods" expresses the unhurried lifestyle of the locale.

OBERLIN. *Inexpensive:* **Oberlin Inn.** Locally popular.

TOLEDO. *Inexpensive:* **Bill Knapp's.** Chicken a specialty; child's plates.

ZANESVILLE. *Moderate:* **Old Market House Inn.** Shrimp, aged meats, Italian dishes.

WISCONSIN

Milwaukee and Lush Resortlands

Milwaukee, with a population of three-quarters of a million within the city limits, is the state's center of trade. Built mainly by German immigrants, it also has a large Polish population as well as the usual potpourri of nationalities. Somehow it retains a small-town friendliness despite its changing skyline. Steel and glass highrises were late to arrive, and residents still value their carefully maintained, older neighborhoods as much as the new additions bordering the lake.

Its lake-front residential district is one of the most beautiful in the nation, and the city has long been known for its orderly good government and its comparative lack of crime. Milwaukee has a beautiful art center and war memorial in an unusual modern structure on the lake front, a fine zoo, an ornate old public library (considered to be, along with the capitol at Madison, one of the state's most impressive buildings), lovely parks, and boulevards.

It probably is best known, though, for beer and baseball. Several breweries, including the giants—Pabst and Miller—offer a conducted tour through their plants with a frothy glass of free refreshment in an attractive tavern at the end of the trip. The Milwaukee Brewers of the American League play home games at County Stadium, which is also used for Green Bay Packer home games during the pro football season.

PRACTICAL INFORMATION FOR MILWAUKEE

HOW TO GET AROUND. *By bus:* The city-owned system operates around the clock throughout Milwaukee County, although runs are abbreviated after weekday evening rush hours and on weekends. They operate June-September sightseeing city tours. Call 344–4550 for information. Special wheelchair lift buses for handicapped. Call 344–6711. *By car: Avis, Budget, Econo-Car,* and *Hertz* maintain offices downtown and at the airport. *By boat: Iroquois Boatline* offers 2-hour harbor cruises. Call 354–5050.

TOURIST INFORMATION. *Greater Milwaukee Convention & Visitors Bureau* is at 756 North Milwaukee St. Two additional centers are at 201 North Mayfair Road, Wauwatosa, May to Sept., and Upper Level of General Mitchell Field. For daily listings of what's happening in town, call Milwaukee Fun Line 799–1177, 24-hours a day.

MUSEUMS AND GALLERIES. *The Milwaukee Art Center and War Memorial,* 750 Lincoln Memorial Dr., a piece of art in itself, designed by Saarinen; the *Experimental Aircraft Association Museum,* 11311 Forest Home houses unique aviation collections and vintage planes. The *Milwaukee Public Museum,* 800 Wells St., the fourth largest natural history museum in the U.S.; the *Milwaukee County Historical Center,* 910 N. Third St.; the *Pabst Mansion,* 2000 West Wisconsin Ave., an extraordinary residential landmark of famed beer baron.

GARDENS. At the *Horticultural Conservatory* in Mitchell Park, 524 Layton Blvd., you can walk through several continents of gardens, and at *Alfred Boerner Botanical Gardens* in Whitnall Park, 5879 S. 92nd St., you can wander about nature trails and formal gardens. New is *Schlitz Audubon Center,* 200 acres under development by National Audubon Society.

SPORTS. Milwaukee has variety for both spectator and participant. Professionally, there's the Milwaukee Brewers, *baseball;* the Milwaukee Bucks, *basketball;* and the Green Bay Packers, *football.* Summer: For the sportsman, there are *sailboat races* on Lake Michigan; supervised sandy *beaches* all along the lakeshore; *pleasure boat* rental, again along the lakefront; *fishing* (fighting coho salmon abound in Lake Michigan); nearly 30 *golf* courses; *scuba* and *skin diving; bike riding* on nearly 200 miles of trails and bikeways; *polo* at Uihlein Field, North 70th St. at W. Good Hope Rd., and *auto racing* at Hales Corners and the State Fairgrounds.

Winter: Rugby and *soccer* are popular. In October, pheasant *hunting*—in November, deer hunting. *Skiing* enthusiasts will find themselves on fine slopes within an hour's drive of the city, and *ice skaters* have numerous city and county parks to choose from.

WHAT TO DO WITH THE CHILDREN. The number one attraction is Milwaukee's *zoo* at 10001 Blue Mound Rd. Its construction keeps natural enemies apart—via hidden moats—yet it appears as if the animals are roaming common ground. Miniature train. Weekend lectures and movies are offered at the *Public Museum,* 800 W. Wells, and the *Central YMCA* also has an array of weekend programs. *Marriott's Great America* is a popular day trip.

HOTELS AND MOTELS in Milwaukee are many and varied. Price categories (for double occupancy) start *up* from following figures: *Moderate,* $35–50 and *Inexpensive,* under $35.

Moderate: **Chalet.** 10401 N. Port Washington Rd., Mequon. Special rates for senior citizens.

    Golden Key Motel. 3600 S. 108th St. Pleasant. Free Breakfast.

    Pine View. 5050 S. 108th St. Park at your door.

    White Court Motel. 4400 S. 27th St. Very nice rooms.

    Inexpensive: **Exel Inn.** 115 N. Mayfair Rd. 24-hour restaurant nearby.

    Safari Motel. 6798 Appleton. Pleasant rooms, some efficiencies.

    Sleepy Hollow. 12600 W. Blue Mound Rd. Continental breakfast.

DINING OUT in Milwaukee reflects the varied ethnic make-up of the city. There is much good German food, as well as French and Italian. Seafood and good midwestern beef are staples. Restaurant price categories (averages) are as follows: *Moderate,* $12–18, *Inexpensive,* under $10. Price includes complete meal, excluding drinks, tax and tip.

    Moderate: **John Ernst Café.** 600 E. Ogden Ave. Excellent German food.

    Karl Ratzsch's. 320 E. Mason St. Serving German favorites since 1904.

    Maders. 1037 N. Third St. Medieval-style dining room with flavorful German menu. A local favorite.

    Old Town Serbian Gourmet House. 522 W. Lincoln. Well known locally for Serbian specialties.

    Public Natatorium. 1646 S. 4th St. Conversation-stopper in an imaginatively refurbished onetime city bathhouse. Giant hanging baskets, dolphin show.

    Inexpensive: **Balistreris.** 68 & Wells. Old house. Try the fried eggplant.

    La Joy's Chinese Restaurant. 49th & North Ave. Pressed duck, egg rolls.

    Pagoda. 72nd & North Ave. Re-celebrates Chinese New Year every couple weeks. All-you-can-eat specials.

    Palate Pleasers. Plankinton, 1st & Wells. On 2nd floor of landmark Germania Bldg. Homemade soups, marvelous cream puffs.

    Sherlock's Home. 111 E. Wisconsin. English pub atmosphere.

EXPLORING WISCONSIN

Nearly 1.5-million choice acres compose the wilderness of the two national forests in Wisconsin, both of which are in the northern region. Chequamegon National Forest is in the northwest and Nicolet National Forest is in the northeast.

Both forests offer the best in outdoor living and recreational activities. Contact the Forest Supervisor for details, road maps, literature, times, and schedules of events at Chequamegon, U.S. Forest Service, Park Falls, 54552; Nicolet, U.S. Forest Service, Federal Building, Rhinelander, 54501.

Lake Superior Shoreline and the Apostle Islands

Wisconsin has about 125 miles of shoreline on Lake Superior, which forms the northwest boundary of the state. The peninsula, which thrusts out into the big lake, is heavily forested and little settled. It is here that the historic town of Bayfield is located. Once again coming to the fore as a fishing village, it is also the gateway to the Apostle Islands.

There are 22 Apostle Islands, chief of which is Madeline, settled first by the Chippewas, who stayed for 120 years, welcoming such notables as Father Jacques Marquette.

Madeline Island is the only one of the Apostles with a permanent settlement. Two ferries, each carrying nine cars and about 150 people, make frequent crossings from Bayfield.

These wild, remote, scenically spectacular islands are now part of the National Park Service. Campfire lectures and nature walks are regularly conducted by park rangers in season.

Door County and Madison

The Door County peninsula extends about 70 miles right out into Lake Michigan. Swept by water-freshened breezes from all directions, it began to gain fame nearly 100 years ago as a naturally air-conditioned summer retreat. It remains so today, and the miles of narrow land are dotted with summer resorts and loaded with charm.

Often called the New England of the Midwest, Door County boasts a personality all its own—one with heavy Scandinavian overtones. Scandinavian restaurants and gift shops abound. There are an abundance of rustic fishing piers and old docks, beautiful shoreline drives, excellent golf, swimming, boating, and a very special mood.

Touring Madison, you're bound to be impressed by the capitol, standing on a hill in the center of the city. It is one of the most resplendent of the domed edifices which characterize most state capitals. Here, too, is the gorgeous thousand-acre campus of the University of Wisconsin. Madison itself is beautifully situated. It stands on a narrow neck of land between Lake Mendota on the north, Lake Monona on the south, and Lakes Waubesa and Kegonsa to the southeast. About 30 miles east of Madison is Spring Green. Here for a nominal fee you can tour the Frank Lloyd Wright architecture school Taliesin. Also here, the American Players Theatre performs classics in a magnificent outdoor setting. (For schedule and reservations contact APT, Rte. 3, Spring Green 53588, [608–588–7401]).

The Greatest Show on Earth

"The Greatest Show on Earth" got its start in Baraboo, 10 miles south of the Dells. All that's left here now is the Circus World Museum, but it is one of the most interesting sights in the state. Opened in 1959, it is partly housed in the old buildings used by the Ringling Bros. Circus as winter quarters. From mid-May until mid-September the museum puts on a real one-ring show every day. And that isn't all! Many of the fabulous old circus wagons are here, as is John Zweifel's famous animated miniature circus and countless other priceless circus treasures. Bring your tape recorder . . . the circus music is remarkable.

The Great River Road

From Baraboo, if you drive a few miles south to the junction of US 12 and State 60, you should turn west on 60 for the 90-mile ride along the north bank of the Wisconsin River all the way to the Mississippi. It's one of the most beautiful drives in the state.

Then, when you reach Prairie du Chien, at the confluence of the two big rivers, you're not only in historic country, but on the threshold of the Mississippi's most spectacular stretch as well.

PRACTICAL INFORMATION FOR WISCONSIN

HOW TO GET THERE. *By air:* The main carriers to Milwaukee are: *Republic, Simmons Airlines,* and *Continental.By bus: Greyhound* is the major long-distance carrier serving Milwaukee.

By train: Amtrak has scheduled service to Milwaukee, Portage, Wisconsin Dells, Tomah, and La Crosse and offers occasional package tours.

TOURIST INFORMATION. The *Wisconsin Division of Tourism* maintains information centers on main highways leading into the state and distributes detailed maps without charge, in addition to an assortment of literature on statewide attractions and accommodations. This information may also be obtained by writing to that office at Box 7606, Madison 53707.

MUSEUMS AND GALLERIES. The museum buff's first stop should be at the headquarters of the *State Historical Society of Wisconsin,* 816 State St., Madison. Free maps are available, listing more than 100 museums with their descriptions. Furthermore, the Society's museum is one of the best in the state and offers State exhibits from prehistoric times to the present.

In Green Bay, the *Hazelwood Museum* is the former home of Morgan L. Martin; the *Packer Hall of Fame* highlights the glory years of Green Bay Packer football; and the *Railroad Museum* displays vintage railroad engines and cars from all eras.

The *Elvehjem Art Museum* on the University of Wisconsin campus in Madison, at 800 University Ave., displays a fine collection of historical and contemporary art in a beautiful building. Sunday afternoon chamber music concerts. Free.

In Eau Claire, visit the *Paul Bunyan Logging Camp,* which features an 1880 logging camp, and *Sunnyview School,* from the same period. Both in Carson Park.

Chalet of the Golden Fleece at 618 2nd St. in New Glarus contains Swiss antiques and jewelry, while the *Swiss Village Museum* at 6th and 7th Sts. is a replica of a pioneer Swiss village with 12 buildings.

Children always enjoy viewing toys of yesterday inside the *Little Red School House Free Museum* in the city park of Weyauwega.

In conjunction with the *House on the Rock* on State 23 south of Spring Green is a museum with a number of unique collections including dolls, antique guns, model trains, and nickelodeons.

Madeline Island Historic Museum in the Apostle Islands has an intriguing, wide-ranging collection from beaded Indian deerskins to a horse-drawn sleigh hearse.

Lovers of the sea will enjoy the *Manitowoc Maritime Museum* at 402 8th St.

Mid-Continent Railroad Museum at North Freedom attracts train buffs.

At Shullsburg is the *Badger Mine and Museum,* with mine tours.

The *Peshtigo Fire Museum* at 400 Oconto Ave. re-creates the fire which claimed 1,000 lives the same day as the Chicago fire in 1871.

The *Rhinelander Logging Museum* in Pioneer Park on US 8 and State 47 has re-created an actual logging camp, complete with bunkhouse and kitchen.

Webster House at 9 Rockwell St. in Elkhorn is the former home of 19th-century composer Joseph P. Webster, who wrote "Sweet Bye and Bye."

The *Meteor* is a whale of an attraction. This last remaining "whaleback" ship is a unique marine museum on Barker's Island near Superior.

HISTORIC SITES. Wisconsin lives with history. Among its plentiful attractions are: The *Circus World Museum* at Baraboo, located on the grounds of the first winter home of the Ringling Bros. Circus, offering daily circus acts (mid-May to mid-September), a circus train, plus restored old circus wagons.

The *Old Indian Agency House*, a mile east of Portage off State 33 on Portage Canal Road, features Indian and early Wisconsin history in 1832 homestead.

The *Old Ft. Crawford Military Hospital* at Prairie du Chien has exhibits of Indian medicine men.

In Watertown is the famed *Octagon House*, completed in 1854.

Old Wade House, midway between Fond du Lac and Sheboygan on State 23, is an old stagecoach inn built by Sylvanus Wade. The complex includes the *Jung Carriage Museum*, featuring 70 elegant carriages.

Galloway House and Village is located in Fond du Lac. The home is a farm house remodeled into a Midwestern version of an Italianate villa.

Villa Louis at Prairie du Chien is the mansion of the state's first millionaire, and *Old World Wisconsin* is a 565-acre, outdoor, ethnic museum in Kettle Moraine State Forest tracing residents' heritage. *Pendarvis* at Mineral Point is a complex of restored Cornish miners' homes of the 1830s. *Stonefield* near Cassville is an 1890's village in Nelson Dewey State Park, onetime farm site of Wisconsin's first governor. Many historic houses are open to the public. Among headliners are Janesville's *Lincoln-Tallman Mansion*, Wisconsin Dells' *Greek Revival Bennett House* and West Salem's *Hamlin Garland Homestead*.

TOURS. You can find out about them by contacting the following: *Wery Travel Service*, 5343 W. Forest Home, Milwaukee; *Travel & Tour Service*, 722 N. 3rd, Milwaukee; *On the Scene Tours*, 6951 N. Crestwood Dr., Milwaukee.

Cruises are available throughout the state and information may be obtained from the docks in the respective towns. Some standouts are in the Apostle Islands out of Bayfield; Door County; Lake Superior from Superior; along the Mississippi from the larger river towns, and along the chains of lakes which dot the Northwoods area.

For information concerning one-day car tours in southern Wisconsin contact *Wisconsin Division of Tourism*, P.O. Box 7606, Madison, 53707 for their free booklet on one- and two-day tours, and for the Guide to Wisconsin Attractions.

SUMMER SPORTS. Nearly 15,000 lakes and over 1,700 rivers and streams, make "outdoors" synonymous with Wisconsin. *Fishing* is the number one activity, but *scuba* and *skindiving* are fast gaining ground. There's a *bikeway across the entire state*, and heavy *canoeing* on both quiet- and whitewater rivers. Information on both is available from the Wisconsin Division of Tourism, P.O. Box 7606, Madison 53707.

The *hiker, camper*, and *backpacker* will find a bit of heaven throughout the state, and the *golfer* will find ample opportunity to swing.

WINTER SPORTS. Winter means one thing in Wisconsin and that's snow. When the white stuff falls, the sportsmen rise to meet its challenges. Ice hockey runs (rather skates) rampant. Big game hunting—whitetail deer and black bear—is popular.

There are more than 60 ski locations within the state lines and an ever-growing number of private and public cross-country ski trails, extensive snowmobile trails. *Wisconsin Division of Tourism,* Box 7606, Madison 53707, will forward facts.

HOTELS, MOTELS, AND RESORTS throughout Wisconsin range from glamorous old-line hotels and plush resorts to new motels and homey family-owned establishments. Most resort areas have facilities which operate on various plans—European, Modified American and American. The price categories in this section, for double occupancy, will start and range up as follows: *Moderate,* $35–50; *Inexpensive,* under $35.

BARABOO. *Inexpensive:* **Highlander.** Inviting rooms. Nice playground.

BAYFIELD. *Moderate:* **Rittenhouse Inn.** Lumber baron's former summer home decorated with antiques. Exceptional dining rooms.

DELAVAN. *Moderate:* **Lake Lawn Lodge.** Frontier woodsy decor in popular rambling resort. Marina, golf, tennis, horses. Wonderful rustic mood.

FOND DU LAC. *Inexpensive:* **Motel 6.** Pool, pay TV.

GREEN BAY. Motel 6. Modest prices, pay TV, pool. Crib is free.

LAKE GENEVA. *Moderate:* **Lake Geneva.** Nice setting.

MADISON. *Moderate:* **Roadstar Inn.** 2 locations: 5 mi. E. and 7 mi. S.E. Children under 12, crib and coffee free.
Trails End. 2 ½ mi. south. Some kitchens, free coffee, free airport bus.
Inexpensive: **Exel Inn.** Family prices.
Motel 6. Pool, pay TV.
Red Roof Inn. Free crib.

MANITOWOC. *Moderate:* **Thrifty Scot.** Serves a free continental breakfast.

NEW GLARUS. *Moderate:* **Swiss-Aire Motel.** Very nice, pleasant rooms.

SUPERIOR. *Moderate:* **Manning.** Off-season rates, picnic table and grill for picnickers.

WISCONSIN DELLS. *Moderate:* **Birchcliff Lodge.** Wooded grounds, fine accommodations. Some fireplaces, tennis, beach.
Luna. Modern, comfortable. Seasonal rates. Pool and playground, picnic area.

DINING OUT in Wisconsin covers the gamut of eating establishments, from Scandinavian to lumberjack, from country cafés to elegant restaurants. Restaurant price categories are as follows: *Moderate,* $9–15; *Inexpensive,* $6–9. Prices include a complete meal, excluding drinks, tax and tips.

DOOR COUNTY PENINSULA. Inquire locally about traditional outdoor fish boils scheduled in communities summer into fall.

EAGLE RIVER. *Moderate:* **Pine Gables Gast Haus** on Hwy. 70. Quality German food served in log cabin setting.

FONTANA. *Moderate:* **Stevensons Three.** Sit in stalls of 1836 timbered barn and eat hearty.

HAYWARD. *Inexpensive:* **Logging Camp Cook Shanty.** All you can eat—better come hungry. Checkered tablecloths, tinware, mountains of food.
Summer. A fun place with lumberjack atmosphere.

LAKE GENEVA. *Moderate:* **The Hayloft.** 1½ mi. from town on County BB. Fun place in posh stables of Old Lorimar estate.
Inexpensive: **Golden Buddha.** Tasty Chinese food in unusual barn setting.

MADISON. *Moderate:* **Quivey's Grove.** Off Hwy. 18 and 151 on Nesbitt Rd. Restored farmhouse dining rooms are connected by tunnel to bar in barn. Outdoor fish boil in summer.
Inexpensive: **The Avenue Bar.** E. Washington Ave. A bit too crowded, but fun if you're feeling raucous. Nightly specials—especially Friday fish boils—are some of the best deals in town.
Chi Chi's. Lively Mexican atmosphere, peso prices.
University of Wisconsin Student Union. Modest campus prices. Eat outside on lake in summer.

MANITOWISH WATERS. *Moderate:* **Little Bohemia.** 2 mi. S of US 51. Stop for a meal or a cocktail at the lakefront resort where John Dillinger once hid out. Personal belongings left behind when he escaped lawmen are still there.

MINOCQUA. *Inexpensive:* **Paul Bunyan Lumberjack Restaurant.** Recaptures flavor of state's lively logging past. Good food, lots of it.

WISCONSIN DELLS. *Inexpensive:* **Henny Penny Kitchen Inn.** Good food and ambience.
Paul Bunyan Lumberjack Restaurant. Nostalgic logging camp atmosphere. All you can eat, family-style.

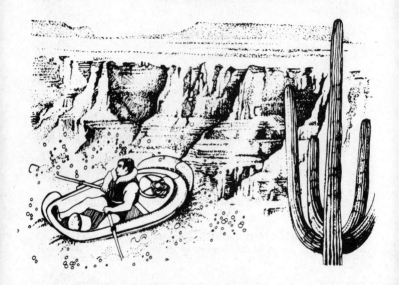

ARIZONA

Phoenix, Tucson and Shangri-La

Phoenix, with surrounding Maricopa County, is the heart of Arizona. The main points of interest in the city are midtown Encanto Park, Pueblo Grande, Papago Park with the Phoenix Zoo and Desert Botanical Garden, the State Capitol, South Mountain Park, Civic Plaza, and several museums, including the noted Heard Museum, devoted to different aspects of Arizona's art, anthropology, Indian culture and history.

Adjacent Scottsdale is so closely wrapped up in the Phoenix resort picture as to be an integral part of it, and, in addition, it is a thriving art and crafts center, with elegant homes, town houses, resort hotels, smart stores, art galleries, crafts shops, and outstanding restaurants.

Traveling via routes I–19, US 89 and 89A not only reveals the many diverse landscapes, from southern deserts through the higher plateaus and grass prairies to pine-clad mountains, but also is a key to many of the state's major cities, unusual sights, sports, and historic locales. The routes run north from the Mexican border at Nogales through Tucson, Phoenix, and Prescott, thence past cattle lands, ghost towns, piney mountains and Oak Creek Canyon to Flagstaff, and then across the Navajo Reservation to Page and Glen Canyon Dam. No other Arizona highways match their variety and magnitude of lures.

In the northwestern section of Arizona, the Lake Mead National Recreation Area attracts millions of visitors annually. The interior of

726-foot-high Hoover Dam, one of the world's largest, can be toured, as can its power plant.

Side roads lead to developed sports sections like Temple Bar and Willow Beach. If desired, take US 93 to Kingman, then south on I-40 to State 95 and Lake Havasu. A prime lure is Lake Havasu City, where London Bridge has been reconstructed with an adjoining "English Village"; state park facilities, water sports, and other recreation add much appeal.

Northeast of Kingman stretches the million-acre Hualapai Indian Reservation, whose headquarters and trade center, on the Old Route 66, is Peach Springs. Near Ash Fork, the highway enters Kaibab and Coconino National Forests, which have some of the state's loveliest stands of ponderosa pine and aspen.

Northward, Glen Canyon National Recreation Area contains 186-mile Lake Powell with a shoreline of about 1,800 miles, much of it accounted for by an incredible number of side canyons that create imposing landscapes for boaters. The lake has both pleasure boating and sightseeing trips, as well as excellent fishing.

US 160 running northeastward to the Four Corners area (the only place in the United States where four state lines meet) rolls over vast, lonely expanses dotted with occasional Navajo hogans and sheep herds.

Six-hundred-acre Navajo National Monument contains some of the biggest and most intricate of the state's 13th-century cliff dwelling ruins. Easiest to reach is the Betatakin Area, in a spur of Segi Canyon, where a steep trail of slightly more than a mile leads from the monument Visitor Center to a prehistoric apartment house that probably had 135 rooms.

In central Arizona, the old territorial capital of Prescott still reflects the mining, farming, and ranching endeavors that made it important in the late 1800s. Indians and cowboys are common sights in town, and the Smoki Ceremonials and Frontier Days Rodeo each summer intensify the atmosphere of yesteryears. The old section—with the log Governor's Mansion, Old Fort Misery, Shalot Hall Museum and other lures—is one of the state's foremost centers for viewing the paraphernalia of frontier days in a setting where the first Territorial Legislature met over 119 years ago.

Southward, just outside Coolidge, Casa Grande National Monument is one of the choicest surviving remnants of the Hohokam culture that flourished more than six hundred years ago. The main ruin, a four-story apartment house–watchtower, is protected by a huge steel umbrella. Self-guided tours through this Big House reveal such things as calendar holes, strange designs, pioneer inscriptions, and the waist-high passageways between the maze of rooms. A deep appreciation of the area, its people, and their civilization can be obtained by examining exhibits in the monument's museum in the Visitor Center.

Tucson

The vacation lures of southern Arizona—for which Tucson is the touring center—are much more concentrated, the majority of them being located in and around Old Pueblo's environs, and in the region southeastward. Many of them are along or quite near the principal routes: Interstate 10 and 19; US 80 and 89. In Tucson the Spanish influence can still be seen and felt despite the rapid development as a winter resort and its ranking as Arizona's number-two city. Many sections of Tucson are browner than any in Phoenix since there is not the same widespread irrigation system. The desert comes closer to the city's mid-section, yet it's a pleasing, not harsh, meeting. Tucson's central area has the greenest look, and one of the nicest spots is the 312-acre University of Arizona campus. Points of interest on the campus are the Arizona State Museum, with its comprehensive archeological exhibits; the University Art Gallery, which features the Kress Collection of Renaissance Art; The Grace Flandrau Planetarium; and the Mineral Museum, with a collection of specimens from all over the world. Across from the campus, the Arizona Historical Society offers a complete Southwestern research library and pioneer museum. Nearby is the University's Center for Creative Photography, the nation's first, with library, memorabilia, and pictures of famous photographers.

Around the downtown section, some of the adobe buildings from the early American period—when architecture more closely reflected the heritage from south of the border—still stand. The most famous, The Old Adobe Patio, now a historic site, was erected in 1868 and shows the charm of pioneer patio-style living.

Tucson is a town for exploring especially around the fringes, where a small bonanza of sights and pastimes awaits. The Santa Catalina Mountains, rising to the 9,157-foot summit of Mt. Lemmon, and their foothills, hide a wealth of vacation pursuits. Beneath the summit lies rocky Sabino Canyon, where tall pines shade trout pools, a cool clear stream, picnic and camp facilities, and nature trails that give intimate glimpses of the countryside. Tucson's old Fort Lowell, a key point in the Apache warfare during the 1870s and 1880s, has been partially restored, though many adobe walls still stand. Artist Ted DeGrazia's Mission in the Sun, constructed by him and Yaqui Indians entirely from desert materials, is an expression of both artistic ability and religious faith. The mission is part of the artist's gallery.

On the Tucson west side, at the Arizona-Sonora Desert Museum, emphasis is placed on desert life. Larger animals are kept in open paddocks while smaller ones—insects, reptiles, and the like—are shown in three-dimensional dioramas. Trails lead through a desert garden, a walk-in aviary, along Water Street, through the above- and underground Beaver-Otter-Bighorn Sheep complex, the Congdon Earth Sciences Center (underground cave geology), and into the tunnel exhibit, where visitors can watch various animals living underground as they normally do. Other exhibits, from fish to minerals, also are featured.

Mission San Xavier del Bac, the White Dove of the Desert, founded about 1700 by Father Kino, represents a major breakthrough in early missionary work, and has remained important ever since it was created. The present structure dates to 1783 and is a gem of Spanish Colonial architecture, with carved stone portals, Indian-painted murals, and elaborate altar. It fell into disrepair in later years, but now has been faithfully restored.

The Grand Canyon, Flagstaff, and Vicinity

The arrival at Grand Canyon, north via State 64 from Williams or US 180 from Flagstaff, is breathtaking since thick pine forests give little hint of the awesome gorge until you are on its southern edge. Although only a relatively small portion of the 277-mile-long canyon is visible from the South and North rims, it is the most spectacular part, with widths varying from one to fourteen miles between rims and with depths of up to 5,750 feet from North Rim points. The climate change within the canyon—it has six of the Northern Hemisphere's seven botanical life zones—is, from top to bottom, the same as one would encounter traveling from Canada to Mexico. However, without doubt, the most striking feature of Grand Canyon is its geological story and scenery. There is nothing like the canyon anywhere else on earth. Its saga is estimated to be one and one-half billion years old; some of the multicolored strata, for instance, took more than 170 million years to be formed, and each layer was built upon the top of a lower one that took about as long for its creation. Parts of the canyon even formed the bed of an ancient sea, and one can see marine fossils along Bright Angel Trail as it snakes from Grand Canyon Village down to the Colorado River.

If the mighty gorge seems unbelievable, like a two-dimensional stage backdrop, don't be surprised. Only through repeated meetings can one begin to appreciate its vastness. A trip into its heart—via foot or mule—helps to create a greater sense of reality. Even so, one can leave wondering if all the scenes were not part of a dream. If you can, go in autumn—after the summer crowds are gone and before the first snow falls. It's then that the crisp air and the chance for solitude can heighten the canyon's grandeur so that you can get a better feeling for the scope of this wonder.

The majority of travelers view Grand Canyon only from the South Rim, since it is open year-round and is most accessible from the major northern Arizona tourist centers. To reach the North Rim, only 14 miles away, means a 200-mile drive, unless one wants to hike or ride a mule on a jaunt of at least two days to canyon bottom, across the river, and up the other side. But, assuming it is not the season (from October to April) when heavy snows prevent a visit, try to include it. For the North Rim vistas—from high points like Point Imperial, Cape Royal, Point Sublime, and others—lend an entirely different interpretation to Grand Canyon's depths and citadel-like formations.

South Rim sightseeing, other than excursions to Phantom Ranch or to Plateau Point, halfway down, is chiefly confined to the so-called East and West Rim drives, the former being part of State 64 to Cameron. Focal point is Grand Canyon Village, where, in addition to nature walks and forest bridle trails, viewpoints overlooking the canyon are popular. The eight-mile West Rim Drive goes by several panoramic view-points and ends at Hermits Rest with its curio-snack shop; during crowded summer months, it is closed to vehicles except for free National Park Service shuttle buses.

The 25-mile East Rim Drive from Grand Canyon Village to Desert View is the real motoring gem. There are about a half-dozen major lookout points, the best of which—for its expansive vistas up and down the canyon-cutting Colorado far below—is Yavapai Point. It has binoculars aimed at important gorge features, a small museum dealing with fauna and flora, a relief map of the canyon, and ranger-naturalist talks on the creation of the canyon. This point is about a half-mile east of the Visitor Center, where there is another, larger museum describing all aspects of the region. About three miles before reaching Desert View, the Tusayan Ruin and Museum, near the south side of the road, gives an insight into how early man lived in the area and how he built his small stone pueblos. At Desert View, the Watchtower overlooks canyon views as well as part of the western section of the Painted Desert.

Tourists seeking remote, off-the-beaten-path locales should try Havasu Canyon near the southern boundary of the national park. Access, via a good-to-rough sixty-two-mile road, is best from US 66 about five miles east of Peach Springs. Entrance to this isolated canyon —where Havasupai Indians live amid dashing streams, waterfalls, green fields, and ruby walls—is Hualapai Hilltop. From here you can hike or take a horse down (advance arrangements are essential) the twisting, eight-mile trail to Supai, the main village, where the white man's civilization has only recently begun to make an impression. Some people have called this canyon America's Shangri-la; certainly there's no better place to completely get away from the sometimes frantic tempo of today—if you don't mind plain accommodations or, more likely, camping out.

Flagstaff is a tourist-trade center, a popular outdoor locale, and the home of Northern Arizona University. The salient sights on the outskirts of town are two. One is Lowell Observatory, where the planet Pluto was discovered in 1930; the other is the Museum of Northern Arizona, about three miles northwest on Fort Valley Road, where the whole picture of this region—from geology through prehistoric Indians to natural science and modern crafts—is vividly revealed. See, too, annual displays by Hopi and Navajo craftsmen (who demonstrate their techniques); the museum shop, with moderate prices, has one of the choicest selections of handicrafts produced by northern Arizona Indians.

South of Flagstaff, off I–17, are two points of interest. One is Montezuma Castle National Monument, whose principal feature is a five-story, twenty-room cliff dwelling built into the face of a steep limestone wall; it is one of the Southwest's best-preserved 13th-century Pueblo structures of its type, being about 90 percent intact. Some seven miles northeast, Montezuma Well is a round limestone sinkhole having smaller cliff home ruins. The other place is Camp Verde, where the Fort Verde Museum, now part of a state park in part of the original army outpost, displays Indian, military, and pioneer relics.

US 89A winds southward from Flagstaff through Coconino National Forest and Oak Creek Canyon, called by many residents the most beautiful in the state. Reddish-brown and grayish-white weather-sculptured rock formations rise dramatically above pine and oak forests, campgrounds, rustic lodges, and the dashing creek to form a gorge some 1,500 feet deep and about twelve miles long, opening into a gorgeous amphitheater with monumental, brilliantly tinted formations all around. Beyond is Sedona, an art colony where over 200 artists live and work plus Tlaquepaque, Sedona's "Mexican village" of arts and crafts.

Petrified Forest National Park.

Situated 15 miles east of Holbrook, this park is one of the most unusual national parks in the country. Ancient trees which have turned to rock are colored with every hue of the rainbow. The park is divided into six general areas: *Long Logs, Giant Logs, Rainbow Forest, Blue Mesa, Crystal,* and *Jasper Forests.* Rainbow has stone logs more than 100 feet long. The petrified wood is protected against pilferage by park authorities. Pieces from other areas can be purchased at one of the shops. The petrified wood can also be gathered outside the preserve. It is not the only item of interest here. *Agate House,* constructed by Indians from petrified wood more than 900 years ago, is of interest, as is *Newspaper Rock,* which contains petroglyphs of an ancient civilization. *Puerco Ruin* here is the remains of a 14th-century Indian village. *Rainbow Forest Museum* contains fossilized skulls found in the vicinity in addition to fossils, minerals, and other artifacts.

PRACTICAL INFORMATION FOR ARIZONA

HOW TO GET THERE. *By car:* Major routes are: *east-west*—Interstate 40, 10, and 8, U.S. 60, US 70; *north-south*—US 666, US 89, Interstate 17 and 19, US 93 and State 95.

By air: Phoenix is served by *American, Continental, Cochise, Delta, Eastern, Frontier, Northwest, Pan Am, PSA, Republic, TWA, United, USAir,* and *Western.* Airport terminal facilities for handicapped persons are excellent.

By bus: Greyhound and *Continental Trailways* have northern, central, and southern passages across the state.

By train: Amtrak's Sunset Limited stops in Benson, Tucson, Phoenix, and Yuma. Its *Southwest Limited* serves Winslow, Flagstaff, Seligman and Kingman.

TOURIST INFORMATION. State of Arizona Office of Tourism, 3507 N. Central Ave., Phoenix, AZ 85004. Telephone: (602) 255–3618.

MUSEUMS AND GALLERIES. There are worthwhile museums of Arizona's natural features, Indian culture, and white man's history in Flagstaff, Prescott, Tombstone, Tucson, Yuma, Jerome, Bisbee, Patagonia, Page, Fort Huachuca, and Camp Verde, in addition to the important museums and galleries concentrated in the Phoenix area, and in National Park Service areas.

HISTORIC SITES. Twenty national parks, monuments, historic sites, and memorials protect exceptional scenic and geological areas, rare and beautiful plants, and outstanding Indian cultural remains. Some 19 state parks present relics of pioneer days, abundant recreational outlets and unusual scenery.

TOURS. In Tucson there is *Gray Line,* 180 W. Broadway Blvd. Phoenix has *Gray Line,* 600 E. Jefferson, and the Sept.–May low-cost travelcades of the non-profit *Phoenix Dons Club,* P.O. Box 13493, Phoenix 85002. Flagstaff has *Gray Line (Nava-Hopi Tours),* 401 Malpais Lane.

 DRINKING LAWS. Legal drinking in any licensed bar, restaurant, hotel, or inn from 6:00 A.M. to 1:00 A.M. weekdays, noon to 1:00 A.M. on Sundays. Most package stores close by 11:00 P.M. There are no state liquor stores. Minimum legal age is 19. Many markets and drug stores also sell alcoholic beverages.

SUMMER SPORTS. These include archery, camping, horseback riding, boating, bowling, fishing, golf, hiking, hunting, river tubing, swimming, surfing, scuba diving, snorkeling, water skiing, soaring, hang-gliding, ballooning, and tennis.

WINTER SPORTS. *Skiing:* The *Arizona Snow Bowl* near Flagstaff; *Mount Lemmon,* an hour's drive from Tucson; *Sunrise Ski Area* outside Springerville. Season and conditions vary widely.

 SPECTATOR SPORTS. *Baseball:* Major league ball in exhibition games in Cactus League in Mar. to Apr. *Cleveland Indians* train in Tucson, *San Francisco Giants* at Scottsdale and the Oakland A's at Phoenix, *Chicago Cubs* in Mesa, *Milwaukee Brewers* at Sun City, *Seattle Mariners* at Tempe, and *San Diego Padres* at Yuma.

Boxing, Basketball: NBA Phoenix Suns, many lower-priced college games. Phoenix and Tucson offer bouts.

Racing dogs: Parimutuel betting at Phoenix. Other tracks near Apache Junction, Amado, Black Canyon, Tucson and Yuma. *Horse racing:* summer meets at Prescott and at county fairs. Fall, winter, and early spring racing at Turf Paradise, Phoenix, and Rillito Downs, Tucson. *Horse shows:* Tucson and Valley of the Sun regularly host shows during the winter.

Rodeos: Major sites are Prescott and Payson.

Other: The Fiesta Bowl, a major month-long (actually part of Nov. and all of Dec.) series of sporting events (about 33), culminates in the nationally televised Fiesta Bowl football game on New Year's Day.

 WHAT TO DO WITH THE CHILDREN. *Tombstone's* famous landmarks are the *OK Corral, Wells Fargo Office, Boot Hill,* and many others around which stories have been told and retold.

Indian villages always interest children, particularly those of the *Hopi Indians,* where tribal dances are staged frequently.

There are also the ghost towns, various frontier forts, the old jails like those in *Wickenburg, Clifton* and *Yuma,* the *Smoki Museum* at *Prescott. Old Tucson,* a converted movie set outside Tucson and *Rawhide,* north of Scottsdale, offer various Western-style amusements and staged gunfights in the streets. The *Arizona Sonora Desert Museum* in Tucson has special appeal for any age.

 HOTELS AND MOTELS. The price categories in this section, for double occupancy, will start up from following prices: *Moderate,* $25–30, and *Inexpensive* below $25.

FLAGSTAFF. *Moderate:* **Chalet Lodge.** 1990 E. Santa Fe. Pleasant, color TV, pool, adjacent café.

Inexpensive: **Regal 8 Inn.** 2440 E. Lucky Lane. Chain member. Color TV, pool.

GRAND CANYON PARK. *Moderate:* **Grand Canyon Lodge.** At canyon's north rim. Open mid-May to Oct.

LAKE HAVASU CITY. *Moderate:* **Sandman Inn.** Pool, some housekeeping units. Near Colorado River recreation.
Inexpensive: **Easy 8.** 41 Acoma. 64 units. Heated pool, Jacuzzi. Restaurants in area.

NOGALES. *Inexpensive:* **Motel 6.** 2210 Tucson Hwy. Chain member.

PHOENIX. *Moderate:* **Bali Hi.** 1515 Grand Ave. Large motel, family accommodations. Dining room, restaurant, lounge.
Cocoanut Grove. 2012 W. Van Buren. Small motel, family units.
Days Inn. Two locations on Int. 17. Part of a chain, with seasonal rates, reasonably priced coffee shop.
Friendship Inn 6 Motel. 201 N. 7th Ave. International chain. 2-story motel with kitchenettes, color TV, pool, adjacent restaurant.
Pyramid Motel. 3307 E. Van Buren St. 2-story spot with large rooms, color TV, pool, adjacent restaurant, family rates.
Rodeway. 3400 Grand Ave. 3 in Phoenix.
Sandman Motel. 2120 W. Van Buren St. Kitchen units, heated, pool.
Tropics Motor Hotel. 1902 E. Van Buren St. 2 levels, lounge, restaurant, pool.
Western Village Motor Hotel. 1601 Grand Ave. Attractive western-motif units, good dining, cocktail lounge, pool.
Inexpensive: **Motel 6.** 2323 E. Van Buren; 5315 E. Van Buren. 2 levels, modern, pay TV. 4 others in Phoenix area.
Western 6. 4130 N. Black Canyon Highway; 214 S. 24th St. Chain.

PRESCOTT. *Moderate:* **Auto Rest Motor Motel.** Nearest in-town. Nice family units.
Inexpensive: **Motel 6.** 1111 E. Sheldon St. Chain.

SCOTTSDALE. *Inexpensive:* **Motel 6.** 6848 E. Camelback Rd. Pay TV. Chain member.

SEDONA. *Moderate:* **Cedar Motel.** In-town. Varied units, most have color TV, informal mood, café opposite.

TEMPE. *Inexpensive:* **Regal 8 Inn.** 1720 S. Priest Dr. TV, pool. Chain.
Western 6 Motel. 513 W. Broadway Rd.; 1612 N. Scottsdale Rd. Chain.

TUCSON. *Inexpensive:* **Motel 6.** 1031 E. Benson Hwy.; 960 S. Freeway. Chain member.
Regal 8 Inn. 1222 S. Freeway. Chain.
Western 6 Motel. 1388 W. Grant Rd.; 755 E. Benson Hwy. Chain.

YOUNGTOWN. *Inexpensive:* **Motel 6.** 11133 W. Grand Ave. Pool, pay TV. Chain.

DINING OUT in Arizona means chiefly American and Continental cuisine, but it can also mean Mexican, German, Chinese, Italian, Polynesian, and many other types. Restaurant price categories are as follows: *Moderate* $5–10, and *Inexpensive* $3–$5. These prices are for salad or soup, entree, and dessert. Not included are drinks, tax, and tips.

FLAGSTAFF. *Moderate:* **Gables.** 602 Mike's Pike. Bar. Children's plates. Entertainment. Popular with both tourists and residents.

PHOENIX. *Moderate:* **Alpine Village Inn.** 5025 N. 7th Ave. Bavarian atmosphere. American and Bavarian dishes. Cocktails.

Macayo. 4001 N. Central and 2 other locations. Mexican specialties, American food served. Aztec decor. Bar.

Paulo's International Cuisine. 605 E. Missouri Ave. Specialties include shrimp, breast of chicken, scallops, stuffed pork chops plus basic beef. Dancing and entertainment Thurs., Fri., Sat.

Victoria Station. 1720 E. Camelback Rd. Good steaks and prime rib in a whimsical setting—a choice of Victorian or early boxcar.

Inexpensive: **Carrows Restaurants.** 4 in Phoenix and 2 in Sun City and Tempe.

Jordan's Mexican Foods. 2633 N. Central Ave. American, Mexican cuisine. Children's plates. Closed Tues. evenings. Also at 6247 N. 7th Ave. **The Spaghetti Company.** 1418 N. Central Ave. and 4th St. and Mill, Tempe. An attractive, sometimes noisy conglomeration of rooms. Good food in hearty portions with emphasis on Italian specialties. Bar.

NOTE: The Valley of the Sun (Phoenix, Scottsdale, Tempe, Mesa, etc.) has a large and fine variety of inexpensive to moderately priced American-style chain restaurants serving good food in pleasant settings. These include *Black Angus, Coco's, Guggy's, Jolly Roger,* and *Furr's* and *Picadilly* Cafeterias. There is also an abundance of cheaper fast food, drive-in establishments.

NOGALES. *Moderate:* **Cavern Cafe.** Part of restaurant is in a cave, a former gold mine and jail in which Geronimo was imprisoned. In Mexico.

Inexpensive: **Zula's.** Mexican and American menu.

SCOTTSDALE. *Moderate:* **Los Olivos Mexican Patio.** A full range of Mexican dishes in a wonderfully evocative atmosphere; American dishes, too.

Inexpensive: **King's Table Buffet Restaurants.** 4 locations in Phoenix, Peoria, Mesa. Good, varied, ample American dishes.

TUCSON. *Moderate:* **El Corral.** Limited but good Western menu. Bar. 2201 E. River Road.

Inexpensive: **Sutter's.** Café with wide selection of American foods. Own baked goods. 534 N. 4th Ave.

Furr's. Another popular American food café. Fine selection. Non-smoking section. 5910 E. Broadway.

ARKANSAS

Land of Opportunity and the Ozarks

In drawing up your travel budget for a trip to or through Arkansas, make a list of all the places you should see and the things you should do, and then try and find the time to do at least half of them. The state offers quite a variety of attractions—they call them "opportunities" in Arkansas—and many of them are free or inexpensive.

There are the Ozarks and the Ouachitas mountains in the north and west. Here the visitor finds scenic beauty, a chance for relaxation, and the opportunity to meet delightful people. The lakes and rivers are lovely places where the fishing is great and the going can be rugged.

Within an hour you can exchange hills for flatlands and be in the land of cotton and among the flooded paddies of the Grand Prairie. There you will find catfish farming, this country's greatest rice fields, and the finest duck hunting in the nation.

Along the eastern border flows the Mississippi, with its adjoining swamps, bayous and cotton plantations reminiscent of the colorful Old South. Across the western boundary is the great southwest, with its memories and reconstructed relics of frontier days.

The past can be met and known. The Arkansas Post National Memorial on the Arkansas River near Gillette carries the story of DeSoto, LaSalle, Father Marquette, Joliet, de Tonti of the Iron Claw, the Louisiana Purchase, the "Mississippi Bubble"—almost 450 years of history. Fort Smith was a jumping-off place for wagon trains heading west, and its saga is told in the reconstructed National Historic Site.

Include in your itinerary the two health spas, Hot Springs, a national park, and Eureka Springs, an exotic town up in the mountains; Pea Ridge National Battlefield; Dogpatch, U.S.A.; Crater of Diamonds State Park near Murfreesboro; and Little Rock, the lovely state capital.

Fort Smith, with its blend of Deep South and Far Western atmosphere, is a good starting point for a tour. It gives you a choice of a diagonal Arkansas River run or a more comprehensive loop over the Ozark Mountains or the pine country of the scenic Ouachitas. Around and near the shady courthouse square, tourists stroll, reading historical markers depicting the time when gold seekers gathered before crossing the nearby Poteau River and heading west to California in 1849. Other markers designate sites of the last encampments of Cherokees east of the Arkansas at what is termed "End of the Trail of Tears." Bronc riders and roundup clubs bring the Old West to exciting life at Fort Smith's Harper Stadium and along historic Garrison Avenue in late May and early June.

Old Fort Days during the late May and early June Arkansas-Oklahoma Rodeo include authentic exhibition riding, shooting and saber action on horseback by Texas Cavalrymen, a reenactment of the 1896 trial of Cherokee Bill and his hanging, and tours of pre-Civil War and post-Civil War homes in the restoration area of historic old Belle Point.

The famed Judge Parker Courtroom, the "Dungeon Jail," and the hanging gibbet are "must stops," and inside a large brick structure on the corner of Third and Garrison is one of the finest museums of its kind in the nation, the Old Fort Museum.

East of this historic river city, you have the choice of a circular junket across the Boston Mountains or a central run through the state. Both routes offer abundant scenery and history. Try I-40 first, skirting the Arkansas River Valley and beautiful Lake Dardanelle, for the central diagonal run. Just east of Ozark is St. Mary's Mountain, where grape-growing and wine-making have been traditional among the descendants of Swiss and German immigrants for almost a hundred years. Tour the Wiederkehr Wine Cellars and enjoy food and refreshments at the Wein Keller Cafe.

Eureka Springs is probably Arkansas' most unusual city. Dozens of streets loop about the mountainsides below businesses and homes which have been constructed in tiers on sites literally blasted out of the cliffs. The main traffic artery is Spring Street, a narrow, picturesque thoroughfare where houses, and staircases ascending to dwellings further up, seem to lean out over the streets. The Historical Museum has local 19th-century items on display, while the Miles Mountain Musical Museum exhibits old musical instruments, as well as historic items. The last home of temperance crusader Carrie Nation contains personal memorabilia.

The *Christ of the Ozarks* statue atop Magnetic Mountain is sixty-five feet tall, and depicts Christ standing with outstretched arms. In an amphitheater nearby, The Great Passion Play is performed nightly during the warmer months, and on US 62 you will find the Christ Only Art Gallery with an enormous collection of documents in foreign languages—some dating to before Christ.

Eastward from Eureka Springs is Berryville, a gem of a little mountaintop city, with a panoramic view of neighboring mountains. There's good fishing in the nearby Table Rock Lake area, and also in Greers Ferry, Beaver and Norfork Lakes.

Bull Shoals Lake is another of the finer recreational areas of Arkansas; from there, wind your way through the hills to Yellville and southward on State 14 through rugged mountain country along the Buffalo National River, which stretches some 150 miles between magnificent vistas. Limestone bluffs tower above most of its length, and the white rapids offer a challenge to canoeists and floaters. High on a bluff above the river, just off State 14, is Buffalo River State Park. Relax in the shade along natural beaches, swim in the blue pockets of water or enjoy such sites as Pebble Springs and the Indian Rock House, a gigantic overhanging cliff under which you may ramble to your heart's content. Other nearby attractions are Lost Valley and the old ghost town of Rush.

America's greatest new cave find is Blanchard Springs Caverns, a large and amazing subterranean wonderland. Guided tours leave every twenty minutes for a visit to the cavern's Cathedral Room and Coral Room.

Fifteen miles south of Blanchard Springs, the Ozark Folk Center at Mountain View offers a lively showcase for traditional country music. During peak visitor seasons, performances are held each evening except Sunday in the center's 1,060-seat auditorium. Authentic Ozark arts and crafts are exhibited in the Center's 15 buildings. In late April the Center hosts the famed Arkansas Folk Festival. The gala Family Harvest Festival is held there mid-October to early November, as autumn burnishes the surrounding woodlands.

Little Rock

This elegant city stands between the northwestern mountains and the flatlands to the southeast, almost exactly at the state's topographical center. Recreational and historical attractions are abundant both in and around the city, and three municipal parks add to Little Rock's congenial atmosphere.

The Arkansas Territorial Restoration, on a large downtown tract, encompasses 13 original structures, among them the Hinderliter House, last used as a meeting place of the legislature in 1835. Other notable structures here include Noland House; Conway House, home of the state's fifth govenor; and the Woodruff Group, restored home and office of the founder of the Arkansas Gazette, oldest newspaper west of the Mississippi River.

Hot Springs National Park

Almost surrounding the attractive resort city of Hot Springs, these 4,500 acres in the Ouachita Mountains of central Arkansas have 47 thermal springs flowing at temperatures of an average of 143 degrees F. The bathhouses on "Bath House Row" attract visitors from all over the world who come for the "cure." For the more energetic there are miles of trails and bridle paths along the slopes of the park. National

Park Service offers summer evening programs and nature walks; there's camping in Gulpha Gorge.

The sixty-five-day horse racing season at Oaklawn Park, usually held from early February until early April, draws the greatest number of visitors; but tourists congregate here at all seasons.

Other diversions are boating, fishing, swimming, and water-skiing on the surrounding chain of lakes, and hiking or auto tours to the lookout tower atop Hot Springs Mountain. From here a panoramic view of lakes and pine-covered hills stretches before you.

Hot thermal baths may be taken at numerous bath houses. Some are operated by hotels or hospitals, others are ranged along downtown Central Avenue's "Bath House Row." All are supervised by the Federal government, which sets rates (moderate). A doctor's advice is recommended.

The fine futuristic Mid-America Museum features lively exhibits about Arkansas, Perception, Energy, Matter, Life and Focus. Adjoining amphitheater offers professional outdoor dramas and musicals each summer. Many other special events are held here during the year, including an *Easter* Sunrise Service; the Arkansas Fun Festival in early *June;* the Arkansas Oktoberfest in *October;* and the Christmas Pageant, held in the Convention Auditorium in early *December*.

PRACTICAL INFORMATION FOR ARKANSAS

HOW TO GET THERE. *By air:* There are airports at Little Rock, Fayetteville, Harrison, El Dorado, Jonesboro, Pine Bluff, Hot Springs and Ft. Smith. *By car:* All of Arkansas's interstate highways are complete. They provide access into the state from Missouri, I–55; from Tennessee, I–40; from Texas, I–30; from Oklahoma, I–40. US highways provide entries from Mississippi and Louisiana.

By bus: Major bus lines serving Arkansas include *Trailways, Greyhound, Arkansas Motor Coaches, Great Southern Motor Coaches* and *Oklahoma Transportation Lines. By rail:* Amtrak serves Walnut Ridge, Newport, Little Rock, Malvern and Texarkana.

TOURIST INFORMATION. Arkansas Dept. of Parks & Tourism, One Capitol Mall, Little Rock, 72201; Hot Springs Chamber of Commerce, P. O. Box 1500, Hot Springs National Park, 71901. Tourist Information Centers on major highways leading into the state are at Ashdown (US 71–59); Texarkana (I–30); Bentonville (US 71); near Corning (US 67); Fort Smith (I–40); near El Dorado (US 167); Lake Village (US 65); Blytheville (I–55); and West Memphis (I–40). The Arkansas State Police, with district headquarters all over the state, is also a dependable source of information.

MUSEUMS AND ART GALLERIES. Historical: *Saunders Museum,* 314 E. Madison, Berryville, one of world's largest historic gun collections; *Greathouse Home,* ca. 1830, restored farmhouse, inn, Conway; *Eureka Springs Historical Museum,* 95 S. Main St.; *University of Arkansas Museum,* U. of Arkansas, Fayetteville is a natural history museum. In Fort Smith, *Old Fort Museum,* 320 Rogers Ave., displays Indian, pioneer artifacts; *Robinson Heritage Center,* on US 65SE, Harrison. *Museum of Automobiles,* atop Petit Jean Mtn., Morrilton; *Jimmy Driftwood Barn and Folk Hall of Fame,*

Mountain View; *Lum & Abner Museum,* Pine Ridge; *Daisy International Air Gun Museum,* US 71 S. Rogers; *Arkansas County Agricultural Museum,* 921 E. 4th & Park Ave., Stuttgart; *Hampson Museum* (Indian relics, artifacts), Wilson.

Art: *Christ Only Art Gallery,* Mt. Oberammergau, off US 62, Eureka Springs; *Fine Arts Center,* University of Arkansas campus, Fayetteville. *Fort Smith Art Center,* 423 N. 6th St. *Southern Artists Association Fine Arts Center,* 815 Whittington Ave., Hot Springs which also stages productions of the Community Players. *The Arkansas Arts Center,* MacArthur Park, Little Rock; *Southeast Arkansas Arts & Science Center,* 8th St., Pine Bluff.

HISTORIC SITES. *Fort Smith National Historic Site,* 1839–71, soldiers' barracks and commissary, "Hanging Judge Parker's" courtroom, Rogers and S. 2nd Sts., Fort Smith. *Arkansas Post National Memorial,* south of Gilette via Rtes. 1 and 169. *Old State House,* Little Rock, capitol of Arkansas from 1836 to 1912. Arkansas *Territorial Restoration,* 214 E. 3rd St., Little Rock. Buildings portray life in the 1820's. *Pea Ridge National Military Park,* adjacent to US 62, near Rogers.

Historic houses: *Clayton House,* 514 N. 6th St., Fort Smith, headquarters of Belle Grove Historic District; *Wildwood,* 808 Park Ave., Hot Springs, handsome Victorian mansions; *Villa Marre,* 1321 Scott St., *Angelo Marre House,* 1881, Little Rock—*Italianate Victorian* home is headquarters of Historic Quapaw Quarter; *Du Bocage,* 4 Ave. & Linden St., Pine Bluff, Greek Revival Mansion; *Martha Mitchell's Home,* W. 4th Ave. & Elm Sts., Pine Bluff; *Pott's Tavern,* I–40 & US 64, Pottsville, home of early settlers; Annual Belle Fort Smith Tour of beautifully restored antebellum and mid-Victorian homes occurs last of April and first of May in Fort Smith, and Little Rock's Quapaw Quarter Spring Tour is also late April-early May.

TOURS. *Bus: Trailways* and *Greyhound* provide coach tours of many popular visitor areas. *Gray Line Sightseeing Tours* offers a wide variety of trips from Eureka Springs, Hot Springs and Little Rock. Some resorts also will arrange area sightseeing packages.

Boat: In Little Rock, Allison Queen Cruises runs day cruises on the Arkansas River aboard an 18-passenger "party barge." *The White Duck* is an amphibious landing craft rebuilt for touring the Hot Springs and Lake Hamilton area. *Floating down the White River:* Float trips in 20-foot, flat-bottomed wooden boats have been popular with Arkansas fishermen since shortly after the turn of the century. Today, some 20 concerns operate 200 boats.

SUMMER SPORTS. *Boat rentals:* You'll find Arkansas lakes, such as Bull Shoals, Norfork, Dardanelle, Beaver, and Greers Ferry complete with marinas. Boat-rental fees are moderate.

Fishing: A license is required for fishing. Write: Arkansas Game & Fish Commission, 2 Natural Resources Dr., Little Rock 72201. The White, Little Red, and Spring Rivers, Lakes Millwood and Ouachita, and the Buffalo National River are good areas.

You can find *fishing, boating* and *water sports* at Lake Hamilton, Norfork Lake, Greers Ferry Dam & Reservoir, Lake Greeson, near Murfreesboro. For *fishing* and *swimming:* Blanchard Springs; you can also swim at Ozark National Forest and most state parks. There are *water sports* at Lake Dardanelle, near Russellville.

Hunting: A license is required for hunting. Write Arkansas Game & Fish Commission, Little Rock, 2 Natural Resources Dr., Arkansas 72201. Hunting is Arkansas's primary participant sport in autumn, especially duck and turkey in the Grand Prairie area near Stuttgart.

Golf: Seven courses are recommended by "Golf Digest": The *Hot Springs G. & C.C.; Hot Springs Village C.C.;* also in Hot Springs, *Belvedere C.C.;* the *Dawn*

Hill C.C., Siloam Springs; *Paradise Valley G.C.,* and Cherokee Village G.C., in Fayetteville; *Eden Isle G.C.,* Little Rock.

Horseback riding: Devil's Den State Park, Bull Shoals, Eureka Springs, Hot Springs, Blanchard Springs and Little Rock all have stables.

SPECTATOR SPORTS. *Sailboat racing* on Lake Oua-chita, from Brady Mountain Point, off State 270. *Out-board Racing* on Lake Hamilton. *Car racing,* Stuttgart Municipal Airport, State 11. *Stock Car Racing* in West Memphis. *Thoroughbred racing,* Oaklawn Jockey Club, Hot Springs, *Greyhound racing* at West Memphis. *Golf:* Open Invitational, Hot Springs Country Club in May. *Arkansas-Oklahoma rodeo,* Fort Smith, end May and beginning June at Exposition Park. *State Fair Rodeo,* Little Rock, on W. Roosevelt Rd., a part of the Arkansas Livestock Exposition in early Oct.

Collegiate games: Arkansas Univeristy *Football* either in War Memorial Stadium in Little Rock or at Razorback Stadium in Fayetteville. *Basketball games, horse shows* at Barton Coliseum, Little Rock.

WHAT TO DO WITH THE CHILDREN. In Fort Smith: *Ben Geren Park,* just off State 22T; *Central Mall,* at the junction of old State 22 and Waldron Rd.; *Tilles Park* on Grand Ave.; *Creekmore Park,* just off Jenny Lind Rd.

Hot Springs: *Arkansas Alligator Farm,* 847 Whittington Ave. *Tiny Town,* 374 Whittington Ave., a miniature village, featuring mechanized figures. *Animal Wonderland,* US 270 W., *Hot Springs National Park,* campfire programs, quarry hikes. *I.Q. Zoo,* 380 Whittington, performances by trained small animals. *Josephine Tussaud Wax Museum,* 250 Central Ave. *Magic Springs Family Fun Theme Park,* US 70E, rides, shows, arts and crafts, restaurants, shopping, new looping roller coaster.

In Little Rock: the zoo in *War Memorial Park* and the adjacent amusement park area. In North Little Rock, *Burns Park* playground facilities. The *Arkansas Arts Center,* at MacArthur Park in Little Rock, features a special gallery geared to young visitors. Next door, the *Arkansas Museum of Science and History* has a planetarium and special exhibits.

In Malvern: *Reader Railroad* offers rides on woodburning steam train May-Oct.

HOTELS AND MOTELS. Hotels are based on double occupancy and listed in alphabetical order by city and price category: *Moderate:* $30–45; *Inexpensive:* under $30.

BERRYVILLE. *Moderate:* **Fairway Motor Inn.** 1 mi. W on US 62. Color TV, pool. Restaurant near. Attractive rural setting adjacent to golf course.

BULL SHOALS RESORT AREA (12 mi. W. of Mountain Home). *Moderate:* **Bay Breeze Resort Motel.** Overlooks lake and boat docks a mile below dam.

Crow-Barnes Resort. White River float and overnight camping trips.

Imperial Resort. Overlooks lake. Open Mar.-Nov. Pool. Cafe near.

Inexpensive: **Theodosia Marina Resort.** At lake. Lodge and cottage units. Pool, playground, lighted tennis, boats, guides. Restaurant adjacent.

EUREKA SPRINGS. (All rates higher mid-May–Oct. 31.) *Moderate:* **Alpen Dorf Motel.** US 62, 3¾ mi. E. of US 62B & AR 23 jct. Color TV, some kitchen units.

Joy Motel and Cottages, US 62 W. Pool, restaurant.

Inexpensive to Moderate: **Le Roi.** 27 Van Buren. Picnic tables, free coffee; restaurant nearby.

Travelers Inn. 1 mi. S. on US 62.

Rustic Manor Motel. 1 mi. W. on US 62. Color, cable TV, pool, restaurant. Cottage units.

FAYETTEVILLE. *Moderate:* **Best Western Inn,** US 71 Bypass & US 62B. Color TV, handicapped facilities. Dining room, swimming pool. Senior citizen rates, children under 12 free in same room with parents.

Holiday Inn. 2402 N. College. Daily buffet, lounge. Golf, racquetball.

FORT SMITH. *Moderate:* **Best Western Trade Winds Inn.** 101 N. 11th. Dining room, cocktail lounge, swimming pool. Senior citizen rates, under 12 free in room with parents.

Best Western Kings Row Inn. 5801 Rogers Ave. Color TV, pool, free coffee; restaurant adjacent.

Holiday Inn. 301 N. 11th St., in historic Belle Grove District. Restaurant, lounge.

Inexpensive: **Motel 6.** 6001 Rogers Ave. Pool.

HOT SPRINGS. (All rates higher during racing season.) *Moderate:* **Anthony Island Motel.** AR 7 S. Good family facility. Some efficiencies. Operates Feb. to Nov. Water sports. Pool. Restaurant.

Arlington Hotel & Baths. Central Ave. at Fountain St., popular large resort with some studios and suites. Complete social program; dancing in season. Thermal baths, pools (heated). Shops. Excellent food.

Grand Central Motor Lodge. 1127 Central Ave. Color TV, pool, pets. Restaurant.

Hot Springs National Park Downtowner. 135 Central Ave. Thermal bath house and massage parlor. Coffee shop, dining room.

Majestic Hotel and Apartments. Park & Central Aves., also Lake Hamilton Lodge, new Lanai Towers. Lakeside lodge and new Lanai towers. Wide choice of rooms and suites, some poolside or with mountain view. Nightly entertainment. Pool (heated). Water sports at lodge on Lake Hamilton. Thermal baths.

Shorecrest Resort. 230 Lakeland Dr. On lake. Attractive resort cottages, some kitchens and efficiencies. Pets. Boating, fishing, lawn games, pool, swimming beach. Restaurant near.

Travelier Motor Lodge. 1045 E. Grand Ave. Pool, wading pool, color TV. Pets. Restaurant.

Inexpensive: **Brady Mountain Lodge.** On Lake Ouachita. Perfect for families. Pool, water sports. Pets allowed. Restaurant. Some cottages.

Margarette Motel. 216 Fountain. One two-room unit, kitchens.

LITTLE ROCK / NORTH LITTLE ROCK. *Moderate:* **Best Western Heritage House.** 7500 S. University Ave. Color TV, pool, restaurant, lounge, free coffee.

Best Western Interstate Inn. 400 W. 29th. St., N. Little Rock. Restaurant, lounge; live entertainment. Pool; indoor tennis; jogging track nearby.

Coachman's Inn. E. Capitol at Ferry St. Color TV, pool, wading pool. Dining room, lounge, entertainment, dancing.

Little Rock Downtowner. 6th & Center Sts. French Quarter Lounge and Norman's Restaurant. Near metro-center shopping mall and central business district.

Sam Peck Hotel-Motel. 625 W. Capitol Ave. Color TV, pool, dining room, entertainment. Locally popular.

Inexpensive: **Days Inn.** 2 locations: 2508 Jacksonville Hwy, North Little Rock; 3100 N. Main, Little Rock, Dining rooms, service stations. Pets. September Days Club honored.

Magnolia Inn. 3601 Roosevelt Rd. Color TV, pool. Pets. Some kitchenettes. Restaurant near.

Motel 6. 8322 New Benton Hwy. Pool, pay TV.

Red Roof Inn. 7800 Scott Hamilton Dr. (At jct. I–30.) Color TV, pets. Restaurant near.

DINING OUT in Arkansas can be a lot less expensive than in the more heavily populated states. Look for Arkansas favorites such as fried chicken, hickory-smoked and/or barbecued meats, and hot apple or huckleberry pies.

Restaurants are listed in order of price category, based on price of a complete dinner without drinks, i.e., *Moderate:* $10–15. *Inexpensive:* under $10.

BULL SHOALS RESORT AREA. *Moderate:* **Gaston's White River Resort.** Lakeview, AR. Prime rib, trout dinners, barbecued ribs.

EUREKA SPRINGS. *Moderate:* **Ozark Gardens.** US 62, AR 23 SE. Local fish dishes and home baking.
  Bit o' Sweden. You'll like the Swedish décor and owner-cooked Swedish & German dishes.
  Ozark Village. US 62 SE. Native fish, country ham. Apr.-Nov.

FORT SMITH. *Moderate:* **Emmy's.** German Restaurant & Gift Shoppe. 602 N. 16th St. German menu.
  Red Bar Restaurant and Steak House. Newland Rd. Dinners only. Steak, quail, chicken.
  Taliano's. 201 N. 14th St. Superb Italian specialties in converted 1887 residence. Child's menu. Reservations requested.
  Inexpensive: **Lewis Cafeteria.** 3400 Rogers Ave. Fine food. Near sparkling fountains in north wing of Fort Smith's Central Mall. Highway 22 East.

GREERS FERRY. *Moderate:* **Ferryboat Restaurant.** End of The Narrows Bridge. Delicious lunch and dinner salad bar, Lavish seafood buffet.
  Maxine's Restaurant and Music Hall. Hwy. 16 at The Narrows Bridge. Thurs.-Sat. live country music show for the entire family; restaurant open Mon.-Sat.

HEBER SPRINGS. *Moderate:* **The Stockholm Restaurant.** 600 W. Main St. Wide selection of salads and entrées, sumptuous Friday night seafood buffet. À la carte breakfast, lunch and dinner buffet, and table service.

HOT SPRINGS. *Moderate:* **Mollie's.** 538 W. Grand Hwy. American and kosher foods. Own baking. Dining room displays paintings by local artists.
  Inexpensive: **Franke's Cafeteria.** 510 Central Ave. Very good selection of salads, entrees, vegetables, desserts. Locally popular.

LITTLE ROCK/NORTH LITTLE ROCK. *Moderate:* **Browning's.** 5805 Kavanaugh Rd. Mexican. Open for lunch & dinner. Takeout orders filled.
  Bruno's Little Italy. 1309 Old Forge Rd. Dine Italian style by candlelight. American dishes, too.
  Barleycorn's. I-40 & Rodney Parham Rd. Scrumptious food, salad and soup bar. Eclectic decor includes World War I bunker, British library, Model T truck.
  Inexpensive: Cafeterias: **Franke's Cafeteria.** 3500 S. University, 3929 McCain Blvd. (McCain Shopping Center), 300 S. University, N. Little Rock.

MOUNTAIN VIEW. *Moderate:* *Ozark Folk Center Lodge.* Traditional Ozark fare—catfish, fried chicken, smoked ham, homemade pies.

SPRINGDALE. *Moderate:* **A. Q. Chicken House.** US 62 N. In the heart of chicken country, a famous chicken restaurant.

WINSLOW. *Inexpensive:* **Burns Gables.** On a mountaintop. Country ham, sausage, trout. Closed Dec.-Feb.

KANSAS

Center of Middle America

Kansas lies in the approximate geographical center of the contiguous U.S. The exact geographical center is two miles NW of Lebanon.

When Kansas became a territory in 1854 (pop. 700), it had been home of the Wichita, Pawnee, Osage and Kansa Indians, and had been traded back and forth between France and Spain in a real life Monopoly game.

Today Kansas City alone has a population of about 174,000. The twin sister to Kansas City, Mo., Kansas City is a major livestock marketing center.

The oldest Army post west of the Mississippi River is Fort Leavenworth, situated on a bluff overlooking the Missouri River. It was established in 1827 for protection against Indians and as a starting point for wagon trains, eventually becoming the fountainhead for the Oregon and Santa Fe trails. Relics from its early era can be seen in the Post Museum, which features an excellent exhibit of 19th century horse-drawn vehicles, including one in which Lincoln rode.

The adjoining city of Leavenworth, where Buffalo Bill Cody grew up, has numerous historical buildings, such as the magnificent mansion built by restaurateur Fred Harvey or the elegant Victorian home now housing the Leavenworth Historical Society Museum. A federal prison also is in Leavenworth.

The museum containing thousands of mementos of Gen. Eisenhower's military and political career is situated in Abilene, where the late President and his brothers were reared. The Eisenhower Center is the official U.S. memorial to the late Dwight D. Eisenhower, and contains his home, library and "The Place of Meditation," burial site of the former President. Near the center is an attraction of a different type, the reconstructed wild west town, "Old Abilene Town."

For those with an interest in Indian lore, between Abilene and Salina (four miles E. of Salina) are the Indian burial grounds and museum. Other relics are displayed at Smokey Hill Historical Museum in Oakdale Park in Salina.

If you're hungry for fried chicken and hot biscuits, detour 14 miles west of Salina on Hwy. 140 to Brookville. The Brookville Hotel Dining Room, built in 1870, is famous for its country food served family-style in a frontier atmosphere. Reservations are suggested. After filling up on the bountiful country fare, you may go upstairs to see a parlor and bedrooms furnished in Kansas frontier period furniture. For over 100 years, until 1972, the hotel also was in operation, and it is said that Buffalo Bill stayed in Number 7.

Topeka, the state capital (population approximately 140,000) boasts a Statehouse with murals by John Steuart Curry and grounds dotted by statues depicting its pioneer past. It is also home of the Kansas State Historical Society Museum with its collection of aircraft, autos, and stagecoaches, and is the site of the famed Menninger Clinic.

Northwest of Topeka is the village of Wabaunsee where abolitionist Henry Ward Beecher spewed fire and brimstone from the pulpit of the Beecher Bible and Rifle Church—which still stands today, serving its congregation.

Northwest of Topeka is the original capital of Kansas, Manhattan. Ft. Riley was established between Manhattan and Junction City—the junction of the Republican and Smokey Hill rivers—in 1853. The Ft. Riley Museum contains memorabilia of military history.

William Allen White, the well-known editor and founder of the Emporia Gazette, lived in Emporia, south of Topeka on the Kansas Turnpike. A memorial sculpture in his honor is in Peter Pan Park, and his mementos are in the William Allen White Library on the campus of Emporia State University.

Wichita, profiting from the advent of the railroad in a "cow town boom," grew rapidly and is the state's largest city, with a population of 270,000. In memory of its beginnings, there is a "Cow Town," containing replicas of 1872 Wichita with many original buildings. Wichita is proud of its historical museums, art galleries, some 28 parks and a very fine zoo. Also based here is the Wichita State University, Sacred Heart College and the McConnell Air Force Base. Beech, Boeing, Cessna and Learjet plants are located in Wichita, making the city a world leader in the manufacture of private airplanes and an important military aircraft manufacturing center. Some of the plants can be toured.

If you'd like to "wet your whistle," stop by the Long Branch Saloon in Dodge City, on US 56, where every night from June 1 to Labor Day, Miss Kitty and her can-can girls entertain while visitors drink sarsaparilla and red-eye. You'll probably also find Doc Holliday, Wyatt Earp and Bat Masterson ambling along the Old Front Street of the authentic frontier town that was known as the "Cowboy Capital of the World" because millions of Texas longhorns were driven through in the late 1870s and '80s. Another title it earned was "The Wickedest Little City in America" because of the mixture of soldiers, railroaders, buffalo hunters, trail drivers and settlers who came to town. Some are remembered in the Boot Hill Memorial Cemetery, built on the site of the original Boot Hill.

Another city along US 56, Council Grove, preserves its part in history, too. It is the site of the Post Office Oak, a huge tree where letters were "mailed," awaiting pickup by passing wagon trains. While there, drop by the Kaw Indian Mission, once an Indian school, now a museum.

PRACTICAL INFORMATION FOR KANSAS

HOW TO GET THERE. *By air: United, TWA* and *Continental* fly into Wichita and Kansas City (Mo.). *By train: Amtrak. By bus:* Kansas is served by *Trailways, Greyhound* and numerous other smaller lines, including *Short Way, North Star* and *Missouri Transit.*

TOURIST INFORMATION. You may write *Kansas Department of Economic Development,* 503 Kansas Avenue, Topeka, 66603; or chambers of commerce in major cities. State universities at Lawrence and Manhattan have information on sports events, museums, drama, lectures. Write the president's office.

MUSEUMS AND GALLERIES. *Clark County Pioneer Museum,* Ashland; *Baker University Old Castle and History Museum, Baker University Quayle Collection* (a 17th-century room from Urishay Castle, England), Baldwin; *Safari African Museum* (items from expeditions of explorers Martin and Osa Johnson), Chanute; *Beeson Museum* (pioneer and Indian relics), *Boot Hill Museum,* Dodge City; *Ft. Scott Historical Museum* (old dresses), Ft. Scott; *Bridget Walker Art Collection* (works of John Steuart Curry and Henry Varnum Poor), Garnett; *Ft. Larned National Landmark* (military & Indian relics), Larned; *University of Kansas Wilcox Museum* (Greek & Roman antiquities), Lawrence; *Pony Express Museum,* Marysville; *Dalton Gang Hide-out Museum,* Meade; *El Quartelejo Kiva Indian Museum* (Cheyenne & Pueblo), Scott City; *Menninger Foundation Museum and Archives* (psychiatry museum), Topeka; *Mid-American All-Indian Center Museum,* Wichita.

HISTORIC SITES. In addition to those already mentioned are the *Madonna of the Trail* statue at Council Grove which was the last stop on the Sante Fe Trail; the *Pioneer Adobe House and Museum* in Hillsboro, a replica of the Mennonite pioneer homes; *W.T.C.U. Museum* in Medicine Lodge, hometown of the spirited (and anti-"spirits") Carry Nation.

DRINKING LAWS. Liquor may be purchased in package stores. Private club membership may be obtained for a nominal fee through some hotels and motels.

SPORTS. *Fishing* at numerous federal, state and county lakes. *Hunting* in season. *Trap shooting* at Winchester Center, Bucyrus, 30 mi. S. of Kansas City. All *water sports* at Lake Waconda.

CAMPING OUT. There are camping facilities at the state parks in: Fall River near Chanute, Elk City near Independence, Milford near Junction City, Meade near Liberal, Tuttle Creek near Manhattan, Lovewell near Mankato, Lake Crawford near Pittsburg, Wilson near Russell, Lake Scott near Scott City, Perry near Topeka, Cedar Bluff near Wakeeney, Cheney near Wichita, and Toronto near Yates Center.

WHAT TO DO WITH THE CHILDREN. The major cities have interesting *zoos.* The *wild west towns* at Abilene and in Dodge City provide background for shoot-'em-up fantasies, complete with stagecoach rides. *Old Cow Town* in Sims Park, Wichita, has an 1875 log cabin, saloon and blacksmith shop.

HOTELS AND MOTELS. You'll have your choice, from comfortable old-style hotels to modern motels. The price categories in this section average: *Moderate* $30–41 and *Inexpensive* $29 and under.

DODGE CITY. *Inexpensive:* **Astro Motel.** Pets accepted. Swimming pool. **Western Inn Motor Lodge.** Restaurant, pool. Pets accepted.

FT. SCOTT. *Inexpensive:* **Colonial Motel.** Playground, restaurant.

HUTCHINSON. *Inexpensive:* **Scotsman Inn.** Has 48 rooms.

JUNCTION CITY. *Moderate:* **Hilton Inn.** Club. Restaurant. 102 rooms.

KANSAS CITY area. *Moderate:* **Mission Inn.** Hwy. 50 & 63 St. Restaurant. **White Haven.** 8039 Metcalf. Free coffee. Restaurants adjacent. **Flamingo Best Western.** 4725 State Ave.

TOPEKA. *Moderate:* **Ramada Inn.** 420 E. 6th Ave. Club. Restaurant. Excellent. 340 rooms. **Best Western Meadow Acres.** 2950 S. Topeka Ave. Has 90 rooms.

WICHITA. *Moderate:* **TraveLodge.** 3900 W. Kellogg. Restaurant. Pets accepted. *Inexpensive:* **Motel 6.** 5736 W. Kellogg.

DINING OUT in Kansas means plenty of good country food. Restaurant price categories are: *Moderate,* $7–12, *Inexpensive,* under $7. Prices are for a complete meal, excluding drinks, tax and tip.

DODGE CITY. *Moderate:* **Dodge House.** Prime rib, steak and daily buffet. Children's menu.

JUNCTION CITY. *Moderate:* **Cohen's Chicken & Steak House.**

KANSAS CITY. *Moderate:* **Leona Yarbrough's.** 2800 W. 53rd St. Home-cooked meals. Family atmosphere. Excellent.

John Francis Restaurant. 7148 W. 80 St. Open for breakfast, lunch and dinner. Fried chicken specialty. Smorgasbord Tuesday, Thursday and Sunday.

SALINA. *Moderate:* **Brookville Hotel Dining Room.** 14 miles W on Hwy. 140. Family-style chicken dinners. Family owned and operated. Excellent.

WICHITA. *Moderate:* **Brown's Grill East.** 545 N. Hillside. Family atmosphere.
Hickory House. 1625 E. Central. Smoked meats and seafood. Williamsburg atmosphere. Children's menu.

MISSOURI

St. Louis, Kansas City, Ozarks and More

A new spirit pervades St. Louis, one of the most historic communities in the nation. The St. Louisan of today walks with a brisk stride, proud of recent civic accomplishments, foremost of which has been the construction of the Gateway Arch—sometimes called the "Giant Wicket"—of the Jefferson National Expansion Memorial. Towering 630 feet above the city's riverfront redevelopment area, it is the nation's tallest monument, and was designed by Eero Saarinen.

This arch, built of stainless steel, commemorates the westward march of America. Each leg houses a stairway and trains. Carrying forty passengers at a clip, the trains rise to the top of the arch to give passengers a panoramic view of St. Louis and the surrounding areas from an observation deck.

The Old Cathedral, the Basilica of St. Louis, completed in 1834, still stands and receives worshippers near the Jefferson National Expansion Memorial grounds. St. Louis' Old Courthouse, of Greek Revival architecture, is also near the Gateway Arch. Here slaves stood on the auction block and in 1847 Dred Scott's lawyers first pleaded for his freedom from slavery.

The (new) St. Louis Cathedral, some five miles away, is worth a special trip. The golden dome covering the main altar reflects the images of the twelve apostles ranged on its interior. A large dome rises 207 feet above the surface of the church and is visible from the exterior.

The mosaics that adorn the cathedral's interior are masterpieces of their kind—and the collection is reported to be one of the largest in the world.

Inside Forest Park are the St. Louis Art Museum and the Missouri Historical Society in the Jefferson Memorial Building, which features the Charles A. Lindbergh Gallery. So is the McDonnell Planetarium, one of the nation's finest for research and study of the stars, and an 83-acre zoo, and over 2,000 animals in habitat settings.

Southeast of here is another unique attraction, the Missouri Botanical Garden. In a geodesic-domed greenhouse visitors may view a variety of flora and see special displays year-round. The largest traditional Japanese Garden in the U.S. is the newest attraction. The site is often referred to as Shaw's Botanical Garden after its founder, Henry Shaw, whose restored home is open for viewing.

PRACTICAL INFORMATION FOR ST. LOUIS

 HOW TO GET THERE. *By car:* I–70 (US 40) runs east-west through St. Louis. Points of reference on I–70 are Terre Haute, Indiana, to the east and Kansas City to the west. On a north-south axis, I–55 begins at Chicago, passes through St. Louis and enters Arkansas near the juncture of Missouri, Arkansas and Tennessee. I–44 runs from the northeast corner of Oklahoma to St. Louis,

By train: St. Louis has regular service on *Amtrak.*

By bus: As a gateway to the west, St. Louis is a major bus terminal. It is served by *Trailways, Greyhound,* and several local lines.

By air: St. Louis is served by ten major airlines including *American, Delta, Eastern, Frontier,* and *TWA.*

By boat: The *Delta Queen* and the newer *Mississippi Queen* use St. Louis as a point of departure and/or return on Delta Queen Steamboat Co. Mississippi River cruises.

 HOW TO GET AROUND. *By bus:* St. Louis has an extensive bus system that covers both the downtown area and the suburbs. Maps of the system are available from Bi-State Transit Co. at 3869 Park Ave. *By taxi:* The taxi fare is comparable to fares in other large cities.

From the airport: Limousines run from Lambert-St. Louis International Airport to downtown hotels on a regular schedule. Taxis are also available.

TOURIST INFORMATION. The *Convention and Visitors Bureau of Greater St. Louis* is located at 500 N. Broadway on the 15th floor. They have maps and information of all kinds for the visitor.

 MUSEUMS AND GALLERIES. The *St. Louis Art Museum* in Forest Park has a wide range of paintings, sculpture, drawings and prints. There are also Oriental and African collections. The *National Museum of Transport,* at 3015 Barrett Station Road, displays more than 50 locomotives and cars, streetcars and buses and other types of transport spanning the last century. *Steinberg Art Gallery* at Washington University has a fine collection of modern art, as well as changing exhibits. The *Missouri Historical Society,* at Lindell Blvd. and De Baliviere Ave., has a collection of frontier artifacts and the Lindbergh collection. The USS *Inaugural,* at Wharf St. near the Gateway Arch, has been converted into a naval museum.

HISTORIC SITES. The *Jefferson National Expansion Memorial,* better known as the "Gateway to the West," ranks with New York's Empire State Building and Houston's Astrodome as one of the most familiar landmarks in an American city. The 630-foot arch, designed by Eero Saarinen, is open every day, except Thanksgiving, Christmas and New Year's. Also see the *Old Courthouse,* in the Jefferson National Expansion Memorial, the *Old Cathedral* nearby, and the birthplace of famed poet Eugene Field. *Grant's Farm,* at Grant and Gravois Rds., contains a log cabin built by Ulysses S. Grant when he lived here as a farmer from 1854 to 1860. Also, *Jefferson Barracks Historical Park,* south of St. Louis on Grant Rd. at Kingston, was one of the pioneer military establishments of the west, in use from the early 19th century through World War II. Now it's a county park with restored buildings containing two military history museums.

SPECTATOR SPORTS. St. Louis is possibly the most *soccer*-conscious city in the country. The University of St. Louis almost always has a nationally ranked team. The St. Louis Stars play professional soccer at Francis Field, Washington University. Busch Memorial Stadium is the home for the Cardinals, both *baseball* and *football* teams. Incidentally, the Sports Hall of Fame is at the Stadium, too. The National *Hockey* League St. Louis Blues play at the Arena. Fairmount Park, 10 minutes east of the Gateway Arch, off I–55 and I–70, has *harness racing* and thoroughbred *horse racing.*

WHAT TO DO WITH THE CHILDREN. The zoo and children's zoo at the *Zoological Gardens* have about 3,000 animals. There are animal shows, and a railroad circles the zoo. *Six Flags Over Mid-America* is about 30 miles southwest of the city in Eureka, Mo.; but the kids will certainly think it worth the trip. There are over 80 rides, including one of the world's famous roller coasters, The Screamin' Eagle, puppet shows, re-creations of frontier towns and a porpoise pool, among other attractions. *Strekfus Steamers* has narrated sightseeing harbor cruises on the Mississippi River.

HOTELS AND MOTELS in St. Louis range from quite simple but clean and comfortable to luxurious with many amenities. Some of the older, more famous establishments have excellent restaurants on the premises. The price categories, for double occupancy, average as follows: *Moderate:* $30–45 and *Inexpensive* $29 and under.

Moderate: **Drury Inn.** Three facilities in St. Louis area, each with restaurant. Airport, 10800 Pear Tree Lane; Northeast, I–55 and I–70 in Collinsville, Ill., and Southwest, I–44 and Bowles in Fenton.

Regal 8 Inn. *Inexpensive:* 3651 Pennridge Rd., Bridgeton. Has 155 rooms, restaurant.

Red Roof Inn. Two in the St. Louis Area: In Bridgeton at 3470 Hollenberg Dr., and in Florissant at 309 Dunn Rd.

DINING OUT in St. Louis can mean an enjoyable evening in the elegant atmosphere of the city's downtown restaurants or fine food in one of the city's more casual, ethnic spots. Although St. Louis is noted for its German traditions, it has surprisingly few restaurants specializing in German cuisine.

Price categories are divided as follows: *Moderate* $8–15 and *Inexpensive* $7 and below. Prices are for complete meal, excluding drinks, tax and tip.

Moderate: **Casa Gallardo.** 462 West Port Plaza. This place, in the lively new suburban West Port business/entertainment center, seems right out of Old

Mexico. Menu includes authentic chiles rellenos, burritos, tacos and enchiladas. Mariachi musicians. Casual attire.

Catfish & Crystal. 409 N. 11th St. Families enjoy this small, comfortable establishment in the heart of Downtown. Varied cuisine in 19th-century setting.

Miss Hulling's Cafeteria. Downtown. Open 'til 8 P.M.

La Sala. 513 Olive St. As the name implies there is living-room atmosphere in this delightfully decorated spot where the specialties are stuffed peppers, tacos and tamales.

EXPLORING KANSAS CITY

Kansas City, "The Heart of America," is progressive. For example, city fathers claim that there is more per capita construction here than in other U.S. cities. They cite the recently completed $250,000,000 Kansas City International Airport, a 5,000-acre facility of revolutionary design, and the unique twin-stadium Harry S. Truman Sports Complex, with a combined seating capacity of nearly 120,000. Crown Center, a short distance from the heart of downtown, is a long-range $350,000,000, 85-acre shopping, residential, business and hotel complex. Another major hotel and office building recently were completed across from Crown Center.

Before beginning your tour around the city, you may want to get an overall view. Perhaps the most impressive is that from the top of the Liberty Memorial, a 217-foot shaft erected on a hill overlooking the downtown area in front of Union Station. Built in memory of those who served in World War I, it was dedicated in 1921 by Marshal Foch of France, Admiral Beatty of England, General Jacques of Belgium, General Dias of Italy, and Missouri's own General "Black Jack" Pershing.

Maybe you'll want to spend part of the day shopping downtown or visiting the top of the 423-foot-high City Hall for a view of the city's expanse. (Kansas City, by the way, has more 30-story-plus skyscrapers than any interior city west of Chicago.) Near the Civic Center, with its Courthouse (also a skyscraper) and handsome Public Library, is "Petticoat Lane," also known as 11th Street, heart of the downtown shopping district. The new H. Roe Bartle Exposition Hall and adjacent 1930s-style Municipal Auditorium provide space for conventions and exhibits.

From here, take the Southeast Freeway or Truman Road east to Independence. There, you can see the Harry S. Truman Home, the Truman Memorial Library and the Jackson County Jail of frontier days.The Reorganized Church of Jesus Christ of Latter Day Saints has its headquarters in Independence. One of the largest houses of worship in the world, its auditorium has a magnificent pipe organ, which is used for annual recitals of the *Messiah* at Christmas. Also here is the site on which the church members believe the Temple of Zion will be built.

Northeast of Independence a few miles, at Sibley, is restored Fort Osage, a former outpost of the early 19th century. Blockhouse, barracks, store, and stables are all here to see.

Back in Kansas City is famed Country Club Plaza, a world-renowned shopping center of distinctive Spanish architecture, with attractive fountains and parkway greenery. Many of the fountains were sculpted in Italy. One of the most impressive is the huge one at the corner of 47th Street and Broadway, a memorial to J. C. Nichols, creator of the Plaza. The first totally planned shopping center in the United States (1922), it is still considered by many to be the most beautiful. Its display of Christmas lights is spectacular and an excellent subject for camera fans.

After lunch, you should visit the Nelson-Atkins Museum of Art, two institutions combined into one magnificent building at the north end of a sweeping mall. The museum is known for its especially fine collection of Chinese art (the tomb figures in particular). It also has a fine assortment of European and American works and an ambitious educational program. Next door is the Kansas City Art Institute, which also has galleries open to the public.

South of the Plaza are Kansas City's most impressive residential districts, areas which Francois Mauriac was thinking of when he called Kansas City "the most beautiful city in the world." Loose Memorial Park and its adjoining residential districts show the older influence; Mission Hills, Kansas, across the border, boasts elegant mansions and has continuously ranked among America's premier residential areas. Also on the Kansas side (the state line is a street, named "State Line"), you can visit the historic Shawnee Indian Mission in Fairway.

PRACTICAL INFORMATION FOR KANSAS CITY

HOW TO GET THERE. *By car:* Kansas City is on I–70, an important east-west highway. To the west of Kansas City on I–70 is Topeka, Kansas, and to the east, across Missouri, is St. Louis. From the north, I–35 runs from Des Moines, Iowa, to Kansas City, and from Oklahoma City in the south, I–44 connects with US 71 near Carthage, Missouri, to head due north for Kansas City.

By train: Kansas City is on the *Amtrak* line; the station is at Main and Pershing Sts. Tel. (816) 421–3622.

By air: Ten major airlines fly into Kansas City International Airport (often called "KCI"), one of the most modern and convenient in the country. These include *Continental, Frontier, Ozark, TWA,* and *United.*

By bus: Trailways and *Greyhound* are the major carriers to Kansas City but there are many other local lines.

HOW TO GET AROUND. *By car:* Driving around Kansas City is slightly complicated by the Kansas and Missouri rivers, which lie to the west and north of the city. The Missouri separates Kansas City from North Kansas City. Main bridges across the Missouri are the Broadway Bridge on Broadway (Richards Rd. in N. Kansas City), the A.S.B. Bridge on U.S. 71 (Burlington Ave.), and the Paseo on I–35. To the west of the city, Seventh St., off Southwest Blvd., crosses the Kansas River.

By taxi: Cab fare is 90¢ to start the meter and 80¢ for each additional mile.

By bus: Municipal fare begins at 60¢, with additional charge for each zone crossed. Special 10¢ fare for downtown area. Maps of the system are available from the Convention and Tourist Council, 1212 Wyandotte St.

From the airport: A bus from the airport to downtown hotels will cost $7.50; a taxi ride for the same trip will run about $20.

TOURIST INFORMATION SERVICES. The *Convention and Visitors Bureau of Greater Kansas City* is at 1221 Baltimore, (816) 221–5242.

MUSEUMS AND GALLERIES. The *Nelson-Atkins Museum of Art* is one of the country's most impressive settings for a justly famous and wide-ranging art collection. Chinese and Japanese rooms outstanding. 45th and Oak Sts. (near US 50, 56) about 4 mi. S. of mid-city. The *Museum of History and Science,* Gladstone Blvd. at Indiana Ave., has a collection of natural history and anthropology including American Indian and pioneer villages populated by life-scale figures. There's also a planetarium in this mansion of seventy-two (!) rooms. The *Kansas City Art Institute,* almost next door to the Nelson Gallery, holds its own with a permanent roster of painting and sculpture, complemented by periodic shows.

SPORTS. *Swope Park* has two 18-hole golf courses. For spectators, Kansas City has acquired major franchises in *baseball* (Royals), *football* (Chiefs), *basketball* (Kings) and, recently, *soccer* (Comets). Baseball and football are played in the Truman Sports Complex; basketball in Kemper Arena. *K.C. Rodeo* at Benjamin Stables, 6401 E. 87 St., in mid-summer.

In early November the *American Royal Horse Show* brings top riders and their show horses to the city to compete in matinee and evening performances.

WHAT TO DO WITH THE CHILDREN. *Worlds of Fun,* at I–435 and Parvin Rd., has rides and entertainment of all kinds for the kids. One admission price. Open April to October. *Line Creek Park,* 60th St. and Waukomis Dr., has deer, buffalo and elk roaming around its 35 acres. Riverboat tours on the Missouri River in summer. Phone 842–0027.

HOTELS AND MOTELS in Kansas City cover the gamut from the inexpensive to the luxurious. Price categories are divided as follows: *Moderate* $30–40 and *Inexpensive* $29 and under. For a more complete explanation of these categories see the *Hotels and Motels* section of *Facts at Your Fingertips.*

Moderate: **Antioch Motor Inn.** I–35 & Antioch. Suites with kitchen available.

Blue Valley Manor. I–70 & 7 Hwy. in Blue Springs. Pool and restaurant. Near sports stadium and Worlds of Fun.

Red Roof Inn. Three facilities in Kansas City area: North, I–435 at Randolph Rd.; Overland Park, Ks., I–435 at Metcalf and Independence, I–70 at Noland Rd.

Inexpensive: **Interstate Inn.** I–70 & Woods Chapel Rd.

DINING OUT in Kansas City means steak and the cut doesn't matter as long as it's "Kansas City steak." A real "KC" steak is a strip sirloin. There are a number of restaurants specializing in other types of food but when you order steak in this town you will generally not go wrong. Price categories are divided as follows: *Moderate* $7–12 and *Inexpensive* $7 and under. Prices are for complete meals, excluding drinks, tax and tip. For a more complete explanation of restaurant categories refer to *Facts at Your Fingertips.* Some restaurants offer reduced prices in early evening hours or on week nights. These are advertised in the newspaper.

Moderate: **Annie's Santa Fe.** 100 Ward Parkway. Authentic Mexican artifacts add color to the south-of-the-border atmosphere. Specialties: crabmeat de la Concho, pizzas, and burritos. Cocktails.

Berliner Bear. 7815 Wornall. A hofbrau house with various schnitzel specialties. German beer available.

Italian Gardens. 1110 Baltimore. A family-owned restaurant since 1925, it
has a warm, hospitable atmosphere. Italian food expertly prepared.

Sam Wilson's Restaurant and Bar. 3 locations: 1029 W. 103; 9545 Antioch,
Overland Park; and 3706 S. Noland Rd., Independence. Country store atmosphere. Chicken, barbecued meats, salad bar.

Inexpensive: **André's.** 5018 Main St. Charming Swiss atmosphere near the
Country Club Plaza. Luncheon only. Choice of two entrees, plus wide selection
of delicious French pastries at one fixed price. Tempting candy and pastry retail
counter.

Arthur Bryant's Bar-B-Que. 1727 Brooklyn. Writer Calvin Trillin raved
about the food here, and even Presidents have eaten the barbecue here. Carry-
out suggested.

Forum Cafeterias. Independence Center, I–70 & M291; Antioch Shopping
Center, 5407 N. Antioch in North Kansas City. Selection of meats, vegetables,
salads, and desserts. Child's plate.

Gold Buffet. 503 E. 18th Ave., North K.C. 80 items and tantalizing dessert
cart.

Meierhoffs. 3800 Broadway. Beer and hot potato salad are good here, with
food other than German available. Sandwiches are the thing here. One of the
city's older eateries, it has the atmosphere of a neighborhood pub.

Old Washington Street Station. 900 Washington St. Trolley car theme interi-
or. Spaghetti specialty. Children's menu.

Patricio Mexican Food. 9849 Holmes. Casual, family atmosphere. Mountainous tostados.

Putsch's Coffee House. 333 W. 47th St. Baking done on premises. Charming
sidewalk café.

Putsch's Cafeteria. 300 W. 47th St. Tasty simple food. Baking on the premises.

EXPLORING MISSOURI

Of all Missouri's delightful and unusual communities, one merits
special attention—the friendly Mississippi River town of Hannibal.
Samuel Clemens was born near here (at Florida, 30 miles away, west
on US 24 and south on State 107), and grew up here in an environment
that provided a rare assortment of childhood experiences. The river
front, woods, caves, and slopes of Hannibal gave Clemens a natural
setting for his stories about Tom Sawyer and Huck Finn. Clemens, who
took the name Mark Twain, became one of America's first literary
giants.

Today, Hannibal loves to recall the Twain heritage. A steamboat still
anchors at the riverside dock, and occasionally other traffic up and
down the mammoth stream recalls the paddlewheel days. A city of
nearly 20,000, Hannibal has achieved significant industrial rank, but
the recollections of Mark Twain still remain its primary claim to national attention. In fact, a popular annual event is Tom Sawyer Days,
with a fence painting contest, raft races, etc., held early in July.

Southeast Missouri

An area of Missouri with the atmosphere of the Old South may be
found in the southeastern Bootheel region. Cotton is grown here in
what seems like Mississippi Delta country.

Ste. Genevieve, Missouri's oldest town, was founded by the French in the 1720s. By that time, lead miners had already been in the area for a number of years. Many of the town's old buildings date back to the 1700s and are open for modern visitors. Every August Ste. Genevieve holds "Jour de Fete," a commemoration of the town's French heritage.

Journey to the Springs

Missouri's diverse and beautiful scenery can be especially enjoyed on a tour of the south central region that might be termed "a journey to the springs." Missouri's range of ancient mountains, now shrunken by geologic metamorphosis, left behind a rich legacy of springs, caves, cliffs, and bluffs.

Just 55 miles southwest of St. Louis on I-44 are some of America's most popular caverns, the Meramec Caverns, in Stanton. Famous as a hideout of the Jesse James gang in the 1870s, this attraction claims to be the only five-story cave in the world. There are an underground river, a cave called the "Jungle Room," an onyx mountain, and groupings of rocks which look like stage curtains, subterranean gardens, and grapes, not to mention a wine table, all in a nature-controlled year-round temperature of 60 degrees. Nearby is Meramec State Park, second largest in Missouri, for boating, fishing, swimming, and camping.

America's first scenic riverway, the Ozark National Scenic Riverways preserves rivers in the region in their natural state. Among those directly concerned with this conservation program are Missouri's float fishermen. Float fishing is as typical of Missouri as mules, and the best-known float rivers are in the Big Springs region. Rivers such as the Current, the Jacks Fork, and the Eleven Point are well-known for float trips. These pleasant, peaceful journeys, by canoe or John Boat (a long, flat-bottom boat), can take one day or several, and they offer the beauty and isolation of the Ozark backwoods, all wrapped up in a simple fishing trip.

The Capital and a Big Dragon

Jefferson City ranks as one of America's finest capital cities. The massive state capitol, built of native Carthage marble, has long been a Missouri River landmark. The capitol building houses a museum that recalls the state's history and has many craft, geographical, and industrial exhibits. Near the capitol is the Cole County Historical Museum and the restored mercantile buildings of the Jefferson Landing Historic Site. You also may want to visit the governor's mansion nearby.

Continuing south from the capital, you reach the huge Lake of the Ozarks, also known as the Big Dragon. The lake has become a year-round attraction for Missourians and visitors alike. Near Camdenton are Bridal Cave (where many weddings have taken place), and Ozark and Stark caverns, farther north.

Southwestern Missouri

Missouri explorers also may consider a tour of the western and southwestern sections of the state and their several major lakes and prime resort areas. A section of the nearly 1.5 million acres which now comprise the Mark Twain National Forest is near Rolla. This area boasts almost 800,000 acres of oak and pine, clear waterways for float trips (fishing or just relaxing) and some small game. Some other sections are south of Springfield, including the popular Table Rock area which borders on Arkansas.

St. Joe and Jesse James

St. Joseph was one of the authentic frontier towns of a century ago. It was a rendezvous of Jesse James, the outlaw who roamed over much of this area. Visitors may visit the cottage in which Jesse was shot in the back in 1882. St. Joe has the Pony Express Stables Museum, located on the spot where the original express mail service to the West began. Lewis and Clark State Park on the Missouri River is southwest of St. Joseph.

For a taste of home cooking in a quaint atmosphere a detour east of St. Joseph on Hwy. 6 to Gallatin is well worth the scenic drive. In 1931 the McDonald Tea Room was opened by a Texas transplant named Virginia McDonald who had grown up with southern cooking and southern tradition. She died in 1969 and Jim and Dottie Stotts bought the restaurant in 1979. Glazed ham, fried chicken and catfish taste as good today as in Mrs. McDonald's day, and the homemade pastries are delicious. The main dining room retains its 1930s aura with a checkerboard floor, Roseville pottery and plants. Reservations are suggested on weekends and in summer.

PRACTICAL INFORMATION FOR MISSOURI

HOW TO GET THERE. *By Car:* I–70, from Vandalia in central Illinois, enters the state at St. Louis and connects it with Kansas City via Fulton, Columbia and Boonville. It continues to Topeka, Kansas, and beyond. From Oklahoma City and Tulsa, take I–44 to Joplin, Springfield, Rolla and St. Louis. I–55 follows the undulations of the Mississippi River from Memphis to St. Louis, looking in on Cape Girardeau and Ste. Genevieve; then it veers northeast to Springfield, Illinois. Motorists bound for Bull Shoals or Lake of the Ozarks from Little Rock may use US 65, which continues to Springfield. Southeastern Missouri is served by US 67, also out of Little Rock. It goes to Poplar Bluff and joins I–55 at Festus. In the northwest quadrant, Kansas City is express-linked to Omaha and Des Moines by I–29 and I–35 respectively.

By air: After St. Louis and Kansas City the busiest airports are at Springfield and Joplin, both of which have direct service from cities in neighboring states. Most of this service is provided by *Ozark,* complemented by *Frontier* and *Delta.*

By train: Amtrak's *National Limited* serves St. Louis and Kansas City on its New York-Los Angeles route, and St. Louis has rail links to Springfield, Illinois, and Chicago. The route of the old *Chief* is a diagonal across northern Missouri from Fort Madison, Iowa, to Kansas City.

By bus: Coast-to-coast *Greyhound* and *Trailways* expresses stop in St. Louis, Springfield and Joplin. Kansas City and northern Missouri are on east-west routes that stretch through Chicago and Omaha. *Trailways* has a diagonal route from Memphis serving Thayer, Cabool, Springfield, Osceola, Warrensburg and Kansas City.

TOURIST INFORMATION SERVICES. The larger offices offering information are *Missouri Tourism Commission,* Box 1055; *Missouri Dept. of Conservation,* Box 180; and *Missouri Division of Parks & Recreation,* Box 176; all are in Jefferson City, Missouri 65101.

 MUSEUMS AND GALLERIES. The *Springfield Art Museum* has American sculpture and paintings and relics of the westward movement. St. Joseph reflects its former role as the first point of the Pony Express route and Missouri's first railroad. *The Pony Express Stables Museum* and the *Doll Museum* are open to the public during the summer. Students of history and architecture will want to spend time at the *Winston Churchill Memorial and Library,* on the campus of Westminster College in Fulton. Here the British statesman delivered his "Iron Curtain" address just 10 months after the Allies had triumphantly entered Berlin. A London, England, church was moved here, stone by stone, and reconstructed in 1966. The church had been restored by Sir Christopher Wren in 1666, when it was already 500 years old. The library proper contains manuscripts, letters and paintings by Sir Winston.

 HISTORIC SITES. In Sibley, off US 24, visit the *Fort Osage Restoration.* A trading post and barracks for defense against Indian attacks, it was established in 1808 by William Clark after his return from exploring the Louisiana Territory. The *Harry S. Truman Shrine Birthplace* in Lamar has the restored family home, through which guided tours are available. Independence is where the *Truman Library and Museum* is located.

As one might expect, there are more historic houses in the state's oldest permanent community, *Ste. Genevieve,* than in any other community except Kansas City and St. Louis. The *George Caleb Bingham House* near Arrow Rock is open during the summer. Mark Twain, Bingham's contemporary, is, of course, the most famous citizen of *Hannibal,* and the Samuel Clemens Boyhood Home preserves local relics and family memorabilia. One of the state's most beautiful antebellum mansions is Linwood Lawn in *Lexington,* huge and elaborate with over 230 acres of grounds. *Defiance* is the site of the Daniel Boone Home. Daniel oversaw the building of this home and lived here the last 10 years of his life.

 TOURS. Sightseeing tours within individual communities in Missouri often focus on lakes and rivers. Lake Taneycomo in the southwestern region offers a Pirate Cruise from the Sammy Lane dock in Branson. A similar excursion on the *Lake Queen* puts out from Fisherman's dock, also in Branson. The huge Lake of the Ozarks has its cruise boats too, and they leave from Casino Pier near Bagnell Dam. Daytime trips and evening dance socials are available. Hannibal has sternwheeler tours on the Mississippi River and a "trackless" train ride around town. These all operate in warm-weather months. Tourists also enjoy a free tour year-round of Bagnell Dam in Lake Ozark. The dam, completed in 1931, formed one of America's largest man-made lakes, the Lake of the Ozarks.

DRINKING LAWS. Liquor laws vary from town to town. Generally, liquor may be bought by the drink from 6 A.M. to 1:30 A.M. except Sunday, when the hours are 1 P.M. to midnight. Package sales are prohibited on Sunday; other days they are legal from 6 A.M. to 1:30 A.M. Legal drinking age is 21.

 **SUMMER SPORTS.** "Golf Digest" recommends several courses: Lake Valley, near Camdenton, is public, and the Lodge of the Four Seasons Course, on the Lake of the Ozarks, is a layout by that Michelangelo of course design, Robert Trent Jones. The fishing in Ozark waters is famous, with walleye, rainbows, panfish, bluegill and bass the prized catches. Waterskiing and row-

boating are available on the region's lakes, and canoeing, too, is healthy and relaxing, especially on the beautiful, quiet streams that lace the southern tier. Horseback riding is among the activities available at some resorts and state parks.

WINTER SPORTS. Include the fall and you've got tremendous opportunities for hunting, if that's what you like; small game roams in great abundance: squirrel, rabbit, skunk, raccoon, fox and varieties of fowl. There are several Ozark resorts now offering ski slopes, but if you're used to Colorado or Switzerland, it might seem a little tame.

SPECTATOR SPORTS. Horse and auto races, with no regular seasons in rural Missouri, are special events for state and county fairs. Of course the University of Missouri, Columbia, has a full athletic program, including football, basketball, track, swimming and wrestling.

WHAT TO DO WITH THE CHILDREN. Missouri's most unique natural attraction is its extensive series of caves. Nevada has the *Bushwhacker Museum,* a former jail complete with inmates' graffiti and cuts, scraping, chippings and holes recording their efforts at escape. Mementos of two famous native sons may interest youngsters. The *George Washington Carver National Monument,* off County Rd. V, southwest of Diamond, has exhibits and a diorama plus a self-guiding pathway through the neighborhood where Carver grew up. Hannibal has several houses, exhibits and events of interest to readers of Mark Twain. Near Excelsior Springs, in *Watkins Mill State Park,* visit the woolen factory and see the equipment used over 100 years ago. By all means, plan on a day's entertainment at the state's two major theme parks: *Six Flags Over Mid-America* near St. Louis and *Worlds of Fun* in Kansas City.

HOTELS AND MOTELS outside St. Louis and Kansas City range from the lavish Lodge of the Four Seasons in the Lake Ozark region to clean and comfortable establishments in smaller towns. Price categories for double occupancy average as follows: *Moderate* $20–30 and *Inexpensive* $20 and under. Many smaller motels in the Ozarks close during the winter months, and spring and fall rates often are less than summer rates.

BRANSON. *Moderate:* **Bridgeport Resort.** On lake. Seventh day free. Kitchenettes available.
Blue Haven Resort. Cottages with kitchenettes. Playground, pool, fishing.

COLUMBIA. *Inexpensive:* **Regal 8 Inn.** There are 84 rooms. Restaurants nearby.

JOPLIN. *Moderate:* **Capri.** Comfortable setting. Pool, restaurant.

OSAGE BEACH. *Moderate:* **Hilltop.** Pool, playground, restaurant next door. Grills, picnic tables and great view of lake. Marina adjacent.

SPRINGFIELD. *Moderate:* **Kentwood Arms.** An older hotel with a motel operation added on. 2 pools, restaurant, beauty shop.
TraveLodge. Pool, restaurant nearby.
Inexpensive: **Interstate Inn.** Has 144 rooms.

DINING OUT in Missouri can provide unique experiences to anyone willing to go off the beaten track. Eating in a plush dining room overlooking the Lake of the Ozarks is a real pleasure, as is sitting down to a plain table of simple, good food. Price categories are divided as follows: *Moderate* $7–12 and *Inexpensive* $7 and under. Prices are for a complete meal, excluding drinks, tax and tip.

ARROW ROCK. *Inexpensive:* **The Old Tavern.** A museum and restaurant on the Old Santa Fe Trail built in 1834 and furnished in the style of the period. Reservations required.

ST. GENEVIEVE. *Moderate:* **The Old Brick House.** 3rd & Market. German and American bill-of-fare served in charming, restored, 200-year-old building. Liver dumplings and kettle beef are specialties.

SPRINGFIELD *Inexpensive:* **Heritage Cafeteria.** Popular for simple American cooking, homemade bread.

NEW MEXICO

Santa Fe, Albuquerque and Indian Country

The best (but expensive) base for seeing New Mexico is Santa Fe (pop. 48,963), but the many affluent summer people who flock in for the cool climate and the Santa Fe Opera make reservations essential.

The Plaza is worth several hours. Its north side is formed by the Palace of the Governors. Under this block-long porch, Indians from nearby pueblos traditionally hold a daily open-air market, spreading their silver-and-turquoise jewelry, pottery, leather goods, and other handicrafts on the brick sidewalk. The Palace is now part of the Museum of New Mexico. Its cool, dim, thick-walled rooms are filled with exhibits displaying the panorama of the state's history and prehistory. A superb example of adobe construction, with walls up to six feet thick, it was the official residence of one hundred appointed governors—Spanish, Mexican, and U.S.—from 1610 until 1910, and is by far the oldest public building in the country. Its exhibits offer a pleasant way to get a feeling for New Mexico's Indian, Spanish and Anglo-American cultures.

Just down Palace Avenue from this historic structure is the state's Fine Arts Museum, housed in Pueblo-style architecture.

In the block up Palace Avenue from the Palace of the Governors is Sena Plaza, the palatial former home of the Sena family. Stand at the fountain in its interior courtyard to get some feeling of how the rich lived in days gone by.

Just across Palace are the grounds of St. Francis Cathedral, a 19th-century Romanesque structure begun by Archbishop Jean Baptiste Lamy in 1869. The cathedral's Sacred Heart Chapel houses *La Conquistadora,* a statue of the Blessed Virgin Mary that Captain-General Don Diego de Vargas brought with him when he reconquered Santa Fe from the Indians in 1692.

Around the corner from the cathedral is another of Santa Fe's interesting churches—the tiny Loretto Chapel, modeled after the church of Sainte-Chapelle in Paris and best known for its beautiful staircase that climbs in a tight spiral to its choir loft. According to local legend, a stranger appeared when the church was nearing completion, performed this superb piece of carpentry, and then vanished without being paid.

Santa Fe's "Oldest Church" is two blocks away across the Santa Fe River. The Mission of San Miguel was built in 1636, burned by Indians in 1680, and rebuilt after the reconquest.

Adjoining this chapel across De Vargas Street is what may be the oldest house in the United States, an often-restored structure of puddled adobe which houses a curio shop.

A block west down the Santa Fe River Park on narrow De Vargas Street and you are on the State Capitol grounds. The Executive-Legislative Building is a controversial building which locals call "The Roundhouse"; it's the nation's only round capitol building, and a symbol of what happens when a state tries to compromise between modern and traditional.

Canyon Road, on the south side of the Santa Fe River, is one of the city's oldest and most exclusive neighborhoods. The street is lined with the studios and galleries of painters, sculptors, and craftsmen. Browsers are welcome (and buyers even more so). An association of Canyon Road artists usually has an updated map available at hotels and the Chamber of Commerce office.

Just off Canyon is Cristo Rey (The Church of Christ the King), the largest adobe structure in the United States, with stark white walls and a high ceiling supported by wooden *vigas.* The screen behind the altar was carved in stone in 1751 and is considered a priceless example of Spanish-colonial religious art.

The Museum of International Folk Art on the southeast side of the city includes the largest collection of international folk art ever assembled by a private benefactor. Don't miss the Alexander Girard Collection housed in its own wing.

The Folk Art Museum, one of the very few of its kind in the world, is devoted to the beauty found in everyday costumes, carvings, furniture, toys, weapons, and tools of common people.

Santa Fe is also an excellent base for brief side excursions. A few hours of round-trip driving will take you through colonial-vintage villages in the mountains, ghost towns, thriving Indian pueblos, a ski basin complete with Hudsonian Life Zone fir, spruce, and aspen—and a rushing stream cold enough to numb your hand on the hottest day of summer.

Albuquerque and the Rio Grande Valley

Another excellent base for exploring is Albuquerque (pop. 328,837), New Mexico's only large city.

The Old Town Plaza looks pretty much as it did when Albuquerque began. The fortresslike San Felipe de Neri Church, along with its convent, makes up its north side. Inside is a choir-loft stairway that spirals its way around the trunk of a spruce tree. Mass has been said in the building every day since it opened in 1706.

The city's most spectacular attraction is the Sandia Peak Aerial Tram, with a view that defies description. The altitude is 10,678 feet and all of north-central New Mexico lies around and below you: Albuquerque and some 10,000 square miles of river valley and mountain ranges. You can also see Santa Fe and, if the weather is as clear as it usually is, mountain ranges as far north as Colorado, into the Navajo country near Arizona, and stretching southward toward Mexico.

Acoma, one of the most remarkable settlements in the Western Hemisphere, may be the oldest continuously occupied town in the United States. It is a tidy and compact village atop a sheer-walled table of stone that juts out of surrounding grazing country for 357 feet, the height of a 40-story skyscraper. A look at the great mission church, the neat row of houses, and the natural cistern that provides the residents with their water supply on their flat sandstone perch is something to remember.

The landscape on the Acoma Reservation, and through much of this part of New Mexico, features great sandstone cliffs; pink, white, gray, salmon-colored, and bloody red, carved into grotesque shapes, or streaked with all the shades of red and often undercut into echo caves.

The colorful old art colony of Taos is an ideal base for exploring the northern mountain portion of New Mexico. It's an almost purely adobe place, easy to tour on foot. Its galleries and studios are nearly all centered within a few blocks of the plaza. The D. H. Lawrence ranch is maintained by the University of New Mexico and is open to visitors. It offers a superb view, of which Lawrence wrote: "I think the skyline of Taos is the most beautiful of all I have ever seen in my travels around the world."

The Kit Carson House, where the famous frontiersman lived, is now a museum. (Carson, incidentally, is considerably less idealized in these days of Indian militancy. The Navajos remember his role in the scorched-earth campaign that starved them from the Dinetah and led to their infamous "Long Walk" into exile.)

Taos Pueblo, just north of Taos, is the northernmost of the pueblos. It is a thriving village of some nine hundred people and is dominated by its principal five-story apartment building which was ancient when the white men first saw it in the 16th century. It hasn't changed since.

St. Francis of Assisi Mission, at Ranchos de Taos, a suburb village four miles south, is probably the most-depicted church this side of St. Patrick's Cathedral in New York. Made of adobe, with massive abutments and buttresses, it has an odd, stark beauty that neither painters nor photographers seem able to resist.

Just north of Taos is some of the West's most beautiful mountain scenery. The lay of the land makes it possible to see a lot of it in a circle drive of 90 miles via US 64 over Palo Flechado Pass, then via State Road 38, Red River Pass, and Questa. The route is spectacular.

US 84 and State 17 bring you to Chama, an old lumber, sheep and railroad town; it is also the departure point for the Cumbres and Toltec Scenic Railroad, an ancient narrow-gauge railroad formerly operated by the Denver and Rio Grande as a freight line and now purely a sightseeing train. The old steam engines puff their way up Cumbres Pass, 10,022 feet above sea level, and then across the lush, high meadows of Wolf Creek into the Los Pinos River canyon, through Toltec Gorge and onto the Rio Grande plateau at Antonito, Colorado. It's a wonderful ride. There are picnic and photography stops, and since some of the round trips sell out early, check in advance on tickets and schedule (brochures from the State Tourist Bureau).

Aztec Ruins National Monument is just north of US 550 and shouldn't be missed. Here, about A.D. 1106, Indians built one of their largest pre-Spanish pueblos beside the Animas River. It's a massive (Pueblo III Period) five hundred-room apartment complex, with the largest underground kiva (48-foot diameter) ever excavated. No one knows why the great pueblo was abandoned about 1300.

Gallup (pop. 18,232) calls itself the "Indian Capital of the World" with considerable justification. A former coal and railroad town, it has gradually become the trading center for the most populous part of the Navajo nation, Indians from the nearby Zuni Reservation and from the other western pueblos. It's another good place to buy Indian-made articles.

If you happen to be in New Mexico early in December, check on the schedule of the Zuni "Shalako," the annual return of the Zuni "Council of the Gods" to the Pueblo. This is the most dramatic and colorful ceremonial in the Western Hemisphere. The council is accompanied by its six messenger birds (the Shalako) personified by Zunis wearing great bird-form masks ten feet tall; the event is the occasion for twenty-four hours of dancing and feasting and annually draws thousands of spectators. The hospitable Zunis try to feed and provide for everyone. You are welcome at all such ceremonials (at Zuni and the other Pueblos), but photography is absolutely forbidden, and so are sketching and the making of tape recordings.

The emptiest part of New Mexico is the southwest. In the 19th century this country buzzed with mining fever, but today the lodes are exhausted and the towns have fallen into ruin.

Silver City, where Billy the Kid became a juvenile delinquent and killed his first man, now survives on copper, cattle, and on New Mexico Western University. It's the center of a complex of mining communities —Bayard, Santa Rita, Hurley, Central, Hanover, and Tyrone. It also serves as the entrance to the Gila Wilderness Area—the oldest and most isolated in the nation. While no roads or wheeled vehicles are allowed in a Wilderness, this one wraps around a pre-existing access route to the Gila Cliff Dwellings National Monument. The route takes you through the old mining town of Pinos Altos, and then through 37 miles of empty, untouched forests.

If you turn toward the river at San Marcial, you pick up old US 85 which leads to the Bosque del Apache Wildlife Refuge. Here the ancient San Marcial marshes, once a favored wintering place for Apache war parties, have been converted into a sanctuary that attracts ornithologists from around the world. It's one of the few nesting places for the rare Mexican ducks. The winter bird count soars past the half-million level, including the majestic whooping crane, Sandhill cranes, immense flocks of Canada and Snow Geese, and scores of other bird species. The old marsh is also home for deer herds, beaver, coyotes and other wildlife.

At Lincoln the old Lincoln County Courthouse from which Billy the Kid escaped after killing two guards is now a state monument. The young outlaw and 18 companions shot it out with some 40 lawmen of the Murphy-Dolan faction, using the Alex McSween house as their fortress. Seven died in that scuffle; Billy was credited with killing 21 before he was shot to death at age twenty-one. The museum here is intriguing for those interested in frontier badmen.

US 70 leads down off the mountain to Tularosa and the Tularosa Basin. The big town is Almogordo (pop. 24,018), an attractive little city. Its big tourist appeal is White Sands National Monument, 230 square miles of snowy white gypsum dunes, some as high as 100 feet. The back side of these great dunes is hard because it is carved endlessly by the southwesterly winds. The face is as soft as fine sand, great for rolling down (if you're in a playful mood).

The Carlsbad Caverns

There are caves here big enough to contain the whole of the Capitol in Washington. Guided tours, ($3.00 per private vehicle) take you through many of the caverns on a 3½-mile exploration—the full extent of the caverns has never been completely discovered. A jacket or sweater is comfortable down here, where the temperature is always exactly 56 degrees F. If you don't feel like so much walking, a 750-foot-drop elevator will drop you down into one of the caverns, where you can patronize one of the world's strangest lunchrooms if you like. Besides thousands of visitors, the caverns contain millions of bats whose ancestors have lived in here for 15 centuries—at least 100,000 tons of guano had been hauled out of the caves before the National Park Service took possession here. A very early visitor was identified by a sandal he left behind 4,000 years ago—a prehistoric Basketmaker Indian. For the patient traveler, one of the strangest sights in the world is that of the midnight flight of tens of thousands of these bats who flap and clatter their way into the sky and then return at dawn. Fifteen miles southwest of Carlsbad. Accommodations and tourist services at Carlsbad.

PRACTICAL INFORMATION FOR NEW MEXICO

HOW TO GET THERE. *By car:* There are good roads into and across New Mexico from all the bordering states. *By air:* Albuquerque has direct service from the country's half-dozen major air centers. *By bus:* The New York–Los Angeles express buses of *Trailways* and *Greyhound* serve Tucumcari, Albuquerque and Gallup, along I-40. North-south expresses are Trailways' buses from Durango, Greyhound buses from Pueblo, Colorado. *By train:* Amtrak's *Super Chief* goes via Albuquerque and Santa Fe, and the *Sunset Limited* via Deming and Lordsburg.

TOURIST INFORMATION. Write to the *Department of Development,* State of New Mexico, Bataan Memorial Bldg., State Capitol, Santa Fe, N.M. 87501 Phone: (505) 827–5571.

MUSEUMS AND GALLERIES. Santa Fe is the museum capital by virtue of the *Museum of New Mexico's* four units: The *Palace of the Governors, Wheelwright Museum of the American Indian, Fine Arts Museum, Museum of International Folk Art.* All museums are open daily, May to September.

Many other special-interest museums enrich the state: In Albuquerque some free museums: *Museum of Albuquerque, National Atomic Museum* at Kirtland Air Force Base, the University of New Mexico's *Maxwell Museum of Anthropology, Geology Museum* and *Meteorites Museum;* at Abiquiu, *Ghost Ranch;* the *Old Mill Museum* and *Ernest Thompson Seton Memorial Library,* at Cimarron; the *Pancho Villa Museum,* at Columbus; the *Los Alamos Historical Museum* (for atomic-science buffs); and the *Confederate Air Force Museum,* at Hobbs.

HISTORIC SITES. In addition to the pueblo missions, there are several other churches of great antiquity and historical value: *Church of St. Francis of Assisi* at Ranchos de Taos, *San Miguel Mission* and *St. Francis Cathedral* in Santa Fe, the *Church of San Felipe de Neri of Albuquerque,* the *Mission of San Miguel* at Socorro, the *Chimayo Santuario* and the *Church of the Twelve Apostles* at Las Trampas. The *Palace of the Governors* in Santa Fe was built in 1610 and is the oldest public building in the United States.

TOURS. Both *Gray Lines* and *Thunderbird Tours* offer a list of regular sightseeing tours to various parts of New Mexico. Albuquerque and Santa Fe are the main centers; tours cover both the cities themselves and large areas around them.

DRINKING LAWS. Liquor, beer, wine retailers and dispensers are open daily except Sundays. Age limit is 21, or 18 when accompanied by parent, legal guardian, or spouse of legal age. (Sundays, by local option, by drink only, noon to midnight.)

SPORTS. In lakes administered by the Department of Game and Fish, *boating* without motors is permissible. Some of these lakes are: Clayton Lake, twelve mi. N of Clayton on State 370; Fenton Lake, twenty-four mi. N of Jemez Springs on State 126; Bear Canyon Dam, six mi. NW of San Lorenzo on State 61; Lake Van, two mi. E. of Dexter on State 190. *Golf* courses are in Santa Fe, Los Alamos, Albuquerque, Cloudcroft, Hobbs, Carlsbad, Farmington, Las Cruces, Roswell, Socorro and Truth or Consequences.

Horseback riding instructions, *hay rides, pack trips,* and *hunting safaris* are available at dude ranches, resorts, and riding academies.

Skiing: twelve ski areas attract buffs from all states and from Europe. Generally, it's a Thanksgiving-to-Easter season.

WHAT TO DO WITH THE CHILDREN. In Carlsbad, in addition to the caverns, are the *Zoological and Botanical Gardens* and the *President's Park* (which has an old paddlewheel steamboat and miniature train). North of Abiquiu is the *Ghost Ranch Museum;* it is devoted particularly to local animals, plants and geology. In Albuquerque is the *Rio Grande Zoological Park,* where exotic species please the children and adults alike. The *Cumbres & Toltec Scenic Railroad* is a narrow-gauge train pulled by a steam locomotive.

HOTELS AND MOTELS. Accommodations range from American-Standard in towns of little tourist interest to colorful, charming, and unique in places like Taos and Santa Fe.

In all these places, however, it's a good idea to have reservations.

The price categories in this section, for double occupancy, will start *up* from following prices: *Inexpensive* $16–25, and *Moderate* $25–35.

ALBUQUERQUE. *Moderate:* **Aladin Inn.** 13400 Central Ave. Coffee shop; lounge with entertainment; buffet patio. Game room; sauna.

Inexpensive: **Desert Sands Motel.** 5000 Central Ave. SE. Centrally located on Route 66. Restaurant; pool.

Note: Albuquerque is served by virtually every motel chain and has more than a hundred motels available. The older and less expensive ones tend to be located along Central Ave., the former route of the Los Angeles-to-Chicago highway. Its famous downtown hotel, the Alvarado, has been demolished.

SANTA FE. *Moderate:* **El Rey Motel.** Comfortable rooms, pool, restaurants nearby.

Stagecoach Motor Inn. Caters to families. Quiet.

Inexpensive: **De Vargas Hotel.** Downtown Santa Fe.

Note: New Mexico's capital city is now served by most of the major motel chains and has unusually good hotels for a city of its small size. It also has a chronic shortage of accommodations during the summer. Don't count on finding a room unless you have reservations.

TAOS. *Moderate:* **El Pueblo Motel.** Informal. Indoor pool.

Taos Inn. Old Spanish hacienda.

DINING OUT. In theory, traditional dishes of New Mexico are Mexican. Actually, the years have brought a totally unique evolution to New Mexican recipes, and traditional dishes have come to blend Spanish, Indian, and Anglo-American styles.

Restaurant price categories are as follows: *Moderate* $6–10, and *Inexpensive* $3.25–6. These prices are for dinner and do not include dessert, drinks or tips.

ALBUQUERQUE. *Moderate:* **High Noon.** Historic adobe structure. Good place to stop for lunch when visiting Old Town.

El Pinto. Mexican menu.

Inexpensive: **Bella Vista.** Twenty-minute scenic drive from Albuquerque in the Sandia mountains. Steaks, chicken, seafood. Inexpensive family dining.

Mi Casita. Small, unassuming family operation serving authentic Southwestern food.

CARLSBAD. *Inexpensive:* **Cortez Café.** Excellent New Mexican foods.

ROSWELL/RUIDOSO. *Moderate:* **Tinnie's Silver Dollar.** One of the West's most colorful, in the old Tinnie Mercantile Building beside US70/80. Like dining in 1880. Open 5 to 11 P.M.

Other 19th-century frontier recreations by the same operator, and about as good, are the **Double Eagle** in Mesilla (near Las Cruces), the **Palace** in Raton, and the **Legal Tender** in Lamy (near Santa Fe).

LAS CRUCES. *Moderate:* **La Posta.** One of New Mexico's famous old restaurants. Patios, birds, flowers, and a good Mexican menu.

SANTA FE. *Moderate:* **El Farol.** Corner of Canyon and Camino de Monte Sol. An excellent menu including shrimp stuffed with crabmeat. Typically Santa Fe in atmosphere.

La Tertulia. Operated by an old Santa Fe family in the former Guadalupe Parish buildings. Delicious Mexican food, fine décor, fine service.

Shoko Cafe. Exceptional Japanese food; delicious sushi. Japanese beer and saki available.

The Shed. In Sena Plaza at Palace Avenue and Cathedral Place. A favorite spot for lunch only. It is noted for its blue corn tortillas, fine fresh mushroom soup and New Mexico foods. No cocktails.

Guadalupe Café. Located across from the historic Guadalupe Church. New Mexican and Italian specialties well-prepared. Ample portions. Good value for the money.

TAOS. *Moderate:* **Kachina Lodge Dining Room.** Varied menu in a lovely setting, bar.

Michael's Kitchen. Generous helpings of food that seems home cooked.

TUCUMCARI. *Moderate:* **Pow Wow Restaurant.** In the Pow Wow Inn. Standard menu, relaxing setting.

OKLAHOMA

"Home of the Indians"

Many Indian artifacts and other items from Oklahoma's rich history are found across the boulevard from the capitol in Oklahoma City, at the State Museum of Oklahoma. Other facets of its history are documented and displayed at the Oklahoma Heritage Center, the National Cowboy Hall of Fame and Western Heritage Center, the Forty-Fifth Infantry Museum, the National Softball Hall of Fame, the Oklahoma Firefighters Museum and the 1889ers Harn Homestead Museum. All are located within five miles of each other.

Probably one of the West's most famous museums in the West is the National Cowboy Hall of Fame and Western Heritage Center. This unique institution, dedicated to the memory of the heroic pioneers of the Old West, was established through the cooperative efforts of seventeen states: Texas, Oklahoma, Kansas, Nebraska, South Dakota, North Dakota, Montana, Wyoming, Nevada, Utah, Colorado, New Mexico, Arizona, California, Oregon, Idaho, and Washington. Life-size dioramas re-create an Indian camp, a roundup chuck wagon camp, and the frontier cavalry. A taped narration capsules the pioneer history as synchronized lights trace the pioneers' westward trek across a large relief map. The Heritage Center opened on June 26, 1965, and was proclaimed a national memorial by an Act of Congress in 1967. The institution contains books and documents on the frontier development, western art, and exhibits of early clothing and vehicles. The Rodeo Hall

of Fame is devoted to exhibits commemorating the national championships. Although better known for his rope tricks, it was by capturing
a rampant steer from Zach Mulhall's Wild West Show in Madison
Square Garden that Will Rogers got his start in show business in New
York; the show was from Mulhall, Oklahoma. Another Oklahoma
company, Pawnee Bill's Wild West Show, toured the world in combination with Buffalo Bill Cody's show.

Other notable museums are the Museum of Arts, the Science and Art
Foundation, and the Kirkpatrick Center, which houses three unusual
art galleries—the African Gallery, the American Indian Gallery and
a Japanese Gallery. Also at the center are the Omniplex, a "hands-on"
science and technology museum; the Air Space Museum, which highlights the history of U.S. aviation; and the Kirkpatrick Planetarium, a
space and time machine that lets visitors discover the universe.

PRACTICAL INFORMATION FOR

OKLAHOMA CITY

HOW TO GET THERE. *By air: American, United, Eastern, Delta, Southwest, Frontier, Continental,* and *Trans
World Airlines* serve Oklahoma City. There are direct
flights to Oklahoma City from both coasts. *By bus: Greyhound* and *Trailways* both have through service from other states. The best
regional service is provided by *M.K.&O.* (918–582–2261) and *Oklahoma Transportation* (405–239–6831).

HOW TO GET AROUND. *By car: Rent-A-Car* facilities are available from
Avis, Hertz, and independent dealers.

TOURIST INFORMATION. Tourist brochures and information can be obtained by writing the *Oklahoma Tourism and Recreation Department,* 500 Will
Rogers Building, Oklahoma City 73105, or from the information center in the
Capitol Rotunda. A traveler information center is also located on I–35 at the
intersection of NE 50th Street.

Three major events in Oklahoma City are the *Festival of the Arts* every April,
the *Oklahoma State Fair,* in September, and the *National Finals Rodeo* held each
December.

MUSEUMS AND GALLERIES. *Firefighters Museum,*
2716 NE 50; *National Cowboy Hall of Fame & Western
Heritage Center,* 1700 NE 63; *National Softball Hall of
Fame,* 2801 NE 50; and the *Kirkpatrick Center,*
planetarium and fascinating science complex, at Lincoln Park, home of the
city's fabulous zoo. All of the foregoing are clustered within a square mile in
the city's northeast quadrant. The *State Museum of Oklahoma* is a few steps
southeast of the south door of the State Capitol Building. The *Oklahoma Art
Center,* 1400 Nichols Road, is located in Buttram Mansion.

HISTORIC SITES. *Oklahoma Heritage House,* near the
State Capitol Building in the historic preservation area,
was the home of an early-day city father and contains
many antiques and imported items. Mon.–Sat. 9–5, Sun.
and holidays 1–5. The *State Capitol,* NE 23rd St. at Lincoln Blvd., is the only
statehouse with working oil wells right on its grounds. Guided tours available.

WHAT TO DO WITH THE CHILDREN. New in 1982, *White Water* is America's largest water park. On Reno, east of I–40 at Meridian, White Water offers body and mat surfing in Wave Pool, slippery water sliding and just plain swimming. Tiny tots enjoy supervised play on Little Squirt's Island with cannons, swings, and tunnels. For bigger kids, there's Pirate's Cove, Diving Rocks, Boom Swing, Corkscrew Slide, and 80-foot Cable Slide. Visitors will like riding the rapids in oversized inner tubes. Certified lifeguards, Red Cross trained, are on duty.

 HOTELS AND MOTELS. The price categories in this section, for double occupancy, will average: *Moderate* $23–28. All have private clubs for drinking purposes.

Moderate: **Brass Lantern.** 700 N.W. 9th St.
Holiday Inn East. I–40 at 5701 Tinker Diagonal.
Holiday Inn North. I–35 at 12001 NE Expressway.
Holiday Inn West–Airport. I–40 at Meridian.
Holiday Inn NW. 3535 NW 39 Expressway.
Pebbletree Inn. 2200 N.W. Expressway.
Sieber. 1305 N. Hudson.
Southgate Inn. 5245 S. I–35.
Inexpensive: **Dream House Motel.** 4600 S. Shields.

DINING OUT. The price categories in this section are for a complete meal without drinks, tax or tip and will average: *Moderate* $7–10, *Inexpensive* under $7. Most have private clubs (for drinking).

Moderate: **Butterfield Overland Express.** 4217 NW 63. Lunch and dinner. Interesting variety of food. Funky atmosphere.

Classen Grill. 5124 Classen. Soup, sandwiches, unusual specialties.

Furr's Cafeteria. 2842 French Market. Take your pick in this eatery with a homey atmosphere.

Hoe Sai Gai. 5201 N. Shartel. Lunch and dinner. Cantonese, Polynesian, and American specialties. Interesting decor.

Queen Anne Cafeteria. Ground flr., United Founders Life Tower (just NW of NW Expressway & May Avenue intersection). Widely varied menu, pleasant atmosphere.

Surrey House. 12026 NE Expressway (I–35). Southern specialties and homemade pastries.

Inexpensive: **Cattleman's Café.** 1309 S. Agnew in Stockyards City. Open round the clock. Charbroiled steaks and home-style cooking. Where the cowboys chow down.

Lady Classen Cafeteria. 6903 N. May Ave. Local hangout featuring Dutch apple pie, country-style fried chicken and old-fashioned roast beef. Colonial atmosphere.

Johnnie's. 2652 W. Britton Rd. Some of the best hamburgers in town.

EXPLORING THE REST OF OKLAHOMA

Oklahoma is a land of lakes, with many state parks, and is the home of 67 Indian tribes. Remnants of numerous tribes pushed from their original homes by white conquest finally settled in the state; many still bear the tribal names.

The Five Civilized Tribes—Cherokee, Chickasaw, Choctaw, Creek, and Seminole—were granted most of the eastern half of the state. In Tahlequah, once capital of the Cherokee Nation, is Tsa-La-Gi, a restored Cherokee village. Each summer *The Trail of Tears,* an outdoor drama about the tragic forced march of the Cherokees to Oklahoma, is performed here.

Sequoyah State Park is named for the Cherokee Indian leader who devised an alphabet for the Cherokee language. (California's great Sequoia redwoods are also named after him.) His cabin is preserved in Sallisaw.

Although each area has its local Indian festivals, Indians from all over the nation converge on Anadarko the third week in August for the annual American Indian Exposition. The city also houses the permanent exhibits of the American Indian Hall of Fame, the Southern Plains Indian Exhibit and Craft Center and Indian City, USA, with re-created, authentic Plains Indian huts and dwellings.

The Oil Capital

A major event in Tulsa is the International Petroleum Exposition, held every five years (next, 1986). The campus of Oral Roberts University with its futuristic architecture is a popular tourist attraction. The Philbrook Art Center and the Gilcrease Institute of American History and Art are both legacies of prominent Tulsa oilmen. The collection at Philbrook includes outstanding works by North and South American Indians. Gilcrease Institute contains art by western painters, sculptures by the Cherokee artist Willard Stone.

Will Rogers Remembered

The life and works of Will Rogers are commemorated at the Will Rogers Memorial in Claremore with dioramas, exhibits, and voice recordings. The Will Rogers Memorial Rodeo is held in Vinita in mid-August.

If Oklahoma has Indian settlements, it also has forts. Fort Gibson, once the westernmost outpost of the United States, has many of its original buildings remaining; others have been rebuilt. In the nearby National Cemetery is a grave said to be that of Tiana Rogers, Sam Houston's Cherokee wife.

General W. B. Hazen put down the Kiowa and Comanche rebellion from Fort Cobb, where there is now a lake and recreation area. At Fort Sill, the guardhouse where Geronimo was prisoner still stands. And General Custer attacked the Arapaho, Cheyenne and Kiowa Indians from Fort Supply. At that time the land around the fort was arid; today it contains the third largest lake in western Oklahoma.

Oklahoma's largest lake is Lake Eufaula in east central Oklahoma with 102,500 acres. Lake Texoma on the southern border of the state boasts a 93,000-acre lake and 2,600-acre Lake Texoma State Park are one of Oklahomans' favorite recreational areas.

Alabaster Caverns State Park, in the northwest, has the world's largest known alabaster cave open for public tour. Throughout its many chambers, special lighting effects enhance the transparent beauty of the alabaster.

The Chickasha National Recreation Area

This smallest of all National Parks has many bromide and sulphur springs, all running cold, that should be taken on a doctor's advice only. Saddle horses are available in the town of Sulphur for use on the park's bridle trails, and there is an eight-mile circuit drive that links three modern campgrounds. The park was once part of the holdings of the Chickasaw Indians, who traditionally drank these waters for therapeutic reasons. Thousands of redbuds emerge in April make a delightful sight for springtime travelers here, and there are several streams with waterfalls and cascades easily reached in short walks on trails. There is a nature trail, as well, and in summer a naturalist leads guided tours. Accommodations and tourist services at nearby Sulphur.

PRACTICAL INFORMATION FOR OKLAHOMA

HOW TO GET THERE: *By air:* There are direct flights to Oklahoma City and Tulsa from most major U.S. cities. *By bus: Greyhound* and *Trailways* serve the major cities.

TOURIST INFORMATION. Brochures and information are obtainable from the *Oklahoma Tourism and Recreation Department,* 500 Will Rogers Building, Oklahoma City 73105. There are also traveler information centers along major highways.

  MUSEUMS AND GALLERIES. *Tom Mix Museum,* Dewey; *No Man's Land Historical Museum,* Goodwell; *Seay Mansion & Chisholm Trail Museum,* Kingfisher; *Pioneer Woman Statue & Museum,* Ponca City; *Jim Thorpe Home,* Yale.
Woolaroc Museum, J. M. Davis Gun Museum, Antiques, Inc. Car Museum, Thomas Gilcrease Institute of American History and Art, Philbrook Art Center, Rebecca and Gershon Fenster Gallery of Jewish Art, Tulsa.

HISTORIC SITES. Anadarko: *Indian City, USA,* authentic restoration of Plains Indians' villages. El Reno: *Fort Reno* and *General Sheridan cabin.* Fort Gibson: *Fort Gibson Stockade,* 1824. Fort Supply: Established by Custer. Gore: *Cherokee Council House.* Guthrie: *Territorial capital* of state, with numerous landmarks. Heavener: *runestones* thought to be carved by early Viking explorers. Hugo: winter quarters for *circuses.* Lawton: *Fort Sill National Historic Landmark,* grave of Geronimo. Madill: *Fort Washita,* established by Zachary Taylor as area Confederate headquarters during Civil War. Okmulgee: *Creek Nation Council House.* Pawhuska: capital of Osage nation. Pawnee: home of Pawnee Bill who, with Buffalo Bill Cody, took wild west shows to Europe. Ponca City: *Marland mansion.* Sallisaw: *Cabin of Sequoyah,* inventor of Cherokee (the only) Indian alphabet. Spiro: Prehistoric *Indian mounds* built between A.D. 800 and 1350. Tahlequah: Landmarks of *Cherokee National Capital* and *Murrell House,* antebellum mansion. Tishomingo: *Chickasaw Council House,* erected in 1856. Tuskahoma: *Choctaw Council House.* The state is dotted with nearly 2,000 ghost towns waiting to be explored. Information available through the Dept. of Tourism.

DRINKING LAWS. Liquor is available in package stores, 10 A.M.–10 P.M. except Sundays, holidays, and election days. Where mixed drinks are not served, you may "bring your own bottle."

SPORTS. There is almost limitless opportunity for *water sports;* dozens of *golf* courses, and ample *tennis* facilities.

WHAT TO DO WITH THE CHILDREN. Tulsa has an excellent zoo with a separate Children's Zoo featuring Nocturnal Animal Building, Chimpanzee Colony, and African Savanna. The Robert J. LaFortune North American Living Museum is the newest zoo facility with Indian artifacts, fossils and minerals. Children's playgrounds exist in almost all state parks and municipal parks.

 HOTELS AND MOTELS. Many have private clubs (the Oklahoma version of a bar) on the premises; guests automatically become members upon registering. The price categories in this section, for double occupancy, will average: *Moderate* $25–30, and *Inexpensive* $25 and under.

ALTUS. *Moderate:* **Sagamar.** 1501 E. Broadway.

ARDMORE. *Moderate:* **Lake Murray State Resort.** 7 miles south in Murray State Park.
Inexpensive: **Chief.** 911 S. Commerce.
Corral. 1611 N. Commerce.

CLAREMORE. *Moderate:* **Long's Holiday.** 1000 W. Will Rogers Blvd.

CLINTON. *Moderate:* **Glancy.** 217 Choctaw.

DUNCAN. *Moderate:* **Chisholm Trail.** N. on Hwy. 81.

ENID. *Moderate:* **Midwestern Inn.** 200 N. Van Buren.

McALESTER. *Moderate:* **Arrowhead State Resort.** 18 miles North on Highway 69.
Mayfair. 1500 S. Main St.

MUSKOGEE. *Moderate:* **Curt's Inn.** 2360 E. Shawnee Bypass.
Holiday Inn. 800 S. 32 St.

SHAWNEE. *Moderate:* **Cinderella Motel.** 2 mi. S. of I–40 on US 177 & 270.

STILLWATER. *Moderate:* **Student Union Hotel.** On campus of Oklahoma State University.

TAHLEQUAH. *Moderate:* **Oak Park.** 706 E. Downing St.

TULSA. *Moderate:* **Best Western Roadside Inn.** 7475 E. Admiral Palce. Most amenities.
Holiday Inn West. 6109 New Sapulpa Road (I–44).
Trade Winds Central. 3141 Skelly Dr.

WOODWARD. *Moderate:* **Wayfarer Inn.** S. of city on US 270.

DINING OUT. Price categories in this section are for a complete dinner without drinks, tax or tips, and will average: *Moderate* $5–10, *Inexpensive* under $5.

NOTE: The lodges listed in the *Hotels* section, above, for Altus, Ardmore, and McAlester, are state-owned resorts with restaurants serving generally good food at moderate prices.

ARDMORE. *Inexpensive–moderate:* **Eden's.** 205 W. Main. Steak, chicken, boneless catfish, own baking.

Moderate. **El Palacio.** In the Chief Motel, 912 S. Commerce. Mexican/American cuisine.

BARTLESVILLE. *Moderate:* **Murphy's Steak House.** Hamburgers, steaks. Baking done on premises.

BLACKWELL. *Inexpensive–moderate:* **Plainsman.** I-35 at Hwy. 11.

CLAREMORE. *Moderate:* **Hammett House.** 1616 W. Will Rogers Blvd. "Pampered" fried chicken, steak, pecan pie.

ENID. *Moderate:* **Richill's Cafeteria.** Downtown at 221 W. Randolph. Excellent, varied menu.

MARIETTA. *Moderate:* **McGeehee's Catfish Restaurant.** 2½ m. W. of town on Hwy. 32, then S. 3 mi.

McALESTER. *Moderate:* **Gia Como's.** 1 m. SE on 69 Bypass at cloverleaf. Charbroiled steaks.

Isle of Capri. 1 block N. of 270. Italian-American. Family-run.

MUSKOGEE. *Moderate:* **Baker's Fish House.** Seven miles N. of Muskogee on Hwy. 69. Catfish and frog legs.

Okie's Dust Bowl Diner. 219 S. 32 St. Local favorite. Try the marinated chicken breast.

NORMAN. *Moderate:* **Interurban.** 105 W. Main. Soup and sandwiches.

SHAWNEE. *Moderate:* **Mandarin Gardens.** 1814 N. Harrison. Cantonese and Szechuan.

Van's Pig Stand & Charcoal Room. 717 E. Highland.

TULSA. *Moderate:* **Heritage House Smorgasbord.** 3637 Memorial Avenue. Everything under the sun, in nice atmosphere. American cuisine.

Peking Garden. 6625 S. Lewis. Mandarin and Szechuan cuisine.

Sutphen's Barbeque. 3966 S. Hudson.

Inexpensive: **Grandy's Country Cookin.** 6801 E. Admiral Place. American eaterie serving breakfast, lunch and dinner.

Village Inn Pancake House. 3302 S. Memorial Ave., also 5230 S. Yale Ave. Open 24 hours.

TEXAS

Big Cities, Big Parks, Big Everything

Since Houston is the largest and most cosmopolitan city in Texas, it seems only fitting that its two most important sightseeing attractions are massive, both in size and in social implication. The one—the National Aeronautics and Space Administration Lyndon B. Johnson Space Center—played a key part in the nation's space missions, from the early Mercury flights to the orbiting Skylabs, and now is the nerve center for the space shuttle program; the other—Astrodomain, comprising Astrohall, Astroarena and Astrodome—plays a huge role in entertaining Texans and those who are young of heart, for it is a play world of huge proportions and scope.

Astrohall, one of the world's largest exhibit halls—500,000 square feet—is a home-away-from-home for conventions, and a home on the range for the cowboy during the mammoth Houston Livestock Show. Astroarena serves as a basketball and tennis center as well as for the Pin Oak Horse Show. The Astrodome is home for the Houston *Astros* baseball team and the Houston *Oilers* footballers.

Astroworld, a 70-acre theme park now a part of the Six Flags family, is among the nation's outstanding parks for rides, shows, attractions, and musical entertainment for the entire family and it attracts nearly two million guests annually.

But currently, it is growth to which Houston seems most attuned. The nation's fourth largest city has been absorbing newcomers at an astounding rate, and some concern is voiced about where to put everyone in a county area encompassing only 1,723 square miles and with a population estimated at 2.5 million.

Fly Me to the Moon

If your first question about NASA's Lyndon B. Johnson Space Center is "Can I see the Mission Control Center?" the answer is "Yes." Several phases of NASA's remarkable operations 25 miles south off I–45 at NASA Rd. 1 are open to the public without prior arrangement or charge. Cameras are invited.

It was here, to Houston Central, that Neil Armstrong reported his "one short step for man" as he first set foot on the moon. The Houston site was headquarters and control center for Uncle Sam's Mercury, Gemini, and Apollo efforts; and it is now the training center for NASA's new Space Lab and Space Shuttle programs.

About three hours should be allowed for tour time. The hours are 9 A.M. to 4 P.M. and the Center is closed only on Christmas. There is ample parking and visitors are encouraged to drive along a marked route to view some of the exhibit buildings. Keep in mind that late afternoon traffic can be hectic.

Downtown, the Sam Houston Park area, fronting on Bagby, harbors City Hall, the Coliseum, the Music Hall and, northward, the Albert Thomas Convention and Exhibit Center. Jones Hall, permanent home of the Houston Symphony Orchestra, is a block east on Capitol, and the Alley Theater is a block north on Texas. Between Preston and Congress, bearing north and east of the Alley Theater, is old Market Square, popular historic night spot and restaurant area.

Half an hour's ride from Houston—La Porte Freeway via Texas 134—brings you to the San Jacinto battleground, where a gigantic iron and concrete pinnacle, the tallest masonry monument in the world, rises to a height of 570 feet to commemorate the spot where Sam Houston valiantly conquered Mexico's Gen. Santa Anna. The battleship *Texas* is moored nearby.

PRACTICAL INFORMATION FOR THE
HOUSTON AREA

HOW TO GET THERE. *By car:* Houston, like Dallas, is a focal point of many major roads. Clockwise from the north use: I–45 (Dallas, Huntsville); I–30 (Texarkana); I–20 (Shreveport, La., Longview and south via Texas 59); I–10 (Beaumont, Port Arthur); I–10 (San Antonio); US 290 (Austin).

By air: Houston has two airports, the Intercontinental and older William P. Hobby. Twelve international airlines, 15 domestic airlines, and 10 commuter airlines offer service. There are direct flights from such world points as Amsterdam, London, Toronto, and Paris. There is comprehensive service to Mexico. Over a dozen cities within Texas are directly linked, and the 50-minute run from Dallas takes place 50 times a day.

By train: Amtrak. Sunset Limited three times weekly New Orleans—Houston—El Paso—Phoenix—Los Angeles.

HOW TO GET AROUND. *Bus:* Basic charge for the rapid transit bus line is 40 cents, with an additional 10 cents for each zone entered. Within the downtown area the fare is 10 cents on all buses. *By taxi:* $2.10 first mile and 88 cents each added mile. *Airport service: Trailways* to or from five ground terminals $6. Average cab fare $19.

TOURIST INFORMATION. For literature, information, and directions about the numerous attractions in Houston, visit the *Greater Houston Convention and Visitors Council,* 3300 Main. Tel. 713–523–5050, or toll free, outside Texas 800–231–7799, inside Texas 800–392–7722.

MUSEUMS AND GALLERIES. The *Museum of Fine Arts,* 1001 Bissonnet established in 1900, houses some of the finest examples of world art and attracts over 750,-000 visitors annually. The multistoried, glassfronted *Brown Pavilion* surveys contemporary architecture. Open daily except Monday, guided tours on daily schedule. Free.

Bayou Bend: early American furnishings from the former home of the late Miss Ima Hogg, daughter of the first native-born governor of Texas, part of the Museum of Fine Arts Collection and located at 1 Westcott St. *Contemporary Arts Museum:* contemporary statements in art and industrial design. Tours. 5216 Montrose Blvd. *Museum of Medical Science,* a world first in exhibits, displays animated models of the human body. Part of the *Museum of Natural Science* in Hermann Park. Tours.

HISTORIC SITES. Allen's Landing, where Houston originated. Shortly after the Battle of San Jacinto, brothers August and John Allen of New York founded a townsite on Buffalo Bayou, naming it after the victorious Gen. Sam Houston; Main and Commerce. Christ Church Cathedral, founded 1839, but not on its present site, 1117 Texas Ave.; Sam Houston Park, an outstanding work of the Harris County Heritage Society displaying historical buildings. Tours daily, nominal fee. Park admission free.

TOURS. Sightseeing: Printed schedules of daily tours may be obtained from *Grayline Tours* (757–1252) and *Adven-Tours* (522–6390).

HOTELS AND MOTELS. Foreign languages present few barriers, but it may be wise to phone ahead and secure your lodging. Children in the same rooms with parents usually admitted free. Rates for double occupancy will average: *Moderate* $35–60, *Inexpensive* under $35.

Best Western Greenspoint, 11211 North Frwy. Near Mall.
Chief Motel, 9000 S. Main. In the Astrodome area.
Greenway Inn, 2525 Southwest Frwy. Near Summit Arena.
Helena Motor Hotel, 2401 S. Wayside. On Gulf Frwy.
Holiday Inn Eastex, US 59. Lounge, Truck parking.
Holiday Inn–Gulf, 2391 S. Wayside. East side of town.
Holiday Inn—I-10, 7611 Katy Frwy. At I-610 Loop.
Howard Johnson's, 6161 Gulf Frwy. On way to Galveston.
La Quinta–Airport, 6 N. Belt E. Intercontinental Airport.
La Quinta–Sharpstown, 8201 Southwest Frwy. Near Mall.
Martinique Lodge, 4223 Southwest Frwy. Near Summit.
Rodeway, 17607 Eastex Frwy. Intercontinental Airport.
Surrey House, 8330 S. Main. Near Astrodome.
Towers Hotel, 2130 W. Holcombe. Near Medical Center.
TraveLodge, 8700 S. Main. Close to Astrodome.
White House, 9300 S. Main. Astrodome area.
Inexpensive. **Alamo Plaza,** 4343 Old Spanish Trail.
Bestway Motor Inn, 4115 Gulf Frwy. I-45 south.

Camp Manison, FM 528 at 518. Resort area.
Crestwood Tourist Hotel, 9001 S. Main.
Grant Motel, 8200 S. Main. Rollaways, cribs.
Houstonian Motor Lodge, 6319 North Frwy. North side.
Mitchell Inn, 10015 S. Main. Astrodome area.
Ranger Motel, 2916 Old Spanish Trail. Astrodome.
Roadrunner Motor Inn, 8500 S. Main. 24-hour café.
Sun-Tex Services, 770 Greens Rd.
Texas State Hotel, 720 Fannin at Rusk.
Vagabond Motor Hotel, 4815 North Frwy.
Rodeway, 3135 Southwest Frwy. Rice Stadium, Astrodrome.
Rodeway, 7905 S. Main. Food, golf, tennis.
Rodeway, 5820 Katy Frwy. Family units, suites.

DINING OUT. Considered Texas' most cosmopolitan city, Houston increases that prestige with its restaurants. Seafood, quite naturally, is a favorite, and delicacies from the nation's lakes and the world's oceans arrive daily. A center of ranching, beef and barbecue add their flavor to many menus.

And Cajun, Creole, Greek, Mexican, and Far Eastern dishes add their mystique to the city's menus.

Price categories: *Moderate:* $10–15, *Inexpensive* under $10. Prices generally include salad or soup, entree and vegetables. These prices are for complete dinner, but do not consider dessert, drinks and tips.

Moderate: **Angelo's Fisherman's Wharf,** 10200 S. Main, 6396 Richmond. Variety of seafood items including all the favorites served family-style.

Benihana of Tokyo. 9797 Westheimer and 1318 Louisiana (downtown). The Japanese chefs put on a show at your table.

Black Angus. 2925 Weslayan. Restful atmosphere and well-prepared food.

Bordman's Seafood. 2706 Westheimer. Delights from the world's oceans. Reservations.

Capt. Leon's. 9263 Gulf Frwy. Lobster, crab, oysters, and shrimp from the Gulf. Ribs and steaks. Entertainment.

Cody's. 3400 Montrose. Diners can view the skylines of downtown, midtown and uptown while enjoying a pleasant meal.

Gaido's, 9200 S. Main. Serving Houston since 1911. A tradition in the finest of Gulf and seafood. Steaks. Casual atmosphere.

Hebert's Ritz, 1214 McGowen. Personalized service in old Houston mansion. Cajun dishes, seafood, steaks. Over 40 years on scene.

Old San Francisco Steak House, 8611 Westheimer. For a starter your own free block of cheese. Steaks and seafood featured. See the girl in the red velvet swing.

Ruggles, 903 Westheimer and 6540 San Felipe. Westheimer location lunch crowd favorite and has theater following.

Inexpensive: **Athens Bar & Grill,** 8037 Clinton. Called Houston's most exciting Greek restaurant and nitespot. Native dishes at very affordable prices. Across from port.

Bavarian Gardens. 3926 Feagan. German goodies like wiener schnitzel and sauerbraten. Lunch buffet. American dishes.

China Garden. 1602 Leeland. Serving downtown Houston for 10 years.

Dos Gringos. 7525 S. Main. Setting of a Mexican casa; several dining rooms. Cantina upstairs.

El Chico. 7707 S. Main. The very successful chain operation based in Dallas. Try chicken enchiladas with sour cream.

Felix's. 5208 Bissonnet. One of three Mexican restaurants as this family goes into its second 50 years.

Glatzmaier's Seafood. 809 Congress. The catch is bound to be good with Glatzmaiers serving as both a market and restaurant.

Lennox Barbecue. 5420 Harrisburg. Welcoming customers from Southeast Texas for over 20 years.

Longhorn Café, 511 Louisiana. It's Texas on Louisiana St. with real Texas cookin'—chicken-fried steak, chili, burgers.

Luther's. 1001 Gessner. One of four places specializing in hickory-smoked beef, sausage and ribs. Excellent hamburgers.

Molina's. 7933 Westheimer. The Molinas have been serving fine Mexican food to Houstonians 30 years. Nightly music.

Old Spaghetti Warehouse. 901 Commerce. Maybe you'll spend your time looking the first visit. Next time you'll discover the food.

Pacific Ten Fathoms, 740 Polk. Lunch specials attract following. For dinner look over the Chinese menu.

Poor Charles Sandwich Shop. 910 Clay St. Downtown. One of those places you like to discover. Hot maple ham with Swiss cheese is great.

Tamborello. 1615 Main. The restaurant is family-owned and operated and the Italian food homemade.

EXPLORING DALLAS AND FORT WORTH

Dallas is the Southwest's largest banking center, ranks second nationally as an insurance home headquarters, and is one of the nation's top three fashion centers. It also ranks among the first five cities nationally as a convention site.

Showcasing the city's worldwide mercantile standing is Market Center, 150 acres or more five minutes from downtown. Spaced among fountains and courtyards, Market Center's six spacious buildings cater to buyers and sellers in 26 annual shows, attracting over 400,000 buyers, who spend some $4.5 billion. The Center represents the world's largest display of merchandise on one site and still grows. A small hotel, theater and restaurants are being built. Loew's Anatole Dallas, a 1,000-room hotel wonder across the Stemmons Frwy.

Downtown, the glass-encased Hyatt Regency Hotel, sided by the 570-foot Reunion Tower, its "lighted moon," rotating dining room, lounge, observation deck look down on Reunion Sports Arena, and the nearby expanded Convention Center, City Hall, and public library.

Presiding over development in the northeast quadrant of downtown, the Plaza of the Americas brings a European touch to Dallas with a Trust Houses Forte-managed 442-room hotel, two office towers surrounding a 15-story atrium with ground-level ice arena and shopping.

The cities jointly operate 17,500-acre Dallas/Fort Worth Regional Airport, the nation's largest and fourth busiest in the world. The Aviation Safety Institute rates it fifth safest in the world. There are nonstop flights to most world points. The airport hotel, AMFAC, is the world's largest facility of that type. There are other area hotels, including two by Marriott.

Both cities enjoy outstanding colleges and universities and support several museums of national import.

Four new hotels complement the popular Tarrant County (Fort Worth) Convention Center downtown, set off by a spectacular Water Garden Park. Hotels include the Hyatt Regency, Americana, an expanded Fort Worth Hilton, and a Best Western.

Fort Worth's Stockyards area sparkles again for visitors, with shops crafting Western attire, weekly rodeos, cattle auctions and good restaurants. Special events are highlighted by the State Fair of Texas each October in Dallas and the Southwestern Exposition and Fat Stock Show, a Fort Worth attraction in February now past its 85th year.

The Kennedy Memorial

Dallasites have remembered the November 22, 1963 assassination of President Kennedy with a stately John F. Kennedy Memorial, at Main, Commerce and Market Sts. The memorial is in the form of a 30-foot-high marble cenotaph. Site of the tragedy is two blocks northwest.

Playground of the South

Six Flags Over Texas people talk of the 200-acre complex of some 100 thrill rides and shows as a "theme" park, delightfully contrary to the concept of an amusement park. The contention may be well taken since over 40 million people have visited the park since opening day in 1961. It is Texas' top tourist attraction.

You can spend a day—or several—at this park where Texas history walks the streets in a style distinctive of the six nations that at times have ruled: Spain, France, Mexico, the Confederacy, the Republic of Texas, and the United States. Even the shops and the rides carry out this theme. For instance, the Conquistador, a replica of an ancient ship, "sails" in the park's Spanish section.

Nearby interests include International Wildlife Park, where exotic animals graze alongside your car; Southwestern Historical Wax Museum, displaying life-size likenesses of Texas' famous and infamous, and Texas Rangers baseball park. Two water sports parks are new—White Water and Wet 'n Wild—and both just north off I–30.

PRACTICAL INFORMATION FOR

DALLAS-FORT WORTH

HOW TO GET AROUND. *Dallas.* By bus: 70-cent fare, charge for additional zones. Correct change required. Bunny-marked Hop-a-Bus operates downtown, 25 cents. Information, Dallas Transit Service, tel. 826–2222. *Fort Worth.* City-operated Citran buses charge 75-cent fare. Exact fare required. Any bus downtown free. Texas Motor Coaches operate between the two cities.

By taxi: Base fare in Dallas is $2 first mile with 80 cents each added mile. Fort Worth charges $1.30 first ¼ mile, 20 cents each additional ¼ mile. Airport: Surtran buses serve both cities and charge $5 to terminal or $7 to hotel.

TOURIST INFORMATION. *Dallas* Chamber of Commerce maintains a Visitors Information Center in renovated Union Station, Houston and Young Sts., tel. 214–747–2355. For the *Fort Worth* area, contact the Convention and Visitors Bureau, 700 Throckmorton, tel. 817–336–8791. Arlington Convention and Visitors Bureau, 1801 Stadium Dr. E. Tel. 817–265–7721.

 MUSEUMS, GALLERIES AND LIBRARIES. Dallas: Several important museums are at *Fair Park,* Parry and First Avs., including the Hall of State, erected for the 1936 Texas Centennial. *Dallas Health and Science Museum and Planetarium,* life-size transparent figures of man and woman which talk. *Museum of Natural History,* changing exhibits, guest lecturers, slides of animal and plant life. *Dallas Aquarium,* marine, tropical and freshwater fish. *Age *of Steam Railroad Museum,* early passenger station, engines, cars. *Old Tige's Dallas Firefighters Museum,* horse-drawn steam pumper, other antiques. Most open daily, admission, if any, about $1. *Dallas Museum of Fine Arts,* new building scheduled to open in early 1984.

Fort Worth: *Kimbell Art Museum,* 1101 Will Rogers Rd., traveling and permanent exhibits; *Fort Worth Art Museum,* 1309 Montgomery, permanent and changing exhibits. *The Western Company Museum,* 6100 Western Place, oil field exhibits. *Museum of Science and History and Planetarium,* 1501 Montgomery, interesting for children. *Amon Carter Museum of Western Art,* 3501 Camp Bowie Rd., for the Western art lover but other interests.

 HISTORIC SITES. *John F. Kennedy Plaza,* block-wide area containing 30 ft. high, 50 ft. square concrete memorial to the 35th President of the U.S. near the site of his assassination in Dallas, Nov. 22, 1963.

Across Main St., looking north from Memorial, is the restored cabin of John Neely Bryan, first citizen of Dallas.

Old City Park, S. Ervay and Akard Sts. at Gano. Turn-of-the-century homes and buildings recreate a living village.

Fort Worth: A military detachment assigned to protect settlers, founded Fort Worth on a Trinity River bluff in 1849.

TOURS. Dallas: *All Around the Town,* 9:30 A.M. departure. Panoramic downtown view from observation tower, trip to Fair Park, Cotton Bowl. *Dallas Then and Now,* 2 P.M. Market Center, SMU campus, residential areas. Each tour 3 hrs., adults $10.50, children (4–11) $5.25. Board at Hyatt Regency, Holiday Inn, Dallas Hilton.

Fort Worth: The *Gray Line* schedules 10 daily tours (two require eight passenger minimums) of city and area points of interest, including Southfork Ranch of TV notoriety. Fares range from $10.75 to $22.75.

 SPECTATOR SPORTS. *Baseball:* Texas Rangers, American League, play at Arlington Stadium. *Basketball:* Dallas Mavericks play at Reunion Arena. *Football:* Dallas Cowboys play at Texas Stadium off US 183 at Loop 12. On New Year's Day the Southwest Conference football champion meets an invited opponent in the Dallas Cotton Bowl. *Golf:* The Byron Nelson Golf Tournament is played at Cottonwood Valley Country Club in Irving. In Fort Worth, the Colonial Invitational is at Colonial Country Club. *Rodeo:* The Mesquite Rodeo performs Friday and Saturday night, April through September. The arena is at Military Parkway and Scyene Road. Cowtown Coliseum is the setting Saturday nights for rodeo in Fort Worth. *Tennis:* Avon Championships (Women), March, SMU; WCT Finals, Reunion Arena. *Wrestling:* Matches are staged Tuesdays at the Sportatorium at Corinth and Industrial in Dallas, and on Mondays at Will Rogers Coliseum in Fort Worth.

 WHAT TO DO WITH THE CHILDREN. Dallas: *Marsalis Park Zoo,* a 50-acre city park at Clarendon off Thornton Frwy. The complete zoo. Open all year, daily. See 2,000 amphibians, birds, mammals, reptiles, $1 admission. *Fair Park,* First and Parry Avs. Educational museums, Hall of State, midway open weekends in summer.

Arlington: *Six Flags Over Texas, International Wildlife Park, Southwestern Historical Wax Museum, Fire Museum of Texas, Sports Hall of Fame, Sesame Place.*

Fort Worth: *Children's Museum,* 1501 Montgomery, cultural center, planetarium. *Log Cabin Village,* 2100 Log Cabin Village Lane, restored, furnished cabins in realistic 1850s setting. *Forest Park,* 2112 Forest Park Blvd., miniature train. *Fort Worth Zoological Park* in Forest Park. Outstanding display of reptiles, rare birds, spectacular rain forest.

HOTELS AND MOTELS. Accommodations are located convenient to the Interstate and expressway arteries as well as within the city. Senior citizen organization members are often accorded special rates. Establishments in Fort Worth may be slightly less expensive than in Dallas while Arlington counts over 25 hostelries with 2,850 rooms.

Price categories, for double occupancy, will average: *Moderate* $35–60; *Inexpensive* under $35.

ARLINGTON. *Moderate:* **Quality Inn.** 1601 E. Division (Texas 80). 338 units.

Inexpensive: **Days Inn.** 1195 N. Watson Rd. Food, gas, pets. **Motel 6.** 2626 E. Randol Mill Rd. Restaurant. Pool.

Red Carpet Inn. 1175 N. Texas 360. North of Six Flags.

Value Inn. Texas 360 at Six Flags. Fifty efficiencies, 114 units.

DALLAS. *Moderate* **Best Western Market Center.** Off I–35 at Industrial exit. Restaurant, pool.

Circle Inn Motor Hotel. 2560 W. Northwest Hwy. Dining, pool. Pets.

Grenelefe Hotel, formerly **Ramada Inn-Convention Center.** 1011 S. Akard. Pool, lounge, restaurant with view of city.

Holiday Inn-Downtown. 1015 Elm. Very comfortable, convenient. Pool.

Holiday Inn-Market Center. 1955 N. Industrial, at I–35.

Howard Johnson's. 7201 Ferguson exit off Thornton Freeway (I–20, 30). Convenient; restaurant.

NorthPark Inn. 9300 N. Central Expressway. Very large. Near major shopping center.

Plaza Hotel. 1933 Main at Harwood, across from old City Hall.

Quality Inn. 2015 N. Industrial. Dining, pool.

La Quinta. 1625 Regal Row. Take Regal Row exit off I–35 E. Restaurant.

Rodeway-Central. 4150 N. Central Expressway. Near downtown.

Sheraton Inn-Oak Cliff. 321 W. Kiest. Club entertainment, restaurant.

TraveLodge-Market Center. 4500 Hines Blvd. Pool, restaurant, lounge. Wheelchair accommodations. Spanish spoken.

Inexpensive: **Days Inn.** 3817 US 80 at Town East exit. Restaurant, pool, playground. I–35 East at Camp Wisdom Rd.

La Quinta-East. 8303 Thornton Freeway (I–20, 30). Restaurant, club.

Rodeway Market Center. 2026 N. Industrial. Family units. Dining.

Travelers Inn-Dallas. Off I–20, 30 (Thornton Expressway) at Dolphin exit. Close to downtown

FORT WORTH. *Moderate:* **Best Western Convention Center Hotel.** 600 Commerce St. New. Sun dome, whirlpool.

Best Western Park Central Inn. 1011 Throckmorton off I–20.

Holiday Inn Midtown. 1401 S. University. Handy to park.

Howard Johnson's Motor Lodge. 5825 S. Freeway.

TraveLodge. 6855 E. Lancaster. Six Flags 15 minutes away.

Ramada Inn South. 4201 South Freeway. Downtown 4 miles.

Inexpensive: **Best Western Fort Worther.** 4213 South Freeway. Restaurant. Pool.

Days Inn. 812 E. Felix.

Friendship Inn. 3518 South Freeway.

La Quinta Motor Inn. 7920 Bedford-Euless Rd.

La Quinta. 7888 I–30 West. Exit on Cherry La. Dining.

Rio Motor Hotel. 6600 Camp Bowie Rd. Pool.

TraveLodge. 6855 Lancaster. 130 rooms. Kitchenettes.

DINING OUT. The budget-minded diner, before being seated, may find it prudent to inquire about house specials, entrées for two, even all-you-can-eat offerings. If there is a bar, some hearty appetizer may be your dish. And for the kiddies, most places offer children's plates. Price categories for soup or salad, entrée and vegetables usually are: *Moderate* $7–12, *Inexpensive,* under $7. Drinks, tax, tip not included.

ARLINGTON. *Moderate:* **Red Lobster.** 1212 E. Division. Many seafood selections.

Steak & Ale. 916 Six Flags Dr. at Texas 360. Ask about specials.

Inexpensive: **Bonanza Sirloin Pit.** 1108 E. Division. Well known.

El Chico. 1315 N. Collins (Texas 157). Popular Mexican food chain.

DALLAS. *Moderate:* **Campisi's.** 5610 E. Mockingbird. Longtime following.

Casa Dominguez. 2127 Cedar Springs. Get the Pete Dominguez story.

Highland Park Cafeteria. 4611 Cole. Famous for years.

Hong Kong. 9055 Garland Rd. Clean, friendly. No liquor.

Ianni's. 2230 Greenville. Sort of hidden in small shopping area.

India House. 5422 E. Mockingbird. Authentic Indian dishes; spicy.

Jägerstube. 7811 Inwood. All the German favorites.

Jay's Marine Grill. 3020 W. Mockingbird. Love Field entrance.

Kirby's. 3715 Greenville. Has reputation for steaks.

Le Boul' Mich. 2704 Worthington. Limited French dishes.

Michelino's. 6312 La Vista. Italian family operated.

Oyster House. 108 N. Akard. Across from Adolphus.

Papa Zaby's. 2114 Greenville. Family-run, breakfast special.

Pietro's. 5722 Richmond. Popular neighborhood Italian spot.

The Torch. 2620 W. Davis. The souvlaki is patented.

S&D Oyster Co. 2701 McKinney. Some New Orleans flavor.

Inexpensive: **Banno's Seafood.** 1516 Greenville. Menu not extensive.

Blue Front. 1310 Elm. 100-year-old favorite. Lunch.

Dixie House. 2822 McKinney. Home-cooking, hot rolls, cornbread.

Dunston's. 5423 W. Lovers La. Steaks cooked over mesquite.

Farmer's Grill. 1101 S. Pearl Expressway. Food's always ready at the market.

Fuji-Ya. 13050 Coit Rd. This one's a sleeper.

Lucas B&B. 2520 Oak Lawn. Full menu, 24 hours.

New China. 4218 Lemmon. Wide selection of Chinese dishes.

Ojeda's. 4011 Cedar Springs. Mexican food. Comfortable dining.

Old Spaghetti Warehouse. 1815 N. Market. The kids love it.

Shanghai. Preston at I–635. The best of Mandarin and Szechuan fare.

Shed. 9600 Overlake off Northwest Hwy. One menu, all you can eat.

Stuart Anderson's. 7102 Greenville. Moderately priced steak menu. Salad.

FORT WORTH. *Moderate:* **Bogard's Bar & Bistro.** West Side. Appetizers a meal. beef entrées. New.

Four Winds. 5650 E. Lancaster. Owner Joe Daniel is a past president of the Texas Restaurant Association.

Joe T. Garcia. 2201 N. Commerce. Mexican food, served family-style.

Petta's. 4255 Camp Bowie. Family place. Dinner prepared when ordered.

Richelieu Grill. 415 Main. Since 1885. Homemade chili, stew, pit BBQ.

Winfield '08. 301 Main in Sundance Sq. Popular showplace.

Inexpensive: **Colonial Forest Park Cafeteria.** 1700 Rogers Rd. Features "no line" service. Some like this best of three local establishments.

Continental. 6855 E. Lancaster. General menu. Open 24 hours.

Jimmie Dip's. 1500 S. University Dr. Chinese dishes, steaks, seafood.

Mi Charrito Ray. 5693 Westcreek Dr. Home-cooked Mexican food. Also American dishes. Well recommended.

Old Spaghetti Warehouse. 600 E. Exchange. Unusual décor. Like going to a 1900s garage sale. Homemade bread a treat.

Terry's. 902 Houston. Only breakfast and lunch served. Many go back for the chocolate pie.

EXPLORING EL PASO

El Pasoans consider their city a crossroads and oasis for travelers—some of whom will decide to stay—and this has proved to be true for years. Spanish gold seekers first trekked to the area in 1581. The city was the site of outposts of European civilization long before the Pilgrims set sail from England. Several early missions still stand. One of these, Ysleta, is the base of Texas' oldest ethnic community—the Tigua Indian Reservation. International bridges connect El Paso with Juarez, a few steps across the Rio Grande.

A three-minute cable car ride goes 5,632 feet to Ranger Peak atop the Franklin Mountains. From that vantage point one may view three states and two nations, along with the rapidly spreading outlines and contours of El Paso and Juarez themselves.

PRACTICAL INFORMATION FOR EL PASO

HOW TO GET AROUND. *Bus:* Within the city the fare is 50¢. Sun City Area Transportation, tel. 533–3333, will supply information. *Cab:* Fare is 90¢ to board and 70¢ per mile. *Airport service:* Taxi fare costs about $6 and there is a limousine at El Paso International Airport. Fares cost less from Juarez airport.

MUSEUMS. *Wilderness Park Museum,* 2000 Trans Mountain Rd. Tracing primitive man in the Southwest. *El Paso Museum of History,* 12901 Gateway West. Era of the pioneers. *El Paso Museum of Art,* 1211 Montana. Displays of European masters.

HISTORIC SITES. *Fort Bliss* was originally established in 1848 as a defense post against hostile Indians. It was headquarters for the Confederate forces in the Southwest. Today it is the site of the U.S. Army Air Defense Center. A replica of the original adobe fort is maintained as a museum of the frontier military era. The *Ysleta, Socorro,* and *San Elizario missions,* built in the 1600s, are still in use. The *Tigua Indian Reservation* represents Texas' oldest identifiable ethnic group. All are located in the El Paso Lower Valley. Visitors are welcome.

TOURS. Escorted tours of either El Paso or Juarez are offered morning and afternoon. There are nightclub tours to Juarez and trips to the bullfights and greyhound races. El Paso Convention & Visitors Bureau, Five Civic Center Plaza, tel. 915–544–3650, will supply information.

SPORTS. *Parimutuel horse racing.* Betting is illegal in Texas, but there is a winter and spring racing season at Sunland Park, New Mexico, six miles from El Paso. Bullfights, in season, and greyhound races, where there is betting, are lures in Juarez. The Sun Bowl *football* game in El Paso at end of the year is nationally televised.

WHAT TO DO WITH THE CHILDREN. *Western Playland,* family amusement park located in El Paso's beautiful Ascarate Park. Accessible from either the 6900 block of Delta or the 6900 block of Alameda. *El Paso Zoological Park,* 4201 Paisano.

HOTELS AND MOTELS in El Paso are not as flashy or as expensive as in Dallas or Houston, but they are comfortable and convenient. The price categories, for double occupancy, will average as follows: *Moderate* $35-60; *Inexpensive* under $35.

Moderate: **Best Western Cabellero Motor Hotel.** 6400 Montana. Near shopping center, theater, airport.

Best Western Tom Penny Inn. 7144 Gateway East.

Holiday–Airport, 6655 Gateway W.; **Holiday–Downtown,** 113 W. Missouri; **Holiday,** I-10 at Gateway E. Restaurants, entertainment at airport and downtown locations and golf and tennis at Airport.

Howard Johnson's Motor Lodge. 8887 Gateway West. Near airport; 140 rms.

Ramada–East, 6099 Montana. Airport courtesy van, playground, lounge and disco.

Sheraton El Paso, 325 N. Kansas. Restaurant, lounge, airport limo. 117 rooms, suite. New.

TraveLodge Downtown, 1301 Mesa; **TraveLodge East,** 6308 Montana. Restaurant, pool.

Inexpensive: **Beverly Crest Motor Inn.** 8709 Dyer. Restaurant, pool, kitchenettes.

Colonia Motor Hotel–Best Value. 8601 Dyer. Restaurant, lounge, pool. Kitchenettes. Truck parking. Near Fort Bliss.

Del Camino Motor Hotel. 5001 Alameda Ave. Downtown convenience. Bullfight Museum.

Executive Inn-Mesa. 4501 N. Mesa. Restaurant, lounge with entertainment, heated pool. Courtesy car to Sunland track.

Friendship Inn–La Posta Motor Lodge, 4111 N. Mesa. Heated pool, spa.

Gardner Hotel. 311 E. Franklin. Range of accommodations at very low rates.

La Quinta Motor Inn. 6140 Gateway east. Airport area.

Stardust Motel–Best Value. 6210 Montana Ave. Kitchens, pool.

YMCA. 315 E. Franklin St. Single rooms, European backpackers $9.50.

DINING OUT in El Paso is enhanced by the Mexican influence on most menus or by simply crossing into Juarez to patronize one of the excellent restaurants there. One surprise in El Paso is authentic German food brought about by the presence of German troops training there. Price categories are as follows: *Moderate* $7–12, *Inexpensive* under $7. Prices are for a complete dinner but do not include drinks, tax or tip.

Moderate: **Billy Crew's.** 3164 Doniphan. Steaks are the house specialty.

Cinders. 2280 Trawood. Fresh seafood, steaks and prime rib.

Gunter's Edelweiss. 11055 Gateway West. Bavarian goodies for lunch or dinner.

Happy Bavarian. 8168 Alameda. German food at its very best, and plenty of it. Reservations a day ahead advised.

Iron Tender. I-10 and McCrae. Steaks and seafood. Bar entertainment very pleasant.

Jaxon's. 508 N. Stanton. Daily soup special, sandwiches, salad.

Jersey Lily. 5411 N. Mesa. Crepes are the specialty.

Montana Mining Co. 6238 N. Mesa. Steak is very much king in El Paso, and the "mine" ranks among the best. Also another location at 5710 N. Montana.

Miguel. Shadow Mts. at N. Mesa. Disco. Steaks and seafood.

Inexpensive: **Bella Napoli.** 6331 N. Mesa. One of two good Italian spots.

Casa Juardo. 226 Cincinnati. Mexican food consistently good.

Griggs. 5800 Doniphan. Mexican food enthusiasts are in for a treat and a new taste. There is another located at 9007 Montana.

La Hacienda. 1722 W. Paisano. Get the location story.

Leo's Mexican Food. Six locations, and the food is uniform and plentiful. Beer, wine.

EXPLORING SAN ANTONIO

San Antonio is Spanish and Mexican, not only in its heritage, but in its daily routine. But while its setting is palm trees and banana plants, and parts of the city seem basically sleepy in its outlook on 20th-century life, the lure of San Antonio lies in its resistance to easy description. It is an amalgam of old and new, or ox-cart and intercontinental missile, of broiled cabrito and steaks tartare: and to understand the city you must accept the contradictions.

Your tour of San Antonio—whether you choose a sightseeing bus, your own car, or a walking visit to downtown points—will begin, of course, with the Alamo, alive with the story of Travis' arrogant defiance of the Mexicans, of Crockett and Bowie and the rest of the reckless and valiant 188 men who made a shambles of a mighty army before they fell under sheer weight of numbers. Your sense of the spirit of the outgunned and outnumbered defenders of the mission will be enhanced with a pre-tour sound-and-sight presentation at the Remember the Alamo Theatre-Museum across the street.

From the Alamo you'll find the River Walk, or Paseo del Rio, as it is now referred to, with due regard for the melodious Spanish equivalent. If you have an eye for tropical splendor, walkways bordered by quaint shops, art galleries and eating places, you'll love the Paseo del Rio. The cuisine features Mexican, Italian, and French food and a couple of elegant steak houses, not to mention the dining rooms of several fine riverside hotels. Outside dining is enjoyable every month of the year.

You can hire a pedal boat—and pedal yourself up and down the river, seeing all its sights at leisure—or board one of the many sightseeing boats for relaxed enjoyment or to make an impressive entrance at the city's Convention Center. Again, you may relish an evening of dining on the boats serenaded by Mexican musicians.

You'll especially enjoy the Arneson River Theater, where performers undertake every kind of production on one side of the river, and the audience applauds from the other. Some of the most dramatic passages are interrupted from time to time by the passage of some kind of riverboat—but this only adds to the gaiety.

It's still walking distance to La Villita—where you'll cross suddenly over into 18th-century Spanish Texas. La Villita (pronounced Lah Vee-YEE-tah) is a charming city within a city, standing in the very shadow of downtown skyscrapers, a block-square restoration of San Antonio as it was in the time of Bowie and Travis or even before. Many of the skills and crafts of the very early San Antonio days are still practiced at La Villita—and if you have an eye for blown glass, pottery bowls and the like, you'll find a beautiful assortment here. Free brochures describe nearly 20 fascinating structures, sites, and places of interest. The Starving Artists show comes to La Villita in April.

On Military Plaza, directly behind City Hall, is the old Spanish Governor's Palace; a statue of Texas pioneer Moses Austin stares down on the palace. Inside the adobe walls that surround the palace the Spanish governors of Texas brightened a wilderness frontier with fantastically colorful balls and parties.

East from La Villita is HemisFair Plaza, site of the 1968 world's fair, HemisFair '68. This area is marked by the 750-foot Tower of the Americas, with an entertaining restaurant on top that revolves every hour.

An important legacy of the Fair is the impressive Institute of Texan Cultures, a continuing representation through displays, sound film and all forms of communication, of the 26 ethnic cultures that constitute Texas.

The Institute is open to visitors and guided tours year around, except for a few days in early August when thousands of visitors bring all these cultures together with an annual Texas Folklife Festival.

Also on HemisFair Plaza, the Museum of Transportation displays early-vintage automobiles and all the forms of avoiding walking; the Hall of Texas Wax Museum presents dioramas reflecting chapters in history, and the Mexican Cultural Institute shows works of Mexican and South American artists.

At N. Presa and W. Market Sts., in the original Public Library, you can go to the circus—a most unusual circus. Here is housed the Hertzberg Circus Collection, which includes circus artifacts and scale-model replicas of all of the thrills from the era of the Big Tops. The collection begins with the circus pretentions of King George III of England, and continues through the heyday of Phineas T. Barnum. You'll find Tom Thumb's original carriage. And a full miniature circus!

El Mercado, a Mexican area on W. Commerce St., exudes charm with a variety of shops and restaurants, among the latter an inviting indoor-outdoor oyster bar housed in a restored turn-of-the-century building on Produce Row. The City of San Antonio and private enterprise are each active in blending early-era structures with new construction. New or expanded hotels and motels in the picturesque Riverwalk area are examples.

And, tying the downtown points together, small but brightly colored El Centro buses run north-south and east-west schedules for 10 cents.

You can spend a day at Brackenridge Park on North Broadway with its miniature train a touring convenience, and Skyride giving an overhead view. And you can walk about the marvelous Sunken Gardens. In the park, too, the San Antonio Zoo is nationally acclaimed. There are motorized tours.

The military influence upon the city is considerable and you can visit historic Fort Sam Houston and the four air bases. The musty missions —in all their 18th-century glory—will also be on your visiting list.

If you are so fortunate as to be in San Antonio for Fiesta—10 days in late April—it will be a memorable experience. Events include a Battle of Flowers Parade, the Fiesta King's River Parade, Flambeau Night Parade, and the unforgettable "A Night in Old San Antonio," which goes on for four nights.

PRACTICAL INFORMATION FOR SAN ANTONIO

HOW TO GET AROUND. *By bus:* via Metropolitan Transit Authority, 800 W. Myrtle, tel. 227–2020, operates air-conditioned buses to city areas and communities. El Centro buses run Monday–Saturday days. Fare 10 cents. *By taxi:* Metered rates average $1.85 the first mile and 80 cents each added mile. *Airport:* Limousine to downtown hotels $4 per person, taxi about $8.25, bus 6 A.M. –8 P.M., 75 cents.

TOURIST INFORMATION. The Convention & Visitors Bureau maintains an information booth in Alamo Plaza or calls and mail may be directed to the Bureau at P.O. Box 2277, San Antonio 78298. Tel. 800–531–5700 outside Texas and 800–292–1010 inside Texas.

SEASONAL EVENTS. Though perhaps more accustomed to sombreros, the San Antonians don 10-gallon hats for 10 days in *February* for the San Antonio Livestock Exposition and Rodeo at Freeman Coliseum. Fiestas are held for any occasion, and so San Patrick's Day is celebrated—for a week—with green dye coloring the San Antonio River and bars along the Paseo del Rio adding green coloring to their beer. Starving Artists next display their crafts and canvasses at La Villita. Fiesta San Antonio, a week of fun and festivity, pageanty and parades, attracts national attention for ten days around April 21. The Arneson River Theater comes alive in June and July with thrice-weekly Fiesta Nocha del Rio programs. The Texas Folklife Festival at the Institute of Texan Cultures attracts thousands for four days in *August.* Mexican Independence Day, *September 16,* is celebrated with a fiesta and parade. In *October* a River Art Show displays arts and crafts by local and regional artists. And in *December* the River Walk glitters each night with Christmas lights, the lighting of candles, the singing of carols from river barges, and a pageant depicting the Holy Family's search for lodging. A Fiesta Navidena also is observed for a week in Market Square.

MUSEUM AND GALLERIES. A charmingly renovated old brewery is the site of the well-supported *San Antonio Museum of Art.* McNay Art Institute, 6000 N. New Braunfels. Picasso and Van Gogh are among artists whose works may be seen. *Witte Memorial Museum,* 3801 N. Broadway. Local history and cultures. A flashback to early life is shown in a visual presentation, "San Antonio is . . . " *Buckhorn Hall of Horns,* 600 Lone Star Blvd. An impressive collection of horns, antlers and tusks of Southwestern game, along with an outstanding fin and feathers collection.

HISTORIC SITES. *The Alamo,* built in 1718 and often referred to as the "Cradle of Texas liberty," is in the downtown area. Other missions of circa 1700 are to be found along "mission row." The *Spanish Governor's Palace,* an 18th-century structure, is typical of the buildings in Colonial Spain. Moses Austin came here in 1820 for permission to bring a colony of U.S. citizens into Spanish Texas. *King William Historic District,* at King Williams St. and S.

TEXAS 471

St. Mary's St., comprises restored Victorian and early Texas homes of the 1870s. *Jose Antonio Navarro State Historic Site,* 228 S. Laredo, was the home of the Texas patriot and signer of the Texas Declaration of Independence.

SPORTS. *Baseball:* San Antonio fields a team in the Texas League. *Basketball:* The Spurs are a power in the National Basketball League. *Golf:* The Texas Open lures top names in September. Four 18-hole public courses are available. The San Antonio Recreation Dept. maintains McFarlin *Tennis* Center, which offers 22 courts and is available for night play. And the stables in Brackenridge Park rents horses for use on the park bridle paths.

WHAT TO DO WITH THE CHILDREN. *Brackenridge Park,* 2800 block N. Broadway, is an adventure for a full day or several. There are 343 acres and something exciting with every step—a miniature train, the Brackenridge Eagle, runs sightseeing trips through the park all year. Also there are stables for horseback riding, and the Sunken Gardens for beauty, a Skyride by cable car for thrills, and the Zoological Gardens and Aquarium. And the San Antonio Zoo is right at hand and rated one of the best in the country. Some 4,500 animals, birds, and reptiles. The *Hertzberg Circus Collection,* 210 W. Market, is for circus lovers of all ages. And your youngster will get a better understanding of his visit to the Alamo by first seeing the sight-and-sound drama "Remember the Alamo" just across the street at 315 Alamo Plaza. There are rides and amusements for children, along with a miniature golf course in *HemisFair Plaza.*

HOTELS AND MOTELS. Several new or renovated establishments downtown embrace the river's charm, but many comfortable locations rim the city within Loop 410. Price categories for two persons average: *Moderate* $35–60, *Inexpensive* under $35. Seniors, military discounts common.

Moderate: **Alamo TraveLodge.** 405 Broadway downtown. Also TraveLodges on River location, 100 La Villita and 1616 St. Mary's St.

Broadway Plaza Motor Hotel. 1111 NE Loop 410. Dining, pool.

Days Inn. 4100 E. Houston St. Four miles downtown. Restaurant.

El Tropicana. 110 Lexington. On river downtown. Bar, shops.

Granada Inn. 402 S. St. Mary's. Restaurant, lounge, pool. Handicapped aids.

Holiday Inn. 318 W. Durango in Alamo area.

Howard Johnson's. I-35 north at Loop 410. Lounge, pool.

Menger. 204 Alamo Plaza. History sleeps with you here.

Ramada–Airport. 333 NW Loop 410. Pool, lounge. Also 1131 Austin Hwy. and 3645 N. Pan Am Expy. locations.

Sheraton Resort and Conference Center. 1400 Austin Hwy. Tennis, golf.

Quality Inn. 601 E. Elmira. Completely remodeled. Dining, pool.

Inexpensive: **Best Western Townhouse Motel.** 942 NE Loop 410. Near airport. 60 rooms. Pool, TV.

Downtowner. 902 E. Houston. Alamo area. Pool.

Elmira Motor Inn. 1126 E. Elmira. Minutes to airport, downtown.

La Quinta Inn. Founded here. Two representative locations: 1001 E. Commerce St. downtown offers restaurant, lounge, pool. 6511 Military Dr. near Lackland AFB. Restaurant, pool. Total of nine inns in city.

Park Plaza Motel. 2908 Broadway. A block from Breckenridge Park entrance. Pool, pets.

Rodeway Inn Downtown. 900 N. Main. Pool, 128 rooms.

Town & Country Lodge. 6901 San Pedro. North area of city.

KOA Kampground. 602 Gambler Rd. Between I-35 and I-10.

DINING OUT. There are many family-operated restaurants, which usually tend to be modest in price and generous in servings. While Mexican places are in the majority, dishes representative of much of the world are at hand. Price categories are: *Moderate* $7–12, *Inexpensive* under $7, and are for salad or soup, and entree. Drinks, tax, tip not included.

Moderate: **Bayou.** 2617 Wagon Wheel. Cajun-flavored charm wafted from East Texas.

Christie's, 3130 Broadway. A seafood house serving a following for nearly 40 years. Trout, flounder, shrimp, steaks, chicken.

El Jarro. 13421 San Pedro. North side of town. Mexican dishes.

El Mirador. 722 S. St. Mary's. Downtown area spot with a following.

Magic Time Machine. 902 NE Loop 410. American food. Fun place. Serve yourself soup from an MG.

Le Fromage. 4011 Broadway. Lunch only. French country-style food.

Mama's Hofbrau, 9903 San Pedro. They go in big for eating at Mama's. The steaks are large and the potato pancakes great.

Maximillian's. 135 E. Commerce. Breakfast, lunch. American food.

Naples. 3210 Broadway. Good Italian food. Near Brackenridge Park.

Night Hawk. 7202 San Pedro. American menu for lunch, dinner.

Ninfa's. 8023 Vintage Dr. A newcomer from Houston. Hear the Ninfa story.

Stuart Anderson Cattle Co. 3731 NW Loop 410. Reasonable steaks.

The Stockman. 409 E. Commerce. Downtown area.

Tower of America's. HemisFair. High up dining in revolving room.

Inexpensive: **Avery's.** 2030 N. Main. Menu changes daily, but delicious hamburgers always offered.

La Margarita. 120 Produce Row. Mexican dishes. Lunch, dinner served.

Mi Tierra and Bakery. 218 Produce Row. Pan dulce from the bakery and nachos from the kitchen will get you started in this unusual family operation.

Royal Street Crossing. 526 River Walk. American dishes.

Schilo's Deli. 424 E. Commerce. Serving lunch only. German, American fare.

Valerio's. 3820 Broadway. Italian favorites.

EXPLORING THE REST OF TEXAS

Moving west from Dallas through Fort Worth along combined I–20, US 80 and US 180, you'll find yourself on a gently rolling plain. Sticking to US 180, you'll shortly arrive in Weatherford, the hometown of actress Mary Martin. Near the courthouse citizens have erected a statute of her as Peter Pan.

A slightly zigzag trail northward from Weatherford brings you to Wichita Falls, scene of Indian massacres and the U.S. Calvary riding to the rescue. Wichita Falls is now home of Sheppard Air Force Base, a vital U.S. training center. In 1979, a devastating tornado struck the city.

Just 150 miles southwest of Wichita Falls lies Abilene, itself a strange mixture of modern enterprise and Old West flavor. Three denominational colleges call the city home: Hardin Simmons University (Baptist), McMurry College (Methodist), and Abilene Christian University (Church of Christ). The city has an outstanding zoo that will fill young eyes with wonderment. History buffs will revel in the ruins of old Fort Phantom Hill. Abilene State Park provides camping, fishing, swimming.

Moving up from Wichita Falls on US 287 past Childress, brings you into the Panhandle plains which, up to 1870, supported no human life at all. Here the Conquistadores searched for the mythical Seven Cities of Cibola, and the last of the food-giving bison was slaughtered.

Modern-day taming of the Panhandle, and the booming of Amarillo, began with the discovery of oil and natural gas. Today the city claims title as "helium capital of the world," and a Futuristic Helium Monument with Time Capsules is a sightseeing attraction. Lake Meredith is a recreational paradise and the Alibates Flint Quarry National Monument an historical treasure trove. Nearby Boy's Ranch is nationally known. Visitors are welcome to the big tri-weekly cattle auctions.

Twenty-seven miles southeast, you come to the town of Canyon and to 120-mile long Palo Duro Canyon, a spectacular color attraction. Here in Palo Duro Canyon State Park, from mid-June through mid-August, the outdoor musical drama "Texas," which has attracted visitors from over the nation and several foreign countries, is performed nightly except Sundays. The large cast of local people and ambitious collegians plays to audiences of 100,000 each summer.

And on, via I–27, to Lubbock, where, so the story goes, a group of buffalo hunters around a campfire in 1878 took turns making up phrases to the song we now know as "Home on the Range." Regardless, Lubbock is "home" to the prairie dog, with Prairie Dog Town at MacKenzie State Park. It is also home to some 22,000 students attending Texas Tech University. The Ranching Heritage Center at the university shows ranch homes, buildings and equipment in a setting of several acres.

There is a story that the city of Midland actually grew from an industrious hunter's selling of antelope meat from an abandoned box-car. However, it was to be oil, not antelope meat, that would mean prominence and prosperity for Midland and its neighbor city, Odessa. Both are south of Lubbock via US 87, along with Lamesa, an oil, ranching, and agricultural community, and Big Spring, where Indians once battled for control of the life-giving spring.

The huge Permian Basin oil discovery was made in 1923 and takes its name from a prehistoric inland sea, the Permian. Grateful citizens have erected the Permian Basin Petroleum Museum, Library and Hall of Fame to tell the story of this development. Visit a sea 230 million years old. Exhibits let children participate. It is located on I–20.

Down the road a piece is Odessa and a replica of William Shakespeare's original Globe Theatre where the bard's plays and other productions are presented in season. Odessa likes to be called the Southwest hub of entertainment and stays up late to earn the reputation. Odessa is blue-collar; Midland, office-oriented.

Moving southward from Odessa along I–20 you come to a 4,000 acre sandpile with dunes reaching as high as seventy feet where adults and children happily cavort. Monahans Sandhills State Park has many attractions. Legend holds there's a treasure in gold lost somewhere in the windblown sand, buried seconds before an Indian massacre.

The Pecos

Bearing on southwestward you'll cross the Pecos River and come to the town where early-day cowboys staged shoot-'em-ups to relieve the monotony, and where the world's first rodeo occurred in 1883. Shortly beyond Pecos, the land roughens and purple mountains rise out of the plain. If you peer northward from your car window at Van Horn, you can imagine yourself atop 8,749-foot Guadalupe Peak—Texas' highest point—in Guadalupe Mountains National Park, some fifty miles distant.

Travelers on US 62, 180 between El Paso and Carlsbad, N.M., have 40 miles of scenic wonderment while driving the southern edge of the Guadalupes. A principal point is craggy, 2,000-foot cliff El Capitan. For visitors, park attractions are limited to camping and backpacking over miles of marked trails. Outdoor enthusiasts should write the Superintendent, National Park Service, 3225 National Parks Highway, Carlsbad, N.M. 88220.

The motorist you wave to where where Texas 54 crosses your path in Van Horn may be on his way to the Guadalupes. I–10 continues west through Sierra Blanca, then forks right to begin a gradual descent into El Paso, described earlier.

From I–10 southeastward via Texas 118 is Fort Davis (pop. 900), seat of Jeff Davis County, and hub for Fort Davis National Historic Site and 1,800-acre Davis Mountains State Park, a few miles west. A museum at the reconstructed fort traces 175 years of history and a sound recording of a military retreat thrills daylight hours visitors. Camping, campsites, showers and restrooms are available at the park and there is some lodging and food. Fort Davis itself boasts a café, hotel and gift shop. A 70-mile circular tour of the mountains is mapped, including the University of Texas McDonald Observatory open to visitors.

Your visit to Big Bend National Park—even for a day, though distance alone makes that improbable—must be well planned for your own safety and comfort. The 708,000-plus acres of scenic delights are reached from Marathon by US 385, from Alpine over Texas 118, and from Marfa traveling US 67 to Presidio, often the nation's hottest summer point, and via FM 170 to the park. Marathon, the closest of these starting points, is 80 miles distant, so check your vehicle for gas, oil and water. Carry some drinking water. A phone call to the park beforehand is advisable.

Overnight accommodations are limited to the Chisos Mountain Lodge in the basin, and although some expansion has been recently made, reservations well in advance are necessary. Contact National Park Concessions, Inc., Big Bend National Park, TX 79834, tel. (915) 477–2291. Rates are moderate and food is served at the lodge.

Big Bend National Park

Once there, this vast sloping desert reaching up into the Chisos Mountains along the Rio Grande in southwest Texas gives the traveler a marvelous sense of isolation in stark, arid beauty. There are the fantastic shapes and colors of the cactuses and other desert plants, and the sweeping, shadowy, changing colors of the mountain faces; and then, when you get well into the park and find your own way along the paved roads through passageways down to the river, you come to one of the two wondrous canyons reachable by car—Santa Elena, to the east, and Boquillas, to the west. Except at flood time you can walk along the sandy edge of the riverbed alongside the looming canyon walls, and take a rowboat across to a Mexican village—this is the international border, of course—where quartz prisms are sold for a dollar (and you can buy a welcome cold beer, Mexican from Monterrey, as well). Back up in the Chisos basin there is a stable of good horses for mountain treks far up into the high reaches from where you can see for many miles down in the Chihuahua Desert of Mexico. A short trip to a fine scenic hole in the mountain wall, called the "window," spices your morning.

Boquillas Warm Springs adds to the contrast of Big Bend with mineralized waters where temperatures vary from 95 to 105 degrees. And some 20 miles west and on the north edge of Big Bend is the ghost town of Terlingua. In this area a national chili cook-off is held each fall, attended by contestants from all over the nation. Nearby on Texas 170, a developer is modernizing Lajitas, a Pancho Villa–era trading post, with condos, residences and fun spots.

From the Marfa, Alpine, Marathon gateway to Big Bend, a 100-mile drive on US 90 takes you to Langtry, stomping ground of the flamboyant Judge Roy Bean, known as "The Law West of the Pecos" and an admirer of actress Lillie Langtry. The judge held court in the bar of the Jersey Lilly Saloon, brandishing a six-shooter to keep order instead of a gavel. His unusual judgments included fining a corpse $40 for carrying a concealed weapon. The Texas Highway Department maintains the Judge Roy Bean Visitor Center at Langtry where the original saloon is one of the attractions.

US 90 south takes you across Lake Amistad and a look upstream where the United States and Mexico jointly operate giant Amistad Reservoir, impounding waters of the Rio Grande for flood control and recreation. A Port of Entry connects Ciudad Acuna in Mexico and the city of Del Rio. Visitor interests center on the state's oldest winery, and a restored trading post turned museum. It is also Judge Bean's burial site.

Gateway to Mexico

Highly spiced Laredo enjoys luxury hotels and exciting cuisines amid the splendor of centuries-old structures and cultures. The historical district and shopping areas are in leisurely walking distance. Nuevo Laredo, just across the International Bridge, sparkles with a new $9 million horse and dog racetrack, along with a downtown Turf Club accepting bets on U.S. sports events. Laredo is the southern anchor for daily Amtrak service from Chicago and connecting with Mexican trains. Established in 1755, Laredo has known seven national flags. The short-lived (1839–41) Republic of the Rio Grande capitol still functions as a museum. Since 1898 Laredo and Nuevo Laredo have observed George Washington's birthday with a several-day celebration.

Lower Rio Grande Valley

On US 83 south from Laredo you will pass the Falcon Reservoir, a flood and water conservation facility financed jointly by the United States and Mexico, and an important tourist source of income for the cities of Zapata and Rio Grande City. Deer and white wing dove lure hunters in season, and fishing is excellent.

You are now in the Rio Grande Valley, a citrus-rich world of contrasting Mexican-American cultures and the setting for a bevy of cities catering to winter visitors from the North. Most of the sparkle is provided by the cities of McAllen, Harlingen, and Brownsville, and across-the-border neighbors Reynosa and Matamoros. Hotels and motels, mobile-home and travel-trailer parks abound in the Valley.

Imagine a half hundred American combat planes of the World War II era being assembled in a single museum, restored in the colors and with the insignia and personal sketches and slogans. Incredible? More important is that they fly! The self-named Confederate Air Force—some 4,500 World War II pilots, crewmen and enthusiasts, all self-proclaimed "colonels"—is based at Harlingen and open daily. The colonels are dedicated to the preservation of the vintage planes. Some are former enemy craft. An "Airsho" is staged yearly. Valley Historical Museum is on the same site.

And, in Brownsville, you reach Texas' southernmost point, a port city established in 1846 as a fort. Here the first shots of the Mexican War were fired, as well as the last shots of the Civil War—a month after surrender. Five fort buildings remain on Texas Southmost College campus. Cageless Gladys Porter Zoo is widely acclaimed. Brownsville and Matamoros, Mexico, observe Charro Days, a costumed pre-Lenten four-day fiesta. The 1851 Port Isabel Lighthouse is open daily; its interior is thrilling to photographers. Admission. See the Yacht Club Hotel.

Of course you'll want to see Padre Island, one-time pirate hangout and a "graveyard" in past years for craft swept ashore by vicious winds and currents in the adjoining Gulf. Despite its association with pirates and shipwrecks, the island took its name from a padre who operated a ranch there in the early 1800s. It's now sometimes called a little Miami, crowded with condominiums and luxurious hotels.

The Queen Isabella Causeway above Brownsville at Port Isabel takes you to South Padre. Camping is to be found at Isla Blanca Park, or the South Padre Island Tourist Bureau will help you find lodging and dining. An abandoned causeway becomes a lighted fishing pier at night.

Of Horses and Ships

On US 77 back through Harlingen, you'll pass the King Ranch near Kingsville. Consisting of 805,259 acres, it is said to be the largest working ranch in the world. Visitors are welcome 8 A.M. to 4 P.M. on a 12-mile road passing ranch points and may get orientation maps at ranch headquarters.

Past Kingsville swap US 77 for Texas 44 and breeze 40 miles into Corpus Christi, a crisp, clean city of white buildings and smart saloons at an upper level, while imposing hotels, motels and eating spots rim the bay's blue waters. Here pleasure craft bob restlessly at their moorings and cruise and fishing boats board their passengers. Commercial fishermen display their catches for public sale.

Swimmers splash year-round at the beach, and the port ranks ninth nationally. Also on the bay are the Bayfront Plaza Convention Center and Harbor Playhouse. An easy drive southward over the Kennedy Causeway and you're on Padre Island.

Here, too, Padre is condos, hotels, costly homes, expensive boats, even a country club. Malaquite Beach, the public area of Padre, bobs up 14 miles south. There's a covered pavilion with refreshments, restrooms, beach equipment rentals and paved parking. All right on the gulf.

If you must leave this "sparkling city by the sea," and some never do, the driver may choose between I-37 and go north to meet US 281 up from the Valley to San Antonio, or, US 181, crossing Corpus Christi Bay's spectacular bridge, and on to San Antonio. For the Whooping Crane admirer, Texas 35 visits Aransas National Wildlife Refuge up coast at Austwell. Whooper season is mid-October to early April.

In San Antonio take Texas 16 to Bandera and casually move through dude-ranch territory (some have their own airstrips) north to Kerrville, there crossing I-10 but sticking with Texas 16 on to Fredericksburg, home of the late Adm. Chester Nimitz of World War II fame. The Adm. Nimitz Center there is worth a visit. From Fredericksburg take US 290 to Stonewall and on to Johnson City where the birthplace and home of the late President Lyndon B. Johnson may be seen. US 290 goes on to Austin, the state capital.

Three of Texas' six spectacular commercial caves can be visited by driving north from San Antonio on I-10 to Boerne to see Cascade Caverns, then on Texas 46 east to meet US 281 and dip south to FM 1863 and east to Natural Bridge Caverns. Leaving Natural Bridge, follow FM 1863 east into New Braunfels and I-35. Wonder World Caverns and Aquarena Springs, year round water show, are located at San Marcos, farther north on I-35.

If you arrive in Austin by night, you will see its renowned tower lighting system in action—basically 26 towers casting a blue arc light glow Austinites have dubbed "artificial moonlight." Outstanding landmarks include the 311-foot-high 100-year-old domed capitol built of native pink stone, the University of Texas tower, and the newest pride —the Lyndon B. Johnson Memorial Library, whose extensive archives and presidential museum pieces include a replica of the White House Oval Office.

East from Austin, along US 290 on the way to Houston, you will cross the Brazos River. It was at Washington-on-the-Brazos, a few miles north, where a group of Texans gathered in March 1836 to declare independence from Mexico and approve a Constitution, even as the Battle of the Alamo was nearing its climax.

And on to Galveston where The Strand, a section of the city known in the 19th century as the "Wall Street of the West," for cotton and shipping dealings, is now prospering anew. At Galveston Island State Park an adopted Texan named Sam Houston is the principal figure in an outdoor summer drama, "The Lone Star," alternating nightly except Mon., late May through August, with "Annie Get Your Gun."

Marineworld, the multimillion-dollar showplace, features performing fish and animals and displays of birds and fowl in their natural habitat. The 32 miles of sandy beach, the pier and deep-sea fishing, historic homes, the Bishop's Palace, and the archives and view of Galveston from the 20-floor American National Tower add to the lure of this charming city.

From Galveston you can retrace I–45, but a fun route (Texas 87) crosses to Port Boliva via the state-operated free ferry, then hugs the coast before turning north on Texas 124 and entering Beaumont on I–10.

In whatever order your interests lie you'll want to see Gladys City Spindletop Boom Town for an idea of Beaumont when oil was discovered Jan. 10, 1901; the city's inland port, the Babe Didrikson Zaharias Memorial, and the new civic center. Interesting tours are on tap.

Northward, US 69–287 showcases the Big Thicket 40 miles to Woodville, where we turn left on US 190 to view Heritage Garden, a restored early times village and the neighboring Alabama Coushatta Indian Reservation. "Beyond the Sundown," an outdoor drama of reservation history, plays in summer. At Livingston a turn north (right) on US 59 splits the Davy Crockett and Sabine national forests to the lumbering center of Lufkin and on to history-steeped Nacogdoches. Here US 259 sweeps to the important oil city of Longview. Take old US 80 to Marshall, where the capital of Missouri functioned in the Civil War, and pick up US 59 again toward Texarkana, with a peek along the way at Caddo Lake and the early cities of Jefferson and Atlanta.

PRACTICAL INFORMATION FOR TEXAS

HOW TO GET THERE. *By car:* Interstate and U.S. highways enter Texas from the west, north and east and from Mexico. *By air:* Dallas-Fort Worth, El Paso, Houston, Laredo, San Antonio boast regional or international airports. Service is worldwide, often direct. Full interstate service. *By bus:* *Greyhound* and *Trailways Bus System* serve Texas. *By train:* Check *Amtrak.*

TOURIST INFORMATION. The State Department of Highways and Public Transportation maintains tourist bureau stations at Amarillo, Anthony, Austin, Denison, Gainesville, Langtry, Laredo, Orange, Texarkana, the Valley, Waskom and Wichita Falls. They provide maps and information about roads, camper and trailer regulations, the latest weather and location of state-maintained roadside rest areas, state parks and campsites.

For advance planning, write Texas Tourist Development Agency, Box 12008, Dept. DB, Austin, Texas 78711. They will send you free, colorful material about vacationing in Texas.

MUSEUMS AND GALLERIES. Museums listed here by city generally are open daily, except Mon., afternoons Sat., Sun. Admission, if any, is small. *Alpine.* Sul Ross University Museum of Big Bend. Pioneer artifacts. *Austin.* Daughters of Confederacy and Daughters of Republic of Texas Museums. Boom towns live again. *Bonham.* Sam Rayburn Library. Possessions of the late Speaker of the House. *Brownsville.* Stillman House. In 1850's home of the town founder. *Canadian.* Hemphill County Pioneer Museum. *Canyon.* Panhandle Plains Museum on West Texas University campus. *Childress.* Childress County Heritage Museum. Artifacts, period rooms.

Dallas. Hall of State. Dedicated to the famed of Texas history. *Del Rio.* Whitehead Memorial Museum. Judge Roy Bean's grave on grounds. *Devine.* Big Foot Wallace Museum. Possessions of Texas Ranger, Indian fighter. *Groesbeck.* Limestone County Historical Museum. Old Fort Parker data. *Haskell.* Railroad Museum. Fittingly, in old depot. *Hillsboro.* Confederate Research Center. Hillsboro Junior College campus. *Huntsville.* Sam Houston Museum in Houston Memorial Park. His home is there.

Jasper. Jasper County Museum. Local material on Civil War. *Jefferson.* Jefferson County Historical Museum in old Federal Building. *Kilgore. East Texas Oil Museum. Levelland.* South Plains Museum. Recalls days of the big cattle ranches. *Longview.* Caddo Indian Museum, 18th-century relics. *Lufkin.* Forestry Museum. Early logging equipment. *McKinney.* Heard Natural Science Museum. Tours arranged. *Marshall.* Harrison County Historical Society Museum in old courthouse. *Midland.* Permian Basin Petroleum Museum. Devoted to oil discovery, development.

Nederland. Windmill Museum. Three-story windmill houses Dutch community history. *Odessa.* Presidential Museum. Possessions, collections of some U.S. presidents. *Panhandle.* Square House Museum. Outdoor-indoor lectured tours. Very good. *Pecos.* West of the Pecos Museum. Housed in restored hotel saloon. *Plainview.* Llano Estacado Museum. Some artifacts date back 10,000 years. *Port Arthur.* Port Arthur Historical Museum shows Santa Anna debt paper. *Richmond.* Fort Bend County Historical Museum. Traces settlement period. *Snyder.* Western Heritage Museum. Ranch house, chuck wagon, Indian relics. *Tulia.* Swisher County Historical Museum. Pioneer tools, utensils. *Waco.* Texas Ranger Museum. An active Ranger station, houses Ranger Hall of Fame, Waco Tourist Information Center. *Weatherford.* Texas Railroad Museum. Presidential car of Texas and Pacific Railroad among displays.

HISTORIC SITES. Texas has a plethora of historical sites of national as well as local importance, such as *Pres. Dwight David Eisenhower's Birthplace* at S. Lamar and Day Sts., Denison; the *John F. Kennedy* assassination site in Dallas; the *Alamo* in San Antonio; the *Battle of San Jacinto* Monument east of Houston; graves of *Col. James W. Fannin Jr.* and 342 men at Goliad, where they were massacred on orders of Santa Anna on March 27, 1836; and *Gonzales,* where the museum tells the story of the first battle of the Texas Revolution.

TOURS. *Air:* Major airlines seasonally join with cities, tour agencies and car rentals in fly/drive tours. *Train:* check *Amtrak* for Texas tour packages. *Bus: Gray Lines* operates sightseeing tours in major cities and arranges charter tours. *Boat:* Fishing and sightseeing excursions are offered from Corpus Christi, Galveston, Houston, Port Aransas, Rockport, and South Padre Island.

DRINKING LAWS. Legal age for purchase of spirits is 19. Hours for legal sales are set by state law, but each county—even precincts within counties—can determine by local option election whether to permit sales. Such elections also decide what spirits may be sold. For instance, some counties or precincts may limit sales to beer and wine only and decide if they may be consumed at the place of sale. Liquor by the bottle is sold only at package stores, and on-premise consumption is unlawful. Package stores are open between 10 A.M. and 9 P.M. Monday through Saturday. In legal areas, restaurants and taverns may sell spirits between the hours of 7 A.M. and midnight Monday through Friday and until 1 A.M. Sunday. Legal hours for Sunday sales are from noon until midnight. Restaurants and taverns in the major cities may purchase special permits allowing operation until 2 A.M. daily. Generally, beer, wine, and liquor can be purchased in the larger cities, but you may do well to ascertain the laws in the town ahead. A case of beer or a quart of liquor can be legally carried in your car.

SPORTS. *Baseball:* American League Texas Rangers play in Texas Stadium while the National League Houston Astros perform in the Astrodome. In the Texas League, Amarillo, El Paso, Midland and San Antonio field entries.

Basketball: Texas teams in the National Basketball Association and their home court: Dallas Mavericks, Reunion Arena; Houston Rockets, the Summit; and San Antonio Spurs, Center Arena.

Football: National Football League teams Dallas Cowboys play at Texas Stadium and the Houston Oilers in the Astrodome.

Golf: Professional Golf Association tournaments include the Byron Nelson in Irving, Fort Worth's Colonial Invitational Tournament, the Texas Open at San Antonio and the Houston Open. Austin sponsors a Legends of Golf play. The Ladies Professional Golf Association plays a Dallas tournament.

Auto racing: Principal track is the Texas World Speedway near College Station. Headline event is the Texas 500 run in June.

Tennis: World Championship Tennis Finals at Dallas Reunion Arena. Women compete in Avon Championship, Moody Coliseum, Southern Methodist University.

Golf courses and tennis courts open to the public, or hospitable country clubs extending privileges to visitors will be found in many cities and towns.

Texas Sports Hall of Fame, adjacent to I–30 in Grand Prairie. New two-story building honors feats of great Texas athletes.

WHAT TO DO WITH THE CHILDREN. There will be a public park and playground for children almost every place you visit in Texas. Here are some biggies and smallies:

Alamo Village, 6 mi N of Brackettville on Ranch Rd. 674. A western town setting, with jail, general store, cantina, blacksmith shop, Indian store used in a number of movies (the most famous being "The Alamo," with John Wayne), television shows, and other programs. Food and drink at cantina, cowboys and cowgirls are around, and there are live shows and gun fights during June and August. One price admission.

Alabama-Coushatta Indian Reservation, US 190 between Livingston and Woodville. Life in a real Indian village, rides by Indian Chief train, tour of Big Thicket, museums, curio shops, Indian dances. Closed December–February. One price admission. "Beyond the Sundown," outdoor historical drama, nightly, mid-June through August. Admission. Modern campground at reservation.

Aquarena Springs, San Marcos off I–35. Underwater spectacle, with audience viewing performance while submerged in spacious theater. Glass-bottomed boats for tour of springs. Swiss sky ride, Texana village, early buildings. Beautiful inn for guests. Open all year.

Gladys Porter Zoo, 6th at Ringgold, Brownsville. Most areas of zoo contain wildlife indigenous to that area. Zoo walks circle the park. Over 1,500 birds, reptiles, and mammals in lush, botanical display. Open daily. Adults $1.50, children under 12, $.50.

Heritage Garden Village. Woodville near Indian Reservation. Early settler village with many buildings and furnishings has been created. Perhaps the state's largest collection of early-Texas memorabilia. Open daily. Meals served.

Institute of Texan Cultures, San Antonio. Depicts lifestyles of 26 ethnic groups populating the state using sound, sight, films, and slides as mediums. Closed Monday. Admission, parking free except four days early August for statewide Festival.

Prairie Dog Town. Mackenzie State Park, Lubbock. Known as the last stand for the prairie dog, the "town" is only a part of this attractive park. Natural showmen, the prairie dogs entertain children and adults alike with their antics. Camping, camp sites, restrooms, showers.

Six Shooter Junction, Expressway 77, 83 South, Harlingen. 1880 steam train, rides for children, shops, early buildings. Frontier Jamboree Theatre features western music at night on weekends.

"Texas," Palo Duro Canyon State Park near the city of Canyon. Outdoor drama presented in natural amphitheatre tells history of area in story, song, and dance. Nightly except Sunday, mid-June through late August. Admission $3 to $6. Children $1.75 to $6. Tent, trailer camping, $3 per car.

Texas State Railroad glorifies the era of the steam locomotive with passenger runs between the East Texas cities of Rusk and Palestine. A tourist attraction operated by the Texas Parks and Wildlife Department, the four-car TSR chugs a weekend schedule mid-March through mid-May and early September through late October. Summer runs Mon., Thurs., Fri. and weekends. Round trip requires four hours.

Children's Zoo, 125-acre tract in Tyler. Both native and wild animals. Petting zoo, burro rides, Shetland pony rides, goat cart, and farm wagon rides—also circus train rides for small charge. Open daily. Free.

 HOTELS AND MOTELS. Recognized chains, usually with uniform rates and services, dot the state. They will book reservations ahead for your convenience. Privately owned operations are often bargains. Seasonal rates prevail in some areas and for important sports events.

Price categories, for double occupancy, average: *Moderate* $35–60, *Inexpensive* under $35.

ABILENE. *Moderate:* **Holiday Inn.** I–20 and Texas 351, near airport.
Sheraton Inn–Abilene. 505 Pine St. Downtown, full accommodations.
Inexpensive: **American Best Western.** Impact exit off I–20.
Hotel Windsor. N. 4th & Pine. Restaurant, air conditioning.

AMARILLO. *Moderate:* **Best Western–Trade Winds.** Fillmore and Pierce. Heated pool.
Howard Johnson Motor Lodge–East. T-Anchor Blvd. and I–40. Courtesy car.
Rodeway Inn. 2015 Paramount. Food, golf, tennis. Adjoining lounge.
Inexpensive: **Plainsmen Hotel.** 1503 Amarillo Blvd.cafe.

AUSTIN. *Moderate:* **Holiday Inn Town Lake.** 20 N. Interregional. Lake view.
The Bradford. Formerly Stephen F. Austin. $15-million new look.
Inexpensive: **Austin Motel–Best Value.** 1220 S. Congress. Some kitchens.
Days Inn. 8214 N. Interregional.
Imperial 400. 901 S. Congress. Small, friendly.
State Motel. 2500 S. Congress Ave.

BEAUMONT. *Moderate:* **Ramada Inn–North.** 1295 N. 11th St. Spacious. Pool, lounge. Pets.
Red Carpet Inn. 55 I–10 North. Lounge, dancing. Convenient for Houston travelers.
Inexpensive: **La Quinta.** 220 I–10 North. Restaurant, lounge.

BROWNSVILLE. *Moderate:* **Fort Brown Motor Hotel.** 1900 E. Elizabeth. A showplace.
Valley Inn & Country Club. Restaurant. Pool, golf, tennis.
Inexpensive: **El Jardin.** Restaurant, TV. 150 rooms.
Motel 6, 190 rooms. Pool, TV.

CORPUS CHRISTI. *Moderate:* **Best Western Sandy Shores.** 3200 Surfside Blvd. Dining, lounge, beach.
La Quinta Royale. 601 N. Water St. 200 rooms.
Quality Inn–Bayfront. 411 N. Shoreline. Babysitting. Restaurant, lounge.

Inexpensive: **Catalina Motel and Apartments,** 4333 Ocean Dr.; **Motel,** 2100 block Agnes St.; **Modern Motel,** 3421 S. Padre Island; **Tally-Ho Motel,** 3901 Leonard St. Accommodations vary, all Best Dollar properties.
Dunes Motel. 10545 Padre Island Dr.
Sea Ranch Motel. 4401 Ocean Dr. Some kitchens; restaurant near.

GALVESTON. *Moderate:* **Anchorage Motor Hotel,** 2620 Seawall Blvd.
Gaido's Motor Inn. 38th and Beach Blvd. Near all activities.
Islander Beach Motel. Sixth St. and Seawall. 193 rooms, located on beach.
La Quinta. 1402 Seawall. Beach front, 115 rooms.
Rodeway, 845 N. Expressway. Exit Price Rd.
Inexpensive: **Motel 6.** 7404 Broadway. Pool, 114 rooms.

HARLINGEN. *Moderate:* **Rodeway Inn.** 1821 W. Tyler. Lounge, family units.

KERRVILLE. *Moderate:* **The Inn of the Hills.** Hill Country showplace.

LAREDO. *Moderate:* **La Posada Motor Hotel.** 1000 Zaragoza. Near International Bridge.
Inexpensive: **La Quinta,** 3600 Santa Ursula. 24-hour Denny's Restaurant, lounge.

LUBBOCK. *Inexpensive:* **Best Western Brass Lantern,** 5912 Avenue H. Shopping nearby, downtown seven miles.
La Quinta–Civic Center. 601 Avenue Q. Restaurant.

McALLEN. *Inexpensive:* **La Quinta.** 1100 S. 10th. Dining, lounge. Paraplegic room.

MIDLAND. *Moderate:* **Holiday Inn.** Downtown convenience.

NACOGDOCHES. *Inexpensive:* **Quality Inn Fredonia.** 200 N. Fredonia St.

ODESSA. *Moderate:* **Hospitality Lodge.** 5901 E. US 80. Pool, dining, lounge.

PALESTINE. *Moderate:* **Holiday Inn.** Near National Balloon Flight Station.

SALADO. *Inexpensive:* **Stagecoach Inn.** Exits off I–35. Early stagecoach stop lives again. Good food.

TEXARKANA. *Inexpensive:* **Coachman Inn.** 4415 State Line Ave. Restaurant, lounge, heated pool.

TYLER. *Inexpensive:* **Best Western–Kingsway Inn.** 3209 Gentry Pkwy. Near Rose Gardens.
Red Carpet Inn. 2828 NW Loop 323. Dining, private club, pool.

WACO. *Moderate:* **Holiday Inn.** On I–35, bypassing downtown. Convenient.

WICHITA FALLS. *Moderate:* **Best Western–Towne Crest Inn.** 1601 Eighth St. One block off US 277–281–287.

DINING OUT. With modern highways tending to skirt cities and towns, many chain and franchise operations on exit and frontage roads have gained popularity. Yet, it's often fun to drive into town and get a local view. Price categories are: *Moderate* $7–12, *Inexpensive* under $7. This will include soup or salad, entree and vegetables.

ABILENE. *Moderate:* **Buffalo Gap Steak House.** South of Abilene. Worth the trip.
  Guiseppi's Italian Station. 4109 S. Danville. On the track here.
  Town Crier. 818 I–20 East, at US 80 North.
  Windsor Hotel. 4th and Pine. Steaks, complete menu.
  Inexpensive: **Bonanza Family Restaurant.** 4223 N. First. Steaks.
  China Hut. 4205 N. First. Large helpings.
  El Chico. Abilene Mall. Dallas-based Mexican chain.
  Saddle & Sirloin. 3901 S. First. Varied menu. Open 24 hours.

AMARILLO. *Moderate:* **Best Western Tradewinds.** 1001 N. Pierce. Breakfast, lunch, dinner served.
  Big Texan. 7700 I–40 East. Steaks in an 1800s setting.
  Rhett's. 2805 W. 15th. The Old South is alive here.
  Seafood Galley. 2921 S. Virginia. Seafood treats with shore dinners a house specialty.

AUSTIN. *Moderate:* **Convict Hill Restaurant.** US 290 and Texas 71 at Oak Hill. Salad bar, homestyle bread.
  Hill's Café. 4700 S. Congress. Chicken-fried steak a specialty.
  Hoffbrau. 613 W. Sixth. Grilled steaks in lemon butter. Reservations.
  Lock, Stock & Barrel. 2700 W. Anderson Lane. Steaks, seafood. Entertainment.
  Montana Mining Co. 1601 Oltorf. It used to be that the cattlemen sold steaks to the miners, but now . . .
  Old Pecan St. Café. 310 E. 6th. French touch, courtyard and bar.
  Inexpensive: **Cisco's.** 1511 E. Sixth. Widely known for Mexican specialties and pastries.
  Night Hawk. 336 S. Congress. Several places, college favorites. Frisco hamburger special, steaks, seafood.
  Scholz Garden. 1607 San Jacinto. German food. Started in 1866.

BEAUMONT. *Moderate:* **Catfish Kitchen.** 1080 S. 11th St. All the catfish you want.
  Cody's. 6680 Calder. Steaks, hamburgers a specialty.
  Don's Seafood & Steak House. 2290 I–10 South. Around a long time.
  Inexpensive: **Carlo's.** 2570 Calder. Italian food.
  Luby's Cafeteria. 745 Gaylynn Shopping Center. The Luby-Romano cafeterias, started in San Antonio, operate in many Texas cities.

BROWNSVILLE. *Moderate:* **Beacon Harbor.** 3505 Boca Chica. Located on leading boulevard.
  Lavio's. 2474 Boca Chica. Mexican dishes prepared from 38 special recipes.
  Leonardo's Fiesta Restaurant. 1004 Central Blvd.
  Inexpensive: **Mr. Q. Family Restaurant.** 1104 International Blvd.
  Texas Café. Market Square. Operating since 1912, the café has never closed —not even when a fierce storm struck in August 1980.
  White Owl Café, 2045 E. 14th. Known to utility workers.

CORPUS CHRISTI. *Moderate:* **Astor.** 5533 Leopard. Charcoal steaks, seafood.
  J. B.'s Crab Pot. 10649 S. Padre Island Dr. Friendly surroundings. Ask for J.B.

Nolan's. 4425 Weber Rd. Steaks are the feature of several locations.

Old Mexico Restaurant. 3329 Leopard. A puffed taco is the house pride.

Peking Restaurant. 601 S. Shoreline. Chinese and American dishes.

Rusted Rail. 5102 S. Padre Island Dr. Prime rib, lamb, seafood. Wine list a restaurant pride.

Ship Ahoy. 1017 N. Water. A downtown favorite.

The Torch. 4425 S. Alamedo. Redfish a house specialty.

Inexpensive: **Black Diamond Oyster Bar.** 5712 Gallagner. Half shell oysters, frog legs, shrimp.

Frank's Spaghetti House. 2724 Leopard. Homemade Italian dishes.

Mi Tierra. 2319 Morgan. Mexican specialties, American dishes.

Ray's. 920 Louisiana. Variety menu, breakfast any time.

Spanish Kitchen. 3117 Surfside. Versatility here. Steaks, seafood, Mexican and Italian treats.

Whataburger. 222 S. Staples. Based in Corpus Christi, this hamburger chain is found in many Texas cities.

GALVESTON. *Moderate:* **Candy's.** 2112 Mechanic. Italian fare.

Christie's Beachcomber, 401 Seawall. Your dinner may swim by.

Corrella's Corral, 2528 61st. Mexican dishes in this corral.

Captain's Galley, 5224 Seawall. Charcoal shrimp has followers.

Cattlemen's. 2404 61st. Steak and barbecue and good.

Happy Buddha. 2827 61st. Chinese.

Hill's. 35th and Seawall. Owners operate their own market and fishing boats.

Inexpensive: **El Zarape.** 1615 39th St. Mexican food.

Shrimp & Stuff. 3901 Avenue Q. and 6801 Stewart Place. Place your own order.

Tong's Happy Buddha. 4400 Seawall. For the Chinese lover.

JACKSBORO. *Moderate:* **The Green Frog.** Near Fort Richardson State Park.

JACKSONVILLE. *Inexpensive:* **Saddler's.** 402 S. Jackson. Like stepping into a farmer's dining room.

LAREDO. *Moderate:* **Chez Mauricette.** 1001 Park. Impressive. French specialties.

Eduardo's Continental. 7005 N. Expressway. A touch of Italian and French wizardry.

Favarato's. 1916 San Bernardo. Catering to the gourmet appetite.

Golding's. 1702 Santa Maria. Old favorite. Seafood, Mexican delights.

Inexpensive: **Giuseppe's.** 4413 San Bernardo. Italian all the way.

Hungry Farmer. 802 Juarez and 620 Calton Rd. Good menu selection. 24 oz. steak feature.

Mi Tierra. 4309 San Bernardo. Steak ranchero a leader.

LONGVIEW. *Moderate:* **Jamil's.** 2103 E. Marshall. The Lebanese touch with steaks.

Madden's. 309 Sabine. Two decades of barbecue and steak fans.

LUBBOCK. *Moderate:* **Chelsea Street Pub.** South Plains Mall. Proud of its prime rib.

Depot. 1801 Avenue G. Dining delights in a landmark location.

Golden China. 3626 50th. Chefs are brought from Hong Kong.

Gridiron. 4413 50th. Home-owned and operated, specializing in steaks.

Harrigan's. 3801 50th. Crepes with an Irish touch.

Pelican's Wharf. 7202 Indiana. Seafood with wharf atmosphere.

MARSHALL. *Moderate:* **Gables Restaurant.** 304 E. Pinecrest. Years of followers for home-baked bread.

MIDLAND. *Moderate:* **Eden Restaurant.** 3303 N. Midkiff. Prime rib a treat.

NEW BRAUNFELS. *Moderate:* **The Smokehouse.** Off I–35 at Texas 46. Smoked sausages, ham, turkey, bacon. German cooking.

ODESSA. *Moderate:* **Barn Door & Pecos Depot.** 2140 N. Grant. Atmosphere from the past.
    Oliver's. Permian Mall. Prime rib, seafood. Sandwiches, too.
    Inexpensive: **Manuel's.** 1404 E. 2nd. Solid Mexican fare.

SALADO. *Moderate-Expensive:* **Stagecoach Inn.** Marked route off I–35. Entrée price includes complete dinner. Historic place.

TEMPLE. *Moderate:* **The Matterhorn.** 7-story "mountain" restaurant park complex on I–35 west of Temple, between Salado and Jarrell.

TEXARKANA. *Moderate:* **Acadian Seafood House.** 114 E. Broad. Cajun cooking at its best.
    Hush Puppy Restaurant. Hwy. 71 North. Catfish the specialty.
    The Line and Hook Restaurant. 110 E. 36th. Seafood including frog legs, oysters, butterfly shrimp and crab claws.
    Inexpensive: **La Casa Rosa,** 1824 State Line. Mexican dishes. Fresh daily.

TYLER. *Moderate:* **Monterey House.** 2506 E. Fifth. Mexican food:
    Red Ackers. 2500 E. Fifth. Steaks are the specialty.
    Inexpensive: **Liang's.** 3400 S. Broadway. Oriental menu.
    Lee's Restaurant. 1816 N. Gentry Pkwy. Fresh catfish.
    Western Sizzlin. 3521 S. Broadway. Chain steak operation.
    Wyatt's Cafeteria. Broadway Square Mall.

WACO. *Moderate:* **Sun Blossom's.** 4201 Franklin in Ramada Inn.
    Nick's. 4508 W. Waco. Steaks, specialty Greek food.
    The Outpost. 7000 Sanger. West of downtown.
    The Sirloin. 2803 Franklin. Steak and seafood.

WICHITA FALLS. *Moderate:* **Frontier Steak House.** 1210 Lamar. Big salad bar, steaks and fine aged cheese.
    Carrow's. 4310 Kemp. Popular restaurant.
    Old Town Steak House. 4022-B Callfield. Plate for children.
    Pelican. 2719 Southwest Pkwy. For the seafood farer.
    Inexpensive: **L&M Restaurant.** 3064 Seymour Hwy. Open 24 hours.
    Zeno's. 4600 F Southwest Pkwy. Italian standards.

COLORADO

Denver, Mining Towns and Ski Paradise

Perhaps the best place to start a tour of the mile-high city of Denver is the Colorado Visitor's Bureau at 225 West Colfax Avenue, across from the city hall (known as the City and County Building), where visitors can find information about the city and the state.

North of the City and County Building is the United States Mint, where automatic machinery stamps out pennies, nickels, dimes, quarters, and half dollars. Tours are offered throughout the year, except from mid-June through July 4.

From the City and County Building a grassy mall, dotted with shade trees, stretches eastward to the gold-domed Colorado State Capitol. The capitol, constructed of Colorado gray granite, is a miniature version of the U.S. Capitol in Washington, D.C. Fountains, a Greek theater for public gatherings, and monuments to Colorado pioneers grace this popular public area.

On Bannock Street is the Denver Art Museum, noted for its contemporary and traditional American, European, and Oriental exhibits. The building, next to the Civic Center, is composed of more than one million faceted-glass tiles. Across from the museum is the Denver Public Library. The library's Western History department is considered one of the nation's best.

Capitol Hill, once the site of luxurious homes of mining tycoons, still has a number of mansions that can visited. Among them is Molly

486

Brown's House, which was the home of the real-life folk heroine of "The Unsinkable Molly Brown."

A panoramic view of Denver is available from the restaurant atop the 30-story Security Life Building. And the ride to the top in the glass-enclosed outside elevator is an exciting experience.

East of the downtown area is the Denver Museum of Natural History situated in the 640-acre City Park. You can view fossilized bones of prehistoric animals found in the Rockies. Other exhibits show Rocky Mountain, Arctic, and South American animals mounted in lifelike settings. City Park itself has a large zoo. Also in east Denver, adjoining Cheesman Park, are the Denver Botanic Gardens, featuring a million-dollar conservatory for tropical flowers and plants.

In the northwest, on 44th Avenue, is the Colorado Railroad Museum, which will please the rail buff.

PRACTICAL INFORMATION FOR DENVER

HOW TO GET AROUND. *By bus:* RTD buses running centrally and into the suburbs. *By taxi:* cabs are plentiful. *From the airport:* Airport taxi; airport limousine service to major hotels.

TOURIST INFORMATION. Denver & Colorado Convention & Visitor's Bureau, 225 W. Colfax Ave., Denver 80202.

SEASONAL EVENTS. *January:* National Western Stock Show and Rodeo. *April:* Easter Sunrise services at Red Rocks. *May:* Lakeside Amusement Park open for summer. *June:* Elitch Gardens opens. *October:* Larimer Square Oktoberfest. Denver Symphony begins its season. *December:* Denver Civic Center Christmas Display. Colorado Biennial art exhibit at the Denver Art Museum.

MUSEUMS AND GALLERIES. *Denver Museum of Natural History* in City Park has realistic dioramas of prehistoric and present-day animals, *Colorado Heritage Center,* 1300 Broadway. *Denver Art Museum,* noted for its American, European, and Oriental collections, on 14th Ave. The city has several cooperative, contemporary art galleries on the west side.

HISTORIC SITES. The *Governor's Mansion,* 400 E. 8th Ave. *Molly Brown's House,* 1340 Pennsylvania St.

TOURS. *AA Tours, Inc., Back Roads Mountain Tours,* and *Gray Line Tours* offer daily excursions. *Historic Denver Walking Tours,* 1340 Pennsylvania, organizes interesting city walks and van tours.

The most famous special-interest tour is of the *U.S. Mint* at Colfax and Delaware Sts.

GARDENS. The *Denver Botanic Gardens* is one of the best in the western U.S. Library and greenhouse open to the public.

SUMMER SPORTS. Two dozen public golf courses; tennis in city parks. Sloans Lake and nearby Cherry Creek Reservoir have boating and water-skiing facilities. Jogging paths and bicycle routes are plentiful.

WINTER SPORTS. Major skiing at more than thirty Colorado areas and resorts. If you ski "low season," before Dec. 16 and after April 1, savings can be made on lodging. Also consider special group package rates for air fares— inquire with your travel agent. Condominiums needn't be expensive if there is a group of six or more; otherwise try motels, hostels and pensions in the area—most resorts operate a free shuttle bus service to the slopes. Ski equipment can be rented in Denver. Finally, beginners should avoid the more famous ski meccas, such as Vail and stick to lesser-known ones like Winter Park or Crested Butte.

SPECTATOR SPORTS. Englewood and Lakeside Speedways offer drag and sports car racing. Denver Bears in AA baseball league. Denver Nuggets, basketball. Denver Broncos, football. Colorado Rockies, hockey. Rodeo at the National Western Stock Show and Rodeo in January. Horse racing at Centennial Racetrack; dog racing at Mile High Kennel Club.

WHAT TO DO WITH THE CHILDREN. The *Children's Museum, City Park* with its zoo, children's zoo, and the Denver Museum of Natural History and Planetarium. The *Forney Transportation Museum* and the *Wax Museum* are of interest. The *Colorado Railroad Museum* is good for exploring. *Elitch Gardens* has a kiddie area, and Lakeside Amusement Park features rides.

HOTELS AND MOTELS. Price categories, for double occupancy, will start *upward* from the following: *Moderate* $21–34; *Inexpensive* $14–20.

Moderate: **Broadway Plaza.** Broadway at 11th Ave., 4 blks. south of State Capitol. In addition to clean rooms, there is a rooftop sundeck. 24-hour cafés nearby.

Colburn Hotel. 980 Grant Street, close to downtown area. All 150 rooms with baths. Some kitchenettes and facilities for permanent guests.

Denver Central TraveLodge. I–25 at Speer Blvd. This motel offers free coffee, sundeck. 24-hour coffee shop nearby.

Inexpensive: **Anchor.** 2323 S. Broadway, Small motel, free coffee, pets, sundeck. 24-hour cafe nearby.

Motel 6. 480 Wadsworth Blvd. (Westside). Excellent value.

Rosedale Motel. 3901 Elati, off I–25 at 38th Ave. Modest with clean rooms.

DINING OUT Price categories are: *Moderate* $6–9; *Inexpensive* $3–5. Drinks, tax, and tips not included.

Moderate: **The Apple Tree Shanty.** 8710 East Colfax. Ribs a house specialty. Sizable dessert menu.

Hungry Farmer. 6925 W. Alameda, in Lakewood. Hearty farm food served in a large barn. Prime rib, steak, barbecued ribs, chicken are part of Granny's selection.

North Woods Inn. 6115 S. Santa Fe Dr. Cowboy dinners.

Inexpensive: **White Fence Farm.** 6236 W. Jewell. Well-known, Colonial-style, family dinners.

Casa Bonita. 6715 W. Colfax Ave. Mexican and American food. Popular with large families.

EXPLORING COLORADO

A number of attractions and scenic areas are within range of one-day excursions from Denver.

As you approach Boulder, home of the University of Colorado, the tilted slablike Flatirons rock formations tower on your left. Head west from Boulder, up Boulder Canyon and along the edge of Barker Reservoir, to the mountain town of Nederland. State 72, the scenic Peak to Peak Highway, winds through lodgepole pine forests toward Estes Park, a recreation gateway to Rocky Mountain National Park. On the other side of the Continental Divide is Granby, noted for its lakes and abundance of dude ranches.

From Golden, site of the first territorial capital and home of the Colorado School of Mines, a good highway leads to Central City, an old gold-mining community whose Opera House, Teller House Hotel, and private Victorian homes have been preserved and restored. Opera companies and Broadway shows perform here each summer. Well-maintained highways to Idaho Springs and gemlike Echo Lake at 10,600 feet provide breathtaking views. For the adventuresome there is a further drive up Mount Evans on the nation's highest automobile road.

South from Denver are Colorado Springs and Pikes Peak, elevation 14,110 feet. At Castle Rock, en route, there are mountain views in all directions. Various areas of the Air Force Academy are open to the public; best known is the many-spired glass and aluminum chapel. Colorado Springs is the state's second largest city, long famous as a summer resort. There are a Fine Arts Center with collections of southwestern art and a Pioneer Museum. The nearby Garden of the Gods is noted for its imposing red rock formations. Pikes Peak looms above Colorado Springs. Pass through Manitou Springs for the toll road to the summit. A cog railway also ascends the mountain from Manitou Springs. In the hills behind Pikes Peak are the once-booming gold-mining towns of Cripple Creek and Victor—now home to only a few hundred people.

On a longer, several-day tour of Colorado, head southwest from Denver through the Kenosha Pass to Fairplay. This pass affords a fine panorama of the broad South Park valley. From Fairplay drive north to the Dillon Reservoir and turn west toward Vail. Vail, created out of a sheep meadow in 1962, is fast becoming a year-round vacation center. Former President Ford's continuing visits to Vail for skiing and golf hasn't hurt its popularity.

Continuing west, the road parallels the Eagle River, which joins the Colorado in Dotsero, and follows spectacular Glenwood Canyon—a 1,000-foot chasm between slate-colored cliffs—to Glenwood Springs. North of the Colorado lies the White River wilderness area, heavily wooded and virtually unscarred by roads.

South of Glenwood Springs is Aspen, Colorado's top ski center and an old silver-mining town transformed into a mountain cultural mecca. The summer Aspen Music Festival and School and the Aspen Institute for Humanistic Studies are widely known. The surrounding area has trout lakes and streams, plus countless miles of hiking and riding trails.

Farther west is Grand Junction, important as a uranium center and western Colorado's largest city. Ten miles outside of town is Colorado National Monument, an area of weirdly eroded stone spires, canyons, and fossil beds.

Mesa Verde National Park

Some 800 years ago the prehistoric Indians who lived and farmed this "green tabletop" were forced to abandon it after a long drought. They left behind stone cities built into cliffs that fascinate archeologists, both professional and amateur. Although some of the dwellings were modest—the pithouses had tiny rooms and housed a single family—there are remains of great structures as well. The Cliff Palace was built into the cliffside 200 feet up the wall and had 200 "rooms"; the Spruce Tree House had 114. An excellent museum at park headquarters helps to bring alive this old civilization and, besides evening campfire talks by rangers and archeologists, neighboring Navahos give regular demonstrations of their chants and dances. As for the original Mesa Verdeans, nobody knows where they may have gone after having lived here for 1,300 years. They left unfinished a temple to the sun, and may simply have gradually mingled with other tribes to the south. Lodges provide restaurants, rooms, and cabins from May to October, and there is a year-round campground.

The museum at Park Headquarters will add to the visitor's understanding of Mesa Verde and her people of long ago. Mesa Verde may be reached by car on US 160, thirty-eight miles west of Durango, then on twenty-one miles on park roads from the park entrance. Bus service is available for those who do not wish to drive into the park; Frontier Airlines serves Durango and Cortez ten miles west of Mesa Verde. A limited number of overnight accommodations are available at the park entrance, as are improved facilities for house trailers. A restaurant, service station, AAA road service, and tire agency are available. The Far West Motel offers lodging in the park itself. Accommodations and tourist services at Cortez, 10 miles west, and at Durango, 38 miles east.

You can return to Denver by way of Durango, where a narrow-gauge train drawn by a steam locomotive makes a 45-mile run to Silverton; Ouray, heart of the "Switzerland of the Rockies"; Black Canyon of the Gunnison National Monument; Canon City, location of Royal Gorge, where the world's highest suspension bridge crosses the 1,000-foot-deep gorge of the Arkansas River; and Pueblo, center of the state's steel industry. Or, swinging farther south, go through Alamosa in the center of the richly productive San Luis Valley to Great Sand Dunes National Monument at the foot of the starkly beautiful Sangre de Cristo Mountains.

Two major areas have not been included in this tour: the eastern plains with the rich agricultural South Platte and Arkansas river valleys; and the sparsely populated northwest, a region with trout fishing streams, skiing at Steamboat Springs, and Dinosaur National Park, where one can see paleontologists at work unearthing dinosaur fossils.

Rocky Mountain National Park

Rocky Mountain National Park is a 405-square-mile reserve of towering peaks and untouched forests first set aside for public enjoyment and as a national treasure back in 1915. The wilds of the park can be explored afoot at leisure, or one can drive through it over the nation's renowned Trail Ridge Road, skirting chasms a thousand feet deep, and winding over the wind-swept tundra above the timberline. Near the top of Milner Pass, 10,758 feet high (where you cross the Continental Divide), is a museum of tundra ecology that displays the diverse flora and fauna of this climatically inhospitable land. Summer comes late to the high country, but brings with it a profusion of exquisite, tiny wildflowers. Trail Ridge Rd. is usually closed by snow in late October or early November and not reopened until Memorial Day or June 1st, when young athletes celebrate the event by skiing on the snow that blankets the top. In midsummer, however, the country above the timberline is delightfully cool after the heat of the plains. Grand Lake (8,380 feet) is considered the world's loftiest yacht marina.

The gateway town of Estes Park has a year-round population of only about 1,600, but in summer tens of thousands of visitors flock to the resort hotels, dude ranches, motels, and campgrounds in the area. Estes Park is not really a park—"park" is an old western term for a mountain valley, and this was Joel Estes' domain in 1860. When two other families moved in to share this huge rugged hollow in the Rockies, Estes moved out, complaining about the crowds. An aerial tramway to the top of 8,896-foot Prospect Mountain offers a sweeping view of the peaks and valleys. Boating and fishing on Lake Estes, scores of miles of riding and hiking trails, and hundreds of miles of trout streams are other attractions in this area. The summit of Long's Peak (14,256 feet) can be scaled via trail by hardy hikers and its sheer East Face is one of the nation's most challenging climbs.

PRACTICAL INFORMATION FOR COLORADO

ROCKY MOUNTAIN NATIONAL PARK

HOW TO GET THERE. *By car* to Rocky Mountain National Park: from south on State 72, Peak to Peak Highway. From Loveland, via Highway #34. From Grand Lake, via Trail Ridge Road (summer only).

SEASONAL EVENTS. *April:* Estes Park Hobby Show. *August:* Shadow Mountain Sailboat Regatta at Grand Lake.

SPECTATOR SPORTS. Estes Park has the Long's Peak Scottish Highland Festival in September.

SUMMER SPORTS. Area noted for fishing, sailing, boating (Grand Lake has the highest altitude yacht club in America), horseback riding, hiking.

HOTELS AND MOTELS. Price categories for double occupancy average: *Moderate* $21–34; *Inexpensive* $14–20.

ESTES PARK. *Moderate:* **Trail Ridge Motel.** Comfortable motel with restaurant.

GRAND LAKE. *Moderate:* **Daven Haven Lodge.** Summer resort, with beach, all water sports.
Inexpensive: **Riverside Guest Houses.** Well-appointed cabins near lake.

 DINING OUT. *Moderate* ($6–9) prices are for a complete dinner without drinks, tax or tip.

ESTES PARK. *Moderate:* **Old Plantation.** Yankee pot roast and rainbow trout are specialties.

THE REST OF COLORADO

 HOW TO GET THERE. *By air:* Denver, Colorado Springs, Pueblo, and Grand Junction have major service. *By rail: Amtrak* from Chicago or San Francisco to Denver. *By car:* I–25 from Wyoming in the north and New Mexico in the south; I–70 from Utah in the west and Kansas in the east; and I–80S/I–76 from Nebraska in the northeast.
By bus: Greyhound and *Continental Trailways.*

TOURIST INFORMATION. *Denver & Colorado Convention & Visitor's Bureau,* 225 W. Colfax Ave., Denver 80202.

 MUSEUMS AND GALLERIES. The *University of Colorado Museum and Art Gallery* and the *Boulder Center for the Visual Arts,* both in Boulder. Central City has the *Opera House* and the *Gold Mine Museum.* Colorado Springs has the *Fine Arts Center, Prorodeo Hall of Champions,* and the *National Carvers Museum. Matchless Mine* and *Tabor Opera House* in restored Leadville. Vail: *Ski Museum.*

 HISTORIC SITES. *Old Fort Garland,* west of Walsenburg, is a restored Army post once commanded by Kit Carson. *Fort Vasquez,* an 1830's fur-trading post, is near Platteville. Colorado has more than 300 mining ghost towns; the best known are in the Central City–Black Hawk region, Nevadaville, Apex, and the Cripple Creek–Victor region.

 TOURS. *AA Tours, Inc.,* and *Back Roads Mountain Tours* in Denver, and *Gray Line Tours* in Denver and Colorado Springs.

DRINKING LAWS. Over 18 for "3.2" beer. The age for hard liquor and regular beer is 21.

 SUMMER SPORTS. Fishing, especially for trout, is a big seasonal sport. Nonresident licenses are obtainable. Mule deer and elk are major hunting quarry. Boating, water skiing, and rafting on lakes and rivers. Colorado also attracts hikers and backpackers. For state park campsite information and reservations contact TeleCheck Minnesota, 5275 Edina Industrial Blvd., Edina, Minn. 55435 (800–328–6338).

WINTER SPORTS. Aspen is one of the largest ski complexes in the country. Ski areas close to Denver are Loveland Basin and Winter Park. Other major centers are Keystone, Copper Mountain, Steamboat Springs, Vail, and Beaver Creek.

SPECTATOR SPORTS. *Auto racing:* the Pikes Peak Auto Hill Climb every July 4. *Dog racing* at Cloverleaf Kennel Club in Loveland, at Pueblo Kennel Association and the Rocky Mountain Kennel Club in Pueblo. *Rodeos* in Colorado Springs, Pueblo, Estes Park, Steamboat Springs, Canon City, Boulder, Grand Junction and Glenwood Springs and in several smaller communities.

WHAT TO DO WITH THE CHILDREN. Colorado Springs has the *Cheyenne Mountain Zoo,* the *North Pole* and *Santa's Workshop,* the *Garden of the Gods* and *Cave of the Winds.* From Antonito, Colorado, to Chama, New Mexico, runs the *Cumbres & Toltec Scenic Railroad.*

HOTELS AND MOTELS. Price categories, for double occupancy, average: *Moderate* $21–34; *Inexpensive* $14–20. Colorado resorts charge more, especially in season.

ASPEN. *Moderate:* **Jerome Hotel.** Historic hostelry. Central.

BOULDER. *Moderate:* **University Inn.** 1632 Broadway. Small, pleasant.

COLORADO SPRINGS. *Moderate:* **Imperial 400.** At 714 N. Nevada. **Imperial 400.** 1231 S. Nevada. Modern, small chain motel with heated pool, basic necessities, cafe nearby.
Inexpensive: **Motel 6.** At exit 64, Interstate 25. Basic but great value.

CRIPPLE CREEK. *Moderate:* **Imperial.** Restored relic of 1891 gold rush. Open summer only.

DURANGO. *Expensive–Moderate:* **General Palmer House.** Gay '90s restored hotel.
Inexpensive: **Silver Spruce.** Comfortable motel.

VAIL. *Moderate:* **The Roost Lodge.** Popular with groups. On Frontage Road, 15 minutes from downtown.

DINING OUT. Price categories are: *Moderate* $6–9; *Inexpensive* $3–6. Drinks, tax, and tips not included.

ASPEN. *Moderate:* **Chart House.** Steak. Nice salad bar. Open all year.

BOULDER. *Moderate:* **Pizza Hut.** 3053 Arapahoe. Italian franchise food. *Inexpensive:* **Tico's.** Mexican and American.

CANON CITY. *Moderate:* **Merlino's Belvedere.** Locally popular Italian restaurant with bar.

COLORADO SPRINGS. *Moderate:* **Flying W Ranch Chuckwagon.** Famous suppers with show (summer only).

Piche's Stagecoach Inn. 702 Manitou Ave., in Manitou Springs. Chicken, prime rib, rainbow trout.

The Village Inn. 217 E. Pikes Peak Ave. Located in an old church, this restaurant serves good food. Cocktail lounge.

Inexpensive: **Mission Bell Inn.** Mexican.

IDAHO

Outdoor Adventures

Boise is the capital and largest city of Idaho. A flourishing agricultural, horticultural, and stock-raising region lies about the city, and rich mines abound in the surrounding mountains. It is also one of the most important wool-trade centers in the U.S.

Among the unique points of interest in Boise is the Basque dancing, a feature here because the state of Idaho still has more Basques than any place other than their homeland.

There is also the classical state capitol, historical Ft. Boise, and Julia Davis Park containing the Idaho Historical Museum, Boise Art Gallery, and Pioneer Village.

Coeur d'Alene's Lovely Lake

This particular drive ought to be made slowly, for there is enchantment every yard of the winding overlook. The lake is lovely to the point of disbelief. No lake in all the Northwest evokes such imagery, has such color range, seems so ethereal.

An excursion boat runs short trips daily from the city dock in summer. There are also 20-minute seaplane flights from 1st St. Dock.

Located at the lowest point in the state, 738-foot elevation, Lewiston is at the confluence of the Snake and Clearwater Rivers, and is flanked by steep hills. A trading center for the rich grainlands and fruit orchards, it is also Idaho's only "seaport."

There is much to see and do here. Potlatch Forests offers free tours. Luna House Museum, a pioneer residence, displays ancient Indian artifacts, and one of the more famous Western rodeos, the Lewiston Roundup, is held here the first weekend after Labor Day.

One of the outstanding riverboat trips in the West begins and ends in Lewiston. Tourist boats go up the Snake River, as far as 93 miles, to within 17 miles of Hells Canyon Dam. Shorter trips and cruises are also available. For information contact the Greater Lewiston Chamber of Commerce.

An Eastern Tour

An eastern tour of the state will take you to Gooding, the gateway to Mammoth Cave, Shoshone Ice Caves, Sun Valley, and Craters of the Moon; Thousand Springs, where waterfalls cascade down the glistening banks above the road; Twin Falls, south-central Idaho's largest city; and Shoshone Falls, a spectacle in the spring when the Snake takes a sheer 212-foot drop over the basaltic horseshoe rim nearly 1,000 feet wide.

If you continue eastward, you'll come to Pocatello, eastern Idaho's largest city, and Ft. Hall, agency headquarters for the Shoshone, Bannock, and other tribes of the Ft. Hall Indian Reservation. Two Sun Dances are held in July on the Ft. Hall Reservation, and in August, on the same reservation, there is the 4-day Shoshone-Bannock Indian Festival. All three include a buffalo feast. Palefaces admitted.

A World-Famous Resort

Long recognized as one of the world's famous winter resorts, Sun Valley has, for some years, also been popular as a summer playground. In addition to the usual ice skating, swimming, riding, tennis, and fishing, there are mind-shattering trips into the wilderness.

Beyond Sun Valley is Craters of the Moon National Monument. This utterly desolate 83-square-mile area is a fantastic, grotesque Dante's inferno of basaltic features. A seven-mile loop drive passes by some of the volcanic landscapes, while a variety of trails leads to others.

National Forests

Several words about Idaho's national forests: fascinating, unparalleled, fantastic, adventurous, and beautiful.

Eight national forests lie entirely within the boundaries of Idaho and seven others partly within, giving the state more than 20 million acres of National Forest lands.

Major forests include: *Boise,* the state's largest; *Caribou, Challis, Clearwater, Coeur d'Alene, Kaniksu, Nez Percé, Payette, Salmon, St. Joe National Forest,* and *Targhee.*

PRACTICAL INFORMATION FOR IDAHO

HOW TO GET THERE. *By air:* United serves Boise from Denver and Salt Lake City; *Republic* and *Pacific Express* serve Boise from Portland; *Cascade* serves Boise, Idaho Falls, Pocatello, Lewiston and Moscow; *Western* serves Boise from Salt Lake City; *Frontier* serves Boise from Portland and Denver. *Wien Air Alaska* serves Boise from Seattle. *By bus: Greyhound* or *Trailways. By train: Amtrak.*

TOURIST INFORMATION SERVICES. Best source: *Idaho Tourism,* Room 108, State House, Boise. For hunting and fishing information write: *Idaho Fish & Game Dept.,* P.O. Box 25, Boise, 83707.

 MUSEUMS AND GALLERIES. Historical: *Idaho State Historical Museum,* Boise; *Blaine County Historical Museum,* Hailey, contains an American Political Items Collection; *Luna House Museum,* Lewiston, displays Indian artifacts; *Pioneers Historical Museum,* Montpelier; *Bannock County Historical Museum,* Pocatello; *Lemhi County Historical Museum,* Salmon; and *Twin Falls County Historical Museum,* Twin Falls. Art: *Boise Gallery of Art* and *Herrett Arts and Science Center,* Twin Falls.

 HISTORIC SITES. Many of Idaho's historic sites parallel the trails of history through the state—the *Oregon Trail* in the south, *Lewis and Clark Route* in the north-central section, and *Mullan Road* in the panhandle. The visitor may retrace these famous routes on modern highways.

Other sites include the gold-mining ghost towns of Centerville, Placerville, and Pioneerville, and a replica of Ft. Hall, built in 1834, in Pocatello.

TOURS. *By boat:* Boat trips from Lewiston go into Hells Canyon. The adventurous can go down the Snake through Hells Canyon or down the Middle Fork of the Salmon, the "River of No Return," on float trips or jet-boat excursions. For detailed information write: *Idaho Outfitters and Guides Association.* P.O. Box 95, Boise, 83701.

 SUMMER SPORTS. Idaho is sheer heaven for the outdoor sportsman. *Fishing:* The fishing is good in all parts of Idaho. Record-size trout, steelhead, and sturgeon. *Boating:* The lakes, rivers, and streams provide water highways for small-boat operators. Special thrills are offered on the white-water trips down the Snake, Salmon, and Selway. *Hunting:* Small and big game, with the many miles of wilderness and forests providing a special opportunity for hunting big game.

WINTER SPORTS. In a word, skiing. For all information contact the *Idaho Tourism,* Room 108, State House, Boise.

SPECTATOR SPORTS. Rodeos are scheduled in Idaho throughout summer and fall. Motorcycle and drag races are held throughout the state and there is horse racing during the summer.

WHAT TO DO WITH THE CHILDREN. In a state abounding with lakes, streams, and trails, children will find activity nearly every time the family car pauses. In addition, there's the *miniature power station* in Trenner Memorial Park at American Falls, and the *Island Park Music Circus,* at Macks Inn, in Idaho's legendary *Mountain Man* country.

HOTELS AND MOTELS. Based on double occupancy, categories and price ranges are as follows: *Moderate* $20 –25; *Inexpensive* under $20.

BOISE. *Moderate:* **Cabana Inn.** Attractively furnished, close to downtown, charming management.
The Boisean. Two-room cottages, garden setting for swimming pool, relaxing atmosphere.
Travelers Motel. Airy, neat, restful.
Idanha Hotel. Modern and antique decor. Historic air (Senator Borah lived here).
Inexpensive: **Skyline.** Comfortable, lovely grounds. Genteel, rustic airiness.

COEUR D'ALENE *Moderate:* **Flamingo Hotel.** Small, with many conveniences. Friendly, concerned management.
Pines Motel. Another lodging where the latch string is out.
Inexpensive: **Motel 6.** Convenient, comfortable, clean.

IDAHO FALLS. *Moderate:* **Sundown Motel.** Medium-size, nice setting, charming ambiance.
Thrifty Lodge. Quiet, restful, informal.
Inexpensive: **Evergreen Motel.** Weekly rates. Play area for children. Truck parking. Cozy.

KETCHUM–SUN VALLEY. *Moderate:* **Wood River Motel.** Rustic log cabins, kitchenettes, quiet, close to lifts and town.
River Run Motel. Overlooks Sun Valley Ski runs. Informal atmosphere.

LEWISTON. *Moderate:* **El Rancho Motel.** Quiet, modest-size motel with heated pool.
Hollywood Inn. Heated pool and good view of Clearwater River.
Sacajawea Lodge. Large motel with variety of units.

POCATELLO. *Moderate:* **Bidwell Motel.** Medium-size motel across from Idaho State University. Campus atmosphere.
Idaho Motel. Across from Idaho State University. Insulated.
Oxbow Motor Inn. Two heated pools, pets allowed, kitchens.
Thunderbird Motel. Comfortable, heated pool, guest laundry.

SALMON. *Moderate:* **Suncrest Motel.** Some kitchen units; playground for youngsters; near cafe.

SANDPOINT. *Moderate:* **Sandpoint Inn.** Rural motif. Small, kitchens, sprightly.
Travelers Motel. Comfortable rooms; dining room and cocktail lounge. "Family" hospitality.

TWIN FALLS. *Moderate:* **Capri Motel.** Medium-size, utilitarian, feel-at-home place.
Deluxe Motor Lodge. Homey atmosphere; kitchens, playground.
Imperial "400" Motel. Medium-size, heated pool, comfortable.

Monterey Motor Inn. Quiet, medium-size, on spacious grounds; family units, heated pool; picnic and playground areas.
Twin Falls TraveLodge. Free coffee, two-story, heated pool.

WALLACE. *Moderate:* **Stardust Motel.** Downtown, medium-size, family units, ski-waxing room, free coffee.

WEISER. *Moderate:* **Colonial Motel.** Comfortable units; some kitchens; close to restaurant and coin laundry.

 DINING OUT. Restaurants are listed by categories. *Moderate* $5–10; *Inexpensive* under $5. Drinks, tax and tip are not included.

BOISE. *Moderate:* **The Boarding House.** Cuisine with a Basque flavor.
Kowloon Family Restaurant. Great Cantonese dining.
Pengilly's Saloon. Unusual lunches served in a unique turn-of-the-century atmosphere.

COEUR D'ALENE. *Moderate:* **North Shore Plaza Restaurants.** Lakeshore complex, with plush rooftop dining, casual atmosphere of Shore Restaurant, or chicken-to-go from Templin's.

IDAHO FALLS. *Moderate:* **Sizzler.** Family steak house with excellent salad bar. Children's menu.
Stardust Restaurant. Well patronized. Westbank Coffee Shop. Varied menu and exhilarating river view.

KETCHUM–SUN VALLEY. *Moderate:* **The Ore House.** On the mall. Informal, tasty. Eat in an alpine environment.
Warm Springs Ranch Restaurant. Outdoor dining with a mountain view.

LEWISTON. *Moderate:* **Cedars III.** Famous for juicy salad bar and hand-cut steaks.
Helm Restaurant. Mouth-watering prime ribs, steaks, and shrimp. Children's menu.

POCATELLO. *Moderate:* **Elmer's Pancake and Steak House.** Twenty-one varieties of pancakes. Located across from Idaho State University.

SANDPOINT. *Moderate:* **Garden Restaurant.** Outdoor dining; specialties range from fresh seafoods to roast duck and Oriental-style dishes.

TWIN FALLS. *Moderate:* **Depot Grill.** Smorgasbord in the Caboose Room. 55 different specialties. Children's prices.
Morgan's Rogerson Restaurant. Long-established restaurant for good food. Warm hospitality has a boarding-house nostalgia.

MONTANA

Yellowstone and Riches of the Earth

The Yellowstone River has been the dominant highway of the region for years. Generations of Montanans have looked to it for protection, direction, and a sometimes reliable drink for man, cow, or crop.

The Tongue River forks into the Yellowstone at Miles City, and just north of Miles City you can see the Fort Peck Dam and the Missouri River where Lewis and Clark first entered Montana.

Custer's Last Stand is the Montana incident most familiar to Americans, and at Custer Battlefield National Monument, 13 miles southeast of Hardin, a government museum tells the story of the ill-fated Yellow Hair, as the general was called.

Billings, northwest of the Custer Battlefield, is the largest city in Montana. Named for Frederick Billings, president of the Northern Pacific Railway that gave it life, Billings has sugarbeet and oil refineries, livestock yards, and two small colleges.

Among the Billings sights is the statue of the Range Rider of the Yellowstone, posed for by William S. Hart, cowboy hero of silent movies. This is along Black Otter Trail, which follows the rim above the city to the north. Five miles from Billings, a Pictograph Cave contains the most important scratchings of prehistoric man on the Great Plains.

From Billings, a breathtaking ride along the Beartooth Scenic Highway cuts through the western portion of Custer National Forest.

500

If you go west from Bozeman to Three Forks, you'll find the Missouri River Headquarters State Park, where three rivers meet: the Jefferson, the Madison, and the Gallatin. One of Montana's leading natural attractions, Lewis and Clark Caverns, is 13 miles beyond Three Forks. This is a safe, underground limestone cavern where guided tours operate daily.

Williamsburg of the West

Virginia City, a fully restored boom town, captures the feel of those post-Civil War gold rushes that first drew the hordes upriver and overland to the mountainous West. Because it was such a productive mining center—over $300 million in gold dust was found here from 1863 to 1937—the visitor will see more authentic details of the mining frontier than anywhere else in the West.

Butte and Helena

Butte was settled in 1864. First gold and then silver were discovered around Butte, but the big fortunes were made after 1870 in copper. From beneath these five square miles of bleak hilltop have come more than $17 billion in ores.

Today Butte is an industrial and distributing center, and an international Port of Entry. While you are there, be sure and see the Old Town and the Mining Museum.

Helena, the state capital, got its start when some discouraged miners took their "last chance" in 1864 on what is now the main street of the city—and made a strike. The area subsequently produced $20 million in gold. It is said that by 1888 Helena had fifty millionaires and was the richest city per capita in the country.

Today, the city has some large industry, but the main business is government, and the trappings of politics are the real attraction.

Sixteen miles north of Helena is the Gates of the Mountains, a 2,000-foot gorge in the Missouri River, named by Lewis. Also north of Helena is Great Falls, a large Montana industrial boom town and the state's second largest city.

Great Falls is historically famous as home base for cowboy artist Charlie Russell, and his work may be seen in his old studio cum gallery in the center of town. Another must-see in the Great Falls area are the falls themselves, and the nearby springs which flow at a rate of 388 million gallons daily.

Glacier National Park

There are still some 40 glaciers among the peaks and ridges of the 1,600 square miles of this great scenic area that adjoins a Canadian section to make up the Waterton-Glacier International Peace Park.

The park season runs from approximately June 15 to September 10, when most hotels and cabin camps are open. The main roads, however, may stay clear until mid-October, depending on the weather.

Most of Glacier Park is accessible only by its 1,000 miles of foot and horse trails; on-the-spot inquiry and attention to park regulations is essential—this is rugged country. When the road itself is closed, US 2 may be used to the south from Browning to West Glacier. Local inquiry is advisable if the weather looks threatening. And, under no circumstances, feed the bears.

Starting from Browning, you'll visit the Glacier Park Lodge at East Glacier on US 2. This hotel, like its sisters, Many Glacier Hotel and Lake McDonald Lodge, in West Glacier, offers a variety of riding, hiking, golf, and fishing (no license needed in the park). Be sure to inquire about guided tours and lectures offered by the National Park Service naturalists to increase your enjoyment of this alpine beauty spot.

From St. Mary you can also swing north to Waterton-Glacier International Peace Park in Canada, an extension of the mountain terrain you find on the American side. Also note on the north route the access road to Many Glacier Hotel on Swiftcurrent Lake; you leave the highway at Babb and drive a few miles west to what many consider the park's most varied center of activity. All recreation activities are available here, with trails to Grinnell Lake and Glacier. George Bird Grinnell, the naturalist, was instrumental in the establishment of the park.

On a quick tour, you'll want to see Two Medicine Valley and Lake. Turn west about four miles north of East Glacier on State 49. A seven-mile road leads to a lake (launch trips during the season) ringed by high peaks. There is a trail at Running Eagle, a safe, quick introduction to Glacier.

There's a good campground at St. Mary Lake and another at Rising Sun on the north shore highway. Four miles west of the latter at Sun Point there are self-guiding trails. The frontal range of the Rockies at this point is known as Lewis Range.

The most spectacular drive through Glacier is over the Continental Divide via the Going-to-the-Sun Road. From Browning and East Glacier, drive north on State 49 and 287 to St. Mary, and then turn westward for the 50-mile drive over Logan Pass to the west end of the park. If you are hauling a camper, and your rig is over thirty feet in length—including your car—you had better make arrangements to leave your camper and pick it up later. Park rules prohibit longer vehicles on this road: you will quickly realize why when you begin your climb.

From St. Mary Lake in the east to Lake McDonald in the west the highway crosses 6,664-ft. Logan Pass. It is a spectacular spot to stop and view the park, for from here you have 100-mile vistas. Ask about the trail to Granite Park Chalet (reservations required for overnight stays).

After Logan Pass, descend west along the Garden Wall, one of America's greatest mountain roads. Below at Avalanche Campground, there is an easy two-mile trail to Avalanche Basin, a natural amphitheater with walls two thousand feet high and waterfalls for a backdrop. The red cedars and the rushing streams give you a sense of what the park must be like deep in the interior if you haven't the time for longer hikes or rides.

Lake McDonald is ten miles long and a mile wide. Lake McDonald Lodge near the head of the lake on our highway is the center. There are public campgrounds here and at the foot of the lake at Apgar, as well as several classes of accommodations at both spots. The hike to

Sperry Glacier and Chalet is popular. Here, too, reservations are a must.

Accommodations and tourist services at Hungry Horse and Whitefish.

PRACTICAL INFORMATION FOR MONTANA

HOW TO GET THERE. *By air: Western, Frontier,* and *Northwest Orient. By train: Amtrak* serves northern Montana to Glacier National Park and Havre.

MUSEUMS AND GALLERIES. The *Montana Historical Museum & C. M. Russell Art Gallery,* Helena, presents a capsule history of Montana and a collection of C. M. Russell's art. *Charles M. Russell Original Studio and Museum,* Great Falls, exhibits Russell's works as well as his own collection of Indian costumes and gear. *J. K. Ralston Museum & Art Center,* Sidney, spotlights historical artifacts from the region and original Ralston paintings. The *Museum of the Rockies* in Bozeman contains exhibits that highlight the physical and social heritage of the Northern Rockies. *World Museum of Mining,* Butte, shows mining relics. *Range Riders Museum,* Miles City, highlights the days of the open range. *The Museum of the Plains Indians,* in Browning, is also worth visiting.

HISTORIC SITES. *Fort Union Trading Post National Historic Site,* 23 miles north of Sidney, is a fort built in 1828 by the American Fur Company. *Custer National Monument,* southeastern Montana, is the scene of the famous last stand. *Pompey's Pillar,* near the town of the same name, is a towering sandstone rock that was a Lewis and Clark Expedition landmark. *Montana Territorial Prison,* Deer Lodge, was the first of its kind in the Western U.S. It's now a museum. *Original Montana Governor's Mansion,* Helena, was built in 1885 and has housed nine governors since 1913. *St. Mary's Mission,* Stevensville, is the oldest church in the Pacific Northwest. *Virginia City,* southwest of Bozeman, is a restored pioneer mining boom town and political capital.

TOURS. *Glacier Park, Inc.* offers two- to six-day tours of Glacier National Park and Waterton Lakes National Park, Canada from May through September. For complete information write Glacier Park, Inc., East Glacier, Montana 59434.

DRINKING LAWS. Legal drinking age is 19 and bars are open until 2 A.M.

SUMMER SPORTS. *Fishing:* Almost every type of fish can be caught in Montana. The season usually starts in May and ends around Nov. 30. Local inquiry to the State Fish, Wildlife and Parks Dept. yield information about laws, and locations of the types of fish you want.

Hunting: Hunting licenses for nonresidents vary. A license entitles you to a variety of game, but the nonresident must put in for drawings, by regions, in order to get the appropriate tags. Applying in time does not insure you of your first-choice region. Most areas also require that you hunt with a resident who can double as guide.

Golfing: There are three dozen courses in Montana, in most principal cities.

Riding: At any of the many guest ranches. For an up-to-date list of riding ranches, contact the Montana Travel Promotion Bureau, Helena, Montana

59620. Also, the bigger towns have saddle clubs which can help you find riding facilities.

Rock hunting: Montana is a rockhound's paradise. The Travel Promotion Bureau has a special pamphlet about the subject.

Boating: Water-skiing and power-boating are common on the larger lakes and reservoirs. River-rafting is also popular.

WINTER SPORTS. *Skiing:* Write for a complete guide on skiing from the Travel Promotion Bureau, Helena, Mont. 59620. Major ski areas are as follows: *Big Sky,* located 45 miles from Bozeman, in the heart of the Gallatin Canyon; *Big Mountain Ski Area,* Whitefish, and *Red Lodge Mountain,* 65 miles southwest of Billings.

WHAT TO DO WITH THE CHILDREN. The opportunities to see animals in their natural habitats are excellent. Near Ronan, the *Ninepipe* and *Pablo National Wildlife Refuges* are particularly good spots to see waterfowl. At the *National Bison Range,* 300–500 head of buffalo roam over an 19,000-acre range. Maiden, Kendall, and Gilt Edge, all near Lewiston, are *ghost towns* left over from the mining days of the 19th century. Helena's *Frontier Town* is a replica of a pioneer village, hewn out of solid rock and cut from giant trees. Virginia City is a restored *gold boom town,* and the Nevada City Depot has a *railroad museum* with antique engines and cars. Glacier National Park is bear country—be sure to read a bear information folder.

HOTELS AND MOTELS. The price categories in this section, for double occupancy, will average as follows: *Moderate* $30–40; and *Inexpensive* $15–29. For additional information on Montana's hostelries and restaurants, call 1–800–548–3390.

BILLINGS. *Moderate:* **Rimrock Inn.** Near Airport. Western atmosphere.

BOZEMAN. *Moderate:* **Alpine Lodge.** Small budget motel.

BUTTE. *Moderate:* **Copper King Inn.** Close to airport. Indoor pools, sauna. **Mile Hi Motel.** Heated pool, restaurant adjacent.

GLACIER NATIONAL PARK. *Moderate:* **Rising Sun Motor Inn.** Restaurant, playground on lake.
Swift Current Motor Inn. On lake with camp store, resort activities.
Inexpensive: **Tamarack Lodge.** Flathead River float trip.

GREAT FALLS. *Moderate:* **Starlit Motel.** Heated pool.

HELENA. *Moderate:* **Park Plaza.** Elevator, restaurant, entertainment.
Super 8 Lodge. 56 rooms.
Inexpensive: **Motel 6.** Pool, 24-hr. café.

MISSOULA. *Moderate:* **Ponderosa Lodge.** Close to town and university.
Inexpensive: **Family Inn.** Caters to families.

VIRGINIA CITY. *Inexpensive:* **Fairweather Inn.** Old West décor.
Terrace Motel. Clean.

DINING OUT. Steak, prime ribs, and local game (in season) are the big favorites in this area. Restaurant price categories are for a complete dinner but do not include drinks, tax or tip; as follows: *Moderate* $9–14, and *Inexpensive* $4–8.

BILLINGS. *Moderate:* **Black Angus.** Steak.

BOZEMAN. *Moderate:* **Topper.** 1235 N. 7th. Good meats.

BUTTE. *Inexpensive:* **4 B's Restaurant.** Locally popular restaurant.

GLACIER NATIONAL PARK. *Moderate:* **Many Glacier.** Own baked goods.

GREAT FALLS. *Moderate:* **Black Angus Steak House.** Pleasant.
The Freight House. American food. Dancing.
Inexpensive: **Hong Kong Restaurant.** Oriental food reasonably priced.

HELENA. *Moderate:* **Jorgenson's.** Family-style food.
On Broadway. Italian.

MISSOULA. *Moderate:* **Ming's.** Chinese-style dinners.
Montana Mining Co. Beef, wine.

NEBRASKA

Westward Ho, the Wagons

Today's Nebraska was the pathway to the West in the pioneer days. It was the land where the buffalo roamed and the deer and the antelope played. It is the land where history was made and the future of the country was laid down in the tortuous travels of the wagon trains and the arduous construction of the Union Pacific Railroad.

You can relive those days today, and probably more inexpensively than on any other similar trip in the country. The Oregon Trail, the Mormon Trail, and the Pony Express route were traced across the southern part of the state, following the course of the Platte River. Interstate 80 keeps pretty much to this same pathway. The first transcontinental railroad, the U.P., was built along these trails. The first cross-country telegraph line also followed this route. And Lewis and Clark made their way up the state's eastern boundary, following the Missouri River as they explored the Louisiana Territory.

You can see, and almost feel, these dominant westward sweeps of our nation's progress in the well-preserved reminders of our pioneer past maintained throughout the state. There are the ruts of wagon wheels at Windlass Hill near Brule; the one-room sod house where a pioneer family lived at Paxton; the complete pioneer village at Minden. You can relive the Indian wars at Fort Robinson (Crawford), where the great leader, Crazy Horse, was slain, or at reconstructed Fort Kearny, near Kearney. Buffalo Bill Cody's ranch near North Platte is a must

506

for the Western buff. (The buffalo don't roam the plains any more, but there is a herd of them, along with a prarie dog town and other plains animals, at the Fort Niobrara National Wildlife Refuge near Valentine.) Scenic delights include Scotts Bluff National Monument, an 800-foot pioneer landmark; Chimney Rock, near Bridgeport; and the towering state capitol in Lincoln.

Omaha is the largest city and the home of the Joslyn Art Museum, considered the country's foremost center of early Western art and literature. The city is headquarters for the Strategic Air Command with its underground control system and the adjacent Strategic Aerospace Museum; for the Union Pacific, with its museum of pioneer railroading; and for world-famed Boys Town.

For idle moments or a trip destination there are more than 60 recreation areas, and dozens of man-made and hundreds of natural lakes teeming with fish. And most of this can be enjoyed at little expense—or even free.

PRACTICAL INFORMATION FOR NEBRASKA

FACTS AND FIGURES. Nebraska ranks 35th among the states, with a population of 1½ million. Omaha, the largest city, has a metropolitan population of 590,000; Lincoln, the capital city, 178,000; Grand Island, third city, 36,000. Principal industry, agriculture. Climate is marked by definite seasonal variations from hot summers to cold winters.

HOW TO GET THERE: *By air: Republic, Midway, United, Continental, Eastern, TWA, Frontier, Northwest, Ozark,* and six commuter airlines. *By train: Amtrak. By bus: Continental Trailways* and *Greyhound.*

TOURIST INFORMATION. Department of Economic Development, 301 Centennial Mall, Lincoln 68509. Game and Parks Commission, and Nebraskaland, 2200 North 33 St., Lincoln 68503. Douglas County Tourism Dept., Omaha/Douglas County Civic Center, Suite 1200, 1819 Farnam St., Omaha, NE 68183.

CAMPING OUT. More than 60 recreation areas plus other special-use and wayside sites. Larger campgrounds: *Bridgeport* (Bridgeport), *Branched Oak Lake* (Malcolm), *Fremont Lakes* (Fremont), *Lewis and Clark* (North of Crofton), *Two Rivers* (Venice), *Lake McConaughy* (Ogallala).

MUSEUMS AND ART GALLERIES. *Stuhr Museum of the Prairie Pioneer,* Grand Island; *Museum of the Fur Trade,* Chadron; *Hastings Museum* (Indian, wildlife exhibits), Hastings; *Joslyn Art Museum, Union Pacific Museum, Strategic Air Command Museum,* Omaha. At the University of Nebraska: Lincoln, *University of Nebraska State Museum, State Historical Society Museum, Sheldon Memorial Art Gallery and Sculpture Garden.*

HISTORIC SITES. *Agate Fossil Beds National Monument,* 9 mi. NW of Scottsbluff on US 26 to Mitchell, then 34 mi. N. on State 29, is an area where the fossils of animals alive 20 million years ago are concentrated. *John Brown's Cave,* in Nebraska City, was a major station of the famed "Underground Railroad." *Arbor Lodge State Historical Park,* Nebraska City, is Nebraska's oldest state historical park. *Fort Kearny State Historical Park,* 8 mi. SE of Kearney on State 10, re-creates the frontier outpost as it was a century ago. *Buffalo Bill Ranch State Historical Park,* at North Platte, was William F. Cody's ranch and winter quarters. *Homestead National Monument,* near Beatrice, is the site of the U.S.'s first homestead.

DRINKING LAWS. Liquor by the drink or bottle, 6 A.M. to 1 A.M. Beer and wine only on Sundays. Local option. Minimum drinking age, 20.

SUMMER SPORTS. *Fishing:* Game fish abundant— black bass, trout, northern pike, walleye, catfish. *Hunting:* Ring-neck pheasant is the prime target. There are seasons for other small game. Inquire: State Game and Park Commission, 2200 North 33 St., Lincoln 68503.

Boating, swimming, water skiing—large lakes formed behind dammed rivers provide plenty of water sports.

SPECTATOR SPORTS. *Rodeos* are held in many parts of the state during summer and fall. *Horse racing.* Parimutuel thoroughbred racing opens in Grand Island in late March, then to Ak-Sar-Ben in Omaha in May, to Lincoln in July, Columbus in September, and the season ends in South Sioux City in November. *Omaha Royals,* Class AAA baseball, in Omaha early April to early September. *College World Series,* in Omaha, early June.

WHAT TO DO WITH THE CHILDREN. In Lincoln, the Children's Zoo and the State Fair in early September. In Brownville, cruise the Missouri River on the *Belle of Brownville.* In Omaha, the Children's Museum, Puppet Museum, Henry Doorly Zoo, and Peony Amusement Park.

HOTELS AND MOTELS. The price categories for double occupancy will average: *Moderate* $25–30; *Inexpensive* under $25.

ALLIANCE. *Moderate:* Frontier Motel; Rainbow Lodge. *Inexpensive:* McCarroll's Motel; Super 8.

BEATRICE. *Moderate:* Holiday House; Holiday Villa Motel. *Inexpensive:* Super 8.

BELLEVUE. *Moderate:* Sandman Motel; Whitehouse Inn.

CHADRON. *Moderate:* Friendship Inn Grand Motel; Roundup Motel. *Inexpensive:* Super 8 Motel; Westerner Motel.

COLUMBUS: *Moderate:* Rosebud Motel; Gembol's Friendship Inn. *Inexpensive:* Royal Motel; Seven Knights Motel.

CRAWFORD. *Inexpensive:* Hilltop Motel; Town Line Motel.

FREMONT. *Moderate:* Modern Aire; Holiday Lodge; Lake Sunset Motel.

GOTHENBURG. *Inexpensive:* Smitty's Dun Rovin Inn; Western Motor Inn.

GRAND ISLAND. *Moderate:* Island Inn; Erin Rancho Motel.
Inexpensive: Conoco Motel; Regal 8 Inn; Super 8 Lodge; Lazy V Motel.

HASTINGS. *Moderate:* Grand Motel.
Inexpensive: Rainbow Motel; Redondo Motel; X-L Motel.

KEARNEY. *Moderate:* Hammer Motel; Western Inn South.
Inexpensive: Motel 8; Fort Kearney Inn; Pioneer Motel.

LEXINGTON. *Moderate:* Motel Royal; L R Ranch.
Inexpensive: Hollingsworth Motel; Toddle Inn.

LINCOLN. *Moderate:* Days Inn, 2410 N.W. 12 St.; Clayton House, 10th and O St.; Congress Inn, 2801 West O St.,; Great Plains Motel, 2732 O St.
Inexpensive: Motel 6, 3001 NW 12 St.; Buffalo Motel, 347 N. 48 St.

McCOOK. *Moderate:* Chief Motel; Royal Motel; Cedar Motel.

MINDEN. *Inexpensive:* Pioneer Motel.

NORFOLK. *Moderate:* Capri Motor Hotel; Sey-Crest Motel; Blue Ridge Motel; Best Western Villa Inn; Super 8; Skyline Motel.

NORTH PLATTE. *Moderate:* I-80 Inn; Best Western Chalet Lodge; Sands Motor Inn; Rambler Motel; TraveLodge; Sanford Lodge.
Inexpensive: Park Motel; Triangle Motel; Friendship Inn; Motel 6.

OGALLALA. *Moderate:* Lazy M Motel; Lee's I–80 Motel; Erin Plaza Motel.

OMAHA. *Moderate:* Ben Franklin Motel, I–80 & Highway 50; Best Western Shamrock, 120 & Dodge Sts.; Hiway House Motor Inn, I–80 & Highway 370; Imperial 400, 2211 Douglas St.; TraveLodge, 3902 Dodge St.
Inexpensive: Motel 6, 10708 M St.; Leisure Inn, 4815 L St.; Satellite Motel, 6006 L St.; Thrifty Scot, 7101 Grover.

SCOTTS BLUFF. *Moderate:* Capri Motel; Lamplighter Motel; Sands Motel.
Inexpensive: Park Motel; Coach House Motel; Overland Cabins.

SIDNEY. *Moderate:* El Palomino; Fort Sidney Motor Hotel.

SOUTH SIOUX CITY. *Moderate:* Midtown Motel; Park Plaza Friendship Inn.

VALENTINE. *Moderate:* Super 8; Fountain Inn; Ballard Motel.

YORK. *Moderate:* Camelot Inn; Palmer Inn.
Inexpensive: Buzz's Motel; Staehr Motel.

 DINING OUT. Price categories: *Moderate:* $5–10; *Inexpensive* below $5. Prices are for a complete meal but do not include drinks, tax or tip.

ALLIANCE. *Moderate:* Iron Horse; Grampy's; West Roads. Café.

COLUMBUS. *Moderate:* Wunderlich's Good Eatin' Kitchen. *Inexpensive:* DeFreece's; Valentino's; Stack 'n Steak.

GRAND ISLAND. *Moderate:* Dreisbach's; Atch's Grand Restaurant. *Inexpensive:* Bosselman and Eaton Café.

FREMONT. *Moderate:* Brestwoode Inn; Valentino's; The Prospector.

HASTINGS. *Moderate:* Bernardo's; Atch's; LoRayne's.

KEARNEY. *Moderate:* Grandpa's Steak House; Chef's Oven.

LEXINGTON. *Inexpensive:* Norm's Café.

LINCOLN. *Moderate:* Miller and Paine Tea Room; Bishop Buffet; Valentino's; Lee's Chicken; Tony & Luigi's; The Rose; Peking Garden.

McCOOK. *Moderate:* Chief Restaurant. *Inexpensive:* Midwest Café.

NEBRASKA CITY. *Moderate:* Embers. *Inexpensive:* Ulbrick's.

NORFOLK. *Moderate:* Villa Inn; Brass Lantern. *Inexpensive:* Sirlion Stockade; Valentino's.

NORTH PLATTE. *Moderate:* Talk of the Town. *Inexpensive:* Valentino's; Farm Fare; Bonanza.

OGALLALA. *Moderate:* La Paloma; Hoke's Café; Stagecoach.

OMAHA. *Moderate:* Kenny's; Bishop Cafeterias; Mr. C's; Jack & Mary's Cliff House; Bohemian Cafe; House of Genji; House of Cathay; Valentino's; Dugger's; Gorat's Steak House; La Fonda de Acebo; Golden Apple; Jerico's.

O'NEILL. *Moderate:* Town House.

SCOTTSBLUFF. *Moderate:* The Loft; Gaslight. *Inexpensive:* Sirloin Stockade; The Woodshed.

WAHOO. *Moderate:* Fairview Café.

WAYNE. *Moderate:* Black Knight Steak House.

WEST POINT. *Inexpensive:* L & M Café; Scharpen's Café.

NORTH DAKOTA

Roughrider Country

North Dakota is known as Roughrider Country because of the horseback antics of Teddy Roosevelt, the state's well-remembered "temporary" resident.

Fargo is the main portal to this broad plainsland, via I-94. It is the state's largest city, with a population of more than 60,000, almost twice that of its sister city of Moorhead, Minnesota, just across the Red River. It was named for William G. Fargo of the Wells Fargo Company, and features the 2,100-acre campus of North Dakota State University.

West on I-94 is Jamestown, site of the popular Jamestown Dam Recreation Area with its 14-mile lake. Upstream thirty miles, the Arrowwood National Wildlife Refuge is a nesting and feeding ground for migratory birds and various kinds of wildlife. Twice a year the skies over Jamestown are almost blackened by millions of migrating ducks and geese. To the southwest, Gackle is known as the "Mallard Capital of the World."

The West truly begins at Bismarck, where the skyscraper state capitol rises 18 stories above the prairies. Across the Missouri River is Mandan, and five miles to the south is Fort Abraham Lincoln from which Lt. Col. George A. Custer and the Seventh Cavalry began their ill-fated trek to disaster at Little Big Horn.

Northwest of Bismarck, Garrison Dam on the Missouri River creates 200-mile-long Lake Sakakawea, a versatile recreation area. Once quiet prairies now bustle with oil and lignite coal production. The Little Missouri River, which flows northward through much of the state's western extremity, has sculpted the spectacular North Dakota Badlands in Custer National Forest.

Theodore Roosevelt National Park

The stark, shadowy Badlands pockmark the plains where Teddy Roosevelt set up as a ranchman in 1883, branding his stock with the sign of the Maltese cross. For 15 years he stuck with the difficulties and disasters of raising cattle through the killing winters of this land that only the doughty bison could survive with any certainty. Finally, before going to Cuba with his famed Rough Riders, he ended his operation here, but he always kept a strong affection for this bleak country. Today a visitors' center recalls TR's life, and hiking and motor trails lead through the isolated grasslands where a herd of bison again has possession of its domain.

There are two major units to the Park: the South unit whose attractions include prairie dog towns, nature trails, columnar junipers and a variety of wildlife; and the North unit, 65 mi. N on US 85, which offers a majestic view of a more rugged section of the Badlands. A third unit, Teddy Roosevelt's Elkhorn Ranch site on the Little Missouri River north of Medora, is accessible only over rough dirt roads. Consult Park Headquarters in Medora before setting out.

Medora itself is now a rebuilt cowtown at the entrance of the South unit. It was founded originally by the fabled Marquis de Mores, a Frenchman who established a short-lived cattle dynasty there in the 1880's. The restored Chateau de Mores is a special attraction.

Elsewhere in the State

North of Fargo lies Grand Forks, on the northward-flowing Red River, and home of one of the state's two universities. Site of a major Air Force base, the city is also near one of the nation's most important missile complexes.

Westward along the Canadian border is the International Peace Garden, a series of landscaped gardens in both Canada and the US, surrounded by 2,000 acres of park. The Garden celebrates what both nations like to call "the longest undefended border in the world."

About one hour south by car is the exact geographical center of North America, at Rugby, on US Highway 2. A monument marks the spot.

Strasburg, in Emmons County, is the birthplace of Lawrence Welk, and Wimbledon, northeast of Jamestown, is the hometown of singer Peggy Lee. Louis L'Amour, the prolific writer of Western stories, spent his early years in the Jamestown area.

PRACTICAL INFORMATION FOR
NORTH DAKOTA

HOW TO GET THERE. *By air: Northwest, Republic,* and *Frontier* airlines fly into North Dakota.

By train: Amtrak passenger service is available from Minneapolis in the east and from Billings and Havre in the west.

By bus: Greyhound, Continental, and *Interstate Transportation Co.* are the major interstate carriers in North Dakota.

By car: I–94 and US 2 provide access to the state from Minnesota in the east and from Montana in the west. US 85, 83, 281 and 81 reach the state from South Dakota in the south. I–29 and US 281 are major routes to and from Manitoba.

TOURIST INFORMATION. The North Dakota Tourism Promotion Division, Economic Development Commission, Bismarck 58505, provides a brochure and other material of interest to the visitor. A national WATS line is available: 1–800–437–2077.

MUSEUMS AND GALLERIES. Historical: *Bismarck —Heritage Center,* on the capitol grounds; The *Camp Hancock Museum; Medora—De Mores Interpretive Museum.* Art: *Grand Forks—University Art Gallery.* U. of North Dakota. *Medora—Gallery of Western Art.*

HISTORIC SITES. Many sites and remnants of forts remain from the Indian wars. Custer commanded the 7th Cavalry at *Fort Lincoln,* near Mandan. Sitting Bull surrendered at *Fort Buford,* 5 mi. west of Williston. In the same vicinity is *Fort Union,* once the largest fur-trading post on the Missouri River. The Fort Mandan Historic Site overlooks the site of the *Lewis and Clark winter camp.*

The *Whitestone Battlefield Historic Site,* near Ellendale, was the site of the largest major battle between U. S. troops and Sioux Indians east of the Missouri River.

DRINKING LAWS. Liquor can be purchased by the drink at bars and by the bottle at liquor stores from 8:00 A.M. to 1:00 P.M..

TOURS. *Theodore Roosevelt National Park,* located in the western North Dakota Badlands, has a 49-mile circle drive through spectacular scenery in both North and South units.

The *Lewis and Clark Trail* parallels Lewis and Clark's famous Missouri River expedition.

STATE PARKS. North Dakota boasts nine year-round and five seasonal state parks. Annual or one-day permits are required for camping; permits may be obtained at the parks.

SPORTS. *Fishing:* Major year-round sport. Many species available. Huge Lake Sakakawea behind Garrison Dam is especially productive. *Hunting:* Whitetail deer throughout state; mule deer in west, antelope in southwest. One of the best duck areas in the country. *Golf:* Challenging courses at or near all major cities. Sand greens in west. *Skiing:* There are six areas scattered throughout the state. Cross-country skiing is booming.

SPECTATOR SPORTS. *Rodeo* is a big event here, and many towns sponsor one or more throughout the year. *Curling:* The National Curling Finals are held annually in Grand Forks. *Auto racing:* Stock car racing takes place at the Grand Forks Speedway from mid-May to mid-Sept.

WHAT TO DO WITH THE CHILDREN. In Bismarck, the *Sertoma Riverside Park* is located near the Missouri River. Next to the Park is the *Dakota Zoo*, with over 100 species of native animals. Jamestown features the world's largest buffalo (in concrete and steel) and *Frontier Fort* for the children. In Minot, the *Roosevelt Park and Zoo* includes not only many animals but an amusement park.

HOTELS AND MOTELS The price categories in this section have an *Inexpensive* to *Moderate* range of from $16–30 for double occupancy. The economy-minded traveler should be on the lookout for new "budget motels" which are appearing at small towns and intersections along the Interstates.

BISMARCK. *Moderate:* **Bismarck Motor Hotel.** Medium-sized, family rates.
Fleck House Motel. Downtown, large, attractive.
Colonial. Medium-size; heated pool.

BOTTINEAU. *Moderate:* **Norway House.** Viking motif; comfortable.

DEVILS LAKE. *Moderate:* **Artclare.** With lounge and restaurant.

DUNSEITH. *Moderate:* **Dale's Motel.** Near International Peace Garden.

FARGO. *Moderate:* **Doublewood Inn.** En route to West Fargo and popular Bonanzaville.
Oak Manor. For the family. Pets allowed.

GRAND FORKS. *Moderate:* **North Star Inn.** Attractive; excellent restaurant.
Plainsman Motel. Medium-size.

JAMESTOWN. *Moderate:* **Tumbleweed.** Restaurant and lounge.
Inexpensive: **Jamestown.** Medium-size; 24-hour café nearby.

MEDORA. *Moderate:* **Badlands Motel.** In unique Badlands town.

MINOT. *Moderate:* **Sandman.** Opposite city golf course.

VALLEY CITY. *Moderate:* **Midtown Motel.** Comfortable, near site of gigantic Winter Agricultural Show.

DINING OUT. Restaurant price categories are as follows: *Moderate* $4–7; and *Inexpensive* under $4. Not included are drinks, tax and tip. There are also numerous fast-food franchises throughout the state.

BISMARCK. *Moderate:* **Kroll's Kitchen.** Family dining treat.
The Wood House Restaurant. Interesting decor.

BOWMAN. *Moderate:* **Gene's Restaurant.** Highly rated in its price range.

DEVILS LAKE. *Moderate:* **The Ranch.** In remodeled barn.

DICKINSON. *Moderate:* **Jack's Family Restaurant.** Homemade soups and pastries a specialty.

DRAYTON. *Moderate:* **The Spinning Wheel Restaurant.** Steaks a specialty.

FARGO. *Moderate:* **Embers.** Featuring North Dakota steaks.
Haugen's. Old-fashioned ice cream parlor and family restaurant.

GRAND FORKS. *Moderate:* **The Bronze Boot.** Features steaks, chops, Chinese food.
La Campana. Mexican dishes in appropriate setting.

JAMESTOWN. *Moderate:* **Chuckwagon Restaurant.** Near the "world's largest buffalo."

MANDAN. *Moderate:* **Gourmet House.** Charming, widely known. Across Missouri River from Bismarck.

MINOT. *Moderate:* **The Roll'n Pin.** Family dining. Large breakfast menu.
El Tios Mexican Restaurant. American entrees also available.

RUGBY. *Moderate.* **Cornerstone Café.** Family fare, near center of North America monument.

WEST FARGO. *Moderate:* **The Brothers Deli.** Soup and sandwich specialties.

WILLISTON. *Moderate:* **Bavarian Inn.** German-American restaurant and lounge, in oil, lignite coal region.
Red Fox Restaurant. Family dining, full menu.

SOUTH DAKOTA

Black Hills, Badlands and Prairies

South Dakota is unique among the 50 states in its capacity to test the timbre and temperament of those who have called it home. It has been dubbed a "land of savage extremes," with temperatures ranging from 40 degrees below zero to 116 or more above. That is why the nickname *The Challenge State* is so appropriate and inspiring. It describes and dramatizes the continuing struggle for an unshackled life by Indians, homesteaders, farmers, and entrepreneurs who have pitted themselves against nature on the prairie arena. The state is 16th among the 50 in size, 45th in population, first in the production of gold, and its people are noted for their longevity.

The major geographical features are the broad prairies, the Black Hills, the Badlands, and the Missouri River. Of the four, the historic stream undoubtedly has had the greatest effect on the most citizens over the longest period of time. Today the dam-harnessed river divides the state into two distinct sections, geographically and philosophically.

Sioux Falls, the largest city, is the bustling home of more than 80,000 residents on the eastern border. Yankton, in the southeastern corner, is called the Mother City of the Dakotas and is near Gavins Point Dam, southernmost of the four barriers on the Missouri which create the Great Lakes of South Dakota. South Dakota State University at Brookings specializes in agriculture, engineering, and sciences. The University of South Dakota at Vermillion features law, medicine, and liberal arts. Mitchell is the site of the "world's only" Corn Palace; and Wall, near the Badlands, boasts one of the world's most unusual drugstores. Pierre (pronounced "Peer") is the state capital and is in the middle of ranching country on the Missouri. De Smet in Kingsbury County is Laura Ingalls Wilder's famed "Little Town on the Prairie."

The Badlands

From the city to the Badlands is an incredible contrast. The latter are reached by turning south off I–90 on SD 240, just eighteen miles west of Kadoka. The headquarters are at Cedar Pass, nine miles southwest, where exhibits and audio-visual programs illustrate this fantastic area of wind- and water-eroded rocks. Millions of years ago, this jagged and desolate area was a flat grassland and the home of prehistoric beasts such as saber-toothed tigers and hairy mammoths. Then the earth's crust rose and volcanic ash drifted down. Rivers carved gorges, and the winds of thousands of centuries slowly wore away the softer rock and left sharp spires, rounded cones, and grotesque designs. The Badlands are a rich fossil bed, but it is illegal to remove specimens. Picture-taking, however, will provide a thrill almost equal to the finding of a tiger bone. Subtle colors, especially striking in early morning and late afternoon, are difficult to capture but are worth many hours of trying. As for the fossils, they can be seen under plexiglass along the fossil trail.

The Black Hills

The fabled Black Hills—so named because of the ebon hue created by thick growths of various coniferous trees—are entered from Rapid City, rebuilt following a tragic flood in 1972 which claimed 238 lives. The city's growth was stimulated during World War II by the establishment of Ellsworth Air Force Base on the flatlands to the east. The Dahl Arts Center, near mid-city, is noted for its 200-foot mural of U.S. progress. The Chapel in the Hills is a replica of Norway's eight-centuries-old nail-less Stavkirke.

The Black Hills National Forest consists of nearly 1¼ million acres, featuring towering spires, magnificent forests, and dramatic scenery. Harney Peak, at 7,242 feet, is the highest mountain. A whole spectrum of year-round recreational activities is available. The two-hour 1880 train ride from Hill City to Keystone is a special treat. So is a drive on the spectacular Needles Highway.

In 1876 the region was populated virtually overnight after the Custer Expedition revealed the discovery of gold. Today, after more than a century of operation, the Homestake Mine in Lead (pronounced "Leed") still produces more gold than any mine in the Western Hemisphere. Tours are conducted, but only on the surface. Just four miles away the historic "naughty" city of Deadwood features Mount Moriah Cemetery where Wild Bill Hickok and Calamity Jane are buried.

Mount Rushmore, about 25 miles southwest of Rapid City on US 16, is the area's leading man-made attraction. Carved into the granite face of the mountain is the "Shrine of Democracy," 70-foot-high likenesses of Washington, Jefferson, Lincoln, and Theodore Roosevelt.

This masterpiece of sculptor Gutzon Borglum is a "must" stop for everyone, especially on the first trip to the Hills.

South of Mount Rushmore is Custer State Park, where one of the largest buffalo herds in the country can be viewed. The Game Lodge, once President Coolidge's Summer White House, is also located in the park. West of Custer, Jewel Cave National Monument is a 1,300-acre area covered with ponderosa pine and wildflowers. Jewel Cave itself consists of a series of subterranean chambers and limestone galleries whose calcite crystals produce unusual effects. Guided tours and picnicking facilities are available.

Spearfish, home of the internationally famous Passion Play, is the logical place of departure from the Black Hills going north or west. Hot Springs, which features the largest indoor natural warm-water pool in the world, is the southern exit. North of the historic spa city is Wind Cave National Park, where rangers conduct safe tours of the vast underground caverns, seven miles of which have been explored. Above ground, buffalo, deer, antelope, and prairie dogs inhabit the park.

Other South Dakota Attractions

Custer National Forest is north of the Black Hills and extends into Montana. This vast expanse of rolling hills and grasslands offers camping areas, picnic facilities, and hiking trails.

Bear Butte State Park, northeast of Sturgis, is dominated by a huge volcanic bubble which rises abruptly 1,400 feet above the plains. Indians still regard it as a religious shrine.

Fort Sisseton State Park, in the lake region of the northeastern corner of the state, is the site of an excellent example of a stone frontier military installation built in 1864.

North of Sioux Falls, near Garretson, is the Earth Resources Observation Systems project (EROS), a data center for recording and disseminating information received from orbiting satellites.

Huron is the home of the South Dakota State Fair and is in the center of the pheasant hunting country.

PRACTICAL INFORMATION FOR

SOUTH DAKOTA

HOW TO GET THERE. *By air:* Service to South Dakota is limited beyond Sioux Falls, Pierre, and Rapid City. Check current scheduling for carrier availability to other locales.

By bus: Greyhound, *Continental Trailways, Jack Rabbit Lines,* and *Midwest Coaches* provide the bulk of the passenger service into the state, serving Sioux Falls, Aberdeen, Rapid City, Pierre, and other towns.

By car: I–90 enters South Dakota from Minnesota in the east and from Wyoming in the west. I–29 is the principal access from Nebraska and Iowa in the south and North Dakota in the north.

TOURIST INFORMATION. Free travel information and leaflets are available from the South Dakota Division of Tourism, Pierre 57501, which also has a national WATS line: 1–800–843–1930.

MUSEUMS AND GALLERIES. The *Museum of Geology* in O'Harra Memorial Building on the campus of South Dakota School of Mines and Technology, in Rapid City, has excellent exhibits of rocks and minerals from the Black Hills and fossils from the Badlands.

Prairie Village, at Madison, is a "living museum" which features turn-of-the-century buildings and pioneer activities.

The *Robinson Museum* opposite the State Capitol in Pierre has pioneer, Indian and historic exhibits and houses the *South Dakota State Historical Society,* a repository for genealogical study.

Shrine to Music, Vermillion, contains the nationally renowned Arne B. Larson collection of antique and foreign musical instruments.

South Dakota Memorial Art Center, in Brookings, features a collection of Harvey Dunn paintings. The major collection of paintings by the Sioux artist, Oscar Howe, is at the *W. H. Over Dakota Museum* in Vermillion.

Not to be overlooked are the *Blue Cloud Abbey Museum,* Marvin; *Buechel Memorial Lakota Museum,* St. Francis; *Pettigrew Museum,* Sioux Falls; *Agricultural Heritage Museum,* Brookings; *Museum of Pioneer Life,* Mitchell.

HISTORIC SITES. *Mount Rushmore* is a most impressive sight, by day or by night. Meanwhile, at *Thunderhead Mountain,* 5 mi. N of Custer off US 16, 385, the family of Korczak Ziolkowski carries on the late sculptor's dream of carving the world's largest statue. It will depict the fabled Sioux chief, Crazy Horse, astride an enormous steed.

The *Sitting Bull Monument,* on a hill near Mobridge overlooking the Missouri River, marks the controversial burial site of the famous Sioux medicine man.

The *Dells of the Sioux* near Dell Rapids feature craggy formations of red rock known locally as "Sioux Falls granite."

TOURS. *Gray Line, Stagecoach West,* and *Jack Rabbit* offer a varied program of tours of the Black Hills and Badlands, including the Passion Play. Free pickup and return service to hotels and motels is available. *Golden Circle Tours* visit points of interest in the southern Black Hills, including an evening schedule to the lighting program at Rushmore, an inspirational treat.

DRINKING LAWS. Liquor may be purchased both by the bottle (in stores) and by the drink. Liquor may be sold in stores from Mon. to Sat., 7:00 A.M. to midnight; by the drink to 2:00 A.M.; Sun. 1:00 to 10:00 P.M., subject to local option. Legal drinking age is 18 for beer, 21 for all other alcoholic beverages.

SUMMER SPORTS. *Fishing:* The four huge lakes created by damming the Missouri River have made South Dakota one of the finest sport-fishing areas for walleye. The reservoirs and streams of the Black Hills offer excellent trout fishing, and there are many largemouth bass in stock ponds across the state. *Hunting:* Many consider South Dakota the Pheasant Capital of the World; and grouse, prairie chicken, quail and partridge are plentiful. *Boating and waterskiing:* The same four reservoirs on the Missouri which offer exciting fishing provide ample space for boating and skiing. *Golf:* There are numerous courses, although many are 9-hole, and some still have sand greens. *Gold-panning* and *rock-collecting* are other interesting Black Hills diversions.

WINTER SPORTS. *Skiing:* Best known of South Dakota's ski areas is Terry Peak in the Black Hills, whose 1,200-foot vertical drop from over 7,000 feet makes it the highest ski area west of the Rockies. Facilities include chair lifts and cross-country trails. Other areas include Great Bear Ski Valley near Sioux Falls, Deer Mountain Ski Area near Lead, and Inkpa-du-ta near Big Stone City. Ski season generally runs from Thanksgiving to April. Snowmobiling and cross-country skiing are popular statewide.

SPECTATOR SPORTS. *Horse racing:* Park Jefferson in Jefferson offers parimutuel racing from June to Sept. *Greyhound racing:* The Black Hills track at Rapid City and Sodrac Park in N. Sioux City have races from June to Sept. *Drag racing:* Thunder Valley Dragway at Marion.

WHAT TO DO WITH THE CHILDREN. Sioux Falls is a good place to bring children because the small but excellent *Great Plains Zoo* is next to *Dennis the Menace Park.* A short drive leads to *Terrace Park,* where children may fish in a stocked lake. In Rapid City, *Dinosaur Park* on Skyline Dr. has life-size models of prehistoric dinosaurs; eons ago these beasts romped on this spot. At Aberdeen is the fabled *Land of Oz.*

At *Reptile Gardens,* 6 mi. S. of Rapid City on US 16, children may view an extensive reptile collection which includes an underground snake den. There are performing animals, and children may ride giant tortoises. *Story Book Island* is a fairyland park in Rapid City where nursery rhymes come to life. Animals are erected in gigantic living color especially for children's enjoyment.

HOTELS AND MOTELS in South Dakota, because they are generally smaller then those in the east or west, offer a homey, friendly atmosphere. A tip: When traveling the sparsely populated interior, make advance reservations. Out-of-season rates are usually available in the Black Hills region.

The price categories in this section have an *Inexpensive* to *Moderate* range of from $16–30 for double occupancy.

ABERDEEN. *Moderate:* **Avalon Motel.** Near shopping centers, airport. **Riverview Motel.** Well kept; convenient location.

BROOKINGS. *Moderate:* **Wayside Motel.** Accessible to South Dakota State University.

CUSTER. *Moderate:* **Rocket Motel.** Comfortable accommodations. **Valley Motel.** Western atmosphere; near hunting and fishing.

DEADWOOD. *Moderate:* **Franklin Hotel & Motel.** Historic facility on "gold rush" main street.

KADOKA. *Moderate.* **Budget Host Cuckleburr.** Near entrance to Badlands.

KEYSTONE. *Moderate.* **Miners Motel.** Minutes away from Mt. Rushmore and other attractions.

MITCHELL. *Moderate:* **Lawler Motor Inn.** Near world's only Corn Palace.

MOBRIDGE. *Moderate:* **Wrangler.** Overlooking Lake Oahe.

PIERRE. *Moderate:* **Fawn Motel.** Accessible to Lake Oahe and walleye fishing.

State. Very pleasant, not far from state capitol.

RAPID CITY. *Moderate:* **Plaza Motel.** Municipal pool, parks, golf nearby.

Tip-Top Motor Hotel. Center of town location.

SIOUX FALLS. *Moderate:* **Lindendale Motel.** Country setting on edge of city.

Town House. Downtown, convenient.

SPEARFISH. *Moderate:* **Downtown McColley.** Highly rated; convenient.

Hilltop Motel. Near Passion Play amphitheater.

VERMILLION. *Moderate:* **Lamplighter.** Very nice accommodations. Near university.

YANKTON. *Moderate:* **Flamming Court.** Accessible to historic and recreational attractions.

Skyline Motel. Lounge and cafe. Near shopping mall.

(Larger cities and towns now have a number of economy motels such as Super 8, Econotel, Thrifty Scot, etc. Check locally.)

 DINING OUT. The number of tourists visiting South Dakota has increased dramatically in recent years, and as a result many of the newer restaurants have been built in conjunction with the motels intended to accommodate this influx of visitors. But there remain a number of restaurants, not associated with any lodging establishments, which serve good, moderately priced food.

Restaurant price categories are as follows: *Moderate* $4–7; and *Inexpensive* $3–4. These prices usually are for salad bar or soup, entrée, and dessert. Not included are drinks, tax, and tips.

ABERDEEN. *Moderate:* **Centurion Restaurant.** Family dining, extra-large salad bar.

CHAMBERLAIN. *Moderate:* **Al's Oasis.** Buffalo burgers a specialty.

CUSTER. *Moderate:* **Skyway Café.** Well recommended, on Main St.

HILL CITY. *Moderate:* **Chute Roosters.** Old barn, a dining treat.

KEYSTONE. *Moderate:* **Buffalo Room.** View of the Mt. Rushmore Memorial.

MURDO. *Moderate:* **Star.** Wholesome food, steak the specialty.

PIERRE. *Moderate:* **Kings Inn.** Walleye a house specialty.

Inexpensive: **State Capitol Cafeteria.** In basement of statehouse building.

RAPID CITY. *Moderate:* **Chuck Wagon.** Western décor, fun for children.

Tally's. In historic downtown Rapid City.

Sacora Station. Old railroad décor. Exit 46 or 48 for I–90 at Piedmont.

Westwood. Attractive, modern; beef specialties.

SIOUX FALLS. *Moderate:* **Minerva's Corner Creperie.** Specialties are Brittany crepes.
Stockyards Café. Eat well with ranchers and truckers here.
Wilson's Town 'n Country. A variety of home-cooked foods.

SPEARFISH. *Moderate:* **Latchstring Inn.** In beautiful Spearfish Canyon.

SPRINGFIELD. *Moderate:* **Sandbar Marina.** Fish specialties, on scenic Lewis & Clark Lake backwater.

VERMILLION. *Moderate:* **The Prairie.** Broad general menu, near university campus.

WALL. *Moderate:* **Wall Drug Store.** Varied fare in unusual setting. Still 5¢ coffee.

YANKTON. *Moderate:* **Captain Norm's.** Catfish featured; near federal aquarium and Gavins Point Dam.
JoDean's Steak House. Large South Dakota steaks a specialty.

UTAH

Salt Lake City and Magnificent Vistas

Salt Lake City serves three essential functions. First, and eternally foremost, it is the headquarters—the Mecca, the Vatican, the Jerusalem—of an international religion: the three-million-member Church of Jesus Christ of Latter-day Saints. Next, but not necessarily in that order, it is Utah's economic drive wheel. Finally, it is the state's capital city. From any approach to Salt Lake City, the setting is impressive.

Temple Square

Salt Lake City's greatest single attraction for visitors is the Temple Square area, the sacred ground of Mormonism. Here, on two 10-acre blocks flanking Main Street, in the middle of town, are the central religious shrines of Latter-day Saint worship. The Temple block, on the west, is surrounded by a 15-foot-high masonry wall. On the grounds stand the Temple, Tabernacle, Assembly Hall and Visitors Center. Visitors are welcome in all these buildings except the Temple, which is for sacred rites, such as marriages and devotional chores, known as "temple work," done by church members in good standing.

The Tabernacle houses the famous Temple Square pipe organ and hosts the Sunday concerts performed by the Mormon Tabernacle Choir. This is an elongated structure with rounded ends that resembles a grounded dirigible. The choir, 375 mixed voices, was organized in the early 1850s and can be heard during its Thursday evening rehearsals as well as on Sundays, when the formal program is presented in its entirety.

Overwhelming everything in Temple Square is the Temple itself. Although there are seven other LDS temples in Utah, the Salt Lake City Temple has a majesty and singularity about it denied the others. Its architectural style is imprecise. Some have called it "Mormon Gothic." In appearance it is not unlike Europe's medieval cathedrals, yet it departs from that design, too. In any case, the building was dedicated in 1893, exactly 40 years to the day after ground was broken for the foundation. Granite for its 167-foot-high walls was quarried from the nearby mountains and first dragged by oxen and mules to the building site. Later, rails were used for transportation. At each end of the 163-foot-long, 100-foot-wide edifice rise three spire-tipped towers, the highest, 204 feet in the air, centered above the east facade. Balanced on that point is a gilded statue of the angel Moroni, heralding toward the east with a long-stemmed trumpet. According to Joseph Smith, it was Moroni (pronounced Morown-eye) who led him to the golden plates engraved with hieroglyphics described as "Reformed Egyptian." Smith testified that with heavenly aid he was allowed to translate the record into English. Two years of laborious writing became the Book of Mormon. By 1830, Smith had six followers and the beginning of the Church of Jesus Christ, which eventually lengthened into the Church of Jesus Christ of Latter-day Saints.

Skiing around Salt Lake City

Skiing is the area's chief winter pastime. East from the city, up two adjacent canyons, are four ski areas that rival any in the U.S. for snow depth and consistency. Salt Lake City residents have been skiing at Park City, on the east side of the mountains, for the last several years. Originally a mining town, Park City made a comeback from "ghost" status when its recreational potential was discovered. Downtown Park City has retained much of its old mining character. As a "Gentile" town, Park City differs markedly from other Utah communities. Its streets are two-lane and its past is charred by horrendous fires that repeatedly leveled homes, stores, bars, churches and schools. Most of the mine owners, who took their riches from hills around Park City, lived in Salt Lake City. Deer Valley, on the east flank of Park City, is Utah's newest, most elegant ski area.

The four ski areas nearest Salt Lake City are Brighton Ski Bowl and Solitude, located in Big Cottonwood Canyon, and Alta and Snowbird, in Little Cottonwood Canyon. All offer excellent skiing conditions and facilities for the beginner and advanced skier, and reach altitudes from 8,500 to 10,000 feet.

Skiing season usually begins mid-Nov. and ends mid-May, depending on the weather. Generally, Utah's downhill skiing is priced low, compared to most Western States resorts. Park City and Snowbird are the exceptions. Both are fully tourist-oriented and lift-ticket prices are scaled accordingly.

PRACTICAL INFORMATION FOR

SALT LAKE CITY

HOW TO GET THERE. *By car:* I–80, probably the most heavily traveled transcontinental highway, passes through Salt Lake City. From the north I–80N runs southeast through Salt Lake from Portland, Oregon. I–15 comes from the Los Angeles area through Cedar City, Utah, and up to Salt Lake.

By air: Salt Lake City is the major terminal. Among the long-distance carriers serving it are *Frontier, Delta, American, United,* and *Western.*

By train: Amtrak's *Rio Grande Zephyr* runs from Denver to Ogden, Utah, about 30 miles north of Salt Lake City. The *Amtrak Pioneer* connects Salt Lake City and Seattle, with stops at Ogden, Pocatello, Boise, and Portland in between. The *Denver Rio Grande* also provides service between Salt Lake and Denver, Colorado.

By bus: Continental Trailways and *Greyhound* are the major carriers to Salt Lake City, but the area is also served by numerous other lines. *Utah Transit Authority,* the publicly financed bus system, runs inexpensive service between Salt Lake City and Ogden.

SEASONAL EVENTS. *January:* The drama season is still in full swing, with productions at Promised Valley Playhouse and Theatre 138. Utah's Central Hockey League team, the Golden Eagles, and the National Basketball Assn. Utah Jazz are in mid-season at the Salt Palace. *June:* The Salt Lake City municipal band starts its Sunday concerts in Liberty Park. *July:* On the 24th the "Days of '47" parade is held in downtown Salt Lake City; rodeo at the Salt Palace. *August:* County fair time. *September:* The Utah State Fair is held at the state fairgrounds. *December:* Utah Symphony and Ballet West launch season. The Salt Lake Oratorio Society's annual performance of *The Messiah* is performed in the Salt Lake City Tabernacle.

MUSEUMS AND GALLERIES. The Utah Museum of Natural History, located on the University of Utah campus, houses prehistoric fossils and Indian relics. Also on the University of Utah campus is the University Fine Arts Museum, exhibiting a variety of art forms. Art exhibits may also be seen at the Salt Lake Art Center at the Bicentennial Symphony Hall, in the Salt Palace complex, downtown Salt Lake City.

HISTORIC SITES. Salt Lake City is packed with historic reminders. Prominent among them are *Lion House,* Brigham Young's office, and *Beehive House,* right next door, which was one of his homes. Also, there are the *"This Is the Place" Monument,* the *Daughters of the Utah Pioneers Museum and Council Hall.* The last two are on Capitol Hill.

SPECTATOR SPORTS. The Central Hockey League *Golden Eagles* and National Basketball Assn. *Utah Jazz* play at the Salt Palace, and the minor league baseball team, the *Gulls,* play at Derks Field. A full range of intercollegiate sports are contested on the University of Utah campus in Salt Lake City; at Brigham Young University, Provo; Utah State University, Logan; and Weber State College, Ogden.

OTHER PLACES OF INTEREST. *Hanson Planetarium,* 15 South State Street, offers simulated journeys to the moon or anywhere in the universe. Excellent for the whole family. Group rates available.

Hogle Zoo, Emigration Canyon and Sunnyside Avenue, houses hundreds of specimens of wildlife. Children's Zoo, where some animals may be touched, has a Miniature Train and refreshment stands.

Trolley Square, 602 East 5th South, is a delightful shopping mall that used to house Salt Lake's trolley cars and buses. The many shops, stores, and restaurants include the Spaghetti Factory and even a "Farmer's Market." One square block blending the old Salt Lake with the new, it is recognized as a Utah Historical Site.

 HOTELS AND MOTELS. Double occupancy rates for hotels and motels in Salt Lake City are: *Moderate* $25–30; *Inexpensive* under $25.

Moderate: **Ramada Inn.** 999 South Main St. Near downtown area. 24-hr. restaurant, game room, liquor store, disco dancing.

Inexpensive: **Country Club Motor Inn.** 2665 Parleys Way. Medium-sized, scenic view.

KOA Salt Lake Valley Campgrounds. 1400 W. North Temple. Near I–80.

Scenic. 1345 Foothill Drive. Opposite convenient shopping center.

Temple Square Hotel. 75 W. South Temple. Downtown Salt Lake City, across from Temple Square. Has restaurant.

 DINING OUT. Salt Lake City is beginning to acquire a distinctive cuisine, but the going is slow because of the conservative liquor laws. But specialty places, offering French, Spanish and German dishes, are increasing. Some of the best menus will be found up nearby canyons. Price categories are for a complete dinner but do not include drinks, tax or tip: *Moderate* $5.50–10; and *Inexpensive* under $5.50.

Moderate: **Balkan Village.** 1500 W. North Temple. Excellent Greek food.

Canton Kitchen. 870 S. Main. Authentic Chinese with variety and tradition.

Le Parisien. 417 S. 3rd East. French and Italian food, done with care. Downtown.

Tampico. 167 Regent St. downtown. Mexican fare in sidestreet atmosphere.

Inexpensive: **Spaghetti Factory.** 189 Trolley Sq. Fun family setting.

TOURIST INFORMATION. Information about Salt Lake City and its surrounding areas can be obtained from the Salt Lake Valley Convention and Visitors Bureau, Salt Palace, Suite 200, Salt Lake City, Utah 84101. Phone (801) 521–2822.

EXPLORING UTAH

Great Salt Lake is indeed a natural wonder. Approximately 1,500 square miles in area, it is the nation's largest inland sea. Twenty-five percent saline, the lake is five times saltier than any ocean. Utah's relationship with the lake has changed through the years, just as the waterline has fluctuated.

Except for a species of tiny shrimp, no fish live in Great Salt Lake, so it had little practical value to the pioneers. Eventually, wood-hauling sternwheelers plied its waters. Some were converted to early-day cruise ships. Lakeside resorts, dance halls and amusement parks have been operated around Great Salt Lake's eastern and southern shores through the years, but all have either burned or been abandoned. The last, giant Saltair, with its Arabian Nights-inspired pavilion, disappeared in flames during 1972. A new, smaller version is now open for business.

It's true that a swimmer can bob on the lake surface "like a cork," without any effort, but some bathers suddenly discover they are allergic to salt in such concentrated solution. The reaction is a stinging sensation over that part of the skin immersed in the water. By all means shower under available fresh-water tanks after leaving the lake water.

Dinosaur National Monument, east of Vernal, is particularly fascinating. The area has supplied the largest collection of prehistoric vertebrates in the U.S. Entire skeletons have been excavated intact by several archeological institutions. Some are kept at a small museum for visitors to inspect.

Railroad Run

During summer months, a steam engine, known as the Heber Creeper, and Thanksgiving to New Year's Day in fall and winter, hauls passengers from Heber City to Bridal Veil Falls in Provo Canyon. The round trip meanders through meadowland, along streams and reservoirs while penetrating a mountain pass. It's a quaint way to sightsee.

Bridal Veil Falls, a double cataract, splashes in steep descent down Provo Canyon's sheer mountain walls. It's viewable from along US 189, if that's the route selected out of Heber City. Provo Canyon is one of the principal passes slicing through the Wasatch Range, and, most of the way it follows the Provo River, a premier trout stream. Also off US 189 in Provo Canyon is Sundance Resort, a development led by film actor Robert Redford. It features skiing during the winter and camping or horseback riding through the other seasons.

Provo and BYU

Located at the foot of 11,000-foot-high Provo Peak, the city of Provo is typically Mormon, with clean, wide streets and well-tended landscaping. It is a combination agricultural, educational and industrial center. The Mormon Church's biggest and best college campus graces Provo—Brigham Young University. Handsome and sprawling after a massive 1960s construction program, BYU (or "The Y," as it is colloquially called by many Utah admirers) attracts 25,000 students from LDS families throughout the U.S. and foreign countries. Its rigid and obeyed code of conduct rivals its nationally ranked athletic teams for far-flung recognition.

To the north, near Lehi, is Timpanogos Cave National Monument. Located in American Fork Canyon, the cleverly lighted caves were formed by a now-vanished underground river. The monument visitor center is open from May to October and the setting is spectacular. The cave is at the head of a long uphill walk not recommended for the aging or infirm.

Colorado River Canyon Country

Capitol Reef National Park, 61 square miles in area, includes 20-mile stretches of cliff. A road along the base meets spurs and graded trails leading to impressive Grand and Capitol gorges, Chimney Rock, Hickman Natural Bridge, petrified forests and Indian petroglyphs engraved on stone 1,200 years ago.

The Capitol Reef escarpment marks the southern boundary of Wayne Wonderland, a desert region of canyons, basins and sheer cliffs, the most awesome work produced by natural upheaval and erosion. Here stand Cathedral Valley, Walls of Jericho, Hoodoo Arch and the surrealistic Valley of the Goblins. Ask about road conditions before exploring these sites in standard model cars.

East of Bluff, southeastern Utah's first white settlement, are the widely scattered prehistoric ruins of Hovenweap National Monument. The two Utah sections are reachable by partly paved, partly graded roads. South from Mexican Hat, on US 163, travelers enter the northern rim of the 25,000-square-mile Navajo Indian Reservation, largest in the U.S. Here, on the Utah-Arizona border, is awesome, incredible Monument Valley. Mile after mile, the pavement passes huge red sandstone buttes, pillars, columns and needles soaring more than a thousand feet above the wide desert floor. The unforgettable shapes have been given such names as Totem Pole, Castle, Stagecoach, Brigham's Tomb and Mitten Buttes. Indians still spend summers amid these wonders, living much as their ancestors did centuries ago.

Arches and Towers

Crossing the Colorado, US 163 passes Arches National Park, featuring a 53-square-mile area with rock spires, pinnacles and narrow fins pierced by 88 naturally formed openings. One is a 291-foot bridge, the largest known natural arch. You may drive on paved roads to the finest specimens, but some walking is necessary to see the rock-formed skyscrapers of Park Avenue, Landscape Arch, The Devil's Garden and whimsical Delicate Arch. The last, called Schoolmarm's Britches by local cowhands, is the most beautiful and remarkable of the bunch. Rising more than 100 feet high, it stands alone and unsupported in a setting of slickrock domes, with the gorge of the Colorado River and the 12,000- to 13,000-foot peaks of the La Sal Mountains in the distance.

Bryce Canyon National Park

The painted canyon country of Utah can be dazzling in the yellow light after dawn, the Pink Cliffs here looking like fairyland. A drive of 34 miles takes motorists along the high rim parkway, where overlooks are starting points for hiking trails into this land of fantasy. As the altitude of the drive is around 9,000 feet, hikers should take it easy to keep from getting out of breath. Horses can be hired to make things simpler.

There are roads in the park, but some sections are accessible only on a mule or horse. For those without cars, the park provides transportation at a nominal charge. In addition to a hotel and lodge the park has improved camp sites. Camping is limited to 14 days. Bryce Canyon also has a well-organized museum with lectures and illustrations explaining the origins of its outstanding features. Accommodations and tourist services at Panguitch, 26 miles away.

Canyonlands National Park

The wild, colorful, rocky scenery of this wilderness has not been invaded by paved roads or tourist facilities. Travel is on foot or horseback, or by four-wheel-drive vehicle. The Green and Colorado Rivers, in their natural gorges, meet within the park in settings of excitingly stark isolation. The town of Green River has boat trips into the park. There are primitive campsites.

Many Jeep camp tours are available for a good, close look at Utah's newest National Park. They can be engaged at Moab, Blanding or Monticello. This park is divided roughly into the Needles Section at the southern end and the Island in the Sky at the northern end. Between the two are fascinating formations in The Maze, Land of Standing Rocks, Doll House, Salt Creek, Horseshoe Canyon and White Rim. In the south lies Chesler Park, a secluded valley completely ringed by fingers of rock jutting skyward.

Autos are advised to proceed with advance knowledge about conditions ahead. Local pilots have offered sightseeing flights over the area and information on such trips is available at the Arches Visitor Center.

For a less expensive bird's-eye view of the Canyonlands region, a black-topped county road leads west from US 163, north of Moab, to Dead Horse Point State Park, a magnificent overlook on the Colorado gorge. Accommodations and tourist services in Moab and Monticello.

Zion National Park

The lavish coloration of rockface everywhere in the Southwest is at its best here in a wonderland of canyons, mesas, and spindly stone towers. Hanging gardens of columbine, shooting star, and cardinal flowers are at their height of color in springtime. A specialty is the famous Zion moonflower that grows two feet high or taller on the floor of the canyon, with white horn-shaped flowers opening at night and closing in the morning sun. Early Basketmakers were followed by Cliff Dwellers, in turn displaced by the Paiute Indians still here when the Spaniards finally arrived in the 1780s. Later the Mormons arrived and named the area Dixie Land, hoping, without any success, to attract cotton planters from the South. The park has many trails, and is open all year, with lodge rooms and cabins available in summer only. There is a dining room and campground.

Zion National Park is located directly south of Cedar City, off I–15 and then along state routes that take motorists through small prim Mormon settlements named Toquerville, LaVerkin and Virgin. A tranquil, wooded camping site east of Cedar City off State 14 is Navajo Lake. The lake is cold enough for good trout fishing and big enough for boating. Accommodations and tourist services at Springdale.

PRACTICAL INFORMATION FOR UTAH

TOURIST INFORMATION. Detailed information about anything in the state may be obtained from the *Utah Travel Council,* Council Hall, Capitol Hill, Salt Lake City 84114, telephone (801) 521–8102.

MUSEUMS AND GALLERIES. *Pioneer Museum,* Provo, contains a particularly extensive assortment of pioneer utensils, tools and weapons used in the early West. The *Springville Museum of Art,* Springville, Utah County, is Utah's most well-known art center. Outdoor art festivals are held annually at many of Utah's resort areas. *Park City* closes its Main Street for such an occasion, usually sometime in August.

HISTORIC SITES. The state's oldest house, the *Miles Goodyear Cabin,* is on display in Ogden. Built around 1841, the log-hewn house was used by the first white family settling permanently in what became Utah. *Ghosttown* prowling has become a popular Utah pastime, principally because there are so many abandoned settlements throughout the state and it's another enjoyable way to see the countryside. Stephen L. Carr, in a 1972 publication, listed 150 ghost towns marking Utah's landscape. Just outside Brigham City is the Golden Spike Historical Site, where on May 10 of every year the driving of the golden spike connecting the Transcontinental Railways is reenacted. It is easily reached by I–15 North.

OTHER PLACES OF INTEREST. *Lagoon Amusement Park,* Farmington, is a favorite fun spot of the people of Utah. 34 rides, including a roller-coaster; picnic areas, miniature golf, games, and a heated outdoor pool. Open daily from mid-May to Labor Day.

Pioneer Village, in the Lagoon Amusement Park, includes reconstructed buildings, complete with furnishings from several periods of U.S. history, and stores stocked with original inventories. Enjoyable and educational. Free with paid admission to Lagoon.

Bonneville Salt Flats, near Wendover, is the home of the land speed records. For further information contact the Utah Travel Council.

Bingham Copper Mine, Bingham, the world's largest man-made copper pit. Visitors can view the mine from an observation platform while hearing a recording of its history.

TOURS. *Gray Lines* offers tours to Bryce Canyon National Park, Zion National Park and Cedar Breaks National Monument, as well as a Canyonland tour. *Trailways* schedules tours from Salt Lake City to Zion, Bryce, and Cedar Breaks National Monument. Boat tours are offered on Flaming Gorge Reservoir behind Flaming Gorge Dam by *Hatch River Expeditions.* Similar outings are available at *Lake Powell* behind Glen Canyon Dam, at Page in Arizona. For white-water river running on the Green and Colorado rivers, float trips are conducted by *Worldwide River Expeditions* at Vernal and Moab. *Hatch Expeditions* has river-running headquarters at Vernal, *Tag-a-long Tours* is in Moab.

DRINKING LAWS. Utah's liquor control laws beg the visitor's tolerance. Beer is the only alcoholic beverage served in all public bars. Certain licensed restaurants also serve two-ounce "mini-bottles" of the most commonly preferred cocktail or highball liquor; but they can only be ordered with food. That applies to wine as well. Retail liquor is only sold in state stores or package agencies. The legal age is 21.

SUMMER SPORTS. Some 200 *fishing* waters are open year-round. The state's most popular and regularly caught fish is the rainbow trout. Frequently taken from many waters are brook, native cutthroat, brown, Kokanee salmon, Mackinaw or lake trout, grayling, largemouth and white bass, channel catfish and walleyed pike. Nonresident license fee: 1 day, $5; 5 days, $15; season, $35. All trout fishing requires a $4.30 "stamp" for adults, $2.30 for youngsters under 12.

There are 45 public *golf* courses in operation around Utah. Many are nestled in unique mountain or desert settings.

Hunting is widely practiced in Utah, whether for deer, elk, antelope, jackrabbits, badgers, woodchucks and gophers or quail, pheasant, chukar partridge, ducks and geese. A nonresident big game license costs $120 for one deer. Small game nonresident license is $30.

WINTER SPORTS. Utah's mountain winters are long, snow-covered and, though cold, often sunny for extended periods. The official state guidebook lists 14 ski resorts, but not all excel. Snowmobiling and cross-country skiing are catching on in Utah's snow country. Both are allowed in certain areas of local canyons.

HOTELS AND MOTELS in Utah are relatively inexpensive. Highest rates are in effect for the "in-season" period, which, according to the locale, is either ski season (November to April) or the summer months that bring tourists to the national parks and forest lands. Based on double occupancy, the rate categories for Utah are: *Moderate* $25–35; and *Inexpensive* under $25.

ALTA. Alta Lodge. Scenic mountain atmosphere.

BRYCE CANYON. *Moderate:* **Ruby's Inn.** Café, laundromat.

CEDAR CITY. *Moderate:* **Astro.** Queen-size beds. Indoor pool; free coffee served.

HEBER CITY. *Moderate:* **Homestead.** Many activities; including horseback riding.

MEXICAN HAT. Friendship Inn San Juan Motel. Scenic tours; restaurant.

MONTICELLO. *Moderate:* **Navajo Trail.** Family style.

PROVO. *Moderate:* **Holiday Inn.** 45 minutes from ski resorts; near municipal golf course. Beer available.
Inexpensive: **Safari Motel.** 250 S. University. New and convenient in downtown.
Uptown. Small but serviceable.

DINING OUT. Mormon cooking is neither different nor unique. It's possible to discover especially tasty fare in out-of-the-way locations, but don't count on it. State-wide restaurant quality has improved considerably, however, since tourism has developed into such a big, booming business. Price categories are for a complete dinner without drinks, tax or tip: *Moderate* $5.50–10; and *Inexpensive* under $5.50.

CEDAR CITY. *Moderate:* **Sugar Loaf Café.** Roasted chicken, steak.

HEBER CITY. *Inexpensive:* **The Hub.** Open 24 hours.

LOGAN. *Moderate:* **Country Kitchen.** Good family style.

OGDEN. *Moderate:* **Olde Country Bar.** Old-fashioned American food, served family style.

PROVO. *Moderate.* **Jedediah's Famous Dining,** at the Rodeway Inn. 1292 University Ave. Family dinners and lunches.

ST. GEORGE. *Moderate:* **Atkins' Sugar Loaf Café.** Chicken, steak.

WYOMING

The Cowboy State

Wyoming sits in the lap of the broadest part of the Rocky Mountains. Rectangular in shape, on a plateau four to seven thousand feet above sea level, Wyoming is at a higher average altitude than all other states except neighboring Colorado.

A big loop tour of the state can begin at Newcastle near South Dakota's Black Hills. Newcastle is a trading center for surrounding ranches, and cowboys in high-heeled boots and cowboy hats give a sense of the Old West. Proceeding northwest, near Moorcroft, is Devils Tower National Monument, a stump-shaped cluster of volcanic rock columns 1,000 feet across at the bottom and 275 feet at the top. In 1906, it was set aside as America's first National Monument. Farther west is Buffalo and nearby Indian-U.S. Cavalry battlegrounds and the Bradford Brinton Memorial Ranch near Big Horn.

Sheridan is the largest city in northern Wyoming and headquarters for Bighorn National Forest. Sheridan's rodeo in mid-July and All-American Indian Days the last weekend in July are authentic relics of earlier frontier days. Over the Bighorn Mountains lies Cody, named after the scout, Buffalo Bill Cody. The town is packed with mementos of this famed westerner, including an historic center and boyhood home.

Laramie, in the southwest, is over one hundred years old and has flourished since its inception as a Union Pacific Railroad station. Nearby is Old Fort Sanders, a stopping place for Western pioneers and Mormons. Laramie is also home of the University of Wyoming.

Cheyenne, the state capital and now a peaceful prosperous community, was known as "Hell on Wheels" in the days of the Old West. Once a year, during the last full week of July, the spirit of the bygone era is revived with Cheyenne Days, a festival of grade A rodeos, parades and cowboys playing cowboys.

From Cheyenne are three suggested day tours. The first loop takes in "Old Bedlam," Fort Laramie and the Oregon Trail National Historic Site. Indian, U.S. Cavalry and settler artifacts and remains are found along the way. A second loop tour takes in the Medicine Bow National Forest, Curt Gowdy State Park and Laramie. The third trip includes stops at Scotts Bluff National Monument, which commemorates a stopping point for both the Pony Express and Oregon and California bound settlers; Chimney Rock National Historic Site, Lusk, home of the annual Rawhide Pageant in August; and the Glendo Recreation area.

Yellowstone Park

So vast is Yellowstone National Park—3,472 square miles—that several weeks are needed to explore all of its scenic and varied attractions. Most outstanding among attractions in America's first national park are the world's largest geyser basins and the thundering falls and canyon of the Yellowstone River. The park may also be the world's most varied wildlife sanctuary—with binoculars still the safest way to observe the bear, elk, buffalo, moose, deer, antelope and birds prevalent in the region.

Starting out from Fishing Bridge, a loop road leads to Canyon Village at Canyon Junction and one of the park's most spectacular sights, the Grand Canyon of Yellowstone. This twenty-four mile long, 1,200 foot deep gorge is aglitter with shades of red and yellow rocks and is surrounded by emerald green forests. Inspiration Point, on the north rim, is the best place for viewers and photographers to see the two largest waterfalls.

The road to Tower Junction passes Mt. Washburn (10,317 ft.) and slips through Dunraven Pass and to the rustic accommodations of Roosevelt Lodge at Tower Falls. Mammoth Hot Springs, at the North entrance, has the impressive travertine terraces of the geological domes —some vividly colored, some snow white.

South past Norris and Madison Junctions is geyser land. Some erupt in rage and fury spewing thousands of gallons of water over one hundred feet in the air, others merely splash up a few inches. Most beloved is Old Faithful. It "blows" every hour on the hour and has not missed a performance in over eighty years. The visitor center here describes the unique geological wonders. Those wishing to see more geysers should go to Shoshone Geyser Basin or Heart Lake Geyser Basin, near West Thumb Junction.

Yellowstone may be visited year-round and there are always accommodations (though not always available at the Old Faithful Inn, open May–October.) Different ways to see the park are by hiking the Howard Eaton or smaller trails, horseback riding on the 700 miles of trails, or by snowmobiling or snowshoeing in during the winter. Accommodations, although excellent, are far from adequate, especially in peak season. Early reservations are advised at lodges and inns.

Yellowstone's five entrances are: from the north, via Livingston and Gardiner, Montana and I–90; from Billings and Silver Gate, Montana on the northeast; on the east, from Cody, Wyoming; from Jackson on the south; and via West Yellowstone on the west.

The Grand Tetons

The magnificent scenery of the Grand Teton National Park extends continuously from the lakes and valleys skyward to 13,000-foot mountain peaks. Snowcapped and glacier covered, the towering mountains are a backdrop to the placid, emerald lakes, to craggy canyons and pristine forests.

The 485-square-mile park is quite a compact area with possibilities for the traveler to spend several weeks, with each day revealing something new.

Scattered throughout Teton National Park are a variety of facilities and campgrounds. In fact, one of the most interesting ways of touring the park is to hedgehop from one accommodation to another. First stop could be Colter Bay Cabins and Signal Mountain Lodge, set in the natural wooded area on the shores of Jackson Lake. Facilities include well-appointed cabins (some with kitchens), opportunities for fishing outings or horseback riding, and a fully equipped marina. By way of contrast, the Jackson Lake Lodge has 385 luxurious rooms, and features a floor-to-ceiling picture window in the lodge that frames the lake and the Grand Teton Range. Down the road toward Jackson is the Jenny Lake Lodge where the peak of Grand Teton Mountain rises almost from the front porch. Most of these areas also have ample campgrounds. However, both the indoor and outdoor vacationer is advised to reserve in advance if possible.

The other major way to experience the Tetons is to reach the back country by hiking or by horseback. The Park Service maintains a wide assortment of routes—some designed for a few hour's hike, some for both horse and foot trips, and some for hikers with only good hiking shoes and strong legs. One famous trail reaches the 11,000-foot summit of Static Peak Divide. Another climbs to the contemplative, glacier-formed Lake Solitude. The lowland regions can be traversed via the Lakes Trail or paths through Death Canyon, Cascade Canyon, or Indian Paintbrush Canyon.

If water is your element, full- and half-day float trips down the Snake River are available at the Lake or from Jackson. Along the route the majestic bald eagle may be seen high in the trees in one of its few remaining natural habitats.

Gateway to the Tetons and the National Parks is Jackson. Located at the southern entrance to the parks, Jackson is headquarters for the Teton National Forest, an area of 1,701,000 acres of wilderness bordering on both Grand Teton and Yellowstone National Parks. This resort community offers year-round recreational opportunities, abounding in dude ranches, motels and entertainment centers, good fishing and hunting, and three exceptional ski slopes—Snow King, Jackson Hole, and Targhee. There is a modern airport with transportation to hotels and motels in Jackson, Teton Village, and Jackson Lake Lodge. The culture and historic sides of Jackson on one hand remain entirely western and on the other boast 15 art galleries, a summer fine arts festival, a summer symphony, and summer stock theater. The Silver Dollar Bar in the Wort Hotel is world famous, and the Pink Garter Theater is home of the performing arts. For sheer natural beauty, don't miss seeing the huge elk herd which winters right on the edge of town. Beginning in November, as many as 10,000 elk come into the refuge and remain into early May.

Nearby Pinedale offers a slightly slower pace than the well-trafficked Jackson area. Pinedale is a true western community and is surrounded by working cattle ranches, but also offers modern motels, dude ranch accommodations, and restaurants. Pinedale is also gateway to the Bridger Tetons National Forest and some beautiful, relatively under-visited camping and hiking areas.

Another major attraction in the Jackson region is the Dubois area, located on the upper Big Wind River and surrounded on three sides by Shoshone National Forest, and one of the richest places in the nation to prospect and search for rocks. Found in the region are gem-quality, agatized, opalized wood, cast material, pine and fir cone replacements, amethyst-lined trees and limb casts, and all types of agate equal to any found elsewhere.

Bordering the Dubois area is the big Shoshone and Arapahoe Indian Reservation. In July, first the Shoshone and then the Arapahoe Indians hold their sun dances. Dressed in full costumes, they dance continuously for three days and nights without taking food or water. Nearby is Crowheart Butte, a monument commemorating the scene of the great battle between the Shoshone and Crow Indian chiefs. In Riverton, located in the center of the Reservation, the Riverton Museum has Indian displays. Three Indian missions are in the vicinity: St. Stephen's on State 789; St. Michael's mission at Ethete; and Ft. Washakie, the Indian headquarters in Ft. Washakie. Sacajawea, the Indian guide of the Lewis and Clark expedition from the Missouri River to the Pacific Coast and back during 1805–06, is buried in the Indian cemetery at Wind River.

John D. Rockefeller, Jr., Parkway

Linking Grand Teton and Yellowstone National Parks is a short stretch of highway along the Snake River that, with its adjoining forest land, makes up another National Park Service property. Besides the spectacular mountain views, the area has hot springs and bridle trails—and a number of campgrounds.

PRACTICAL INFORMATION FOR WYOMING

YELLOWSTONE

HOTELS AND MOTELS. Based on single room, double occupancy, the rates are: *Moderate* $25–45; *Inexpensive* under $25.

Canyon Village. *Moderate:* All facilities, horses. **Mammoth Hotel and Cabins.** *Moderate:* North end. Open late May–late Sept. **Old Faithful Inn.** *Moderate:* 350-room lodge. Across from the geyser.

DINING OUT. All hotels have dining facilities. Most are *moderate* ($5–12) for a meal, excluding drinks, tax or tip), in price. Yellowstone concessions are operated by the Yellowstone Park Co.

GRAND TETONS

HOW TO GET THERE. *By air: Frontier* and *Transwestern Airlines* to Jackson, which has a modern airport. *By car:* US 89 and 287 from Yellowstone or good highway from Moose. *By rail: Amtrak* to Rock Springs, then connections. *By bus: Continental Trailways, Greyhound,* or *Jackson-Rock Springs Stages.*

TOURIST INFORMATION. Wyoming Travel Commission, Cheyenne, Wyo. 82002.

FARM VACATIONS AND GUEST RANCHES. Full list available from state Travel Commission. *CM Ranch* near Dubois and *Triangle X Ranch* in Teton Park are two of best known in area; the *Heart Six* is another good spot.

MUSEUMS AND GALLERIES. Jackson has many art galleries, Riverton Indian relics in an old church. Another worthwhile stop is the Lander Pioneer Museum.

HISTORIC SITES. Wind River Indian Reservation is the home of Shoshone and Arapahoe tribes. Missions at St. Stephen's, St. Michael's, and Ft. Washakie, Fort Bridger, in Bridger, is worth inspecting.

TOURS. Package tours through Jackson Lake Lodge. Special interest tours offered of national park by the Old West Tours, Jackson.

SUMMER SPORTS/WINTER SPORTS. Boat trips, fishing, rafting, hiking, backpacking, canoeing, horseback riding all possible in the area. Skiing: major activity in Jackson Hole, both downhill and cross-country. Also snowshoe expeditions, ice skating.

WHAT TO DO WITH THE CHILDREN. All parts of Teton Park are OK for children, with proper supervision. Stagecoach rides in Jackson. Indian dances in Jackson and at Jackson Lake Lodge.

INDIANS. Arapahoe and Shoshone preserves offer many native customs on some of nation's largest reservations. Many local spots to see and celebrations to observe. Consult Riverton Chamber of Commerce guidebook.

HOTELS AND MOTELS. Rates are based on single room, double occupancy, as follows: *Moderate,* $25–45; *Inexpensive,* $15–24. Summer reservations should be made far in advance. Rates higher in season.

DUBOIS. *Inexpensive:* **Branding Iron Motel.** Downtown.

JACKSON. *Moderate:* **Horseshoe Motel.** Open all year. **Wort Hotel.** Cocktail lounge, entertainment.

GRAND TETON NATIONAL PARK. *Moderate:* **Hatchet Motel.** In Moose. **Signal Mountain Lodge.** On edge of Jackson Lake.

RESTAURANTS. Prices are for a complete meal excluding drinks, tax or tip: *Moderate,* $8–14; *Inexpensive,* under $7.

JACKSON. *Moderate:* **Silver Spur.** Family-style food. Downtown. **The Westerner.** Favorite local hangout.

THE REST OF WYOMING

HOW TO GET THERE. *By air: Frontier* flies to Cheyenne, Casper and Laramie from Denver; *Rocky Mountain Airways* offers service to Cheyenne. *By rail: Amtrak* to Cheyenne. *By car:* I–80 passes east-west in the southern part of state, I–90 in the north. I–25 from Colorado in the south. *By bus: Continental Trailways* and *Greyhound.*

TOURIST INFORMATION. *Wyoming Travel Commission,* Cheyenne 82002.

MUSEUMS AND GALLERIES. In Cody, *Buffalo Bill Historical Center,* with *Buffalo Bill Museum* and *Whitney Gallery of Western Art. Bradford Brinton Memorial Ranch,* near Big Horn, with western pioneer relics. *University of Wyoming Art Museum* and *Plains Museum* in Laramie. The *Wyoming State Museum* in Cheyenne with artifacts, Indian and military collections and the Frontier Days Museum. *Fremont County Pioneer Museum* in Lander.

HISTORIC SITES. *Fort Laramie* has been restored to the days when it served as Calvary headquarters. *South Pass City* near Lander has rebuilt the authentic western gold ghost town from 1867–68. Most famous of the forts are: *Fort Bridger,* in Fort Bridger State Park, named after the famous trapper and guide; *Fort Phil Kearney* near Story in the Sheridan area; *Fort Caspar* in Casper. Best-known of pioneer sites are: *St. Mary's Stage Station,* near South Pass City, where 90 Mormons perished in a blizzard; *Buffalo Bill Statue* near Cody; and *Independence Rock* near Casper.

TOURS. *Jackson Lake Lodge* and *Yellowstone Park Co.* arrange tours of park areas. Also look into *Old West Tours* in Jackson.

DRINKING LAWS. Minimum drinking age is nineteen.

SUMMER SPORTS. *Boating,* rafting, canoeing on lakes and reservoirs, state and national recreation areas. Trout is most prevalent *fish* in 20,000 miles of streams and 264,000 acres of lakes. *Hunting* seasons for various animals—consult state Game and Fish Commission. Horseback *riding* and *pack trips* throughout the state.

WINTER SPORTS. Better known *ski* areas at: Jackson; Grand Targhee in the Tetons; Medicine Bow, both near Laramie; Hogadon Basin, near Casper. *Snowmobiling* is growing in popularity.

SPECTATOR SPORTS. *Rodeos* held in Cody, Cheyenne, Casper, Lander, Riverton, Douglas. Consult state commission for dates and times. Gillette has *stock car racing* and Meadowlark Downs in Riverton has *quarter horse racing.*

SHOPPING. *Welty's Store* in Dubois is a large trading post. Most towns have shops selling leather and buckskin jackets, hunting and camping equipment.

WHAT TO DO WITH THE CHILDREN. All parks, of course, offer delights for children. Special *stage coach rides* for children from Town Square in Jackson as well as nightly "shootouts." See separate section on Yellowstone Park earlier in book.

HOTELS AND MOTELS. Rates are based on single room, double occupancy as follows: *Moderate,* $21–40; *Inexpensive,* $14–20.

CASPER. *Inexpensive:* **Travelier Motel.** Small, but adequate.

CHEYENNE. *Moderate:* **Cheyenne TraveLodge.** Open all year. **Home Ranch Motel.** Medium size. *Inexpensive:* **Motel 6.** Open all year.

CODY. *Moderate:* **Irma Motor Hotel.** Downtown Old West landmark. *Inexpensive:* **Uptown.** Comfortable rooms.

LARAMIE. *Moderate:* **Motel Eight.** Open all year. **Wyo. Motel.** Across from University.

RIVERTON. *Moderate:* **Tomahawk Motel.** Downtown motel.

SHERIDAN. *Moderate:* **American Inn.** Modern. **Trails End Motel.** Attractive, own cocktail lounge.

DINING OUT. Prices are for a complete meal without drinks, tax or tip. *Moderate:* $8–16; *Inexpensive,* $5–7.

CHEYENNE. *Moderate:* **Carriage Court.** Elegant. *Inexpensive:* **Longhorn Café.** Buffet-style. Good value.

CODY. *Moderate:* **Green Gables.** Western food.

EVANSTON. *Moderate to Inexpensive:* **Freeman's Cafeteria.** Hot meals from 7 A.M. to 11 P.M.

LARAMIE. *Moderate:* **Diamond Horseshoe.** Chinese and American.

ALASKA

America's Last Frontier

State capital Juneau, in southeast Alaska, started with an 1880 gold strike. Now, downtown high-rises tower over narrow, winding streets and wooden stairways leading to homes seemingly gouged out of the mountain backdrop.

Visitors should see the Indian and Eskimo artifacts at the Alaska State Museum, and follow the walking tour map to nearby marked historic places. The log cabin Visitor Center, near the modern State Capitol Building, was built in 1980, Juneau's Centennial year. Pick up free maps, brochures and information there.

But the area's key attraction is Mendenhall Glacier, a spectacular receding ice river only 14 miles from downtown, with trails, campgrounds, and a fine, interpretive Visitors Center.

Glacier Bay National Park and Preserve, 2,803,840 acres of deep fjords, tidewater glaciers, jutting icebergs, and rare species of wildlife, is in the Fairweather Range of the St. Elias Mountains, and 55 miles northwest of Juneau.

The 65-mile-long Glacier Bay is reached only by air and sea.

At the northern end of the Inside Passage, air and overland routes connect Haines and Skagway with interior and northern destinations. The Haines Highway meets the Alaska Highway south of Whitehorse, capital of Yukon Territory. From Skagway, Highway 2 via Carcross is open summer only. The 1898 White Pass & Yukon Railroad was closed down in 1983, but by 1984, railroad buffs are counting on again riding the narrow-gauge rails, switchbacking up mountains and over-looking vestiges of the Trail of '98.

Gold-founded Fairbanks is at the northernmost point of the Alaska Highway. The state's second largest city has grown to a military center, seat of the University of Alaska, an important center of space communication from unmanned satellites, and supply hub for the Interior and Arctic regions. After a breather upon completion of the oil pipeline, Fairbanks is now accelerating North Slope activity. Visitors mix with transient oil experts, slope workers, and scientists along with the residents, many of them original homesteaders and prospectors.

Temperatures may range from above 90° in summer to 60° below zero in winter. Highlight of long midsummer days is midnight baseball, no lights needed.

North of Fairbanks, where the Yukon River makes its northernmost bend above the Arctic Circle, Athabascan Indians live at Ft. Yukon. Eskimos live in small villages along the Artic Ocean and the Bering Sea.

Denali National Park (Formerly Mt. McKinley National Park)

There is a no more impressive sight in North America than the double peaks of Mt. McKinley, the highest one rising to 20,320 feet in the Alaska Range southwest of Fairbanks. The 2-million-acre park is traversed by a 90-mile highway that is like a giant natural museum of mountain, tundra, and wildlife.

The park can be reached by plane (a 3,000-foot airstrip is maintained for light aircraft); by rail, from Anchorage or Fairbanks, which is paved and passes by the park entrance. The gravel, summer-only Denali Highway winds 135 miles from Paxson on the Richardson Highway to join the Anchorage-Fairbanks highway near the park portal. Charter flights are available from Anchorage or Fairbanks, and there is scheduled bus service.

Travel by private vehicle is restricted, but frequent free shuttle buses traverse the park road. Also, Tundra Wildlife Tours, are conducted daily by experienced driver-guides. Some carry tourists to Eielson Visitor Center, 65 miles west, and back. Frequent stops are made to photograph flowers, birds, mountains, and animals, particularly grizzlies, caribou, Dall sheep and moose. The fare, (about $25; children half) includes a picnic lunch.

On clear days, the north summit of Mt. McKinley, 19,470 feet, is visible 31 miles off, to the southwest. In the foreground is Muldrow Glacier, which drops from the mountain and spreads out over the valley floor.

There are several campgrounds within the park. Since firewood is scarce, campers should bring a camp stove with plenty of fuel, as well as all supplies. You can drive to the first two campgrounds, which have space available on a "first-come" basis. To camp beyond, especially at popular Wonder Lake, make reservations and get permits from rangers at Park Headquarters.

Accommodations outside the Park include McKinley Village Hotel, McKinley Chalets, a KOA Kampground, Denali Cabins (with hot tub), and Jere-e-Tad Lodge boasting a supper club. Reserve ahead to stay within the Park at the Denali Park Station Hotel, North Face Lodge, or Camp Denali, both near Wonder Lake.

Camp Denali, 90 miles from park headquarters, is rustic plumbing-wise, but geared to true nature lovers. These several-day-long Sourdough Vacations and Wilderness Workshops (P.O. Box 67, Denali Park, Alaska 99755) require advance reservations.

Besides being an air crossroads of the world, Anchorage is a takeoff point for remote areas in Western Alaska and the Arctic. The semivolcanic, treeless Aleutian Island chain stretches more than a thousand miles into the North Pacific. Air tours visit the Pribilof Islands, breeding grounds for fur seal and the largest settlement of Aleuts at St. Paul; Nome on the Bering Sea coast; and the Katmai National Park.

From Anchorage, roads lead to Interior destinations, the Alaska Highway, and popular recreation areas on the game- and fish-filled Kenai Peninsula.

Kenai, on Cook Inlet, and Kodiak Island, were both settled by the Russians during the last half of the eighteenth century. The city of Kodiak is the oldest permanent settlement in Alaska.

Perhaps Kodiak is most famous for the Kodiak brown bear and king crab. The continent's largest carnivore can weigh up to 1,200 pounds. The sea monster may reach four feet, pincer to pincer.

PRACTICAL INFORMATION FOR ALASKA

HOW TO GET THERE. *By air:* Scheduled U.S. airlines jet direct to Alaska from gateway cities in the United States and Canada. Several foreign and domestic airlines touch down on international flights. Reliable travel agents and tour operators keep informed on the best fares from home cities. Promotional air fares also offer substantial savings. Ask about *Alaska Airlines'* "Buy Alaska" fare, and *Wien Air Alaska's* "Passport."

By car: The Alaska Highway is open year-round. Car travelers should buy a guide to facilities and services, and despite the generally good road conditions, special precautions and preparations may be needed. U.S. citizens need no passport at the Canadian border, but some personal papers as proof are advisable. Bus systems serve major Alaskan cities from U.S. and Canadian points.

By sea: Alaska State Ferries operate year-round between Prince Rupert, B.C., Seattle, Wash., and Southeastern Alaska ports along the Inside Passage. For schedules, fares, and reservations (needed in peak-season summer travel) contact the Alaska Marine Highway System, Pouch R. Juneau, AK 99811. Contact the B.C. Ferry Corp, 1045 Howe St., Vancouver, B.C. Canada V6Z 2A9, about Canadian ferries operating between Vancouver, Vancouver Island, and Prince Rupert. Most cruise ships leave from Vancouver, B.C.; a few sail from San Francisco and Los Angeles. Combination land, air, and Marine Highway trips are popular.

TOURIST INFORMATION SERVICES. The *Alaska Division of Tourism* Pouch E, Juneau, AK 99811, offers a free Alaska Travel Brochure. Send $2 for their "Alaska Travel Planner." Almost every community has a tourist contact center which can supply information about overnight accommodations and attractions.

Alaska Highway travelers may get information every day from 7 A.M. until 12 P.M. at the *Tok Alaska State Visitor Center* at Mile 1314.

MUSEUMS AND GALLERIES. *The Anchorage Historical and Fine Arts Museum,* 121 W. Seventh Ave., exhibits arts and artifacts of Alaska, as do the *University of Alaska Museum* at Fairbanks, and Juneau's *Alaska State Museum.* Ketchikan: Southeast Alaska Indian art and artifacts at *Tongass Historical Society Museum,* and at the *Totem Heritage Cultural Center.* Knik: 50 miles from Anchorage in the Matanuska Valley is the unusual *Dog Musher's Hall of Fame.* Kodiak: *Baranof Museum* is in Erskine House, the oldest structure remaining in Alaska. Nome: *The Carrie McClain Memorial Museum* has gold rush relics. The *Arctic Trading Post Museum* features ivory carving and Eskimo life. A fine bronze sculpture "Fisk" in front of the Clausen Memorial Museum portrays all of Petersburg's fish. *Sheldon Jackson College Museum* in Sitka has a collection from Tlingit Indian and Russian-American times. The *"Trail of '98" Museum* is in Skagway. Kotzebue: the *Living Museum of the Arctic* combines dioramas of Arctic life and environment with live Eskimo dancing and demonstrations of skills.

Art: Numerous galleries represent Alaskan artists and welcome visitors, from far north University of Alaska Fine Arts Center in Fairbanks to art-minded Homer, near the tip of the Kenai Peninsula.

HISTORIC SITES. Over a hundred places are listed in the National Register. Some are National Historic Landmarks, such as the town of Eagle. Buildings are restored, including Judge Wickersham's First Judicial Courthouse, from 1901.

Fairbanks hoards history in 44-acre Alaskaland, a free outdoor museum. The *Pedro Creek Discovery Claim* marks the beginning of the 1902 gold rush.

Haines: Vintage buildings surround parade grounds of 1903 Fort William H. Seward at adjacent Port Chilkoot, also a center for Alaska Indian arts.

Juneau: The house museum of turn-of-the-century statesman and historian, Judge Wickersham, has outstanding Alaskana. (Admission fee)

Kenai: Site of *Redoubt St. Nicholas,* a fortified Russian fur-trading post (1791). The Russian Orthodox Church (1894) is an Historic Landmark.

Ketchikan: *Totem Bight State Historical Site* contains excellent totems.

Sitka: *St. Michael's Cathedral* has religious relics and treasures on display. *Sitka National Historical Park* with totem poles and Visitor Center commemorates site where Russians defeated Indians in the final "Battle for Alaska" in 1804.

Skagway and nearby ghost town Dyea, overland starting points for the rugged mountain and river route to Canadian goldfields, are part of the new *Klondike Gold Rush National Historical Park.*

TOURS. Package tours cover big Alaska using assorted land/sea/air transportation. Prices range from budget to deluxe. They allow for optional tours, which add up to good savings. Also, during early spring and autumn, tour prices may be 10–15% lower. Most firms listed here grew up with Alaska tourism. They work closely with airlines, cruise ships, ferries, motorcoaches, railroads, local Alaskans, and your local travel agent.

Alaska Exploration Holidays & Cruises (ATMS), 1500 Metropolitan Park Bldg., Olive Way at Boren Ave., Seattle, WA 98101. They round up the best of Alaska and the Yukon in summer destinations ranging from the remote Pribilofs to the Arctic. Their brochures describe fly-out fishing trips and boat charters, naturalist/photography "safaris," fly/drive programs for independent travelers, and programs of their "Exploration Cruise Lines."

The 88-passenger *Majestic Alaska Explorer* sails the Inside Passage, and explores fjords and wilderness areas where bigger cruise ships cannot go. She port calls and lands passengers—even next to a glacier—during day-long cruises in Glacier Bay National Park. From the Park Lodge, her smaller sister ship, the *Glacier Bay Explorer,* overnights at a glacier, and the *Thunder Bay* makes day trips up-Bay for wildlife and glacier watching.

Airlines offering tours: *Alaska Airlines,* Box 68900, Seattle WA 98168; *Wien Air Alaska Tour Office,* 4797 Business Park Blvd. G, Anchorage AK 99503;

Northwest Orient Tour Sales, Minneapolis-St. Paul International Airport, St. Paul, MN 55111; *Western Airlines,* P.O. Box 92931, Los Angeles, CA 90009.

Kneisel Travel, Inc., 345 N.E. 8th Ave., Portland, Oregon 97232, long has offered "Mr. K's Alaska Treasure Chest" of air/sea tours for independent travelers, and the Green Carpet program for escorted groups. *Maupintour's* Alaska adventures are also escorted. Write Box 807, Lawrence, KS. 66044. *TravAlaska Tours, Inc.* 555 4th & Battery Bldg., Seattle, WA 98121, headed by Alaska travel pioneer Chuck West, feature economy all-season tours by ferry and motorcoach, and custom-designed itineraries. Their *Alaska-Yukon Motorcoaches* are scheduled from Seattle.

Alaska Campout Adventures, 938 P St., Anchorage AK 99501; *Alaska Travel Adventures,* 200 N. Franklin St., Juneau AK 99801, and *Questers,* 257 Park Ave. S., NY, NY 10010 feature small group wilderness trips.

City tours include *Alaska Sightseeing, Gray Line, American Sightseeing,* and local companies. Taxi and city bus drivers can be used on-your-own exploring; they are eager to "show and tell." *Princess Tours,* 4th & Blanchard Bldg., Suite 1800, Seattle, WA 98121, and *Westours,* 300 Elliot Ave. W., Seattle, WA 98119.

SUMMER ACTIVITIES. *Animal Watching.* Keep an eye out—everywhere. Deer, black bear, brown bear, moose and mountain goat are in southeastern Alaska. Bear, moose, caribou, wolf, Dall sheep and other game are found in the interior and the mountains. Trophy Alaska brown bear hang out on Kodiak Island and the Alaska Peninsula. Moose are far-ranging, with the largest in the world living on the Kenai Peninsula. Visitors are likely to see the most in the Park & Monument wildernesses.

Hunting them may run into considerable expense. All nonresidents must possess a valid hunting license and tags. Write the Alaska Department of Fish and Game, Subport Bldg., Juneau, AK 99811 for current regulations on both hunting and fishing.

Fishing. The season is literally year-round. Trout, shellfish and grayling provide excellent fishing also.

Major salmon derbies run from January through September. A bargain for visitors is a special one-day license for $5 or a 10-day for $15, available at sporting goods stores throughout Alaska.

Boating. Boats are available for rent or charter in some communities. Kayaking, canoeing, and rafting expeditions are offered on all kinds of rivers and lakes.

Scuba and *skin diving* are popular along the coast. *Swimmers* find coastal waters chilly, but lakes are warm enough. Hotels in larger cities may have pools. Some towns have community swimming pools.

Hiking. Of about 500 miles of trails in the national forests alone, the most famous is the Chilkoot Pass Trail from Skagway.

Mountain climbing. From afternoon climbs to the highest peak in North America. But be prepared in every respect—and have guides on any extended climb.

Golf. 5 greens in the Anchorage area; 2 at Fairbanks; and a course at Soldotna on the Kenai Peninsula.

Glacier skiing, high on the Juneau Ice Field and in mountains benind Mt. Alyeska near Anchorage, is for diehards.

Flightseeing tours by small plane and helicopter are reasonable when the cost is shared. Ask in communities from Ketchikan to Kotzebue about the possibilities.

WINTER ACTIVITIES. Alaskans frequent many local ski runs and tows, but the best-developed ski area is *Mt. Alyeska Ski Resort,* about 40 miles from Anchorage, with heli-skiing, cross-country ski touring, and dogsledding via the "Chugach Express," chairlifts, ski school, day lodge, overnight accommodations, and restaurants. Two easily accessible ski slopes are near *Fairbanks.* Juneau's Eaglecrest ski area, across the bridge on Douglas Island, has a day lodge, chairlift and rope tows. *Turnagain Pass Area,* 59 miles from Anchorage on the Seward Highway, is popular with cross-country skiers and snowmobilers; snowfall frequently exceeds 12 feet. *Ice skating* and *ice fishing* are popular on many suitable frozen lakes, December through March. *Curling.* This Scottish favorite is played in Anchorage, Fairbanks, and in Whitehorse, YT.

SEASONAL EVENTS. Alaskans are prone to celebrations year-round, and for almost any reason. The best excuse in 1984 is the 25th Statehood Anniversary. In the summer season, roughly May through September, you can count on being entertained by assorted continuous community "specials." For events and festivals and exact dates, write the area Chamber of Commerce and consult the listings in the Alaska Yukon Travel Directory, free on request from the Division of Tourism, Pouch E, Juneau, AK 99811.

February: Cordova holds an *Iceworm Festival;* Homer, a *Winter Carnival.* The Anchorage Fur Rendezvous features *World Championship Sled Dog Races.*

March: Fairbanks holds more *Championship Sled Dog Races.* Nome sponsors the 1000-mile Iditarod *Sled Dog Classic.*

April: Kotzebue, *Archie Ferguson Memorial Snow Machine Race* and *Eskimo games.*

May: Petersburg's *"Little Norway"* Festival; Kodiak *King Crab Festival.*

June: Highlighting the solstice: Nome's *River Raft Race;* Fairbanks' *Midnight Sun Baseball Game,* and the *Yukon 800 Riverboat Race.* The Anchorage Historical and Fine Arts Museum holds a *Festival of Native Arts;* and nearby Palmer features *Scottish Games* and a *Horse Show.* Sitka revels in a three-week *Summer Music Festival,* and watches the all-Alaska *Logging Championships.* There are *whaling festivals* at Barrow and Point Hope.

July: The 4th of July is a bang-up celebration from Ketchikan to Kotzebue; *Alaska Logging Championships* at Sitka; *Loggers Rodeo,* Ketchikan; *horse races,* Palmer; *foot race* up Mt. Marathon, Seward; and all sorts of fun and *Eskimo games* in Arctic towns. Fairbanks "Golden Days" is biggest summer celebration with the *World Eskimo, Indian, Aleut Olympic Games.*

August-September: Gold Rush Days at Valdez, and *Silver Salmon Derbies* at Valdez and Seward. *Fairs* at Haines, Fairbanks, and Palmer, and a *Buffalo Barbeque* at Delta. *Outdoor drama* "Cry of the Wild Ram" at Kodiak, and also a *Rodeo and State Fair.* In Anchorage they celebrate a mid-September *Festival of Music.*

October: Alaska Day Festival (Oct. 18) at Sitka.

The rest of the year Alaskans celebrate the usual holidays; visitors are welcome to join in.

 WHAT TO DO WITH THE CHILDREN. The gold mines, ghost towns, old forts, museums, sled dogs, sawdust-floor saloons, ferry boats, glaciers, nights without darkness, sourdough breakfast, salmon bakes—in all these and more Alaska offers an unlimited opportunity for a child's delight and wonder.

At *Denali National Park,* free-roaming wildlife, birds and flora will amaze and instruct. More animals are on view in the free museum at *Elmendorf Air Force Base* and at the *Alaska Children's Zoo* near Anchorage. *Alaskaland,* at Fairbanks, is designed for all ages.

There will be memorable rides on the sternwheeler *Discovery* paddling gold trails from Fairbanks, or rides on the *Alaska Railroad,* as it tunnels through mountains or traverses wilderness spiced with glimpses of wildlife.

Fishing streams, especially those with salmon spawning, will attract the curious. Indians, Aleuts and Eskimos will leave indelible impressions.

Use "Around and About Anchorage with Children" as a guide while there. It's full of ideas for family fun, many free or inexpensive. Ask at bookstores or write P.O. Box 3762-S, Downtown Station, Anchorage, AK 99510.

HOTELS & MOTELS. There's a variety, from frontier to plush, and with prices now about the same as in the "lower 48" states. In smaller towns they may be less expensive than in the big cities, but fewer choices. In general, prices for lodging are higher than in the "lower 48" states. Reserve ahead in summer, unless you are self-sufficient with camper, trailer, or tent. Stop by visitor information centers and Chambers of Commerce wherever you are, for local lodging leads and prices. These are based on double occupancy. *Moderate:* $45–60, and *Inexpensive:* Under $45.

ANCHORAGE. *Moderate:* **Best Western Barratt Inn** and the **International Inn,** both near the airport; **Mush Inn** near Merrill Field; the **Northern Lights Inn,** the **Red Ram Motor Lodge** and the **Voyager Hotel** downtown.
Inexpensive: **The Inlet Inns;** the **Hillside Motel.** and **Johnson's Motel,** both with camper parks, and in the suburbs.

FAIRBANKS. *Moderate:* **Klondike Inn; Maranatha Inn; Tamarac Inn Motel.**
Inexpensive: **Alaska Motel & Apts; Cripple Creek Resort,** with mining camp atmosphere, 11 miles from town; **Aurora Motel** near University of Alaska. **Alaskan Motor Inn,** downtown.

HOMER. *Moderate:* **The Baycrest Motel;** and the **Heritage Hotel.**
Inexpensive: **Anchor River Inn** (16 miles from Homer); and in Homer, the **Driftwood Inn** near the beach.

JUNEAU. *Moderate:* **Driftwood Lodge; Tides Motel.**
Inexpensive: The **Bergmann,** the **Alaskan,** and the **Summit** hotels are vintage and reflect "early Juneau."

KETCHIKAN. *Moderate:* **Hilltop Motel** across from airport and ferry terminal; and the **Ingersoll Hotel,** in the heart of downtown overlooking the waterfront.
Inexpensive: The **Gilmore** downtown adjacent to the Mall. **Ketchikan Bed & Breakfast,** P.O. Box 8515, Ketchikan AK 99901; phone (907) 225-3331.

KODIAK. *Moderate:* **Kodiak Star Motel;** and the **Shelikof Lodge.**

SITKA. *Moderate:* **Potlatch House,** several blocks from downtown; **Sitka Hotel** in the heart of town.

SKAGWAY. *Moderate:* **Irene's Inn; Taiya Lodge; Skagway Inn.**
Inexpensive: **The Bunkhouse,** a step above camping out with showers and laundry facilities.

TOK. *Moderate:* **Golden Bear Motel; Tundra Lodge; Tok Lodge;** Young's **Husky Lounge & Motel.**

VALDEZ. *Moderate:* **Totem Inn; Village Inn; Valdez Motel.**

YOUTH HOSTELS. These are located in Anchorage, Cordova, Juneau, Ketchikan, Denali National Park, and Nome. For more information on facilities and membership, write American Youth Hostels, Delaplane, VA 22025. Alaska Bed & Breakfast Association, 114 So. Franklin, #102, Juneau AK 99801. Phone (907) 586-2959.

DINING OUT. You'll get your money's worth—the portions served are most generous. Don't hesitate to ask the "natives" where they eat—when they want to splurge, and when they want to eat inexpensively, but well. Sometimes eating at "the only place in town" turns out to be delightful, friendly, and delicious. Sourdough and seafood are Alaskan specialties. Larger cities have infinite variety in cuisine, including chains like Colonel Sanders and H. Salt, McDonald's, etc., to aid the food budget. These categories will give a clue to the tab of complete dinners in a sampling of restaurants around the state. Not included are drinks, tax, and tip. *Moderate:* $10–15; and *Inexpensive:* under $10.

ANCHORAGE. *Moderate:* Long a favorite is **Peggy's Airport Café** (Merrill Field); **The Cauldron** and the **Downtown Deli** (healthful things); the **Rice Bowl** (Oriental); and there's no doubt about the myriad specialties at **One Guy from Italy.**

Inexpensive are **Thirteen Coins,** with amazing variety and daily specials; and **The Balcony,** University Center; **Huggebuns,** 6th & I St.

FAIRBANKS. *Moderate:* **Tiki Cove; Hungry Dog** (vegetarian). **The Pump House** has atmosphere and antiques. Besides Mexican food, **Los Amigos** is famous for its ham-cheese sandwich.

Inexpensive: **Arctic Pancake House** across from Log Cabin Visitor's Center; **Star of the North Bakery** has meals, too.

HAINES-PORT CHILKOOT. *Moderate:* **The Bamboo Room, The Lighthouse, Kitchen Restaurant,** and **Sourdough Pizza** in Haines; and **Hotel Halsingland** in Port Chilkoot, with super family-style meals.

HOMER. *Moderate:* They eat well in town and out at the **Willow Wind Restaurant, Ebbtide Dinner House, Porpoise Room** on the Spit, **Putter Inn, Sterling Café,** and **Waterfront Bar and Dining.**

Inexpensive: **Parfait Shoppe,** across from the school, hamburgers, shakes; **Soup Bowl Café & Deli,** Lakeside Mall; **Reel House** for food and movies.

JUNEAU. *Moderate:* **City Café; El Sombrero** (in town) and **Fernando's** (out the Glacier Highway) for fine Mexican dishes; **Mike's Place** across the bridge in Douglas; **Glacier Restaurant & Lounge** at the airport; **Pattie's, Etc.,** a deli-type, take-with or eat there; **Summit Café** serves only 18 at a time, try the tempura and prawns.

Inexpensive: **Bullwinkle's Pizza; Sally's Kitchen;** the **Fiddlehead** in the Driftwood Hotel features vegetarian and home-baked goodies.

KETCHIKAN. *Moderate:* **Kay's Kitchen;** the **Narrows;** the **Fireside; Charley's Restaurant** in the Ingersoll Hotel.

Inexpensive: **The Galley; Harbor Inn; Diaz Café; Angela's Delicatessen.**

KODIAK. *Moderate:* **El Chicano; Sollies; Harvester Food Cache.**

NOME. *Moderate:* **Polar Cub** (lunch and breakfast).

PETERSBURG. *Moderate:* **Sandy's,** near Fisherman's Wharf.

SITKA. *Moderate:* **The Nugget Saloon,** airport; **Revards,** by Cathedral Circle.

Inexpensive: **Fish Factory; Marina Pizzeria.**

SKAGWAY. *Moderate:* **Irene's Inn,** Alaskan food; **Salmon & Sourdough Shedde** across from the Klondike; **Northern Lights Café; Sweet Tooth Saloon; Klondike Barbecue.**

VALDEZ. *Moderate:* **Hangar 9** at airport; **Pizza Palace,** view of pipeline terminal site; **Valdez Café** downtown; **Lamplighter Hotel, Totem Inn** restaurants; and the **Village Inn Dining Room.**

WRANGELL. *Moderate:* The **Dockside** in the Stikine Inn is noted for tiny shrimp in season; Steak and seafood are mainstays in the Totem Bar's **Timber Room.** Try the **Hungry Beaver** at Wrangell's oldest site. The **Roadhouse,** out of town, sends a courtesy car for diners.

CALIFORNIA

America's Future, Today

Those who come to Southern California thinking that they will spend all their time sightseeing within the city limits of Los Angeles are in for a pleasant surprise. Los Angeles proper is a microcosm. It is a large city—some 463.7 square miles—with countless things to see and do here. Furthermore, Los Angeles is merely the center of a much larger area—the Los Angeles basin—extending into Los Angeles County, into Ventura, Orange, Riverside and San Bernardino counties, providing numerous scenic attractions.

Principal attractions in downtown Los Angeles include the Civic Center near the original site of the city, the Old Plaza, now preserved in Olvera Street. There are few remnants of the city's romantic past here, yet to see this monumental civic-center complex of theaters, industry, and commerce is to feel the vigor and vitality of this young city. It has the largest concentration of public buildings west of Washington, D.C.

Downtown's skyline has been dramatically altered in just the past five years. New hotels like the ultra-modern Westin Bonaventure and multi-story office building complexes often in excess of 50 stories now punch the air. Previously no building could be taller than the now-squat City Hall.

At First Street and Grand Avenue is one of the country's most enlightened, municipally supported developments—the Music Center.

Composed of three handsomely designed buildings, it is interconnected by a large landscaped plaza and crowned by Jacques Lipschitz's symbol of peace—an impressive sculpture entitled *Peace on Earth.*

The splendid Dorothy Chandler Pavilion, home of the Los Angeles Philharmonic, where opera, ballet, symphonies, and musical comedies are performed, is also venue for the Academy Awards each year.

The Ahmanson Theater features the Civic Light Opera, musical dramas, and plays. It is a major center of popular entertainment. The Mark Taper Forum features experimental and intimate theater. A number of the Taper's productions, like *Children of a Lesser God,* go on to Broadway.

To orient yourself to Los Angeles, visit the 25th-floor observation area in the City Hall. A clear day provides a panorama of the entire city—Mt. Wilson in the San Gabriel Mountains, the Pacific Ocean, and the Los Angeles Harbor. You may also ascend to the revolving restaurant atop the Hyatt Regency, or to one of several other high-altitude vantage points.

Nearby, facing the Plaza, is Olvera Street, now part of the 42-acre El Pueblo de Los Angeles State Park, a mall of open booths, Mexican restaurants and strolling musicians. Walk and browse; they sell souvenirs, Mexican candies, and handicrafts. Worthwhile bargains in candles, onyx bookends, and sandals. Frequently there is outdoor entertainment. It is no wonder that this is the city's number one tourist attraction, for Los Angeles holds the honor of having the second-largest Spanish speaking population of any city in the world. Many of this metropolis' Spanish-speaking community live in East Los Angeles, where murals of famous Chicano artists adorn the walls, speaking in vibrant colors of California's heritage, her people's struggles, hopes and dreams.

Nearby, at First Street, is Little Tokyo, the Japanese quarter of downtown Los Angeles. The city has one of the largest Japanese populations in the United States. There are unusual gift shops, an ornate Buddhist temple, a few Oriental food markets, fine Japanese book stores and good restaurants. Weller Court, adjacent to the luxurious New Otani Hotel, boasts fine department stores, specialty shops and restaurants.

Chinatown, located off North Broadway near College Street, is a collection of Chinese curio shops and restaurants, the cuisine ranging from mediocre to excellent. Some are so popular that long waits are required for tables, increasing the popularity of local picture galleries, curio shops, and the typical amusement-park entertainment. Travelers can find excellent values in fine silk (by the yard), brocades, lacquerware, soapstone and jade novelties, and kimonos. While not quite as exciting as the New York or San Francisco Chinese quarters, the Los Angeles Chinatown does have lively nighttime activities.

Reaching northwest toward Hollywood, you pass the edge of Griffith Park, the country's largest city park, with over 4,000 mountainous acres. Griffith Park boasts an imposing observatory-planetarium (seen from almost all points in the city and an easily recognizable white art deco building); the open-air Greek Theater (set in a natural canyon below pine-covered mountains), where summer performances play to capacity audiences; golf courses; five tennis courts; baseball fields; and miles of hiking and riding trails. In the center of the park is the Los

Angeles zoo with its 2,000-plus animals. They are grouped by their five continental origins, in areas resembling their natural environments. There's also a Children's Zoo, and Travel Town, featuring vintage transportation. Here, children can explore a Victorian railroad station, antique trains, planes, cable cars, and a swimming pool.

The Los Angeles Municipal Art Gallery is in Barnsdall Park (near corner of Hollywood Blvd. and Vermont Ave.), cached in Frank Lloyd Wright-designed Hollyhock House.

Hollywood

Hollywood is still synonymous with the movies and television. As the glamour capital of the world, it retains much magic because of the stars who work, live and play in this vicinity. For anyone who has not been into a large motion-picture studio, Universal Studios invites you into Never-Never Land (you can catch Hollywood in the act, for a price). Guided tours through the back lot and sound stages are available also at nearby Burbank Studios and NBC.

Hollywood Boulevard brings to mind visions of glamour and excitement few hometowns can equal. Some visitors are disappointed by its honky-tonk. Others are thrilled by famous names and places. The Walk of Fame is a roll call of entertainment's "greats," commemorated in concrete and bronze stars in miles of sidewalks. Check to see when the next unveiling of a new star along the Boulevard will take place. A media event free to the public, the Greater Los Angeles Visitors and Convention Bureau (at 213-488-9100) can tell when and who is set to star next on Hollywood Boulevard's sidewalks.

The celebrated Mann's Chinese Theatre, 6925 Hollywood Boulevard, started the dramatic custom of preserving concrete footprints and handprints of theatrical personalities back in 1927 with Norma Talmadge. By now, millions of tourists have matched their footprints with those of leading cinema personalities. Lasky Studios now stands at 1221 Highland Blvd., in a parking lot across the street from the Hollywood Bowl; that's where the first major motion picture, *The Squaw Man,* was made. It has become the Hollywood Studio Museum, opening to the public this spring and packed with movie memorabilia.

The famous Hollywood sign, which stands 45 feet high, weighing over 480,000 pounds, watches over the city from atop the Hollywood Hills. (See it from the top of a double-decker bus on the Hollywood Fantasy Tour, a two-hour jaunt filled with 87 different attractions.) First erected in 1928, the sign fell into disrepair over the years. Its significance to the community, however, was not forgotten, and a massive fund-raising campaign to reconstruct the sign was launched with a new sign officially rededicated in 1978. It can be seen from the Hollywood Freeway to the now chic Sunset Strip, curving through the city below.

Western Los Angeles

The western section of the city includes Beverly Hills, Century City, Westwood, Brentwood, and Bel Air. These suburbs became part of the vast Los Angeles metropolis in the early 1900s. Most visitors to Southern California have a great desire to see TV and movie stars, who frequent the chic shops, supermarkets, and celebrity haunts of these elegant communities. Starting from the early 1920s, many of the movie colony moved to these suburbs, and it is still a popular area among celebrities. An evening stroll along Wilshire Boulevard in Beverly Hills is perfectly safe.

Century City is a pacesetter for urban development. It is a handsome, well-planned "city within a city." This complex includes Century Plaza Hotel, an elevated shopping mall, (a great place to find trendy Los Angeles fashions and great gifts all under one roof) the ABC entertainment center, towering office buildings and apartments, the Playboy Club, restaurants, and a hospital. The development is built on the grounds that were once Twentieth Century-Fox Studios.

Northwest of Los Angeles, near Beverly Hills, is Westwood, a unique cosmopolitan center, that has retained much of the strolling village atmosphere, with 15 movie theaters and a variety of restaurants. Westwood is the center of much of Los Angeles' night life. One block north of the village is the sprawling campus of the University of California at Los Angeles. UCLA has outstanding departments of medicine, chemistry, theater arts, environmental design and athletics. For a special afternoon, walk through the University's Franklin D. Murphy Sculpture Garden, the Japanese Gardens and the newly expanded Frederick S. Wright Art Galleries, which displays contemporary and historical art, archeological and anthropological artifacts and the reknowned Grunwald Collection.

West of the village are Santa Monica and Venice, two popular beachside communities which offer an exciting variety of activities ranging from body surfing and roller skating to antique hunting, gallery hopping and nighttime entertainment and dining on the reconverted and charming Main Street.

From Pasadena to San Gabriel

Pasadena is located northeast of Los Angeles and is the well-known home of the annual Tournament of Roses (The Rose Bowl) each January 1. The city is famed for its fine residential district, stately old homes, leisurely and aristocratic way of life, and the sprawling Huntington-Sheraton hotel, built at the turn of the century by railroad tycoon Henry E. Huntington.

The site of the Rose Bowl—open throughout the year in the bottom of the Arroyo Seco just west of town—and of the California Institute of Technology, on California Boulevard at Hill Avenue, Pasadena has become even more famous recently as the home of NASA's Jet Propulsion Laboratory. Many of the complicated moon- and Mars-scanning satellites sent aloft from Cape Kennedy in Florida were designed at Pasadena's Jet Propulsion Laboratory by local technicians. Pasadena is also the home of the magnificent Norton Simon Museum (Thurs.–Sun., noon–6 P.M.), and the Pasadena Historical Museum, a 1905 mansion with Pasadena memorabilia.

In La Canada, five miles west, are lovely Descanso Gardens, 1418 Descanso Dr. Each month features floral beauties, from camellias in January to roses, begonias, and fuchsias in June. The 165-acre horticultural haven is part of Rancho San Rafael, located on a 1784 Spanish

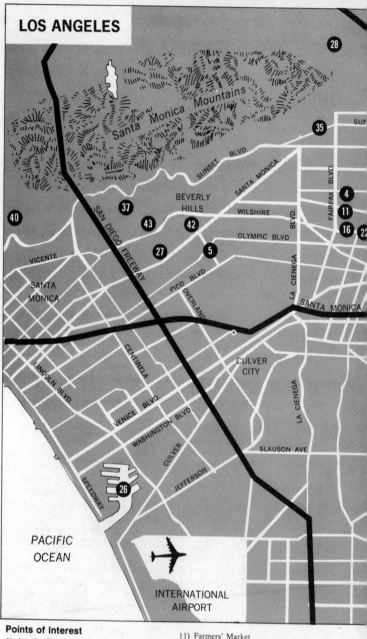

LOS ANGELES

28

35

SUN

Santa Monica Mountains

SUNSET BLVD.

SANTA MONICA

4

FAIRFAX BLVD.

11

BEVERLY HILLS

WILSHIRE

37

16

BLVD.

40

43

42

OLYMPIC BLVD.

27

5

LA CIENEGA

VICENTE

SANTA MONICA

SANTA MONICA

PICO BLVD.

OVERLAND

CENTINELA

CULVER CITY

LINCOLN BLVD.

LA CIENEGA

VENICE BLVD.

SLAUSON AVE.

WASHINGTON BLVD.

CULVER

26

SPEEDWAY

JEFFERSON

PACIFIC OCEAN

INTERNATIONAL AIRPORT

Points of Interest

1) Angelus Temple
2) Atlantic Richfield Plaza
3) California Museum of Science and Industry
4) CBS Television City
5) Century City, Shubert Theater
6) Chinatown
7) City Hall (Los Angeles)
8) Civic Center (Los Angeles)
9) Dodger Stadium
10) Exposition Park

11) Farmers' Market
12) Forest Lawn Memorial Park
13) Mann's Chinese Theater
14) Greek Theater
15) Griffith Park Zoo
16) Hancock Park
17) Hollywood Bowl
18) Hollywood Star Sidewalk
19) La Brea Tarpits, George C. Page Museum
20) Lawry's California Center
21) L.A. Convention Center

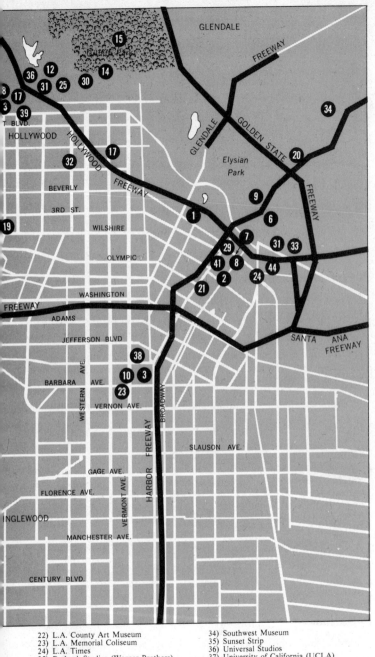

22) L.A. County Art Museum
23) L.A. Memorial Coliseum
24) L.A. Times
25) Burbank Studios (Warner Brothers)
26) Marina del Rey
27) Mormon Temple
28) Mulholland Drive
29) L.A. Music Center
30) Observatory and Planetarium
31) Olvera Street
32) Paramount Studios
33) Pueblo de Los Angeles State Historical
Park

34) Southwest Museum
35) Sunset Strip
36) Universal Studios
37) University of California (UCLA)
38) University of Southern California
39) Wax Museum
40) Will Rogers State Historic Park
41) World Trade Center
42) Beverly Hills
43) Westwood
44) Little Tokyo

Land Grant. Paths wind through the lovely woods, which are threaded by a running stream. More than 150 species of birds find refuge here.

Valleys, Gardens and Show Farms

In Pomona, the Los Angeles County Fairgrounds stage the Los Angeles County Fair each September. There are miles of vineyards in this corner of the Pomona Valley, around Cucamonga and Guasti. There are numerous wineries in the area, most with tasting rooms. It is a colorful sight in the fall to watch the grapes being harvested, and at the winery you can smell the perfume of new wine. At Pomona is California Polytechnic College and the Kellogg Arabian Horse Ranch, where demonstrations by the fine horses are given. Also to be seen in this eastern San Gabriel Valley-Pomona Valley-San Bernardino Valley complex are the last of the great groves of citrus that once blanketed all of this area. Each spring, San Bernardino hosts an 11-day National Orange Show.

Knott's Berry Farm, on Beach Boulevard in Buena Park, is an amusement center theme-park built up from the original industry of raising boysenberries and selling boysenberry jam and pies from a roadside stand. Today the spreading farm has restaurants, still featuring the famous berry pies, and a host of amusements. Shops and rides have a frontier motif. You can pan for gold. Holdups are staged on the narrow-gauge railroad. New at Knotts is the multi-million-dollar remodeling of its famed fiesta village. Included in this bright new package are two unique rides; the Soapbox racers and the Dragon Boat (riding a Viking-style ship), which carries its passengers on an unforgettable boat ride for the brave at heart.

Also on Beach Boulevard in Buena Park is the Movieland Wax Museum, a collection of more than 230 waxen images of famous motion-picture and TV stars in actual onstage settings. Buena Park also has Movie World, featuring Cars of the Stars and movie memorabilia.

Westward, beyond Point Fermin and Cabrillo Beach, is Southern California's Disneyland, and Hanna-Barbera's Marineland, situated right on the ocean in an area where smugglers and pirates used to put ashore. Presented here are the antics of trained whales in a giant seawater tank. There is a larger tank, as well, with viewplates around its circumference at various levels. This vast tank contains all manner of Pacific Ocean fish. Divers frequently visit this large tank and hand-feed the fish. Sharks and barracuda are among the residents. There are also smaller, jewel-case display aquariums, with more delicate and rare fish on display. New is the Adventure Family Swim. Here, guests can swim in half million-gallon tank with 4,000 fish. Visit the film theater and the Fred Flintstone Fun Factory. Enjoy the antics of the Brass Barnacles band. Penguins and cranes decorate the grounds.

Fabulous Disneyland

Disneyland, the "Magic Kingdom," is Walt Disney's legacy to Southern California's amusement and entertainment world. Located at 1313 Harbor Blvd., Anaheim, Disneyland has appealed to visitors of all ages since it opened in 1955. From the entrance into Main Street, a typical thoroughfare in the United States in the 1890s, the various "lands" of Disneyland—Tomorrowland, Frontierland, Fantasyland and Adventureland—open up.

Tomorrowland is typified by the great gleaming monorail that whisks passengers around the park. There is a miniature reproduction of the freeways of the future with scale automobiles that can be driven, as well as a sky ride and a rocket ride to the moon.

Fantasyland is highlighted by the freshly painted Sleeping Beauty's Castle, the most photographed site in all the park. There are a number of "in the dark" rides, such as Mr. Toad's Wild Ride and Peter Pan's flight over the world of fantasy. In this area, too, there are more conventional rides—a gay merry-go-round, a Teacup ride, a bobsled ride down the replica of the Matterhorn, and small boat and train rides.

Frontierland recaptures yesterday. A train ride takes you back into Gold Rush days, past a drowsy little mining camp, into the desert and through a mine lit with myriad-colored waterfalls. There are rivers of America on which two boats, the stern-wheeler *Mark Twain* and the sailing vessel *Columbia,* take visitors on a tour around Tom Sawyer Island. And there are burro-back rides, rides on rafts and in canoes, caves to explore and Indians to fight. In the summer, entertainers perform on the dock and on the two boats that sail around the lagoon.

In Adventureland the most popular rides are the Jungle River Cruise and the Pirates of the Caribbean. Other "theme" lands that are favorites include the "Haunted Mansion," the recently reopened "Matterhorn" with its bobsled run, and the mysterious Abominable Snowman. The park celebrated its 25th anniversary in July 1980, marked by spectacular daily parades and the opening of a new ride, "Big Thunder Mountain." This runaway mine train gives a spine-tingling roller-coaster ride as it travels unleashed down twisting mountain tracks.

When you want to take a break or a rest, you can head for one of the curio shops or eating spots. Merchandise in the shops ranges from inexpensive gifts to exquisite, expensive items. You can take your choice of dining—there are many refreshment stands and fancy restaurants.

No matter when you visit Disneyland, you'll be impressed by its freshness and cleanliness, as well as the friendliness and courtesy of its staff. The park is open year-round (though it keeps shorter hours in the winter). Plan on a good six hours to see everything—there's well over $100 million worth of magic. And do inquire about special prices on ticket books and special events.

PRACTICAL INFORMATION FOR THE

DISNEYLAND AREA

HOW TO GET THERE. *By air:* The John Wayne Orange County Airport is 14 miles south from Anaheim with daily local flights from Los Angeles and San Diego. The airport services *Aircal, Frontier, Golden West, PSA, Republic* and *Sun Aire Airlines.*

Some 35 miles from downtown Anaheim, Los Angeles International Airport (LAX) is easily accessible to Orange County. LAX can be reached from any point in the United States, including Puerto Rico, as well as from major cities in Canada and Mexico.

By car: The Santa Ana Freeway is the major artery running through Orange County. Anaheim is 27 miles (or a 45-minute drive) from downtown Los Angeles.

By train: The *Santa Fe Railroad* operates two passenger trains daily on the San Diego-Orange County-Los Angeles route. *Amtrak* offers six departures daily from Los Angeles south to San Diego with several stops.

HOW TO GET AROUND. *By car: Avis* and *Hertz* have airport offices. Transportation to Disneyland: A number of motels offer transportation to Disneyland for guests.

TOURIST INFORMATION SERVICES. Visitor & Convention Bureau, 800 W. Katella Ave., Anaheim 92802, has booklets, brochures and maps. Buena Park Visitors & Convention Bureau, 6696 Beach Blvd., Buena Park, CA 90621 has information on attractions and accommodations. Automobile Club of Southern California (affiliated with the American Automobile Association) provides members with maps and pertinent information. AAA has offices in all major cities. Headquarters: 2601 S. Figueroa St., Los Angeles 90054.

TOURS. Sightseeing boat trips depart from the piers and docks at Newport Beach.

OLD MISSIONS. San Juan Capistrano, founded in November 1776, is renowned for the legend of its swallows, which reputedly return faithfully to a mission ruin every St. Joseph's Day (March 19). The classic beauty of the "Jewel of the Missions," its gardens and its flocks of white pigeons draw many visitors, especially photographers.

SPORTS. *Fishing:* Newport Beach offers sportfishing services. *Surfing:* Huntington Beach is a surfing center, with Championship Meets in September. *Boating:* Boat marinas and yacht harbors line the Newport Beach shore.

SPECTATOR SPORTS. *Baseball:* Anaheim Stadium, 2000 State College, is the home of the Angels. *Football:* Anaheim Stadium is also the new home of the Los Angeles Rams. Their first home games can be seen August through November. *Boating:* Newport Beach hosts the Flight of the Snowbirds Regatta, in which Snowbird-class catboats race, in July; "Character Boat Parade" in August. *Soccer:* The California Surf hold home games at the Long Beach Arena. *Racing:* Drag racing, time trials and grudge racing, as well as motorcycle races, may be seen at the Orange County International Raceway, Santa Ana Freeway at Sand Canyon Ave.

DRINKING LAWS. California drinking laws are rigidly enforced. The legal drinking age is 21, and, if you're youthful looking, you may be asked for an identification card. Stores and bars are allowed to sell liquor from 6 A.M. to 2 A.M. every day, including holidays.

WHAT TO DO WITH THE CHILDREN. *Disneyland* is the center of a vacation playground designed to delight kids of all ages. *Knott's Berry Farm and Ghost Town,* Beach Blvd. (State 39), Buena Park, takes you back to the Old West and Gold Rush eras. You can pan for gold, ride ore cars and stagecoaches and witness a holdup on the narrow-gauge railroad. The "berry"

is the boysenberry, the original crop, now featured in pies at Knott's restaurants. Across the street is the *California Alligator Farm,* the world's most extensive collection of reptiles. You can take a guided tour to see alligators, crocodiles, snakes and turtles.

Movieland Wax Museum is close by at 7711 Beach Blvd. Over 200 images of famous movie and television stars are displayed in actual on-stage settings. Sample the unusual sandwiches, salads, and soups in their new California Plaza Restaurant.

Movieland of the Air, John Wayne Airport, Santa Ana, preserves a $2 million air force, from Jennies to jets. Kids can climb into real planes and ride in a Waco open bi-plane at rates based on a passenger's weight. Many of the planes have been used in motion pictures, and one former owner, the late aviation pioneer Paul Mantz, was killed flying an experimental model plane for the movie *Flight of the Phoenix.*

Lion Country Safari, African Wildlife Preserve, in Irvine, fronts on the San Diego Freeway at Moulton Parkway. Drive your own car along jungle trails and view African animals in their natural habitat. Cars are allowed within the preserve until dark.

Experience Center at 3531 Main St. in Irvine is a tactile science museum which gives children "hands-on" experience with electronics, space-age technology and computers.

 HOTELS AND MOTELS. Because this area is the locale of Disneyland, Lion Country Safari, aircraft plants and the Anaheim Stadium, Orange County abounds in fine, modern motels. Many have off-season rates from September to May, and offer such fringe family benefits as free cribs, wading pools, rollaway cots, kitchenettes, babysitters, play areas and free shuttle bus service to nearby attractions.

Listings are in order of price category. For a more complete explanation of hotel and motel listings, see *Facts At Your Fingertips.* Based on double occupancy, the price categories and ranges are as follows: *Moderate:* $20–30; and *Inexpensive:* under $20.

ANAHEIM. *Moderate:* **Alamo Motor Lodge.** 1140 W. Katella Ave. Pools, free coffee.

Alpine Motel. 715 W. Katella Ave. TV, swimming, sitters.

Anaheim Travelodge. 1116 W. Katella Ave. Attractive. Pools.

Best Western La Palma Inn. 2691 W. La Palma Ave. Cocktail lounge, kitchens.

Galaxy Motel. 1735 S. Harbor Blvd. Swimming pool, shuttle to Disneyland.

Holiday Inn. 1850 S. Harbor Blvd. Pool. Pets permitted.

Mecca Motel. 1544 S. Harbor Blvd. Swimming pool, Disneyland Hospitality Ticket books.

Park Vue Motel. 1570 S. Harbor Blvd. Pools. Family rates.

Inexpensive: **Ana-Lin Motel.** 2123 W. Lincoln Ave. Pool, low winter rates.

The Mediterranean Inn. 733 S. Beach Blvd. Pool. No pets. 29 rooms.

Polynesian Motel. 641 S. Brookhurst. Pool, coffee shop near property.

HUNTINGTON BEACH. *Moderate:* **Huntington Shores Motor Hotel.** 21002 Ocean Ave., on Calif. 1. Opposite beach. Pleasant.

Sun 'N Sands. 1102 Pacific Coast Hwy. Opposite the beach. Pool, café.

LAGUNA BEACH. *Moderate:* **Vacation Village.** 647 So. Coast Hwy. Good beach location with pool and jacuzzi.

Seacliff Motel. 1661 So. Coast Hwy. Great ocean view.

NEWPORT BEACH-BALBOA BAY. (Reservations necessary in summer and during Easter Week, when teenagers take over the town.)

Moderate: **Newport Channel Inn.** 6030 South Coast Hwy. On the water, quaint.

Newport Beach Travelodge. 6208 W. Pacific Coast Hwy. Opposite beach. Pool.

SAN JUAN CAPISTRANO. *Moderate:* **La Golondrina.** 32232 El Camino Capistrano. Attractive. Sitters, free coffee.

 DINING OUT. The Disneyland visitor will find many good restaurants conveniently located in Orange County. Within an hour's drive is a host of restaurants that will satisfy your yen. Additional listings for restaurants close by, but not in Orange County, are included in the Los Angeles Dining Out section.

It is advisable to call for reservations. Restaurants are listed in order of price category within each city. Price categories and ranges for a complete dinner without drinks, tax or tip are as follows: *Moderate* $7–12; and *Inexpensive* under $7. Restaurants featuring à la carte menus would, of course, be more expensive. For a more complete explanation of restaurant categories, see *Facts At Your Fingertips* at the front of this volume.

ANAHEIM. *Moderate:* **Bessie Walls.** 1704 N. Tustin Ave. This former mansion is now a restored restaurant. Early California food is featured; chicken and dumplings, rabbit Madeira and enchiladas.

Mr. Stox. 1105 E. Katella Ave. Continental, à la carte menu; cocktail lounge with entertainment. Section for non-smokers. Great wine list.

Inexpensive: **Acapulco.** 1410 S. Harbor Blvd. Authentic Mexican cuisine featuring creative concoctions. Casual.

Chalet Pancake and Steak House. 721 W. Katella Ave. Family restaurant near Disneyland.

CORONA DEL MAR. *Moderate:* **Five Crowns.** 3801 E. Coast Hwy. Sunday brunch. Attractive. Old English atmosphere. Very popular.

The Quiet Oman. 3224 East Coast Hwy. Continental cuisine, local favorite.

LAGUNA BEACH. *Moderate:* **Andree's.** Swiss, French cuisine. Old World service.

Ben Brown's Restaurant. Continental menu, entertainment, dancing.

Inexpensive: **El Lugar.** 213 Ocean Avenue. Mexican-American restaurant. Sunday champagne brunch.

ORANGE. *Moderate.* **D'Amico's.** 2710 E. Chapman Ave. Cheerful Southern Italian cooking, cioppino a specialty. Papa D'Amico, waiters and waitresses are always singing, everything from opera to folk.

Inexpensive: **No No's Italian Restaurant.** 1866 Tustin Ave. Great value for hungry pasta lovers and big families with small budgets.

SAN JUAN CAPISTRANO. *Inexpensive:* **Mission Gardens.** 31481 Camino Capistrano. Small, family-style restaurant serves typical Mexican fare. Beer, wine.

Swallows Inn. 31786 Camino Capistrano. Local hangout. Western-style Mexican eatery. Two bars; live entertainment.

Walnut Grove Restaurant. 31688 El Camino Real, Mission San Juan Capistrano exit off US 101. Family-type foods.

CALIFORNIA

PRACTICAL INFORMATION FOR THE
LOS ANGELES AREA

HOW TO GET AROUND. *By air: Golden West Airlines* serves Orange County and Fullerton Airports with commuter flights from Los Angeles. *Air California* has daily flights to and from Palm Springs, as does *Republic. PSA* has daily flights on convenient schedules from Los Angeles International Airport, and also from Hollywood-Burbank Airport.

By car: Avis, National, Budget, Dollar-A-Day and *Hertz* have many offices.

By bus: Continental Trailways and *Greyhound* operate out of the central bus terminal, 6th and Los Angeles Sts., Los Angeles, and out of Hollywood and Santa Monica.

By train: Amtrak has four departures daily to San Diego, and vice versa. Stops at San Clemente, Santa Ana, Fullerton, San Juan Capistrano, and north.

TOURIST INFORMATION SERVICES. *Los Angeles Convention and Visitors Bureau,* 505 S. Flower St., level B, Atlantic Richfield Plaza, provides printed material, helpful information. Another branch is found at 6801 Hollywood Blvd. on the corner of Hollywood and Highland. *Visitor & Convention Bureau,* 800 W. Katella Ave., Anaheim 92802. *Beverly Hills Visitors and Convention Bureau,* 239 S. Beverly Dr., Beverly Hills 90212 (tel. 271–8174).

Automobile Club of Southern California (affiliated with the American Automobile Assn.) provides maps, brochures, booklets and information on highway conditions, special events, theaters, hunting and fishing. For ACSC and AAA members only. Offices in all major cities. Headquarters: 2601 S. Figueroa St., Los Angeles 90054. Tel. 213-746-4070.

Santa Monica Chamber of Commerce, 200 Santa Monica Blvd. (tel. 393–9825), distributes self-guided tour maps of the city, movie-TV personalities' homes, and Palisades Park, where there's a visitors' information booth.

Some useful publications are: *Southern California Guide,* a free monthly guide available at leading tourist spots, packed with info about attractions, accommodations, movies and restaurants.

Where Magazine is a weekly distributed in the better hotel and motel lobbies.

Los Angeles Magazine and *California Magazine* list attractions.

Two free weekly newspapers, the *L.A. Weekly* and *Reader,* offer entertainment guides for Los Angeles and surrounding areas; they're available at most newsstands, and some bookstores, shops and restaurants.

Los Angeles *Sunday Times,* Calendar Section. This supplement to the Sunday *Times,* which comes out Saturday mornings, lists every interesting cultural event of the week to come.

Key Magazine. A pocket-sized weekly guide, free, on counters everywhere. For the *1984 Olympics,* an information center is operated at the Los Angeles International Airport.

MUSEUMS AND GALLERIES. Los Angeles museums maintain fine permanent collections and display significant changing exhibitions. Take your choice of museum displays such as science and natures, ethnic artifacts, fine arts, furniture, technology, crafts and designs. Call the museums, check the Los Angeles *Times,* or *Los Angeles Magazine,* for information on exhibits, lectures, films, dance and special museum programs, hours and admission fees. Gallery viewing may be done on La Cienega Blvd.

Art: *University Galleries,* University of Southern California, 823 Exposition Blvd. Paintings, sculpture, graphics, archaeology. *Municipal Art Gallery,* 4804 Hollywood Blvd. Houses general collection. *Los Angeles Art Association and Galleries,* 825 No. La Cienega Blvd. Changing exhibits of local artists. *Los Angeles County Museum of Art,* 5905 Wilshire Blvd., Hancock Park. Housed in three separate buildings. The Ahmanson Gallery is the main building. Traveling exhibitions can be seen in the Frances and Armand Hammer Wing. The Leo S. Bing Center has an Art Rental Gallery. *Otis Art Gallery,* 2401 Wilshire Blvd. Exhibits and sells the works of the students of the Otis Art Institute semiannually. *Frederick S. Wight Art Galleries,* U.C.L.A., 405 Hilgard Ave. The *Fowler Foundation Museum,* 9215 Wilshire Blvd., Beverly Hills. *J. Paul Getty Museum,* 17985 Pacific Coast Hwy., Malibu (reservations essential). *Lace Gallery,* 243 S. Broadway, *Craft and Folk Art Museum,* 5814 Wilshire Blvd. and *Self-Help Graphics,* 3802 Brooklyn Ave. present the works of some of L.A.'s outstanding artists.

Norton Simon Museum, Colorado and Orange Grove Blvds., Pasadena. The nucleus of the permanent collection is 20th-century works. In addition, the museum showcases sculpture and paintings from the Norton Simon Foundation. There is also a charming restaurant and bookshop. Entrance ticket is exchanged for a free museum print.

San Marino: *Huntington Library, Art Gallery and Botanical Gardens,* 1151 Oxford Rd. Once the home of railroad magnate Henry E. Huntington, this estate boasts many of the world's "only, finest, and earliest," including Thomas Gainsborough's painting, *The Blue Boy,* the world's largest garden of desert shrubs and growths, one of the world's 47 copies of the Gutenberg Bible, early editions of Chaucer and Shakespeare, handwritten works by Benjamin Franklin, George Washington and Edgar Allan Poe. Admission free.

George C. Page Museum, Hancock Park (Wilshire Blvd. next to Los Angeles County Museum of Art). Fascinating collection of Ice Age mammal skeletons (saber-toothed cats, mammoths) displayed at the site of the tar pits (still active) where they were trapped 35,000 or more years ago.

La Cienega Blvd. Art Walk. If it's Tuesday, join the evening art buffs browsing and buying in the 30-odd galleries, boutiques, and antique shops between Melrose and Santa Monica blvds.

Special Interest: *Hollywood Studio Museum,* 1221 Highland Blvd. To be open 1984. Hollywood movie memorabilia housed in Lasky Barn, where the first talking picture was made. *Natural History Museum of Los Angeles County,* 900 Exposition Blvd. *California Museum of Science and Industry,* 700 State Dr., Exposition Park. Space show of missiles and capsules, scientific do-it-yourself gadgets, incubator that hatches 100 chicks. *Ferndell Ranger Station and Nature Museum,* 5375 Red Oak Dr. Collections of insects, reptiles, mammals, and birds, geology, local plants. *Southwest Museum,* 234 Museum Dr., Highland Park. Comprehensive collection of Indian artifacts from North, South, and Central America. *Mount Wilson Observatory,* Hwy. 2 to Mount Wilson Rd. Visitors are admitted for a view of the heavens through the 100-inch telescope. Exhibits of work done at Hale's Observatory. *Marineland of the Pacific,* Palos Verdes Peninsula. World's largest oceanarium. One of the most unique facets of Los Angeles art is the muralist movement. Murals of every imaginable nature—on grocery stores or the Tujunga Wash—can be seen throughout the city. To obtain a map and list of murals in East Los Angeles, Venice and Santa Monica, write SPARC (Social and Public Art Resource Center), 685 Venice Blvd., Venice, California 90291.

Others: *Movieland Wax Museum and Palace of Living Art,* 7711 Beach Blvd., Buena Park. More than 200 waxen images of stars and scenes that made them famous. The *Motorama Museum,* 7001 Hollywood Blvd., showcases famous racing and movie and T.V. stars. *Queen Mary Museum* and *Captain Jacques-Yves Cousteau's Living Sea Museum,* Pier J (at the end of the Long Beach Freeway), Long Beach. In Van Nuys visit *Busch Bird Sanctuary.* It offers 30 acres of tropical gardens and exotic bird life, plus a new multimedia show, "Day of the Balloons." *Magic Mountain* is the state's newest amusement park, and its thrill rides are increasingly popular with all ages.

 HISTORIC SITES. *Avila Adobe,* 14 Olvera St., 1818 historic house. Antique furnishings. *El Alisal,* another historic home, once occupied by the late author, editor and poet Charles F. Lummis, is at 200 E. Avenue 43, east of N. Figueroa, L.A. *Pueblo de Los Angeles,* Olvera St. and the Old Plaza, is a 42-acre state park, undergoing extensive restoration. The adobe *Pio Pico Mansion,* in Whittier, is also an historical monument.

OLD MISSIONS. *San Gabriel Arcangel,* on the outskirts of eastern Los Angeles at 537 W. Mission Dr. in San Gabriel, was the fourth mission to be founded (1771). It is famous for its bells and museum of religious and historical treasures of early California and holds regular church services. Handsome *San Fernando Rey de Espana* is in a valley two miles west of suburban San Fernando at 15151 Mission Blvd. It includes one of the largest single structures of the Mission era.

San Juan Capistrano, the "Jewel of the Missions," founded in November 1776, is known the world over for the legend of its swallows, which return faithfully to a mission ruin every St. Joseph's Day (March 19th). The classic beauty of the mission, its gardens and its flocks of white pigeons attract visitors and photographers in great numbers.

TOURS. *By bus: California Parlor Car Tours.* Overnighters to: Carmel & Monterey, the wine country, South Lake Tahoe and Yosemite Valley. Largest of the sightseeing companies in the Southland is *Gray Line Tours Company* of Los Angeles. There are offices, branches, and travel desks in hotels throughout Southern California. Listed under Sightseeing Tours in the yellow classifed pages are many smaller companies offering individualized tours, multilingual guides, personal chauffeurs in your car or theirs, etc.

Gray Line will, for a large enough group and with enough advance notice, plan any special tour anywhere you want to go. All Gray Line tours make pick-ups at major hotels in Hollywood and Beverly Hills, then join up for a mass departure from the Gray Line, 1207 W. 3rd St., L.A.

Among the tours offered are: Pasadena and Huntington Library; Hollywood, Beverly Hills and Ocean; Universal Studio Tour, includes studio tour plus many of the things in Hollywood and Beverly Hills. Also goes to Forest Lawn, Los Angeles and Hollywood, and Marineland of the Pacific, San Diego and Tijuana, Mexico.

Hollywood Fantasy Tours. 1721 N. Highland Ave., Hollywood 90028; 469-8184. Double-decker bus stops by 87 different attractions.

Starline Sightseeing Tours, 6845 Hollywood Blvd., Hollywood 90028, goes to moviestars' homes in Beverly Hills, as well as Universal Studios.

By boat: Sightseeing boat trips are available from the piers and docks at Malibu, Pierpoint Landing at the Port of Long Beach and at the foot of Mangolia Ave. in the City of Long Beach itself, and from Fisherman's Wharf at Redondo Beach.

Catalina Terminals, Inc., has tours via ship from San Pedro to Santa Catalina Island which include glass-bottomed boat, inland motor trips, seal colony, scenic drives.

Long Beach/Catalina Cruises offers one of three modern boats to Catalina Island. There are also harbor tours at Long Beach, including close-up water view of the *Queen Mary.*

Exciting Los Angeles—Long Beach Harbor helicopter tours lift off from San Pedro's Ports o' Call Village.

SPECIAL INTEREST TOURS. *Stars' Homes Tours.* If time is limited, join either a Starline or Gray Lines bus tour, which highlights celebrities' homes in Beverly Hills and Bel Air.

Architecture Buff's Tour. Everywhere you look, there are sleek, handsome high-rise buildings surging upward—that's L.A. today. However, intermingled with these new structures are older ones that reflect the tastes and styles of the city during different stages. Many are exceptional works and were designed by such world-famous architects as Frank Lloyd Wright and Richard Neutra. They have Spanish, Southern, New England and Far Eastern overtones. Here is a sampling of some of the most fascinating of these: Frank Lloyd Wright's Hollyhock House, built 1917–20, Barnsdall Park; Bradbury Building, 304 S. Broadway, L.A., outstanding iron decoration; Cathedral of Saint Sophia, 1324 S. Normandie Ave., L.A., ornate, Byzantine architecture; Gamble House, Pasadena, Greene, luncheon served and reservations are necessary, charming example of the California bungalow-style; La Casa Pelanconi, 33–35 Olvera St., first brick house in L.A., dates back to 1855, presently a restaurant; Lovel House, 4616 Dundee Ave., the 1929 home that established Richard Neutra's reputation; Queen Anne Cottage, 301 N. Baldwin, part of the Los Angeles State and County Arboretum; fabulous Watts Tower, 33 years in the making, 1765 E. 107 St., L.A. Casa de Adobe, 4605 N. Figueroa St., L.A., duplicates a Spanish hacienda.

There is an annual home tour into private homes designed by master builders and architects. Check with information at the *Los Angeles County Museum of Art* to find out when this is scheduled.

Nature Tour. For a closer look at the migrating gray whales, there are scheduled excursion boats which leave the pier at Long Beach and San Pedro. Best time for whale sightings is Dec. and Jan., when 70 or 80 a day have been counted splashing and sounding their way south.

STUDIO AND ENTERTAINMENT TOURS. On the *Universal Studios Tour,* you'll enjoy a behind-the-scenes look at the world's largest television and movie studio. Guided tour aboard a tram will take you through the back lots and sound stages. You'll peek into star's dressing rooms, survive encounters with the Incredible Hulk and come face-to-face with Universal Studios' most frightening monsters inside the new Castle Dracula. This latest addition is designed to show you how movie techniques are used to build suspense, tension and terror. The *NBC* studios in Burbank also offers a guided tour through the television stages and sets where some of the most popular shows have been filmed. Tickets to admit you free to any live shows open to the public may be obtained at the studio where the show is being filmed. Do call in advance to make sure that seats are still available, as some of the more popular shows fill up quickly. Tickets to ABC shows can be obtained—but not reserved—by calling 213-557-7777. To pick up tickets, visit network ticket booths at ABC TV Center (4151 Prospect Ave.), ABC Vine Street Theater (1313 N. Vine, Hollywood), and ABC Entertainment Center (Plaza Level—2040 Avenue of the Stars, Century City).

CBS programs can be attended by sending a written request to CBS Ticket Office, 7800 Beverly Blvd., LA 90036. Include a return envelope. In Hollywood, you can visit another entertainment-field industry: *Capitol Records,* Tower, 1770 N. Vine St., which is in a unique circular building north of Hollywood Blvd. The visitor is shown the top-floor executive offices and a film history of record making.

 GARDENS. *Exposition Park Rose Gardens,* Exposition Blvd. between Figueroa St. and Vermont Ave., has 150 species of roses on 15,000 bushes in seven areas. They bloom with heavenly scent and color during spring and summer. One of the world's most complete cactus gardens is found at the *Cactus Gardens* on the north side of Santa Monica Blvd. between Camden and Bedford Drives in Beverly Hills.

And there's U.C.L.A. *Botanical Garden,* southeast end of campus near Le Conte and Hilgard Aves. Printed trail guide available at entrance tells about each numbered tree and other flora and fauna. For botany buffs, a guided group tour may be arranged by calling U.C.L.A. Visitors' Center. The university also offers the serene and authentic Japanese Gardens, a most rewarding experience.

At the *Descanso Gardens,* in La Canada, camellias are in bloom from late Dec. thru March.

In Pasadena, the gardens at the Huntington Library, Art Gallery and Botanical Gardens is a superb spot, possibly the finest gardens in California. The 130 landscaped acres include the Shakespeare Garden, the desert garden, and the Japanese garden. Free, but Sunday visitors must phone ahead to make reservations.

SPORTS. *Fishing:* You will find the best ocean sportfishing services at Malibu, Redondo Beach, San Pedro and Santa Monica.

Surfing: The entire city of Huntington Beach is directed toward surfing. Walk out on the Huntington Beach Pier, catch the Championship Meets in Sept., watch in amazement as they "shoot" (means "going through" in surfers' language) the pier pilings. The "Wedge" in Corona del Mar is the most famous body-surfing beach in California—waves up to 20 feet! Malibu Beach is always crowded—the "real" surfers say that it has the best point break in California, meaning that the swell is in the right direction. At Leo Carrillo Beach in Malibu, the surfers take off next to 10-foot rocks and surf waves up to seven feet. The oceanfront is part of Leo Carrillo State Park; it has picturesque rocky-sandy beaches and camping areas.

Boating: There are boat marinas and yacht harbors in Playa del Rey just south of Santa Monica, in San Pedro, Long Beach, Newport Beach, Laguna Beach. An annual Grand Prix Power Boat Race takes place from Long Beach in Sept.

Golf: According to "Golf Digest," the Riviera G.C., at Pacific Palisades, ranks among the second ten best of U.S.A.'s 100 greatest golf courses; Los Angeles G.C., among the third ten. El Rancho is an excellent public course; there is also one at Griffith Park.

Other courses in the Los Angeles area (all of them municipal) recommended by "Golf Digest" are: Rancho Park G.C., Los Angeles; Brookside G.C., Pasadena; Costa Mesa. *Pala Mesa Golf/Tennis/Health Resort,* near Escondido, also boasts one of the best courses in the U.S.A.

Jogging: Jogging has become a tradition in California. Join other joggers in open spaces, along the waterfront at the beaches, on special paths in the parks, during the winter or summer. A favorite jogging stretch is along San Vincente Blvd., from the Pacific Palisades Park, along a wide grassy strip with coral trees through Brentwood and also at UCLA in Westwood. If you prefer the use of showers and other facilities, try the *YMCA,* 11311 La Grange, Westwood, Uniturf jogging track on roof; or the *YMCA,* 1553 N. Hudson, Hollywood, men and women, 1/16th-mile roof track.

Bicycling: For information on bicycling clubs, contact the *American Youth Hostels,* 7603 Beverly Blvd.

You can play *tennis, hike, ride* at Griffith Park. There are numerous tennis courts in Long Beach's 35 municipal parks.

Tennis: There are hundreds of free municipal and pay-for-play courts in Los Angeles, where tennis is more popular than any other sport. Also some of the top private tennis clubs in the country are here.

Roller Skating: This fun-filled albeit risky activity has become one of the most popular sports in town. People of all ages and sizes are renting skates at the roller rinks and more popular "Speedway" rental booths in Santa Monica and Venice.

 WINTER SPORTS. Ski areas offer all types of slopes. Rentals range from skis to snowmobiles, depending on location. Novice to expert runs can be found at Blue Ridge Ski Area, Holiday Hill Ski Lifts, which also has a toboggan run, Kratka Ridge, Mt. Waterman and Table Mountain Ski area.

 SPECTATOR SPORTS. *1984 Olympics:* The games will run July 28, 1984–August 12, 1984. For detailed information contact Los Angeles Olympic Organizing Committee, Los Angeles 90084; (213) 209–1984. *Baseball:* Dodgers, April through September, at Dodger Stadium in L.A.; Anaheim Stadium, Anaheim, home of the Angels, and adding further to the build-up of this Orange County area as a major economic sector in the state of California.

Basketball: The modern Inglewood Forum, a 15,000-seat-capacity sports palace, is where the pros (Los Angeles Lakers) and the collegiates dribble. Track meets and other sports spectaculars show off here, plus circuses. UCLA's championship squad goes at it at Pauley Pavilion on the campus.

Football: Now that the Los Angeles Rams have moved to Anaheim, the U.S.C. Trojans and U.C.L.A. Bruins offer the best spectator football in the city. The famous Rose Bowl follows the Rose Parade each New Year's Day, and is played at the Rose Bowl Stadium in Pasadena.

Golf: Annual Andy Williams PGA Tournament, Pasadena; Glen Campbell-L.A. Open Golf Tournament, Rancho Park Golf Course.

Auto Racing: A big sport in Southern California—very well-attended year-round at Ascot Park in Gardenia and Riverside International Raceway, Riverside. The Long Beach Grand Prix in early April, draws more than 30 of the world's top Formula One drivers for three days of celebrity and pro racing. (Ticket information: Long Beach Grand Prix Association, 110 W. Ocean, Suite A, Long Beach, CA 90802).

Horse Racing: Santa Anita Racetrack, Arcadia, (at the junction of Huntington Dr. and Colorado Pl.) Dec.–early April. Oak Tree Thoroughbred Racing, Oct. through Nov., Santa Anita Park; $500,000 Santa Anita Handicap, early March. Thoroughbred racing at Hollywood Park Racetrack, Inglewood. April through July and night Harness Racing at Los Alimitos Sept. through Dec.

Ice Hockey: From October–March, fans are out at the Forum for the Los Angeles Kings.

Drag races are at Orange County International Raceway, Santa Ana Freeway at Sand Canyon Ave., and San Diego Freeway, Moulton Parkway. Also, monthly *motorcycle races* and the Super Bowl of Motocross, held annually at the Coliseum. In Sept., the Ontario Motor Speedway near Pomona is the site of the annual California 500. *Boxing:* At the Olympic Auditorium in downtown Los Angeles and at the Forum.

WHAT TO DO WITH THE CHILDREN. *Hanna-Barbera's Marineland* is about 30 miles from downtown L.A. on Palos Verdes Peninsula. Adjoining restaurant and motel. Renamed and remodeled, it features new sealife displays and animal shows. The Adventure Family Swim is new at Marineland. Here, guests can swim in a half million-gallon tank with 4,000 fish.

Lion Country Safari, African Wildlife Preserve, in Irvine, fronting on the San Diego Freeway at Mouton Parkway. Drive your own car along jungle trails and view African animals in their natural habitat.

Los Angeles Zoo, 5333 Zoo Dr., Griffith Park, reached via Ventura and Golden State Freeways. Across from the zoo is the new *Equestrian Center,* an Olympic-caliber center with frequent horse shows. Call (213) 840–9063.

Queen Mary, Long Beach. In addition to a museum and self-guided tour, visit *Jacques Cousteau's Living Sea,* a marine museum. Also new on the scene is *Howard Hughes' Spruce Goose. Magic Mountain,* Valencia. 85 acres of rides and attractions.

Busch Bird Sanctuary, Van Nuys. Guided monorail tour of brewery. Boat cruise through 20-acre landscaped bird paradise.

STAGE. The theater scene is growing in Los Angeles. In fact, some refer to this city as the Broadway of the West. To better facilitate travelers on a budget, Los Angeles' first half price ticket booth opened in 1982. Located in Westwood (near UCLA) and similar to operations in New York, London, and Chicago, tickets go on sale the day of performance at a 50 percent discount, plus service charge. All major Los Angeles theaters are participating. Tickets also available to dance, opera, and concert happenings. At 1093¼ Broxton Ave. in the Patio next to Wherehouse Records and also at a new location at the Sherman Oaks Galleria, 15301 Ventura Blvd.

From mid-July to the end of August, take in the Free Public Theater Festival at the Gallery Theater in Barnsdall Park. Schedule available from Theater Festival LA, 6523 Hollywood Blvd., Suite 222, Los Angeles 90028.

HOTELS AND MOTELS. Listings are in several sections: first is the downtown (central) area of the city, followed by the leading outlying areas and distinctive neighborhoods, such as Hollywood, Beverly Hills, West Los Angeles and Santa Monica, listed in alphabetical order. Listings are in order of price category. For a more complete explanation of hotel and motel listings, see *Facts At Your Fingertips,* earlier in this book. *Note:* The Olympics will be in LA July 28–August 12, 1984, and accommodations will be unusually hard to come by.

Based on double occupancy, the price categories and ranges are about as follows: *Moderate* $25–45; and *Inexpensive* under $25.

DOWNTOWN LOS ANGELES. *Moderate:* **Alexandria.** Spring St. at Fifth St. Restored 1905 hotel.

Gala Inn Towne. 925 So. Figueroa St. Large spacious rooms.

L.A. Downtown Travelodge. 1710 W. 7th St. Pleasant rooms.

Park Plaza Lodge. 6001 W. 3rd St. Attractive.

Vagabond Figueroa Motor Hotel. 3101 S. Figueroa St. Handsome rooms.

Inexpensive: **Cloud Motel.** 3400 W. Third St. Centrally located.

Downtowner Motel. 944 S. Georgia St. Double-story.

Holiday Lodge Motels. Downtown locations; 811 N. Alvarado St., 1631 W. Third St. (more elaborate).

Milner Hotel. 813 S. Flower at 8th across from the Broadway Plaza.

Oasis Motel. 2200 W. Olympic Blvd. Quiet, attractive.

Royal Viking. 2025 W. 3rd St. Restaurant.

WEST LOS ANGELES. *Moderate:* **L.A. West Travelodge.** 10740 Santa Monica Blvd., Westwood Village. Complimentary extras.

Stardust Motor Hotel. 3202 Wilshire Blvd. near UCLA and Westwood.

AVALON (CATALINA ISLAND). *Moderate:* **Pavilion Lodge.** 513 Crescent Ave. Across from beach.

Zane Grey Pueblo. Chimes Tower Rd. Former home of Zane Grey.

BEVERLY HILLS. *Moderate:* **Beverly House.** 140 S. Lasky Dr. Complimentary continental breakfast Sundays.

Inexpensive: **Beverly Vista.** 120 South Reeves near Wilshire Blvd. and Beverly Dr. Hostel-type accommodations. Choice of many European visitors.

HOLLYWOOD. More expensive Hollywood motels generally are in the Sunset Strip area. Farther out, the rates are apt to be lower.

Moderate: **Best Western Hollywood Franklin Motor Hotel.** 6141 Franklin Ave., between Gower and Argyle St. Comfortable. Some kitchens.

Hollywood Travelodge. 7370 Sunset Blvd. "Sleepy Bear" member.

Sahara Motor Hotel. 7212 Sunset Blvd. Pool; plenty of free parking.

Inexpensive: **Highlander Motor Inn.** 2051 N. Highland Ave. Coffee shop.

Saharan Motor Hotel. 7212 Sunset Blvd. near La Brea. Swimming pool.

INGLEWOOD. *Moderate:* **Airport Hotel.** 600 S. Prairie Ave. Airport transportation.

Hacienda. 525 N. Sepulveda Blvd. Airport transportation.

Ramada Inn. 9620 Airport Blvd. Airport transportation.

LONG BEACH. *Moderate:* **Downtown TraveLodge.** 80 Atlantic Ave. Near ocean, Queen Mary.

Holiday Inn. 2640 Lakewood Blvd. at Willow St. Attractive, multi-story circular.

Ramada Outrigger Inn Motor Hotel. 5325 E. Pacific Coast Hwy. Polynesian mood.

PASADENA. (Reservations mandatory during Tournament of Roses and Rose Bowl Game on New Year's Day.)

Moderate: **Pasadena Motor Hotel.** 2131 W. Colorado Blvd. Some cottages, swimming pool.

Inexpensive: **Pasada Motel.** 3625 E. Colorado Blvd. near Santa Anita, visitors attractions.

SANTA MONICA. *Moderate:* **Roman Inn.** 530 Pico Blvd. and 6th Ave. Swimming pool, jacuzzi, game room, coffee shop.

Santa Monica TraveLodge. 1525 Ocean Ave. Overlooks the ocean.

HOSTELS. Los Angeles International Hostel. 1502 Palos Verdes Dr. N., Harbor City. Self-service, kitchen, TV room. French and German staff.

 DINING OUT. Dining in the Los Angeles area has become sophisticated and international in accent. The gourmet can dine on superb continental cuisine in a variety of elegant settings—some quiet and intimate, others *a la Français,* with strolling musicians. There are the chic eateries that attract "the beautiful people," and there is the gamut of ethnic restaurants. So whether your preference is for Mexican, Polynesian, Greek, Japanese, Chinese, or just good, tasty traditional food, you'll be able to please your palate in the City of the Angels. It is advisable to call for reservations.

Restaurants are listed in order of price category within each type of cuisine. Price categories and ranges for dinner for two, without wine, are: *Moderate* $15–20; and *Inexpensive* $7–15. Restaurants featuring á la carte menus are more expensive. For a more complete explanation of restaurant categories, see *Facts At Your Fingertips* at the front of this volume.

Chinese. Moderate: **Liu's.** 140 S. Rodeo Dr., Beverly Hills. Mandarin and Szechuan cuisine.

Continental. Moderate: **The Egg and the Eye.** 5814 Wilshire Blvd. Across the street from the Los Angeles County Art Museum is this delightful restaurant specializing in omelets and crepes. Reservations suggested. Closes at 5 P.M.

French. Moderate: **L.A. Nicola.** 4326 Sunset Blvd. Nouvelle Cuisine at incredible prices. Hi-tech décor. Great hors d'oeuvres. Chef excels with fish, chicken dishes. Around the corner from ABC Studios.

American. Inexpensive: **Phillippe, The Original.** 1001 North Alameda near Union Station. Great French-dip sandwiches, casual atmosphere, sawdust on the floor. Coffee is still 10 cents.

Japanese. Moderate: **Benihana of Tokyo.** Hibachi-style Japanese cuisine (cooked at your table); delicious, too. 38 N. LaCienega Blvd. Also: 16226 Ventura Blvd., Encino; 14160 Panayway, Marina Del Rey.

Mexican. Inexpensive: **Lucy's El Adobe.** 5536 Melrose Ave. Known for its excellent food; in a charming atmosphere. A Jerry Brown L.A. hangout.

Thai. Moderate: **Chao Praya.** In Hollywood at Yucca and Vine. Unquestionably the best Thai restaurant in the greater Los Angeles area, at amazingly low prices. The beef and pork satay drenched in a delectable peanut sauce is scrumptious; the garlic chicken a delight. Comfortable, homey atmosphere.

The Fez. 1508 N. Vermont Ave. Arabian belly dancers, audience participation.

Polynesian. Inexpensive: **Kelbo's Hawaiian Barbecue.** 101 N. Fairfax Ave. Island atmosphere.

WEST HOLLYWOOD. *Moderate:* **Oscar's.** 8210 Sunset Blvd., West Hollywood. English-style bistro. Chicken and parsley pie, Stilton quiche or steak and kidney pie.

Butterfield's. Alfresco or indoor dining of "healthy" edibles. Picturesque setting at 8426 Sunset Blvd.

The Ginger Man. Bedford Dr., off Wilshire Blvd. Beverly Hills. Chic décor, great hamburgers. Happy hour draws singles.

La Masia. 9077 Santa Monica Blvd., West Hollywood. Spanish. Epicurian dishes served in an elegant atmosphere. Classical guitarist.

Old World. 8782 Sunset Blvd. The outdoor patio faces the Strip is good for people-watching.

La Villa. 5724 Melrose. Serves specialties of 21 Latin American countries. Unique restaurant, good value.

SANTA MONICA. *Moderate:* **The Famous Enterprise Fish Company.** 174 Kinney St., Santa Monica. A great place to relax and enjoy a hearty seafood dinner after a day at the beach. All fish is served charcoal-broiled.

Gladstone's 4 Fish. 146 Entrada Dr., Santa Monica Canyon. Wide selection of fresh seafood. Char-broiled over mesquite. Enormous-sized desserts. Friendly young waiters.

Inexpensive: **El Tepa.** 1426 Pico Blvd., Santa Monica. Don't let the small cantina atmosphere fool you; this restaurant offers some of the best northern Mexican food in town, at the right price.

COFFEEHOUSES AND CAFÉS. Catering to the appetite needs of the "traveler on the go," they are conveniently located throughout the city near theaters, at the beaches, parks, and entertainment centers. Some stay open around the clock.

Two lively coffee houses with Hollywood atmosphere are *City Cafe,* 7407½ Melrose, Hollywood, and *Figaro,* 9010 Melrose Ave., West Los Angeles. Both have excellent food, informal atmosphere. You'll find a truly bohemian atmosphere and fine entertainment at the *Deja Vu Coffeehouse,* 1705 N. Kenmore in Hollywood. Among French cafés are *Michel Richard* (310 S. Robertson) on the edge of Beverly Hills, and *La Poubelle* (5909 Franklin) in Hollywood.

For the best chili-dogs—a California specialty—you must try *Pink's* at Melrose and La Brea. Great hamburgers are made at *Carney's* on the Sunset Strip, *Tommy's* on Beverly Blvd. *Fat Jack's* on Ventura Blvd. in Studio City or *The Apple Pan* on Pico Blvd, West L.A.

If you're out in Pasadena, you shouldn't miss the *Espresso Bar,* 34 S. Raymond Ave. Monday night, there's jazz in the alcove. Persian rugs and fireplace create a unique café atmosphere comparable to Europe or South America.

Check the *Los Angeles Times* Calendar section, *Los Angeles Magazine* and the *L.A. Weekly* and *Reader* for a more extensive rundown on the inexpensive and moderately priced entertainment in town. This includes the many new small theaters of the highest quality, jazz nightclubs and disco dancehalls, comedy clubs and of course, movies.

EXPLORING SAN DIEGO

San Diego, the "Harbor of the Sun," ranks second among California's natural harbors, and is home port for the Eleventh Naval District, with approximately 125 active U.S. Navy ships. A lighthouse tips Point Loma, the land arm hugging the bay on the west. It is Cabrillo National Monument, the No. 1 National Monument among visitors, outpacing the Statue of Liberty in popularity. Park also includes visitor center, walking trail, whale-watch station, Cabrillo statue.

North Island, power-packed with the U.S. Naval Air Station, is the geographic fist of the southeastern arm protecting the bay. The adjoining community of Coronado is a favorite anchorage for retired Naval officers. "The Del," dowager queen of California's hotels, has crowned Coronado since 1888. Formally known as the Hotel del Coronado, this resort and convention site has drawn a royal clientele. Guests have included the Prince of Wales, the Maharajah of Jaipur, and eight presidents of the United States. The skinny arm of barrier beach extends southward toward the city of Imperial Beach. Silver Strand State Park's beach facilities are along the route.

The Coronado Bay Bridge connects San Diego and Coronado. Harbor excursion boats leave the Broadway pier for one- and two-hour cruises around San Diego Harbor. The excursions head toward Shelter Island and Point Loma, passing cargo vessels and Navy ships. The *Star of India* has been restored and is moored alongside the Embarcadero as part of a three-ship maritime museum. The vessel, launched in 1863, is now the oldest ship afloat. Much of San Diego's cultural and recreational life centers on Balboa Park. The 1,400-acre garden spot is one of the country's finest city parks. Gracious Spanish Baroque buildings house many attractions, including the Fine Arts and Timken Galleries, displaying Old Masters' works, Russian icons, exceptional changing exhibitions; the Reuben H. Fleet Space Theater and Space Center, Aero-Space Museum, Museum of Man, Natural History Museum, and the Botanical Building. A new 750-seat Festival Theater is scheduled to replace the arson-destroyed Old Globe. Meanwhile, the Shakespeare Festival is staged in a temporary amphitheater. The 5,000-pipe Spreckels organ is one of the world's largest outdoor organs; Sunday recitals are presented regularly. The House of Pacific Relations is a quaint collection of 15 cottages representing 20 nationalities, their folkways and traditions. The San Diego Zoo also is in Balboa Park. Most of the 5,500 animals of 1,600 species live outdoors in simulated natural habitats. There are huge walk-through, free-flight cages for viewing some of the zoo's 2,850 birds, including condors with 10-foot wingspreads.

Sea World is the home of several dolphins, assorted seals and a killer whale, plus marine shows and attractions.

The San Diego Wild Animal Park is 30 miles northeast of downtown but still within city limits. An electric monorail train takes visitors through the 1,800-acre site where 1,000 animals live in near-natural habitats. Presidio Park and the Junipero Serra Museum (historical relics of the Southwest) mark the site where Spanish padres founded the first of California's missions in 1769. Mission San Diego de Alcala later was relocated five miles up Mission Valley. The mission's original five bells still hang from the belfry. The University of San Diego's archeological research is unearthing fascinating artifacts, on display in the mission's museum. Old Town State Historic Park is around the plaza below Presidio Park. Adobe buildings of the later Spanish rancho era and Early California restaurants dot Old Town. Seaport Village is San Diego's newest attraction. Located in the shadow of the San Diego –Coronado Bridge at the foot of Harbor Drive and Pacific Highway, Seaport Village has three connected sections: Old Monterey, Victorian San Francisco, and traditional Mexico. Appropriate architecture pinpoints each section, and Northern Pacific-style five-story lighthouse guards the edge of the quarter-mile boardwalk. Featured are 50 boutiques and many restaurants. Adjacent to Seaport Village is the eight-acre Embarcadero Marine Park.

PRACTICAL INFORMATION FOR SAN DIEGO

 HOW TO GET THERE. *By air: Republic, Golden West, American, Delta, Air California, National, Pacific Southwest, United, Ozark, Continental,* and *Western Airlines* serve San Diego. *By car: Avis, Budget, Dollar-A-Day, Hertz,* and *National* have car rental offices in San Diego. *By bus:* City buses are your best bet. You can take them up to La Jolla, down to the Mexican border, and to Coronado, Point Loma, La Mesa and El Cajon.

By train: Amtrak operates from Los Angeles and Orange County, with several stops en route. The downtown Santa Fe Amtrak Station is located at Kettner Blvd. and Broadway.

 TOURIST INFORMATION SERVICES. Write to or visit the *San Diego Convention & Visitors Bureau,* 1200 3rd Ave., Suite 824, San Diego 92101, for maps and booklets on tours, golf, restaurants, hotels, motels, and what to do and where to go in San Diego and vicinity. Call (714) 232–3101 from 9 A.M. to 5 P.M.; after hours, (714) 239–9696. The *San Diego Union* and *Evening Tribune,* 350 Camino de la Reina, San Diego, hands out a San Diego Facts Book. *San Diego Magazine* has current input on attractions, dining and shopping.

 MUSEUMS AND GALLERIES. *San Diego Historical Society, Serra Museum, Library and Tower Gallery,* 2727 Presidio Dr., Presidio Park, honors the Franciscan founder of California's missions. Located on the site of the first mission, founded in 1769 by Fray Junipero Serra and Gov. Capt. Gaspar de Portola. The museum contains relics and documents concerning the history of San Diego and environs. Setting and view are magnificient.

Whaley House, 2482 San Diego Ave., displays historical items.

Villa Montezuma, 1925 K St., is a restored Victorian era home.

In San Diego's 1,400-acre Balboa Park: the *Museum of Man* traces mankind's history with emphasis on American Indian cultures; the *Natural History Museum* contains exhibits of birds, fish, reptiles, mammals and prehistoric animals; the $4 million *Reuben H. Fleet Space Theater and Science Center* features a futuristic space adventure shown on the largest projection dome in the U.S. and a scientific do-it-yourself exhibit hall; the *House of Pacific Relations* is a folk museum representing 20 nationalities; the *Fine Arts Gallery* of San Diego features changing and permanent exhibitions of Flemish, Renaissance, Italian, Spanish and contemporary art. The *San Diego Art Institute* offers both exhibits and competitions of institute members. When visiting Balboa Park, you can obtain maps, brochures and information at Park Information Center, House of Hospitality.

Others: Two other art museums are the *La Jolla Museum of Contemporary Art,* 700 Prospect in La Jolla, and the *Mingei International Museum of World Folk* at 4405 La Jolla Village Dr. One of the largest model railroad operations in the country is at *House of Charm,* Balboa Park. A maritime museum at the complex (Embarcadero, Harbor Drive at Broadway) includes the merchant windjammer *Star of India,* 1800s ferryboat *Berkeley* and WW I-vintage yacht *Medea.*

HISTORIC SITES. San Diego harbors an entire historical *Old Town State Park,* "where California began." Follow a painted green line, your guide through history, for glimpses of the early days, with stops at Early California restaurants. Daily ranger-led tours. The *Cabrillo National Monument* commemorates the discovery of the West Coast. Seaport Village, a shopping and dining complex located in the shadow of the San Diego–Coronado Bridge, reflects San Diego's harborside as it was a century ago, complete with authentic architectural styles and furnishings.

 OLD MISSIONS. *Mission San Diego de Alcala,* the first of 21 links in the California mission chain stretching north along El Camino Real (The King's Highway) to Sonoma, was founded by the Franciscan padre, Junipero Serra. Today, peaceful gardens grace the site where the state's first palm and olive trees were planted. The mission museum contains religious relics and items from that era.

San Luis Rey de Francia, about five miles east of Oceanside, was founded in 1798. The 18th and largest mission now is a seminary. Dates back to 1789, called the "King of Missions." Self-guided tours.

San Antonio de Pala, constructed in 1816 near Palomar Mtn., Hwy. 76, as an *asistencia* to San Luis Rey.

Santa Ysabel, an *asistencia* to Mission San Diego de Alcala, built in 1818; Hwy. 79, north of Julian.

 TOURS. San Diego offers a wide variety of tours and packages such as "golf " outings, San Diego Zoo and Sea World Trips. Write: San Diego Convention and Visitor's Bureau, 1200 Third Ave., Suite 824, San Diego 92101.

Bike Tours: Bike tours are a natural for Southern California. One possibility, covering approximately eight miles, combines "a ride back into California history" and a pleasant view of San Diego's surrounding bay, sea and landscape. Start at Pepper Grove Dr., in Balboa Park. Ride along El Prado, pedal to Upas St., ride west to a connection with Third Ave., continue along University Ave. and Ft. Stockton Dr. to Presidio Park—the site of the original mission. The view from this vantage point encompasses Point Loma, San Diego Bay and Mission Valley. Then ride down the slope to Old Town where you can relax in Old Town Plaza, follow the painted green line leading to historical sights, or lunch at one of the excellent Mexican restaurants.

The *Fun Bus* operates between Anaheim and San Diego three times a day. In addition, seven days a week, the company runs excursions to both Los Angeles and Las Vegas. Contact Fun Bus at 304 Katella Way, Anaheim, 92802.

A 3.6-mile *La Jolla bike tour* runs along the ocean. Start at La Jolla Cove, pedal along Coast Blvd., ride along Neptune Place, continue to Chelsea St., and follow the well-marked route to its end at Turquoise St. Stops along this tour will allow you to explore La Jolla caves, view charming seaside homes, and see Bird Rock, at times covered with flocks of sea gulls, pelicans and cormorants.

Horseback, sightseeing hikes and jeep tours: Available at *Anza Borrego Desert State Park.* Best season is mid-January through April.

By *boat:* One- and two-hour excursions around the San Diego Harbor depart from the Broadway Pier. Whale-watching excursion boats depart from the San Diego Bay and Mission Bay piers, generally Dec. through April.

Across the border is the Mexican city of Tijuana, offering a wide variety of colorful shops, restaurants, Mexican festivals and sporting events. The newest mode of transportation between San Diego and Tijuana is the *San Diego Trolley.* Comparable to a San Francisco cable car, it makes a 40-minute trip through town, beginning at the Amtrak train station, ending at San Ysidro on the U.S. side of the border. (Price: $1). Buses or taxis there complete the trip into town. Daily tours from San Diego to Tijuana are offered by Gray Line and Mexicoach. More extensive trips through Baja California can be arranged through El Pasco tours. Contact the San Diego Convention and Visitors Bureau to find out which of the many tourist services to Mexico provide the type of guided trip you desire.

NATURE: *San Diego Zoo.* One of the world's largest zoos. Guided bus tour and Skyfari aerial tramway. Also children's zoo. *San Diego Wild Animal Park* is an 1,800-acre preserve within city limits. Exhibits, snack bars, shops and guided five-mile monorail tour. *Sea World,* 1720 S. Shores Rd., Mission Bay, has daily shows, Hydrofoil boat ride, Japanese Village, and Skytower ride.

SPORTS. *Surfing* is popular along the 10 miles of beaches in the county, with La Jolla's Wind 'n' Sea Beach said to be the best this side of Hawaii. To learn where the surfing is good, telephone 714–225–9494.

Fishing: If there's a fisherman's paradise, it's the San Diego area. Take your pick of fishing surface, bottom, surf, rock, bay, shell and freshwater for albacore, barracuda, bluefin tuna, bonita, grunion, mackerel, kelp bass, white sea bass, marlin, swordfish and yellowtail. Ocean sport-fishing services are offered year-round by a number of operators. For further information, contact the San Diego Convention and Visitors Bureau.

Boating: Boat marinas and yacht harbors ring Mission Bay, Harbor Island and Shelter Island.

Water sports: Full range of facilities are available at Mission Bay Park, Carlsbad, Shelter Island and Harbor Island.

Tennis: The La Jolla Beach & Tennis Club has eight championship courts. But tennis is booming everywhere in this area, with the Parks and Recreations Dept. operating 145 public courts, and 1200 public courts counted in the county. Morley Field in Balboa Park has 25 two-tone cement courts, a stadium court, pro shop, and clubhouse. *Free courts* include those at Mesa, Grossmont, Palomar, Mira Costa and Southwestern College, Escondido, Helix, Poway, Vista and Chula Vista high schools.

Golf: San Diego is "Golfland, U.S.A.," with 70 year-round courses. Among the many recommended by "Golf Digest" are: Pauma Valley C.C., Pauma Valley; Torrey Pines G.C., S. La Jolla; and La Costa C.C., Carlsbad. All are ranked among the second 50 of America's great golf courses.

Bicycling: Most of the clubs are affiliated with the American Youth Hostels. For details, contact the A. Y. H., 1031 India St., San Diego.

Jogging: Groups for men and women: San Diego Parks and Recreation Dept.; Y.M.C.A., 1115 8th Ave.

SPECTATOR SPORTS. *Football:* The Chargers play at San Diego Stadium.

Soccer: Catch the San Diego Sockers at the San Diego Sports Arena for the winter indoor season; outdoor spring games are at San Diego Stadium.

Basketball: The Clippers play home games at the San Diego Sports Arena.

Baseball: Spring Padres games are at San Diego Stadium.

Horse Racing at Del Mar Race Track, 15 mi. north of San Diego. The season is mid-July to mid-Sept. Also horse and dog racing all year at Agua Caliente Racetrack in Tijuana, 15 miles south of San Diego.

At Torrey Pines State Park you can watch the Annual Pacific Coast *Glider Soaring Championship* in late March or early April. Tijuana, Mexico, offers year-round jai alai and summer bullfighting.

Rough water swims Sept. at La Jolla Cove, July 4 at Coronado, Oct. at Oceanside. *Golf:* Andy Williams San Diego Open, Torrey Pines, Jan. or Feb.; Tournament of Champions, La Costa, April. *Tennis:* La Jolla Tennis Championship, July.

WHAT TO DO WITH THE CHILDREN. San Diego Zoo at Balboa Park is a five-minute ride from downtown. World's largest collection of rare and wild animals housed in enclosures duplicating their native habitat.

Separate Children's Zoo. Seal shows, aviaries, guided bus tour; restaurant, refreshment stands, picnic areas, curio shop.

Sea World, Mission Bay Park, San Diego, is an oceanarium like Marineland, but the shows, features, and concepts are different, so don't miss one simply because you have seen the other.

Visit the *Scripps Institution of Oceanography,* with its new T. Wayland Vaughn Aquarium Museum exhibiting local and tropical aquatic specimens. Inspect the San Diego–La Jolla Underwater Park (an ecological reserve, extending nearly two miles along the shoreline) and view the television monitor for a Cousteau-view of aquatic life.

San Diego also offers 6-hr. guided trips to Coronado Islands to observe migration of grey whales (Jan. weekends only).

HOTELS AND MOTELS in the San Diego area are listed in order of price category. For double occupancy, categories and ranges are as follows: *Moderate* $20–35; and *Inexpensive* under $20. For a more complete explanation of hotel categories, see *Facts At Your Fingertips* at the front of this volume.

Moderate: **Fabulous Inns of America.** 2485 Hotel Circle Place.

Hotel Churchill. 827 C. St. Downtown, near Balboa Park. Jacuzzi; golf and tennis nearby.

Inexpensive: **Pickwick Hotel.** 132 W. Broadway. Central San Diego, in the Greyhound bus terminal. Undergoing remodeling.

DINING OUT. San Diego offers an unusually broad range of choices for dining. The oceanside location of the city means a ready supply of fresh seafood, and the proximity to the Mexican border accounts for the spicy, Mexican influence. San Diego's eating establishments reflect a cosmopolitan heritage. Categories: *Moderate* $15–20 per couple and up; *Inexpensive* $7–15. (Prices do not include wine or cocktails.) À la carte menus more expensive. For more complete explanation of categories, see *Facts at Your Fingertips* earlier in book.

Moderate: **Bali Hai.** 2230 Shelter Island Dr. Cantonese specialties, all served in a pleasant environment overlooking the bay. A long and exotic drink list complements dining. Floor show. Located close to many hotels. Luau luncheon buffets and Cantonese specialties. Also char-broiled steak and lobster.

Boom Trenchard's Flare Path. 2888 Pacific Highway. American cuisine. Tasty entrees. Overlooks airport.

Kelly's Steak House. 248 Hotel Circle N. Great steaks.

Lino's—Bazaar del Mundo. 2754 Calhoun St., Old Town. Italian. Veal specialties.

Mandarin House. 6765 La Jolla Blvd. Locally popular, chef-owned.

Inexpensive: **Reuben's.** 880 Harbor Island Dr., near airport. Boat docked on San Diego Bay. Steak, seafood. Scenic dining.

The Spice Rack. 4315 Mission Blvd., Pacific Beach. Indoor garden dining with hearty, fresh breads, biscuits and waffles. No reservations.

San Francisco

Some of the best places for you to savor this maritime center's salty flavor are along the Embarcadero, where ships of all flags are constantly disgorging cargo; beside the Fisherman's Wharf lagoon in the late morning when the fishing fleet puts in; and looking shoreward from the deck of one of the sightseeing boats that cast off at frequent intervals from Pier 43½. A backward glance at San Francisco's romantic seafaring past is possible at the Maritime Museum at Aquatic Park, aboard the museum's three-masted *Balclutha* at Pier 43, or the turn-of-the-century coastal vessels berthed at Hyde Street Pier.

Pier 39, on the Embarcadero near Fisherman's Wharf, is two stories and 45 acres of shops and restaurants on the waterfront.

Not to be missed across the street from the Maritime Museum is Ghirardelli Square, a fascinating collection of shops, galleries, restaurants, and plazas concocted out of a 19th-century chocolate factory. Nearby at Fisherman's Wharf is The Cannery, a comparable complex housed in an old fruit-processing plant. A look at "The Coast" in Gold Rush days can be had at the Wells Fargo History Room at 420 Montgomery Street.

There are three distinct and captivating cities within the city: Chinatown, the largest settlement of its kind outside of Asia; North Beach, San Francisco's "Little Italy"; and Japantown, in the Post–Buchanan Streets sector, newly landmarked by the $15-million Japan Center.

Following the Seagull

An excellent introduction to San Francisco's charms is the 49-Mile Scenic Drive. It's well marked. Follow the blue, white and orange sign of the seagull by car or sightseeing bus, then return to the spots that intrigue you.

The starting point is Civic Center, where the fountain-dappled plaza is surrounded by public buildings, including domed City Hall, the elegant Opera House, and the Civic Auditorium. Beneath the plaza is Brooks Hall, a gigantic exhibition arena linked underground to the auditorium. Heading downtown past the new George R. Moscone Convention Center and well-groomed Union Square, you'll plunge into the Far East. Chinatown's mainstream, Grant Avenue, is lined with up-curved roofs, dragon-entwined lamp posts, shops crammed with Oriental merchandise, and restaurants serving exotic dishes. Grant Avenue leads straight to North Beach, the city's predominantly Italian "Latin Quarter," dotted with delicatessens, pizzerias, ristorantes and cabarets where operatic arias are served along with the *cappuccino.* Upper Grant Avenue is easily recognizable as the center for the Beach's free spirits by its far-out art galleries, handicraft shops, coffee houses, and offbeat bistros. Japantown, the sector around Post and Buchanan Streets, is an ethnic neighborhood that affords the finest view of Japan this side of the Pacific. Nearby is the famous observation area commanding a fabulous four-way view from the top of Telegraph Hill, site of Coit Tower.

The 49-Mile Drive skirts the festive hubbub of Fisherman's Wharf and brushes the Bay at Aquatic Park. Beyond is the Marina, a Spanish-style residential stretch overlooking a public green and a private yacht harbor. Continuing on, you'll catch sight of the terra-cotta rotunda of the Palace of Fine Arts, a carefully restored souvenir of the 1915 Panama-Pacific International Exposition. Close by is the Presidio, an active military post since 1776 and an especially scenic setting for viewing the Golden Gate Bridge. (For closer inspection of this engineering marvel, park at the Bridge Toll Plaza or Vista Point on the Marin side of the span.)

Eventually, via northwestern cliffs and beaches, you reach the Cliff House. Offshore is Seal Rock, a landmark nearly everyone knows. Below, the Great Highway sweeps along the oceanfront for three miles to the Zoo and Lake Merced. Doubling back to the vast, wooded reaches of Golden Gate Park, you can visit such "musts" as the Japanese Tea Garden, Steinhart Aquarium, Morrison Planetarium, and de Young Museum. Continue on to Twin Peaks for a panoramic view of the city and Bay. Then dip down to Mission Dolores, which was founded by the Franciscan fathers in 1776. The 49-Mile Drive leads through the outer Mission district and back to the Bayfront via the James Lick Freeway and the Embarcadero. The latter passes the deepwater piers and the Ferry Building, once a teeming trans-Bay terminal, now the port's World Trade Center. Also en route is the Golden Gateway Center, a $150-million waterfront-renewal project comprised of high-rise apartments, townhouses, office towers, shopping facilities, and parks. Next door is the $150-million, five-building Embarcadero Center commercial-cultural complex.

From the financial district you may climb Nob Hill. Here you can enjoy cocktails along with intoxicating views atop the Hill's two highest hotels. Here, too, Anglican tradition is upheld by the exclusive Pacific Union Club and Grace Cathedral, seat of the Episcopal Bishop of California. The route back to City Hall, completing the loop, includes Gough Street's Victorian dwellings and the new, architecturally dramatic St. Mary's Cathedral, at Gough and O'Farrell Streets.

The East Bay Area

Even the casual observer would be amazed at how much the East Bay has changed within the past decade. Once the poor stepchild of San Francisco, Oakland has added some major attractions of its own. The Port of Oakland boasts excellent facilities. The attractive Oakland-Alameda sports complex is home to the Oakland Raiders and the Oakland Athletics. Tour the Oakland Museum, with its new Breuner Gallery, or attend the Oakland Symphony, which has a beautiful performing center. Lake Merritt, in the heart of downtown Oakland, has excellent facilities; boats may be rented, and special events are held frequently.

Berkeley, Oakland's next-door neighbor, is the site of the magnificent University of California. Its impressive buildings include a new, architecturally important University Art Museum.

Not quite the radical town of the Sixties, Berkeley's coffeehouses and street people still abound in a calmer atmosphere.

The North Side of San Francisco Bay

Drive across the Golden Gate Bridge and you're in a different world. Sausalito (Little Willow) is situated on the Mediterranean side of the Golden Gate, eight miles north of San Francisco. Its rustic houses cascade down steep slopes to the bay; its shops and restaurants hug the waterfront; its winding, wooded streets look down on a thicket of masts and a colony of houseboats.

Tiburon (Shark) lies eight miles east of Sausalito on Raccoon Strait. Its villagelike Main Street is a blend of Cape Cod and early California.

Its colorful harbor shelters the venerable Corinthian Yacht Club and a cluster of open-deck restaurants.

Angel Island (dramatically domed by summer fog) looms like a pocket-size Corsica seven-eighths of a mile across Raccoon Strait from Tiburon. The bay's biggest island, Angel has a crescent cove leading to a grassy rise, with picnic tables and 12 miles of roads and hiking trails.

A 130-foot, $1.5-million, 800-passenger sightseeing boat, the *Countess,* is the sixth tour boat operated by Harbor Tours. She'll make the Tiburon-Angel Island run.

To the delight of commuters, shoppers, and joyriders, the *Golden Gate* operates round trips daily year-round. The blue-and-white cruiser casts off from the north side of the San Francisco Ferry Building, at the foot of Market Street. She comes about in the shadow of the San Francisco-Oakland Bay Bridge, skirts the towering hulls of liners loading along the Embarcadero, and then strikes a course past Alcatraz. The crossing takes 30 minutes. Snacks are served on the saloon deck, and the bar is open all day. In Marin County, passengers disembark into the town plaza, a few steps from Sausalito's mainstream, Bridgeway.

San Francisco's inland sea resorts are apt to be as crowded as Capri on weekends. The best time to sample the charms of the Willow, the Shark, and the Angel is during the week.

PRACTICAL INFORMATION FOR

SAN FRANCISCO

TOURIST INFORMATION SERVICES. General information is available from *San Francisco Convention and Visitors Bureau,* 201 3rd; 415–974–6900. Call (415) 391-2000, 24 hours, for a recorded message on day's events. For bus tours, contact: *Gray Line of San Francisco,* 420 Taylor St., San Francisco.

Visitors in need of guidance should go to the bureau's San Francisco Visitors Information Center, which is located at lower level Hallidie Plaza, Powell & Market Streets, Benjamin H. Swig Pavilion (the cable-car turn-around point). The Redwood Empire Association also is headquartered in San Francisco, at One Market Plaza. Besides information on the Bay Area, the Redwood Empire Association represents nine surrounding counties. Services are free. There is also a *Visitor Service Representative* on duty in the International Arrival Area at San Francisco International Airport to provide information and assist with customs and languages difficulties.

 HOW TO GET AROUND. *By foot:* San Francisco is surprisingly compact. Many of its most interesting sights are within easy walking distance of each other. From Union Square, it's an easy stroll through Chinatown to Jackson Square and North Beach—and wherever you are there are things to see.

By car: If you are driving your car during your stay in San Francisco, there are three points to remember: 1) cable cars have the right of way, 2) cars parked on any grade or hill must have wheels set to the curb to prevent rolling, 3) watch parking signs—there are many tow-away zones during certain hours, and cars parked illegally are towed away.

Points of Interest

1) Alcoa Building
2) Balclutha
3) Bank of America
4) Cannery
5) City Hall
6) Civic Center
7) Coit Tower
8) Curran Theater
9) Embarcadero Center
10) Ferry Building
11) Fisherman's Wharf
12) Flood Building
13) Geary Theater
14) George R. Moscone Convention Center
15) Golden Gate Center
16) Grace Cathedral
17) Hilton Hotel
18) Hyatt Hotel
19) Hyde Street Pier
20) Lotta's Fountain
21) Maritime Museum
22) Municipal Pier
23) Museum of Modern Art
24) Old U.S. Mint
25) Opera House
26) Pier 39
27) St. Mary's Cathedral
28) St. Patrick's Church
29) Stock Exchange
30) Transamerica Pyramid
31) Victorian Park
32) Visitor Information Center

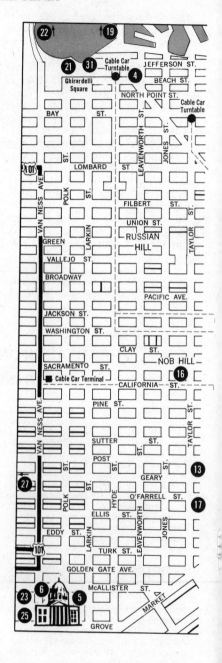

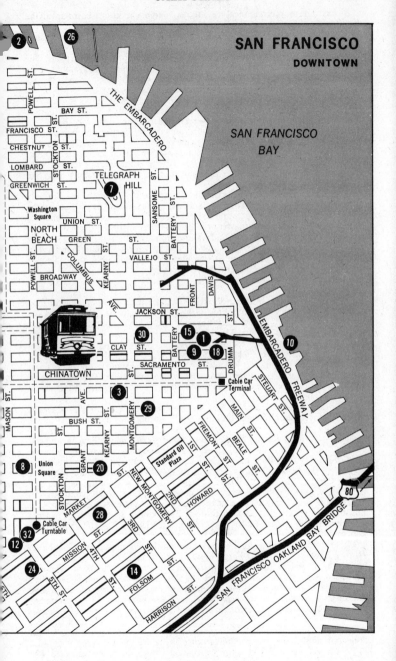

By bus: The most economical ways to reach points in the city beyond walking distance are cable cars, streetcars and buses. Bus maps are at the front of the Yellow Pages in the telephone book. Transfers are available at many points. Basic fare is 60 cents.

Beyond the city limits, trains and buses will carry you most anyplace. The *Bay Area Rapid Transit System* (BART) is now in operation; *Greyhound* offers regular commuter service to most points. *AC Bus Transit System* operates between San Francisco and many points in the East Bay.

By ferry: MV *Golden Gate* makes 10 round trips weekdays, seven on week-ends and holidays, between Sausalito and San Francisco. The Tiburon-San Francisco commuter run is covered by ferries of *Harbor Tours, Inc.,* Pier 43½; it takes 35 min. Harbor Tours also operates cruises around the bay all year round. From May through October, champagne cruises from San Francisco to Oakland's Jack London Square, with dining at a wharf restaurant, are popular.

By bridge: San Francisco-Oakland Bay Bridge is the world's longest: over eight miles. Golden Gate Bridge, accessible to autos and pedestrians, links San Francisco and the north.

By cable car: There used to be 600 cars, operated by 10 companies. But only one company remains, operating 39 cars (sometimes called "grips") over three sets of tracks. Cable cars, buses and streetcars are often tied into one system with a standard fare and liberal transfer privileges. There's an all-day excursion ticket good for unlimited travel on Sundays and holidays. In September 1982, the entire cable-car system was shut down temporarily for a $58.6 million facelift. At press time, buses follow cable car routes, but by June 1984, the cable cars are expected to be back in operation.

 MUSEUMS AND GALLERIES. There are several good art museums in the city. In the Civic Center is the *San Francisco Museum of Art,* which frequently changes exhibits. The *M. H. deYoung Museum* is in Golden Gate Park. Its spacious galleries enclose a landscaped court. Included are paintings by Rembrandt, El Greco, Titian and Rubens. Also at the deYoung Museum, be sure to see the magnificent $30 million collection of Asian art, one of the finest in the western world, donated by Avery Brundage, president of the international Olympic Committee. The collection is housed in the Asian Art Museum, a wing of the deYoung building.

The best in contemporary art is at the *San Francisco Museum of Modern Art* in the War Memorial Veterans Building, with paintings by Calder, Klee, Pollock and others.

The *California Palace of the Legion of Honor* is in Lincoln Park, at the end of California Street. A beautiful museum inside and out, it offers a magnificent view of the city from the terrace. There's a small restaurant. It's worthwhile to get out to the *Oakland Art Museum* at the Municipal Auditorium, 10th and Fallon Streets, Lake Merritt. There's a large collection of California art, including early engravings by the Spanish explorers, and Gold Rush paintings.

Arts and crafts may be seen at the Union Street galleries, between several unusual restaurants. *The Nathan Gallery,* 2124 Union St., specializes in local as well as Israeli artists. *Artists' Cooperative,* 2224 Union St., exhibits paintings and sculpture for sale by the artists themselves, who take turns as hosts.

Other kinds of exhibits may be seen at the following museums: *Wells Fargo History Room,* in the Wells Fargo Bank at 420 Montgomery St., has a varied collection of objects that figured in the development of the West. The *San Francisco Wine Museum,* across from The Cannery, at 633 Beach Street, offers a collection of sculptures, paintings, goblets and crystal depicting the mythology and history of wine. The *Mexican Museum of San Francisco,* 1855 Folsom St., houses contemporary and historic works by Chicano artists. There is the *Academy of Sciences* in Golden Gate Park, housing a collection of American and African mammals (stuffed), as well as the *Steinhart Aquarium,* with its great fish collection, and the *Morrison Planetarium.* The *Maritime Museum,* at the foot of Polk Street, has seafaring exhibits with model ships, old figureheads, etc. *The Museum of Paleontology,* at the University of California in Berkeley (Hearst Memorial Building and Bacon Hall), houses the largest such collection on the

Pacific Coast. A good geology museum displays rocks, minerals and dioramas depicting what life was like in various ages. The *Chinese Historical Society of America*, at 17 Adler Place in Chinatown, features artifacts, documents and photographs of the Chinese community during the Gold Rush.

The *Balclutha* is a museum ship, last of the square-sail fleet that sailed around Cape Horn to San Francisco in the late 19th century. Exhibits aboard include photo displays and relics. The *Cable Car Barn* has a visitors' gallery and museum with 19th-century photos of the cars that are the only national landmarks on wheels. The *California Historical Society*, 2090 Jackson St., has a library and small museum.

HISTORIC SITES. San Francisco itself has the *Presidio*, the *Mission Dolores*, and the *Opera House* was the site of the official organization of the United Nations. *Ft. Point*, the city's most northern point, was built to protect the Bay during the Civil War. Its unique architecture lies beneath the Golden Gate Bridge and the views are superb. *Portsmouth Square* is a small historic park in Chinatown, where the U.S. flag was raised in July 1846. Short trips outside the city will take you to a few other historic spots. *Ft. Ross* is one. Ten miles north of the junction of State Highways 1 and 12 at Jenner, north of San Francisco, it is a 19th-century fort that was used by Russian fur traders.

GARDENS. The sidewalk flower stands of San Francisco have been a tradition since the 1880s. Specialties: daphne in the spring, tiny Pinocchio roses in summer, chrysanthemums in fall and holly in winter. At Golden Gate Park, see the *Japanese Tea Garden,* with its camellias, magnolias and red-leafed Japanese maples. It's a fairyland of cherry blossoms in the spring (usually at their best in early April). See also the *Conservatory.* Modeled after Kew Gardens in England, it's a fascinating hothouse. Sections of the building were brought around Cape Horn by clipper ship. Out front, a floral design honors contemporary events of local or national importance. The *University of California's Botanical Garden* is a 33-acre site located in Strawberry Canyon. The emphasis is on world-wide desert plants.

In Watsonville, see *Rod McLellan Gardens,* at 2352 San Juan Road. There are orchids as far as the eye can see, as well as greenhouses filled with carnations, gardenias, anthuriums and poinsettias, all aligned in uniform rows under laboratory-like conditions. The gardens at *Sunset Magazine,* Menlo Park (down the Peninsula), have all the outstanding trees, shrubs and flowers native to all sections of the Pacific coast. Take a tour or stroll about on your own.

Lakeside Nursery Gardens, at Lake Merritt, Oakland, has a show garden and a propagating nursery for the many Oakland parks. In *Santa Cruz* (Antonelli Bros.) and in *Capitola* (Vetterle & Reinelt Hybridizing Gardens), begonia nurseries are at their most spectacular in August and September. Capitola has a Begonia Festival every September.

TOURS. *Gray Line* offers a deluxe three-hour city tour of San Francisco several times daily; a *Chinatown Dinner Tour* and a *Chinatown After Dark* tour (nightly, all year); an *Oakland-Berkeley-University of California* tour (daily in summer, three times a week the rest of the year); a tour across the Golden Gate Bridge to *Muir Woods,* the nearest redwood grove to San Francisco (daily, all year); a *Three-Bridge* tour combining Muir Woods with Oakland and Berkeley (daily in summer, three times a week the rest of the year); *Monterey-Carmel* and the *17-Mile Drive* (daily in summer, three times a week otherwise); a tour of the *Valley of the Moon* wine country April 1–Oct. 15 (three times a week); a *Night Life Party,* nightly all year (except New Year's Eve); and a tour of the *Peninsula,* including Menlo Park and Palo Alto (once a week, year-round). Gray Line also offers four-day tours combining *Yosemite, Monterey, and Carmel,* weekly, all year (reservations required).

The *Harbor Tours* sightseeing boats make short (1¼-hour) cruises around San Francisco Bay constantly, every day, all year round. Departures are from Fisherman's Wharf. Weekly, from late April through October, one of the boats makes a Champagne Dinner Cruise to Tiburon, fare including the round-trip ferryboat ride, champagne party on board and dinner at your choice of excellent Tiburon restaurants.

The new *Blue and Gold Fleet* also sails the Bay daily. Year-round from the Pier 39 shopping complex on the Embarcadero.

SUMMER SPORTS. *Golf:* According to "Golf Digest," the Olympic Club ranks among the first 10 of America's 100 greatest courses. Others recommended by "Golf Digest" are: Lew F. Galbraith G.C., Oakland, a municipal course, and the Harding Park G.C., an outstanding municipal course. There are also excellent courses at Golden Gate Park (nine holes only), Lincoln Park, Hardin Park, and down the Peninsula at Sharp Park.

Tennis: There are good public courts at Funston playground in the marina and in Golden Gate Park. In Burlingame, down the Peninsula, are a number of public courts.

Sailing: San Francisco offers sailing all year in the Oakland Estuary, and on Lake Merced, Lake Merritt, Richardson Bay, and Tomales Bay, as well as at Palo Alto and Redwood City.

Fishing: Just go casting off San Francisco's municipal pier at Aquatic Park (all year, no license), or try Lake Merced.

SPECTATOR SPORTS. Professional matches may be seen year-round: *football* games of the San Francisco 49ers and the Oakland Raiders; the Giants and A's play *baseball* games; *basketball* matches feature the Golden State Warriors. The Annual Open *Skeet and Trap Shoot* of the Pacific Rod and Gun Club takes place at Lake Merced in late April. *For horse racing,* Bay Meadows is the major spot, with three seasons: roughly, mid-January through February, mid-May to mid-June, and early November to mid-December. *Indoor Soccer* with the San Francisco Fog is at the Cow Palace and the San Jose Earthquakes play home games during the winter at the Oakland—Alameda Coliseum. There is also racing in the East Bay at Golden Gate Fields from mid-September to late October. See the annual Pacific Coast International.

Tennis Championships at the Berkeley Tennis Club in September. *Rodeo* buffs will want to see the Grand National, in October. Opening Day *yachting* parade is held the first Sunday in May. In addition, the Yacht Racing Association holds about 20 races a year, most of them in the Bay. Good vantage points are along the Marina or the Vista View area on the Sausalito side of the Golden Gate Bridge. And in October, there's the International *Ski & Winter Sports Show,* held at the Cow Palace.

WHAT TO DO WITH THE CHILDREN. At the end of the cable-car line (temporarily shut down for major rehabilitation) on the north side of Nob Hill, the entire fleet of cable cars rests. Here a visitors' gallery provides historical remembrances with a restored 1887-style cable barn, corner of Washington and Mason, inside of which is a museum with the first cable car, built in 1873, plus 57 scale model examples of cable cars used in the past 100 years in San Francisco.

Stroll across the *Golden Gate Bridge.* Try to time your walk to coincide with the sailing of a ship beneath. Then you'll realize how very high you are (220 feet) and how very huge the bridge is. Take them aboard the *Balclutha,* the handsome old three-masted sailing ship near Fisherman's Wharf. They'll enjoy inspecting the wheelhouse, the red-plush chart house, the captain's cabin and the ship's galley. Take them *sailing* on easy-to-navigate Lake Merritt in Oakland or Lake Merced in San Francisco. They can fish in Lake Merced, too.

Take them to the *San Francisco Zoo.* The easiest way to get around is by the Elephant Train, which makes frequent departures from the Giraffe Barn. Show them the buffalo in the paddock at Golden Gate Park; the buffalo seem to be roaming at large. If the children are very young, visit *Storyland,* with permanent exhibits including the Gingerbread House, Cinderella's Coach and the Old Lady's Shoe. (Storyland is open weekends January through mid-March; daily at other times.)

Visit the Exploratorium, 3601 Lyons St., a museum for touching, hearing, seeing and exploring exhibits in the science, technology and human perception fields. Open Wed. through Sun., 1 to 5.

Marina Green is a grassy waterfront recreation area with a beautiful view of the Bay. *James D. Phelan Beach,* at 28th and Sea Cliff Avenues, is a six-acre park with beach frontage; it's a great place for sunbathing and picnics. Ocean Beach has plenty of sand and surf with a superb view.

From Pier 43, catch a sightseeing boat to cruise the Bay. Launches leave every 45 minutes between 9 and 3—and later in the summer—to pass beneath the Golden Gate and Bay Bridges to the island of Alcatraz. Special children's prices.

 HOTELS AND MOTELS. San Francisco's accommodations are many and varied. Catering to a wide variety of tastes, they range all over the compact city. San Francisco is a very popular city with tourists and convention groups, so be sure to reserve your rooms as soon as your travel plans are set.

Hotel rates are based on double occupancy. Categories determined by price start *up* from following price figures: *Moderate* $20–30, *Inexpensive* under $20. For a more complete explanation of hotel and motel categories, see *Facts At Your Fingertips* at the front of this volume. *Note:* The Democratic National Convention is planned for July 16–20, 1984, and hotel space may be unusually difficult to come by during that period.

Moderate: **Baywood Motel.** 385 9th Street. Family plan, free parking.

Bellevue. Geary and Taylor. Refurbished.

Best Western Carriage Inn. 140 7th St. Whirlpool, continental breakfast included.

Californian. 405 Taylor. Family plan.

Cartwright. 524 Sutter. European ambience.

Chancellor. 433 Powell. Steps from cable cars.

David. 480 Geary St. Charming café on premises.

The Eldorado. 150 Ninth St. A renovated Victorian pensione. Continental breakfast.

Friendship Inn Oasis. 900 Franklin St. Large beds.

Manx. 225 Powell. Movies. Family plan.

Mark Twain. 345 Taylor. Downtown, near theaters.

Mason. 111 Mason. Family plan.

San Francisco Residence Club. 851 Calif. Nob Hill. Modified Amer. plan.

Stewart. 351 Geary. Free parking. Pool.

Inexpensive: **Carlton.** 1075 Sutter. Union Square. Pets.

Embarcadero YMCA Center. 166 The Embarcadero. Singles and doubles, men and women. Packages avail. Pool.

Executive Motel. 465 Grove. Civic Center.

Geary. 610 Geary. Family plan.

Golden State. 114 Powell. Kitchenettes.

Oxford. Mason & Market. Downtown.

Stratford. 242 Powell. Family plan.

Sutter. 191 Sutter. Family plan.

Yerba Buena. 55 Fifth St. European style, no color TV. Private bath or phone. Excellent value.

YMCA Hotel. (Men & women). 351 Turk. Pool.

DINING OUT. San Francisco's more than 2,600 restaurants offer visitors a round-the-world ticket to dining pleasure. Practically every ethnic taste can be satisfied at every price range. Among the unique regional foods to be sampled are abalone, Dungeness crabs, sand dabs, bay shrimp, crusty sourdough French bread, artichoke dishes and excellent cheeses. All these may be accompanied by fine California wines from vineyards within an hour and a half of the city.

Particularly good areas for low-cost eating are Chinatown with its many *dim sum* restaurants, Polk Street between Geary and Union, Japantown and the 1600–2200 blocks of Union Street (Cow Hollow).

Restaurants are listed according to the price of a complete dinner, starting *up* from following figures: *Moderate* $7–10, *Inexpensive* under $7. Prices do not include drinks, tax or tip. A la carte will, of course, be more expensive.

Moderate: **Castagnola.** 289 Jefferson St. on Fisherman's Wharf. Many varieties of seafood, mostly fresh.

Castle Brand Brasserie. 1600 Folsom, Civic Center area. Lunch and dinner.

Coachman. 1057 Powell St. Continental, English menu.

North Beach. 1512 Stockton St. Italian food. Big on pastas.

Sam's Grill and Seafood Restaurant. 374 Bush St. Fresh fish, homemade cheesecake.

Scoma's. Pier 47 (at the foot of Jones St.). It's probably easier to be disappointed on Fisherman's Wharf than any other place in S.F., but this restaurant is a notable exception. Make reservations well in advance. Try the Olympia oysters and the incredible crabs.

Vanessi's. 498 Broadway. Continental-American menu, but stay at counter.

Inexpensive—Moderate: **Yet Wah.** A number of locations: Pier 39, the newest; 1801 Clement; 2140 Clement; 5238 Diamond Heights Blvd. 301 items to choose from in these neighborhood restaurants.

Inexpensive: **Enrico's.** 504 Broadway. Salads, sandwiches.

El Sombrero. At the Cannery. Mexican cuisine, super margaritas.

Iron Pot. 639 Montgomery St. Bohemian atmosphere.

Nam Yuen. 740 Washington St. Chinese cuisine, great Mongolian lamb.

The Beginning. 2020 Filmore St. Menu from the Old South featuring chitlins, chicken gumbo and cornbread. Authentic "soul food."

Tommaso's. 1042 Kearny, North Beach. The eatery that introduced pizza to San Francisco. Formerly known as Lupo's. Oak-burning ovens. Popular.

Also in the *Inexpensive* category are dozens of interesting Chinese restaurants in Chinatown, including *Sun Ya,* 823 Clay; *Asia Gardens,* 772 Pacific; and many others on Jackson, Clay and Washington, off Grant. All offer mostly Chinese cuisine in the Cantonese style, with individual dishes from $1.50 to $3 and up. Several good, inexpensive restaurants border the Japanese Cultural Center. Many of the Chinese restaurants in this category also can provide a good, filling Chinese rice dish from around $1.50. North Beach, San Francisco's "Little Italy," is bursting with inexpensive Italian restaurants, like *Little Joe's.* Most Italian restaurants in this area serve terrific pasta and veal dishes as well as espresso or cappucino.

COFFEE HOUSES AND OUTDOOR CAFÉS. San Francisco has a preponderance of small cafés, many of which are charming and atmospheric, as well as easy on the pocketbook. Particularly good areas for finding them are Broadway and Columbus (and surrounding side streets); Polk St. between Geary and Union; the "1800" to "2000" blocks of Union St.; and Lombard St. between Laguna and Broderick. To name some: *Enrico's Sidewalk Cafe* (504 Broadway), *Caffe Roma* (414 Columbus) and *Caffe Puccini* (411 Columbus).

Good dependable counter-type restaurants include *The Hippo, Manning's, Zim's, Pam Pam East,* 398 Geary, in the Raphael Hotel, and *The Noble Frankfurter,* in two downtown locations.

In Sausalito, check the terrace at the *Alta Mira,* as well as the *Trident,* an indoor-outdoor restaurant directly on the waterfront (it's the lower floor of

Ondine's). Don't miss *Valhalla*, it was run by San Francisco's famous former madam, the late Sally Stanford, who furnished her café in the style of a turn-of-the-century high-class brothel.

In Tiburon, you can eat outdoors at a ramshackle place called *Sam's*, and at the very modern and attractive *Dock* and *The Windjammer*.

EXPLORING THE REST OF CALIFORNIA

California abounds in attractions and the lures are not confined to major cities. Today US 101 closely parallels the historic Mission Trail, one of the state's most popular tourways. In 1768, when the Russian interest in Alaska was seen as a possible prelude to southward expansion, King Charles of Spain ordered the colonization of California. His decree launched the missions which provided the seminal growth for California. Under the astute leadership of Father Junipero Serra and Father Fermin Lausen (each founded nine missions), the gray-robed Franciscans moved slowly northward. By 1823 a chain of 21 missions extended 600 miles from San Diego to Sonoma along the coastal route, El Camino Real (The King's Highway).

On California 76, a replica of Mission San Antonio de Pala, originally Asistencia, or outpost of the Oceanside Mission, still serves the Indians' religious needs and provides schooling for seven neighboring reservations. Thus, it is the only California mission still serving its original purpose.

Mission San Buenaventura, at Ventura, was the ninth mission founded and the last to be dedicated by the Franciscan padre, Father Serra. The date was Easter Sunday, 1782, two years before his death.

Mission Santa Barbara, "Queen of the Missions," on a height overlooking sea and city, is considered the state's most photographed building. Its museums and gardens are outstanding. This is the only one of California's missions never abandoned by the Franciscans. A candle has been kept burning on the altar since December 4, 1786. Mission Santa Ines, 35 miles north of Santa Barbara, is only a bell's call from the Danish-inspired town of Solvang. The beautifully restored mission housed California's first seminary, the College of Our Lady of Refuge. Santa Ines was founded in 1804 and dedicated to the martyred Saint Agnes. Still in use are carved wooden crucifixes, hand-hammered copper and silver pieces, and other religious articles crafted on the premises by Indian neophytes. The original mural decorations are rivaled only by those at San Miguel.

Mission La Purísma Concepción is a faithful restoration of the impressive mission that was sadly neglected after the Mexicans sold it at auction in 1854 for $1,000. When the mission was being restored in the 1930s, young men of the Civilian Conservation Corps (CCC) molded more than 100,000 adobe bricks in the manner of the original Indian builders. The mission was founded in 1787, but the original buildings were destroyed in an 1812 earthquake. The hero of the earthquake, Father Mariano Payeras, is buried on the premises.

San Luis Obispo de Tolosa, in the center of the city of San Luis Obispo, was Father Serra's fifth mission, dedicated in 1772. It is believed that tile roofs had their beginning here after the flaming arrows of Indians continually set fire to the original roofs of tule or rush. Father Serra's vestments and other rare religious items are preserved in the mission museum.

San Miguel Arcángel Mission, about 10 miles north of Paso Robles, adjacent to the town of San Miguel, is noted for its murals, arches and a donkey named Ramona. Founded in 1797, it is the sixteenth mission.

Other missions, with the town nearest each one, are: San Antonio de Padua, King City; Nuestra Senora de la Soledad, Soledad; San Juan Bautista, San Juan Bautista; San Jose de Guadalupe, San Jose; Santa Clara de Asis, Santa Clara; San Francisco de Asis, San Francisco; San Rafael Archangel, San Rafael; and San Francisco Solano de Sonoma, Sonoma.

State Parks

California counts its blessings in having five National Parks and eight National Monuments. Today, California's State Park system involves more than 258 sites, with almost 900,000 acres of mountains and valleys, lakes and plateaus, rivers, forests, and beaches. It also embraces many landmarks of historical heritage.

Noteworthy state parks include:

Big Basin Redwoods State Park, the first of the redwood groves to be declared a protected state park, usually is visited en route to Carmel. You can hike, picnic, or camp here, take advantage of planned recreation facilities, or just enjoy the magnificent giant trees. Only restrictions: no horses and no dogs allowed overnight.

Caswell Memorial State Park is five miles west of US 99, 16 miles south of Stockton. The park is one of the few remaining primeval groves of valley oaks that once were abundant in the Great Central Valley. It is a pleasant picnic spot and always cool in summers.

Del Norte Coast Redwoods State Park is the one forest preserve in Northern California that has been left alone (no campgrounds or visitor centers as yet). There are magnificent drives through rugged inland forest, with views of the Pacific from high points.

Henry Cowell Redwood State Park, just south of Felton, is another forest preserve. Picnic areas are outside the grove of big trees. Take a ride on the old train here.

East Bay Regional Parks are 8,200 acres of beautiful California countryside set aside for daytime recreation. The parks practically overlap each other with miles of hiking and bridle trails and picnic spots. Charles Lee Tilden Regional Park has the most recreational facilities. Try Lake Temescal Regional Park, Round Top, Redwood and Grass Valley.

Humboldt Redwoods State Park is 35 miles of forest bordering US 101 between Garberville and Redcrest. Highlights are the Rockefeller Forest, Founder's Grove, and the Avenue of the Giants, where you can drive on the wide pebble beach of the Eel River.

Mount Diablo State Park is behind Oakland. According to Indian superstition, the mountain was the dwelling place of an evil spirit, a "puy." Bret Harte stated that the peak was named when a Mexican muleteer on a missionary expedition first espied it and cried: "Diablo!" (Devil). The Creek-Clayton Road gives the most diabolic impression—dark shadows in deep ravines, sharp and craggy contours.

Mount Tamalpais is back of Mill Valley, across the Golden Gate Bridge from San Francisco. It's one of the few places close to downtown that can really be termed pastoral. You may drive to the top—also an easy hike. Part of the land is in Muir Woods National Monument; the rest is state park.

Russian Gulch State Park is along the coast just north of Mendocino. It has a wave-scarred headland pocked with coves, pools with good campsites, and the lure of skin diving for abalone. It is foggy here in the summer. A more protected park a few miles inland, Paul A. Dimmick Memorial State Park, is nine miles from the coast on Calif. 128 and has camping facilities.

Sand Harbor State Beach Park is at Lake Tahoe, 10 miles north of the US 50 junction, just off Calif. 28. It offers good picnic spots with an area reserved for swimmers or waders. Camping and boating are prohibited.

Sonoma Coast Beaches State Park is great for views of the Pacific, especially from the Russian River approach at Jenner, where Calif. 12 and Calif. 1 intersect.

Santa Catalina and the Beaches

In the southern part of the state, Santa Catalina Island is 22 miles offshore and accessible from the Santa Catalina terminal in San Pedro by amphibian airlines and cruise ships, which operate daily. In the summer months, there is additional boat service from the Balboa Pavillion in Newport Beach. To receive schedules and routes, contact the Catalina Island Chamber of Commerce. Avalon is the island's only settlement. It's a quiet village, a sports-fishing capital, fronting a crescent bay and scaling the slopes inland. The flying fish (May to October) are, according to authorities, the world's largest, some growing to 18 inches. Glass-bottom boats cruise over the California State Marine Preserve, which covers a scenic stretch of protected sea life.

Back on the mainland, and more southerly, is Huntington Beach, site of annual September Surfboard Championships. Newport Beach and Harbor are next. Most people live on seven islands dotting the bay. Newport's boat population is more than 8,000. There are seven yacht clubs and a regatta practically every weekend of the year.

Next along the coast is Laguna Beach. Its cliffs are flowery and studio-clustered and the area is often compared to the Normandy coast. The artistic center of Laguna Beach comes alive during the summer months when the Festival of the Arts takes place.

Missions and Sports

A few miles beyond is Mission San Juan Capistrano, founded by the Spanish Franciscan padres in 1775. Its legend says that its flock of swallows always flew off on the mission patron saint's day, October 23, and returned "miraculously" on St. Joseph's Day, March 19. An inquiring young priest studied swallows and found that they all come and go at fairly regular dates, but the discovery failed to dampen the local Spanish Californians' beliefs.

San Clemente is farther down the coast. The town once was restricted to Spanish-style red-tiled roofs and white walls. Many of the early buildings still dot the town today. The city gained national prominence when Richard Nixon retired here after he resigned his presidency in August 1974.

At La Jolla, a nearby art and resort colony, and home to University of California, San Diego, seven caves have been carved out of the soft cliffs by waves over the centuries. One may be explored via an inland tunneled stairway and the other six must be entered from the ocean. La Jolla has been a tennis center for generations. The venerable La Jolla Tennis Tournament, held since 1916, includes some 30 events for all ages. The La Jolla Beach and Tennis Club has ten championship tennis courts. In the oceanside Marine Room restaurant and Spindrift lounge, picture windows of tempered plate glass are slapped by Pacific waves. The aquarium museum at Scripps Institution of Oceanography, 8602 La Jolla Shore Dr., is one of two such in the world. The research base for Jacques Cousteau, it is open to visitors. Picnics areas and beaches are nearby.

Mission Bay Park's 4,600-acre aquatic wonderland is a sunny play-ground between La Jolla and San Diego. The bay area, the marine parks, the grassy, tree-lined coves, and the resort hotels offer boating, swimming, fishing, water-skiing, golfing, camping and trailer sites. Sea World is one of the highlights at Mission Bay. Trained dolphins per-form at its Theater of the Sea. Also on exhibit are elephant seals, trained killer whales and demonstrations by Japanese pearl divers. While here, take a skyride, a hydrofoil ride or catch a 360-degree view from the skytower.

Palm Springs-Mojave Desert-Death Valley

The resort of Palm Springs sprawls in the Colorado Desert, south-ernmost of California's desert lands. From the vacation oasis, the warm, low-level desert stretches east to the Colorado River and south to the Mexican border.

The Colorado Desert passes through navel orange country and below the flat-topped wall of the San Bernardino Mountain Range, where a chain of resort lakes and winter snow slopes dot the mile-high Rim o' the World Highway. San Gorgonio Pass divides the desert from the orange country and is a great trough beneath mountain peaks towering more than two miles high.

Palm Springs nestles in the lee of one of the peaks, Mt. San Jacinto. Rising 10,831 feet, Mt. San Jacinto is in the steepest mountain escarp-ment in the United States. "Old San Jack," as it is called, protects Palm Springs from the wind blasts that sometimes whistle down the pass. The melting snows from its summit supply water for the resort's nu-merous pools and green grass golf courses.

The 80-passenger Palm Springs Aerial Tramway runs to the top of Mt. San Jacinto, where there are gift and apparel shops, a game room, restaurant and picnic area. (Keep in mind that the Aerial Tramway is closed for two weeks in August.) The Moorten Botanical Gardens display 2,000 varieties of desert plants, Indian lore, petrified wood and relics.

Much of Palm Springs life centers around more than 5,000 swim-ming pools of all shapes and sizes. Some are entirely within houses.

Shapes run the gamut from the frequently photographed, double-oval pool at the Tennis Club, to square, oblong, egg- or fiddle-shaped.

Palm Springs with its 37 grass golf courses, has become known as the "Golf Capital of the World." It has been a favored golfing site for political figures, motion-picture and television stars. Stars owning local business establishments occasionally are seen waiting on customers. Palm Springs has many exclusive shops, a number of them branches of Los Angeles' larger stores. You may shop in a casual sun outfit.

Other activities at Palm Springs include horseback and chuckwagon breakfast rides, tennis, hikes, drives over the nearby desert to such spots as Tahquitz Falls and Palm Canyon, and fishing at nearby Whitewater Canyon. At Palm Canyon a grove of 3,000 palms along a trickling stream is a mute reminder of the great groves that once covered much of the country in prehistoric times. Palm Canyon is on a reservation. About 30,000 acres of the Palm Springs desert is reservation land, some of it right downtown. The land, freed for sale or lease by an act of Congress and now worth several million dollars, is owned by 166 members of the Aqua Caliente band of the Coahuila Indians.

Well worth visiting is the Palm Springs Desert Museum, a sprawling split-level, cantilever structure exhibiting desert dioramas, folk and fine art, and Cabot's Indian Pueblo, a four-story building with 35 rooms, constructed single-handedly by Cabot Yerxa over a 20-year period.

A scenic route to Palm Springs is over the Pines-to-Palms Highway. This starts near Riverside at Hemet, where hundreds of townsfolk take weekend roles in the Ramona Outdoor Play, staged in a mountainside bowl each spring. The story dramatizes Helen Hunt Jackson's novel of the California rancho girl and her Indian lover. The country called the "Arabia of America" starts a few miles from Palm Springs, in the Colchella Valley. Here they grow dates better than Arabia's, and even have a town called Mecca. Indio, in the Palm Springs area, is the "Date Capital" and site of the National Date Festival, held in February in an Arabian Nights setting, complete with a Slave Girl Mart plus nightly ostrich and camel races.

After leaving Palm Springs, you may notice the drop in elevation. Calipatri calls itself the "Lowest Down City in the Western Hemisphere." The lowest dip of the Salton Sea is 235 feet below the surface of the Pacific Ocean, 80 miles away. The Sea, 24 miles long and 10 miles wide, was formed when the Colorado River broke loose in 1905 and flooded Salton Sink. Today Salton Sea is favored for swimming, boating, water-skiing and fishing for corvina. A state park is on its shore and resorts are becoming numerous.

Joshua Tree National Monument, northeast, was established to protect the diminishing stands of the Joshua tree, a species of the lily family, which grows 20 to 40 feet high and, in some cases, to be as much as 300 years old. The Joshuas, which bloom with waxy greenish-white flowers in March and April, are havens for desert life—lizards, wood rats and birds.

Northernmost desert in this area is the Mojave (pronounced mo-hav-ee). It is known as the "High Desert" because of its elevation, ranging up to more than 6,000 feet. The Mojave Desert is a vast expanse of natural desert beauty, with traces of century-old ghost towns, wildlife and softly hued plants. The flashy color of the California golden poppies, which bloom in the spring of a rainy year, can be seen 10 miles away. Much of the Mojave Desert is mining country. Near the town of Mojave, once the terminus of the 20-mule-team-borax wagons out of Death Valley, is the lonesome hump of Soledad Mountain. The mountain is pocked by mine shafts that were closed after giving up millions in gold. Tropic Mine is behind the mountain and now a visitors attraction. A Gold Town and museum of relics are interesting to explore. The gold town of Randsburg is what a movie set of an old mining town should look like. Some of the walls of buildings are made of old dynamite boxes. The Old Time Mining Celebration is held in late August. At Boron, visitors can observe borax mining operations. And Calico, an old silver town, has been restored as a visitors' attraction.

Death Valley, north of the Mojave Desert, is the lowest and, in summer, one of the hottest and driest spots in the United States. At more comfortable times of the year, many regard the valley as one of the more geologically fascinating places on earth. Third largest of the national monuments, Death Valley is a trough in the northern reaches of the Mojave Desert, 140 miles long and six to 20 miles wide. The annual rainfall averages about two inches, and the National Park Service has recorded the hottest summertime temperature ever.

The sun-blasted valley was called Tomesha, which means "ground afire," by the Paniment Indians. Its present name is supposed to have originated in 1849 when a party of gold rushers were rescued after wandering the sea of salt for 80 days. One emaciated member of the group is supposed to have looked back and said, "Goodbye, Death Valley!" Today the valley is a well supervised monument, with excellent highways, plenty of water and a wide range of accommodations.

Among the interesting features to be seen in Death Valley are brilliantly colored canyons and mountains, freakish natural formations, and authentic artifacts of the Old West. Zabriskie Point is an awesome lookout over miles of golden-brown hills, and Mosaic Canyon has varicolored pebbles embedded in the gray rock of the floor. The Devil's Golf Course is a bed of rugged salt crystals rising to pinnacles as high as four feet and still growing. Ubehebe Crater is an 800-foot pit formed by a volcanic eruption between 1,000 and 2,000 years ago. The National Park Service maintains the Death Valley Museum at Death Valley National Monument. Natural-history exhibits, charcoal kilns and Harmony borax works are featured.

North of Los Angeles

North of Los Angeles and a few miles inland you'll find lemon groves covering the valleys. The world's largest lemon grove, 1,800 acres, is near Santa Paula, and known as the "Lemon Capital." Lemons are picked every six weeks and in a single year, a well-bearing tree may produce 3,000 lemons. Trees are trimmed, giving the impression of a uniform flat top, to increase the yields.

The stretch of freeway entering Santa Barbara is regarded as the most beautifully landscaped in the California system. Santa Barbara climbs the mountain slopes from the yacht harbor and palm-fringed beach, almost all of it grassed-over public park. This was the gracious social center of old Spanish California. Today's residents, many of them wealthy, retired Easterners, attempt to retain the old atmosphere. The Spanish-Moorish County Courthouse is rated as one of the most beautiful public buildings in North America. The Santa Barbara Museum houses excellent exhibits of Greek, Roman and Egyptian sculptures. The Museum of Natural History, in a wooded canyon behind the Mission, is notable for, among other things, the mounted specimens of the California Condor, the largest flying bird in North America. A sanctuary for the last band of the 10-foot winged Condors is tucked in the mountains behind Santa Barbara.

Santa Barbara's many Spanish adobes were built with massive bricks made from local adobe clay. The rounded red-clay roof tiles were molded on the thighs of Indian women. Numerous adobes are in active community use today. The Spanish influence is quite apparent in the city. Streets bear such names as Indio Muerte (Dead Indian), Los Olivos, (The Olives), and Camino Cielo (Street of the Sky). The University of California is up the coast a few miles. It overlooks the sea at Goleta and is a gem of California architecture. San Marcos Pass is an easy jump inland, offering panoramic marine views out over the coast and the chain of Channel Islands.

The village of Solvang, meaning "Sunny Valley," has sought to make itself a bit of transplanted Denmark. It was founded by Lutheran clergymen who called for Danes throughout the country to help establish an old-country "folk" school here. Danish bakeries come three to a block, and stores selling imports such as pewter, tiles and cloth goods also abound. There's even a windmill for authenticity. Danish festivals are held every September.

For a scenic and leisurely trip, drive along Route 1 to Pismo Beach, home of giant clams. Years ago the beach literally was paved with clams and farmers plowed them up for chicken and hog feed. Today there's a daily limit and no clam less than five inches in diameter can be taken. Local shops and motels carry schedules of the tide and limit.

San Luis Obispo is an old town, epitomized by the Sinsheimer Brothers Drygoods Store, founded in 1876 and still doing business with the same old fixtures. This also is the home of the California State Polytechnic College, which has model stock farms worth a visit. The San Luis Obispo Nuclear Center has many exhibits and a nuclear theater presenting a 14-minute program on nuclear power.

About 40 miles north of San Luis Obispo along Calif. 1, watch the mountains for the first sight of what appears to be a towered European castle. La Casa Grande is just that. It's the castle built by the late William Randolph Hearst and depository of millions of dollars worth of his worldwide art collection. The 159-acre estate is a state historical monument, presented to California by the Hearst family. San Simeon crowns La Cuesta Encantada (the Enchanted Hill) in the Santa Lucia Range. Traveling over a five-mile road to the castle, you'll pass through the former Hearst ranchland for Herefords and a game preserve of zebra, fallow deer, aoudads, axis, sambar deer and tahr goats. Scheduled tours visit some of the castle's 100 rooms (38 are bedrooms, 31 are bathrooms and 14 are sitting rooms). One of the floors of the castle is of Pompeiian mosaic tile dating to 60 B.C. Some of the carved and decorated ceilings were dismantled in Europe and shipped here to be reassembled by European craftsmen.

Gold Rush Towns

The Mother Lode Country lies along a state route appropriately numbered 49. Running along the western slope of the Sierra from Mariposa to Sattley, much of this 266-mile stretch has reassumed the lazy, back-country look California must have had before the Gold Rush.

The most authentic and best restored of all the bonanza towns is Columbia. It's above Sonora on a side road just off 49. California keeps Columbia in its original Gold Rush Days state and classifies it officially as a State Park. Here you'll see drugstores with their shelves stocked with roots, herbs, and simples once used for cures.

Remember Mark Twain's "The Celebrated Jumping Frog of Calaveras County"? The jumping contest was held in a nearby town, Angels Camp. A commemorative Jumping Frog Jubilee is held annually in May.

There's a Gold Rush Museum at Amador, a good place to see many Gold Rush days items. Gold was first found by James Marshall, John Sutter's hired carpenter working on his mill race at Coloma. There's a state park here with a fine statue of Marshall.

The Andes' Lake Titicaca in Bolivia is the highest lake in the world. Tahoe is the second highest. Nevada borders the eastern side of Tahoe and contributes gambling casinos to the lake's other resort attractions. A 70-mile road around Tahoe provides an easy way to view the lake's many coves, forested peninsulas, and broad reaches of water.

From Tahoe City on the lake, Calif. 89 takes you to the 1960 Winter Olympic site—Squaw Valley. Ski lifts operate in summers here.

Sacramento and Nevada City

In Sacramento, California's capital, everything important seems to be named Sutter, after the city's adventuresome founder. At 28th and K streets you'll see a reconstructed Sutter's Fort. It's an entire little village. The new $14 million California State Railroad Museum at 1100 14th St. houses several exhibits, and the Crocker Art Museum, 216 O St., is the oldest museum in the West. Modern day Sacramento is a paradox. Sutter's son laid out the town after Washington, D.C.—yet the former governor's mansion, with its turrets, towers, and gingerbread trim, looks like the original haunted house.

East and northeast of Sacramento lie the Gold Rush towns with the most picturesque and the most improbable names. Some examples are You Bet, Confidence, Red Dog, Rough and Ready, Fairplay. Nevada City is another Gold Rush ghost town that looks the part perfectly. It's set on seven hills, has fantastically shaped houses and a typical old hotel.

Two great rivers, the Sacramento and the San Joaquin, form a maze of sloughs, canals, and marshes locally called the Delta. It's a favorite of San Francisco yachtsmen since it is only 50 miles northeast of San Francisco Bay. Its thousand miles of navigable waterways are plied by vessels from rowboats to ocean freighters. Some of the world's richest farmland lies on either shore. During the Gold Rush, sailing ships and side-wheelers carried miners and supplies to Sacramento, Stockton, and other jumping-off points. At one time, there were 28 steamboats regularly moving up and down the river. The automobile and good roads announced the close of the era here. Within the Delta there are areas much like the early Everglades. Best known is The Meadows at Snodgrass Slough (north of Walnut Grove), a favorite gathering place for boaters and houseboat renters.

Mt. Shasta, a 14,162-foot-tall landmark, is visible for more than a hundred miles in each direction. Take Calif. 89 from Lassen to Mt. Shasta and on the way you'll pass McArthur-Burney Falls State Park, with picnic and camping facilities and a split waterfall fed by an underground river. US 99 takes you through Castle Crags, sheer rocks rising 6,000 feet, the Lake Shasta Caverns, which can be reached only by boat, and the Shasta Dam.

At Redding, king salmon flip up fish ladders in the Sacramento, providing a great show. Pick up Calif. 299, which parallels the Old Trinity Trail—first an Indian path, then a pioneer trail, then a Gold Rush wagon road. Within six miles you're back in gold country in the small town of Shasta. Today, in the streams of this area, you can still see prospectors panning the gravel. French Town is another "gold" mining town which sprang into existence overnight. But it was silver that supported this settlement. More active is Lewiston, on the banks of the Trinity River, which is headquarters for the Trinity Dam project and a fishing center. The rustic Lewiston Hotel, once a stagecoach stop, is still popular. The Trinity Alps' chief attraction is isolation—for its access is pretty much limited to sturdy hikers with packs on their backs and to horses.

A colorful relic of early California is the Joss House at Weaverville. It is a state museum and one of the few structures recalling the role of the Chinese in the Gold Rush and the building of California.

From Junction City, it's 12 miles to Canyon Creek. From here you can hike through mining country to excellent fishing and picnic spots on the Canyon Creek Lakes. Another road strikes off from the Coffee Creek Ranger Station at the northern end of Trinity Lake. To really experience Trinity Alps, however, you should pack in. There are 15 major resort-ranches in the area, most of which offer pack trips. Guides will accompany your party or meet you at specified times. The Yurok, Karuk, and Hoopa Indians live in the town of Hoopa. Game laws permit the tribes to scoop-net the salmon from the falls in the ancient way.

At Klamath, you can camp in the redwoods and photograph the Roosevelt elk in Prairie Creek State Park. This is rugged country, battered by storms in winter, shrouded by fogs in summer. New Englanders first settled here to log and fish. The Victorian charm of Eureka, Arcata and Ferndale is well preserved in architecture and history. Eureka's Old Town on the waterfront has shops and restaurants as well as the Old Town Art Guild. Ferndale, which hosts the annual Humboldt County Fair each August, also has some spectacular restored Victorian homes.

At Pepperwood, on 101, watch for the turnoff to the Avenue of the Giants, a spectacular 31-mile stretch of redwoods in the Humboldt Redwoods State Park. Near Redcrest is another turnoff leading to Rockefeller Redwood Forest, often called the "world's finest forest." You can drive through a giant tree near Legget.

Fifty years ago, Mendocino was a dying, two-street town—there being no more call for ship-building timber. Now the town is having a rebirth, this time as an artists' colony. The tourist peak in this picturesque village runs from Memorial Day to Labor Day. At the beginning of the season, Mendocino is ablaze with azaleas, fuchsias, and rhododendrons. Art works of community residents are on display at galleries and at the Art Center on Little Lake Street. Three powerful lighthouses here are also open to visitors. Mendocino's ancestral heritage is traceable to New England through its architecture, a blend of both pure and improvised Victorian. Surf at most beaches is too rough for swimming, though skin diving for abalone is allowed.

Monterey-Carmel-Big Sur

Monterey is a quaint old town, but brace yourself for initial disillusionment, particularly if you have driven south from San Francisco along State 1. The route runs along the 30-mile seashore of San Mateo Beach State Park and will lead to or allow convenient access to such places as Montara, a picturesque artists' colony; swank suburbs like Burlingame, Hillsborough and Atherton; Santa Cruz and its bustling resort atmosphere; Santa's Village tucked in the Santa Cruz Mountains, and scenic redwood country. After the coastal route, Monterey's entrance is particularly unenchanting.

But just turn off the main drag and look for the line of orange dots painted on the by-street pavements. The line is Monterey's "Path of History." It will guide you to the parts of town which are the most attractive and interesting. They're the parts that have been reconstructed in their original styles. You'll see more than 40 buildings built before 1850. The Old Custom House dates back to Spanish Colonial days. Other points of interest include the ancient Presidio; the first theater; the Larkin House—home of the first American Consul here, with the old-time handsome furniture gleaming in it; the government document house, Colton Hall, and a dwelling where Robert Louis Stevenson lived briefly. The History and Art Associations, 550 Calle Principal, offers guided tours through some of the historic buildings to view costume and painting exhibits. San Carlos Cathedral, 550 Church St., offers guided tours of its 18th- and 19th-century Spanish paintings and sculptures. The United States Army Museum is housed in a 1908 cavalry-supply depot.

After you've seen these sights, you'll want to inspect the bay. Drive to City Wharf first. Fishermen here unload their silvery catch—herring, cod, anchovy, kingfish, tuna and salmon. If you have read John Steinbeck's *Cannery Row,* you'll want to inspect it. It's one section of Ocean Boulevard, renamed in honor of the novel. There is little fish canning here, but the Row still has atmosphere. You'll find good restaurants, shops and a cinema.

Depending on your interests and the season, there are other attractions in Monterey. Monterey holds its county fair in August and a jazz festival in September. Laguna Seca Golf Course in Monterey is recommended by *Golf Digest.*

En route to Carmel, you may opt for an interesting sidetrip. Head for Del Monte Forest on the Seventeen-Mile Drive. You can pick up a map at the Forest's entrance. Maps indicate that you should follow the yellow line—you won't get lost and you'll almost surely see deer, and certainly, on the ledges, wind-twisted cypresses. Get as close as you can to the sea. At Big Basin Redwoods State Park, usually visited en route to Carmel, you'll see the first of the redwood groves declared a protected state park. You can hike, picnic or camp here.

Years ago a saying proclaimed, "No village is simpler than Carmel." But as you'll soon notice, things have changed a great deal. Today at least 150 shops lure thousands of weekend visitors to buy goods, from locally made arts and crafts items to gourmet foods. Even so, Carmel remains charming in appearance. Hundreds of artists and writers live here. Of interest to literature students is Tor House, the stone residence built personally by poet Robinson Jeffers. In addition, Carmel has a great sense of the past. One of Padre Junipero Serra's missions stands here: San Carlos Borromeo de Carmelo. It's alongside State 1, below the town. The padre whose vision and energy blazed the pioneer Mission Trail, with the 21 mission hostels from Baja California north to Sonoma, lies buried in the mission compound. The Carmel Mission and Gift Shop is an historical museum, with sculpture, Indian artifacts and textile collections.

For golfers, "Golf Digest" recommends the Carmel Valley Golf and Country Club in Carmel. For those interested in tours, California Parlor Car Tours Co. operates four- and five-day circle tours of Yosemite, Monterey and Carmel, on a weekly, year-round basis. Gray Line of San Francisco offers Monterey-Carmel and Seventeen-Mile Drive tours year-round. Point Lobos Reserve is a delightful little park of only 354 acres. Visitors from all parts of the globe come to watch and photograph the sea lions off the rugged shoreline and the gaunt Monterey cypresses. A herd of sea-dwelling otters occasionally appears. A whaler's cottage and a whale skeleton are on exhibit. The name "Lobos," incidentally, comes from the barkings of the offshore seals, which the early Spaniards thought sounded like wolves.

The Big Sur Highway runs some 30 miles south from Carmel to Big Sur. The road is one of the most breathtakingly beautiful in the world. The rugged Big Sur area is popular with artists and writers and here you'll find Nepenthe, one of the West's outstanding restaurants. Folk dances and music bring it alive at night. In this area you'll be in Carmel Valley, which many Californians prefer to Carmel proper. The climate is less foggy, and there are far fewer visitors milling about. Good horseback riding and swimming are available here.

An interclub horse show is held in early May at the Carmel Valley Trail and Saddle Grounds. The Carmel Valley Horsemen's Roundup is held in mid-August. While in Carmel Valley, you may want to visit Hanssens' Begonia Gardens. And for golfers, the Rancho Canada Golf Course has a *Golf Digest* recommendation. When you leave the valley, follow the signs to Salinas: California's biggest rodeo is held there every July.

Concentrated into four days, the rodeo is a gigantic Western celebration known locally as Salinas Big Week. It includes such events as a night parade through downtown with bands, drill teams and clowns; a Sweetheart Contest open to high school girls who are judged on personality, horsemanship and appearance in riding clothes; a street dance and a public breakfast. More than one thousand horses and riders parade down Main Street prior to each day's rodeo. The four standard events are calf roping, saddle-bronc riding, steer wrestling and bull riding.

Twenty miles from Salinas is the San Juan Bautista State Historical Monument. You get a brochure recounting the history of the place when you enter the mission. Of particular interest are the mission and its bell tower, the stable and carriage house, and the Plaza Hotel, once a gourmet's delight.

Sequoia and Kings Canyon National Parks

Sequoia and Kings Canyon National Parks are a pair of natural beauties running wild from the gentle foothills of the San Joaquin Valley to the splintered crest of the Sierra Nevada. Although the parks were established 50 years apart, they adjoin and are referred to as a team. Their combined area covers 1,314 square miles.

Sequoia Park's noble stands of its namesake tree *(Sequoia gigantea)* began reaching for the California heavens about the time Troy fell to the Greeks. Largest of the park's sequoias is the General Sherman Tree in the Giant Forest, over 36 feet through and 101 feet around at the base. It soars to just over 272 feet—higher than a 20-story office building—and is estimated to be 3,500 years old. A man could lie crosswise on some of its massive branches. The tree's weight has been estimated at 2,145 tons (as heavy as a small ocean-going steamship), and it also has been estimated that the General Sherman Tree could produce 600,000 board feet of lumber—enough to build a small town.

Kings Canyon Park also has giant sequoias. The General Grant Tree is only five feet shorter than the Sherman and exceeds the Sherman's base circumference by six feet. In 1965, Kings Canyon Park, already noted for its lakes, canyons, waterfalls and rushing rivers, was greatly enhanced when President Lyndon B. Johnson signed into reality the dream of naturalist John Muir, adding the Cedar Grove tract and the Tehipite Valley to the national park area.

Other notable sights in these parks include Tharp Log (where the road goes through, rather than around, the trunk), the Fluted Column and Chimney Tree. Moro Rock, which you can climb on a safe, 300-foot stairway for a view over the Great Western Divide, and Crystal Cave, a marble cave with elaborate limestone formations, may also prove fascinating. Crystal Cave is open during the summer, with guide service available.

There is a museum at the ranger station. Stop by the Lodgepole and Grant Grove Visitor Centers for expert advice on organizing your sightseeing, park data and campfire information. Highways to the parks are kept open year-round, and accommodations are available year-round. Bus tours are available from Tulare and Visalia.

Yosemite National Park

Yosemite National Park is a meadowlike valley threaded by mountain streams, noble groves of trees, and waterfalls; it is surrounded by almost vertical walls taking the shapes of great domes and pinnacles.

You can approach the park through either the Merced route, State 140, or by the slightly longer State 41, which passes through such small towns as Kismet, Coarsegold and Ben Hur. Following the latter, you enter the park through a magnificent stand of big trees, the Mariposa Grove. Jack London recalled the impression the sight of the first monster in the grove made on his otherwise imperturbable cook. "Gee! Chop'm up four foot ties, make'm one dam railroad!" This "slow" route has the advantage of showing you the highlights of the park en route to Yosemite Village. If you come this way, be sure to stop at Wawona (the entrance) and visit the log cabin Pioneer Yosemite History Center.

When you reach Yosemite Village itself, you're suddenly in a land where giant forests clothe the mountains' flanks and waterfalls leap off craggy cliffs. Recommended point for a panoramic view is Glacier Point, from which one can see majestic El Capitan, the world's largest mass of visible granite; Half Dome, rising almost 9,000 feet; Yosemite Falls, best viewed in spring; and Lost Arrow Rock.

Although the valley gorge is seven miles in extent, it is not large enough for the almost three million yearly visitors who come to stay at the many lodges and campsites. You can get away from the people by hiking or driving into the higher mountains, especially in the area called Tuolumne Meadows, accessible by car. Other high-country places in Yosemite require horseback or hiking. Trips in the saddle in the High Sierras go up Tuolumne Meadows and usually do only 10 miles per day. You ride through alpine meadows, vast stands of pine, along trails sprayed by waterfalls. Lakes abound, large and small, hidden away in the mountains. Accommodations are adequate and well arranged. At night you bunk down at park campsites in the tents. Meals are served under canvas too, family-style.

If you want to do the Yosemite High Sierras on foot, you can join one of the guided hiking expeditions. Seven-day treks are offered weekly in summer. Buses take hikers to May Lake, and the walking starts from there.

You may bicycle in Yosemite if you wish. Both wheels and horses may be rented at the stables in Yosemite Valley, as well as at sites at Wawona, Tuolumne Meadows and White Wolf.

Best season to visit the park? Autumn or spring. Next best, winter. Beginning skiers find the Badger Pass slopes superb. Winter also brings the Christmas banquet pageant, very Old English, at Ahwahnee Hotel. This event is so popular that one has to make reservations a year ahead. Although Yosemite is beautiful in summer, the crowds of tourists make it the least enjoyable visiting season.

Wine Country

Calistoga is an excellent central point from which to explore California's wine country. Before imbibing, be sure to take in the geysers, where there is an "Old Faithful" and the petrified forest. There are approximately 60 wineries in Napa County and fifty-plus in neighboring Sonoma County. Most give conducted tours and the walking distances, from one winery to the next, are moderate. Two of the most interesting ones are Inglebrook, which gets its staves for its wine casts from German Black Forest oaks, and Beringer Brothers, where Chinese coolie labor dug out the tunnels in the hills where the barrels of wine are aged. Both are in St. Helena. Santa Rosa has a unique arboreal-architectural curiosity—a whole church built from the wood of one tree. The church is now the Ripley "Believe It or Not" Museum. Jack London State Park is in nearby Glen Ellen. London is buried beneath a giant boulder near the burnt ruins of his Wolf House.

East of Sonoma is the Buena Vista winery. The largest of the annual autumn vintage festivals are held here in the Valley of the Moon. There are band concerts, dancing on the green, parades for children and a religious ceremony of the blessing of the grapes. Only soft drinks are served at this Sonoma festival staged in the shadow of the big eucalyptus tree. The winery has ivy-covered stone walls and a tasting room that is candlelighted. Agoston Haraszthy, a Hungarian, was responsible for establishing Buena Vista. He brought the vine cuttings for planting from Europe's best vineyards.

The town of Sonoma is historical. Successors of Padre Junipero Serra built the last of the 21 missions here. In 1846 Americans proclaimed Californian independence from Mexico and the establishment of the California Republic. There are some European touches here; one of them is the Swiss Hotel where you can get an excellent meal. At "Train Town," one mile south of the Sonoma main square, steam-powered locomotives make 15-minute runs through a reproduction of an old mining town. The country around Sonoma is enchanting. There are rolling hills, and one can wander amongst oak, eucalyptus and pine groves.

Back in the coastal area, Sebastopol is the sole survivor of five California communities that once bore this name. Sebastopol is apple-growing country. An apple blossom festival and tour of the orchards takes place there every year near Easter. Just a bit north of Sebastopol is Guerneville, "capital" of the Russian River, a congested holiday center in summer. The Korbel winery is located here. One of the best producers of California champagne, it offers tours daily in the summer, or any time by appointment. Follow the river west, imagining the days when it teemed with Alaskan colonists. It bring you out to Jenner, a coastal fishing center.

Eleven miles north of here are the stout wooden buildings of Fort Ross. A state monument, it was the American outpost for Russian fur traders during the 19th century. They used it as a base for hunting sea otters and for raising crops to feed their Alaskan allies.

Continuing down the coast, you'll see a 10-mile stretch of spectacular beaches. The surf is treacherous and swimming is prohibited. Pebble collecting is great. Some lucky fossickers have uncovered jade pebbles. The beaches bear such names as Salmon Creek, Arch Rock, Portuguese, Shell and Goat Rock. They make up the Sonoma Coast Beaches State Park.

Angling west through pine forests and sand dunes leads you eventually to Point Reyes Lighthouse, the tip of California's only National Seashore. There is swimming at Drake's Beach and four backpack camping sections. Retracing your steps from Point Reyes National Seashore, you can have the dubious thrill of knowing you're driving on top of California's infamous San Andreas Fault.

Lassen Volcanic National Park

Bumpass Hell, stinking of sulphur and bubbling and fuming, is a reminder of the volcanic explosions that blasted out of the top of Lassen

Peaks for some three years, between 1914 and 1917, here in the Cascade Range of Northern California. Hot lava poured down upon the snow-pack, melted it, and caused an avalanche and a landslide. There are several hot springs, and in the clear, cold lakes, good catches of rain-bow, eastern brook, and German brown trout are to be had. There are four campgrounds, and, at Manzanita Lake, cabins for rent. Accommodations and tourist services at Mineral also.

Park snowed-in most of the year, highway impassable. Best time to visit is summer or early fall.

Redwood National Park

This rare combination of sea and forest is 46 miles long and up to seven miles wide, and besides its magnificent redwood forests it has 30 miles of Pacific coastline here in Northern California, with its own cliffs and sand and pebble beaches. The redwoods creep down some of the steep slopes overlooking the seashore, where mounds and scatterings of driftwood attract beachcombers. There are campgrounds in the park and in the adjoining Six River National Forest. Accommodations and tourist services at Eureka.

PRACTICAL INFORMATION FOR CALIFORNIA

PALM SPRINGS-MOJAVE DESERT-DEATH VALLEY AREA

HOW TO GET THERE. *By Air:* The largest airport in the area is at Palm Springs served by *American, Alaska, TWA, Western, Republic, Pacific Express,* and *Pan Am. Sun Aire,* a commuter airline, is also available.

By car: The major artery serving the area is I–10.

TOURIST INFORMATION SERVICES. Local Chambers of Commerce will provide information, as will the *Palm Springs Convention and Visitors Bureau,* Municipal Airport Terminal, Palm Springs.

SEASONAL EVENTS. Palm Springs is the site of the *Mounted Police Rodeo* in January, the *Bob Hope Desert Golf Classic* in February, and *The Dinah Shore Championship* at Mission Hills Country Club in April.

NATIONAL PARKS. *Death Valley National Monument,* covering almost two million acres, is weird, spooky and memorable. Death Valley is actually a lively place with many facilities, ranging from rough to resort. The Mesquite Spring and Texas Spring *campgrounds* have water and sanitary facilities. The Visitor Center is open year-round.

Joshua Tree National Monument, a 557,992-acre sprawl, preserves the unique yucca species. The Visitor Center is at Twenty-nine Palms, and there are campgrounds. Fill the gas tank before entering.

STATE PARKS. The giant in California's extensive state park system is *Anza–Borrego Desert Park,* boasting over 200 camping and picnic sites across its 488,000 acres. The most popular self-guided tour explores *Palm Canyon.* For guided nature walks, visit the park on a weekend.

GUEST RANCHES. White Sun Guest Ranch, located in the Palm Springs suburb of *Rancho Mirage,* serves family-style meals and offers varied sports activities.

MUSEUMS. *Death Valley Museum,* Death Valley Monument, includes the Natural History Museum, Harmony Borax Works and Scotty's Castle. *Palm Springs Desert Museum,* 135 E. Tahquitz-McCallum Way, features sculpture gardens, Indian artifacts and a 450-seat theater. (Admission $1.50, closed Monday.) Randsburg's *Desert Museum,* Butte St., houses a mineralogy collection. *Cabot's Old Indian Pueblo Museum,* 67–616 E. Desert View Ave., Desert Hot Springs. Hopi Indian-style structure hosting art galleries and trading post.

DRINKING LAWS. The legal drinking age is 21, and the law is rigidly enforced. Liquor may be purchased in stores and bars from 6 A.M. to 2 A.M. daily.

SPORTS. The Palm Springs area offers the *golfing* enthusiast a choice of over 30 courses to play and over 100 tournaments to watch. *A fishing* trip to Salton Sea, the "Sea in the Desert," might yield a 15-pound corvina. *Hiking* trails are plentiful at Palm Canyon for bicycling and horseback riding.

TOURS. Palm Springs Aerial Tramway, located off State 111 north of Palm Springs, takes visitors on a 2½-mile trip to the summit of Mt. San Jacinto. This is a popular picnicking and camping spot in summer. The tram now operates in the winter months a Nordic ski center which offers cross-country skiing, equipment rental and instruction. One favorite tour during the warmer season is the "Ride and Dive," featuring a western outdoor barbecue when passengers reach the mountain peaks. Guided excursions through Palm Springs can be arranged through Celebrity Tours in that city.

Gray Line Tours has an office in Palm Springs.

WHAT TO DO WITH THE CHILDREN. Visit the Living Desert Reserve in Palm Desert. This 300-acre Colorado Desert Reserve offers nature walks, and a Visitor's Center includes displays of desert plants and small live animals. Tour the shafts and stopes of Tropico Mine at *Soledad Mountain* in the Mojave Desert. You can pan for gold and explore a Gold Town. *Calico,* an old silver town, is a ghost town restored by Walter Knott of Knott's Berry Farm fame. Take them to the *Salton Sea* State Recreation Area, a water-and-sand playpen formed by the overflowing Colorado River in 1905. You can water-ski, swim and fish. Best time to go is early or late in the year (it's hot in the summer!).

HOTELS AND MOTELS. Listings are in order of price categories. Based on double occupancy, price categories and ranges are as follows: *Moderate* $20–25; *Inexpensive* under $20. For a more complete explanation of hotel and motel categories, see *Facts at Your Fingertips* at the front of this volume.

DEATH VALLEY. *Moderate:* **Stovepipe Wells Hotel.** On State 190, 82 miles east of Lone Pine. Open Oct.–Apr. Units, rooms, cottages.

DESERT HOT SPRINGS. *Moderate:* **Desert Inn.** 10805 Palm Dr. Mineral spa. Sauna, golf, tennis.

HEMET. *Inexpensive:* **Best Western Hemet.** 2625 W. Florida Ave. Pool. Restaurant near.

INDIO. *Moderate:* **El Morroco.** 82–645 Miles Ave. at King St. Attractive rooms, grounds. Many facilities.

PALM SPRINGS. Don't attempt to visit this famous resort during holiday season without advance reservations. Also, some of the hotels will not accept children as guests. It is advisable to check beforehand for age minimums. The off-season in Palm Springs affords some tremendous bargains, and is worth checking into.
Moderate: **Westwood Ho.** 701 E. Palm Canyon Dr. Therapeutic pool.
Royal Inn. 1700 S. Palm Canyon Dr. Attractive. Restaurant opposite.
Tiki Spa Hotel & Apts. 1910 S. Camino Real. Sauna, hot tub, isolated atmosphere, not pretentious.
Tuscany Manor Apartment-Hotel 350 Chino Canyon Rd. Pool; hot tub. Esther Williams swam here for a film she made in the forties.
Inexpensive: **The Monkey Tree Hotel.** 2388 E. Racquet Club Rd. Swimming pool, some kitchens. Pets allowed.

 DINING OUT. Price ranges for a complete dinner excluding drinks, tax or tip are as follows: *Moderate* $7–12; *Inexpensive* under $7. Restaurants featuring à la carte menus would, of course, be more expensive. Check hotel listings for other worthwhile restaurants. For a more complete explanation of restaurant categories, see *Facts at Your Fingertips* at the front of this volume.

DESERT HOT SPRINGS. *Moderate:* **Eriksen's.** 6121 Peirson Blvd. American, Scandinavian. Family-oriented.

HEMET. *Moderate:* **The Embers.** 828 W. Florida Ave., on State 74. Weekday buffet lunch.

INDIO. *Moderate:* **El Morocco Dining Room.** 82–645 Miles Ave. In motor hotel; beef and lamb specialties.

PALM SPRINGS. *Moderate:* **Banducci's Bit of Italy.** 1260 S. Palm Canyon Dr. Italian dishes, seafood, steak.
Burgett's. 960 S. Palm Canyon Rd. American cuisine.
C.B.'s Fish Joint. 203 N. Palm Canyon Dr. Fresh seafood, homemade bread.
Don the Beachcomber. 1101 N. Palm Canyon Dr. Outstanding Cantonese, American menus. Long list of tropical drinks.
Las Casuelas. 368 N. Palm Canyon Drive. Delicious food served in a fun and traditionally Mexican ambience. A new Las Casuelas restaurant, **Las Casuelas Nuevas,** is located at 70–050 Highway 111 in Rancho Mirage.
Lyons English Grill. 233 E. Palm Canyon Dr. English fare with fair serving wenches, prime rib a specialty.
Sorrentino's Seafood House. 1032 N. Palm Canyon Dr. French, Italian. Steaks, chops. Continental variations of fresh seafood.
Inexpensive: **Louise's Pantry.** 124 S. Palm Canyon Dr. Popular. Fabulous desserts. Closed June–September. Down-home cooking, home-baked pastries.
Nate's Delicatessen. 283 N. Palm Canyon Dr. Since 1948, serving deli-delicacies. Sandwiches are a mile-high, corned beef is a true delicacy. Nine-course budget dinner served between 4 P.M. and 6 P.M.

MONTEREY-CARMEL-BIG SUR AREA

HOW TO GET THERE. From San Francisco, you can reach Monterey and Carmel via US 101, the faster route, or State 1, the scenic route following the coastline.

HOW TO GET AROUND. *By air:* Monterey Airport, on the southern outskirts of Monterey, off Monterey-Salinas Hwy. 68, is served by*Air California, United* and *Golden West.*

By car: The famous Seventeen-Mile Drive between Monterey and Carmel offers panoramic views.

By train: The *Roaring Camp & Big Trees Railroad,* operating out of Felton in the Santa Cruz Mountains, is one of the few remaining steam railroads in the nation. Passengers are carried in open cars and a caboose for a six-mile round trip.

TOURIST INFORMATION SERVICES. Local Chambers of Commerce will send you information about their cities. (In Monterey, at 380 Alvarado St.), (408) 649–3200.) For tours, contact Gray Line of San Francisco, 420 Taylor St., San Francisco. Carmel Business Association, P.O. Box 4444, Carmel 93921, offers information; (408) 624–2522.

SEASONAL EVENTS. *July* is rodeo month. There's a Fiesta Rodeo in San Juan Bautista which has a barbecue and a horse show, and Salinas is the home of the California Rodeo. Monterey holds its county fair in *August* and a Jazz Festival in *September.*

NATIONAL PARKS. Big Basin Redwoods State Park, the first of redwood groves to be declared a protected state park, is usually visited en route to Carmel. You can hike, picnic or camp here. Only restrictions: no horses, and no dogs allowed overnight.

MUSEUMS AND GALLERIES. Carmel: *Carmel Mission and Gift Shop,* 3080 Rio Rd., is a historical museum, with sculpture, Indian artifacts and textile collections. Monterey: *Allen Knight Maritime Museum,* 550 Calle Principal; *History and Art Association,* also at 550 Calle Principal, offers guided tours of three historic buildings and its painting and costume exhibits. *Monterey Peninsula Museum of Art,* 559 Pacific St. *Old Monterey Jail,* Dutra St., Civic Center. *Robert Louis Stevenson House,* 530 Houston St. *San Carlos Cathedral,* 550 Church St., offers guided tours of its 18th- and 19th-century Spanish painting and sculpture. *United States Army Museum,* Presidio of Monterey, is housed in a 1908 cavalry-supply depot. California's first theater is in Monterey, corner of Scott and Pacific streets, where in 1847 Jack Swan, an English sailor, gave the first performance before soldiers. Preserved in 1906; informal tours are conducted.

HISTORIC SITES. San Juan Bautista State Historical Monument is a chapter of early California history that ended with the coming of the railroad.

TOURS. *Four- and five-day circle tours* of Yosemite, Monterey and Carmel are offered weekly, year-round, by California Parlor Car Tours Co. Gray Line of San Francisco operates *Monterey-Carmel* and the *Seventeen-Mile Drive* tours year-round. Also touring these areas are California Heritage Tours ([408]373–6454), Monterey Peninsula Tours ([408]375–1550) and Steinbeck Country Tours ([408]625–5107.)

MISSIONS. The San Juan Bautista Mission is one of many historical California missions on the Mission Trail, which parallels US 101 and is one of the state's most popular tourways.

GARDENS. In Carmel Valley, see Hanssens' Begonia Gardens. A mile east of San Juan Bautista on Hollister Rd. is the Ferry-Morse Flower Farm, with 900 acres of blooms.

DRINKING LAWS. You must be 21, and the youthful looking should have identification to prove their age. Legal hours for dispensing drinks in public places are from 6 A.M. to 2 A.M.

SPORTS. Golf: "Golf Digest" recommends Rancho Canada G.C., *Carmel Valley;* Laguna Seca G.C., *Monterey;* and Carmel Valley G. & C.C., *Carmel.* Rodeos: The California Rodeo at *Salinas* in July is one of the "Big Four" of the rodeo world. Horse shows: An interclub show is held at the Carmel Valley Trail and Saddle Club grounds in early May. In mid-August, see the *Carmel Valley* Horsemen's Roundup.

WHAT TO DO WITH THE CHILDREN. Go to Santa's Village, seven miles north of *Santa Cruz.* Charming wooded acres with Santa's House, the old boy himself, and his workshops. Santa Cruz Beach-Boardwalk offers a seashore playland, with rides, games and a mile-long beach.

HOTELS AND MOTELS. Listings are in order of price category. Based on double occupancy, price ranges are as follows: *Moderate* $20–25; *Inexpensive* under $20.

MONTEREY. *Moderate:* **Bel Air Motel.** 2050 Fremont. Pool, fireplace.
Cypress Gardens. 1150 Munras Ave. Complimentary coffee, rolls.
El Adobe. 936 Munras Ave. Whirlpool.
Inexpensive: **Motel 6.** 1278 Munras Ave. Good value.

CARMEL. *Moderate:* **Cypress Inn.** Lincoln and 7th. Fireplaces.
Wayside Inn. Mission & 7th. Kitchenettes. Family units.
La Playa Hotel. P.O. Box 900. Near the beach, pool.
Village Inn. Ocean and Junipero Avenues. Adobe charm in center of town.

BIG SUR. *Moderate:* **Big Sur Lodge.** On State 1, 30 miles south of Monterey. In Pfeiffer Big Sur State Park. Check season in operation.
Glen Oaks Motel. On State 1, two miles north of State Park. Adobe motel resort.

DINING OUT. Cuisines, restaurant setting and décor vary. So do business hours. Many establishments are closed on certain holidays and particular days of the week. Some close during brief periods annually. Telephone beforehand to avoid disappointment. Restaurants are listed according to categories: *Moderate,* $10–15; *Inexpensive,* under $10. Prices are for a complete meal but do not include drinks, tax or tip. À la carte meals will cost more. For a more detailed explanation of restaurant categories, see *Facts at Your Fingertips* at the front of this volume.

MONTEREY. *Moderate:* **Neil DeVaughn's.** Long-time Cannery Row favorite for steaks and seafood.
Inexpensive: **The Cellar.** Italian fare, homemade desserts.

BIG SUR. *Moderate:* **Nepenthe.** Three miles south of Big Sur on Hwy 1. Great view of coastline, terrific gift shop stocked with local crafts. Area landmark.

CARMEL. *Moderate:* **French Poodle.** Mission, between Fourth and Fifth. French. Good value.

Raffaello. Mission, between Ocean and Seventh. Northern Italian menu.

Swedish Restaurant. Dolores Street, between Seventh and Ocean. Swedish-American menu.

SEQUOIAS-KINGS CANYON

HOW TO GET THERE. State 180 and 198 lead to the parks from Fresno and Visalia, respectively.

TOURIST INFORMATION SERVICES. Sequoia has a Visitor Center that will provide you with advice on sightseeing. Helpful data and photographs are on display.

 NATIONAL FORESTS. Sierra National Forest, Sequoia's neighbor to the north, features ponderosa pines and blue oaks. This area offers winter and summer recreation in rough or resort fashion.

 DRINKING LAWS. California drinking laws are enforced rigidly. Youthful-looking men and women are often asked for identification to establish that they are 21, the legal drinking age. Liquor may be sold and served in stores and bars from 6 A.M. to 2 A.M. every day, including all holidays.

 SPORTS. Fishermen will find excellent trout *fishing* in many lakes and streams. And hikers will find *trails* appropriate to their abilities. The more experienced may want to climb Mount Whitney, 14,495 feet, the highest point in the continental United States with the exception of Alaska. One warning: if you're hiking without a guide, go prepared with map and compass. Trail directions, and maps can be purchased at visitor centers. For safety, register at trailheads. Tell a responsible person where you are going and when you expect to return. On long hikes, carry rainwear, extra woolen clothing and food. If lost, hurt or caught by fog or darkness, don't panic. Just wait. Before you do anything, collect yourself. If you keep your cool, the chances of being found soon are excellent. Build a fire and stay by it. Rescuers will find you.

TOURS. Inquire in Tulare and Visalia about bus tours of the parks.

 HOTELS AND MOTELS. In *Sequoia National Park,* housekeeping cabins (European plan) are located at Camp Kaweah, where there are also a coffee shop, grocery store, gas station and gift shop, all open year-round. *Giant Forest Lodge* (American and European plan) and *Grant Grove Lodge* (European plan) are open from May to October.

At *Kings Canyon,* the lodge, cabins and housekeeping camps keep approximately the same dates and have similar facilities. For additional information, write: Sequoia Kings Canyon National Parks, Three Rivers, Calif. 93271.

Motel prices are based on double-occupancy rates as follows: *Moderate* $20–30; *Inexpensive* under $20.

VISALIA. *Moderate:* **Lamp Liter Inn.** Calif. 198 at 3300 W. Mineral King Ave. Restaurant, TV, pool.

Inexpensive: **TraveLodge Motel.** 4645 W. Mineral King Avenue. Two-story property. TV, pool. Pets welcome.

YOSEMITE NATIONAL PARK

HOW TO GET THERE. Yosemite National Park may be reached by State 140, the Merced gateway, or State 41, a somewhat slower route passing through several small towns.

TOURIST INFORMATION SERVICES. Information about tours to Yosemite may be obtained from *Gray Line of San Francisco*, 420 Taylor St., San Francisco.

FARM VACATIONS AND GUEST RANCHES. Yosemite National Park has six-day *guided saddle trips*, departing several days a week in summer and making a tour of the High Sierra camps. There are four-day trips, too, out of Tuolumne Meadows. Write Yosemite Park and Curry Company.

Hunewill Circle H Ranch is in *Bridgeport*, northeast of Yosemite and fairly close to the Nevada border. This is a real working cattle ranch. Activities include breakfast rides, steak fries, square dancing, picnics, hiking, swimming, pack trips, fishing, and hunting. Guests are accommodated in the main ranchhouse or cabins, and meals are served family-style, with all you can eat.

Diamond D Ranch is in *Lakeshore* in the high Sierras, southeast and over a very wiggly road from Chowchilla or Coarsegold. Open only from mid-June to mid-October, this ranch is in an extremely remote and grandiose location. You can take many easy pack trips into scenic canyons and over mountain passes. Bring your own bedroll. Camping is in log cabins or tents, with modern plumbing. For information, write Box 167, Auberry, Calif.

TOURS. *Four- and five-day circle tours* of Yosemite, Monterey and Carmel are offered weekly, all year, by California Parlor Car Tours Co., using modern air-conditioned motor coaches. *A six-day trip* combines the above with Lake Tahoe, plus Santa Barbara and Los Angeles in Southern California; this trip is offered weekly in summer only. Gray Line of San Francisco offers *four-day tours* combining Yosemite, Monterey and Carmel also; advance reservations are required for this weekly tour, given year-round.

SPECIAL INTEREST TOURS. Seven-day guided *hiking trips* leave Yosemite Valley every Sunday in summer for a tour of the park. Guided six-day *horseback trips* around the High Country of the park leave the valley several days a week in summertime.

DRINKING LAWS. You must be 21—and if you look young, be sure to carry proof of your age, for you're bound to be asked to show it. Legal hours for dispensing drinks in public places are from 6 A.M. to 2 A.M.

SPORTS. *White-water* enthusiasts can run the Tuolumne River in three days. Information may be obtained from the American River Touring Association, 1016 Jackson St., Oakland, Calif. 94607. Badger Pass offers good *skiing*, including competitive racing. Twain Harte hosts the *High Sierra Trail Horseback Ride* in mid-August. And, of course, the *hiking, fishing, swimming* and *boating* are excellent.

Hikers should take special precautions if hiking without a guide. Go prepared with map and compass. Do be safe and register at trailheads. Tell a responsible person where you are going and your expected time of return. On longer hikes, it's best to take along rainwear, extra woolen clothing and food. If the unanticipated happens, don't panic. Collect yourself before you do anything. If you keep your cool, you'll be able to help rescuers locate you. Build a fire and stay by it.

 ACCOMMODATIONS in Yosemite National Park are priced for every budget. They range from rustic free campgrounds to hotels equipped with such amenities as heated pools, tennis and sitter lists. One campground (Camp 4) and two hotels *(Ahwahnee* and *Wawona)* are open year-round; other accommodations are seasonal. For information, write to the Yosemite Park and Curry Company, operators of all accommodations within the park. Advance reservations are recommended and may be made through offices at the park, in San Francisco or in Los Angeles.

YOUTH HOSTELS. The Yosemite Institute Youth Hostel offers tents with beds at nominal fees. The season extends from mid-June to mid-September.

 DINING OUT. Yosemite visitors have a choice of dining fare, too. Campers who wish to dine alfresco by their campfires will find provisions at a grocery store in Yosemite Valley. Pack trippers dine heartily family-style in tents. And both hotels have dining facilities.

THE REST OF CALIFORNIA

 HOW TO GET THERE. *By air: TWA, United, American Airlines, Delta, National, Continental, Northwest* and *Republic* service both San Francisco and Los Angeles from various major points in the U.S. *Eastern, Texas International, Western, Golden West, Pacific Southwest, Commuter Air Lines, China Airlines, British Airways* and *Korean* also serve Los Angeles. Airlines and service from other points to Los Angeles are: *Pan Am,* Honolulu; *Delta,* Puerto Rico; *Air Canada,* Montreal and Toronto; *Republic* and *Western,* Calgary; *Aeromexico, Mexicana, Republic* and *Western,* Mexico. You can reach Sacramento via *United* and *Republic.* The Burbank Airport is served by *Continental, Republic, Pacific Southwest* and *Commuter Airlines.* Long Beach Airport may be reached via *Republic, Pacific Southwest, Western, Golden West, Catalina,* and *Catalina Seaplanes, Inc.* San Diego is served by several major airlines.

By car: Interstate 80 runs from the east to San Francisco, Interstate 5, from Washington through California. The main freeways delivering traffic through and into downtown Los Angeles are: Pasadena, from the San Gabriel Valley; Hollywood, servicing Hollywood and the San Fernando Valley; San Bernardino Freeway, from eastern areas, Riverside and San Bernardino counties. The Santa Ana Freeway reaches down toward beach communities and Orange County. The Santa Monica Freeway links Los Angeles and Santa Monica on the Pacific. The Harbor Freeway covers the San Pedro/Wilmington route. The Golden State Freeway runs toward eastern San Fernando Valley, Burbank and Glendale.

By train: Amtrak provides a relaxing and enjoyable mode of travel to California from many parts of the United States. The most popular route is the "Coast Starlight" from Seattle to Los Angeles, running through the scenic Washington and Oregon countryside, and covering over 100 miles of the California coastline. Another delightful journey is the "Southwest Limited." Originating in Chicago, it winds its way through the Painted Desert towards its final destination of Los Angeles. San Francisco and San Diego can also be reached via connecting routes from several other major cities.

TOURIST INFORMATION SERVICES. Most local Chambers of Commerce will send you material on their cities. The *San Francisco Convention & Visitors Bureau,* 1390 Market, has a supply of general information. Also in San Francisco, the *Redwood Empire Association* welcomes visitors at its office, 360 Post St. Information on specific subjects is available from such services as these:

California Chamber of Commerce, 455 Capital Mall, Sacramento, CA. 95814; *Wine Institute,* 139 Market St., San Francisco; *Shasta-Cascade Wonderland Association,* Redding; *Lake Tahoe Chamber of Commerce,* P.O. Box 884, Tahoe City; *Golden Chain Council of Mother Lode,* P.O. Box 206, Soda Springs, and *Division of Beaches and Parks* (send $1 for its booklet), P.O. Box 2390, Sacramento 95814. For information on the *National Forest Campgrounds,* write the Regional Forester, 630 Sansome St., San Francisco 94111. *Pacific Gas and Electric Co.,* San Francisco, issues an excellent booklet, *California's Historical Monuments.* For tour information, you may also contact *Gray Line of San Francisco,* 420 Taylor St., San Francisco. The *Napa Chamber of Commerce* at 1900 Jefferson St. provides maps and picnic facilities, while the *Wine Institute,* 165 Post St., San Francisco, points out the wineries in the state.

MUSEUMS AND GALLERIES. Hours and admission fees vary. Some exhibits are open only seasonally. It is advisable to check locally for up-to-date information. Amador City: *Gold Rush Museum,* Fleeheart and Main Sts., is a small, privately owned museum with a collection of mining equipment, Indian artifacts.

Bakersfield: *Kern County Museum,* 3801 Chester Ave. Indian artifacts, firearms.

Berkeley: *Art Center,* 1275 Walnut St. Paintings and sculpture; films, gallery talks. *Judah L. Magnes Memorial Museum,* 2911 Russell St., houses an impressive collection of Jewish ceremonial art, rare books, a holocaust collection. *University Art Museum,* 2626 Bancroft Way, offers guided tours and gallery talks, paintings, sculpture, drawings, prints.

Carmel: *Carmel Mission and Gift Shop,* 3080 Rio Rd., is a historical museum, with sculpture, Indian artifacts and textile collections.

Crescent City: *Del Norte County Historical Society,* 710 H St., is housed in an old jail building.

Death Valley: *Death Valley Museum,* Death Valley National Monument, Natural History Museum, charcoal kilns, Harmony Borax Works and Scotty's Castle.

Desert Hot Springs: *Cabot's Old Indian Pueblo,* 67–616 East Desert View, is a Hopi Indian-style structure with a museum, art gallery and trading post. *Eastern California Museum,* 155 Grant St. Indian artifacts, narrow-gauge steam locomotive.

Eureka: *Clarke Memorial Museum,* 240 E. St., has anthropology, archeology, costume, Indian lore and natural history exhibits.

Fresno: *Arts Center,* 3033 E. Yale Ave. *County Historical Society,* 7160 W. Kearney Blvd., is a general history museum with a blacksmith shop, carriage house and 1890s home.

Laguna Beach: *Laguna Beach Art Gallery,* 307 Cliff Dr. Paintings by early Calif. artists.

Malibu: *J. Paul Getty Museum,* 17985 Pacific Coast Hwy. J. Paul Getty collection; much Greek and Roman sculpture.

Monterey: *Allen Knight Maritime Museum,* 550 Calle Principal. *History and Art Association,* 550 Calle Principal, offers guided tours of three historic buildings and its painting and costume exhibits. *Monterey Peninsula Museum of Art,* 559 Pacific St. *Old Monterey Jail,* Dutra St., Civic Center. *Robert Louis Stevenson House,* 530 Houston St. *San Carlos Cathedral,* 550 Church St., offers guided tours of its 18th- and 19th-century Spanish religious painting and sculpture. *United States Army Museum,* Presidio of Monterey, is housed in a 1908 cavalry-supply depot.

Palo Alto: *Department of Nature and Sciences,* 250 Hamilton Ave.

Redding: *Museum and Art Center* specializes in Indian lore, crafts.

Sacramento: *California State Indian Museum,* 1218 K St., is located on the site of Sutter's Fort. *E. B. Crocker Art Gallery,* 216 O St.

San Jose: *State University Art Gallery,* 20th-century painting, sculpture, graphics. *Civic Art Gallery,* 110 S. Market St. Regional artists. *Historical Museum,* 635 Phelan Ave. Mining, transportation, historic houses.

San Luis Obispo: *County Historical Museum,* 696 Monterey St.

Santa Barbara: The *Santa Barbara Museum of Art,* 1130 State St.

Stockton: *Pacific Center for Western Historical Studies,* Univ. of the Pacific. Western Americana, John Muir papers. *Pioneer Museum and Haggan Galleries,* 1201 N. Pershing Ave.

Special Interest: Bishop: *Laws Railroad Museum,* 5 miles N.E. on U.S. 6. Port Hueneme: *Civil Engineer Corps Seabee Museum,* a fascinating memorial to the U.S. Navy Construction Battalions, Naval Base. Palm Springs: *The Palm Springs Desert Museum,* 135 E. Tahquitz-McCallum Way, has exhibits devoted to the desert. Randsburg: *Desert Museum,* Butte St. Mineralogy collection. Santa Barbara: *Museum of Natural History,* 2559 Puesta del Sol Rd. *County Courthouse,* 1220 Anacapa & Anapamu Sts. Spanish-Moorish structure. Santa Paula: *The California Oil Museum,* 1003 Main St., is a gusher of oil information. Morrow Bay: *The Museum of Natural History,* State Park Rd.

HISTORIC SITES. Scattered along the 780-mile length of California are about 44 official State Historical Monuments and nearly 900 Historical Landmarks. There is also the "Father Junipero Serra Rosary" of 21 missions. *Columbia,* four miles from Sonora, is the best preserved of the Gold Rush towns. Its buildings are marked for easy identification and the town has an excellent museum.

Donner Memorial Park, two miles west of Truckee on US 40, has a very impressive monument, commemorating members of the Donner party who camped there during the winter of 1846–47.

San Juan Bautista State Historical Monument, off US 101 between Gilroy and Salinas, is a chapter of California history that ended with the coming of the railroad.

Sutter's Fort (Sacramento), where gold was discovered, has California's greatest collection of Gold Rush and Pioneer relics.

Be sure to visit Santa Barbara's adobe *Casa de la Guerra.* It houses the Chamber of Commerce in the center of El Paseo, a quaint restoration of an old Spanish shopping center at 19 E. de la Guerra St.

Hearst San Simeon Historical Monument has castles, mansions, statuary, art treasures, historical structures, an indoor gold-inlaid Roman pool and magnificent gardens on its 123-acres.

A note on Monterey: Be sure to visit the famous surviving adobes of historic old Monterey, in the new Monterey State Historic Park.

TOURS. *California Parlor Car Tours* has year-round four- and five-day circle tours of Yosemite, Monterey and Carmel. Six-day versions, offered in the summers only, include Lake Tahoe, Santa Barbara and Los Angeles. The *California Western Railroad* operates a small train, the Skunk, between Ft. Bragg and Willits. The 80-mile round trip runs through redwood forests, over 33 bridges and trestles and through two tunnels.

Western Greyhound Lines offers four-day Redwood Empire tours monthly in July, August and September, covering Frank Lloyd Wright's Marin Civic Center, Sonoma, St. Helena, Santa Rose, Mendocino, Ft. Bragg, the Avenue of the Giants, the Pacific Lumber Mill at Scotia, Eureka and the Rockefeller Redwoods State Park.

By boat: Some options are sightseeing excursions available from piers and docks at Santa Barbara and Newport Beach.

At the California State Marine Preserve, you may observe sea life on glass-bottom-boat cruises. And at Mission Bay, hydrofoil rides are available.

Cable car rides: Palm Springs Aerial Tramway, located at Tramway Dr., Chino Canyon, off Hwy. 111 North, operates seasonally. Adult and children prices. There are also special ride and dinner tickets.

DRINKING LAWS. The state rigidly enforces its drinking laws. You must be 21—if you're youthful-looking, be sure to carry proof of your age. Legal hours for dispensing drinks in public places are from 6 A.M. to 2 A.M. daily.

SUMMER SPORTS. For *skiing* and *boating* in general, California is loaded with lakes. Some major ones are Tahoe, Berryessa and Mendocino. Year-round water sports may be enjoyed along California's southeast border, from Parker to Blythe, and among many places, at Salton Sea, Lake Gregory, Lake Arrowhead, Big Bear Lake and June Lake. You can dig for clams at Morro Bay; for giant clams at Pismo Beach.

Fishing: Inland, the lakes, reservoirs, rivers and mountain streams yield bluegill, bullheads, channel and white catfish, crappie and rainbow trout. There's trout fishing at Whitewater Canyon and Bishop. Salton Sea is populated with corvinas weighing up to 15 lbs. Oxnard is a port for fishing the Channel Islands for halibut. There is good sportfishing at Catalina Island. Ocean sportfishing services are available at Santa Barbara, Avila Beach, Morro Bay, Port Hueneme, San Simeon and Ventura. There are many choice fishing spots at such places as Lake Tahoe, along the Upper Sacramento River and in the Castle Crags State Park area.

White-water enthusiasts can run the Tuolumne River in three days. For information contact The American River Touring Association, 1016 Jackson St., Oakland, Calif. 94607.

Riverboating: After an absence of 100 years, in 1980 riverboats once again began to ply the Sacramento River adjacent to the Old Sacramento Historic Area. Modern riverboat cruises between Sacramento and San Francisco are run by Delta Travel, 1240 Merkely Avenue, P.O. Box 813, West Sacramento, CA. 95691.

Golf: California is teeming with courses. The Palm Springs area alone has 37. Pebble Beach G. Links, Pebble Beach, ranks among the top 10 of America's 100 greatest courses; Spyglass Hill, Pebble Beach, among the fourth 10, and Cypress Point Club, Pebble Beach, among the fifth 10. Some of the many others recommended by *Golf Digest* include: Lake Shastina, Mt. Shasta, a Robert Trent Jones course; Alameda, in Alameda, a renovated course with five artificial lake hazards; Pasatiemo, in Santa Cruz, overlooking Monterey Bay; Laguna Seca, Monterey, a Trent Jones course; Avila Beach, a resort course; Alisal, a resort course at Solvang; Ojai Valley, a resort course at Ojai; Soboba Springs, San Jacinto, a challenging Muirhead creation; Desert Island, Cathedral City, private Muirhead course; Pala Mesa Inn, Fallbrook, a championship course; San Vincente, Ramona, semi-private Ted Robinson course; Rancho Santa Fe, Santa Fe, a fine, interesting course.

Boating: California's most popular boating park is the Salton Sea State Recreational Area.

Houseboating: On the Sacramento River (the Delta), you can rent a houseboat and tie up at night to any convenient tree. There are many primeval water mazes where you'll hear nothing but the bulrushes clattering softly in the wind. Ocean-going freighters use the Delta, too. For more information, and to be placed on a newsletter mailing list, write Houseboats, P.O. Box 9140, Stockton, CA 95208.

Surfing: Surfing is a big sport in Southern California. There are about 125 beaches between Morro Bay and San Diego. For exciting participation or observation, head for the beaches early—best time is between 6 A.M. and 9 A.M. You'll find lots of surfers during the summers in the arty community of Laguna; the main spot is at Thalia St. During the winters (it's a year-round sport) you'll see some of the world's best surfers at Rincon in Ventura and at Jalama State Park in Santa Barbara.

Bicycling: There are many bicycling clubs in Southern California, most of them affiliated with the American Youth Hostels.

Hiking: Sturdy shoes are recommended for trails at Andreas, Murray, Palm Canyons and up Mt. Whitney.

Pack trips: There are guided pack and saddle animal trails in summer at Mammoth Lakes.

WINTER SPORTS. *Skiing* is another big sport in California. Good areas are Squaw Valley, eight miles from Tahoe City; Alpine Meadows, a mile south of Squaw Valley turnoff; Sugar Bowl, Badger Pass, in Yosemite; Lassen Park Ski Area; Mount Shasta Ski Bowl. In the Ontario/Riverside/San Bernardino area, there's skiing at Lake Arrowhead. Novice and intermediate runs are at Blue Horizon Resort, Happy Hill Resort, Rebel Ridge Resort, all of which have a toboggan run. Novice to expert runs also are at Green Valley Snow Bowl, Goldmine Ski Area at Moonridge, Mt. Baldy Ski Lifts, Inc., Snow Forest, Snow Valley, Inc. and Snow Summit.

 SPECTATOR SPORTS. *Rodeos:* California is second only to Texas in number of rodeos. More than 60 are sanctioned each year by the Rodeo Cowboys Association. Major ones are at Red Bluff in April. The California Rodeo, the biggest of them all, is held at Salinas in July.

Equestrian events include: the Interclub Horse Show at Carmel Valley Trail and Saddle Club in May; the Shasta Wonderland Three-Day Non-Competitive Trail Ride in July, and the Equestrian Trails and Western American Cup, preceded by a big public breakfast and a parade at the Pebble Beach Stables in early September.

Races: Ontario Motor Speedway, Ontario. California "500" Grand Prix Motorcycles, N.H.R.A. Supernationals Drag Race, Miller 500 Stock Car Race. Year-round. Riverside Raceway, Riverside. Five major races yearly. And in Indio, a few miles from Palm Springs, camel and ostrich races are held every winter during the National Date Festival.

Tennis: The annual Ojai Tennis Tournament is held in April.

Boating: The flight of the Snowbirds Regatta is held at Newport in July; "Character Boat Parade" in August.

Soccer: The Sacramento Gold pro team has its season April through August and plays at Hughes Stadium, Sutterville Road between Franklin and Freeport Blvd. The San Jose Earthquake play their spring season at Sparton Stadium.

Jai Alai (pronounced *Hi Lie*): The betting is heavy and the crowds gather during scheduled weeknights at Fronton Palacio, Tijuana, Mexico, 16 miles below San Diego.

 WHAT TO DO WITH THE CHILDREN. *Marine World/Africa U.S.A.* Sixty-five-acre complex of sea and jungle citizens. Among the animal community is Lancelot, the only known unicorn in existence who closely resembles the New York Metropolitan Museum of Art's renowned unicorn tapestry. The unicorn's mom is of angora goat stock—but there's no telling who the father is. Phone (415) D-O-L-P-H-I-N for information. Just south of San Francisco. *Child's Estate Zoological Gardens,* Santa Barbara, is a unique park, playground and zoo. Its Sealarium has underwater portholes for viewing. A miniature railroad tours the park.

Movieland of the Air, Orange County Airport, Santa Ana, preserves a $2-million air force of airplanes, from Jennies to jets. There are real planes that kids can climb into and rides in a Waco open bi-plane.

Marriott's Great America, 45 miles south of San Francisco, is a 65-acre amusement park dedicated to recalling America's history (Orleans Place, Hometown Square, Yukon Territory). Debuted in 1976. World's largest and probably most beautiful carousel. Super-sensational roller coaster. 28 rides, ditto eateries. Open late May-early Sept., daily. Check for other seasonal weekend opening days.

Santa's Village, seven miles north of Santa Cruz on Calif. 17, is situated on wooded acres with Santa's house, the old boy himself and his workshops.

In *Happy Hollow Park,* San Jose, children may feed seals and pet the ponies, donkeys, lambs, goats and ducks. Also in San Jose, you can paddle an Indian war canoe through the muddy waters of *Frontier Village.* San Jose's *Winchester Mystery House* is a 160-room dwelling with trapdoors and secret passageways.

Another favorite spot with youngsters is Oakland's *Fairyland,* as well as the *Oakland Zoo* in Knowland State Park.

The *Sacramento Science Center and Junior Museum* at 3615 Auburn Blvd. lets kids explore animals, science labs and has special classes during the summer.

The *Frontier Historical Center* in Temecula contains the world's largest collection of Old West memorabila. Open daily 9:30 A.M. –5:00 P.M. Admission: $4.95 adults; $3.95 children 5–11 and senior citizens; free for children under 5.

HOTELS AND MOTELS. In *Northern California* accommodations range from plush seaside establishments to the cozy chalet-type digs found in Carmel, to the rustic and far-from-rustic rooms available in and around the national parks. Accommodations are plentiful in *Southern California,* where you are apt to find some good bargains. Motels compete vigorously for the tourist trade—most have one swimming pool, several have three. The luxury hotels are as elaborate as those in Florida, though not all of them are beachfront.

Based on double occupancy, prices throughout California start *upwards* from figures given, as follows: *Moderate* $20 and up; *Inexpensive* under $20.

For a more complete explanation of hotel and motel categories, refer to *Facts at Your Fingertips* at the front of this volume.

BAKERSFIELD. *Moderate:* **Best Western Oak Inn.** Pool, pets.
Best Western Casa Royale Motor Inn. 251 S. Union Ave. 24-hour coffee shop, comfortable.
Downtowner Inn. Friendly.
Holiday Inn. Attractive rooms.
Ramada Inn. Pleasant, large.
Inexpensive: **Motel 6.** Nicely decorated rooms.

BERKELEY. *Moderate:* **Best Western Berkeley House Motor Hotel.** 920 University Avenue. Pool, convenient.
Hotel Durant. 2600 Durant. Downtown, near campus.

BIG BEAR LAKE. *Moderate:* **Robinhood Inn.** Year-round. Fireplaces.

FRESNO. *Moderate:* **Fresno Hilton.** Downtown. Rooftop bar.
Holiday Fresno Airport. 5090 E. Clinton Ave. Sauna, miniature golf, indoor-outdoor pool. Nicely decorated rooms.
Hyatt Tradewinds. Usual amenities.
Water Tree Inn. Spacious rooms.
Inexpensive: **Motel 6.** Attractive. Two locations.

MENDOCINO AND FT. BRAGG. *Moderate:* **Mendocino Inn.** Refurbished Victorian ambience.
Pine Beach Inn. Tennis, beach.
Trade Winds Lodge. Comfortable.

OAKLAND. *Inexpensive:* **Motel 6.** Heated pool.
Townhouse Travelodge.

PALO ALTO. *Moderate:* **Flamingo Motor Lodge.** Restaurant, lounge.

SACRAMENTO. *Moderate:* **Holiday Inn.** Two locations.

Mansion Inn. Opposite Governor's Mansion.
Inexpensive: **Lemon Tree Hotel.** Pets.

SAN BERNARDINO. *Moderate:* **Holiday Inn San Bernardino.** 666 Fairway Dr. Free in-room movies, gift shop. Convention facilities.
Inexpensive: **Villa Viejo.** Sauna, whirlpool.

SAN JOSE. *Moderate:* **Holiday Inn.** Golf available.
Howard Johnson's. Restaurant, lounge. Pool.
Inexpensive: **Campus Motel.** 404 Santa Rosa Street. Playground for the kids.
Pepper Tree Inn. Family-oriented.

SAN LUIS OBISPO. *Moderate:* **Howard Johnson's Motor Lodge.** Tastefully furnished.
Madonna Inn. Unusual decor. Reservations a must usually six months in advance.
San Luis Obispo TraveLodge.
Sands Motel. Heated pool.
Vagabond Motor Hotel. Comfortable.

SAN SIMEON. (Reservations advisable during summer season, when tourists flock to see Hearst's Castle.)
Moderate: **Cavalier Inn by the Sea.** Neat. Oceanfront.
Green Tree Inn. Near Hearst Castle.
San Simeon Pines. Near Hearst Castle.

SANTA BARBARA. *Moderate:* **Ambassador by the Sea.** Free continental breakfast.
Miramar By the Sea. 1555 S. Jamisen Lane. Beautifully landscaped hotel by the Pacific.
El Prado Motor Inn. Downtown.
Encina Motor Lodge. Spacious, nicely furnished.
Holiday Lodge. Queen-size beds, near Mission.
Howard Johnson's Motor Lodge. Tasteful décor.
La Casa del Mar. Faces beach, near Stearns Wharf.
Petite Chateau Inn. French Provincial décor, free coffee. Quaint.
Inexpensive: **Tides Motel.** One block from beach, overlooks Pershing Park.

 DINING OUT. Restaurants throughout California are prepared to please all palates and pocketbooks. Generalizing is impossible as the array runs from gourmet to good, plain fare. You should have no trouble selecting an interesting place to have lunch or dinner. If you're in *Southern California,* try some of the dishes from south of the border. And, since you are on the Pacific Coast, look into specialties from China, Japan and Polynesia. Some of the best Oriental restaurants are in this part of the United States.

The range is as wide in *Northern California,* where fish, particularly the hard-to-find abalone, is the specialty of many seaside restaurants. In that part of the state, you'll also note a range of settings—from waterfronts to an old firehouse, tea rooms, Spanish missions and restaurants with stagecoachy decor.

Price ranges for a complete dinner excluding drinks, tax and tip start *upwards* from the following figures: *Moderate* $8–12, *Inexpensive* under $8. For à la carte meals, double the figure.

For a complete explanation of restaurant categories, see *Facts at Your Fingertips* at the front of this volume.

BAKERSFIELD. *Moderate:* **Maison Jaussaud.** Gallic touch. Excellent.

BERKELEY. *Moderate:* **Spenger's Fish Grotto.** Popular seafood restaurant.
Warszawa. Polish cuisine. Fine wines.

LAKE TAHOE AREA. *Moderate:* **The Edelweiss.** 945 Ski Run Blvd. South Lake Tahoe. German-inspired mood and menu.

OAKLAND. *Moderate:* **Sea Wolf.** Jack London Square flavor.
Khyber Pass. Mideastern mood & food.

PALO ALTO. *Moderate:* **Ming's.** Chinese menu. Popular.
Proud Popover. Stanford Shopping Center. Colonial decor; quiches, popovers. American menu.

SACRAMENTO. *Moderate:* **The Delta Queen.** 1107 Front St., and **Old Sacramento.** 1112 Second St. Nostalgic. Excellent service, popular with locals and visitors alike.
Frank Fat's. 806 L St. Cantonese. Favorite of politicians & lobbyists.

SAINT HELENE. *Moderate:* **La Belle Helene.** Tiny French treasure.

SANTA BARBARA. *Moderate:* **Paula's Place Restaurant.** 2700 De La Vina St. Salad bar, complimentary glass of sherry.
Inexpensive. **The Eggception.** 1208 State Street. One hundred varieties of omelettes plus other light choices. Breakfast, lunch.
Skandi Buffet. 2911 De La Vina St. Authentic Scandinavian smorgasbord. Open 7 days.

SOLVANG. *Moderate:* **The Belgian Cafe.** 475 First Street. Belgian waffles, Solvang fruit wines. Breakfast, lunch.
Danish Inn. Own baked goods; wonderful Danish pastries.

SONOMA. *Moderate:* **Swiss Hotel.** Family-style dinners.

VACAVILLE. *Moderate:* **Nut Tree.** Super breakfast, salad treats. A legend in Northern California.

NEVADA

Las Vegas, Reno and Lake Tahoe

Las Vegas, which calls itself "The Entertainment Capital of the World," is truly one of the world's most exciting cities. Located in the Southern Nevada desert near the tip of the "Silver State," Las Vegas annually plays host to some 12 million visitors, who come to this famous resort to see the top stars of show business and try their luck in the city's numerous legal casinos. Although casino-style gambling was legalized in Nevada in 1931, the phenomenal growth of Las Vegas did not start until after World War II. But it has continued unabated since that time.

The largest concentration of luxury resorts is along the three-and-one-half-mile "Strip." But another casino complex is located downtown, in what is called "Casino Center." The latter is along famous Fremont Street, the main street of the city when it was founded in 1905.

Today, Las Vegas is one of the country's leading convention cities. A 825,000-square-foot, one-level, air-conditioned Convention Center is the site of over 300 conclaves yearly, and also is used for a number of sporting and special events.

Boulder City & Hoover Dam

Stop at the Visitor's Center in Boulder City or at the headquarters of the Lake Mead National Recreation Area for exhibits and a schedule of tours and other activities. If you want to explore on your own, start with the tour of Hoover Dam, then drive on to Willow Beach on the Arizona side of Lake Mohave. Here you will develop a fast appreciation for the effort it required to tame the rampant Colorado in such a rugged setting. Return to Hoover Dam and proceed along the shore of Lake Mead to the marina for swimming, boat rides and sweeping views. (In March there are superb wildflower displays throughout the desert.)

Death Valley

Starting from Las Vegas, head out for a long day's drive on US 95 north, detouring up to Mt. Charleston, the highest range in the vicinity. This road carries you through heavy stands of yucca and cactus up to elevations where evergreens dominate and where substantial snowfall allows skiing in winter.

Returning to US 95, continue north to Lathrop Wells, then take State 373 west to Death Valley Junction. From here take State 190 (Cal.) north through this desolate desert basin to Scotty's Castle, an odd bit of architecture now open to the public as a museum. From Scotty's make your return via State 374 into Nevada and proceed to Tonopah. En route you pass through Goldfield, a pitiful remnant of the Tonopah-Goldfield boom 60 years ago.

PRACTICAL INFORMATION FOR LAS VEGAS

HOW TO GET THERE. *By air:* There are direct flights on 15 lines from major cities all over the U.S., and from western Canada by *Eastern, Republic* and *Western. By train: Amtrak* from Los Angeles or Chicago-Salt Lake City.

TOURIST INFORMATION SERVICES. For Las Vegas information, hotel and show reservations, stop at the *Travel Center* on Interstate 15, southwest of the city, the *Las Vegas Tourist Center* on Hwy. 95 southeast of town or at the *Greater Las Vegas Chamber of Commerce,* 2301 E. Sahara Ave.

SEASONAL EVENTS. Desert Inn National Pro-Am Golf Tournament, mid-March; Alan King Caesar's Palace Tennis Classic, mid-April; Mint 400 Off-Road Race, beginning of May; Helldorado (Western events), mid-May; Jaycee State Fair, mid-September.

 MUSEUMS AND GALLERIES. There are galleries in many of the Strip hotels. Shows are also held year-round at the *Grant Hall Art Gallery,* on the campus of the University of Nevada. There is also the *Desert Research Institute* on the same campus. *The Las Vegas Art Museum* is located at 3333 W. Washington Ave.

 TOURS. *American Sightseeing* and *Gray Line* operate bus tours of Las Vegas and its nightclubs, Hoover Dam, the Grand Canyon and Death Valley. *Las Vegas Airlines* and *Scenic Airlines* fly tours to and through the Grand Canyon.

NIGHTCLUBS. Las Vegas has the reputation of being the entertainment capital of the world. There are million-dollar extravaganzas, Broadway productions, and shows starring Hollywood headliners, all playing simultaneously on the three-and-one-half-mile stretch of boulevard known as the Las Vegas "Strip." The usual pattern among the showroom restaurants is to present a dinner show at about 8 P.M., then a late show around midnight; however, some hotels have a cocktail show in place of the dinner show. Reservations are recommended for all shows. The average cost of a "headliner" show is $35 a person, which often includes dinner. To keep the fun going, all the hotels also have shows in the lounges (actually part of the casinos) that also provide a continuous stream of name entertainment from dusk until dawn.

CASINOS. Nevada is all one big gambling casino; slot machines are at airplane, train, and bus terminals, at restaurants, grocery stores, even gas stations. Las Vegas standouts along the Strip, a carnival-like glittering 3 ½-mile section, are *Caesars Palace, Circus Circus,* the *Desert Inn,* the *Dunes, Hacienda,* the *Flamingo Hilton,* the *Riviera,* the *Sahara,* the *Sands,* the *Stardust,* the *Frontier,* the *Holiday Inn,* the *Landmark,* the *Las Vegas Hilton,* the *Imperial Palace,* the *El Rancho,* the *Maxim,* the *Marina,* the *MGM Grand Hotel,* and the *Tropicana.*

Games of chance include 21, craps, roulette, blackjack, poker, baccarat, and keno. Pretty cocktail waitresses hover about the tables, offering free drinks to the more serious-looking players. You don't have to order liquor; you can just have a soft drink if you would prefer. (There is something about the casinos that makes you terribly thirsty; you will be glad of this special service.) Most of the above-named casinos also maintain (very close to the playing rooms) bountiful buffet tables, where you can have breakfast, lunch, or dinner at a very modest price.

Outstanding casinos in downtown Las Vegas (Fremont St.) are the *Mint,* the *Union Plaza,* the *Fremont,* the *Sundance,* the *Las Vegas Club,* the *Golden Nugget* and *Binion's.* "Glitter Gulch," as this section is called, is only three blocks long, but the light is so bright from a dozen hotels that you can read a newspaper at 3 A.M.! This section of Las Vegas has been more photographed than the Strip and is the site of much VEGA$ action. The big-name stars do not work here, but many tourists feel the casino odds are better than those on the more luxurious Strip.

SUMMER SPORTS. Golf is readily available. The best courses are the Sahara Country Club, the Dunes Country Club, the Tropicana Country Club and the Desert Inn Country Club. Public courses are Winterwood, Craig Ranch, Las Vegas City and Paradise Valley.

WINTER SPORTS. Skiing is found at Lee Canyon (Mt. Charleston), Las Vegas.

SPECTATOR SPORTS. Rodeos highlight *Helldorado,* the big annual Western pageant in Las Vegas in May.

WHAT TO DO WITH THE CHILDREN. From Las Vegas there are several nearby outings. *Old Nevada,* a replica of an old Western town, complete with shootouts in the streets, is only a 40-minute drive west of Las Vegas on Charleston Boulevard. In Las Vegas, children seem to enjoy the live circus acts at the Circus Circus Hotel, and the electronic games rooms found in most of the major hotels, particularly the MGM Grand and the Hilton, which has a children's hotel of its own. Another big and inexpensive hit is the Omnimax Theatre at Caesars Palace, which shows films on a huge wraparound screen.

Hoover Dam is an exciting sightseeing venture that no child can resist; tours are offered daily. (The huge dam was constructed in 1931–35 and backs up the Colorado River for 115 miles, as Lake Mead.)

 HOTELS. The famous Las Vegas "Strip" is the world's most concentrated area of luxury hotels. The hotels are designed to keep the guests inside and entertained 24 hours a day and so have a half-dozen restaurants each, many shops, varied entertainment—and no clocks. Rates are *Moderate,* $40 and up, and *Inexpensive,* under $40.

ON THE "STRIP." *Moderate:* The **Stardust** and **Hacienda** hotels.

OTHER HOTELS AND MOTELS. *Moderate:* **Golden Inn.** In downtown area. Medium-sized with family rates.

Gold Key. Family rates. Pets allowed.

Imperial "400." Large chain member.

Las Vegas Strip Travelodge. Large, chain-operated.

Royal Las Vegas. Near the Strip. Moderate.

Rodeway Inn. Good choice of accommodations with family rates.

Showboat Hotel. 500 rooms and 110 lanes of bowling.

Inexpensive: **Downtown Travelodge.** Medium-sized chain member with family rates.

Mini-Price Inn. Two locations in the city. Some rooms have double-double beds.

Western 6 Motel. Near Interstate 15 and Tropicana. Some family units.

 DINING OUT. The offerings range from exotic and foreign gourmet cuisine to buffet budgeter's bonanzas. The latter refers to the practice of most Las Vegas hotels of offering buffets, where you can eat all you want for a reasonable price. The restaurants vary in price and menus—you'll find moderately priced cafes, coffee shops, health food store counters, and pancake houses all around town. Food is served at all hours of the day and night.

An average dinner costs between $15 and $25 at the hotel showrooms, and a marvelous show is included. Some hotels serve no dinner at the shows, but do have cocktail service. (Casual tourists should be prepared to stand in line for about an hour to be seated.)

The principal showrooms are at the *Caesars Palace,* the *Desert Inn,* the *Dunes,* the *Riviera, Sahara, Sands, Stardust, Frontier, Aladdin, MGM Grand, Hilton, Flamingo Hilton* and the *Tropicana.* In "Casino Center" downtown, the *Union Plaza* also features dinner-theater with Broadway plays.

Restaurants are listed by price ranges of a complete meal, without drinks: *Moderate* $10–15. *Inexpensive* under $10.

Moderate: **Alpine Village.** Authentic Swiss and German food in a mountain inn atmosphere. Across from the Hilton.

Battista's Italian. More fun than a barrel of opera singers. Wonderful Italian food. Across from the MGM Grand.

The Tillerman. On Flamingo St. Excellent seafood, good service.

Inexpensive: **Cattleman's Steak House.** Reasonable "Early Bird" specials from 4 to 7 P.M.

Old Heidelberg. Authentic Bavarian food in a warm and friendly atmosphere. Near the Sahara.

Ricardo's. At Tropicana and Eastern. Best Mexican food in town.

The Vineyard. In the Boulevard Mall. Simple but hearty Italian fare at reasonable prices.

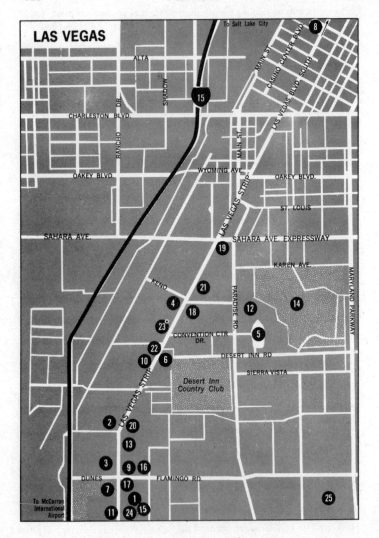

Points of Interest

1) Aladdin
2) Castaway's Hotel
3) Caesar's Palace
4) Circus Circus Hotel Spa
5) Convention Center
6) Desert Inn Hotel
7) Dunes Hotel
8) Downtown hotels
9) Flamingo Hilton
10) Frontier Hotel
11) Hacienda
12) Hilton Hotel
13) Holiday Inn
14) Las Vegas Country Club
15) Marina Hotel
16) Maxim Hotel
17) MGM Grand Hotel
18) Riviera Hotel
19) Sahara Hotel
20) Sands Hotel
21) El Rancho Hotel
22) Silver Slipper
23) Stardust Hotel
24) Tropicana Hotel
25) University of Nevada

EXPLORING RENO–LAKE TAHOE AND NORTHERN NEVADA

At Virginia City you are in one of the West's most fascinating towns. Boardwalks, sagging facades, Victorian mansions (several open to the public), and honky-tonk saloons vividly transmit the spirit of the Comstock days. Take a walking tour and really poke—you can spend two hours pleasantly, or an entire day, in this very lively ghost town.

In Carson City, visit the State Museum. See the impressive Indian and period exhibits and go through the realistic underground mine. Then take the tour of old houses and mansions of Nevada's capital, and have a quick look at the quaint old Victorian Capitol.

PRACTICAL INFORMATION FOR RENO–LAKE TAHOE AND NORTHERN NEVADA

HOW TO GET THERE. *By air:* Reno is now served by nine major airlines. *By car:* The Reno-Lake Tahoe region via U.S. Hwy. 50 and I–80 from San Francisco and Sacramento; U.S. Hwy. 395 from Los Angeles; I–80 from Salt Lake City and points east. *By train: Amtrak* has service to Reno from San Francisco and Chicago.

TOURIST INFORMATION SERVICES. *Reno: Reno Visitors Service,* 704 S. Virginia St. *Sparks: Sparks Chamber of Commerce,* 1880 Prater Way. *Virginia City: Virginia City Visitors Bureau,* South Virginia City *Carson City: Carson City Chamber of Commerce,* 1191 S. Carson St.

MUSEUMS AND GALLERIES. *Nevada State Historical Society,* 1650 N. Virginia St., Reno. Early settlement days of Nevada, Indian artifacts, Victorian costume, mining artifacts. *Sierra Nevada Museum of Art,* 549 Court St., Reno. Local and regional artists and traveling exhibitions of national importance. *Fleischmann Atmospherium-Planetarium,* N. Virginia St., Reno. Star shows, 180-degree motion picture projection. Stunning presentations. *Nevada State Museum,* 600 N. Carson St., Carson City. Formerly a branch of the U.S. Mint. Mineral exhibits and a replica of a full-scale mine.

HISTORIC SITES. Historical markers, some three dozen in all, were erected throughout the state during the Centennial year of 1964. For a listing of locations, write the *State Park Commission,* Carson City, Nevada 89701. *The Nevada Department of Highways* also makes them easy to locate. Its official highway map, published annually, circles the major places of interest; by a dotted trail, the map also pinpoints the early pioneer trails and ghost towns.

Outstanding are *Virginia City,* the most tourist-conscious and once the richest city in America; *Manhattan* and *Belmont,* on State 69, are semi-ghost towns, relics of past glories and riches; *Austin,* on State 50, is an interesting ghost town of deteriorating old buildings (Stokes, Castle, Courthouse, churches, stores, and hotel); *Eureka,* State 50, is another relic of mining days, while *Tuscarora,* on State 11, also exhibits remains of an early mining camp.

TOURS. *Reno Tahoe Tours,* 2503 E. Second St., Reno, 322–6343. Personally guided tours in an air-conditioned limousine. Special-interest tours. *Gray Line Scenic Tours,* 1675 Mill St., Reno. Tours of Reno, Lake Tahoe and Virginia City. M.S. *Dixie Cruiseship,* Zephyr Cove. Tour of Lake Tahoe.

DRINKING LAWS. There are no restrictions on hours for legal drinking, nor on where drinks and bottles can be ordered and consumed. Age minimum is 21.

SUMMER SPORTS. *Fishing* is best from November through April at Pyramid Lake (cutthroat and rainbow trout), Lake Tahoe (giant mackinaw, rainbow, and cutthroat), Walker Lake (cutthroat and Sacramento perch), lakes Mead and Mohave (bass, bluegill, catfish, black crappie, stripers, coho, and rainbow trout). Licenses are $10 for the special three-day visitor's permit or $20 annually. For Mead and Mohave there are also $3 special-use stamps.

Swimming, boating and water sports are year-round activities in southern parts of the state, but are enjoyed in the summer only at Lake Tahoe and other northern regions. Water-skiing is especially good on Lake Tahoe, and on lakes Walker, Pyramid, Topaz, Mead, and Mohave.

Golf: The best courses are: Brookside Municipal, 700 S. Rock Blvd., Reno; Washoe County, Hwy. 394 north; Lakeridge, 1200 Razorback Rd., Reno; Sierra Sage, Stead Turnoff, 8 mi. N. of Reno; Northstar at Tahoe, Hwy. 267 and Northstar Dr., Truckee; Wildcreek, 3500 Sullivan La., Sparks; Incline Village.

Hiking is enjoyed throughout the state, particularly in the National Forest areas. Here are good, established trails, awaiting the outdoorsman.

Horseback riding can be found at Stateline Stables, South Shore, Lake Tahoe, and Corky Prunty's Stable, 10199 Mogul Rd., Reno.

Hunting is richly varied. Deer hunting lasts from early October through mid-November; non-resident licenses cost $50 plus $50 for a deer stamp; state duck stamp is $2; pheasant stamp $2. Bow-and-arrow hunts can be held before the regular rifle season, usually the first three weeks of September; license is $10 with a $50 tag fee. Hunting seasons for ducks and upland game are mid-October until early January; mid-September to late January is the season too for small game, except mid-November for pheasant.

WINTER SPORTS. Skiing is excellent. In the Reno-Lake Tahoe area, more than a dozen large, well-equipped ski resorts lie within an hour's drive from Reno. Among the big ones are Alpine Meadows, Heavenly Valley, Mt. Rose, Northstar, Ski Incline, Squaw Valley and Tahoe Donner.

SPECTATOR SPORTS. Rodeos are the favorite. The Reno Rodeo, the state's richest, occurs in June. The Nevada Rodeo, the biggest and most traditional, takes place in Winnemucca in September.

HOTELS AND MOTELS. Prices quoted are double-occupancy in-season rates: winter rates are slightly lower. *Moderate* $25–35; *Inexpensive* under $25. Hotels are listed by price category.

BOULDER CITY *Moderate:* **Nevada Inn.** Heated pool, sauna, therapy pool.

CARSON CITY. *Moderate:* **Carson City Travelodge.** Medium-sized chain member with fireplaces in some special units. Family rates.

RENO. *Moderate:* **Cavalier Motel.** Close to clubs.
Best Western Kings. 152 rooms, family rates.
Colonial Motor Inn. 100 rooms, sauna.
Golddust West Motor Lodge. Some family units; 24-hour restaurant.
Golden Road Motor Inn. Pool, 142 rooms.
Wonder Lodge. 65 rooms, pool.

TONOPAH. *Moderate:* **Mizpah Hotel.** A historic hotel beautifully restored.

VIRGINIA CITY. *Moderate:* **Comstock.** Comfortable, small motel.

 DINING OUT. Dining out in Nevada often means dining and dancing and show-watching, especially in the gambling towns of Reno-Lake Tahoe. Most of the hotel-casinos have buffets, where you can eat all you want for a reasonable price. You should also try to sample the cooking of the Basque shepherds in northern Nevada; Elko and Gardnerville have good, representative Basque restaurants.

Restaurants are listed by price ranges of a complete meal without drinks: *Moderate:* $10–15; *Inexpensive* under $10.

CARSON CITY. *Moderate.* **West Indies.** Polynesian and American cuisine.

ELKO. *Inexpensive:* **Nevada Dinner House.** Family-style dinner specializing in Basque food.
Star Hotel. One of the best Basque restaurants in Nevada.

GARDNERVILLE. This tiny town has two excellent and inexpensive popular Basque restaurants that serve dinner starting at 6 P.M. They are the **J. and T.** and the **Overland.**

RENO. *Moderate.* **Stuart Anderson's Black Angus.** Steak dinners.
Louie's Basque Corner. A unique dining experience, family-style.
Miguel's. Fine Mexican food.
Micasa. Authentic Mexican.
Stan Yee's Chinese. Authentic Cantonese.

SPARKS. *Moderate:* **Siri's.** Authentic homemade Italian food.

OREGON

Portland, the Gorgeous Coast, and Wilderness

Portland is not only Oregon's largest, but also its sole metropolitan city. As such, it is the proper starting point for tours of the state. But first, Portland itself invites exploration.

The best way to see the "City of Roses" is to take the fifty-mile Scenic Drive, whose most convenient starting point is the Visitors Information Center (Chamber of Commerce Building) at S.W. Fifth and Taylor streets.

The Scenic Drive leads motorists to the summits of three hills—Council Crest, Rocky Butte, and Mount Tabor (an extinct volcano)—which afford awesome panoramas of Oregon and Washington. Clearly visible from these vantage points are Mount Rainier, the Fujiyamalike Mount St. Helens, and Mount Adams, all in Washington; and the great peaks of the Oregon Cascades: Mount Hood, Mount Jefferson, and the Three Sisters.

Other attractions on the route are the famed International Rose Test Gardens, Rhododendron and Azalea Test Gardens, and Peninsula Park's Sunken Gardens; Reed College, which has turned out more Rhodes scholars than either Yale, Harvard, or the University of Chicago and whose reputation for intellectual freedom is worldwide; the fun-in-learning Oregon Museum of Science and Industry (OMSI); the Western Forestry Center; the Portland Zoo, with its famed elephants and streamlined Zooliner, which carries riders on a mile-long journey through Washington Park; Japanese Gardens; Hoyt Arboretum; the opulent Pittock Mansion; and many old homes and some of the city's most beautiful neighborhoods.

The city's biggest event is its Rose Festival, an annual celebration since 1909. The fiesta, generally held the second week of June and as colorful as a Mardi Gras, features the Rose Show; the Golden Rose Ski Tournament (on the slopes of Mount Hood, 62 miles east); and numerous cultural, carnival, and outdoor stage and entertainment activities—all climaxed by the Grand Floral Parade, which draws floats and bands from as far as 1,500 miles away.

PRACTICAL INFORMATION FOR PORTLAND

 HOW TO GET THERE. *By air:* Portland, which has about half the state's population in its metropolitan area, is served by 14 airlines. From the city's modern international airport, DART buses take visitors to the downtown area. *By train: Amtrak* runs passenger trains from several West Coast cities and the East via Boise. *By car:* Route I-5 runs to Portland from Washington and California. *By bus: Trailways* and *Greyhound* have continental service to Portland.

HOW TO GET AROUND. *By car:* Oregon has a fine, toll-free highway system. The main north-south route (Interstate 5) runs stoplight-free through the heart of the state. *By bus:* Portland's municipal bus system, Tri-Met, costs 75¢, in-city, with free transfers.

TOURIST INFORMATION SERVICES. In Portland, the *tourist center* is at Interstate 5 (north, near the Interstate bridge). It is open from May 1 to Oct. 30. The *Portland Visitors Service* is at 824 S.W. Fifth Ave., in Chamber of Commerce Bldg.

SEASONAL EVENTS. The top attraction on Portland's crowded calendar of events is the *Rose Festival* in June. Other highlights include the *Pacific International Livestock Exposition,* an all-breed *dog show* in July, and *Neighborfair* in August.

 MUSEUMS AND GALLERIES. Historical: *Oregon Historical Society,* 1230 S.W. Park Ave. The French Renaissance *Pittock Mansion,* 3229 N.W. Pittock Dr. Art: *Portland Art Musuem,* 1219 S.W. Park Ave. Northwest Indian artifacts. Special Interest: *Oregon Museum of Science and Industry,* 4015 S.W. Canyon Rd.; *Western Forestry Center,* 4033 S.W. Canyon Rd.

TOURS. Several sightseeing tours are available from *Gray Line.*

SPECIAL INTEREST TOURS. *The Sierra Club, Audobon Society* and *Mazamas* offer inexpensive, varying length tours to the rivers, lakes, woods and mountains. Portland Park Bureau has inexpensive hiking tours to the coast, hills and woods.

SUMMER SPORTS. There are 29 golf courses in the Portland area, most open to public play.

WINTER SPORTS. The largest ski crowds gather at Mt. Hood's *Timberline Lodge,* which has the most complete facilities in the area.

SPECTATOR SPORTS. A range of offerings from minor league *baseball* to pro *basketball, horse racing* at Portland Meadows and *greyhound racing* at nearby Gresham, in the summer.

WHAT TO DO WITH THE CHILDREN. The parks system has daily children's programs in the summer, the *zoo* is famous for its elephants, and the *Oregon Museum of Science and Industry* is a daily fun-in-learning wonderland.

HOTELS AND MOTELS. Hostelries listed here are given in price categories based on double occupancy without meals: *Moderate* $25–30; *Inexpensive* under $25.

Moderate: **Ara Bel Motel.** 11324 N.E. Sandy Blvd. Kitchens, water beds, relaxed air.

Cameo Motel. 4111 N.E. 82nd, near airport. Cheerful atmosphere.

Caravan Motor Hotel. 2401 S.W. 4th. Good choice of rooms. Heated pool. Near Health Sciences Center medical complex.

Chumaree Motor Inn/Holgate. 4512 S.E. 82nd Ave. Clean, airy. Rooms for the handicapped.

City Center Motel. 3800 N.E. Sandy Blvd. Family units. In Hollywood shopping district, near Memorial Coliseum. Caring management.

Continental Motel. 800 E. Burnside. Across bridge from city center.

Corsun Arms Motor Hotel. 809 S.W. King. Quiet, roof garden. In historic section of Portland.

Imperial Hotel. 400 S.W. Broadway. Well-kept, convenient. Old West atmosphere, a favorite for stockmen.

Lamplighter Motel. 10207 S.W. Parkway. Suburban motel near shopping center.

Mallory Motor Hotel. 729 S.W. 15th Ave. At edge of downtown. An old hotel revitalized.

Portland Rose Motel. 8920 S.W. Barbur Blvd. Pool, playground. Wheelchair units.

Rose Manor Motel. 4546 S.E. McLoughlin Blvd. Family units, kitchens, family rates.

Econo Lodge. 4810 N.E. Sandy Blvd. Family units, kitchens. A place with a grin on its face.

Inexpensive: **Danmoore Hotel.** 1217 S.W. Morrison. Older, quiet. At edge of downtown.

Motel 6. 3104 S.E. Powell Blvd. Comfortable. Big, but generally quiet.

Poolside Motel. 19224 S.E. McLoughlin Blvd., Gladstone, just outside Portland. Indoor heated pool.

Union Ave. Motel. 59 N.E. Gertz Road at Union Ave. Small, quiet, kitchens.

DINING OUT. Restaurants are listed in order of price category: *Moderate* $6–10; *Inexpensive* under $6. Drinks, tax and tip not included.

Moderate: **Dan & Louis Oyster Bar.** 308 S.W. Ankeny. Seafood in nautical-style dining room. Popular for ages.

Hung Far Low. 112 N.W. 4th. Specializing in Chinese cuisine since 1928.

Old Spaghetti Factory. 126 S.W. 2nd. Zany atmosphere, fun, Italian favorites.

Pier 101. In Galleria, 931 S.E. Morrison. Seafood, hamburgers with flair.

Poor Richard's. 3907 N.E. Broadway. Bargain steak dinners draw throngs.

Rose's. 315 N.W. 23rd. and 12329 NE Glisan. Kosher-style. Nasher's Plate for 2 is big enough for 3 or 4.

Sumida's. 6744 N.E. Sandy Blvd. Authentic Japanese atmosphere.

Tortilla Flats. 9010 S.E. 82nd St. Reputed to have the best Mexican food north of the Oregon border.

Inexpensive: **Dragon's "I."** 28 N.W. 4th Ave. Lovely decor. Heaps of wholesome food.

The Organ Grinder. 5015 S.E. 82nd Ave. Pizza to the accompaniment of the world's largest organ—and a surprise a minute.

Red Robin. 2020 S.W. Morrison. Every kind of burger conceivable.

EXPLORING OREGON

The Oregon Coast

Of all sections of Oregon, the coast is the most famous and the most visited. It has often been termed the most scenic marine border drive in the world, and for good reason; none who sees it is disappointed.

Take hundreds of miles of shore fronting the Pacific, fill with rolling sand dunes, mouths of swift rivers, fresh-water lakes, craggy cliffs, toppled mountainside, battered headlands, hills bursting with greenery, secret coves, deep inlets, picturesque lighthouses, broad beaches, herds of sea lions, grassy state parks, millions of wildflowers, leaping waterfalls—and you have the Oregon coast. To the purple-shadowed range skirting the shores and the virgin stands of giant firs, add the unsurpassed vistas of surf and sea—and you have one of the nation's grandest terrains. Add to all of this a salubrious climate, fabulous fishing, the taste of world-famous cheese in the valley where it is produced, colorful seashore towns, and a wealth of recreational opportunities—and the pleasure is double.

Almost all of the tideland of the coast belongs to the people; only a few miles are privately owned. More than thirty state parks, including the choicest scenic spots, are reserved for public use. In addition, there are many national forest camps.

It is a bit ironic, perhaps, that the most scenic and historical route linking Portland to the coast should be the longest and most time-consuming; nevertheless, US 30, which skirts the Columbia River, is a storybook way to reach Astoria (the northern terminal of the littoral). On the other hand, US 26, the most popular route, is also the most crowded.

Astoria sits at the mouth of the Columbia River—its northern shore is the southern border of Washington. In 1966 a spectacular 4.1-mile-long toll bridge ($1.50 per car and passengers) was completed, crossing to Megler. Astoria calls itself the "Oldest American City West of the Missouri." It possesses, in this respect, many firsts, including the first post office west of the "Big Muddy." Local historians claim that there has been "more history made within twenty miles of Astoria than all the rest of Oregon put together." This claim is disputed by others, but Astoria is so steeped in history that some citizens would like to turn the city into a "Williamsburg of the West."

Seaside, further down the coast, has the finest beach in the state, boasting in addition a two-mile-long concrete promenade. More people swim in the ocean here than anywhere else on the Oregon coast. There are also more tourist facilities—and their variety is legion—than in any town twice its size. The "Miss Oregon" pageant is staged here, which seems appropriate since many people in the state think of Seaside as the Coney Island of the coast because of its main street, hurdy-gurdy atmosphere. For years Seaside was the chief resort community in Oregon, but in the past few years it has lost much of its luster.

Not lacking the least in luster is Salishan Lodge at Gleneden Beach, the innkeeper's Taj Mahal of the Oregon coast. The swankiest resort in the state and the prime convention center of the coast these days, Salishan contains a fine collection of coastal art and spells the finest in taste and the highest in price to most Oregonians.

In the five miles between Salishan and Depoe Bay, there are three excellent state parks: Gleneden, Fogarty Creek, and Boiler Bay. Depoe Bay, long-settled but incorporated only in 1973, is geographically the most exciting town on the coast. It over looks a rockbound bay, usually jammed with fishing boats.

Two miles south of Depoe Bay, US 101 encounters the north junction of the Otter Crest Scenic Loop, which rejoins the highway at Otter Rock after winding along the rugged shore to Otter Crest View Point.

Otter Crest Wayside, 1.6 miles south of the junction, is a must stop for anyone who wants to appreciate the glory of the Oregon coast and imbibe a heady draught of beauty. From the 50-car parking area on the promontory, miles of scalloped, battered, gossamer coastline is visible. The Lookout, 500 feet above the sea on Cape Foulweather, faces Oregon's most photographed seascape. Large observatory telescopes are available. Sometimes, focusing on offshore rocks, one sees more than the riled or rhythmic ocean: namely, sea lions, Oregon penguins, and sea turkeys.

The area between the coast towns of Yachats and Florence is a camper's paradise—no fewer than seven state parks and forest camps. There are also in this stretch several freshwater lakes for boating, swimming, and fishing. Florence, on the Siuslaw River, is the shopping center of a beautiful lake and sand-dunes area. In spring and early summer, rhododendrons run riot over hills and lowlands.

Little more than three miles south of Florence is what is probably Oregon's most-used state park, Jessie M. Honeyman. It has 313 campsites and 66 trailer spaces, electric stoves, showers, laundry, boat ramp, and many other facilities including an outdoor theater. Day-use facilities include picnic tables, toilets, and bathhouses. The 522-acre tract includes a dense forest, swarms of rhododendrons and Cleawox Lake. Trails lead from the park into the cool forest or up to the undulating sand dunes. The dunes area, extending south about 50 miles to the Coos Bay country, is now the Oregon Sand Dunes National Recreational Area, Oregon's only one of this kind.

The dunes, mutable and mysterious, rise to heights of more than 250 feet. Commercial sand buggies—motorized vehicles that range in size from jeep to bus—grind across the dunes with absolute safety. Drivers halt frequently to permit passengers to take pictures.

Mile-long McCullough Bridge, 11 miles down from Lakeside Junction, spans the channel of Coos Bay and leads into North Bend, a virile lumber town. This is myrtlewood country, and by taking drives off the main road to the southeast you will see the myrtle groves. They grow nowhere else in the nation. The hub of the myrtle area is Coquille, 17 miles south of Coos Bay, reached via US 101 and 42.

The prime scenic package in the Coos Bay-North Bend area is the Empire-Cape Arago excursion. Empire, three miles from either Coos Bay or North Bend, boasts a sportfishing fleet, crabbing, and clamming. Charleston, five miles below Empire, is a busy fishing village. Within six miles south of Charleston are clustered three of Oregon's grandest state parks: Sunset Bay, Shore Acres, and Cape Arago.

On the last 15 miles to Brookings, six miles above the California state line, is some of the grandest scenery along the entire coast—including Whaleshead Beach, where at incoming tide the rock formation resembles a whale spouting. Spectacular indeed is the seaward view from 350-foot-high Thomas Creek Bridge, higher than San Francisco's Golden Gate Bridge.

Heading inward from Oregon's famed coast, visitors may venture toward the Rogue River Valley. En route is Cave Junction, 14 miles above the California line. This is the gateway to Oregon Caves National Monument, "The Marble Halls of Oregon." The monument consists of a group of weirdly beautiful caverns at an elevation of 4,000 feet in the heart of the Siskiyou Mountains.

Grants Pass, 30 miles east of Cave Junction, sits on the banks of the Rogue and is the takeoff point for runs down the frothing, wicked waters; runs range from a few hours to five days.

About 33 miles from the town of Rogue River, en route to Medford, is Jacksonville, Oregon's most picturesque historical settlement, founded on the heels of a gold rush in the early 1850s. Brought back to its previous state, the town is a 19th-century Western portrait.

Crater Lake National Park

Crater Lake, a two-square-mile circle of an unforgettable blue that is nearly 2,000 feet deep, is fed only by melting snows, and has no outlet. Sometimes visitors have to wait for an hour or two until a cloud settling close down over the surface of the water decides to move away and let them have a look. Every morning a ranger leads a "caravan" of visitors in their cars around the lake, stopping frequently. Launches also make tours of the lake and stop at the strangely formed volcanic islands.

The lake was created thousands of years ago when Mt. Mazama, a 15,000-foot volcano, erupted and formed a crater now filled by the lake. First seen by white men in 1853. Drives through the 250-square-mile park, especially the 35-mile route around the rim, bring a succession of spectacular views: Wizard Island, a symmetrical cone rising 760 feet above the surface of the lake; Phantom Ship, a mass of lava resembling a ship under sail; Llao Rock, a lava flow on the north rim that fills an ancient glacial valley. The view from Cloudcap, on the east rim, is considered the best of many excellent views. There are many fine mountain viewpoints, but even the athletic are liable to be short of breath after climbing to the cap of 8,060-foot Garfield Peak or to the 8,926-foot lookout station atop Mt. Scott.

The northern entrance drive, off Oregon 138, opens about June 14, and Rim Drive about July 4. Vehicle permits—good for all passengers —are $2 per day. Overnight accommodations, meals, garage and gasoline services are available from about June 15 to September 15. In addition to the 75-room lodge there are sleeping cottages. (Sites in the campground, if available, are included in the daily vehicle fee.) There are daily lectures by park naturalists, guided drives and hikes, and geological exhibits. During the off-season the coffee shop serves skiers. Reached by Oregon 62 from Medford, Oregon 138 from Roseburg, or off US 97 onto Oregon 138 or Oregon 232.

Oregon's second largest city, Eugene, is the seat of the University of Oregon. The Oriental Art Museum on campus is visited by scholars from around the world.

Salem, the state capital, lies 24 miles north of Albany. Murals depict the state's history and from the capitol dome—above the murals—there is a marvelous overlook of the Willamette Valley and the Cascade foothills. On the grounds of the old Thomas Kay woolen mill, at Twelfth and Ferry Streets, stand what could be the two oldest buildings in Oregon: the Jason Lee House and Parsonage, both reputedly built in 1841.

Less than 40 miles from Salem is the state's most historic town, Oregon City. The municipality was first called Willamette Falls, the settlement having been located where the river drops 42 feet from a basaltic ledge. Oregon City was the first community incorporated west of the Missouri River and was Oregon's first provisional and territorial capital.

East from Portland, the first point of significant interest is Multnomah Falls, 24 miles from the city's heart. Second highest in the United States (620-foot drop in two steps), the falls are set in a sylvan glen against the cliffs of the Columbia River Gorge.

Eastern Oregon's largest city is Pendleton, home of the internationally renowned Pendleton Rodeo. The four-day affair, held each September, transforms the city into a Western camp. There are more events than most rodeos, with all the leading cowboys from the United States and Canada competing here.

Many regard Hells Canyon as eastern Oregon's most spectacular attraction. Here black walls erupt from the river to a height of 2,000 feet, reach a bench, then soar 2,000 feet to a second bench. Hells Canyon Park, on the reservoir en route to the canyon dam, has trailer-camper hookups with water and electricity. Jet boats, shooting the boiling rapids, penetrate the canyon for seven miles below the dam.

Another of the most impressive explorations in the state is Century Drive, also known as the Cascades Lake Highway. Taking off at the town of Bend, this 97-mile loop passes through high and rugged mountains, lava flow, lakes, reservoirs, and waterfalls.

Just 100 miles from Portland is Warm Springs, administrative center of Warm Springs Reservation. Turn north and drive 10 miles to Kahnee-ta, a resort operated by the Indians. In an Indian encampment, tepees are for rent. There are also a swimming pool complex, hiking trails, riding horses, a golf course, a fine restaurant, convention facilities, picnic grounds, and sites for trailers.

PRACTICAL INFORMATION FOR OREGON

THE OREGON COAST

HOW TO GET THERE. *By car:* From California you can take Interstate 5 to the state line below Ashland or the scenic US 101 to Astoria. *By bus:* Two transcontinental bus lines (*Greyhound* and *Trailways*) have service to Portland with intra-state buses running from the capital.

TOURIST INFORMATION SERVICES. Headquarters for travel and tourist information is the Travel Information division, located on the first floor of the Oregon State Transportation Building in the capitol complex of Salem. The Oregon coast is supplied by the Oregon Coast Association, P.O. Box 670, Newport, Oreg. 97365.

NATIONAL PARKS AND FORESTS. The Siuslaw National Forest, divided into two major areas along the coast, contains the Oregon Dunes National Recreation Area, which was established in 1972 with 32,237 acres. The undulating dunes cover everything in their path, even forest, but conservationists are attempting stabilization with beachgrass and broom.

STATE PARKS AND FORESTS. Fort Stevens, 10 miles west of Astoria, was the only mainland U.S.A. military installation to suffer an armed attack (by the Japanese) during World War II. The 3,670-acre Fort Stevens state park is a coast lake area with beach access near historic Fort Stevens. Farther south is Cape Lookout, an unusually scenic area of Sitka spruce with a fine ocean beach and a headland projecting 1.5 miles into the ocean. The ever-heaving sand dunes provide the recreational backdrop at Jessie M. Honeyman, 2.5 miles south of Florence.

MUSEUMS AND GALLERIES. Astoria: Flavel Mansion, Museum of Clatsop Historical Society in home of 19th-century sea captain. Tillamook: Tillamook Country Pioneer Museum. Natural history and pioneer artifacts. Coquille: Coquille Valley Art Assn.

HISTORIC SITES. Astoria, in the northwest corner of Oregon, is an excellent starting point for the visitor seeking state historic spots. At Port Orford, toward the California line on US 101, is Battle Rock, where Indians battled a party of white men trying to establish a settlement in 1851.

TOURS. The *Gray Line* has an 8-hour Oregon Coast tour, departing Portland daily in summer, weekly in winter.

SUMMER SPORTS. Beachcombing for shells, rocks, and Japanese glass floats and driftwood collecting seem almost an occupation along the entire coast. Area between Yachats and Florence fine for aquatics. The spring and fall runs of chinook are best on the Columbia.

WHAT TO DO WITH THE CHILDREN. At Astoria, kids (and adults) can climb without cost the 166 steps leading to the top of the Astoria Column; board the old lightship *Columbia,* the key feature of the Columbia River Maritime Museum; go through Ft. Clatsop National Memorial; and tour a salmon-packing plant (for free). Newport is full of things for children—the Old Yaquina Bay Lighthouse, Undersea Gardens, and more.

HOTELS AND MOTELS. Price categories are based on double occupancy without meals. *Moderate* $25–35; *Inexpensive* under $25.

ASTORIA. *Moderate:* **Crest Motel.** Located on a hilltop, small, well-maintained with splendid view of Columbia River.
City Center Motel. Small, trimly-kept, on US 30.

BANDON. *Moderate:* **Sunset Motel.** Two levels, some units with ocean view, some with kitchens.
Windermere Motel. Small, oceanfront motel.
Inexpensive: **Table Rock Motel.** Well-kept, smaller motel overlooking ocean.

CANNON BEACH. *Moderate:* **Major Motel.** Smaller motel on beach, with well-kept units.

COOS BAY. *Moderate:* **Holiday Motel.** Center of town, 1 block from covered shopping mall.
Bay Park Motel. Kitchenettes, well-maintained.
Inexpensive: **Timberlodge Motel.** Medium size. Free morning coffee. Near 24-hour restaurant.

DEPOE BAY. *Moderate:* **Bonnie View Motel.** Kitchens. Quiet, near beach, easy walking distance to restaurants.

FLORENCE. *Moderate:* **Park Motel.** Comfortable smaller motel, a few kitchens. Restaurant near.

GOLD BEACH. *Moderate:* **Nimrod Motel.** Small, comfortable; some larger suites.

LINCOLN CITY. *Moderate:* **Coho Inn.** Overlooking ocean.
City Center Motel. Short walk to beach.

NEWPORT. *Moderate:* **7 Seas Motel.** Medium-size, restaurant adjacent.

NORTH BEND. *Moderate:* **Pony Village Lodge.** Large, comfortably equipped, located at distinctive Pony Village Shopping Center.

SEASIDE. *Moderate:* **White Caps Motel.** On the beach. Sparkling neat.

TILLAMOOK. *Moderate:* **El Rey Sands Motel.** Smaller; comfortable units, restaurant near.

YOUTH HOSTELS. Lodgings for young people traveling on limited budgets have increased in recent years. Call ahead for information. At *Cannon Beach,* there is a youth hostel operated by the *Conference Center.* And at *Coos Bay,* the Presbyterian Church at 1st and Elrod operates *The Sea Gull Youth Hostel* summers only.

DINING OUT. Price categories and ranges for a complete dinner are: *Moderate:* $6–10; and *Inexpensive:* $6 and under. Drinks, tax and tip not included.

ASTORIA. *Inexpensive.* **Ship's Inn.** On Fishermen's Wharf. English cooking, featuring luscious fish 'n chips, by Australian owners.

LINCOLN CITY. *Moderate:* **Pixie Kitchen.** Fresh seafoods a specialty, along with steaks. Disneyland atmosphere.

NEWPORT. *Moderate:* **Mo's.** Famous for clam chowder, and fine seafood.

SEASIDE. *Moderate:* **Crab Broiler.** Excellent seafood restaurant.

THE REST OF OREGON

HOW TO GET THERE. *By air:* Portland is served by 13 airlines *(Aircal, Alaska, American, Continental, Delta, Eastern, Frontier, Northwest Orient, Pacific Express, Republic, United, Western* and *Wien Air Alaska). By train: Amtrak* runs passenger trains from Seattle, San Francisco, Oakland, Los Angeles, San Diego and from the East on the Union Pacific line. *By car:* From the east, Interstate 84N enters the state from Idaho at Ontario. From California, you can take Interstate 5 to the state line below Ashland or U.S. 101 along the scenic coast to Astoria. *By bus: Greyhound* and *Trailways* have service into the state.

TOURIST INFORMATION SERVICES. Headquarters for travel and tourist information is the *Travel Information Division,* on the first floor of the Oregon State Transportation Bldg., in the Salem capitol complex. There are six port-of-entry *information centers* to aid travelers. *Tourist information services* are also offered at more than 45 Certified Centers located in local chamber of commerce offices throughout the state. Travelers can look for the blue directional signs adjacent to the major highways for reference to the centers.

MUSEUMS AND GALLERIES. Several Oregon towns, some only a few ghostly buildings, are maintained as museums. They are scattered about the state.

Historical. Astoria: *Flavel Mansion.* Museum of Clatsop County Historical Society in the home of a 19th-century sea captain.

Canyon City: *Herman and Eliza Oliver Museum.* Well-displayed relics of the gold rush days.

Champoeg: *Robert E. Newell House,* D.A.R. Museum.

Haines: *Eastern Oregon Museum.* Wide assortment of 19th-century articles.

Jacksonville: *Jacksonville Museum.* Historical displays of famous gold country and studio of great photographer, Peter Britt.

Klamath Falls: *Favell Museum of Western Art and Artifacts;* gorgeously displayed life of the Old West.

Salem: Archives of the *Oregon State Library* on the capitol mall—a wealth of precious documents and other historical materials.

Tillamook: *Tillamook County Pioneer Museum.*

Art. Eugene: *Museum of Art,* University of Oregon, Oriental collection; *Maude I. Kerns Art Center,* full schedule of arts and crafts exhibits.

Salem: *Salem Arts Ass'n,* art gallery and collection of costumes.

TOURS. Despite its many attractions and brisk tourist trade, Oregon has surprisingly few commercial travel tours. The visitor who drives to the state is best off with a do-it-yourself tour service—selecting specific areas or attractions, then plotting a course.

Launches circle Crater Lake or go to Wizard Island and Phantom Ship. A bus also makes daily trips around the lake. A thrilling way to view the Wallowa Mountains is to take the *High Wallowas Gondola Lift,* which rises 3,700 vertical ft. in 15 minutes to 8,020-foot Mt. Howard.

DRINKING LAWS. Nearly all bars in Oregon serve to the legal limit of 2:30 A.M. The minimum age for consumption of alcohol is 21. Motor Vehicles Dept. issues ID cards for anyone who doesn't have a driver's license.

SUMMER SPORTS. *Swimming:* Most popular spa swimming is at Kah-nee-ta, on the Warm Springs Reservation. Most popular coastal swimming is at Seaside, and the most popular river swimming is at Rooster Rock State Park on the Columbia. *Boating:* All kinds on lakes and scenic rivers. Water-skiing also popular. *Fishing* draws more than half a million fishermen a year to 15,000 miles of angling streams and hundreds of lakes.

Golf: Oregon boasts over 130 courses, active all year in mild western areas.

Hiking and packing: Natural sites in the numerous national forests and primitive areas. Indian-style hiking at Kah-nee-ta and at Rooster Rock State Park is available.

Horseback riding: Fine resources in all areas. Organized packhorse trips appealing to many through the mountainous country of central and eastern Oregon.

Hunting: The best game hunting is in the mountain country of central and eastern Oregon, and birds are also more plentiful east of the Cascades.

WINTER SPORTS. Widely acclaimed for its fine powder snow and as training site for the 1972 Olympic team is Mt. Bachelor, 22 mi. west of Bend. Outstanding skiing and a breathtaking panoramic view can be found at Hoodoo Bowl Ski Area, 88 mi. southeast of Salem. Other areas: Mt. Hood, with the greatest concentration of ski areas in the state; Spout Springs in the Blue Mountains; Anthony Lakes Ski Area in the Alkhorn Range; and Mt. Ashland Ski area, south of Ashland.

SPECTATOR SPORTS. *Football:* Oregon plays its home games at Eugene and Oregon State at Corvallis.

WHAT TO DO WITH THE CHILDREN. Everything. The unlimited possibilites include: building sand castles, collecting driftwood and looking for Japanese glass floats, agates, and shells on the beaches of the coast; rockhounding throughout the state; swimming in lakes and rivers; hiking forest trails; looking at waterfalls and wildflowers and caves and canyons and Indian pictographs; splashing in Portland's *Forecourt Fountain;* angling for a trout at *Small Fry Lake* (14 is the upper age limit) seven mi. southeast of Estacada; goggling at the *Lakeview geyser;* tracing the steam to the hot mineral outlets at *Austin Hotel Springs,* on the Upper Clackamas River; watching the *fishing boats* come in at Astoria, Depoe Bay, Warrenton, Newport, and other ports; playing on an extinct volcano and walking through huge lava fields; rodeos, dune-buggy rides, and much more.

HOTELS AND MOTELS. Oregon has many fine local hotels and motels that complement those operated by, or under franchise with, the larger regional and national chains. While price and luxury generally go hand-in-hand, the traveler will frequently find excellent accommodations and facilities in the moderate and inexpensive price ranges. Seasonal price variations are more likely to be found along the coast and in a few other prime tourist areas than in the larger cities, where prices tend to be more constant the year round. Hostelries listed here are given in order of price category, highest first, within each city or town group. Cities are listed in alphabetical order.

Price categories are based on double occupancy without meals. *Moderate* $25–35; *Inexpensive* $25 and under. For a more complete examination of hotel and motel categories see *Facts At Your Fingertips* at the front of this volume.

ALBANY. *Moderate:* **Al-Ray Motel.** Attractive, heated pool.
Swept-Wing Motel. Near Albany Airport.

ASHLAND. *Moderate:* **Knight's Inn Motel.** Medium-size, seasonal rates.
Inexpensive: **Columbia Hotel.** Charming European style. Intimate.

BAKER. *Moderate:* **Green Gables Motel.** Full-sized kitchens.
Inexpensive: **Western Motel.** Small; playground area for youngsters.

BEND. *Moderate:* **Maverick Motel.** Pool, restaurant, quiet, neighborly ambiance.
Westward Ho Motel. Some kitchens; play area.
Inexpensive: **Edelweiss Motor Inn.** Some kitchen facilities. Great view of mountains.
Rainbow Motel. Some kitchens, playground area, coffee bar.

BURNS. *Moderate:* **Silver Spur Motel.** Smaller motel, comfortable. Western folksiness.

CORVALLIS. *Moderate:* **Country Kitchen Motel.** North of business center, near Oregon State Univ. Pool, restaurant.

CRATER LAKE. *Moderate:* **Crater Lake Lodge.** Lodge-type, comfortable, activites.

EUGENE. *Moderate:* **Downtown Motel.** Near prize-winning mall.
Eugene Hotel. In center of picturesque desert hamlet.
TraveLodge. Medium size, close to downtown. Pool, restaurant.
The Timbers Motel. Convenient central location.
Willow Tree Motel. Large, heated pool; snazzy.
Inexpensive: **Budget Host Motor Inn.** Sparkling clean, companionable.
City Center Lodge. Medium-size, close to downtown mall.
66 Motel. Medium-size, comfortable units.

GRANTS PASS. *Moderate:* **Redwood Motel.** Small, comfortable, some kitchens, playground.
Regal Lodge. Well-maintained; long beds.

JOHN DAY. *Moderate:* **Little Mac's Motel.** Small, family-oriented.

JORDAN VALLEY. *Moderate:* **Sahara Motel.** In center of picturesque desert hamlet.

JOSEPH. *Moderate:* **Indian Lodge Motel.** Small, well-maintained.

KLAMATH FALLS. *Moderate:* **Molatore's Motel.** Well-furnished, well-kept.

LA GRANDE. *Moderate:* **Royal Motor Inn.** Medium-size, comfortable units, restaurants nearby.

LAKEVIEW. *Moderate:* **Lakeview Lodge Motel.** Quiet location off highway. Neat throughout.

MEDFORD. *Moderate:* **Cedar Lodge Motel.** Medium-size; heated pool. **Capri Motel.** Some kitchen facilities. Good beds.

ONTARIO. *Moderate:* **Holiday Motor Inn.** Free in-room movies, heated pool.
Inexpensive: **Stampeder Motel.** In north-center of town.

OREGON CAVES. *Moderate:* **Oregon Caves Château.** Beautiful mountain locale at Oregon Caves National Monument.

PENDLETON. *Moderate:* **Chaparral Motel.** Kitchenettes, color TV, latch-string hospitality.

ROSEBURG. *Moderate:* **Rose-etta Motel.** Cozy, family atmosphere.
Inexpensive: **Shady Oaks Motel.** Small; spacious units.

SALEM. *Moderate:* **City Center Motel.** Medium-size, cozy.
Inexpensive. **Western \$aver Motel.** Pool, air-conditioning.

THE DALLES. *Moderate:* **Mill Creek Motel & Trailer Park.** On Mill Creek. Kitchens, automatic heat, near restaurants.
Inexpensive: **Shamrock Motel.** Small, close to city center, neat.

DINING OUT in Oregon means an opportunity to savor fresh salmon and other seafood, as well as river-fresh fish from the state's many streams. The all-time favorites—steak, fried chicken, and prime ribs—are also easily found. But there are also many foreign favorites that can be found here, and the exotic treats of Oriental, European, Middle East, and Polynesian cooks have made dining out in Oregon a cosmopolitan experience. Restaurants are listed in order of price category.

Price categories and ranges for a complete dinner are: *Moderate* \$5–10; and *Inexpensive* under \$5. *À la carte* meals would cost a little more. Drinks, tax and tip not included.

BEND. *Moderate:* **Tumalo Emporium.** Old-time atmosphere at museum-like restaurant.

BURNS. *Moderate:* **Pine Room Café.** Delightful surroundings.

COTTAGE GROVE. *Moderate:* **The Cottage.** Nourishing food in innovative solar building. Clean; courteous service.

LAKEVIEW. *Moderate:* **The Indian Village.** Beautiful decor.

ONTARIO. *Moderate:* **East Side Café.** Oriental-American food.

PENDLETON. *Moderate:* **Judy K's Steak Chalet.** Fill-up meals.

ROSEBURG. *Moderate:* **Duffy's.** Seafood, steaks.

WASHINGTON

Seattle, Sound, Sea and Mountains

From the Space Needle's observation tower, newcomers can quickly orient themselves to Seattle and its entire setting. Clockwise from Queen Anne Hill (north) are the marinas and houseboats of Lake Union with the University District behind them, Capitol Hill, Beacon Hill, the central business district, Elliott Bay and its shipping activity, and to the west, Puget Sound, its islands, and the Olympic Mountains as the backdrop. To the east are glimpses of the city's eastern boundary, 24-mile-long Lake Washington, and, in the distance, the Cascade Range. On a clear day you can see 10,778-foot Mt. Baker, 14,410-foot Mt. Rainier, 12,307-foot Mt. Adams and, 165 miles away, 9,677-foot Mt. St. Helens.

Mt. St. Helens, the active volcano, is the state's newest attraction. The volcano exploded in March 1980, after a 123-year rest, and nobody knows how long it will remain active, or *how* active it may become.

Pioneer Square, at First and Yesler, gives its name to the district around the totem pole and south to Kingdome, the huge covered stadium. Here the city began in 1852 when Henry Yesler built the first steam sawmill on Puget Sound and skidded logs to it. As business moved on uptown, the old hotels, taverns, and cafes became the haven of transient workers and people down on their luck. The area was called "Skid Road," and the name spread to other cities (where, lacking the same logging background, it often changed to "Skid Row"). Now

636

protected by preservation ordinances, the pioneer Historic District is full of small shops, galleries, and restaurants.

Up Yesler Way from Pioneer Square, in an area bounded roughly by 4th and 8th Avenues and Main and Lane Streets, is the International District. Here, along with many Chinese and Japanese restaurants and shops, are the "Benevolent Society" buildings with their ornately carved balconies. Daily tours begin at 622 S. Washington. At the August festival of Bon Odori, with its costumed street dances, the International District is transformed into a huge bazaar.

The downtown waterfront, stretching some 20 blocks, is perhaps the greatest tourist attraction of all. Shipping moved down the harbor to more modern facilities, and the old piers are devoted to shops, restaurants, bars, sightseeing boats, a new aquarium, and harbor viewpoints in two waterfront parks (the second one being a path north of Pier 70). Pike Place Market, at Pike and 1st, is a covered warren of shops and stalls deep with vegetables, fruit, and fish fresh from salt and fresh waters. The market, started in 1907, has undergone renovation—by voters' decree—to save it from extinction. It has many small restaurants, some overlooking the harbor.

A short distance north of mid-city lies Lake Union, with its marinas, boat moorages, and houseboats. Lake Union is connected to Lake Washington and to Puget Sound by a ship canal and the Hiram M. Chittenden Locks, one of the largest in the Western Hemisphere and another tourist attraction. Crowds constantly watch the parade of boats passing through the inland waterway. At the locks are gardens, a salmon fish ladder, and an interpretive center, all free.

Lake Washington, the largest of the metropolitan lakes, is spanned by two long floating bridges connecting to eastside suburbs, the largest of which is Bellevue, with a population of 70,000. The west side of the lake is dotted by moorages, playgrounds, beaches, and parks. The biggest parks are Seward and a brand new one at Sand Point. In August, the famous hydroplane races of Seafair are staged on Lake Washington.

PRACTICAL INFORMATION FOR SEATTLE

HOW TO GET AROUND *By air:* From Seattle-Tacoma International Airport several commuter lines lead to Spokane, Pullman, Walla Walla, Tri-Cities (Pasco, Richland and Kennewick), Yakima, Bremerton, Whidbey Island, Bellingham, Port Angeles, and the San Juan Islands.

Air-taxi and charter service—available at Boeing Field, Lake Union, Renton, Paine Field (Everett) and Cedar Grove Air Park, Kenmore Air Harbor.

Car rental: Avis, Hertz, and *National,* plus a dozen or more other firms.

By ferry: From Pier 52, foot of Marion St. to Bremerton; and to Winslow, Bainbridge Island. From Fauntleroy, West Seattle to Vashon Island and to Southworth, Kitsap Peninsula. From Edmonds, north of Seattle, to Kingston and to Port Townsend on the Olympic Peninsula.

By bus: Metro Transit serves city, surrounding county, and waypoints to Everett and Tacoma. No fare charged in the central business district.

A *monorail* whisks passengers from downtown to Seattle Center in less than three minutes.

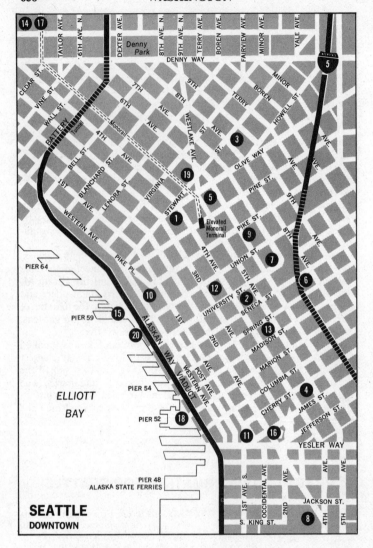

Points of Interest

1) Bon Marche
2) Four Seasons Olympic Hotel
3) Central Bus Terminal
4) City Hall
5) Frederick & Nelson
6) Freeway Park
7) Hilton Hotel
8) King Street Station (Amtrak)
9) Seattle Sheraton

10) Pike Place Market
11) Pioneer Square
12) Post Office
13) Public Library
14) Seattle Center
15) Seattle Public Aquarium
16) Smith Tower
17) Space Needle
18) State Ferry Terminal
19) Westin Hotel
20) Waterfront Park

TOURIST INFORMATION SERVICES. The *Seattle–King County Convention & Visitors Bureau,* 1815 Seventh Ave., provides schedules of events and brochure-maps of the four loop drives. For ferry information, write the *Washington State Ferry System,* State Ferry Terminal, Seattle 98104

 MUSEUMS AND GALLERIES. Historical: *Museum of History and Industry,* 2161 E. Hamlin. History, transportation, aerospace, fashion, furnishings, maritime and wildlife collections. Art: *Charles and Emma Frye Art Museum,* 704 Terry—Munich School paintings, 1850–1900; American School, 19th and 20th centuries. *Seattle Art Museum,* Volunteer Park—Asian art; pre-Colombia collection; European and American paintings. *Seattle Art Museum Pavilion,* Seattle Center—Rotating exhibits, generally contemporary. *Henry Art Gallery,* U. of Washington—19th-and 20th-century American and European paintings; contemporary prints; American ceramics; modern Japanese folk pottery. There are also more than a hundred recognized private galleries in Seattle and its suburban cities.

Special Interest: *Pacific Science Center,* 200 2nd Ave. N. *Thomas Burke Memorial Washington State Museum,* U. of Washington—ethnology, geology, paleontology, zoology. *Fire Station No. 5,* foot of Madison Street, waterfront. *Wing Luke Memorial Museum,* 414 8th St. S.—Chinese history and culture. *Kirkland Historical Museum,* Kirkland (a suburb)—three old ships.

 TOURS. *Seattle Harbor Tours*—from Pier 56 downtown. *Canadian Pacific* summertime daily cruise from Seattle to Victoria, B.C, via the *Princess Marguerite,* Lenora St. Terminal, Pier 69.

Boat to Tillicum Village, Blake Island (summer), Pier 56.

Gray Line of Seattle, 4th and University—a variety of tours by bus or boat, daytime and nighttime.

Bill Speidel Underground Tours—guided walking tour of Pioneer Square area (682–4646 for reservations).

Trident Tours—Four self-guiding, drive-yourself tours, following street signs.

GARDENS. *U. of Washington Arboretum,* Lake Washington Blvd. 250 acres including *Japanese Tea Garden. Woodland Park Zoological Gardens,* 95 acres including extensive rose garden. *Volunteer Park* and its conservatory. *Carl S. English, Jr. Gardens,* Hiram M. Chittenden Locks.

 SPORTS. *Boating:* See Yellow Pages in telephone directory for rentals of rowboats, kickers, canoes, sailboats, cruisers and yachts for charter. *Bicycle riding:* Miles of designated streets and paths. Best areas for bike rentals are Alki (West Seattle), Green Lake, University District, Seward Park, and Kenmore. *Fishing:* From downtown piers, in city lakes and in Puget Sound. License required for freshwater but not for saltwater, except salmon. Boathouses at Ballard, West Seattle, and in suburban shore towns. *Golf:* Municipal 18–27-hole courses in Seattle and a dozen other public links in the suburbs. *Hiking:* Many trails in and around the city. Myrtle Edwards Park is a 2-mile path along Elliott Bay. Nature trails in Arboretum–Foster Island; Seward, Schmitz, Lincoln, and Discovery Parks. Burke-Gilman Trail runs 12½ miles from Lake Union to Kenmore, north end of Lake Washington. (It's also for bicyclers.) *Picnicking:* In almost all city and county parks. *Swimming:* City and county beaches, very cold freshwater and saltwater. Twenty more-comfortable public pools in city and suburbs. *Tennis:* City parks have many courts, but with current tennis madness, call Seattle Parks & Recreation Dept. for reservation, 625–4672.

SPECTATOR SPORTS. For schedules consult daily papers or Seattle Visitors Center. *Baseball:* Seattle Mariners, American League. *Basketball:* Seattle SuperSonics, National Basketball Association; college contests. *Football:* Seattle Seahawks, NFL; U. of Washington Huskies. *Boxing:* Seattle Center Arena. *Hockey:* Seattle Breakers, Western Hockey League. *Soccer:* Major league's Seattle Sounders. *Auto Racing:* Pacific Raceways at Kent; Evergreen Speedway at Monroe; Puyallup International Dragway. *Horse Racing:* Longacres, Renton (mid-May–late September). *Hydroplane Racing:* Lake Washington, early August.

WHAT TO DO WITH THE CHILDREN. There is an abundance of parks and beaches. The most unusual playground is the new Gas Works Park, north side of Lake Union. You'll never see another one like it, nor happier children as they clamber over and into what was once industrial equipment. Ferry rides and the Monorail appeal to the young. In Seattle Center are the Space Needle, Skyride, Pacific Science Center (with special exhibits for youngsters only), an amusement area, and children's shows at Piccoli Theater. Children also enjoy Tillicum Indian Village on Blake Island; the Lake Washington Ship Canal and locks; Woodland Park Zoo; and the waterfront with its curio shops, fire station, fire boats, and aquarium. They can fish from a pier at the downtown Waterfront Park.

HOTELS AND MOTELS. There are few low-cost accommodations within a dozen miles of the city center. If any are to be found, they are on the two "motel strips," Aurora Avenue running north, and Highway 99 south of the airport. Figure *Moderate* at $20–25 and *Inexpensive* anything under that. Bed-and-breakfast is a growing industry here. Check with the Convention & Visitors Bureau for listings.

Moderate: **Bridge Motel.** Handy to downtown. 3650 Bridge Way N.
Imperial 400 Motel Downtown. Pool. 325 Aurora Ave. N.
La Hacienda Motel. Some kitchens. 5414 First Ave. S.
Max Ivor Motel. Some 2-room units. Some kitchens. 6188 Fourth Ave. So.
Park Plaza Motel. 4401 Aurora Ave. N.
University Inn. Some kitchens. Coffee shop. Laundry. 4140 Roosevelt Way N.E.
West Wind Motel. Some kitchens. 110 Rainier Ave. S., in the center of Renton.
Moderate–Inexpensive: **Thunderbird Motel.** Some 2-room units with kitchens. Pool. 4251 Aurora Ave. N.
Inexpensive: **Marco Polo Motel.** 1- and 2-room units, some with kitchens. 4114 Aurora Ave. N.
Motel "6". Pool. No credit cards. 18900 47th St. (South, off I–5.)
Seattle Downtown YMCA. Daily or weekly rates. 242 rooms. 909 Fourth Ave.

DINING OUT. *Moderate* dinner: $8–10. *Inexpensive:* There's a chance of $6 or less, starting with $4.50. Coffee or tea is usually extra. Add sales tax and tip and a $4.50 meal becomes $6. Same for "moderate"—A $6.95 entree ends up about $8. Buffets and counter service, usually inexpensive, offer the advantage of no tipping.

Moderate: **Andy's Diner.** 2963 Fourth Ave. S. Prime-quality beef only
Black Angus. 208 Elliott West and five others: 12255 Aurora N. and in Bellevue, Burien, Crossroads (Bellevue), and Renton. One-price steak house.
Dungeness Dan's. On Pier 52, foot of Marion St., in Seattle Ferry Terminal. Seafood specialties and meat. Children's portions.

Italo Casa Roma. 6400 Empire Way S. Excellent and inexpensive Italian food.

Ivar's Acre of Clams. On Pier 52, at foot of Marion St. Fried and steamed clams, baked salmon.

Ivar's Salmon House. 401 N.E. Northlake Way. Indian-style barbecued salmon. Children's portions.

Olympia Oyster House. Excellent seafood as well as other dishes. Nice view from the top of the First and Cedar Branch of the SeaFirst Bank. 2701 First Ave.

Inexpensive: **The Old Spaghetti Factory.** Alaskan Way & Broad St. Special sauces, sourdough bread.

Royal Fork. Extensive buffet. All you can eat. Special prices for children. 310 15th Ave. E., 2205 N. 45th, 10342 Aurora Ave. N., 2222 California St., 1545 Market St, and in Burien at 137 S.W. 160th.

The Sizzler Family Steak House. A new chain of steak-and-salad restaurants with 9 locations around the state. Seattle location is in Southcenter shopping center complex.

Chinese. Inexpensive: **Orchid Villa.** Very good Cantonese and American food. Children's and Seniors' menus. Next to University Village Shopping Center at 4530 Union Bay Ave. N.E.

Mexican. Inexpensive: **Guadalajara Café.** 1429 Fourth; 1718 N. 45th; 2nd and Main; and in Bellevue.

EXPLORING WASHINGTON

Tacoma

Washington's third-largest city (second in metropolitan population) is so devoted to business, industry, and seaport activities that most of its hotel-motels and leading department stores are out in shopping centers rather than downtown. However, there are outstanding tourist attractions which families can visit at little or no expense.

Most obvious is Point Defiance Park, with its zoo, aquarium, gardens, beach, marine view drives, outdoor museum of logging equipment (called Camp Six), a nursery-rhyme "land" for children, and old Fort Nisqually, partially original, part replica. Nearby is the Tacoma Narrows suspension bridge, the only bridge crossing Puget Sound.

These sights can be reached by motorists following "Klahowya Trail" signs, or by a modestly priced summertime bus tour run by Travelines morning and afternoon, starting at the old Union (railroad) Station.

The Washington State Historical Society Museum is at 315 N. Stadium Way. Art galleries of note are the Tacoma Art Museum, 12th and Pacific, and Handforth Gallery, Public Library, 1102 S. Tacoma.

Hub of the Inland Empire

Spokane, the second-largest city in Washington, is known as the "Hub of the Inland Empire." It lacks the scenic backgrounds of Seattle or Tacoma, but is, in its own way, close to nature. Lakes and countless streams surround the city. Northeast by 34 miles is the highest point in the "Inland Empire"—a 5,878-foot peak at the center of Mt. Spokane State Park. The park, the largest in the state, with almost 21,000 acres, offers views in the summer, sports in the winter.

Spokane itself has more than 60 parks and gardens, including the famous Duncan Gardens and Japanese Tea House in Manito Park. The 100-acre city-center site was cleared by the city for its Expo '74 World's Fair. It is on riverbanks and islands, by the waterfalls of the Spokane River. Spokane's museums include Cheney Cowles Memorial Museum, a history museum of plateau Indian art and culture, and also an art gallery; Ft. Wright College Historical Museum, with items relating to the military occupancy of the fort (1899–1958); and Clark Mansion, W. 2208 Second, an elegant old residence with Tiffany glass, carved wood-work, murals and period furniture. Adjoining Cheney Cowles Memori-al Museum is Campbell House, a late 19th-century mansion of 19 rooms and 10 fireplaces that has been restored to its former glory. Pacific Northwest Indian Center is one of the best of its field.

Grand Coulee Dam is about a 1½-hour drive from Spokane. Huge dams are abundant in the West, but this is the granddaddy of them all. Everything about it—the hydroelectric power it produces, the 151-mile lake it backs up, the 2,000 square miles those waters irrigate, the setting among desert coulees—comes in superlatives. You can be both awed and educated for no cost. At a visitors' center with a grandstand, you get the whole picture, geological to mechanical.

Coming or going to the dam, stop at Dry Falls, near Coulee City. Dry Falls supplements the story, with the aid of an excellent interpre-tive center. A cataract many times larger than Niagara once plunged down sheer cliffs here when the river's course was changed.

Mt. Rainier National Park

Mighty Mt. Rainier, the state's best known and highest mountain, is an ice-clad, dormant volcano on the southeast horizons of Seattle and Tacoma. It rises 14,410 feet, and its gleaming mantle of ice is composed of more glaciers than there are on any other single mountain in the United States south of Alaska.

The park is the best known tourist attraction in Washington. It symbolizes the region's wealth of natural wonders—glaciers, water-falls, forests, wildflowers, lakes, abundant wildlife, and stunning vistas. For hikers and climbers, the park offers a variety of trails, some for experts only. Motorists can get a close look at Emmons Glacier, on the east slope of the mountain, by taking the winding road that twists west to Sunrise, off US 410. For extended visits to the park, there are campgrounds, an inn, and varied eating facilities.

North Cascades National Park

This park, lying along the northern boundary of Washington, has the most outstanding alpine scenery in the U.S. within its 1,053 square miles. There are hundreds of icefalls, hanging valleys, waterfalls, jagged peaks, and lakes caught within glacial cirques. Three dams that provide power for Seattle form lakes of considerable size, one 24 miles long.

The park is divided into four units—North and South Units of the Park, and Ross Lake and Lake Chelan National Recreation Areas. The only through-route for motorists is the North Cascades Highway, Wash. 20. In one stretch of 75 miles, it has no facilities. The highway is closed during mid-winter due to heavy snowfall. Outdoor recreation can be enjoyed from early April to mid-October at lower elevations. At higher elevations, the season is from mid-June to mid-September. The western side of the North Cascades gets more rain, has more lakes and streams, and more abundant vegetation.

There is no motel or lodge inside the North and South Units of North Cascade National Park. The larger towns and cities near the North Cascades group have the usual tourist accommodations, but are 2- to 3-hour drives from area boundaries. Smaller communities within Ross Lake NRA and Lake Chelan NRA or adjacent to the areas have limited guest accommodations. Chambers of commerce for each of the towns surrounding the North Cascades group have information on packers, guides, and other outdoor services.

Hiking access and roadside views of the northwest corner are offered from Wash. 542 from Bellingham. A picturesque way to enter the area is from Stehekin, reached by boat from Chelan, 55 miles southeast. (Daily boat services; 2 lodges at Stehekin.) There is scheduled boat service on Diablo Lake as well. Permits, required for all back-country camping, are obtainable at any Park Service office or ranger station. Colonial Creek and Goodell are developed drive-in campgrounds off Wash. 20 in Ross Lake NRA, but apart from these, campsites are pretty primitive. There are no campgrounds in the North Unit of the national park, and only 2 in the South Unit. Ross Lake NRA has some campgrounds that are reached by boat. Fishing is principally for rainbow, Eastern brook, Dolly Varden, and cutthroat trout. Swimming is not suggested—the waters of the lakes and rivers are quite chilly. For further information, write: Superintendent, *North Cascades National Park*, Sedro Woolley, WA 98284.

Olympic National Park

Unlike most stretched-out Western ranges, the Olympic Mountains occupy an area as wide as it is long, taking up the entire center of the Olympic Peninsula. Bordered on three sides by saltwater, with elevations running from sea level to nearly 8,000 feet, the peninsula has been called "a continent in miniature" because entire cycles of nature are self-contained in this geographical unit.

A highway loops the peninsula, all but a few miles of it outside the 1,400-square-mile Olympic National Park. No road crosses the park, but a few dead-end inside its boundaries, notably at Hurricane Ridge south of Port Angeles (the view is into the center of the Olympics and out across the Strait of Juan de Fuca) and in the Hoh River Rain Forest off US 101 south of Forks.

The park's Ocean Strip, a 60-mile stretch of primitive coast, is tapped by sideroads to Ozette and La Push. Highway 101 follows the coast for 13 miles, and short easy trails lead to ocean beaches. As for trails into the mountains, they are long and arduous. Experienced backpackers are about the only ones who ever glimpse the much-touted Roosevelt elk herds.

The visitors' center at park headquarters is open all year (address Superintendent, Olympic National Park, 600 E. Park Ave., Port Angeles, WA 98362), and so is the one at Hoh Rain Forest. Storm King Center at Lake Crescent is open in summer. Drive-in campgrounds in the park are greatly augmented by state and Forest Service sites around the entire perimeter.

PRACTICAL INFORMATION FOR WASHINGTON

HOW TO GET THERE. *By air: Alaska Airlines, American, British Airways, Continental, Delta, Eastern, Evergreen International, Finnair, Mexicana, National, Northwest, Pacific Western, Pan Am, Reeve Aleutian, Republic, SAS, Thai Airways, Trans World, United, Western* and *Wien Air Alaska.* Commuter airlines include *Air Oregon, Cascade, Harbor, Pearson* and *San Juan,* all at Seattle-Tacoma International Airport. *Northwest, United, Republic* and *Cascade* have been serving Spokane, and some of the new ones at Sea-Tac have said they will add Spokane, too.

By train (Amtrak): From the east, to Spokane and Seattle; West Coast route from San Diego to Seattle.

By car: The main east-west route, Interstate 90, enters from Idaho, just east of Spokane. US 101 enters at Astoria, Ore., and the main arterial, I–5, at Portland or from British Columbia.

By bus: Greyhound, Trailways.

By ferry: Black Ball between Victoria (British Columbia) and Port Angeles. *Alaska State Ferries* run once a week summers, twice weekly in winter, between Southeast Alaska and Seattle.

TOURIST INFORMATION SERVICES. There are *Visitor Information Centers* at border points and chambers of commerce throughout the state. *Travel Development Division,* General Administration Building, Olympia, WA 98504—tourist attractions. *U.S. Forest Service,* Regional Office, P.O. Box 3623, Portland, OR 97208—camping. *Washington State Dept. of Natural Resources,* Public Lands Bldg., Olympia, WA 98501—camping. *Superintendent, Mt. Rainier National Park,* Ashford, WA 98304. *Superintendent, Olympic National Park,* Port Angeles, WA 98362. *Superintendent, North Cascades National Park,* Sedro Woolley, WA 98284. *State Parks and Recreation Commission,* P.O. Box 1128, Olympia, WA 98504. *Washington State Dept. of Fisheries,* General Administration Bldg., Olympia, WA 98504—saltwater fishing. *Washington State Game Dept.,* 600 N. Capitol Way, Olympia, WA 98504—hunting and freshwater fishing.

MUSEUMS AND GALLERIES. Some of these have been mentioned in connection with Seattle, Spokane and Tacoma. Almost all of the 39 counties have their historical societies and a museum, usually at the county seat. Inquire locally for the address. Exhibits run from the usual heirlooms of local pioneer families to some rather impressive collections.

Other museums worthy of note are *Fort Lewis Military Museum; Olympia State Capital Museum,* 2111 W. 21st Ave.; *Port Townsend Rothschild House,* 19th-century furnished, a State Parks operation; Vantage, *Gingko Petrified Forest State Park Museum;* Walla Walla, *Fort Walla Walla Museum Complex.*

Fair to excellent handcrafts and paintings appear in small shops and galleries in the most unexpected places. Somehow an "art colony" (or an outstanding individual) has developed there. Gig Harbor, Langley on Widbey Island, Stanwood, and Anacortes are a few examples. Best guide to these is to look for them where you find them.

HISTORIC SITES. Lately, these proliferate (in recognition) as Americans become conscious of their heritage. Among a few not mentioned elsewhere are Ellensburg: *Olmstead Place Heritage Site,* 4 miles east of town. 1875 log cabins.

Olympia: *Crosby House,* Des Chutes Way, built in 1860.

Port Townsend: *Fort Worden,* 1 mile north of town. Site of *Old Fort Townsend,* 3 miles south of town. Rosalia: *Steptoe Battlefield.*

Spokane: *Site of Spokane House,* 1810 fur-trading post.

Vancouver: *Fort Vancouver* (founded in 1824) replica being built on the site. Wallula: *Site of Fort Walla Walla; Whitman Mission National Historic Site.* Blaine: *International Peace Arch.* White Swan: *Fort Simcoe. Port Gamble,* where the whole town is registered as a National Historic Site; Suquamish, *Chief Seattle's grave* and site of *Old Man House,* a 600-foot-long, pre-white Indian "condominium."

TOURS. *Gray Lines* runs sightseeing tours year-round in Seattle, and during the summer in Spokane and Port Angeles. Summer excursion boats in the harbors and lakes of Seattle. Excursions into the Snake River's Hell's Canyon start in Clarkston. River float trips on the Skagit, and out of Spokane.

DRINKING LAWS. Bars, all in conjunction with a restaurant, can stay open until 2 A.M. every day. Taverns dispense beer and wine, which is also sold by the bottle in grocery stores. Hard liquor at state stores, usually open 10 A.M.–8 P.M., closed Sundays. Some big-city stores stay open later and also on holidays (except Christmas). Minimum drinking age, 21.

SUMMER SPORTS. Bicycle riding, swimming, tennis are found throughout the state. *Golf:* For details on golf courses, write to area chambers of commerce. *Fishing:* River fishing—licenses required for steelhead. Lakes—8,000, with trout, bass, and other whitefish. Saltwater—salmon in summer. Charter boats and equipment at Westport (Grays Harbor), Ilwaco (mouth of Columbia River), Neah Bay and Sekiu (outer end, Strait of Juan de Fuca), Port Angeles and other coastal towns. *Clam digging*—Pacific beaches.

No license is needed in national parks.

Hiking: Trails within an hour of all cities. Longest are Cascade Crest Trail and Olympic National Park trails crossing Olympic Peninsula.

Horseback Riding: inquire locally.

Hunting: Deer, elk, black bear, mountain goats. Pheasants, ducks, geese, grouse, quail and partridge. Rabbits. Licenses are purchased from sport stores or request application from the Game Department.

Mountain Climbing: Mountains cover half the area of state, some with glaciers. (A guide is required at Mt. Rainier.)

WINTER SPORTS. *Skiing:* In the Cascades, drawing skiers from both sides of the range, the fully equipped areas are at or near the passes: Stevens, US 2 at Stevens Pass; Alpental, Snoqualmie Summit, Ski Acres and Hyak, I–90 at Snoqualmie Pass; Crystal Mountain, Wash. 410, approaching Cayuse Pass; White Pass Village, US 12 at White Pass. Mt. Baker, 60 miles from Bellingham on Wash. 542, has a westside entrance only. The doorway to Mission Ridge is Wenatchee (12 miles). From Spokane skiers head to Mt. Spokane (34 miles) and 49° North at Chewelah (45 miles). There are numerous others in the state, if not as big, not as crowded, either.

Skating: Unique to the state is the outdoor Pavilion in Spokane's Waterfront Park. Open mid-November to mid-April. Indoor rinks are found in a few other cities.

SPECTATOR SPORTS. (Other than in Seattle area.) *Baseball:* Pacific Coast League baseball in Tacoma, Spokane. *Football:* Washington State U and other university and college games. *Basketball:* Collegiate games—Washington State U and other universities and colleges. *Horse Racing:* Playfair at Spokane—July to late Oct. Yakima Meadows—March to early May; Oct. to end of Nov.

WHAT TO DO WITH THE CHILDREN. Most large cities have zoos, parks and playgrounds. Along the coast, nothing beats *beachcombing. Gingko Petrified Forest* is unique.

Tacoma: *Point Defiance Park*—Aviary, Never-Never Land, Old Ft. Nisqually, Aquarium; *Children's Farm Animal Zoo.* Steam Shea Locomotive at *Camp Six,* replica of logging camp. Totem Pole.

Bremerton: *U.S.S. Missouri*

Lake Chelan: *Boat ride.*

Largest zoo is in Seattle. Spokane is developing a cageless zoo. *Northwest Trek* at Eatonville is a branch of the Tacoma zoo. Animals roam freely, viewed from quiet motor trams. Near Sequim is *Loboland,* with many species of wolf, and *Olympic Game Farm,* where famous animal characters are kept and filmed for TV and Disney "nature" movies. Walk through with guide or drive around the extensive compound.

Throughout the state, children can climb, swim, throw snowballs in August, watch rodeos, dance to Indian drums, ride horses, and have a good chance of seeing animals in the forest. The state is a children's playground.

HOTELS AND MOTELS. Prices in towns and small cities tend to vary more than they do in metropolitan areas. When there is a choice among "vacancy" signs, inquire before signing up. Two motels of equal quality can differ from $2 to $4 a night. Don't overlook old, well-kept ones. They often offer the best rates and are most likely to have kitchenettes for an extra $2–3. *Moderate,* $22–30; *Inexpensive,* under $22.

ANACORTES. *Moderate–Expensive:* **San Juan Motel.** Kitchens. Small pets. *Inexpensive–Moderate:* **Island Motel.** 1- and 2-room units. Some kitchens.

BELLINGHAM. *Inexpensive:* **Motel "6".** Pool.

BREMERTON. *Moderate–Expensive:* **Chieftain Motel.** Some kitchens. Pool.

EVERETT. *Inexpensive:* **Motel "6".** Pool.

MOSES LAKE. *Moderate:* **Interstate Inn.**
Maples Motel.

OAK HARBOR. *Inexpensive–Moderate:* **Alpen Haus Motel.** Some kitchens. Seasonal rates.

OLYMPIA. *Moderate:* **Golden Gavel Motel.** Just 3 blocks north of the capitol campus.
Inexpensive: **Motel "6".** Pool. Pets. In Tumwater.

PORT ANGELES. *Moderate–Deluxe:* **Angie's Inn.** Wide choice of accommodations.

PORT TOWNSEND. *Moderate:* **Port Townsend Motel.**

SHELTON. *Inexpensive–Moderate:* **City Center Motel.**

SPOKANE. *Moderate–Expensive:* **Desert Motel.** Downtown. 123 Post St. **Clinic Center Motel.** 702 McClellan.
Moderate: **Tiki Lodge.** Pool. W. 1420 2nd Ave.
Inexpensive: **Motel "6".** Pool. 1508 So. Rustle St.

TACOMA. *Moderate:* **Nendel's.** 1- and 2-room units. Pool. Restaurant. 8702 So. Hosner. South, off I–5.
Inexpensive: **Motel "6".** North, off I–5. 5201 20th St., Fife.

VANCOUVER. *Moderate:* **Aloha Motel.** Pool and playground. Pets. 3 miles north of town.
Fort Motel. Pool. East side of town.
Riviera Motel. Pool. 3 blocks from business center.

WALLA WALLA. *Moderate:* **Walla Walla TraveLodge.** Pool.
Inexpensive: **Midtown Motel.** Downtown.

WENATCHEE. *Moderate:* **Imperial 400 Motel. Scotty's Motel.** Pool. **Uptown Motel.** All units have kitchens. Pool. Downtown.

YAKIMA. *Inexpensive:* **Motel 6.** Pool.

 DINING OUT. Budget-minded travelers, especially those with families, know the fast-food and restaurant chains that operate nationally. Not so familiar in name are some that started on the West Coast and are best known there. The following chain restaurants in Washington state have kept their prices *moderate* ($8–10) or *inexpensive* (under $8).

Moderate: **Black Angus** (Stuart Anderson's). Began in Seattle but is fast spreading to other states. Quality steak dinners. Also in Bellingham, Everett, Lakewood (Tacoma), Pasco, Spokane, Vancouver, Walla Walla and Yakima.

Inexpensive–Moderate: **Turkey House.** Named for its specialty. Four in Seattle area plus Bellingham and Tumwater (Olympia).

VIP's. General menu. Besides Seattle area, they're in Chehalis, Everett, Kelso, Kennewick, Mount Vernon, Olympia, Richland, Spokane, Tacoma, Union Gap (Yakima) and Vancouver, Wash.

Inexpensive: **Old Spaghetti Factory.** See Seattle. Also in Spokane and Tacoma.

Royal Fork. Buffet, good variety. Flat price under $4 includes tax. Children charged by age, 22 cents a year up to 10. Chain has expanded from Seattle to Bellingham, Bremerton, Everett, Federal Way, Lynnwood, Olympia, Tacoma (2) and Yakima.

Inexpensive chains below deal in specialty goods. Majority of trade is dine-in, but many also offer take-out service.

Herfy's. Hamburgers, roast beef, some fish. Huge West Coast chain with 41 outlets in western Washington.

Skipper's. Variety of seafoods, also chicken. From Bellevue start, has grown to 50 in state. Found in Aberdeen, Bellingham, Chehalis, Everett, Lacey (Olympia), Marysville, Mount Vernon, Oak Harbor, Pasco, Port Angeles, Richland, Spokane, Tacoma and Yakima.

Taco Time. Began in Oregon, has many outlets in Washington. Good Mexican food prepared to order.

HAWAII

Honolulu and Four Beautiful Islands

Headquarters for your Honolulu sightseeing is probably a poolside chair or a mat on Waikiki Beach, and you may be tempted to do all your sightseeing from here in a supine position. There is much to be said for this method. It will leave an indelible impression of three things Hawaii is famous for: sun, surf, and girls. However, the inherent problem in this method is that you miss the thousand other things that make Hawaii Hawaii. So, do yourself a favor; roll over, stand up, and see what there is to see.

Walking in Waikiki

Though most Honolulans ride—via bus or car—there is no law against walking. In fact, pedestrians in Honolulu have a sort of favored status. And, should you decide to hoof it, there are a number of places in Honolulu where you can stroll and enjoy the local scenery.

The first of these places is Waikiki, which, despite its many new hotels, smart shops, and crowds, remains in essence a kind of provincial village. The veneer of sophistication is pretty thin here, and you will probably enjoy the International Market Place, the Waikiki Shopping Plaza, King's Village, Eaton Square or Hilton Hawaiian Village, as well as the rest of the passing show on Kalakaua Avenue. But beware, there's plenty of hustle on Kalakaua these days.

Chinatown

The area between Nuuanu Avenue and River Street is where many of the respected Chinese merchants have their stores and restaurants. There are herb shops, Oriental dry goods shops, and fascinating Chinese food shops. Don't hesitate to sample the little Chinese restaurants in this neighborhood—you'll go a long way before you find better soup and noodles.

One block beyond Maunakea Street is River Street, which flanks the Nuuanu Stream as it winds its way into Honolulu Harbor. Once the scene of legalized houses of prostitution, River Street has now blossomed with the completion of the River Street Mall, a promenade walk along the stream, that features the Chinese Cultural Plaza. Chinatown's attractions are still there, but be warned that the residents today are largely Filipino, and porno shops along Hotel Street have caused something of a cultural blight.

PRACTICAL INFORMATION FOR HONOLULU

 TRANSPORTATION. *Air:* Many major airlines around the world serve the Hawaiian Islands. For inter-island travel there are three major airlines: *Hawaiian, Aloha* and *Mid-Pacific.*

Bus: Public transportation in the capital is by modern Mass Transit Lines buses. There are 30 different lines crisscrossing the city, cutting into the residential valleys and climbing to the heights which separate them. All buses carry signs showing their route number and destination, and the driver will issue a free transfer for another route if you must change. For information call The Bus 531–1161.

Cabs: Taxi cabs are plentiful, driven by qualified drivers, and metered at $1.20 for the first sixth of a mile and 20¢ for each additional one-sixth mile. Since random cruising is not allowed, don't stand on a street corner, pick up a phone instead.

U-Drive Cars: You can hardly take two steps on Kalakaua Avenue, the main drag of Waikiki, without stumbling over a drive-yourself car for rent. The range of cars for hire runs just about the whole gamut of the automotive industry, both domestic and foreign. *Avis* will rent to anyone over 21, if they have a driver's license and a major credit card. *Robert's Hawaii Rent-A-Car* will rent to 18-year-olds if they're married. The major firms in Honolulu are: *Avis,* 148 Kaiulani Ave., in the Hilton Hawaiian Village; *Budget Rent-A-Car,* 2379 Kuhio Ave. and other Waikiki locations as well as all major airports; *Hertz,* Honolulu International Airport, Hilton Hawaiian Village and 8 other major hotels, and *National Car Rental,* 2160 Kalakaua Ave. Less expensive cars can be obtained from *Greyhound Rent-A-Car,Sears Rent-A-Car* and *Mal Mat Leasing.* To go a little slower and get more sun exposure, try the mopeds that rent in Waikiki. Slower yet are pedicabs.

GUIDED TOURS. A number of tour and travel services are engaged in conducting tours of the city by bus. Limousines are also available. The major companies are *Gray Line* and *Trade Wind.*

SPORTS. *Golf:* There are 28 good courses on Oahu, counting military and par-3s. There are three city-county courses, with weekday greens fees of only $2.50, and one, Kahuku, charges $1.75. Not a bad buy. *Tennis:* There are 108 public tennis courts on the island. Visitors are welcome to play any of them. There are 10 courts at Ala Moana Park, 8 at Keehi Lagoon, 7 at the Diamond Head Tennis Center, 6 at Koko Head, another 4 in Kapiolani Park. Thirty-seven courts are lighted for night play. Public tennis, as public golf, sometimes means a lot of waiting around.

Deep-Sea Fishing: Best waters are off the Waianae Coast, off Koko Head, off Kaneohe Bay, and along the Penguin Banks southwest of Molokai across the Molokai Channel from Oahu. Charter boats available at Kewalo Basin. The trouble with deep-sea sailing and most water activities is that they're expensive. Swimming is great on the pocketbook. For a twilight dinner sail on ship or catamaran, check in Kewalo Basin.

Hiking: There are about two dozen trails on Oahu. Maps showing the trails may be obtained both from the state and City Hall. There are hikes scheduled nearly every Sunday by the *Hawaiian Trail and Mountain Club* (telephone, 734–5515) from the Church of the Crossroads grounds at 8 Sunday morning. In recent years, the *Sierra Club* has been offering alternate hikes. They meet at 8 Sunday morning in the Bishop Museum parking lot.

Skindiving: Call Ken Taylor, *South Seas Aquatics.* 1050 Ala Moana Blvd.

If you just want to look at the fish wiggle by under your toes, take the glass-bottom boat that tours off Waikiki 5 times a day. It leaves from Fisherman's Wharf at Kewalo Basin.

Hunting: Oahu quarry includes wild pigs and goats in the Waianae and Koolau Mountains. The *State Fish and Game Division* at 1151 Punchbowl St. can provide you with complete information on hunting in Oahu.

Camping: There are 18 parks on Oahu for those renting motor homes. Beach Boy Campers rents vans. Permits for a week are required and renewable. Telephone the Parks Department at 523–*525.

Audubon Society: The *Hawaii Audubon Society,* P.O. Box 5032, Honolulu, is headquarters for bird watchers. They have Sunday morning bird hikes every month, leaving from The Library of Hawaii. Visitors welcome.

HOTELS. Rates are for single rooms—for doubles add 15–25%. Categories are as follows: *Moderate,* $30; *Inexpensive,* $20–30; *Rock Bottom,* for under $20.

Moderate: **Hawaiian King.** 417 Nohonani, Waikiki. Attractive suites with lanai, sitting room, and kitchen.

Ilima. 445 Nohonani St., Waikiki. All units with kitchen. Restaurant and pool.

Inexpensive: **Nakamura.** 1140 South King St., Honolulu. Midway between downtown and Waikiki.

Reef Lanais. 225 Saratoga Road, Waikiki. Restaurant, pool, cocktail lounge.

Royal Grove. 151 Uluniu Ave., Waikiki. Small, with pool and patio.

Waikiki Circle. 2464 Kalakaua Ave., Waikiki. Good locale, wide-range views from rooms.

Waikiki Surf. 2200 Kuhio St., Waikiki. Restaurant, pool, bar.

Waikiki Surf West. 412 Lewers St., Waikiki. Attractive units with kitchenettes and private lanais.

Rock Bottom: **Waikiki Terrace.** 339 Royal Hawaiian Ave. In the heart of Waikiki.

OTHERS. Near the airport is the **Holiday Inn-Airport** and **Ramada Inn,** both on Nimitz Highway. Rates are *moderate.*

Laniloa Lodge Hotel. 55–109 Laniloa St., Laie. Private beach across the road.

DINING OUT. The cuisine of contemporary Hawaii is basically American, spiced with the adopted dishes of the many nations which have amalgamated in Hawaii. However, ethnic restaurants flourish, and Japanese, Korean and Chinese eateries naturally abound. Dinner in a *moderate* restaurant will cost from $6–10; in an *inexpensive* restaurant from $5–6. Prices are for a complete dinner, but do not include drinks, tax or tip.

Our list of reasonable restaurants in Honolulu follows.

Moderate: **Café Colonnade.** Princess Kaiulani Hotel. Mediterranean décor.

Columbia Inn. 645 Kapiolani, at the Top of the Boulevard. And at 98–1226 Kaahumanu St. in Waimalu. Likes newsmen and athletes.

Flamingo Chuckwagon. 1015 Kapiolani. Eat all you want, with prime rib the feature.

M's Coffee Tavern. 124 Queen St. Downtown financial district. Lunches only.

Specialty Houses. Chinese. **King Tsin.** 1486 S. King St. Features Mandarin cooking in intimate setting.

Wo Fat. 115 N. Hotel St. Downtown, elegant, serving authentic Cantonese cuisine.

Japanese. **Kanraku Tea House.** 750 Kohou St. in Kalihi. Sit on the floor as the locals do.

Suehiro's. 1824 S. King St. Again, popular with the locals.

Korean. **Kal Bi House.** In Kaimuki. A tiny spot next to a pool hall. But what short ribs!.

Italian. **Matteo's.** 364 Seaside in the Marine Surf Hotel and downtown. Another fine Italian spot.

Trattoria. Cinerama Edgewater. Fine Italian food.

Mexican. **Jose's.** In Kaimuki. Another good, hot spot.

Mama's Mexican Kitchen. 378 North School St. Most popular Mexican place in city. Bring your own beer.

Hawaiian. **Ono Hawaiian Foods.** 726 Kapahulu Ave. Locals crowd in for local kaukau

Jewish. **Lyn's Kosher-Style Delicatessen.** Ala Moana Center. Good pastrami.

EXPLORING HAWAII ISLAND

Hawaii's greatest claims to fame are its flowers (more than 22,000 varieties of orchids) and its flames. The island is in fact composed of five volcanic mountains. (In 1983, the mountain Kilauea exploded into activity and the condition of the area around the eruption is still uncertain at press time.)

Kailua-Kona is the oldest and most developed of the Big Island's resort areas, though there is little beach anywhere on the island. Resting on a blue bay at the foot of 8,000-foot Mount Hualalai, its single winding street is lined with hotels, small shops, and old churches. Allow yourself time here. Its climate is warm, its pace languid, and historical remnants can be seen in the old stone walls, the petroglyphs, the paved "highway" across the lava, the holua sled runs for the dangerous sledding contests, and the crumbling platforms of Hawaiian temples, called heiaus.

Special stops in Kona: The Mokuaikaua Church, built by young missionaries in 1837, and the Hulihee Palace, across the street from Mokuaikaua. Once the summer palace of Hawaiian kings, it is now a museum displaying artifacts of the Victorian-influenced Hawaiian court.

About 100 miles from Kona is a cool tropical highland called The Volcano. It can be reached by well-paved roads that take you through very interesting country—an area, in fact, that many discerning travelers consider the most fascinating in the Pacific.

Hilo, the only standard-looking city on the island, has a population of 32,000. It is the business, banking and shipping center of the island, as well as the seat of the county government, the law courts and branches of the state government. In addition, it has an international airport.

There are a variety of things to see and do: Rainbow Falls, the Lyman House Museum (built in 1839), the sampan fishing fleet, the early-morning fish auctions. But the favorite diversion of Hilo is visiting the orchid and anthurium nurseries. About 200,000 packages of orchids, anthuriums and other exotic blooms are air-mailed out each year.

Off the highway, close to Hilo, is an interesting macadamia nut orchard which welcomes visitors, and there is another at Honokaa on the Hamakua Coast near Waipio, a deep, verdant valley.

Worth investigating also is the open ranchland country at Waimea, headquarters of the Parker Ranch. This little bit of Montana includes a lovely tree-covered, cool road over Kohala Mountain to Hawi.

EXPLORING MAUI

Best bases for touring the Valley Isle are Kahului, the principal sea and airport, and Wailuku, the county seat three miles away, both of which are in the valley.

Wailuku, nestling at the base of the West Maui Mountains, is a charming provincial town. Its white-steepled church is a bit of New England transplanted by the missionaries in 1837. Hale Hoikeike, the historical museum, was built in 1841, and stands on Iao Road at the mouth of Iao Valley, a beautiful gorge known as the Little Yosemite of Hawaii. The road runs inland to Iao Valley Park and Iao Needle, a volcanic monolith rising in green splendor 2,250 feet straight up from the valley floor.

The most celebrated of Maui's tourist attractions lies forty-one miles southeast of Wailuku and 10,000 feet above it. It is Haleakala, House of the Sun. Haleakala's last volcanic outburst occurred two centuries ago. All of Manhattan Island could be deposited within the crater's twenty-one-mile circumference, and the tallest of skyscrapers would not rise above its rim.

Lahaina is no longer the "plantation town" it once was, picturesquely huddled between the sea and 5,800-foot Puu Kukui. Lahaina is actually the Williamsburg of Hawaii.

For a quarter of a century, 1840–1865, it was the center of the whaling industry, and many a whaler found temporary housing in Hale Paahao, the old prison whose massive coral walls have been standing since 1851. The *Carthaginian II*, an old German cargo ship cum museum, was built by Krupp in 1920.

In addition, you will want to visit the coral stone courthouse, built in 1857, behind which stands the largest banyan tree in the islands, planted in 1873. Nearby is the Old Baldwin House, built by the missionaries early in the 19th century. The house is now a museum.

Even more interesting as a relic of missionary days is Lahainaluna High School, the oldest school west of the Rockies, founded in 1831.

EXPLORING KAUAI

Lihue, your base for exploring the Garden Island of Kauai, is the county seat, and one of the oldest plantation towns in the islands (founded in 1849).

Wailua River

A trip on the Wailua River is something you should not miss. The place is redolent of history and romance as well as a tropical daydream. You are standing on the spot where the first Polynesians may have landed in Hawaii 1,000 years ago. You are also standing in the middle of Kauai's fastest-growing tourist resort. Near here is Heiau Holo-Holo-Ku, one of the most ancient and impressive temples in Hawaii.

Waimea Canyon

The town of Waimea was a focal point in history. It was here that Captain Cook first set foot on Hawaiian soil more than 200 years ago; here that the first missionaries settled on Kauai, and here that the sandalwood trade flourished. Today, Waimea is a busy plantation town, famous for its magnificent Waimea Canyon.

The two roads up to the Canyon—one from Waimea, one from Kekaha—wind through forests of koa, silver oak, eucalyptus and lehua trees. On your left you will have views of the sea and Niihau; on your right are glimpses of the canyon and, finally, numerous lookouts.

Beyond Puu Ka Pele, whose summit is 3,687 feet high, you reach Kauai's wonderful gorge which, at this point, is more than half a mile deep and a mile wide. Its length is ten miles.

For another striking vista into the gorge and across it to the Alakai Swamp, stop at Kaana Ridge. At this point, you are at the gateway to Kauai's wonderful Kokee district, a tropical rain forest. The Kokee region is a state forest reserve and it has an interesting Natural History Museum with exhibits of local plants, wildlife, rocks and petroglyphs.

From here, it is a three-mile drive through a dense tropical forest to the end of the road and two lookouts for the view of forbidden Kalalau. Four thousand feet below you, a ribbon of sand separates the green floor of Kalalau Valley from the sea. Do not miss this incredible spectacle.

PRACTICAL INFORMATION FOR THE ISLANDS

(Practical information for Oahu is included in the Honolulu section, earlier.)

THE ISLAND OF HAWAII

HOW TO GET THERE. There are more than a dozen flights daily from Honolulu to the Big Island, plus a number of special weekend flights. This includes nonstops to either Hilo or Kailua-Kona and limited service to Waimea. *United Air Lines* also has direct service from California.

 BIG ISLAND TOURS. There are a number of these, all originating either in Hilo or Kailua-Kona. The *Gray Line* conducts four different tours with limousines or custom-built Grayliners. The U-Drive firms have guided tours.

Captain Cook Cruises leave the Kailua-Kona wharf every morning and cover all historic points of Kealakekua Bay.

If you want to see what's under the surface of Kailua Bay, take the *Captain Cook VI* glass-bottom boat.

If you want to feel what's under the surface of Kailua Bay, check out scuba tanks and snorkels with *Jack's Diving Locker,* telephone 329-7585.

SPORTS. *Deep-Sea Fishing at Kona:* The waters off the Kona Coast teem with fighting game fish, and everything is available here for the fisherman's pleasure. *Hunting:* If you want to arrange a hunting expedition for wild sheep, boar, or game birds, get in touch with the Hawaii Visitors Bureau. *Hiking and Camping:* The Elysian fields for these activities are in the Volcano district, and source of trail information and permission to camp and hike is the *National Park Headquarters* opposite the Volcano House.

For a wide range of camping gear, check *Travel/Camp Inc.* in Hilo. Information on the county and state parks is available from the *Department of Parks and Recreation* in Hilo and the *Division of Parks,* Department of Land and Natural Resources, P.O. Box 936, Hilo 96720. *Golf:* Two miles from Volcano House is a good course. In Hilo there is the Municipal Golf Course. At Kona the best course is the new Keauhou Kona Golf Club. Newest courses in Hawaii are Seamountain near the southern tip of the island and the Mauna Lani and Waikaloa Beach courses near Waimea. But most resort courses are expensive, like $30 for a share of a cart; walking through Hilo's Municipal course, however, costs only $3. *Tennis:* There are 41 public courts in the county—10 in Hilo and many more at the hotels, with 9 of these at Mauna Kea.

 HAWAII HOTELS. Rates are for single rooms—for doubles add 15–25%. Categories are as follows: *Moderate,* $25; *Inexpensive,* $20–25; *Rock Bottom,* under $20.

Moderate: **Dolphin Bay.** In Hilo's Puueo district. Very homey.

Inexpensive: **Crescent Manor.** Hilo. In heart of Hilo's business district.

Hilo Hukilau. Hilo. Filtered freshwater pool. Restaurant.

Rock Bottom: **Kamuela Inn.** Kamuela. In heart of famous Parker Ranch land. Small country inn. Great views. Or **Manago's** in the coffee uplands above Capt. Cook.

Luke's, in Hawi at the north end of the island, is simple living.

HAWAII DINING OUT. Fine Chinese restaurants are **Sun Sun Lau** and **Canton Garden.** For Japanese fare in Hilo try **K. K. Tei,** on the Kona side. **Teshima's** restaurant, up the hill at Honalo, is also good.

THE ISLAND OF MAUI

HOW TO GET THERE. Maui is served by 49 flights a day and eight airlines, including the air taxis. *U-Drives:* At Kahului Airport many firms will provide you with a late-model vehicle. Reservations in advance will help.

TOURS. *Gray Line* has a tour of Iao Valley and Haleakala; *Holo Holo* has a tour to Hana. All tour information is available at the hotels and through the *Hawaii Visitors Bureau* in Wailuku. In Lahaina, the *Lahaina Restoration Foundation* has a tour.

SPORTS. *Horseback Riding: James Aki, Jr.,* has horses at Kipahulu and so does *Thompson Ranch* at Kula. *Fishing:* There are charter boats at Kahului, Lahaina, and Maalaea. The *Hawaii Visitors Bureau* can help you make charter arrangements. *Skindiving:* Maui Divers in Lahaina have skindiving equipment and boats for rent, and offer lessons for divers. *Hunting:* Kula Game Management Area is open on weekends and holidays, and you can take pheasants, quail, and doves during the season. Wild pigs and goats may be hunted all year around. *Golf:* There are nine golf courses for public play: the seaside course at Waiehu; the two courses at the Kaanapali development; two more at Kapalua; two at Wailea in the Kihei development, another at Makena Beach, and the Maui Country Club at Spreckelsville. *Tennis:* There are nine lighted county public courts and eleven at the hotels, with the six at the Royal Lahaina Hotel open to the public.

HOTELS AND RESTAURANTS ON MAUI. (Restaurants are within the hotels.) There is almost nothing available now on Maui for less than $30. But consider: **Hale Kai O Kihei,** near the beach at Kihei.

Maui Palms Resort. Built around a freshwater pool. Guest rooms are spacious and well-appointed.

Pioneer Inn. A delightful hotel with high-ceilinged and spacious rooms.

THE ISLAND OF KAUAI

HOW TO GET THERE. *Aloha Airlines, Mid-Pacific* and *Hawaiian Air* with between seven and ten flights a day from Honolulu, and there are air taxis. *U-Drives:* All companies have stands at the Lihue Airport: *Hertz, Islander U-Drive, Avis* and *Robert's U-Drive & Tours.*

TOURS. *Robert's* has guided tours of Kauai. There are boat trips on the Wailua River, day and night. *Paradise Pacifica,* located on the south side of the Wailua River, is a coconut plantation turned into a village of Polynesian huts and many exotic trees and flowers.

Remember the beach is free, so is the moon as it shimmers on the water or outlines the palm fronds. That's so on Oahu or any of the islands. On Oahu many things are free, such as the Kodak Hula Show, the Pearl Harbor trip, the views from the Capitol, Nuuanu Pali, Punchbowl, Aloha Tower. The zoo is free and there are free trips to a clothes or nut factory, and the art in many galleries. And Foster Garden, the University, the Royal Mausoleum, Kawaiahao and the many other churches. Your Hawaii trip needn't be expensive.

SPORTS. *Horseback Riding:* Horses can be rented at *Higates Ranch* and *Pooku Stables. Fishing:* Rainbow trout season opens on the first Saturday of August and remains open for 16 days. After that, fishing is permitted only on weekends and holidays through the end of September. Other fish, such as bluegill, are open daily, year-round. *Hunting:* There are four hunting areas: Wailua, Puu Ka Pele, Kakaha, and Kalepa. For all information, call the Lihue offices of the *Division of Fish and Game,* phone 245–4444.

Mammal hunting seasons are set by the *State Board of Land and Natural Resources.* Visitors should inquire at the *Lihue Fish and Game* office for current seasons.

HOTELS AND RESTAURANTS IN KAUAI. (Restaurants within the hotels.) **Kahili Mountain Park** has cabins in a very rustic setting.

    Poipu Village is on the beach, cottage-type.

Inexpensive: **Tip Top Motel.** A mile from from the airport.

Rock Bottom: **Hale Pumehana.** Across from Lihue Shopping Center.

Kokee Lodge. Wake up with the chickens and make your own bed.

INDEX

INDEX

General

Air travel
  discount travel 43
  from abroad 38-9
  within the U.S. 22-3
Auto travel
  from Canada & Mexico 40
  within the U.S. 18-21
British students 44
Bus travel
  discount travel 43-4
  from Canada & Mexico 40
  within the U.S. 24-6
Camping 30-2
Children 26-7
Climate 8-13
Clothing 17-18
  sizes 50-1
Cosmetics 51
Costs 3-5
Credit cards 8
Currency & exchange 46-7
Customs 41-3
Discount & bargain travel 43-4
Drinking laws 33
Electricity 48
Farm vacations 30
Fly/drive vacations 21-2
Food products regulations 43
Foreign visitors 43-53
Geography 40-1
Handicapped travelers 127
Health requirements 42
Hiking 30-2
Holidays 15-16
Hospitality programs 44
Hotels & motels 27-30
  discount accommodations 44
Hours of business 47-8
Immigration requirements 41-2

Insurance 18
Interpreter services 44-6
Legal aid 53
Letters of credit 47
Mail 36
Measurements 47
Medical assistance 51-2
National parks 37-8
Nightlife 33
Packing 17-18
Passports and visas 41-2
Pets 42-3
Places of worship 35
Rail travel
  from Canada & Mexico 39-40
  within the U.S. 23-4
Restaurants 32-3
Sales taxes 50
Seasonal events 13-15
Ship travel 39
Shopping 48-50
  Discount stores & factory outlets
  49-50
Special travel rates 5-6, 43-4
Sports 33-5
Telegrams 37
Telephones 36-7
  telephone & telegraph facilities 51
Time zones 13
Tipping 6-7
Tobacco 51
Tour packages 44
Traffic signs & road markings 20-1
Travel agents 17
Traveler's checks 46-7
Trip planning 16-17
Vaccinations 42
Weights & measures 42
Youth hostels 31

The letters H and R indicate hotel and restaurant listings.

ALABAMA

Alexander City H253
Birmingham 250, H253, R254
Children's entertainment 253
Decatur H253, R254
Drinking laws 252
Florence H253, R254
Gadsden H253, R254
Gulf Shores H253
Guntersville H253, R254
Historic sites 252
Huntsville 251, H254, R254
Information sources 252
Mobile 251-2, H254, R254
Montgomery 251, H254, R255
Museums & galleries 252
Russel Cave Natl. Mon. 251
Sports 253
Tours 252
Transportation 252
Tuscumbia 250-1
Wilson Dam 251

ALASKA

Anchorage 543, H547, R548
Children's entertainment 54-6
Denali (Mt. McKinley) Natl. Pk. 542-3
Fairbanks 542, H547, R548
Glacier Bay Natl. Park 541
Haines-Port Chikoot R548
Historic sites 544
Homer H547, R548
Information sources 543
Juneau 541, H547, R548
Ketchikan H547, R548
Kodiak 543, H547, R548
Museums & galleries 544
Nome R548
Petersburg R548
Seasonal events 546
Sitka H547, R548
Skagway H547, R549
Sports 545-6
Tok H547
Tours 544-5

659

MAP OF
THE UNITED STATES

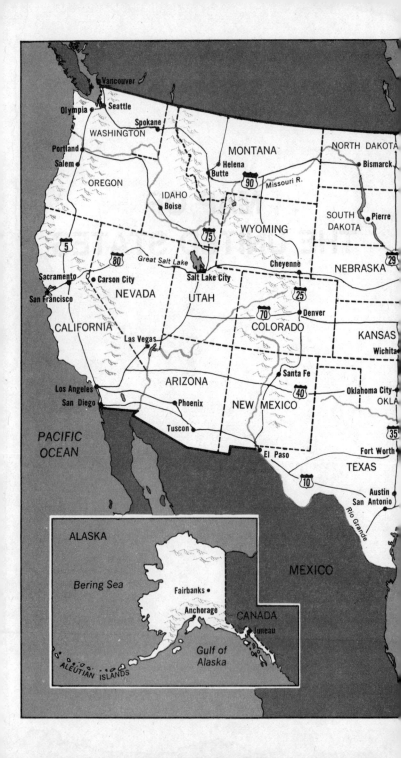

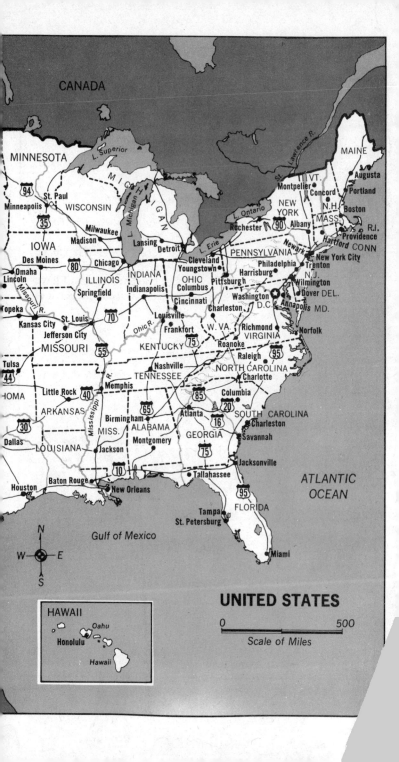

CANADA

MINNESOTA

L. Superior

MAINE
Augusta

94
St. Paul
Montpelier
VT.
Concord
Portland

Minneapolis
WISCONSIN
NEW YORK
N.H.
Boston

35
Madison
Milwaukee
Lansing
L. Ontario
Rochester
Albany
MASS.
R.I.

IOWA
Detroit
L. Erie
90
Hartford
CONN
Providence

Des Moines
Chicago
Cleveland
PENNSYLVANIA
Philadelphia
Newark
New York City

Omaha
80
INDIANA
Youngstown
Harrisburg
Trenton

Lincoln
ILLINOIS
Indianapolis
OHIO
Columbus
Pittsburgh
N.J.
Wilmington
Dover
DEL.

Springfield
Cincinnati
Washington
D.C.
Annapolis
MD.

Topeka
St. Louis
70
Louisville
Charleston
Richmond
Norfolk

Kansas City
Frankfort
Ohio R.
W. VA.
VIRGINIA

Jefferson City
55
KENTUCKY
75
Roanoke
95

MISSOURI
Nashville
Raleigh

Tulsa
44
TENNESSEE
NORTH CAROLINA
Charlotte

Little Rock
40
Memphis
85
Columbia

OKLAHOMA
ARKANSAS
65
Atlanta
20
SOUTH CAROLINA

30
Birmingham
16
Charleston

Dallas
MISS.
ALABAMA
GEORGIA
Savannah

LOUISIANA
Jackson
Montgomery
75
Jacksonville

10
Tallahassee
ATLANTIC
OCEAN

Houston
Baton Rouge
New Orleans

Tampa
95
FLORIDA

St. Petersburg

N
Gulf of Mexico
W—E
S
Miami

HAWAII
Oahu
Honolulu
Hawaii

UNITED STATES

0   500

Scale of Miles

L. Michigan

MICHIGAN

Missouri R.

Mississippi R.

St. Lawrence R.